AVATARS AT WORK AND PLAY

Computer Supported Cooperative Work

Volume 34

Avatars at Work and Play

Collaboration and Interaction
in Shared Virtual Environments

Edited by

Ralph Schroeder
Oxford University, Oxford, U.K.

and

Ann-Sofie Axelsson
Chalmers University, Gothenburg, Sweden

 Springer

A C.I.P. Catalogue record for this book is available from the Library of Congress.

ISBN-13 978-90-481-6989-4
ISBN-10 1-4020-3898-4 (e-book)
ISBN-13 978-1-4020-3898-3 (e-book)

Published by Springer,
P.O. Box 17, 3300 AA Dordrecht, The Netherlands.

www.springer.com

Printed on acid-free paper

List of Contributors

Ann-Sofie Axelsson, Department of Technology Management and Economics, Chalmers University of Technology, SE-412 96 Gothenburg, Sweden annaxe@ chalmers.se

Jeremy N. Bailenson, Department of Communication, Stanford University, Stanford CA 94305-2050, USA bailenso@stanford.edu

Andrew C. Beall, Department of Psychology, University of California Santa Barbara, Santa Barbara CA 93106-9660, USA beall@psych.ucsb.edu

Marek Bell, Department of Computer Science, University of Glasgow, Glasgow G12 8QQ, UK marek@dcs.gla.ac.uk

Jim Blascovich, Department of Psychology, University of California Santa Barbara, Santa Barbara, CA 93106-9660, USA blascovi@psy.ucsb.edu

Barry Brown, Department of Computer Science, University of Glasgow, Glasgow G12 8QQ, UK Barry@dcs.gla.ac.uk

Lars Bråthe, Volvo Powertrain, SE-405 05 Gothenburg, Sweden Lars.Brathe@volvo.com

Katy Börner, School of Library and Information Science, Indiana University, Bloomington, IN 47405, USA katy@indiana.edu

Mari Siân Davies, Childrens Media Center and Department of Psychology, UCLA, Los Angeles, CA 90095, USA marisian@ucla.edu

Maia Garau, Department of Computer Science, University College London, London WC1E 6BT, UK.garau@cs.ucl.ac.uk

Patricia M. Greenfield, Childrens Media Center and Department of Psychology, UCLA, Los Angeles, CA 90095, USA greenfield@psych.ucla.edu

Ilona Heldal, Department of Technology Management and Economics, Chalmers University of Technology, SE-412 96 Gothenburg, Sweden ilohel@chalmers.se

Mikael Jakobsson, Arts and Communication, Malmö University, SE-205 06 Malmö, Sweden mikael.jakobsson@k3.mah.se

Oliver Otto, The Centre for Virtual Environments, University of Salford, Manchester M5 4WT, UK o.otto@salford.ac.uk

Susan Persky, Department of Psychology, University of California Santa Barbara, Santa Barbara, CA 93106-9660, USA persky@verizon.net

Shashikant Penumarthy, School of Library and Information Science, Indiana University, Bloomington, IN 47405, USA sprao@indiana.edu

David Roberts, The Centre for Virtual Environments, University of Salford, Manchester M5 4WT, UK D.J.Roberts@salford.ac.uk

Ralph Schroeder, Oxford Internet Institute, University of Oxford, Oxford OX1 3JS, UK ralph.schroeder@oii.ox.ac.uk

Diane H. Sonnenwald, The Swedish School of Information and Library Science, Gothenburg University & University College of Borås, SE-501 90 Borås, Sweden diane.sonnenwald@hb.se

Maria Spante, Department of Technology Management and Economics, Chalmers University of Technology, SE-412 96 Gothenburg, Sweden marspa@chalmers.se

Anthony Steed, Computer Science, University College London, London WC1E 6BT, UK A.Steed@cs.ucl.ac.uk

Francis F. Steen, Childrens Media Center and Department of Communication Studies, UCLA, Los Angeles, CA 90095, USA steen@commstds.ucla.edu

Brendesha M. Tynes*, Childrens Media Center and Department of Psychology, UCLA, Los Angeles, CA 90095, USA btynesb@ucla.edu

Nick Yee, Department of Communication, Stanford University, Stanford, CA 94305-2050, USA nyee@stanford.edu

Robin Wolff, The Centre for Virtual Environments, University of Salford, Manchester M5 4WT, UK r.wolff@salford.ac.uk

---

* Currently African American Studies and Educational Psychology, University of Illinois, Urbana-Champaign, IL 61820, USA

Contents

WORK AND PLAY IN SHARED VIRTUAL ENVIRONMENTS: OVERLAPPING THEMES AND INTERSECTING RESEARCH AGENDAS

Ralph Schroeder and Ann-Sofie Axelsson

This volume, like its predecessor *The Social Life of Avatars: Presence and Interaction in Shared Virtual Environments* [1], aims to provide a state-of-the-art overview of research about how people interact in shared virtual environments (SVEs). Unlike the first volume, which covered a wide variety of topics, the essays collected here focus on two applications of SVEs; collaborative work and online gaming. These two areas are rapidly emerging as key drivers of SVE development. (Sometimes work applications are discussed under the label of collaborative virtual environments—or CVEs—but SVE is a broader term since it includes online gaming and socializing, so SVE is more suitable here.)

One reason for examining the two areas or work and play jointly is that although they are often treated in different academic arenas, in fact many issues overlap. As argued in the introduction to *The Social Life of Avatars*, certain issues—presence and copresence, communication between people in the environment, the appearance of the avatar and the environment, differences in the size of groups interacting, and how technology and the offline world shape the interaction—apply to *all* SVEs. Yet despite common themes, several academic disciplines are represented in this volume to tackle them—including psychology, sociology, computer science, and information sciences. Clearly, the study of SVEs requires that a number of disciplines work together.

This volume begins with two essays that investigate the important topic of avatar appearance, the appearance of the person inside the SVE. The essays by Bailenson and Beall and by Garau come at this from quite different perspectives. While Bailenson and Beall explore the plasticity of avatars, or the way in which the manipulation of appearance and behavior of avatars can be exploited for different purposes, Garau investigates the fidelity of avatar appearance with special reference to behavioral realism and eye gaze.

Bailenson and Beall demonstrate that it is easy to manipulate people's appearance. Changing facial appearance, allowing people to appear to be looking at several other people at the same time (non-zero sum gaze), and giving avatars virtual trainers that others cannot see—these and many other possibilities exist in SVEs that are not possible in face-to-face interaction. Their research, which they call "transformative social interaction", opens the way for investigating a host of social science questions in settings that can be controlled and manipulated. Their chapter makes a start in this direction (though there is some earlier related work by Blascovich [2] and by Slater and Steed [3]) by investigating, for example, how people respond when their own face is blended into that of the group they interact with, or when people are able to direct their gaze at two conversational partners simultaneously.

Eye gaze may seem like a very specialized topic, but as anyone who has studied interaction between people will know, in many instances eye gaze is the single most important form of non-verbal communication (and non-verbal communication may, of course, be more important than verbal communication). It is also very difficult to reproduce accurately in SVEs, though as Garau's chapter shows, it will be more important to focus on behavioral realism than on representational realism (or photorealism), which will have major implications for the design of SVE systems. Further, her findings suggest that, as there will always be trade-offs in implementing eye gaze and avatar fidelity, it may be that there are easier ways to provide more effective means for believable social interaction than is often thought.

One advantage of SVEs is that the interaction between people in the environments can easily be captured and analyzed. The next chapter by Penumarthy and Börner gives an excellent demonstration of this. Their essay is also a good example of investigating larger groups of people interacting in SVEs rather than the small groups of two or three that are typically studied. Put differently, their chapter addresses the area beyond the micro of small group encounters. This level is often difficult to capture and analyze in social science about the *real* world. In virtual worlds, however, the analysis is easily scalable (for some other examples, see [4, 5])—although, as the authors point out, patterns of interactions in virtual worlds will be different from real world ones.

We can also see in Penumarthy and Börner's essay, as in the one that follows by Sonnenwald, the beginnings of the systematic investigation into some basic building blocks of social interaction in SVEs; such as cooperation and competition, leadership (see also [6]) and status. As Sonnenwald shows, collaboration over the course of time with larger groups across a number of sites requires not only smoothly functioning technology, but even more importantly the social coordination of people and their adaptation to new roles in SVE settings. A key issue that emerges in this and several other papers in this volume—and one that has not been studied sufficiently since many SVE trials and experiences have been for shorter periods—is that a different dynamic sets in with longer-term routine collaboration (see also [7, 8]).

Sonnenwald also reports, in relation to another study of collaboration in which two participants used a haptic system for a science lab exercise and which compared pairs working side by side and pairs working across a network—that the latter is in many ways superior to the former. This is an important result since it is often claimed that distributed collaboration can never be as good as face-to-face collaboration. The only previous result (to our knowledge) which shows that collaboration in a SVE is practically as good as working face-to-face is our own study of pairs solving a spatial task with a Rubik's cube-type puzzle using networked immersive projection technology systems [9].

The study of SVEs has to a large extent focused on presence, copresence and on doing different tasks with different systems. Much less is known so far about the patterns of how the bodies of avatars interact with each other and with the environment. The chapter by Heldal, Bråthe, Steed and Schroeder analyzes this interaction in detail, focusing on pairs of users using networked immersive projection technology systems doing a number of tasks together. By analyzing their movements and conversation in great depth, the authors are able to highlight certain common successful and less successful forms of interaction. It is clear from this analysis that some elements that one might expect to be problematic are not; for example, going through each other's avatar bodies and through objects during certain phases in the collaboration (and despite the fact that these are "unnatural" forms of interaction). Conversely, some forms of interaction that one might expect to find unproblematic in fact present obstacles to smooth interaction; such as moving a non-tracked arm to point to objects, or navigating together and orienting oneself in a large space. These findings can only be obtained by means of closely examining such small sequences of interaction. The problem for future research, as they point out, will be to find out how general lessons can be drawn from these very brief and specific sequences.

For open-ended and less true-to-life tasks (such as those in the chapter just described) these issues may not be so pressing since participants can develop workarounds for many of the problems. Roberts, Otto and Wolff's essay addresses a different type of collaboration; working together with objects on a closely coupled task which requires close coordination in building a small structure together. One of their aims is to show, as some others have done, the advantages of handling objects in an immersive SVE as opposed to a desktop one. Another is to highlight that for this type of—again, closely coupled task—a lot of decisions need to be made about how, in the virtual world, objects can be passed from one person to another (who "owns" them?) and how objects and tools are used (how is "gravity" implemented? How to indicate when a screw has been successfully screwed in?).

These are some problems that do not exist for physical world collaboration. Roberts, Otto and Wolff also describe how implementing the technical aspects of simultaneously handling objects and using tools is by no means a trivial task in terms of handling network traffic and software design—since time and coordination are critical. Still, the main point of their essay is that they demonstrate that even for a scenario in which people need to work closely and accurately together, which is perhaps the most demanding scenario to implement in immersive SVEs, solutions can be found for very difficult problems, such as delays, consistency of objects, and the like.

As we saw earlier, it is important how "truthful"—in behavioral terms—avatars are. The chapter by Spante, Axelsson and Schroeder deals with a related issue for people collaborating with others via different systems; namely, that it is important to let users know what the capabilities of each others' systems are. Unless this information is made explicit, users will often make assumptions about the other person's avatar or system that are incorrect, and this can lead to misunderstandings. Spante, Axelsson and Schroeder argue that greater transparency by means of more information will improve interaction and learning about the other person's system—or, that "putting yourself into the other person's shoes" can lead to an enhanced experience of collaboration. It should be noted, however, that there are also drawbacks to this: for example, the user will need to bear this information about the other person's system in mind throughout the interaction, and this means that another piece of information is added to concentrating on the task and other aspects of interaction.

Here, it can be recalled that the whole point of Virtual Reality (VR) technology is supposed to be that this is a "natural" interface, or that SVEs do away with the interface; that is, that the interface is so realistic that the user does not need to worry about commands or other pieces of information. So keeping in mind what kind of system the other person is using will put information between the user and the interface. These issues will also apply to the kinds of artificially enhanced or altered scenarios in Bailenson and Beall's paper: knowing that the encounter has "artificial" features could either detract from "realism", or it could be made transparent—but in this case detract from the naturalness of the interaction or add to the "cognitive load" of the participants.

The essay by Persky and Blascovich about immersive gaming provides an interesting transition between the two parts of the book—since immersive SVEs have to date been almost exclusively used for work or research purposes. Online gaming, on the other hand, is almost invariably associated with desktop computers. Nevertheless, it can be envisaged that online games will become increasingly immersive. Persky and Blascovich's experiments supply a number of findings which anticipate this development: one is that playing a violent game in an immersive SVE—as one might expect—has a more powerful effect on aggressive feelings than playing a non-violent one, and that these feelings are stronger in an immersive than in a non-immersive (desktop) SVE. The same does not apply to an art-themed game; in this case creative feelings are not heightened by playing on an immersive VR system. (Again, one of the limitations of these findings is that they apply to short-term experiences of VEs.) Nevertheless, although violence and addiction have been obvious topics for online gaming on desktop computers, they will take on a new dimension with immersive SVE systems.

Yee's chapter about the massively multiplayer online role playing game (MMORPG) Everquest is intended to go beyond the study of violence and addiction in long-term online gameplay. With his extensive questionnaire responses from 30000 MMORPG players, we begin to have a better understanding of what attracts people to interacting online. Apart from steering us away from the stereotype of the a-social male teenager, his findings are also relevant to why people are drawn to immerse themselves in virtual worlds—which is closely related to the question of "presence" and "copresence" analyzed in the other contributions in the volume. Yee shows, to give just a small example, that women are more motivated by the "relationship", "immersion" and "escapism" factors than men. Another interesting finding is the possibility raised by his research that partners or parents and their children can learn about aspects of each others' personalities that they may not been able to discover in face-to-face relations with each other. These findings could be relevant not only to the design of online games, but also to collaborative work and other applications of SVEs.

Everquest is one of the online games in Yee's study, and this popular game is also the focus of Jakobsson's chapter. Like Yee, Jakobsson is interested in why people are attracted to virtual worlds, but his approach is quite different: He charts, in the manner of an ethnographic participant observer, how the relationship to the game and to others changes over the course of time. He points out that few people, and certainly not game designers, have thought about questions to do with longer-term engagement with virtual worlds, such as how to maintain relations with friends when leaving a particular game and the continuity between different worlds ("continuity" is a problem for the economies of virtual worlds, see Castronova's essays [10]). Jakobsson also describes how gameplay increasingly entails more "managerial" functions at the more advanced levels, such as coordinating team play with others. In the end, however, even this more complex level faces the problem of where to take player progression—ultimately, towards being able to leave the game in a suitably rewarding way.

The last two chapters overlap in that they both focus on the social glue that makes online social interaction pleasurable—mostly successfully in the case of *There*, and mostly unsuccessfully, it seems, for *The Sims Online*. Brown and Bell's chapter about the online virtual world *There* argues for example that the design of the text bubbles for conversational turn-taking and how objects can be handled together provide a shared focus that enhances sociability. They also argue, like the first two chapters in this volume, that embodiment in online gaming plays an important role in facilitating social interaction (see also [11]). Their chapter is a good counterpoint to Steen, Davies, Tynes, and Greenfield's account of *The Sims Online*. Steen et al. argue that *The Sims Online* incorporated precisely the wrong elements—that is, the elaborate social structure—from the (highly successful) offline *Sims* game, and that the designers did not build enough features facilitating more immediate sociability around conversation and interaction with objects into the online version.

The essay by Steen et al. does not deal with SVEs in the strict sense that is used in the other contributions (for definitions of SVEs and Virtual Reality, see the introductory chapter in [1]), since control over one's first-person visual perspective and direct manipulation of the environment is lacking. Still, this environment is interesting because it is a large-scale and much discussed environment which hoped to replicate many of the complex features and depth of the real-world social interaction more thoroughly than other online social spaces.

As we have seen, this question—of the artificiality of the environment and the "structuredness" of interpersonal interaction—is one that is addressed in different ways in earlier chapters. Brown and Bell are thus surely correct to say that designers of collaborative work environments will benefit from studying online games. A further reason for this is that online gaming needs to engage the user over a long period of time. The interaction that is described in several of the work related chapters would, if it were to take place over longer periods, not only need smooth interaction with devices, but also promote a sense of sociability and of the participants enjoying each other's company.

Many other connections between these essays could be made. In the end, they are all linked by a common goal—of better understanding the uses of SVEs for practical work purposes and for leisure or socializing purposes. The first volume of essays *The Social Life of Avatars* was mainly exploratory and mapped out different research directions. With this volume, our hope is that research on SVEs is well on its way towards better insights into what makes them more effective and enjoyable—and to improved SVE design.

References

1. Schroeder, R. (Ed.) (2002). *The Social Life of Avatars: Presence and Interaction in Shared Virtual Environments*. London: Springer.
2. Blascovich, J. (2002). Social influence within immersive virtual environments. In R. Schroeder (Ed.), *The Social Life of Avatars: Presence and Interaction in Shared Virtual Environments*. London: Springer, pp. 127–145.
3. Slater, M. & Steed, A. (2002). Meeting people virtually: Experiments in shared virtual environments. In R. Schroeder (Ed.), *The Social Life of Avatars: Presence and Interaction in Shared Virtual Environments*. London: Springer, pp. 146–171.
4. Craven, M., Benford, S., Greenhalgh, C., Wyver, J., Brazier, C.J., Oldroyd, A., & Regan, T. (2001). Ages of Avatar: Community building for inhabited television. In E. Churchill & M.

Reddy (Eds.), *CVE2000: Proceedings of the Third International Conference on Collaborative Virtual Environments*. New York: ACM Press, pp. 189–194.

5. Schroeder, R., Huxor, A., & Smith, A. (2001). Activeworlds: Geography and social interaction in virtual reality. *Futures: A Journal of Forecasting, Planning and Policy 33*: 569–587.

6. Slater, M., Sadagic, A., Usoh, M., & Schroeder, R. (2000). Small group behaviour in a virtual and real environment: A comparative study. *Presence: Journal of Teleoperators and Virtual Environments 9*(1): 37–51.

7. Hudson-Smith, A. (2002). 30 Days in Activeworlds—Community, design and terrorism in a virtual world. In R. Schroeder (Ed.), *The Social Life of Avatars: Presence and Interaction in Shared Virtual Environments*. London: Springer, pp. 77–89.

8. Steed, A., Spante, M., Schroeder, R., Heldal, I., & Axelsson, A.S. (2003). Strangers and friends in caves: An exploratory study of collaboration in networked IPT Systems for extended periods of time. In *ACM SIGGRAPH 2003 Symposium on Interactive 3D Graphics*. New York: ACM Press, pp. 51–54.

9. Schroeder, R., Steed, A., Axelsson, A.S., Heldal, I., Abelin, Å., Wideström, J., Nilsson, A., & Slater, M. (2001). Collaborating in networked immersive spaces: As good as being there together? *Computers & Graphics 25*: 781–788.

10. Castronova, E. (2005). Available at http://mypage.iu.edu/~castro/

11. Taylor, T.L. (2002). Living digitally: Embodiment in virtual worlds. In R. Schroeder (Ed.), *The Social Life of Avatars: Presence and Interaction in Shared Virtual Environments*. London: Springer, pp. 40–62.

Chapter 1

TRANSFORMED SOCIAL INTERACTION: EXPLORING THE DIGITAL PLASTICITY OF AVATARS

Jeremy N. Bailenson and Andrew C. Beall

1.   Introduction

What does it mean to be you? How drastically can a person change and still remain, in the eyes of either themselves or their peers, the same person? Until recently, these questions were typically asked in the context of philosophy, psychoanalysis, or science fiction. However, the increasingly common use of avatars during computer-mediated communication, collaborative virtual environments (CVEs) in particular, are quickly changing these once abstract questions into practical quandaries that are fascinating, thought-provoking, potentially paradigm shifting for those who study social interaction, and potentially devastating to the traditional concept of human communication.

Historically, even before the advent of computers, people have demonstrated a consistent practice of extending their identities. As Turkle [1, p. 31] points out:

> The computer of course, is not unique as an extension of self. At each point in our lives, we seek to project ourselves into the world. The youngest child will eagerly pick up crayons and modeling clay. We paint, we work, we keep journals, we start companies, we build things that express the diversity of our personal and intellectual sensibilities. Yet the computer offers us new opportunities as a medium that embodies our ideas and expresses our diversity.

Extending one's sense of self in the form of abstract representation is one of our most fundamental expressions of humanity. But abstract extension is not the only manner in which we manipulate the conception of the self. In addition to using abstract means to extend one's identity, humans also engage in the practice of using tangible means to transform the self. Figure 1-1 demonstrates some of these self transformations that occur currently, without the use of digital

R. Schroeder and A.S. Axelsson (Eds.), Avatars at Work and Play, 1–16.
© 2006 *Springer.*

	Appearance	Nonverbal Behavior	Verbal Behavior
Short term	Haircuts Makeup	Mimicking Ingratiating Gestures	Lying Word Choice
Long term	Plastic Surgery Dieting	Habit Suppression Table Manners	Oratory Training Language- Acquisition

Figure 1-1. Non-digital transformations of self currently used.

technology. Before the dawn of avatars and computer-mediated communication, this process of self transformation was minor, incremental, and required vast amounts of resources.

However, given the advent of collaborative virtual reality technology [2–5], as well as the surging popularity of interacting with digital representations via collaborative desktop technology [6], researchers have begun to systematically explore this phenomenon of *Transformed Social Interaction* [7]. TSI involves novel techniques that permit changing the nature of social interaction by providing interactants with methods to enhance or degrade interpersonal communication. TSI allows interactants themselves, or alternatively a moderator of the CVE, to selectively filter and augment the appearance, verbal behavior, and nonverbal behavior of their avatars. Furthermore, TSI also allows the interactants to filter the context in which an interaction occurs. In our previous work outlining the theoretical framework of TSI, we provided three dimensions for transformations during interaction.

The first dimension of TSI is transforming *sensory abilities*. These transformations augment human perceptual abilities. For example, one can have "invisible consultants" present in a collaborative virtual environment, ranging from other avatars of assistants rendered only to you who scrutinize other interactants, to algorithms that give you real-time summary statistics about the movements and attentions of others (which are automatically collected in a CVE in order to render behaviors). As a potential application, teachers using distance learning applications can have "attention monitors" that automatically use eye gaze, facial expressions and other gestures as a mechanism to localize students who may not understand a given lesson. That teacher can then tailor his or her attention more towards the students higher in need. As another example, teachers can render virtual nametags (displayed to the teacher only) inserted over their students' avatars. Consequently, even in a distance learning classroom of hundreds, the students' names will always be at an instructor's disposal without having to consult a seating chart or a list.

The second dimension is *situational context*. These transformations involve changes to the temporal or spatial structure of an interaction. For example, each interactant can optimally adjust the geographical configuration of the room—in a distance learning paradigm, every single student in a class of twenty can sit right up front, next to the teacher, and perceive his or her peers as sitting behind. Furthermore, real-time use of "pause" and "rewind" during an interaction (while one's avatar exhibits stock behaviors produced by an "auto-pilot" algorithm) may be quite an effective tool to increase comprehension and productivity during interaction. Another example of transforming the situational contexts is to utilize *multilateral perspectives*. In a normal conversation, interactants can only take on a single perspective—their own. However, in a CVE, one can adopt the visual point of view of any avatar in the entire room. Either by bouncing her entire field of view to the spatial location of other avatars in the interaction, or by keeping "windows" in the corners of the virtual display that show in real time the fields of views of other interactants, it is possible for an interactant to see the behavior of her own avatar, as they occur, from the eyes of other interactants. Previous research has used either role playing scenarios [8] or observational seating arrangements [9] to cause experimental subjects to take on the perspectives of others in an interaction, and has demonstrated that this process is an extremely useful tool for fostering more efficient and effective interactions. Equipping an interactant with the real-time ability to see one's avatar from another point of view should only enhance these previous findings concerning the benefits of taking other perspectives.

The third dimension of TSI is *self-representation*. These transformations involve decoupling the rendered appearance or behaviors of avatars from the human driving the avatar. In other words, interactants choose the way in which their avatars are rendered to others in the CVE, and that rendering can follow as closely or as disparately to the actual state of the humans driving the avatars as they so desire. The focus of this chapter will be to discuss this third dimension in greater detail. While transforming situational contexts and sensory abilities are fascinating constructs, thoroughly discussing all three dimensions is beyond the scope of the current work.

This idea of decoupling representation from actual behavior has received some attention from researchers previously exploring CVEs. For example, [10] as well as [11] discussed *truthfulness* in representation, Biocca [12] introduced a concept known as *hyperpresence*, using novel visual dimensions to express otherwise abstract emotions or behaviors, and, moreover, numerous scholars debate the pros and cons of abstract digital identities [1, 13]. Furthermore, Jaron Lanier, considered by many to be one of the central figures in the history of immersive virtual reality, often makes an analogy between the human using immersive virtual reality and the "aplysia", a sea-slug that can quickly change its surface features such as body shape and skin color. Before virtual reality, humans had to resort to makeup, plastic surgery, or elaborate costumes to achieve these goals. William Gibson [14, p. 117] may have put it best when he declared that, once the technology supports such transformations, it is inevitable that people take advantage of "the infinite plasticity of the digital".

In sum, the idea of changing the appearance and behaviors of one's representation in immersive virtual reality has been a consistent theme in the development of the technology. The goals of the Transformed Social Interaction paradigm are threefold: (1) to explore and actually implement these strategies in collaborative virtual environments, (2) to put human avatars in CVEs and to measure which types of TSI tools they actually use during interaction, and (3) to examine the impact that TSI has on the effectiveness of interaction in general, as well as the impact on the specific goals of particular interactants. In the current chapter, we provide an overview of the empirical research conducted to date using avatars to examine TSI, and then discuss some of the broader implications of these digital transformations.

2.   Transforming Avatar Appearance

This section reviews a series of TSI applications concerning the static appearance of one's avatar, some of which have been already tested using behavioral science studies in CVEs, others that have yet to receive empirical examination.

2.1.   Identity Capture

The nature of a three-dimensional model used to render an avatar lends itself quite easily to applying known algorithms that transform facial structure according to known landmark points on the head and face. Once a face is digitized, there are an infinite number of simple morphing techniques that alter the three-dimensional structure and surface features of that face. This practice can be a powerful tool during interaction.

For example, persuaders can absorb aspects of an audience member's identity to create implicit feelings of similarity. Imagine the hypothetical case in which Gray Davis (the past governor of California, depicted in the leftmost panel of figure 1-2) is attempting to woo the constituents of a locale in which the voters are primarily fans of Arnold Schwarzenegger (the governor of California that ousted Davis) depicted in the rightmost panel of figure 1-2.

Research in social psychology has demonstrated large effects of similarity on social influence, in that a potential influencer who is more similar to a given person (compared to a less similar influencer) is considered more attractive

Figure 1-2. A digital morph of the two-dimensional avatars of Gray Davis (left) to Arnold Schwarzenegger (right).

[15] and persuasive [16], is more likely to make a sale [17], and is more likely to receive altruistic help in a dire situation [18]. Consequently, using digital technology to "absorb" physical aspects of other interactants in a CVE may provide distinct advantages for individuals who seek to influence others, either in a positive manner (e.g., a teacher during distance learning), or in a manner not so wholesome (e.g., a politician trying to underhandedly co-opt votes). Moreover, this type of a transformation may be particularly effective in situations in which the transformation remains implicit [19]. In other words, the effect of the transformation may be strongest when CVE interactants do not consciously detect their own face morphed into the face of the potential influencer.

To test this hypothesis, we brought Stanford University undergraduate students into the lab and used a simple morphing procedure with MagicMorph software [20, 21] to blend their faces in with an unfamiliar politician, Jim Hahn, a mayor of Los Angeles. Figure 1-3 depicts images of two undergraduate students as well as two blends that are each compromised of 60% of Jim Hahn and 40% of their own features.

The main hypothesis in this study [22] was that participants would be more likely to vote for a candidate that is morphed with their own face than a candidate that is morphed with someone else's face. In other words, by capturing a substantial portion of a voter's facial structure, a candidate breeds a feeling of familiarity, which is an extremely effective strategy for swaying preference [23].

Our findings in this study demonstrated two important patterns. First, out of 36 participants, only two detected that their own face was morphed into the candidate, even when we explicitly asked them to name one person like whom the candidate looked. Interestingly, their responses often demonstrated an implicit similarity (e.g., "He looks like my grandfather," or "He looks really familiar but I am not sure who he is"), but very rarely indicated a detection of the self. Second, overall there was a preference for candidates that were morphed with the self over candidates that were morphed with others, though the effect was strongest for white male participants (who were similar enough to the picture of Jim Hahn to create a successful morph) and for people interested in politics (who ostensibly were more motivated to pay attention to the photograph of the

Figure 1-3. Pictures of the participants are on the left; the blend of 60% of an unfamiliar politician and 40% of the given participant is on the right.

candidate). In sum, very few participants noticed that their face was morphed into the political candidate, but implicitly the presence of themselves in the candidate gave the candidate a greater ability to influence those participants.

2.2. Team Face

A related study [24] examined the use of TSI for collaborative teams by creating a "Team Face". Given the underlying notion that teams function more cooperatively when they embrace commonalties (e.g., dress codes, uniforms) it is logical to consider that organizations would consider extending these team features to the rendering of avatars. Consider the faces in figure 1-4.

Figure 1-4. Four participants (left four panels) and their team face (far right), a morph that includes 25% of each of them.

The face on the far right is a morphed avatar that includes the faces from all four of the participants at equal contributions. In our study, participants (32 in total: four sets of four participants of each gender) received two persuasive messages: one delivered by their own team face, and one delivered by a team face that did not include their own face.

In this study, only three participants noticed their own face present inside the team face when explicitly asked to name one person like whom the face looked. In regards to persuasion, our results indicated that when participants received a persuasive message from an avatar wearing the team face, they were more likely to scrutinize the arguments. Specifically, arguments that were strong (determined by pre-testing) were seen as stronger when received by one's own team face than when received by a different team face, and the opposite pattern occurred for weak arguments.

This pattern is quite consistent with what would be predicted by the elaboration-likelihood model of Petty and Cacioppo [25]. According to that model, people processing a persuasive message utilize either the central route (i.e., dedicate cognitive resources towards actually working through the logical strengths and weaknesses of an argument) or the peripheral route (i.e., analyze the message only in terms of quick heuristics and surface features). In the study using team faces, participants were more likely to process a message centrally when the message was presented by their own team face than when presented by another team face—they were more likely to accept a strong argument and less likely to accept a weak argument. In sum, these preliminary data indicate that interacting with an agent wearing one's own team face causes that person to dedicate more energy towards the task at hand.

These two studies [22, 24] have been utilized solely with two-dimensional avatars in non-immersive displays. Current projects are extending this work to three-dimensional avatars in immersive virtual reality simulations that feature not only the texture being morphed between one or more faces but the underlying shape of the three-dimensional model as well. Previous research has demonstrated that three-dimensional models of a person's head and face built with photogrammetric software is sufficient to capture a majority of the visual features of one's physical self, both in terms of how people treat their own virtual selves [26] and in terms of how others treat familiar virtual representations of others [27].

2.3.   *Acoustic Image*

While the majority of research and development in virtual environment technology has focused on stimulating the visual senses, the technology to richly stimulate the auditory senses is not far behind and possibly holds as much promise in its ability to transform social interactions amongst individuals as does its visual counterpart. Just a few years ago the process to render accurate spatialized (three-dimensional) sound required specialized and expensive digital signal processing hardware. Today, all this processing can be done on consumer-class PCs while easily leaving enough system resources left-over for the user's primary applications. In day-to-day living, we all take spatialized sound for granted just as we take binocular vision for granted. Only when you stop and reflect on the acoustical richness of our natural environments do you realize how much information is derived from the sensed locations of objects: without looking you know from where behind you your colleague is calling your name or that you better quickly step to one side and not the other to avoid being hit by a speeding bicyclist. Spatialization is partly what enables the "cocktail party phenomena" to occur—namely the ability to selectively filter out an unwanted conversation from an attended conversation. As such, our ability to synthetically render these cues in correspondence to three-dimensional visual images enables accurate reconstruction of physical spaces.

More interesting, however, are the possibilities arising from purposely altering the correspondence between the visual and acoustic images. By "warping" relational context, one can hand pick targets that are made maximally available along different channels. Research in cognitive psychology shows that human information processing is capacity limited and that these bottlenecks are largely independent for the visual and auditory channels. This means that by decoupling the visual and auditory contexts one could potentially empower a CVE user with the ability to maximize her sensory bandwidth and information processing abilities. For instance, in a meeting scenario one might place two different persons centered in one's field of attention, person A centered visually and person B centered acoustically. This way both A and B could be monitored quite carefully for their reactions to a presentation, albeit along different dimensions.

Just as it is possible to spatialize sound in real time, it is also possible to alter the characteristics of human speech in real time. Various software and hardware solutions are available on the consumer market today that can be used to alter one's voice in order to disguise one's identity. While it is not typically easy to transform a male voice into a female voice or vice versa, it is easy to alter a voice with a partial pitch and timbre shift that markedly changes the characteristics so that even someone familiar with the individual would unlikely recognize his identity. The implications of this regarding transforming social interaction are considerable. First, this technology enables the use of duplex voice as a communication channel while still maintaining the anonymity that digital representation allows. Already users in the online gaming community are using this technology to alter their digital personas.

But changing voice to disguise is just one possibility; voice can be transformed in a way that captures the acoustic identity just as the photographs can be morphed to do the same. One form of voice cloning is to sample a small amount of another's voice (e.g., 30 seconds or so) and analyze the frequency components to determine the mean tendencies and then use those statistics to modestly alter the pitch and timbre of your own voice using tools available today. In this way, you could partially transform your voice. While we know of no research that has done so, we believe the end result would be similar to the studies we have discussed in the visual domain. Perhaps a closer analogy to visual morphing is a voice cloning technology recently commercialized by AT&T Labs known as "concatenative speech synthesis." From a sample of 10–40 hours of recorded speech by a particular individual, it is possible to train a text-to-speech engine that captures the nuances of a particular individual's voice and then synthesize novel speech as if it came from that individual [28]. While the technology is impressive, it certainly still has a "robotic" ring to it—but its potential in CVE use is considerable.

As the next section demonstrates, extending TSI into immersive virtual reality simulations in which interactants' gestures and expressions are tracked bring in a host of new avenues to explore, and allow for extremely powerful demonstrations of strategies that change the way people interact with one another.

3.   Transformations of Avatar Behavior

One of the most powerful aspects of immersive virtual reality, and in particular naturalistic nonverbal behavior tracking, is one that receives very little attention. In order to render behaviors onto an avatar as they are performed by the human, one must record in fine detail the actual behaviors of the human. Typically, the recordings of these physical movements are instantly discarded after they occur, or perhaps archived, similar to security video footage. However, one of the most powerful mechanisms behind TSI involves analyzing, filtering, enhancing, or blocking this behavior tracking data in real time during the interaction. In the current section, we review some previous research in which interactants have transformed their own nonverbal behavior as it occurs, and discuss some of the vast number of future directions for work within this paradigm.

3.1.   *Non-Zero-Sum Gaze*

One example of these TSI "nonverbal superpowers" is *non-zero-sum gaze (NSZG)*: providing direct mutual gaze at more than a single interactant at once. Previous research has demonstrated that eye gaze is an extremely important cue: directing gaze at someone (compared to looking away from him or her) causes presenters to be more persuasive [29] and more effective as teachers [30–32]; it increases physiological arousal in terms of heartbeat [33], and generally acts as a signal for interest [34]. In sum, people who use mutual gaze increase their ability to engage a large audience as well as to accomplish a number of conversational goals.

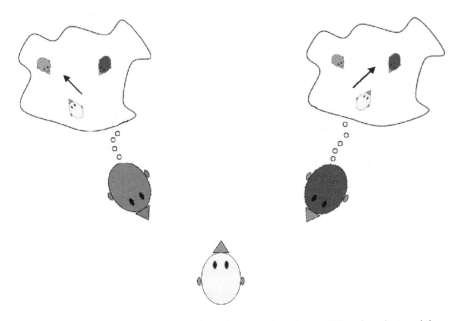

Figure 1-5. Non-zero-sum Gaze: Both the interactant on the top left and on the top right perceive the sole mutual gaze of the interactant on the bottom.

In face-to-face interaction, gaze is zero sum. In other words, if interactant X looks directly at interactant Y for 80% of the time, it is not possible for X to look directly at interactant Z for more than 20% of the time. However, interaction among avatars using TSI is not bound by this constraint. In a CVE, the virtual environment is individually rendered for each interactant locally at extremely high frame-rates. Consequently, with digital avatars, an interactant can have his avatar rendered differently for each other interactant, and appear to maintain mutual gaze with both Y and Z for a majority of the conversation, as figure 1-5 demonstrates.

NZSG allows a conversationalist to maintain the illusion that he or she is looking at an entire roomful of interactants. Previous research has implemented avatars that use "non veridical" algorithms to drive eye movements. For example, [35] implemented eye animations that were inferred from the verbal flow of the interaction. In other words, while head movements of interactants were tracked veridically, animation of the eyes themselves were driven not by the people's actual movements, but instead based on an algorithm based on speaking turns. These authors found that the conversation functioned quite well given this decoupling of rendered eye movements from actual eye movements, out-performing a number of other experimental conditions including an audio-only interaction.

Moreover, there has been research directly examining the phenomenon of NZSG. Two studies [36, 37] have utilized a paradigm in which a single presenter read a passage to two listeners inside an immersive CVE. All three interactants were of the same gender, wore stereoscopic, head-mounted displays, and had their head movements and mouth movements tracked and rendered. The presenter's avatar either looked directly at each of the other two speakers simultaneously for 100% of the time (augmented gaze) or utilized normal, zero-sum gaze. Moreover, the presenter was always blind to the experimental condition; in the augmented condition an algorithm automatically scaled down the magnitude of the presenter's head orientation movements (pitch, yaw, and roll) by a factor of 20 and redirected it at the eyes of both listeners.

Results across those two studies demonstrated three important findings: (1) participants never detected that the augmented gaze was not in fact backed by real gaze, despite being stared at for 100% of the time, (2) participants returned gaze to the presenter more often in the augmented condition than in the normal condition, and (3) participants (females to a greater extant than males) were more persuaded by a presenter implementing augmented gaze than a presenter implementing normal gaze.

The potential to use this tool should be extremely tempting across a number of conversational contexts ranging from distance education to sales pitch meetings to online dating chatrooms. Given the preliminary evidence described above, it is clear that avatar-gaze powered by algorithms, as opposed actual human behavior, can be at the very least innocuous, and most likely quite effective, during conversation.

3.2.   Digital Chameleons

Chartrand and Bargh [38, p. 893] describe and provide empirical evidence for the Chameleon effect: when a person mimics our nonverbal behavior, that person has a greater chance of influencing us:

> Such a Chameleon effect may manifest itself different ways. One may notice using the idiosyncratic verbal expressions or speech inflexions of a friend. Or one may notice crossing one's arms while talking to someone else who has his or her arm's crossed. Common to all such cases is that one typically does not notice doing these things—if at all—until after the fact.

Data from Chartrand and Bargh's studies demonstrate that when people copy our gestures we like them better, interact more smoothly with them, and are more likely to provide them favor.

Given that typical rendering methods require capturing extremely detailed data concerning their gestures and actions, CVEs lend themselves towards utilizing mimic algorithms at very little added cost. Either from a "nonverbal profile" built from user historical archive data, or from slight adjustments to real-time gestures, it is quite easy for interactants to morph (or even fully replace) their own nonverbal behaviors with those of their conversational partners. There are many motives for interactants to implement the digital chameleon in CVEs, ranging from subtle attempts to achieve influence to powering their avatar with some type of "autopilot" while the user temporarily abdicates his or her seat in the CVE.

Previous research [37] demonstrated that participants often do not detect their own head movements when those movements are rendered at a delay onto other interactants in a CVE. Consequently, to test the digital chameleon hypothesis, Bailenson and Yee [24] ran an experiment in which undergraduate students sat in an immersive virtual environment, at a virtual table, across from an embodied agent. The agent proceeded to read a persuasive passage approximately four minutes long to the participants, whose head orientation movements were tracked while the scene was rendered to them stereoscopically through a head-mounted display. For participants in the *mimic condition*, the agent's head movements were the exact same movements (on pitch, yaw, and roll) as the participants with a lag of 4 seconds. In other words, however the participant moved his or her head, the agent mimicked that movement 4 seconds later. For a separate group of participants in the *recorded condition*, the agent's head movements were simply a playback of one of the other participants from the mimic condition.

Results of this study demonstrated a huge difference between groups. Agents that mimicked the participants were far more successful at persuading the participants and were seen as more likable than recorded agents. This effect occurred despite the fact that hardly any of the participants detected their own gestures in the behavior of the agents when given a variety of post-experiment questionnaires. These findings are extremely powerful. In order to render the behaviors of an avatar effectively, one must record in high detail all of the actions of the interactants. However, by doing so, the door is opened for other interactants (as well as embodied agents) to employ many types of nonverbal chameleon strategies. In this way, all interactants, some with less than altruistic motives, may achieve a new level of advantage in interaction.

Mimicry is also possible in the auditory channel. Recently, a team at ATR Media Information Science Laboratories in Japan succeeded in doing so [39]. Their idea was to avoid the obstacles of speech recognition and semantics and instead to mimic the overall rhythm and intonation of a speaker. To see if this idea would work, participants were asked to work with an animated agent whom they were told in advance would possess the speech skills of a 1-year-old child. The participants' task was to make toy animals out of building blocks on the computer screen and to teach the agent the names of the toys being built. The agent child would then produce humming like sounds that responded in ways that mimicked the participants' speech rhythms, intonations, and loudness. In a formal study, the levels of mimicry were varied and the effect on the participants' subjective ratings of the agent were then assessed. Ratings were taken that measured cooperation, learning ability, task achievement, comfort, friendliness, and sympathy. The avatar that mimicked 80% of the time scored highest in user ratings. Just as with the studies reported above on head motions, these findings show that by isolating low-bandwidth dimensions of an interaction it is possible to create a sense of mimicry that does not require a top–down understanding of the interaction.

3.3. *Other Behavioral Transformations*

There are countless other ways to envision using TSI with the behavior of an avatar. For example, during interaction in CVEs, the automatic maintenance of a "poker face" is possible; any emotion or gesture that one believes to be particularly telling can just be filtered out, assuming one can track and categorize that gesture. Similarly, troubling habitual behaviors such as nervous tics or inappropriate giggles can be wholly eliminated from the behaviors of one's avatars. On the other hand, behaviors that are often hard to generate in certain situations, such as a "genuine smile", can be easily rendered on one's avatar with the push of a button.

4. Implications and Outlook

The Orwellian themes behind this communication paradigm and research program are quite apparent. Even the preliminary findings discussed in this chapter concerning identity capture, face-morphing, augmented gaze, and digital mimicry are cause for concern, given the huge potential for misuse of TSI by advertisers, politicians, and anyone else who may seek to influence people via computer-mediated communication. On a more basic level, not being able to trust the very pillars of the communication process—what a person looks like and how they behave—presents interactants with a difficult position. One may ask whether or not it is ethical to keep the behaviors and appearance of your avatar close enough to veridicality in order to prove your identity to other interactants, but to then pick and choose strategic venues to decouple what is virtual from what is real. Is TSI fundamentally different from nose jobs, teeth-whitening, self-help books and white lies?

The answer is unclear. Currently, digital audio streams are "sanitized" over cell phone lines such that the digital information is transformed to present an optimal voice stream using simple algorithms. While this is an extremely mild form of TSI, it is important to point out that very few users of cell phones mind or even notice this transformation. Moreover, the potential ethical concerns of TSI largely vanish if one assumes that all interactants in a CVE are aware of the potential for everyone to rampantly use these transformations.

On a more practical note, an important question to consider is whether or not interactants will bother to pay attention to each other's behavior if there is no reason to suspect those behaviors are genuine. These strategic transformations utilized in CVEs may become so rampant that the original intent of a CVE—fostering multiple communication channels between physically remote individuals—is rendered completely obsolete. People may completely ignore the nonverbal cues of avatars, given that there is no reason to suspect the cue is genuine. On the other hand, as certain cues become non-diagnostic (e.g., it becomes impossible to infer one's mental state from one's facial expression), one can make the argument that interactants will always find the subtle conversational cues that are in fact indicative of actual behavior, appearance or mental state. For example, anecdotal evidence suggests that interactants speaking on the telephone (who do not have any visual cues available) are much more sensitive to slight pauses in the conversation than face-to-face interactants.

CVE programmers may be able to create an extremely persuasive illusion using an avatar empowered with TSI, but will it be possible to mask all truth from an interaction? If there is a lesson to be learned by various forms of mediated communication, it is that people adapt quite well to new technologies. Kendon [40] describes a concept known as *interactional synchrony*, the complex dance that occurs between (1) the multiple channels (i.e., verbal and nonverbal) of a single person during an interaction, and (2) those multiple channels as two interactants respond to one another. Kendon's studies indicated that there are extremely rigid and predictable patterns that occur among these channels during interaction. However, despite this consistent complexity of behavior during conversation, humans are quite adept at maintaining an effective interaction if a channel is removed, for example speaking on the telephone.

Taking away a channel of communication is one thing, but scrambling and transforming the natural correlation among multiple channels is another level of disruption entirely. Transformed social interaction does exactly that, decoupling the normal pairing of behaviors during interaction and, at the whim of interactants, changing the rules of the conversational dance completely. One would expect conversations to completely break down given such an extreme disruption to the traditional order of conversational pragmatics. However, given the results from the empirical investigations of TSI to date, which admittedly are quite limited and preliminary, this has not been the case. Interactants do not seem particularly disturbed by any of the TSI strategies discussed in this paper, and for the most part remain completely unaware of the breakdown among conversational channels.

As future research proceeds, and researchers and systems developers tamper more and more with the structure of interaction, we will provide a true test of the endurance of this conversational structure. One can imagine an equilibrium point in which sufficient amounts of conversational synchrony is preserved, but each interactant is utilizing TSI to the fullest advantage. As systems employing avatars that use these algorithms become widespread, it is essential that this balance point between truth and transformation is achieved. Otherwise, if actions by conversational partners are ships passing in the night, the demise of CVEs and computer-mediated interactions is inevitable.

References

1. Turkle, S. (1995). *Life on the Screen: Identity in the Age of the Internet.* New York: Simon & Schuster.
2. Schroeder, R. (2002). Social interaction in virtual environments: Key issues, common themes, and a framework for research, in R. Schroeder (Ed.), *The Social Life of Avatars: Presence and Interaction in Shared Virtual Environments*, (London: Springer), pp. 1–18.
3. Blascovich, J., Loomis, J., Beall, A., Swinth, K., Hoyt, C., & Bailenson, J. (2002). Immersive virtual environment technology: Not just another research tool for social psychology. *Psychological Inquiry, 13*: 103–124.
4. Slater, A. Sadagic, M. Usoh, R., & Schroeder, R. (2000). Small group behaviour in a virtual and real environment: A comparative study. *Presence: Teleoperators and Virtual Environments, 9*(1): 37–51.
5. Normand, V., Babski, C., Benford, S., Bullock, A., Carion, S., Chrysanthou, Y., *et al.* (1999). The COVEN project: Exploring applicative, technical and usage dimensions of collaborative virtual environments. *Presence: Teleoperators and Virtual Environments, 8*(2): 218–236.
6. Yee, N., chapter in this volume.
7. Bailenson, J.N., Beall, A.C., Loomis, J., Blascovich, J., & Turk, M. (2004). Transformed social interaction: Decoupling representation from behavior and form in collaborative virtual environments. *Presence: Teleoperators and Virtual Environments, 13*(4): 428–444.
8. Davis, M.H., Conklin, L., Smith, A., & Luce, C. (1996). Effect of perspective taking on the cognitive representation of persons: A merging of self and other. *Journal of Personality and Social Psychology, 70*: 713–726.
9. Taylor, S.E. & Fiske, S.T. (1975). Point of view and perception of causality, *Journal of Personality and Social Psychology, 32*: 439–445.
10. Benford, S., Bowers, J., Fahlen, L., Greenhalgh, C., & Snowdon, D. (1995). User embodiment in collaborative virtual environments. In *Proceedings of CHI'95*, New York, ACM Press, pp. 242–249.
11. Loomis, J.M., Blascovich, J., & Beall, A.C. (1999). Immersive virtual environments as a basic research tool in psychology. *Behavior Research Methods, Instruments, and Computers, 31*(4): 557–564.
12. Biocca, F. (1997). The cyborg's dilemma: Progressive embodiment in virtual environments. *Journal of Computer-Mediated Communication Online, 3*(2). Available at http://www.ascusc.org/jcmc/vol3/issue2/-biocca2.html
13. Rheingold, H. (2000). *The Virtual Community: Homesteading on the Electronic Frontier.* Revised Edition. Cambridge: MIT Press.
14. Gibson, W. (1999). *All Tomorrow's Parties.* Ace Books.
15. Shanteau, J. & Nagy, G. (1979). Probability of acceptance in dating choice. *Journal of Personality and Social Psychology, 37*: 522–533.
16. Byrne, D. (1971). *The Attraction Paradigm.* New York: Academic Press.
17. Brock, T.C. (1965). Communicator-recipient similarity and decision change. *Journal of Personality and Social Psychology, 1*: 650–654.
18. Gaertner, S.L. & Dovidio, J.F. (1977). The subtlety of white racism, arousal and helping behavior. *Journal of Personality and Social Psychology, 35*: 691–707.

19. Bargh, J.A., Chen, M., & Burrows, L. (1996). Automaticity of social behavior: Direct effects of trait construct and stereotype priming on action. *Journal of Personality and Social Psychology, 71*: 230–244.

20. Blanz, V. & Vetter, T. (1999). A morphable model for the synthesis of 3D faces. *SIGGRAPH'99 Conference Proceedings*, pp. 187–194.

21. Busey, T.A. (1988). Physical and psychological representations of faces: Evidence from morphing. *Psychological Science, 9*: 476–483.

22. Bailenson, J.N., Garland, P., Iyengar, S., & Yee, N. (2004). The effects of morphing similarity onto the faces of political candidates. Manuscript under review.

23. Zajonc, R.B. (1971). Brainwash: Familiarity breeds comfort. *Psychology Today, 3*(9): 60–64.

24. Bailenson, J.N. & Yee, N. (2004). *Transformed Social Interaction and the Behavioral and Photographic Capture of Self.* Stanford Technical Report.

25. Petty, R.E. & Cacioppo, J.T. (1986). *The Elaboration Likelihood Model of Persuasion.* New York: Academic Press.

26. Bailenson, J.N., Beall, A.C., Blascovich, J., Raimundo, M., & Weisbuch, M. (2001). Intelligents agents who wear your face: User's reactions to the virtual self. In A. de Antonio, R. Aylett, D. Ballin (Eds.), *Lecture Notes in Artificial Intelligence*, 2190: 86–99.

27. Bailenson, J.N., Beall, A.C., Blascovich, J., & Rex, C. (2004). Examining virtual busts: Are photogrammetrically-generated head models effective for person identification? *Presence: Teleoperators and Virtual Environments, 13*(4): 416–427.

28. Guernsey, L. (2001). Software is called capable of copying any human voice. *New York Times.* July 31: Section A, Page 1, Column 1.

29. Morton, G. (1980). Effect of eye contact and distance on the verbal reinforcement of attitude. *Journal of Social Psychology, 111*: 73–78.

30. Sherwood, J.V. (1987). Facilitative effects of gaze upon learning. *Perceptual and Motor Skills, 64*: 1275–1278.

31. Otteson, J.P. & Otteson, C.R. (1979). Effect of teacher's gaze on children's story recall. *Perceptual and Motor Skills, 50*: 35–42.

32. Fry, R. & Smith, G.F. (1975). The effects of feedback and eye contact on performance of a digit-encoding task. *Journal of Social Psychology, 96*: 145–146.

33. Wellens, A.R. (1987). Heart-rate changes in response to shifts in interpersonal gaze from liked and disliked others. *Perceptual & Motor Skills, 64*: 595–598.

34. Argyle, M. (1988). *Bodily Communication.* (2nd ed.). London, UK: Methuen.

35. Garau, M., Slater, M., Bee, S., & Sasse, M.A. (2001). The impact of eye gaze on communication using humanoid avatars. *Proceedings of the SIG-CHI Conference on Human Factors in Computing Systems*, March 31–April 5, Seattle, WA, USA, pp. 309–316.

36. Beall, A.C., Bailenson, J.N., Loomis, J., Blascovich, J., & Rex, C. (2003). Non-zero-sum mutual gaze in immersive virtual environments. *Proceedings of HCI International 2003*, Crete.

37. Bailenson, J.N., Beall, A.C., Blascovich, J., Loomis, J., & Turk, M. (2004). Non-Zero-Sum Gaze and Persuasion. Paper presented in the Top Papers in Communication and Technology Session at the 54th Annual Conference of the International Communication Association, New Orleans, LA.

38. Chartrand, T.L. & Bargh, J. (1999). The chameleon effect: The perception-behavior link and social interaction. *Journal of Personality & Social Psychology, 76*(6): 893–910.

39. Suzuki, N., Takeuchi, Y., Ishii, K., & Okada, M. (2003). Effects of echoic mimicry using hummed sounds on human-computer interaction. *Speech Communication, 40*(4): 559–573.

40. Kendon, A. (1977). *Studies in the Behavior of Social Interaction.* Indiana University: Bloomington.

Chapter 2

SELECTIVE FIDELITY: INVESTIGATING PRIORITIES FOR THE CREATION OF EXPRESSIVE AVATARS

Maia Garau

Recent works of cyberfiction have depicted a not-so-distant future where the Internet has developed into a fully three-dimensional and immersive datascape simultaneously accessible by millions of networked users. This virtual world is described as having spatial properties similar to the physical world and its virtual cities are populated by digital proxies of people, called avatars. The multisensory sophistication of this shared space is such that it supports interpersonal communication on a level of richness interchangeable with face-to-face interaction. The vision presented encapsulates two of the central goals not only of collaborative virtual environments (CVEs), but also of any communication medium. First, to enable groups of people to collaborate and interact socially in an efficient and enjoyable way, and second, to foster the illusion that people are together when in reality they are in distinct physical locations.

CVEs have the makings of a potentially powerful medium of communication that heralds new promises and challenges. It is their inherently spatial property that sets them apart from other collaborative media. Though videoconferencing and groupware systems allow users to interact visually, the 3D context of each person's physical environment is lost. This can pose difficulties in small group interaction where conversation management can be disrupted by ambiguous eye gaze cues. The loss of 3D context can also be particularly problematic in tasks for which it is essential to preserve spatial relationships, such as remote acting rehearsals. CVEs can begin to address these concerns by placing geographically dispersed users in a shared, computer-generated space where they can interact with the environment and with other users represented by avatars. Immersive interfaces can also offer multimodal, surrounding experiences that can create a strong sense of being inside that artificial space (presence), and sometimes of being there with others (copresence). As mediators of users' actions and appearance, avatars are likely to play a significant role in social interaction in CVEs.

One of the central challenges in the development of CVEs is the creation of expressive avatars capable of representing users' actions and intentions in real time. This chapter focuses on the issue of avatar fidelity, arguing for the need to explore priorities by investigating the impact of avatar appearance and behaviour on the experience of interaction. It presents research on minimal fidelity, and discusses its implications for the future development of CVEs as a viable communications medium.

1.   CVEs as a Communication Medium

CVEs are networked, computer-generated environments capable of supporting human-to-human communication by allowing users to interact with the space and with each other via graphical embodiments called avatars. CVEs can be used explicitly for work-related purposes, but also for social interaction and play; applications can range from conferencing, simulation and training, shared visualisation and collaborative design, to social communities and multiplayer games. Avatars play a significant role in all of these contexts because they embody the user in a shared space, opening multiple possibilities for interaction.

Virtual environments (VEs) can be experienced non-immersively using a desktop, or immersively using a head-mounted display (HMD) or Cave (CAVE^{TM}is a trademark of the University of Illinois at Chicago, but the term "Cave" is used here to describe the generic technology as described in [1] rather than to the specific commercial product). Non-immersive desktop VEs can suffer from the same limitations in field of view as videoconferences. Immersive VEs (IVEs), however, combine stereoscopic images with head-tracking to produce a sense of being surrounded by the virtual world [2]. In IVEs, avatars representing interaction partners are experienced not as 2D images on a screen, but as life-size, 3D entities occupying a shared, surrounding mediated space (figure 2-1).

CVEs have several properties that make them suited to group interaction. They are:

- *multi-user*, supporting multiple, geographically dispersed users;
- *synchronous*, enabling people to interact with each other in real time;
- *navigable*, allowing users to freely navigate the 3D space;
- *embodied*, representing users by digital proxies called "avatars";
- *spatial*, providing a shared 3D interaction context.

It is their inherent *spatiality* that sets CVEs apart from other groupware systems such as video-mediated communication (VMC) and media spaces.

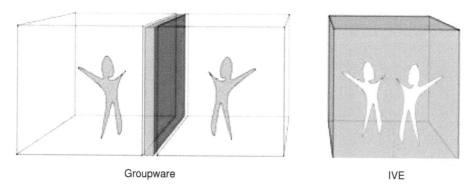

Groupware   IVE

Figure 2-1. Using groupware systems such as VMC, people remain in separate physical contexts and interact with each other via video projection. Using IVEs, people interact in a shared, computer-generated 3D context where they are represented by digital proxies called "avatars".

Though media spaces enable people to share visual information from their physical environment [3], they fail to preserve the spatial context of each user's physical environment [4]. The portrayal of space in CVEs has two practical advantages for remote collaboration: the provision of a shared interaction context for geographically dispersed users, and the portrayal of directed attention.

While it is not the aim of this chapter to compare the relative merits of video and avatar-mediated communication, three key distinctions help to highlight some potential strengths of CVEs as a medium (figure 2-2). Videoconferencing portrays participants' real appearance and actions as well as views of their real environment, and is therefore high in *fidelity*; however, it is experienced on a 2D screen and is therefore low in *spatiality* and *immersiveness*. Conversely, IVEs provide a 3D surrounding experience and are high in *spatiality* and *immersiveness*. However, they are lower in *fidelity* because they portray artificial, computer-generated scenes as opposed to real scenes captured from the physical world. In the context of group interaction, the degree of fidelity of a CVE hinges on its capacity to portray a convincing context and process for collaboration. The ambiguous relationship between an avatar and the person represented therefore poses complex challenges in terms of creating expressive embodiments that contribute meaningfully to the ongoing interaction. One key aim of CVE research is to increase fidelity with a view to bridging the gap between virtual and face-to-face interaction.

2.   The Need for Avatar Fidelity: Goals for Expressive Avatars

One of the underlying assumptions behind research in both VMC and CVEs has been that the inclusion of visual information can improve mediated

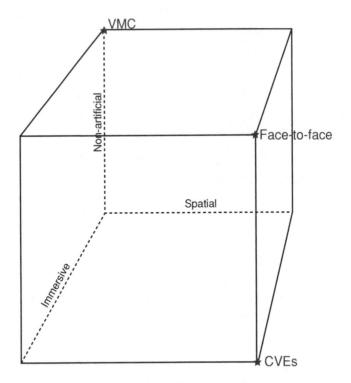

Figure 2-2. Comparison between VMC and IVEs along the dimensions of fidelity, spatiality, and immersion.

interaction by harnessing our natural ability to read meaning into the human form. Short, Williams and Christie have argued that all attempts at producing visual communications media are "primarily directed at remedying what is the most obvious defect of the simple telephone—the fact that one cannot see the other person or group" [5, p. 43]. The question that arises with the advent of CVEs is, what happens when both the environment and the people in it are not portrayals of the real world, but computer-generated representations? One significant barrier to interaction in current CVEs is in the paucity of avatar expression compared with live video of real people. One of the challenges in developing CVEs as a communications medium is therefore the creation of expressive avatars that enrich, rather than hinder, communication between remote participants.

In face-to-face interaction people rely heavily on nonverbal cues such as eye gaze, facial expression, posture, gesture and interpersonal distance to supplement the verbal content of conversation [6]. Indeed some argue that nonverbal signals not only constitute a separate channel of communication, but that they often override verbal content [7]; in other words "how" something is said can be more important than "what" is said.

Nonverbal behaviours serve at least two central functions in face-to-face interaction: conversation management and the communication of emotion. Conversation management concerns the use of paralinguistic cues to ensure the smooth flow of conversation. Movements such as eyebrow raises, head nods and posture shifts give structure and rhythm to the conversation and are essential to maintaining a sense of mutual understanding. The communication of emotion is itself integral to the regulation of communication and interaction [8, 9]. Picard explains that in addition to enriching the quality of interaction, emotion is crucial in the communication of understanding, and speakers continually monitor listeners' body language and facial expression for confirmation that they are being understood [8].

Given the central function played by nonverbal behaviours in face-to-face conversation, avatars' ability to convey such nonverbal cues is likely to affect how they are perceived as well as their contribution to social interaction. In works of cyberfiction such as Neal Stephenson's *Snow Crash* [10], avatars are both highly photorealistic and expressive. They perform seamlessly in real time, and are so reliable in conveying intended behaviour that businessmen happily substitute face-to-face meetings with interactions in the "Metaverse". In comparison, avatars in today's CVEs are extremely limited in their expressive potential.

3.   Constraints on Avatar Fidelity

There are key technical constraints and theoretical concerns affecting the degree of avatar fidelity possible in current CVEs. The first consideration, in terms of the avatar's static appearance (visual fidelity), is the tension between *realism* and *real time*. The second, in terms of its dynamic animation (behavioural fidelity), is the tension between *control* and *cognitive* load.

3.1.   The Tension between Realism and Real Time

Visual fidelity concerns not only the avatar's morphology and level of photorealism, but also the degree to which it resembles the person represented (referred to by Benford *et al.* as "truthfulness" [11]). Figure 2-3 illustrates three key dimensions of visual fidelity.

This chapter is concerned exclusively with humanoid avatars, and the issue of "truthfulness" is beyond the scope of the present discussion. For simplicity, visual fidelity will refer here to the avatar's level of photorealism. Typically, avatars used for communication purposes are relatively cartoonish. Cheng *et al.* [12] suggest that this may be partly dictated by user preference. However, restrictions related to rendering and bandwidth also mean that there is a tension

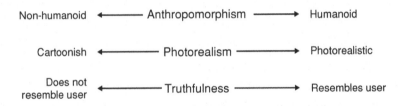

Figure 2-3. The dimensions of visual fidelity include anthropomorphism, photorealism and truthfulness.

between real-time performance and the level of realism achievable. Increased photorealism introduces computational complexity, resulting in significant and unwanted delays to real-time communication. Morningstar and Farmer cite this as a particular concern in the design of graphical chats [13]; for the same performance-related reasons, Hindmarsh *et al.* advocate using recognisable but simplistic humanoid avatars for small group communication purposes [3].

3.2.   The Tension between Control and Cognitive Load

Being computer-generated, avatars afford control not only over appearance but also over behavioural expression, thereby potentially avoiding the pitfalls of nonverbal leakage that can occur in both face-to-face and video-mediated communication. However, avatars in existing graphical chats have been widely critiqued for their insufficient and sometimes misleading behaviours [14].

Avatar behaviours can be driven in a variety of ways. Manual driving through menu selection, mouse movement, pen gesture [15] and hand gesture [16] afford control over the avatar's actions but require continuous attendance to its state. Several alternative approaches have been proposed in response to the problem of enriching avatar communication while reducing cognitive load. Cuddihy and Walters [17] suggest a solution involving high-level control through a dynamic interface that clarifies what actions are available to users at any given time. This would make it possible to direct a "waving" action at an approaching avatar rather than manually orienting the avatar and then raising its arm, as was the case in Slater *et al.*'s acting rehearsal experiment [18]. A similar high-level approach is taken by Vilhjálmsson and Cassell in the BodyChat system [19]. Here, users choose whether to be available for conversation, and their avatars automate appropriate cues such as smiles, eyebrow raises and glances to indicate a willingness to approach or depart. Analogously, Tromp and Snowdon suggest the use of automated behaviours to enhance group interaction, for instance locking gaze to the speaking avatar to denote attention [20]. However, the drawback is that automation may result in misleading behaviours.

A radically different approach involves mapping the person's real-life expression onto the avatar's. Durlach and Slater indicate two possible approaches: the use of "direct, pass-through video of the participants" [21, p. 216], or using tracking data to manipulate the avatar's 3D mesh. Body and facial tracking makes it possible to animate an avatar using motion data from a real person. Tracking equipment can, however, be expensive as well as intrusive for users. On a theoretical level, it is also questionable whether full tracking will be desirable in a medium that is prized for the control it offers users over their own embodiment.

Overall, there are significant challenges in driving appropriate behaviours for avatars. In addition to technical challenges, there remain open questions about the appropriateness of tracking or automating behaviours in the quest to reduce cognitive load without sacrificing users' control over avatar actions.

4.   Setting Priorities: The Trade-off between Visual and Behavioural Fidelity

Combined, these technical and theoretical concerns mean there is a need to make trade-offs and establish priorities for avatar fidelity. Fraser *et al.* have stated that many designers of CVEs and virtual characters operate on the premise that more realistic environments and avatars should result in qualitatively better experiences in CVEs: "virtual environments—models, avatars, interfaces and so on—are often designed with realism in mind" [22, p. 30].

The need for literal portrayals in VEs is, however, a matter of debate. As Zeltzer argues, given current technical limitations, the priority is to develop selective fidelity based on contextual needs, and further research is needed to understand how to measure selective fidelity. Similarly, Fraser *et al.* propose a shift in priorities away from literalism and realism, particularly given the crudeness of current interfaces for conveying human movement [22]. Benford *et al.* argue that improving avatar expressiveness necessarily involves compromises [23], later adding that the streamlining of avatars and the use of more "abstract" approaches to their design may be more appropriate [11]. They therefore advocate incremental, context-driven improvements to fidelity rather than an absolutist drive towards photorealism.

Several authors share the assumption that rather than attempting to maximize realism, the priority is to focus on improving behavioural fidelity for communication purposes. For instance, Sallnäs argues that in collaborative tasks realistic appearance is secondary to the support of body positioning, pointing and object manipulation [24] . Similarly, Swinth and Blascovich reason that both anthropomorphism and photorealism are separate from, and secondary to, behavioural realism, which they define as "the extent to which avatars and other objects in an virtual environment behave like their counterparts in the physical world" [25, p. 329].

The assumption that visual fidelity is secondary to behavioural fidelity is partly supported by lessons from animation. Disney animators translated films of actors' body language and facial expression into simple line drawings and discovered it was possible to achieve effective emotional portrayals in visually simplistic characters, provided the movement was convincing [26]. More recently, Katsikitis and Innes' study on line drawings of a smile illustrated that even a cartoonish representation of an expression can be decoded accurately down to its five phases of development [27].

Recent studies on the transmission of nonverbal cues in mediated communication add further support to the argument favouring behavioural fidelity. Ehrlich *et al.* [28] point out that the same bandwidth restrictions constraining CVEs also apply to VMC. They suggest that the standard approach of preserving spatial and colour resolution at the expense of temporal degradation is counterproductive. Their experimental findings indicate that preserving motion information is critical to the recognition of facial expression and may compensate for significant losses in image resolution.

Considering that the transmission of nonverbal cues can be severely affected by temporal delays and inconsistencies, they suggest that "if a bandwidth trade-off is required, one should consider preserving high-fidelity motion information at the expense of image realism, not the other way around" [28, p. 252]. In a separate study on facial affect recognition, Schiano, Ehrlich, Krisnawan, and Sheridan [29] compared a low-fidelity robot enacting the six "basic" emotions with video of human actors enacting the same emotions. Though scores for the robot were lower, the expressions were decoded in a pattern that closely followed the human faces. This further supports the argument prioritising behaviour over accurate appearance in the transmission of nonverbal cues.

Bente and Kramer [30] describe a related study on person perception, this time comparing silent video clips of dyadic interactions between human actors with equivalent clips of identically animated computer-generated agents. Their findings indicate a remarkable correspondence in responses to both conditions, despite the lower-fidelity appearance of the agents. In summary, technical limitations have forced the need to set priorities in avatar design. Findings from different media experiences partially support the notion that behavioural fidelity may be more pressing than visual fidelity for communication purposes.

5.   Exploring the Impact of Minimal Fidelity

The argument for exploring the lower boundaries of fidelity is not born exclusively out of technical necessity. Reeves and Nass [31] document a series of studies suggesting that people respond to media as social actors, and tend to anthropomorphise even the simplest of text-based interfaces. This theory of the "medium as social actor" is of direct interest to avatar design because it suggests that minimal cues can elicit social responses.

Biocca, Harms and Burgoon [32] maintain that interaction in CVEs may be built on minimal cues because the automatic interpretation of humanoid forms and nonverbal behaviour can lead people to attribute a degree of sentience to virtual humans. This tension between automatic social responses and the rational knowledge that virtual humans are artificial entities represents a fundamental and engaging issue that has been addressed in a selection of studies in different research institutions.

Studies on fear of public speaking [33,34] and spatial interaction with humanoid agents [35] support this notion that people can respond socially to virtual humans even in the absence of two-way verbal interaction, and despite knowing rationally that they are not "real". In our research we sought to explore the impact of minimal fidelity on communication experiences in CVEs, investigating one key behaviour, eye gaze, in the context of dyadic interaction.

6.   Experiments on Eye Gaze and Photorealism

One of the central problems in mediated communication is the portrayal of directed attention. The advantage of CVEs is that participants' embodiments can be seen in spatial relation to each other and to the objects they are interacting with. Unlike videoconferencing and media spaces where camera positions are fixed, participants in CVEs are free to control their point of view (POV) by navigating through the environment. As Bowers, Pycock and O'Brien point out [36], this alone allows a degree of awareness of the others' focus of attention. However, the granularity of this understanding depends largely on the fidelity of the embodiment, on its level of visual detail (photorealism) and behavioural accuracy. There are significant challenges involved in portraying accurate eye gaze in CVEs, particularly in an immersive setting where participants' faces are partially obscured by stereoscopic goggles, making tracking more problematic.

Gaze is a richly informative behaviour in face-to-face interaction. It serves at least five distinct communicative functions [37, 6]: regulating conversation flow, providing feedback, communicating emotional information and the nature of interpersonal relationships, and avoiding distraction by restricting visual input. Research on gaze in mediated communication has been concerned mainly with issues of conversation management in multiparty interaction. One of the perceived limitations of telephony-based videoconferencing systems is that they do not support selective gaze [38–40]. Various media space systems have attempted to address this limitation by distributing individual audiovisual units in physical space to represent each user (see [40] for a review).

Studies in CVEs have attempted to address the problem of how to support selective gaze in multiparty interaction within a shared 3D space. The GAZE groupware system [40] is designed to ease turntaking by conveying gaze direction in a shared virtual space using VRML2. This system uses an advanced desk-mounted eye-tracking system to measure where each person is looking. The gaze information is then represented metaphorically in the form of a 2D texture-mapped "persona" that moves about its own x- and y-axes in the 3D environment.

Taylor and Rowe [4] argue that the GAZE groupware system is problematic for two reasons. First, using a snapshot instead of video precludes any possibility of expressing other nonverbal cues through the persona. Second, the use of a plane makes it difficult to generate the kinds of profile views useful in multiparty communication. They address these limitations by rendering video of the facial region on a generic 3D model of a face. Their system animates the head movement by tracking the two earphones and microphone to obtain head position information for each user. The eye movement is contained in the video image. Their system renders avatars from an asymmetric viewpoint that corresponds to the position of the real participant, who typically sits 20 inches away from a 14-inch desktop screen. They conclude that this system improves group interaction by preserving the semantic significance of gaze. However, integrating video as a part of gaze animation fails to address the needs of users who prefer to remain visually anonymous behind a synthetic avatar.

Both of the above systems are concerned with supporting selective gaze in groups of three or more. In terms of two-person (dyadic) communication, Colburn, Cohen and Drucker [41] present findings from an experiment comparing visual attention to the screen during 20 conversations using an avatar. Participants were presented with three 3-minute visual stimuli in random order: a blank screen, a fixed-gaze avatar and an avatar with a functioning eye gaze model, based on who was speaking and whether or not the participant was looking at the screen. Participants looked at the screen more when the avatar was present and most of all when the gaze model was active. The experiments presented in the remainder of this chapter extend this research by investigating the impact of eye animations on a range of subjective responses, including perceived quality of communication and copresence.

6.1.   *Behavioural Fidelity: Exploring the Impact of Eye Gaze*

Our first 100-person experiment was designed to investigate the importance of eye gaze in humanoid avatars representing people engaged in conversation. The experiment was conducted using a video-tunnel setup and was therefore not immersive (figure 2-4); this was done deliberately to isolate gaze behaviour from any other factors, such as spatial, gestural or postural cues

Figure 2-4. Participants in the video condition speaking with each other via the video-tunnel.

that might have confounded results. In the avatar condition, participants saw a face-on head-and-shoulders view of the avatar representing their conversation partner.

We compared responses to dyadic conversation in four mediated conditions. An avatar with "random" head and eye movements was compared to a visually identical "inferred-gaze" avatar that combined simple head-tracking with "while speaking" and "while listening" eye animations inferred from the audio stream. The design of these eye animations was informed by social psychology research on the differences in gaze patterns while speaking and while listening in face-to-face interaction [37, 42, 6]. Both avatar conditions were then compared to video (with audio) and audio-only baseline conditions. The impact of each condition on the perceived quality of communication was assessed by comparing participants' subjective responses along four dimensions: how natural the conversation felt, their degree of involvement in the conversation, their sense of copresence, and positive or negative evaluation of the conversation partner.

The goal of the experiment was two-fold: firstly, to test whether an avatar with minimal behavioural fidelity could contribute to the perceived quality of communication between two remote users. The second, more specific goal was to examine the role of gaze: when the avatar's gaze was directly related to the conversation, would this improve the quality of communication compared to a visually identical avatar with random gaze?

The perception of eye gaze depends on a combination of head and eye orientation [43, 6]. In the random-gaze condition, both the head and eye movements were designed to appear natural but were in no way tied to the content or flow of conversation. For the inferred-gaze avatar, the head movements were tracked using a single Polhemus sensor attached to the headphones. The eye movements were inferred from the audio stream. One of the fundamental rules for gaze behaviour in face-to-face dyadic interaction is that people gaze at their communication partner more while listening than while speaking [44, 42, 6].

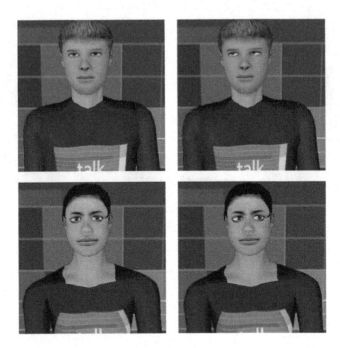

Figure 2-5. Male and female avatars looking "at" and "away".

Drawing on this principle, "while speaking" and "while listening" eye animations were implemented based on timing and frequency information taken from
face-to-face dyadic studies. Figure 2-5 shows the male and female avatars in
"at" and "away" gaze.

In order to assess the avatar's impact on perceived quality of communication, a task was needed in which participants would be sensitive to visual
feedback. It has been suggested [45, 39] that users benefit most from having
visual feedback when performing equivocal tasks that have no single "correct"
outcome but require negotiation. Short, Williams and Christie [5] argue that
tasks involving conflict and negotiation are particularly suited to testing perceptions of communications media. A role-playing negotiation task was developed
specifically for the study, requiring participants to come to a mutually acceptable agreement to avoid a family scandal breaking out in a small town. It was
also thought that the emotional content of the scenario combined with the negotiation requirements of the task would mean that results could speak both to
social and business contexts.

Participants' responses were elicited by means of the post-experiment questionnaire, each response being on a 9-point Likert scale.

The results showed that the random-gaze avatar did not provide a significant improvement over pure audio, suggesting that the simple introduction of
an avatar does not automatically improve participants' perception of communication. Rather, the avatar must have certain behaviour characteristics in order
to be useful. The inferred-gaze avatar outperformed the random-gaze avatar

and the audio-only condition on several response measures. This suggests that an avatar whose behaviours reflect an aspect of conversational flow can indeed make a contribution to improving remote communication. Finally, the inferred-gaze avatar significantly outperformed the random-gaze avatar on all measures, indicating that an avatar whose behaviours are related to the conversation can present a marked improvement over an avatar that merely exhibits liveliness.

These findings had encouraging implications for inexpensive approaches to improving avatar fidelity. However, a central question remained unanswered. In the inferred-gaze condition, the avatar's gaze behaviour was being driven by two separate channels of information: its eye movement was based on inference from the audio stream, while its head movement was based on tracking the participant's real head movement. The open question was whether the significant impact on participants' perceptions was due to tracked motion data or from inferences about the eye movement based on research from face-to-face interaction. Answering this question would have significant implications for providing inexpensive ways to improve eye gaze based on information readily available from the audio stream.

Moreover, the experiment was conducted in a non-immersive setting. The question remained of how the inferred-gaze model would perform in a more demanding immersive setting, where participants were free to wander about a shared 3D space. A second experiment was therefore designed to address these concerns.

Between the publication of results from the first eye gaze experiment [46] and the second experiment [47], Lee, Badler and Badler published a similar study comparing subjective responses to a humanoid agent with static, random and inferred gaze [48]. Their agents' inferred-gaze animations were consistent with the timings from the face-to-face literature detailed above, but were refined using a statistical model developed from their own gaze tracking analysis of real people engaged in dyadic interaction. Their results from a 12-person evaluation are consistent with those from our first study, in that the inferred-gaze model results in more positive perceptions. The inferred-gaze agent significantly outperforms the visually identical random-gaze agent in terms of perceived interest, engagement, friendliness, and liveliness. However, it is not clear whether participants were engaged in two-way verbal communication with the agent, or whether they simply viewed the animations on a screen.

In terms of eye gaze and photorealism, two studies by Fukayama *et al.* are also directly relevant [50]. The first is a 13-person study concerning the impact of eye animations on the impressions participants formed of an interface agent [50]. Their gaze model consists of three parameters: amount of gaze, mean duration of gaze and gaze points while averted. Their comparative analysis of responses to nine different gaze patterns suggests that agent gaze can reliably influence impression formation. For this particular study they isolated the agent's eyes from any other facial geometry. In a related study, they investigate whether the impact of the gaze patterns is affected by the photorealism of the agent's face [49]. Their findings suggest that varying the appearance from visually simplistic to more realistic has no effect on the impressions produced. The interaction is one-way, with participants viewing a pre-recorded agent animation. It is therefore difficult to know whether the findings would generalise to a sustained verbal interaction.

6.2.   *Visual and Behavioural Fidelity: Exploring the Impact of Eye Gaze and Photorealism*

One aspect of the studies described above was that participants were shown a limited, head-and-shoulders view of the virtual human, and that the spatial relationship was fixed by the 2D nature of the interaction. They therefore left open the question of how these gaze models might hold up in an immersive situation where participants are able to wander freely around a shared space, and where they can interact with a full-body, life-size avatar. Our follow-up experiment was designed with these questions in mind.

The goal for this second experiment was threefold. Firstly, to disambiguate between the effect of inferred eye movements and head-tracking, both of which may have contributed to the results reported in the first study. Secondly, to test how the inferred-gaze model performs in a less forgiving immersive setting where participants were free navigate in the 3D IVE. Finally, to explore the relative impact of two logically distinct aspects of avatar fidelity: appearance and behaviour.

As previously discussed, one assumption made by several researchers is that convincing behaviour is a higher priority than realistic appearance in the development of expressive avatars. We wished to test this assumption by investigating the impact of the (higher-fidelity) inferred-gaze model with the (lower-fidelity) random-gaze model on avatars whose appearance represented different levels of photorealism. The initial hypothesis was that behavioural realism would be independent in its effects on perceived quality of communication from the impact of visual realism, and that it would be of greater importance. The inferred-gaze model was expected to outperform the random-gaze one for both the higher-realism and lower-realism avatar. One open question concerned the extent to which the gaze animations would impact on the lower-realism avatars, or how the two avatars would perform in comparison with each other.

Participants were represented to their conversation partner as a life-size avatar, as illustrated in figure 2-6. Both participants in each pair were represented by a visually identical avatar to avoid differences in facial geometry affecting the impact of the animations.

Since one of the central aims of this experiment was to disambiguate the impact of head-tracking and the inferred eye animations, participants' heads were tracked in all conditions, and only the eye animations were varied. The

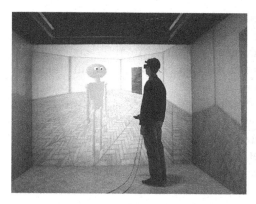

Figure 2-6. Participants saw their conversation partner as a life-size avatar. The avatar was either lower realism (left) or higher realism (right).

random-gaze eye animations were identical to the first eye gaze experiment, but the inferred-gaze animations were refined based on newly published information [48].

Our previous four indicators of perceived communication quality of communication were considered in the analysis, along with a number of additional responses including:

- *Gaze fidelity*: The sense of mutual gaze with the conversation partner;
- *Avatar fidelity*: The degree to which the avatar's appearance and behaviour were seen to be realistic;
- *Social-copresence*: Consisting of the following subcomponents:
- *General copresence*: The sense of being "in the company of" another person;
- *Spatial copresence*: The sense of being in the same space as the conversation partner;
- *Personal contact*: The degree of personal contact experienced with the partner.

Again, participants' subjective responses were elicited by means of a postexperience questionnaire. Our analysis revealed a very strong interaction effect between the *type of avatar* and the *type of gaze*. In other words, the impact of the gaze model is different depending on which type of avatar is used. For the higher-realism avatar the (more realistic) inferred-gaze behaviour *increases* perceived effectiveness for several response measures. For the lower-realism avatar, the (more realistic) inferred-gaze behaviour *reduces* effectiveness. This seems to indicate a need for consistency between the visual appearance of the avatar and the type of behaviour that it exhibits. With respect to eye gaze, low-fidelity appearance demands low-fidelity behaviour, and correspondingly higher-fidelity appearance demands a more realistic behaviour model.

The findings clear up the ambiguity from the first experiment regarding whether the significant differences in performance between the gaze models were due to head-tracking or eye animations inferred from the audio stream. They indicate that independent of head-tracking, inferred eye animations can have a significant positive effect on participants' responses to an immersive interaction. The caveat is that there should be some consistency between visual and behavioural realism, since the lower-realism avatar did not appear to benefit from the higher-realism, inferred-gaze model. This finding has implications for inexpensive ways of improving avatar expressiveness using information from the audio stream and suggests avenues for interim solutions for the difficult problem of providing robust eyetracking in Cave-like systems.

Findings from an in-depth qualitative analysis of the interviews from the first eye gaze study indicate that avatar fidelity does not work in isolation in shaping interaction experiences. Both communication context and personal character-istics such as everyday social anxiety, prior media experiences, and technical expertise shape perceptions of the avatar's role in interaction. The quantita-tive findings suggest that simply adding "liveliness" to the avatar's behavioural repertoire does not add value to the interaction. They further suggest that users would benefit from information about how "truthful" the animations are, be-cause in the absence of priming, people are likely to interpret the significance of the avatar's behaviour according to their own technical assumptions about how it is driven. These assumptions are sometimes illogical and uninformed, and may work to the detriment of the avatar by leading users to discard as in-significant even those selected behaviours that are in fact informative. Overall this analysis signals the importance of educating users about the behavioural capabilities of the avatar.

Interviews with participants indicated that it is possible to rationally think of avatars as computer-generated and therefore not "real", while simultaneously exhibiting social responses towards them. This is consistent with Reeves and Nass' [31] theory of the medium as social actor that predicts people will tend to anthropomorphise media and treat them as social entities. This finding also supports Blascovich and colleagues' hypothesis that there are at least two levels of response to virtual humans: higher-level rational responses, and lower-level involuntary responses [51]. This opens avenues for future research on the com-plex multi-level responses of people to virtual humans in the context of small group communication in CVEs.

7.   Conclusions and Future Work

One key barrier to effective communication in current CVEs is the relative paucity of avatar expressiveness as compared to live video. Increasing the ex-pressive potential of avatars involves significant challenges. In terms of their appearance, the tension between realism and real time means that photorealism comes at the expense of unwanted delays to real-time communication. Visual fidelity must therefore be traded-off against available computing resources. In terms of behaviour, the tension between control and cognitive load under-lines the difficulty of transparently driving avatar behaviours that appropriately represent the user. Full manual control of avatar behaviour would entail an unacceptable level of cognitive load. On the other hand, full tracking can be expensive and invasive, and may not be desirable in a medium that is prized for the control it affords over visual identity.

Given these constraints, the approach taken in our research was to explore the lower boundaries of avatar fidelity. The overarching goal was to investigate whether minimal increments in fidelity could contribute to participants' inter-action experience in CVEs. Fidelity was considered in terms of both dynamic behaviour (behavioural fidelity) and static appearance (visual fidelity).

The findings from the first experiment on eye gaze indicate that an avatar with minimal fidelity can make a positive contribution to interaction. However, simply adding "liveliness" to its behavioural repertoire does not add value to the interaction. In the case of gaze, the avatar's animation should reflect some aspect of the ongoing conversation, even something as simple as turntaking. Concerning the relationship between visual and behavioural fidelity, we dis-covered a significant and overwhelmingly consistent interaction effect between visual and behavioural realism. The findings from the experiment on eye gaze and photorealism indicate that the effect of identical eye animations changes in relation to the avatar's appearance. The higher-realism avatar benefited from the higher-fidelity inferred-gaze animations, whereas the opposite was true for the lower-realism avatar. This suggests the need to align behavioural fidelity with avatar appearance. The conclusion is that the impact of behaviour is not independent of appearance and points to a more complex picture than was pre-viously envisaged. Simply privileging behavioural over visual fidelity may not necessarily lead to optimal improvements for expressive avatars.

Bowers, Pycock and O'Brien suggest that "a viable and systematic research strategy for developing useful CVEs is to incrementally add further sophistica-tion to very simple embodiments *as and when* analysis reveals that it is called for in the support of social interaction" [36, p. 65]. Varying individual dimen-sions allows researchers to explore their individual impact on the perceptual and social impact of avatars. This is a logical approach given the need to priori-tise which aspects of fidelity might be traded-off against available computing resources.

Our experiments attempted to focus on the impact of a single nonverbal be-haviour. We chose eye gaze because of its central function both in conversation management and in the directed expression of emotion. The isolation of a sin-gle behaviour is potentially problematic, however, because it compromises the "gestalt" of nonverbal expression that characterises face-to-face interaction.

Short, Williams and Christie point out the danger of treating behaviours individually: "In attempting to assess the functions of the visual channel, it is dangerous to confine attention at any one time to individual cues such as posture, eye-gaze, proximity and the like. The channels do interact.... Studies of media must look at relevant combinations of channels. Important overall properties of communication may be missed if attention is restricted to individual channels" [5, p. 7–8]. Additional behaviours should therefore be investigated in conjunction with gaze and with each other, with a view to exploring their interdependencies.

Our research focused on participants' subjective responses to their interaction experience. Although interviews and in-depth qualitative analysis go a step further than questionnaires in understanding users' perceptions, they necessarily only capture the rational level of experience. The findings reported here indicate that it is important to further explore both higher-level and lower-level social responses to virtual humans. Previous research has indicated that minimal fidelity can affect lower-level involuntary responses such as spatial behaviour in response to an agent [35]. Potentially fruitful avenues for research include the observation of involuntary behaviours, as well as the use of psychophysiological measures to study objective responses. Future work will build on these findings by combining subjective and objective approaches to understand how avatars can be further improved for richer multiparty interaction in CVEs.

There are numerous application areas for VEs, from simulation to training to the treatment of phobias. At present, CVEs are primarily used for research and entertainment purposes and have yet to come into mainstream use as a communication medium. They have the potential to extend beyond their present usage to address the practical collaborative needs of geographically dispersed users. One of their chief attractions lies in their ability to combine 3D spatial interaction with a high degree of multisensory immersion. In *Simulacra and Simulation* [52], Baudrillard argues that science fiction is nothing more than an exaggeration of the possibilities inherent in present circumstances. If recent films such as the Matrix [53] and works of cyberpunk literature [10] are anything to go by, then we face a future where communication in CVEs will become part of the fabric of our everyday lives. Avatars, the visual representations of people in CVEs, therefore deserve careful consideration as they will play a pivotal role in enriching the communicative possibilities of this medium.

It is possible to imagine a day when avatars will, like those in the novel *Snow Crash* [10], communicate users' intentions so reliably that people will willingly use CVEs for social interaction and for serious collaborative purposes. In 1998 Allbeck and Badler argued that every aspect of avatar design, motion and appearance described in Snow Crash had already begun to be tackled by different research groups throughout the world [54]. It is encouraging to think that all of these various branches of research may converge to create truly compelling communicative avatars.

Avatars are computer-generated and therefore, unlike video, free us from the need to present a faithful visual replica of real places or real people. Like masks, they preserve our visual anonymity and open up the possibility for new and potentially different forms of interaction. Existing technical limitations have meant that it is not currently possible to model human appearance and behaviour in all its complexity for real-time interaction. This has dictated a need to explore minimal and selective fidelity with a view to gradually increasing the expressive potential of avatars.

The ability of humans to decode caricature and cartoons indicates that we do not require exhaustive photorealistic depictions to decipher the human form. The research and ideas discussed in this chapter have rested on the assumption that our common goal is to enhance avatar animation to harness our natural ability to decode nonverbal behaviours. It is conceivable, however, that a move away from photorealism might be accompanied by a parallel move away from behavioural literalism. Just as the lack of sound in silent films made actors instinctively "turn up the volume" on their visual performances, perhaps current constraints will lead to ways of "emoting" through avatars that do not precisely mirror everyday nonverbal communication. Freed from the need to mimic the real world, avatars can distort, change colour and morph into new forms to express emotional states in non-literal ways. As the medium matures it will be interesting to see how current constraints will give rise to creative emergent solutions, and how people will choose to use their avatars to express themselves in new and possibly more magical ways.

Acknowledgements

My warmest thanks to my advisors Mel Slater, Angela Sasse and Simon Bee for their precious guidance over the past few years. Special thanks to my collaborators at University College London (UCL) for making the research possible: David-Paul Pertaub, Anthony Steed, Andrea Brogni, Vinoba Vinayagamoorthy, Pip Bull and David Swapp. I am also very grateful to Tim Child, Sanja Abbott and Marcus Tutt for giving me use of their Televirtual avatars for the first study on eye gaze, and to the people at BT Exact who helped in so many ways with the study: Dickon Povey, Alex Bourret, Michelle and Jim Tasker, Paul Bowman, Tim Stevens, Mike Hollier, Dan Ballin and Dan Argent.

References

1. Cruz-Neira, C., Sandin, D.J., & DeFanti, T.A. (1993). Surround-screen projection-based virtual reality: The design and implementation of the CAVE. In *Proceedings of the 20th Annual Conference on Computer Graphics and Interactive Techniques*. Anaheim, CA: ACM Press, pp. 135–142.

2. Barfield, W. & Weghorst, S. (1993). The sense of presence within virtual environments: A conceptual framework. In G. Salvendy & M. Smith (Eds.), *Human Computer Interaction: Software and Hardware Interfaces.* Amsterdam: Elsevier, pp. 699–704.

3. Hindmarsh, J., Fraser, M., Heath, C., Benford, S., & Greenhalgh, C. (1998). Fragmented interaction: Establishing mutual orientation in virtual environments. In *Proceedings of the ACM Conference on Computer Supported Cooperative Work.* Seattle, WA: ACM Press, pp. 217–226.

4. Taylor, M.J. & Rowe, S.R. (2000). Gaze communication using semantically consistent spaces. In *Proceedings of the SIGCHI Conference on Human Factors in Computing Systems.* The Hague, The Netherlands: ACM Press, pp. 400–407.

5. Short, J., Williams, E., & Christie, B. (1976). *The Social Psychology of Telecommunications.* London: John Wiley & Sons.

6. Argyle, M. & Cook, M. (1976). *Gaze and Mutual Gaze.* Cambridge: Cambridge University Press.

7. Forgas, J.P. (1985). *Interpersonal Behaviour: The Psychology of Interpersonal Interaction.* Oxford: Pergamon Press.

8. Picard, R. (1997). *Affective Computing.* Cambridge, MA: MIT Press.

9. Goleman, D. (1996). *Emotional Intelligence.* London: Bloomsbury Publishing Plc.

10. Stephenson, N. (1992). *Snow Crash.* London: ROC.

11. Benford, S., Bowers, J., Fahlén, L.E., Greenhalgh, C., & Snowdon, D. (1995). User embodiment in collaborative virtual environments. In *Proceedings of the SIGCHI Conference on Human Factors in Computing Systems.* Denver, CO: ACM Press, pp. 242–249.

12. Cheng, L., Farnham, S., & Stone, L. (2002). Lessons learned: Building and deploying shared virtual environments. In R. Schroeder (Ed.), *The Social Life of Avatars: Presence and Interaction in Shared Virtual Environments.* London: Springer, pp. 90–111.

13. Morningstar, C. & Farmer, R. (1990). The lessons of Lucasfilm's Habitat. In M. Benedikt (Ed.), *Cyberspace: First Steps.* Cambridge, MA: MIT Press, pp. 273–302.

14. Vilhjálmsson, H. & Cassell, J. (1999). Fully embodied conversational avatars: Making communicative behaviours autonomous. *Autonomous Agents and Multi-agent Systems, 2*: 45–64.

15. Barrientos, F. & Canny, J.F. (2002). Cursive: Controlling expressive avatar gesture using pen gesture. In *CVE '02: Proceedings of the 4th International Conference on Collaborative Virtual Environments.* Bonn, Germany: ACM Press, pp. 113–119.

16. Lee, C., Ghyme, S., Park, C., & Wohn, K. (1998). The control of avatar motion using hand gesture. In *Proceedings of the ACM Symposium on Virtual Reality Software and Technology.* Taipei, Taiwan: ACM Press, pp. 59–65.

17. Cuddihy, E. & Walters, D. (2000). Embodied interaction in social virtual environments. In *Proceedings of the Third International Conference on Collaborative Virtual Environments.* San Francisco, CA: ACM Press, pp. 181–188.

18. Slater, M., Howell, J., Steed, A., Pertaub, D-P., Garau, M., & Springel, S. (2000). Acting in virtual reality. In *Proceedings of the Third International Conference on Collaborative Virtual Environments.* San Francisco, CA: ACM Press, pp. 103–110.

19. Vilhjálmsson, H. & Cassell, J. (1998). Bodychat: Autonomous communicative behaviors in avatars. In *Proceedings of the 2nd Annual ACM International Conference on Autonomous Agents.* Minneapolis, MN: ACM Press, pp. 269–276.

20. Tromp, J. & Snowdon, D. (1997). Virtual body language: Providing appropriate user interfaces in collaborative virtual environments. In *Proceedings of the ACM Symposium on Virtual Reality Software and Technology (VRST).* Lausanne, Switzerland: ACM Press, pp. 37–44.

21. Durlach, N. & Slater, M. (2000). Presence in shared virtual environments and virtual togetherness. *Presence: Teleoperators and Virtual Environments, 9*(2): 214–217.

22. Fraser, M., Glover, I., Vaghi, I., Benford, S., Greenhalgh, C., Hindmarsh, J., & Heath, C. (2000). Revealing the realities of collaborative virtual reality. In *Proceedings of the Third International Conference on Collaborative Virtual Environments*. San Francisco, CA: ACM Press, pp. 29–37.

23. Benford, S., Bowers, J., Fahlén, L.E., Mariani, J., & Rodden, T. (1994). Supporting cooperative work in virtual environments. *The Computer Journal, 37*(8): 653–668.

24. Sallnäs, E.L. (2002). Collaboration in multi-modal virtual worlds: Comparing touch, text, voice and video. In R. Schroeder (Ed.). *The Social Life of Avatars: Presence and Interaction in Shared Virtual Environments*. London: Springer, pp. 172–187.

25. Swinth, K. & Blascovich, J. (2002). Perceiving and responding to others: Human-human and human-computer social interaction in collaborative virtual environments. In *Fifth Annual International Workshop on Presence*. Porto, Portugal: ACM Press, pp. 310–340.

26. Thomas, F. & Johnston, O. (1981). *Disney Animation: The Illusion of Life*. New York: Abberville Press Publishers.

27. Katsikitis, M. & Innes, J.M. (1997). Encoding and decoding of facial expression. *The Journal of General Psychology, 124*(4): 357–370.

28. Ehrlich, S.M., Schiano, D., & Sheridan, K. (2000). Communicating facial affect: It's not the realism, it's the motion. In *Proceedings of the ACM Conference on Human Factors in Computing Systems*. The Hague, The Netherlands: ACM Press, pp. 251–252.

29. Schiano, D., Ehrlich, S.M., Krisnawan, R., & Sheridan, K. (2000). Face to interface: Facial affect in (hu)man and machine. In *Proceedings of the ACM Conference on Human Factors in Computing Systems*. The Hague, The Netherlands: ACM Press, pp. 193–200.

30. Bente, G. & Kramer, N. (2002). Virtual gestures: Analysing social presence effects of computer-mediated and computer-generated nonverbal behaviour. In *Fifth Annual International Workshop on Presence*. Porto, Portugal: ACM Press, pp. 233–244.

31. Reeves, B. & Nass, C. (1996). *The Media Equation: How People Treat Computers, Television and New Media Like Real People and Places*. Cambridge: Cambridge University Press.

32. Biocca, F., Harms, C., & Burgoon, J.K. Criteria for a theory and measure of social presence. (Submitted). *Presence: Teleoperators and Virtual Environments*. Available at: http://www.mindlab.org/networkedminds/

33. Pertaub, D-P., Slater, M., & Barker, C. (2001a). An experiment on fear of public speaking anxiety in response to three different types of virtual audience. *Presence: Teleoperators and Virtual Environments, 11*(1): 68–78.

34. Pertaub, D-P., Slater, M., & Barker, C. (2001b). An experiment on fear of public speaking in virtual reality. In D. Stredney, J.D. Westwood, G.T. Mogel and H.M. Hoffman (Eds.), *Medicine Meets Virtual Reality 2001: Outer Space, Inner Space, Virtual Space*. Newport Beach, CA: IOS Press, pp. 372–378.

35. Bailenson, J.N., Blascovich, J., Beall, A.C., & Loomis, J.M. (2001). Equilibrium theory revisited: Mutual gaze and personal space in virtual environments. *Presence: Teleoperators and Virtual Environments, 10*(6): 583–598.

36. Bowers, J., Pycock, J., & O'Brien, J. (1996). Talk and embodiment in collaborative virtual environments. In *Proceedings of the SIGCHI Conference on Human Factors in Computing Systems*, Vancouver, Canada: ACM Press, pp. 58–65.

37. Kendon, A. (1967). Some functions of gaze-direction in social interaction. *Acta Psychologica, 26*: 22–63.

38. Buxton, W. (1992). Telepresence: Integrating shared task and person spaces. In *Proceedings of the Conference on Graphics Interface*. Vancouver, Canada: ACM Press, pp. 123–129.

39. Sellen, A. (1995). Remote conversations: The effect of mediating talk with technology. *Human-Computer Interaction, 10*(4): 401–444.

40. Vertegaal, R. (1999). The GAZE groupware system: Mediating joint attention in multiparty communication and collaboration. In *Proceedings of the SIGCHI Conference on Human Factors in Computing Systems.* Pittsburgh, PA: ACM Press, pp. 294–301.

41. Colburn, A., Cohen, M., & Drucker, S. (2000). The role of eye gaze in avatar-mediated conversational interfaces. Technical Report MSR-TR-2000-81, Microsoft Research.

42. Argyle, M. & Ingham, R. (1972). Mutual gaze and proximity. *Semiotica, 6:* 32–49.

43. Gibson, J.J. & Pick, A. (1963). The perception of another person's looking behaviour. *American Journal of Psychology, 46:* 386–394.

44. Argyle, M., Ingham, R., Alkema, F., & McCallin, M. (1973). The different functions of gaze. *Semiotica, 7:* 10–32.

45. Straus, S. & McGrath, J.E. (1994). Does the medium matter? The interaction of task and technology on group performance and member reactions. *Journal of Applied Psychology, 79:* 87–97.

46. Garau, M., Slater, M., Bee, S., & Sasse, A. (2001). The impact of eye gaze on communication using humanoid avatars. In *Proceedings of the SIGCHI Conference on Human Factors in Computing Systems,* Seattle, WA: ACM Press, pp. 309–316.

47. Garau, M., Slater, M., Vinayagamoorthy, V., Brogni, A., Steed, A., & Sasse, A. (2003). The impact of avatar realism and eye gaze control on perceived quality of communication in a shared immersive virtual environment. In *Proceedings of the SIGCHI Conference on Human Factors in Computing Systems.* Ft. Lauderdale, FL: ACM Press, pp. 529–536.

48. Lee, S.H., Badler, J.B., & Badler, N.I. (2002). Eyes alive. In *Proceedings of the 29th Annual Conference on Computer Graphics and Interactive Techniques.* San Antonio, TX: ACM Press, pp. 637–644.

49. Fukayama, A., Sawaki, M., Ohno, T., Murase, H., Hagita, N., & Mukawa, N. (2001). Expressing personality of interface agents by gaze. In *Proceedings of INTERACT Conference on Human-Computer Interaction.* Tokyo, Japan: IOS Press, pp. 793–794.

50. Fukayama, A., Takehiko, O., Mukawa, N., Sawaki, M., & Hagita, N. (2002). Messages embedded in gaze of interface agents: Impression management with agent's gaze. In *Proceedings of the SIGCHI Conference on Human Factors in Computing Systems.* Minneapolis, MN: ACM Press, pp. 41–48.

51. Blascovich, J. (2002). Social influence within immersive virtual environments. In R. Schroeder (Ed.), *The Social Life of Avatars: Presence and Interaction in Shared Virtual Environments.* London: Springer, pp. 127–145.

52. Baudrillard, J. (1994). *Simulacra and Simulation.* (Translated by S.F. Glaser *Simulacres et Simulation.* English). Ann Arbor: University of Michigan Press.

53. The Matrix. 16 mm, 136 min. Burbank: Warner Bros., 1999.

54. Allbeck, N. & Badler, N. (1998). Avatars à la Snow Crash. In *Proceedings of Computer Animation.* Philadelphia, PA: IEEE Computer Society, pp. 19–24.

Chapter 3

ANALYSIS AND VISUALIZATION
OF SOCIAL DIFFUSION PATTERNS IN
THREE-DIMENSIONAL VIRTUAL WORLDS

Shashikant Penumarthy and Katy Börner

1.   Introduction

In order to indicate how difficult it is to orient oneself and navigate in virtual worlds, let us begin with an example—the story of John. Just having finished an hour of e-mail, John looks at his watch and realizes that it is time to switch identities. A few mouse clicks, the brief appearance of a splash screen and faster than one can say "Avatar!", the monitor screen fills up and one world is replaced by another.

Exit John, enter PringleCrow. As LinkWorld (one of several three-dimensional virtual worlds that John has access to) fades into view, PringleCrow waits to orient herself (today John has chosen a female avatar). She waits for her world to manifest itself, one object at a time. The network isn't very fast and PringleCrow is suddenly "lost", the connection to her life-force severed, as John's consciousness comes back to the real world wondering why the graphics are so jerky. Back again to PringleCrow, the life-force restored! This time, though, enough of the world has loaded ensuring that PringleCrow won't be lost again soon. An extension of consciousness takes over, as the human and his avatar are unified. Today, PringleCrow is going to be part of a treasure hunt that is designed to test how well the inhabitants of the virtual world under-stand the principles of physics. When she teleports to the meeting point for the participants, she realizes that the other avatars are already there, the chatter almost "deafening". She spots a chat utterance by CyberDog, her team-mate for the treasure hunt, who has been waiting for PringleCrow for a few minutes. A few more chat utterances later ("I am a blue puppy", "Let's meet near the waterfall", "It's at coordinates 10 west 56 north I think"), they finally meet. At this point neither avatar is aware of where the rest of the avatars are or even how many of them are in the world. They walk together to the podium where the avatar StrazyFoure, who is the moderator for the hunt, is reviewing the rules. After the rules are done, StrazyFoure raises his hand to signal the start of the treasure hunt and PringleCrow and CyberDog begin looking for clues. They are careful to communicate through "whispers", rather than chat to ensure that everything they say is "inaudible" to the avatars from competing teams.

At the end of the day, StrazyFoure goes to each team to find out what they think about the hunt and is a little concerned to discover that not everyone has succeeded to find all answers. While some found the clues very difficult to decipher, others complain that they sometimes could not figure out if they were going the right way. The virtual world is so big that some lost sense of how far they had come from the starting point.

At what point did the unsuccessful avatars get lost? Which clues were easy and which ones were difficult? Did the avatars interpret the clues correctly? What did the avatars talk about during the whole period? Could some of the clues have been placed in locations that were easier to access? These are just a few of the interesting questions that could be asked in order to determine how successful the treasure hunt was and how to support information foraging in 3D virtual worlds.

The avatars of the virtual world as well as researchers that study them need to be able to quickly obtain a broad overview of activities in the virtual world, as well as examine local details. Researchers must also be able to discover patterns of behavior, of movement, chat and interaction on a local and global scale. Some questions are short term such as "What paths did the avatars take?" or "Which avatars' movement trails deviated most from the average of the entire group?" Other questions are: "Which areas of the world are most used?", "What topics are the inhabitants talking about and where?", or "Who talked/interacted with whom?"

In this chapter we describe how advanced data mining and information visualization techniques [1–4] can be advantageously applied to augment, evaluate, optimize, and study collaborative 3D virtual worlds and to study their evolving communities [5]. We begin by discussing related work in the area of analysis and visualization of spatial and social data. After briefly commenting on the nature of virtual world data, we outline types of user groups and their tasks in virtual worlds. The use of patterns for analysis of virtual world behavior is detailed. We then show how techniques developed in areas as diverse as data analysis [6, 7] and information visualization can be combined to create simple yet powerful means for answering some of the questions posed above. A toolkit [8] for the analysis and visualization of social diffusion patterns in virtual worlds is presented. The chapter concludes with directions for future research in analysis and visualization in virtual worlds.

2. Related Work

Several highly diverse research areas have developed theories, techniques and systems for analysis and visualization of data possessing a distinct spatial component. The well-developed area of scientific visualization deals with applying computer graphics to scientific data "for purposes of gaining insight, testing hypothesis, and general elucidation" [9]. Scientific data usually takes the form of measured values obtained from a system or a phenomenon, in addition to three-dimensional coordinates associated with each measurement. Scientific visualization typically consists of data that can be accurately represented using three-dimensional geometry and is being used in such diverse areas as designing aircraft and constructing complete three-dimensional views of the human anatomy [10].

Another mature field that makes extensive use of visualization of spatial patterns is geography. Today's Geographic Information Systems (GIS) contain a large number of spatial analysis methods that enable one to analyze, model and query spatial data. Cartographers, in particular, have developed a number of techniques to visualize spatio-temporal diffusion patterns. Pioneering work by Dorigo and Tobler [11] represents and visualizes diffusion potentials and gradients as vector fields computed using a continuous spatial gravity model. By overlaying population density information over a geographic map, they have shown that New York, being densely populated, exhibits the highest outward pressure, i.e., it acts as a source, while Florida has the highest inward pressure, i.e., it acts as a sink.

The work that relates most closely to ours comes from the area of social visualization. Social visualizations are a special type of information visualization that focus on analysis of social behavior. For example, lifeline visualizations reveal migrations, transitions and trajectories of users or user groups [12]. Other research aims at the visualization of large-scale conversations, such as those that take place on the Usenet [13] or visualization of access patterns of users on the Web [14]. There also exists work on visualizing and supporting social interactions in text-based or 2D graphical systems. For example, Chat Circles [15] is a 2D graphical interface for synchronous conversation that visualizes the non-textual components of online chatting, such as pauses and turn-taking behavior, which are typically not available in chat log files. Another piece of work analyzes gestures and movement of users in VChat, a graphical chat system [16], in which a comparison is made between average distance and orientation of users in relation to users targeted in their chat and randomly selected users. Naper [17] was among the first to analyze chat text logged in a 3D virtual worlds and called for the use of visual semiotics for the analysis of computer mediated communication.

A very interesting body of work that analyzes social patterns exists in the area of urban studies. Whyte [18] determined the influence of steps, fountains, green spaces, sitting places, building arrangement, etc. on the crowd flow and social interaction in New York plaza. The company Space Syntax Limited (http://www.spacesyntax.com/) undertakes projects that aim to quantify the degree to which urban planning influences socio-economic factors such as pedestrian flow, crime patterns and land value. Results augment strategic design as well as the selection of design alternatives that best serve the needs of a particular segment of population.

Work on mapping MUDs and 3D virtual worlds is a relatively new area. The section on MUDs and Virtual Worlds in Dodge's and Kitchin's "Atlas of Cyberspaces" [19] provides a beautifully illustrated overview of this area. The well-known AlphaWorld Mapper (http://mapper.activeworlds.com/aw/) by Greg Roelofs and Pieter van der Meulen provides access to an impressive zoomable 2D map of a virtual world that is roughly the size of the state of California (429,025 km^2) [20]. However, the scale of hardware and other resources required to generate such a map is beyond the reach of most virtual world researchers. Until recently, it was not possible for researchers and users of virtual worlds to create a map of a virtual world or to analyze and visualize user interaction data collected in virtual worlds. The toolkit described in this chapter allows researchers to do this on a regular basis and in a consistent manner. The results have been shown to provide new insights about the evolution and usage of virtual worlds and the activities of their users [8, 21, 22].

3.   Data in Virtual Worlds

It has been estimated that 80% of all data that exists in our world today has a spatial component [23]. This suggests that using spatial analysis and visualization techniques is essential in order to gain a fuller understanding of social patterns in real as well as virtual spaces. However, in the real world, collecting information about pedestrian flow, traffic or building utilization is difficult and often requires invasive and expensive methods such as the placement of sensors or cameras at various locations. The task of data collection is greatly simplified in virtual environments due to the ease with which user behavior can be recorded in a manner that does not interfere with the activities of inhabitants of the virtual world. The monitoring methods used in virtual worlds also have the inherent advantage that they result in data that is clean and consistent across time and space. The data therefore readily lends itself to analysis using data mining methods. In particular, the ActiveWorlds SDK (http://www.activeworlds.com/sdk/) offers ways to collect information such as movement, orientation, chat text, interactions such as clicks and even gestures using programmed software agents known as "bots". Information on the structure of virtual worlds is obtained using what are known as "propdump" and "registry" files, which respectively describe relative and absolute geometry of objects in the virtual world. The availability of such rich data eases the study of the interplay among space and social behavior. However, before one can begin addressing these questions, one must first identify the subjects of such a study, i.e., the user groups and the tasks that they perform within or related to the environment under consideration. This is the focus of the next section.

4. User Groups and Tasks

Our work in virtual worlds is embedded primarily in educational settings. Our users consist of kids from primary schools exploring information in the virtual world, performing scientific experiments, taking part in team-based games and engaging in other social activities—always with *learning* as the underlying goal. In this context, we aim to support three user groups:

Inhabitants: These are the core users who actually use the virtual world for activities such as exploring an art exhibition or participating in a treasure hunt. In our case, this usually consists of school kids who take part in the learning activity and their teachers who act as moderators or guides. This user group has all the needs and problems associated with using virtual worlds for collaborative work such as navigation, communication and coordination.

Designers: These are professionals who design the virtual world, set up the "infrastructure" and mentoring strategies to perform various kinds of activities. They also configure the environment so that it is suitable for diverse events to be held in the virtual world. This user group consists of technical designers who use computer and artistic skills to create the virtual world as well as teachers who aid the designers in creating an environment that supports a certain learning goal. This user group defines the overall design of the virtual world; placement of objects, locations of teleports, colors, textures, and behaviors of objects in response to user actions such as clicking or movement. This user group can benefit from answers to questions pertaining to patterns of usage in virtual worlds, such as the influence of the age of buildings in the virtual world on their usage, characteristics of objects that attract a high amount of interaction versus those that are ignored, etc.

Researchers: This user group is primarily concerned with asking and answering questions about social and technological aspects of virtual worlds such as "What are the effects of the environment on user behavior?", "What is the extent of influence of interface devices on the navigation capabilities of users?" and "What role does spatial reference play in the interaction between avatars?".

As is evident, each of these user groups has distinct roles to play either inside virtual worlds, outside or both. The specific nature of problems that each user group encounters varies widely. However, one can see that answering any of these questions needs information that synthesizes data about local and global patterns of activity. For example, in order to understand how often particular areas of the world are used, one needs to step back and look at the global pattern of density of usage of the virtual world. At the same time, to understand why such a pattern exists, one needs to zoom-in to specific regions of the world and examine interaction data or chat text to identify what the avatars in those regions have been exploring or talking about. Observations about such local and global activity can then be combined with the analysis of learning outcome but also pre and post-test questionnaires to obtain a comprehensive picture of a virtual world event.

5.   Patterns of Social Activity

The term "pattern" can be defined as: a perceptual structure, a customary way of operation, a model worthy of imitation, a decorative or artistic work. Patterns occur in nature due a variety of physical, chemical and biological mechanisms. Many of these patterns manifest themselves as concrete physical phenomena and lend themselves to immediate perception in a sensory manner. At the same time, we find a number of patterns that are hidden, sometimes due to their existence on a plane other than the physical or sensorial, requiring a serious cognitive effort to uncover them, at other times due to their recursive nature, which reveals only the gross manifestation, while the intricacies are hidden away within the structure. Curiously, patterns of social activity in virtual worlds may be found to be of both types—visible as well as obscure. Geospatial patterns such as patterns of user trails are highly visible and fairly simple to visualize, while patterns in semantic space such as those found in chat activity are more difficult to uncover.

5.1.   Social Diffusion Patterns

In a virtual world, avatars perform activities in isolation or in the immediate presence of (or collaboration with) other avatars. We use the term *group* to denote a set of users that perform an activity together. The characteristics that define a group are similar to those necessary for the existence of a community [24], including "a common interest" and "being rooted in the same geographical space". However, in educational settings, a group is usually a short-term congregation of avatars who share a common goal. For example, the group of all researchers exploring ways to improve a virtual world for education form a community, while the set of students that take part in a short-term science experiment, form a group within the context of the experiment. A lone user exploring a virtual world in a random manner does not share a common purpose with other avatars and hence does not form part of a group in our sense. Note that this notion of a *group* is different from the way we refer to it in the term *user groups*.

We define social activities as activities that are carried out by a group of avatars as part of a larger objective. In our research, this larger objective is usually *learning* and the activities may be a play, a college-recruitment event, a treasure hunt, etc. The patterns that emerge as a result of these activities, hence, are also social in nature.

The Webster's New Millennium Dictionary of English defines the term *diffusion* in several ways, one of them being "the process by which a cultural trait, material object, idea, or behavior pattern is spread from one society to another". For such a diffusion process, two things are necessary: (1) the diffusing element and (2) the diffusion medium. In the above definition, the cultural trait, material object or idea is the diffusing element. This is the element that actually propagates through society possibly changing the structure of society as it diffuses. The diffusion medium in the above case is society itself, which consists of a large number of discrete units (people) that all share some common characteristic that enables the diffusion of ideas or material objects. Although homogeneity of the diffusion medium is not a pre-requisite for a diffusion process, a heterogeneous diffusion medium presents a complicated case and hence, here we consider diffusion only in a homogenous diffusion medium. We can then classify types of diffusion on the basis of whether the avatars of the virtual world act as (1) the diffusing element, or (2) the diffusion medium.

5.1.1. Users as Diffusing Element

Users in a virtual world move in diverse ways in accordance with their personal goals or the requirements of their group. Members of a group of users move towards areas that are most suitable to their tasks. For short-term activities, this process is not evident, since the quick succession of movements and teleports can hardly be termed diffusion. However, in the case of large worlds such as the *Avatars* world (see http://ccon.org), which is 2 kilometers long and 2 kilometers wide, we see that over time, there is a non-uniform distribution of users through the world due to certain areas of the world being used more often than others. Such a pattern is also reflected in the evolution of virtual world buildings over time, where we see distinct building patterns that seem to suggest that certain parts of the world are more preferred than others (figure 3-1).

5.1.2. Users as Diffusion Medium

An interesting way of looking at user behavior in virtual worlds is obtained by viewing users of virtual worlds as actors and a medium for the diffusion of ideas. Users in a virtual world communicate with each other in a variety of ways,

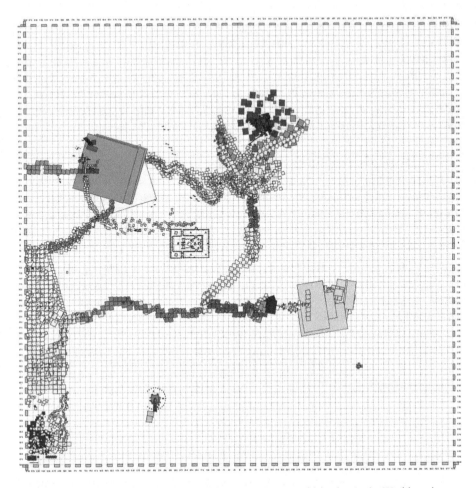

Figure 3-1. Map showing the structure of the "Avatars" world in the ActiveWorlds universe. Grid lines are used to indicate the size of the virtual world: the distance between two grid lines corresponds to 25 meters in the virtual world. The rectangles represent buildings and other structures in the virtual world and are color-coded by age. Older buildings are shown in darker color while younger buildings are shown in lighter color.

including whispering, chatting, gesturing, etc. with chat being the dominant method of communication. In fact, many users show very little movement during the entire duration of their visit to a virtual world and restrict their activity almost exclusively to chatting.

Today, virtual worlds offer a variety of ways to control the effect of the environment on the users and their activities; among the most common being configurable limits on the "visibility" of objects and the "hearing range" of chat. Visibility places a limit on how far an avatar can see in the virtual world. Objects that are farther away can be made less visible (by blurring them or hiding them by fog) or not visible at all, while objects that are closer to the avatar are made clearly visible. Hearing range limits how far away an avatar can move from a sound source (or an avatar uttering chat phrases) before it stops "hearing" sounds or receiving chat text. An avatar must be within a particular distance from another avatar to be able to receive chat-text from the latter. These limits ensure that awareness of events in a virtual world is not *broadcast* to all the users; there is clearly a diversity of awareness or knowledge of events among users. Thus, if an idea or a concept (or simply a word) appears in the chat text of one user, it spreads to the other users subject to the limitations posed by visibility and hearing range. This spread will depend—as with any diffusion process—on a variety of factors including the density and distribution of users, the "strength" of an idea or its relevance to subsets of users. Here the idea becomes the diffusing element, while the avatars become the diffusion medium.

5.2. *Emergence of Patterns in Group Situations*

There is a great deal of diversity in the kinds of groups that are found in virtual worlds and they vary from short-term task based groups such as the ones we encounter in our research—to longer-term communities such as the "E-Church" world studied by Schroeder, Heather and Lee [25]. Research on groups in virtual worlds is in its infancy and much research is needed before we will achieve a comprehensive picture of groups, roles and interactions in virtual worlds. This task is not simple because groups in virtual worlds have different dynamics compared with groups in the real world. Therefore, one cannot assume that communities in virtual environments are a mere projection of communities in the real world [26]. Keeping this in mind, we caution the reader to view the subsequently discussed types of user groups as a personal observation coming out of looking at large amounts of virtual world data, rather than a complete list.

Leader-Follower: This type of group is characterized firstly by the presence of a single avatar that is automatically accepted as the leader and secondly by the existence of prescribed paths and actions. Members of the group (not including the leader) are the followers which obey orders, follow instructions given by the leader or simply copy her actions. Some examples of such a group include a group taking a guided tour (the tour guide being the leader) or a group of students working on a building project (the leader of the group being their teacher). The followers in the group are not expected to significantly deviate from the pattern set by the leader.

Moderated: This type of group is different from the one outlined above in that there are no real followers in the group. The group consists of autonomous members free to do as they wish within the scope of the activity which the group is involved in. In a way, the moderator *could* be considered the leader of the group, since the moderator holds the right to decide upon the range and variety of actions that can fall within the scope of that particular group activity. An example of such a group is a research discussion group on virtual worlds led by the organizer of the event. In this particular group, researchers are free to discuss issues related to research in virtual worlds. However, if a heated debate gets underway or if the group begins to digress away from the main theme of discussion, the moderator can step in and restore order and focus. Typically such groups also possess the trait that its members all share a personal goal that is a subset of or is related to the common goal of the group. For example, every virtual world researcher has his/her own research agenda. However, a common thread of interest in virtual worlds binds the group together.

Competitive: This type of group is characterized by the presence of sub-groups within the main group, each of which competes against the other for some reward. All members of the sub-group share with each other a sense of belonging and a group identity. At the same time, each sub-group member maintains a sense of separation from the competing sub-groups, while they may all belong to the same super-group. In the geospatial sense, this group is usually seen to have fixed destinations but variable paths as each sub-group takes varying approaches to achieve their goals. A treasure hunt played by kids of a class is an example of a situation where such groups are encountered.

Ad-hoc: This group is characterized by its short-term existence. Members of this group do not usually possess a shared objective outside the context of the group activity being performed. For example, in the case of a group of school kids taking part in a role play, the kids may or may not have a common goal related to stage-performance. In this particular case, the group is brought together for the sake of the play and is usually dissolved as soon as the task ends. Each child in the group associates himself/herself with the group activity only as long as the activity is being carried out.

The traits described above are not mutually exclusive. Two avatars can collaborate in order to perform a task and this group might be competing against other similar groups, all of which belong to the one bigger group that is led by a single avatar. Also one might notice that the above listed traits result in progressively more decentralized groups. The level of decentralization and more importantly the concurrence of objectives of the members of the group can play a significant role in the paths taken by members of the group during an activity. Geospatially speaking, the trail of a member of a group or the group as a whole can vary depending on how coherent the behavior of the members of the group is with respect to each other and the group as a whole. Looking at the patterns of avatar trails in virtual worlds with this idea in mind reveals that we can classify group trails into the following four types in terms of the variation of their geospatial distribution over time [8] (see figure 3-2):

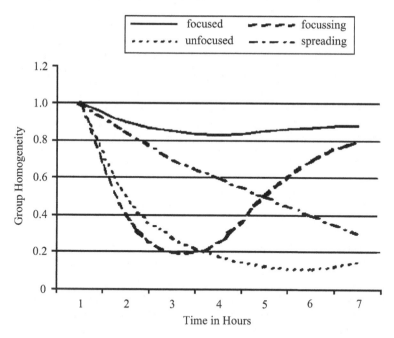

Figure 3-2. A hypothetical example showing the diffusion behavior of groups of avatars. The four types of behavior can be represented by a function that captures the variation of group homogeny over time.

— *Focused*: This group remains tightly knit and the members of the group do not deviate much from each other's paths.
— *Unfocused*: The members of this group move as they wish, resulting in quite random trail patterns.
— *Focusing*: This group starts out dispersed all over space but over time tends to congregate as the trails of the group members become increasingly similar to each other.
— *Spreading*: This group starts out with all its members on a common trajectory, but over time, the members of the group diverge, resulting in very diverse trail patterns.

One can now see that specific kinds of events can result in specific types of diffusion behavior. An art exhibition where all visitors follow pre-set paths around the exhibits results in focused group trails. A random group of users in a public virtual world results in unfocused diffusion behavior, as each member explores the world individually. An event where members of the group are assigned set regions of the world which they scan results in focusing or spreading group trails. Identifying the type of group trail resulting from an event can give researchers a good idea of whether the event went as planned. This idea is elaborated in the next section.

6.   Analysis and Visualization

Any study on patterns requires tools for repeated and consistent analysis of data. A good toolkit can facilitate this by providing researchers with a wide variety of perspectives from which to analyze and view a data set. An effective visualization can summarize the data, highlight anomalies or outstanding features and even reveal patterns that are impossible to identify by looking at data in its raw form. In this section we describe how visualization can support the study of social behavior.

6.1.   The ActiveWorld Toolkit

The ActiveWorld Toolkit (available for download at http://ella.slis. indiana.edu/~sprao/research/virtualworlds/) is a free toolkit that helps researchers to analyze and visualize world structure and user behavior data in virtual worlds built with ActiveWorlds technology. The toolkit allows one to load world data (*propdump* and *registry* files) and data about activity of avatars in the virtual world (bot log files). The world data is usually obtained by using an administrative utility for the virtual world which can export data about location, orientation, size and information on how the objects react in response to user actions such as movements or mouse clicks. User data is collected in the virtual world using bots which continuously monitor user activity such as movements, chats, clicks, teleports, etc.

To analyze how this toolkit can help researchers analyze virtual world events, consider an educational treasure hunt in a virtual world where the idea is to let kids follow clues to find treasures, picking up bits of information about issues such as environmental pollution, conservation of natural resources, etc. This requires designing the clues for the hunt in a way that is appropriate to the level of the users' cognitive abilities. One cannot incorporate clues so complex that kids get frustrated and quickly lose interest. On the other hand, the clues must be complicated enough to ensure that not all kids immediately figure them out. Hence, the ideal set of clues for the hunt would help the kids "stay in the flow" [27] of the hunt.

Also critical to the success of such an event is the ability to successfully navigate through the world. Navigational clues must be placed in strategic locations to ensure that the kids can find their way around the world, but at the same time they should not give away the locations of the clues themselves. Some questions about the treasure hunt that can be asked are "Were most of the users able to follow the clues and find their way through the world?", "Which group of users was most focused?", "Which users were lost and at what point?", "Which parts of the treasure hunt were most or least challenging?" etc. These are some questions which can be answered using visualization of user data.

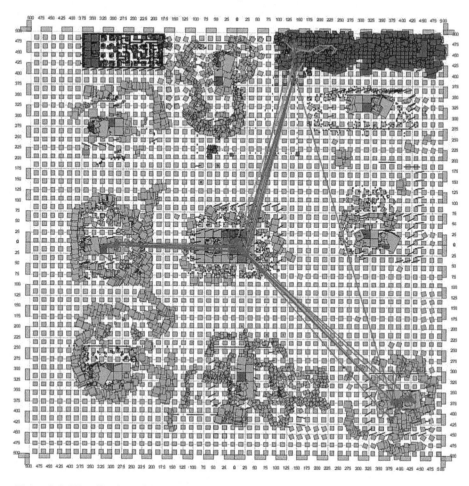

Figure 3-3. Visualization of the trails of the participants of three parallel Spanish learning sessions in LinkWorld. The three sessions are taking place in the north, south-east and west. The trails of the participants (avatars) are represented by lines. The rectangles represent buildings and other structures in the virtual world.

An example of such a visualization is shown in figure 3-3. This visualization shows the trails of users that took part in three parallel Spanish learning sessions in LinkWorld, with the treasure hunt being held in the northern part of the world. This map gives us an overview of where avatars went and where they have been most active, i.e., where they have chatted the most or where they have clicked and interacted with objects the most. In order to answer specific questions, however, one needs to be able to examine the interactions of each individual user. This is facilitated in the toolkit using the zoom function, which allows one to focus on the area of interest. The toolkit allows one to smoothly move between overview and detail mode, thus helping the user maintain her orientation while working with the toolkit.

50   75   100   125   150   175   200   225   250   275   300   325

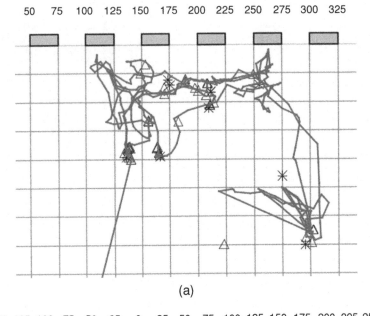

(a)

175 150 125 100 75 50 25   0   25 50   75 100 125 150 175 200 225 250 275

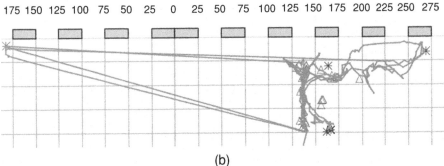

(b)

Figure 3-4. Two participants who have strayed away from the main treasure hunt area during the event. Triangles show locations where participants chatted, stars show locations where they clicked objects in the world, while trails show the path that these two participants took. The numbers at the periphery indicate the distance in meters from the centre of the virtual world along the *x*-axis.

6.2.   *Analysis of Geo-Spatial Patterns*

Figure 3-4a and b show zoomed-in views of the trails and chats (triangles) of two users who seem to have strayed significantly from the area where the treasure hunt was being held. In both cases an examination of the chat text revealed that the moderator of the treasure hunt realized that two participants were lost and made an attempt to bring them back. One can also look at the chat text of the participants to understand when they themselves realized that they were not in the right area. There are several reasons why such confusion could have arisen: the clues for the hunt were not right, or perhaps the placement of

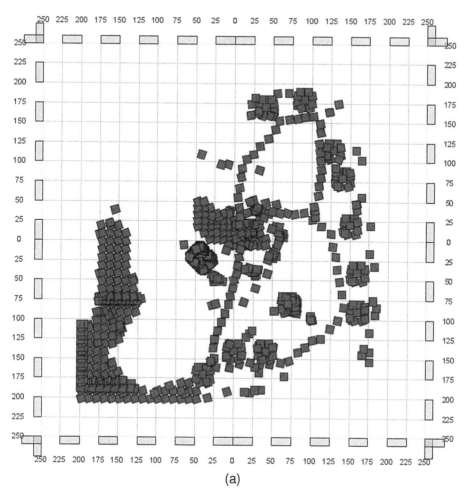

(a)

Figure 3-5. Three views of an art show in the Avatars world. (a) Structure of the world showing positions of objects. (b) Trails of avatars viewing the art show (represented by lines). (c) Locations where users chatted (triangles) and clicked objects (stars).

objects was such that the participants were misled into following a path that was out of bounds for the event, or maybe the participants were curious to explore other areas in the world. A conclusion of the latter type is especially useful when a statistical analysis is planned; one can quickly decide whether or not the behavior of the user in question is an anomaly and accordingly exclude or include him/her in the analysis. A quick peek at the chat text of these avatars revealed that one of them (figure 3-4a) spent a considerable amount of time in an area out of bounds of the actual hunt before coming back to the main area, while the other avatar (figure 3-4b) was brought back to the main area almost immediately after they left the group.

Figure 3-5 shows another set of visualizations that uncover behavioral patterns in virtual worlds. These are visualizations of an art show held during the

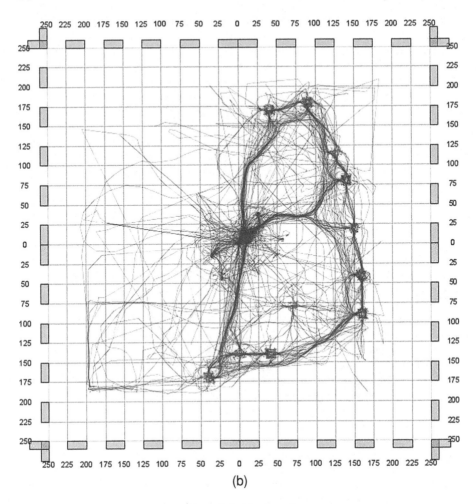

Figure 3-5. (Continued)

Avatars! Conference in 2002 (see http://www.ccon.org). Figure 3-5a shows the structure of the world. The art exhibits are placed roughly in the shape of the letter "B". Figure 3-5b shows the trails of the avatars as they explored the exhibition. From these two figures, it is clear that the avatars followed the path of exhibits very well. The trails which deviate from the center were found to belong to avatars who, after seeing all the exhibits, decided to explore the world a bit more and then exit. Finally, figure 3-5c shows the locations of chat (triangles) and clicks (stars) overlaid over the structure of the world (dark objects). This final figure gives us a clear picture of the exhibits near which people chatted with each other or interacted with objects. This information can be used along with post-event questionnaires to determine what aspects of those locations or exhibits encouraged people to talk to each other.

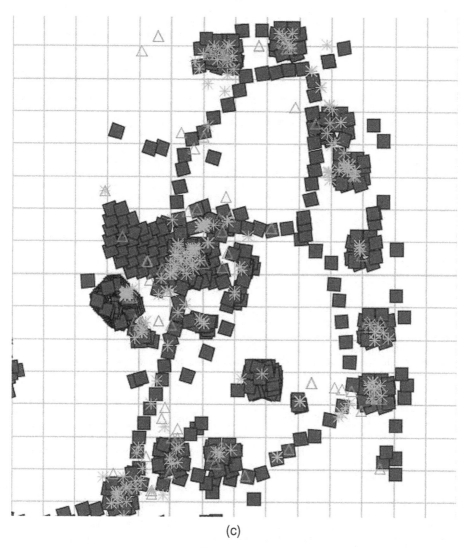

(c)

Figure 3-5. (Continued)

6.3.   *Analysis of Chat Data*

Chat data in virtual worlds is especially interesting because it can potentially reveal patterns about users' thought processes while they performed activities inside the virtual world. Chat data collected over a long period of time give us a picture of the evolution of the topics discussed among the inhabitants of the virtual world. A particularly interesting analysis is the detection of changes in the frequency of usage of particular words. The results enable us to make inferences about the emergence of topics in a conversation among avatars.

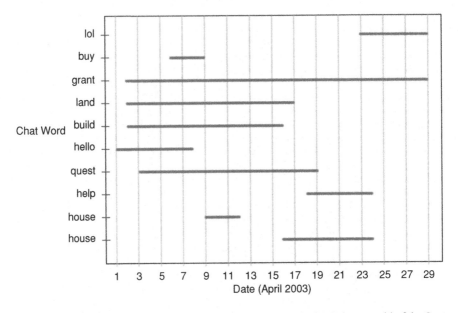

Figure 3-6. Top ten bursty words over the month of April 2003 in the Culture world of the Quest Atlantis universe. The vertical (Y) axis shows the burst words, while the horizontal (X) axis shows the dates during which the bursts occurred. For each word, a horizontal line is drawn starting from the date that the burst began till the date that burst ended.

Such an analysis demands that we do not restrict our search to any particular set of words, but rather that we let the analysis itself determine the set of most popular words. Specifically, we are looking for words which suddenly "burst on the scene", generate a lot of activity and then die down. We believe such *bursty* words are good indicators of popular topics in chat.

In order to identify bursty words, we can use a predictive model such as Kleinberg's burst detection algorithm [7]. Simply speaking, this algorithm considers a word to be bursty if it appears with a high frequency over a time period that is short compared to the total time span of the complete data set. Note that the set of words identified using this analysis are not simply the set of words which have high frequency of usage; in fact a word that constantly keeps appearing in chat will not be recognized as a bursty word.

Figure 3-6 shows the result of such an analysis performed on chat data collected over the month of April 2003 for the Culture world in Quest Atlantis universe (http://questatlantis.uni.activeworlds.com). The "X" axis shows the bursty words. The "Y" axis represents the dates in the month of April. Each horizontal line begins at the date at which the word started to burst and ends at the date at which the usage of that word died down. Table 3-1 shows the strength of the burst for these words. The "strength of burst" indicates the amplitude of the burst of that word, i.e., how intense the usage of that word was. Table 3-1 shows us that the word "lol" (an acronym for Laugh Out Loud), appears with very high

Table 3-1. Strength of burst of the top ten bursty words in chat data over the month of April 2003 in Culture world in the Quest Atlantis universe.

Word	lol	Buy	Grant	Land	Build	Hello	Quest	Help	House
Strength of burst	88.213	50.387	45.257	33.25	31.555	30.492	29.879	29.481	28.694

amplitude compared to other words such as "grant" or "hello". However, the latter category of words have a longer life-span: the word "lol" remains in the conversation for 7 days but the word "land" and "build" remain dominant for 15 and 16 days, respectively. Note that the word "house" appears twice, meaning that this word appeared as the dominant word twice in one month—the first time between April 9 and 12 and the second time between April 16 and 24.

From figure 3-6, we know exactly what day the burst of a particular word occurred and therefore we can go back to the original data and determine the cause for that burst. In this case, the reason for the sudden burst of the word "lol" was traced back to a kid who kept welcoming every new visitor into the virtual world with strange and funny welcome messages. The messages were written in a way that made them look as if they were coming from an automated bot. Every time this kid made a fool of a new user, everyone assembled in the virtual world would burst out in laughter. The other words have a more serious tone and clearly indicate building and trading activities going on very actively for a period of about 15 days. One can also take advantage of the starting and ending dates of the burst and make inferences about the chain of events that took place. So we see that "hello" is one of the first words that burst— probably a time for introductions—after which users got down to business talking about "quest", "build" and "land", ending with "lol". One can see that simple analyses like these can lead to interesting inferences that can then be verified using questionnaires and interviews.

The sequence of chat data can be visualized to show trends in the rise and fall of the word frequency over time. One of the most frequently used words in chat text which did not appear in the analysis outlined above was the word "you". This word was consistently used with very high frequency and hence was ignored by the burst algorithm. Figure 3-7 shows the frequency of usage of the word "you" over time in the same data set analyzed above visualized using TimeSearcher [28]. From the figure, the pattern of usage over time is immediately evident: the word started off at a low frequency, its average increased slowly over time, it took a big jump after the half-way point through the time period of observation and maintained a relatively high average frequency until finally the frequency dropped very suddenly. This pattern of frequency can then be compared to changes in the user group, environment or activity in the virtual world to yield additional clues.

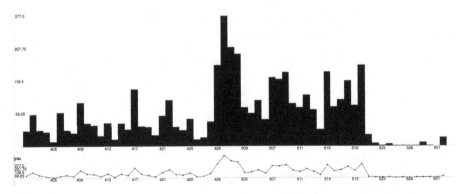

Figure 3-7. Visualization of the frequency of usage of the word "you" in a two-month sample of chat data in Culture world in the Quest Atlantis universe. The vertical axis (*Y*) indicates the frequency of usage of this word, while the horizontal (*X*) axis indicates time. The bar graph (top) and the line graph (bottom) provide the same information. However, in the TimeSearcher application, the bar graph allows users to zoom in and out as well as query for details over a particular time period, while the line graph acts as a constant reference.

7.   Outlook

In this chapter, we have seen how one can combine diverse methods of analysis and visualization in order to create powerful ways to analyze user behavior data and discover patterns in them. The use of patterns for social research in virtual worlds is not only powerful, but necessary in order to truly understand the impact of space and time on the behavior of individual users and groups in virtual worlds. Visualizations provide researchers with effective means to discover these patterns and enable efficient communication of analysis results to peers.

In the future, we hope to apply these analysis and visualization techniques to gain an understanding of virtual world behavior in real-time. One can imagine a tool that provides continuous real-time summaries of activity patterns of users as they perform tasks in a virtual world. Such a real-time map could provide navigational support to users, present a real-time summary of chat topics emerging in different areas of the virtual world, or even display a dynamically-generated social network of avatars as they interact in the virtual world. We believe that such tools will prove to be essential for determining the influence of spatial, semantic, and social factors on dynamic group behavior.

Another line of research that looks promising is the development of techniques to automatically identify roles that avatars take in a group based on spatial patterns, chat utterances and interaction data. For example, we can ask the question, "From the patterns of social behavior, is it possible to identify automatically which avatar emerged as the leader?" Such a question calls for an intelligent synthesis of theories and techniques developed in computer supported cooperative work, information visualization, spatial analysis, clustering methods, computer-mediated communication [29], social network analysis [30], and others.

Acknowledgements

We would like to thank Bonnie DeVarco of the BorderLink project (http://www. borderlink.org) for her support throughout this research and for access to the LinkWorld data. Thanks also to Sasha Barab and Bob Carteaux of the Quest Atlantis project (http://questatlantis.uni.activeworlds.com) for their valuable comments and for permitting us to log Quest Atlantis log data and Bruce Damer of Digital Space Commons (http://www.digitalspace.com) for granting us permission to log the "Avatars!" Conference and generate maps of the Avatars world. Thanks also to Rich Bernstein of Cornell University whose helpful suggestions led to several improvements to the ActiveWorld Toolkit. This work is supported by a National Science Foundation grant under Role-0411846.

Figure 3-2 reprinted with permission from "Social Diffusion Patterns in 3D Virtual Worlds", Information Visualization Journal, Vol. 2, Issue 3, Sept. 2003. Copyright Palgrave-Macmillan, UK.

References

1. Chen, C. (1999). *Information Visualisation and Virtual Environments*. London: Springer Verlag.
2. Card, S., Mackinlay, J., & Shneiderman, B. (Eds.) (1999). *Readings in Information Visualization: Using Vision to Think*. San Francisco: Morgan Kaufmann.
3. Ware, C. (2000). *Information Visualization: Perception for Design*. Morgan Kaufmann Interactive Technologies Series. San Francisco: Morgan Kaufmann.
4. Spence, B. (2000). *Information Visualization*. Reading, MA: Addison-Wesley.
5. Börner, K. (2002). Twin worlds: Augmenting, evaluating, and studying three-dimensional digital cities and their evolving communities. In M. Tanabe, P. van den Besselaar, & T. Ishida (Eds.), *Digital Cities II: Computational and Sociological Approaches*. Japan: Springer Verlag, pp. 256–269.
6. Rabiner, L.R. (1989). A tutorial on hidden Markov models and selected applications in speech recognition. In *Proceedings of the IEEE, 77*(2), February, pp. 257–286.
7. Kleinberg, J. (2002). Bursty and hierarchical structure in streams. In *The 8th ACM SIGKDD International Conference on Knowledge Discovery and Data Mining*, July 23–26.
8. Börner, K. & Penumarthy, S. (2003). Social diffusion patterns in three-dimensional virtual worlds. *Information Visualization, 2*(3): 182–198.
9. Aref, H., Charles, R.D., & Elvins, T.T. (1994). Scientific visualization of fluid flow. In C.A. Pickover & S.K. Tewksbury (Eds.), *Frontiers of Scientific Visualization*. Hoboken, NJ: Wiley Interscience.

10. Senger, S. (1996). Digital cadavers (TM): An environment for the study and visualization of anatomic data. In *Proceedings of the Visible Human Conference*, National Institutes of Health, Bethesda, Maryland, p. 127.

11. Dorigo, G. & Tobler, W. (1983). Push pull migration laws. *Annals Association of American Geographers, 73*(1): 1–17.

12. Plaisant, C., Milash, B., Rose, A., Widoff, S., & Shneiderman, B. (1996). *Life lines: Visualizing personal histories*. In the *ACM CHI '96 Conference Proceedings*. New York: ACM Press, pp. 221–227.

13. Donath, J.S., Karahalios, K. & Viegas, F. (1999). Visualizing conversation. *Journal of Computer Mediated Communication, 4*(4). Available at http://www.ascusc.org/jcmc/vol4/issue4/donath.html

14. Hochheiser, H. & Shneiderman, B. (2001). Using interactive visualizations of WWW log data to characterize access patterns and inform site design. *American Society for Information Science, 52*(4): 331–343.

15. Donath, J.S. (1995). Visual Who: Animating the affinities and activities of an electronic community. *In Proceedings of the Third ACM International Conference on Multimedia*, San Francisco, CA, pp. 99–107.

16. Smith, M., Farnham, S., & Drucker, S. The social life of small graphical chat spaces. In R. Schroeder (Ed.), *The Social Life of Avatars: Presence and Interaction in Shared Virtual Environments*. London: Springer, pp. 205–220.

17. Naper, I. (2000). System features of an inhabited 3-D virtual environment supporting multimodality in communication. In *Proceedings of the 34th Annual Hawaii International Conference on Systems Sciences*. Maui, Hawaii: IEEE Computer Society.

18. Whyte, W.H. (1980). *The Social Life of Small Urban Spaces*. Washington, DC: The Conservation Foundation.

19. Dodge, M. & Kitchin, R. (2001). *An Atlas of Cyberspaces*. Reading, MA: Addison Wesley.

20. Schroeder, R., Smith, A., & Huxor, A. (2001). Activeworlds: Geography and social interaction in virtual reality. *Futures, 33*: 569–587.

21. Börner, K., Penumarthy, S., DeVarco, B. J., & Kerney, C. (2004). Visualizing social patterns in virtual environments on a local and global scale. In *Digital Cities 3: Local information and communication infrastructures: Experiences and challenges*. To be published by Springer Verlag.

22. Börner, K., Jun Lee, G., Penumarthy, S., & Jones, R. J. (2004). Visualizing the VLearn3D 2002 conference in space and time. In *Visualization and Data Analysis*, San Jose, CA. SPIE-IS&T, Vol. 5295: 24–32.

23. *Federal Geographic Data Committee, Geospatial Standards*. Available at http://www.fgdc.gov/publications/documents/standards/standards.html

24. Becker, B. & Mark, G. (2002). Social conventions in computer-mediated communication: A comparison of three online virtual environments. In R. Schroeder (Ed.), *The Social Life of Avatars: Presence and Interaction in Shared Virtual Environments*. London: Springer, pp. 19–62.

25. Schroeder, R., Heather, N., & Lee, R. (1999). The sacred and the virtual: Religion in multi-user virtual reality. *Journal of Computer-Mediated Communication, 4*(2). Available at http://www.ascusc.org/jcmc/vol4/issue2/schroeder.html

26. Wellman, B., Salaff, J., Dimitrova, D., Garton, L., Gulia, M., & Haythornthwaite, C. (1996). Computer networks as social networks: Collaborative work, telework, and virtual community. *Annual Review of Sociology, 22*: 213–238.

27. Bederson, B. (2004). Interfaces for staying in the flow. *Ubiquity, (5)*27, Sept. 1–7. Available at http://www.acm.org/ubiquity/views/v5i27_bederson.html

28. Keogh, E., Hochheiser, H., & Shneiderman, B. (2002). An augmented visual query mechanism for finding patterns in time series data. In *Proceedings of the Fifth International Conference on Flexible Query Answering Systems*, October 27–29, Copenhagen, Denmark. *Lecture Notes in Artificial Intelligence*. London: Springer.

29. Herring, S.C. (2002). Computer-mediated communication on the Internet. *Annual Review of Information Science and Technology, 36*: 109–168.

30. Wasserman, S. & Faust, K. (1994). *Social Network Analysis: Methods and Applications*. Cambridge: Cambridge University Press.

Chapter 4

COLLABORATIVE VIRTUAL ENVIRONMENTS FOR SCIENTIFIC COLLABORATION: TECHNICAL AND ORGANIZATIONAL DESIGN FRAMEWORKS

Diane H. Sonnenwald

1.   Introduction

Collaboration among scientists is human behavior that facilitates the sharing of meaning and completion of tasks with respect to a mutually shared scientific goal, and which takes place in social settings. Scientific collaboration across geographic distances began centuries ago, when scientists began utilizing postal and shipping services to exchange ideas as well as samples of plants and animals. More recently, collaborative virtual environments have brought new opportunities—and challenges—for scientific collaboration across distances. This chapter discusses two different challenges: designing collaborative virtual environment software tools, and designing organizational structures and practices to facilitate collaboration across geographical distances. To address the first challenge, a technical design framework that focuses on supporting situation awareness is proposed. The framework is based on research conducted by designing and evaluating a scientific collaboratory system, called the nano-Manipulator Collaboratory, that allowed scientists to synchronously conduct experiments, collecting and analyzing data from an atomic force microscope. To address the second challenge, an organizational design framework based on a two-year case study of a distributed scientific organization is proposed. These two frameworks may be relevant for a wide range of distributed scientific work.

Today, many scientists often use multiple collaborative virtual environment (CVE) tools in various combinations to facilitate collaboration. Examples of tools that support synchronous collaboration are the telephone, video conferencing, instant messaging, chat, shared electronic whiteboards, virtual networked computing, shared access to scientific instruments, and

R. Schroeder and A.S. Axelsson (Eds.), Avatars at Work and Play, 63–96.
© 2006 *Springer.*

shared applications, such as shared data visualization programs. Examples of tools that support asynchronous collaboration are e-mail, file transfer programs, WIKIs, electronic lab notebooks, project management tools, and listservs. Examples of tools that support individual access to information or a device include web pages that provide information about scientific research and outcomes, digital libraries and search programs that allow scientists to contribute, find and/or comment on scientific publications and data, and single-user remote access to scientific instrumentation and data.

No one tool today provides all features needed to fully support collaboration across distances during the entire scientific research life cycle. One challenge facing collaborative virtual environment tools is the ability to fully support shared situation awareness. Situation awareness has been defined as: "continuous extraction of environmental information, integration of this information with previous knowledge to form a coherent mental picture in directing further perception and anticipating future events" [1, p. 11].

It is a general sense of knowing about things that are happening in the immediate environment and includes having both an accurate understanding of the situation and the knowledge to respond appropriately as the situation evolves [2]. Based on previous research and our empirical studies, the types of information needed to develop and maintain situation awareness include contextual, task and process, and socio-emotional information. Research in virtual reality systems suggests that control, sensory, distraction and realism attributes of technology contribute to a sense of presence [3]. Consideration of these attributes with respect to contextual, task and process, and socio-emotional information provides insights to guide technical design decisions. The resulting framework was used when designing a CVE for scientific collaboration [4]. Results from a controlled experimental evaluation of the collaboratory system help illustrate the framework's utility.

It has long been known that organizational structures and practices influence technology adoption and use [e.g., 5, 6]. In addition to supporting situation awareness through technology, scientific collaboration in collaborative virtual environments may often require new organizational practices, especially when larger numbers of scientists need to collaborate across distances. Thus providing a framework to help design CVE tools should be augmented by a framework to help design organizational structures and practices in which the tools will, ideally, be embedded.

The organizational design framework to facilitate scientific collaboration proposed in this chapter is based on a two-year case study of a group of over 100 scientists. The scientists were primarily chemists and chemical engineers at four universities in the USA who were members of a research centre. They collaborated during all phases of the scientific process, including sharing knowledge during proposal development, scientific instrument design and construction, experiment design, data collection and analysis, and dissemination of results through papers and presentations. The case study began during the beginning stages of the centre and continued for 2 years. While conducting the case study, the author was a participant observer, having both complete and peripheral membership roles, collecting case study data and providing advice regarding collaboration technology and collaborative practices. Case study data included interviews, observations of meetings, sociometric surveys, and centre documents. These data were analyzed in the ethnographic and grounded theory traditions [7, 8], and the organizational design framework discussed in this chapter emerged from this analysis.

The organizational design framework introduces a new concept, called the conceptual organization. A conceptual organization has characteristics in common with traditional organizations, invisible colleges, collaboratories and virtual teams. However, it uniquely combines a management structure that is interwoven across other organizations, collaborative work practices based on collaboration technology, and use of integrative, economic and destructive organizational power. It has few employees in the traditional sense; most members are scientists who join the organization because they wish to contribute to its vision and goals. Benefits of a conceptual organization include its ability to discover solutions, quickly and effectively contributing to relevant dynamic knowledge bases and meeting diverse stakeholder needs with minimum capitalization and start-up costs [9].

This chapter first presents the technology design framework and, second, the organizational design framework. In presenting the technology design framework, the type of information needed to develop and maintain situation awareness in scientific collaboration, and features of technology to support the acquisition and sharing of these types of information are discussed. The application and evaluation of the framework in the context of the nanoManipulator collaboratory is also discussed. In presenting the organizational design framework, it is defined and compared to other organizational designs. Details regarding management structure, organizational membership, stakeholders, and collaborative knowledge management practices and use of technology are presented. Potential benefits and an evaluation of the organizational design framework are also presented. In sum, this chapter is a first effort to consider both technology and organizational design relevant for a wide range of future distributed scientific work.

2.   A Technical Design Framework Focusing on Supporting Situation Awareness

2.1.   *Information to Develop and Maintain Situation Awareness*

To develop an understanding of situation awareness in scientific collaborative work, 27 interviews with faculty, postdoctoral and graduate student scientists actively collaborating with one another were conducted. The average

length of these interviews was 1.5 hours, with a minimum duration of an hour
and a maximum duration of 2.75 hours. Study participants were also observed
on nine occasions as they conducted experiments while working alone and
with others. Analysis of the data and previous research suggest that situation
awareness in scientific research collaboration requires several types of information, including contextual, task and process, and socio-emotional information.
Distinguishing between these types of information facilitates our understanding of situation awareness and technical requirements for collaborative virtual
environments.

Contextual information is a broad sense of the context in which things are
happening. Context can be defined as a "framework of meaning" [10, p. 8] or a
"framework of understanding" [11, p. 52]. Contextual information includes information regarding norms of scientific practice, research goals, organizational
culture and work environment. Contextual information can vary between collaborators, as one scientist described:

> The person that we were collaborating with was so much into "let's hurry up
> and publish this before so-and-so beats us and we won't get credit if they beat
> us."... And in the end, we found out the results weren't reproducible. I resisted
> all of the ideas this collaborator had to publish and in the end, it was the best thing
> I ever did because if we had published it we would have been wrong.

In a sense, contextual information includes the "rules of the game" and the
"players in the game," and how to apply the rules. A scientist stated:

> I don't mind the political games necessary to see a few things come together... To
> get an idea... going... you have to get the blessings of various people.

When collaborators work face-to-face in the same context, they may already
know most of the contextual information relevant to the situation, reducing
the amount of contextual information that must be mediated by technology.
However, when collaborators come from different contexts, they need to be able
to discover differences and similarities in their understanding of the context,
and possibly discuss or negotiate those differences.

Task and process information is defined as information about current and
relevant task activities and work processes. It includes information about tasks
currently being performed and who is performing them. It also includes information about what tasks should be performed, how they can be performed,
who can perform them and where and when they can be performed. Task and
process information assists an individual in understanding what collaborators
are doing. It also assists in creating expectations regarding what collaborators
might do. When two collaborators share an in-depth understanding of processes, they may appear to function as one with work responsibilities passing
smoothly between them.

An individual may increase his or her task and process information by observing the sequence of tasks another person or group of people are performing and by discussing tasks and processes with them. As one scientist explained:

> Every now and then, she would look at us over the shoulder, I guess, and see how the experiment was going. And we talked with her too, every now and then.

Collaborators may have different task and process information, especially when collaborators come from different disciplines or have different expertise. For example, a scientist told us:

> [My collaborators] will generate data and then they'll go "we're going to run this through our computer software to see blah, blah, blah".... I have no sense of what that involves. Is that a week of running a mainframe or is this something you put on there and click it and it comes back and says here's your picture?

Socio-emotional information is interpersonal information about collaborators. It includes information about their skills, work styles, approach to science, likes and dislikes, personality and emotional state. Several scientists discussed the important role socio-emotional information plays in their collaborative work:

> The best collaborations I have are the ones where the person I'm collaborating with thinks differently than I do ... [this] is much more important than just getting experiments done more quickly.
> Interviewer: How do you judge whether somebody would be a good collaborator? What criteria do you use?
> Scientist: [The] kind of behavior they have towards other people. Do they behave ethically? Are they forthright? Do they openly discuss their research or are they secretive? Are they, it may sound silly, but do I like them? ... Do I find them interesting people with sort of the same kind of values that I have towards the science?

Bales [12] and Nardi, Whittaker and Bradner [13] have shown that groups, working both face-to-face and remotely, communicate socio-emotional information. They show tension, tension release, antagonism, enthusiasm, solidarity, agreement, disagreement and empathy through a variety of mechanisms including jokes, questions, assertions and body language.

Contextual, process and task, and socio-emotional information can be interrelated. Information or a lack of information of one type can enhance or limit one's understanding of other information. For example, a scientist described collaborating with a professional and not understanding why the professional did not complete several tasks. The scientist lacked contextual and socio-emotional information about his collaborator, and could not understand the task and process information at hand:

> [He] is a clinician that deals with children who have this lethal disease...I just cannot seem to ever get him to come over or respond to e-mails...[is] he so inundated with clinical stuff that he can't carve out of his day what he needs to do the scientific?...I don't understand that...He can treat these patients for his whole career. Here's an opportunity to potentially bring a cure to them, and I don't understand why [he] can't say this is a priority.

This lack of contextual and socio-emotional information not only hindered the immediate collaboration but also future collaborations.

In summary, research suggests that situation awareness is built on a foundation of contextual, task and process, and socio-emotional information from previous situations. Poorly designed collaborative virtual environments that do not adequately support the development and maintenance of situation awareness may not only reduce the quality of current work but also of future work.

2.2.   *Technology Features to Enable Situation Awareness*

When scientists collaborate face-to-face, they share an immediate environment and can develop situation awareness using contextual, process and task information gained through exploring, and experiencing, the (local) environment independently and/or collaboratively. However, when collaborating across distances, this exploration must occur across multiple environments (local and remote). The exploration of the remote environments is no longer a direct experience, but is mediated by technology. It is important to design systems that enable scientists to obtain contextual, task and process, and socio-emotional information about the remote environments independently and/or collaboratively.

Substituting "virtual" for "remote" in the previous sentence makes an obvious link to virtual reality (VR) technology. For CVE tools, the goal is to enable users to create and maintain situation awareness at the remote and local sites; in virtual reality technology, the goal is for users to create and maintain a sense of presence, or "being there" in a place other than where she is physically.

Virtual reality research suggests several attributes, or factors, of virtual reality systems that contribute to providing a sense of presence [3, 14–16]. More recent research [e.g., 17, 18] investigates the impact of these types of system attributes on task effectiveness.

Witmer and Singer [3] organize VR system attributes into four groups: control, sensory, distraction, and realism. *Control attributes* describe how well the user can interact with and change the virtual or remote environment. *Sensory attributes* are concerned with delivering information about the remote environment to the remote user, allowing the user to move through the remote

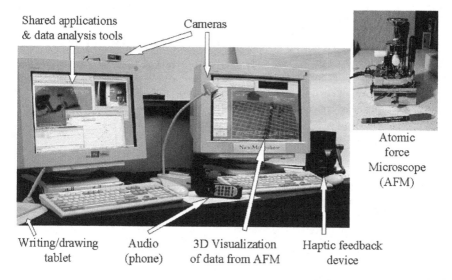

Figure 4-1. The nanoManipulator Collaboratory System.

environment and to actively and purposefully explore it. Just as systems must provide appropriate sensory stimuli, they must also minimize irrelevant external stimuli, or *distraction attributes*, that are not a part of, and particularly are inconsistent with, the stimuli from a remote environment. *Realism attributes* concern how much the remote world is like the natural world, i.e., the degree of consistency between the users' experience of the real world and their experience of the remote place. [Two of Witmer and Singer's realism attributes, meaningfulness of experience and separation anxiety/disorientation, are not dependent on technology design, but rather the application domain. Thus these factors are excluded from the design framework.]

We propose that, when designing a system, these attributes should be considered with respect to their ability to facilitate access to contextual task and process, and socio-emotional information. A table, with each row representing an attribute and each column representing a type of information, can be created to assist in this process (table 4-1). Each blank cell in the table represents something to consider during the design process.

2.3. Applying the Framework

2.3.1. The nanoManipulator Collaboratory

The framework was applied to the design of a CVE tool, the nanoManipulator collaboratory (figure 4-1). The goal of the nanoManipulator collaboratory is to provide shared remote access to a specialized scientific instrument, called a nanoManipulator (nM), and to support small groups of scientists as they

Table 4-1. Technical design framework.

		Information needed for situation awareness		
Technology attributes		**Contextual**	**Task & process**	**Socio-emotional**
Control	Degree of control Immediacy of control Anticipation Mode of control Physical environment modifiability			
Sensory	Modality Environmental richness Multimodal presentation Consistency of multimodal presentation Degree of movement perception Active search			
Distraction	Isolation Selective attention Interface awareness			
Realism	Scene realism Information consistent with objective world			

conduct research that utilizes the nM instrument. The single-user nM provides haptic and 3D visualization interfaces to a local (collocated) atomic force microscope (AFM), providing a natural scientist with the ability to interact directly with physical samples ranging in size from DNA to single cells [19, 20].

Hardware elements in the collaboratory system include two PCs. One PC is equipped with a Sensable Devices Phantom™ force-feedback device. This PC and its associated software provide haptic and 3D visualization interfaces to a local or remote atomic force microscope (AFM) and support collaborative manipulation and exploration of scientific data. Scientists can dynamically switch between working together in *shared* mode and working independently in *private* mode. In shared mode, remote, i.e., non-collocated, collaborators view and analyze the same (scientific) data. Mutual awareness is supported via multiple pointers, each showing the focus of attention and interaction state for one collaborator. Collaborators can perform almost all operations synchronously. Because of the risk of damage to an AFM, control of the microscope tip is explicitly passed between collaborators. In private mode, each collaborator can independently analyze the same or different data from stream files previously generated. When switching back to private from shared mode, collaborators return to the exact data they were previously using.

Another PC supports shared application functionality and video conferencing (via Microsoft NetMeeting™) and an electronic writing/drawing tablet. This PC allows collaborators to work together synchronously using a variety of domain-specific and off-the-shelf applications, including specialized data analysis, word processing and whiteboard applications. Video conferencing is supported by two cameras. One camera is mounted on a gooseneck stand so it can be pointed at the scientist's hands, sketches, or other physical artifacts scientists may use during experiments; the other is positioned to primarily capture a head and shoulders view of the user. Collaborators have software control of which camera view is broadcast from their site. A wireless telephone headset and speakerphone connected to a commercial telephone network provides high quality audio communications for collaborators.

2.3.2. Making Design Decisions

Following is a discussion of the technology attributes, and their importance to contextual, task and process, and socio-emotional information. Examples of design decisions that were made using the framework are provided. However, due to space limitations not all design decisions made based on the framework are presented here.

2.3.2.1. Control Attributes

Degree of control: Degree of control refers to the number of elements in the remote and local environments that the user can control and the extent of that control. The more control that collaborators have over the remote environment, the greater their situation awareness. The more control that collaborators have over the local environment, the easier it is to proactively provide contextual, task and process, or socio-emotional information to a remote collaborator. For example, controlling the focus of a local camera on task activities can help increase a remote collaborator's task and process information. The capability to reserve a system for an experiment and to learn about what experiments are planned will increase contextual information. Thus, the nM system was designed with these features.

Immediacy of control: Immediacy of control focuses on system responsiveness. The smaller the delay between initiating a system function (in the local or remote environment) and seeing the function's impact, the greater the sense of presence afforded. This enhances situation awareness by providing the means by which scientists can confirm actions. Software mechanisms that provide feedback as well as efficient algorithms and high network transmission speeds with low latency are typically needed to support this feature.

Anticipation: Anticipation is supported through media richness and consistency. When scientists conduct experiments while working face-to-face, they can recognize the activities being done and the status of those activities, and anticipate subsequent activities. For example, they can gather socio-emotional information, such as frustration and excitement, and anticipate responses, such as encouragement. This was addressed by providing multiple (high resolution and low latency) video camera views of the remote scientists.

Mode of control: In a collaborative system, a person may need to perform an action in one environment in order to cause a responding action in the other environment. Situation awareness is facilitated when that action is natural and similar across environments. For example, actions to change parameters for a data visualization should be exactly the same at all locations.

Physical environment modifiability: Situation awareness is enhanced when collaborators are able to modify the same artifacts in the remote environment as they could if co-located. For the nM system, this includes actions such as pushing, touching and/or modifying a sample during an experiment. In the stand-alone nM system, a scientist could perform these actions locally. The nM collaboratory system allows a scientist to perform the same actions when working remotely.

2.3.2.2. Sensory Attributes

Sensory modality: This attribute implies that systems should avoid forcing users to substitute one sensory mode for another. For example, although audio communication is closely related to collaborative task accomplishment, visual information is a strong source of socio-emotional, task and contextual knowledge [e.g., 21], and its absence in a collaborative virtual environment system would diminish the effectiveness of the system. In the nM system, haptic feedback is also provided when the microscope tip is pushed against a sample.

Environmental richness: Environmental richness implies that systems should gather and display a variety of contextual, task and process, and socio-emotional information at adequate resolution and update rates. This implies a need for high quality video connections that show facial expressions, gestures and local objects; high quality audio connections; and shared applications to increase the richness of the environment. In addition, a "window within a window" to view a collaborator's remote screen while still viewing your local screen may enhance contextual and process knowledge.

Multimodal presentation: When the senses of sight, hearing, smell and touch are stimulated in an integrated and complete manner, situation awareness may be increased. Our observations of scientists engaged in audio–video conferences reveal that the more artifacts brought into the discussion (such as shared drawing tools or shared documents), the more the participants become engaged in the discussions. In a collaborative virtual environment, such senses may include touch integrated with sight and sound. In the nM collaboratory system, haptic feedback is integrated with visual information coming from the visualization screen, contributing task and process knowledge.

Consistency of multimodal presentation: When visual, audio and haptic information are consistent and synchronized, people can more easily understand information. This can increase their confidence in, and use of, the information.

Time synchrony across data presentation modes is an important component of consistent multimodal presentation.

Degree of movement perception: This attribute focuses on self-motion within an environment. Zahorik and Jenison [22] believe that presence is enhanced when one understands the result of an action in an environment, whether that environment is virtual or real. Ideally, a collaborator should be able to clearly see and hear actions that occur in the remote location as a result of a local action.

Active search: Active search capabilities allow users to control sensors at remote locations to obtain desired information. When collaborators can modify sensors to effectively search the remote environment, their socio-emotional, task and process, and contextual information can increase. The scientists interviewed indicated that they would like to have multiple, pre-set video views of a remote collaborator's environment and the ability to modify those views dynamically using remotely controlled pan-tilt-zoom camera mounts and/or automatic tracking cameras. Previous research [e.g., 23, 24] has also illustrated the importance of providing the ability to switch between multiple camera views, as well as repositioning and refocusing cameras.

2.3.2.3. *Distraction Attributes*

Isolation: Isolation refers to the extent that the user is physically shielded from non-relevant, or distracting, information or activities in the local and remote environments. For example, devices that isolate a scientist from non-relevant aspects of the local environment can enhance his or her ability to gather and understand information from a remote environment. An example is the use of headphones to reduce ambient noise in the local environment so that a user may fully concentrate on the interaction with a remote collaborator. However, observations of scientists using desktop audio–video conferencing tools such as NetMeeting™ also show that they like to hear auxiliary conversations arising in the local and remote environment to increase their contextual situation awareness. A solution is to provide options regarding audio headsets and audio speakers.

Selective attention: This attribute focuses on the extent users ignore non-relevant information. For example, a collaborator's willingness to ignore distractions in the local environment should enhance their awareness of the remote environment. This is a psychological issue.

One method to capture and focus the attention of another person, particularly with respect to information on a monitor, is through pointing. We frequently observed scientists pointing to computer screens with their mouse pointer, fingers and pens to selectively focus a collaborator's attention. Thus, the nM system was designed to enable each scientist's pointer to be viewable by all collaborators.

Interface awareness: This attribute focuses on human–computer interface design. The human–computer interface for all types of information should be natural and easy to use. This has been previously proposed for all types of systems, and widely discussed in the human computer interaction literature [e.g., 25].

2.3.2.4. Realism Attributes

Scene realism: Scene realism, or the realistic rendering of the remote environment, addresses the validity of information from the remote environment used to develop situation awareness. Scene realism can be developed using real-world content, such as video, and simulated content, such as computer animation or graphical representations. It is affected by camera resolution, light sources, field of view, as well as the connectedness and continuity of information being presented [3]. Emerging technology, such as 3D telepresence, has the potential to increase scene realism.

Consistency of information with the natural world: Information about the remote environment provided by the system should be consistent with information learned through first-hand experiences. For example, if a scientist had previously visited a collaborator's lab then information about the lab, e.g., a floor plan, provided by the system should be consistent with the scientist's existing knowledge of the lab. Even when scientists have not had the opportunity to visit a collaborator's environment, they have expectations regarding that environment based on their previous experiences. Information provided by the system should be consistent with these expectations.

2.4.   Evaluating the Design Framework

2.4.1.   Controlled Experiment Evaluation

To investigate the validity and utility of the framework, we can evaluate the systems it helps to create. This is an indirect measure, and conclusions from the evaluation should be interpreted with caution.

The evaluation conducted was a repeated measures, or within-subjects, controlled experiment comparing working face-to-face and working remotely, with the order of conditions counterbalanced. The hypotheses followed previous research [e.g., 26] and would predict that task performance and perceptions of the system when using it to collaborate across distances would be lower because collaborators would lack the richness of collocation and face-to-face interaction, including multiple and redundant communication channels, implicit cues, and spatial co-references. This lack of richness is often thought to impair situation awareness and subsequently have a negative impact on task performance and perceptions of technology.

In the evaluation, twenty pairs of study participants (upper level under-graduate natural science students) conducted two realistic scientific research activities each requiring 2–3 hours to complete. Ten pairs of study participants worked face-to-face first and, on a different day, worked remotely (in differ-ent locations). Another ten pairs worked remotely first and, on a different day, face-to-face. When face-to-face, the participants shared a single nM collabo-ratory system; when collaborating remotely, each location was equipped with a complete nM collaboratory system.

The scientific research activities completed by the participants were de-signed in collaboration with natural scientists. The tasks were activities the scientists actually completed and documented during the course of their re-search. To complete the tasks the participants had to engage in the following activities typical of scientific research: operate the scientific equipment prop-erly; capture and record data in their (electronic) notebook; perform analysis using scientific data analysis software applications and include the results of that analysis in their notebooks; draw conclusions, create hypotheses and sup-port those hypotheses based on their data and analysis; and prepare a formal report of their work.

Task performance was measured through graded lab reports. The informa-tion participants were asked to provide in the reports mirrored the information scientists record in their lab notebooks. Each pair of study participants collab-oratively created a lab report under each condition, generating a total of 40 lab reports; 20 created working remotely and 20 created working face-to-face. In ad-dition, each participant was interviewed after each session. The post-interviews focused on participant's perceptions of the collaboratory system and their work patterns. The lab reports were graded blindly, and the post-interviews were analyzed using both open and axial coding [27]. During open coding, the in-terviews were read thoroughly and carefully and coding categories, or frames, were identified. During axial coding, the final step, all interviews were re-read and analyzed using the coding categories. Additional details regarding the ex-periment can be found in Sonnenwald *et al.* [28, 29].

2.5.   Evaluation Results

The average lab report scores for the first task session were identical (70/100) for both the face-to-face and remote condition (table 4-2). Although a null result statistically, the comparable scores between the two conditions on the first task are encouraging.

Data analysis further indicated that in this study collaborating remotely first had a positive effect on the second, face-to-face interaction. Using a mul-tivariate analysis of variance (MANOVA) test, the differences in scores for the face-to-face and remote conditions were not statistically significant at the

Table 4-2. Graded lab report statistics.

| | Graded lab report scores (max. score = 100) | | | | | | | | | |
| | Collaborated FtF first (*n* = 20) | | | | | Collaborated remotely first (*n* = 20) | | | | |
Condition	Mean	SD	Max	Min	Range	Mean	SD	Max	Min	Range
Face-to-face	70.0	16.75	88	42	46	86.4	10.52	98	70	28
Remote	75.1	10.49	89	56	33	70.0	8.89	80	55	25

$p \leq 0.05$ level. However, when order is taken into account, participants who collaborated remotely first scored significantly higher on task 2 than did those who collaborated face-to-face first (df $= 1$, $F = 9.66$, $p < 0.01$). Due to available resources, we did not study the cases where participants completed the two task sessions under the same condition, e.g., both face-to-face or both remotely, and thus we are unable to eliminate the possible effect of task differences between the two sessions. However, these results suggest that the scientific tasks conducted remotely were of similar quality as those conducted face-to-face. The results further suggest that working remotely, each scientist having full access to the system at all times, may facilitate their learning about the system and scientific tasks at hand, and this possibly influenced subsequent scientific work in a positive way.

Participants' perceptions regarding control, sensory, distraction and realism attributes of the nM collaboratory system emerged from the analysis of the interview data. Participants requested several features the framework predicted would be important but were not implemented due to technical constraints; they reported negative perceptions of features that did not conform to the framework; and they reported positive perceptions regarding features the framework predicted would be important and which were implemented.

An example of features suggested by the framework and not implemented are automatic tracking or remotely controlled pan-tilt-zoom camera capabilities. These features were originally suggested when considering the active search (sensory) attribute. In post-interviews, several participants requested these features, e.g., one participant commented: "We didn't want to waste our time always adjusting the camera . . . have the camera follow you."

Similarly, a participant requested the capability to view a collaborator's remote screen while viewing their local screen, a feature suggested by the environmental richness (sensory) attribute. The participant explained:

> It would be good . . . if you're both in your private state [if] you could each see what the other's doing . . . if you have two different ideas of how to go about something, then you each can try it and see if you get to the same point without having to flip back and forth between [states.]

Study participants also reported negative perceptions of features that did not conform to the framework. For example, the consistency of multimodal presentation (sensory) attribute emerged as problematic for study participants. In particular, the video would "freeze" and be out of sync with the audio. Participants commented: "The video window froze and that was slightly aggravating." And, "[the video] kept stopping . . . his picture would freeze . . . the audio would be far ahead of where the video was." Other participants commented: "[The video] was extremely helpful . . . I couldn't really describe [a scientific phenomenon] as well as I could just move my hands . . . in front of the camera." Also, "I liked the video conferencing . . . I like seeing people as I interact with them and they react."

Thus the video had utility, but the multimodal presentation of the video and audio was not effective. This particular problem can be addressed through improvements in networking infrastructure and algorithms that provide faster and more reliable video transmission and coding and decoding. These types of issues are typically outside the scope of any single collaborative virtual environment, yet they impact users' perceptions of the environment.

Participants also reported positive perceptions of features that were suggested by the framework and implemented. This was particularly evident with respect to the mode of control attribute. In the nM visualization software component, all users can execute system functions concurrently. Thus the model of control is identical when working individually and collaboratively. Participants commented: "The best thing was . . . the ability to work on the same thing at the same time with the nM." And, "[we] never fought over the nM because . . . both of us [could] use it at the same time."

In comparison, the mode of control differed when using the off-the-shelf shared application software, NetMeeting™. In NetMeeting users were required to explicitly take control of a shared application by double-clicking on the application window. One participant explained:

> [It] became exceedingly frustrating . . . to share control . . . When I wanted to do something and my partner wanted to do something at the same time, we . . . went back and forth double-clicking to gain control, and . . . it took us a few seconds to even acknowledge that. Essentially . . . we were fighting over control.

Task performance as measured by graded lab reports and perceptions of the system as discussed in post-interviews help demonstrate the appropriateness of the features suggested by the framework and provide some insights regarding the validity and utility of the framework.

2.6. Limitations of the Technical Design Framework

It may not be possible or necessary for a CVE to equally support the acquisition and dissemination of contextual, task and process, and socio-emotional information. Emphasizing one or two types of information may help prioritize design and implementation decisions. The framework presented in this chapter identifies types of information to support situation awareness but it does not prioritize them. For example, due to technical and budget constraints, some design decisions suggested by the framework could not be implemented.

Furthermore, it is not known if the list of attributes in the framework is exhaustive. Additional categories of attributes and additional attributes within categories may emerge as technology and our understanding of human information processing evolves. Future research is needed to investigate guidelines for prioritization.

3.   An Organizational Design Framework

As mentioned earlier, technology adoption and use is not solely influenced by features of the technology but also by organizational structures and practices. These organizational factors become increasingly complex when a large group of scientists needs to collaborate across distances, not only by sharing data and instruments but also by actively discussing ideas, identifying problems and solutions. Increasingly scientific problems require such collaboration among groups of scientists, many of who often work in different organizations, geographic locations and disciplines. How can such scientific research be best organized?

To address this issue, a two-year field study of a large, distributed group of scientists was conducted. Analysis of organizational documentation, sociometric surveys, interviews and observation data suggests that a new type of research and development (R&D) organization, called the conceptual organization, is one solution [9, 30].

3.1.   Research Methodology

The conceptual organization framework is based on an in-depth two-year case study of an R&D centre in the US. Initially, the Centre had approximately 30 faculty scientists and 82 students and postdoctoral fellows, and three full-time staff members physically located at four different universities in the US. Membership has changed over the years, and after 3 years there were approximately 45 faculty scientists, 70 students and postdoctoral fellows and three full-time staff members located at five US universities. The R&D centre was first funded late 1999, with a five-year $15 million dollar commitment from a national funding agency with matching support from several participating universities, corporations and a non-profit foundation.

The case study began during the beginning stages of the centre and continued for 2 years. While conducting the case study, the author was a participant observer, having both complete and peripheral membership roles. As a complete member, the author had functional, in addition to research, roles in the research setting. The author served as the Centre Coordinator of Social Science Research Efforts and a member of the Centre management team. She actively participated in the management meetings, contributing to discussions and participating in decision-making. However, when the meetings and decision-making focused on research in natural science and engineering topics, topics not in the author's areas of expertise, she assumed the role of a peripheral member. She observed the activity, taking notes and audio-recordings, and occasionally discussed events and outcomes with meeting participants but she did not actively participate in the discussions and decision-making. Seventy-three management team meetings were held during the two-year study, and the author observed and participated in these meeting. The author was also a peripheral member participant in centre-wide weekly research meetings, generally observing discussions and only completely participating when discussions regarding collaboration and collaboration technology took place. Centre members were made aware of the author's roles.

Observation data included transcribed audio-recordings of meetings, video-recordings of videoconferences, meeting and centre documentation and researcher notes. These data were analyzed in the ethnographic and grounded theory traditions [7, 8]. Using semantic content analysis [31] patterns and meanings behind the observations were sought. That is, a theoretical framework was not imposed on the data a priori but rather the data were thoroughly analyzed for patterns within the data and the meaning of those patterns. Results were subsequently shared with several centre members (informants) and their feedback was incorporated.

Two sociometric surveys were also conducted to provide quantitative data regarding collaboration within the centre. The surveys investigated current collaboration among centre members, and took place approximately 12 and 24 months after the centre was established. Response rates for the two surveys were 68% and 73%, respectively. The data were analyzed using sociometric techniques [32] to investigate the number of collaborations among scientists and students, collaborations across universities and changes in collaborations over time. To further investigate collaboration and organization effectiveness, co-authorship of journal publications and research funding data over 3.5 years was collected and analyzed.

Although the technology used in the case study was not a CVE in the strictest sense, components of the technology used had features, such as synchronous applications and voice over IP, that overlap with CVEs. Furthermore, we know that issues regarding the use of CVEs are often organizational in nature. Getting people to participate in CVEs, sharing information equally, are typically more serious and harder to resolve than technical issues, and thus this case study has relevance for CVEs.

3.2.   *The Conceptual Organization*

3.2.1.   *Definition of a Conceptual Organization*

A conceptual organization is a new type of research and development (R&D) organization that has emerged to facilitate collaboration among large groups of geographically distributed scientists in order to tackle large, complex and challenging problems of national and global importance. Its purpose is to discover solutions, quickly and effectively contributing to relevant dynamic knowledge bases and meeting diverse stakeholder needs with minimum capitalization and start-up costs. It has a conceptual organizational structure in addition to a physical structure, both of which are interwoven across other external organizational structures. It has few employees in the traditional sense; most members are scientists who join the organization because they wish to contribute to its vision and goals. These scientists are typically employed full time by universities or an R&D laboratory, and have a part-time affiliation with the conceptual organization. The conceptual organization provides a management structure and organizational practices that facilitate collaboration among members working towards its vision and goals. The power of the conceptual organization is primarily integrative in nature.

3.2.2.   *Synthesis of Multiple Organizational Forms*

The conceptual organization has characteristics, or features, in common with traditional organizations, invisible colleges, scientific collaboratories and virtual teams. For example, similar to traditional R&D organizations, conceptual organizations need physical space, including offices for researchers and staff as well as laboratories to house specialized scientific equipment and conduct scientific experiments. For the conceptual organization, however, these needs are often negotiated and met through relationships with other organizations, such as universities, with which their members are affiliated. Conceptual organizations and traditional R&D organizations also have aspects of management in common, such as a management team that includes directors and an external advisory board who reviews the organization's progress. However, as discussed below the management structure of a conceptual organization has a more diversified membership.

Similar to invisible colleges [33], members elect and are selected to participate in a conceptual organization based on their knowledge and expertise. However, in a conceptual organization the selection and participation process is more formal than in an invisible college. Participation in an invisible college is often a matter of knowing its members and thereby gaining entry and acceptance through interaction with them. In a conceptual organization, there is a formal invitation or application process in addition to the informal process.

This is because conceptual organizations typically provide research funding or other costly resources for its members whereas invisible colleges do not.

A scientific collaboratory is a laboratory without walls [34]. A conceptual organization has many characteristics in common with a collaboratory, e.g., a conceptual organization may provide remote (electronic) access to data sources, artifacts, tools and experts. However, the primary goal of a conceptual organization is to address a specific, complex and challenging research issue, while the primary goal of a typical collaboratory is to provide remote access to data sources, artifacts, tools and experts to facilitate scientists' individual research initiatives. The nature and emphasis of these goals are slightly different, although the implementation of these may have aspects in common. For example, a conceptual organization and collaboratory may use similar technology, such as a CVE, to facilitate collaboration across geographic distances. However, a conceptual organization focuses on, and is evaluated with respect to, the results of its research and educational activities; whereas a collaboratory typically focuses on, and is evaluated with respect to, the utilization of its resources.

Virtual teams are groups of individuals who may not meet face-to-face but work together towards a common goal at a distance. Often the team is brought together to address a specific goal and disbanded after that goal is met or when the goal is no longer deemed important [35]. In corporate settings, these teams may cross organizational boundaries and include individuals from different corporations. A conceptual organization may encourage teams to form to address goals related to the vision, and some of these teams may be virtual. For example, a virtual team could be formed to help coordinate all proposed research efforts going on in two locations on a particular topic. However, a virtual team is more limited in scope and size than a conceptual organization.

Thus, a conceptual organization has characteristics in common with traditional organizations, invisible colleges, collaboratories and virtual teams. However, it also appears to be a unique organizational form. As described below, its management structure, use of organizational power, types of stakeholders, benefits and challenges combine to represent a new organizational form that facilitates collaboration across organizations and geographic distances.

3.3. Description of a Conceptual Organization

As discussed previously, the conceptual organization has characteristics in common with other types of R&D organizations, and it employs an innovative combination of organizational practices found in them. These organizational practices are presented in this section to provide a detailed portrayal of a conceptual organization.

3.3.1.   *Management Structure and Organizational Membership*

The management structure of a conceptual organization includes a director who sets the overall prioritization for the centre and is responsible for leading the strategic vision and planning process. In addition, the director takes a lead in organizing the research as well as the dissemination of the research in "real time" by organizing the centre-wide group meetings. As director, this person also leads the interactions with the external stakeholder groups, such as the national funding agency, an external advisory board, affiliate university administrations and the media. In addition to these responsibilities, the director teaches and conducts research.

A conceptual organization typically also has a co-director and a deputy director. The co-director's primary responsibility is financial leadership and leadership in strategic planning. The co-director is also the leader of the external industrial affiliates group and conducts research. In the organization studied, the co-director was a close research collaborator to the director and was essentially interchangeable with the director in many functions. The deputy director is a position created explicitly to help with the numerous administration requirements associated with the centre. The deputy director plays an organizational lead position for the strategic plan and its implementation and accountability. The deputy director is also responsible for leading the generation of the annual report and overall compliance with the cooperative agreement between the universities and the funding agency. In a supporting role, the deputy director also assists with the numerous outreach programs and represents the organization at external venues on numerous occasions.

Thus the directors share in the responsibility of creating and communicating the vision of the organization, as well as administrative tasks. This helps to alleviate common burnout, which often leads to a degradation of management's ability to create and maintain a strategic vision and vibrant research program.

To further broaden participation in organization management, the directors are assisted by a management team that includes a site coordinator for each participating university, a coordinator of collaborative efforts, a higher education outreach coordinator, a kindergarten through 12th grade (K-12) education outreach coordinator, a scientific program committee and an office manager. Site coordinators handle location-specific administrative issues, ranging from reserving a videoconference room for weekly meetings to distributing allocated budget funds. The coordinator of collaborative efforts manages socio-technical activities to support collaboration within the centre and coordinates social science research done in the centre. The higher education and K-12 outreach coordinators oversee the educational outreach activities done by centre members and their staff. The scientific program committee provides input regarding natural science research and development.

The participation of site coordinators, i.e., representatives from each physical location, provides ongoing dialog about challenges, progress, perceptions and ways of working at each location. It is a way to interweave the conceptual organization among multiple physical locations and the external organizations at those locations. It eliminates the need for individual scientists to take sole responsibility of coordination and cooperation between their local and remote organizations (in this case, between their local university and a conceptual organization). It also facilitates learning about different ways of working and collaborative problem solving when members from different locations suggest how practices at their location may solve problems at other locations. For example, one team member suggested a possible solution to a colleague at a different location:

> Another thing you can do ... to magnify your undergraduate help is that you can have undergraduates getting paid for a certain amount of their research but then getting credit for a certain amount, so that you only have to pay for part of it ... We pay [our undergraduate students], but ... we also want them to take two semesters of [research credits].

Similarly, the participation of K-12 outreach, social science, minority and technical program coordinators on the management facilitated coordination and collaboration among these diverse domains.

Scientists and students in a conceptual organization typically have a primary affiliation with the university at which they are physically located. They become members by proposing research projects and activities that would help the conceptual organization achieve its vision, mission and goals. Faculty scientists (current and potential members) may submit proposals that outline research projects that, ideally, support the conceptual organization's vision and mission. The proposals are typically reviewed and discussed by members of the conceptual organization's management team. Primary evaluation criteria may include: fit to strategic plan, potential impact and scientific merit. Secondary evaluation criteria may include: collaboration plan, K-12 outreach record and plan, and outside funds attracted.

3.3.2. Power within the Conceptual Organization

Boulding [36] describes three types of organizational power: destructive, economic and integrative. Destructive power, the power to destroy things, can be used for carrying out a threat and as a prelude to production, where things are destroyed or altered to make way for production. An example of destructive organizational power is the firing of employees who are seen as resisting change in an organization. Economic power is used in all organizations. It involves the creation and acquisition of economic goods, including intellectual property, through production, exchange, taxation or theft. Integrative power involves the capacity to build organizations, inspire loyalty, to bind people together and to develop legitimacy. It has a productive and destructive aspect. In a negative sense it can create enemies and alienate people. All organizations have some integrative power or they could not survive. Some, however, rely on integrative power more than others; these include religious organizations, political movements, volunteer organizations and clubs. Their existence and growth are influenced by the extent to which the objectives of these organizations match the dynamic value structures within a larger population.

The conceptual organization uses a combination of integrative, economic and destructive power; however, its primary source of power appears to be integrative. It solicits funding and participation based on its vision, mission and goals. That is, it attracts funding from corporations, government agencies and other institutions by convincing them that its vision, mission and goals are valid and achievable. A conceptual organization cannot promise an economic return on investment although it may offer some hope to funding corporations that it will effectively educate students who may become future employees and generate patents and other knowledge that may have economic value. Conceptual organizations attract scientists and students similarly, i.e., by convincing them that the organization's vision, mission and goals are exciting and participation in the organization can provide great personal satisfaction.

A conceptual organization may use integrative power in developing its vision, mission and goals. For example, when describing the process of developing a vision, the executive director commented:

> It's intended to be an inclusive process. We've included most of the [faculty] here in the centre in this process. Certainly our external advisory board had a part to play. It's iterative... We made our first draft of the vision, mission and goals, and reviewed those with [the faculty]... We then reviewed those with [industrial partners] and with our external advisory board. We got their input, what they thought we should be doing in a strategic direction... we integrated these comments.

A conceptual organization augments integrative power with economic power, providing some funding to scientists and students. For example, in the conceptual organization studied scientists typically receive one month's summer salary, funding for one graduate student or 50% funding for a postdoctoral fellow, up to $4,000.00 for supplies, and $500 for travel. However, these amounts are by themselves not necessarily sufficient to attract and retain high-caliber scientists who often receive government and corporate funding in much larger amounts. A vision that scientists believe in is also required.

As in any organization, destructive power is used when members do not meet expectations or keep commitments. This may be implemented in the conceptual organization through decisions not to continue funding scientists whose work is judged not in alignment with the conceptual organization's vision, mission and goals. For example, during a meeting deciding funding, participants supported and criticized proposals using comments such as: "This [proposed project] was not the lowest on my list, but I really miss the connection to objectives, goals, mission, etc. here. I could not see where this is going to lead."

These decisions, however, should be reached through integrative power. In the conceptual organization studied, the review was done collaboratively with the scientific program committee, consisting of a lead scientist from each location and the conceptual organization's director, co-director and deputy director. This group also developed the call for proposals. The call included the conceptual organization's vision, mission, goals and critical needs as well as the proposal process and evaluation criteria. The process included a preliminary proposal in which faculty were requested to provide a title and a brief statement of research objectives (six to eight lines in length.) The committee provided feedback to the faculty on their preliminary proposals. The preliminary proposals were: "A mechanism for earlier dialogue... The benefits are... to attempt to avoid excess overlap [between projects];... to identify opportunities for collaboration... not only within a given university, but also between universities;... to identify any unmet needs."

Thus, through interaction with faculty and collaboration among management team members, integrative and destructive powers were used.

3.3.3. Stakeholders of a Conceptual Organization

All organizations, including conceptual organizations, have stakeholders, i.e., individuals or organizations who have a stake in a given organization's success. The case study suggests that stakeholders in a conceptual organization include society, scientific disciplines or paradigms, government funding agencies, businesses and academic institutions.

It appears that society is a primary stakeholder of a conceptual organization's vision in that society legitimizes the government, corporations and institutions that ultimately fund the conceptual organization. For example, the vision of the conceptual organization in the case study supports green chemistry. Green chemistry in general is currently valued by American society. The need to develop new processes and products that do not pollute the environment are recognized as important throughout American society. Even with this general support, results and justification of the government's investment is needed. For example, the conceptual organization directors have made presentations to the US Congress and met with Senators and Representatives. These activities are necessary in part because if citizens in democratic societies do not approve of a conceptual organization's goal, they may organize to limit its funding.

Scientific disciplines are also stakeholders interested in the mission of a conceptual organization. Disciplines typically wish to see knowledge created and students trained in certain scientific areas. This is motivated by collectively held belief systems and yearning for self-preservation and perpetuation of a discipline or scientific paradigm [37], and the mission of a conceptual organization has the potential to contribute to the growth of knowledge in particular scientific disciplines and/or paradigms.

Government funding agencies, businesses and academic institutions are stakeholders who are typically interested in a conceptual organization's vision, mission and goals. For these stakeholders the vision and mission is necessary but not necessarily sufficient. They are also interested in how the vision and mission will be achieved and measured, i.e., the organization's goals. They are typically concerned about justifying their investment in the conceptual organization to their stakeholders, e.g., federal and state governments, and upper management. For example, the conceptual organization studied produced a 226-page report detailing its activities and accomplishments during the preceding 12 months to help justify its government funding. Quantitative measures reported included publications, presentations, patents, supplemental funding, students supported, students graduated, K-12 and minority students reached through outreach activities, and K-12 teachers reached.

Businesses do not appear to seek a return on investment from a conceptual organization in the same way when investing in a company because they anticipate other benefits. For example, in a survey of 249 corporations who participated in industrial-university research centers, Gray, Lindblad and Rudolph [38] found that professional networking, including enhanced student recruitment and improved cooperation with scientists, was the primary factor influencing corporate decisions to maintain their relationship with and support of an industry-academic centre. Quality of the research and technical benefits, such as commercialization impact, were not found to impact corporate support of the centers. A conceptual organization should hold bi-annual or annual meetings that showcase students for its external industrial affiliates group.

3.3.4.   *Knowledge Management: Interaction among Members*

A conceptual organization must utilize CVE and other technology as mechanisms to support its vision and mission, or incur expensive monetary and temporal travel costs. For example, in the conceptual organization studied video conferencing and shared electronic whiteboards were used for organization-wide meetings, weekly centre-wide research meetings, and weekly project team meetings. Organization-wide meetings were held relatively infrequently (e.g. once every 6–8 months); these meetings included all members at all universities and have been used to share information among all members. For example, a conceptual organization-wide meeting was held that introduced the organization's mission, management structure and conceptual organization-wide activities several months after the organization was established.

In the organization studied, centre-wide research meetings were held weekly; all members were invited to attend these meetings, however, students were required to attend. Each meeting typically lasted 1.5–2 hours, and at each university participating in the centre, small groups of 2–25 students and faculty would be in attendance. During the meetings, students and postdoctoral fellows presented and discussed their work at least once per year, responding to questions and comments from other participants.

The format and technology used in these meetings evolved over time. New social protocols, including the introduction of sharing interpersonal information, were introduced to compensate for constraints imposed by the technology. New operations protocols to help reduce technical problems were developed and implemented working with centre members and technical staff [39].

The video-conference technology used for centre-wide meetings included: a large electronic whiteboard and PC running shared application software to display slides and create and capture notes in real time; two large (120 inch) display screens that showed an overview shot of participants in each location and multiple views of one or several individuals in each location; microphones for each participant to capture and broadcast anything they wish to say; stereo audio speakers to enable each participant to clearly hear what is said by others; multiple cameras at each location to capture views of the audience, especially the person currently speaking; and a combination of networks such as ISDN/H.320, local state government analog video network, and video over IP (internet protocol) and required muxes. The technology used for project team meetings was similar but smaller in scale, e.g., it included the large electronic whiteboard but not the large display screens. Although these are not CVE tools in the strict sense, there are many similarities with CVEs if used for large meetings.

Initially, the technology increased the formality of the meetings. Students were concerned about using technology that was new to them and discussing their work with such a large audience; thus they initially prepared more before the meetings and gave formal talks. The initial meetings were also plagued with technical problems and this frustrated many participants. However, after these issues were resolved through new social and technical protocols [39], the meetings became very interactive and increased members' awareness of one another's work. In particular, students received important feedback on their work, and faculty learned about ongoing research efforts. The latter was achieved through minimal effort. If a presentation and discussion was not relevant to a member's work, the member could unobtrusively do other work during the discussion. However, problems originating from a lack of trust among members can still occur and need to be managed. Discussions regarding this issue can be found in Sonnenwald [30].

3.4.   *Benefits of a Conceptual Organization*

A benefit of a conceptual organization is its ability to contribute to and respond to dynamic needs for new knowledge. This is achieved through multiple
mechanisms. One such mechanism used is the dynamic incorporation of scientific experts in emerging relevant areas. For example, the centre has a call for
proposals on a two-year cycle. This enables the incorporation of new scientists
and research topics every other year. Another mechanism that supports the dynamic incorporation of scientific experts and emerging relevant areas is "seed
funding" which is available on a yearly basis. In other R&D organizations,
such efforts have been called "skunk works" but these are limited to existing
organizational members and are hidden from other parts of the organization. In
conceptual organizations, such efforts can be proposed by existing or potential
members. These efforts are not hidden from view, and may be fully integrated
in the organization through activities such as review meetings. Thus, all results
are shared among centre members so everyone can learn from them. A third
mechanism is matching funding. Scientists can use funding from the conceptual organization as matching funds in other grant proposals that may include
additional scientists and students as well as emerging relevant research topics.
This brings additional resources to bear in addressing the vision, mission and
goals of the conceptual organization.

An additional benefit provided by the conceptual organization appears to be
lower capitalization or start-up costs. These lower costs are achieved through
the re-use of existing physical spaces and equipment at the associated universities and organizations, limited term and partial commitment to members
and the inclusion of students and postdoctoral fellows. A conceptual organization may rely on space and equipment at its associated universities to support the research being conducted by its members, scientists and students. In
return, the organization may purchase new equipment that scientists and students at the universities but not associated with the conceptual organization
may also access. The conceptual organization also provides funding to enable students to attend the universities. A limited (2 or 1 year) and partial
commitment to scientists (only one month summer salary is typically provided to scientists) further reduces the start-up costs of a conceptual organization. Of course, the inclusion of students and postdoctoral fellows who
are by definition limited term also reduces or limits start-up costs for it as
well.

A further benefit of a conceptual organization may be found in its ability
to meet diverse stakeholders' and members' needs. As discussed previously,
a conceptual organization's stakeholders can include society, scientific disciplines or paradigms, government funding agencies, corporations and academic
institutions. This diverse and important set is an outgrowth of a variety of political, social and economic forces; no other type of R&D entity has a similar

broad set of stakeholders. Furthermore, the infrastructure at academic institutions is typically based on department and disciplinary boundaries with fierce competition for resources, authority and territory [40]. This is often a barrier when addressing large complex and challenging problems of national and global importance where the best scientists irrespective of discipline, department or institution affiliation are required.

3.5.   Evaluation of the Conceptual Organizational Framework

To evaluate the effectiveness of the conceptual organizational design framework, data regarding collaborations, co-authorship, and funding in the organization studied were collected and analyzed.

As previously mentioned, two sociometric surveys were conducted asking organization members to identify other members they were currently collaborating with. The first survey took place 1 year after the conceptual organization was established; the second took place 1 year later. The number of collaborations reported among faculty scientists increased from an average of 2.37 per scientist to 3.36 per scientist; a 41.7% increase from year 1 to year 2 (see table 4-3.) A larger increase was seen in the growth of collaborations among scientists at different universities than among scientists at the same university (61.1% versus 27.6%). This indicates that collaboration among scientists within the organization developed across universities (and distances).

Another effectiveness measure is co-authorship of journal publications. Table 4-4 shows the number of co-authored and single-authored journal articles published over 3.5 years. Not surprisingly, there were fewer articles published in year 1 due to the start-up time lag that naturally occurs in research. From year 2 on, there were more articles published by co-authors from different universities than published by authors at the same university or published by single authors. On average, 48% of the total articles published were by authors from different universities. These data further suggest that the organizational structure and practices within the conceptual organization studied facilitated collaboration.

A third measure of research effectiveness is the ability to attract funding. The centre studied was initially successful in obtaining research funding from a government agency. Over the next 3 years, the organization also procured $1 million per year in funding from the participating universities, $1 million per year from other sources, e.g., corporations and non-profit organizations. The participating faculty also procured an additional 128 grants for a total of $47 million. These data combined with data regarding the quantity of self-reported collaborations and co-authorship trends provide insights regarding the utility of the conceptual organizational framework.

Table 4-3. Reported collaborations in the centre.

Type of collaboration	Collaborations						
	After 1 year		After 2 years		Change between 1st and 2nd year		
	Total	Per person	Total	Per person	Total	Per person	% change per person
Among all scientists	71	2.37	148	3.36	+77	+0.99	+41.7
Among scientists at the same university	37	1.23	69	1.57	+32	+0.34	+27.6
Among scientists at different universities	34	1.13	80	1.82	+44	+0.69	+61.1
Among all scientists & students	191	1.71	223	1.96	+32	+0.25	+14.6
Among scientists & students at the same university	42	0.38	68	0.60	+26	+0.22	+57.9
Among scientists & students at different universities	139	1.24	155	1.36	+16	+0.12	+9.7

Table 4-4. Co-authorship of journal articles by centre members.

Publication year	Co-authors from						Total
	Same university		Different universities		Single author		
	#	%	#	%	#	%	
Year 1	3	75	1	25	0	0	4
Year 2	2	14	10	71	2	14	14
Year 3	10	34	12	41	7	24	29
First 6 months of year 4	8*	28	16**	55	5	17	29
Yearly averages		*38*		*48*		*14*	

* Includes 3 published and 5 submitted.
** Includes 5 published and 11 submitted.

3.6. Challenges for a Conceptual Organization

One challenge for a conceptual organization involves reconciliation with existing academic and disciplinary cultures. As discussed, a conceptual organization is embedded within existing academic and disciplinary cultures; its members must also be active and accepted participants in their university departments and disciplines. Conflict among these can emerge with respect to job performance evaluation and career paths.

For example, one critical job performance evaluation in research universities in the US occurs when an assistant professor is reviewed for tenure and promotion to associate professor. Typically, an assistant professor is required to leave the university where they are employed if tenure is not granted. Decisions regarding tenure are initially decided by colleagues in the same department and discipline (who may not be members of the conceptual organization). These decisions are based on several evaluation criteria, including: an individual's ability to establish a research agenda or vision; an individual's record of research funding; and recognition of the individual's research contributions in the larger academic community. All of these may be negatively perceived in cases where an assistant professor is a member of a conceptual organization. For example, an assistant professor's research agenda or vision may be perceived by colleagues as lacking originality or insight because it is linked to the conceptual organization's vision, which would not be credited to the assistant professor. Research funding through a conceptual organization does not have the same requirements or review process as found with national and other funding agencies, and thus may not be as highly valued. Furthermore, a conceptual organization's vision may require expertise from multiple disciplines. When an assistant professor collaborates with others not in the same discipline, it can limit the opportunity for colleagues in her or his discipline to learn about and understand the assistant professor's research contributions. This lack of knowledge or understanding may also contribute to a negative evaluation. Thus, the tenure evaluation process may discourage or even conclude an assistant professors' participation in a conceptual organization, with negative consequences for both the assistant professor and conceptual organization.

Associate and full professors must also be active participants in their local university departments and discipline. Activities encouraged by a conceptual organization, e.g., participation in weekly video-conference meetings providing students at other universities feedback on their research and helping a colleague at another university set up research lab equipment, may not be encouraged or valued by one's local university department and colleagues in the same discipline. Individuals have time constraints and, as a result, a faculty member may find they must make difficult choices between contributing to a local department and their career versus contributing to a conceptual organization.

4.   Discussion

Scientific collaboration is complex, yet critical to addressing complex problems that cannot be solved by any one individual, discipline or organization. Collaborative virtual environments can facilitate scientific collaboration but care should be taken when designing both the technology and the organization for which the technology is intended. Traditionally technology design occurs independently of organizational design. Indeed, research in these areas also typically occurs in different disciplines, e.g., computer science and business. However, in practice technology and organizational design are interdependent; each influences and helps shape the other. This chapter is a first effort to consider both technology and organizational design for scientific collaboration.

To address the technical design challenge, we built on previous research in situation awareness as well as interviews and observations of scientists to illuminate the complexity of situation awareness in scientific research and to propose that contextual, task and process, and socio-emotional information is needed to create and maintain situation awareness. Research in virtual reality systems suggests control, sensory, distraction and realism attributes of technology contribute to a sense of presence. We suggest that consideration of these attributes with respect to contextual, task and process, and socio-emotional information provides insights to guide design decisions.

The framework was used to guide decisions regarding technology to support situation awareness for the nM collaboratory system. As a result, the nM collaboratory system includes: consistent shared and private work modes, or spaces; the ability to dynamically switch between those shared and private work modes; the ability to customize an individual view of a shared work space; and multiple pointers that indicate each collaborator's focus of attention, interaction mode and actions simultaneously to all remote sites when in shared mode. The results of a repeated measures, or within-subjects, controlled experimental evaluation of the nM collaboratory system help illustrate the validity and utility of the framework, yet should be interpreted with caution because they are indirect measures of validity and utility.

In addition to considering new frameworks to support technology design, it is important to consider organization design, i.e., how the structure and practices of an organization can be designed to facilitate scientific collaboration. To address the organizational design challenge, we built on previous research as well as an in-depth two-year case study of a successful group of approximately

100 geographically distributed scientists. The resulting framework is the conceptual organization. A conceptual organization should have a long-term vision that addresses large complex and challenging problems of national and global importance. Its goal is to works towards this vision, quickly and effectively contributing to relevant dynamic knowledge bases and meeting diverse stakeholder needs with minimum capitalization and start-up costs. To achieve this, it has an explicit conceptual organizational structure in addition to a physical structure, both of which are interwoven across other external organizational and physical structures. Conceptual organizations engage scientists through the appeal of their vision and management structure and practices that encourage and facilitate collaboration. Challenges for conceptual organizations may arise due to conflicts with traditional norms and practices embedded in university and R&D settings. Social network, co-authorship publication and funding data from the case study setting provide initial evidence of the effectiveness of the conceptual organizational framework.

Additional research, utilizing both the technical and organizational design frameworks in a single setting, would provide increased insight regarding the interplay between the frameworks. However, seldom do researchers get such opportunities; our disciplinary, institutional and funding structures today do not encourage such efforts. Yet as we move towards greater understanding of both technical and social aspects of collaborative virtual environments perhaps such new opportunities may emerge. In the meantime, the technical design framework can help guide the development of CVE technology, in particular its ability to support the creation and maintenance of situation awareness across distances. The organizational design framework can help guide the design of research organizations that are geographically distributed. Both frameworks offer new ways of facilitating distributed scientific collaboration.

Acknowledgements

This chapter is based on research funded by the NIH National Center for Research Resources, NCRR 5-P41-RR02170, and the NIH National Institute of Biomedical Imaging and Bioengineering, P41-EB-002025, and by the STC Program of the National Science Foundation under Agreement No. CHE-9876674. Parts of this chapter were originally published in [4, 9].

Thanks to all study participants; to the team that built the nanoManipulator collaboratory system, including Frederick P. Brooks, Jr., Martin Guthold, Aron Helser, Tom Hudson, Kevin Jeffay, David Marshburn, Don Smith, Richard Superfine, and Russell M. Taylor II; thanks to Kelly Maglaughlin, Ron Bergquist, Bin Li, Atsuko Negishi, Leila Plummer and Eileen Kupsas-Soo who assisted in the nM collaboratory project. I would also like to give special thanks to Mary Whitton for her valuable work during the nM controlled experiment and her assistance in an earlier publication on this work, to Joe DeSimone for his comments on an earlier version of the section on conceptual organizations, and to Ralph Schroeder for his helpful comments on this chapter.

References

1. Vidulich, M., Dominquez, C., Vogel, E., & McMillan, G. (1994). Situation awareness: Papers and annotated bibliography. AL/CF-TR-1994-0085, Air Force Material Command, Wright-Patterson Air Force Base. OH: Armstrong Laboratory.
2. Endsley, M.R. (2000). Theoretical underpinnings of situation awareness: A critical review. In M.R. Endsley & D.J. Garland (Eds.), *Situation Awareness Analysis and Measurement*. Mahwah, NJ: Lawrence Erlbaum, pp. 3–32.
3. Witmer, B.G. & Singer, M.J. (1998). Measuring presence in virtual environments: A presence questionnaire. *Presence: Teleoperators and Virtual Environments, 7*: 225–240.
4. Sonnenwald, D.H., Maglaughlin, K.L., & Whitton, M.C. (2004). Designing to support situation awareness across distances: An example from a scientific collaboratory. *Information Processing and Management, 40*(6): 989–1011.
5. Rogers, E. (1995). *Diffusions of Innovations*. New York: Free Press.
6. Orlikowski, W. (1993). Learning from notes: Organizational issues in groupware implementation. *The Information Society, 9*(3): 237–250.
7. Glaser, B. (1978). *Theoretical Sensitivity: Advances in the Methodology of Grounded Theory.* Mill Valley, CA: Sociology Press.
8. Straus, A. (1998). *Basics of Qualitative Research: Techniques and Procedures for Developing Grounded Theory.* Thousand Oaks, CA: Sage.
9. Sonnenwald, D.H. (2003). The conceptual organization: An emergent collaborative R&D organizational form. *Science Public Policy, 30*(4): 261–272.
10. Cool, C. (2001). The concept of situation in information science. In W.E. Williams (Ed.), *Annual Review of Information Science and Technology*, Vol. 35. Medford, NJ: Information Today, pp. 5–42.
11. Klein, G. (2000). Analysis of situation awareness from critical incident reports. In M.R. Endsley & D.J. Garland (Eds.), *Situation Awareness Analysis and Measurement*. Mahwah, NJ: Lawrence Erlbaum, pp. 51–72.
12. Bales, R. (1950). *Interaction Protocol Analysis*. Cambridge, MA: Addison-Wesley.
13. Nardi, B., Whittaker, S., & Bradner, E. (2000). Interaction and outeraction: Instant messaging in action. In *ACM 2000 Conference on Computer Supported Cooperative Work*. NY: ACM Press, pp. 79–88.
14. Held, R. & Durlach, H. (1992). Telepresence. *Presence: Teleoperators and Virtual Environments, 1*(1): 109–112.
15. Sheridan, T. (1992). Musings on telepresence and virtual presence. *Presence: Teleoperators and Virtual Environments, 1*(1): 120–125.
16. Witmer, B.G. & Singer, M.J. (1992). *Measuring Presence in Virtual Environments* (DTIC Reference Number AD A286 183 DTIC TR 1014), Ft. Belvoir, VA: DTIC, Defense Technical Information Center.
17. Basdogan, C., Ho, C., Srinivasan, M., & Slater, M. (2000). An experimental study on the role of touch in shared virtual environments. *ACM Transactions on Computer–Human Interaction, 7*(4): 443–460.

18. Usoh, M., Arthur, K., Whitton, M., Bastos, R., Steed, A., Slater, M., & Brooks, F. (1999). Walking > walking-in-place > flying in virtual environments. In *Proceedings of the 26ᵗʰ Annual Conference on Computer Graphics and Interactive Techniques*. NY: ACM Press, pp. 359–364.

19. Finch, M., Chi, V., Taylor II, R.M., Falvo, M., Washburn, S., & Superfine, R. (1995). Surface modification tools in a virtual environment interface to a scanning probe microscope. In *Proceedings of the ACM Symposium on Interactive 3D Graphics—Special Issue of Computer Graphics*. NY: ACM Press, pp. 13–18.

20. Taylor II, R.M. & Superfine, R. (1999). Advanced interfaces to scanning probe microscopes. In H.S. Nalwa (Ed.), *Handbook of Nanostructured Materials, Vol. 10.* Norwood, NJ: Ablex, pp. 217–255.

21. Daly Jones, O., Monk, A., & Watts, L. (1998). Some advantages of video conferencing over high-quality audio conferencing: Fluency and awareness of attentional focus. *International Journal of Human Computer Studies, 49*: 21–58.

22. Zahorik, P. & Jenison, R.L. (1998). Presence as being-in-the-world. *Presence: Teleoperators and Virtual Environments, 7*: 78–89.

23. Bellotti, V. & Dourish, P. (1997). Rant and RAVE: Experimental and experiential accounts of a media space. In K. Finn, A. Sellen, & S. Wilbur (Eds.), *Video-Mediated Communication.* Mahwah, NJ: Lawrence Erlbaum, pp. 245–272.

24. Harrison, S., Bly, S., & Anderson, S. (1997). The media space. In K. Finn, A. Sellen, & S. Wilbur (Eds.), *Video-Mediated Communication.* Mahwah, NJ: Lawrence Erlbaum, pp. 273–300.

25. Shneiderman, B. (1998). *Designing the User Interface.* Reading, MA: Addison Wesley.

26. Olson, G.M. & Olson, J.S. (2000). Distance matters. *Human–Computer Interaction, 15*(2–3): 139–178.

27. Berg, B.L. (1989). *Qualitative Research Methods for the Social Sciences.* Boston: Allyn and Bacon.

28. Sonnenwald, D.H., Whitton, M.C., & Maglaughlin, K.L. (2003). Evaluating a scientific collaboratory: Results of a controlled experiment. *ACM Transactions on Computer–Human Interaction, 2*(10): 150–176.

29. Sonnenwald, D.H., Maglaughlin, K.L., & Whitton, M.C. (2001). Using innovation diffusion theory to guide collaboration technology evaluation: Work in progress. In *IEEE 10ᵗʰ International Workshop on Enabling Technologies: Infrastructure for Collaborative Enterprise (WET ICE).* NY: IEEE Press, pp. 114–119.

30. Sonnenwald, D.H. (2003). Managing cognitive and affective trust in the conceptual R&D organization. In M. Iivonen and M. Huotari (Eds.), *Trust in Knowledge Management and Systems in Organizations.* Hershey, PA: Idea Publishing, pp. 82–106.

31. Robson, C. (2002). *Real World Research.* Oxford, UK: Blackwell Publishers.

32. Wasserman, S. & Faust, K. (1994). *Social Network Analysis.* NY: Cambridge University Press.

33. Crane, D. (1972). *Invisible Colleges: The Diffusion of Knowledge in Scientific Communities.* Chicago: University of Chicago Press.

34. Wulf, W.A. (1989). The National Collaboratory: A White Paper. Appendix A in *Toward a National Collaboratory*, unpublished report of a National Science Foundation invitational workshop held at Rockefeller University.

35. Duarte, D. & Snyder, N. (1999). *Mastering Virtual Teams.* San Francisco: Jossey-Bass Publishers.

36. Boulding, K. (1989). *The Three Faces of Power.* Newbury Park, CA: Sage.

37. Kuhn, T. (1970). *The Structure of Scientific Revolutions.* Chicago: University of Chicago Press.

38. Grey, D., Lindblad, M., & Rudolph, J. (2001). Industry-university research centers: A multivariate analysis of member retention. *The Journal of Technology Transfer, 26*: 247–254.

39. Sonnenwald, D.H., Solomon, P., Hara, N., Bolliger, R., & Cox, T. (2002). Collaboration in the large: Using video conferencing to facilitate large group interaction. In A. Gunasekaran and O. Khalil (Eds.), *Knowledge and Information Technology in 21st Century Organizations: Human and Social Perspectives.* Hershey, PA: Idea Publishing, pp. 155–136.

40. Salter, L. & Hearn, A. (1996). *Outside the Lines.* Montreal, Canada: McGill-Queen's University.

Chapter 5

ANALYZING FRAGMENTS OF COLLABORATION IN DISTRIBUTED IMMERSIVE VIRTUAL ENVIRONMENTS

Ilona Heldal, Lars Bråthe, Anthony Steed and Ralph Schroeder

1.   Introduction

Working together at a distance has been a long-standing research goal of collaborative virtual environments (CVEs). While desktop-based CVEs have come into widespread use for online games and to some extent for distributed work, immersive projection technology (IPT) systems [1] are still relatively rare and they are typically used in specialized applications such as oil exploration, molecular visualization, and architectural walkthroughs. Using IPT systems in networked mode, so that people can share the environment with life-size avatars representing other people in another location, is even more rare. However, it can be envisaged that this kind of distributed collaboration, with highly immersive and surrounding displays, will become more widespread in the future. This prognosis is partly based on technological developments, which are bringing ever-larger screens, more intuitive interface devices and more powerful network connections. It is also based on the increasing need for co-visualization of complex data and large-scale models. Since it is clear that networked immersive systems have distinctive benefits [2, 3], it is useful to make a start on identifying the advantages and disadvantages of these types of virtual environments for distributed collaboration.

One feature of new and highly specialized technologies is that, unlike widespread commercial products, they have not undergone extensive usability testing. Although existing usability evaluation methods have been applied to single-user virtual environments [4–6], these will not be adequate for multi-user or collaborative environments [7, 8]. It is not just the complexity and novelty of the networked immersive technologies that makes evaluations difficult, but also the fact that social processes within the group add a further layer

R. Schroeder and A.S. Axelsson (Eds.), Avatars at Work and Play, 97–130.
© 2006 *Springer.*

of complexity. It has been shown that both the experience and the effectiveness of collaboration in CVEs are substantially affected by groups' characteristics and the interpersonal dynamics [9, 10].

The aim of this chapter is to take some first steps towards demonstrating a method for analyzing social and technical interactions in immersive CVEs. The method consists of analyzing sequences of interactions which we call "interaction fragments". Interaction fragments usually last only a few seconds and often recur in a similar form several times per session. They either support or disturb the process of collaboration for solving the task. Fragments can be classified as mainly involving interaction via the interface technology, interaction with each other (social interaction), or fragments involving problem solving (or reaching the goals of the tasks). One question that then arises is whether generalizations can be derived from these very brief snippets of interaction. In the conclusion, we will return to the question regarding the lessons that can be learned from these fragments, as well as their broader usefulness.

2.   Background

There have been several attempts to classify the experience in virtual environments in order to understand what makes their use more effective and enjoyable [11–13]. Moreover, a number of factors have been identified such as presence, immersion, interaction, etc., that influence the experience of—and performance in—virtual environments [14, 15]. Additional factors that need to be taken into account include the levels of realism of the representation of self (the embodiment), of the objects, and the surrounding space. It has been argued that the aim of virtual reality systems should not necessarily be to reproduce physical artifacts or achieve graphical realism [16], nor to reproduce natural interaction in these environments for all situations [17]. For example, although a more realistic embodiment may support better collaboration, simple embodiments can often be sufficient for interaction [18, 19]. Here, we will leave realism and embodiment mostly to one side, and concentrate instead on how people collaborate with each other.

Presence can influence interaction in different ways. For example, several studies show that presence is correlated in different ways with task performance [20, 21]. Task performance and usability issues also depend on the applications [9] or settings [22, 23]. Nevertheless, we will argue that it is possible to identify some common usability issues if we break interaction down into social interaction, interaction via technology, and interaction in order to reach the goal [24]. Apart from the work of Heldal, the analysis here can draw on several kinds of previous studies: studies of single-user environments [17] and of orientation and navigation [6, 25]. For social interaction, some of the main mechanisms or elements (conversation, coordination and awareness) have been identified by Preece [26] and by Tromp [7] for collaboration and usability, and by Tromp, Steed, & Wilson [10] for social conduct (verbal/phatic communication, turn-taking, etc.). To examine how participants reach their goals, it is also necessary to take into account the strategies of task-focused collaboration, proxemic shifts, as well as observations of changes over the course of time.

This chapter is based on a trial in which the aim was to examine collaboration and interaction in networked IPTs. A number of papers discuss other results related to this trial: one discusses the differences in interaction between strangers and friends, i.e. people who do or do not know each other [27]. Another examines some usability issues and the importance of the awareness of one's partner's intentions during collaboration based on questionnaires and interviews with the participants [9]. A third study examines the successes and failures in collaboration in the immersive networked IPT setting with those that have previously been identified for desktop-based CVE systems for object-focused interaction [28]. In this chapter, we will concentrate on the usefulness of examining fragments of interaction for understanding people's collaboration. (Note that interaction fragments should not be confused with the "fragmented interactions" which Hindmarsh, Fraser, Heath, & Benford [29] identified when they analyzed interruptions in the flow of collaboration in desktop CVEs. In their work, Hindmarsh *et al.* showed that problems arose when the technology got in the way and disturbed the users, who were then unable to collaborate successfully.)

3.   Study Design

We examined six pairs of users working together via two IPT systems in different locations. Five pairs spent at least 210 minutes each doing five tasks together in networked immersive virtual environments over the course of a day. For one pair, the trial was stopped approximately halfway through because both partners experienced severe nausea and anxiety. The subjects took a break of between 15 and 20 minutes between tasks, and had a longer lunch break of 60–90 minutes between the first two and the other three tasks. The times that pairs spent for each task session were between a minimum of 25 minutes and a maximum of 70 minutes. The order of the tasks was the same for each group, so that they were exposed to the same experience, and could thus be compared:

1.   Puzzle—the task was to do a small-scale version of the popular Rubik's cube puzzle, with eight blocks having different colors on each side so that each side would have a single color (i.e. four squares of the same color on each of the six sides, see figure 5-1).
2.   Landscape—the environment in this case was a small townscape with surrounding countryside ringed by mountains (see figure 5-2). Subjects

Figure 5-1. Puzzle.

were instructed to familiarize themselves with this landscape and count the number of buildings. They were also told that they would be asked to draw a map of the environment at the end of the task.

3. Whodo—the task was based on a popular game, in this case the murder mystery board game Cluedo. The subjects were asked to find five murder weapons and five suspects in a building with nine rooms (see figure 5-3).

Figure 5-2. Landscape.

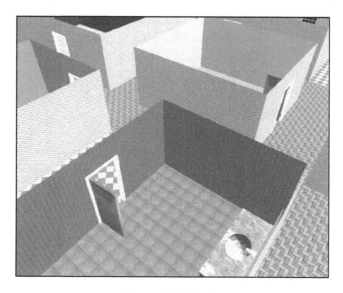

Figure 5-3. Whodo.

They needed to locate the murder victim's body and to find and eliminate
weapons and suspects.

4. Poster—this environment consisted of a room with ten posters stuck on
    the walls (see figure 5-4). The posters each contained a list of six sentence
    fragments. When all the fragments were put in the right order, they would
    make a popular saying or proverb.

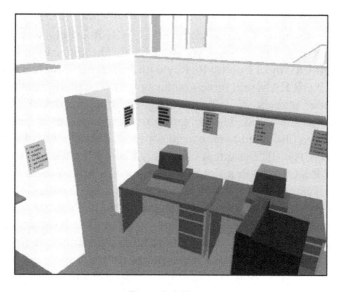

Figure 5-4. Poster.

Figure 5-5. Modeling.

5. Modeling—this environment contained 96 shapes (square blocks, cones, etc.) in six different colors. The subjects were told to make a building, or model of a building, to be entered in an architectural competition. They had to use at least three colors and the building had to be a single object. The result was to be their joint "architectural masterpiece" (see figure 5-5).

One of the goals of this study was to cover a wide range of tasks (for a more detailed description, see [27]).

The IPT system at Chalmers University in Gothenburg was a five-sided (no ceiling) 3 m × 3 m × 3 m TAN VR-CUBE. The application was run on a Silicon Graphics Onyx2 Infinity Reality with fourteen 250 MHz R10000 MIPS processors, 2 GB RAM and three graphics pipes. The participants wore Crys-talEyes shutter glasses. A Polhemus magnetic tracking device tracked both the glasses and the wand. The rendering performance was at least 30 Hz in the applications discussed here, except for the Landscape world where it was around 10 Hz. The IPT system at University College London was a four-sided Trimension ReaCTor with a floor of 2.8 m × 2.8 m and three 2.8 m × 2.2 m walls. It was powered by a Silicon Graphics Onyx2 with eight 300 MHz R12000 MIPS processors, 8 GB RAM and four Infinite Reality2 graphics pipes. The participants wore CrystalEyes stereo glasses. The head and wand were tracked by an Intersense IS900 system. Rendering performance was at least 45 Hz in the applications discussed here, except for the Landscape world where it was around 10 Hz. Both applications were implemented in a customized version of the Distributed Interactive Virtual Environment (DIVE) system [30, 31].

Each participant was portrayed to the other by the use of a simple avatar with a jointed left or right arm. The participant could not see his or her own avatar, except for a virtual hand drawn in the same position as the physical hand. Although local tracker updates perform at the fastest rate provided by the tracker driver, updates to the remote avatar are only sent at 10 Hz to avoid congestion. The network latency between the two sites was approximately 180 ms. Locomotion was effected by a "move in the direction of gaze" metaphor. The object manipulation metaphor was a ray-casting technique but using a short ray of about 10 cm. The subjects could talk to and hear each other by using a wired headset with microphone as well as earphones. The Robust Audio Toolkit (RAT) was used for audio communication between the participants.

4.   Method

For this study, we examined video and audio recordings and referred to some data collected via questionnaires. It is difficult to examine the exact occurrences of certain activities or complete actions in an IPT system because it is not possible to record the activities from all angles [6]. Thus, we recorded the activities from one angle from a camera on top of one corner of the IPT system in Gothenburg and from behind the participant in the IPT system in London. In this way we could watch and listen to details of problematical or supporting sequences over and over again.

We use the following notations in what follows:

LxGx   The xth couple ($x = 1, \ldots, 6$), where one partner Lx is working in the IPT system in London and Gx in the IPT system in Gothenburg.

LxGx Task yy:zz The xth couple working on the task indicated has worked for yy minutes and zz seconds on the task. For example, *L2G2 Puzzle 10:30* means that L2G2 has worked for 10 minutes and 30 seconds (approximately) with the Rubik-cube type puzzle.

Lx:blabla   Lx saying "blabla"

Lx ⇒Wait   Lx interrupts Gx by saying "Wait" or says very quickly "Wait"

Figure 5-6. A subject locomotes straight ahead in the virtual environment. The subject's face and glasses are in the direction of the small line on the circle.

Figure 5-7. A person locomotes backwards.

For the Poster task only we use UPPER-case letters for the sayings on the posters. The lower-case letters are the participants' own words (the notations for how subjects move are shown in figures 5-6 and 5-7).

It is worth mentioning that it is essential to view interaction fragments repeatedly in order to be able to break the interaction down into its significant and detailed parts. For reasons of space we will often present only the transcribed text of particular fragments, including enough description of the actions to provide the context—but ideally the video and audio recordings, and transcriptions of text and movements should be analyzed and presented in conjunction to arrive at a complete understanding of how the collaboration works (some examples are available online at www.mot.chalmers.se/tso/ilona/fragments.html).

5.   Interaction Via Technology

5.1.   *Orientation and Locomotion*

The following observations refer to orientation and locomotion fragments, and fragments identified when people responded to and handled the virtual and the real objects around themselves.

For the Puzzle and the Poster tasks, people hardly had to orient themselves or get their bearings since they had a view of the whole virtual space. The orientation in the Landscape, on the other hand, was considered very difficult by all couples. One reason was that the environment contained many similar buildings with a generic background. It was hard to differentiate reference points, which resulted in the pairs using trial-and-error strategies and taking a long time to familiarize themselves with the environment. The conversations show that it took at least 20 minutes for participants to get an approximate feeling of the size of the environment, and to establish facts such that the main road was circular:

L6G6 Landscape 12:30
L6: It feels that we are going in circles.
G6: Yes. The problem is that the horizon everywhere looks the same . . . All
    the time . . . .

Many pairs said that locomotion in the next task (Whodo) was easier. The corridors and rooms with different appearances helped locomotion and helped

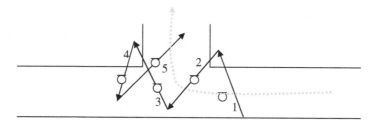

Figure 5-8. L1 tries to follow the gray trajectory, but his movements follow the black arrows. He goes into the wall (1), goes backward (2), tries again and goes into the wall (3), goes backward (4), tries again straight ahead (5) and at this point he is in the corridor going upward (L1G1 Whodo 10:30).

to identify reference points. Some of the people did not follow the corridors and just went through the walls. Those who tried to follow the corridors were constantly colliding with the walls. Figure 5-8 shows the trajectory of one person who tried to go right in a T-junction.

In the Modeling world it was easy to orient oneself even though the space was quite large. This was because the differently colored and shaped objects provided reference points.

For all the tasks we observed that people had difficulties in locomoting straight ahead, and this persisted over long periods of time. They had problems following each other and following the roads (for the Landscape) and the corridors (for the Whodo) tasks. These two tasks were the most locomotion-intensive. Since the task in the Landscape was collaborative exploration, they had to follow each other a lot, but they had a hard time doing this at a constant distance. They often "ran through" each other during a straightforward locomotion or followed the other subject's avatar in a zigzag manner. They commented on this mainly in the beginning of the task, as in the example below, or when they were not preoccupied with the task:

L1G1 Landscape 8:00.
L1: It is fun. It's really like racing.
G1: Yes, it would be funny to [be able to] run so fast!
L1G1 8:40.
L1: Sorry, I'm running through you again.

Just a short while later, between 9:30 and 10:30, L1 ran through G1's avatar four times again, but without mentioning it at all. This is true for other couples too; L6G6 mentions only once that they crossed each other in the beginning of the task, as when L6 apologizes:

L6G6 Landscape 3:00
L6: I think it is hard to go straight ahead... Oops!... Sorry! [she crosses G6]. I don't think I can go straight ahead.

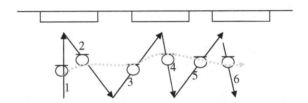

Figure 5-9. Instead of following the gray arrow and locomoting sideways, the subjects usually locomoted back and forth in zigzag in front of the walls with the posters.

In this task the participants could locomote quite fast, which also contributed to the difficulty of adjusting the movements to each other. Among all couples only one person mentioned that he liked it—"it is like racing" (see earlier quote). Several others said that it would be good if they could take a bus or a car to travel with. In the following example, G3 several times asks his partner to slow down.

L3G3 Landscape 6:40
G3 has a hard time following L3.
G3: Can you slow down? . . . So I can adjust . . . .

L3G3 Landscape 9:25
L3 has problems locomoting, but he and G3 ignore this. G3 is only bothered that he cannot follow L3.
G3: Can you slow down? . . . I cannot see you any longer.

Figure 5-9 points to another frequently observed behavior in locomotion. For all tasks, people frequently and easily locomoted backwards. This could be observed in open spaces (Landscape and Modeling), closed spaces (Whodo), as well as smaller places (Puzzle and Poster). In the Poster world, instead of turning somewhat and locomoting sideways, almost all subjects locomoted in a zigzag manner.

In the Modeling world, the subjects often locomoted from the middle of the virtual space, where they built their building, to the border of the environment where the required objects were situated. They did this only by using their joystick; physically they did not move in the IPT system. In other words, they locomoted straight ahead, fetched the object and backed up, rather than turning around physically in the space.

5.2.   *Using the Interface Technologies*

We examine here both the treatment of the virtual objects and the handling of real objects (technical devices and constraints of the surrounding space).

In the subjects' interactions with the technology in this regard, we observed disturbances on three different levels. The first were small interruptions such as usability problems (for example when the subject could not grab an object on the first attempt but could do so on the second), short audio disturbances, inconsistencies in texture updates, and the like. These problems with the system were rarely mentioned at all during the collaboration. An example here is when menu windows were accidentally displayed in the environment by the experimenters (for couple L5G5 Puzzle, 29:39). The subjects did not react at all, probably because the windows disappeared quickly.

A second type of technical disturbances comprised those that were observed and mentioned by one of the subjects but where the partner did not react. For example, the projected hand of one subject got stuck in the bedroom door and the subject complained—even though her partner did not observe the problem at all. In fact this happened because the displayed images become frozen for some seconds when the London tracker lost synchronization for a while:

L6G6 Whodo 4:00
G6 speaks about the task.
L6: My hand got stuck in the door... [Some seconds] Now it lets me go.
G6 continues to talk about the task as if nothing had happened.

Another example of this type is when L6 (L6G6 Poster 17:33) mentioned audio problems, and he asked his partner if she heard the "strange noise", but the partner did not answer and no further attention was paid to it.

The third type of technical disturbance affected both partners. For example, if a subject complained for a long time to her or his partner, asked them for help, or informed them explicitly. Here is an example of the latter:

L1G1 Poster 30:00
G5 has problems with his glasses; the operator changes the batteries in his glasses. L5 is solving the problem; he almost does not notice that G5 has problems.
G5: OK. Now it is a little bit clearer. But still blurred a bit. I have to adapt to it more.
L5 [observes that something is wrong with G5]: OK.
G5: This is technology.
L5: Are your glasses a little bit heavy as well? [He speaks about *his own* problem.]
G5: Unfortunately they cut on one of my ears... But the problem is that they are blurry.
L5 ⇒ Move on! You are in my way! [He is eager to continue with the task.]
G5: OK.
L5: TO RIGHT stays here.

Sometimes longer breaks occurred in the audio connection. In these cases the subjects usually worked alone and tried not to care too much about the interruption:

L5G5 Poster 5:00–8:45
The couple did not observe that the audio had come back, only when G5
 started whistling and L5 heard it did he say:
L5: Hi! Are you back?
G5: Yes, I'm back. But I do not have "buttons" [joystick]. Now I have. Wait,
 I have to put on the clothes [the glasses].

Even though both subjects were using IPT systems, the images displaying the virtual environment were not completely symmetrical since the two IPT systems were not entirely the same. For the tasks where the subjects had to differentiate colors in order to solve the task properly (Puzzle, Posters), the subjects in London found it easier. This was probably due to the better projection system. For those tasks where the subjects had to manipulate more (Puzzle, Whodo, Modeling), the subjects in the IPT in London again found this easier. In this case it was because of the better tracking system. For some tasks, a more surrounding experience was more valuable, particularly in the Landscape, Whodo, Poster, and Modeling tasks, which were better supported in the IPT in Gothenburg with its five walls. The walls were made of fabric in the IPT in Gothenburg and of acrylic in London. Even this slight difference caused differences in the users' reactions: since the users were supposed to handle the surrounding virtual space separately from the real space, the constraints of the physical surroundings disturbed them, e.g. when one subject collided with the real walls. The subjects in London mentioned these collisions much more often, especially in the beginning of the trials:

L1G1 Posters 11:08
L1: Oh s!&%...! I'm just going straight into the walls of the CAVE again,
 I think.
G1 [mumbling]: Be careful.

One of the reasons why they mentioned it more often may be that they could hurt themselves more than people in Gothenburg, who collided only with a fabric wall.

For L2G2, it was the person in Gothenburg who often collided with the walls of the IPT system. In the beginning he mentioned this but his partner never answered. We observed that it was generally in the beginning of the tasks that the subjects paid more attention to disturbances caused by colliding with the walls, getting in a muddle with the cables, or complaining about using the 3D glasses. This was not so later on.

Figure 5-10. Working for 20 seconds with the hands outstretched, but not touching the walls to avoid possible collision.

As figure 5-10 shows, one can focus on solving the task, work on fetching objects, and at the same time reach out the other hand to avoid potentially colliding with the wall of the IPT system for a longer period.

During the fourth task, the Posters, only one subject (G5) mentioned the furniture in the room where the Posters were on the walls. This person said that it was a pity that the chair in the middle was not real, since he was tired and he would like to sit down:

L5G5 Poster 41:00

G5: I would like to sit down. We have a chair here. I would like to sit on it. But of course I cannot. Irritating . . . .

L5: Try out! So . . . .

G5: Is this a TV in front of me?

G5: I think that these are mainly computers. But maybe this one is a TV. I'll take it home. Should we jump on the 9 [9th list of words in the Puzzle] now? This is irritating.

L5: [in a higher voice] But this is nearly done! WHERE EVERYTHING IS . . . No, this EVERYTHING cannot be.

The following example shows that the users ignored those objects that were not important for task solving. They would just locomote through them and hardly mentioned them at all if they were not relevant for solving the problems.

Figure 5-11. Ignoring objects (L5G5 Posters 9.00).

In the example above, the couple had already finished three tasks and had worked for approximately 40 minutes on the fourth, indicating that they could have been physically tired and bored in the environment. Otherwise, every user completely ignored the furniture. They just went through the objects or stayed for substantial periods inside them, as the figure above (figure 5-11) shows where someone just stands in the middle of a shelf.

The virtual walls were more often mentioned for the Poster task, both because it was difficult to locomote to and from the posters (see figure 5-9 above) and because the subjects unintentionally and by mistake went through the walls and left the room (too much locomotion straight ahead). Usually, they did not discuss this, but sometimes a subject looked for her or his partner who could be hidden by the walls:

L1G1 Posters 11:22
L1: Are you outside as well?
G1: No, I'm inside.

Even though the objects are important for solving the problems, the couples merely adapt to these virtual objects' non-material structure and pass through them easily. This is true for all tasks. However, they were often aware of the objects. This is shown best in the Whodo application, where the couples were

Figure 5-12. L1G1 Whodo 17:56–18:10. L1 goes to the table (picture 1) through the table (picture 2), turns back, bends down, looks under the chair, and goes down on the knees under the table looking upward (picture 3).

looking for a hidden murder weapon. They went through a bed, sofa, chair, and table in one second, in such a way that the observer had the feeling that they did not consider that there were any objects in the environment. Yet, seconds later one participant just looked under or crawled completely under a virtual object, to see if there was a weapon hidden under or behind it (see figure 5-12).

Despite the fact that the objects had neither mass nor gravity, the subjects handled them almost like real objects. It was possible, as the following example shows, that one person could mark an object, move it to her or his partner, and leave it (the object would stay suspended in the space), while the other "took it" and moved it where she or he wished. This is clearly hard to perform in non-immersive CVEs.

L6G6 Puzzle 16:30
L6: What is happening if I try to take this from you?
G6: I don't know. Oops [surprised as she hands over a cube and L6 takes it] . . . do you have a red one at your place?

A problem that affected collaboration was that many subjects, for all tasks, kept pointing with non-tracked hands. In many cases they failed to observe that their partners could not possibly see what they were pointing at. They did this on several occasions for short or long periods.

Except for the Puzzle task when the cubes snapped together if they were close enough to each other, the objects were quite difficult to adjust into a correct position relative to each other.

L6G6 Modeling 17:30–50
L6 tries for several seconds to fix a cylinder straight in the right place.
L6: How stubborn it is! OK, then. This can be inclined, then [leaves the cylinder at an angle rather than straightened].

5.3.   *Handling the Partner's Avatar*

There was a difference in how subjects handled the partner's avatar during the different stages of collaboration (introductory phase, proper collaboration, end phase). During the introductory phase they often briefly discussed each other's appearance, the colors of their clothes, the sizes of their avatars, the name tags on the top of the other's head and the like. They were also interested in their own appearance, and whether, for example, they looked as "slim" as their partners. They often combined this short information with "real information"—where the other was situated physically, how the weather was in that city, or about their occupations.

During the proper collaboration, when each subject was focused on solving the task, the subjects did not care about their avatars except as points of reference. If they stopped solving the task and talked with each other about general matters, and about the task, they handled the others' avatars almost like real people. For example they would face each other when speaking to each other (figure 5-13).

In the intermediate phase, during proper problem solving, they would locomote through each other more often. There were instances for most of the tasks when one went through the other's avatar several times in the course of one minute, or also worked standing inside the other person's avatar for several

Figure 5-13. L5G5 speaking to each other.

seconds. In these cases they mentioned the other's avatar only if it disturbed problem solving, for example by blocking each other's view. In the following example, L5 tells G5 to move out of his way, and immediately afterwards continues with the puzzle:

L5G5 Poster 32:00
L5 ⇒ Move on! You are in my way.
G5: OK.
L5: TO RIGHT stays here.

A key benefit of using immersive VR technology is that a person can quickly glance at what the partner is doing. These are very small movements that may not have been noticed by the participants. However, they occurred frequently, especially in the large spaces (Landscape, Modeling) where people worked for longer time periods on their own by observing, counting and carrying objects (but also with the Poster task).

Finally, many of the pairs who succeeded with a task "shook" each other's hand (tried to move their virtual hand to the partner's hand), and L6G6 waved goodbye to each other at the end of almost every task, and when they succeeded with the Puzzle, they lifted their hands over their head and tried to "high five" each other.

6.   Social Interaction

Here we present fragments that illustrate being-at-ease or having difficulties in the course of social interaction. These are sequences of actions that show how a person in a pair handles her or his partner during conversation and communication, and to what extent one subject is aware of the other.

6.1.   Conversation

Small appreciative phrases, e.g. "Great", "Precise", "Cool", "Fine", "Perfect", etc. were effective in supporting collaboration. When one subject in the couple encouraged the other, the collaboration went fine, even though the partners seldom reacted to these phrases. They did not necessarily react to short acknowledging sentences, like "this is nice/hard/right", "I'm here", etc. or questions like "How are you?", "All well?". Nevertheless, these played an important role in keeping the conversation going. By the same token, people who often complained about how difficult the task was, or that they did not think they could manage it, or who were silent—disturbed the collaboration, even though their partner did not necessarily acknowledge these complaints directly:

L3G3 Puzzle 16:20
G3: I still haven't learned how to operate. How to get them. . . .
L3 [silence].
G3: Aha. What happened with that one?
L3 [silence].
G3: Do you think we'll make this in 20 minutes?
L3: Hah [strange laugh]. No. I don't think so!

How quickly a subject answered the partner was very important and directly influenced the success of collaboration. Longer periods of silence confused the partners because they did not know whether the partner was listening at all, intentionally or unintentionally ignoring their comments, or if they were experiencing a technical failure. For L2G2, the subject from Gothenburg constantly made more efforts that kept the conversation going, and the collaboration went much better than for L3G3:

L2G2 Puzzle 6:00
G2: We are going to run out of the cubes soon [says this in a joking way].
L2: I think we may each have a side of different color.
G2: Yes, I think so.
L2 [silence].
G2: OK, black is no color. Maybe you tried to tell me that?
L2 [no answer].
G2: "Ah."

The conversation was problematical for L2G2, but G2 pushed it forward. L2 was passive, but at least he responded with "OK", "Sure", "Right". As a result, they were one of only two pairs who succeeded in putting together all the 11 sayings on the posters (correctly or not). For example, G2, the Swede, often asked his English partner if he had trouble understanding:

L2G2 Poster 34:00
G2: EVERYBODY. MEMOIRS. What does that mean? Remember?
L2: MEMOIRS? . . . Is that . . . like a book of personal experiences?
G2: Ah! Memoirs!

For L3G3, even though G3 had problems with the language, he never asked his partner for help. The following conversation sequences show how L3 gets frustrated because of his passive partner, who often took a long time to respond—and when he did so, it was in an unhelpful way:

L3G3 Whodo 35:00
L3: OK. Ah . . . Last time, when you clicked the rooms, what criteria did
     you follow to click on the rooms?

G3: Ah, Ah . . . .

L3: You see, you have done it well. So? . . . I don't know . . . what did you do with the rooms?

G3: Last time? Do you mean last game?

L3: Yapp.

G3: [does not respond].

L3: Yes?

G3: Do you mean . . . ? [short pause].

L3: Yes. [upset].

G3: . . . what I did with the rooms last game? [pause].

L3: Yees! [upset].

G3: Jaha. Here I can see you. I'm right behind you.

L3: OK . . . [he gives up].

G3: I can see the dead body again. [pause] I just clicked on the posters.

G3 also had problems with using the devices and seeing objects in 3D, which made him talk in Swedish (to himself, or to the operator), which, in turn, made L3 upset:

L3G3 Whodo 25:00

L3: Hello!

G3: Yes.

L3: So, we have to do it again!

G3 [talks in Swedish to the operator].

L3 [irritated]: He is talking Swedish!

Conversation played different roles during the different phases of problem solving. During the introductory phases for each task, it was especially important to suggest strategies, ask the partner about suggestions, acknowledge the partner's suggestions quickly, and show that one was active and interested in the task. L6G6, a pair who solved the tasks effectively, had intense conversation periods at the beginning of each task, as the Landscape example shows:

L6G6 Landscape 3:30

G6: I think is quite hard to see where a house begins and ends. Should we go nearer to see better?

L6: OK.

G6: Should we go near?

L6: Should we traverse the lawn?

G6 ⇒ Yes, I think we should go straight over.

Frequent acknowledgment and turn-taking were important. However, quick comments sometimes resulted in confusion. By not having gestures, facial expressions or eye glances, the conversation was occasionally stopped by unnecessary breaks and starts when partners did not know who should continue speaking:

L6G6 Landscape 30:00
L6 ⇒ This has to be . . . [she stops and waits].
G6 ⇒ Is this . . . [she also stops and waits].
L6: An airfield.
G6: Or something. . . .

Speaking simultaneously was not just distracting but also, on some occasions, supported collaboration. For the Posters, people often read the words at the same time by dividing the posters between themselves, and each subject read the words from the posters located in her or his part of the room. Hearing several words belonging in one way or another to the same saying helped them to put together the proverb more quickly. They often recited the sayings, or possible variants, together. This seemed to be an effective method for all couples in this task:

L6G6 Poster 20:00
L6 and G6 together: DIPLOMACY IS TO SAY THE NASTIEST THINGS IN THE NICEST WAY.
G6: No. TO DO, we have here.
L6 and G6 together: DIPLOMACY IS TO DO THE NASTIEST THINGS IN THE NICEST WAY.

The following example shows an adaptation to the "problematical partner" encountered earlier. L3 in a way got used to G3's complaints and to the fact that from time to time he spoke in Swedish. He filtered the unnecessary words out and tried to put the right sayings together:

L3G3 Poster after 20:00
G3: OK. Seems that I had some problems with my glasses, but now it is OK.
L3: Should we do the number one? A CRITIC IS A MAN WHO KNOWS.
G3 ⇒ THE WAY har jag hittat här [He says in Swedish: "har jag hittat här", which means "I found here"].
L3: Yes! A CRITIC IS A MAN WHO KNOWS THE WAY.
[It seems that he does not care about Swedish being spoken.]

6.2.   Communication

It is difficult to separate communication from conversation, awareness, or problem solving that supports collaboration. Treating the other's avatar as discussed earlier can be regarded as (non-verbal) communication. Conversely, people could speak in the environment without communicating with each other. For example G3 sometimes spoke Swedish, or spoke with the operator. G1 sometimes spoke with the objects. Some people described certain movements without being interested in whether the partner answered or not. Finally, one person could be aware of the other without necessarily communicating with her or him. For example, when one subject became frustrated that the other was too quiet. Collaborative problem solving is both an internal and external process [32]. One must communicate with one's partner in order to work together, but thinking about new strategies or understanding strategies that have been suggested does not necessarily entail that one should communicate with one's partner. And engaging with the other's avatar is not necessarily communication— as, for example, when one locomotes through the other's avatar several times without mentioning it.

Besides speaking to each other, as presented in the section on technical interaction, the subjects could easily see their partner's location in the environment during most of the tasks and they could note what the partner was doing. By taking a short glimpse of one's partner, one could ascertain that everything was all right. Immersive technologies also make it possible for participants to easily relate to their partners' size, position in the environment, and direction of movement [28].

Gesturing and pointing was important for collaborating effectively on the tasks, so as to help each other if needed. Seeing what the partner was doing and speaking at the same time enabled a subject to assist the partner in handling the technical devices or to do things instead of her or him:

L3G3 Puzzle 15:30
G3: . . . I don't know how to drop this.
L3: You just release the button.

The real-time communication also created possibilities to discuss inconsistencies in the environment. Even though the subjects could not be sure whether their partner's environment and the devices they used were exactly the same, they appeared to assume this. Here G6, who went through the floor of the simulated environment (due a software inconsistency), tried to help her partner by telling her how she managed to come back after having experienced the same problem:

L6G6 Landscape 27:00–28:00
L6: Now I'm coming up again.
G6: I think it is only to go backward. Anyway, when you are falling down through the texture . . . Are you there somewhere? Or are you stuck?
L6: ⟹ How did you came back before? Did you go backward . . . or so . . . ?
G6: I just went backward. I stayed and went backward.

L6 [to herself]: We should go straight backward. I can't. Failed. Ah, now I'm going backward.

G6: Yes, I see that you are . . . .

L6 ⇒ I'm going out to the road instead . . . I refuse to go further in the quicksand.

For the modeling world, the participants often had to help each other because if one person grabbed an object this person "owned" it and the partner could not grab it. The following is a case when a subject asks her partner for help to move an object. In addition, she instructs the partner to put it in the right place and the correct position.

L6G6 Modeling 46:30

L6: Could you please help me with the red one? This is one that I definitely cannot move. Please put it round this one [pointing with the wrong hand].

L6G6 Modeling 47:30

L6 is giving instructions to G6 where she should put an object.

L6: A little more . . . A little more on my side . . . Now straight . . . Straight . . . a little more straight away . . . A little more . . . Yes!

Here, we have to stress that both partners would use their non-tracked hand for pointing throughout all tasks. Sometimes they noticed their mistake and commented on it:

L5G5 Puzzle around 7:00

G5: Here, here . . . against me . . . Do you see my . . . Of course, you can't see my hand. Damn, I'm waving with my real hand, hmmmm. . . .

L5: Sure, yes . . . If you point with the joystick hand I'll see it.

6.3.   *Awareness of the Partner*

The partners were aware of each other since they helped each other directly (when a subject asked for help) or indirectly (when they were looking around and monitoring what the partner was doing or what was happening). For the Puzzle and the Modeling applications, because the environments were small and open, each user could constantly see their partner. The only exceptions were for the participants in the IPT system in London who would occasionally face out towards an open wall. This did not cause any major disturbances in collaboration. For the other applications, there were times when one person could not see the other's avatar. In these cases, the subjects often reported to each other verbally on where they were and what they were doing.

Almost all subjects in the experiment helped their partners occasionally during the tasks. For the Puzzle task, the subjects often asked their partners about the colors of the hidden sides; that is, the sides that they could not see but that they knew their partners could see. Even though manipulating the cubes was easy, the subjects could get a sense of the colors of objects more quickly by asking their partners rather than by manipulating the object to see themselves.

Many of the subjects also verbally described what they were doing in the environment. They followed their own movements and thoughts with a "trail of words". Such behavior was especially prominent for the Whodo task, probably because the subjects were in different virtual rooms and could not see each other but where the task required keeping the partner informed of progress. "Now I'm in the room" was a typical phrase in Whodo. For this task, they often jointly discussed the rooms, weapons and suspects that they had to eliminate.

Saying things together perhaps gave a feeling of being acknowledged by the partner. In the Poster task the couples often said the sayings jointly. In the Landscape, they often jointly counted the houses:

L1G1 Landscape 19:00
L1: How many houses do we have now? Fifteen, or?
G1 and L1 [counting out loud together]: We had 11 before.
L1: Yes, we had 11 so it might be 16. . . .

Two things that seemed to be particularly important were being able to do things together and being able to see what the partner was doing. However, this requires implementation awareness from designers. Designers could, for example, implement objects that support collaboration so that they can be used or viewed simultaneously by both partners. However, when people got to know certain benefits of their partner's technology that they did not have themselves, often in the middle of a task, they got frustrated. Almost all subjects in Gothenburg observed relatively late during the task that they could see the posters on the walls just by turning around. When they mentioned this to the partners from London, who usually knew it already, they felt disadvantaged and frustrated:

L5G5 Poster 17:00
G5: I try a smart strategy here. I just missed a thing at the beginning. This room, the Cube I'm inside in, is almost exactly the same size as this room [the virtual]. Also I do not have to move [locomote] around. I can go forwards and backwards instead.
L5: Yes . . . I do so. . . .
G5: Really? You don't use your "remote control" [joystick] at all?
L5: No, I'm moving instead.
G5 [somewhat irritated]: OK. Well . . . Number 5 [he turns to the task instead].

The following example is another illustration of how a person becomes frustrated when he becomes aware of the advantages that the other person has. This is an example of when the partner is able to manipulate objects much more easily:

L3G3 Whodo 15:00
G3: But you? Don't have any problem, do you?
L3: Well, no. . . .
G3: You understand the task?
L3: Yes. And you?
G3: [sighs] I hope so . . . I don't know how to drop this.
L3: You just release the button.
G3: . . . The one that I was working with is now in front of you [irritated].

7.   Problem Solving

To examine how people reached their goals in the environments, we can consider the flow of collaboration in different phases of problem solving. In this trial, the subjects had to solve problems in all five applications. For two tasks (Puzzle, Whodo), they got visual responses and knew whether they solved the problem correctly or not. For the Landscape and Poster task, they did not know, even though many of them were curious about the results. The Modeling was an open-ended task. In examining problem solving, we were interested in how they began to solve the problems, what they did to choose strategies, whether they repeated the same strategies or changed them, and how they acted when they got partial results.

There were very short discussions about choosing strategies before the first task. Almost everyone used trial and error, just attempting to put the cubes together by building one side from four small cubes with the same color. All of the couples ended up redoing their first side. For almost all couples (except one) the strategy they then adopted was to continue in the same vein—to begin with one side of the same color, or sometimes a second simultaneously, and adjust the rest to it. Only two couples (L1G1, L6G6) chose a different strategy at a later stage.

In the Landscape, when people looked around, they often observed that the size of the environment was huge. Many of them suggested, as an initial strategy, to divide the environment between themselves so that each should explore half of the city. However, all couples changed this strategy because it was difficult to communicate the results. Also, they could not easily delimit half of the environment so that they would know what was assigned to them.

For the Whodo task, the couple often discussed how they should proceed since different tasks and investigations took place in different rooms. The importance of continually acknowledging correct strategies, while actively contributing to influence the solution and modify it if necessary, is shown in the following example:

L5G5 Poster around 13:00

L5: WHEN . . . THEY . . . NAME . . . SPELL . . . and . . . YOU ARE. What can this mean?

G5: One more time! Take it again. I did not find any 5 yet.

G5: And I have YOUR here.

L5: OK. YOU ARE FAMOUS WHEN THEY CAN SPELL YOUR NAME. It is done!

G5: OK.

L5: YOU ARE FAMOUS WHEN THEY CAN SPELL YOUR NAME.

G5: YOU ARE FAMOUS WHEN THEY CAN SPELL YOUR NAME.

L5: Perfect. We took this in 10 seconds.

G5 ⇒ No! Wait a minute! I have here...Yes, that is true.

L5 ⇒ No. Then we begin. It was the fifth, or? YOU ARE FAMOUS WHEN THEY CAN SPELL YOUR NAME.

G5: No! It says here: IN KARACHI. Says here. Wait! We did not reach this before. YOU ARE FAMOUS WHEN THEY CAN SPELL YOUR NAME IN KARACHI.

L5G5 [they read together]: YOU ARE FAMOUS WHEN THEY CAN SPELL YOUR NAME IN KARACHI.

L5: OK. YOU ARE FAMOUS IN KARACHI WHEN THEY CAN SPELL YOUR NAME.

G5: No, the opposite! YOU ARE FAMOUS WHEN THEY CAN SPELL YOUR NAME IN KARACHI.

It can be seen here that both partners are constantly repeating to each other what they are saying and thus sharing which part of the problem they are working on. Another example can illustrate a different approach to problem solving: even in cases when a subject mentions a technical problem and the partner reacts, it may happen that the first person does not want to pursue it further but prefers to concentrate on problem solving. This occurred several times for a number of couples, and often followed different technical interruptions. Here, L5G5 contributed to efficient task solving by keeping the partner's attention on the task:

L5G5 Poster 11:20

There are several occasions when L5 works and G5 either works or not because he is commenting on problems with the technology or making observations about the environment, etc.

L5: Could you take your 3's [the words with the number 3 in front of them]?

G5: It is so bad that they are so low.

L5: Low???

G5: Yes, I have to bend down.

L5: Come along [with the task]! Did you find any?

[A few minutes later:].

L5 and G5 "read" together their words: A MAN WHO DOES NOT MAKE MISTAKES DOES NOT USUALLY DO ANYTHING.

This couple chose an efficient strategy in solving the Posters from the start. They took positions in a room such that L5 could easily see half of the room and read the posters well while G5 could do so with the other half. Many of the other couples took similar positions at some point during the problem solving.

The following example also shows that it is important to push the problem solving forward, even though one is not completely sure of the results. For the Landscape task, the couples were rather unsure on several occasions whether they had counted the buildings correctly or not. This was hard without feedback, references, and marking possibilities.

L6: "The 34th was this. Or?"

G6: "OK. But... we are going to continue. Straight away...".

Active participants and strong opinions often caused conflicts, as in the following example, where G6 does not agree on the same solution as L6. They stand in front of each other, face each other and argue. Neither of them backed down or wanted to continue with another proverb.

L6G6 Poster 48:30

L6: WHEN EVERYTHING IS BAD IT IS GOOD TO KNOW THE WORST.

G6: No. In the opposite way. WHEN EVERYTHING IS THE WORST THE BAD CAN BE GOOD.

L6: Here you have THE WORST. Because of that I think WHEN EVERYTHING IS BAD IT MUST BE GOOD TO KNOW THE WORST.

G6: Noooo!... I think it is one....

L6 ⇒ But I think so!

G6: I don't understand why this should be a proverb in this way! If....

L6 ⇒ [explaining] WHEN EVERYTHING IS BAD IT MUST BE GOOD TO KNOW WHAT IS WORST....

G6: Hah! Hah!

L6: [agree] Yes, a strange proverb, I should say. [She still believes that she is right.] For example: There is sun today. Hmmm. OK. Today... Yes, today.

G6: No! Yes, no! TO KNOW IT ... TO KNOW IT GOOD ... You cannot say "TO KNOW IT GOOD".

L6: TO KNOW IT GOOD.

G6 ⇒ Can't we say ...?

L6: We must say WHEN EVERYTHING IS BAD because the only verb we have is ...

[L6 and G6 argue with each other. L6 does not give up with her version.] 50:00

L6: I'm positive. I'm sticking to this absolutely!

The next example shows a conflict between L3 and G3. At the beginning, L3 wishes to explore the village alone, but G3 wants to do it together. After approximately half an hour G3 suggests that he should do it alone, which frustrates L3 since it was his idea all along.

L3G3 Landscape 15:00

G3: Do you think this is a circular road?

L3 Yes. This village is not so big.

At this point G3 modifies the strategy again.

L3: Let's count the houses, G3!

[But G3 suggests that they should follow the road in opposite directions and see if they meet again. L3 does not like it but agrees. He makes shortcuts through the lawn and becomes impatient.]

L3: Should we start counting now?

G3: Yes, this is the middle of nowhere. [He is irritated.]

L3: How would you like to proceed now? [Tries to be polite anyway.]

[G3 indicates that he does not care. He suggests again that they should go on their own and each count half the village.]

L3. Yes. Can you count the houses? [Sarcastically.]

G3: Yes, I will count the houses. [At this point G3 follows the strategy that originally was suggested by L3 although he had earlier disapproved of it.]

L3: I leave you to explore this part. I go back to the center of town. OK?

G3: Yes.

L3: Then we meet again.

G3: OK.

Sometimes people changed their methods in problem solving because of technical problems. For example, L6 had problems locomoting over a grassy lawn; she stopped G6 even though they had decided previously to locomote to some part of the town through the lawn.

L6G6 Landscape 28:00

L6 ⇒ I'm going on the way instead. I refuse to go out in the quicksand.

G6: Hah. Hah. Do you see me? I'm staying with the traffic sign on the way.

L6. This lawn seems to be dangerous.

G6: Hah. Then we should keep to the asphalt.

We can now turn to the end stage of the collaboration. L5G5 were generally eager to solve the tasks. The following example shows a short sequence with rapid conversation. The participants are speaking to each other and arguing, not bothering if they make mistakes and they are speeding up the work at the end to solve the puzzle:

L5G5 Puzzle approx 27:00

L5: Only a cube wrong.

G5: And it is right on two sides, only here. . . .

L5 ⇒ Do you see a white one here? Yes, I must. . . .

G5 ⇒ Were there any white ones here? On the wrong one?

L5: No. . . .

G5 ⇒ Yes, it is white on this side!

L5: No!

G5: Yes.

L5: No, but watch this. I didn't see this before. Yes, but then . . . Look at this, boy! This is done now!

G5 ⇒ Wait a little bit now! Wait a little bit now! Is this so?

L5 ⇒ So! This is done!

G5: Yes, this is right in all directions. I see it now!

L5: Me too! Me too!

G5 ⇒ Then we can . . . Then we can shake hands now!

L5: Yes, it is done! Yes, we can!

[They try to shake hands. Then, after several minutes:]

L5: You . . . you are in the middle of the cube . . . you. [for the first time they comment that they can go through the objects] . . . do you feel it?

[Both are laughing.]

People followed the convention of saying goodbye, but also commented more on the simulated avatars and objects at the end too—in other words, they can focus on these elements once the task is finished.

8.   Discussion

8.1.   *Interaction Via Technology*

What lessons can be learned from analyzing fragments of interaction in collaborative situations? For interaction via technology we have identified several problems in locomotion, orientation and handling the tasks. Many of the problems for locomotion and orientation showed how people experience clumsy movements, disorientation, problems in following each other, and the like. Other problems in interacting with technology were to due to shortcomings in the operation of the system. Such shortcomings are quite common with a complex new technology that is not yet robust. These included problems with grasping and aligning objects, poor audio, and colliding or passing through objects leading to disorientation. These are immediate usability problems that can be treated in the design of CVEs. One point to highlight is that these problems were often not noticed, or they were mentioned by participants but ignored.

Another type of problem are those arising from the asymmetrical technological settings. Examples here include the person using the Gothenburg IPT having problems manipulating or identifying objects. In these cases the participants often did not know that their partners did not have the same kinds of problems, and this created frustration when they found out that they were handicapped. The misunderstandings about interaction with technology, in turn, had an impact on social interaction and problem solving (see also chapter 7 in this volume for a further discussion of technical inequalities and social effects).

One important set of fragments illustrates how people treated virtual objects: Sometimes participants ignored objects as if they did not exist but seconds later they would treat them as real objects. Similarly, sometimes they treated the partner's avatar as if it was not there, going through it forward and backward, but at other times they apologized when colliding with it. This observation was true for all tasks and all couples (a previous study has also mentioned this, though without explanation, see [10]). This phenomenon raises questions for the study of presence, but it also raises questions about how objects and people should be represented if they can be ignored in one moment but in another treated as if they were real. If participants do not need consistency in this respect, then under what conditions is one or the other mode (treating people and objects as real, or the opposite) or switching between the two problematic? It can be noted here that it is often possible to tell from a participant's focus of attention whether they will treat avatars and objects as real or not.

At the same time, again, participants often easily coped with or ignored difficulties in interacting with technology, including difficulties with devices, with audio, or with interruptions due to technical problems. This includes using the constraints of the real environment in an odd way: figure 5-8 shows a person who focused on the task, using the devices, and automatically using her right hand to avoid collision with the wall. Does this mean that she has less presence since she knew about the walls? Or does it mean that she has higher presence because she had learned to "use the walls" in a similar way as she learned to use the devices? In short, participants learned during the tasks how to use devices, to adjust to the audio, and accept interruptions. At the end of the day, people had also adapted to the technical constraints, cables and working within the walls of the IPT systems.

8.2.   Social Interaction

As for social interaction, we have highlighted the role of small conversational fragments. These can be easily overlooked unless recordings are viewed repeatedly, but they also often play an important role. They were more frequently identified as beneficial in that they kept the conversation going. Moreover, encouraging each other and acknowledging each other had a positive effect on problem solving. We have also seen that keeping the conversation going can help problem solving, but that missing communication cues can cause confusion as participants do not know who should speak next. Long periods of silence, especially for the first four tasks, were confusing (perhaps less so in the final task because both could work alone or engage with each other as required). Counting houses together in the Landscape task, on the other hand, and reading words aloud to each other for the Posters and Whodo tasks, helped problem solving.

In this trial there were problems when people did not share the same skills, for example with different language backgrounds, or if they regarded their partner as clumsy or unwilling. However, good intentions and effort promoted the collaboration. For problem solving more specifically, keeping the conversation going (for example, not letting long periods occur without any feedback, especially in the beginning of conversation) increased the effectiveness for problem solving. A frequent pattern of behavior that was observed was that the subjects occasionally glanced at each other in order to maintain awareness. In between conversation, pointing and helping the partner (non-verbally) also contributed to efficient collaboration.

Awareness of their partners was also achieved by asking where the other was if they did not see her or him, discussing their appearances (mainly in the beginning), apologizing if they collided with the other's avatar, and mentioning when they went through each other's avatar. We also observed that the partners could adapt to one another's behavior, for example if the partner always complained because of technical disturbances. This means that the awareness of the other partner, and what one must do to have sufficient contact with the partner, influences both problem solving and technical interaction. To foster better awareness of each other and avoid frustration, a first step would be to make known from the start the differences in technology and the main differences in each other's backgrounds. Simply letting the partner know at the outset that the other needs more help with the language or the technology, for example, would counteract unnecessary frustration during problem solving.

8.3.   *Problem Solving*

We have presented evidence that people interact with each other differently in the different phases of collaboration. Further, we have focused on strategies during problem solving. We highlighted that the main difficulties that directly influence effectiveness and experiences are related to strategies. It is too easy to choose the "trial-and-error" strategy first. Misunderstandings were caused by difficulties in following through on the strategies, changing strategies, and continuing with the same strategy with very little modification.

There were situations when people did not have any clear strategy and hence did not know how to proceed with the task. There were also confusions around collaboration, misunderstanding each other's intentions, and frustration when one could not make the other person aware of one's situation (see also [10]). In a successful situation, people would check a strategy, follow up steps to reach their goal with each other, and have enough feedback to be sure that they performed correctly. All these ways of handling strategies have an impact on supporting or disturbing task-focused collaboration.

9.   Conclusions

This chapter has presented a detailed study of collaboration in a CVE using immersive VR systems by examining three processes: interaction via technology, social interaction, and problem solving. Through numerous examples of fragments, we have illustrated the benefits of examining fragments very closely for the design of more usable CVEs. Clearly, the three areas that we have kept analytically distinct are interrelated in practice. We suggest, however, that the distinction between the three can help to address, if not overcome, the problem that analyzing CVEs always seems to depend on the context—including different technologies and different tasks or applications. By separating these three areas, we can perhaps find common properties in different contexts; for example if interaction with a certain type of technology always causes certain problems regardless of task or collaborators.

These observations raise larger issues about how to improve the usability of CVEs. Is it better to improve the systems and features of the environment, or to improve the users' awareness of their activities and settings? Our observations also raise broader questions about the aims, development and uses of CVEs, such as whether the aim should be more intuitive devices and greater realism, and what purposes CVEs are best suited for. One lesson that can be derived from the fragments that we have analyzed is the greater importance of social problems and task-solving problems as opposed to problems associated with technology. We saw, for example, how the subjects often ignored or got used to interacting with the technology. The implication is that potential solutions to these problems should also focus on these two areas rather than on technology issues. However, there may be technological solutions to problems in social interaction and problem solving. For example, it may be possible to develop tools for synchronizing the activities of the participants, or to create computer-aided awareness.

This leads to a more general point, which is that the successes and failures in these processes are something that the outside observers can easily become aware of through the method presented here. These same processes, however, are something that the participants were not necessarily aware of. This can be seen in the examples when the participants successfully coped with the various "unnatural" aspects of this setting and when they failed to overcome problems that they could easily avoid if they became more aware of the situation.

One of the benefits of analyzing fragments over the course of a longer collaboration is to examine whether, in the CVE, people follow conventions of interactions from their everyday experiences in the physical world. Since participants in this case collaborated over a longer period, we can argue that breaks with these conventions are unlikely to have been due to the novelty effect of the technology or the situation. Our examples show that whether or not conventions are maintained might depend on the focus of attention of the participants, what they are preoccupied with, how long they have collaborated and what phase of collaboration they are in.

In future work, it will be useful to gauge the relative weight or importance of these three processes more closely and to systematize the fragments according to the conditions in which they have wider applicability. Many of the fragments that have been analyzed here within each of the three areas will be found in a range of tasks in immersive spaces. By examining these fragments closely, we have highlighted some typical problems and successes. In view of the fact that working together in distributed systems is likely to become ever more widespread and complex, it is all the more urgent to develop systematic approaches for improving the usability of immersive CVEs.

References

1. Cruz-Neira, C., Sandin, D., & DeFanti, T. (1993). Surround-screen projection-based virtual reality: The design and implementation of the CAVE. In *Proceedings of SIGGRAPH 93*. New York, pp. 135–142.
2. Slater, M., Sadagic, A., Usoh, M., & Schroeder, R. (2000). Small-group behavior in a virtual and real environment: A comparative study. *Presence: Teleoperators and Virtual Environments, 9*(1): 37–51.
3. Schroeder, R., Steed, A., Axelsson, A.S., Heldal, I., Abelin, A., Wideström, J., Nilsson, A., & Slater, M. (2001). Collaborating in networked immersive spaces: As good as being there together? *Computers & Graphics, 25*(5): 781–788.

4. Gabbard, J.L. & Hix, D. (1997). *A Taxonomy of Usability Characteristics in Virtual Environments.* Report. Blacksburg, Virginia Polytechnic Institute and State University.

5. Kaur, K. (1998). *Designing Virtual Environments for Usability.* Doctoral dissertation. City University, London.

6. Bowman, D., Gabbard, J., & Hix, D. (2002). A survey of usability evaluation in virtual environments: Classification and comparison of methods. *Presence: Teleoperators and Virtual Environments, 11*(4), 404–424.

7. Tromp, J. (2001). Systematic *Usability Design and Evaluation for Collaborative Virtual Environments.* Doctoral dissertation. University of Nottingham.

8. Heldal, I. (2003). *Usability of Collaborative Virtual Environments. Technical and Social Aspects.* Licentiate thesis. Chalmers University of Technology.

9. Steed, A., Spante, M., Heldal, I., Axelsson, A.S., & Schroeder, R. (2003). Strangers and friends in caves: An exploratory study of collaboration in networked IPT systems for extended periods of time. In *Proceedings of ACM SIGGRAPH 2003 Symposium on Interactive 3D Graphics April 27–30,* Monterey, California, pp. 51–54.

10. Tromp, J., Steed, A., & Wilson, J. (2003). Systematic usability evaluation and design issues for collaborative virtual environments. *Presence: Teleoperators and Virtual Environments, 10*(3): 241–267.

11. Robinett, W. (1992). Synthetic experience: A proposed taxonomy. *Presence: Teleoperators and Virtual Environments, 1*(2): 229–247.

12. Zeltzer, D. (1992). Autonomy, interaction, and presence. *Presence: Teleoperators and Virtual Environments, 1*(1): 127–132.

13. Schroeder, R. (2002). Copresence and interaction in virtual environments: An overview of the range of issues. *Fifth International Workshop on Presence, October 9–11,* Porto, Portugal, pp. 274–295.

14. Draper, J.V., Kaber, D.B., & Usher, J.M. (1998). Telepresence. *Human Factors, 40*(3): 354–375.

15. Steed, A., Slater, M., Sadagic, A., Tromp, J., & Bullock, A. (1999). Leadership and collaboration in virtual environments. In *Proceedings of the IEEE Virtual Reality*, 13–17 March, Houston, Texas; USA, pp. 112–115.

16. Stanney, K.M. (Ed.). (2002). *Handbook of Virtual Environments: Design, Implementation, and Applications.* London: Lawrence Erlbaum Associates.

17. Bowman, D.A. (1999). *Interaction techniques for common tasks in immersive virtual environments. Design, evaluation, and application.* Doctoral dissertation. Georgia Institute of Technology.

18. Bowers, J., Pycock, J., & O'Brien, J. (1996). Talk and embodiment in collaborative virtual environments. In *Proceedings of Conference on Human Factors in Computing Systems, CHI'96,* April 13–18, Vancouver, British Columbia, Canada, pp. 58–65.

19. Bente, G., & Krämer, N.C. (2002). Virtual gestures: Analyzing social presence effects of computer-mediated and computer-generated nonverbal behaviour. *Fifth International Workshop on Presence, October 9–11,* Porto, Portugal, pp. 233–244.

20. Heldal, I. & Schroeder, R. (2002). Performance and collaboration in virtual environments for visualizing large complex models: Comparing immersive and desktop systems. In *Proceedings of Virtual Systems and Multimedia, VSMM'2002,* 25–27 September, Gyeongju, Korea, pp. 208–220.

21. Sadowski, W. & Stanney, K. (2002). Presence in virtual environments. In K.M. Stanney (Ed.), *Handbook of Virtual Environments: Design, Implementation, and Applications.* London: Lawrence Erlbaum Associates, pp. 791–806.

22. Heldal, I., Schroeder, R., Steed, A., Axelsson, A.S., Spante, M., & Wideström, J. (2005). Immersiveness and symmetry in copresent situations. In *Proceedings of IEEE Virtual Reality*, 2005, Bonn, Germany, pp. 171–178.

23. Yang, H. & Olson, G.M. (2002). Exploring collaborative navigation: The effect of perspectives on group performance. In *Proceedings of Collaborative Virtual Environments, CVE 2002*, 30 September- 2 October, Bonn, Germany, pp. 137–142.

24. Heldal, I. (2004). Usability development for collaborative virtual environments. *VIRART workshop: Designing and Evaluating Virtual Reality Systems*, 22–23 January, Nottingham, England.

25. Stanney, K.M., Mollaghasemi, M., & Reeves, L. (2000). Development of MAUVE, the multi-criteria assessment of usability for virtual environments system (Final Report, Contract No. N61339-994-C-0098). Orlando, FL: Naval Air Warfare Center-Training Systems Division.

26. Preece, J., Rogers, Y., & Sharp, H. (2002). *Interaction Design: Beyond Human-Computer Interaction*. New York: John Wiley & Sons.

27. Spante, M., Heldal, I., Steed, A., Axelsson, A.S., & Schroeder, R. (2003). Strangers and friends in networked immersive environments: Virtual spaces for future living. In *Proceedings of HOIT 2003, Home Oriented Informatics and Telematics*, April 6–8, Irvine, CA, USA.

28. Heldal, I., Steed, A., Spante, M., Schroeder, R., Bengtsson, S., & Partanen, M. (2005). Successes and failures in copresent situations. Forthcoming in *Presence: Teleoperators and Virtual Environments*.

29. Hindmarsh, J., Fraser, M., Heath, C., & Benford, S.J. (1998). Fragmented interaction: Establishing mutual orientation in virtual environments. In *Proceedings of ACM conference on computer supported cooperative work, CSCW'98*, 14–18 November, Seattle, WA, USA, pp. 217–226.

30. Frecon, E., Smith, G., Steed, A., Stenius, M., & Stahl, O. (2001). An overview of the COVEN platform. *Presence: Teleoperators and Virtual Environments, 10*(1): 109–127.

31. Steed, A., Mortensen, J., & Frecon E. (2001). Spelunking: Experiences using the DIVE System on CAVE-like Platforms. In B. Frohlich, J. Deisinger, H-J. Bullinger (Eds.), *Immersive Projection Technologies and Virtual Environments*. Wien: Springer-Verlag, pp. 153–164.

32. Fjeld, M., Lauche, K., Bichsel, M., Voorhorst, F., Krueger, H., & Rauterberg, M. (2002). Physical and virtual tools: Activity theory applied to the design of groupware. *Computer Supported Cooperative Work, 11*(1–2): 153–180.

Chapter 6

THE IMPACT OF DISPLAY SYSTEM AND EMBODIMENT ON CLOSELY COUPLED COLLABORATION BETWEEN REMOTE USERS

David Roberts, Robin Wolff and Oliver Otto

1.   Introduction

Trends towards greater collaboration between organisations increase the need for effective, efficient and safe ways to collaborate within distance teams. Technology has already greatly reduced the need for face-to-face meetings. Telephones, text messaging, email, web, and classical video conferencing have all thrived in supporting specific aspects of tele-working. There is, however, still a need for face-to-face meetings, even though the cost to business individuals and the environment can be significant. The holy grail of tele-collaboration is to support the full range of communication used within a co-located group.

Psychologists categorise social communication between humans as verbal, non-verbal, the role of objects and that of the environment [1]. Immersive displays surround the senses within an information world, which, compared to desktop systems, is believed by some to increase the feeling of presence and by others to increase task performance. Immersive Collaborative Virtual Environments (ICVE) allow a number of people to share an interactive synthetic experience from a true first person perspective. The use of these technologies in tele-immersion allows geographically separated people to interact using a variety of verbal and non-verbal communication within a shared meaningful environment and through shared information objects. We believe that this is the first technology to support these four primary categories of social human communication in a natural and intuitive way.

Linking walk-in displays, such as Caves, supports unprecedented naturalness of communication between physically remote people by placing them together in a shared scene in which they can naturally move around, talk, gesture and manipulate shared objects. We have investigated the impact of display device and embodiment on the perception and performance of collaboration during a shared task requiring various forms of social human communication and ways of sharing objects. The task, building a garden gazebo, has been routinely evaluated in sustained trials between as many as four linked interactants, distributed between four sites in the UK and Austria.

1.1.   Placing People in an Information and Social Context

Inhabited Information Systems (IIS) encapsulate the principle of placing people within an information context [2]. Immersive virtual reality technology is well suited to this, as it physically places a person within a 3D scene where one can naturally look around and move. Geographically separated people are able to interact and communicate with each other when linking such immersive display interfaces through a CVE, which usually represent a remote user by a human-like articulated character, the avatar. A tracking system placed on the head allows natural control of gaze, while another on a hand can allow an object to be pointed at or reached for. Within the physical confines of the display and tracking system, participants are able to naturally walk around, walk up to and face each other and objects, thus supporting natural social behaviour such as proxemics, communicational gaze and gross gesturing. In the natural world, gaze is extremely important for controlling conversational turn taking, representing attention and emotion. Most immersive systems track gaze to control the viewpoint and this may be communicated to remote participants. However, most present systems do not distinguish between head and body rotation, thus communicating horizontal gaze movement by moving the avatar's torso.

The predominant method for immersion was for many years the Head Mounted Display (HMD). Large screen display systems, such as cubic walk-in (Cave-like) displays, Workbenches and Panoramas, have gradually gained acceptance and are now predominant in industrial applications. Like HMDs, these place people within the scene and offer natural control of gaze and reach, but Panorama and walk-in displays offer far greater field of view than typical HMDs, additionally reducing the risk of motion sickness and nausea. Another important distinction between HMD and walk-in displays is that the user can observe his physical body within the scene, which is thought by some to increase the feeling of presence [3].

1.2.   Level of Cooperation

Levels of cooperation within CVEs have been categorised by a number of research groups in similar ways: Ruddle *et al.* described the different levels of cooperation as level 1—co-existence and shared-perception; level 2—individual modification of the scene; and level 3—simultaneous interactions with an object [4]. A similar taxonomy was presented for haptic collaboration that describes the respective levels as Static, Collaborative and Cooperative [5]. Our studies provide a more detailed taxonomy of level 3, which will be described later.

1.3.   Impact of Display Configurations

Closeness of collaboration depends upon the supported level of communication. We now look at the impact of display configuration on characteristics associated with the feelings of presence and co-presence across the forms of social human communication described above. The majority of CVEs have been experienced through desktop interfaces. The limited field of view and unnatural viewpoint–control characteristic of desktop interfaces introduced problems in navigation and observation. A technique for increasing the field of view by introducing an avatar to represent the local participant and attaching the viewpoint behind the head has become well established through the computer games industry. However, this approach does not utilize a human's peripheral vision and is difficult to control from natural head gaze. The former may be addressed by providing a desktop surround display, e.g. from three monitors joined in an arc [6]. The latter can be addressed through an immersive display with head tracking. Our studies attempt to address both former and latter by using a walk-in display with head tracking.

Significant problems in communicating the referencing of objects of interest within a crowded environment were experienced through desktop interfaces [7]. When participants were given the task of relocating furniture in a shared virtual room, more talking was dedicated to identifying objects than to deciding where to put them. This problem was reduced but not removed by again placing the viewpoint behind the local avatar.

Several studies have investigated the effect of linking various combinations of display systems for collaboration. It was found that immersed users naturally adopted dominant roles versus desktop users [8]. A study by Schroeder *et al.* investigated the effect of display type on collaboration of a distributed team [9]. Their work extended the concept of a Rubik's cube by splitting the composite cube such that two people could concurrently interact with individual component cubes while observing each other's actions. The study compared three conditions based on display combinations: two linked walk-in displays; face-to-face; and a walk- in display linked to a desktop. The primary finding was that the asymmetry between users of the different systems affects their collaboration and that the co-presence of one's partner increases the experience of the CVE as a place.

1.4.   Naturalness of Interaction

Immersive displays are typically imbalanced in terms of input and output bandwidth to the senses. We have observed that most people seem very impressed on entering a walk-in display and observing the immersive rendering but become quickly disappointed when they attempt to interact with the scene. There is considerable scope to improve the naturalness and intuitiveness of interaction in today's systems. Two important factors are multi-sensory alignment and responsiveness.

A walk-in display system gives a perfect alignment of visual and kinematical senses as the user can see his or her own body moving within the space. It is well accepted that the feeling of touch through the haptic sense improves the realism of many simulated tasks, for example in medical training. Multi-user haptic systems are now gaining maturity with control systems used to stabilise interaction in the face of network delays. However, haptic rendering requires considerably higher and less jittery frame rates than vision and combining the two senses in multi-user worlds has proved problematic [10].

Responsiveness is of prime importance. Latency in viewpoint changes following head movements appears to increase feelings of motion sickness and disorientation. Latencies in interacting with objects cause frustration. Responsiveness to interactions with the scene can be improved through localisation and replication. That is, each display system has a dedicated computer that contains a replication of at least part of the object database. The effect of a user's actions on the scene, including their viewpoint, can be calculated and rendered locally. Changes to the scene are sent across the network to update other replications. Consistency control is required to ensure that replications do not diverge to an unstable degree.

2.   Experimental Set-Up

In order to investigate the effect of the display system and user embodiment on closely coupled collaboration in virtual environments as well as its impact on human communication and the CVE system, we designed a benchmark application that involves various forms of coordinated shared object manipulation.

2.1.   Benchmark

Our benchmark allows the analysis of each form of social human communication across a variety of collaborative scenarios, including various forms of shared object manipulation. The task, the construction of a garden gazebo,

Figure 6-1. The Virtual Gazebo application.

cannot be done alone. The time taken to complete each scenario is a measure of the success of collaboration. Scenarios include planning, passing, carrying and assembly, each requiring a distinct mix of non-verbal communication and method of object sharing. Figure 6-1 shows a snapshot of the Virtual Gazebo and figure 6-2 shows a user accessing the application through a walk-in display.

The experiment starts by situating the user in a virtual garden setting, along with all the necessary building materials and tools scattered on the ground. Avatars that represent remote users appear as the rest of the team enters the garden. A user can pick up material and start to build the gazebo. However, constructing a gazebo on your own is not possible. The simulation of gravity intentionally prohibits leaving materials in thin air. Beams have to be held by one person while another fixes them with screws and a screwdriver tool. Moving, positioning and joining of beams require teamwork. Other tasks, such

Figure 6-2. A local user (left) interacting with a remote user (right) within a walk-in display.

as gathering materials, can be done sequentially, but still require coordination between the sub-tasks. The limited set of tools provokes competition for shared resources.

2.2.   Collaborative Scenarios

We now examine the four scenarios of planning, passing, moving and fixing, as summarised in table 6-1. In the planning phase, users reference and discuss shared objects. For example, deciding which material to start with, where to get it from and where to carry it, will make use of both spoken word and

Table 6-1. Scenarios of object sharing.

Scenario	Figure	Description	Method of sharing
Planning	6-3a	Discussing how to proceed.	Referencing objects and environment.
Passing	6-3b	A tool or material is passed from one user to another.	Sequential sharing and manipulation of the same object attribute.
Moving	6-3c	A wooden beam is too heavy to lift alone requiring one user to lift each end.	Concurrent sharing of an object through the same attribute.
Assembling	6-3d	A wooden beam must be held in place by one user, while another fixes it by drilling a hole and inserting a screw.	Concurrent sharing of an object through distinct attributes.

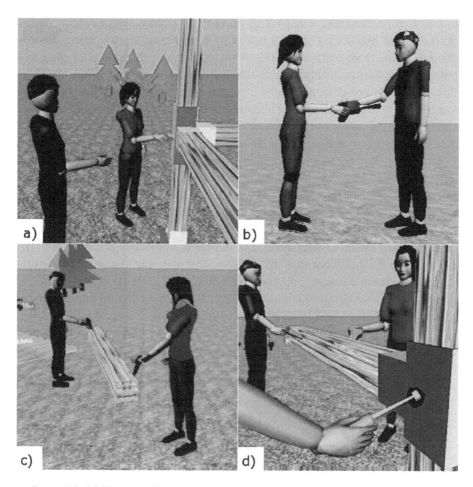

Figure 6-3. (a) Planning, (b) passing a tool, (c) moving a beam, (d) assembling an object.

referential gesturing. Passing an object, for example a screwdriver, between people requires sequential manipulation of the same object attribute, movement in this case. Moving an artificially heavy object, such as a beam, requires two people to share the manipulation of the movement attribute. Assembly often requires one person to hold a material while another drills a hole or inserts a screw. The existence of a hole or screw is defined as an attribute and so the object must be shared through distinct attributes if held while fixed. The effectiveness of communication of intention, attention and emotion, all impact on the performance of each scenario (see figure 6-3).

2.3. Referencing Objects

The performance of collaboration focussed on shared objects is dependent on the efficiency of communicating objects of attention. Other work has shown that this is problematic when using desktop interfaces [7]. We have earlier proposed the hypothesis that problems in referencing objects using desktop displays arise from restricted field of view and indirect control of gaze and pointing. We further proposed that the use of walk-in displays should reduce this. Although not designed for the purpose, the gazebo application is well suited to test our hypotheses. The construction site environment is similarly cluttered as the room of furniture in Hindmarsh *et al.* [7], but has a greater diversity in size of objects and scale of environment. The task of building the gazebo routinely requires communication of the referencing of objects as well as the place within the environment that they are to be taken. Communication of referencing must reflect nuances of speech and gesture and the interface must not restrict the recipient from capturing these. When using a walk-in display, control of gaze and pointing are driven through a tracking system and the user is surrounded by the display surface to the front, both sides and the floor. The complexity of the task requires the collaborative planning of a number of steps, which may involve several collaborators and objects. A wide field of view and direct control and communication of gaze and pointing should allow efficient referencing, location and identification of each.

A typical conversation between two collaborators—Bob and Lara in this case—engaged with moving a heavy beam using carry tools, is reproduced below.

> Bob: Hey, let's move this beam over there. [Points with his hand to the beam in front of him and to the left.]
> Lara: [Rotating to see Bob and then follows his hand movements.]
> Lara: Ok, I will take this carry tool here. [Points to the tool and moves to pick it up.]
> Bob: I'll take the other tool then. Where is that?
> Lara: Just next to you.
> Bob: Ah, ok. [Rotates and picks up the tool.]
> Lara: I have my end of the beam now.
> Bob: Yup, I am right with you. Ok now let's move it over there.
> Lara: I am following your direction.

2.4.   Implementation

The Virtual Gazebo has been implemented on top of the established CVE platform DIVE [11] in version 3.5. Each remote user is embodied through a human like avatar. A non-jointed avatar represents the non-immersed desktop user, whereas the immersed user's avatar shows dynamic head and arm-articulation controlled from head and hand tracking data. Our application included various interactive objects that imitated the behaviour of building materials and tools.

An object's behaviour has been implemented in the form of DIVE/Tcl scripts that describe a set of procedures to change an object's state in a specific way. For example, when a screwdriver intersects with a screw, all objects intersected by the screw are fixed together. All behaviour scripts are reactive and triggered by specific events. These are update messages generated by the CVE system to update replicated versions of the distributed virtual environment. DIVE supports several event types. These include object transformation events, such as movement or rotation; object interaction events, such as grasp, release or select events; object collisions; and changes to object-specific properties and flags. Most functionality of the Virtual Gazebo is triggered by collisions of material and tool objects. For example, when a drill tool is held closely to a material object so that they collide, the resulting collision event would trigger a procedure in the material object's behaviour script to increment the property that counts the number of holes in the object.

Certain object behaviour scripts additionally provide a level of consistency control within the application level. For example, during most interactions a user-defined flag is set to signal a definite object state as an acknowledgment of the successful action of a tool. Hence, a level of causal ordering and discarding of events is realised by constraining the order of manipulations through such flags and properties that must be set in a certain order. For example, a hole must be drilled between two materials and then a screw inserted through both, before they can be fixed together with a screwdriver. The material conditions of possessing a hole and being fixed are each achieved in the code through setting a respective flag. If such a condition was not fulfilled the action would not be successful and the current event discarded, forcing the user to repeat the step.

Early research claimed that generic concurrent manipulation of shared objects would be not possible unless the CVE system fulfils hard real time and reliability constraints [12]. We relaxed these constraints and, again, provided some level of concurrency control through the application level. Allowing script procedures to set several distinct properties concurrently has enabled the concurrent object manipulation of distinct attributes, avoiding exclusive object ownership. For instance, a counter attribute of an object could be set while its position was continuously updated. In contrast, concurrent manipulation of the same attribute has been realised through intermediate procedures that gather and process events before updating the actual attributes of the manipulated object. For example, carrying a beam together with a remote user would be performed with help of specialised carry tools, used at each end of the beam to attract its transformation. These tool objects send their current position to the carried object, which in turn attempts to find an average transformation between them and finally communicates the result to the remote peers that update the scene accordingly. Instead of manipulating the carried object directly, the users interact through intermediate objects that, due to their relatively little overhead in behaviour scripts, show responsive feedback. Hence, carry tools are used also to hide the effect of network latency while concurrently sharing the manipulation of objects.

2.5.   *Effects of Remoteness*

All four scenarios of collaboration have distinct requirements on responsiveness and consistency of the system. For example, the representation of gestures must be sufficiently complete to be recognised and their subtleties understood. Nuances, relating to referencing or manipulating objects, must be sufficiently communicated. This requires timely capture and synchronisation. Communication of events across a switched network, such as the Internet, introduces the possibility of delay, loss and disorder of events. Although this can be addressed by reliable protocols, these introduce dependencies between sender and receiver that can increase jitter and, thus, affect synchronisation. The vast majority of events in most CVE applications represent movement. As movement can be communicated atomically, synchronisation can be increased by discarding all but the most current movement event for each object.

Excessive delay in communication between users can confuse concurrent manipulation of objects, turn taking in conversations, as well as sequential object manipulation. Although reductions in consistency in avatar representation may result in confusion and lower the performance of collaboration, they are unlikely to produce unwanted outcomes in the overall task, unless understood. The loss of events, such as the drilling of a hole, insertion of a screw and tightening the screw with a screwdriver, can cause significant confusion, as can the loss of ordering between them. Furthermore, it becomes confusing if the movement events for an object are delayed and displayed after it has been fixed. Ideally, such events should be discarded before they affect the model. If not, the effect must be overridden quickly.

3.   **User Trials**

Our benchmark has been used to support routine user trials over a two year period between four sites in Europe. Typical configurations of the involved display types can be seen in table 6-2. Initial trials, linking three walk-in displays at Reading and London in UK and Linz in Austria, demonstrated that supporting both verbal and natural non-verbal communication during shared object manipulation was achievable with today's CVEs, but not without significant network-induced inconsistencies [13]. For example, our initial prototype induced around two seconds of delay which was clearly noticeable, as actions appeared to lag behind their words. This problem was due to the CVE system becoming overwhelmed by the scale of tracking events and was fixed in a later

Table 6-2. Display configurations.

Display type	View	Input	Audio	Avatar*
Walk-in (CAVE-like)	Stereo	Tracked head & hand	Yes	Medium realism, dynamic body
Workbench	Stereo	Tracked head & hand	Yes	Medium realism, dynamic body
Desktop	Mono	Mouse & keyboard	Yes	Medium realism, static body

* Avatar: The remote representation of the local user.

prototype with a simple filter mechanism based on the magnitude of movement allowed to generate an event. We found that a good compromise between sufficient detail to support understandable non-verbal communication and sufficient synchronisation to achieve shared object manipulation was to only send movements of above 1cm. Many events below this seemed to be caused by tracking jitter rather than real human movement.

A second and more substantial problem was the loss of event messages vital to causal state changes of the shared objects during manipulation. Although intermediate movement events may often be lost without causing undue confusion, vital events, such as the fixing of a beam to a foot, cause considerable confusion when lost on a remote site. Although we found that the collaborators quickly learned to detect and rectify the problem by carrying out that part of the task again, this did cause frustration, a reported reduction in the feeling or realism and in productivity.

3.1. Experimentation

The subjects were all higher degree students from the three participating universities. Most were aged between twenty and thirty and were studying computer science related subjects. Teams of two or three people, in distinct locations, were given a short tutorial in using the application, told the goal of the task and left to plan and undertake it together. An average session took between a half and one hour, during which, both quantitative and qualitative measurements were taken for each scenario or sub-task. Quantitative measurements included the time to complete each sub-task along with the resultant event traffic. Qualitative measurements of the impression of collaboration were obtained through a post-questionnaire. Most questions were based on those of Usoh *et al.* [14]. Answers could be given on a scale of 1–7, where 7 represents total agreement and 1 total disagreement. Asking sets of related questions reduced errors arising from a user's misinterpretation of a question. Overall, more than one hundred students helped us to gather data and to study different aspects of such close collaboration.

We adapted our application to reduce the dependency on vital events and reduced the goal of the task to building one corner of the gazebo, thus eliminating redundancy in the scenarios. The first of these revised trials were undertaken between a walk-in display and two desktop systems at the University of Reading [15]. The purpose of the trial was to test the impact of asymmetric displays on supporting non-verbal communication including the shared manipulation of objects in comparison to a study by Schroeder *et al.* [9]. We found that novice users adapt quickly to the interface and remoteness of peers. Typically, after three sessions of approximately 15 minutes their performance doubles, approaching that of expert users (5 minutes to perform the task). Immersive users undertook most parts of the task far more efficiently than their desktop counterparts.

3.2.   User Performance

Our benchmark requires close collaboration at numerous points. This means that a faster worker must often wait for the slower before beginning the next step. Schroeder *et al.* found that the perception of collaboration is affected by asymmetry between users of the different systems [9]. Our results showed that the time taken to complete a collaborative task is also affected. When roles in the collaborative task are ill-defined, the performance of the team equals that of the weakest link. However, the performance is greatly increased when the immersed user undertakes the more difficult part of every sub-task. The results of our questionnaire confirmed that the perception of contribution is affected by asymmetry of linked displays when carrying a beam [15]. However, this is clearly not the case when fixing a beam. This suggests that the interface plays a major role during the sharing of an object's attribute and a minor role when sharing an object through distinct attributes.

Surprisingly, neither the interface, nor the form of object sharing, is perceived to affect the level to which the remote user has hindered the task. This appears to contradict the results of the performance analysis above. From the perspective of immersed users, collaboration is considerably easier with a symmetric user. Desktop users, however, found the type of remote display to play little part in the degree of collaboration. Another finding of this trial was that walk-in displays are much more efficient than desktop systems in terms of team performance, especially when positioning objects. In some cases, however, a basic desktop interface may be easier to use, such as when holding an object in the air, as this is just a mouse click. The extent of usability and natural interaction, though, depends on application and interface.

Figure 6-4. A desktop interface with headset for verbal communication.

One would have expected verbal communication between remote users to become more natural when the technology is transparent, that is when the microphone and speakers are hidden. However, we observed a significant increase in verbal communication when the user is constantly aware of a familiar communication device, such as a headset with microphone and earphones [1]. When this was introduced in the trials (see figure 6-4 for a desktop set-up), the team worked together more successfully and each participant made greater use of the non-verbal communication influences. Verbal communication, compared with non-verbal communication, was perceived to be of the greatest importance. Little difference was perceived in the importance of the other influences.

The current state of technology is still some way from providing natural social human communication between remote participants. Novice users commonly commented that the lack of a feeling of touch made interaction with objects unintuitive. We addressed this in an extended study by placing a haptic system within the walk-in display [16]. In addition to possibly being the first group to do this, the exercise resulted in two important findings: Firstly, decoupling graphics and haptics rendering onto separate machines can maintain suitable frame rate, latency and jitter characteristics for both visual and haptic senses, while maintaining sufficient consistency between them. Secondly, the frame rate of visual representation affects the usability of the haptic interface.

3.3.   Event Traffic

In order to design a consistency management scheme it is vital to have a detailed understanding of the requirements of interaction and collaboration and the characteristics of event traffic that is likely to be generated while supporting these between particular interfaces. We also used the Virtual Gazebo to study the event traffic across all three levels of collaboration, and across various symmetric and asymmetric display configurations, paying particular attention to the form of object sharing in levels two and three [17]. We looked at the impact of the four categories of collaboration on event traffic within a local area network at University of Reading through both a desktop system and a walk-in display system. The frequency of specific event types to update avatar movement, object manipulations and consistency control, were measured, analysed and compared.

We found that the interface provided by a particular display device, as well as the form of object sharing, have significant impact on the frequency of generated events. Event bursts, arising from greater magnitudes of human movement, occurred during shared object manipulation that often resulted in event queuing. This was often manifested through the jumping around of the shared object, with the magnitude of discontinuity depending on a combination of interface and type of object sharing. The bursts were exacerbated by events generated to ensure consistency of shared objects by bringing them to an objective state. We found that concurrent object manipulation can result in more traffic than sequential manipulation, whereas concurrent manipulation of the same attribute impacts more than distinct attributes. Again, erroneous results arose from the delay or loss of vital events, such as those that change the hierarchy of the scene graph. Vital events were rare but tended to coincide with or bound bursts of non-vital events. We concluded that a CVE does not yet exist which is capable of supporting applications like the Virtual Gazebo across walk-in displays, without unnaturally constraining the application and laboriously tuning event passing.

3.4.   Relating Event Characteristics to Semantics

Another set of trials investigated the relationships between event characteristics and the semantics of human movement. These trials were undertaken between linked walk-in displays at the University of Reading and Johannes

Kepler University in Linz [18]. Again, the event traffic has been measured in terms of event frequency. But this time we focused on the motion of the tracked head and hand during collaboration and the resulting effect on the event traffic. We found that supporting natural interaction and non-verbal human communication implies increased event traffic for detailed movement representation of avatar and shared objects. The magnitude and importance of movements was shown to depend on the kind of collaborative scenario. Within our trials, the frequency of avatar movement events is fairly continuous and constitutes 64% of event throughput. Object movement events only occur during or shortly following interaction. The highest peaks in frequency of events come from shared object attribute manipulations and are caused by the added effect of the consistency mechanism. Vital events, which synchronise or trigger actions and are essential for steering the application, often bound the manipulation of a shared object attribute and sometimes coincide with it. Tracing movement across the various collaborative scenarios (figure 6-5) has revealed interesting results that

Figure 6-5. Traced head and hand motion of avatars.

offer potential for optimisation to reduce overall event traffic. Although the form of collaboration seems to play little part in the frequency of head and hand movement events, it plays a considerable role in the magnitude of change described by the events. Furthermore, only one member of the team seems to be highly animated at any one time.

The exclusive use of walk-in displays significantly improved the observable naturalness and performance of a distributed team, compared to the exclusive use of desktop, or of an asymmetric pair of both display types, as used in previous trials. As with the above furniture moving application [7], we observed considerable verbal communication related to the referencing of objects. However, we did not observe this leading to excessive or unnatural delays. However, when linking walk-in and desktop displays, we have observed such problems encountered by desktop users. Furthermore, we have found that users in walk-in displays perform much better than those using desktop systems in object placement tasks. We suspect there to be a number of factors behind this. Firstly, the walk-in displays have a much wider field of view than a desktop display and secondly, objects and others can be located through natural head glance which is much quicker and easier to control than moving the view of an avatar; thirdly, placing people within the environment, as opposed to allowing them to "look into" it, is likely to encourage natural proxemic behaviour including a sense of the relative position of people temporarily out of one's field of view.

4.   Conclusion

Although advances in technologies, such as tele-conferencing, threaten the justification for the full-size avatars of immersive systems, they still offer considerable advantages in supporting social human communication, especially through and around shared objects. A variety of organisations have expressed a strong need for such tools to meet the growing demands of collaboration fuelled by globalisation. One example is in Aerospace, where engineers, often in different countries, need to discuss the routing of pipe work around an engine. Here, it is necessary to efficiently communicate which pipe is under discussion and what is thought about the route it follows. Different solutions may need to be explored by manipulating the pipe work in real time and a reliable collective opinion must be reached.

There is currently no commercial system capable of communicating sufficient levels of naturalness in attention, understanding and emotion to remove the need for a face-to-face meeting. Technologies such as tele-conferencing and pure tele-immersion can communicate gestures, posture and facial expression, however, neither objects of interest nor the environment are truly shared. Extensions, such as Access Grid, allow data to be presented in an adjacent window, but then the whole team is physically removed from it. Furthermore, participants are usually constrained to face into one direction. Collaborative Computer Aided Design and digital mock-up systems allow a model to be shared and some allow it to be collaboratively updated and annotated, but again they separate the people from the data. Although CVEs allow a fairer and more powerful method of sharing objects, previous trials have indicated problems referencing these objects between a team.

We hypothesised that the combination of walk-in display technology and CVEs would better overcome the separation of people and data by placing people within it such that they could use and see their own bodies interacting with data and others. We further hypothesised that the characteristics of these displays and their tracking interfaces would reduce problems in referencing objects. We classified various forms of closely coupled collaboration and related this to a set of distinct collaborative scenarios and built a benchmark application.

Our studies have shown that combining the characteristics of walk-in displays and collaborative virtual environments allow people to interact through and around shared objects with unprecedented levels of naturalness. We have demonstrated that even a particularly demanding application of this genre can be supported with current technology. Major failings reported of CVE technology were found to be mostly overcome using walk-in displays. Both qualitative and quantitative measures showed walk-in displays to perform better than desktop displays. Developing this application was hard work using current technology. A detailed investigation of the relationships between interaction scenarios and event traffic demonstrated requirements for consistency control and suggested optimisations for increasing scalability. In summary, this technology appears to take us considerably closer to removing the need to travel to support teamwork involving shared artefacts.

Future work that follows on from what has been presented here and that deserves exploring more closely includes communicational eye gaze, closely coupled visual-haptic collaboration and applications within health, culture and engineering.

Acknowledgements

The authors would like to particularly thank Anthony Steed, both for porting the DIVE CVE to immersive devices and for his high level input on the drawbacks of current technology. Thanks also goes to David Swapp at University College London, Dieter Kranzlmueller, Christoph Anthes, Paul Heinzlreiter, Jens Volkert and Johann Messner at Johannes Kepler University in Linz, Vassil Alexandrov, Ali Al-Khalifah and Detlef Krischker at the University of

Reading, all students, lecturers and everyone else involved in the user trials and the creators and developers of DIVE at The Swedish Institute of Computer Science.

References

1. Otto, O. & Roberts, D.J. (2003). Importance of communication influences on a highly collaborative task. In *Proceedings of The Seventh IEEE International Symposium on Distributed Simulation and Real Time Applications (DS-RT)*. Delft, The Netherlands, pp. 195–201.
2. Snowdon, D.N., Churchill, E.F., & Frécon, E. (Eds.) (2004). *Inhabited Information Spaces: Living with Your Data*. London: Springer, 2004.
3. Schuemie, M.J., Straaten, P.v.d., Krijn, M., & Mast, C.A.P.G.v.d. (2001). Research on presence in VR: A survey. *CyberPsychology & Behavior, 4*(2): 183–202.
4. Ruddle, R.A., Savage, J.C., & Jones, D.M. (2002). Verbal communication during cooperative object manipulation. In *Proceedings of the ACM Conference on Collaborative Virtual Environments (CVE)*, pp. 120–127.
5. Buttolo, P., Oboe, R., & Hannaford, B. (1997). Architectures for shared haptic virtual environments. *Computers & Graphics, 21*(4): 421–429.
6. Lessels, S. & Ruddle, R.A. (2004). Changes in navigational behaviour produced by a wide field of view and a high fidelity visual scene. In *Proceedings of the 10th Eurographics Symposium on Virtual Environments (EGVE'04)*, Aire-la-Ville, Switzerland, pp. 71–78.
7. Hindmarsh, J., Fraser, M., Heath, C., Benford, S., & Greenhalgh, C. (2000). Object-focused interaction in collaborative virtual environments. *ACM Transactions on Computer–Human Interaction (ToCHI), 7*(4): 477–509.
8. Slater, M., Sadagic, A., Usoh, M., & Schroeder, R. (2000). Small group behaviour in a virtual and real environment: A comparative study. *Presence: Teleoperators and Virtual Environments, 9*(1): 37–51.
9. Schroeder, R., Steed, A., Axelsson, A.S., Heldal, I., Abelin, Å., Wideström, J., Nilsson, A., & Slater, M. (2001). Collaborating in networked immersive spaces: As good as being there together? *Computers & Graphics, 25*(5): 781–788.
10. Park, K.S. & Kenyon, R. (1999). Effects of network characteristics on human performance in a collaborative virtual environment. In *Proceedings of IEEE Virtual Reality*, Houston TX, March 13–17, pp. 104–111.
11. Carlsson, C. & Hagsand, O. (1993). DIVE—A platform for multi-user virtual environments. *Computers & Graphics, 17*(6): 663–669.
12. Broll, W. (1995). Interacting in distributed collaborative virtual environments. In *Proceedings of the IEEE Virtual Reality Annual International Symposium (VRAIS)*, Los Alamitos, CA, pp. 148–155.
13. Roberts, D.J., Wolff, R., & Otto, O. (2004). Pushmepullyou: The reality of interaction with shared objects in networked walk-in displays. In *Proceedings of the 17th International Conference on Parallel and Distributed Computing Systems (PDCS)*, San Francisco, CA, USA, no pp.
14. Usoh, M., Catena, E., Arman, S., & Slater, M. (2000). Using presence questionnaires in reality. *Presence: Teleoperators and Virtual Environments, 9*(5): 497–503.
15. Roberts, D.J., Wolff, R., & Otto, O. (2003). Constructing a Gazebo: Supporting team work in a tightly coupled, distributed task in virtual reality. *Presence: Teleoperators and Virtual Environments, 12*(6): 644–657.

16. Seelig, M., Harwin, W., Roberts, D., Otto, O., & Wolff, R. (2004). A haptic interface for linked immersive and desktop displays: Maintaining sufficient frame rate for haptic rendering. In *Proceedings of 17th International Conference on Parallel and Distributed Computing Systems (PDCS)*, San Francisco, CA, USA, 2004, no pp.
17. Wolff, R., Roberts, D.J., & Otto, O. (2004). A study of event traffic during the shared manipulation of objects within collaborative virtual environments. *Presence: Teleoperators and Virtual Environments, 13*(3): 251–262.
18. Roberts, D.J., Wolff, R., & Otto, O. (2004). Supporting social human communication between distributed walk-in displays. Forthcoming in *Proceedings of ACM Symposium on Virtual Reality Software and Technology (VSRT)*, Hong Kong, November 10–12.

Chapter 7

THE GOOD INEQUALITY: SUPPORTING GROUP-WORK IN SHARED VIRTUAL ENVIRONMENTS

Maria Spante, Ann-Sofie Axelsson and Ralph Schroeder

1.   Introduction

Most of our daily social interaction takes place face-to-face—this applies to work meetings as well as to personal encounters. Yet, in recent years, mediated interaction of various kinds and for various purposes has become more common, including the use of email, videoconferencing, tele-meetings, instant messaging, and online computer games—to mention just some of the main ones. In recent years virtual reality technologies (VR) have been increasingly used for distributed work and play, making it possible for people physically distributed to interact with each other and with a spatial graphical 3D interface in real time. In order to be able to connect to and interact with the Shared Virtual Environment (SVE) generated by the VR technology, the user must use some kind of VR system; for example a high-end immersive projection technology system (IPT, also known as Cave-type system) or, more commonly, a desktop system. All VR systems provide the user with some kind of output from the SVE, most commonly visual and audio output, and the possibilities to make input into the SVE by using some kind of tool (e.g., a mouse, a pointer, or a joystick) for interaction with the graphical environment and with other users.

When people interact with each other in a SVE, they do not necessarily use the same kind of VR system—for example, desktop computers or Head-Mounted Displays (HMDs). Or again, it could be that members of a group use the same kind of output technology (for example, two networked Caves) but different types of input technology (for example, a 3D joystick at one end and a cyberglove at the other).

R. Schroeder and A.S. Axelsson (Eds.), Avatars at Work and Play, 151–166.

As has been pointed out in previous writings in relation to system differences in distributed group-work [1], users are seldom aware of these differences. The reasons for this are mainly two: (1) since the users only see each other as graphical representations (avatars) in the SVE, they are not aware of the physical surroundings—including technical system setup—of the other group members, and (2) since people have a tendency to overestimate other peoples' similarity to themselves on attitudes, behaviors, and personality traits (the so called "false consensus effect" [2]), they also see themselves as the norm technically; that is, when working together in a distributed group, they believe that the other group members have the same technical capabilities as they do themselves and do not bother to ask about what kind of technology the other group members are using. As has been reported elsewhere [3], the use of different VR systems (different input and output features) in distributed group-work gives the group members unequal possibilities to interact with the SVE and with each other, something which often causes confusion, misunderstandings, and difficulties in collaboration. However, due to the unawareness of the situation that causes these problems of inequality, collaborators seldom discuss this problem or solutions to it. This means that, instead of jointly tackling the collaboration problems that occur, they try, not always successfully from a group-work perspective, to handle the problems individually.

It is highly unlikely that distributed collaborators will be using exactly the same VR systems for group-work in SVEs in the future, for example for reasons of costs (highly immersive systems can be provided for a limited number of participants). Thus, there will continue to be a serious need for managing the collaborative problems that an unequal technical setup causes. One way to manage this is simply to make the collaborators familiar with each others' systems in order to reduce the misunderstandings about what the different systems can and cannot do, and perhaps even to take advantage of the system differences and distributing the labor in a way that makes better use of the two or more VR systems.

This chapter reports on a trial where individuals worked together in pairs on a collaborative problem-solving task in a SVE using very different VR technologies; a desktop VR system on one side and a high-end immersive VR system on the other. Half-way through the task (after approximately 10 minutes) they were asked to switch system with their partner. The hypothesis was that the change of perspective would lead to better possibilities of dealing with issues that are related to distributed group-work and thereby improving the group-work process. It was found that there are several advantages with experiencing different and unequal systems when dealing with a collaborative task of this kind. Partners learn not only about the strengths and limitations of the different systems, but also about collaborating with others and about the implications of using different technologies. The chapter concludes with the implications of this "good inequality" for the design and use of SVEs.

2.   **Background and Previous Research**

Even though many researchers have shown the benefit of face-to-face collaboration in comparison with mediated interaction [4], distributed collaboration is becoming increasingly common. Various technologies have contributed to this development, including tools for text-based computer-supported collaborative work, videoconferencing as well as SVEs [4, 5]. However, mediated collaboration faces both technical and social challenges. Access to technology varies within and between countries [6] as well as within and between groups [7]. Even within organizations it is often the case that different sites have access to different technologies, and practices in using technologies for mediated collaboration can vary between sites (see, for example, [8] for videoconferencing). So when people work together at a distance via computers, videoconferencing systems or in SVEs, they often use systems with different capabilities.

The consequences of this asymmetry can be problematic or they can go unnoticed. Partners may "divide the labor" between themselves, taking on different tasks without being aware of this (for SVEs, see [9]). Or the consequences may be problematical insofar as the differences between systems can lead to inequalities in leadership or in status and thus in how people interact and work together—again, without the collaborators being aware that this inequality has been introduced or shaped by the technology and its different capabilities.

One reason for this effect is the absence of social cues in computer-mediated communication. This effect has been studied at least since Short, Williams and Christie's studies [10], which compared different communication technologies and face-to-face communication in terms of "social presence". A SVE can be considered as a "rich" medium in terms of social presence, compared to for example text chat, since the SVE generates a strong sense of "being there together" (for definitions of presence and co-presence, see [11–13]). How people take advantage of the lack of social cues and of the social cues they have available in SVEs in comparison with face-to-face situations is critical for this kind of mediated collaboration.

Previous research on collaboration in SVEs involving different systems has shown a variety of effects. A study by Slater and colleagues [14] of small group collaboration involving three people where one used a HMD and the other two used ordinary desktop computers, showed that the person who used the HMD was considered the leader, without knowing what kind of system the others were using. Schroeder and colleagues made similar findings for pairs working together, one using an IPT system and the other person using a desktop system [15]. Again, the person using the IPT was considered the leader and as contributing the greater share to the task. When doing the same task face-to-face, desktop-to-desktop, or IPT system networked with another IPT system, no such leadership or unequal contribution tendencies were found. An additional finding was that the subjects "naturally" divided the labor between themselves, with the immersed subject taking a more active role in the spatial aspects of the task and in manipulating objects, and the non-immersed subject taking a more "supervisory" role—again, without being aware of the differences between the two systems [9]. Finally, Axelsson [3] has analyzed the findings from a number of studies of interaction between people using immersive and non-immersive systems, and discussed the different problems that occur when people use asymmetrical technologies.

Findings by Hindmarsh, Fraser, Heath, & Benford [16] showed that problems of working together using networked desktop systems for a spatial task occur because of the restricted field of view and because the collaborators are not aware of what their partners can and cannot see. Heldal, Steed, Spante, Schroeder, Bengtsson, & Partanen [17] by contrast found that this problem on the whole does not apply to collaboration using networked IPT systems. The benefit of using symmetrical technological set-ups to facilitate equal collaboration has thus been shown by a number of studies.

3.   Method

In contrast to the studies mentioned in the previous paragraph which used a between subject design, the current study used a within subject design, giving users an experience of both types of technologies. Eighteen subjects arranged into nine pairs participated in the trial. Each pair met in a SVE to solve a Rubik's-cube type puzzle (see figure 7-1) using an immersive and a non-immersive VR system. The trial was limited to 20 minutes and the subjects changed systems half-way through the trial. The subjects were 17 postgraduate students taking a pedagogical course at a technical university and their teacher. There were 4 females and 14 males from various disciplines at the university. The subjects had all met during the course, but they had no previous experience of working together.

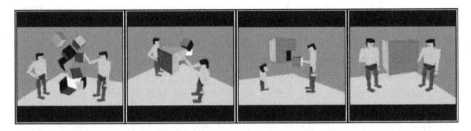

Figure 7-1. Two subjects (visible as human-like avatars) involved in a puzzle-solving task in a SVE using an IPT and a desktop system.

3.1. Technology and Task

The immersive system used was a $3 \times 3 \times 3$ meter TAN VR-CUBE with stereo projection on five walls (no ceiling). The application was run on a Silicon Graphics Onyx2 Infinity Reality with 14 250 MHz R10000 MIPS processors, 2 GB RAM and 3 Infinite Reality2 graphics pipes. The subjects wore CrystalEyes shutter glasses and used a 3D wand for object manipulation. A Polhemus magnetic tracking device tracked the head via the glasses and the hand via the wand. The non-immersive desktop system consisted of a Silicon Graphics O2 with one MIPS R10000 processor and 256 MB RAM and a 19-inch screen display. The dVise 6.0 software was used.

The task was to solve a puzzle involving eight blocks with different colors on different sides and to rearrange the blocks such that each side of the finished cube would display a single color. The colors on the sides of the 8 blocks were red, blue, green, orange, yellow, white, and black.

Using the IPT system, the subjects could move the virtual blocks by putting their virtual hand into a block, pressing the button of the 3D wand and moving the wand in the desired direction. Navigation was purely by moving around physically and pointing with the 3D wand. Using the desktop system, the subjects navigated by pressing the middle mouse button. In order to move a block, the subjects had to first select a block by clicking on it with the left mouse button, then keep the right mouse button pressed and move the mouse in the desired direction. By pressing the right mouse button combined with the shift key, the subject could rotate the virtual block. When selecting a virtual block as described above, the outlines of the block appeared as dotted lines (also visible to the partner). Whereas the avatar in the immersive system (representing the immersed subject) was dynamic and represented the subject's actual movements, the avatar in the desktop system was static (e.g. no gestures) since the subject's physical body was not tracked. We used the Robust Audio Toolkit (RAT) for audio communication between the subjects via headsets with microphones and earphones.

3.2. Procedure and Experimental Design

Before each trial session, the two subjects were given verbal instructions concerning the aim of the task and the various functions of the input- and output devices. The subjects were deliberately not informed about their partner's system. They had 5 minutes to familiarize themselves with the system but were not allowed to start communicating with the partner. The total time for the task was 20 minutes and halfway through the subjects changed system. Post-trial interviews with the subjects took between 5 and 15 minutes and focus

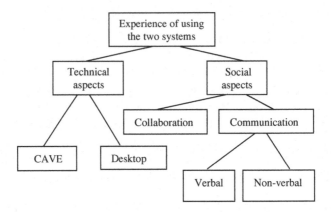

Figure 7-2. The different technical and social aspects that the subjects reflected upon during the post-trial interviews.

group discussions involving 4–6 subjects were held which took between 45 and 60 minutes.

3.3.   Data Collection and Analysis

The trial sessions were audio- and videotaped and the post-trial interviews and discussions were audiotaped. The analysis presented here is based only on the transcribed post-trial interviews. In order to interpret the interviews we used content analysis as described by Altheide [18]. We were particularly interested in how the subjects experienced the change of VR systems; how that influenced their sense of collaboration and their experience of the two VR systems. During the post-trial interview we asked the subjects to reflect on the task, the collaboration and the change of VR systems with specific reference to the technical aspects on the one hand and the social aspects on the other. These aspects were operationalized as described in the above scheme (figure 7-2).

4.   Results

In the following section we present, first, the data where the subjects reflect on their experiences in relation to technical aspects, which will be followed by reflections in relation to social aspects. Quotes from subjects are coded as follows: "I1" informs us that the quotation comes from the first subject who started the trial using the IPT system, and "D1" informs us that the quotation comes from the first subject who started the trial using the desktop system—and so forth.

4.1. Experiences of Using Different Systems: Technical Aspects

One question concerned how the subjects experienced the use of the two different systems during the trial. Typically, the subjects remarked on the different technical functionalities. In general, they experienced the IPT system as more intuitive to use and the manipulation of the virtual blocks as easy. The desktop system was experienced as more difficult to use because of the need for button pressing to manipulate the objects. Typically subjects commented on similarities and differences:

> I started at the workstation [referring to the desktop system]...When I came down here [to the room where the IPT system was located] it was more intuitive in a way what I should do. I saw where I was and I had only one type of control apart from my own movements. The only thing I needed to do was to grasp and release. There I could twist and do the turns. At the workstation I had to do it with control –alt-shift or control-shift and a mouse click so it was harder for me to do the task there. I thought I noticed that for [name of the partner] as well. When she came up there [to use the desktop system] she didn't really know how to move either. (D1)

> One was more handicapped there [on the desktop system]. One cannot do everything. The function one could have is to stand aside and look since one does not have the same functionalities. Here [IPT system] one is much smoother. (D7)

> I think you get a better view from here, from the computer [desktop system], but you cannot handle the things from here very well. I don't know if there is a problem with a cable or with the special joystick. But I think when you are there on the stage [IPT system] it is easier to move and manipulate objects. (I11)

Regardless of which system the subjects started with, most subjects shared the same view, that the IPT system was more intuitive and easy to use. However, in contrast to the majority opinion, one subject said:

> I think that the computer [desktop system] was easier, but one is used to computers. At the same time, here [IPT system], some things were easier to do here such as walking around faster and seeing the colors. That one could do faster down here, but the mere use of it, the computer was easier, but that is surely a habit issue, one is used to control [with the keyboard]. Here, it was more of trying to see the hand and, well, click on the right spot. I experienced that as harder. (D6)

The majority of the subjects could intuitively and easily use the IPT system even though they had no previous experience of the technology. A few subjects expressed minor difficulties grasping objects with their virtual hand using the wand, but the general experience was that it was easy to manipulate the virtual objects using the IPT system in comparison with the desktop system.

Another experience in relation to the technology was the difference in immersion. Even though the majority of the subjects said that the IPT system was more intuitive to use in comparison with the desktop system for actions such as rotating the virtual blocks, some subjects experienced the IPT system as being too immersive:

> My feeling is that you can manage better the system through the computer [desktop system]. That cube [the IPT system] is ... it ... causes a lot of difficulties. You feel surrounded by cubes. And you sort of ... you can grab one of them. But for me from this monitor [desktop system] I can see everything and probably I can manage my tools. I think so. (I13)

> There they [the virtual blocks] are all around you so it is hard to get a real overview. (I16)

Even subjects that did not mention the feeling of being "surrounded by cubes" said that the desktop provided a better overview of the puzzle. The following two quotes illustrate the general view of the subjects concerning the advantage of using the desktop in comparison with the IPT system:

> I think it was easier in front of the desktop using the mouse and keyboard to have an overview and perhaps help out a bit and check it out and think a bit. (D9)

> I think you get a better view from here from the computer but you cannot handle the things from here [desktop system] very well. (I11)

It was not the case that the subjects were completely in favor of one system compared to the other. The subjects appreciated the two different systems in different ways. The different technical functionalities of the IPT and desktop systems were useful for different purposes in solving the puzzle together. The IPT system was seen as useful for manipulating objects and the desktop system for obtaining a clearer overview of the puzzle. At the same time, the different technical functionalities also caused different types of difficulties: the desktop system was associated with problems in moving and manipulating the virtual blocks due to the need for button pressing; using the IPT system, on the other hand, was experienced as easy to use in relation to navigation and object manipulation but difficult in relation to getting an overview of the puzzle. This yields the following picture (table 7-1).

Table 7-1. Difficulties associated with the two different VR systems.

	IPT	Desktop
Manipulation	Easy	Difficult
Overview	Difficult	Easy

4.2.   Experiences of Using Different Systems: Social Aspects

The subjects were also asked a number of questions concerning their experience of using the two systems in relation to different social aspects. We will present, first, their views on collaboration and then their views on communication.

The majority of the subjects experienced the trial as a highly collaborative situation and expressed themselves in a positive way about working together. Regardless of whether they solved the puzzle or not, working with a partner on a task like this was seen as a good thing. However, although 11 out of 18 subjects had a positive experience of the collaboration, three subjects felt that they could have very well solved the task without a partner. Only two subjects reported that their collaboration was not working.

Most subjects thought that their collaboration improved after they had changed systems, and thought that they could use this knowledge about how the different systems worked to improve their collaboration:

> I thought it [the collaboration] worked well. I thought it worked very well when one knew, when one had tried out each other's tools. In the first instance one did not know what kind of capabilities the other had. I noticed that he could move around much easier but I did not know if that was because of him being better to manage the terminal [the desktop system] or what it was. I didn't know that he was down here [IPT system], that he had a tool like this. It became much easier after, when one knew, then we could divide the work better between us. (D7)

> I think the collaboration with my partner was really fruitful and especially because we had two different views. From the computer I can see above better, and he can handle better the cubes, so I think the collaboration is necessary to solve the task faster. (I11)

> You know, we started with no strategy at all. That was actually bad because we didn't see what next. But during this final stage we understood each other better and that was a relief. (I13)

Even subjects who thought that they did not really make active use of their knowledge about the different technologies believed that changing systems had improved their collaboration.

> I think it is better than working on my own because obviously there are some tasks that are more difficult to do from the computer [the desktop system] but it is easier for me to move around and he can turn around more easily different sides of the block. So I think that it is good to compensate but all we need is to have a better plan if we know the task earlier or in the middle. We should have some time in the beginning to just [talk about]—how we should do the task . . . It's easier to control when you sit here in front of your computer [desktop system] of course. So maybe it is good to have a strategy and then do some work from the computer first and then go downstairs [IPT system] to make the detail. (I10)

In relation to the experience of collaboration, most subjects thought that collaboration was useful and that it was improved by the fact that they had changed systems. The change of system led to an increased understanding of each other's perspectives and capabilities. This understanding enabled them to divide the labor between themselves based on the capabilities of the technology—such that the IPT person took a more active role in manipulating and moving the virtual blocks, and the desktop person had an overview and took a more "supervisory" role.

As for communication, subjects regarded verbal communication via the audio channel as crucial, but they also considered it to be as important to see their partner's avatar movements and actions. Typically they commented on the way their partner moved around in the environment. In particular, those who started off using the desktop system found it remarkable that their partner moved around so easily and smoothly in comparison with themselves:

> In some way I realized that he had a different tool. One understands that at once when one can see how smoothly he can move. One understood that quite quickly. Then it took a while before we talked about what kind of tool the other one had, but that became obvious when we changed. (D7)

This quote also illustrates how some subjects attributed the differences in movements to the technology without any knowledge about the differences between the systems. Some subjects, however, associated this to their partners' skills:

> I thought it was a superman I had met that could do exactly as he pleased with his keyboard. (D3)

The ability to refer to objects by pointing at or moving them back and forth facilitated communication concerning which block was being handled at the moment. However, as one subject noticed, the ability to refer to objects was different in the two systems:

> He was there in a way. It was really hard to express when one was upstairs [desktop system]. Then one had to grab a cube and say—"I am over here". But for him [in the IPT system] he could say "here I am", or, "I am going here". In some way he was there but I was not. (D8)

This quote demonstrates the subtle mix of verbal and non-verbal communication in a SVE which is further complicated by an asymmetrical setup. The possibility of referring to objects depended on the system: when using the desktop system the subject had to select a virtual block to indicate to the partner what object s/he was talking about. When using the IPT system the subject could refer to a block by simply pointing at it. Movement could be conveyed by means of the dynamic avatar, which showed the physical movements of the user, something which was not possible on the desktop system. Not only was action more intuitive in the IPT system, but language use was also more intuitive in the sense that "here" and "there" could be conveyed through the interface in the same sense as in the physical world. Subjects realized that knowledge of the two different systems also improved the way they communicated:

> [Changing systems halfway through] was fun. One could see these different possibilities. But that also meant, given that one had tried both systems, that one could more easily communicate with the systems and [also] communicate better with each other. (D6)

Changing systems was thus important for a better understanding of each other's possibilities and constraints, which helped subjects to agree on who should do what.

Finally, the experience of collaboration and communication is also reflected in the subjects' comments related to "being there together" or co-presence:

> Without voice communication it would have been difficult, so it was crucial. (D8)

However, this same subject also felt that he sometimes forgot his partner while busy handling the objects using the IPT system:

> But also, since I did not see him, or rather he was over there so to speak, he was not close to the cubes. Then it was very easy to forget [him]... not until I was working alone I thought: oops, now I'm doing too much! (D8)

This quote also illustrates that it is the avatars that subjects respond to (not to the "real" partner), and in this case, when the subject was busy with the virtual blocks, he felt that he lost awareness of his partner.

5.   Discussion

Previous studies have highlighted the disadvantages of asymmetrical setups. But as shown in this chapter, if users can be made aware of the differences entailed by different systems, users can obtain a better understanding of the possibilities and constraints of the systems, and collaboration can in this way be enhanced. The subjects in this study clearly thought that changing systems was positive and that they could collaborate and communicate better after the change. They also thought that they made use of the different capabilities of the technology and that this improved their strategy for solving the task. They recognized that the IPT system provided them with better possibilities for object manipulation and the desktop system provided them with a better overview of the puzzle.

Interestingly, subjects recognized the benefits as well as the drawbacks of each system. These were insights that they in some cases were able to implement immediately, during the ongoing trial, after having changed systems, and in other cases these new insights occurred to them only after they had completed the session, insights that they should be able to make use of in similar future collaborative situations.

Research that points to the importance of face-to-face meetings for distributed work typically highlights the importance of shared knowledge about the situational context in which the collaboration takes place—such as knowledge regarding what it looks like at the other site and "getting a feel for" the work culture that may vary from site to site [19, 20]. As in many previous studies, the present study underscores that shared knowledge enhances collaboration. However, in addition to the shared knowledge about the context in which the collaboration takes place, it is also, as the current study shows, important to facilitate knowledge-sharing regarding the capabilities of the technical systems, since this knowledge is hidden to the users.

Before we discuss the implications of these findings further, it will be useful to recall some of the disadvantages of unequal systems. One of the main disadvantages is that the collaborators may not be aware of the unequal technical capabilities that they and their partners have, which may lead to misunderstandings since they will communicate and collaborate with each other on the basis of their own technical system. Although users will experience co-presence in the SVE, they will still not be able to see or do things in the same way. Hence, the users may adopt a poor strategy for solving the task since they believe that they can contribute fairly and equally, which is not the case. In addition, people who collaborate using unequal technical systems can obtain incorrect impressions of their partner since the partner's way of handling the technology is interpreted as an indication of personal skills and character rather than of the technology the partner is using.

However, overcoming the disadvantages of different technologies by "trading places" will often not be possible. The point of distributed work is usually that partners should work together at a distance without meeting face-to-face, in order, for example, to save time or travel costs. However, when the technical set-up is so different as when an IPT system is linked to a desktop system, there may be a trade-off between this disadvantage and effective collaboration. A further insight from this study is that one should consider whether it is worthwhile to invest in and use a costly immersive system for an object manipulation task when the partner on the opposite site has a non-immersive system. The drawbacks with this set-up might actually be greater than the benefits. However, although previous research has shown the benefit of symmetrical set-ups for object manipulation [14, 15] collaboration *can* and *must* work with asymmetrical set-ups of VR systems. Some of the disadvantages of asymmetrical set-ups can be overcome with enhanced knowledge about the possibilities and constraints that the systems provide. If people know about the system differences, they can make use of them in their collaboration.

It is also worth mentioning that there may be advantages for two or more participants to have different technologies and actually take on different roles—for example, when people need to perform different complementary tasks. One result of using unequal systems is that, as mentioned earlier, even when collaborators are unaware of the type of system that their partner is using, they may be able to divide the labor between themselves. In the present study, when the participants found out about the reason for their unequal participation, they said that they could make use of this knowledge to figure out a better strategy for carrying out the task. In other words, creating a "common ground" in a situation of missing social cues allowed them to collaborate better [21]. It can be seen that VR technology is not only a tool *for* social interaction, but also an important feature *in* social interaction [22].

6.   Conclusion and Future Work

The finding that distributed group-work via VR technology can be enhanced by increased awareness of the technological capabilities will have obvious relevance for the design of VR systems and their uses. How then can VR systems provide knowledge about different capabilities? Can knowledge be built into the systems, or should task sessions be structured so as to allow for "putting on the other person's virtual shoes"? One suggestion that one is tempted to make in response to this study is that the differences between the VR systems—the technical capabilities—should be made obvious to users, and that this can easily be done with VR technology. For example, avatars could have labels that specify what type of system and input/output devices the users possess.

Note, however, that this solution would also have drawbacks: for example, such labels might create a cognitive overload on the users' part (how much information can the user "take in"?). Moreover, the whole point of VEs is that they are supposed to be natural interfaces, without the need to bring extraneous information into the environment—information that the users then need to maintain awareness of. It may also be that by focusing on figuring out what capabilities their partners have, collaborators lose the ability to "naturally" divide the labor between themselves and thus add to rather than reduce the time they need in order to carry out the task. As in everyday work life, we collaborate with people with various capabilities that are not made explicit, and this seldom causes collaboration difficulties. On the contrary, different capabilities often increase collaboration between people [23].

In the case of SVEs, however, the present study showed the benefit of being made aware of the various capabilities of technology by means of trading places.

Another suggestion for improving collaboration in SVEs might therefore be that users develop a verbal protocol whereby they talk about what tools they have access to instead of displaying this information. Developing a verbal protocol could be that after: "Hi how are you?" it might become a convention to ask: "What does the technology look like at your end and how does it work?". Mark [24] has demonstrated the benefits of explicit shared conventions in computer-supported collaborative work whereby users save both time and effort by using these.

One limitation of our trial was that it was short and that the subjects had only one opportunity to solve the task together. It may be that collaborators could easily adapt to the different capabilities or to the absence of social cues which could make them aware of these differences, over the course of time [25] (for time effects in text-based communication and collaboration, see also [26]). It would be interesting in future research to test whether such adaptation takes place, as well as whether longer sessions with different systems could mitigate the need for "trading places"—or if doing so could be even more valuable during longer sessions. It would also be interesting to examine whether simply communicating the different capabilities verbally or by means of the partners demonstrating them to each other remotely could be just as effective as experiencing the different systems.

To sum up: putting yourself into the other person's virtual shoes can enhance the interaction and the strategy in a collaborative task, as well as providing people with valuable insights into the use of VR systems. In other words, knowing about the different capabilities of technologies can enhance collaboration, thus creating "the good inequality". As the discussion has shown, however, such a setup for "trading places" may not always be possible or desirable to implement. Future research will show under what circumstances it can be useful to change VR systems—for designers of VR systems, and to participants involved in distributed group-work beyond the trial setting of this study.

Acknowledgements

This research was part of the project "Living in Virtual Worlds: Implications of the Uses of Virtual Reality in Long-Term Settings" supported by VINNOVA, and the Chalmers C-SELT project "Engendering Good Learning".

References

1. Axelsson, A.S. (2004). *Framing Social Interaction in Shared Virtual Environments: The Influence of Technical and Social Factors*. Doctoral Dissertation. Chalmers University of Technology.

2. Ross, L., Greene, D., & House, P. (1977). The false consensus effect: An egocentric bias in social perception and attributional processes. *Journal of Experimental Social Psychology,* *13*: 279–301.

3. Axelsson, A.S. (2002). The digital divide—Status differences in virtual environments. In R. Schroeder (Ed.), *The Social Life of Avatars: Presence and Interaction in Shared Virtual Environments,* London: Springer, pp. 188–204.

4. Hinds, P. & Kiesler, S. (Eds.) (2002). *Distributed Work.* Cambridge Massachusetts: The MIT Press.

5. Churchill, E., Snowdon, D., & Munro, A. (Eds.) (2001). *Collaborative Virtual Environments: Digital Spaces and Places for Interaction.* London: Springer.

6. DiMaggio, P., Hargiatti, E., Neuman, R., & Robinson, J.P. (2001). Social implications of the Internet. *Annual Review of Sociology,* (27): 307–336.

7. Haythornthwaite, C. & Wellman, B. (Eds.) (2002). *The Internet in Everyday Life.* Oxford: Blackwell Publishing.

8. Sonnenwald, D.H., Solomon, P., Hara, N., Bollinger, R., & Cox, T. (2002). Collaboration in the large: Using video conferencing to facilitate large group interaction. In A. Gunasekaran & O. Khalil (Eds.), *Knowledge and Information Technology in 21ˢᵗ Century Organizations: Humans and Social Perspectives.* Hershey, PA: Idea Publishing Co, pp. 155–136.

9. Axelsson, A.S., Abelin, Å., Heldal, I., Nilsson, A., Schroeder, R., & Wideström, J. (2001). Cubes in the cube: A comparison of a puzzle-solving task in a virtual and real environment. *CyberPsychology & Behaviour,* *4*(2): 279–286.

10. Short, J., Williams, E., & Christie, B. (1976). *The Social Psychology of Telecommunications.* London: John Wiley & Sons.

11. Scheumie, M.J., van der Straaten, P., Krijn, M, & van der Mast, C. (2001). Research on presence in virtual reality: A survey. *CyberPsychology & Behaviour,* *4*(2): 183–201.

12. Schroeder, R. (Ed.) (2002). *The Social Life of Avatars: Presence and Interaction in Shared Virtual Environments.* London: Springer.

13. Biocca, F., Harms, C., & Burgoon, J.K. (2003). Towards a more robust theory and measure of social presence: Review and suggested criteria. *Presence: Teleoperators and Virtual Environments,* *12*(5): 456–480.

14. Slater, M., Sadagic, A., Usoh, M., & Schroeder, R. (2000). Small group behaviour in a virtual and real environment: A comparative study. *Presence: Teleoperators and Virtual Environments,* *9*(1): 37–51.

15. Schroeder, R., Steed, A., Axelsson, A.S., Heldal, I., Abelin, Å., Wideström, J., Nilsson, A., & Slater, M. (2001). Collaborating in networked immersive spaces: As good as being there together? *Computers & Graphics,* *25*(5): 781–788.

16. Hindmarsh, J., Fraser, M., Heath, C., & Benford, S. (1998). Fragmented interaction: Establishing mutual orientation in virtual environments. *Proceedings of CSCW'98,* pp. 217–226.

17. Heldal, I., Steed, A., Spante, M., Schroeder, R., Bengtsson, S., & Partanen, M. (in press). Successes and failures in co-present situations. *Presence: Teleoperators and Virtual Environments.*

18. Altheide, D. (1996). *Qualitative Media Analysis.* Thousand Oaks: Sage Publications.

19. Kraut, R., Fussell, S., Brennan, S., & Siegel, J. (2002). Understanding effects on proximity on collaboration: Implications for technologies to support remote collaboration. In P. Hinds, & S. Kiesler (Eds.), *Distributed Work.* Cambridge Massachusetts: The MIT Press, pp. 137–162.

20. Nardi, B. & Whittaker, S. (2002). The place of face-to-face communication in distributed work. In P. Hinds & S. Kiesler (Eds.) *Distributed Work.* Cambridge Massachusetts: The MIT Press, pp. 83–110.

21. Axelsson, A.S., Abelin, Å., & Schroeder, R. (2003). Communication in virtual environments: Establishing common ground for a collaborative spatial task. *The 6th International Workshop on Presence.* Aalborg, Denmark, October 6–8.

22. Spante, M. (2004). *Shared Virtual Environments: Technology, Social Interaction, Adaptation and Time.* Licentiate Thesis. Chalmers University of Technology.

23. Albrecht, M.H. (2001). *Managing Diversity in the Workplace.* Oxford: Blackwell Publishers.

24. Mark, G. (2002). Conventions for coordinating electronic distributed work: A longitudinal study of groupware use. In P. Hinds, & S. Kiesler (Eds.), *Distributed Work.* Cambridge Massachusetts: The MIT Press, pp. 259–282.

25. Nilsson, A., Heldal, I., Schroeder, R., & Axelsson, A.S. (2002). The long-term uses of shared virtual environments. An exploratory study. In R. Schroeder (Ed.), *The Social Life of Avatars: Presence and Interaction in Shared Virtual Environments.* London: Springer, pp. 112–126.

26. Walther, J.B. (2002). Time effects in computer-mediated groups: Past, present, and future. In P. Hinds, & S. Kiesler (Eds.), *Distributed Work.* Cambridge Massachusetts: The MIT Press, pp. 235–257.

Chapter 8

CONSEQUENCES OF PLAYING VIOLENT VIDEO GAMES IN IMMERSIVE VIRTUAL ENVIRONMENTS

Susan Persky and Jim Blascovich

1.   Immersive Virtual Environments versus Desktop Platforms

One way to gauge the implications that immersive virtual environments (IVEs) hold for research, work, and play is to compare participant experiences using IVE platforms with participant experiences using non-immersive platforms. Hence, virtual environment (VE) researchers have increasingly investigated platform type as an important factor influencing media impact. Experimental researchers can and have evaluated platform effects on participants' interactions and experiences experimentally by varying platform type or configurations, such as IVE systems and non-immersive systems (e.g., desktop computers), while holding content constant across platforms. The outcomes of such experimental studies can help investigators determine the added value of IVE technologies in various domains. Such outcomes can be positive, contributing an important research tool for behavioral, biomedical, and social scientists; increasing productivity and efficiency in the workplace, and providing desirable leisure experiences. However, such outcomes might also be negative, causing researchers to alert users to potential hazards of various platform types and identifying application-platform combinations in which caution should be exercised and care taken in development and distribution.

Immersive virtual environment technology is increasingly used to simulate relevant environments for government and military training, for performance assessment of various activities such as driving an automobile or piloting an airplane, and for research in the behavioral and computer sciences. Research supports the value of IVE use in such arenas. Empirical studies have shown that IVEs are more effective than non-immersive platforms for various types of training and learning purposes. For example, participants who were trained

R. Schroeder and A.S. Axelsson (Eds.), Avatars at Work and Play, 167–186.
© 2006 *Springer.*

on a simple search and navigation task in a simulated environment using an IVE platform that incorporated a head mounted display (HMD) and tracking system later performed the same task in a non-simulated environment more quickly and consistently than participants who were trained using either of two non-immersive platforms [1]. In a more complex search task, participants who were trained using a digital IVE training simulation later performed better in an analogous physical simulation than did participants who were initially trained using a desktop computer version of the digital training simulation or who received no prior simulation training [2]. In addition to transfer of training skills, research shows improved performance via IVEs compared to desktop platforms as a medium for spatial and navigation training and tasks. For example, participants asked to learn about configuration and movement of 3D chess pieces demonstrated better performance if the learning phase took place via an HMD-based IVE rather than via a desktop monitor screen [3].

Use of IVE systems has also been shown to produce benefits for collaborative task performance in terms of general efficiency, productivity and leadership. In a small study in which one of three participants in a collaborative group was immersed in a shared IVE using an HMD and in which the other two participants shared the environment via desktop monitors, the immersed participant consistently emerged as a leader during the criterion task [4]. Other researchers have also reported a positive correlation between use of IVE technology and leadership in a molecular visualization task [5]. In terms of task performance, in a study in which participants collaborated in a virtual building task in either a Cave-type IVE or desktop platform, researchers reported a performance increase for users of the Cave-type interface, particularly for the more difficult tasks [6]. In addition, performance has been shown to suffer when one of two cooperating participants uses a desktop rather than an IVE. Furthermore, studies comparing collaborative performance in an IVE to performance in a physical environment have found little or no differences in performance between the two [7] suggesting that IVE collaborative groups are able to function at a high level.

Immersive virtual environment use may not always result in the highest levels of task performance, however. In one study, participants were assigned to perform tasks in a single-user map-based battlefield simulation using four types of platforms including a desktop computer and a Cave-type IVE system. In this study, researchers reported the best task performance for users of the desktop computer system [8]. However, the battlefield simulation used in this type of simulation provides little advantage or immersion for users in IVEs compared to desktop platforms. Indeed, other work has suggested that presence in an IVE is a major factor in the advantages conferred by IVE use. Tasks involving environments that require unrealistic viewpoints and actions might be more appropriate for and therefore benefit more from a non-immersive interface. Clearly, then, IVE use will not confer an advantage in all situations, however, for the tasks that are enhanced by IVE use, it is important to consider why this particular type of platform confers such an advantage.

Simulations in IVEs can be quite compelling and can be experienced as more realistic than on other platforms. When IVEs include advanced tracking and orientation systems, users can interact seamlessly with media content, ignore the physical environment in which they are located, and interact within the environment in a naturalistic way. In many contexts in which IVEs are used, enhanced realism and opportunity for naturalistic interaction within these environments can prove beneficial to users. In other contexts, however, enhanced realism and naturalistic interaction can prove problematic.

One of the most obvious arenas in which IVE technology may prove problematic is in situations in which it involves violent content. The increased immersion produced via IVE platforms is particularly relevant to the study of violent video games in which users act aggressively and perform the violent actions necessary for game play. Before discussing the particulars of how immersion, presence, and violent content can interact to produce heightened anti-social outcomes, a review of the video game violence literature will be helpful.

2.   Violent Video Game Effects Research

Compared with the study of other types of media violence, research on violent video game effects is relatively young with a small but growing research literature. A spate of narrative review papers was published between 1998 and 2001, advancing varying conclusions as to the richness of the video game violence literature [9–14]. At the time of their publication, most suggested that it was too soon to draw broad conclusions about the potentially problematic effects of violent video games, and cited mixed results in the available body of literature. Also at issue were common methodology and demand problems, and a general dearth of experimental publications.

Two meta-analyses were published during the same period, each reporting a small-to medium effect size of violent video game play on various aggression-related outcomes [15, 16]. One of these analyses found that year in which a study was performed was the strongest positive indicator of overall effect size and suggested that the technological advancement of games over time was responsible in large part for mixed experimental findings [16]. As game technologies became more advanced over time, they led to more realistic, more intense, and ultimately more violent games that, in turn, appear to have led to increases in aggressive outcomes.

More recent experimental studies of violent video games have resolved many of the previous methodological issues. These recent studies also tended to use contemporary games replete with high levels of realistic violence. With few exceptions [17], these studies contributed to increasing evidence of detrimental outcomes resulting from violent video game play including aggressive behavior [18–20], aggressive cognitions [18], increased hostility [21, 22], and implicit associations between the self and aggressive traits [23]. The consistency of these latest studies support the proposition that the mixed results in the early video game violence literature may stem, at least in part, from the inconsistent levels of realism in the violent games used in experiments.

Clearly, if technological advancement and increasing realism in violent video games underlies an increase in aggression resulting from game play, these technological developments are an important focus for research. Immersive virtual environment technology is one such development that promises to contribute to increasing realism in violent video games and indeed is already beginning to do so.

3.   Video Game Playing in IVEs

Immersive virtual video games are not new. Such games have been popular since the 1990s when they first appeared at arcade gaming centers in shopping malls, amusement parks, and entertainment complexes. Immersive virtual video games generally took one of two forms, a vehicle simulation pod in which a user would sit and watch a screen that acted as his or her window to the virtual world, or a head mounted display system with various forms of tracking. IVE games varied in content, but shooting or battle-themed games were quite prevalent. Many of the original VE game centers have since closed, but newer centers, such as Disney Quest in the United States, have opened to take their place.

Still, IVE games are not as widespread as might be expected given the levels of enjoyment and repeated use reported by players [24]. Perhaps this is due in part to a disconnect between what inexperienced users would expect of virtual reality given its representation in popular media and the actual sophistication of the technology in its current state. Technology for IVE simulations continues to advance, however, due not only to the work of researchers and game manufacturers, but due also to the development of training simulators for military purposes. Furthermore, arcade game devices have begun to include aspects of immersive technology such as motion tracking that does not create full immersion but comes close. These developments promise not only more advanced IVE games in public spaces and centers, but also a move toward more immersive gaming experiences in the home [25] where video games are played most frequently.

As we move closer to widespread diffusion of IVE games, it is essential to consider the ways in which this IVE technology will change gaming experiences for the better and also, importantly, for the worse. Examination of how platforms, violent video games, and presence might interact will help us understand what a move toward immersive technologies for gaming might mean for post-play outcomes.

4. Immersive Virtual Environments, Violent Video Games, Presence, and Aggression

4.1. Implications of Virtual Violent Video Games for Presence

We define presence as a psychological state in which one perceives one's self as existing in an environment. Presence, then, exists as a phenomenological state independent of any particular hardware system. Researchers have identified many antecedents to, and consequences of, the experience of presence within IVEs both theoretically and empirically [26]. By investigating the ways in which immersive virtual violent video games influence antecedents to presence, we can arrive at a clearer understanding of the mutually reinforcing nature of this relationship.

Media characteristics in a given context are influenced by their content, in this case violence. Visual display characteristics such as image quality, motion, color, and dimensionality can all enhance presence. These characteristics are often quite rich and realistic in modern video games, especially those with violent content. Such games are typically designed to visually represent high levels of violence realistically with high image quality. Auditory display characteristics operate similarly. Sound quality in games continues to improve, as home stereo systems continue to grow and designers create more graphic sounds designed to accompany and amplify the violent visual images that users see. Enhancement of the stimuli (e.g., haptic, olfactory) sent to other senses can also increase presence though their implementation is not widespread. That many immersive virtual video games allow user movements to directly control character movements engages the kinesthetic and orienting systems leading to an increase in both breadth and depth of stimulus quality. Thus, in the realm of media characteristics, the way that contemporary violent video games are designed serves to increase users' experiences of presence.

User characteristics that can increase presence are particularly relevant in the context of immersive violent video games. The experience of presence should increase when the user experiences meaningful content and motivation to engage in that content. So, if a user is prone to violent or aggressive cognitions and is well suited to process such information, as users who voluntarily and recreationally choose to play violent video games may well be, then the user should be more likely to experience a heightened sense of presence when playing such games. Finally, as users gain practice with IVEs, feelings of presence may increase [27]. Video games are popular among adolescents and young adults; perhaps even addictive in certain cases [28, 29]. Video game users are likely to engage in high frequency play because of the enjoyable and/or addictive nature of the games. As these games are increasingly played using an IVE platform, heightened experiences of presence should result.

Because of media characteristics such as visual and auditory display, and user characteristics such as dispositional tendencies for aggressive cognitions and behavior, using IVEs to play violent video games should increase experiences of presence over other types of content. While violent video game content is expected to lead to heightened aggression in IVEs, a user's level of presence in violent games is also expected to affect the relationship between immersive violent video games and resulting aggression.

4.2.   *Implications of Presence for Playing Virtual Violent Video Games*

Presence is central to the prediction of differences in the consequences of playing violent video games using IVEs versus traditional platforms (e.g. desktop computers, arcade units). On a conceptual level, the better a situation is simulated, the less likely individuals will activate a media schema to interpret the situation [30]. Media schemata signal that what one is experiencing is artificial and that responses that would be appropriate in natural situations may not be appropriate. Hence, more realistic simulations should lead to greater presence increasing the likelihood that individuals will experience a simulation situation naturally and thereby be less likely to activate media schemata to control their behaviors.

Other factors have previously been identified as affecting aggression and presence in the violent game playing literature. Early writings and research proposed that video games would lead to increased aggression over other less participatory or interactive media in part because video game players generally take an aggressor's viewpoint [10]. Media violence research supports the claim that identification with the aggressor in a media context increases later aggression against another individual [31]. Increase in the potential for individuals to identify with the aggressor in video games is apparent in two trends. First, modern video games often adapt a viewpoint in which the player's view is identical to an aggressors' view. The player sees through the eyes of the aggressor, experiencing virtually what the aggressor experiences when committing violent, hostile acts. A second development adding to increased likelihood of identification with the aggressor is the ability of players to choose their own (i.e., the aggressor's) representation from a pool of characters who differ in race, sex, build, and other individualizing characteristics. Players therefore have the opportunity to construct a character and an identity.

Virtual environments can further increase identification with the aggressor vis-à-vis presence. When using a virtual platform, not only is the player's view an aggressor's view, the player's body motions are the aggressor's body motions.

Identification with the aggressor and presence are clearly connected as the more an individual experiences presence in the game environment, the more he or she should feel connected to the aggressor's actions.

Other work suggests that aggression should increase as the realism of violent acts increases. The most important type of realism is behavioral realism capturing violent movements, sounds, and even facial expressions. Though, as evidenced by studies of early video games, photographic realism is not a necessary condition for linking violent game play and subsequent aggression, links between increased realism and increased aggression have been found (see below). With new technological advances not only has behavioral realism increased but so has photographic realism likely adding to players' experiences of presence. Game development in the 1990s (e.g. Mortal Kombat) brought more photographically realistic depictions of decapitation and other gruesome actions. Contemporary games bring more photographically realistic blood, screams, wounds, and other such features of violent encounters.

There is some evidence that increases in realism engender increases in violent behavior [32]. Also as mentioned above, more recent studies of violent video games and aggression demonstrate larger effect sizes than earlier studies [16]. Increases in realism, both behavioral and photographic, are likely responsible in large part for increased findings of post-game aggression among video game players. In the case of IVEs, again it follows that heightened realism will play an important part in any increased aggression effects. Environments, opponents, and objects as seen in IVEs are more realistic behaving and looking. In IVEs, players experience objects and characters as three-dimensional. Because presence in a violent game will in turn make experiences in the game environment more realistic, those experiences should lead to increases in aggression.

Tamborini et al. [33] proposed that the strength of the impact of violent content on aggression-related cognition and behavior should be determined by the level of presence experienced during game play. More specifically, Tamborini et al. suggested that a game's impact rides on its ability to enhance involvement and immersion. Involvement and immersion are two critical features of presence [27] where involvement stems from focus on and attention to the environment and immersion results from an environment's ability to isolate and interactively engage the user.

Tamborini et al. suggested that because video games with high-resolution graphics can engage multiple sensory systems, they have increased vividness over other media forms. Because users can almost instantaneously influence the form and content of the game environment, video games are also more interactive than other media. These qualities, vividness and interactivity, share a positive relationship with involvement and immersion such that increases in the former lead to increases in the latter. Therefore, video games in general are a medium that should lead to heightened involvement and immersion, and the addition of IVE technology should increase that involvement and immersion to an even higher level. Tamborini et al. suggested that one of the mechanisms by which immersion in a multi sensory environment would lead to increased aggression is that it should facilitate the learning of more complete aggressive scripts by increasing available and salient cues. The cues in response to which actions are performed should also seem more realistic and should be more easily recognized in the future. According to a cognitive neoassociationist theory of media violence effects, recognizing cues to violence that were present in violent media can underlie violent behavior outside of the game context by priming related cognitions and increasing their accessibility.

All of the routes from immersive video games to increased presence and, in turn, to increased aggression provide strong reason to believe that playing violent video games in IVEs will lead to heightened aggressive responses. Though one study was previously conducted by Tamborini and his colleagues to investigate this possibility [33], the results were mixed, failing to replicate some of the most well established findings in both the presence and the media violence literature. Reasons for the inconsistencies were likely due to characteristics of the VE platform used because the interface was found to be non-intuitive and difficult to master. Convinced of our own and Tamborini et al.'s reasoning, we sought to eliminate this methodological shortcoming. We therefore undertook a series of studies aimed at answering the basic empirical question, does playing violent video games in IVEs increase aggression more than playing these games on traditional platforms?

5.   Effects of Immersive Virtual Violent Video Games

5.1.   *Effects of IVE Platforms versus Traditional Platforms*

We conducted two studies [reported in detail in 34] both of which shared the same basic procedure. Participants were asked to play a specific video game either on a desktop computer platform, or using an IVE platform. On the desktop platform, participants viewed the game on a 17″ monitor; they played in a standing position using a hand-held arcade gun controller both to move in the game and to aim and shoot at opponents. On the IVE platform, participants viewed the game in a Virtual Research V8 stereoscopic HMD; they moved in the game using natural body movements while their location and head orientation were tracked. These participants also used the hand-held arcade gun controller, but here they only used it to aim and shoot at opponents.

We developed a gun fight-themed violent video game that could be played on either an IVE or desktop platform. The players' experience was designed to be as identical as possible between the desktop and IVE platforms with

Figure 8-1. Screenshot of the violent gun fight-themed video game created for our experimental studies.

the obvious exception of the differences inherent in the two platforms (e.g., wearing an HMD or not). The game was designed to be simple and easy to play to eliminate issues of differences in playing interface. In the game, players simply shot at two opponents located at the opposite end of the virtual room and were able to hide behind any of three virtual walls to dodge opponents' bullets (see figure 8-1).

To attempt to answer the question of whether playing violent video games in IVEs would lead to increases in aggression compared to the desktop platform, we recorded several types of dependent measures. We included a self-report measure of aggressive feelings composed of a multi-item scale as well as a multi-item presence scale and items assessing playing experience. In addition to our self-report measures, we included two measures to assess behavioral aggression. The first measure was the proportion of head hits to opponents because shooting at the head is arguably more violent than shooting elsewhere on opponents' bodies.

We also, however, wanted to use a more established behavioral measure, one that measured aggression outside of the game context. For this purpose we included a computer-based competitive game. This measure was essentially a reaction time contest with a partner. Participants were told that it was a competition to see who could respond faster to a stimulus. The loser on any given trial was punished by a blast of white noise, the level of which was set by his or her opponent. Participants played against the computer, there actually was no opponent, and noise levels and win/loss trials were randomized. The overall measure here was how high participants set the aversive noise, from no noise at all to the highest setting of about 105 dB, to be delivered to their partner.

In addition to the traditional self-report and behavioral aggression measures, we believed it was important to include a measurement paradigm that was invulnerable to demand and participant manipulation. For this reason we included physiological measures in our experiment, specifically cardiovascular indices of challenge and threat based on the work of Blascovich and his colleagues [35]. Although challenge and threat do not directly measure aggression, challenge and threat do point to benign versus malignant ways of coping with a situation, and furthermore, threat and aggression can be closely tied conceptually, as reactive aggression can be a response to threat. In the challenge and threat paradigm, we looked for three cardiovascular indices to differentiate the motivational states of challenge and threat. Challenge is defined as the condition that exists when resources to perform a particular task outweigh the demands, and threat is defined as the condition when demand outweighs resources.

To index challenge and threat, we examined cardiac performance (indexed by heart rate and ventricular contractility), cardiac output, and total peripheral resistance. The challenge pattern is indexed by increased cardiac performance, large cardiac output increases, and decrease in total peripheral resistance. The threat pattern is indicated by increased cardiac performance, small increase or no change in cardiac output, and small increase or no change in total peripheral resistance.

5.1.1. Findings and Implications

First, enjoyment and satisfaction with the game playing experience as measured by self-report questionnaire items was found to be higher for participants who played the game using an IVE platform versus a desktop platform [detailed results can be found in 34]. This result lends support to the proposition that IVE technology is more enjoyable and a preferred way to play video games and is therefore likely to expand in popularity and use in the coming years.

Our self-reported aggressive feelings measure, reported after the game play period, indicated that participants reported significantly more aggressive feelings after playing the exact same game in an IVE versus on a desktop computer. Our measures of behavioral aggression produced the same results, participants in the IVE condition had a significantly higher proportion of head hits than participants in the desktop condition. In terms of the competitive reaction time measure, participants who played the violent video game in an IVE administered significantly higher levels of aversive noise to a partner than participants who had played on a desktop computer platform.

Our physiological results were slightly complicated by the fact that we had considered the possibility that being attached to physiological measuring equipment, ambulatory though it was, might substantially change the experience of immersion in an IVE, possibly by creating breaks in presence. To examine this possibility and, hopefully, demonstrate that use of physiological measures was appropriate for our paradigm, we varied their inclusion as an independent variable, analyzing the responses of participants who had and had not been hooked up to physiological equipment. These analyses revealed no differences in self-report or behavioral measures by physiological measure inclusion, satisfying us that inclusion of the measures did not alter participants' experiences of the game environment. Analysis of the physiological data from those participants who had been hooked up to the measuring equipment revealed that participants who played the violent video game using an IVE platform displayed the threat pattern of response. Participants who had played the violent game on a desktop platform, however, were not significantly physiologically influenced by the experience.

Taken together, our four measures of aggression and aggression-related outcomes clearly suggest that playing violent video games using an IVE platform results in more detrimental aggression-related outcomes than does playing an identical game using a traditional platform. As previously suggested, we had reason to believe that this difference might be caused by differences in presence in the game environment. This hypothesis was partially supported by our data. We found full statistical mediation by self-reported presence of the relationship between playing platform and our self-report measure of aggression. Though presence fully explained the relationship between platform and our self-report measure, statistically, it did not explain the relationship for either of our behavioral measures. We suspect that this disconnect in mediating construct between our self-report and behavioral measures may be due to the explicit, self-report nature of our particular presence measure in these experiments, though this has not yet been experimentally confirmed.

These experiments support our hypothesis that playing violent video games using IVEs lead to increases in aggression over play using traditional desktop platforms, as well as lending support to our proposal that presence is responsible for this effect. Still at issue though, is whether the content of the game matters, as the previous experiments assessed only play in a violent game. Conventional wisdom would suggest that IVE use should intensify only content-related outcomes, in this case aggression from violent games. If this is the case, playing a nonviolent game in an IVE should not lead to increases in aggression. This prediction, however, had not yet been tested. Also yet unexplored was whether nonviolent themes might similarly be intensified through experiences in an IVE game with related content.

Figure 8-2. Screenshot of the nonviolent art-themed video game created for our
experimental studies.

5.2.   *Effects of Violent versus Non-Violent Games*

To address questions of game content-specific intensifying effects, we designed a second, nonviolent game with art-themed content [fully reported in
36]. The non-violent game was designed to remain as similar as possible to
the violent gun fight-themed game, including a similar game environment and
identical body movements. In this game, players shot paint at a canvas located
across the virtual room to create an abstract painting. Players selected paint
colors by moving to different locations in the virtual room. By randomly assigning participants to play either the violent or new nonviolent game using
either a desktop computer or an IVE platform, we were able to investigate
content effects (see figure 8-2).

In this particular experiment, we included two types of dependent measures,
self-report and physiological. Our self-report measures included a multi-item
scale of aggressive feelings, as well as a multi-item scale of artistic and creative
feelings which were content-specific to the art-themed game. Physiological
measurement for challenge and threat states was included for all participants.

5.2.1.   *Findings and Implications*

As expected, our self-report aggressive feelings measure revealed a significant interaction between game violence content and game playing platform

[detailed results can be found in 36]. Participants who played the violent game in an IVE reported the highest level of aggressive feelings whereas participants who played a nonviolent game in an IVE reported the lowest level. This result confirmed that IVEs, at least in this case, only intensify aggressive outcomes for games with violent content. Additionally, analysis of the cardiovascular psychophysiological data revealed a pattern consistent with our self-report aggressive feelings measure. Specifically, only participants who had played the violent game on an IVE platform exhibited increases in physiological responsivity indicative of threat influenced during game play.

On our self-report measure of artistic and creative feelings, however, we found no differences by condition. Neither game content type nor game playing platform influenced how creative and artistic game participants reported feeling after the game play period. This suggested that artistic and creative feelings did not seem to be transferred when playing an art-themed game, nor were these feelings intensified by IVE use. Because of the nature of these results, it is difficult to draw a firm conclusion as to their implication. It may be that our particular art game did not engender strong artistic feelings to begin with, or that these particular nonviolent feelings do not tend to transfer from video game play. These results might also suggest, however, that there is something special about aggression and violence that transfers and is intensified particularly easily by IVE game play.

5.3.   *Research Conclusions*

Overall our program of research on video games played in IVEs has allowed us to clarify various issues related to advances in video game technology. We have shown that IVE use for violent video game play does lead to increased aggression and physiological threat over play on a traditional desktop computer platform. Further, we have shown that presence is apparently the critical factor by which IVE use leads to increases in self-reported aggressive feelings as well as congruent physiological responses. Furthermore, this intensifying effect of IVE game play is limited at present to violent and aggressive game content.

6.   **Virtual Violent Video Game Effects in Multiplayer Games**

Though findings with respect to the effects of IVE video game play in single-player environments are important and useful in and of themselves, networked gaming is becoming quite popular. Multiplayer networked games appear to be a major direction in which mainstream video gaming is headed. How multiplayer IVE violent video games might affect players' interactions with one another, then, is not simply an academic issue. To date, however, very little research has been performed in this area, and in particular there has been no research specifically addressing any distinct effects of multiplayer games and potential unique patterns of resultant anti-social responses.

Though there may not be much in the way of research focusing on unique effects of multiplayer games, we do know that the outcomes following multi-player games are similar to the effects of single-player games such that violent games played in a multiplayer context also lead to more aggressive outcomes than nonviolent multiplayer games [37]. In terms of multiplayer IVE violent games, then, it would follow that playing against an avatar (i.e., a representation of an actual human other) rather than against an agent (as in the study reported here) would tend to evoke the same sorts of aggressive responses.

A single study performed by Buckley and her colleagues examined effects of playing a violent video game in a multiplayer IVE [38]. In this study, participants played either a two-player shooting-themed game or a two-player game of virtual tennis. Findings from this experiment were mixed. Results from a post-game behavioral reaction time competitive task, similar to the one we used, revealed that participants administered more noise to opponents if they had played the violent game using an IVE (i.e. Cave-type) platform rather than a desktop platform. Researchers also reported an interaction such that levels of noise administered after playing the nonviolent game on a desktop system were by far the lowest. Results from written story completion task responses rated for aggressive cognitions revealed an interaction such that participants completed the highest proportion of stories aggressively after playing the desktop violent game and the IVE nonviolent game. Story completion results were inconsistent both with the behavioral results in the same study and with previous work. However, in general, results of the behavioral measure do show a similar pattern to results found for single-player IVE games.

More interesting than general aggression effects from the standpoint of a multi-user environment, however, is the question of whether there might be special consequences of playing against an avatar, particularly for a post-game shared IVE experience. One way we can look at this question is through the lens of Blascovich's [39, 40] threshold model of social influence in IVEs.

7.   Social Influence in Virtual Environments

The threshold model of social influence posits that social influence will increase as social presence increases. According to this model, social presence itself varies as a function of four factors, two of which are internal and two external to the target of influence. According to the model, behavioral realism and agency (whether interaction partners are believed to be agents or avatars) are the two external factors influencing social presence. The internal factors are self-relevance of the situation and whether the social influence response in

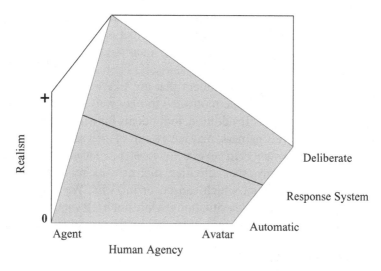

Figure 8-3. The three-dimensional threshold surface of social influence as a function of behavioral realism, human agency, and response system level.

question is a high versus low-level response. The threshold of social influence will be lowest when the target is interacting with what he or she believes is an avatar in a non-self-relevant situation where the response in question is low-level or automatic (see figure 8-3).

Previous research has used the model to determine both deliberate, or high-level social influence effects, and non-deliberate, or low-level social influence effects. The model has been used to identify the level of certain social responses based on the conditions under which a given response was elicited. For example, because a conformity response was elicited by both an agent and an avatar in a particular simulation, conformity was determined to be a lower-level response than social comparison which was elicited only by an avatar (and not elicited by an agent) in an identical situation [41]. According to the model, because conformity in this situation can be elicited by social interaction with an agent whereas social comparison cannot, we are able to conclude that conformity is the more automatic response. When the level of the social influence response behavior in question is held constant, however, the threshold model can also be used to examine the effect of variations in one of the other three factors affecting the social influence threshold.

In terms of our investigation of immersive virtual violent video games, aggression is the relevant social influence outcome. Aggression, particularly behavioral aggression, can be considered a low-level behavior when it is activated without awareness, as is often the case [42]. In the model, low-level processes such as aggression result in a lower threshold for social influence. Examination of the other three contributing factors can help us understand how likely such social influence aggression outcomes are, given the typical characteristics of the violent video game play situation.

Self-relevance, the other internal factor, involves the extent to which an interaction involves a central aspect of the self. There are some aspects of a virtual violent video game environment that are likely to be somewhat high in self-relevance as one might be motivated to play well so as to be favorably evaluated by one's opponent. In addition, individuals for whom video games are a large part of their life (i.e. gamers) may have a part of their self-esteem wrapped up in video game performance. In general, however, playing games is likely to be less self-relevant than many other activities, such as work-related collaboration and interpersonal interaction, which can occur in IVEs. We therefore would consider violent video game play situations, while not irrelevant, to be relatively low in self-relevance, which again is predicted by the model to lead to a lower threshold for social influence.

Examining the third factor, behavioral realism, it is important to note that while not all violent video games are the same, it is likely that there are more commonalities than differences in terms of behavioral realism. Inherent in video games is both a limited context and a limited range of player actions and responses. Though behavioral realism of a game opponent is partially tied up in the complexity of artificial intelligence programming, given context and input limitations, it does not take much for an agent or avatar in most games to appear to be enacting realistic behaviors. In most video games, then, particularly those of a violent nature where the context is often extremely limited, behavioral realism is likely to be relatively high. As behavioral realism increases, the threshold of social influence becomes lower.

The final factor, agency, is where we focus our examination on how the model can inform us as to the likely effects of multiple versus single-player IVE violent video games. Agency speaks directly to this issue as in single-player games one's opponent is by definition an agent whereas in multiplayer games, one's opponent is almost always an avatar. Because characteristics of virtual violent video game environments and of virtual violent video game play, overall, should result in low-to-moderate self-relevance and high behavioral realism, and because aggression, our social influence outcome, is relatively low-level, we would expect a low, shallow threshold of social influence. Given the configuration of factors we have outlined, therefore, we would not expect agency to matter in the majority of cases. In other words, whether a game opponent is or is believed to be an agent or an avatar, immersive virtual violent video games are expected to result in an aggression response. This interpretation is supported by the studies presented earlier where violent video game play against agent opponents resulted in aggressive social responses within the IVE (an increased proportion of head hits). The experiment also found increased behavioral aggression in a supposedly unrelated computer-mediated competitive game (the competitive reaction time/noise-blast game) which though in this case occurred outside of the IVE, may be somewhat analogous to a post-game interaction within the IVE.

We would also expect, however, that in the case where any of the other three variables, level of response, self-relevance, or behavioral realism should change such that social presence was decreased, the agency of the gaming opponent might begin to matter. For example, if we were to use a very high-level measure of anti-social feelings as our social influence response or if we were to limit the opponents' range of actions so as to reduce their behavioral realism, we might increase the threshold such that agency would become a crucial variable. Therefore, we would expect that playing a violent VE video game against an avatar would be more likely to result in aggression than playing against an agent, and would also be more likely to result in higher level, more intentional, forms of aggressive and hostile behavior.

8. Conclusion

The threshold model of social influence predicts that playing violent games in a networked multiplayer game environment versus a single-player environment should make a difference for aggressive outcomes within IVEs. Though not specified in the model, it would be logical to expect unique or intensified responses to one's game opponent over other unrelated individuals. Whether playing against avatars versus agents will prove to lead to heightened aggression and whether that aggression will be more acutely experienced by a gaming opponent versus an unrelated other, however, are still open empirical questions. Questions such as these highlight important themes for future research both in the area of video game effects and in the area of IVE research.

In a practical sense, however, it is unclear how often and in what situations game playing opponents currently have contact with one another either within IVEs outside of the game context or outside of IVEs following the game period. At present, VE video games are generally played in busy public spaces in situations where one might not even be aware of one's gaming opponents' identities. Furthermore, as technology advances, it brings closer the promise of combining immersive virtual technology and networked gaming where opponents will be separated by physical space, as in the networked non-immersive games of today. In these situations, too, it at first seems unlikely that gaming opponents will have much opportunity to interact outside of a gaming context. However, the same technology that brings distributed gaming promises to bring non-physically located social interactions, so perhaps more and more we may be meeting our gaming opponents in social VEs. Based on our investigations reported here, it seems likely that when these social interactions follow multi-player violent video games, they will be marked by aggressive social influence.

For now though, we know that in both single and multi-player contexts aggression resulting from virtual violent video game play can be diffuse in nature and directed toward non-opponent targets. This alone seems to be reason enough to begin to expand our awareness to include the content of material experienced in IVEs and effects of the immersive nature of IVEs when considering their social or potentially anti-social effects.

References

1. Boyd, C. (1997). Does immersion make a virtual environment more usable? *CHI'97 Electronic Publications*. Available at http://www.acm.org/sigchi/chi97/proceedings/short-talk/cb.htm
2. Youngblut, C. & Huie, O. (2003). The relationship between presence and performance in virtual environments: Results of a VERTS study. In *Proceedings of IEEE Virtual Reality Conference 2003*, pp. 277–278.
3. Slater, M., Linakis, V., Usoh, M., & Kooper, R. (1996). Immersion, presence and performance in virtual environments: An experiment with tri-dimensional chess. In *Proceedings of the Virtual Reality Software and Technology*, pp. 163–172.
4. Tromp, J., Bullock, A., Steed, A., Sadagic, A., Slater, M., & Frecon, E. (1998). Small group behavior experiments in the COVEN project. *IEEE Computer Graphics and Applications, 18*: 53–63.
5. Axelsson, A.S., Abelin, Å., Heldal, I., Nilsson, A., Schroeder, R., & Wideström, J. (1999). Collaboration and communication in multi-user virtual environments: A comparison of desktop and immersive virtual reality systems for molecular visualization. In *Proceedings of the Sixth UKVRSIG Conference*, pp. 107–117.
6. Roberts, D.J., Wolff, R., & Otto, O. (2003). Constructing a gazebo: Supporting team work in a tightly coupled, distributed task in virtual reality. *Presence: Teleoperators & Virtual Environments, 12*: 644–657.
7. Schroeder, R., Steed, A., Axelsson, A.S., Heldal, I., Abelin, Å., Wideström, J., Nilsson, A., & Slater, M. (2001). Collaborating in networked immersive spaces: As good as being there together? *Computers & Graphics, 25:* 781–788.
8. Gabbard, J.L., Hix, D., Swan, J.E. II., Livingston, M.A., Höllerer, T.H., Julier, S.J., Brown, D., & Baillot, Y. (2003). Usability engineering for complex interactive systems development. Paper presented at *Engineering for Usability, Human Systems Integration Symposium*, June, Vienna, VA.
9. Bensley, L. & Van Eenwyk, J. (2001). Video games and real-life aggression: Review of the literature. *Journal of Adolescent Health, 29*: 244–257.
10. Dill, K.E., & Dill, J.C. (1998). Video game violence: A review of the empirical literature. *Aggression and Violent Behavior, 3*: 407–428.
11. Freedman, J.L. (2001). Evaluating the research on violent video games. Paper presented at *Playing by the Rules: The Cultural Policy Challenges of Video Games*, University of Chicago, Chicago, IL.
12. Griffiths, M. (1999). Violent video games and aggression: A review of the literature. *Aggression and Violent Behavior, 4*: 203–212.
13. Ivory, J.D. (2001). Video Games and the Elusive Search for their Effects on Children: An Assessment of Twenty Years of Research. Paper presented at the *National AEJMC Conference*, August. Available at http://asuwlink.uwyo.edu/~poison/video_games_and_children_.htm

14. Unsworth, G. & Ward, T. (2001). Video games and aggressive behaviour. *Australian Psychologist, 36*: 184–192.
15. Anderson, C.A. & Bushman, B.J. (2001). Effects of violent video games on aggressive behavior, aggressive cognition, aggressive affect, physiological arousal, and prosocial behavior: A meta-analytic review of the scientific literature. *Psychological Science, 12*: 353–359.
16. Sherry, J.L. (2001). The effects of violent video games on aggression: A meta-analysis. *Human Communication Research, 27*: 409–431.
17. Funk, J.B., Buchman, D.D., Jenks, J., & Bechtoldt, H. (2003). Playing violent video games, desensitization, and moral evaluation in children. *Journal of Applied Developmental Psychology, 24*: 413–436.
18. Anderson, C.A., Carnagey, N.L., Flanagan, M., Benjamin, A.J., Eubanks, J., & Valentine, J.C. (In press). Violent video games: Specific effects of violent content on aggressive thoughts and behavior. *Advances in Experimental Social Psychology*.
19. Anderson, C.A. & Murphy, C.R. (2003). Violent video games and aggressive behavior in young women. *Aggressive Behavior, 29*: 423–429.
20. Bartholow, B.D. & Anderson, C.A. (2002). Examining the effects of violent video games on aggressive behavior: Potential sex differences. *Journal of Experimental Social Psychology, 38*: 283–290.
21. Bushman, B.J. & Anderson, C.A. (2002). Violent video games and hostile expectations: A test of the general aggression model. *Personality and Social Psychology Bulletin, 28*: 1679–1686.
22. Panee, C.D. & Ballard, M.E. (2002). High versus low aggressive priming during video-game training: Effects on violent action during game play, hostility, heart rate, and blood pressure. *Journal of Applied Social Psychology, 32*: 2458–2474.
23. Uhlmann, E. & Swanson, J. (2004). Exposure to violent video games increases automatic aggressiveness. *Journal of Adolescence, 27*: 41–52.
24. Heeter, C. (1995). Communication research on consumer VR. In F. Biocca & M.R. Levy (Eds.), *Communication in the Age of Virtual Reality*. Hillsdale, NJ: Lawrence Erlbaum Associates, Inc., pp. 191–219.
25. Pham, A. (2004). Eye toy springs from one man's vision. *Los Angeles Times*, January 18. Available at http://www.latimes.com/business/la-fi-eyetoy18jan18,1,4576015.story?coll=la-home-business
26. Lombard, M. & Ditton, T. (1997). At the heart of it all: The concept of presence. *Journal of Computer Mediated Communication, 3*, Available at http://jcmc.huji.ac.il/vol3/issue2/lombard.html
27. Witmer, B. & Singer, M. (1998). Measuring presence in virtual environments: A presence questionnaire. *Presence: Teleoperators and Virtual Environments, 7*: 225–240.
28. Funk, J.B. (1993). Reevaluating the impact of video games. *Clinical Pediatrics, 32*: 86–90.
29. Griffiths, M.D. & Hunt, N. (1995). Computer game playing in adolescence: Prevalence and demographic indicators. *Journal of Community and Applied Social Psychology, 5*: 189–193.
30. Ijsselsteijn, W. (2002). Understanding presence. Paper presented at the *Fifth Annual International Workshop PRESENCE*, October, Porto, Portugal.
31. Leyens, J.P. & Picus, S. (1973). Identification with the winner of a fight and name mediation: Their differential effects upon subsequent aggressive behavior. *British Journal of Social and Clinical Psychology, 12*: 374–377.
32. Geen, R.G. (1990). *Human Aggression*. Belmont, CA: Brooks/Cole Publishing Co.
33. Tamborini, R., Eastin, M., Lachlan, K., Fediuk, T., Brady, R., & Skalski, P. (2000). The effects of violent virtual video games on aggressive thoughts and behaviors. Paper presented at the

86*th* *Annual Convention of the National Communication Association*, November, Seattle, WA.

34. Persky S. & Blascovich J. (Under review). Violent video games and aggression: Effects of immersion and presence.

35. Blascovich, J. & Tomaka, J. (1996). The Biopsychosocial model of arousal regulation. *Advances in Experimental Social Psychology, 28*: 1–51.

36. Persky S. & Blascovich J. (Under review). Platform and gender effects on violent and non-violent video game play.

37. Ballard, M.E. & Wiest, J.R. (1996). Mortal Kombat™: The effects of violent videogame play on males' hostility and cardiovascular responding. *Journal of Applied Social Psychology, 26*: 717–730.

38. Buckley, K.E., Tapscott, R.L., Sidhartha, R., Rypma, C.A., Gentile, D.A., Anderson, C.A., Nacin, C., Sannier, A., Oliver, J.H., & Bushamn, B.J. (2004). The effects of violent virtual reality games on aggressive behavior and cognitions. Paper presented at the *American Psychological Society Annual Meeting*, Chicago, IL.

39. Blascovich, J. (2002). Social influence within immersive virtual environments. In R. Schroeder (Ed.), *The Social Life of Avatars: Presence and Interaction in Shared Virtual Environments*. London: Springer, pp. 127–145.

40. Blascovich, J. (2002). A theoretical model of social influence for increasing the utility of collaborative virtual environments. *CVE 2002: Proceedings of the 4*th* International Conference on Collaborative Virtual Environments*, pp. 25–30.

41. Swinth, K.R. & Blascovich, J. (2001). Conformity to group norms within an immersive virtual environment. Paper presented at the *American Psychological Society Annual Meeting*, Toronto, Ontario.

42. Todorov, A. & Bargh, J. (2001). Automatic sources of aggression. *Aggression and Violent Behavior, 7*: 53–68.

Chapter 9

THE PSYCHOLOGY OF MASSIVELY MULTI-USER ONLINE ROLE-PLAYING GAMES: MOTIVATIONS, EMOTIONAL INVESTMENT, RELATIONSHIPS AND PROBLEMATIC USAGE

Nick Yee

1.   Introduction

Every day, millions of users [1, 2] interact, collaborate, and form relationships with each other through avatars in online environments known as Massively Multi-User Online Role-Playing Games (MMORPGs). For example, in a planetary system known as Corbantis, geological surveyors are busy inspecting their chemical harvesting installations to maintain their daily quota for a cartel of pharmaceutical manufacturers. These manufacturers, allied with a rebel faction, are struggling to research and supply key medical supplies to the front lines of the conflict. Corbantis is an incredibly sophisticated online environment capable of supporting thousands of users at a time. Users log on to the server from remote locations independent of each other, and interact with each other through graphical avatars to accomplish complex goals. But Corbantis is merely one planetary system out of many other equally complex worlds. These online environments offer tantalizing glimpses of how millions of avatars interact on a daily basis outside a laboratory setting and what users derive from that experience.

The study of MMORPGs is highly relevant to research on social interaction in Shared Virtual Environments (SVEs) and avatars at work and play in these environments. Although many of the theoretical implications of social interaction in virtual environments have been explored in the artificial confines of Virtual Reality (VR) research laboratories [3–8], MMORPGs are the only existing naturalistic setting where millions of users voluntarily immerse themselves in a graphical virtual environment and interact with each other through avatars on a daily basis. The opportunity to study what

R. Schroeder and A.S. Axelsson (Eds.), Avatars at Work and Play, 187–207.
© 2006 *Springer.*

people actually do when they choose to be in a virtual environment with thousands of other people cannot be overstated, and the results and implications of a survey study of 30,000 MMORPG players will be presented in this chapter.

In the following section, the history and structure of MMORPGs will be presented, followed by an overview of the methodology used in the survey study. The demographics, usage patterns and motivations of users will then be presented. A combination of quantitative and qualitative data will guide the discussion of relationship formation, role exploration, skill transfer, and problematic usage in these environments. Finally, potential uses of these environments for social science research will be discussed.

2.   History of MMORPGs

MMORPGs are a new class of Multi-User Domains (MUDs) – online environments where multiple users can interact with each other and achieve structured goals. The first MUD—an adventure game in a persistent world that allowed multiple users to log on at the same time—was created in 1979 by Roy Trubshaw and Richard Bartle [9]. While it is commonly thought that MUDs descended from table-top role-playing games (RPGs) such as Dungeons and Dragons, the two genres emerged around the same time and co-evolved beginning in the early 1970s [10] and became popular during the 1980s. Both games allow users to create characters based on numerical attributes (i.e. Strength, Dexterity, Intelligence) and templated roles (i.e. Warrior, Cleric, Druid) with different strengths and weaknesses. Game-play typically revolved around a combination of interactive story-telling and logistical optimizations under the guise of slaying monsters and attaining higher levels and skills. In RPGs, a designated Game Master controlled the outcome of events based on dice-rolls and references to charts and tables. In MUDs, this is controlled by the server.

As the graphical and processing capabilities of the modern personal computer increased, and as accessibility to the Internet became widely available, it became possible in the early 1990s to build MUDs with graphical front-ends. *Ultima Online*, launched in 1997, is recognized to be the first MMORPG—a persistent, graphical, online environment that allowed thousands of users to be logged on at the same time. The number of active users that Ultima Online could support was what distinguished MMORPGs from existing graphical MUDs. The second MMORPG, *EverQuest*, launched in 1999, quickly achieved a sustained user base of 400,000 and remains the most popular MMORPG in North America as of 2004 [2] even though at least 10 competing MMORPGs have emerged since then.

3.   Details of MMORPGs

Users must purchase or download the specific MMORPG client and pay a monthly subscription fee (around 10–15 USD) to access the central servers. Users view the world in real-time 3D graphics, and use an avatar (a humanoid graphical representation of the user/player in the game) to interact with the environment and each other through a combination of a mouse-driven user interface and keyboard commands. Communication between users occurs through typed chat and animated gestures and expressions. The worlds of MMORPGs are vast and presented in rich, graphical detail. It typically takes several hours to traverse the entire world of an MMORPG, although different types of transportation are available to teleport users to different locations in the world. Users are given a large degree of control over the appearance of their avatars. For example, in the recent MMORPG *Star Wars Galaxies*, users are able to manipulate their avatar's gender, race (Wookie, Human, Rodian, etc.), skin tone, age, height, weight, musculature, cheek prominence, jaw prominence, brow prominence, nose shape, eye shape, eye color, hair style, hair color, mouth shape, lip fullness, and the presence of body markings or freckles.

Users choose from a set of professions or roles that the MMORPG provides. The permanence or fluidity of roles varies depending on the design of the environment. Each role has varying strengths and weaknesses and most MMORPGs are designed such that users must often collaborate to achieve goals within the environment. While early MMORPGs were based on fantasy medieval worlds made popular by RPGs and contained only combat-oriented roles (i.e. Warrior, Archer, Healer, etc.), recent MMORPGs have offered more diverse profession alternatives. For example, in *Star Wars Galaxies*, one can become a skilled musician, chef, hair stylist, pharmaceutical manufacturer, or politician.

Goals and rewards in MMORPGs typically use a random-ratio reinforcement schedule based on operant conditioning. Early achievements are quick, almost instantaneous, and gradually take more and more time and effort until progression becomes almost imperceptible. Most forms of advancement in MMORPGs require increasing cooperation or dependency on other users, oftentimes mutually beneficial. In *Star Wars Galaxies*, surveyors locate deposits of chemicals and minerals across different planets. To harvest these resources in bulk, surveyors must purchase mining installations from architects. Alternatively, surveyors can choose to sell the locations of rich deposits (i.e. the information itself) to miners rather than harvesting the resources themselves. Surveyors who choose to harvest resources may then become resource brokers who market those resources to artisans and manufacturers who need those resources to produce goods. Combat, medical or fashion goods then are sold on the open market and bought by mercenaries, doctors and other members of the general public.

Ultimately, each user decides which form of advancement they will pursue, and the richness and complexity of the environment eliminates the need for super-ordinate goals or storylines. Every user is motivated by a different combination of the possible rewards. The result is that adventures, stories, and most importantly, meaningful interactions and relationships between users emerge. Functional constructs within the environment facilitate these social networks— combat groups (temporary collaboration between a few users), guilds (persistent user-created membership organizations), and ideological alliances (agreements between guilds or "racial" groups).

4.   Collaboration in MMORPGs

Combat-oriented collaborations in MMORPGs become incredibly complex once users have advanced beyond beginner levels. In typical battle-oriented scenarios, groups of 4–8 users are confronted by multiple enemy agents based on fairly sophisticated AI. These groups of users are typically composed of a balanced combination of roles and must communicate and perform effectively as individuals using a predetermined group strategy. Consider a fairly typical crisis situation. Certain enemy agents will run away and elicit help from allied agents when they are badly wounded. In a dungeon setting, these enemy agents typically run towards deeper, more dangerous locations. If the agent succeeds, he will return with several stronger agents. But if one user chases the agent, while the others decide not to, then that jeopardizes the group as well. This situation typically occurs while the group is still engaged with other half-wounded agents. Also remember that different users have different personalities (risk-taking propensities, assertiveness, and so on) and different stakes at this point of their adventure, and differ in their loyalty to the group and each other. In the span of 5–10 seconds, the risk-analysis, opinions and decisions of the group communicated over typed chat, or the solitary actions of a particular user, will determine the life or death of all members of the group. This particular type of crisis is also embedded into the larger context of existing tensions such as emergent leadership, group polarization, and personality differences.

More recent MMORPGs such as *Star Wars Galaxies* have also created collaboration scenarios of an entirely entrepreneurial nature. All non-basic goods in the environment (clothing, housing, pharmaceuticals, etc.) are produced by users. Unlike earlier MMORPGs, users cannot sell goods back to the server itself. All transactions, and the resulting supply, demand, and pricing of specific goods, are user-driven. The environment has mechanisms allowing users to survey for resources, harvest those resources, research schematics for assembling resources into sub-components, construct factories to mass-produce finished goods, and market those goods to the public. The process is so complex, time-consuming, and distributed over several skill sets that users typically specialize as resource brokers, manufacturers, or retailers, and typically form quasi-business entities with other users to facilitate that process. These entities have to communicate effectively, develop a coherent product strategy, assess market competition, and ensure that the production chain is running smoothly. Many users comment that being part of such entities feels like having a second job.

5.   Existing Literature on MMORPGs

More than a decade has passed since Dibbel [11] pondered the significance of a virtual rape in *LambdaMOO* as it was embroiled in a political reform. The academic interest in MUDs it sparked was almost entirely driven by qualitative scholars. Turkle [12] articulated how these environments revealed the fluid and decentralized nature of identities. Others [13] have challenged the utopian visions of cyberspace, arguing that online communities do not foster racial equality but merely make racial minorities easier to suppress. The behavioral sciences have kept their distance from these online environments. With regards to video gaming in general, the field of psychology seems fixated on whether video games cause real-life aggression [14–23]. Considering that new forms of social identity and social interaction are emerging from these environments, is aggression the only thing worth our attention?

Academic attention in MMORPGs has largely been driven by economic and legal scholars. Castronova [24] has calculated the Gross National Product of the world of *EverQuest* by aggregating e-Bay sales of virtual items and currency, and has also shown that male avatars sell for more than female avatars of exactly the same capabilities [25]. Legal scholars [26] have examined the ownership of virtual property and whether avatars have enforceable legal rights. Griffiths [27] has also aggregated online poll data at websites catering to *EverQuest* players to provide the basic demographics and preferences of *EverQuest* players.

In essence, there has been very little research available that has explored the social interactions, relationship formation and derived experiences of the users of MMORPGs. Since the spring of 2000, the author has carried out an extensive survey study of over 30,000 MMORPG users that has examined who uses MMORPGs, what motivates their use, and the salience and impact of the experiences that emerge in these environments. While a previous paper [28] focused on presenting statistical findings from the data set, the following chapter summarizes and elaborates on those findings with qualitative data to provide a richer perspective of these online environments.

6.   Methodology of Survey Study

The survey study consisted of a series of online surveys that were publicized in web portals that catered to MMORPG users from the years 2000 to 2003. The approximate number of active subscribers to each existing MMORPG was publicly available [1], and it was usually clear which MMORPGs comprised the bulk of all MMORPG players. Therefore, users of the four most popular environments were targeted for the study—*EverQuest, Dark Age of Camelot, Ultima Online,* and *Star Wars Galaxies*. A survey with new content was usually publicized every two to three months. Each survey took about 5–10 minutes to complete, and typically 2000–4000 respondents would complete each survey. In each survey, respondents were asked to provide their email if they were interested in participating in future surveys. At the beginning of each survey phase, in addition to the recruitment at websites, respondents already in the database were contacted via email to notify them of the new survey in which they could participate. Over the course of four years, 30,000 unique users participated in the survey study.

Lack of motivation and integrity in web-based surveys are two potential concerns, but studies have shown that web-based respondents are typically highly-motivated due to self-selection and anonymity does not have an adverse affect on data integrity (for review, see [29]). Sampling bias is also a concern. In particular, a skewed representation of dedicated and heavy users is possible. Because of market competition, demographic information about users of these environments is not publicly available; however, informal communication with representatives of some of these companies has corroborated the basic demographic representativeness (average age and average hours per week) of the sample. Also, the sampling bias in using a large, non-random sample of MMORPG users to generalize to other MMORPG users is probably not any riskier than the standard practice in experimental psychology of using small, non-random samples of mostly Caucasian students between the ages of 18–22 who are enrolled in introductory psychology courses to generalize to all of humanity (for example, see [30]).

7.   Only For Teenagers?

The stereotype that only teenagers partake in these environments discourages broader interest in studying these environments. Indeed, the Journal of Adolescence recently dedicated an entire special issue to the topic of video game violence (February, 2004), fostering the stereotype that adults do not engage in these kinds of activities, or that somehow adolescents interact with video games in an entirely different way from how adults interact with them. Data from Griffiths' study [27] as well my survey study [28] challenge that stereotype. The average age of MMORPG respondents was 26.57 ($n = 5509$, SD $= 9.19$); the median was 25, with a range from 11 to 68. The lower and upper quartile boundaries were 19 and 32, respectively. Thus, in fact only 25% of MMORPG users are teenagers.

Many MMORPG users have stable careers and families of their own [28]. 50% of respondents ($n = 2846$) worked full-time, 36% were married, and 22% had children. The data showed that teenagers, college students, early adult professionals, middle-aged homemakers, as well as retirees were part of these environments. Indeed, these seemingly disparate demographic groups would oftentimes be collaborating and working together to achieve the same goals similar to the ones mentioned earlier. This finding is particularly striking given that these disparate demographic groups seldom collaborate in any real life situation.

8. Time Investment

The demographic reality of these environments is important to establish to frame the significance of the following data on usage patterns. Users spend on average 22.72 hours ($n = 5471$, SD $= 14.98$) each week in their chosen MMORPG. The lower quartile and upper quartile boundaries were 11 and 30 respectively. The distribution showed that about 8% of users spend 40 hours per week or more in these environments—the equivalent of a normal work week. The significant amount of time that users are willing to invest in these environments is further highlighted by the finding that 60.9% of respondents ($n = 3445$) had spent at least 10 hours continuously in an MMORPG. The correlation between age and hours spent per week was not significant, implying that the appeal of these environments is comparable for high-school students, middle-aged professionals and retirees.

9. Emotional Investment

The appeal and salience of these environments is further demonstrated by the degree that users are emotionally invested in their avatars and the environment. When respondents were asked whether the most positive experience they had experienced over the period of the past 7 days or the past 30 days occurred in an MMORPG or in real-life, 27% of respondents ($n = 2170$) indicated that the most satisfying experience over the past 7 days occurred in the game, and 18% of respondents indicated the same when the wording was changed to "over the past 30 days". With regards to the most negative event, 33% of respondents indicated that the most negative experience over the past 7 days occurred in the game, and 23% of respondents indicated the same when the wording was changed to "over the past 30 days".

Open-ended questions asking users to elaborate on examples of these experiences drew responses that revolved around interactions with other users [31]. Typical positive experiences involved an unexpected altruistic or courageous action by another user.

> He showed rare courage by staying until everyone was clear, including me, knowing that he would probably not make it out alive. That was the most selfless thing I had seen done before or since. He stayed, knowing the corpse retrieval that awaited him, the experience he would lose, and the wasted time he was about to experience because of it. He could have run and lived, but he did n't for our sakes. When you make sacrifices for people, they will remember, and the best groups are those built on loyalty, self-sacrifice, and courage. [male, 32]

On the other hand, typical negative experiences involved the selfish actions of other users, or actions or behaviors that constituted an attack on the competence or self-worth of a user.

> I was playing my enchanter at the time, and his partner turned out to be an enchanter, a level higher than I was. I was medding up after buffing the group and switching my spells back to hunting/guarding spells, when the new enchanter started casting everything I had just cast, overwriting everything I had done, telling the group what to do and commenting on how they obviously hadn't had a chanter with them who knew how to take care of their group and they were lucky he was there, he'd make sure they didn't get into TOO much trouble. I disbanded and headed for the zone, in tears of frustration. To be overwritten, pushed aside, and belittled was unbearable. [female, 36]

What is clear is that these environments encourage both time and emotional investment from the users, and that users derive salient emotional experiences from these environments.

10.   Motivations

The usage patterns of users force us to examine what makes these environments so appealing. What motivates users to become so invested in these environments? User responses expose the varied and multi-faceted reasons for why users engage in these environments.

> After many weeks of watching I found myself interested in the interactions between people in the game, it was totally absorbing!!!! The fact that I was able to immerse myself in the game and relate to other people or just listen in to the "chatter" was appealing. [female, 34]

> I play MMORPGs with my husband as a source of entertainment. Overall it can be a cheaper form of entertainment where you can spend quite a bit of time with a significant other. To play well you end up developing more ways of communicating. [female, 31]

I like the whole progression, advancement thing ... gradually getting better and better as a player, being able to handle situations that previously I wouldn't have been able to. [male, 48]

No one complains about jobs or other meaningless things. It's a great stress reducer. I like that I can be someone else for a couple hours. [female, 28]

Currently, I am trying to establish a working corporation within the economic boundaries of the virtual world. Primarily, to learn more about how real world social theories play out in a virtual economy. [male, 30]

Having an empirical framework of articulating motivational differences between users is the foundation to understanding the emergence of more complex behaviors and interactions in these environments. This framework provides the foundation to explore whether different sections of the demographic are motivated differently, and whether certain motivations are more highly correlated with usage patterns or in-game preferences or behaviors.

In an attempt to create an empirical framework for articulating motivations for MMORPG usage, a series of 40 statements covering a broad range of motivations were generated based on open-ended responses as well as Bartle's [32] theoretical framework of "Player Types" based on his experiences in MUDs. Examples of the resulting items include: "I like to feel powerful in the game," and "I like to be immersed in a fantasy world." These statements were presented using a 5-point Likert-type scale and then analyzed using an exploratory factor analysis to arrive at a parsimonious representation of the associations among the 40 items [28].

The analysis produced five factors. The "Relationship" factor measures the desire of users to interact with other users, and their willingness to form meaningful relationships that are supportive in nature, and which include a certain degree of disclosure of real-life problems and issues. The "Manipulation" factor measures how inclined a user is to objectify other users and manipulate them for his personal gains and satisfaction. Users who score high on the "Manipulation" factor enjoy deceiving, scamming, taunting and dominating other users. Users who score high on the "Immersion" factor enjoy being in a fantasy world as well as being "someone else". They enjoy the story-telling aspect of these worlds and enjoy creating avatars with histories that extend and tie in with the stories and lore of the world. The "Escapism" factor measures how much a user is using the virtual world to temporarily avoid, forget about and escape from real-life stress and problems. And finally, the "Achievement" factor measures the desire to become powerful in the context of the virtual environment through the achievement of goals and accumulation of items that confer power.

It was found that male users score higher than female users on Achievement and Manipulation, whereas female users scored significantly higher on the Relationship, Immersion and Escapism factors. In other words, male users are more likely to engage in these environments to achieve objective goals, whereas female users are more likely to engage in MMORPGs to form relationships and become immersed in a fantasy environment. These gender differences resonate with findings by Cassell and Jenkins [33] and suggest that MMORPGs do not have one set of factors that appeals to everyone equally well, but instead, have a host of appealing factors each of which draws in users with different motivations. With regard to how these motivations related to usage patterns, among male users, age was inversely correlated with the Manipulation ($r = -0.33$, $p < 0.001$) and Achievement ($r = -0.27$, $p < 0.001$) factors, implying that younger male users tend to objectify both the environment and other users for their own personal gains. Among female users, age was inversely correlated with the Manipulation ($r = -0.15$, $p < 0.001$) and Immersion ($r = -0.13$, $p < 0.001$) factors.

The articulation of the different reasons why users engage in these environments allow researchers to explore usage preferences and behaviors in relation to the motivations of the user in addition to gender and age differences. It is simply not the case that all users engage in these environments for the same reason.

11.   It's All Pretend?

Because these environments are labeled "role-playing games", it is easy to assume that users treat it as a simplistic game of pretend-play. The emotional investment that these environments derive from users is one way of countering that assumption. Users in fact take these environments very seriously. Other survey data also show that the majority of users indicate that the way they behave and interact with others in these environments is very close to how they behave and interact with others in the material world [31]. In other words, most users are simply being themselves rather than experimenting with new identities or personalities. It is also easy to assume that nothing serious or meaningful happens in or can be derived from these environments because they are merely semi-sophisticated forms of play. The following sections provide multiple lines of evidence to argue that many different kinds of serious social phenomena occur in these environments.

12.   Relationships in MMORPGs

When asked to compare the quality of their MMORPG friendships with their material world relationships, 39.4% of male respondents ($n = 2971$) and 53.3% of female respondents ($n = 420$) felt that their MMORPG friends were comparable or better than their material world friends [28]. Furthermore, 15.7% of male respondents ($n = 2991$) and 5.1% ($n = 420$) of female respondents had physically dated someone who they first met in an MMORPG [28]. Thus, both platonic and romantic relationships seem to occur with significant frequency in MMORPG environments. This finding resonates with Walther's [34] notion of the hyperpersonal effects of computer-mediated communication (CMC).

Indeed, the ingredients that Walther proposed for hyperpersonal interactions—interactions that are more intimate, more intense, more salient because of the communication channel—all exist in MMORPGs. First, the communication channel allows the sender to optimize their self-presentation because interactants do not have to respond in real-time. Second, the receiver forms an impression of the sender by inflating the few pieces of information that the sender has optimized. Third, participants can reallocate cognitive resources typically used to maintain socially acceptable non-verbal gestures in face-to-face interactions and focus on the structure and content of the message itself, which comes across as more personal and articulate. Finally, as interactants respond to personal messages with equally personal and intimate messages, the idealized impressions and more personal interactions intensify through reciprocity. The cumulative effect is that the interaction becomes more intimate and positive.

It has also been suggested that there are factors unique to MMORPGs that facilitate relationship formation [35]. The kind of high-stress crisis scenario outlined earlier in the chapter occur with great frequency in these environments under different guises. When paired with the degree of emotional investment users place in these environments, many relationships are in fact triggered by these trust-building scenarios, analogous to boot camps and fraternity initiations in the material world.

> To succeed in EQ you need to form relationships with people you can trust. The game does a wonderful job of forcing people in this situation. Real life rarely offers this opportunity as technological advances mean we have little reliance on others and individuals are rarely thrown into life-or-death situations. [male, 29]

While it may appear that meeting other users with compatible personalities and interests seems like finding a needle in a haystack in these environments, users are in fact pre-selected for compatibility. 36% of employed respondents ($n = 1099$) work in the IT industry, and 68% of respondents ($n = 3415$) have experience with table-top role-playing games. IT workers are typically analytical and rational; RPG players are typically imaginative and idiosyncratic. Both tend to be non-conformist. MMORPG environments are a very specific form of entertainment—gradual advancement via avatars in a fantasy medieval or futuristic world with other users. Thus, in fact, MMORPG users are probably similar in more ways than not.

And finally, the fantastical metaphors employed in these environments encourage idealizations that parallel cultural myths of chivalric romance—knights in shining armor, clerics with glowing auras. Thus, these metaphors also encourage idealization in addition to the underlying inflated sense of compatibility due to hyperpersonal interactions. MMORPGs are environments where users are in fact falling in love with knights in shining armor:

> The MMORPG relationship is inexplicably more romantic, more epic, more dramatic... [female, 16]

MMORPG environments allow us to think about how the mechanics and functional constraints of a constructed world could be used to engineer the relationships that form [36]. User dependencies, the mechanics of death, and other structures all play a role in encouraging or discouraging relationships to form in these environments. MMORPGs allow us to ask questions about how the mechanics of a world influence the communities that form instead of focusing on individual interactions.

13.   Romantic Partners and Family Members

There is a very different kind of relationship "formation" that can be explored in MMORPGs. Many MMORPG users participate in the environment with a romantic partner or family members. 15.8% of male respondents ($n = 1589$) and 59.8% of female respondents ($n = 311$) participate in the environment with a romantic partner, while 25.5% of male respondents and 39.5% of female respondents participate in the environment with a family member—a sibling, parent or child [28]. Open-ended responses from these users indicate that their online relationships shape, influence and allow them to explore their material world relationships.

Many romantic couples who participate in the environment together commented on how the environment highlighted their individual differences. For these users, the MMORPG environment reflected and accentuated differences in their personalities and worldviews.

> Our styles are totally different. For instance, I will rather play in a group just for company, even if the exp gain is minimal, whereas my partner tends to literally AVOID other players. I am often a pushy role-player, forcing others to RP or get out of my face. Thus I am unafraid of starting an argument, whether in /say, /tell or even /shout. This seems to make my partner very uncomfortable. For these reasons, if we are playing together we try very hard to compromise. However, I insist on having "solo" characters that I only play on my own. I tend to find his gaming style restrictive. [female, 23, engaged]

> I would say rather than having learned something new about him, it was more like it emphasized differences between us that I already knew about. He is very patient, I am very impulsive, etc. And these differences are a lot more apparent in a game situation. [female, 27, dating]

For other romantic partners, the MMORPG environment not only reveals individual differences, but it also comes to shape the relationship itself.

> Like children who play dolls to explore social situations and different perspectives, EQ enables us to look at issues of dependence/independence, and gender perceptions. It's increased the equanimity between us, and brought us closer through exercises in trust that transcend in game terms, class, level, and gender. We will discuss game scenarios and learn from each others perception (i.e., when to run). After 3 years of playing together we are a well-oiled machine, and can lead a group, follow or solo together or apart. [female, 34, married]

> Our relationship has definitely been enhanced. We're better now at working together towards goals. And we both really enjoy growing, learning and adventuring together. It's exciting to be involved in each other's triumphs. [female, 29, married]

Parents and their children who participate in these environments provide another perspective on how the MMORPG environment interacts with existing relationships. Many parents commented on how the environment allowed them to observe their children in social interactions that they usually had no access to in the material world. For them, the MMORPG environment became a window into parts of their children's identity that they had not known about before.

> I learned that my son is a very good strategist. I knew that to a degree before, but it has been eye opening to watch him lead a group. I did not know he had these skills. [female, 49]

> It added depth and clarity to many traits that I knew they had to see how they presented themselves in a different environment. Since I am pretty much removed from their circle of friends and can't watch them at school, EQ provides a window into their behavior outside of the house [female, 37]

> I found that my son handles himself in a very mature manner. (He's 13 now). I have also been told by many other players that know of our relationship how courteous and well spoken he is. [male, 49]

Other parents commented that the MMORPG environment has allowed them to transcend the strict roles of parent-child relationships in a rewarding way. The MMORPG environment not only shapes these relationships, but in fact restructures them by allowing the participants to redefine the boundaries of their material world roles.

> I think it has enhanced our relationship, we both treat each other more like equals and partners in our private life. It is much easier to talk to her now and I have found her talking to me about much more of her life and ideas. [female, 40]

> Yes, playing EQ with my daughter has been very enjoyable, and I have learned more about my daughters personality as she treats me as a friend on EQ and not a parent. [female, 40]

Thus, MMORPG environments are not only places where new relationships are engineered, but in fact are windows into existing relationships as well as catalysts for the restructuring of roles in those relationships.

14.   Role Exploration and Skill Transfer

Turkle [12] articulated how MUDs allow users to explore new roles and identities. MMORPG environments are also used for these purposes.

> In reality I'm an Army Officer, very assertive and aggressive. In MMORPGs I'm more like I wish I could be, quiet, introspective and sensitive of other's feelings. Taking on different roles has also taught me to "walk a mile" in other shoes before judging—not useful as an army officer, perhaps, but very useful in becoming a quality human being. [male, 42]
>
> When I play my male characters, other male members of the party will listen to me better, take me more seriously. In my male form I could give orders and have them listened to, where as a female, my characters aren't always taken quite as seriously. Also, where my female characters were given many gifts by random players when they were young, I didn't see it happening with my males, which I didn't mind at all. I've enjoyed the higher level of "respect" for my abilities that seems to come with playing in a male body. [female, 22]

But beyond exploring how MMORPGs can shape the identities of individuals, these highly social and structured environments also allow us to explore whether certain valuable skills learned in an MMORPG can transfer to the material world.

Personal advancement in MMORPGs typically involves collaboration among groups of users in an attempt to achieve a challenging task. Thus, a prime candidate for acquired skills is leadership skills. In emergent groups within the MMORPG environment, leaders deal with both administrative as well as higher-level strategy issues, most of which arise and have to be dealt with spontaneously. Administrative tasks include: role assignment, task delegation, crisis management, logistical planning, and how rewards are to be shared among group members. Higher-level strategy tasks include: motivating group members, dealing with negative attitudes, dealing with group conflicts, as well as encouraging group loyalty and cohesion. These issues are even more salient in long-term social groups, such as guilds, which have formalized membership and rank assignments. In other words, MMORPGs provide many opportunities for short-term and long-term leadership experiences. As one user notes:

> I've never been one who is particularly comfortable with a leadership role in real life. In the game, friends and I left another guild that no longer suited us for various reasons and formed our own. I was approached by several of these friends

to assume leadership of the guild and agreed, even though I was uncertain of my suitability. I've grown more accustomed now to directing various aspects of running the guild and providing a vision and leadership to the members. Follow-up and assertiveness now feel more natural to me even in real life. It has been an amazing opportunity to push myself beyond my boundaries and a rewarding experience. [female, 46]

This sentiment is shared by many users. In the survey study [28], 10% of users felt they had learned a lot about mediating group conflicts, motivating team members, persuading others, and becoming a better leader in general, while 40% of users felt that they had learned a little of the mentioned skills. This is striking given that these environments are not structured pedagogically to teach leadership. Acquisition of leadership skills in these environments is in fact an emergent phenomenon. But more importantly, these findings demonstrate that real-life skills can be acquired or improved upon in these environments. Certainly, self-reported assessments are not robust assessments, but these findings lay the foundation for more controlled studies of the acquisition of complex social skills in these environments.

15.   Problematic Usage

As mentioned in the section on time investment, 8% of users spend 40 hours or more in these environments, and 70% have spent at least 10 hours continuously in an MMORPG in one sitting. Both quantitative and qualitative data suggest that a small, but significant, group of users suffer from dependence and withdrawal symptoms [37].

I am addicted to EQ and I hate it and myself for it. When I play I sit down and play for a minimum of 12 hours at a time, and I inevitably feel guilty about it, thinking there a large number of things I should be doing instead, like reading or furthering my education or pursuing my career. But I can't seem to help myself, it draws me in every time. I have been out of work now for over a month and now find myself in a stressful, depressed state that is only quelled when I am playing EQ, because it's easy to forget about real world troubles and problems, but the problem is when you get back to the real world, problems and troubles have become bigger, and it's a bad, bad cycle. I've tried quitting seriously on several occasions. There are serious withdrawal pangs, anxiety, and a feeling of being lost and not quite knowing what next to do with yourself. [male, 26]

On 5-point Likert scales, 15% of respondents ($n = 3989$) agreed or strongly agreed that they become angry and irritable if they are unable to participate. 30% agreed or strongly agreed that they continue to participate in the environment even when they are frustrated with it or not enjoying the experience. And

18% of users agreed or strongly agreed that their usage patterns had caused them academic, health, financial or relationship problems. Agreement with the mentioned statements was significantly positively correlated with average weekly use of the environment. Even more striking, 50% of respondents ($n = 3166$) considered themselves addicted to an MMORPG in a direct "yes"/"no" question. While it may be difficult to draw a line between healthy and unhealthy usage of these environments, it is clear that certain users are engaged in problematic usage of these environments.

While the design of these environments, such as the sophisticated reward cycles based on operant conditioning paradigms [38], certainly plays a role in engaging users in problematic usage, it would be overly-simplistic to focus entirely on the architecture of the environment itself. After all, that perspective fails to account for why only certain users engage in problematic usage. It also fails to take into account that different users are motivated to participate in the environment for different reasons. One proposed model of problematic usage [37] approaches the environment as a place where many common anxieties can be overcome. For example, users who have low self-esteem can become powerful and competent in these environments and they are driven to achieve in these environments as a way of overcoming anxieties they have in the material world. Or for example, users who feel undervalued in the material world can become needed and valued members of groups or guilds. Users with poor self-image can choose to be as attractive and physically fit as they desire. Users with low internal locus-of-control gain a stronger sense of agency in these environments. Users with stressful problems can use these environments as escape. In short, these environments are seductive for some users because they empower them in ways specific to their anxieties.

16. Online Environments as Potential Social Science Research Platforms

The structure and design of these environments make them good candidates for a host of alternative uses for social scientists. For example, traditional personality assessment techniques are typically transparent and reactive. Because actions in massively multi-user online environments can be tracked unobtrusively by the server, every users' attitudes and personalities may be tracked using behavioral measures. And because users are personally invested in their avatars and the environment, every decision they make is personally revealing. The length and frequency of utterances, as well as the breadth and depth of a user's social network can all be meticulously measured and tracked over long periods of time. This database of measures provides rich longitudinal profiles of individual users as well as how they rank amongst a large sample of other users. One could think of MMO environments as a gold-mine of personality data as well as a platform to develop unobtrusive personality assessment tools.

The arguments that Blascovich *et al.* [39] make for the use of immersive virtual reality technology as a methodological tool for social psychology can also be applied to MMORPG environments. The movements, interactions and preferences of large numbers of users can all be tracked unobtrusively and recorded. For example, one could implement a transformed social interaction ([40], see also Bailenson and Beall's chapter in this volume), such as non-zero-sum gaze, on one MMORPG server and use another server for control, and track the aggregate changes in mean length of utterances or topology of social networks. The MMORPG environment allows us to answer social psychology questions on a social level rather than an individual level. How does non-zero-sum gaze or other transformed social interactions reshape social networks, alter the flow of information, or affect trust in a social organization? As social organizations proliferate in MMORPG environments, research in transformed social interactions becomes even more important as it will inform us of how designers could engineer these environments to encourage the formation of strong and trusting social networks.

17.   Conclusion

As scholars who studied MUDs [11, 12] pointed out, our virtual identities and experiences are not separate from our identities and experiences in the material world. They co-evolve as they shape each other. MMORPGs are not a new form of play as much as a new communication medium that affords new forms of social identity and social interaction.

While typical VR environments try to replicate human avatars in contemporary physical locations, MMORPGs offer fantastical avatars and worlds. After all, if you could be anyone anywhere, would you choose to be exactly who you were? This tension begs the broader question—given that we are not constrained to human forms or modes of movement and interaction that are bound by laws of physics, why do we insist on replicating them? If the body is merely the original prosthesis [41], can we not think "outside of the body"? Insisting on visual veridicality also forces us to abandon interesting issues in self-representations. What might decisions in virtual self-representation tell us about users?

The strong appeal of these environments also has interesting implications. MMORPGs do not only appeal to teenagers. They are online environments where young professional adults, middle-aged home-makers and retirees interact and collaborate on a daily basis. More importantly, the average MMORPG user spends more than half a work week in these environments. As more people engage in online environments instead of watching TV, it raises interesting questions with regard to Gerbner's cultivation theory [42]. Gerbner found that heavy TV viewers have a worldview that overestimates violence and the percentage of legal-enforcement workers in the general population due to their over-representation in TV content. Might certain worldviews be cultivated by heavy exposure to online environments? For example, users are given a high degree of control and agency in MMORPGs, and all events are based on underlying numeric variables. So it might make sense to ask whether heavy users have a stronger internal locus of control, or apply a more closed-system perspective on thinking about events in the material world.

The data presented also explored how virtual environments impact relationship formation in different ways. Not only can these environments facilitate formation of relationships, but they are also windows into and catalysts in existing relationships. More importantly, relationships can be thought of as being engineered by the architecture of the environment. For example, what are the potential effects of transformed social interaction [40] on social interactions at a community level? It also leads us to wonder how a community in the material world could be shaped by allowing them to interact in an engineered virtual environment.

The excessive usage exhibited by certain MMORPG users might appear problematic at first, but in fact forces us to ask whether the mechanisms of appeal in MMORPGs could be harnessed for pedagogical purposes. Story-path curriculums, used in certain schools, embed the syllabus of each term in an ongoing hypothetical setting, such as an iron-forging village in 19th century England. Every student takes on the role of a member of the village, such as blacksmith, pastor or farmer, and the syllabus material is woven into relevant tasks that the villagers encounter. For example, basic algebra may be embedded into a task that tried to optimize ratios of profitable crops, while social policy material may be embedded into a town meeting over a local epidemic of scarlet fever. The goal is to increase interest in learning by making the material personally relevant to students. The structure of MMORPGs are well-suited for story-path curriculums, and in fact, would also allow classes from different schools to inhabit different villages and create a larger social community that worked together to resolve conflicts or achieve common goals.

Finally, MMORPGs also blur the distinction between work and play in intriguing ways. Case studies of virtual real-estate brokers [43] are one of many compelling examples of how digital media blur the distinction between work and play. These users sell virtual real-estate (as well as virtual weaponry and currency) for real-life currency on auction sites such as eBay. More compelling are the "sweatshops" in developing nations that hire youths to generate profit by accumulating these virtual goods and currency and then selling them for real-life currency [44]. In this case, work and play are indistinguishable. As Andrejevic [45] has pointed out, interactive media creates digital enclosures that allow work to be performed under the guise of entertainment. For example, in There.com, brand-name fashion designers use the environment as a marketing test-bed for new clothing designs. Sales of the test products and whether users who have large social networks buy them are aggregated automatically. The irony is that not only do these users have to pay a monthly fee to subscribe to the environment, but they are performing free labor for a third-party corporation. As these environments become more sophisticated, we can imagine them transforming into predominantly sites of economic activity under the guise of interactive entertainment.

We have seen that MMORPG users become highly invested in these environments, and that serious social phenomena occur in these environments that can create, shape and restructure relationships in the material world. Every day, millions of users log on to worlds like Corbantis, performing highly-specialized and complex tasks, interacting and collaborating with each other through avatars. Some of them are accumulating virtual real estate to trade for US dollars. Some are married to people they have never met. Some are collaborating with their children to produce advanced pharmaceuticals, while others are planning a mayoral campaign. Indeed, if we are interested in the social lives of avatars, the citizens of worlds like Corbantis have a great deal they can tell us.

References

1. Woodcock, B. (2003). An Analysis of MMOG Subscription Growth. Available at http://pw1.netcom.com/~sirbruce/Subscriptions.html
2. Corpnews.com, MMOG Roundup: Depressing 2004 Edition. (2004). Available at http://www.corpnews.com/news/fullnews.cgi?newsid1081411764,6286
3. Bailenson, J.N. & Blascovich, J. (2002). Mutual gaze and task performance in shared virtual environments. *Journal of Visualization and Computer Animation, 13*: 1–8.
4. Leigh, J., DeFanti, T., Johnson, A., Brown, M., & Sandin, D. (1997). Global telemersion: Better than being there. In *Proceedings of ICAT '97*, no pp.
5. Mania, K. & Chalmers, A. (1998). A classification for user embodiment in collaborative virtual environments. In *Proceedings of the 4th International Conference on Virtual Systems and Multimedia*. IOS Press—Ohmsha, Ltd., pp. 177–182.
6. Normand, V., Babski, C., Benford, S., Bullock, A., Carion, S., Chrysanthou, Y., Farcet, N., Harvey, J., Kuijpers, N., Magneat–Thalmann, Raupp–Musse, S., Rodden, T., Slater, M., & Smith, G. (1999). The COVEN project: Exploring applicative, technical, and usage dimensions of collaborative virtual environments. *Presence: Teleoperators and Virtual Environments, 8*: 218–236.
7. Slater, M., Sadagic, A., Usoh, M., & Schroeder, R. (2000). Small group behavior in a virtual and real environment: A comparative study. *Presence: Teleoperators and Virtual Environments, 9*: 37–51.
8. Zhang, X. & Furnas, G.W. (2002). Social interactions in multiscale CVEs. In *Proceedings of the ACM Conference on Collaborative Virtual Environments 2002*, Bonn, Germany, September 30–October 2, pp. 31–38.
9. Bartle, R. (1990). Early MUD history. Available at http://www.mud.co.uk/-richard/mudhist.htm

10. Koster, R. (2002). Online world timeline. Available at http://www.legendmud.org/-raph/gaming/mudtimeline.html

11. Dibbel, J. (1993). A rape in cyberspace. Village Voice, Vol. XXXVIII, No. 51, December 21.

12. Turkle, S. (1995). *Life on the Screen: Identity in the Age of the Internet.* New York: Simon and Schuster.

13. Nakamura, L., Rodman, G., & Kolko, B. (2000). *Race in Cyberspace.* New York: Routledge.

14. Anderson, C.A. & Bushman, B.J. (1997). External validity of "trivial" experiments: The case of laboratory aggression. *Review of General Psychology, 1*(1): 19–41.

15. Bushman, B.J. & Anderson, C.A. (2002). Violent video games and hostile expectations: A test of the general aggression model. *Personality & Social Psychology Bulletin, 28*(12): 1679–1686.

16. Anderson, C.A. & Dill, K.E. (2000). Video games and aggressive thoughts, feelings, and behavior in the laboratory and in life. *Journal of Personality & Social Psychology, 78*(4): 772–790.

17. Anderson, C.A. & Bushman, B.J. (2001). Effects of violent video games on aggressive behavior, aggressive cognition, aggressive affect, physiological arousal, and prosocial behavior: A meta-analytic review of the scientific literature. *Psychological Science, 12*(5): 353–359.

18. Ballard, M.E. & Lineberger, R. (1999). Video game violence and confederate gender: Effects on reward and punishment given by college males. *Sex Roles, 41*(7–8): 541–558.

19. Funk, J.B. & Buchman, D.D. (1996). Playing violent video and computer games and adolescent self-concept. *Journal of Communication, 46*(2): 19–32.

20. Funk, J.B., Hagan, J.D., Schimming, J.L., Bullock, W., Buchman, D.D., & Myers, M. (2002). Aggression and psychopathology in adolescents with a preference for violent electronic games. *Aggressive Behavior, 28*(2): 134–144.

21. Griffiths, M. (1999). Violent video games and aggression: A review of the literature. *Aggression & Violent Behavior, 4*(2): 203–212.

22. Scott, D. (1995). The effect of video games on feelings of aggression. *Journal of Psychology, 129*(2): 121–132.

23. Ferguson, C.J. (2002). Media violence: Miscast causality. *American Psychologist, 57*(6–7): 446–447.

24. Castronova, E. (2002). Virtual worlds: A first-hand account of market and society on the cyberian frontier. Available at http://ssrn.com/abstract=294828

25. Castronova, E. (2002). The price of "man" and "woman": A hedonic pricing model of avatar attributes in a synthetic world. Available at http://ssrn.com/abstract=415043

26. Lastowka, G. & Hunter, D. The laws of virtual worlds. (2003). Available at http://ssrn.com/abstract=402860

27. Griffiths, M. (2003). Breaking the stereotype: The case of on-line gaming. *CyberPsychology and Behavior, 6*: 81–91.

28. Yee, N. (2004). The demographics, motivations, and derived experiences of users of massively multi-user online graphical environments. Submitted for publication.

29. Gosling, S.D., Vazire, S., Srivastava, S., & John, O.P. (2004). Should we trust web-based studies? A comparative analysis of six preconceptions about Internet questionnaires. *American Psychologist, 59*(2): 93–104.

30. Bailenson, J.N., Shum, M.S., Atran, S., Medin, D.L., & Coley, J.C. (2002). A bird's eye view: Triangulating biological categorization and reasoning within and across cultures. *Cognition, 84*: 1–53.

31. Yee, N. (2004). The Daedalus project. Available at http://www.nickyee.com/daedalus

32. Bartle, R. (2003). Hearts, clubs, diamonds, spades: Players who suit MUDs. Available at http://www.mud.co.uk/richard/hcds.htm

33. Cassell, J. & H. Jenkins (Eds.). (1998). *From Barbie to Mortal Kombat: Gender and Computer Games*. Cambridge, MA: MIT Press.

34. Walther, J.B. (1996). Computer-mediated communication: Impersonal, interpersonal, and hyperpersonal interaction. *Communication Research, 23*(1): 3–43.

35. Yee, N. (2003). Inside out. Available at http://www.nickyee.com/daedalus/archives/-000523.php

36. Yee, N. (2003). Engineering relationships. Available at http://www.nickyee.com/-daedalus/archives/000429.php

37. Yee, N. (2002). Ariadne: Understanding MMORPG addiction. Available at http://www.nickyee.com/hub/addiction/home.html

38. Yee, N. (2001). The Virtual Skinner Box. Available at http://www.nickyee.com/-eqt/skinner.html

39. Blascovich, J., Loomis, J., Beall, A., Swinth, K., Hoyt, C., & Bailenson, J.N. (2002). Immersive virtual environment technology as a methodological tool for social psychology. *Psychological Inquiry, 13*(2): 103–124.

40. Bailenson, J.N., Beall, A., Loomis, J., Blascovich, J., & Turk, M. (2004). Transformed social interaction: Decoupling representation from behavior and form in collaborative virtual environments. *Presence: Teleoperators and Virtual Environments, 13*(4), 428–441.

41. Hayles, K. (1999). How we became Posthuman: Virtual bodies in Cybernetics, Literature, and Informatics. Chicago: University of Chicago Press.

42. Gerbner, G. (1973). *Communications Technology and Social Policy: Understanding the New Cultural Revolution*. New York: Interscience Publication.

43. Dibbell, J. (2003). The unreal estate boom. *Wired, 11*(01).

44. The Walrus. (2004). Game theories. Available at http://www.walrusmagazine.com/-04/05/06/1929205.shtml

45. Andrejevic, M. (2002). The work of being watched: Interactive media and the exploitation of self-disclosure. *Critical Studies in Media Communication, 19*(2): 230–248.

Chapter 10

QUESTING FOR KNOWLEDGE—VIRTUAL WORLDS AS DYNAMIC PROCESSES OF SOCIAL INTERACTION

Mikael Jakobsson

1.   Introduction

In this chapter I will discuss the nature of social interaction and game-play in the massively multi-player online game *Everquest*. Based on my studies of this particular type of virtual world, I will address the question of how the experience of participating in virtual worlds changes over the course of time and the implications of this on how we conceive virtual worlds from a design perspective. In parallel, I will also address some methodological implications of performing ethnographic studies in an environment where new levels of interacting with the world and its participants continuously reveal themselves—like new levels in a platform game.

For social interaction to exist within a virtual environment there have to be social actors in it. This book as well as its predecessor [1] covers a wide range of cases of social interaction from separate individuals all the way up to large groups of people. In this volume, yet another dimension is added as this and Nick Yee's (chapter 9) look at a fully three-dimensional graphical environment that attracts and supports participants on a massive scale averaging several thousands of participants in the same virtual world.

In a previous essay (in [1]) I argued for the importance of an *inside view* in order to grasp the unique properties of the social environments of virtual worlds. In this chapter my focus is on the vantage point of a participant embedded in the world. I will describe the game from four different points in the process of progressing through the game as a player and through the empirical study as a researcher. These discrete reference points will then be connected in an attempt to reveal a richer picture of the processual qualities of virtual worlds in terms of understanding the object of study as well as the process of studying it.

R. Schroeder and A.S. Axelsson (Eds.), Avatars at Work and Play, 209–225.
© 2006 *Springer.*

While it is generally a bad idea to recount a study in chronological terms, I will do exactly that here with the explicit purpose of showing how the understanding of an object of study can change when looked at over an extended period of time. In this way I wish to uncover the research process rather than hiding it beneath the surface of the text.

Until recently, there were no systems of this scale and complexity in existence—but that changed with the arrival of the game *Everquest* in 1999. Built on a real-time three-dimensional graphics system similar to e.g. Active Worlds but with a closed graphics library, *Everquest* took the role-playing genre of computer games to a new level of technological sophistication. The response from the gaming community was overwhelming and a flood of similar games has followed establishing a new genre of computer games, the massively multiplayer online game MMOG. (This kind of game is sometimes referred to as MMORPGs, or role playing game, but since the role-playing element is often very weak and some games lack it completely, the RP part of the acronym is becoming ever less appropriate).

Everquest continues to be one of the most successful games in the genre with over 2.5 million copies of the game sold and currently having over 400,000 paying subscribers of which around 100,000 play simultaneously at peak times [2]. Operating via a client/server architecture, the world of *Everquest* is a fairly elaborately rendered three-dimensional space in which players battle a variety of characters and creatures. The world of *Everquest* is inhabited by participants who wander a vast terrain covering a number of continents. Much like old-style tabletop role-playing games, players create a character to play by selecting a "race" such as human, halfling or troll, a class such as warrior, shaman or wizard, and setting a few other parameters defining their character. On special servers players can engage in combat against other players or in more formalized role-playing, but the overwhelming majority play against the monsters in the world without bothering with the role-playing aspects of the game.

2.   The Beginner Level: Everquest as a Single-Player Game

To say that the *Everquest* world is vast feels like a bit of an understatement. The amount of places to visit and monsters to battle is almost endless. Most of this is, however, out of reach for a beginner. When a player first enters the world, it is in the designated hometown. Before the player has put a few experience levels under her or his belt and acquired some basic equipment, it is impossible to venture very far beyond the city gates without falling prey to the creatures that roam the game world.

The very first obstacle that the player has to overcome is, however, the user interface. Before being able to interact with the environment, with non-player characters, or with other participants, the technical aspects of interaction have to be mastered. A crucial part of this interaction is the communication with other players. All text-based communication is carried out in different chat channels. As long as the player has not selected a channel for the text input, the keys on the keyboard work as shortcuts to different commands. This means that if you target a non-player character and start typing to say something to it without indicating the appropriate channel, the keystrokes will be interpreted as commands. This will in turn prove deadly if the intended message includes the character "A" since that key by default is set to trigger the command "auto-attack", and the non-player characters in the game are powerful enough to quickly eradicate a beginner player. (Measures are continuously taken to make the system more forgiving to the beginners, including a recent move of the default key for auto-attack from typing the "A" key to typing the significantly less used "Q" key.)

One of the promises of three-dimensional graphics was the possibility of making interaction interfaces more intuitive and easy to use for beginners. What we see in the user interface of *Everquest* should not necessarily be interpreted as an indication that these promises were incorrect. Instead, it speaks of the powerful impact of history in technology development. Despite the ocean-wide difference in complexity and experience of play between the early text-based MUDs and today's MMOGs, many designers as well as players have come to today's MMOGs via the MUDs, bringing their history of previous influences and experiences with them. *Everquest* displays a number of technological and cultural traces to these earlier systems.

The command interface is so reminiscent of the DIKU (Datalogisk Institut, Københavns Universitet) MUD system that people coming from a MUD of that variety testify to feeling right at home in *Everquest*. The *Everquest* team at one point had to release a sworn statement that they had not used any actual code from DIKU MUD which resulted in the following response: "The DIKU group is proud that 'the DIKU feeling' has found its way into a game as enjoyable and award winning as Everquest" [3]. *Everquest* also borrows from other sources. Many of the sites and monsters bear a striking resemblance to those in fantasy fiction in general and Tolkien in particular. The game system is heavily influenced by Dungeons and Dragons [4]. There are also technical solutions and modes of navigation originating from predecessors within the field of three-dimensional graphical environments.

The notion of a beginner becomes more complex when the history of the players—and the ways it coincides with the history of the game—is taken into account. A Tolkien reading MUD veteran with previous experience of virtual worlds is a very different kind of beginner than the person without this background.

After a few fatal encounters with merchants and other non-player characters in the hometown, the player will avoid at least the more devastating interaction mistakes. There will, however, still be a barrier between the beginner and the other players in the game. One very palpable factor that keeps beginners separate from other players is the geography. While the beginners cannot stray very far from the guarded cities, the more experienced players have to find other hunting grounds in order to find strong enough monsters to gain experience points from slaying them.

Besides the geographically imposed obstacles to playing the game together with the more experienced players, there is the lack of strategic knowledge. The abilities of different characters are designed in a way to make it beneficial for players to form groups and hunt together. The safety and efficiency of the group is dependent on the participants performing their tasks correctly and being able to efficiently communicate with the other group members. These skills take time to learn and a beginner lacks both the knowledge and the ability to communicate that is required. To accommodate for this, the developers have made it possible for all classes to easily defeat monsters on their own the first ten or so experience levels. A player who decides to start a second character will on the other hand have the required knowledge set and ties to the social networks between players [5] to be able to traverse the isolation of the beginner player.

After having played *Everquest* for a week or so and gained around ten experience levels, I could claim to have gained first-hand experience of the object of study and my notes were full of impressions from the intense experience. But what had I really seen? My perception of the game was that it was a fairly repetitive hack and slash game mainly played solo in a fairly confined space. I knew there was much more of the world to explore out there and that the game was full of other players, but I had no way of knowing if the experience of being in the game world and playing the game would change significantly or if it was going to be more of essentially the same thing. The only way to experience this for myself was to continue playing.

3.   The Intermediate Level: Everquest as a World of Personal Communities

Just like a player bursting out in a triumphant "ding" signaling that a new experience level has been reached, I remember feeling a sense of elation when I stepped into the world of interconnected personal networks that signifies participation in the world of *Everquest* at an intermediate level. In my case it was not so much a question of being rewarded after a long hard struggle, as having contacts outside the game that helped me get "connected" on the inside. In [5], Taylor and I give a detailed description of the structure and importance of social networks in the game and the process of socialization. There we describe how social networks share structural properties with the mafia (as we understand its organization from popular fiction). Everything from initiations, pledges of trust and allegiance, vows of silence and favor systems exist both in the mafia and the social networks of *Everquest*. They both also seem to have their origin in a need for protection in an environment of insufficient control of law and order. Here, I will concentrate on describing the way the experience of the game and the world changes as a result of moving from the outside to the inside.

While the beginner stage is passed fairly quickly, the second stage will take months, sometimes years, and ranges approximately from level twenty to sixty. For the majority of the players most of the time is spent in groups at this stage of the development of the character. The gaming session typically begins with the player spending some time looking for a group to join, or starting a group and gathering the other five players needed. These players will then pick a place to set up camp and start killing the monsters there. When a monster is killed a new one will emerge at the same spot after a set time so the group will not run out of things to kill no matter how long they stay. Normally, a session lasts a couple of hours.

Although the players can move around more freely in the world at this stage, they do so to a very limited degree. Since the monsters you kill have to be on par with your own experience level to yield good experience earnings, there are only a few zones to choose from at any given experience level. The activity of camping around the same monsters for hours on end—sometimes referred to as experience grinding—might seem repetitive and even a bit boring. But with a fairly routine task to perform to keep the development of the character in motion, the players have plenty of time to socialize with the other group members and other friends in the game. Some people have social ties to other players already when they come to the game in the form of family members or friends. Others start from scratch in making friends through playing and hanging out together and before long, almost all players have created a social network of friends and acquaintances within the game.

From essentially being a single-player game on the first few levels, the gaming experience transforms into a rich social experience for the intermediate player. The game play stays basically the same. Instead it is the context around the actual monster killing that has changed. Just as in non-game virtual worlds, it turns out that the social interaction is the very foundation for the appeal of the world (see chapter 9 in this volume for more about social interaction as game motivation). At this stage of the game, the social networks are still loose and informal for the most part. Every player has his own web of contacts primarily organized by the friends list function in the game. The players perceive belonging to a community but each player's community looks different; in other words, they are personal communities as defined in [6]. With continued playing this will, however, change.

4.   The High-End Game: Organized Play

Somewhere around level fifty to sixty and after perhaps a year or so in the game, players start feeling that there is something—more specifically their epic weapon—that they are missing and that it is time to try to do something about it. All classes in the game can take on an epic quest that will result in an epic weapon as reward if it is completed successfully. The epic quests are designed to require the help of more than just a handful of friends to complete. Besides the monsters that need to be defeated for the epic quest, the high-end game also includes many other tasks that require a raid force of up to seventy strong players to conquer.

The personal communities that players create during their time as intermediate players are not strong enough to support the level of organization that the high-end game requires. There are many reasons to be in a guild—such as belonging to a community and protection of the gaming experience from disruptive forces—but it is not until the high-end game that it becomes more or less a necessity. Guilds are formalized social networks managed by the players with the support of a few in-game tools. To start a guild, a minimum of ten players have to commit to joining. The person starting the guild becomes guild leader and chooses which other players to authorize as officers. The guild gets a dedicated chat channel and a tag under their names showing which guild they belong to.

The role of an officer in a guild differs depending on the size and type of guild. The bigger guilds have officers dedicated to specific tasks such as organizing raids or handling recruitment while the officers of smaller guilds tend to all do a bit of everything. I am a member of a medium sized guild with approximately three hundred registered characters. For about a year I have been involved in managing the guild as an officer, raid leader and for a brief time guild leader. We are a social guild which means that we do not make any particular requirements on our participants in terms of experience level, abilities, play time or attendance and we only raid once a week.

We do, however, require that our members adhere to our guidelines for social behavior within the game. These guidelines—posted on the guild website— cover topics of honorable and fair behavior towards other players and helping guild members achieving their goals. We also keep a fairly strict norm on language use in the guild channel since many of the participants are combining playing with looking after their kids. The social guilds tend to attract a more mature type of players while raiding guilds often appeal to a younger crowd. Older players may still put a significant number of hours into the game every week but often cannot commit to playing in the way a raiding guild demands. Out of these differences in appeal grows a difference in culture between the two types of guilds.

The downside of not belonging to a raiding guild is that some parts of the world require persistent raiding and these zones are the ones where you can find the best items to equip your character with. An alternative to joining a raiding guild is to join a raid channel. These channels are set up and administered by one or more guilds that wish to raid but lack the critical mass of players within their own guild. They therefore offer access to the channel to players who do not have a guild or are in a non raiding guild but still wish to raid occasionally. The raid channels are of course established to benefit the guilds behind them, but work as a kind of community service to social players with a taste for raiding.

At one particular raid we picked up a person along the way who said that he was looking for a guild to join and asked if he could tag along. Since he was a high level character of a class that we had use for, we were happy to bring him with us. While he handled his job of bringing monsters to the rest of us very well, he was also a little too eager to get a cut of the items we were getting by killing the monsters, suggesting that he had special needs for some of the items and that they should be defaulted to him instead of letting the luck of the draw decide who would get it. The officers running the raid and handling the looting and distribution of items that dropped from the monsters, however, paid no attention to these requests.

When we headed home at the end of the evening he mentioned that he wanted to join our guild. At the time the rules for inviting people into the guild were that at least three officers had to agree that a person was suitable for membership before issuing an invitation. Since there were more than three officers present at the raid we could immediately make a decision and he was invited. This was to be the last time someone was invited to the guild this way.

It only took until the next day before our guild leader received a private chat message from another player in the game issuing a complaint against our recently invited guild member. The complaint regarded a case of "ninja looting" which means that a player takes an item from a defeated monster that she or he does not rightfully deserve (see [5] for more on social consequences of the possibility to "ninja loot").

The guild leader then proceeded to interview the accused, the person issuing the complaint and one more person who had been in the same group at the time of the incident. He then posted all this material in the officer-only section of the guild website and requested comments from the other officers. After a few postings back and forth between the officers it was the guild leader who decided that the person should be removed from the guild.

The last thing a guild wants is rumors of questionable behavior to start spreading on the server, since the reputation of a guild affects the reputation of all its members and will make it harder for the guild to form alliances with other guilds. So as a direct consequence of the incident the officers decided to tighten up the recruitment process. Now applicants to the guild have to post an application on the guild website and then spend some time in a special recruitment channel in the game before they can be invited. This increase in rules, guidelines and formalized procedures is typical of guilds growing in numbers and reputation on a server. It also leads to that the officers of the guild spend more and more of their game-time on community management.

As an officer in general and a guild leader in particular, the nature of play shifts dramatically from mostly minding your own business and helping out others when needed, to management responsibilities that take up more time than the actual monster killing. Besides making sure that the guidelines of the guild are adhered to, officers spend much of their time reading up on how to tackle certain monsters, screening guild applicants, managing guild bank money and items and keeping the guild website in shape.

Somewhere in the middle of all this, the actual killing of the monsters still works more or less the same way as at level one, but the scale and complexity of what it means to play the game has reached a level that makes the gaming experience completely different from that of a beginner player.

5.   The Endgame: Players Turning Against Players

Before the first expansion of *Everquest* was released there was a very limited selection of monsters to kill at the very high-end level of the game. The guild leader of one of the first raiding guilds on one of the first *Everquest* servers told me that after having done all the other content in the game, there were only two monsters left of interest to them. It was the two dragons Lady Vox and Lord Nagafen. His guild was the first to defeat the dragons but another was not far behind. Despite a fair amount of rivalry between the two guilds they managed to stay out of trouble by taking turns killing the two dragons. The situation became more complicated when a third guild on the server became strong enough to challenge the dragons. The limited resources in the game had created a volatile situation.

At one point, one of the guilds failed in an attempt to kill one of the dragons and when they came back later for a new attempt, the next guild scheduled was already there setting up for their turn. The exact details of what happened that night may differ depending on who you ask, but everybody agrees that things got ugly. Players tried to get players from the other guild killed and the verbal exchange between the raid forces was harsh and abusive. The incident led to an outright war between the guilds and both sides lost members as a result of it. Peace finally came when all the involved guilds agreed to follow a web-based event calendar operated by neutral players. With the aid of this calendar, guilds could make reservations for a monster they wanted to kill and the others would stay away from it until their turn came. The event calendar was successful in making rival guilds share the limited resources equally. But eventually one guild decided that they were not going to honor the calendar any more and would try to kill any of the dragons whenever they would see fit to do so. This guild could be described as a rogue guild, a guild that thrives on gaining a reputation—but not for being good and honorable but for being bad and doing whatever they feel like.

Most servers have one or a few of these guilds and they are always the source of huge amounts of discussions and complaints on the community message boards. While the majority of players harbor negative attitudes towards the rogue guilds, there are also players who are attracted by their boldness and attitude. The impact of these guilds on the servers is undisputable. Once a guild had publicly declared that they were not going to honor the event calendar, the initiative was in effect dead since it required backing from all parties to work as intended.

Things had, however, changed in the game world. New continents and monsters had been added to the game and the two dragons were no longer the most rewarding or prestigious targets. Since there were more possible targets to choose from, the need to take turns for the monsters was no longer as pressing. The issue of bottlenecks still existed though.

When the epic quests were introduced in The Ruins of Kunark—the first expansion of the game—many players wanted to kill the particular monsters that held the pieces they needed to complete the quest and receive the epic weapon for their class of player. At the time, the dragon Zordakalicus Ragefire, needed for the cleric epic, took several days to spawn again after it had been killed. The discrepancy between supply and demand created a severe bottleneck and according to [7] the waiting list for a shot at killing Ragefire was over a year on some servers. Other servers had no waiting list, but instead had to deal with large groups of players waiting around, hoping to engage the dragon first whenever it would spawn, leading to a situation reminiscent of the one with Vox and Nagafen.

While the developers tried to eliminate some of the problems stemming from players fighting over limited resources by simply adding more content and making the end-game more diverse, they were reluctant to shorten the spawn time of Ragefire with the motivation that the cleric epic is a powerful item and that "in Everquest power and rarity usually go hand-in-hand." [7].

The designers continuously have to deal with the trade-off between frustration and sense of accomplishment. If a quest is too easy in terms of time investment or manpower, the items gained from it will not be regarded as very special by the players. On the other hand there are players who know that they will never see large parts of the content of the game since they cannot make the commitment required. This leads to an ever changing environment where the developers try to find new ways of accommodating different styles of play with every new expansion of the game—at the same time as older content is under constant revision.

One of the defining traits of Everquest is that players exclusively fight against non-player characters and not against each other as in many MUDs and other MMOGs. In the endgame, however, when the selection of attractive targets becomes narrower, the guilds tend to turn against each other. While players still cannot directly fight each other, the competition for monsters between raiding guilds can be fierce at times and disputes often lead to trash talking and open animosity between members of the rivaling guilds. Many players who initially were attracted to the game partly because of its focus on collaboration rather than direct competition are deterred by this development. Although their character has become strong enough to pass the entry requirements for a raiding guild, some players choose not to join one, thus excluding themselves from a large number of zones and even larger number of monsters. Others thrive under these conditions and claim that it is at this point that the game truly begins.

6.   The Final Level: Death

The following interaction took place in Plane of Knowledge, a hub in the game world that always is full of players, on a Saturday in September 2004. The names of the characters have been replaced with generic names. Since the communication in the game more or less constitutes a language of its own, I have added some explanatory remarks. All of this was said in the out of character channel which is a way of reaching all players in a zone without having to use the more intrusive shout channel.

Monk says, "Bye bye Everquesters ... monk gona go FD [feign death is a monk specific ability used to fool monsters that you are dead] one last time in Qeynos [one of the hometowns] .... if i knew you, well met ...... see you on EQ2 [Everquest 2] or WoW [World of Warcraft]"

Player 1 says, "Bye Monk!"
Player 2 says, "Take Care Monk ... gl [good luck] man"
Player 3 says, "Fare Well MOnk!!!"
Player 4 says, "Bye Monk"
Player 5 says, "Be safe mon"
Player 6 says, "MONK NOOOOoooo not EQ2"
Player 7 says, "Farewell friend"

Death is a constantly present part of life in *Everquest*. A character that dies in the game respawns at a predetermined location and can run back and reclaim the possessions from the dead body, only suffering a minor penalty to the experience level. But since there is no final goal to the game, the player will sooner or later have to make the decision to stop playing the game altogether.

While the *Everquest* game system is constantly evolving and many additions have been made following requests from the player community, there is not a single line of code or advice written to help players who want to quit.

Once a player stops paying the monthly subscription fee, the character lingers on in a kind of limbo for an undisclosed period of time before eventually risking deletion from the database and being gone forever without a trace. I have come across many examples of how players react to and try to deal with this issue. Some players sell their characters for real money [4]. Others keep paying without playing or give away their characters. I have also encountered players paying for other people's accounts to keep those characters alive. There is even a guild called Zombies of EQ that works as a support group for former *Everquest* players [8].

When Sony announced that the Planes of Power expansion to *Everquest* was going to include something called graveyards, my first thought was that they finally had addressed the issues of the inevitable death of characters in the game, but unfortunately these were only designated areas for corpses to re-spawn in order to make them easier to retrieve. But what if graveyards where players really could bury their characters when they are done with the game were implemented? Maybe a culture of funeral ceremonies would develop within the player community where friends and guild members could say farewell to the character in a way that would provide a sense of closure both for the player who is leaving the game as well as those who have developed a relationship to the player within the game. While a high score list is a fitting way for gamers to leave a trace from their encounter with a coin-op game, and a "hall of fame" website is a suitable addition to a racing game, the persistent nature of MMOGs creates special needs for the kind of traces the gamers should be able to leave behind them when they go.

7. Discussion and Conclusions

7.1. *The World as a Process*

Everquest is both a game and a virtual world. As a game, it needs to drive the process of playing forward. Exactly what that process is can only be determined individually and at given points in time since different players have different motivations for playing and these motivations change over time. The most important driving force in the game, however, is to increase the abilities and experience level of one's character. The pursuit of experience points could be regarded in terms of a number of possible paths traversing geographical space. Right outside all hometowns are beginner areas with low level monsters that players can kill to gain the first few levels, but soon they need to move on through the world in order to keep the experience points rolling in. The issue

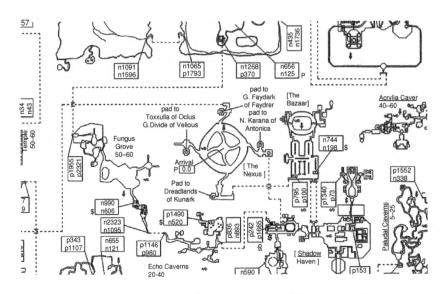

Figure 10-1. Area of a spatially oriented map of the moon Luclin.

of where to go next once the experience gain starts dropping off is a constantly hot topic among the players.

This gives rise to a need from the players to map the game landscape in two different ways. The first is the traditional geographical maps which show which zones are adjacent to each other and how to get from one place to another (figure 10-1). The second is a process-oriented description showing which zones provide the best trade-off between difficulty of the monsters and gain in experience.

While the first map shows the shortest way from one place to another in the virtual landscape, the second way of describing the world focuses on the optimal way to develop the statistics of your character. The process-oriented progression through the game becomes even clearer in the high-end game. In figure 10-2, the high-end zones are ordered in a flow-chart telling players how to progress through the zones to finally get to the Plane of Time, the most rewarding zone in the game at the time when this illustration was made. It also tells us that this world can be understood as a flow of people through the environment working their way towards their goals.

In the case of Everquest, the process that the world is there to support—or provide a pleasurable resistance against, depending on how you look at it—is the development of the player's characters. The process-oriented nature is, however, nothing unique for the MMOG game worlds. In earlier studies of general purpose virtual worlds, I have come to the conclusion that virtual worlds need an activity of some kind to keep them going. The activity provides the driving force that propels the process on which the world depends forward. This should both help us understand the success of MMOGs

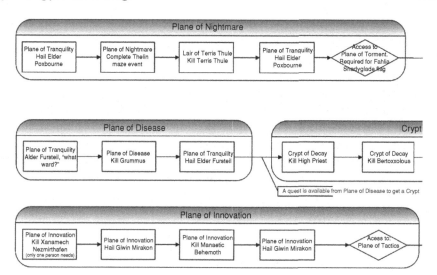

Figure 10-2. Excerpt from a process-oriented map showing how to get to the Plane of Time.

and tell us something about how to create successful virtual worlds for other purposes.

7.2.   One World?

From the very beginning *Everquest* has struggled with the problem of its own popularity. For one thing, the number of players wanting to be in the same world at the same time leads to technical problems. Without any restrictions to the number of players that can be present at the same location at the same time, the fact that all the player's movements and actions alter the state of the world which has to be distributed to everybody puts a big strain on the networking and processing power of both clients and servers. On top of that, the fairly advanced graphics in the game put a strain on the rendering capabilities of the participants' computers. All these factors contribute to a lag between the issuing of an action by the player and the actual execution of that action. This lag is of course especially annoying if your life is in the balance, which it often is when fighting monsters is on the agenda.

Besides making the technology handle all the people who want to play the game, there is also the issue of having enough content in the world for everyone as was discussed in Section 5. With the release of a number of expansions that all add more territory to explore and more monsters to fight, the developers have tried to reduce some of the bottlenecks on the paths of progression through the virtual landscape and create an alternative solution to the same problem as the event calendar aimed to resolve. In the fourth expansion—Planes of

Power—the trend towards creating alternate progression routes was broken with the introduction of the so called flag progression path: The new zones were divided into tiers and access to higher tier zones was given by killing certain monsters in the lower tier zones giving the character a "flag"—an intangible check mark that works as a key to the next zone. The beginning of the flag progression path can be seen in figure 10-2. In the figure we can for instance see that a player has to kill the Manaetic Behemoth in the Plane of Innovation—a tier one zone—to get access to the tier two zone Plane of Tactics.

Again the focus of many players was turned towards the same monsters with traffic jams as the result. The rogue guilds found a particularly sinister way of benefiting from the situation. Since a guild cannot go to any zones beyond the zone they try flagging their members for, a rogue guild that already has that flag can reduce the competition in the zones they are hunting in by making sure that they kill the monster that gives the flags to get there whenever it spawns, an activity known as "cock blocking."

The developers again reacted to the situation, but this time with a new strategy. Instead of creating a wider range of content, something called instanced zones was introduced. What makes the instanced zones special is that a new copy of the zone is created every time a group of players enter it. In Gates of Discord—the seventh expansion—progression through the new zones is based on the completion of a number of "trials." These trials take place in instanced zones—which means that a guild can begin a particular trial and another guild can arrive five minutes later and start the same trial. For each guild, an instance of the same zone with the same monsters in it is created. The need to wait for particular monsters to re-spawn is thereby eliminated, as is the possibility of blocking other guilds by keeping monsters inaccessible.

The instanced zones, however, break one of the more fundamental principles of virtual world design. This principle—we can call it the singular world rule—states that all the participants are part of the same geographical world and if two participants go to the same place in that world, they will meet each other. This rule was in one sense broken already from the beginning of *Everquest* since there are a number of servers all running their separate copy of the game world. But the instanced zones further weaken the concept of a singular world that all participants are part of. Here the players can still communicate with each other and thus share the same social space, but if they are not part of the same instance, they cannot meet with each other.

In the eighth and latest (as of this writing) expansion—Gates of Discord—the developers have once more adjusted the direction of the development of the world and moved away from instanced zones. Alan Crosby, Community manager of *Everquest*, explains the change like this: "We do feel that the task system [quests given on demand] is a better solution than instanced zones, as they will not remove you from the community and isolate you in a little area by yourself. With tasks you remain a part of the world at large" [9].

The singular world rule has not been debated much in the past. It has always been seen as desirable by the virtual world design community; maybe because it seems to dominate virtual world fiction completely. But when a world becomes as large as the worlds the science fiction authors write about, we realize that there is a distinct difference between design ideals and the best solution in practice. In this regard, *Everquest* works as an interesting test-bed for virtual world design concepts.

7.3. Researchers at the Doorstep

In game reviews and research presentations alike, it is very common to hear references to character creation, exploration of the hometown and endless killing of low-level monsters such as rats, snakes, and spiders. The problem with these descriptions of the game is that they do not capture the typical experience of the game of the people who actually play it. You only create your character once, and although you can make more characters, most players only ever make a few and put substantial play time into even fewer. Once the character is created, however, it can be developed for years and years within the game. By character development I do not just mean the way the statistics of the character such as experience level, skills and abilities are developed. More importantly, the social networks within the game that are slowly developed over time contribute significantly both to the possibilities of success in the game as well as a rich and rewarding gaming experience.

As I have tried to show in this text, the experience of the game changes dramatically based on where in the process the player is. This is easily overlooked since the layers existing beyond the current position are in many ways hidden to the player. I myself have several times thought that I had reached a status quo where the gaming experience would not change dramatically again—only to be proven wrong by continued play. The understanding of the properties of the game world goes hand in hand with a more developed experience of the game as a player. I understand that not everyone can spend years on the same object of study and I do believe that there is a place for snapshot observations of game worlds and game cultures. My point is rather that there are things to be seen that cannot come through any other process than immersion over long periods of time.

7.4. It is All about Learning

If you ask *Everquest* players why the game appeals to them you will find a more or less even mix between exploration, achievement, socialization, empowerment and escapism. This list pretty well corresponds to the typical ideas of what games in general provide to their players. If you instead look at what the players do, you realize that much of the activities revolve around learning more about the game world and passing on that information to other players.

Studying tactics for how to defeat certain monsters or how to get to a certain place is typically thought of as a meta-activity by the gamers themselves. It is something that is needed to do in order to advance in the game, but not considered as gaming as such. It is perhaps not surprising that the learning aspect is diminished when gaming pleasures are discussed since learning can be connected to work, school and studies—which is exactly what a significant portion of the *Everquest* players want to get away from when they play. It is nevertheless always present in the gaming activities and a substantial time is spent on learning more and more about the game world. Reputation in the game is also closely associated with the knowledge a player has about zone geography, the value of tradable items, tactics for killing monsters or the history of other guilds and players.

After two years of playing and studying the game I have started to take interest more and more in questions connected to leaving the game and have begun to interview people who contemplate or have decided to leave the game after having played for a long time. In these interviews the issue of learning plays a strong, almost dominating, role. Most players connect the loss of passion for the game with having seen as much of it as they can hope to see at their level of play and having so much knowledge about the game that it has in some regard become transparent to them and therefore lost its mystical appeal.

This is where my two roles in the game merge. Both the quest of satisfying my needs as a player and my quest to grasp the structures of the game are tightly connected to knowledge and understanding of the world, and to reaching a point where my experiences have reached a state of saturation. I have several times experienced that I have reached a point where I know what I need to know and that it has become time to move on to the next study. But every time I have found new information or some aspect of the game that I had been previously unaware of, and I have been pulled back in again. After years of playing more than an hour every day on average I have to conclude that virtual worlds not only can be seen as processes and places but also that these are processes in a constant state of change and development; they are dynamic. This means that the inside view always can be developed further by continued participation as long as the world continues to exist.

References

1. Schroeder, R. (Ed.) (2002). *The Social Life of Avatars: Presence and Interaction in Shared Virtual Environments*. London: Springer.
2. Sony Online. Everquest press release. (2003). Available at http://sonyonline.com/corp/press_releases/030503_EQ_growth.html

3. DIKU Group, The DIKU MUD Homepage. (2003). Available at http://www.dikumud. com/everquest.aspx

4. Taylor, T. (2002). Whose game is this anyway?: Negotiating corporate ownership in a virtual world. In F. Mäyrä (Ed.) *Computer Games and Digital Cultures Conference Proceedings.* Tampere: Tampere University Press.

5. Jakobsson, M. & Taylor, T. (2003). The Sopranos meets Everquest—Social networking in massively multiuser networking games. fineArt forum, 17:8, August 2003.

6. Croon, A. (1997). R U out there? On personal communities in cyberspace. In K. Braa & E. Monteiro (Eds.), Proceedings of the 20th IRIS Conference Social Informatics, Oslo: Department of Information and Computer Science, University of Oslo, pp. 591–604.

7. BBC News. (2002). Cyber heroes forced to wait for glory. Available at http://news.bbc. co.uk/1/hi/technology/2129912.stm

8. Zombies of EQ. (2002). Available at http://www.guildportal.com/Guild.aspx?GuildID=1669 &TabID=1417

9. Crosby, A. (2004). Omens of War Chat #2. Available at http://eqforums.station.sony.com/ eq/board/message?board.id=Crier& message.id=38&no_redir=true

Chapter 11

PLAY AND SOCIABILITY IN THERE: SOME LESSONS FROM ONLINE GAMES FOR COLLABORATIVE VIRTUAL ENVIRONMENTS

Barry Brown and Marek Bell

1.   Introduction

While online games have become increasingly popular in recent years, there has been very little overlap between games research and virtual environments researchers. Indeed, one could argue that for a number of years, the design of video games have been ahead of virtual environment research, not only in technical aspects such as graphics or networking, but also in how game designers have managed their online worlds as social environments. Designers of online games have had to take seriously both the details of social interaction between individuals, but also how these interactions play out in the broader socio-economic balance of their online worlds [1].

In this chapter, we explore the lessons which collaborative virtual environments (CVEs) could derive from online gaming environments, focusing on *mundane interaction.*

Our activities and experiences in the real world depend in many ways upon mundane interaction for their operation [2]. Organisations whatever their size, in meetings and elsewhere, rely on talk [3]. Even the market transactions of currency traders depend upon chat for their coherence and reproducibility [4]. In a similar way in virtual environments it is in avatar-to-avatar interaction that experiences are configured. For virtual environments to be successful, we need to be able to interact with others around objects, refer to objects in our talk and share our awareness of other players and their movements [5].

This chapter focuses on these interactions, exploring how in the seemingly simple building blocks of talk and interaction around objects, enjoyable experiences are formed. We focus on the study of one game in detail, the social environment *There*, examining how its flat displays of colour come to form

R. Schroeder and A.S. Axelsson (Eds.), Avatars at Work and Play, 227–245.
© 2006 *Springer.*

meaningful social experiences for its players. As with other virtual environments, *There* moves beyond text chat to support acting together around objects. These shared activities generate a qualitatively different experience to the textual interactions common in MUDs and MOOs.

We focus on how these interactions build two key features of social life: *play* and *sociability*. Play is a prevalent feature of our experiences both in leisure and work. Indeed, although often presented as distinct from work, play is an integral part of work as well as leisure. Play gives us an ability to rest, learn, or experience and experiment with new activities and experiences. In online games, play is a focal concern. In particular, in *There*, we discuss how its noncompetitive nature makes it a more playful online environment than other, more competitive online environments. Yet this can present a challenge to players in deciding what to do next, and co-ordinating their activity with others.

The second feature we address is the role of *sociability*. While it is hardly surprising to see online environments as social environments, the more conventional meaning of "social"—as in "sociable"—has been somewhat neglected. We argue that the key issue is not necessarily what sorts or number of social relationships are formed online, but rather how those relationships are performed in online spaces. We use Simmel's discussion of sociability to give traction on understanding what it is about online environments that does (or does not) allow us to socialise online. In particular, we will argue that since in online virtual environments we can *do things with others*, we can "perform" our friendships in these environments.

2.   Method: Studying *There*

Our original interest in *There* came from its innovative design for supporting social interactions [6]. *There*'s designers paid special attention to supporting avatar to avatar interactions, and chat more generally. This environment was therefore from the start designed as a social environment. *There* (www.there.com) has been open to the public since October 2003, although at that time it had been in beta testing for over a year, and development for over six. It is an online commercial environment, charging around $4 a month for access. *There* shares many of the features of other online virtual environments, such as "Active Worlds" (www.activeworlds.com), "Second Life" (www.secondlife.com), and other online, persistent role-playing games such as Everquest or Star Wars Galaxies. *There* is a persistent world with objects which can be manipulated, customisable avatars representing each user, and various facilities for interactions between avatars, and between avatars and objects.

Rather than as a competitive game as such, *There* is marketed as a "virtual getaway"—a world where social interaction and play are the main activities. There is no overall goal to *There* and its environment supports a range of

Figure 11-1. A screenshot from There.

activities such as buggy races, paintball, flying jetpacks, treasure hunts, card games and even playing with virtual pets. Avatars are capable of expressing emotional gestures, and chat is displayed in speech bubbles within the game world, word by word, rather than in the complete lines of text displayed in instant messaging (figure 11-1). *There* also has a rich range of features for organisation that sit outside the 3D space in separate 2D web browser windows. This augments *There's* virtual world with support for instant messaging (both text and audio), forums, tools for organising virtual "events", and forming groups. The interface of *There* is therefore split between a conventional set of webpages and a 3D virtual environment.

We have studied *There* for nine months, playing *There* for two hours each week. Our methods are informed by an emerging approach to studying online activity characterised as "virtual ethnography" [7]. This approach involves the familiar techniques of ethnography with a significant amount of time spent online in the research setting, observing, participating and taking field notes. As with all ethnographic work, the researcher's own experiences are taken as key data, yet due to the persistent nature of online data, virtual ethnography also makes extensive use of textual materials such as webpages, screenshots and videos.

A special focus of our study was the interactions between players in the game. Most ethnographic studies of online worlds have sought, in a broadly anthropological way, to study online culture. In comparison in this study we focused much more on the details of the interactions between players. Like any online world, *There* is an unusual conversational environment. We were particularly interested in how the resources (such as speech bubbles) were appropriated by users to support their interactions.

Accordingly, in studying *There* we collected videos of our experiences inside *There*, and our interactions with other players. These videos could be viewed repeatedly to look in detail at how certain interactions were carried out. To analyse the video data we broadly followed an interaction analysis approach [8]. This involved shared data analysis sessions where we observed key incidents recorded from our time in *There* over and over again. One of the key inspirations we used for this work was Sacks' observations on ordinary interaction [2], allowing us some useful comparison between *There* and real-world naturally occurring interactions and conversation.

3.   Themes: Play and Sociability

As with other online games, *There* is a complex social environment where a host of different activities and actions take place. However, *There* is distinct in two ways. First, *There* is explicitly presented as a "playful" environment. Unlike games such as Everquest or Star Wars Empires, there is no overall goal to using *There*. The focus is much more on play—non-competitive activities which exploit features of the environment. As we will see, at times this can present problems to players in terms of finding what to do in *There*—actions are not directed by an overall goal. Second, with its focus on social interaction, *There* has been presented, and has some success as, an environment for socialising. Much of the business of *There* is chatting with others, "making new friends" as *There*'s own advertising hopefully presents it.

3.1.   Play

As playful experiences, games present a number of challenges to a conventional HCI (human computer interaction) and design focus on optimising behaviour. With games, optimising the efficiency of behaviour makes little sense, since it is the *experience* rather than an end goal that is key. The pleasure of games can come from features such as aesthetics, narrative, or even the connection with a broader culture—topics difficult to address under the troika of effectiveness, efficiency and satisfaction. Yet research into HCI often suffers from a "negative utilitarianism" [9]—the goal in design is usually to minimize the "pain" that a system produces—for example, by replacing a difficult phone collaboration with a more effective interaction using a media-space (e.g. [10]). There is little concern with the "pleasure" that systems can produce.

With games, enjoyment comes from play. Recent research on games (the so called "ludology" approach) has argued that we need to move beyond considering the game itself (and in particular games' narratives) to consider how users "play" with games [11]. That is, studying users' behaviour and exploration of games rather than treating games as a static text. This makes the flow of gameplay, and user activities, into the key research object, rather than seeing games as a cultural object. In some senses, this is a very standard ethnographic move—from studying text to studying action. Within cultural studies it has some similarities with the moves made in the study of television [12], from considering television programs (such as newsbroadcasts) as texts in their own right, to understanding more how television programs were received and understood by viewers.

Focusing on play can move us from the (at times arbitrary) re-description of games to their treatment as social objects. Yet conceptually, play is a difficult activity to define and demarcate. Salen and Zimmenman [13], for example, describe play as "free movement within a more rigid structure" and although this captures the flexibility of play, it gives us very little purchase on the different forms which play might take in different settings. One approach could be to define play by differentiating it from activities done as part of paid employment or work. The problem with this definition is that it ignores much of the variety in work. While we use terms such as "at work" to account for our activity to others, this can hide many aspects of our activity [14]. For example, Roy's classic study of horseplay at work, "Banana Time" [15], shows how monotonous work is made tolerable through "mucking around" or playing at work. Although "work" contains considerable play, professionalism often relies upon *denying* this play since it can conflict with accounts of work as a serious, professional, well managed enterprise. In particular, defining work and play as opposed loses an important area for design—the space of playful work technologies [16].

An alternative approach is to build typologies of play, and a number of authors have attempted to describe play and its different features in that way (e.g. [17]). As ethnographers, however, we would be sceptical of the ability to define play *a priori*. Play can instead be seen as a varied yet similar set of practices which lead into but also conflict with each other—a family resemblance of activities. For example, research into slot machines [18] has shown how these games fit into individuals' lives by occupying time while waiting for others, and how this is not necessarily the same as play in the office, or play amongst children.

Despite these issues with conceptually describing play, and accepting it as a varied set of practices, a focus on play does give us traction on the variety of activities that have been very much ignored in design—the open, flowing and non-utilitarian. As in our other studies of leisure [19, 20], we start our enquiry by asking what leisure is in this specific case—what form does play take for the inhabitants of *There?* How is play organised?

3.2.   Sociability

The second theme we address concerns the sociability of *There*. While studies of technology for the last twenty or so years have been deeply concerned with the social (e.g. [21]), research on technology has tended to ignore the more colloquial meaning of social—the experience and enjoyment of companionship with others. Even work on technologies such as instant messaging [22], while considering the pleasures of communication, has seldom addressed what effects IM has on friendship.

One of the few classic sociologists to consider the importance of friendship was Simmel [23]. In his paper about "the sociology of sociability", he argues for the value of "sociability", social experiences where their purpose is not external to that experience but rather *is* that experience itself. We engage in the company of others (in its purest form) when we engage for that company itself. Yet, while in these exchanges we are separated from everyday external conflicts and concerns, sociable encounters have within them a shadow of these conflicts and concerns. As Simmel [23, p. 261] puts it, they intrude in a "play form":

> All sociability is but a symbol of life, as it shows itself in the flow of a lightly amusing play; but, even so, a symbol of *life*, whose likeness is only so far alters as is required by the distance from it gained in the play, exactly as also the freest and most fantastic art, the furthest from all reality, nourishes itself from a deep and true relation to reality, if it is not to be empty and lying.

For Simmel, play, sociability and real life were entangled but at a distance— sociability was the play form of life where we could experience and experiment with the concerns of the world. While sociability never loses its lightness and justification in itself, it does not become sterile and removed from our lives. Indeed, it relies upon reflecting our concerns and battles to maintain a substance.

There are few sociologists who have taken Simmel's lead in considering sociability. While a number of recent ethnographic studies—particularly recent auto-ethnographic studies and research in the sociology of the emotions [24], have explored companionship, there is little discussion of the experience of sociability *per se*. Indeed, the study of friendship in sociology has been dominated by social network approaches which apply more quantitative methods to social relations—the research question becomes "how many friends, what type, and what support do they give you?" [25], rather than the questions of activity or action in friendship. Indeed, discussions of the activity involved in sociability are more prevalent in social psychological discussions of friendship. For example, Duck argues that it is through experiencing enjoyable activities together that we perform our friendships and relationships [26]. This is a view of social relationships as collective action. By choosing to do leisure activities with certain people they become our friends.

Computer gaming has always been a social affair—the original video game "Pong" was, after all, a two player game [13]. The massively multi-player environments of *There* and other games bring this even more to the fore. This is at the heart of what makes *There* enjoyable—it supports, in a crude though still enjoyable form, many of the ordinary activities that we engage in as part of our social lives. Conversation is perhaps the most obvious, but *There* also supports travelling, buying goods, exploring new places and playing conventional games (such as cards). While many of these activities are possible in single player games, multiplayer features make these activities sociable, supporting a community around these activities.

In the CVE community, this has been recognised in the notion of "social presence"—the sense in which users of a CVE feel that there are real people present in the online environment [27]. Alternatively, in the game literature the social ties formed in online games have also been a focus [28]. However, we would argue that both these approaches ignore the importance of *social action* as a focus of CVEs. That is to say, a key advance of CVEs is their support for doing things together with others over the internet. A focus on "social bonds" misses the importance of the shared activity together—such as chat, or interaction around objects, where we perform our friendships. Research on friendship underlies the importance and enjoyment of leisure activities carried out in the company of others. We would argue that it is this shared activity in itself which is pleasurable and a goal for players, rather than necessarily making new social bonds.

4.   The Building Blocks of *There*

Play and sociability rely upon a number of interactional "building blocks" for their operation. Interaction around objects, talk, topic and identity, all work together to make play and sociability possible. As an environment distinct from the ordinary and unexplicated, *There* constantly foregrounds simple interactions such as answering a question, or leaving a conversation. Without successful interaction, it is difficult for play to reach its potential, and without conversation, sociability is near impossible. Each of these blocks contributes to the accomplishment of broader activities.

4.1.   Interactions around Objects

The starting point to playing *There*, as with all online games, is mastering the interface. Indeed, there are a number of subtle design decisions which the developers of *There* have made which differentiate it from CVEs as convention-ally studied and designed. First, and of perhaps surprising importance, is that the avatar control method uses the standard gaming control method, combining the use of the mouse (for direction of gaze) and keyboard (for movement). This dual control method allows users to quickly move their gaze with their mouse, and then slow that movement to rest their gaze on a particular object. As their gaze moves, this action is visible to other players by the turning of their avatar's head and body. By holding down a control key, a mouse pointer can also be made to appear, along with arrows over objects in the scene. These arrows can be clicked to display a menu to carry out different actions on these objects. *There* also places its default view above the head and some distance back. This increases the field of view allowing easier interaction with objects that are close to the avatar. It also goes some way to smoothing the interactions that take place in *There* between avatars, and in particular around objects.

There supports some remarkably smooth, although not unproblematic, in-teractions around objects. In the example in figure 11-2, the first author (known as "Ba") is giving a tour to a new player ("Bo"). Earlier the users had landed a hoverboat to look round a forest and after deciding to get back in the boat, the users search around to locate the boat once again. After a minute of searching, Ba resorts to "retrieving" the boat—an in-game function that retrieves objects to where the player is. When he sees that Bo has noticed the retrieved boat, he climbs onboard, followed by Bo, and they take off.

While this interaction may not seem a source of enjoyment or a form of play in itself, interactions around objects are a key part of everyday activity [29]. Most real world games feature some sort of interaction around an object—such as a football. The players in this clip co-ordinate their activities (search, retrieval and discovery) without having to explicitly describe to each other what they are doing—both users search the local area, and are seen by each other to be searching. At the end of the clip, after beckoning Bo, Ba sees Bo walking towards the boat—he does not need further confirmation to jump on the boat. The orientation of each avatar in this example allows what each user sees to be predictable. A key part of this short interaction is how the object of the hoverboat exists not as a single user object but as an object shared between the two players.

When seen together, this short episode can be easily described—the two players look for a boat, retrieve it, get in and fly off. Yet a textual description does not do justice to the interaction, since it is much more than a textual experience. It both has unusual features which add to its enjoyability—we

1) Ba: Wana get back on the boat?

2) Bo: yes

3) Ba: Where did we leave it?
   Bo: '?

4) Bo: I don t know
   (Ba retrieves the boat)

5) Ba: Hey Bo!

6) *(Ba gets on boat, Bo gets on boat and Ba takes off)*

Figure 11-2. Conversation around a boat.

don't usually fly around in boats—but it is also ordinary (looking for an object collaboratively).

Not all interactions around objects are as unproblematic in *There*. In particular, gaze and orientation is only grossly available so, for example, an avatar's orientation towards a particular seat on the boat would be unavailable (and on other occasions we observed this causes problems with negotiating who sits where). Yet this is an example of a straightforward successful collective social action, analogous to a real world situation where we drop our keys and find them again with a friend's help. That players can reliably interact around objects is a crucial building block in enabling more complex interactions in *There*.

Along with their use in the 3D environment, objects have a less collaborative existence in an e-bay style auction website. This takes the form of a separate 2D web interface that allows players to buy and sell objects. While this 2D web interface is perhaps easier to use than a 3D interface, the move is with some cost. As with real world shopping, aspects of identity creation are performed through the purchasing and display of objects, such as in the form of avatar clothing. Indeed, one of the main activities in *There* is making and selling clothes. Many players have large collections of outfits—one player we spoke to talked about having over one hundred outfits, with each outfit costing around US$ 2 on average. Unfortunately, the buying and selling interface is only a *single* user interface. The move from 3D to 2D interface has been at the cost of the collaborative features of the virtual environment. This makes one of the most important activities in *There*—shopping—a single user activity. Players who wish to shop online together need to constantly switch between the 2D and 3D environments and manage the connection with talk or chat.

The complex uses of objects in *There* builds on the actions shown here—interaction, transportation, trading—to produce complex compound activities such as skydiving into falling cars, or making short films which are recorded in-game. Importantly, objects in *There* have taken on a *social* function, in that they centre the collaborative activities within the game and produce opportunities for social action.

4.2.   Chat

Along with interactions around objects, chat—what players say to each other—is an important part of *There*. As evidenced by the popularity of instant messaging, chat can be a valuable and enjoyable part of online interaction. While previous research has uncovered problems with text chat, such as the out of turn sequencing of turns [30], less attention has been given to the temporal aspects of text chat. That is, the timing of chat as it is typed. These aspects are particularly important in *There* since, unlike IRC or IM, text is displayed in speech bubbles which rise above users as they type each word [6]. In its design, *There* takes the use of speech bubbles in systems such as Habitat [31] or Comic Chat [32], and applies this to a 3D environment. Since sentences are shown as they are typed, the system affords some dynamic features of chat, with overlapping typing visible on screen as turns unfold simultaneously. For example, in this extract a group of users are arranging where to meet up in the UK (the square brackets show overlapping typing, the numbers in round brackets are notable pauses):

Jim: We have arranged Internet meets not for this program but for IRC and worlds.com the best place to (0.5 seconds) hold a (1 second) meet is (9 seconds) [Birmingham]

Sam: [Holland?]

One player suggests meeting in Birmingham, but his pause allows a second player to heckle him, completing the sentence with a joke destination. While in many ways this is a very normal interaction, heckling does need some subtlety in timing. Indeed, although text chat is in many ways a less rich experience than voice, small delays in voice conferencing can disrupt this sort of action [33].

More generally, overlapping talk affords replying to chat as it is produced, rather than waiting to the end of a turn, hastening conversation. Chat in *There* is thus unusual in that, rather than having only one speaker at a time, the system supports overlapping chat. In this extract a user replies while the previous turn is still unfolding:

Jo: Something as simple as town hall meetings should be a [requirement of each subcommittee thing]

Sue: [I agree or more vocal] webpage at there.com would be nice

Sue's reply agrees with Jo's suggestion before she has finished, displaying an assumption about how Jo's suggestion will finish. This display of chat as it is produced limits the time in which players are waiting for others' turns to end and mitigates some of the frustrations of slow typing:

Jo: Maybe they read but don't respond

Sue: Or can't [officially respond]

Gail: [well they used to] really respond and gleam info from the forums

In this extract following Sue's collaborative production of a sentence (as in [43, vol. I, p. 144]), Gail's "really respond" acts as a contrast right after Sue's "officially respond", even though her sentence started before Sue had finished. In this way unfolding overlapping text can be used as a live resource by conversation participants.

The slow movement of the speech bubbles up the screen can also work as a resource when entering a new conversation or walking past conversing groups—the bubbles allow users to see at a glance the previous turns in a conversation and thus quickly gain a rough concept of the topic of the conversation.

However, the use of speech bubbles does not come without cost. Speech bubbles occlude much of the environment as they are relatively large and each bubble may only contain a small segment of the conversation. To prevent overlapping speech bubbles, *There* also needs to put users into a specific "conversation" mode when it detects a stable conversation, moving users into positions where their speech bubbles will not overlap (as in figure 11-1). As with all modes, users need to issue an explicit command to leave. While this does solve problems with achieving positioning of avatars during conversation [27], it also puts limits on the number of participants in a conversation as well as the possibility of interaction around objects. Large groups also lead to problems with speech bubbles overlapping on screen. Simultaneous chat can also lose the sequential positioning of turns. This can cause confusion regarding who players are addressing their talk to, and players often need to use naming (such as in figure 11-1) to disambiguate turns.

4.3.   Topic

The social interaction in chat rooms often disintegrates into "trivial, useless, sex-oriented" babble (Esther Dyson, quoted in the New York Times [34]).

Much of the conversation in *There* concerns *There* itself. For example, glitches (bugs or mistakes in the system) are common topics of conversation with users, often manipulating the glitches to produce bizarre actions that are otherwise impossible. In one "glitch" two users found themselves superimposed upon each other. This allowed the players to appear as a combination of two people, causing much play and conversation around the bizarre combined body. Glitches have become "local resources" for conversation, topics for discussion as much as problems or bugs in the system (see also [2, vol. 2, p.92].

This topicalisation of the game itself can also be seen in how gestures have moved from a *resource* for conversation to a *topic*. Gestures pervade conversation in *There*, and, as with emoticons [35], players have adopted these gestures to communicate lost aspects (e.g. emotions, illocutionary force) of face-to-face conversation. However, gestures have also become a topic of conversation in themselves. Users discuss the different gestures, and tutor each other in using them effectively. Support for gestures has even led users to exchange ways of producing avatar "dances". Using keyboard macro software, different, otherwise unrelated gestures, can be combined to make avatars "dance" on screen. Indeed, "dancing competitions" have even become popular where avatars compete for prizes for elaborate or inventive "dances".

In this way much of the chat in *There* is actually *about There*. As Sacks remarks, in some cultures there are topics that are inexhaustible as topics: they are "intrinsically rich, in the sense that whatever it is that members of that culture tend to talk about [...] they can talk about via that thing." [2, vol.1, p.178] In American youth culture, Sacks observes that topics such as "respect" can be discussed—often at great length—through talking instead about cars. This can also be seen in *There*:

Jo: The advisory board seem really closed [off to the untrained eye.]

Gail: [Well if you have any time Jo get on the IM with them let em] know

Jo: I'm not sure my little voice would make a difference=

Gail: =oh please woman [you are public beta 1 you people get mad respect from *There*]

Sue: [every little bit helps I don't think it is due to a lack of listening] more a slow development turn around.

While the topic here is ostensively the system itself, matters such as showing each other respect and organisational politics are covered through a conversation about the system. So while chat in *There* often concerns *There* itself, like with any group of enthusiasts, other topics are addressed through that topic.

4.4.   *Status and Identity*

In the classic text based MUDs there is often a differentiation between "mortals" [33]—ordinary game players, and "immortals"—players with special abilities who are usually involved in running the game. In newer games such as Everquest or Star Wars Galaxies this has developed into "levelling up"—player characters gaining levels through completing in-game tasks, with different levels having different abilities.

While *There* does have levels for users, such as "socialisation" or "boarding" level, the advantages of higher levels are limited. This makes levelling up less of a goal in *There*. However, one clear visible divide that does exist is between trial users (who play for a limited time for free) and paying users. Trial users have no money to buy clothes, and so are usually adorned with a plain white t-shirt and slacks, in contrast to the colourful outfits of other players.

Indeed, appearance is a major focus in *There*, with avatar clothing used to present an identity in the world and differentiating oneself from others. While much of the research on virtual online worlds has argued that online identity is more flexible and transitory than real world identity [36], with users experimenting with changes such as trans-gendered identities, identity in *There* is a relatively stable and persistent phenomenon. The system itself presents barriers to maintaining multiple identities; users can only have one avatar per account, with a fixed gender and name which is decided before a user even enters the game. *There* also creates a standardized home page for each player (which can be optionally filled in), listing their interests, the clubs of which they are a member, a biography and a virtual and real photo. These features encourage the maintenance and creation of a single online identity, with a fixed gender.

This stability assists the formation of stable relationships—users create virtual relationships listing each other on their "buddy" list. Indeed, our experiences with identity manipulation in *There* was met with considerable resistance from other players. When we experimented with logging into other accounts, this generated hostility from our "buddies" who felt we were misleading them, and subverting the relationships they had built up. Even experimenting with changing our avatar's body shape was a source of complaint.

5.   Discussion

Each of these aspects of *There* help to make *There* a reasonably successful environment. In particular, they contribute to making *There* both a playful environment and a sociable one. Through the "open-ness" of action—the ability to talk in different places, interaction around a range of different objects, *There* supports a wide range of activities. Designing for appropriation is a familiar recommendation for design [37], in that technology should be opened in its design sufficiently that new uses and applications can be discovered by users. Yet it is still a rare feature of computer games. Games are normally constrained around a linear plot based on involving the completion of a set number of tasks [38]. Yet in *There*, much of the play has come from the creation of new activities—heckling, joking, dancing, skydiving and the like. As Hughes' work on playground games [39] shows, children invent whole repertoires of new rules around traditional games, provided sufficient resources are available. For children in a playground this can be as simple as chalk markings, free time, and a ball (e.g. [40]). In *There*, these resources were its flexible support for chat and interaction around a range of objects.

Consequently, this means that *There* is as much a *platform* for gaming and play, as it is a specific game in itself. *There* provides resources for users, but it is users themselves who decide what form their play will take. *There* has been appropriated for play by its users in ways not intended by its designers, such as in how accidental glitches in the system have become opportunities for play and conversation. The social online environment, and fan websites around the game, all produce an environment supportive of appropriation and sharing of new activities.

There's open nature also gives it a more "playful" form than many other games. Sacks [2, vol 1, p. 475] remarks that in children's games mistakes are seldom serious, since the games are short and imaginary. Yet due to the persistent and competitive nature of online games, mistakes, such as losing objects, often have serious consequences. In *There*, however, the consequences of losing objects are minor, since missing objects can be easily "retrieved". In the situations discussed in figure 11-2, although the players lose their hoverboat, Ba can "retrieve" the boat easily. The lack of a competitive goal allows for a safe environment where users can play with different activities without conflict with their overall goals or broader enjoyment.

Yet this flexibility does come at some cost—*There* presents a problem to users in that they need to decide what to do next, rather than have a preset goal or task. Users must find their own activities in the game and negotiate their participation in group activities. Enjoying *There* thus involves some of the commitment and organisation of real world activities. While the open nature of *There* supports playful appropriation, it in turn requires commitment from its users. The key problem for users in *There* is "what will I do next?"

Much of the design effort in *There* has gone into its chat environment, and its rich support for talk and interaction. Of course, chat and talk are already massively popular aspects of the internet—seen in the popularity of chat rooms and message boards. Yet social action online—actions shared by others—has tended to be limited to text communication. While text is an obviously powerful medium, it is very different from face to face interaction. By offering a range of collective activities around objects, *There* expands the opportunity for *social action*. What is crucial here is a sense of acting together around objects—such as skydiving, trading, travelling around the world, playing cards and such, building up a shared history of collective experiences. For example, activities could be designed to require the co-ordination of groups of individuals, encouraging collaboration. Skydiving into a car in *There* involves co-ordination, since one player needs to drop the car from high up, while the second player jumps into the car as it falls. The pleasure of this activity comes in part from the difficulty in co-ordinating actions together. Work on other online games such as Everquest has also suggested the importance of shared activities in producing enjoyable experiences, for example Seay et al. [41] argue that a key feature of guilds is their shared activities in the game.

This suggests a key design goal for future environments will be supporting in game social activities. Economic transactions are one activity that could be enhanced in this way—with greater support for negotiation and interaction during the exchange of objects. Systems could also assist in producing a sense of group activity and belonging amongst users. For example, a system could automatically generate a history of what a group does together (such as in the form of a weblog), or of allocating a special game area to a particular group.

There is also unusual in that it encourages and supports interactions between strangers, something which has proved difficult to support in face-to-face settings [42]. One aspect of this is that presence in the environment shows an availability for talk. This suggests a lesson for the design of systems that require interaction between strangers: these systems should require some sort of commitment from participants to a setting which is differentiated from ordinary interaction. In that way a setting may work to produce an availability for interaction amongst participants. This also suggests that interaction between strangers will be harder around technologies which require little commitment to their use—such as, for example, museum exhibits [42], compared to those where there is a clear divide from ordinary interaction—such as in a tour group. More success may be had in settings where participants show their availability for interaction with others.

We started our discussion of sociability with Simmel's arguments concerning the form of pure sociability. Sociability in *There* follows very much Simmel's description, we interact in *There* not for the benefits to our career or goals, but for sociability in itself. Enjoyment is in the conversation and chat in itself. Yet, as Simmel warns, sociability stripped of its connection with the world, with the shadow of life, can become farce. This highlights a key problem with *There*—as with the problem of finding what to do next—its sociability lacks an orientation to an overall goal. There is no competition in *There*, at least at the level of other online games. *There* loses a close connection with the competitive nature of much of the real world. Its design challenge then is to find a way of connecting its rich support for sociability with a "deep and true relationship to the world" [23].

6.   Conclusion

This chapter has focused on two themes from *There*. First, we have described the nature of play in *There*, and in particular how this depends upon the building blocks of smooth interaction around objects and chat between players. While these are not dramatic features, they enable many of the richer interactions in this game. The open design of *There*, and in particular how users have appropriated features of *There*, allows support for play in unpredictable ways.

Second, we discussed the importance of social action in *There*, and how players can carry out social activities with other players. By offering a range of collective activities around objects, *There* expands the opportunity for social action, and enjoyment for others. *There* also supports social action with strangers, something that has proved difficult in face-to-face settings.

Virtual environments, perhaps more than any other application, have suffered from hyperbolic accounts of their impact and development. Exaggerated claims of "replacing reality" place unrealistic goals onto systems, and may, as Fraser *et al.* argue, undermine the goal of designing compelling CVEs [43]. The nature of *There* and other virtual environments as games should be kept in mind—they do not replace social encounters or life in the real world. Although for some users they can become obsessions, on the whole they fulfil the traditional roles of enjoyment and enrichment, a role that games have traditionally played along with movies, music and fiction.

It is easy to dismiss games as of little significance, certainly when compared with more weighty topics or activities. Yet games occupy our attention for longer time than many of the traditional office applications studied by HCI. It is not only that games are an interesting new application of collaborative systems, but that in looking at games, HCI has the opportunity to consider new purposes for the systems we design, and new social benefits that they can produce.

References

1. Castronova, E. (2001). Virtual worlds: A first-hand account of market and society on the cyberian frontier. *CESifo Working Paper no. 618, 2001*. Available at http://papers.ssrn.com.
2. Sacks, H. (1995). *Lectures on Conversation: Vol 1 & 2*. Oxford: Basil Blackwell.
3. Boden, D. (1995). *The Business of Talk: Organizations in Action*. London: Blackwell.
4. Knorr-Certina, K. & Bruegger, U. (2003). Global microstructures: The interaction practices of financial markets. *American Journal of Sociology, 107*(4): 905–950.
5. Hindmarsh, J., Fraser, M., Heath, C., Benford, S., & Greenhalgh, C. (1998). Fragmented interaction: Establishing mutual orientation in virtual environments. In *Proceedings of computer supported collaborative work (CSCW) 1998, Seattle, WA.*, New York: ACM Press, pp. 217–226.
6. Clanton, C. & Ventrella, J. (2003). Avatar centric communication in There. *Stanford seminar on people, computers and design*, Stanford University. Available at http://stanford-online.stanford.edu/murl/cs547/.
7. Hine, C. (2000). *Virtual Ethnography*. London, UK: Sage.
8. Heath, C. & Luff, P. (2000). *Technology in Action*. Cambridge: Cambridge University Press.
9. Sinnott-Armstrong, W. (2003). Consequentialism. In E.N. Zalta (Ed.), *Stanford Encyclopedia of Philosophy*, Stanford University Press. Available at http://plato.stanford.edu/archives/sum2003/entries/consequentialism/.
10. Gaver, W. (1992). The affordances of media spaces for collaboration. In *Proceedings of Computer Supported Cooperative Work, CSCW'92*. Toronto, Canada., ACM Press, pp. 17–24.
11. Frasca, G. (2003). Ludologists love stories, too: Notes from a debate that never took place. In M. Copier & J. Raessens (Eds.) *Proceedings of LevelUp 2003*, DIGRA.
12. Taylor, A.S. & Harper, R. (2003). Switching on to switch off. In R. Harper (Ed.), *Inside the Smart Home*. London: Springer-Verlag, pp. 115–126.
13. Salen, K. & Zimmerman, E. (2004). *Rules of Play: Game Design Fundamentals*. Cambridge, Mass.: MIT Press.
14. Abramis, D. (1990). Play in work: Childish hedonism or adult enthusiasm? *American Behavioral Scientist, 33*(3): 353–373.
15. Roy, D.F. (1960). Banana time: Job satisfaction and informal interaction. *Human Organization, 18*: 156–168.
16. Boucher, A. (2003). The disuptive office: Mechanised furniture to promote useful conflicts. In *Proceedings of 1AD: First International Conference on Appliance Design*, 6–8 May Bristol, UK, no pp.
17. Caillois, R. (1962). *Man, Play and Games*. London: Thames and Hudson.

18. Sutton-Smith, B. (2001). *The Ambiguity of Play*. Cambridge, MA: Harvard University Press.
19. Brown, B. & Chalmers, M. (2003). Tourism and mobile technology. In K. Kuutti, E.H. Karsten, G. Fitzpatrick, P. Dourish, & K. Schmidt (Eds.). In *Proceedings of the European Conference on Computer Supported Collaborative Work (CSCW) 2003, Helsinki, Finland*, Dordrecht: Kluwer Academic Press, pp. 335–355.
20. Brown, B., Geelhoed, E., & Sellen, A.J. (2001). The use of conventional and new music media: Implications for future technologies. In M. Hirose (Ed.), *Proceedings of Interact 2001*, Tokyo, Japan: IOS Press.
21. Button, G. (1993). *Technology in Working Order*. London: Routledge.
22. Nardi, B. & Whittaker, S. (2000). Interaction and outeraction: Instant messaging in action. In *Proceedings of computer supported collaborative work (CSCW) 2000*, Philadelphia, PA: ACM Press, pp. 79–88.
23. Simmel, G. & Hughes, E.C. (1949). The sociology of sociability. *The American Journal of Sociology, 55*(3): 254–261.
24. Ellis, C. (1995). *Final Negotiations: A Story of Love and Chronic Illness*. Philadelphia: Temple University Press.
25. Wellman, B. & Frank, K. (2001). Network capital in a multi-level world: Getting support from personal communities. In N. Lin, R. Burt, & K. Cook (Eds.), *Social Capital: Theory and Research*. Chicago: Aldine De Gruyter, pp. 233–273.
26. Duck, S. (1991). *Friends: The Psychology of Personal Relationships*. London: Harvester.
27. Becker, B. & Mark, G. (2002). Social conventions in computer mediated communication: A comparison of three online shared virtual environments. In R. Schroeder (Ed.), *The Social Life of Avatars: Presence and Interaction in Shared Virtual Environments*. London: Springer, pp. 19–39.
28. Yee, N. (2002). Mosaic: Stories of digital lives and identities. Available at http://www.nickyee.com/mosaic/home.html
29. Hindmarsh, J., Fraser, M., Heath, C., Benford, S., & Greenhalgh, C. (2000). Object-focused interaction in collaborative virtual environments. *ACM Transactions on Computer-Human Interaction (TOCHI), 7*(4): 477–509.
30. O'Neill, J. & Martin, D. (2003). Text chat in action. In *Proceedings of Group '03*, New York: ACM Press, no pp.
31. Morningstar, C. & Farmer, F.R. (1991). The lessons of Lucasfilm's Habitat. In M. Benedikt (Ed.), *Cyberspace: First Steps*. Cambridge, MA: MIT press, pp. 273–302.
32. Kurlander, D., Skelly, T. & Salesin, D. (1996). Comic chat. In *Proceedings of the 23rd Annual Conference on Computer Graphics and Interactive Techniques*, ACM Press, pp. 225–236.
33. Ruhleder, K. & Jordan, B. (2001). Co-constructing non-mutual realities: Delay-generated trouble in distributed interaction. *Computer Supported Cooperative Work, 10*(1): 113–138.
34. Marriott, M. (2003). Now playing: Reality without the downside, January 9, 2003. *The New York Times*, New York.
35. Guye-Vuillieme, A. & Capin, T.K. (1999). Non-verbal communication interface for collaborative virtual environments. *Virtual Reality Journal, 4*: 49–59.
36. Turkle, S. (1995). *Life on the Screen: Identity in the Age of the Internet*. New York: Simon and Schuster.
37. Randell, R. (2004). Accountable technology appropriation and use. In *Proceedings of the Third ACM NordiCHI conference*, New York: ACM Press, pp. 161–170.
38. Frasca, G. (2003). Sim sin city: Some thoughts about Grand Theft Auto 3. *Game Studies, 3*(2). Avaliable at http://gamestudies.org/0302/frasca/
39. Hughes, L. (1989). Beyond the rules of the game, why are rooie rules nice? In J. Evans (Ed.), *Children at Play Reader*. Geelong, Victoria: Deakin University Press, pp. 81–89.

40. Goodwin, C. (2000). Action and embodiment within situated human interaction. *Journal of Pragmatics, 32*: 1489–1522.
41. Seay, A.F., Jerome, W.J., Lee, K.S., & Kraut, R. (2003). Project Massive 1.0: Organizational commitment, sociability and extraversion in massively multiplayer online games. In M. Copier & J. Raessens (Eds.), *Proceedings of LevelUp 2003*, DIGRA.
42. Hindmarsh, J., Heath, C., vom-Lehn, D., & Cleverly, J. (2002). Creating assemblies: Aboard the ghost ship. In *Proceedings of computer supported collaborative work (CSCW) 2002*, New York: ACM Press, pp. 156–165.
43. Fraser, M., Glover, T., Vaghi, I., Benford, S., Greenhalgh, C., Hindmarsh, J., & Heath, C. (2000). Revealing the reality of collaborative virtual reality. In *Proceedings of the Third ACM Conference on Collaborative Virtual Environments (CVE 2000)*, ACM Press, pp. 29–37.

Chapter 12

DIGITAL DYSTOPIA: PLAYER CONTROL AND STRATEGIC INNOVATION IN THE SIMS ONLINE

Francis F. Steen, Mari Siân Davies, Brendesha Tynes, and Patricia M. Greenfield

1.   Introduction

Around New Year 2004, a quiet year after the official launch, *The Sims Online* hit the global headlines. Disappointingly, the topic was not a celebration of how this "new virtual frontier," this "daring collective social experiment," had succeeded in bringing "our divided nation" together, as *Time* magazine had blithely prophesied [1]. Instead, the media reported that the online game had turned into a Biblical den of iniquity, a Sin City, a virtual Gomorrah—and that the whistleblower who bore witness to this had his account terminated [2–5]. Rivaling mafia organizations were practicing extortion and intimidation, pimps running brothels where underage girls provided sex for money, and con artists scamming newbies out of their start capital. Maxis, the company that designed and operated the game, maintained a relaxed laissez-fair policy of light and somewhat haphazard intervention. The first mafias and in-game brothels had been established already in the early days of beta-testing; they continued to operate unchecked. Pretend crime paid well and recruitment was good, leading to a rapidly mutating series of inventive scams targeting the inexperienced and the unwary.

It wasn't meant to be like this. Gordon Walton, one of the chief designers, had spoken in glowing terms of the game's potential to provide opportunities for better relations between people. While "all of our mass media positions us to believe our neighbors are psychopaths, cheating husbands, and just bad people," *The Sims Online* would short circuit our distrustful negative stereotypes [6]. Echoing McKenna & Bargh [7], who had found that relationships initiated online benefited from transcending the limitations of spatial proximity and

R. Schroeder and A.S. Axelsson (Eds.), Avatars at Work and Play, 247–273.

physical appearance, leaving more room for a creative identity construction that might act as a guide to a real self, Walton envisioned a game where people would "interact with others anonymously, have physical distance, and not be judged on your outward appearance. You interact with people on a pure intellectual and emotional level, devoid of all those filters." If his team did their job right, *The Sims Online* would feel like Disneyland [6].

Careful steps were taken to forestall "griefers", gamers who derive enjoyment from anti-social behavior. In line with the vision of a privately run amusement park as the contemporary image of the good society, The Sims Online would have no common areas or public property where griefers could harass people. The habitable landscape would be divided into lots, each of which would be owned and controlled by an individual gamer. If a player was giving others a hard time on your lot, you could throw him out or permanently ban him. If that seemed too much trouble, you could restrict access to a registry of friends. The programmers even anticipated the problem of one player blocking another's exit from a room; to avoid this they decided the trapped avatar would be able to escape by walking straight through its would-be captor. Implementing Lessig's (1999) dictum that on the Internet "code is law" [8] the makers of *The Sims Online (TSO)* sought to prevent crime by writing software code that made crime impossible.

These twin elements—the redemptive vision of the game's potential for creating friendships across barriers of distrust, and the proactive, structural legislation within the computer code itself to remove the threat of anti-social behavior—represent two of three main pillars of the game's utopian project. The third is more subtle: the freedom of the players themselves to create and to govern their own virtual society. Its spokesman is Will Wright himself, the lead designer and originator of The Sims family of games. Even before the game was released, he had begun imagining a self-governing society, with local governments and elections. But these features would not be built into the game. "All of this political stuff has to come from the bottom up," he insisted from the start. "We can't do it from the top down and dictate structure" [6]. A key inspiration was the architect Christopher W. Alexander's work on the emergence of communities. Alexander speaks of a "pattern language" that evolves organically from people's small acts. The patterns that define a town or community "can never be 'designed' or 'built' in one fell swoop—but patient piecemeal growth, designed in such a way that every individual act is always helping to create or generate these larger global patterns, will, slowly and surely, over the years, make a community . . ." [9]. Could *TSO* also be designed so that each individual act added up to a whole? After putting a basic framework in place and building some incentives into the game, it must be left to the players to establish their own political and civic cultures. According to Wright, "totally planned cities don't work. It's sort of like the Utopian society movement, where there were these guys who went off and started building planned cities. For the most part the cities were total failures" [6].

The uncertainty that such freedom entailed, however, was also a cause for worry: the team was painfully aware that nobody knew how the virtual world within the game would develop. Walton and Wright envisioned a society in which human relations were—paradoxically—more direct, because they transcended space, physical appearance, and entrenched identities, where crime was banished by the very architecture of the game, and where human freedom would express itself in self-organizing cultures. Could this vision be realized? Within the first year, this utopian dream was shattered, at least provisionally, by persistent reports that human relations had taken a turn towards an eerily familiar catalog of exploitative behaviors, where crime flourished and spread in the face of attempts to remove its very conditions of possibility, and where freedom had led not to democracy but to warring mafias. "How would people act if they were freed from real life laws and social constraints?" the BBC asked rhetorically, responding with reports of "child prostitution, rampant crime, mafia-controlled neighborhoods, shadowy self-declared governments struggling to maintain order and runaway inflation" [3]. "Hobbes in Cyberspace: Life in an online game world proves nasty, brutish, and short," *Reason Magazine* concluded [10].

In the following, our goal is to understand the role of the unanticipated outbreak of crime in the dynamics of cultural creation in *TSO*. We start by examining the origins of the game in the single-player offline version of *The Sims*, focusing on the key design features that later become incorporated into the multiplayer online version. In the second section, we examine the three main dimensions of player involvement in the game: the immediate-term mechanical control of the avatar, the medium-term control of strategic moves, and the long-term control of the goals and ultimate meaning of the game. We argue that at all three levels, control is inadequate and tends to produce dissociations between player and avatar. In the third section we discuss the architectonic constraints on cultural development, the scope for rebellion against these constraints, and the significance of the strategy of crime. We end with an overall assessment of the game and the lessons to be learned from this vast and exorbitantly expensive experiment.

2.   The Origins of The Sims Online

In order to understand the surprising dynamics of the online world of *TSO*, we propose to begin by examining its history. The official birthday of the game is the 17th of December 2002, when the game was first released to the general public. At that point, however, *The Sims Online* was already a bustling world, thanks to the activities of tens of thousands of beta-testers. Starting in mid-September, they had been invited to join the game for free, to uncover any show-stopping programming bugs, to ensure that the system scaled adequately, and to populate and settle the vast and virgin electronic landscapes. Paying

users, Maxis reasoned, would prefer to join an existing world to constructing
one from scratch. These beta-testers, in turn, encountered a world that was
already highly structured, even if this structure would become actualized only
by the gamers' own activities. Some of these structural features are odd: key
design decisions of *The Sims Online* make little sense until one realizes they are
the result of code inherited from the earlier, off-line version of the game, *The
Sims*. We will suggest, in our analysis in sections two and three, covering player
control and the higher-level cultural dynamics of the game, that the high degree
of path dependence on code written for an off-line, single-player environment
is a significant contributing factor to the problems that subsequently unfolded.

It was the Oakland fire of 1991 that provided the impetus to what was to
become *The Sims*. Will Wright, a game designer at Maxis, lost his house in the
blaze, and in the following months he became fascinated with the process by
which his family gradually drew up the plans for the new house and its furnishings. Wright abstracted the sequential characteristics of this process and
realized it could be turned into computer code. The program would supplement and extend the power of the imagination, simulating the construction and
decoration of a house. He began to design *Home Tactics: The Experimental
Domestic Simulator*. In 1993, after 2 years of in-house development, he presented a prototype to Maxis executives during a focus session. The idea was
so unlike anything that had been done in computer games up to that point that
they rejected it outright. For the next 4 years, the game was only worked on by
Wright himself in his spare time [6]. When Maxis was acquired by Electronic
Arts in 1997, however, Wright's reputation as the designer of *SimCity* earned
him a blank cheque with his new bosses. *Home Tactics* got all the attention it
needed and was released under the new name *The Sims* in January 2000. Once
scorned, *The Sims* and its expansion packs became the most popular computer
game of all times, selling more than 20 million units over the next 2 years [11].

At the core of *The Sims* is the act of building, landscaping, and furnishing a
suburban house. The natural environment is an invariant subdivision: a rolling
meadow by a brook, a road circling a dozen lots ready for construction. The
game invites the player to build a house, or a succession of houses, and to
move ready-made families into them. The building materials, the plants and
trees for landscaping, and the furnishings and interior decorations are selected
by the player from virtual shopping windows and assembled onto the three-
dimensional canvas of the building site at the click of a mouse. A profusion of
bricks and wood sidings, roof shingles, potted plants, wall papers, chairs, and
kitchen utensils makes this part of the game straightforwardly enjoyable. The
combinatorial possibilities are finite but astronomical; for all practical purposes
infinite. You can move the walls around freely, put in a kitchen, a bedroom, a
bath, a pool, a TV lounge, an exercise room. These practices build design rather
than genuine engineering skills—according to a classic text of structural engineering, "a deep, intuitive appreciation for the inherent cussedness of materials

and structures is one of the most valuable accomplishments" of an engineer [12]. In *TSO* the materials are flawless, each brick or chair the spit image of any other of its kind: there is a perfect and predictable match between the real and the ideal. The very act of design is an act of building. This simplification of reality allows the player to focus singlemindedly on the task of architectural design, maneuvering through a gratifyingly vast possibility space. The task of design is further aided by a series of elegant interface features: while you build and decorate, you can zoom in and out and view your progress from different angles. As you adopt a particular view, the walls in front of you becomes selectively transparent, allowing you to see the entire layout of the house. This aspect of the game bears the quality stamp of sustained iterative design [13] and surprises the player with delightful features.

The second layer of code in the game is the sims, or simulated people. They are the dolls that inhabit the houses built by the player. Controlled by artificial intelligence (AI), the sims are imbued with a rudimentary form of agency. They can walk from one location to another, perform a finite but expandable repertoire of tasks, express emotions, and communicate desires. The player interacts with the sims in a manner very different from that of the building materials. Where the latter move only when the player moves them by clicking and dragging her mouse, the sims behave as if they were alive, folding their arms impatiently if you leave them standing, as if chafing at the bit. While they do not actually move from place to place or perform tasks on their own initiative, you also cannot move them directly, by grabbing hold of them with your cursor and dragging them to a new location, as you can the building materials. For a sim to do something, you must give him an instruction to act. This is done by interacting with the sim's virtual environment. Objects in the sims world are endowed with Gibsonian affordances [14], or activities and behaviors that can involve the sim in some way. By right-clicking on the object, a contextual menu in the form of a cloud of affordances is displayed, and you make your choice. Clicking on the sim itself will give you a menu of possible behaviors valid for that particular location and circumstance, or you can click on a distant object and instruct the sim to interact with it. For instance, you can wake your sim up in the middle of his night and tell him to go for a swim in the pool simply by right-clicking on the pool and selecting "Swim". Like a truculent child in the face of a stern parent, the sim will get out of bed and stamp his foot on the floor repeatedly in a bout of displaced aggression and frustration, a fume of anger rising from his mind. He finds his way through the house and out to the pool on his own, without any player intervention: this shows his behavioral routines are pre-programmed and robotic. As he gets into the pool and begins to swim, the image of a bed floats in a thought bubble above his head, informing you that he is tired and needs to sleep. In the morning, having so rudely been deprived of sleep, he may become unresponsive to the instruction to go to work and require time to regain a functional level of comfort.

These responses create the impression, gratefully accepted in pretense, that the sim is a dynamic, homeostatic system, whose behavior is regulated by a simulation of causally connected mental and physical states such as hunger and the need for food. Dominating a sim's life is the physiological needs at the bottom of Maslow's pyramid [15]: the need to sleep, to eat and drink, to go to the restroom, to be comfortable, and—this is after all suburbia—to take regular showers. Each of these needs is tracked by a bar on the player's screen, turning slowly from green to red if it is neglected; taking care of your sim so that his basic needs are being met is called "greening." Higher needs have a rudimentary presence: if you don't provide your sim with regular social company, he will become despondent and slowly refuse to function. With some variations, this is as far as what Wright calls the "economy of motives" has been elaborated [16]. Sims do not live in a world where they need to worry about safety, and although in some versions of the game they can fall in love and marry, they do not complain if this doesn't happen to them. The built-in motives are of a ground-level nurturing kind. The sims have no aspirations to achieve social recognition through outstanding acts—to kill a dragon, to become president: they don't have a life project, a mission. Nor do they show an interest in learning and understanding the world they live in, though if you make them read employment-appropriate books, their skill levels increase and they get promoted at work. They do not seek to actualize themselves artistically or spiritually. They are, after all, dolls.

What are the design goals realized by creating sims with this particular circumscribed degree of autonomy? A sim has a fixed set of clearly defined needs, in part conveyed directly through emotional responses and through the display of the simplistic and generally predictable content of his mind, yet he is entirely incapable of taking care of even the simplest of these needs himself. Devoid of independent initiative, he relies on you, the player, to instruct him how to meet his own needs. For your benefit, a special "greening" panel tracks the precise progress of the sim's needs from moment to moment. If appropriately instructed, the sim will be healthy, energetic, and promptly carry out your commands; if his needs are not consistently met, however, he will drift towards a non-functional state, become unresponsive to your commands, and eventually die. This design creates—and is clearly aimed at creating—a distinctive dependency relation between the sim and the player. The function of this dimension of the game is to encourage the player to care for and nurture the sim. The game in effect provides opportunities for a kind of practice parenting, similar to playing with dolls, but with a more realistic feedback. By nurturing the sim, the player experiences the systematically differential consequences of proper care and neglect, and acquires skills relating to taking care of others. Care and nurture are behaviors with a deep natural history and they remain vitally important for any society, yet they had never before been the target of a sophisticated computer game. *The Sims* tapped into a vast and hitherto neglected audience of young girls who were left cold by the typical competitive or adversary shooter games favored by the boys [6].

Experienced players of *The Sims*, however, take the game far beyond the elementary task of keeping your sims green. As a player, you are in a position of directing the sims' lives as a dramaturg directs his actors, creating dramatic situations and developing extended narratives. Your capacity for absorbing information, for seeing connections, for opening up new possibilities, exceeds that of your charges by orders of magnitude. Like a god you can control whole neighborhoods of sims, staging their marriages, births, quarrels, reconciliations, and breakups. The writer Monique van den Berg's illustrated Sims diary [17], where a dozen families interact in intricate and often comic situations, provides good examples of the game's potential for staging complex narrative scenarios in richly elaborated environments. If you so choose, the godlike power of the player can even be used in the spirit of Gloucester's "As flies to wanton boys are we to th' gods, They kill us for their sport" [18]: you can command your sim with the terrible voice that the God of the Old Testament used to instruct Abraham to sacrifice Isaac, wall him into a closed room, electrocute him when he changes a light bulb, make him drown in the pool. If you adopt the sim's point of view, the situation is distinctly odd: in the middle of the night, with nobody in view, you are commanded to perform some meaningless act, strongly aversive to you, and you feel the anger welling up in you at the pointless imposition. But the command is as ineluctable as it is mysterious, and you are entirely incapable of disobeying. Such is the power of the player in *The Sims*.

In summary, the immensely successful offline, single-player version of *The Sims* developed out of a program designed to simulate the hands-on building and furnishing of a house, and was elaborated to incorporate robotic agents dependent for their basic welfare and continued existence on the constant nurturing behavior of the player. The game facilitated player psychologies ranging from an architect and interior decorator to a doting mother caring for her family and a movie director staging elaborate narratives. The secret of the game's phenomenal appeal lay in providing players with a godlike power to explore and innovate in two complementary and fully developed permutational spaces: that of building, landscaping, and decorating houses, mansions, and castles, and that of caring for, directing, and narrating the lives of simulated humans in evolving tangles of complex social relations. When *The Sims* was to be taken online, Electronic Arts sought to build on the success of the existing game and reuse tested code by preserving the core features of the game. Just like *The Sims*, *The Sims Online* would present a suburban housing division, albeit a much larger one, where players constructed and furnished houses on lots, using the mature code inherited from the offline game. Just as in *The Sims*, the simulated people within *The Sims Online* would respond robotically to instructions selected by the player from clouds of affordances surrounding in-game objects. The secret of the game's phenomenal appeal lay in providing players with a godlike power to explore and innovate in two complementary and fully developed permutational spaces: that of building, landscaping, and decorating houses, mansions, and castles, and that of caring for, directing, and narrating the lives of simulated humans in evolving tangles of complex social relations. *The Sims* would go online.

Yet massively multiplayer online games rely on a very different dynamic in the relationship between players and on-screen characters. Key to a multiplayer environment is that each player is represented in the virtual world by a single character, his or her avatar. A relatively tractable dimension of this change is that the game now needs to have a unique avatar for each player. Users typically want to control their avatar representation and have input into its design, yet the need to download tens or hundreds of thousands of unique avatar designs onto each player's computer would cause severe network and storage problems [19]. *The Sims Online* solves this problem by providing more than a hundred different heads and bodies with outfits for the user to mix and match. This combinatorial space is sufficiently large to minimize the risk of two avatars looking exactly alike, yet avoids storage problems, as all avatars can be represented by a number referring to the graphics in the selection. While this solution provides sufficient differentiation between avatars, it does not allow players to contribute their own graphics, thus limiting the work the representation can do in defining and channeling a particular identity.

More troublesome than avatar design was the requirement of *The Sims Online* that the player identify with his or her avatar. The mantra of the development group was that in TSO, "the sims are real" [16]. Massively multiplayer online games like *EverQuest* and *Ultima Online* had shown that players became emotionally engaged in their own avatar and formed strong bonds with others through their on-screen representations. Such identification would be absurd and inappropriate in *The Sims*, where each simulated human being was endowed with a carefully circumscribed autonomy, expressed in robot behavior, designed to be endearing and to elicit a caring and nurturing stance. As Will Wright himself put it during the alpha phase of the development process, "That's never been an issue in any of my games before. Most of the time I'm dealing with little simulated AI people that pee on the floor all the time" [6]. In *The Sims*, the player was in charge of the entire virtual world and all its inhabitants; in *The Sims Online*, tens and hundreds of thousands of players would interact with each other. If the player was god in *The Sims*, what would be his role in *The Sims Online?*

The conversion of *The Sims* to *The Sims Online*, starting in 2000, was an enormously complex and expensive undertaking, with a development staff of a hundred programmers, three million lines of code, and a rumored budget of $25 million [6]. It was undertaken at breakneck speed, and achieved its ambitious goal of shipping in time for the Christmas season 2002. Subscription numbers shot up instantly to 40,000 and by New Year to 80,000, continuing to mount until topping out around 105,000 in June 2003, far below the projected numbers [20]. In the following section, we examine two players' responses to the game over the course of the first year, focusing on identification and player control. How did the experience of player control change as the core features of *The Sims* were ported to a radically different, multiplayer environment?

3.   Player Control in The Sims Online

When *The Sims Online* was released in December 2002, Patricia Greenfield, with the collaboration of Brendesha Tynes and the research team at Children's Digital Media Center at UCLA, had already recruited two players and initiated data-collection. The intention was to treat the game as a laboratory in which the spontaneous emergence and evolution of culture could be documented. By starting participants at the game's beginning, Greenfield hoped to be able to observe not just the adaptation to an existing culture, but the actual creation of a culture from scratch. Steen and Davies joined the project in early 2004, and when the assembled team began the task of examining the collected data, it became clear that we needed to change the research focus. In the participants' diaries and captured gameplay we found little or no evidence of the players creating a shared cultural world of meanings, norms, activities, and physical environments through processes of social interaction and communication [21, 22]. The virtual inhabitants of Alphaville, the first city within *The Sims Online*, appeared to have surprisingly little to say to each other, and the game did not provide our study participants with opportunities or tools to engage in sustained collaborative cultural creation. As we observed their interest in the game slowly fade, we shifted our focus to investigate what had gone wrong. In the following, we present a summary of our findings, with selections from the data and some new analytical points; for the full story, see Steen, Greenfield, Davies, and Tynes [22].

A massively multiplayer online role-playing game (MMORPG) can provide its participants with control along a spectrum of time horizons, ranging from the immediate to the long term (figure 12-1).

At the far left of the spectrum we find the immediate-term mechanical control of the avatar. Is there a one-to-one correspondence between the player's manipulation of the game controller and the behavior of the on-screen avatar? Such synchronous control is a mandatory feature of fast-paced shooter games; Kirk [23] argues it is critical for a low-level, physiologically driven player-avatar identification that powerfully enhances game immersion. The code that *The Sims Online* inherited from *The Sims* handles avatar behavior through artificial intelligence, thus removing a base level of support for an immersive experience. In contrast to other MMORPGs, such as *There* [24], you cannot directly control your avatar—you cannot, for instance, use the keyboard or

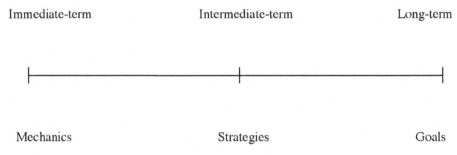

Immediate-term   Intermediate-term   Long-term

Mechanics   Strategies   Goals

Figure 12-1. The spectrum of player control in a MMORPG.

mouse to turn your avatar to face a certain direction, move its arms, or move it step by step in some direction. All control is done through menu interaction, where you give instructions the avatar acts out.

In the diaries and videotaped gameplay of our first study participant, KM, a 23-year-old female graduate student, we found that the lack of synchronous avatar control generated a series of dissociations between the players and their avatars. KM described herself as a recovered addict of the off-line version of *The Sims* and was thus familiar and comfortable with the sims' robotic behavior in the single-player environment. In the spirit of the new multiplayer environment of *TSO*, she began play on 30 December 2002 by creating an avatar to represent herself, an *alter ego*: "I created this character based on myself. It took me a while to go through all of the hair and outfits to pick one that I thought resembled me." (KM, p. 16). In short order, she was confronted with what for all of us was the most surprising feature of *TSO*: the low level of social interaction and conversation. KM began by identifying the avatar she encounters with a real person: "I said 'hi' to the other person playing chess, but little conversation happened. I noticed that no one in this house was talking everyone was just earning skill points." (KM, p. 17). Skill points can be earned through activities such as standing in front of a mirror ("practicing charisma"), playing chess, and cooking. In order to encourage socializing, a key novel feature engineered into the game is that skills are acquired more rapidly if practiced in the company of other avatars. As with other avatar activities in *TSO*, the behavior itself is robotic, and skills points take hours to build. KM's suspicions were soon aroused: "After about 10 minutes of playing chess, and seeing how long it took for the skill meter to go up I could see why no one was talking—probably no one was there!" (KM, p. 19). The substance of this insight is a dissociation between the avatar and the player: the presence of one frequently does not entail the presence of the other. In the absence of synchronous control, avatars in the online chat rooms of *TSO* can be intermittently attended; it is common practice to go "afk" or "away from keyboard" and leave your avatar, robotic slave that it is, stay behind and accumulate points. An unfortunate downstream consequence of this behavior is that players begin to see the presence of other sims in purely utilitarian terms, as an opportunity for earning skill points more rapidly, rather than as a chance to meet people and socialize. This second dissociation separates your own needs for real human social contact from the avatar's more pedestrian need for the proximity of other avatars, attended or not.

The absence of synchronous control also created anomalies in the immediate-term mechanics of social interaction. We analyzed a recorded conversation at Lucky Luc's Slots, where AJ, the proprietor's roommate, gives KM instructions on how to play a particular gambling game. During most of this conversation, the two avatars have their backs to each other, yet it would be incorrect to infer from this that they had lost interest in the conversation. At one point, AJ refers to a game score result that she could not have seen, as it appeared behind her. These incongruities open up a third dissociation, that between the panoptic perspective of the player and the embedded, in-game perspective of the avatar.

Finally, robotic behavior can generate dissociations of intentional states. In one session of recorded game play, we observed KM giving instructions to her avatar to play the guitar. Once instructed, the avatar persists in the task until it is completed. Other sims talk of leaving; half in jest, as she isn't actually playing, she says, "I am going to go too, can't stand listening to my own music." Zooming out of the building, she ends up with a bird's eye view of Alphaville, from which you can see all the different properties and decide where to go next. Her own intentions have dissociated from those of the avatar, who is left behind playing the guitar (see figure 12-2).

In KM's diaries, we begin to understand why so little conversation takes place in *The Sims Online*: typical gameplay is characterized by long absences from the keyboard, as the robotic work of skilling is itself experienced as boring. Our analysis of her game play captured on video indicates that this boredom forms part of a series of dissociations between player and avatar, which act cumulatively to weaken the bond of identification. These dissociations have a primary cause: the absence of immediate-term, synchronous player control.

At the other extreme of the spectrum of player control is the long-term goal or overall purpose of the game. In the single-player, offline version of the game, *The Sims*, the player is comfortably in charge of the purpose of the game, whether it is to build castles in the air (there's a trick to getting them up there), to raise a sim family, or to start a gay karaoke bar [17]. In keeping with the hallmark of Will Wright's game philosophy, the promise of *The Sims Online* was that it, too, would allow the gamer to formulate his or her own goals within the game.

TSO, however, had introduced something co-designer Chris Trottier called "a real secure economy" [6]. In *The Sims*, the economy is insecure. If you enjoy the constraint, you can abide by the rules and hold off on that swimming pool gazebo until your sim has boned up on his mechanical skills,

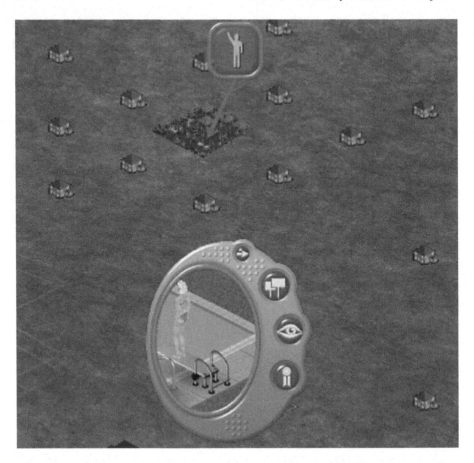

Figure 12-2. Players can leave their avatars behind and—like disembodied spirits—view the world from above. In the meantime, the avatar continues to engage in activities as instructed.

developed some friendships, and can start earning some real money. But if you don't, a Google search for "sims cheat codes" will pull up 283,000 hits. These cheat codes, which are built into the game, allow a player to get unlimited resources with a few keystrokes. The insecure economy of *The Sims* allows players the flexibility of setting their own goals. The secure economy of *The Sims Online*, in contrast, introduces a resource scarcity into the game that tends to swamp all other goals, as illustrated in the following analysis.

Our second study participant was a 28-year-old man (SH), a free-lance producer and part-time actor. On the 19th of January 2003, after spending the first play sessions exploring the game, he creates an avatar, "Sammar", to represent himself:

> I chose to develop this character because he is the closest thing to my alter ego. I needed an outlet for that ego in order to help myself in real day to day life. I'm

hoping that I'll be able to learn from my other self and take those characteristics that I feel I lack and forge them into my real life. (SH, p. 9)

His entry suggests a very rich vision of the game's potential. By creating a virtual self, he imagines he will be able to explore and to cultivate modes of being and responding to the world that he can subsequently incorporate into his own life in a selective manner. This is a goal he sets himself, demonstrating his confidence in being able to control the overall purpose of the game. After recounting Sammar's first day of play, visiting places, getting a roommate, and earning money—"simoleans"—making pizza, he states a subordinate and interim goal in the game, now projected onto his avatar:

His main goal at present is to make enough money to build a party pad by the beach. (SH, p. 11).

His entry contains the key elements of a narrative self: a goal (a party pad), an obstacle preventing him from realizing the goal immediately (not enough money), and a strategy for overcoming the obstacle (making money). The goal itself is envisaged in social terms: his house will be constructed in an attractive location and provide a venue for himself and other players to have a good time together. As he continues playing the game, he maintains a strongly positive disposition:

A lot of the people I've visited at their properties have been exceptionally nice. I imagine it has to do with their visitor bonus. The people I met in the pizza place are not nearly as friendly. It's amazing what greed will do. (SH, p. 13)

The effect of the game's incentive structure on the other players is beginning to transpire. Property owners are paid for the time others spend on their lots; his warm appreciation of their welcoming behavior is qualified by the suspicion that they, just like the unpleasant pizza makers, are driven by greed. A few days later he reports:

Sammar is feeling accepted in this community. He is still figuring out the finer details but it's coming along well. He aspires to make his skills at their peak and make as much money as possible." (SH, p. 19)

SH continues to view *TSO* primarily as a community, a place regulated by norms and common meanings, in which he can feel accepted and welcomed. At the same time, as he begins to master the rules of the game, his visionary goals narrow. The next day, we find him for the first time thinking of friendships in instrumental terms: "He's building a friendship base that's making him money and skill." (SH, p. 23). When SH returns to the game on 18 March 2003, he reports:

> "Sammar" has built his skill levels, mostly mechanical & logical, and is making a decent amount of money making gnomes. He has a home now and is in the process of building it up to be a place where other sims can come to relax and make money. (SH, p. 25)

He now shows little emotional involvement with his avatar, whose activities in this session are directed not towards forming relationships, but on building skills and making money. However, he sees these activities as a temporary means to a more attractive goal of building a house. The purpose of this house is still to provide a place for others, but he no longer imagines they will come to party. Instead, they will come to his house to hang out, and to make money. His basic motivation remains altruistic:

> My characters main goal at present is to be a viable and successful character who can help other Sims in their money and skill earning endeavors (SH, pp. 25 & 27).

At the same time, his interest in *The Sims Online* is starting to flag. The game, he writes, is "somewhat boring" and does not facilitate the social contact he came looking for:

> The game would be more condusive to chatting if email were accessible while playing to swap pics and personal info. A real possibility of meeting these people off line would get the place buzzing. (SH, p. 39)

Avatar encounters, apparently, do not have the emotional and intellectual qualities of real encounters. His suggestions of introducing e-mail, swapping pictures, and meeting people off-line indicates that he experiences the on-screen characters as poor representatives of the players' social agency: identification has become unattractive and the channeling role of the avatars is failing.

When he decides to give the game another try in April, he abandons Sammar and begins Freakstick, a skeleton-like character to "express my off the wall personality" (p. 37). He attempts to reformulate his strategies:

> Now that I've learned the main tricks and tips in succeeding in The Sims, I have a new way of going about things. I plan on amassing large amounts of mechanical and logical skill. Those skills have the greatest amount of financial profitability with the least amount of constant attention. (SH, pp. 37–39)

He soon learns, however, that *TSO* provides very limited opportunities for rapid progress in the game, gets bored, and plays infrequently. On 27 July 2003 he goes on for a brief session to build skills. There were few people online, so the effort didn't pay off as much as he had hoped. "Maybe there will be more people the next time I log on," he comments (SH, p. 45). He is now speaking of people as a simple means to speed up the gaining of skill points; he is no longer interested in socializing or meeting friends. The incentives of the game appears to have ground sociality out of him.

On 4 August 2003, his goal is subtly reconceptualized, even as he represents it to himself as unchanged:

> My ultimate goal, still, is to gain enough skill and money to build the ultimate house where I won't have to work at making money. Rather I earn money by collecting the revenues given to me by the Sims for visitors coming to my house. Also I will get residuals for every dollar that my guests make. (SH, pp. 47, 49)

Shortly after, complaining that the "time it takes to build skill is a little overwhelming, not [to] mention boring" (26 August 2003, p. 51), the record trails off and he abandons the game.

From start to finish, SH displays an active desire to define the long term, overall purpose as well as the intermediate goals of his gameplay. Step by step, he lets go of his own goals and adapts to the goals built into the game. He relinquishes the desire to become a better person by trying out new modes of relationship within the game, he gives up on the idea of helping others succeed and of becoming appreciated by a community of friends. Unable to remain motivated by the time-consuming and mindless activities of skilling and making money, he is drawn towards the ultimate goal provided by the structure of the game: to become a "sim lord" (SH, p. 41) and live off the labor of others. At that point, human relationships have deteriorated beyond the level of instrumentality to something reminiscent of exploitation. An early review spelled out the emerging culture of the game:

> Since a player can earn money simply by enticing other players to congregate on their property, and because all the other players truly want to do is earn money, the object of the game is reduced to building—not a "house" in which your Sim will live, but a labor camp in which other Sims will come to earn money. Providing beds, showers, food and a pool table persuades your guests to stay longer and spend more of the money they are earning, owing their souls to the company store, so to speak, and never truly needing a place of their own. The result is a "city" in which nearly every house is a sweatshop [25].

What *The Sims Online* failed to do, then, was to provide the players with the tools to control the overall purpose of the game. From the early interviews, it is clear that Wright and his development group fully intended to build this freedom into the game. When large numbers of beta-testing citisims started spending their time making pizza, the developers were distressed. "A few weeks ago, we thought we'd have Disney World. But right now, everyone is just making pizza," Trottier lamented. Wright worried that too many people were chasing money in the game—"we might start to lose the creative players" [6]. However, no satisfactory solution appears to have been found (see figure 12-3).

The Sims online involved two major design challenges, one social and one psychological. The psychological challenge was the shift from a godlike player

Figure 12-3. Avatars practicing "charisma" before mirrors in a lavish interior. Clicking on another avatar gives you a "cloud" of interactive options; the sequence of tasks to be carried out by your avatar accumulates in the upper left corner. A needs panel monitors your avatar's state along eight dimensions.

to an embedded avatar. In KM's experience, we see some of the player-avatar dissociations that make this transition unsatisfactory. On the social front, the challenge was to establish some kind of resource scarcity. Kollock's seminal "Design principles for online communities" argues that scarcity is an important dimension of a vibrant online community, not just to keep things lively, but because "moderate amounts of risk are required for the development of trust . . . and encourage the formation of groups and clubs as a way of managing that risk (or exploiting it, in the case of a guild of thieves)" [26]. Using only a "secure economy" to create scarcity, however, backfired. It set up a dominant incentive gradient that funneled most people's energies into mindless and boring money-making routines, destroying the fun and creativity of the game.

The effect of the design choices made in these two major transitions was to curtail player control at both extremes of the spectrum—the immediate-term mechanics of avatar movement, as well as the long-term goals and purposes of the game. There remained, however, the central portion: player control of intermediate-term strategic innovation. This area provided the developers with ample possibilities of expansion, but they were not exploited. A rich set of tools and opportunities for medium-term, strategic innovation would have given players something to focus on, compensating in part for the loss of control at the extremes of the spectrum. We see in SH's diaries a mounting frustration at the ineffectiveness of his actions and his inability to come up with strategic short-cuts, indicating a strategic deficit. Player control at the intermediate, strategic level involves the ability to formulate complex and clever sequences of moves that help further the player's goals in effective and original ways. In *TSO*, plodding along a number of roughly equivalent routes was the only legitimate way forward.

When the players of *TSO* found, to everyone's surprise, that they had nothing to talk about, the explanation may lie in the glaring absence of strategic opportunities. In most multiplayer online games, it is strategy development that provides the gamers with something worth communicating about. Indeed, a distressing effect of the failure to develop the central, strategic portion of the spectrum of player control is that players had no way of becoming uniquely valuable to each other. Human beings are irreplaceable resources for each other in part because each one of us gathers our own information, adopts an idiosyncratic perspective, and develops our own strategies—complex sequences of actions that reliably achieve improbable results. In a society rich in strategic opportunities, information becomes the critical scarce resource. In the next section, we examine how a relatively small number of innovative players found a way of mining this middle of the control spectrum, with dramatic effects.

4. Strategies and Limits of Cultural Evolution in The Sims Online

Full-scale social experiments are expensive. In order to put a new model of social organization to a realistic test, you need tens of thousands of subjects over a period of years. Finding a suitable and willing population is almost impossible; funding the enterprise is prohibitive; gaining human subjects approval is impracticable; the logistics a nightmare. In the initial phases, you will need to insulate your state to some degree from its surroundings, to give it time to develop its own economic practices and civic institutions. The continuity of history must be broken for your ideas to be implemented and given full play. If your experiment goes awry and your ideas turn out to produce a monstrous society, you will be held personally responsible, exposed to the murderous ire of your own captive citizens. Until recently, short of a full-scale revolution or a military invasion, the only viable alternative available to social visionaries was the thought experiment. Where past ages were constrained to choose either the expensive realism of war, colonization, and revolution, or the cheap but fallible instrument of utopian thought experiments, we now have a technology that permits us to create imaginary worlds and to populate them with real people.

What was simulated in the mind for millennia can now be simulated in public, in vast simulated online cities.

The utopian question is not "What emerges from a state of nature?" [5]. A utopia is a social experiment that involves the explicit and deliberate manipulation of certain structural parameters in establishing and running the imagined state. The intricate thought experiments of Plato's *Republic*, More's *Utopia*, and Butler's *Erewhon* exploit the imagination as a cheap and readily available vehicle to explore the possibility space of social arrangements. They ask the question, "How do the choices we make in setting up the structure of society affect the behavior of individuals and thus its course of history?" As computer-mediated active worlds proliferate, this question is pivotal not only for understanding the evolutionary trajectory of a particular multiplayer online game, but also for being able to develop the kinds of worlds we want. The utopian question has become reformulated as a challenge of software design: in an active world, "what features must the environment have in order to enable particular types of social interaction?" [19, p. 8]. The evolution of culture in a massively multiplayer online world cannot develop from scratch; it must necessarily emerge from the complex dynamics of interactions between the programmers, the structural framework of the game they create, and the gaming activities of the players, which may take place both within the game itself and—as we shall see in a moment—extend beyond it. A game is not a clean-room implementation of a new society, untainted by preexisting values, beliefs, and conventions, but imports these dimensions, explicitly or implicitly.

In the case of *The Sims Online*, we begin with a richly featured environment, structured on multiple levels. We argued in section one that the secret of *The Sims'* phenomenal appeal lay in providing players with a godlike power to explore and innovate in two complementary possibility spaces: that of building, landscaping, and decorating houses, and that of caring for and directing the lives of simulated humans in evolving tangles of social relations. In section two we argued that the shift to *TSO* involved two major innovations, on the opposite ends of the spectrum of player control: one social and one psychological. The transition from an insecure to a secure economy effectively barred most players from the joys of building, reducing their game play to sweatshop labor. Adding insult to injury, the transition from the dollhouse to the avatar model barred players from the godlike power to control and stage the lives of the sims within the game. These architectural decisions were in large part forced upon the developers: going online meant that you had to remove the godlike power of the player. In this section, we will argue that *TSO's* critical shortcoming was that these constraints on the extremities of the spectrum of player control were not compensated for by new powers in the middle: by new strategic opportunities.

The co-creation of culture within a multiplayer online game is not necessarily cooperative; the goals of developers and gamers may be only partly overlapping. When the implementation of a game fails to provide attractive avenues to success, inventive players may seize the strategic initiative and attempt to move the game in new and unanticipated directions. The game designers' vision may be incoherent or produce unanticipated results, and the developers may falter in the implementation—in May of 2003, EA spokesman Jeff Brown acknowledged that "The people who make The Sims [Online] believe that its execution isn't what it should have been when it was launched" [27]. As we saw in section two, casual players, working with the tools provided to them within the game, met with repeated frustration and boredom in trying to achieve their goals. Creative players, on the other hand, may extend the boundaries of the game, drawing in resources that supplement the game, and find ways to compensate for its weaknesses.

The absence of a mechanism to import customized graphics into the game, for instance, cut off an important dimension of user creativity and constrained the elaboration of in-game identities. Some of the players responded by creating off-game web sites devoted to their *TSO* avatars, in which they were able to utilize their own art work and draw freely on cultural references that added resonance and power to their role play. A striking example was www.thesimsmafia.com by JC Soprano, played by the 25-year-old Sacramento native Jeremy Chase. It sported dramatic flash animations on the mafia theme and a detailed list of available in-game services, from prostitution and gambling to debt collection and assassinations—"Moe Green Specials" as he called them. Another group of players established the Rose Bush Gardens neighborhood in Alphaville devoted to "Bondage, Discipline, and Sadomasochism," amplifying this theme on the external Black Rose Castle Learning Center web site, with detailed instructions by the avatar Lady Julianna on how to be a dominant without being obnoxious, and how to participate in pony submissive races within the game. Urizenus, played by University of Michigan philosophy professor Peter Ludlow, created *The Alphaville Herald*, an online newspaper covering in-game events. By conducting in-character interviews outside of the game, he raised the profile of the inventive players, created a wider audience for their role play, and provided them and other players with an opportunity to reflect on the significance and impact of their in-game behavior. In these and other ways, the limited opportunities for creating an arresting identity within the game were transcended, as the gamers recruited a range of off-game resources to reinforce and heighten their own game experience.

Expanding the game beyond the confines of *TSO* proper also increased the effectiveness of the in-game character. To circumvent Maxis' Online Community Representatives, the Soprano mafia family members chatted with other players on *Yahoo Instant Messaging (IM)* rather than using the game's own chat feature, logged by the company. This allowed JC and his recruits to refine and develop a string of strategies for mimicking mafia-type activities within the game, without giving them away to the developers. As presented on his web site, these strategies were mysterious, vaguely menacing, and clearly fun. Maxis tried to keep up: "Most of the behavior described in stories about these 'mobs' is no longer possible, actually; we've been improving the game with frequent updates," associate director Kyle Brinx claimed in June 2003 [28], but six months later JC confidently proclaimed, "The city is mine . . . I hate to say it, but I got the juice in AV [Alphaville] and have for awhile" [29]. By figuring out ways to "warp" the built-in features of the game for mafia role-play, he had in effect seized the initiative from the developers and taken a strategic level of control of the game.

The blatantly anti-social character of the mafia role, adopted within a game that set out to simulate a real society, raised the question of how such a virtual society can be policed and governed. By creating a publicly available representation of his in-game activities, JC Soprano made it easy for the non-playing world to participate in contemplating this question. In the summer of 2003, the *Associated Press* did a story on "Sex, mob hits: Sims tests virtual morals" [30], reporting on the exploits of two rivaling mafia groups, the Sopranos and the Sims Shadow Government (SSG). CNN followed up a month later with live coverage [31]. In these interviews, both mafia families defended their activities by claiming that they dispensed a rough justice to discourage griefers. EA simply didn't respond effectively to protect innocent players from abuse. "Griefers . . . find and utilize loop-holes within the game," Jennifer Mathieson of the SSG said, "and it happens very, very quickly. So what we do, we just fight back. We use the same tactics . . . against them." [31]. Jennifer and her husband, who jointly played the avatar Mia Wallace, recounted that they had "ransacked apartments, sent out their 'troops' to urinate on others' lawns, and once drove another player from the game" [30]. By extending role-play into the media, these gamers gave people a new reason to play the game: to experience and to explore the ethical dimensions of online worlds. The "darker side of Sims life," Wright himself conceded, "makes the game more interesting. It is pretty playful and harmless"—and the governance of virtual communities "is something our society is grappling with" [32].

At the same time, *The Sims Online* was revealing its potential as a breeding ground for a wide range of humiliating, anti-social, and exploitative behaviors. In a BBC interview, Ludlow later explained that his make-believe newspaper, created off-game but edited in-character, was founded to document "the emergence of economic, social and political structures in the game" [3]. As events unfolded, *The Alphaville Herald* turned out to be perfectly positioned to become the media hub of the seething underworld of TSO. As Urizenus, Ludlow covered the rise of the mafia families and their increasingly hardball tactics, such as harassing a sim by sending her a new roommate, and then asking him to tear down her house. The interviews show that the players invested considerable emotion in the conflicts. In early December, he conducted a series of instant-messaging interviews with Evangeline, a cyber-prostitute, who had set up a brothel early on in the game as a strategy to avoid the boredom of skilling and working. Describing her business in graphic terms, Evangeline let it slip that she was underage herself, and claimed that several of the girls that provided "sexual services" within the game were also minors. Using the proceeds from the prostitution racket, she had purchased the property at the top of the game's welcome list, naming it Free Money for Newbies. Here she cheated newcomers out of their money, humiliated them by caging them in small rooms and ridiculing black avatars as monkeys [24].

Of course it was just a game. The houses are pixels on a screen, "money" is a play currency called simoleans, and sex between avatars is no more than dirty talk in cartoon bubbles. The CNN anchors kept tongues firmly in cheek and concluded that "this is all taking place in a virtual world. We can hope that it stays there and that if you don't like it you can just leave the game and stop playing" [31]. Electronic Arts, the game publisher and Maxis's parent company, who had long been aware of these activities, handled the publicity angle by an appeal to unreality. Confronted with stories of online prostitution in an interview with *The New York Times*, Jeff Brown, vice president for communications at Electronic Arts, said, "If someone says that is going on in cyberspace, is it lost on anybody that it's not actually happening? No law was violated. It's a game" [4].

Yet the interface between game and world does not present a simple and clean-cut boundary. The motto at Maxis, as we saw in section one, was that in *TSO*, "the sims are real" [16]. A subjective act of identification with the sim is an integral aspect of the design of the game: from your perspective as a player, your sim was intended to function as a virtual self onto which your own subjectivity and agency is displaced, and you become emotionally invested in the sim's changing social relations, reputation, and resources. Equally, in order to interact with and understand the other sims, you need to model the sim as an avatar channeling a real person. Since the sims are real in the sense that each one is a real individual once removed, displaced onto an avatar, then ethical questions that could be entirely ignored as fictive in the offline version of the game have inescapably moved much closer to reality. Add to this the fact that creative players actively widened the boundaries of the game, extending their gameplay far beyond the confines of the game itself, and in various ways integrating their in-game character with the real world. Finally, they found ways of taking strategic control by devising their own methods of earning money within the game, bypassing *TSO*'s intended gameplay. EA continued to treat the game as if everything were happening within their proprietary controlled world, when this clearly was not the case. Ludlow's research assistant, Candace Bolter, pointed out that although prostitution was remunerated using simoleans, the in-game currency of *TSO*, this "fantasy money" was readily convertible into US dollars through money trading at online auction sites such as Gaming Open Market and eBay [33]. Electronic Arts, they argued, had a moral responsibility of governance that they couldn't simply walk away from: *The Sims Online* was not just a game.

Urizenus' *The Alphaville Herald* provides a case in point: it started out as an in-character blog, but in the course of documenting the conflicts and exploitation taking place within the game, it quickly morphed into a project of serious investigative journalism. The significance of this stance towards the game was underlined by the following incident. In October 2003, roleplaying as the priest Urizenus in a *TSO* church, he was contacted by another player:

> A sim IM'ed me claiming to be a 13-year-old boy and started asking me about God and forgiveness. He claimed that he had beaten his 8-year-old sister because she had annoyed him, and that she had gone to the hospital with a broken jaw. I asked if he had reported this, and he said no, and then broke off contact with me [34].

Responding to the reality of the situation and casting aside an implied in-game seal of confession, Ludlow contacted EA to report a real-life crime, repeatedly requesting they pursue the case with the boy's local authorities. EA responded with a string of boiler-plate customer service replies, advising him that they could only take action on Terms of Service violations [34]. Bolter finally threatened to take the case to the media; EA relented and handed the case over to local police. They also terminated Ludlow's account on a technicality. In the following days and weeks, the termination story and the background corpus of interviews was picked up by the international media, from *The Detroit Free Press* to the *Corriere della Sera* and *Izvestia*, featured as an attempt to suppress the public's knowledge of the truth and a possible violation of freedom of speech. In a recent academic paper, Ludlow notes that the real-world press incongruously treated *The Alphaville Herald* as a real newspaper, even though it was produced as an in-character blog as part of a game, and advances the thesis that "there is no such thing as fiction, and there are no such things as fictional objects" [35].

In this section, we have argued that taking *The Sims Online* entailed a loss of player control at both ends of the spectrum (figure 12-1). While large numbers of casual players, including our study participants, appear to have responded to the highly constrained game by attempting to adapt and eventually losing interest, a small number of highly inventive players found a variety of ways of taking charge of the game. They accomplished this by developing intermediate-term strategic control on two fronts. First, they found original ways of bending and twisting the built-in features of the game into complex series of moves to achieve their own defined goals. Second, they extended their gameplay beyond the confines of the game to include web sites, instant messaging, and media outreach, thus embedding their in-game character within a broader matrix of cultural references and meanings. Moving in-character communication out of the game allowed the players to develop their "warped" use of the programmed rules in a conspiratorial spirit of secrecy, away from prying eyes of EA's monitors, thus deepening the gameplay and staying ahead in the conflict of interest between developers and adventurous gamers. Web sites served the function of reinforcing and advertising social role and player identity, creating a community memory of causally connected historical events, or a cumulative repository of instructions.

Because the regular gameplay within *The Sims Online* was so boring, most of what has been recorded about the game on web sites and discussion boards relates to the events generated by the small number of players who played against the grain. These players took charge of the game and moved it in new directions. Evangeline, for instance, who turned out to be a boy, exposed himself and other underage players to forms of adult sexual imagination that may have been harmful and developmentally inappropriate. Jeremy Chase started playing JC Soprano when he was unemployed; his masterful gameplay got him paid work to play online games and design web sites [36]. Peter Ludlow became world famous as the academic that exposed the seamy side of *The Sims Online*, and his career may take a turn towards active worlds research. In each of these cases, it was the originality of the gameplay that created the real-world consequences. The fictional world blended into the real world because the players dragged the real world into the game.

5.   Conclusion and Outlook

The chief creator of *The Sims*, Will Wright, often cites the work of Christopher W. Alexander as an important inspiration for his work, in particular his *A Pattern Language* [37]. Communities, Alexander *et al.* write, emerge out of "a hierarchy of social and political groups, from the smallest and most local groups—families, neighborhoods, and work groups—to the largest groups—city councils, regional assemblies" [9]. The enabling condition that allows such groups to form spontaneously and to constitute communities is that "each group makes its own decisions about the environment it uses in common . . . . Ideally, each group actually owns the common land at its 'level.' And higher groups do not own or control the land belonging to lower groups—they only own and control the common land that lies *between* them, and which serves the higher group" [9]. By assigning resources to be held in common at different levels of organization, people would be challenged to institute appropriate collaborative patterns of governance at each level.

In *The Sims Online*, these architectural principles of community design were never implemented. The community has a flat structure of individual ownership, with no land held in common at any level. In part, this happened by default as the code was ported from *The Sims*; the single-player model of private, suburban lots was simply scaled up to a multiplayer environment. Far from acknowledging this to be a massive design blunder, however, EA championed private ownership of all land as the key to forestalling griefers, as each player could bar any other from their site. The result is distinctly odd: since many players don't own properties, they must meet their avatar's basic needs by entering other player's private houses, using their shower and bathroom, getting food from their fridge, and even sleeping in their beds. This socially anomalous practice is not only tolerated but encouraged, since owners are rewarded for the time other sims spend on their properties. Indeed, as a result, the primary function of a private property is not that of a home planned and decorated to delight its owner and inhabitant. Instead, properties become investments, designed to optimize return on capital by providing the skilling and working equipment, along with food, gyms, motel-style beds, showers, and bathrooms, to attract and retain the maximum number of visitors. As we saw in section two, the incentive structure of this economic model not only produces very boring play but reduces human relationships to one of instrumentality, grinding any real sociality out of the game.

By leaving out the multiple levels of commons recommended by Alexander, the game designers blocked the formation of effective higher-level community structures within the game. It turned out that the hyper-privatized model was not effective in preventing crime and griefing: Evangeline and others set up their bordellos on their own properties, and the mafia leveraged the power of room-mates, harassing chat and e-mail, negative reputation links, and a host of other tools within and outside of the game to achieve their ends. Community-based governing structures, in contrast, had a hard time getting off the ground. Con-sider the case of the Alphaville Government, established by a group of friends in early 2003. This act involved the creation of the avatar Mr-President, played by Arthur Baynes, and the construction of a Capitol in the best neoclassical tradition. Baynes web site at avg.simsgov.com showed an animated graphic of Mr-President waving from the balcony. The focus, then, was on the trappings of power, and since all properties were private, the Capitol, and later the Court, had to belong to an individual player who might at any time decide to quit. The Alphaville Government also aspired to take on the task of maintaining law and order within Alphaville, but they had no legitimate tools with which to enforce city-wide laws and regulations and never became anything like an effective government.

In the fall of 2004, as this manuscript goes to press, there is widespread expectation among the gamers that *The Sims Online* is about to close. The initial prospect of hundreds of thousands of customers paying monthly fees of ten dollars each had made the idea of porting their most popular game to the Internet financially extremely attractive to EA. Suneel Ratan, its former vice president, said informal projections had run as high as a million subscribers for the online version, implying a regular annual revenue of $120 million [27]. Instead, *TSO* subscriptions at the first anniversary were estimated to be around 80,000 [20] and by April of 2004, the company reported 57,500 subscribers [38]. If the attrition rate of 5,000 a month is sustained, *TSO* will dip below 20,000 before the year is out—the level at which EA closed Earth & Beyond [20].

Several of the key players have taken the consequences. After being kicked out of *The Sims Online* in late 2003, Peter Ludlow continued for a while to visit Alphaville through other players' accounts, but soon moved on to *Second Life*, a very differently managed online social space. In July 2004, Jeremy Chase predicted *TSO* would close after a final Christmas season and reported he had joined the online multiplayer game *Star Wars Galaxies*. In August, Simoleanman, one of the main currency traders, announced his closing sale, and The Alphaville Government shut down. It is possible that it's still not too late to rescue the game: the example of the innovative rebels has inspired a host of online newspapers, mafias, and government players, and EA has continued to make significant improvements to the game. A crucial innovation in friendship formation has moved the game closer to a psychology of real relationships. Yet these improvements may have arrived too late.

In its heyday, *The Sims Online* did a spectacular job as a dystopian experiment and remains a rich source of opportunities for social research. Rushed into production, it contains layers of questionable design decisions. Its doll-house ancestry, emphasizing sims driven by artificial intelligence, militated in multiple ways against effective player-avatar identification. The incentive system implicit in its economic structure produced mind-numbingly boring play and purely utilitarian avatar relations. Its lack of strategic opportunities spurred creative players to extend their gameplay beyond the company servers and to bend the built-in features of the game to their own purposes. Finally, the absence of land held in common at different levels prevented the natural emergence of effective layers of governance. Yet precisely by inspiring players to warp the rules and to extend the game to the world-wide web, *The Sims Online* has succeeded in introducing the larger practical and ethical questions of online community governance to the public at large, making us all participants in a virtual utopian experiment.

Acknowledgments

We thank the participants for making a year-long commitment to participating in this study. We also thank the National Science Foundation for funding the Children's Digital Media Center, UCLA, under whose auspices the research was conducted.

References

1. Grossman, L. (2002). Sim Nation. *Time*, 25 November. Available at http://www.time.com/time/magazine/archive/preview/0,10987,1101021125-391544,00.html
2. Seguret, O. (2004). Putsch et Sims. *Liberation*, 27 February. Available at http://www.liberation.fr/page.php?Article=181923#
3. Ward, M. (2003). The dark side of digital utopia. *BBC News*, 22 December. Available at http://news.bbc.co.uk/go/pr/fr/-/1/hi/technology/3334923.stm
4. Harmon, A. (2004). A Real-life debate on free expression in a cyberspace city. *The New York Times*, 15 January. Available at http://www.nytimes.com/2004/01/15/technology/15SIMS.html
5. Manjoo, F. (2003). Raking muck in "The Sims Online". *Salon.com*, 12 December. Available at http://www.salon.com/tech/feature/2003/12/12/sims_online_newspaper/index_np.html
6. Keighley, G. (2002). The endless hours of The Sims Online. *Gamespot.com*, 28 November. Available at http://gamespot.com/gamespot/features/pc/simsonline
7. McKenna, K.Y.A. & Bargh, J.A. (2000). Plan 9 from cyberspace: The implications of the Internet for personality and social psychology. *Personality and Social Psychology Review 4*, *1*: 57–75.
8. Lessig, L. (1999). *Code and Other Laws of Cyberspace*. New York, NY: Basic Books.
9. Alexander, C. W, Ishikawa, S., & Silverstein, M. (1977). *A Pattern Language: Towns, Buildings, Construction*. New York, NY: Oxford University Press.
10. Walker, J. (2004). Hobbes in cyberspace: Life in an online game world proves nasty, brutish, and short. *Reason*, 1 April. Available at http://www.keepmedia.com/ShowItemDetails.do?item_id=387500
11. Electronic Arts (2003). *Annual report*, 31 March. Available at http://ccbn26.mobular.net/ccbn/7/266/277/
12. Gordon, J.E. (1978). *Structures: or, Why Things Don't Fall Down*. New York, NY: Penguin.
13. Salen, K. & Zimmerman, E. (2004). *Rules of Play: Game Design Fundamentals*. Boston, MA: MIT Press.
14. Gibson, J.J. (1979). *The Ecological Approach to Visual Perception*. Boston, MA: Houghton Mifflin.
15. Maslow, A.H. (1943). A theory of human motivation. *Psychological Review, 50*: 370–396.
16. Green, J. (2002). The Sims Online: Indulging your inner weirdo. Gamers.com, May 1. Available at http://www.gamers.com/game/1016135/previews?page=1
17. van den Berg, M. (2004). Simmery and sluttery...the mo pie sims. Available at http://www.mopie.com/sims/simdex.html
18. Shakespeare, W. (2001). *The History of King Lear*. S. Wells (Ed.). Oxford, UK: Oxford University Press.
19. Schroeder, R. (2002). Social interaction in virtual environments: Key issues, common themes, and a framework for research. In R. Schroeder (Ed.), *The Social Life of Avatars: Presence and Interaction in Shared Environments*. London: Springer, pp. 1–18.
20. Woodcock, B.S. (2004). An analysis of MMOG subscription growth. Version 10.0. September. Available at http://pw1.netcom.com/%7Esirbruce/Subscriptions.html
21. Greenfield, P.M. (1997). Culture as process: Empirical methods for cultural psychology. In J.W. Berry, Y. Poortinga, & J. Pandey (Eds.), *Handbook of Cross-Cultural Psychology: Vol. 1. Theory and Method*. Boston, MA: Allyn & Bacon, pp. 301–346.
22. Steen, F.F., Greenfield, P.M., Davies, M.S., & Tynes, B. (In press). What went wrong in The Sims Online? Cultural learning and barriers to identification in a MMORPG. In P. Vorderer & Jennings Bryant (Eds.), *Playing Video Games: Motives, Responses, and Consequences*. Mahwah, NJ: Erlbaum.

23. Kirk, C. (2004). Culling external sensory response: How we feel videogames. Unpublished manuscript, Department of Communication Studies, UCLA.

24. Brown & Bell, this volume.

25. White, A.A. (2003). Chatting for dummies. Game-Revolution.com, January. Available at http://www.game-revolution.com/games/pc/sim/sims_online.htm

26. Kollock, P. (1996). Design principles for online communities. Harvard Conference on the Internet and Society. Available at http://www.sscnet.ucla.edu/soc/faculty/kollock/papers/design.htm

27. Ratan, S. (2003). Sim flop dogs game developers. *Wired*, 12 May. Available at http://www.wired.com/news/games/0,2101,58749,00.html

28. Hopkinson, T.B. (2003). The Sims Online mob interview. *GameGossip.com*, 11 June. Available at http://www.gamegossip.com/comment.php?id=208

29. Ludlow, P. (2004). JC Soprano: Now the city is mine! *The Alphaville Herald*, 14 January. Available at http://www.alphavilleherald.com/archives/000089.html

30. Wadhams, N. (2003). Sex, mob hits: Sims tests virtual morals. *Associated Press*, 5 July. Available at http://www.cnn.com/2003/TECH/fun.games/07/05/misbehaving.online.ap/index.html

31. Sieberg, D. (2003). Next@CNN, *CNN*, 2 August. Transcript available at http://www.cnn.com/TRANSCRIPTS/0308/02/nac.00.html

32. Twist, J. (2004). Simulating life, love and the Universe. *BBC*, 17 September. Available at http://news.bbc.co.uk/1/hi/technology/3645552.stm

33. Ludlow, P. (2003). Evangeline: Interview with a child cyber-prostitute. *The Alphaville Herald*, 8 December. Available at http://www.alphavilleherald.com/archives/000049.html

34. Ludlow, P. (2003). Comment. *The Alphaville Herald*, 11 November. Available at http://www.alphavilleherald.com/archives/000016.html

35. Ludlow, P. (In preparation). From Sherlock and Buffy to Klingon and Norrathian platinum pieces: Pretense, contextalism, and the myth of fiction. Available at http://www.alphavilleherald.com/archives/Fiction.rtf

36. Chase, J. (2004). Bombshell! JC Soprano retires from TSO, but confesses ALL on the way out. *The Second Life Herald*, 20 July 2004. Available at http://www.alphavilleherald.com/-archives/000331.html

37. Cambron, M. (2002). A chat with Will Wright. *GIGnews.com*, April. Available at http://www.gignews.com/goddess_wright.htm

38. Glassman, M. (2004). Braving bullying hecklers, simulants run for president. *The New York Times*, 1 April. Available at http://tech2.nytimes.com/mem/technology/techreview.html

Index

Lecture Notes in Artificial Intelligence   2168

Subseries of Lecture Notes in Computer Science
Edited by J. G. Carbonell and J. Siekmann

Lecture Notes in Computer Science

Edited by G. Goos, J. Hartmanis, and J. van Leeuwen

Springer
Berlin
Heidelberg
New York
Barcelona
Hong Kong
London
Milan
Paris
Tokyo

Luc De Raedt   Arno Siebes (Eds.)

Principles of
Data Mining and
Knowledge Discovery

5th European Conference, PKDD 2001
Freiburg, Germany, September 3-5, 2001
Proceedings

Dedicated to Jan Żytkow

Springer

Series Editors

Jaime G. Carbonell,Carnegie Mellon University, Pittsburgh, PA, USA
Jörg Siekmann, University of Saarland, Saarbrücken, Germany

Volume Editors

Luc De Raedt
Albert-Ludwigs University Freiburg
Department of Computer Science
Georges Köhler-Allee, Geb. 079, 79110 Freiburg, Germany
E-mail: deraedt@informatik.uni-freiburg.de

Arno Siebes
University of Utrecht, Inst. of Information and Computing Sciences
Dept. of Mathematics and Computer Science
Padualaan 14, de Uithof, 3508 TB Utrecht, The Netherlands
E-mail: arno@cs.uu.nl

Cataloging-in-Publication Data applied for

Die Deutsche Bibliothek - CIP-Einheitsaufnahme

Principles of data mining and knowledge discovery : 5th European conference
proceedings / PKDD 2001, Freiburg, Germany, September 3 - 5, 2001. Luc de Raedt ;
Arno Siebes (ed.). - Berlin ; Heidelberg ; New York ; Barcelona ; Hong Kong ; London ;
Milan ; Paris ; Tokyo : Springer, 2001
    (Lecture notes in computer science ; Vol. 2168 : Lecture notes in
    artificial intelligence)
    ISBN 3-540-42534-9

CR Subject Classification (1998): I.2, H.2, J.1, H.3, G.3, I.7, F.4.1

ISBN 3-540-42534-9 Springer-Verlag Berlin Heidelberg New York

Springer-Verlag Berlin Heidelberg New York
a member of BertelsmannSpringer Science+Business Media GmbH

http://www.springer.de

© Springer-Verlag Berlin Heidelberg 2001
Printed in Germany

Typesetting: Camera-ready by author, data conversion by PTP Berlin, Stefan Sossna
Printed on acid-free paper   SPIN 10840371   06/3142   5 4 3 2 1 0

In Memoriam

The PKDD community has learned with great sadness that Jan Zytkow passed away on Jan. 16, 2001. Jan was a well-known researcher in the area of scientific discovery, a pioneer in machine learning, an author of many publications and books, an organizer of many conferences and meetings, the driving force behind the PKDD conferences, a wonderful person, and a friend. Those who knew him will miss him. These proceedings are dedicated to Jan.

Preface

It is our pleasure to present the proceedings of the 12th European Conference on Machine Learning (*Lecture Notes in Artificial Intelligence 2167*) and the 5th European Conference on Principles and Practice of Knowledge Discovery in Databases (this volume). These two conferences were held from September 3–7, 2001 in Freiburg, Germany, marking the first time – world-wide – that a data mining conference has been co-located with a machine learning conference.

As Program Committee co-chairs of the two conferences, our goal was to co-ordinate the submission and reviewing process as much as possible. Here are some statistics: a total of 117 papers was submitted to ECML 2001, 78 papers were submitted to PKDD 2001, and 45 papers were submitted as joint papers. Each paper was carefully reviewed by 3 (in exceptional circumstances 2 or 4) members of the Program Committees. Out of the 240 submitted papers, 40 were accepted after the first reviewing round, and 54 were accepted on the condition that the final paper would meet the requirements of the reviewers. In the end, 90 papers were accepted for the proceedings (50 for ECML 2001 and 40 for PKDD 2001).

We were also aiming at putting together a 5-day program that would be attractive, in its entirety, to both communities. This would encourage participants to stay the whole week and thus foster interaction and cross-fertilization. The PKDD 2001 conference ran from Monday to Wednesday, and the ECML 2001 conference from Wednesday to Friday, with the Wednesday program carefully selected to be of interest to a mixed audience. On each day there was an invited talk by an internationally renowned scientist. Tom Dietterich spoke on *Support Vector Machines for Reinforcement Learning*; Heikki Mannila on *Combining Discrete Algorithmic and Probabilistic Approaches in Data Mining*; Antony Unwin on *Statistification or Mystification, the Need for Statistical Thought in Visual Data Mining*; Gerhard Widmer on *The Musical Expression Project: A Challenge for Machine Learning and Knowledge Discovery*; and Stefan Wrobel on *Scalability, Search and Sampling: From Smart Algorithms to Active Discovery*. In addition, there was an extensive parallel program of 11 workshops and 8 tutorials. Two workshops were devoted to results achieved by the participants in the two learning and mining challenges that were set prior to the conferences.

It has been a great pleasure for us to prepare and organize such a prestigious event, but of course we could not have done it without the help of many colleagues. We would like to thank all the authors who submitted papers to ECML 2001 and PKDD 2001, the program committee members of both conferences, the other reviewers, the invited speakers, the workshop organizers, and the tutorial speakers. We are particularly grateful to the workshop chairs Johannes Fürnkranz and Stefan Wrobel; the tutorial chairs Michèle Sebag and Hannu Toivonen; and the challenge chairs Petr Berka and Christoph Helma for their assistance in putting together an exciting scientific program. Many thanks to Michael Keser for his technical support in setting up the CyberChair website, to Richard van de Stadt for developing CyberChair, and to the local team at Freiburg for the organizational support provided. We would also like to thank Alfred Hofmann of Springer-Verlag for his co-operation in publishing these proceedings. Finally, we gratefully acknowledge the financial support provided by the sponsors; EU Network of Excellence MLnet II, National Institute of Environmental Health Sciences (US), SICK AG, the city of Freiburg, and the Albert-Ludwigs University Freiburg and its Lab for Machine Learning.

Although at the time of writing the event is yet to take place, we are confident that history will cast a favorable eye, and we are looking forward to continued and intensified integration of the European machine learning and data mining communities that we hope has been set in motion with this event.

July 2001   Luc De Raedt
                                                              Peter Flach
                                                              Arno Siebes

Executive Commitees

Program Chairs ECML-2001: Peter Flach (University of Bristol)
Luc De Raedt (Albert-Ludwigs University)
Program Chairs PKDD-2001: Arno Siebes (Utrecht University)
Luc De Raedt (Albert-Ludwigs University)
Tutorial Chairs: Michèle Sebag (Ecole Polytechnique)
Hannu Toivonen (Nokia)
Workshop Chairs: Johannes Fürnkranz (Austrian Research Institute for Artificial Intelligence)
Stefan Wrobel (University of Magdeburg)
Challenge Chairs: Petr Berka (University of Economics Prague)
Cristoph Helma (Albert-Ludwigs University)
Local Chairs: Luc De Raedt (Albert-Ludwigs University)
Stefan Kramer (Albert-Ludwigs University)
Local Organization: Catherine Blocher (K&K Freiburg)
Susanne Bourjaillat (Albert-Ludwigs University)
Dirk Hähnel (Albert-Ludwigs University)
Cristoph Helma (Albert-Ludwigs University)
Michael Keser (Albert-Ludwigs University)
Kristian Kersting (Albert-Ludwigs University)
Walter Koch (K&K Freiburg)
Andrea Kricheldorf (K&K Freiburg)
Advisory Committee : Ramon Lopez de Mantaras (IIIA-CSIC Artificial Intelligence Research Institute)
Heikki Mannila (Nokia and Helsinki University of Technology)
Jan Rauch (University of Economics Prague)
Maarten van Someren (University of Amsterdam)
Stefan Wrobel (University of Magdeburg)
Djamel Zighed (University of Lyon 2)
PKDD Steering Committee : Jan Komorowski (Norwegian University of Science and Technology, Trondheim)
Jan Rauch (University of Economics Prague)
Djamel Zighed (University of Lyon 2)

X

ECML Program Committee

A. Aamodt (Norway)
H. Blockeel (Belgium)
H. Bostrom (Sweden)
I. Bratko (Slovenia)
P. Brazdil (Portugal)
W. Burgard (Germany)
J. Cussens (UK)
W. Daelemans (Belgium)
L. De Raedt (Germany)
M. Dorigo (Belgium)
S. Dzeroski (Slovenia)
F. Esposito (Italy)
D. Fisher (USA)
P. Flach (UK)
J. Fürnkranz (Austria)
J.-G. Ganascia (France)
Y. Kodradoff (France)
S. Kramer (Germany)
N. Lavrac (Slovenia)
R. Lopez de Mantaras (Spain)
D. Malerba (Italy)

B. Manderick (Belgium)
S. Matwin (Canada)
K. Morik (Germany)
H. Motoda (Japan)
V. Moustakis (Greece)
S. Muggleton (UK)
C. Nedelec (France)
E. Plaza (Spain)
G. Paliouras (Greece)
C. Rouveirol (France)
L. Saitta (Italy)
M. Sebag (France)
A. Siebes (The Netherlands)
M. van Someren (The Netherlands)
D. Sleeman (UK)
P. Stone (USA)
P. Turney (Canada)
P. Vitanyi (The Netherlands)
G. Widmer (Austria)
R. Wirth (Germany)
S. Wrobel (Germany)

PKDD Program Committee

Referees

Tutorials

Workshops

Semantic Web Mining
Gerd Stumme, Andreas Hotho and Bettina Berendt

Machine Learning as Experimental Philosphy of Science
Kevin Korb and Hilan Bensusan

Visual Data Mining
Simeon J. Simoff, Monique Noirhomme-Fraiture and Michael H. Böhlen

Integrating Aspects of Data Mining, Decision Support, and Meta-Learning
Christophe Giraud-Carrier, Nada Lavrac, and Stephen Moyle

Active Learning, Database Sampling, Experiment Design: Views on Instance Selection
Tobias Scheffer and Stefan Wrobel

Multi-Relational Data Mining
Arno Knobbe and Daniël van der Wallen

The Discovery Challenge on Thrombosis Data
Petr Berka, Shusaku Tsumoto, Katsuhiko Takabayashi and Shishir Gupta

The Predictive Toxicology Challenge for 2000-2001
Christoph Helma, Ross D. King, Stefan Kramer, and Ashwin Srinivasan

Database Support for KDD
Gunter Saake, Daniel Keim, Kai-Uwe Sattler, and Alexander Hinneburg

Data Mining for Marketing Applications
Wendy Gersten and Koen Vanhoof

Ubiquitous Data Mining: Technology for Mobile and Distributed KDD
Hillol Kargupta, Krishnamoorthy Sivakumar, and Ruediger Wirth

Contents

Invited Papers

Self-Similar Layered Hidden Markov Models

Jafar Adibi and Wei-Min Shen

Information Sciences Institute, Computer Science Department
University of Southern California
4676 Admiralty Way, Marina del Ray, CA 90292
{adibi,shen}@isi.edu

Abstract. Hidden Markov Models (HMM) have proven to be useful in a variety of real world applications where considerations for uncertainty are crucial. Such an advantage can be more leveraged if HMM can be scaled up to deal with complex problems. In this paper, we introduce, analyze and demonstrate Self-Similar Layered HMM (SSLHMM), for a certain group of complex problems which show self-similar property, and exploit this property to reduce the complexity of model construction. We show how the embedded knowledge of self-similar structure can be used to reduce the complexity of learning and increase the accuracy of the learned model. Moreover, we introduce three different types of self-similarity in SSLHMM, and investigate their performance in the context of synthetic data and real-world network databases. We show that SSLHMM has several advantages comparing to conventional HMM techniques and it is more efficient and accurate than one-step, flat method for model construction.

1   Introduction

There is a vast amount of natural structures and physical systems which contain self-similar structures that are made through recurrent processes. To name a few: ocean flows, changes in the yearly flood levels of rivers, voltages across nerve membranes, musical melodies, human brains, economic markets, Internet web logs and network data create enormously complex self-similar data [21]. While there have been much effort on observing self-similar structures in scientific databases and natural structures, there are few works on using self-similar structure and fractal dimension for the purpose of data mining and predictive modeling. Among these works, using fractal dimension and self-similarity to reduce the dimensionally curse [21], learning association rules [2] and applications in spatial joint selectivity in databases [9] are considerable. In this paper we introduce a novel technique which uses the self-similar structure for predictive modeling using a Self-Similar Layered Hidden Markov Model (SSLHMM).

Despite the broad range of application areas shown for classic HMMs, they do have limitations and do not easily handle problems with certain characteristics. For instance, classic HMM has difficulties to model complex problems with large states spaces. Among the recognized limitations, we only focus on complexity of HMM for a certain category of problems with the following characteristics: 1) The uncertainty and complexity embedded in these applications make it difficult and impractical to construct the model in one step. 2) Systems are self-similar, contain self-similar struc

L. De Raedt and A. Siebes (Eds.): PKDD 2001, LNAI 2168, pp. 1-15, 2001.

tures and have been generated through recurrent processes. For instance, analysis of traffic data from networks and services such as ISDN traffic, Ethernet LAN's, Common Channel Signaling Network (CCNS) and Variable Bit Rate (VBR) video have all convincingly demonstrated the presence of features such as self-similarity, long range dependence, slowly decaying variances, heavy-tailed distributions and fractal dimensions [24].

In a companion paper, Adibi and Shen introduced a domain independent novel technique to mine sequential databases through Mining by Layered Phases (MLP) in both discrete and continuous domains [1]. In this paper we introduce a special form of MLP as Self-Similar Layered HMM (SSLHMM) for self-similar structures. We show how SSLHMM uses the information embedded in a self-similar structure to reduce the complexity of the problem and learn a more accurate model than a general HMM. Our result is encouraging and show a significant improvement when a self-similar data are modeled through SSLHMM in comparison with HMM.

The rest of this paper is organized as follows. In section 2 we review the related work to this paper. In section 3, we introduce SSLHMM, its definition and properties. We explain major components of the system and we drive the sequence likelihood for a 2-layers SSLHMM. Section 4 shows the current result with an experimental finding in Network data along with discussion and interpretation followed by the future work and conclusions in section 5.

2   Related Work

HMMs proven tremendously useful as models of stochastic planning and decision problems. However, the computational difficulty of applying classic dynamic and limitation of conventional HMM to realistic problems has spurred much research into techniques to deal with the large states and complex problems. These approaches includes function approximation, ratability consideration, aggregation techniques and extension to HMM. In the following we refer to those works which are related to our approach in general or in specific. We categorize these woks as extension to HMM, aggregation techniques and segmentation.

Regular HMMs are capable of modeling only one process over time. To overcome such limitation there are several works to extend HMMs. There are three major extension which are close to our method. The first method introduced by Gharamani and Jordan as Factorial Hidden Markov Model (FHMM)[12]. This models generalize the HMM in which a state is factored into multiple state variables and therefore represented in a distributed manner. FHMM combines the output of the N HMMs in a single output signal, such that the output probabilities depend on the N dimensional meta-state. As the exact algorithm for this method is intractable they provide approximate inference using Gibbs sampling or variational methods. Williams and Hinton also formulated the problem of learning in HMMs with distributed state representations[23], which is a particular class of probabilistic graphical model by Perl [16]. The second method known as Coupled Hidden Markov Model (CHMM) consists of modeling the N process in N HMMs, whose state probabilities influence one another and whose outputs are separate signals. Brand, Oliver and Pentland described polynomial time training methods and demonstrate advantage of CHMM over HMM [5].

The last extension to HMM related to our approach introduced by Voglar and Metaxas as Parallel Hidden Markov Models (PHMM) which model the parallel process independently and can be trained independently [22]. In addition, the notion of hierarchical HMM has been introduced in [11] in which they extend the conventional Baum-Welch method for hierarchical HMM. Their major application is on text recognition in which the segmentation techniques benefits of the nature of handwriting. The major difference of SSLHMM with most of the above mentioned approaches is that they do not consider self-similarity for data. SSLHMM uses a recursive learning procedure to find the optimal solution and make it possible to use an exact solution rather approximation. In addition, SSLHMM as a specific case of MLP use the notion of phase in which learner consider laziness for the systems which is along with long range dependence and slowly decaying variances. For a detail description of MLP please refer to [1]. In addition, FHMM does not provide a hierarchical structure and its model is not interpretable while SSLHMM is designed toward interpretability. Also, HHMM does not provide the notion of self similarity.

In sequential planning, HMM-in general and Partial Observable Markov Decision Process models (POMDP) specifically have proven to be useful in a variety of real world applications [18]. The computational difficulty of applying dynamic programming techniques to realistic problems has spurred much research into techniques to deal with the large state and action spaces. These include function approximation [3] and state aggregation techniques [4, 8]. One general method for tackling large MDPs is decomposition of a large state model to smaller models [8, 17]. Dean and Lin [8], Berteskas and Tsikits [3] also showed some Markov Decision Process are loosely coupled and hence enable to get treated by divide-and-conquer algorithms. The evolution of the model over time also has been modeled as a semi-Markov Decision Process (SMDP) [18]. Sutton1[20] proposed temporal abstraction, which concatenate sequences of state transition together to permit reasoning about temporally extended events, and form a behavioral hierarchy as in [17]. Most of the work in this direction split a well-defined problem space to smaller spaces and they come up with subspaces and intra actions. In contrast SSLHMM attempt to build a model out of a given data through a top down fashion. The use of hierarchical HMMs mostly has been employed to divide a huge state space to smaller space or to aggregate actions and decisions. MLP in general and SSLHMM in specific are orthogonal to state decomposition approaches.

Complexity reduction also has been investigated through segmentation specially in Speech Recognition literature. Most of the work is based on probabilistic network, Viterbi search for all possible segmentation and using of domain knowledge as hypothesized segment start and end times [6, 7, 15]. Segmental HMMs also has been investigated in [13]. Even though the approach fits in speech recognition applications, but it decompose a waveform to local segments each present a "shape" with additive noise. A limitation of these approaches in general is that they do not provide a coherent language for expressing prior knowledge, or integrating shape cues at both the local and global level. SSLHMM integrates the prior knowledge in the infrastructure of model and as part of knowledge discovery process.

Based on our knowledge, the notion of Self-Similar Layered HMM has not been introduced yet. In addition, the notion of locality and boundary in phases make this work distinguish with similar approaches.

3   Self-Similar Layered Hidden Markov Model (SSLHMM)

Conventional HMMs are enable to model only one process at the time which represent by transition among the states. Fig. 1(a) shows a HMM with 9 states. A HMM λ for discrete symbol observation characterized by the following set of definitions: *state transition matrix: S, observation distribution matrix: B,* a set of *observations M,* a set of *states: n* and *initial distribution* π [19]. Having a set of observation O and a model λ, the old well-known problem is to adjust model parameters to maximize $P(O \mid \lambda)$.

In the modeling of complex processes, when the number of states goes high, the maximization process gets more difficult. A solution provided in other literature is to use of a Layered HMM instead [1, 12]. Layered HMM has the capability to model more than one process. Hence, it provides an easier platform for modeling complex processes. Layered HMM is a combination of two or more HMM processes in a hierarchy. Fig. 1(b) shows a Layered HMM with 9 states and 3 super-states, or macro-states (big circles with shade), which we refer to them as p*hases*. As we can see, each phase is a collection of states bounded to each other. The real model transition happens among the states. However, there is another transition process in upper layer among phases. The comprehensive transition model is a function of transition among states and transition among phases. Layered HMM similar to conventional HMM characterized by the following set of definitions: *a set of observation: M and* a set of *states: n,* a set of *phases: N, state transition matrix: S, phase transition matrix: R, observation distribution in each state: B and observation distribution in each phase :C* and *initial condition for each layer:* π.Learning and modeling follows the well-known Baum-Welch algorithm with some modification in forward and backward algorithm.

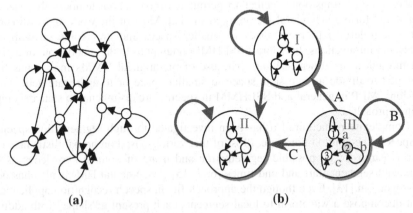

Fig. 1. **(a)** A normal Hidden Markov Model with 9 states, **(b)** Self-Similar Layered Hidden Markov Model with 9 states and 3 phases. As it shows each *phase* contains similar structure

A macro point of view suggests that the overall system behavior is more a trajectory among phases. In particular, system may go from one phase to another and stays in each phase for a certain amount of time. From a modeling point of view, *phase* is a set of properties, which remain homogenous through a set of states of the system and during a period of time. *phase* may be considered as a collection of locally connected sets, groups, levels, categories, objects, states or behaviors. The notion of *Phase* comes with the idea of granularity, organization and hierarchy. An observed sequence of a system might be considered as a collection of a behaviors among phases (rather than a big collection of states in a flat structure), and it may provide enough information for reasoning or be guidance for further details. Hence, a sequence with such property could be modeled through a layered structure. For example in network application domain a phase could define as "congestion" or "stable". A micro point of view shows that the overall system behavior is a transition among the states.

SSLHMM is a special form of Layered HMM in which there are some constraints on state layer transition, phase layer transition, and observation distribution. A closer look at Fig. 1(b) shows that this particular Layered HMM structure indeed is a *self-similar* structure. As it shows, there is a copy of the super model (model consists of *phases* and transition among them) inside of each phase. For instance the probability *A* of going form *phase III phase I* is equal to the probability *a* of transition from *state 3* to *state 1* in *phase III* (and in other phases as well).

The advantage of such structure is that like any other self-similar model it is possible to learn the whole model having any part of the model. Although there are a couple of assumptions to hold such properties but fortunately for a large group of systems in nature self-similarity is one of their characteristics. In the following, we introduce a self-similar Markovian structure in which the model shows similar structure across all or at least a range of structure scale.

3.1 Notation

In the following we describe our notation for the rest of this paper along with assumptions and definitions. We follow and modify Rabiner [19] notation for discrete HMM. A SSLHMM for discreet observation is characterized by the Table 1.

For the simplicity we use $\lambda = (S, B, \pi)$ for the state layer and $\Lambda = (R, C, \pi)$ for a given phase layer structure. In addition we use $\Theta = (\lambda, \Lambda, Z)$ for the whole structure of SSLHMM in which Z holds the hierarchical information including leaf structure and layer structure. Even though the states are hidden but in real world application there is a lot of information about physical problems, which points out some characteristics of state or phase.

Table 1. Self-Similar Layered Hidden Markov Model parameters and definition

Parameter	Definition
N	The number of *Phases* in the model We label individual phases as $\{1,2,\cdots,N\}$ and denote the phase at time t as Q_t.
n	The number of states. We label individual states as $\{1,2,\cdots,n\}$ and denote the state at time t as q_t.
M	The number of distinct observations
$R=\{r_{IJ}\}$	Phase layer transition probability, where $r_{IJ} = P(Q_{t+1} = J \mid Q_t = I)$ and $1 \leq I, J \leq N$
$S=\{s_{ij}\}$	State layer transition probability: where $s_{ij} = P(q_{t+1} = j \mid q_t = i)$ and $1 \leq i, j \leq n$
$C=\{c_J^t(k)\}$	The observation probability for phase layer in which $c_J^t(k) = P[o_t = v_k \mid Q_t = J]$
$B=\{b_j^t(k)\}$	The observation probability for state layer in which $b_j^t(k) = P[o_t = v_k \mid q_t = j]$
$O=\{o_1, o_2, \cdots, o_T\}$	The observation series
$\pi_{il} = P[q_t = i \wedge Q_t = I]$	The initial state distribution in which $1 \leq i \leq n$ and $1 \leq I \leq N$

3.2   Parameter Estimation

All equations of Layered HMM can be derived similar to conventional HMM. However without losing generality we only derive the forward algorithm for a two layer HMM as we apply such algorithm to calculate likelihood in next section. In addition, we assume a one-to-one relation among states and phases for hidden self-similarity. Similar to HMM, we consider the forward variable $\alpha_t(I, i)$ defined as

$$\alpha_t(I,i) = P(o_1, o_2, \cdots o_t, Q_t = I \wedge q_t = i \mid \Theta) \tag{1}$$

which is the probability of the partial observation sequence, $o_1, o_2, \cdots o_t$ at time t at state i and phase I, given the model Θ. Following the *Baum-Welch* forward procedure algorithm we can solve for $\alpha_t(I, i)$ inductively as follows:

Initialization:

$$\alpha_1^\Theta(J, j) = \pi_{(J,j)} P(o_1 \mid Q_1 = J \wedge q_1 = j) \tag{2}$$

Induction:

$$\alpha_{t+1}^{\Theta}(J,j) = \left[\sum_{I=1}^{N}\sum_{i=1}^{n}\alpha_t^{\Theta}(I,i)\cdot W_{(I,i)(J,j)}\right]*P(o_{t+1}\mid Q_{t+1}=J \wedge q_{t+1}=j) \qquad (3)$$

in which $W_{(I,i)(J,j)}$ is the transition matrix form state i and phase I to state j in phase J. We will show how we calculate this transition matrix in a simple way.

Termination:

$$P(O\mid\Theta) = \sum_{I=1}^{N}\sum_{i=1}^{n}\alpha_t^{\Theta}(I,i) \qquad (4)$$

3.3   Self-Similarity Definition and Conditions

In geometry, self-similarity comes with the term *fractal*. *Fractals* have two interesting features. First they are self-similar on multiple scales. Second, *fractals* have a fractional dimension, as opposed to an integer dimension that idealized objects or structures have. To address self-similarity in Layered HMMs, we define three major types of Markovian Self-Similar structures: *structural self-similarity*, *hidden self-similarity* and *strong self-similarity*.

Structural Self-Similarity: The structural self-similarity refers to similarity in structure in different layers. In our example if phase structure transition be equivalent to the state structure transition, we consider model Θ as a self-similar HMM. In this case, we will have $r_{IJ} = s_{ij}$ if $i=I$, $J=j$ and $n=N*2$. This type of self-similarity refers to the structure of the layers. The scale of self-similarity can goes further depends on the nature of the problem. It is important to mention that in general, in modeling via HMM the number of states preferably keep low to reduce the complexity and to increase accuracy. One of the main advantage of SSLHMM as it was described is that it reduces the number of states dramatically.

Hidden Self-Similarity: The Hidden self-similarity refers to similarity in observation distribution in different layers. We define Hidden self-similarity as the following. There is a permutation of I,i, $I = \Psi(i)$ in which $P(o_t \mid \Psi(i)) = P(o_t \mid (\Psi(i),i))$ in which

$$P(o_t \mid (\Psi(i),i)) = \sum_{j=1}^{n}P(o_t \mid (\Psi(i),j))\cdot P(j\mid\Psi(i)) = \sum_{j=1}^{n}P(o_t \mid j)\cdot P(j\mid\Psi(i)) \qquad (5)$$

in our example if we assume $\Psi(1)=I, \Psi(2)=II$ and $\Psi(3)=III$, the above mention property for *state* 1 and *phase I* will be as the following:

$$P(o_t \mid (1,I)) = P(o_t \mid (I,1))P(1 \mid I) + P(o_t \mid (I,2))P(2 \mid I) + P(o_t \mid (I,3))P(3 \mid I) \qquad (6)$$

We refer to this type of self-similarity as *hidden* because it is not intuitive and it is very hard to recognize.

Strong Self-Similarity: A SSLHMM $\Theta = (\lambda, \Lambda)$ is *strong self-similar* if the model satisfies requirements of *structural self-similarity* and *hidden self-similarity*.

3.4   Assumptions

In the following we describe our major assumptions, definitions and lemmas to re-write the sequence likelihood.

Decomposability: we assume layers in a Layered HMM model are decomposable. The probability of occupancy of a given state in a given layer is:

$$P[Q_{t+1} = J \wedge q_{t+1} = j] = P[Q_{t+1} = J] * P[q_{t+1} = j \mid Q_{t+1} = J] \qquad (7)$$

Decomposability property assumes that system transition matrix is decomposable to phase transition matrix and state transition matrix. Considering such assumption, the overall transition probability for a given state to another state is a Tensor product of phase transition and state transition. For a multi-layered HMM the over all transition probability would be equal to *Tensor products* of HMM transition models. Without loosing generality we only explain the detail of a 2-layer SSLHMM. The transition probability among states and phases will be as following:

$$P[Q_{t+1} = J \wedge q_{t+1} = j \mid Q_t = I \wedge q_t = i] = r_{IJ} \times s_{ij} \qquad (8)$$

We show the tensor product with W.

$$W = S \otimes R \quad \text{and} \quad w_{(I,i)(J,j)} = r_{IJ} \times s_{ij} \qquad (9)$$

Example: If we consider the transition probability for state layer and phase layer as

$$S = \begin{bmatrix} .2 & .3 & .5 \\ .7 & .1 & .2 \\ .3 & .1 & .6 \end{bmatrix} \text{ and } R = \begin{bmatrix} .2 & .3 & .5 \\ .7 & .1 & .2 \\ .3 & .1 & .6 \end{bmatrix}, \text{ we will have :}$$

$$W = \begin{bmatrix} .04 & .06 & .1 & .06 & .09 & .15 & .1 & .15 & .25 \\ .14 & .02 & .04 & .21 & .03 & .06 & .35 & .05 & .1 \\ .06 & .02 & .12 & .09 & .03 & .18 & .15 & .05 & .3 \\ .14 & .21 & .35 & .02 & .03 & .05 & .04 & .06 & .01 \\ .49 & .07 & .14 & .07 & .01 & .02 & .14 & .02 & .04 \\ .21 & .07 & .42 & .03 & .01 & .06 & .06 & .02 & .12 \\ .06 & .09 & .15 & .02 & .03 & .05 & .12 & .18 & .3 \\ .21 & .03 & .06 & .07 & .01 & .02 & .42 & .06 & .12 \\ .09 & .03 & .18 & .03 & .01 & .06 & .18 & .06 & .36 \end{bmatrix}$$

Lemma 1: Tensor Product of HMMs: Considering a HMM Model as $\lambda = (W, B, \pi)$, it is possible to decompose λ to smaller models if $\exists W_1, W_2$ of order $|W_1|$ and $|W_2|$ such that $|W| = |W_1| \times |W_2|$ and $W = W_1 \otimes W_2$.

Note: Not all HMMs are decomposable to a Tensor product of smaller models.

Lemma 2: Markov Property of HMMs Tensor Products: If S and R are Markovian transition matrix then $W = R \otimes S$ is Tensor Markov.

$$\sum_{J=1}^{N} R_{IJ} = 1 \text{ for all } I \in R \text{ and } \sum_{j=1}^{n} S_{ij} = 1 \text{ for all } i \in S \tag{10}$$

$$\sum_{J=1}^{N}\sum_{j=1}^{n} W_{(I,i)(J,j)} = \sum_{J=1}^{N}\sum_{j=1}^{n} r_{IJ} s_{ij} = \sum_{J=1}^{N} r_{IJ} \sum_{j=1}^{n} s_{ij} = 1 \tag{11}$$

Any Tensor Markov Model $|W_1| \times |W_2|$ is isomorphic by a Markov Model to order of $|W| = |W_1| \times |W_2|$.

3.5   Re-writing Sequence Likelihood

By using above mentioned assumptions we can re-write the sequence likelihood for a strong self-similar (one-to-one) HMM as following. *Hidden self-similarity* implies:

$$P(o_{t+1} \mid Q_{t+1} = J \wedge q_{t+1} = j) = P(o_{t+1} \mid q_{t+1} = j) \text{ if } J = j \tag{12}$$

Decomposability assumption along with *structural self-similarity* make it possible to calculate W. Hence equation (3) becomes as:

$$\alpha_{t+1}^{\Theta}(J, j) = \left[\sum_{I=1}^{N}\sum_{i=1}^{n} \alpha_t^{\Theta}(I,i) \cdot W_{(I,i)(J,j)}\right] * P(o_{t+1} \mid q_{t+1} = j) \text{ if } i = j \tag{13}$$

$$\alpha_{t+1}^{\Theta}(J, j) = \left[\sum_{I=1}^{N}\sum_{i=1}^{n} \alpha_t^{\Theta}(I,i) \cdot W_{(I,i)(J,j)}\right] * \sum_{j=1}^{n} P(o_t \mid j) \cdot P(j \mid \Psi(i)) \text{ if } i \neq j$$

3.6   The Learning Process

The learning procedure for SSLHMM is similar to traditional HMM via the expectation maximization (EM) [19] except the calculation of $\alpha_t(i, I)$ and $\beta_t(i, I)$ as above. We can choose $\Theta = (\lambda, \Lambda, Z)$ such that its likelihood $P(O \mid \Theta)$ is locally maximized using an iterative procedure such as *Baum-Welch* method. This procedure iterates between E step which fixes the current parameters and computes posterior probabilities over the hidden states and M step which uses these probabilities to maximize the expected log likelihood of the observation. We derived forward variable α in last section, and deriving B, the backward parameter is similar to forward parameter.

4   Result

We have applied SSLHMM approach to synthetic data and a Network domain database. Our implementation is in *MATLAB* programming language and has been tested on Pentium III 450 MHz processor with 384 MB RAM.

4.1   Experiment 1: Synthetic Data

To compare SSLHMM with HMM, we employed a SSLHMM simulator with the capability of simulation of discrete and continuous data. In our simulator, a user has the capability to define the number of sequence in experimental pool, length of each sequence, number of layers, number of states in each phase, number of phases and observation set for discrete environment or a range for continuous observation. We verified that the synthetic data is indeed self-similar with H=.6. In this paper we only report the comparison of *Baum-Welch forward algorithm* for HMM with n_{HMM} states and a 2-layer *strong* SSLHMM with N phases and n states. The main purpose of this experiment is built on the following chain of principles:

Assume there is a sequence of observation O generated by a self-similar structure.

- We would like to estimate HMM parameter for such data (n assume to be known in advance)
- We would like to adjust model parameters $\lambda = (S, B, \pi)$ to maximize $P(O \mid \lambda)$.
- Model could be either a flat HMM or a SSLHMM
- We illustrate that for $O = \{o_1, o_2, \cdots, o_T\}$, $P(O \mid SSLHMM)$ is higher than $P(O \mid HMM)$, the probability of the observation given each model.
- We also observed that if O is not generated by a SSLHMM but by a HMM $P(O \mid SSLHMM) \approx P(O \mid HMM)$. However due to space limitation we do not show the result.

We ran a series of test for a problem consists of pre-selected number of states, up to 15 perceptions and 100 sequence of observation for each run. We assume the number of states and phases are known so *Baum-Welch* algorithm uses n_{HMM} to build the model and SSLHMM use N and n (number of phases and number of states). The assumption of *strong* self-similarity implies that $n = N^2$, as we have a copy of phase structure inside of each phase to present state layer. We repeat the whole experience with a random distribution for each phase but in a self-similar fashion and for a variety of different n and N. First we trained on the 50% of the data and find *P(Model | train)* for both HMM and SSLHMM. In second step we calculate *P(Model | test)* where "*test*" is the remaining 50% of the data. Fig. 2 shows *-log(likelihood)* of different experiments. A smaller number of *-log(likelihood)* indicate a higher probability. We ran HMM with prior number of states equal to 9, 16 and 64, and SSLHMM with

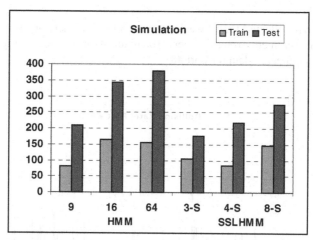

Fig. 2. Negative log likelihood for synthetic data. "x-s" indicates a 2 layers SSLHMM with x as number of state in each layer

number of phases equal to 3, 4 and 8 (shown as 3-s, 4-s and 8-s in the Fig. 4. As we may see the best model of SSLHMM outperforms the best model of HMM. In addition, the average -log(likelihood) of modeling through SSLHMM in all experiences is lower than modeling through HMM by 39%.

4.2   Experiment 2: Network Data

Understanding the nature of traffic in high-speed, high-bandwidth communications is essential for engineering and performance evaluation. It is important to know the traffic behavior of some of the expected major contributors to future high-speed network traffic. There have been a handful research and development in this area to analyze LAN traffic data. Analyses of traffic data from networks and services such as ISDN traffic and Ethernet LAN's have all convincingly demonstrated the presence of features such as self-similarity, long term dependence, slowly decaying variance and fractal dimensions.[10, 14].

In this experiment we applied the same principle similar to synthetic data experiment. A sample of network data is logged by the Spectrum NMP. There are 16 ports p_n on the routers that connect to 16 links, which in turn connect to 16 Ethernet subnets (S_n). Note that traffic has to flow through the router ports in order to reach the 16 subnets. Thus, we can observe the traffic that flows through the ports. There are three independent variables:

- *Load*: a measure of the percentage of bandwidth utilization of a port during a 10 minute period.
- *Packet Rate:* a measure of the rate at which packets are moving through a port per minute.
- *Collision Rate:* a measure of the number of packets during a 10 minute period that have been sent through a port over the link but have collided with other packets.

Data has collected for 18 weeks, from '94 to '95. There are 16,849 entries, representing measurements roughly every 10 minutes for 18 weeks. Fig. 3 illustrates an example of collected data for port #8.

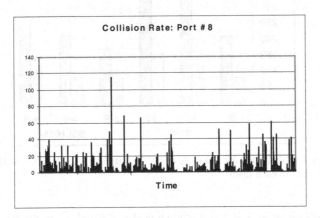

Fig. 3. The number of collisions of port #8. Data show self-similarity over different scales

We applied the HMM and SSLHMM to a given port of database with the purpose of modeling the Network data. We did test our technique through cross validation and in each round we trained the data with a random half of the data and test over the rest. We repeat the procedure for Load, Packet Rate and Collision Rate on all 16 ports. Fig. 4 illustrates the comparison of HMM and SSLHMM for Load, Packet Rate and Collision Rate. Respectively, we ran HMM with prior number of states equal to 2, 3, 4, 9 and 16, and SSLHMM with number of phases equal to 2, 3 and 4 (shown as 2-s, 3-s and 4-s in the Fig. 4). As it shows in Fig. 4 the SSLHMM model with $N=4$ outperforms other competitors in all series of experiments. Our experiment showed - $log(likelihood)$ increases dramatically for models with number of sates grater than 16 as it over fits the data. The best SSLHMM performance beats the best HMM by 23%, 41% and 38% for Collision Rate, Load and Packets Rate respectively.

Our experiments show SSLHMM approach behave properly and does not perform worse than HMM even when the data is not self similar or when we do not have enough information. The SSLHMM provides a more satisfactory model of the network data from three point of views. First, the time complexity is such that it is possible to consider model with a large number of states in a hierarchy. Second, these larger number of states do not require excessively large numbers of parameters relative to the number of states. Learning a certain part of the whole structure is enough to extend to the rest of the structure. Finally SSLHMM resulted in significantly better predictors; the test set likelihood for the best SSLHMM was 100 percent better than the best HMM

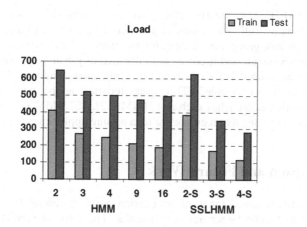

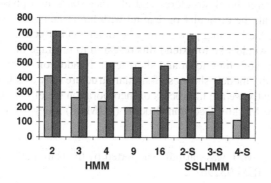

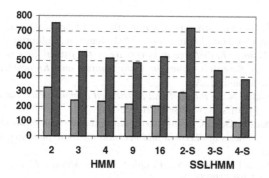

Fig. 4. The comparison of negative log likelihood for Network data for *Load, Packets Rate* and *Collision Rate*. SSLHMM outperform HMM in all three experiments

While the SSLHMM is clearly better predictor than HMM, it is easily interpretable than an HMM as well. The notion of phase may be considered as a collection of locally connected sets, groups, levels, categories, objects, states or behaviors as a collection of certain behavior and it comes with the idea of granularity, organization and hierarchy. As it mentioned before in Network application domain a phase could define as "congestion" or "stable". This characteristics is the main advantage of SSLHMM over other approaches such as FHMM [12]. SSLHMM is designed toward better interpretation as one the main goal of data mining approaches in general.

5   Conclusion and Future Work

Despite the relatively broad range of application areas, a general HMM, could not easily scale up to handle larger number of states. The error of predictive modeling will increased dramatically when the number of sates goes up. In this paper we proposed SSLHMM and illustrate it is a better estimation than flat HMM when data shows self-similar property. Moreover, we introduced three different types of self-similarity along with some result on synthetic data and experiments on Network data. Since SSLHMM has hierarchical structures and abstract states into phases, it overcomes, to a certain extent, the difficulty of dealing with larger number of states at the same layer, thus making the learning process move efficient and effective.

As future work we would like to extend this research to leverage the MLP power for precise prediction in both long term and short term. In addition we would like to extend this work when the model shows self-similar structure only at a limited range of structure scale. Currently we are in process of incorporation of self-similar property for Partially Observable Markov Decision Process (POMDP) along with generalization of SSLHMM.

Acknowledgement. This work was partially supported by the National Science Foundation under grant: NSF-IDM 9529615.

References

1. Adibi, J., Shen, W-M. *General structure of mining through layered phases.* submitted to *International Conference on Data Engineering.* (2002). San Jose, California, USA: IEEE.
2. Barbara, D. *Chaotic Mining: Knowledge discovery using the fractal dimension.* in *ACM SIGMOD Workshop on Research Issues in Data Mining and Knowledge Discovery (DMKD).* (1999). Philadelphia, USA,.
3. Bertsekas, D.C., Tsitsiklis, N. J., *Parallel and distributed computation: Numerical Methods.* (1989), Englewood Clifffs, New Jersey: Printice-Hall.
4. Boutilier, R.I., Brafman, I., Geib, C. *Prioritized goal decomposition of Markov Decision Processes: Toward a synthesis of classical and decision theoretic planning.* in *IJCAI-97.* (1997). Nagoya, Japan.
5. Brand, N., Oliver, N., and Pentland, A.,. *Coupled Hidden Markov Models for complex action recognition.* in *CVPR.* (1997).
6. Chang, J.W., Glass, J, *Segmentation and modeling in segment-based recognition.* (1997).

7. Cohen, J., *Segmentation speech using dynamic programming*. ASA, (1981). **69**(5): p. 1430-1438.
8. Dean, T.L., S.H. *Decomposition techniques for planning in stochastic domains*. in *IJCAI*. (1995). Montreal, CA.
9. Faloutsos, C., Seeger, B., Traina, A. and Traina Jr., C. *Spatial Join selectivity using power law*. in *SIGMOD*. (2000). Dallas, TX.
10. Feldmann, A., Gilbert, A. C., Willinger, W., Kurtz, T.G., *The changing nature of Network traffic: Scaling phenomena*. ACM Computer Communication Review,, (1998). **28**(April): p. 5-29.
11. Fine, S., Singer Y, Tishby N, *The hierarchical Hidden Markov Model: Analysis and applications*. Machine Learning, (1998). **32**(1): p. 41-62.
12. Ghahramani, Z., Jordan, M., *Factorial Hidden Markov Models*. Machine Learning, (1997). **2**: p. 1-31.
13. Holmes, W.J., Russell, M. L., *Probablistic-trajectory segmental HMMs*. Computer Speech and Languages, (1999). **13**: p. 3-37.
14. Leland, W., Taqqu, M., Willinger, W., Wilson, D. *On the self-similar nature of Ethernet traffic*. in *ACM SIGComm*. (1993). San Francisco, CA.
15. Oates, T. *Identifying distinctive subsequences in multivariate time series by clustering*. in *KDD-99*. (1999). San Diego, CA: ACM.
16. Pearl, J., *Probabilistic reasoning in intelligence: Network of plausible inference*. (1988), San Mateo, CA: Morgan Kaufmann.
17. Precup, D., Sutton, R. S., *Multi-time models for temporally abstract planning*, in *NIPS-11*, M. Moser, Jordan, M.Petsche, T., Editor. 1998, MIT Press: Cambridge.
18. Puterman, M.L., *Markov Decision Process: discrete stochastic dynamic programming*. (1994), New Yourk: Wiley.
19. Rabiner, L.R., *A tutorial on Hidden Markov Models and selected applications in speech recognition*. IEEE, (1989). **7**(2): p. 257-286.
20. Sutton, R., Barto, A., *Reinforcement learning: An Introduction*. (1998), Cambridge: MIT Press.
21. Traina, C., Traina, A., Wu, L., and Faloutsos, C. *Fast feature selection using the fractal dimension*. in *XV Brazilian Symposium on Databases (SBBD)*. (2000). Paraiba, Brazil.
22. Vogler, C., Metaxas, D. *Parallel Hidden Markov Models for American Sign Language recognition*. in *International Conference on Computer Vision*. (1999). Kerkyra, Greece.
23. Williams, C., Hinton, G.E., ed. *Mean field networks that leat discriminate temporally distorted strings*. , ed. D. Touretzkey, Elman, J., Sejnowski, T. and Hinton G. (1991).
24. Willinger, W., Taqqu M. S., Erramilli, A., ed. *A bibliographical guide to self-similar trace and performance modeling for modern high-speed networks*. Stochastic Networks: Theory and Applications, ed. F.P. Kelly, Zachary, S. and Ziedins, I. (1996), Clarendon Press, Oxford University Press: Oxford. 339-366.

Automatic Text Summarization Using Unsupervised and Semi-supervised Learning

Massih-Reza Amini and Patrick Gallinari

LIP6, University of Paris 6, Case 169, 4 Place Jussieu
F – 75252 Paris cedex 05, France
{amini,gallinari}@poleia.lip6.fr

Abstract. This paper investigates a new approach for unsupervised and semi-supervised learning. We show that this method is an instance of the Classification EM algorithm in the case of gaussian densities. Its originality is that it relies on a discriminant approach whereas classical methods for unsupervised and semi-supervised learning rely on density estimation. This idea is used to improve a generic document summarization system, it is evaluated on the Reuters news-wire corpus and compared to other strategies.

1 Introduction

Many machine learning approaches for information access require a large amount of supervision in the form of labeled training data. This paper discusses the use of unlabeled examples for the problem of text summarization.

Automated summarization dates back to the fifties [12]. The different attempts in this field have shown that human-quality text summarization was very complex since it encompasses discourse understanding, abstraction, and language generation [25]. Simpler approaches were explored which consist in extracting representative text-spans, using statistical techniques and/or techniques based on superficial domain-independent linguistic analyses. For these approaches, summarization can be defined as the selection of a subset of the document sentences which is representative of its content. This is typically done by ranking the document sentences and selecting those with higher score and with a minimum overlap. Most of the recent work in summarization uses this paradigm. Usually, sentences are used as text-span units but paragraphs have also been considered [18, 26]. The latter may sometimes appear more appealing since they contain more contextual information. Extraction based text summarization techniques can operate in two modes: generic summarization, which consists in abstracting the main ideas of a whole document and query-based summarization, which aims at abstracting the information relevant for a given query.

Our work takes the text-span extraction paradigm. It explores the use of unsupervised and semi-supervised learning techniques for improving automatic summarization methods. The proposed model could be used both for generic and query-based summaries. However for evaluation purposes we present results on a generic summarization task. Previous work on the application of machine learning techniques for summa-

L. De Raedt and A. Siebes (Eds.): PKDD 2001, LNAI 2168, pp. 16–28, 2001.

rization [6, 8, 11, 13, 29] rely on the supervised learning paradigm. Such approaches usually need a training set of documents and associated summaries, which is used to label the document sentences as relevant or non-relevant for the summary. After training, these systems operate on unlabeled text by ranking the sentences of a new document according to their relevance for the summarization task.

The method that we use, to make the training of machine learning systems easier for this task, can be interpreted as an instance of the Classification EM algorithm (CEM) [5, 15] under the hypothesis of gaussian conditional class densities. However instead of estimating conditional densities, it is based on a discriminative approach for estimating directly posterior class probabilities and as such it can be used in a non parametric context. We present one algorithm upon on linear regression in order to compute posterior class probabilities.

The paper is organized as follows, we first make a brief review of semi-supervised techniques and recent work in text summarization (Sect. 2). We present the formal framework of our model and its interpretation as a CEM instance (Sect. 3). We then describe our approach to text summarization based on sentence segment extraction (Sect. 4). Finally we present a series of experiments (Sect. 5).

2 Related Work

Several innovative methods for automated document summarization have been explored over the last years, they exploit either statistical approaches [4, 26, 31] or linguistic approaches [9, 14, 22], and combinations of the two [2, 8]. We will focus here on a statistical approach to the problem and more precisely on the use of machine learning techniques.

From a machine learning perspective, summarization is typically a task for which there is a lot of unlabelled data and very few labeled texts so that semi-supervised learning seems well suited for the task. Early work for semi supervised learning dates back to the 70s. A review of the work done prior to 88 in the context of discriminant analysis may be found in [15]. Most approaches propose to adapt the EM algorithm for handling both labeled and unlabeled and to perform maximum likelihood estimation. Theoretical work mostly focuses on gaussian mixtures, but practical algorithms may be used for more general settings, as soon as the different statistics needed for EM may be estimated. More recently this idea has motivated the interest of the machine learning community and many papers now deal with this subject. For example [19] propose an algorithm which is a particular case of the general semi-supervised EM described in [15], and present an empirical evaluation for text classification. [16] adapt EM to the mixture of experts, [23] propose a Kernel Discriminant Analysis which can be used for semi-supervised classification.

The co-training paradigm [3] is also related to semi supervised training. Our approach bears similarities with the well-established decision directed technique, which has been used for many different applications in the field of adaptive signal processing [7].

For the text summarization task, some authors have proposed to use machine learning techniques. [11] and [29] consider the problem of sentence extraction as a classification task. [11] propose a generic summarization model, which is based on a Naïve-Bayes classifier: each sentence is classified as relevant or non-relevant for the summary and those with highest score are selected. His system uses five features: an indication of whether or not the sentence length is below a specified threshold, occurrence of cue words, position of the sentence in the text and in the paragraph, occurrence of frequent words, and occurrence of words in capital letters, excluding common abbreviations.

[13] has used several machine learning techniques in order to discover features indicating the salience of a sentence. He addressed the production of generic and user-focused summaries. Features were divided into three groups: locational, thematic and cohesion features. The document database was CMP-LG also used in [29], which contains human summaries provided by the text author. The extractive summaries required for training were automatically generated as follows: the relevance of each document sentence with respect to the human summary is computed, highest score sentences are retained, for building the extractive summary. This model can be considered both as a generic and a query-based text summarizer.

[6] present an algorithm which generates a summary by extracting sentence segments in order to increase the summary concision. Each segment is represented by a set of predefined features such as its location, the average term frequencies of words occurring in the segment, the number of title words in the segment. Then they compare three supervised learning algorithms: C4.5, Naïve-Bayes and neural networks. Their conclusion is that all three methods successfully completed the task by generating reasonable summaries.

3   Model

In this section, we introduce an algorithm for performing unsupervised and semi-supervised learning. This is an iterative method that is reminiscent of the EM algorithm. At each iteration, it makes use of a regression model for estimating posterior probabilities that are then used for assigning patterns to classes or clusters. The unsupervised version of the algorithm may be used for clustering and the semi-supervised version for classifying. Both versions will be described using an unified framework. This algorithm can be shown to be an instance of the Classification EM (CEM) algorithm [5, 15] in the particular case of a gaussian mixture whose component densities have equal covariance matrices (section 3.3). In order to show that, we will make use of some basic results on linear regression and Bayes decision, they are introduced in section 3.2. For our application, we are interested in two class classification, we thus restrict our analysis to the two class case.

3.1   Theoretical Framework

We consider a binary decision problem where there are available a set of labeled data D_l and a set of unlabelled data D_u. D_u will always be non empty, whereas for unsupervised learning, D_l is empty.

Formally we will note, $D_l=\{(x_i, t_i)|i=1,\ldots,n\}$ where $x_i \in IR^d$, $t_i=(t_{1i},t_{2i})$ is the indicator vector for x_i and $D_u=\{x_i \mid i=n+1,\ldots,n+m\}$. The latter are assumed to have been drawn from a mixture of densities with two components C_1, C_2 in some unknown proportions π_1,π_2. We will consider that unlabeled data have an associated missing indicator vector $t_i=(t_{1i},t_{2i})$, $(i=n+1, \ldots, n+m)$ which is a class or cluster indicator vector.

3.2 Discriminant Functions

We give below some basic results on the equivalence between Bayes decision functions and linear regression that will be used for the interpretation of our learning algorithm as a CEM method.

3.2.1   Bayesian Decision Rule for Normal Populations

For two normal populations with a common covariance matrix $N(\mu_1,\Sigma)$ and $N(\mu_2,\Sigma)$ the optimal Bayesian discriminant function is [7]:

$$g_B(x) = (\mu_1-\mu_2)^t.\Sigma^{-1}.x + x_0 \tag{1}$$

Where x_0 is a given threshold. The decision rule is to decide C_1 if $g_B(x)>0$ and C_2 otherwise.

3.2.2   Linear Regression

Let X be a matrix whose i^{th} row is the vector x_i and Y be the corresponding vector of targets whose i^{th} element is a if $x_i \in C_1$ and b if $x_i \in C_2$. For a and b chosen such that $|C_1|.a + |C_2|.b = 0$, e.g. $a=\dfrac{|C_1|+|C_2|}{|C_1|}$ and $b= -\dfrac{|C_1|+|C_2|}{|C_2|}$, the solution to the minimization of the mean squared error (MSE) $\left\| Y - W^t X \right\|^2$ is:

$$W = \alpha.\Sigma^{-1}.(m_1 - m_2) \tag{2}$$

The corresponding discriminant function is :

$$g_R(x) = W^t (x-m) = \alpha.(m_1 - m_2)^t.\Sigma^{-1}.(x - m) \tag{3}$$

where m_k and Σ respectively denote the mean and the variance of the data for the partition C_k and α is a constant (see e.g. [7]). and m is the mean of all of the samples. The decision rule is: decide C_1 if $g_R(x)>0$ and otherwise decide C_2.

By replacing the mean and covariance matrix in (1) with their plug in estimate used in (2), the two decision rules g_B and g_R are similar up to a threshold. The threshold estimate of the optimal Bayes decision rule can be easily computed from the data so that regression estimate could be used for implementing the optimal rule if needed. For practical applications however, there is no warranty that the optimal Bayesian rule will give better results.

3.3 Classification Maximum Likelihood Approach and Classification EM Algorithm

In this section we will introduce the classification maximum likelihood (CML) approach to clustering [28]. In this unsupervised approach there are N samples generated via a mixture density:

$$f(x,\Theta) = \sum_{k=1}^{c} \pi_k f_k(x,\theta_k) \tag{4}$$

Where the f_k are parametric densities with unknown parameters θ_k, c is the number of mixture components, π_k is the mixture proportion. The goal here is to cluster the samples into c components $P_1, .., P_c$. Under the mixture sampling scheme, samples x_i are taken from the mixture density (4), and the CML criterion is [5, 15]:

$$\log L_{CML}(P,\pi,\theta) = \sum_{k=1}^{c} \sum_{i=1}^{N} t_{ki} \log\{\pi_k \cdot f_k(x_i,\theta_k)\} \tag{5}$$

Note that this is different from the mixture maximum likelihood (MML) approach where we want to optimize the following criterion:

$$\log L_M(P,\pi,\theta) = \sum_{k=1}^{N} \log(\sum_{i=1}^{c} \pi_k \cdot f_k(x_i,\theta_k)) \tag{6}$$

In the MML approach, the goal is to model the data distribution, whereas in the CML approach, we are more interested into clustering the data. For CML the mixture indicator t_{ki} for a given data x_i is treated as an unknown parameter and corresponds to a hard decision on the mixture component identity. Many clustering algorithms are particular cases of CML [5, 24]. Note that CML directly provides a partition of the data, for MML a partition can be obtained by assigning x to the group with maximal posterior probability $p(P_i/x)$.

The classification EM algorithm (CEM) [5, 15] is an iterative technique, which has been proposed for maximizing (5), it is similar to the classical EM except for an additional C-step where each x_i is assigned to one and only one component of the mixture. The algorithm is briefly described below.

CEM

Initialization : start from an initial partition $P^{(0)}$

j^{th} *iteration*, $j \geq 0$:

E –step. Estimate the posterior probability that x_i belongs to P_k ($i=1,..., N$; $k=1,...,c$):

$$E[t_{ki}^{(j)} / x_i; P^{(j)}, \pi^{(j)}, \theta^{(j)}] = \frac{\pi_k^{(j)} \cdot f_k(x_i; \theta_k^{(j)})}{\sum_{k=1}^{c} \pi_k^{(j)} \cdot f_k(x_i; \theta_k^{(j)})} \tag{7}$$

C – step. Assign each x_i to the cluster $P_k^{(j+1)}$ with maximal a posteriori probability according to (7)

M–step. Estimate the new parameters $(\pi^{(j+1)}, \theta^{(j+1)})$ which maximize $\log L_{CML}(P^{(j+1)}, \pi^{(j)}, \theta^{(j)})$.

CML can be easily modified to handle both *labeled and unlabeled* data, the only difference is that in (7) the t_{ki} for labeled data are known, (5) becomes:

$$\log L_C(P,\pi,\theta) = \sum_{k=1}^{c} \sum_{x_i \in P_k} \log\{\pi_k.f_k(x_i,\theta_k)\} + \sum_{k=1}^{c} \sum_{i=n+1}^{n+m} t_{ki} \log\{\pi_k.f_k(x_i,\theta_k)\} \qquad (8)$$

CEM can also be adapted to the case of semi supervised learning: for maximizing (8), the t_{ki} for the labeled data are kept fixed and are estimated as in the classical CEM (E and C steps) for the unlabeled data.

3.4   CEM and Linear Regression

We will show now that CEM could be implemented using a regression approach instead of the classical density estimation approach. In CEM, parameters $(\pi^{(j)}, \theta^{(j)})$ are used to compute the posterior probability so as to assign data to the different clusters in the C-step. However, instead of estimating these probabilities, one could use a regression approach for directly assigning data to the different clusters during the C-step.

We will show that in the case of two normal populations with equal covariance matrices, these two approaches are equivalent.

For a given partition $P^{(j)}$ corresponding to an iteration of the CEM algorithm, suppose we perform a regression of the input matrix X whose columns are the x_i against the target vector Y whose i^{th} row is a if $x_i \in P_1^{(j)}$ and b if $x_i \in P_2^{(j)}$ with a and b as described in section 3.2.2. In this case, the decision rule inferred from the regression estimation together with an appropriate threshold, will be the optimal Bayes decision rule with plug in maximum likelihood estimates. Using this decision rule derived from the linear regression, we could then assign the data to the different clusters and the partition $P^{(j+1)}$ will be exactly the same as the one obtained from the classical mixture density version of CEM.

Therefore the E-step in the CEM algorithm may be replaced by a regression step and the decision obtained for the C-step will be unchanged.

Because we are interested here only in classification or clustering, if we use the regression approach, the M-step is no more necessary, the regression CEM algorithm could start from an initial partition, the jth step consists in classifying unlabeled data according to the decision rule inferred from the regression. It can easily be proved that this EM algorithm converges to a local maximum of the likelihood function (5) for unsupervised training and (8) for semi-supervised training. The algorithm is summarized below:

Regression-CEM
    Initialisation : start from an initial partition $P^{(0)}$
    j^{th} iteration, $j \geq 0$:

    E-step : compute $W^{(j)} = \alpha.\hat{\Sigma}^{(j)^{-1}}.(m_1^{(j)} - m_2^{(j)})$

    C-step : classify the x_is according to the sign($W^{(j)}x_i + w_0^{(j)}$) into $P_1^{(j+1)}$ or

$P_2^{(j+1)}$.

In the above algorithm, posterior probabilities are directly estimated via a discriminant approach. All other approaches we know of for unsupervised or semi supervised learning rely on generative models and density estimation. This is an original aspect of our method and we believe that this may have important consequences. In practice for classification, direct discriminant approaches are usually far more efficient and more robust than density estimation approaches and allow for example to reach the same performance by making use of fewer labeled data. A more attractive reason for applying this technique is that for non linearly separable data, more sophisticated regression based classifiers such as non linear Neural Networks or non linear Support Vector Machines may be used instead of the linear classifier proposed above. Of course, for such cases, the theoretical equivalence with the optimal decision rule is lost.

Regression CEM can be used both for unsupervised and semi supervised learning. For the former, the whole partition is re-estimated at each iteration, for the latter, targets of labeled data are kept fixed during all iterations and only unlabelled data are reassigned at each iteration. In the unsupervised case, the results will heavily depend on the initial partition of the data.

For our text summarization application we have performed experiments for both cases.

4   Automatic Text Summary System

4.1   A Base Line System for Sentence Classification

Many systems for sentence extraction have been proposed which use similarity measures between text spans (sentences or paragraphs) and queries, e.g. [8, 13]. Representative sentences are then selected by comparing the sentence score for a given document to a preset threshold. The main difference between these systems is the representation of textual information and the similarity measures they are using. Usually, statistical and/or linguistic characteristics are used in order to encode the text (sentences and queries) into a fixed size vector and simple similarities (e.g. cosine) are then computed.

We will build here on the work of [10] who used such a technique for the extraction of sentences relevant to a given query. They use a *tf-idf* representation and compute the similarity between sentence s_k and query q as:

$$Sim_1(q,s_k) = \sum_{w_i \in s_k, q} tf(w_i,q).tf(w_i,s_k).\left(1 - \frac{\log(df(w_i)+1)}{\log(n+1)}\right)^2 \qquad (9)$$

Where, $tf(w,x)$ is the frequency of term w in x (q or s_k), $df(w)$ is the document frequency of term w and n is the total number of documents in the collection. Sentence s_k and query q are pre-processed by removing stop-words and performing Porter-reduction on the remaining words. For each document a threshold is then estimated from data for selecting the most relevant sentences.

Our approach for the sentence extraction step is a variation of the above method where the query is enriched before computing the similarity. Since queries and sentences may be very short, this allows computing more meaningful similarities. Query expansion - via user feedback or via pseudo relevance feedback - has been successfully used for years in Information Retrieval (IR) e.g. [30]. The query expansion proceeds in two steps: first the query is expanded via a similarity thesaurus - WordNet in our experiments - second, relevant sentences are extracted from the document and the most frequent words in these sentences are included into the query. This process can be iterated. The similarity we consider is then:

$$Sim_2(q,s_k) = \sum_{w_i \in s_k, q} \bar{tf}(w_i,q).tf(w_i,s_k).\left(1 - \frac{\log(df(w_i)+1)}{\log(n+1)}\right) \qquad (10)$$

Where, $\bar{tf}(w,q)$ is the number of terms within the "semantic" class of w_i in the query q. This extraction system will be used as a baseline system for evaluating the impact of learning throughout the paper. Although it is basic, similar systems have been shown to perform well for sentence extraction based text summarization. For example [31] uses such an approach, which operates only on word frequencies for sentence extraction in the context of generic summaries, and shows that it compares well with human based sentence extraction.

4.2   Learning

We propose below a technique, which takes into account the coherence of the whole set of relevant sentences for the summaries and allows to significantly increasing the quality of extracted sentences.

4.2.1   Features

We define new features in order to train our system for sentence classification. A sentence is considered as a sequence of terms, each of them being characterized by a set of features. The sentence representation will then be the corresponding sequence of these features.

We used four values for characterizing each term w of sentence s: $tf(w,s)$, $\bar{tf}(w,q)$, $(1-(\log(df(w)+1)/\log(n+1)))$ and $Sim_2(q,s)$ -computed as in (10)- the similarity between q and s. The first three variables are frequency statistics which give the importance of a term for characterizing respectively the sentence, the query and the document. The last one gives the importance of the sentence containing w for the summary and is used in place of the term importance since it is difficult to provide a meaningful measure for isolated terms [10].

4.2.2   The Learning Text Summary System

In order to provide an initial partition $P^{(0)}$, for the semi-supervised learning we have labeled 10% of sentences in the training set using the news-wire summaries as the correct set of sentences. And for the unsupervised learning we have used the baseline system's decision. We then train a linear classifier with a sigmoïd output function to label all the sentences from the training set, and iterate according to algorithm *regression-CEM*.

5   Experiments

5.1   Data Base

A corpus of documents with the corresponding summaries is required for the evaluation. We have used the Reuters data set consisting of news-wire summaries [20]: this corpus is composed of 1000 documents and their associated extracted sentence summaries. The data set was split into a training and a test set. Since the evaluation is performed for a generic summarization task, collecting the most frequent words in the training set generated a query. Statistics about the data set collection and summaries are shown in table 1.

5.2   Results

Evaluation issues of summarization systems have been the object of several attempts, many of them being carried within the tipster program [21] and the Summac competition [27].

Table 1. Characteristics of the Reuters data set and of the corresponding summaries.

Collection	Training	Test	All
# of docs	300	700	1000
Average # of sentences/doc	26.18	22.29	23.46
Min sentence/doc	7	5	5
Max sentence/doc	87	88	88
News-wire summaries			
Average # of sentences /sum	4.94	4.01	4.3
% of summaries including 1st sentence of docs	63.3	73.5	70.6

This is a complex issue and many different aspects have to be considered simultaneously in order to evaluate and compare different summarizers [17].

Our methods provide a set of relevant document sentences. Taking all the selected sentences, we can build an *extract* for the document. For the evaluation, we compared this extract with the news-wire summary and used Precision and Recall measures, defined as follows:

$$\text{Precision} = \frac{\text{\# of sentences extracted by the system which are in the news - wire summaries}}{\text{total \# of sentences extracted by the system}}$$

$$\text{Recall} = \frac{\text{\# of sentences extracted by the system which are in the news - wire summaries}}{\text{total \# of sentences in the news - wire summaries}} \tag{11}$$

We give below the average precision (table 2) for the different systems and the precision/recall curves (figure 1). The baseline system gives bottom line performance, which allows evaluating the contribution of our training strategy. In order to provide an upper bound of the expected performances, we have also trained a classifier in a fully supervised way, by labeling all the training set sentences using the news-wire summaries.

Unsupervised and Semi-supervised learning provides a clear increase of performances (up to 9 %). If we compare these results to fully supervised learning, which is also 9% better, we can infer that with 10% of labeled data, we have been able to extract from the unlabeled data half of the information needed for this "optimal" classification.

Table 2. Comparison between the baseline system and different learning schemes, using linear sigmoid classifier. Performances are on the test set.

	Precision (%)	Total Average (%)
Baseline system	54,94	56,33
Supervised learning	72,68	74,06
Semi-Supervised learning	63,94	65,32
Unsupervised learning	63,53	64,92

We have also compared the linear Neural Network model to a linear SVM model in the case of unsupervised learning as shown at Table 3. The two models performed similarly, both are linear classifiers although their training criterion is slightly different.

Table 3. Comparison between two different linear models: Neural Networks and SVM in the case of Self-supervised learning. Performances are on the test set.

	Precision (%)	Total Average (%)
Self-Supervised learning with Neural-Networks	63,53	64,92
Self-Supervised learning with SVM	62,15	63,55

11-point precision recall curves allow a more precise evaluation of the system behavior. Let For the test set, let M be the total number of sentences extracted by the
system as relevant (correctly or incorrectly), N_s the total number of sentences extracted by the system which are in the newswire summaries, N_g the total number of
sentences in newswire summaries and N_t the total number of sentences in the test set.

Precision and recall are computed respectively as N_s/M and N_s/N_g. For a given
document, sentence s is ranked according to the decision of the classifier. Precision
and recall are computed for $M = 1,..,N_t$ and plotted here one against the other as an 11
point curve. The curves illustrate the same behavior as table 2, semi-supervised and
unsupervised behave similarly and for all recall values their performance increase is
half that of the fully supervised system. Unsupervised learning appears as a very
promising technique since no labeling is required at all. Note that this method could
be applied as well and exactly in the same way for query based summaries.

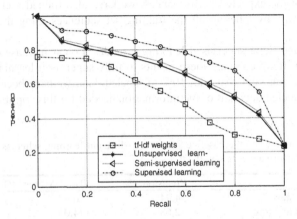

Fig. 1. Precision-Recall curves for base line system (square), unsupervised learning (star),
semi-supervised learning (triangle) and the supervised learning (circle).

6 Conclusion

We have described a text summarization system in the context of sentence based extraction summaries. The main idea proposed here is the development of a fully automatic summarization system using a unsupervised and semi-supervised learning paradigm. This has been implemented using simple linear classifiers, experiments on
Reuters news-wire have shown a clear performance increase. Unsupervised learning
allows to reach half of the performance increase allowed by a fully supervised system,
and is much more realistic for applications. It can also be used in exactly the same
way for query based summaries.

References

1. Anderson J.A., Richardson S.C. Logistic Discrimination and Bias correction in maximum likelihood estimation. *Technometrics*, 21 (1979) 71-78.
2. Barzilay R., Elhadad M. Using lexical chains for text summarization. Proceedings of the ACL'97/EACL'97 Workshop on Intelligent Scalable Text Summarization, (1997) 10-17.
3. Blum A., Mitchell T. Combining Labeled and Unlabeled Data with Co-Training. Proceedings of the 1998 Conference on Computational Learning Theory. (1998).
4. Carbonell J.G., Goldstein J. The use of MMR, diversity-based reranking for reordering documents and producing summaries. Proceedings of the 21st ACM SIGIR, (1998) 335-336.
5. Celeux G., Govaert G. A classification EM algorithm for clustering and two stochastic versions. Computational Statistics & Data Analysis. 14 (1992) 315-332.
6. Chuang W.T., Yang J. Extracting sentence segments for text summarization: a machine learning approach. Proceedings of the 23rd ACM SIGIR. (2000) 152-159.
7. Duda R. O., Hart P. T. Pattern Recognition and Scene Analysis. Edn. Wiley (1973).
8. Goldstein J., Kantrowitz M., Mittal V., Carbonell J. Summarizing Text Documents: Sentence Selection and Evaluation Metrics. Proceedings of the 22nd ACM SIGIR (1999) 121-127.
9. Klavans J.L., Shaw J. Lexical semantics in summarization. Proceedings of the First Annual Workshop of the IFIP working Group for NLP and KR. (1995).
10. Knaus D., Mittendorf E., Schauble P., Sheridan P. Highlighting Relevant Passages for Users of the Interactive SPIDER Retrieval System. in TREC-4 proceedings. (1994).
11. Kupiec J., Pedersen J., Chen F. A. Trainable Document Summarizer. Proceedings of the 18th ACM SIGIR. (1995) 68-73.
12. Luhn P.H. Automatic creation of literature abstracts. IBM Journal (1958) 159-165.
13. Mani I., Bloedorn E. Machine Learning of Generic and User-Focused Summarization. Proceedings of the Fifteenth National Conference on AI. (1998) 821-826.
14. Marcu D. From discourse structures to text summaries. Proceedings of the ACL'97/EACL'97 Workshop on Intelligent Scalable Text Summarization. (1997) 82-88.
15. McLachlan G.J. Discriminant Analysis and Statistical Pattern Recognition. Edn. John Wiley & Sons, New-York (1992).
16. Miller D., Uyar H. A Mixture of Experts classifier with learning based on both labeled and unlabeled data. Advances in Neural Information Processing Systems. 9 (1996) 571-577.
17. Mittal V., Kantrowitz M., Goldstein J., Carbonell J. Selecting Text Spans for Document Summaries: Heuristics and Metrics. Proceedings of the 6th National Conference on AI. (1999).
18. Mitra M., Singhal A., Buckley C. Automatic Text Summarization by Paragraph Extraction. Proceedings of the ACL'97/EACL'97 Workshop on Intelligent Scalable Text Summarization. (1997) 31-36.
19. Nigam K., McCallum A., Thrun A., Mitchell T. Text Classification from labeled and unlabeled documents using EM. In proceedings of National Conference on Artificial Intelligence. (1998).
20. http://boardwatch.internet .com/mag/95/oct/bwm9.html
21. NIST. TIPSTER Information-Retrieval Text Research Collection on CD-ROM. National Institute of Standards and Technology, Gaithersburg, Maryland. (1993).
22. Radev D., McKeown K. Generating natural language summaries from multiple online sources. Computational Linguistics. (1998).
23. Roth V., Steinhage V. Nonlinear Discriminant Analysis using Kernel Functions. Advances in Neural Information Processing Systems. 12 (1999).

24. Scott A.J., Symons M.J. Clustering Methods based on Likelihood Ratio Criteria. Biometrics. 27 (1991) 387-397.
25. Sparck Jones K.: Discourse modeling for automatic summarizing. Technical Report 29D, Computer laboratory, university of Cambridge. (1993).
26. Strzalkowski T., Wang J., Wise B. A robust practical text summarization system. Proceedings of the Fifteenth National Conference on AI. (1998) 26-30.
27. SUMMAC. TIPSTER Text Summarization Evaluation Conference (SUMMAC). *http://www-nlpir.nist.gov/related_projects/tipster_summac/*
28. Symons M.J. Clustering Criteria and Multivariate Normal Mixture. Biometrics. 37 (1981) 35-43.
29. Teufel S., Moens M. Sentence Extraction as a Classification Task. Proceedings of the ACL'97/EACL'97 Workshop on Intelligent Scalable Text Summarization. (1997). 58-65.
30. Xu J., Croft W.B. Query Expansion Using Local and Global Document Analysis. Proceedings of the 19th Annual International ACM SIGIR Conference on Research and Development in Information Retrieval. (1996). 4--11.
31. Zechner K.: Fast Generation of Abstracts from General Domain Text Corpora by Extracting Relevant Sentences. COLING. (1996) 986-989.

Detecting Temporal Change in Event Sequences: An Application to Demographic Data

H. Blockeel[1], J. Fürnkranz[2], A. Prskawetz[3], and F. C. Billari[3]

[1] Katholieke Universiteit Leuven
Department of Computer Science
Celestijnenlaan 200A, B-3001 Leuven, Belgium
Hendrik.Blockeel@cs.kuleuven.ac.be
[2] Austrian Research Institute for Artificial Intelligence
Schottengasse 3, A-1010 Wien, Austria
juffi@oefai.at
[3] Max Planck Institute for Demographic Research
Doberaner Straße 114, D-18507, Rostock, Germany
[fuernkranz,billari]@demogr.mpg.de

Abstract. In this paper, we discuss an approach for discovering temporal changes in event sequences, and present first results from a study on demographic data. The data encode characteristic events in a person's life course, such as their birth date, the begin and end dates of their partnerships and marriages, and the birth dates of their children. The goal is to detect significant changes in the chronology of these events over people from different birth cohorts. To solve this problem, we encoded the temporal information in a first-order logic representation, and employed Warmr, an ILP system that discovers association rules in a multi-relational data set, to detect frequent patterns that show significant variance over different birth cohorts. As a case study in multi-relational association rule mining, this work illustrates the flexibility resulting from the use of first-order background knowledge, but also uncovers a number of important issues that hitherto received little attention.

1 Introduction

In this paper, we study the problem of discovering patterns that exhibit a significant change in their relative frequency of occurrence over time. As was already argued by [8], in many domains the step beyond discovering frequent item sets to the discovery of second-order phenomena like the temporal change in these frequencies is of crucial importance.

The analysis of life courses is such a problem. In the social sciences, and especially in demography and sociology, there has been a diffusion of the so-called *life course approach* [15]. One of the principal interests in that approach is the study of how the lives of humans change as far as the age and the sequencing and the number of crucial events are concerned. To study the evolution of a whole society, it is common to analyze successive *cohorts* of people, i.e., groups

L. De Raedt and A. Siebes (Eds.): PKDD 2001, LNAI 2168, pp. 29–41, 2001.

of people that were born in the same period of time (e.g. the same year or the same decade).

Previous approaches to detecting change mostly propose special-purpose algorithms that had to treat time as special type of variable [12,8]. Instead, we suggest to address this problem by exploiting the power of a general, multi-dimensional data mining system. The system that we use—Warmr [9]—is based on the level-wise search of conventional association rule learning systems of the Apriori-family [1,11]. It extends these systems by looking for frequent patterns that may be expressed as conjunction of first-order literals. This expressive power allows to encode temporal relationships fairly easily. In fact, the system does not need to discriminate between temporal relations and other domain-dependent relations, which is typical for conventional solutions to sequence discovery [3,13], and lets them co-exist in a natural and straight-forward way.

2   The Dataset

The data for our analysis originate from the Austrian Fertility and Family Survey (FFS), which was conducted between December 1995 and May 1996. In the survey, retrospective histories of partnerships, births, employment and education were collected for 4,581 women and 1,539 men between ages 20 and 54. Hence, the Austrian FFS covers birth cohorts from 1941 to 1976. The retrospective histories of partnerships and fertility for each respondent allow us to determine the timing of all births in the current and any previous union. Moreover, information about the civil status of each partnership in any month of observation is available, which allows us to determine whether a union started as a marriage or whether it was transformed into a marriage later on.

We are interested in studying the main features that discriminate between the life courses of older and younger cohorts as far as the number of children, number and type of unions, fertility before and after unions, etc. are concerned. The present study should be considered a first step into that direction.

3   Multi-relational Data Mining – Using Warmr for Discovering Temporal Changes

The dataset under consideration is essentially a multi-relational dataset: a person's life course is not described with a single tuple but by a set of tuples. Most common data mining algorithms expect the data to reside in a single table, and when the data are actually stored in a database with multiple tables they have to be preprocessed: one needs to derive a single table from the original data that hopefully retains as much of the original information as possible. This is a non-trivial task. Two directions are possible: one is to devise automatic pre-processing methods, another is to use data mining methods that can handle a multi-relational database, e.g., inductive logic programming (ILP) methods [10]. Our approach falls into the second category as we employ the ILP system Warmr [9] to detect interesting patterns.

```
female(159).                      subject(I) :- female(I),
birth_date(159,6001).                          birth_date(I,X),
children(159,2).                               X >= 4100, X<=6000.
  child_birth_date(159,7810).     gen40(I) :- birth_date(I,X),
  child_birth_date(159,8706).                 X >= 4100, X<4600.
unions(159,2).                    child_out_of_wedlock_at_age(I,A) :-
  union(159,7805, 8106).             birth_date(I,X),
  union(159,8306, -2).               child_birth_date(I,M),
marriage_date(159,7807).             \+ (marriage_date(I,N), N=<M),
marriage_date(159,8706).             A is (M-X)/100, A =< 35.
```

Fig. 1. On the left, a Prolog encoding of a typical entry in the database is shown. This snapshot represents a female person with id 159 who was born in January 1960. Up to the interview date (≈ December 1995), she had formed two unions. The first lasted from May 1978 to June 1981, and the second started in June 1983 (and has not ended at the time of the interview). Both unions were converted to marriages (July 1978 and June 1987) and in each union one child was born (October 1978 and June 1987).

The right half shows a few predicate definitions that operated on the basic data encoding. The subject/1 predicate served as a key, and could be used to filter the data (in this case to admit only persons from cohorts 1941–60). gen40/1 encodes one of the class values (the cohort 1941–1945), and child_out_of_wedlock_at_age/2 shows an example for abstract background knowledge that can be defined upon the base predicates, as well as an example for censoring events above a certain age.

As multi-relational data mining is a relatively unexplored field, few guidelines exist as to the methodology that should be followed. Consequently, this section describes the complete data mining process that we employed for addressing our problem. On the way, we will also describe the workings of Warmr, the first-order data mining system that we used, as well as the way the data was represented for the use by this system. Although the following sections will only describe the final data representation, it should be noted that this was not the result of a top-down design, but of repeated exploration of several options.

3.1   Data Preprocessing

Data preprocessing consisted of several steps. First, the data were converted into a Prolog format. A typical entry is shown in the left half of Fig. 1. From then on, preliminary experiments could be run, which were helpful to further improve the quality of the domain representation.

To this base representation, we added several pieces of background knowledge in the form of Prolog predicates that operate upon these operational predicates. These were mostly conversions from dates to ages (which is needed when one wants to find, e.g., changes in the average age of marrying etc.), but also included complex high-level predicates such as child_out_of_wedlock_at_age/2, which encodes whether a person had a child out of wedlock. Most importantly, we included the </2 predicate, which allowed the system to compare ages at which

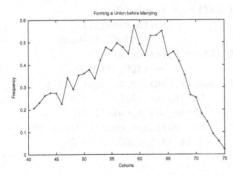

Fig. 2. Relative frequencies of people that had a union before they married. The steady increase up to 1960 is a true regularity, while the decline for the cohorts 1960 — 1975 is due to the fact that for increasingly many individuals of these cohorts, union formation and marriage has not yet taken place in their lives at the time of the interview ($\approx$ December 1995), but will presumably take place later.

events take place in people's life courses, and thus to describe their chronology. Note that this approach does not only allow to find sequences in the strict sense, but also partially ordered events, such as A<B, A<C, where the order of the events B and C is left open (both A<B<C and A<C<B are possible). It is precisely this facility which makes the use of a relational data mining system necessary, because this functionality cannot be achieved with a conventional, propositional association rule finder without using a pre-processing phase that encodes all possible event sequences as separate features. Note that such a procedure would basically reduce the task of the frequent pattern discovery to a single pass over all possible, pre-compiled sequences, which defeats the purpose of the efficient, level-wise search.

In addition, the flexibility of the first-order background knowledge also facilitated *censoring* of the data. In social sciences, this term describes the situation that, when using data collected from interviews where people are asked about their past experience of events, only their life courses up to the age at interview are available to the analyst. Such a situation can, e.g., be seen in the decline of frequencies of people that formed a union before they were married (Fig. 2). As people born after 1965 were, at the time of the interview ($\approx$ December 1995) 30 years or younger, it is quite natural that the probability for these people to have experienced certain events or event sequences in their life course is not the same as for people in their forties or older. Consequently, in preliminary experiments we discovered many rules because of the comparably low frequencies for marriage, union formation, and child birth for people born in the seventies.

After some experimentation, we decided to censor items in the following way:

– only people born in the forties or fifties were retained
– events in people's lives that occurred after the age of 35 were ignored

Censoring was easily done by adding inequations in the relevant definitions of background knowledge (like in the last rule of Fig. 2). Naturally, looking only at events happening before the age of 35 severely limits our study, but increasing this age limit could only be done at the expense of reducing the data set (in order to increase the age limit to 40 and yet avoid artificial patterns, the set of subjects would need to be reduced to those people born before 1956). Our choice is a compromise between keeping as much data as possible and looking at a reasonable set of events in people's lives.

The original dataset contained 6120 entries, 1539 representing male subjects, and 4581 representing female subjects. As the distribution of male and female subjects is obviously skewed, we decided to only work with the larger, female group.[1] Again, this could easily be achieved by adding an appropriate condition in subject/2 (see Fig. 1), which defines the key (as defined below).

3.2 Discovery of Frequent Patterns

Warmr [9] is an ILP system that discovers frequent patterns in a data set, where a "pattern" is defined as a conjunction of first order literals. For instance, in our data set patterns may look like this:

```
subject(S), married_at_age(S,A), child_at_age(S,B), B>A.
subject(S), child_at_age(S,A), child_at_age(S,B), B>A.
```

The first pattern describes a person S who married and subsequently had a child; the second one describes a person who had at least two children (with different ages).

Each pattern is associated with a so-called *key*: the frequency of a pattern is determined by counting the number of key items (i.e., the number of instantiations of the key variable) that satisfy the constraints stated in the pattern. In the above example, it is natural to have the subject S as the key.

Warmr can be considered a first-order upgrade of Apriori [1]; it performs a top-down level-wise search, starting with the key and refining patterns by adding literals to them. Infrequent patterns (i.e. patterns of which the frequency is below some predefined threshold) are pruned as are their refinements. We refer to [9] for more details.

3.3 Discovering Temporal Change

As described above, Warmr finds all patterns that have a frequency above a user-specified threshold. In a second phase, Warmr can combine these patterns into first order association rules; basically, these rules are of the form "*if* LHS *occurs, then* RHS *occurs with probability c*". Contrary to conventional, propositional association rule finders, patterns may be formulated in first-order logic, which allows conditions to be linked together by sharing the same variables.

In order to limit the number of possible rules, the current version of Warmr expects that the user provides a list of possible patterns that can occur on the left-hand side (LHS) or right-hand side (RHS) of a rule. This is done with Warmr's classes setting. More specifically, if there is a frequent pattern P and subsets A and B, such that $A \subset P$ is one of the classes and $B = P \backslash A$, then

---

[1] The over-sampling of female individuals was intentional in the family and fertility survey from which the data originate because fertility is more closely linked to female life courses.

Warmr returns the rules $A => B$ and $B => A$ (assuming they fulfill possible additional criteria, such as achieving a minimal confidence level).

In our application, we used the classes to separate people into different cohorts. After some experimentation, we decided to use four different cohorts, each encompassing a 5-year span. In Warmr, this could be simply encoded using generation literals as classes:

```
classes([gen40(_), gen45(_), gen50(_), gen55(_)]).
```

This tells Warmr that we expect to see rules of the following type[2]

```
gen40(S) => subject(S), child_at_age(S,A), child_at_age(S,B), B>A.
```

The rules are ordered according to their *interestingness*. Interestingness is defined in Warmr as the number of standard deviations the observed frequency of a pattern in an age group differs from the average frequency in the whole data set under consideration. More precisely, for a rule $A => B$, interestingness $d(A => B)$ is defined as

$$d(A => B) = \frac{p(B|A) - p(B)}{\sqrt{\frac{p(B)(1-p(B))}{n(A)}}} \approx \frac{\frac{n(A \wedge B)}{n(A)} - \frac{n(B)}{N}}{\sqrt{\frac{\frac{n(B)}{N}(1-\frac{n(B)}{N})}{n(A)}}}$$

where $p(B) \approx \frac{n(B)}{N}$ is the probability/relative frequency of the pattern B in the entire data set, whereas $p(B|A) \approx \frac{n(A \wedge B)}{n(A)}$ is the probability/relative frequency of the same pattern occurring in the subgroup defined by the class A. Hence, the numerator computes the deviation of the expected frequency of pattern B (if it were independent of A) from its actual frequency of occurrence in the subgroup defined by pattern A. This difference is normalized with the standard deviation that could be expected if $p(B)$ were the true frequency of occurrence of B within A. Thus, $d(A => B)$ computes the number of standard deviations that the actual frequency is away from the expected frequency. In our case, the interestingness measure compares the expected number of individuals that satisfy a certain pattern in a cohort to the expected number of individuals that should satisfy this pattern if the occurrence of the pattern were independent from the birth cohort.

3.4   Filtering of Semantic Redundancy

Many of the discovered rules are syntactically different but semantically equivalent because redundant conditions are added to a rule (if, e.g., a constraint that specifies that a person has more than 3 children is followed by redundant tests for having more than 2 or 1 children) or the same situation is expressed in different

---

[2] As mentioned above, Warmr will also produce rules of the form subject(S), child_at_age(S,A) ...=> gen40(S). because the evaluation of rules $A => B$ and $B => A$ may differ. However, as characteristic rules of the form gen40(S) => pattern are more natural to interpret, we applied a filter to Warmr's output that only retained this kind of rules.

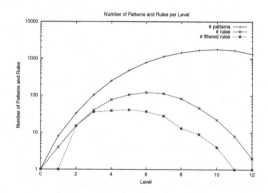

Fig. 3. The number of found patterns, the number of found rules and the number of semantically unique rules that remain after filtering. The scale on the y-axis is logarithmic.

ways (e.g., the above-mentioned constraint on the number of children can also be formulated using an equivalent number of `child_at_age/2` predicates together with inequalities that assure that they refer to successive events). Some (but not all) of these cases can be addressed by Warmr's configurable language bias (e.g., by specifying that only one constraint on the number of children is admissible in a rule) and its constraint specification language (e.g., by specifying that literal `p(X)` must not be added if literal `q(X)` already occurs). We will return to this issue in Sect. 5.

To reduce the number of rules, we employ a simple filtering strategy: for rules that share the same frequencies for all its components ($n(A)$, $n(B)$, $n(A \wedge B)$) and hence have the same measure of interestingness $d(A => B)$, we simply assume that they are semantically equivalent. In such cases we automatically removed all rules except those that were found at the minimum level (i.e., all but the shortest rules).[3]

Figure 3 shows the number of frequent patterns found in one of our experiments, the number of rules generated from these patterns, and the number of rules that survived the filtering process. What also becomes apparent is that the number of irrelevant and redundant patterns increases with the level. At level 10, where the largest number of frequent patterns is discovered (1795), only four rules survive the filtering, and at subsequent levels none remain (0 frequencies are shown as 1 in the log-scale).

3.5   Visualizing the Results

Rules reported by Warmr to be interesting (in the sense that they describe patterns whose frequency in a certain age group deviates significantly from its av-

---

[3] A better approximation of semantical equivalence would be to consider the actual sets of covered instances, instead of just their size. However, after inspecting a number of rules with the same interesting measure, we found no examples where rules with the same interestingness measure were not semantically equivalent, so we did not consider it worthwhile to implement this more accurate approximation. Concerning the choice of the simplest rule, when several rules had the same interestingness measure and the same complexity, we arbitrarily decided for one of them.

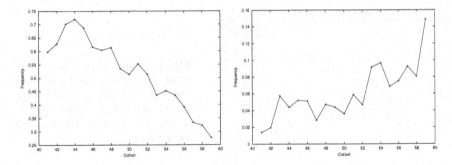

Fig. 4. The trends behind a very simple pattern and a very complex pattern. The left graph shows the negative trend in people that started their first union when they married. The pattern behind the right graph is explained in the text.

erage frequency in the entire population) were inspected manually, looking at the most interesting rules first. The temporal change of interesting patterns was visualized by plotting the frequency of occurrence of the pattern over 1-year cohorts from 1940 to 1960. This was very useful for assessing whether the found anomaly for one age group represented a trend throughout the years or only a temporary change in behavior. This phase could be enriched using a query language for trend shapes, such as the one proposed by [12].

4   Selected Results

In this section, we report on some of the results obtained in our case study. For these experiments we used the Warmr algorithm as implemented in the data mining tool ACE-ilProlog [6], version 1.1.6. We used the default settings for Warmr, except for a minimal support of 0.01 (the default is 0.1). No minimal confidence was specified for the generated rules.

The used background knowledge allowed the system to consider the events of child birth, start of a marriage and start of a union, and to order these events using inequalities, as well as test whether events occurred at the same time. To prevent infinite chains, the latter tests were restricted to ages originating from different event types (e.g., the system was not allowed to test the equality of two marriage dates), and only one equality test per pair of event types was allowed. In addition, all rules were initialized with the date of the first union. With this language, a Warmr run that went 16 levels deep took approximately 6 hours.

Figure 4 shows two discovered trends, one originating from a very simple rule, and the second from a fairly complex rule. The first pattern is the relation that people formed their first union when they married. This pattern was found with a negative deviation of 8.07 for the cohort 1956–1960, and with a positive deviation of 7.05 for the cohort 1941–1945. Together with its counter-part (Fig. 2), this pattern showed the strongest deviation of all discovered rules. Near these two

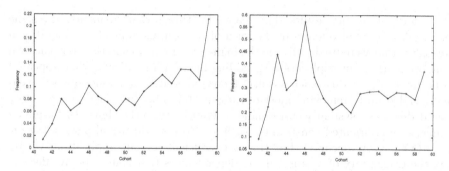

Fig. 5. People that have a child between their first union and a marriage over all people (left) and the same group over those people that had a marriage after their first union.

rules were several similar rules, that add minor restrictions to these rules (e.g., marrying at the time of the first union and having a child at a later time).

The second rule is shown below; it was found at level 7, with negative deviation of 2.17. Only a few rules at levels ≥ 8 survived the filtering process and none of them had a deviation of more than 2 standard deviations.

```
gen55(A) :- subject(A), first_union_at_age(A,B),
     married_at_age(A,C),C>B, child_at_age(A,D),D>C,
     child_at_age(A,E),E>B,
     married_at_age(A,F),F>E, child_at_age(A,G),G>E]
```

The first part of this rule states that persons satisfying this pattern married after their first union and had a child thereafter. The second part specifies that they had a child after their first union and after this child, they had both a marriage and a second child. Note that not all of the events in this rule are strictly ordered, and it is sometimes left open whether they refer to identical or different events. For example, both marriages referred to in the rule could be bound to the same marriage, in which case the pattern describes women that had at least two children, at least one of them before the marriage. However, all 6 event predicates could also refer to different events. The partial ordering of these events makes these patterns more general and may result in interesting combinations of subgroups.

More complicated rules have to be interpreted with caution, as can be seen from Fig. 5. Its left graph shows the trend for people that have a child between their first union and a marriage as discovered by the system, but the second graph, which normalizes this number over the number of people that had their first union before they married, shows that trend was mostly due to the trend in the normalizing pattern.

5   Lessons Learnt

An interesting, somewhat unexpected result of our explorations was that adding domain knowledge not only slows down the system but does not necessarily yield more interesting results. The reason for this is that frequently the same relationships were also found in the form of the conjunctions of the operational predicates that were used to define the high-level predicates in the first place. So while we started our exploration by adding high-level predicates that appeared to be interesting to us (such as `child_out_of_wedlock_at_age/2`), we eventually ended up in removing most of these patterns because they unnecessarily slowed down the system's performance.[4] Warmr currently allows to formulate simple, syntax-oriented constraints (such as "do not add literal `p(X)` if the literal `q(X)` already occurs"), but this is insufficient for our application, where, e.g., the transitivity of < causes many dependencies that cannot be avoided using the current constraint specification language. A more powerful language for expressing semantic constraints is clearly a promising topic for further research.

In particular for higher values of the frequency threshold, we often encountered the problem that negative deviations are often missed by the system. The reason for this is that patterns that occur significantly less frequently than expected are often below the frequency threshold. This is not a big problem in our application because a negative deviation for, e.g., the early cohorts 1941–1945 is typically paired with a positive deviation for the later cohorts 1956–1960, which is easily detected by the system. As we visually inspect the found patterns over all cohorts, it does not matter which deviation is found by the system.

In general, however, these issues may hint at an important shortcoming: in domains where frequency thresholds cannot be applied for effectively reducing the number of candidates (or can only reduce them at the expense of loosing interesting patterns) the level-wise search pioneered by Apriori might in fact not be a suitable choice. In particular if the search is performed in memory, alternative search strategies [5,16] might be considered because of their more flexible pruning strategies. It is an open research problem which strategy is more appropriate for multi-relational data mining systems like Warmr.

6   Related Work

The problem of detecting temporal change in frequent patterns by grouping objects over time was also studied by [4]. In their application, they discovered trends in student admissions to UCI in the years 1993–1998. Their approach was limited to detecting changes in propositional patterns (which they called contrast sets), while we consider change in temporal patterns.

The problem of discovering frequent episodes in event sequences could also be solved by other techniques [3,13]. These could then be post-processed with similar techniques for detecting deviations over time. In fact, [12] discuss such a two-phase solution to the problem of discovering trends in text databases. The first phase consists of discovering frequent phrases in documents, i.e., in sequences of words using the advanced sequence discovery algorithm described in [14]. In the

---

[4] The problem occurs less frequently in propositional tasks, but there too it is recognized that if such dependencies do exist, one needs special techniques to handle them [7].

second phase, the frequencies of the phrases over given time groups are determined, and their shape can be queried using the query language described in [2], which could, in principle, be replaced by our technique of detecting significant deviations from the mean over different periods of time.

The above-mentioned approaches basically treat the problem as a basket analysis problem with time as a special, designated variable that allows to integrate multiple baskets into single rules, as long as certain temporal constraints (e.g., a maximum window size) are followed. Our approach, however, is more general in the sense that it does not give a special role to time. Temporal relations are represented in the same way as other domain-dependent knowledge (even though this was not the main focus of this particular application). As a consequence, we are not only searching for sequential patterns (i.e., strict temporal orders of the form A<B<C), but for more general, graph-like structures (such as A<B and A<C).

Several people have recognized the importance of taking dependencies into account when searching for association rules, and proposed solutions, e.g., in the form of *itemset closures* [7]; some of that work is currently being extended to first-order association rules [De Raedt; personal communication], but we have no knowledge of existing publications in this area.

7 Conclusions

In this paper, we demonstrated a way for exploiting the generality of Warmr, a multi-relational data mining system, for the task of discovering temporal changes in sequential patterns. The generality of Warmr allows a straight-forward encoding of time-dependent information and a seamless integration with additional background knowledge, which facilitates ease of experimentation and flexibility in incorporating new knowledge. In particular, during our experimentation, we frequently changed the system's view of the data, e.g., by censoring recent cohorts and late events in people's life courses. Such changes could be handled by simple changes in the background knowledge, while the underlying data representation could remain the same.

On the other hand, our current experiments clearly show the need for handling dependencies in first order association rule mining in general. A specifically interesting consequence of this is that the use of background knowledge may hurt the performance of systems such as Warmr, rather than improving it. This is an important issue, as the possibility to use background knowledge is one of the advantages of ILP approaches. In the current version of Warmr, dependencies can to some extent be handled using syntactical constraints on clauses, but this is clearly insufficient to handle semantic dependencies between background knowledge definitions (e.g. the transitivity of <). Further research is needed to address such problems in first-order association rule mining.

Acknowledgements. Hendrik Blockeel is a post-doctoral fellow of the Fund for Scientific Research (FWO) of Flanders. The Austrian Research Institute for

Artificial Intelligence is supported by the Austrian Federal Ministry of Education, Science and Culture. The authors wish to thank the Advisory Group of the FFS programme of comparative research for its permission, granted under identification number 75, to use the FFS data on which this study is based. The views expressed in this paper are the authors' own views and do not necessarily represent those of the Max Planck Institute for Demographic Research.

References

1. R. Agrawal, H. Mannila, R. Srikant, H. Toivonen, and A. I. Verkamo. Fast discovery of association rules. In U. M. Fayyad, G. Piatetsky-Shapiro, P. Smyth, and R. Uthurusamy, (eds.) *Advances in Knowledge Discovery and Data Mining*, pp. 307–328. AAAI Press, 1995.
2. R. Agrawal, G. Psaila, E. L. Wimmers, and M. Zait. Querying shapes of histories. In *Proceedings of the 21st Conference on Very Large Databases (VLDB-95)*, Zürich, Switzerland, 1995.
3. R. Agrawal and R. Srikant. Mining sequential patterns. In *Proceedings of the International Conference on Data Engineering (ICDE)*, Taipei, Taiwan, 1995.
4. S. D. Bay and M. J. Pazzani. Detecting group differences: Mining contrast sets. *Data Mining and Knowledge Discovery*, 2001. To appear.
5. R. J. Bayardo Jr. and R. Agrawal. Mining the Most Interesting Rules. In *Proceedings of the 5th ACM SIGKDD International Conference on Knowledge Discovery and Data Mining*, pp. 145–154, 1999.
6. H. Blockeel, L. Dehaspe, B. Demoen, G. Janssens, J. Ramon, and H. Vandecasteele. Executing query packs in ILP. In J. Cussens and A. Frisch (eds.) *Proceedings of the 10th International Conference on Inductive Logic Programming (ILP-2000)*, pp. 60–77, London, UK, 2000. Springer-Verlag.
7. J.-F. Boulicaut and A. Bykowski. Frequent closures as a concise representation for binary data mining. In *Proceedings of the 4th Pacific-Asia Conference on Knowledge Discovery and Data Mining (PAKDD-00)*, pp. 62–73, Kyoto, Japan. Springer-Verlag.
8. S. Chakrabarti, S. Sarawagi, and B. Dom. Mining surprising patterns using temporal description length. In *Proceedings of the 24th Conference on Very Large Databases (VLDB-98)*, New York, NY, 1998.
9. L. Dehaspe and H. Toivonen. Discovery of frequent Datalog patterns. *Data Mining and Knowledge Discovery*, 3(1):7–36, 1999.
10. S. Džeroski and N. Lavrač (eds.). *Relational Data Mining: Inductive Logic Programming for Knowledge Discovery in Databases*. Springer-Verlag, 2001. To appear.
11. J. Hipp, U. Güntzer, and G. Nakhaeizadeh. Algorithms for association rule mining – a general survey and comparison. *SIGKDD explorations*, 2(1):58–64, June 2000.
12. B. Lent, R. Agrawal, and R. Srikant. Discovering trends in text databases. In *Proceedings of the 3rd International Conference on Knowledge Discovery and Data Mining (KDD-97)*, Newport Beach, CA, 1997.
13. H. Mannila, H. Toivonen, and A. I. Verkamo. Discovery of frequent episodes in event sequences. *Data Mining and Knowledge Discovery*, 1(3):259–289, 1997.
14. R. Srikant and R. Agrawal. Mining sequential patterns: Generalizations and performance improvements. In *Proceedings of the 5th International Conference on Extending Database Technology (EDBT)*, Avignon, France, 1996.

15. L. J. G. van Wissen and P. A. Dykstra (eds.). *Population Issues: An Interdisciplinary Focus*. Kluwer Academic/Plenum Publishers, New York, 1999.
16. G. I. Webb. Efficient search for association rules. In *Proceedings of the 6th ACM SIGKDD International Conference on Knowledge Discovery and Data Mining (KDD-2000)*, pp. 99–107, Boston, MA, 2000.

Knowledge Discovery in Multi-label Phenotype Data

Amanda Clare and Ross D. King

Department of Computer Science,
University of Wales Aberystwyth, SY23 3DB, UK
{ajc99,rdk}@aber.ac.uk

Abstract. The biological sciences are undergoing an explosion in the amount of available data. New data analysis methods are needed to deal with the data. We present work using KDD to analyse data from mutant phenotype growth experiments with the yeast *S. cerevisiae* to predict novel gene functions. The analysis of the data presented a number of challenges: multi-class labels, a large number of sparsely populated classes, the need to learn a set of accurate rules (not a complete classification), and a very large amount of missing values. We developed resampling strategies and modified the algorithm C4.5 to deal with these problems. Rules were learnt which are accurate and biologically meaningful. The rules predict function of 83 putative genes of currently unknown function at an estimated accuracy of $\geq 80\%$.

1   Introduction

The biological sciences are undergoing an unprecedented increase in the amount of available data. In the last few years the complete genomes of ~30 microbes have been sequenced, as well as that of "the worm" (*C. elegans*) and "the fly" (*D. melanogaster*). The last few months have seen the sequencing of the first plant genome Arabidopsis [10], and the greatest prize of all, the human genome [11,33]. In addition to data from sequencing, new post genomic technologies are enabling the large-scale and parallel interrogation of cell states under different stages of development and under particular environmental conditions, generating very large databases. Such analyses may be carried out at the level of mRNA using micro-arrays (e.g. [5,8]) (the transcriptome). Similar analyses may be carried out at the level of the protein to define the proteome (e.g. [2]), or at the level of small molecules, the metabolome (e.g. [27]). This data is replete with undiscovered biological knowledge which holds the promise of revolutionising biotechnology and medicine. KDD techniques are well suited to extracting this knowledge. Currently most KDD analysis of bioinformatic data has been based on using unsupervised methods e.g. [8,17,32], but some has been based on supervised methods [4,6,14]. New KDD methods are constantly required to meet the new challenges presented by new forms of bioinformatic data.

Perhaps the least analysed form of genomics data is that from phenotype experiments [25,22,18]. In these experiments specific genes are removed from the

L. De Raedt and A. Siebes (Eds.): PKDD 2001, LNAI 2168, pp. 42–53, 2001.

cells to form mutant strains, and these mutant strains are grown under different conditions with the aim of finding growth conditions where the mutant and the wild type (no mutation) differ ("a phenotype"). This approach is analogous to removing components from a car and then attempting to drive the car under different conditions to diagnose the role of the missing component.

In this paper we have developed KDD techniques to analyse phenotype experiment data. We wish to learn rules that given a particular set of phenotype experimental results predict the functional class of the gene mutated. This is an important biological problem because, even in yeast, one the best characterised organisms, the function of 30–40% of its genes are still currently unknown.

Phenotype experiment data presents a number of challenges to standard data analysis methods: the functional classes for genes exist in a hierarchy, a gene may have more than one functional class, and we wish to learn a set of accurate rules - not necessarily a complete classification. The recognition of functional class hierarchies has been one of the most important recent advances in bioinformatics [29,1,13]. For example in the Munich Information Center for Protein Sequences (MIPS) hierarchy (http://mips.gsf.de/proj/yeast/catalogues/funcat/) the top level of the hierarchy has classes such as: "Metabolism", "Energy", "Transcription" and "Protein Synthesis". Each of these classes is then subdivided into more specific classes, and these are in turn subdivided, and then again subdivided, so the hierarchy is up to 4 levels deep. An example of a subclass of "Metabolism" is "amino-acid metabolism", and an example of a subclass of this is "amino-acid biosynthesis". An example of a gene in this subclass is YPR145w (gene name ASN1, product "asparagine synthetase"). In neither machine learning or statistics has much work has been done on classification problems where there is a class hierarchy. However, such problems are relatively common in the real world, particularly in text classification [16,24,21]. We deal with the class hierarchy by learning separate classifiers for each level. This simple approach has the unfortunate side-effect of fragmenting the class structure and producing many classes with few members - e.g. there are 99 potential classes represented in the data for level 2 in the hierarchy. We have therefore developed a resampling method to deal with the problem of learning rules from sparse data and few examples per class.

Perhaps an even greater difficulty with the data is that genes may have more than one functional class. This is reflected in the MIPS classification scheme (where a single gene can belong to up to 10 different functional classes). This means that the classification problem is a *multi-label* one (as opposed to *multi-class* which usually refers to simply having more than two possible disjoint classes for the classifier to learn). There is only a limited literature on such problems, for example [12,20,30]. The UCI repository [3] currently contains just one dataset ("University") that can be considered a multi-label problem. (This dataset shows the academic emphasis of individual universities, which can be multi-valued, for example, business-education, engineering, accounting and fine-arts). The simplest approach to the multi-label problem is to learn separate classifiers for each class (with all genes not belonging to a specific class used as negative examples for that class). However this is clearly cumbersome and time-consuming when there are many classes - as is the case in the functional hierarchy for yeast. Also, in sparsely populated classes there would be very few positive examples of a class and overwhelmingly many negative examples. We have therefore developed a new algorithm based on the successful decision tree algorithm C4.5 [26].

A third challenge in prediction of gene function from phenotype data is that we wish to learn a set of rules which accurately predict functional class. This differs from the standard statistical and machine learning supervised learning task of maximising the prediction accuracy on the test set. The problem resembles in some respects association rule learning in data mining.

In summary our aim is to discover new biological knowledge about:

- the biological functions of genes whose functions are currently unknown
- the different discriminatory power of the various growth conditions under which the phenotype experiments are carried out

For this we have developed a specific machine learning method which handles the problems provided by this data:

- many classes
- multiple class labels per gene
- the need to know accuracies of individual rules rather than the ruleset as a whole

2 Experimental Method

2.1 Data

We used three separate sources of phenotypic data: TRIPLES [18], EUROFAN [25] and MIPS [22].

- The TRIPLES (TRansposon-Insertion Phenotypes, Localization and Expression in *Saccharomyces*) data was generated by randomly inserting transposons into the yeast genome.
  URLs: http://ygac.med.yale.edu/triples/triples.htm, (raw data)
  http://bioinfo.mbb.yale.edu/genome/phenotypes/ (processed data)
- EUROFAN (European functional analysis network) is a large European network of research which has created a library of deletion mutants by using PCR-mediated gene replacement (replacing specific genes with a marker gene (kanMX)). We used data from EUROFAN 1.
  URL: http://mips.gsf.de/proj/eurofan/
- The MIPS (Munich Information Center for Protein Sequences) database contains a catalogue of yeast phenotype data.
  URL: http://mips.gsf.de/proj/yeast/

The data from the three sources were concatenated together to form a unified dataset, which can be seen at http://users.aber.ac.uk/ajc99/phenotype/. The phenotype data has the form of attribute-value vectors: with the attributes being the growth media, the values of the attributes being the observed sensitivity or resistance of the mutant compared with the wildtype, and the class the functional class of the gene. Notice that this data will not be available for all genes due to some mutants being inviable or untested, and not all growth media were tested/recorded for every gene, so there were *very many missing values* in the data.

The values that the attributes could take were the following:

n	no data
w	wild-type (no phenotypic effect)
s	sensitive (less growth than for the wild-type)
r	resistance (better growth than for the wild-type)

There were 69 attributes, 68 of which were the various growth media (e.g. calcofluor_white, caffeine, sorbitol, benomyl), and one which was a discretised count of how many of the media this mutant had shown a reaction to (i.e. for how many of the attributes this mutant had a value of "s" or "r").

2.2 Algorithm

The machine learning algorithm we chose to adapt for the analysis of phenotype data was the well known decision tree algorithm C4.5 [26]. C4.5 is known to be robust, and efficient [23]. The output of C4.5 is a decision tree, or equivalently a set of symbolic rules. The use of symbolic rules allows the output to be interpreted and compared with existing biological knowledge - this is not generally the case with other machine learning methods, such as neural networks, or support vector machines.

In C4.5 the tree is constructed top down. For each node the attribute is chosen which best classifies the remaining training examples. This is decided by considering the information gain, the difference between the entropy of the whole set of remaining training examples and the weighted sum of the entropy of the subsets caused by partitioning on the values of that attribute.

$$information\_gain(S, A) = entropy(S) - \sum_{v \in A} \frac{|S_v|}{|S|} * entropy(S_v)$$

where A is the attribute being considered, S is the set of training examples being considered, and S_v is the subset of S with value v for attribute A. The algorithms behind C4.5 are well documented and the code is open source, so this allowed the algorithm to be extended.

Multiple labels are a problem for C4.5, and almost all other learning methods, as they expect each example to be labeled as belonging to just one class. For yeast this isn't the case, as a gene may belong to several different classes. In the case of a single class label for each example the entropy for a set of examples is just

$$entropy(S) = - \sum_{i=1}^{N} p(c_i) \log p(c_i)$$

where $p(c_i)$ is the probability (relative frequency) of class c_i in this set.

We need to modify this formula for multiple classes. Entropy is a measure of the amount of uncertainty in the dataset. It can be thought of as follows: Given an item of the dataset, how much information is needed to describe that item? This is equivalent to asking how many bits are needed to describe all the classes it belongs to.

To estimate this we sum the number of bits needed to describe membership or non-membership of each class (see appendix for intuition). In the general case where there are N classes and membership of each class c_i has probability $p(c_i)$ the total number of bits needed to describe an example is given by

$$-\sum_{i=1}^{N} \left((p(c_i) \log p(c_i)) + (q(c_i) \log q(c_i)) \right)$$

where
$p(c_i)$ = probability (relative frequency) of class c_i
$q(c_i) = 1 - p(c_i)$ = probability of not being member of class c_i

Now the new information after a partition according to some attribute, can be calculated as a weighted sum of the entropy for each subset (calculated as above), where this time, weighted sum means if an item appears twice in a subset because it belongs to two classes then we count it twice.

In allowing multiple labels per example we have to allow leaves of the tree to potentially be a set of class labels, i.e. the outcome of a classification of an example can be a set of classes. When we label the decision tree this needs to be taken into account, and also when we prune the tree. When we come to generate rules from the decision tree, this can be done in the usual way, except when it is the case that a leaf is a set of classes, a separate rule will be generated for each class, prior to the rule-pruning part of the C4.5rules algorithm. We could have generated rules which simply output a set of classes - it was an arbitrary choice to generate separate rules, chosen for comprehensibility of the results.

2.3 Resampling

The large number of classes meant that many classes have quite small numbers of examples. We were also required only to learn a set of accurate rules, not a complete classification. This unusual feature of the data made it necessary for us to develop a complicated resampling approach to estimating rule accuracy based on the bootstrap.

All accuracy measurements were made using the m-estimate [9] which is a generalisation of the Laplace estimate, taking into account the *a priori* probability of the class. The m-estimate for rule r (M(r)) is:

$$M(r) = \frac{p + m\frac{P}{P+N}}{p + n + m}$$

where

P = total number of positive examples,
N = total number of negative examples.
p = number of positive examples covered by rule r,
n = number of negative examples covered by rule r
m = parameter to be altered

Using this formula, the accuracy for rules with zero coverage will be the *a priori* probability of the class. m is a parameter which can be altered to weight the *a priori* probability. We used m=1.

The data set in this case is relatively small. We have 2452 genes with some recorded phenotypes, of which 991 are classified by MIPS as "Unclassified" or "Classification not yet clear-cut". These genes of unknown classification cannot be used in supervised learning (though we can later make predictions for them). This leaves just 1461, each with many missing values. At the top level of the classification hierarchy (the most general classes), there are many examples for each class, but as we move to lower, more specific levels, the classes become more sparsely populated, and machine learning becomes difficult.

We aimed to learn rules for predicting functional classes which could be interpreted biologically. To this end we split the data set into 3 parts: training data, validation data to select the best rules from (rules were chosen that had an accuracy of at least 50% and correctly covered at least 2 examples), and test data. We used the validation data to avoid overfitting rules to the data. However, splitting the dataset into 3 parts means that the amount of data available for training will be even less. Similarly only a small amount will be available for testing. Initial experiments showed that the split of the data substantially affected the rulesets produced, sometimes producing many good rules, and sometimes none. The two standard methods for estimating accuracy under the circumstance of a small data set are 10-fold cross-validation and the bootstrap method [15,7]. Because we are interested in the rules themselves, and not just the accuracy, we opted for the bootstrap method, because a 10-fold cross validation would make just 10 rulesets, whereas bootstrap sampling can be used to create hundreds of samples of the data and hence hundreds of rulesets. We can then examine these and see which rules occur regularly and are stable, not just artifacts of the split of the data.

The bootstrap is a method where data is repeatedly sampled with replacement to make hundreds of training sets. A classifier is constructed for each sample, and the accuracies of all the classifiers can be averaged to give a final measure of accuracy. First a bootstrap sample was taken from the original data. Items of the original data not used in the sample made up the test set. Then a new sample was taken with replacement *from the sample*. This second sample was used as training data, and items that were in the first sample but not in the second made up the validation set. All three data sets are non-overlapping.

We measured accuracy on the held-out test set. We are aware that this will give a *pessimistic* measure of accuracy (i.e. the true accuracy on the whole data set will be higher), but this is acceptable.

3   Results

We attempted to learn rules for all classes in the MIPS functional hierarchy http://mips.gsf.de/proj/yeast/catalogues/funcat/, using the catalogue as it was on 27 September 1999. 500 bootstrap samples were made, and so C4.5 was run 500 times and 500 rulesets were generated and tested. To discover which rules were stable and reliable we counted how many times each rule appeared across the 500 rulesets. Accurate stable rules were produced for many of the classes at levels 1 and 2 in the hierarchy. At levels 3 and 4 (the most specific levels with the least populated classes) no useful rules were found. That is, at the lower levels, few rules were produced and these were not especially general or accurate.

The good rules are generally very simple, with just one or two conditions necessary to discriminate the classes. This was expected, especially since most mutants were only sensitive/resistant to a few media. Some classes were far easier to recognise than others, for example, many good rules predicted class "CELLULAR BIOGENESIS" and its subclass "biogenesis of cell wall (cell envelope)".

Some examples of the rules and their accuracies follow. The full set of rules can be seen at http://users.aber.ac.uk/ajc99/phenotype/ along with the data sets used.

The 4 most frequently appearing rules at level 1 (the most general level in the functional catalogue) are all predictors for the class "CELLULAR BIOGEN-ESIS". These rules suggest that sensitivity to zymolase or papulacandin_b, or any reaction (sensitivity or resistance) to calcofluor_white is a general property of mutants whose deleted genes belong to the CELLULAR BIOGENESIS class. All correct genes matching these rules in fact also belong to the subclass "biogenesis of cell wall (cell envelope)". The rules are far more accurate than the prior probability of that class would suggest should occur by chance.

These are two of the rules regarding sensitivity/resistance to Calcofluor White.

```
if  the gene is sensitive to calcofluor white and
    the gene is sensitive to zymolyase
    then its class is "biogenesis of cell wall (cell envelope)"
Mean accuracy:        0.909
Prior prob of class: 0.095
Std dev accuracy:     0.018
Mean no. matching genes: 9.3
```

```
if  the gene is resistant to calcofluor white
    then its class is "biogenesis of cell wall (cell envelope)"
Mean accuracy:        0.438
Prior prob of class: 0.095
Std dev accuracy:     0.144
Mean no. matching genes: 6.7
```

These rules confirm that Calcofluor White is useful for detecting cell wall mutations [28,19]. Calcofluor White is a negatively charged fluorescent dye that

Table 1. Number of genes of unknown function predicted

Level 1			
estimated accuracy	std. deviations from prior		
	2	3	4
≥ 80%	83	72	35
≥ 70%	209	150	65
≥ 50%	211	150	65

Level 2			
estimated accuracy	std. deviations from prior		
	2	3	4
≥ 80%	63	63	63
≥ 70%	77	77	77
≥ 50%	133	126	126

does not enter the cell wall. Its main mode of action is believed to be through binding to chitin and prevention of microfibril formation and so weakening the cell wall. The explanation for disruption mutations in the cell wall having increased sensitivity to Calcofluor White is believed to be that if the cell wall is weak, then the cell may not be able to withstand further disturbance. The explanation for resistance is less clear, but the disruption mutations may cause the dye to bind less well to the cell wall. Zymolase is also known to interfere with cell wall formation [19]. Neither rule predicts the function of any gene of currently unassigned function. This is not surprising given the previous large scale analysis of Calcofluor White on mutants.

One rule that does predict a number of genes of unknown function is:

```
if   the gene is sensitive to hydroxyurea
     then its class is "nuclear organization"
Mean accuracy:        0.402
Prior prob of class: 0.215
Std dev accuracy:     0.066
Mean no. matching genes: 33.4
```

This rule predicts 27 genes of unassigned function. The rule is not of high accuracy but it is statistically highly significant. Hydoxyurea is known to inhibit DNA replication [31], so the rule makes biological sense.

Table 1 shows the number of genes of unassigned function predicted by the learnt rules at levels 1 and 2 in the functional hierarchy. These are plotted as a function of the estimated accuracy of the predictions and the significance (how many standard deviations the estimated accuracy is from the prior probability of the class). These figures record genes predicted by rules that have appeared at least 5 times during the bootstrap process.

It can be seen that analysis of the phenotype growth data allows the prediction of the functional class of many of the genes of currently unassigned function.

Table 2 shows the number of rules found for the classes at level 1. We did not expect to be able to learn rules for every class, as some classes may not be distinguishable given the growth media that were used.

Table 3 shows some general statistics for the rulesets. Due to the nature of the bootstrap method of collecting rules, only *average* accuracy and coverage can be computed (rather than *total*), as the test data set changes with each bootstrap sample.

Table 2. Number of rules that appeared more than 5 times at level 1, broken down by class. Classes not shown had no rules (2/0/0/0, 8/0/0/0, 10/0/0/0, 13/0/0/0 and 90/0/0/0)

number of rules	class no	class name
17	1/0/0/0	METABOLISM
32	3/0/0/0	CELL GROWTH, CELL DIVISION AND DNA SYNTHESIS
3	4/0/0/0	TRANSCRIPTION
1	5/0/0/0	PROTEIN SYNTHESIS
2	6/0/0/0	PROTEIN DESTINATION
1	7/0/0/0	TRANSPORT FACILITATION
21	9/0/0/0	CELLULAR BIOGENESIS (proteins are not localized to the corresponding organelle)
5	11/0/0/0	CELL RESCUE, DEFENSE, CELL DEATH AND AGEING
77	30/0/0/0	CELLULAR ORGANIZATION (proteins are localized to the corresponding organelle)

Table 3. General statistics for rules that appeared more than 5 times. Surprisingly high accuracy at level 4 is due to very few level 4 classes, with one dominating class

	no. rules	no. classes represented	av rule accuracy	average rule coverage (genes)
level 1	159	9	62%	20
level 2	74	12	49%	11
level 3	9	2	25%	18
level 4	37	1	71%	28

4   Discussion and Conclusion

Working with the phenotypic growth data highlighted several learning issues which are interesting:

- We had to extend C4.5 to handle the problem of genes having more than one function, the multi-label problem.
- We needed to select rules for biological interest rather than predicting all examples, this required us to use an unusual rule selection procedure, and this together with the small size of data set led to our choice of the bootstrap to give a clearer picture of the rules themselves.

Biologically important rules were learnt which allow the accurate prediction of functional class for ~200 genes. We are in the process of experimentally testing these predictions. The prediction rules can be easily comprehended and compared with existing biological knowledge. The rules are also useful as they show future experimenters *which media provide the most discrimination between functional classes*. Many types of growth media are shown to be highly informative for identifying the functional class of disruption mutants (e.g. Calcofluor White), others are of little value (e.g. sodium chloride). The nature of the C4.5

algorithm is always to choose attributes which split the data in the most informative way. This knowledge can be used in the next round of phenotypic experiments.

Our work illustrates the value of cross-disciplinary work. Functional genomics is enriched by a technique for improved prediction of the functional class of genes: and KDD is enriched by provision of new data analysis challenges.

Acknowledgments. We would like to thank Ugis Sarkans for initial collection of the data and Stephen Oliver and Douglas Kell for useful discussions.

Appendix: Reasoning Behind Multi-class Entropy Formula

This appendix gives an intuition into the reason for the multi-class entropy formula.

How many bits are needed to describe all the classes an item belongs to? For a simple description, we could use a bitstring, 1 bit per class, to represent each example. With 4 classes {a,b,c,d}, an example belonging to classes b and d could be represented as 0101. But this will usually be more bits than we actually need. Suppose every example was a member of class b. In this case we would not need the second bit at all, as class b membership is assumed. Or suppose 75% of the examples were members of class b. Then we know in advance an example is more likely to belong to class b than not to belong. The expected amount of information gained by actually knowing whether it belongs or not will be:

p(belongs) * gain(belongs) + p(doesn't belong) * gain(doesn't belong)
= 0.75 * (log 1 - log 0.75) + 0.25 * (log 1 - log 0.25)
= - (0.75 * log 0.75) - (0.25 * log 0.25)
= 0.81
where gain(x) = information gained by knowing x

That is, we actually only need 0.81 of a bit to represent the extra information we need to know membership or not of class b. Generalising, we can say that instead of one bit per class, what we actually need is the total of the extra information needed to describe membership or non-membership of each class. This sum will be

$$-\sum_{i=1}^{N}\left((p(c_i)\log p(c_i)) + (q(c_i)\log q(c_i))\right)$$

where $p(c_i)$ is probability of membership of class c_i and $q(c_i)$ is probability of non-membership of class c_i.

References

1. M. Andrade, C. Ouzounis, C. Sander, J. Tamames, and A. Valencia. Functional classes in the three domains of life. *Journal of Molecular Evolution*, 49:551–557, 1999.

2. W. P. Blackstock and M. P. Weir. Proteomics: quantitative and physical mapping of cellular proteins. *Tibtech*, 17:121–127, 1999.

3. C.L. Blake and C.J. Merz. UCI repository of machine learning databases, 1998.

4. M. Brown, W. Nobel Grundy, D. Lin, N. Cristianini, C. Walsh Sugnet, T. Furey, M. Ares Jr., and D. Haussler. Knowledge-based analysis of microarray gene expression data by using support vector machines. *Proc. Nat. Acad. Sci. USA*, 97(1):262–267, Jan 2000.

5. J. DeRisi, V. Iyer, and P. Brown. Exploring the metabolic and genetic control of gene expression on a genomic scale. *Science*, 278:680–686, October 1997.

6. M. des Jardins, P. Karp, M. Krummenacker, T. Lee, and C. Ouzounis. Prediction of enzyme classification from protein sequence without the use of sequence similarity. In *ISMB '97*, 1997.

7. B. Efron and R. Tibshirani. *An introduction to the bootstrap.* Chapman and Hall, 1993.

8. M. Eisen, P. Spellman, P. Brown, and D. Botstein. Cluster analysis and display of genome-wide expression patterns. *Proc. Nat. Acad. Sci. USA*, 95:14863–14868, Dec 1998.

9. J. Fürnkranz. Separate-and-conquer rule learning. *Artificial Intelligence Review*, 13(1):3–54, 1999.

10. The Arabidopsis genome initiative. Analysis of the genome sequence of the flowering plant arabidopsis thaliana. *Nature*, 408:796–815, 2000.

11. International human genome sequencing consortium. Initial sequencing and analysis of the human genome. *Nature*, 409:860–921, 2001.

12. Aram Karalic and Vlado Pirnat. Significance level based classification with multiple trees. *Informatica*, 15(5), 1991.

13. D. Kell and R. King. On the optimization of classes for the assignment of unidentified reading frames in functional genomics programmes: the need for machine learning. *Trends Biotechnol.*, 18:93–98, March 2000.

14. R. King, A. Karwath, A. Clare, and L. Dehaspe. Genome scale prediction of protein functional class from sequence using data mining. In *KDD 2000*, 2000.

15. R. Kohavi. A study of cross-validation and bootstrap for accuracy estimation and model selection. In *IJCAI 1995*, 1995.

16. D. Koller and M. Sahami. Hierarchically classifying documents using very few words. In *ICML 97*, 1997.

17. E. Koonin, R. Tatusov, M. Galperin, and M. Rozanov. Genome analysis using clusters of orthologous groups (COGS). In *RECOMB 98*, pages 135–139, 1998.

18. A. Kumar, K.-H. Cheung, P. Ross-Macdonald, P.S.R. Coelho, P. Miller, and M. Snyder. TRIPLES: a database of gene function in S. cerevisiae. *Nucleic Acids Res.*, 28:81–84, 2000.

19. M. Lussier, A. White, J. Sheraton, T. di Paolo, J. Treadwell, S. Southard, C. Horenstein, J. Chen-Weiner, A. Ram, J. Kapteyn, T. Roemer, D. Vo, D. Bondoc, J. Hall, W. Zhong, A. Sdicu, J. Davies, F. Klis, P. Robbins, and H. Bussey. Large scale identification of genes involved in cell surface biosynthesis and architecture in *Saccharomyces cerevisiae*. *Genetics*, 147:435–450, Oct 1997.

20. A. McCallum. Multi-label text classification with a mixture model trained by EM. In *AAAI 99 Workshop on Text Learning*, 1999.

21. A. McCallum, R. Rosenfeld, T. Mitchell, and A. Ng. Improving text classification by shrinkage in a hierarchy of classes. In *ICML 98*, 1998.

22. H.W. Mewes, K. Heumann, A. Kaps, K. Mayer, F. Pfeiffer, S. Stocker, and D. Frishman. MIPS: a database for protein sequences and complete genomes. *Nucleic Acids Research*, 27:44–48, 1999.

23. D. Michie, D. J. Spiegelhalter, and C. C. Taylor, editors. *Machine Learning, Neural and Statistical Classification*. Ellis Horwood, London, 1994. Out of print but available at http://www.amsta.leeds.ac.uk/~charles/statlog/.

24. D. Mladenic and M. Grobelnik. Learning document classification from large text hierarchy. In *AAAI 98*, 1998.

25. S. Oliver. A network approach to the systematic analysis of yeast gene function. *Trends in Genetics*, 12(7):241–242, 1996.

26. J. R. Quinlan. *C4.5: programs for Machine Learning*. Morgan Kaufmann, San Mateo, California, 1993.

27. L. M. Raamsdonk, B. Teusink, D. Broadhurst, N. Zhang, A. Hayes, M. C. Walsh, J. A. Berden, K. M. Brindle, D. B. Kell, J. J. Rowland, H. V. Westerhoff, K. van Dam, and S. G. Oliver. A functional genomics strategy that uses metabolome data to reveal the phenotype of silent mutations. *Nature Biotech*, pages 45–50, 2001.

28. A. Ram, A. Wolters, R. Ten Hoopen, and F. Klis. A new approach for isolating cell wall mutants in *Saccharomyces cerevisiae* by screening for hypersensitivity to calcofluor white. *Yeast*, 10:1019–1030, 1994.

29. M. Riley. Systems for categorizing functions of gene products. *Current Opinion in Structural Biology*, 8:388–392, 1998.

30. R. Schapire and Y. Singer. BoosTexter: A boosting-based system for text categorization. *Machine Learning*, 39(2/3):135–168, 2000.

31. K. Sugimoto, Y. Sakamoto, O. Takahashi, and K. Matsumoto. HYS2, an essential gene required for DNA replication in Saccharomyces cerevisiae. *Nucleic Acids Res*, 23(17):3493–500, Sep 1995.

32. P. Törönen, M. Kolehmainen, G. Wong, and E. Castrén. Analysis of gene expression data using self-organizing maps. *FEBS Lett.*, 451(2):142–6, May 1999.

33. J. C. Venter et al. The sequence of the human genome. *Science*, 291:1304–1351, 2001.

Computing Association Rules Using Partial Totals

Frans Coenen, Graham Goulbourne, and Paul Leng

Department of Computer Science, The University of Liverpool
Chadwick Building, P.O. Box 147, Liverpool L69 3BX, England
{frans,graham_g,phl}@csc.liv.ac.uk

Abstract. The problem of extracting all association rules from within a binary database is well-known. Existing methods may involve multiple passes of the database, and cope badly with densely- packed database records because of the combinatorial explosion in the number of sets of attributes for which incidence-counts must be computed. We describe here a class of methods we have introduced that begin by using a single database pass to perform a *partial* computation of the totals required, storing these in the form of a set enumeration tree, which is created in time linear to the size of the database. Algorithms for using this structure to complete the count summations are discussed, and a method is described, derived from the well-known *Apriori* algorithm. Results are presented demonstrating the performance advantage to be gained from the use of this approach.
Keywords: Association Rules, Set Enumeration Tree, Data Structures.

1 Introduction

A well-established approach to Knowledge Discovery in Databases (KDD) involves the identification of *association rules* [2] within a database. An association rule is a probabilistic relationship, of the form $A{\rightarrow}B$, between sets of database attributes, which is inferred empirically from examination of records in the database. In the simplest case, the attributes are boolean, and the database takes the form of a set of records each of which reports the presence or absence of each of the attributes in that record. The paradigmatic example is in supermarket shopping-basket analysis. In this case, each record in the database is a representation of a single shopping transaction, recording the set of all items purchased in that transaction. The discovery of an association rule, $PQR{\rightarrow}XY$, for example, is equivalent to an assertion that "shoppers who purchase items P, Q and R are also likely to purchase items X and Y at the same time". This kind of relationship is potentially of considerable interest for marketing and planning purposes.

More generally, assume a set I of n boolean attributes, $\{a_1, \cdots, a_n\}$. and a database table each record of which contains some subset of these attributes, which may equivalently be recorded as a n-bit vector reporting the presence or absence of each attribute. An association rule R is of the form $A{\rightarrow}B$, where A, B are disjoint subsets of the attribute set I. The *support* for the rule R is the number of database records which contain $A \cup B$ (often expressed as a proportion of the total number of records). The *confidence* in the rule R is the ratio of the support for R to the support for its antecedent, A. A rule is described as "frequent" or "interesting", if it exceeds some defined levels of support and confidence. The fundamental problem in association rule mining is the search for

L. De Raedt and A. Siebes (Eds.): PKDD 2001, LNAI 2168, pp. 54–66, 2001.
© Springer-Verlag Berlin Heidelberg 2001

sets which exceed the support threshold: once these frequent sets have been identified the confidence can be immediately computed.

In this paper we describe a class of methods for identifying frequent sets of attributes within a database. For the databases in which we are interested, the number of attributes is likely to be 500 or more, making examination of all subsets computationally infeasible. Our methods use a single pass of the database to perform a partial summation of support totals, with time and space requirements that are linear to the number of database records. The partial counts are stored in a set-enumeration tree structure (the 'P-tree') which facilitates efficient completion of the final totals required. We describe an algorithm for performing this computation, using a second tree structure (the 'T-tree') to store the support-counts. Results are presented which illustrate the performance gain achieved by this approach.

2 Background

The central problem in deriving association rules is the exponential time- and space-complexity of the task of computing support counts for all 2^n subsets of the attribute set I. Hence, practicable algorithms in general attempt to reduce the search space by computing support-counts only for those subsets which are identified as potentially interesting. The best-known algorithm, "Apriori" [3], does this by repeated passes of the database, successively computing support-counts for single attributes, pairs, triples, and so on. Since any set of attributes can be "interesting" only if all its subsets also reach the required support threshold, the *candidate set* of sets of attributes is pruned on each pass to eliminate those that do not satisfy this requirement. Other algorithms, AIS [2] and SETM [9], have the same general form but differ in the way the candidate sets are derived.

Two aspects of the performance of these algorithms are of concern: the number of passes of the database that are required, which will in general be one greater than the number of attributes in the largest interesting set, and the size of the candidate sets which may be generated, especially in the early cycles of the algorithm. The number of passes may be reduced to 2 by strategies which begin by examining subsets of the database [11], or by sampling the database to estimate the likely candidate set [12]. The drawback of these methods is that the candidate set derived is necessarily a superset of the actual set of interesting sets, so again the search space may become very large, especially with densely packed database records. Large candidate-set sizes create a problem both in their storage requirement and in the computation required as each database record is examined. The implementation described for the Apriori algorithm stores the candidate set in a hash-tree, which is searched for each database record in turn to identify candidates that are subsets of the set of attributes included in the record being considered.

The computation involved in dealing with large candidate sets has led researchers to look for methods which seek to identify *maximal* interesting sets without first examining all their smaller subsets. Zaki et al [13] do this by partitioning the search space into *clusters* of associated attributes; however, this approach breaks down if the database is too densely-populated for such clusters to be apparent. Bayardo's [4] Max-Miner algorithm also searches for maximal sets, using Rymon's set enumeration framework

[10] to order the search space as a tree. Max-Miner reduces the search space by pruning the tree to eliminate both supersets of infrequent sets and subsets of frequent sets. In a development from Max-Miner, the Dense-Miner algorithm [5] imposes additional constraints on the rules being sought to reduce further the search space in these cases. These algorithms cope better with dense datasets than the other algorithms described, but again require multiple database passes. For databases which can be completely contained in main memory, the DepthProject algorithm of [1] also makes use of a set- enumeration structure. In this case the tree is used to store frequent sets that are generated in depth-first order via recursive projections of the database. However, because of the combinatorial explosion in the number of candidates which must be considered, and/or the cost of repeated access to the database, no existing algorithm copes fully with large databases of densely-packed records.

In the method we describe here, we also make use of Rymon's set enumeration tree, to store *interim* support- counts in a form that facilitates completion of the computation required. The approach is novel but generic in that it can be used as a basis for implementing improved variants of many existing algorithms.

3   Partial Support and the *P*-Tree

The most computationally expensive part of Apriori and related algorithms is the identification of subsets of a database record that are members of the candidate set being considered; this is especially so for records that include a large number of attributes. We avoid this, at least initially, by at first counting only sets occurring in the database, without considering subsets.

Let i be a subset of the set I (where I is the set of n attributes represented by the database). We define P_i, the *partial support* for the set i, to be the number of records whose contents are identical with the set i. Then T_i, the *total support* for the set i, can be determined as:

$$T_i = \sum P_j \quad (\forall j, j \supseteq i)$$

For a database of m records, the partial supports can, of course, be counted simply in a single database pass, to produce m' partial totals, for some $m' \leq m$. We use Rymon's set enumeration framework [10] to store these counts in a tree; Figure 1 illustrates this for $I = \{A, B, C, D\}$. To avoid the potential exponential scale of this, the tree is built dynamically as the database is scanned so as to include only those nodes that represent sets actually present as records in the database, plus some additional nodes created to maintain tree structure when necessary. The size of this tree, and the cost of its construction are linearly related to m rather than 2^n.

Taking advantage of the structural relationships between sets of attributes apparent from the tree, we also use the construction phase to begin the computation of total supports. As each set is located within the tree during the course of the database pass, it is computationally inexpensive to augment *interim* support-counts, Q_i stored for subsets which precede it in the tree ordering; thus:

$$Q_i = \sum P_j \quad (\forall j, j \supseteq i, \ j \ follows \ i \ in \ lexicographic \ order)$$

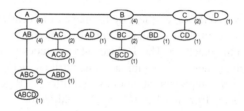

Fig. 1. Tree storage of subsets of $\{A, B, C, D\}$

It then becomes possible to compute total support using the equation:

$$T_i = Q_i + \sum P_j \quad (\forall j, j \supset i, \ j \ precedes \ i \ in \ lexicographic \ order)$$

The numbers associated with the nodes of Fig. 1 are the interim counts which would be stored in the tree arising from a database the records of which comprise exactly one instance of each of the 16 possible sets of attributes; thus, for example, $Q(BC) = 2$, derived from one instance of BC and one of BCD. Then:

$$T(BC) = Q(BC) + P(ABC) + P(ABCD) = Q(BC) + Q(ABC)$$

We use the term *P-tree* to refer to this incomplete set- enumeration tree of interim support-counts. An algorithm for building the P-tree, counting the interim totals, is described in detail in [7]. Because the P-tree contains all the relevant data stored in the original database, albeit in a different form, we can in principle apply versions of almost any existing algorithm to complete the summation of total supports. Use of the P-tree as a surrogate for the original database, however, offers three potential advantages. Firstly, when n is small ($2^n \ll m$), then traversing the tree to examine each node will be significantly faster than scanning the whole database. Secondly, even for large n, if the database contains a high degree of duplication ($m' \ll m$) then using the tree will again be significantly faster than a full database pass, especially if the duplicated records are densely-populated with attributes. Finally, and most generally, the computation required in each cycle of the algorithm is greatly reduced because of the partial summation already carried out in constructing the tree. For example, in the second pass of Apriori (considering pairs of attributes), a record containing r attributes may require the counts for each of its $r(r - 1)/2$ subset-pairs to be incremented. When examining a node of the P-tree, conversely, it is necessary only to consider only those subsets not already covered by a parent node, which in the best case will be only $r - 1$ subsets.

To illustrate this, consider the node $ABCD$ in the tree of Fig. 1. The partial total for $ABCD$ has already been included in the interim total for ABC, and this will be added to the final totals for the subsets of ABC when the latter node is examined. Thus, when examining the node $ABCD$, we need only consider those subsets not covered by its parent, i.e. those including the attribute D. The advantage gained from this will be greater, of course, the greater the number of attributes in the set being considered.

A rather similar structure to our *P-tree* has been described independently by [8]. This structure, the *FP-tree*, has a different form but quite similar properties to the P-tree, but is built in two database passes, the first of which eliminates attributes that fail to reach the support threshold, and orders the others by frequency of occurrence. Each node in the FP-tree stores a single attribute, so that each path in the tree represents and counts one or more records in the database. The FP-tree also includes more structural information, including all the nodes representing any one attribute being linked into a list. This structure facilitates the implementation of an algorithm, "FP-growth", which successively generates subtrees from the FP-tree corresponding to each frequent attribute, to represent all sets in which the attribute is associated with its predecessors in the tree ordering. Recursive application of the algorithm generates all frequent sets. The two structures, the FP-tree and our P-tree, which have been developed independently and contemporaneously, are sufficiently similar to merit a detailed comparison, which we discuss in Sect. 5.

4   Computing Total Supports

The construction of the P-tree has essentially performed, in a single pass, a reorganisation of the relevant data into a structured set of counts of sets of attributes which appear as distinct records in the database. For any candidate set T of subsets of I, the calculation of total supports can be completed by walking this tree, adding interim supports as required according to the formulae above.

We can also take advantage of the structure of the P-tree to organise the computation of total supports efficiently, taking advantage of the fact that the counts for each set in the P-tree already incorporate contributions from their successor-supersets. Figure 2 illustrates the dual of Fig. 1, in which each subtree includes only supersets of its root node which contain an attribute that precedes all those of the root node. We will call this the T-tree, representing the target sets for which the total support is to be calculated, as opposed to the interim-support P-tree of Fig. 1. Observe that for any node t in the T-tree, all the subsets of t which include an attribute i will be located in that segment of the tree found between node i and node t in the tree ordering. This allows us to use the T- tree as a structure to effect an implementation of an algorithm to sum total supports:

```
Algorithm TFP (Compute Total- from Partial- supports)
        for each node j in P-tree do
        begin k = j - parent (j);
              i = first attribute in k;
              starting at node i of T-tree do
              begin if i ⊆ j then add Q_j to T_i;
                    if i = j then exit
                    else recurse to child node;
                 proceed to sibling node;
              end
        end
```

To illustrate the application of the algorithm, consider the node ACD in the tree of Fig. 1. TFP first obtains the difference of this node from its parent, AC, i.e. D, and begins traversing the T-tree at node D. From this point the count associated with ACD

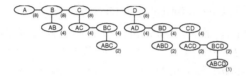

Fig. 2. Tree with predecessor-subtrees

will be added to all nodes encountered that are subsets of ACD, i.e. D, AD, CD and ACD, the traversal terminating when the node ACD is reached. Note that the count for the node BD which is not a subset of ACD will not be updated, nor will its subtree be traversed.

Of course, to construct the entire T-tree would imply an exponential storage requirement. In any practical method, however, it is only necessary to create that subset of the tree corresponding to the current candidate set being considered. Thus, for example, a version of the Apriori algorithm using these structures would consider candidates which are singletons, pairs of attributes, triples, etc., in successive passes. This algorithm, which we will call Apriori-TFP, has the following form:

1. Build level K in the T-tree.
2. "Walk" the P-tree, applying algorithm TFP to add interim supports associated with individual P-tree nodes to the level K nodes established in (1).
3. Remove any level K T-tree nodes that do not have an adequate level of support.
4. Repeat steps (1), (2) and (3); until a level K is reached where no nodes are adequately supported.

The algorithm begins by constructing the top level of the T-tree, containing all the singleton subsets, i.e. the single attributes in I. A first pass of algorithm TFP then counts supports for each of these in a single traversal of the P-tree. Note again that identification of the relevant nodes in the T-tree is trivial and efficient, as these will be located in a (usually short) segment of the level-1 list. In practice, it is more efficient to implement level 1 of the T-tree as a simple array of attribute-counts, which can be processed more quickly than is the case for a list structure. A similar optimisation can be carried into level 2, replacing each branch of the tree by an array, and again this is likely to be more efficient when most of the level 2 nodes remain in the tree.

Following completion of the first pass, the level 1 T-tree is pruned to remove all nodes that fail to reach the required support threshold, and the second level is generated, adding new nodes only if their subsets are contained in the tree built so far, i.e. have been found to have the necessary threshold of support. The new level of the tree forms the candidate set for the next pass of the algorithm TFP. The complete algorithm is described formally in Table 1 (Part 1) and Table 2 (Part 2). This uses a function, $endDigits$, that takes two arguments P and N (where N is the current level) and returns a set comprising the last N attributes in the set P; thus $endDigits(ABC, 2) = BC$. The significance of this is that BC is the last subset of ABC at level 2 that need be considered.

Table 1. Total Support Algorithm (Part 1)

$\forall P \in Ptree \ where \ (numAttributes(P) \geq requiredLevel)$

$\quad P' = P \setminus P_{parent}$

$\forall T_{1,j} \ (nodes \ at \ level \ 1)$

$\quad loop \ while \ P' \neq null$

$\qquad if \ T_{1,j} < P' \ j++$

$\qquad if \ T_{1,j} \equiv P'$

$\qquad\quad if \ (requiredLevel \equiv 1) \ T_{sup} = T_{sup} + P_{sup}$

$\qquad\quad else \ \textbf{Part 2}$

$\qquad\quad P' = null$

$\qquad if \ \left(T_{1,j} \subset P'\right)$

$\qquad\quad if \ (requiredLevel \equiv 1) \ T_{sup} = T_{sup} + P_{sup}$

$\qquad\quad else \ \textbf{Part 2}$

$\qquad\quad P' = P' \setminus firstAttribute(P') \cdot j++$

Table 2. Total Support Algorithm (Part 2)

$P'' = endDigits(P, currentLevel)$

$loop \ while \ T_{i,j} \neq null$

$\quad if \ T_{i,j} < P''$

$\qquad if(T_{i,j} \subset P)$

$\qquad\quad if \ currentLevel \equiv requiredLevel \ T_{sup} = T_{sup} + P_{sup}$

$\qquad\quad else \ recursively call \ Part \ 2 \ commencing \ with \ T_{i++,1}$

$\qquad j++$

$\quad if \ T_{i,j} \equiv P''$

$\qquad if \ currentLevel \equiv requiredLevel \ T_{sup} = T_{sup} + P_{sup}$

$\qquad else \ recursively call \ Part \ 2 \ commencing \ with \ T_{i++,1}$

$\quad stop$

$\quad if \ T_{i,j} > P''$

$\qquad stop$

5   Results

To evaluate the algorithms we have described, we have compared their performance with that for our implementations of two published methods: the original Apriori algorithm (founded on a hash tree data structure), and the FP- growth algorithm described in [8]. In both cases, the comparisons are based on our own implementations of the algorithms, which follow as closely as we can judge the published descriptions. All the implementations, including those for our own algorithms, are experimental prototypes, unoptimised low-performance Java programs.

The first set of experiments illustrate the performance characteristics involved in the creation of the P-tree. Figure 3 shows the time to build the P-tree, for databases of 200,000 records with varying characteristics. The graphs of storage requirements also have exactly the same pattern. The three cases illustrated represent synthetic databases constructed using the QUEST generator described in [3]. This uses parameters T, which defines the average number of attributes found in a record, and I, the average size of the maximal supported set. Higher values of T and I in relation to the number of attributes N correspond to a more densely-populated database. These results show that the cost of building the P-tree is almost independent of N, the number of attributes. As is the case for all association-rule algorithms, the cost of the P-tree is greater for more densely-populated data, but in this case the scaling appears to be linear.

Figure 4 examines the P-tree storage requirement for databases of 500 attributes, with the same sets of parameters, as the number of database records is increased. This shows, as predicted, that the size of the tree is linearly related to the database size. Again, this is also the case for the construction time. The actual performance figures for the P- tree construction could easily be improved from a more efficient implementation, and it would also be possible and probably worthwhile to use this first pass to compute total support counts for the single attributes. However, the construction of the P-tree is essentially a restructuring of the database, the effect of which will be realised in all subsequent data mining experiments.

In Table 3 we examine the cost of building the P-tree in comparison with that for the FP-tree of [8]. The figures tabulated are for two different datasets:

1. **quest.T25.I10.N1K.D10K**: A synthetic data set, also used in [8], generated using the Quest generator (N=1000 attributes, D=10000 records).
2. **fleet.N194.D9000**: A genuine data set, not in the public domain, provided by a UK insurance company. Note that this set is much denser than quest.T25.I10.N1K.D10K

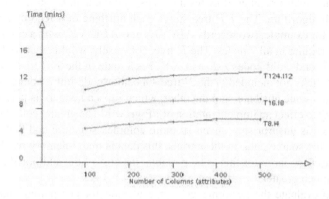

Fig. 3. Graph showing effort (time) to generate P-tree for data sets with number of rows fixed at 200000

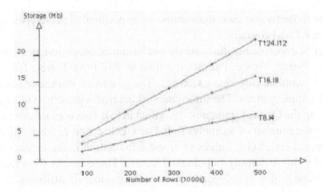

Fig. 4. Graph showing P-tree storage requirements for data sets with number of columns fixed at 500

Table 3. P-tree and FP-tree generation characteristics

	quest.T25.I10.N1K.D10K		fleet.N194.D9000	
	Storage (Bytes)	Time (Mins)	Storage (Bytes)	Time (Mins)
P-tree	1,020,690	0.65	582,196	0.36
FP-tree (Sup 5%)	1,566,838	3.43	767,062	1.24
FP-tree (Sup 4%)	2,283,360	5.53	912,918	1.39
FP-tree (Sup 3%)	3,028,082	9.36	1,334,146	2.04
FP-tree (Sup 2%)	3,974,482	20.00	1,704,990	3.28
FP-tree (Sup 1%)	4,567,480	34.83	1,754,990	3.35

With respect to Table 3 it should be noted that the procedure for building the FP-tree eliminates all single attributes that fail to reach the support threshold, so figures for a range of support thresholds are tabulated against the (constant) characteristics of the P-tree. As can be seen, the P-tree is a significantly more compact structure, and its construction time lower than that of the FP-tree. The greater size of the FP-tree arises from the greater number of nodes it creates, and the additional links required by the FP-growth algorithm. The FP-tree stores each attribute of a record as a separate node, so that, for example, two records $ABCDE$ and $ABCXY$, with a common prefix ABC, would require in all 7 nodes. The P-tree, conversely, would create only 3 nodes: a parent ABC, and child nodes DE and XY. Each node in the FP-tree also requires two additional links not included in the P-tree. One, the "node-link", connects all nodes representing the same attribute, and the other, which links a node to its parent, appears to be necessary to effect an implementation of FP-growth. The greater construction time for the FP-tree is unsurprising, given its more complex structure and that it requires two passes of the source data. In these trials, this data is main-memory resident: in the case of a dataset too large for this to be possible, the cost of the additional pass would of course be much greater.

Finally, to evaluate the performance of the method for computing final support-counts, we have compared the Apriori-TFP algorithm we have described with our implementations of the original Apriori (founded on a hash tree data structure) and of

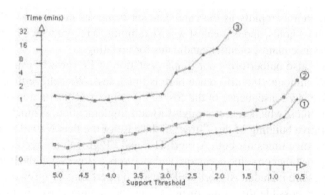

Fig. 5. Graph showing processing time to mine (1) the P-tree, (2) the FP-tree and (3) to perform the same operation using a traditional Apriori algorithm using quest.T25.I10.N1K.D10K

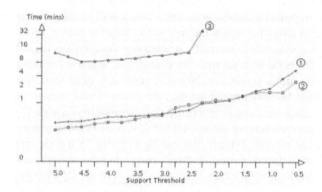

Fig. 6. Graph showing processing time to mine (1) the P-tree, (2) the FP-tree and (3) to perform the same operation using a traditional Apriori algorithm using fleet.N194.D9000

FP-growth. The results are presented in Fig. 5, for quest.T25.I10.N1K.D10K and Fig. 6, for fleet.N194.D9000, In all cases, to give the fairest basis for comparison, we have used data which is main-memory resident throughout. The performance time presented with respect to Apriori-TFP and FP-growth do not include the time to produce the P-tree or FP-tree respectively.

As we would expect, Apriori-TFP strongly outperforms our implementation of Apriori. This improvement arises from a combination of two factors. The first, as described above, is the lower number of support-count updates that will be required when examining a *P*-tree node, as opposed to the number required in Apriori from examination of the records from which the node is made up. This gain will be greatest when there are clusters of records including significant numbers of shared attributes (as we might hope to find when mining potentially interesting data), and, especially, if there are significant numbers of duplicated records. Secondly, the effect is compounded by the more efficient localisation of candidates obtained by using the *T*-tree for the TFP algorithm, as opposed to the hash-tree used by Apriori. The cost of accessing the hash-tree to locate candidates for updating increases rapidly as the candidate set increases in size, as is the case for lower support thresholds, and is greatest when examining a record which includes many attributes and hence many potential candidates for updating.

Apriori-TFP also outperforms our implementation of FP- growth using quest.T25. I10.N1K.D10K although the difference here is much less. We believe that the performance gain here is a consequence of the cost of the recursive construction of successive conditional FP-trees, which, in our straightforward implemention, is much slower than the simple iterative building of the T-tree. In the case of the fleet.N194.D9000 data set similar performance times for both Apriori-TFP and FP growth are recorded with one outperforming the other on some occasions and vice versa. However, if the P-tree/FP-tree generation times are included Apriori- TFP clearly outperforms FP-growth.

Althoughit is possible that some of the advantage is an artefact of our implementations, the results appear to show that the simpler P-tree structure offers at least as good performance as the more complex FP-tree. Moreover, the above experiments use memory-resident data only; we believe that the additional structural links in the FP-tree, and the need for repeated access to generate subtrees, will create problems for efficient implementation in cases for which the tree is too large to hold in main memory. For the simpler P-tree structure, conversely, it is easy to describe an efficient construction process which will build separate trees for manageable segments of the database, prior to a final merging into a single tree. Nor is it necessary, in general, for the P-tree to be retained in main memory throughout the calculation of final support totals. The only structural information necessarily retained is the relationship of a node to its parent. For example, if a node representing the set $ABDFG$ is present in the tree as a child of the node ABD, all the relevant information can be recorded by a node representation of the form $ABD.FG$. In this form, the "tree" can in fact be stored finally as a simple array in any convenient order, depending on the needs of the algorithm to compute the final support totals. In the case of the Apriori-TFP algorithm, the tree/array is processed element-by-element in any order, causing no problems even when it is necessary to hold it in secondary memory.

6 Conclusions

We have presented here an algorithm for computing support counts using as a starting point an initial, incomplete computation stored as a set- enumeration tree. Although the actual algorithm described here to compute the final totals is based on the Apriori algorithm, the method itself is generic, in that, once the P-tree has been created, a variety of methods may be applied to complete the summation. Many of these methods, like the one we have illustrated, will be able to take advantage of the partial computation already carried out in the initial database pass to reduce the cost of further multiple passes.

Note, however, that the advantage gained from this partial computation is not equally distributed throughout the set of candidates. For candidates early in the lexicographic order, most of the support calculation is completed during the construction of the P-tree; for example, for the attributes of Fig. 1, support for the sets A, AB, ABC and $ABCD$ will be counted totally in this first stage of the summation. This observation allows us to consider methods which maximise the benefit from this by a suitable ordering of the attribute set. This is, of course, the heuristic used by [8], and also, in various ways, by [4], [6] and [1].

We could also increase the proportion of the summation which is completed during the initial scan of the database by a partitioning of the P-tree. For example, it would be possible to separate the tree of Fig. 1 into four subtrees, rooted at the nodes A, B, C and D, and for the first pass to accumulate interim supports within each of these subtrees independently. In this case, a record containing the set ABD, for example, would increment the support-counts for ABD within the A-tree, BD within the B-tree, and D within the (single-node) D-tree. Again, the effect of this is similar to that for a set of conditional FP-trees produced by FP-growth. The advantage offered is that is provides a means of reducing the size of trees required for processing. The size of the complete subtree corresponding to an attribute a_i that is in position i in the tree ordering is 2^{n-i}. However, the P-tree construction method we use will produce an incomplete subtree, the size of which will be of order m', where $m' \leq T_{a_i}$, the number of records in the database which contain a_i (again, reduced by the existence of duplicates). Thus, the storage requirement for each subtree is less than or equal to min $\{2^{n-i}, T_{a_i}\}$. The requirement for any single subtree can be minimised by ordering the attributes in reverse order of their frequency, so that the most common attributes are clustered at the high-order end of the tree structure.

Partitioning the tree in this way would allow us (in one pass) to organise the data into sets each of which can be processed independently and may be small enough to be retained in central memory. At the high-order end of the organisation, i.e. for values of i close to n, the 2^{n-i} limit becomes computable. Thus, for large i, it may be more efficient to store partial supports in a complete array of subset-counts, and to use an exhaustive algorithm to compute total supports efficiently. Conversely, for smaller i, the conservative P-tree storage method, and an algorithm such as Apriori-TFP can be applied. We are presently investigating this and other heuristics to produce effective hybrid algorithms of this kind.

References

1. Agarwal, R., Aggarwal, C. and Prasad, V. Depth First Generation of Long Patterns. Proc ACM KDD 2000 Conference, Boston, 108-118, 2000.
2. Agrawal, R. Imielinski, T. Swami, A. Mining Association Rules Between Sets of Items in Large Databases. SIGMOD-93, 207-216. May 1993.
3. Agrawal, R. and Srikant, R. Fast Algorithms for Mining Association Rules. Proc 20th VLDB Conference, Santiago, 487-499. 1994
4. Bayardo, R.J. Efficiently Mining Long Patterns from Databases. Proc ACM-SIGMOD Int Conf on Management of Data, 85-93, 1998
5. Bayardo, R.J., Agrawal, R. and Gunopolos, D. Constraint-based rule mining in large, dense databases. Proc 15th Int Conf on Data Engineering, 1999
6. Brin, S., Motwani. R., Ullman, J.D. and Tsur, S. Dynamic itemset counting and implication rules for market basket data. Proc ACM SIGMOD Conference, 255-256, 1997
7. Goulbourne, G., Coenen, F. and Leng, P. Algorithms for Computing Association Rules using a Partial-Support Tree. J. Knowledge-Based Systems 13 (2000), 141-149. (also Proc ES'99.)
8. Han, J., Pei, J. and Yin, Y. Mining Frequent Patterns without Candidate Generation. Proc ACM SIGMOD 2000 Conference, 1-12, 2000.

9. Houtsma, M. and Swami, A. Set-oriented mining of association rules. Research Report RJ 9567, IBM Almaden Research Centre, San Jose, October 1993.
10. Rymon, R. Search Through Systematic Set Enumeration. Proc. 3rd Int'l Conf. on Principles of Knowledge Representation and Reasoning, 1992, 539-550.
11. Savasere, A., Omiecinski, E. and Navathe, S. An efficient algorithm for mining association rules in large databases. Proc 21st VLDB Conference, Zurich, 432-444. 1995.
12. Toivonen, H. Sampling large databases for association rules. Proc 22nd VLDB Conference, 134-145. Bombay, 1996.
13. Zaki, M.J., Parthasarathy, S. Ogihara, M. and Li, W. New Algorithms for fast discovery of association rules. Technical report 651, University of Rochester, Computer Science Department, New York. July 1997.

Gaphyl: A Genetic Algorithms Approach to Cladistics

Clare Bates Congdon

Department of Computer Science, Colby College, 5846 Mayflower Hill Drive,
Waterville, ME 04901, USA
congdon@colby.edu
http://www.cs.colby.edu/~congdon

Abstract. This research investigates the use of genetic algorithms to
solve problems from cladistics – a technique used by biologists to hypothesize the evolutionary relationships between organisms. Since exhaustive
search is not practical in this domain, typical cladistics software packages
use heuristic search methods to navigate through the space of possible
trees in an attempt to find one or more "best" solutions. We have developed a system called Gaphyl, which uses the genetic algorithm approach
as a search technique for finding cladograms, and a tree evaluation metric from a common cladistics software package (Phylip). On a nontrivial
problem (49 species with 61 attributes), Gaphyl is able to find more of
the best known trees with less computational effort than Phylip is able to
find (corresponding to more equally plausible evolutionary hypotheses).

1 Introduction

The human genome project and similar projects in biology have led to a wealth
of data and the rapid growth of the emerging field of bioinformatics, a hybrid discipline between biology and computer science that uses the tools and techniques
of computer science to help manage, visualize, and find patterns in this wealth
of data. The work reported here is an application to biology, and indicates gains
from using genetic algorithms (GA's) as the search mechanism for the task.

Cladistics [4] is a method widely used by biologists to reconstruct hypothesized evolutionary pathways followed by organisms currently or previously in-
habiting the Earth. Given a dataset that contains a number of different species
(also called taxa), each with a number of attribute-values (also called character states), cladistics software constructs cladograms (also called phylogenies),
which are representations of the possible evolutionary relationships between the
given species. A typical cladogram is a tree structure: The root of a tree can be
viewed as the common ancestor, the leaves of a tree are the species, and subtrees
are subsets of species that share a common ancestor. Each branching of a parent
node into offspring represents a divergence in one or more attribute-values of
the species within the two subtrees. In an alternate approach, sometimes called
"unrooted trees" (and sometimes called "networks"), the root of the tree is not

L. De Raedt and A. Siebes (Eds.): PKDD 2001, LNAI 2168, pp. 67–78, 2001.

assumed to be an ancestral state, and drawing the structures as trees seems to be primarily a convenience for the software authors.

Cladograms are evaluated using metrics such as parsimony: A tree with fewer evolutionary steps is considered better than one with more evolutionary steps. The work reported here used Wagner parsimony, though there are other possibilities, such as Camin-Sokal parsimony. (See [10] or [4], for example, for a discussion of alternatives.) Wagner parsimony is straightforward to compute (requiring only a single pass through the tree) and incorporates few constraints on the evolutionary changes that will be considered. (For example, some parsimony approaches require the assumption that characters will be added, but not lost, through the evolutionary process.) An unrooted tree evaluated with Wagner parsimony can be rooted at any point without altering the evaluation of the tree.

The typical cladistics software approach uses a deterministic hillclimbing methodology to find a cladogram for a given dataset, saving one or more "most parsimonious" trees as the result of the process. (The most parsimonious trees are the ones with a minimum number of evolutionary changes connecting the species in the tree. Multiple "bests" correspond to equally plausible evolutionary hypotheses, and finding more of these competing hypotheses is an important part of the task.) The tree-building approach adds each species into the tree in sequence, searching for the best place to add the new species. The search process is deterministic, but different trees may be found by running the algorithm with different random "jumbles" of the order of the species in the dataset.

The genetic algorithm (GA) approach to problem solving has shown improvements to hillclimbing approaches on a wide variety of problems [5,1,9]. In this approach, a population of possible solutions to the problem "breed", producing new solutions; over a number of "generations", the population tends to include better solutions to the problem. The process uses random numbers in several different places, as will be discussed later.

This research is an investigation into the utility of using the genetic algorithm approach on the problem of finding parsimonious cladograms.

2   Design Decisions

To hasten the development of our system, we used parts of two existing software packages. Phylip [3] is a cladistics system widely used by biologists. In particular, this system contains code for evaluating the parsimony of the cladograms (as well as some helpful utilities for working with the trees). Using the Phylip source code rather than writing our own tree-evaluation modules also helps to ensure that our trees are properly comparable to the Phylip trees. Genesis [6] is a GA package intended to aid the development and experimentation with variations on the GA. In particular, the basic mechanisms for managing populations of solutions and the modular design of the code facilitate implementing a GA for a specific problem. We named our new system Gaphyl, a reflection of the combination of GA and Phylip source code.

The research described here was conducted using published datasets available over the internet [2], and was done primarily with the families of the superorder of Lamiiflorae dataset, consisting of 23 species and 29 attributes. This dataset was chosen as being large enough to be interesting, but small enough to be manageable for this initial study. A second dataset, the major clades of the angiosperms, consisting of 49 species and 61 attributes, was used for further experimentation.

These datasets were selected because the attributes are binary, which simplified the tree-building process. As a preliminary step in evaluating the GA as a search mechanism for cladistics, "unknown" values for the attributes were replaced with 1's to make the data fully binary. This minor alteration to the data does impact the meaningfulness of the resulting cladograms as evolutionary hypotheses, but does not affect the comparison of Gaphyl and Phylip as search mechanisms.

3   The Genetic Algorithm Approach

There are many variations on the GA approach[1], but a standard methodology proceeds as follows:

1. Generate a population of random solutions to the problem. (These are not assumed to be particularly good solutions to the problem, but serve as a starting point.)
2. The GA proceeds through a number of "generations". In each generation:
   a) Assign a "fitness" to each solution, so that we know which solutions are better than others.
   b) Select a "parent" population through a biased random (with replacement) process, so that higher fitness solutions are more likely to be parents.
   c) Use operators such as crossover, which combines parts of two parent solutions to form new solutions, and mutation, which randomly changes part of a solution, to create a new population of solutions.

The algorithm terminates after a predetermined number of generations or when the solutions in the population have converged within a preset criterion (that is, until they are so similar that little is gained from combining parents to form new solutions).

Several factors should be evaluated when considering the utility of GA's for a particular problem:

1. Is there a more straightforward means of finding a "best" solution to the problem? (If so, there is no point in using the GA approach.)

---

[1] As is the custom in the evolutionary computation community, the author distinguishes different forms of evolutionary computation, and is working specifically within the "genetic algorithms" framework.

2. Can potential solutions to the problem be represented using simple data structures such as bit strings or trees? (If not, it may be difficult to work with the mechanics of the GA.)

3. Can a meaningful evaluation metric be identified that will enable one to rate the quality of each potential solution to your problem? (Without such a measure, the GA is unable to determine which solutions are more promising to work with.)

4. Can operators be devised to combine parts of two "parent" solutions and produce (viable) offspring solutions? (If the offspring do not potentially retain some of what made the parents "good", the GA will not be markedly better than random trial and error.)

In the cladistics task, there is a standard approach to forming the cladograms, but that process also has a stochastic element, so the standard approach is not guaranteed to find "the best" cladogram for a given dataset. In the cladistics task, solutions to the problem are naturally represented as trees. In addition, a standard metric for evaluating a given tree is provided with the task (parsimony). However, there is a challenge for implementing the cladistics task using the GA approach: devising operators that produce offspring from two parent solutions while retaining meaningful information from the parents.

4   The GA for Cladistics

The typical GA approach to doing "crossover" with two parent solutions with a tree representation is to pick a subtree (an interior or root node) in both parents at random and then swap the subtrees to form the offspring solution. The typical mutation operator would select a point in the tree and mutate it to any one of the possible legal values (here, any one of the species). However, these approaches do not work with the cladistics trees because each species must be represented in the tree exactly once.

4.1   Crossover Operator

The needs for our crossover operator bear some similarity to traveling salesperson problems (TSP's), where each city is to be visited exactly once on a tour. There are several approaches in the literature for working on this type of problem with a GA, however, the TSP naturally calls for a string representation, not a tree. In designing our own operator, we studied TSP approaches for inspiration, but ultimately devised our own. We wanted our operator to attempt to preserve some of the species relationships from the parents. In other words, a given tree contains species in a particular relationship to each other, and we would like to retain a large degree of this structure via the crossover process.

Our crossover operator proceeds as follows:

1. Choose a species at random from one of the parent trees. Select a subtree at random that includes this node, excluding the subtree that is only the

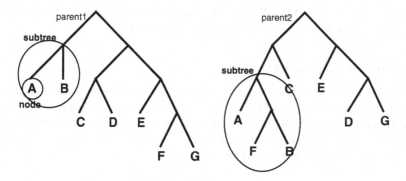

Fig. 1. Two example parent trees for a cladistics problem with seven species. A subtree for crossover has been identified for each tree.

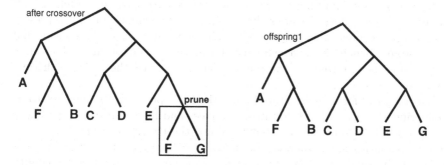

Fig. 2. At the left, the offspring initially formed by replacing the subtree from parent1 with the subtree from parent2; on the right, the offspring tree has been pruned to remove the duplicate species F.

leaf node and the subtree that is the entire tree. (The exclusions prevent meaningless crossovers, where no information is gained from the operation.)

2. In the second parent tree, find the smallest subtree containing all the species from the first parent's subtree.
3. To form an offspring tree, replace the subtree from the first parent with the subtree from the second parent. The offspring must then be pruned (from the "older" branches) to remove any duplicate species.
4. Repeat the process using the other parent as the starting point, so that this process results in two offspring trees from two parent trees.

This process results in offspring trees that retain some of the species relationships from the two parents, and combine them in new ways. An example crossover is illustrated in Figs. 1 and 2. The parents are shown in Fig. 1; Fig. 2 shows first the offspring formed via the crossover operation and identifies the subtree that must now be pruned and second shows the resulting offspring (after pruning species F). (Note that in the cladograms, swapping the left and right children does not affect the meaning of the cladogram.)

4.2   Mutation Operator

The typical GA "mutation" operator takes a location in the solution at random and mutates it to some other value. Again, the standard operator was not suited to our representation, where each species must appear exactly once in the tree. Instead, for our mutation operator, we selected two leaf nodes (species) at random, and swapped their positions in the tree.

4.3   Canonical Form

The Wagner parsimony metric uses "unrooted" trees, leading to many different possible representations of "the same" cladogram that are anchored at different points. Furthermore, flipping a tree (or subtree) left to right (switching the left and right subtrees) does not alter the parsimony of a cladogram (nor represent an alternative evolutionary hypothesis). Therefore, it soon became clear that Gaphyl would benefit from a canonical form, that could be applied to trees to ascertain whether trees in the population represented the same or distinct cladograms.

The canonical form we instituted picks the first species in the data set to be an offspring of the root, and "rotates" the tree (and flips, if necessary) to keep the species relationships in tact, but to reroot the tree at a given species. (To simplify comparisons, we followed the default Phylip assumption of making the first species in the dataset the direct offspring of the root of the tree.) Secondly, the subtrees are (recursively) rearranged so that left subtrees are smaller (fewer nodes) than right subtrees and that when left and right subtrees have the same number of nodes, a preorder traversal of the left subtree is alphabetically before a preorder traversal of the right subtree. This process is carried out when saving the "best" trees found in each generation, to ensure that no equivalent trees are saved among the best ones. Canonical form is illustrated in Fig. 3.

4.4   A Second Mutation Operator

The addition of a canonical form suggested the design of a second mutation operator. The relationships between species in a subtree is potentially useful information for offspring to inherit from parents. But perhaps the subtrees should be connected differently. The second mutation operator picks a random subtree and a random species within the subtree. The subtree is rotated to have the species as the left child of the root and reconnected to the parent.

4.5   Immigration

Early runs with Gaphyl on the larger dataset yielded trees with a parsimony of 280, but not 279 (lower parsimony is better). Reflection on the process and

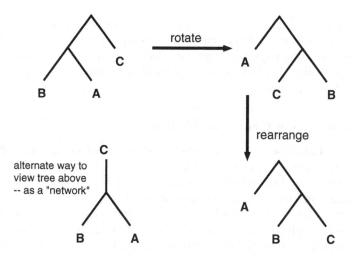

Fig. 3. An illustration of putting a tree into canonical form. The tree starts as in the top left; an alternate representation of the tree as a "network" is shown at the bottom left. First, the tree is rotated, so that the first species is an offspring of the root. Second, subtrees are rearranged so that smaller trees are on the left and alphabetically lower species are on the left.

inspection of the population determined that the process seemed to be converging too rapidly – losing the diversity across individuals that enables the crossover operator to find stronger solutions. "Premature convergence" is a known problem in the GA community, and there are a number of good approaches for combatting it. In Gaphyl, we opted to implement parallel populations with immigration. Adding immigration to the system allowed Gaphyl to find the trees of fitness 279.

The immigration approach implemented here is fairly standard. The population is subdivided into a specified number of subpopulations which, in most generations, are distinct from each other (crossovers happen only within a given subpopulation). After a number of generations have passed, each population migrates a number of its individuals into other populations; each emmigrant determines at random which population it will move to and which tree within that population it will uproot. The uprooted tree replaces the emmigrant in the emmigrant's original population. The number of populations, the number of generations to pass between migrations, and the number of individuals from each population to migrate at each migration event are, of course, all determined by parameters to the system.

5   Experimental Results

Recall that both Gaphyl and Phylip have a stochastic component, which means that evaluating each system requires doing a number of runs. In Phylip, each distinct run first "jumbles" the species list into a different random order. In Gaphyl, there are many different effects of random number generation: the construction of the initial population, parent selection, and the selection of crossover and mutation points. For both systems, a number of different runs must be done to evaluate the approach.

5.1 Comparison of Gaphyl and Phylip

1. With the Lamiiflorae data set, the performance of Gaphyl and Phylip is comparable. Phylip is more expedient in finding a single tree with the best parsimony (72), but both Gaphyl and Phylip find 45 most parsimonious cladograms in about twenty minutes of run time.
2. With the angiosperm dataset, a similar pattern emerges: Phylip is able to find one tree with the best fitness (279) quite quickly, while Gaphyl needs more run time to first discover a tree of fitness 279. However, in a comparable amount of runtime, Gaphyl is able to find 250 different most parsimonious trees of length 279 (approximately 24 hours of runtime). Phylip runs for comparable periods of time have not found more than 75 distinct trees with a parsimony of 279.

In other words, Gaphyl is more successful than Phylip in finding more trees (more equally plausible evolutionary hypotheses) in the same time period.

The first task is considerably easier to solve, and Gaphyl does not require immigration to do so. Example parameter settings are a population size of 500, 500 generations, 50% elitism (the 250 best trees are preserved into the next generation), 100% crossover, 10% first mutation, and 100% second mutation. Empirically, it appears that 72 is the best possible parsimony for this dataset, and that there are not more than 45 different trees of length 72.

The second task, as stated above, seems to require immigration in order for Gaphyl to find the best known trees (fitness 279). Successful parameter settings are 5 populations, population size of 500 (in each subpopulation), 2000 generations, immigration of 5% (25 trees) after every 500 generations, 50% elitism (the 250 best trees are preserved into the next generation), 100% crossover, 10% first mutation, and 100% second mutation. (Immigration does not happen following the final generation.)

We have not yet done enough runs with either Phylip or Gaphyl to estimate the maximum number of trees at this fitness, nor a more concise estimate of how long Phylip would have to run to find 250 distinct trees, nor whether 279 is even the best possible parsimony for this dataset.[2]

Based on these initial experiments, the pattern that is emerging is that as the problems get more complex, Gaphyl is able to find a more complete set of trees with less work than what Phylip is able to find. The work done to date

---

[2] We note that we inadvertently capped the number of trees that Gaphyl is able to find in setting our elitism rate. With a population size of 500 and 50% elitism, 250 is the maximum number of distinct trees that will be saved from one generations into the next.

illustrates that Gaphyl is a promising approach for cladistics work, as Gaphyl finds a wider variety of trees on this problem than Phylip does. This further suggests that Gaphyl may be able to find solutions better than Phylip is able to find on datasets with a larger number of species and attributes, because it appears to be searching more successful regions of the search space.

5.2 Evaluation of Contribution of Operators

To evaluate the contributions of the GA operators to the search, additional runs were done with the first data set (and no immigration). Empirically, crossover and the second mutation operator had been found to be the largest contributors to successful search, so attention was focused on the contributions of these operators.

In the first set of experiments, the first mutation rate was set to be 0%. First, the crossover rate was varied from 0% to 100% at increments of 10% while the second mutation rate was held constant at 100%. Second, the second mutation rate was varied from 0% to 100% at increments of 10% while the crossover rate was held constant at 100%. 20 experiments were run at each parameter setting; 500 generations were run.

Figure 4 illustrates the effects of varying the crossover rate (solid line) and second mutation rate (dashed line) on the average number of generations taken to find at least one tree of the known best fitness (72). Experiments that did not discover a tree of fitness 72 are averaged in as taking 500 generations. For example, 0% crossover was unable to find any trees of the best fitness in all 20 experiments, and so its average is 500 generations.

This first experiment illustrates that in general, higher crossover rates are better. There is not a clear preference, however, for high rates of the second form of mutation. To look at this operator more closely, the final populations of the 20 experiments were looked at to determine how many of the best trees were found in each run.

Figure 5 illustrates the effects of varying the crossover rate (solid line) and second mutation rate (dashed line) on the average number of best trees found. Experiments that did not discover a tree of fitness 72 are averaged in as finding 0 trees. For example, 0% crossover was unable to find any trees of the best fitness in all 20 experiments, and so its average is 0 of the best trees.

As Fig. 5 illustrates, runs with a higher second mutation rate tend to find more of the best trees than runs with a lower second mutation rate.

The impact of the first mutation operator had seemed to be low based on empirical evidence. So another set of experiments was done to assess the contribution of this operator. Figure 6 illustrates two sets of experiments. In both, the crossover rate was set at 100%; in one, the second mutation rate was set at 0% and in the other, the second mutation rate was set at 100%. The figure illustrates the effect of changing the first mutation rate on the average number of generations to find at least one of the best trees.

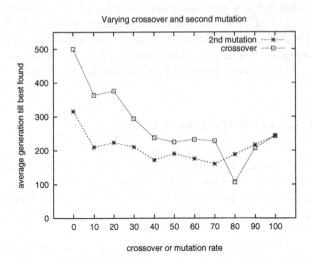

Fig. 4. The effect of varying crossover rate while holding second mutation constant and of varying the second mutation rate while holding the crossover rate constant. The average generation at which the best fitness (72) was found is illustrated.

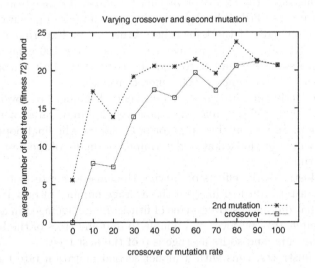

Fig. 5. The effects of varying crossover rate while holding second mutation constant and of varying the second mutation rate while holding the crossover rate constant. The average number of best trees (45 max) found by each parameter setting is illustrated

The results of this experiment clearly indicate that higher rates of this form of mutation are not beneficial. Furthermore, this operator is not clearly contributing to the search.

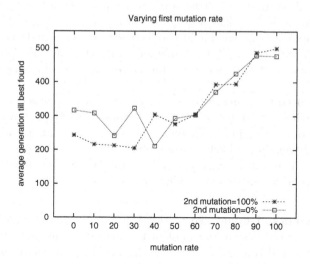

Fig. 6. The effect of varying the first mutation rate while holding crossover and second mutation constant. The crossover rate is 100% for both graphs; second mutation rates of 100% and 0% are shown. The average generation at which the best fitness (72) was found is illustrated.

6   Conclusions and Future Work

The GA search process as implemented in Gaphyl represents an improvement over Phylip's search process in its ability to find more trees than Phylip in the same runtime. One possible facet of this success is that the Gaphyl search process is independent of the number of attributes (and attribute-values); the complexity of the search varies with the number of species (which determines the number of leaf nodes in the tree). Phylip uses attribute information in its search process.

The first mutation operator is perhaps the "obvious" form of mutation to implement for this problem, and yet, its use (at high levels) appears to detract from the success of the search. This points to the importance of evaluating the contributions of operators to the search process.

There is obviously a wealth of possible extensions to the work reported here. First, more extensive evaluations of the capabilities of the two systems must be done on the angiosperms data set, including an estimate of the maximum number of trees of fitness 279 (and, indeed, whether 279 is the most parsimonious tree possible). This would entail more extensive runs with both approaches. Furthermore, as evidenced by the unexpected result with the mutation operator, the effect of the immigration operator in Gaphyl must be explored further.

Second, more work must be done with a wider range of datasets to evaluate whether Gaphyl is consistently able to find a broader variety of trees than Phylip, and perhaps able to find trees better than Phylip is able to find.

Third, Gaphyl should be extended to work with non-binary attributes and to handle data with unknown values. Since the ability to work with missing values and a number of alternative metrics are already part of the Phylip implementation, these changes should be straightforward in the Gaphyl system. This is particularly important in that phylogenetic trees are increasingly used by biologists primarily with the A, C, G, T markers of genetic data. It should also be extended to implement and evaluate alternative evaluation metrics to Wagner parsimony.

Finally, we need to compare the work reported here to other projects that use GA approaches with different forms of cladistics, including [7] and [8]. Both of these projects use maximum likelihood for constructing and evaluating the cladograms. The maximum likelihood approach (which is known as a "distance-based method") is not directly comparable to the Wagner parsimony approach (which is known as a "maximum parsimony" approach).

Acknowledgments. I would like to thank Emily F. Greenfest, who worked with me in the initial design and implementation of this project. Thanks also to Judy L. Stone and Randall Downer for sharing their knowledge of cladistics theory and software. Thanks to Randolph M. Jones, Joshua R. Ladieu, and the anonymous reviewers for comments on previous drafts of this paper.

References

1. L. Davis. *Handbook of Genetic Algorithms*. Van Nostrand Reinhold, New York, NY, 1991.
2. M. J. Donaghue. Treebase: A database of phylogenetic knowledge. web-based data repository, 2000. Available at `http://phylogeny.harvard.edu/treebase`.
3. J. Felsenstein. Phylip source code and documentation, 1995. Available via the web at `http://evolution.genetics.washington.edu/phylip.html`.
4. P. L. Forey, C. J. Humphries, I. L. Kitching, R. W. Scotland, D. J. Siebert, and D. M. Williams. *Cladistics: A Practical Course in Systematics*. Number 10 in The Systematics Association. Clarendon Press, Oxford, 1993.
5. D. E. Goldberg. *Genetic Algorithms in Search, Optimization and Machine Learning*. Addison-Wesley, Reading, MA, 1989.
6. J. J. Grefenstette. A user's guide to GENESIS. Technical report, Navy Center for Applied Research in AI, Washington, DC, 1987. Source code updated 1990; available at `http://www.cs.cmu.edu/afs/cs/project/ai-repository/ai/areas/genetic/ga/systems/genesis/`.
7. P. O. Lewis. A genetic algorithm for maximum-likelihood phylogeny inference using nucleotide sequence data. *Mol. Biol. Evol.*, 15(3):277–283, 1998.
8. H. Matsuda. Protein phylogenetic inference using maximum likelihood with a genetic algorithm. In L. Hunter and T. E. Klein, editors, *Pacific Symposium on Biocomputing '96*, pages 512–523. World Scientific, London, 1996.
9. M. Mitchell. *An Introduction to Genetic Algorithms*. MIT Press, Cambridge, MA, 1996.
10. D. L. Swofford, G. J. Olsen, P. J. Waddell, and D. M. Hillis. *Molecular Systematics*, chapter Phylogenetic Inference, pages 407–514. Sinauer Associates, Inc., Sunderland, MA, 1996.

Parametric Approximation Algorithms for High-Dimensional Euclidean Similarity

Ömer Eğecioğlu*

Department of Computer Science
University of California, Santa Barbara, CA 93106 USA
omer@cs.ucsb.edu

Abstract. We introduce a spectrum of algorithms for measuring the similarity of high-dimensional vectors in Euclidean space. The algorithms proposed consist of a convex combination of two measures: one which contains summary data about the *shape* of a vector, and the other about the relative *magnitudes* of the coordinates. The former is based on a concept called *bin-score permutations* and a metric to quantify similarity of permutations, the latter on another novel approximation for inner-product computations based on power symmetric functions, which generalizes the Cauchy-Schwarz inequality. We present experiments on time-series data on labor statistics unemployment figures that show the effectiveness of the algorithm as a function of the parameter that combines the two parts.

1 Introduction

Modern databases and applications use multiple types of digital data, such as documents, images, audio, video, etc. Some examples of such applications are document databases [6], medical imaging [16], and multimedia information systems [18]. The general approach is to represent the data objects as multi-dimensional points in Euclidean space, and to measure the similarity between objects by the distance between the corresponding multi-dimensional points [13, 6]. It is assumed that the closer the points, the more similar the data objects. Since the dimensionality and the amount of data that need to be processed increases very rapidly, it becomes important to support efficient high-dimensional similarity searching in large-scale systems. This support depends on the development of efficient techniques to support approximate searching. To this end, a number of index structures for retrieval of multi-dimensional data along with associated algorithms for similarity search have been developed [11,19,4]. For time-series data, there are a number of proposed ways to measure similarity. These range from the Euclidean distance to non-Euclidean metrics and the representation of the sequence by appropriate selection of local extremal points [17]. Agrawal, Lin, Sawhney, and Shim [1] considered fast similarity search in the presence of noise, scaling, and translation by making use of the L_∞ norm. Bollobas,

---

* Supported in part by NSF Grant No. CCR–9821038.

Das, Gunopulos, and Mannila [2] considered similarity definitions based on the concept of well-separated geometric sets. It has been noted in the literature however, that as dimensionality increases, query performance degrades significantly, an anomaly known as the dimensionality curse [5,10]. Common approaches for overcoming the dimensionality curse by dimension reduction are linear-algebraic methods such as the Singular Value Decomposition (SVD), or applications of mathematical transforms such as the Discrete Fourier Transform (DFT), Discrete Cosine Transform (DCT), or Discrete Wavelet Transform (DWT). In these methods, lower dimensional vectors are created by taking the first few leading coefficients of the transformed vectors [3].

This paper introduces a spectrum of similarity algorithms which consist of a convex combination of two different measures. A *shape* measure on high-dimensional vectors based on the similarity of permutations through inversion pairs, followed by an associated dimension reduction by bin-score permutations; and a symmetric *magnitude* measure based on the computation of the inner-product and consequently the cosine of the angle between two vectors by a low dimensional representation.

2   The Main Decomposition

An n-dimensional real vector $x = (x_1, x_2, \ldots, x_n) \in \mathbb{R}^n$ can be decomposed as a pair $(s(x), \sigma(x))$ where $s(x)$ is the sorted version of x into weakly increasing coordinates, and $\sigma(x)$ is the permutation of the indices $\{1, 2, \ldots, n\}$ that achieves this ordering. We impose the additional condition that the elements of the permutation $\sigma(x)$ are put in increasing order on any set of indices for which the value of the coordinate is constant. For example when $x = (3, 3, 1, 5, 2, 0, 1, 6, 1)$, $s(x) = (0, 1, 1, 1, 2, 3, 3, 5, 6)$, and in one line notation, $\sigma(x) = 6\ 3\ 7\ 9\ 5\ 1\ 2\ 4\ 8$. Note that in x the smallest coordinate value is $x_6 = 0$, the next smallest is $x_3 = x_7 = x_9 = 1$, etc. Given $x, y \in \mathbb{R}^n$, we aim to approximate the Euclidean distance $\|x - y\|$ as a convex combination

$$\lambda s(x, y) + (1 - \lambda)\pi(x, y) ,\tag{1}$$

where

- $s(x, y)$ is a measure of distance between $s(x)$ and $s(y)$ which is a symmetric function of the coordinates separately in x and y (we refer to this as the *magnitude* or the *symmetric* part),

- $\pi(x, y)$ is a measure of the distance between the permutations $\sigma(x)$ and $\sigma(y)$ (we refer to this as the *shape* part),

- $0 \leq \lambda \leq 1$ is a parameter that controls the bias of the algorithm towards magnitude/symmetry versus shape.

In order for such a scheme to be useful, the individual functions $s(x, y)$ and $\pi(x, y)$ must be amenable to computation using data with reduced dimensionality $\ll n$. In the technique proposed here, this reduced dimension can be selected separately and independently for the two parts. First we discuss the construction of the parts themselves and then present the results of the experiments.

The outline of this paper is as follows. In Sect. 3 we consider the fast approximate calculation of $s(x, y)$ which is based on a novel low-dimensional representation to compute the inner product introduced in [7] and developed in [8]. Section 4 describes how to measure the distance $\pi(x, y)$ on permutations with a low-dimensional representation. This is based on a metric on permutations that we introduce, and the approximation of the metric by *bin-score* permutations. Experiments on labor statistics time-series data are presented in Sect. 5, and conclusions in Sect. 6.

3   The *Magnitude* Part: Power Symmetric Functions

Our representation of data in $\mathbb{R}^n$ with reduced number of dimensions m with $m \ll n$ for the computation of the magnitude part $s(x, y)$ in (1) is based on a novel approximation for the inner product introduced in [7] and further developed in [8]. For integers $n, p > 0$ and $z \in \mathbb{R}^n$, the p-th power symmetric function is defined by $\psi_p(z) = z_1^p + z_2^p + \cdots + z_n^p$. Note that the ordinary Euclidean distance between x and y and the power symmetric functions are related by

$$\|x - y\| = \sqrt{\psi_2(x) + \psi_2(y) - 2 <x, y>} \quad , \qquad (2)$$

where $<x, y> = x_1 y_1 + x_2 y_2 + \ldots + x_n y_n$ is the standard inner-product. Using the $\psi_p(z)$ precomputed for each vector z in the dataset, we look for an estimate for $<x, y>$ by approximating its m-th power in the form

$$<x, y>^m \approx b_1 \psi_1(x)\psi_1(y) + b_2 \psi_2(x)\psi_2(y) + \cdots + b_m \psi_m(x)\psi_m(y) \qquad (3)$$

for large n, where the b_i are universal constants chosen independently of x and y. For each high-dimensional vector x, we calculate $\psi_1(x), \psi_2(x), \ldots, \psi_m(x)$, and keep these m real numbers as a representative of the original vector x. For a given query vector y, we compute $\psi_1(y), \psi_2(y), \ldots, \psi_m(y)$ and approximate $<x, y>$ via (3), and the Euclidean distance via (2).

Our assumption on the structure of the dataset for the computation of $s(x, y)$ by this method is as follows: it consists of n-dimensional vectors whose components are independently drawn from a common (but possibly unknown) distribution with density [12]. In [7] the best set of constants $b_1, b_2, \ldots, b_m$ for the approximation (3) in the sense of least-squares was computed. In particular for the uniform distribution and $m = 2$ the optimal values are shown to be

$$b_1 = -\frac{1}{16} , \qquad b_2 = \frac{45}{64}. \qquad (4)$$

This means that for $m = 2$, $< x, y >$ is approximated by the expression

$$\sqrt{\left| -\frac{1}{16}\psi_1(x)\psi_1(y) + \frac{45}{64}\psi_2(x)\psi_2(y) \right|}$$

In fact in the general case of a density with i-th moment μ_i (about the origin), it can be proved [7] that the constants b_1, b_2 are functions of the first four moments of the density $f(x)$. They are given by the formulas

$$b_1 = \mu_1^2 \cdot \frac{2\mu_2^3 + \mu_1^2\mu_4 - 3\mu_1\mu_2\mu_3}{\mu_2^3 + \mu_1^2\mu_4 - 2\mu_1\mu_2\mu_3},$$

$$b_2 = \frac{\mu_1^4}{\mu_2} \cdot \frac{\mu_1\mu_3 - \mu_2^2}{\mu_2^3 + \mu_1^2\mu_4 - 2\mu_1\mu_2\mu_3}. \tag{5}$$

The moments of the uniform distribution are $\mu_i = 1/(i+1)$, for which the formulas in (5) reduce to the values in (4) above.

A secondary problem of interest in the context of the determination of the best set of constants is dynamic in nature. When the contents of the database changes by adding new data vectors, for example, the parameters used for the approximation problem to the inner-product calculation can be adjusted efficiently. In particular, one *need not* know the density of the distribution of the coordinates in the dataset parametrically. The moments u_i can be estimated as the limit of the N-th estimate $\overline{\mu_i}(N)$ as the dataset is accumulated via

$$\overline{\mu_i}(N+1) = \frac{1}{N+1}\left(N\overline{\mu_i}(N) + t_{N+1}^i\right). \tag{6}$$

where t_N is the N-th sample coordinate observed.

4   The *Shape* Part: Bin-Score Permutations

For a permutation $\rho = \rho_1\rho_2\cdots\rho_n$ of the integers $\{1, 2, \ldots, n\}$ in one-line notation, an *inversion* is a pair $\rho_i > \rho_j$ corresponding to a pair of indices $i < j$. Let $Inv(\rho)$ denote the total number of inversions of ρ. For example for $\rho = 4\ 3\ 5\ 2\ 1$ the set of inversions is $\{(5, 2), (5, 1), (4, 3), (4, 2), (4, 1), (3, 2), (3, 1), (2, 1)\}$ and thus $Inv(\rho) = 8$. For any permutation ρ,

$$0 \leq Inv(\rho) \leq \tfrac{1}{2}n(n-1)$$

with $Inv(\rho) = 0$ iff $\rho = 1\ 2\cdots n$ is the identity permutation and $Inv(\rho) = \frac{1}{2}n(n-1)$ iff $\rho = n\cdots 2\ 1$ is the reverse of the identity permutation. For the details of the underlying partially ordered set see [14]. Inversions arise naturally in the context of sorting as a measure of presortedness [15] when the number of comparisons is the basic measure. The idea of counting inversions is one of many ways of putting a measure of similarity on permutations [9]. Given two permutations ρ and τ, we count the number of inversions ρ would have if we were to use $\tau_1\tau_2\cdots\tau_n$ as the index set. In other words we compute $Inv(\rho\tau^{-1})$. Put

$$\pi(\rho,\tau) = \frac{2}{n(n-1)} Inv(\rho\tau^{-1}) \tag{7}$$

to normalize this measure to the unit interval. Some relevant properties of π are as follows

1. $0 \leq \pi(\rho,\tau) \leq 1$,
2. $\pi(\rho,\tau) = 0$ iff $\rho = \tau$,
3. $\pi(\rho,\tau) = 1$ iff $\rho + \tau_i = n+1$ for $i = 1,2,\ldots n$,
4. $\pi(\rho,\tau) = \pi(\tau,\rho)$,
5. $\pi(\rho,\tau) \leq \pi(\rho,\delta) + \pi(\delta,\tau)$ for any permutation δ.

In particular π is a *metric* on permutations. However, we cannot realistically use the permutations $\rho = \sigma(x)$ and $\tau = \sigma(y)$ introduced in Sect. 2 to compute this distance, since then there is no reduction in the dimension. The question is then whether or not approximations to the permutations ρ and τ by some lower dimensional representation can be made, that would allow us to compute this measure without much deviation from the actual value.

To this end, we consider *bin-score* permutations. For simplicity, assume $n = 2^r$ and ρ is a permutation on $\{1,2,\ldots,n\}$. For any integer $s = 0,1,\ldots,r$, we may divide the index set into $b = 2^s$ consecutive subsets (bins) of length $b' = \frac{n}{b} = 2^{r-s}$ each. The i-th bin is described by the b' consecutive indices

$$i_1 = (i-1)b' + 1, \ \ i_2 = (i-1)b' + 2, \ \ \ldots, \ \ i_{b'} = (i-1)b' + b'.$$

The *score* of this bin is the sum $\rho_{i_1} + \rho_{i_2} + \cdots + \rho_{i_{b'}}$. In this way we construct a myopic version of ρ on $\{1,2,\ldots,b\}$ obtained by placing 1 for the smallest entry among the bin-scores computed, 2 for the next smallest, etc. In case of ties, we make the indices increase from left to right, as in the case of the construction of $\sigma(x)$ described in Sect. 2 (in fact, this permutation is simply $\sigma(x')$ where x' is the b-dimensional vector of bin-scores of x). The bin-score permutation corresponding to $b = n$ is ρ itself, and for $b = 1$ it is the singleton 1. As an example, for $n = 8$, the bin-score permutations of $\rho = 5\ 8\ 2\ 6\ 4\ 3\ 1\ 7$ for $b = 4,2$ are obtained from the scores $13,8,7,8$, and $21,15$ as the permutations $4\ 2\ 1\ 3$ and $2\ 1$, respectively. Note that any bin-score permutation can be obtained by repeated application of the $b' = 2$ case.

5   Experiments

For the experiments, we have used time series data of the seasonally adjusted local area unemployment rate figures (Local Area Unemployment Statistics) for the 51 states supplied online by the U.S. Department of Labor's *Bureau of Labor Statistics*. The monthly rates were extracted for 256 months, covering the period between January 1979 through April 2000 for each state[1]. The dataset we used for the experiments conducted consisted of 51 vectors in $\mathbb{R}^{256}$ of the states, alphabetically ordered as *Alabama* through *Wyoming*, and indexed as $x[1], x[2], \ldots, x[51]$. Thus each $x[i]$ is a vector in $n = 256$ dimensional space. For the query vector y, we used the unemployment rate figures for the same period for the seasonally adjusted national average figures. The purpose of the experiments can be thought of as determining which state in the union has had an unemployment rate history that is closest to the national average for the period of time in question, where closest can be given different meanings by altering the bias parameter λ of the algorithm.

5.1 Estimation of the Parameters: The Magnitude Part

The maximum coordinate over all the vectors in the dataset was found to be 19.5 and the minimum entry as 2.1. Since we have no reason to expect the data to be uniform in this interval, we computed b_1 and b_2 using (5) after a linear normalization to the unit interval.

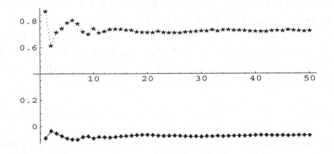

Fig. 1. The estimate to b_1 and b_2 computed for 50 vectors, each of dimension 16 with entries from the uniform distribution on [0,1]. The theoretically obtained asymptotic values are $b_1 = -0.0625$, $b_2 = 0.703125$

To compute the number of sample vectors of dimension 256 required to obtain a meaningful estimate using (5) and the estimates of the first four moments of the density obtained through (6), we first experimented with uniform distribution for which we know the asymptotic values $b_1 = -\frac{1}{16}$, $b_2 = \frac{45}{64}$. Two to three 256-dimensional vectors were enough for convergence. We generated 50 vectors of dimension 16 each. The corresponding values of b_1 and b_2 calculated from the estimates of the moments are shown in Fig. 1. We see that the convergence requires about 20 vectors or about 300 samples. This means that the lower bound on the number of 256 dimensional vectors we need to obtain a reasonable estimates to b_1 and b_2 in the general case is very small.

---

[1] In California unemployment rates, the 1979 year data supplied were 0.0. These were all replaced with the January 1980 value of 5.9.

Computing with $51 \times 256 = 13056$ normalized sample coordinates in the dataset, the approximate moments were calculated by Mathematica to be $\mu_1 = 0.236$, $\mu_2 = 0.072$, $\mu_3 = 0.026$, $\mu_4 = 0.012$. Using the formulas (5) gives

$$b_1 = 0.017 , \quad b_2 = 0.415 \tag{8}$$

With these values, we computed the the summary data $\psi_1(x[1]), \ldots, \psi_1(x[51])$ and $\psi_2(x[1]), \ldots, \psi_2(x[51])$ required.

The following vector of length 51 gives the (approximate) ψ_1 values of the normalized vectors computed in this fashion:

85.3, 95.5, 58.4, 74.1, 74.1, 47.9, 43.7, 48.5, 86.0, 58.3, 52.1, 43.3, 66.6, 73.2, 63.1, 43.3, 36.7, 75.2, 92.3, 58.7, 48.2, 47.1, 90.9, 41.2, 87.8, 56.9, 65.0, 22.7, 60.1, 34.2, 58.6, 78.2, 66.2, 45.0, 34.4, 72.0, 52.1, 74.6, 69.1, 60.4, 60.6, 27.2, 66.7, 62.9, 44.4, 40.5, 40.3, 75.7, 117.7, 51.6, 53.1

and the following the ψ_2 values computed

34.6, 37.6, 15.3, 23.8, 23.5, 10.6, 9.0, 11.8, 31.1, 14.7, 11.5, 8.8, 19.4, 24.6, 21.0, 10.1, 5.8, 25.7, 38.0, 15.6, 10.4, 11.4, 41.6, 8.4, 34.3, 15.0, 17.6, 3.1, 16.5, 6.9, 15.3, 25.3, 18.5, 10.2, 5.5, 25.1, 12.9, 24.9, 22.1, 17.5, 17.2, 3.5, 21.3, 16.9, 9.9, 7.8, 7.5, 25.8, 62.0, 14.4, 13.2

For example for the state of Alabama, the summary magnitude information is

$$\psi_1(x[1]) = 85.3 \quad \text{and} \quad \psi_2(x[1]) = 34.6.$$

We also calculated that for the query vector y of normalized national average rates, the two ψ values are

$$\psi_1(y) = 63.9 \quad \text{and} \quad \psi_2(y) = 17.8.$$

Now for every vector x in the dataset, we calculate the approximation to $< x, y >$ as

$$\sqrt{b_1\psi_1(x)\psi_1(y) + b_2\psi_2(x)\psi_2(y)}$$

where b_1 and b_2 are as given in (8). Therefore as a measure of distance of the symmetric part, we set

$$s(x,y) = \sqrt{|\psi_2(x) + \psi_2(y) - 0.0350342\psi_1(x)\psi_1(y) - 0.82938\psi_2(x)\psi_2(y)|}$$

by using (2).

To see how the approximations to the magnitude part and the actual Euclidean distance values compare, we plotted the normalized actual values and the normalized approximations for the 51 states in Fig. 2. Considering that we are only using the $m = 2$ algorithm for the computation of $s(x, y)$, i.e. the dimension is vastly reduced, the results are satisfactory.

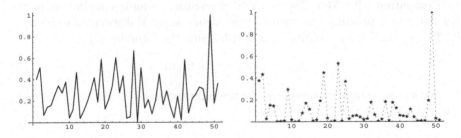

Fig. 2. The magnitude part: normalized actual distances (left), normalized approximations (right)

5.2 Estimation of the Parameters: The Shape Part

To get an idea on the number of bins b to use for the computation of the approximate values $\pi(x, y)$, we calculated vectors of distances $\pi(x, y)$ through the expression (7) with bin-score permutations instead of the actual permutations. Bin-score permutations for each vector $x[1], \ldots, x[51]$ and the query vector y was computed for b ranging from 4 to 256. The resulting distances are plotted in Fig. 3. From the figure, it is clear that even $b = 8$ is a reasonable approximation to the actual curve (i.e. $b = 256$). In the experiments we used the case of $b = 16$ bins.

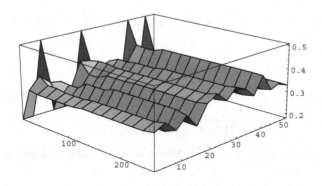

Fig. 3. The shape part: plot of bin–score permutation distances for 4–256 bins

6   Parametric Experiments and Conclusions

In Figs. 5–8, the data plotted is the seasonally adjusted monthly unemployment rates for 256 months spanning January 1979 through April 2000. In each figure, the plot on the left is the actual rates through this time period, and the one on the right is the plot of the rates sorted in increasing order. Consider the function (1) for λ changing from 0 to 1 in increments of 0.01, where for each λ value, $s(x, y)$ makes use of the approximate distance computation described for $m = 2$, and $\pi(x, y)$ is the distance between the bin-score permutations $\sigma(x)$ and $\sigma(y)$ for $b = 16$ bins. For each value of λ in this range we computed the state (i.e. the vector $x[i]$) where the minimum approximate distance is obtained.

- For $0.0 \leq \lambda < 0.5$, the minimum is obtained at $x[15]$, which corresponds to the state of Indiana,

- For $0.5 \leq \lambda \leq 0.9$, the minimum is obtained at $x[46]$, which corresponds to the state of Vermont,

- For $0.9 < \lambda \leq 1.0$, the minimum is obtained at $x[11]$, which corresponds to the state of Georgia.

The observed "continuity" of these results as a function of λ is a desirable aspect of any such family of algorithms.

Figures 5–8 indicate the behavior of the algorithm on the dataset. For small values of λ, the bias is towards the *shapes* of the curves. In these cases the algorithm finds the time-series data of the national rates (Fig. 8, left), resemble most that of Indiana (Fig. 5, left) out of the 51 states in the dataset. On the other extreme, for values of λ close to 1, the bias is towards the *magnitudes*, and the algorithm finds the sorted data of the national rates (Fig. 8, right), resemble most that of the state of Georgia (Fig. 7, right). The intermediate values pick the state of Vermont (Fig. 6) as the closest to the national average rates.

In conclusion, we proposed a spectrum of dynamic dimensionality reduction algorithms based on the approximation of the standard inner-product, and bin-score permutations based on an inversion measure on permutations. The experiments on time-series data show that with this technique, the similarity between two objects in high-dimensional space can be well approximated by a significantly lower dimensional representation.

We remark that even though we used a convex combination of the two measures controlled by a parameter λ, it is possible to combine $s(x, y)$ and $\pi(x, y)$ for the final similarity measure in many other ways,

$$s(x, y)^{\lambda} \pi(x, y)^{1-\lambda},$$

for example. In any such formulation, the determination of the best value of λ for a given application will most likely require the experimental evaluation of the behavior of the approximate distance function by sampling from the dataset.

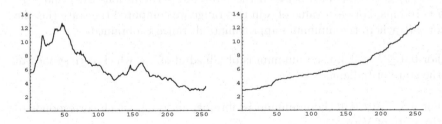

Fig. 4. $x[15] =$ State of Indiana unemployment rate data: actual (left), sorted (right). For parameter λ in the range $0.0 \le \lambda < 0.5$, the algorithm picks the state of Indiana's data as the one closest to the national average data in Fig. 7.

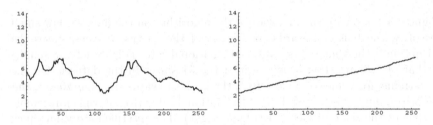

Fig. 5. $x[46] =$ State of Vermont unemployment rate data: actual (left), sorted (right). For parameter λ in the range $0.5 \le \lambda \le 0.9$, the algorithm picks the state of Vermont's data as the one closest to the national average data in Fig. 7.

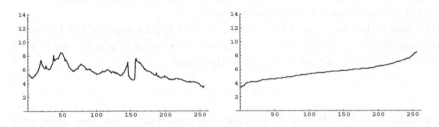

Fig. 6. $x[11] =$ State of Georgia unemployment rate data: actual (left), sorted (right). For parameter λ in the range $0.9 < \lambda \le 1.0$, the algorithm picks the state of Georgia's data as the one closest to the national average data in Fig. 7

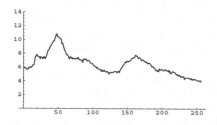 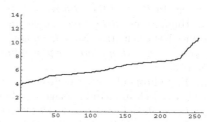

Fig. 7. Query data $y =$ National average unemployment rates: actual (left), sorted (right). The dataset is the seasonally adjusted monthly unemployment rates for 256 months spanning January 1979 through April 2000

References

1. R. Agrawal, K-I. Lin, H. S. Sawhney, and K. Shim. Fast Similarity Search in the Presence of Noise, Scaling, and Translation in Time-Series Databases. *The VLDB Journal*, pp. 490–501, 1995.
2. B. Bollobas, G. Das, D. Gunopulos, and H. Mannila. Time-Series Similarity Problems and Well-Separated Geometric Sets. *Proc. of 13th Annual ACM Symposium on Computational Geometry*, Nice, France, pp. 454–456, 1997.
3. R. Agrawal, C. Faloutsos, and A. Swami. Efficient similarity search in sequence databases. In *4th Int. Conference on Foundations of Data Organization and Algorithms*, pp. 69–84, 1993.
4. S. Berchtold, D. Keim, and H. Kriegel. The X-tree: An index structure for high-dimensional data. In *Proceedings of the Int. Conf. on Very Large Data Bases*, pp. 28–39, Bombay, India, 1996.
5. S. Berchtold, C. Bohm, D. Keim, and H. Kriegel. A cost model for nearest neighbor search in high-dimensional data space. In *Proc. ACM Symp. on Principles of Database Systems*, Tuscon, Arizona, 1997.
6. S. Deerwester, S.T. Dumais, G.W.Furnas, T.K. Launder, and R. Harshman. Indexing by latent semantic analysis. *Journal of the American Society for Information Science*, 41:391–407, 1990.
7. Ö. Eğecioğlu. How to approximate the inner-product: fast dynamic algorithms for Euclidean similarity. *Technical Report TRCS98-37*, Department of Computer Science, University of California at Santa Barbara, December 1998.
8. Ö. Eğecioğlu and H. Ferhatosmanoğlu, Dimensionality reduction and similarity computation by inner product approximations. *Proc. 9th Int. Conf. on Information and Knowledge Management (CIKM'00)*, Nov. 2000, Washington DC.
9. V. Estivill-Castro and D. Wood. A Survey of Adaptive Sorting Algorithms. *ACM Computing Surveys*, Vol. 24, No. 4, pp. 441–476, 1992.
10. C. Faloutsos, M. Ranganathan, and Y. Manolopoulos. Fast subsequence matching in time-series databases. In *Proc. ACM SIGMOD Int. Conf. on Management of Data*, pages 419–429, Minneapolis, May 1994.
11. A. Guttman. R-trees: A dynamic index structure for spatial searching. In *Proc. ACM SIGMOD Int. Conf. on Management of Data*, pp. 47–57, 1984.
12. N.A.J. Hastings and J.B. Peacock. *Statistical Distributions,* Halsted Press, New York, 1975.

13. D. Hull. Improving text retrieval for the routing problem using latent semantic indexing. In *Proc. of the 17th ACM-SIGIR Conference*, pp. 282–291, 1994.
14. J. E. Humphreys. *Reflection Groups and Coxeter Groups,* Cambridge Studies in Advanced Mathematics, No. 29, Cambridge Univ. Press, Cambridge, 1990.
15. D. Knuth. *The art of computer programming* (Vol. III), Addison-Wesley, Reading, MA, 1973.
16. Korn F., Sidiropoulos N., Faloutsos C., Siegel E., and Protopapas Z. Fast nearest neighbor search in medical image databases. In *Proceedings of the Int. Conf. on Very Large Data Bases*, pages 215–226, Mumbai, India, 1996.
17. C-S. Perng, H. Wang, S. R. Zhang, and D. S. Parker. Landmarks: a new model for similarity-basedpattern querying in time-series databases. *Proc. of the 16-th ICDE*, San Diego, CA, 2000.
18. T. Seidl and Kriegel H.-P. Efficient user-adaptable similarity search in large multimedia databases. In *Proceedings of the Int. Conf. on Very Large Data Bases*, pages 506–515, Athens, Greece, 1997.
19. D. White and R. Jain. Similarity indexing with the SS-tree. In *Proc. Int. Conf. Data Engineering*, pp. 516–523, 1996.

Data Structures for Minimization of Total Within-Group Distance for Spatio-temporal Clustering

Vladimir Estivill-Castro[1] and Michael E. Houle[2]

[1] Department of Computer Science & Software Engineering
The University of Newcastle, Callaghan, NSW 2308, Australia
[2] Basser Department of Computer Science
The University of Sydney, Sydney, NSW 2006, Australia

Abstract. Statistical principles suggest minimization of the *total within-group distance* (TWGD) as a robust criterion for clustering point data associated with a Geographical Information System [17]. This NP-hard problem must essentially be solved using heuristic methods, although admitting a linear programming formulation. Heuristics proposed so far require quadratic time, which is prohibitively expensive for data mining applications. This paper introduces data structures for the management of large bi-dimensional point data sets and for fast clustering via interchange heuristics. These structures avoid the need for quadratic time through approximations to proximity information. Our scheme is illustrated with two-dimensional quadtrees, but can be extended to use other structures suited to three dimensional data or spatial data with time-stamps. As a result, we obtain a fast and robust clustering method.

1 Introduction

A central problem in mining point data associated with a Geographical Information System (GIS) is automatic partition into *clusters* [9]. Regardless of the method used, a clustering result can be interpreted as a hypothesis that models groups in the data. Clustering is a form of induction, and uses some bias, in order to select the most appropriate model. The optimization criteria that guide clustering algorithms have their basis in differing induction principles. When these optimization criteria are derived from statistical principles, it is possible to establish formal bounds on the quality of the result, as illustrated by the notion of statistical significance. In this paper, we concentrate on one such criterion studied in the statistical literature, where it was known as the *grouping* [29] and the *total within-group distance* [23], and in the spatial clustering literature as the *full-exchange* [24] — here, we refer to this criterion as the total within-group distance (TWGD). The criterion has several variants widely used in many fields.

Unfortunately, the TWGD criterion is expensive to compute. Attempts in geographical analysis have involved only very small data sets (for example, Murray [17] applied it to less than 152 geographical sites). Minimizing the TWGD

L. De Raedt and A. Siebes (Eds.): PKDD 2001, LNAI 2168, pp. 91–102, 2001.
© Springer-Verlag Berlin Heidelberg 2001

turns out to be an NP-hard problem. Even though it admits a linear programming formulation, the number of constraints is quadratic, making even the use of linear-program solvers infeasible in practice. This leaves the option of using heuristic approaches such as hill-climbing iterative search methods to obtain approximate solutions of acceptable quality. However, traditional hill-climbing interchange heuristics require quadratic time in the number n of data items, again far too much time for data mining applications.

In this paper, we show how a variant of the well-known quadtree data structure can be used to support a hill-climbing interchange heuristic for an approximation of the TWGD optimization problem, in subquadratic time. By computing only an approximation to the traditional TWGD optimization function, great savings in time can be achieved while still producing robust clusterings. The TWGD problem is formally introduced in Sect. 2, and a brief overview of its relationship to other clustering problems is given. After some background on iterative hill-climber searching in Sect. 3, the quad-tree-based heuristics are presented in Sect. 4. The paper concludes in Sect. 5 with remarks on experimental results and a brief discussion of alternative methods.

2 Distance-Based Clustering

We consider partitioning a set of n geo-referenced objects $S = \{s_1, \ldots, s_n\}$ into k clusters. Each object $s_i \in \Re^D$ is a vector of D numerical attributes. Clustering methods typically rely on a metric (or distance function) to evaluate the dissimilarity between data items. In spatial settings, such as those associated with a GIS, the distance function measures spatial association according to spatial proximity (for example, the distance between the centers of mass of spatial objects may be used as the distance between objects [9]). While the analyses of large data sets that arise in such contexts as spatial data mining [19] and exploratory spatial data analysis (ESDA) [21] mostly use the Euclidean distance as a starting point, many geographical situations demand alternative metrics. Typical examples of these are the Manhattan distance, network shortest-path distance, or obstacle-avoiding Euclidean distance. Our method is generic in that it places no special restrictions on d. Typical choices for d in spatial settings are the Euclidean distance $\text{EUCLID}(\boldsymbol{x}, \boldsymbol{y}) = \sqrt{(\boldsymbol{x} - \boldsymbol{y})^T \cdot (\boldsymbol{x} - \boldsymbol{y})}$,[1] the Manhattan distance $\sum_{i=1}^{D} |\boldsymbol{x}_i - \boldsymbol{y}_i|$, or a network distance. When time is introduced, the user may choose a combined measure, for which our methods can also be applied. For example, one possibility is that if $D = 3$, with two coordinates for spatial reference and the third co-ordinate for a time value, the distance metric could be $d(\boldsymbol{x}, \boldsymbol{y}) = \alpha \cdot \sqrt{(\boldsymbol{x}_1 - \boldsymbol{y}_1)^2 + (\boldsymbol{x}_2 - \boldsymbol{y}_2)^2} + \beta \cdot |\boldsymbol{x}_3 - \boldsymbol{y}_3|$, where α and β are constants determining the relative contributions of differences in space and in time. Other alternatives involve cyclic measures in time that arise from the days of the week or the months of the year. In any case, although the distance d could be costly to evaluate, we assume that this cost is independent of n, although dependent on D. A clustering problem is *distance-based* if it makes use

---

[1] For vectors $\boldsymbol{x}$ and $\boldsymbol{y}$, $\boldsymbol{x}^T \cdot \boldsymbol{y}$ denotes their inner product.

of a distance metric in the formulation of its optimization criterion. One such family of criteria is the total within-group distance:

Definition 1. *Let $S = \{s_1, \ldots, s_n\} \subseteq X$ be a set of n objects and $d : X \times X \to \Re^{\geq 0}$ be a metric. The order-a TWGD^a clustering problem for k groups is:*

$$Minimize \ \text{TWGD}^a(P) = \sum_{m=1}^{k} \sum_{i<j \, \wedge \, s_i, s_j \in S_m} w_i \, w_j \, d(s_i, s_j)^a,$$

where $P = S_1| \ldots |S_k$ is a partition of S, a is some constant value (typically 1 or 2) and w_i is a weight for the relevance of s_i, but may have other specific interpretations. If a is not specified, it will be assumed to be 1 by default.

Intuitively, the TWGD criteria not only minimize the dissimilarity between items in a group, but also use all interactions between items in a group to assess group cohesiveness (and thus, use all the available dissimilarity information). Also, they implicitly maximize the distance between groups (and thereby minimize coupling), since the terms $d(s_i, s_j)$ not included in the sum are those for which the items belong to different groups.

In the special case where $d(x, y) = \text{EUCLID}(x, y)$, the literature on parametric statistics has proposed many iterative heuristics for computing approximate solutions to the TWGD^2 problem [7], all of which can be considered variants of expectation maximization (EM) [6] using means as estimators of location. One very popular heuristic that alternates between estimating the classification and estimating the parameters of the model is k-MEANS. k-MEANS exhibits linear behavior and is simple to implement; however, it typically produces poor results, requiring complex procedures for initialization [14]. Other well-known variations of EM are the Generalized Lloyd Algorithm (or GLA), and fuzzy-c-clustering. With the possible exception of k-C-L1-MEDIANS [4,13], all are representative-based clustering methods that use the Euclidean metric.

These EM variants grant special status to the use of sums of squares of the Euclidean metric. This preference for $a = 2$ in the early statistical literature derives from the mathematical need to use differentiation and gradient descent for numerical optimization. However, despite its popularity, the case $a = 2$ has implications for robustness and resistance [25] that ultimately affect the quality of the result. That is, using $a = 2$, rather than (say) $a = 1$, renders the algorithms far more sensitive to noise and outliers. Effective clustering methods can be thus devised by concentrating on the case $a = 1$ (medians rather than means). Still, it is not immediately clear that these methods can be as fast as k-MEANS.

3 Interchange Hill-Climbers

The minimization of $\text{TWGD}^1(P)$ is typically solved approximately using interchange heuristics based on hill-climbers [16,17,18,28]. Hill-climbers search the space of all partitions $P = S_1| \ldots |S_k$ of S by treating the space as if it were a

graph: every node of the graph can be thought to correspond to a unique partition of the data. For the TWGD problem, two nodes P and P' are adjacent if
and only if their corresponding partitions coincide in all but one data point.

Interchange heuristics start at a randomly-chosen solution P^0 (that is, a
random node in the implicit graph), and explore by moving from the current
solution to one of its neighbors. One general interchange heuristic, originally
proposed in 1968 by Teitz and Bart [28], is a hill-climber that is regarded as the
best known benchmark [16]. We will refer to this heuristic as TAB.

TAB considers the data points in a fixed circular ordering $(s_1, s_2, \ldots, s_n)$.
Whenever the turn of data point s_i comes up, it is considered for changing its
group to any of the $k-1$ others. The most advantageous interchange P_j of these
alternatives is determined, and if it is an improvement over the current solution
P^t, then P_j becomes the new current solution P^{t+1}; otherwise, $P^{t+1} = P^t$. In
either case, the turn then passes to the next data point in the circular list, s_{i+1}
(or s_1 if $i = n$). If a full cycle through the data set yields no improvement, a
local optimum has been reached, and the search halts.

Some care must be taken when evaluating the optimization criterion using
TAB. Given a current partition P^t and one of its $k-1$ neighbors P_j, a naive
approach would compute $TWGD(P_j)$ and $TWGD(P^t)$ explicitly in order to
decide whether $TWGD(P_j) < TWGD(P^t)$. A more efficient way computes
the discrete gradient $\triangledown(P^t, P_j) = TWGD(P^t) - TWGD(P_j)$. Since only s_i
is changing cluster membership, $TWGD(P^t)$ and $TWGD(P_j)$ differ only in
$\Theta(n)$ terms, and so $\Theta(n)$ evaluations of the distance metric are required to
compute $\triangledown(P^t, P_j)$. Therefore, the number of evaluations of the distance metric
required to test all interchanges suggested by s_i is in $\Theta(kn)$. The generic TAB
heuristic thus requires $\Omega(n^2)$ time per complete scan though the list. At least
one complete scan is needed for the heuristic to terminate, although empirical
evidence suggests that the total number of scans required is constant.

4   Quad-Trees for Clustering

The clustering heuristic we propose, QUAD, differs from the original TAB heuristic in that, it replaces the discrete gradient $\triangledown(P^t, P_j)$ by a computationally less-
expensive approximation $\triangledown^\approx(P^t, P_j)$. The calculation of $\triangledown^\approx(P^t, P_j)$ is facilitated
by a hierarchical spatial data structure, whose performance depends on the di-
mensionality of the data. For simplicity, we present our method in the context of
two-dimensional spatial data, using a variant of the PR-quadtree [26]. However,
the method is easily extended to spatial and spatio-temporal data in three and
higher dimensions with an appropriate choice of search structure: in particular,
the strategy can immediately be applied to octrees in three-dimensional settings.
Pseudocode descriptions of both TAB and QUAD appear in an extended technical
report [12]. Also, our algorithm is generic in the value of a, since the computation
of $d(s_i, s_j)^a$ can be considered as part of the dissimilarity computation.

The quadtree of a point set encodes a partition that covers the plane. The
coordinates of the point p at the root divide the plane into 4 logical regions by

means of the vertical and horizontal line through p. Then recursively, these four regions are further decomposed until each rectangular region contains a subset of the input of suitable size. The quadtree in QUAD preserves the property that data points are stored at leaves, but internal nodes use data elements as their split points. It also follows the convention that the upper and right bounding sides of each quad-region (including the corners) are open, while the remainder of the boundary is closed. We can easily assume that all data points are distinct, since we can use the weight w_i in Definition 1 to represent the number of copies of point s_i. Using $O(n \log n)$ comparisons, the original instance of TWGD can therefore be reduced to one with no duplicate data points. Also, we can ensure that a particular data element is never used more than once as a split point. These adjustments to the PR-quadtree allow us to represent all data points of the two-dimensional plane independently of the precision at which the points are represented, and to interleave the temporal dimensions in case the metric used is cyclic. Figure 1 shows a data set and a corresponding PR-quadtree, where splits were chosen randomly.

Our quadtree shares the characteristics of other variants in that its expected depth is logarithmic, and thus the routines for insertion, deletion and search require $O(\log n)$ time. We will not elaborate on these data management operations, as their particular implementations can be easily derived from those of other representatives of the quadtree family [26]. Moreover, these data-management operations do not involve distance computations, but only require comparisons with the D coordinates of split points. We will include the cost of constructing the data structure as part of the clustering, but emphasize that the time required does not change with the choice of distance used. Thus, for our purposes, our routine COMPUTE_QUADTREE works by repeated insertion of a random shuffle of the data and requires a total of $O(Dn \log n)$ expected comparisons.

For the operation of QUAD, the internal nodes of the quadtree store additional information pertaining to the current best partition $P^t = S_1^t | \ldots | S_k^t$. For all $1 \leq j \leq k$, each internal node ν stores the total weight $T_\nu[j]$ of points belonging to cluster j under the subtree rooted at ν. Thus, when all weights are 1, $T_\nu[j]$ is the number of points belonging to cluster j under ν. For the root ρ of the quadtree, we have $T_\rho[j] = |S_j^t|$ and $\sum_{j=1}^k T_\rho[j] = n$. Also, for all $1 \leq j \leq k$, each internal node stores the total vector sum $M_\nu[j]$ of the data points under the subtree rooted at ν that belong to cluster j. Note that from M and T we can compute the center of mass $c_\nu[j] = \frac{M_\nu[j]}{T_\nu[j]}$ of all points under ν that belong to cluster j in the current partition P^t. The quadtree in Fig. 1 shows the values of T for the data set shown to its left, in the case where $1 \leq j \leq k = 3$.

Whenever a point s_i changes its current cluster assignment, some of the values of $T_\nu[j]$ and $M_\nu[j]$ must be updated. However, all nodes that may need to be updated lie along the unique path from the root to the leaf corresponding to s_i; also, the only values of j for which this need be done are those corresponding to the clusters between which s_i migrates. More precisely, if s_i migrates from cluster j' to cluster j, then the changes required are (1) $M_\nu[j] \leftarrow M_\nu[j] + w_i s_i$, (2) $M_\nu[j'] \leftarrow M_\nu[j'] - w_i s_i$, (3) $T_\nu[j] \leftarrow T_\nu[j] + w_i$, and (4) $T_\nu[j'] \leftarrow T_\nu[j'] - w_i$,

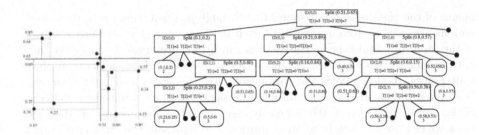

Fig. 1. A partition of the plane according to a two-dimensional data set, and its representation as a quadtree (leaves show cluster labels, internal nodes show T)

for all ν in the path from the root to s_i. Thus, if an interchange occurs, the change in representation of the current partition P^t to the new partition P^{t+1} is performed in $O(\log n)$ time, and does not involve distance computations.

We now turn our attention to $\nabla(P^t, P_j) = \text{MEDIAN}(i, j') - \text{MEDIAN}(i, j)$ where $\text{MEDIAN}(i, j) = \sum_{s \in S_j} w_i d(s, s_i)$. We denote this sum as $\text{MEDIAN}(i, j)$ since its value is an assessment of how well s_i acts as the median of the cluster S_j. The value of $\text{MEDIAN}(i, j')$ is known, having been computed when the most recent change to the partition occurred. Computing $\text{MEDIAN}(i, j)$ exactly, on the other hand, would require $\Theta(|S_j|)$ time. The quadtree-based optimization function $\nabla^{\approx}(P^t, P_j)$ approximates $\text{MEDIAN}(i, j)$ with the value of

$$\text{APPX\_MEDIAN}(i, j) = \sum_{\nu \in \mathcal{N}_i} T_\nu[j] \cdot d(c_\nu[j], s_i), \tag{1}$$

where $\mathcal{N}_i$ is a set of nodes of the quadtree such that every leaf of the quadtree has exactly one element of $\mathcal{N}_i$ as an ancestor. A valid choice of $\mathcal{N}_i$ will be called an *overlay* for s_i, by analogy with the overlay of two layers in GIS. For each node $\nu \in \mathcal{N}_i$, the center of mass $c_\nu[j]$ serves as an approximation of the location of the data points of S_j whose corresponding quadtree leaves have ν as an ancestor. By using the distance from s_i to the center of mass, and counting the distance once for each point of S_j approximated (that is, $T_\nu[j]$ times), the total contribution to $\text{MEDIAN}(i, j)$ can be estimated.

Although there are many possible ways in which $\mathcal{N}_i$ may be chosen, we propose one which limits the error of approximation while still allowing for an evaluation using $O(\log n)$ distance computations. Consider the unique path $\pi_Q(s_i)$ in the quadtree Q from the root to the leaf corresponding to s_i. This path has logarithmic expected length. The boxes in this path will be considered the first input layer to the overlay. Figure 2 illustrates this. The top left region is the first layer corresponding directly with our quadtree Q. The figure in the top-middle corresponds to a virtual set of nodes that constitute a second layer, which we call the virtual neighborhood. This second layer $\mathcal{L}$ is built from the virtual complete tree V as follows. We initialize $\mathcal{L}_i$ to hold the leaf ν_i corresponding to s_i. Then for every node $\nu \in \pi_V(s_i)$ (this is the path from the root in V), ordered from the leaf up to the root, we add to $\mathcal{L}_i$ the siblings of ν in the quadtree V, the nodes representing the neighboring regions of ν at this level, if they exist, and the siblings of these neighboring nodes — provided that none of their descendants have already been added. A node ν' is a neighbor of ν if its region shares a common bounding edge (face boundary in 3D) with that of ν. $\mathcal{N}_i$ is the overlay of $\mathcal{L}_i$ and $\pi_Q(s_i)$ and collects nodes that are deeper in Q but close to s_i.

Indexing techniques allow the neighbors of ν to be determined in constant time [12]. These techniques are well known, having been used for computing linear orders (Morton orders) of the nodes. The virtual neighborhood can be computed in $O(\log n)$ time from Morton order indices. Thus computing our proposed overlay requires time proportional to the length of the path; that is, $O(\log n)$ distance evaluations. Note that all siblings in the tree are neighbors, but not all neighbors are siblings: in the case $D = 2$, a node can have up to 3 siblings and 8 neighbors. Figure 2 shows the construction of the overlay for point $(0.58, 0.53)$ in the example data set of Fig. 1. The top left diagram shows the logical structure for the quadtree of Fig. 1. There are 12 leaves in the quadtree, appearing as white squares (the gray squares correspond to empty nodes). The neighborhood of $(0.58, 0.53)$ across all levels is shown in the diagram in the top center; the diagrams at the bottom show the neighbors at depth 3, depth 2 and depth 1 respectively. The nodes appear in black, while neighbors and siblings of neighbors appear with different patterns.

Since the overlay includes only a constant number of nodes at each level along the path $\pi(s_i)$, the size of the overlay is logarithmic, and therefore the overall time required to determine the overlay is also in $O(\log n)$. Consequently, $\nabla^\approx(P^t, P_j)$ requires only $O(\log n)$ distance computations. In general, for octrees or their higher-dimensional equivalents, the constant of proportionality in these complexities rises exponentially with D. Nevertheless, the constants are sufficiently small for the method to be efficient for two- and three-dimensions.

The proposed overlay construction is such that the area (or volume) covered by a nodes is smaller as the region is closer to s_i. In particular, when $D = 2$, it is not possible to travel in the plane from the (larger) region of an overlay node at depth δ to the point s_i without crossing the (smaller) region of an overlay node at depth $\delta + 2$, unless point s_i is at a leaf with depth less than $\delta + 2$ (in which case the approximation is exact, as its subtree stores only one data point). This property contributes to the accuracy of the proposed approximation in Equation (1). The following lemma illustrates the claim for the Euclidean metric, but can easily be extended to other metrics.

Lemma 1. *Let s and s_i be data items in D-dimensional space such that the Euclidean distance $d(s_i, s)$ is approximated by $d(s_i, c_\nu[j])$, where ν is the unique overlay node to which s is assigned. Then the relative error is no more than 2.*

Proof. We may assume that s_i is at the origin of the D-dimensional space. If ν is a neighbor or sibling in the virtual overlay of the box containing s_i the approximation is exact. If ν is further up the overlay $\mathcal{N}_i$), then the line ss_i cuts at least one virtual neighbor or sibling of s_i. In this case, the worst-case absolute error occurs when s is at a corner of the D-dimensional box (quad) corresponding

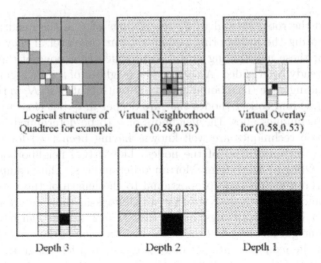

Fig. 2. The logical structure of the quadtree of Fig. 1, the neighborhood and the overlay for $(0.58, 0.53)$

to node ν, and the point $\boldsymbol{c}_\nu[j]$ is at the diametrically opposite corner of the quad (the error is much less in real data sets since $\boldsymbol{c}_\nu[j]$ is the center of mass of all points in the subtree rooted at ν). Also, the absolute error $\|d(s_i, \boldsymbol{c}_\nu[j]) - d(s_i, s)\|$ is maximum when the three points s_i, s and $\boldsymbol{c}_\nu[j]$ are aligned. Let l be the length of side of the D-dimensional box B where s_i is. Then, neighbors and siblings of the parent of B in the overlay are D-dimensional boxes with length $2l$ per side. In general, neighbors and siblings of the i-th ancestor are D-dimensional boxes with length $2^i l$ per side. Thus, if ν is a neighbor or sibling of the h-th ancestor, the maximum absolute error is the Euclidean metric of the vector with all entries equal to $2^h l$. Thus, $\|d(s_i, \boldsymbol{c}_\nu[j]) - d(s_i, s)\| \le \sqrt{\sum_{j=1}^{D}(2^h l)^2} = l 2^h \sqrt{D}$. Because s is in the region covered by the D-dimensional box corresponding to ν, and there is at least one neighbor (or sibling) between s_i and s of side length $2^i l$, for $i = 1, \ldots, h-1$ we have $d(s_i, s)$ is at least the Euclidean norm of the vector who has all entries equal to $\sum_{i=1}^{h-1} 2^i l$. Since the norm of this vector is $l\sqrt{D}(2^h - 1)$ the claim follows

$$\frac{\|d(s_i, \boldsymbol{c}_\nu[j]) - d(s_i, s)\|}{d(s_i, s)} \le \frac{l 2^h \sqrt{D}}{l(2^h - 1)\sqrt{D}} = 1/(1 - 1/2^h).$$

Note that this result is independent of l (which is proportional to the depth of s_i and the dimensions D. This property does not hold for a standard Quadtree since a box may have an arbitrarily larger box as a neighbor. Naturally, the absolute approximation error increases with the distance $d(s_i, s)$; however, the likelihood of s contributing to either cluster containing s_i diminishes with distance.

5   Discussion

Algorithms for TWGD in the case $a = 1$ has been implemented for spatio-temporal clustering [11]. In this context, using the Euclidean distance, the clusterings generated were more robust than when using TWGD^2 or EM. This is not surprising since k-MEANS and EM work well on spherical and ellipsoid-shaped clusters, respectively. Also, experiments show [11] that with a subquadratic algorithm for TWGD, one million data points can be clustered in the same CPU-time that previous quadratic algorithms required for only 10 to 20 thousand points. The subquadratic algorithms presented in [11] are based on a different technique, randomization. While the complexity of those algorithms also does not depend exponentially upon the dimension D, with respect to the number of records n, their complexities are only in $O(n\sqrt{n})$. For the case when D is small (two or three dimensional data with possibly an additional time dimension), the $O(n \log n)$ TWGD algorithms presented here are considerably faster. Of the algorithms proposed, QUAD has been implemented [12]. The experiments

Measurement	File size	
	100	4300
$\Delta = \sharp$ of interchange decisions	902±21	34,440±500
$\Pi = \sharp$ of interchanges performed	127±4.4	5023±115
% of Δ that were suboptimal	0.2%	0.5%±0.1
% of Δ that were counterproductive	0.1%	0.2%
% of Π that were suboptimal	1.04%±0.4	2.0 %±0.5
% of Π that were counterproductive	0.9%±0.3	1.2%±0.4

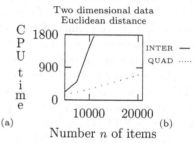

(a)   (b)

Fig. 3. (a) Evaluating the interchange decisions made by QUAD; (b) Illustration of the CPU-time requirements of TAB and QUAD

on CPU-time performance illustrate the scalability of our algorithm even though the metric used was the relatively-inexpensive two-dimensional Euclidean metric (see Fig. 3b). For more complex and expensive metrics, such as network distances or obstacle-avoiding shortest paths, the improvements from our methods would be even more dramatic. Also, the quality of the approximation has been confirmed experimentally [12]. For 10 runs, the outcome of interchange decisions using the approximate gradient computation was contrasted with the decisions using the exact gradient computation. Figure 3a shows 95% percent confidence intervals for the results. From Table 3a we see that only a fraction of one percent of the decisions made by QUAD differ from those that would have been made by TAB.

The techniques for fast approximation of quadratic-time processes presented here have parallels with similar process approximation in other areas, such as the simulation of particle motion [1,5], graph drawing [22] and facility location [2].

For particle motion, approximation of proximity information is used for the computation of the dynamics of the gravitational n-body problem. The goal is to avoid the direct computation of all forces between all pairs of particles, as this number is quadratic. These techniques naturally extend to spring-based graph layout algorithms [15], in which the nodes of the graph are treated as electrically-charged particles and edges as springs. Here, the interplay among the repulsive forces between nodes, and the repulsive and attractive forces along edges, serves to stretch the graph out while keeping the edge lengths reasonably balanced.

Approximation of proximity has also been explored to some extent in two-and three-dimensional clustering settings, where hierarchical structures storing aggregated information have been proposed [27,30,31]. However, these attempts suffer from imposition of a grid on the data where the number of cells grows quadratically in two dimensions, and cubically in three dimensions; also, for some methods, determining an appropriate granularity for the grid can be problematic.

Two of these methods deserve special mention. The BIRCH method saw the introduction of a hierarchical structure for the economical storage of grid information, called a *clustering feature tree* (CF-tree) [31]. The methods of our paper can be adapted to use the information summarized at the nodes of a CF-tree for approximation of the discrete median, also using $O(n \log n)$ comparisons in low dimensional settings. Compared to the quadtree-based method, one would expect that the constants of proportionally for the CF-tree version to be slightly smaller. However, due to the level of aggregation and sampling, one would also expect the quality of the results to be poorer than with quadtrees.

The STING method [30] combines aspects of several approaches. In 2D, STING uses a hierarchical data structure whose root covers the region of analysis. As with a quadtree, each region has 4 children representing 4 sub-regions. However, in STING, all leaves are at equal depth in the structure, and all leaves represent areas of equal size in the data domain. For each node ν, statistical information is computed — namely, the total number T_ν of points that correspond to the area covered by the node ν, the center c_ν of mass, the standard deviation σ_ν, the largest values $\mathbf{max}_\nu$, and so on. The structure is built by propagating information at the children to the parents according to arithmetic formulae; for example, the total number of points under a parent node is obtaining by summing the total number of points under each of its children. When the STING structure is used for clustering purposes, information is gathered from the root down. At each level, distribution information is used to eliminate branches from consideration. As only those leaves that are reached are relevant, the data points under these leaves can be agglomerated. It is claimed that once the search structure is in place, the time taken by STING to produce a clustering will be sublinear. However, as we indicated earlier, determining the appropriate depth of the structure (or equivalently the granularity of the grid) is a considerable challenge. STING would achieve the precision of the QUAD algorithm only when the grid is sufficiently fine for every data point to lie in just one data cell — however, in this case the algorithm would have quadratic complexity.

It should be noted that all the methods mentioned above, including the approximate QUAD method, suffer in that the size of the data structure would expand rapidly with the dimensionality of the data.

An alternative strategy to our approach here is the use of spatial data structures (R^*-trees) to either sample the data set or maintain a Voronoi structure to speed up interchange heuristics [9]. This has been applied with particular attention to I/O operations required since this is the dominant term when clustering is at the interface of spatio-temporal data mining and spatial database system. However, this is restricted to the Euclidean distance and to medoids [9]. Medoid methods are comparable to the case $a = 1$ of the TWGD since they are analogous to the minimization of an L_1-loss function, and since $O(n \log n)$ algorithms have been achieved though approximation for $D = 2$ [10].

The strategy of facility location by aggregation has generated much debate concerning the amount of introduced error (see [3,8] and their references). The common recommendation is to minimize its use; however, this is driven by an interest in optimizing the associated cost rather than the quality of the clustering. While facility location is generally concerned with larger problems, these are usually smaller than those arising in most data mining applications. Approximate solutions using aggregation provide a basis for new aggregation schemes that can again be solved approximately. Iterative refinements of such schemes can result in reduction of the error [3]. Also, algorithms suited to large problems can reduce the proportion of aggregation required to obtain more accurate solutions. In this way, our approximation methods can contribute directly to improvements in existing facility location strategies.

Finally, there is the perception that partitioning algorithms require *a priori* knowledge of the number k of clusters. But, a fast algorithm that can robustly cluster for a given k is an effective tool for determining the appropriate number of clusters. An algorithm that quickly evaluates $L(k)$ [19,20] can be used as the basis of an algorithm with optimization criterion L that uses hill-climbing on k to determine k. Methods such as AutoClass and Snob use hill-climbing with an initial random k_0 to effectively determine an appropriate choice of k.

References

1. J. Barnes and P. Hut. A hierarchical $O(n \log n)$ force-calculation algorithm. *Nature*, 324:446–449, 1986.
2. L. Belbin. The use of non-hierarchical allocation methods for clustering large sets of data. *Australian Comp. J.*, 19:32–41, 1987.
3. R. L. Bowerman, P. H. Calamai, and G. B. Hal. The demand partitioning method for reducing aggregation errors in p-median problems. *Computers & Operations Research*, 26:1097–1111, 1999.
4. P. S. Bradley, O. L. Mangasarian, and W. N. Street. Clustering via concave minimization. *Advances in neural information processing systems*, 9:368–, 1997.
5. J. Carrier, L. Greengard, and V. Rokhlin. A fast adaptive multipode algorithm for particle simulation. *SIAM J. Science and Statistical Computing*, 9:669–686, 1988.
6. A. P. Dempster, N. M. Laird, and D. B. Rubin. Maximum likelihod from incomplete data via the EM algorithm. *J. Royal Statistical Soc. B*, 39:1–38, 1977.
7. R. Duda & P. Hart. *Pattern Classification and Scene Analysis*. Wiley, US, 1973.
8. E. Erkut and B. Bozkaya. Analysis of aggregation error for the p-median problem. *Computers & Operations Research*, 26:1075–1096, 1999.

9. M. Ester, H. P. Kriegel, and X. Xu. Knowledge discovery in large spatial databases: Focusing techniques for efficient class identification. *SDD-95*, 70–82, 1995. Springer-Verlag LNCS 951.

10. V. Estivill-Castro and M. E. Houle. Robust clustering of large geo-referenced data sets. *PAKDD-99*, 327–337. Springer-Verlag LNAI 1574, 1999.

11. V. Estivill-Castro and M.E. Houle. Fast randomized algorithms for robust estimation of location. *Proc. Int. Workshop on Mining Spatial and Temporal Data* (with PAKDD-2001), Hong Kong, 2001.

12. V. Estivill-Castro and M. E. Houle. Spatio-temporal data structures for minimization of total within-group distance. T. Rep. 2001-05, Dep. of CS & SE, U. of Newcastle. http://www.cs.newcastle.edu.au/Dept/techrep.html

13. V. Estivill-Castro and J. Yang. A fast and robust general purpose clustering algorithm. *PRICAI 2000*, 208–218, 2000. Springer-Verlag LNAI 1886.

14. U. Fayyad, C. Reina, and P. S. Bradley. Initialization of iterative refinement clustering algorithms. *4th KDD* 194–198. AAAI Press, 1998.

15. T. M. J. Fruchterman and E. M. Reingold. Graph drawing by force-directed placement. *Software Practice and Experience*, 21:1129–1164, 1991.

16. M. Horn. Analysis and computation schemes for p-median heuristics. *Environment and Planning A*, 28:1699–1708, 1996.

17. A. T. Murray. Spatial characteristics and comparisons of interaction and median clustering models. *Geographical Analysis*, 32:1–, 2000.

18. A. T. Murray and R. L. Church. Applying simulated annealing to location-planning models. *J. of Heuristics*, 2:31–53, 1996.

19. R. T. Ng and J. Han. Efficient and effective clustering methods for spatial data mining. *20th VLDB*, 144–155, 1994. Morgan Kaufmann.

20. J. J. Oliver, R. A. Baxter, and C. S. Wallace. Unsupervised learning using MML. *13th ML Conf.*, 364–372, 1996. Morgan Kaufmann.

21. S. Openshaw. Two exploratory space-time-attribute pattern analysers relevant to GIS. In *Spatial Analysis and GIS*, 83–104, UK, 1994. Taylor and Francis.

22. A. J. Quigley and P. Eades. FADE: Graph drawing, clustering and visual abstraction. *8th Symp. on Graph Drawing*, 2000. Springer Verlag LNCS 1984.

23. M. Rao. Cluster analysis and mathematical programming. *J. Amer. Statistical Assoc.*, 66:622–626, 1971.

24. K. Rosing and C. ReVelle. Optimal clustering. *Environment and Planning A*, 18:1463–1476, 1986.

25. P. J. Rousseeuw and A. M. Leroy. *Robust regression and outlier detection*. Wiley, USA, 1987.

26. H. Samet. *The Design and Analysis of Spatial Data Structures*. Addison-Wesley, MA, 1989.

27. E. Schikuta and M. Erhart. The BANG-clustering system: Grid-based data analysis. *IDA-97*. Springer-Verlag LNCS 1280, 1997.

28. M. B. Teitz and P. Bart. Heuristic methods for estimating the generalized vertex median of a weighted graph. *Operations Research*, 16:955–961, 1968.

29. H. Vinod. Integer programming and the theory of grouping. *J. Am. Statistical Assoc.*, 64:506–517, 1969.

30. W. Wang, J. Yang, and R. Muntz. STING: A statistical information grid approach to spatial data mining. *23rd VLDB*, 186–195, 1997. Morgan Kaufmann.

31. T. Zhang, R. Ramakrishnan, and M. Livny. BIRCH:an efficient data clustering method for very large databases. *SIGMOD Record*, 25:103–114, 1996.

Non-crisp Clustering by Fast, Convergent, and Robust Algorithms

Vladimir Estivill-Castro and Jianhua Yang

Department of Computer Science & Software Engineering
The University of Newcastle, Callaghan, NSW 2308, Australia

Abstract. We provide sub-quadratic clustering algorithms for generic dissimilarity. Our algorithms are robust because they use medians rather than means as estimators of location, and the resulting representative of a cluster is actually a data item. We demonstrate mathematically that our algorithms converge. The methods proposed generalize approaches that allow a data item to have a degree of membership in a cluster. Because our algorithm is generic to both, fuzzy membership approaches and probabilistic approaches for partial membership, we simply name it non-crisp clustering. We illustrate our algorithms with categorizing WEB visitation paths. We outperform previous clustering methods since they are all of quadratic time complexity (they essentially require computing the dissimilarity between all pairs of paths).

1 Introduction

In a top-down view to clustering [3], the aim is to partition a large data set of heterogeneous objects into more homogeneous classes. Many clustering methods are built around this partitioning approach [17]. Because we are to partition a set into more homogeneous clusters, we need to assess homogeneity. The degree of homogeneity in a group is a criterion for evaluating that the samples in one cluster are more like one another than like samples in other clusters. This criterion is then made explicit if there is a distance between objects. The type of clustering that we find here attempts to find the partition that optimizes a given homogeneity criterion defined in terms of distances. Thus, this type of clustering is also distance-based, but rather than looking for the most similar pair of objects and grouping them together, which is the bottom-up approach of hierarchical clustering, we seek to find a partition that separates into clusters. Variants of the partitioning problem arise as we see different criteria for defining homogeneity and also different measures of similarity. Then, within one variant of the problem, several algorithms are possible. Consider the following optimization criteria for clustering which attempts to minimize the heterogeneity in each group with respect to the group representative.

$$\text{Minimize } M^a(C) = \sum_{i=1}^{n} d(u_i, \text{REP}[u_i, C])^a, \tag{1}$$

L. De Raedt and A. Siebes (Eds.): PKDD 2001, LNAI 2168, pp. 103–114, 2001.
© Springer-Verlag Berlin Heidelberg 2001

where $a \geq 1$ is a constant, $C \subset U$ is a set of k representatives, REP$[u_i, C]$ is the most similar representative (in C) to u_i and $d(\cdot, \cdot)$ is a measure of dissimilarity. We underline that $d(\cdot, \cdot)$ does not need to be a distance satisfying the axioms of a metric. In particular, while $d(u_i, u_i) = 0$, we do not require that $d(u_i, u_j) = 0$ implies $u_i = u_j$. Also, we do not require the triangle inequality, however, we do expect symmetry, that is $d(u_i, u_j) = d(u_j, u_i)$. These requirements are satisfied by all similarity measures based on computing the cosine of the angle between attribute-vectors of positive-valued features [16,27,28,32,33]. Note that these similarity functions $sim(\cdot, \cdot)$ have a range in $[0, 1]$ and the corresponding dissimilarity is $d(\cdot, \cdot) = 1 - sim(\cdot, \cdot)$, also in the range $[0,1]$.

Equation (1) is not unfamiliar to statistics nor to the Data Mining community. The case $a = 2$ defines the objective function that the k-MEANS method iteratively approximates. This case is the result of applying an analysis of variance using total sum error squares as the loss function. The case $a = 1$ replaces means by medians and the L_2 loss function by the L_1 loss function (the total absolute error). The case $a = 1$ was brought over from the statistics as medoid-based clustering [21]. However, CLARANS is a randomized interchange hill-climber in order to obtain subquadratic algorithmic complexity. CLARANS can not guarantee local optimality. The best interchange hill-climber [11] is the Teitz and Bart heuristic [31] which requires quadratic time. Only in restricted cases, the time complexity of this type of hill-climber has been reduced to subquadratic time (for example, $D = 2$ and Euclidean distance [9]). Because medians are a more robust estimator of location than means, an algorithm optimizing the case $a = 1$ is more resistant to noise and outliers than an algorithm optimizing the case $a = 2$. However, k-MEANS is heavily used because it is fast [1,24,34], despite its many drawbacks documented in the literature [12].

Clustering algorithms optimizing the family of criteria given by Equation (1) search for a subset $C = \{c_1, \ldots, c_k\}$ of k elements in U. In the case $a = 1$, we use medoids to denote discrete medians; that is, the estimator of location for a cluster shall be a member of the data. Previous to the approach presented here, the classification step for medoids performs a crisp classification. That is, classification computes the representative REP$[u_i, C]$ of each data item u_i and each data item belongs to only the cluster of its representative. It seems that robustness to initialization (as it happens in k-HARMONIC MEANS [34]) comes from a combining relaxation of crisp classification with a boosting technique. It seems that to achieve this, each data item should be able to belong to different clusters with a degree of membership (the degree could be a probability as in EXPECTATION MAXIMIZATION, or a fuzzy membership as in FUZZY-c-MEANS).

Thus, our contribution here is to achieve this degree of membership to different clusters. We will propose algorithms and then show their advantages. We prove mathematically that they converge. We show our algorithms are generic (the degree of membership could be a fuzzy-membership function, a harmonic distribution, or even revert to the case of crisp-membership). We show versions requiring sub-quadratic time by using randomization. We apply our algorithms to a case study where other algorithms can not be used [13,18].

2   Non-crisp Clustering Algorithms

Consider the crisp classification step that computes $\text{REP}[u_i, C]$ for each data item u_i. It requires a simple pass through the data and $O(nk)$ computations of $d(\cdot, \cdot)$. This results in a temporary partition of U into k clusters $U_1, \ldots, U_k$. We can generalize crisp classification by assigning a vector $\boldsymbol{\pi}_i \in [0,1]^k$ to each u_i. We consider that the j-th entry $\boldsymbol{\pi}_{ij}$ denotes the degree by which u_i belongs to the j-th cluster. In parallel with EXPECTATION MAXIMIZATION and FUZZY-c-MEANS, we will normalize the values so that $\sum_{j=1}^{k} \boldsymbol{\pi}_{ij} = 1$. Crisp classification means the closest representative has its entry in $\boldsymbol{\pi}$ set to 1 while all other clusters have their entry set to zero. Non-crisp classification will mean more than one cluster has its entry different from zero.

To detail more our approach we need to introduce some notation. Given a vector $\boldsymbol{x} \in \Re^k$, let $\text{SORT}(\boldsymbol{x}) \in \Re^k$ denote the vector of sorted entries from $\boldsymbol{x}$ in non-decreasing order (entries with equal values are arranged arbitrarily). Thus, if $j < j'$ then $\text{SORT}(\boldsymbol{x})_j \leq \text{SORT}(\boldsymbol{x})_{j'}$. We use the notation e_j^{T} to denote the j-th canonical vector $(0, \ldots, 0, 1, 0, \ldots, 0)$ that has only the j-th entry equal to 1 and all other equal to zero. This notation allows us to rewrite the loss function in Equation (1) because the minimum operator in $\text{REP}[u_i, C]$ can be replaced by $e_1^{\mathrm{T}} \cdot \text{SORT}(\cdot)$ as follows $M^a(C) = \sum_{i=1}^{n} e_1^{\mathrm{T}} \cdot \text{SORT}(d(u_i, c_1), d(u_i, c_2), \ldots, d(u_i, c_k))$. Moreover, we can already describe a Harmonic set of weights as the degrees of membership. Let $K = \sum_{j=1}^{k} 1/j$, the Harmonic loss function is then $M^H(C) = \frac{1}{K} \sum_{i=1}^{n} (1, 1/2, \ldots, 1/j, \ldots, 1/k)^{\mathrm{T}} \cdot \text{SORT}(d(x_i, c_1), d(u_i, c_2), \ldots, d(u_i, c_k))$. Moreover, we propose here an even more general approach, and let $\omega \in \Re^k$ be any vector with non-negative entries and entries in descending order; then, the non-crisp classification loss function with respect to ω is

$$M^\omega(C) = \frac{1}{\|\omega\|_1} \sum_{i=1}^{n} \omega^{\mathrm{T}} \cdot \text{SORT}(d(u_i, c_1), d(u_i, c_2), \ldots, d(u_i, c_k)). \qquad (2)$$

(where we denote the 1-norm of a vector $\boldsymbol{x}$ as $\|\boldsymbol{x}\|_1$ and it equals $\sum_{j=1}^{k} |\boldsymbol{x}_k|$). Note that the first canonical vector e_1 and the Harmonic vector with $1/j$ in its j-th entry are special cases for ω. The vector $\boldsymbol{\pi}_i$ giving the degree of membership of u_i is defined by $\boldsymbol{\pi}_{ij} = d(u_i, c_j)\omega_j / \|\omega\|_1$.

Recently, by using randomization several variants of clustering algorithms for optimizing instances of the criteria in Equation (1) with $a = 1$ have emerged [10]. These variants are subquadratic robust clustering algorithms. These randomized algorithms have been shown mathematically and empirically to provide robust estimators of location [10]. This is because randomization is not sampling. Sampling reduces the CPU-requirements by using a very small part of the data, and the accuracy suffers directly with the size of the sample. Randomization uses the entire data available.

While those algorithms are more robust than k-MEANS to initialization, we produce here a general family of algorithms that optimize Equation (2) and are even more robust to initialization.

2.1   The EXPECTATION MAXIMIZATION Type

Our first family of randomized algorithms carries out an iterative improvement as found in k-MEANS, EXPECTATION MAXIMIZATION, FUZZY-c-MEANS and k-HARMONIC MEANS (refer to Fig. 1). The iteration alternates classifica-

---

ITERATIVE_STEP$(C = \{c_1, \ldots, c_k\} \subset U)$
    CLASSIFICATION_STEP(C)
        For $j = 1, \ldots, k$: find $U_j = \{u_i \in U \mid d(u_i, c_j) \leq d(u_i, c_{j'})j' = 1, \ldots, k\}$
    new $C \leftarrow$ RECONSTRUCTION_STEP
        For $j = 1, \ldots, k$: new $c_j \leftarrow$ new estimator of median for U_j

---

Fig. 1. Body of the iteration alternating between finding a classification for the data given a model, and finding a model given classified data.

tion of data from a current model (classification step) and model refinement from classified data (reconstruction step). We say that is an EXPECTATION MAXIMIZATION type because it follows the alternation between Expectation and Maximization. That is, Expectation because in the statistical sense we estimate the hidden information (the membership to clusters of the data items). Maximization, because we use some criteria (like Maximum Likelihood) to revise the description (model) of each cluster.

Our task now is to describe the iterative algorithms that minimizes the non-crisp classification loss function with respect to a vector ω. The algorithm has the generic structure of iterative algorithms. It will start with a random set C^0. The t-th iteration proceeds as follows. First we note that non-crisp classification is computationally as costly as classification in the crisp algorithms. It essentially requires to compute SORT of the vector of distances of the data item u_i under consideration to each member of the current set of representatives C^t. This requires computations of $d(\cdot, \cdot)$ for the k representatives. Although sorting of k items requires $k \log k$ comparisons, it does not require any more dissimilarity computations and in the applications we have in mind, the computations of dissimilarity values is far more costly than the time required to sort the k values. Thus, classification is performed by a simple pass through the data and $O(nk)$ dissimilarity computations. This results in a labeling of all data items in U by a vector ranking the degrees of membership to the k clusters. That is, for each u_i, we record the rank of $d(u_i, c_j^t)$, where c_j^t is the j-th current representative. We let RANK$_i^t[j]$ denote the rank of u_i with respect to the j-th representative at the t-th classification. For example, if the first current representative is the 3rd nearest representative to u_i then RANK$_i^t[1] = 3$.

The reconstruction step computes new representatives. For each old representative, we have a degree of membership of every data item. Thus, for each $j =$

$1, \ldots, k$ we seek a new representative that minimizes $f_j^t(x) = \sum_{i=1}^n e_{\text{RANK}_i^t[j]}^T \cdot$
$\omega d(x, u_i) = \sum_{i=1}^n \omega_{\text{RANK}_i^t[j]} d(x, u_i)$. Thus, for example, if an item u_i was ranked
first with respect to the j-th representative because it was its nearest represen-
tative, then the distance $d(x, u_i)$ in Equation (2) is multiplied by the largest
weight in ω (which is the value in the first entry). Also, note that in the case of
crisp classification, all weights are zero except the largest (and the largest weight
equals 1). Thus, the minimization of $f_j^t(x)$ above just corresponds to finding the
median amongst the data items in the j-th cluster. Because of this, the data item
u_i such that $f_j^t(u_i)$ is smallest will be called the j-th discrete weighted median.

To detail our algorithm further, we must describe how a new representative
c_j^{t+1} is computed by minimization of $f_j^t(x)$ amongst the data items u_i. The
algorithm we introduce for this task is a randomized approximation inspired in a
sub-quadratic randomized algorithm for computation of the discrete median [10].
For this subproblem of approximating the discrete median we note that $U = \{u_1, \ldots, u_n\}$ is the set of candidates (during the t-th iteration of the algorithm)
for finding the minimum of each function $f_j^t(x)$, for $j = 1, \ldots, k$.

However, for simplicity of the notation, in what follows we drop the super-
index t since it is understood we are dealing with the current iteration. We will
also assume that we know which representative is being revised and we denote by
OLD_MED(j) the previous approximation to the data item that minimizes $f_j(x)$
(during the t-th iteration, OLD_MED(j) is actually c_j^t).

Clearly, the discrete weighted median MED(j) can be computed in $O(\|U\|^2)$
computations of the dissimilarity $d(\cdot, \cdot)$ by simply computing $f_j(x)$ for $x = u_1, \ldots, x = u_n$ and returning the x that results in the smallest value. We will
refer to this algorithm as EXHAUSTIVE. It must be used carefully because it has
quadratic complexity on the size $\|U\| = n$ of the data. However, it has linear
complexity of $\phi(d)$, the time to compute $d(\cdot, \cdot)$. Thus, our use of randomization.

The first step consists of obtaining a random partition of U into approxi-
mately $r = \sqrt{n}$ subsets $U_1, \ldots, U_r$ each of approximately $n/r \approx \sqrt{n}$ elements.
Then, algorithm EXHAUSTIVE is applied to each of these subsets to obtain
$m(j)_s = med\_d(U_s)$, $s = 1, \ldots, r$. These r items constitute candidates for the
j-th discrete weighted median of U. We compute $f_j(m(j)_s)$ for $s = 1, \ldots, r$ and
also $f(\text{OLD\_MED}(j))$. The item that provides the smallest amongst these (at most
$r + 1$) items is returned as the new approximation to the discrete median. The
algorithm has complexity $O(\phi(d)\|U\|\sqrt{\|U\|})$ because EXHAUSTIVE is applied to
$\Theta(\sqrt{\|U\|})$ sets, each of size $\Theta(\sqrt{\|U\|})$; thus this requires $O(\phi(d)\|U\|\sqrt{\|U\|})$ time.
Finally, $f_j(m(j)_s)$ requires $O(\phi(d)\|U\|)$ time and is performed $O(\sqrt{\|U\|})$ times.
This is also $O(\phi(d)\|U\|\sqrt{\|U\|})$ time. These types of randomized algorithms for
finding discrete medians have been shown mathematically and empirically to
provide robust estimators of location [10]. This is because randomization is not
sampling. Randomization uses the entire data available.

We enhance the fundamental results of iterative clustering algorithms by
proving that our algorithm converges. We prove this by showing that both steps,
the non-crisp classification step and the reconstruction step never increase the
value of the objective function in Equation (2).

Lemma 1. *Let* RANK_i^t *be the rank vector for each* $u_i \in U$ $(i = 1, \ldots, n)$ *after the non-crisp classification step in the* t-*th iteration of the algorithm. Let*

$$M^\omega(C^t) = \frac{1}{\|\omega\|_1} \sum_{i=1}^{n} \sum_{j=1}^{k} \omega_{\mathrm{RANK}_i^t[j]} d(u_i, c_j^t). \tag{3}$$

Then, the value of $\frac{1}{\|\omega\|_1} \sum_{i=1}^{n} \sum_{j=1}^{k} \omega_{\mathrm{RANK}_i^t[j]} d(u_i, c_j^{t+1})$ *of the objective function after the reconstruction step is no larger than* $M^\omega(C^t)$.

Proof. First note that, by expanding the dot product $\omega^{\mathrm{T}} \mathrm{SORT}(\cdot)$ and using the RANK vector we have that Equation (2) and Equation (3) are the same. Then, we can reverse the order of the summation signs and also note that $1/\|\omega\|_1$ is a constant. Thus, the objective function is simply $M^\omega(C^t) = \frac{1}{\|\omega\|_1} \sum_{j=1}^{k} f_j^t(c_j^t)$. The reconstruction step finds new c_j^{t+1} such that $f_j^t(c_j^{t+1}) \leq f_j^t(c_j^t)$, for $j = 1, \ldots, k$ (because the previous discrete median is considered among the candidates for a new weighted discrete median). Thus,

$$M^\omega(C^t) \geq \frac{1}{\|\omega\|_1} \sum_{i=1}^{n} \sum_{j=1}^{k} \omega_{\mathrm{RANK}_i^t[j]} d(u_i, c_j^{t+1}).$$

Lemma 2. *The value*

$$M^\omega(C^{t+1} = \{c_1^{t+1}, \ldots, c_k^{t+1}\})$$
$$= \frac{1}{\|\omega\|_1} \sum_{i=1}^{n} \omega^{\mathrm{T}} \mathrm{SORT}(d(u_i, c_1^{t+1}), d(u_i, c_2^{t+1}), \ldots, d(u_i, c_k^{t+1}))$$

after a classification step is no larger than $\frac{1}{\|\omega\|_1} \sum_{i=1}^{n} \sum_{j=1}^{k} \omega_{\mathrm{RANK}_i^t[j]} d(u_i, c_j^{t+1})$ *resulting in the previous reconstruction step.*

Proof. Note that $\frac{1}{\|\omega\|_1} \sum_{j=1}^{k} f_j^t(c_j^{t+1}) = \sum_{i=1}^{n} \frac{1}{\|\omega\|_1} \sum_{j=1}^{k} \omega_{\mathrm{RANK}_i^t[j]} d(c_j^{t+1}, u_i)$. Thus, we can say that the contribution of u_i to the objective function before the next classification is $\frac{1}{\|\omega\|_1} \sum_{j=1}^{k} \omega_{\mathrm{RANK}_i^t[j]} d(c_j^{t+1}, u_i)$. Now, we know that after classification, this contribution by u_i is

$$\frac{1}{\|\omega\|_1} \omega^{\mathrm{T}} \mathrm{SORT}(d(u_i, c_1^{t+1}), d(u_i, c_2^{t+1}), \ldots, d(u_i, c_k^{t+1})).$$

Thus, the terms $d(u_i, c_j^{t+1})$ involved before and after non-crisp classification are the same, it is just that after classification they are in non-decreasing order. Since ω^{T} has entries in descending order we claim that

$$\omega^{\mathrm{T}} \mathrm{SORT}(d(u_i, c_1^{t+1}), d(u_i, c_2^{t+1}), \ldots, d(u_i, c_k^{t+1})) \leq \sum_{j=1}^{k} \omega_{\mathrm{RANK}_i^t[j]} d(c_j^{t+1}, u_i)$$

whatever the order of the set $\{d(u_i, c_1^{t+1}), d(u_i, c_2^{t+1}), \ldots, d(u_i, c_k^{t+1})\}$ given by the permutation encoded in $\text{RANK}_i^t[j]$ (note the rank is the one that resulted in the previous classification, and we are about to perform the $(t+1)$-th classification).

We prove this claim by showing that if $j < j'$ and $d(u_i, c_j^{t+1}) > d(u_i, c_{j'}^{t+1})$, but $d(u_i, c_j^{t+1})$ is ranked earlier than $d(u_i, c_{j'}^{t+1})$ in the t-th ranking, then we can reduce the value of the contribution of u_i by swapping the order in the permutation of j and j'.

This is because if $j < j'$ we have $\omega_j > \omega_{j'}$ and $d(u_i, c_j^{t+1}) > d(u_i, c_{j'}^{t+1})$ implies $\omega_j(d(u_i, c_j^{t+1}) - d(u_i, c_{j'}^{t+1})) > \omega_{j'}(d(u_i, c_j^{t+1}) - d(u_i, c_{j'}^{t+1}))$.

Thus, $\omega_j d(u_i, c_j^{t+1}) + \omega_{j'} d(u_i, c_{j'}^{t+1}) > \omega_{j'} d(u_i, c_j^{t+1}) + \omega_j d(u_i, c_{j'}^{t+1}))$. Thus, swapping j and j' reduces the contribution of u_i. This proves that the sorted array of values reduces the contribution of u_i, and this is for all u_i. Thus, the new non-crisp classification produces a ranking that can not increase the value of the objective function.

Theorem 1. *Our algorithm converges.*

Proof. The domain of the objective function has size $\binom{k}{n}$, since it consists of all subsets of size k of U. Thus, the objective function has a finite range. The algorithm can not decrease the value of the objective function continuously.

This result is in contrast to the problem of the continuous median in dimensions $D \geq 2$ and the Euclidean metric (the continuous Fermat-Weber problem) where fundamental results show that it is impossible to obtain an algorithm to converge [2] (numerical algorithms usually halt because of the finite precision of digital computers). Other algorithms for non-crisp classification, like k-HARMONIC MEANS have not been shown to converge.

2.2   The Discrete Hill-Climber Type

We now present an alternative algorithm to optimizing Equation (2). The algorithm here can be composed with the algorithm in the previous section (for example, the first can be the initialization of the latter). The result is an even more robust algorithm, still with complexity $O(n\sqrt{n})$ similarity computations.

The algorithm in this section is an interchange heuristics based on a hill-climbing search strategy. However, we require to adapt this to non-crisp classification since all previous versions [8,9,11,15,19,20,21,31] are for the crisp classification case. We will first present a quadratic-time version of our algorithm, which we will name non-crisp TAB in honor of Teitz and Bart [31] original heuristic. Later, we will use randomization to achieve subquadratic time complexity, as in the previous section.

Our algorithms explore the space of subsets $C \subset U$ of size k. Non-crisp TAB will start with a random set C^0. Then, the data items $u_i \in U$ are organized in a circular list. Whenever the turn belonging to a data item u_i comes up, if $u_i \notin C^t$, it is used to test at most k subsets $C_j = (C^t \cup \{u_i\}) \setminus \{c_j^t\}$. That is, if u_i is currently not a representative (medoid), it is swapped with each of the k current medoids. The objective function M^ω in Equation (2) is evaluated in $M^\omega(C_j)$, for $j = 1, \ldots, k$ and if any of these values is less than the current $M^\omega(C^t)$, then the swap with the best improvement $M^\omega(C_{j_0})$ is accepted and $C^{t+1} = C_{j_0}$. In this case, or if $u_i \in C^t$ or if no C_j improves C^t, the data item u_i is placed at the end of the circular list. The turn passes to the next data item and the algorithm halts when a pass through the circular list produces no swap.

The algorithm requires $O(kn^2)$ dissimilarity evaluations because evaluating $M^\omega(C)$ requires $O(n)$ distance evaluations and at least one pass is made through the circular list to halt.

Our randomized TAB also partitions U into approximately $r = \sqrt{n}$ subsets $U_1, \ldots, U_r$ each of approximately $n/r \approx \sqrt{n}$ elements. The non-crisp TAB is applied to each of $U_1, \ldots, U_r$. Thus each U_i is clustered into k groups. This requires $O(kn\sqrt{n})$ distance calculations and results in r sets of k representatives. Then, all the resulting rk representatives are placed in a circular list. Then non-crisp TAB is applied in this list but the evaluation of $M^\omega(C)$ is performed with respect to the entire data set U. Since the circular list has length $k\sqrt{n}$, the iteration achieved by the last execution of non-crisp TAB requires $O(k^2 n\sqrt{n})$. If having k^2 in the complexity is a problem, then we can simply chose $r = \sqrt{n}/k$, and obtain an algorithm with linear complexity in k as well.

Clearly, this algorithm also converges.

3   Case Study

The literature contains many illustrations in commercial applications where clustering discovers what are the types of customers [3,4]. Recent attention for WEB Usage Mining [30] has concentrated on association rule extraction [5,23, and references]. There has been comparative less success at categorizing WEB-visitors than categorizing customers in transactional data. This WEB usage mining task is to be achieved from the visitation data to a WEB-site [29]. The goal is to identify strong correlation among users interests by grouping their navigation paths. Paths are ordered sequences of WEB pages. Many applications can then benefit from the knowledge obtained [7,16,27,28,32]. Discovery of visitor profiles is an important task for WEB-site design and evaluation [26,33]. Other examples are WEB page suggestion for users in the same cluster, pre-fetching, personalization, collaborative filtering [25] and user communities [22].

Paths are discrete structures. Several similarity measures have been defined but they all correspond to dissimilarity between high-dimensional feature vectors extracted from the paths [16,27,28,32,33]. Because the length of the path, the order of the WEB pages, the time intervals between links and many other aspects play a role in dissimilarity measures the resulting clustering problems are high dimensional. For example, a measure that has been used for WEB-path clustering is defined as follows [32]. Let $P = \{p_1, \ldots, p_m\}$ be a set of pages, and let the corresponding usage-feature vector USAGE_{u_i} of user u_i defined by

$$\text{USAGE}_{u_i}[j] = \begin{cases} 1 & \text{if } p_j \text{ is accessed by } u_i \\ 0 & \text{Otherwise.} \end{cases}$$

Then, $\text{USAGE}(u_i, u_{i'}) = \text{USAGE}_{u_i}^T \cdot \text{USAGE}_{u_{i'}} / \|\text{USAGE}_{u_i}\| \|\text{USAGE}_{u_{i'}}\|$ is the *Usage Similarity Measure* (the cosine of the angle between the usage-feature vectors).

Clearly the dimension of the vectors involved is the number m of pages in the WEB-site, typically a number higher than 10 and usually much larger. Moreover, the Usage Similarity Measure is the simplest of the dissimilarity measures since it does not consider order, length or time along a visitation path. Other more robust dissimilarity measures are more costly to evaluate and imply feature vectors in even higher dimensions.

Also, the discrete nature of paths removes vector-based operations, like averages (means). Thus, while it is possible to compute the average of two feature vectors like $(\text{USAGE}_{u_i} + \text{USAGE}_{u_{i'}})/2$, it is not clear that the result is the feature vector of a path (a path with such feature vector may actually be infeasible given the links between pages). Also, spaces defined by dissimilarity measures are different form Euclidean spaces, since for all feature vectors v, the similarity between v and itself is maximum (1); however, it is also maximum between v and any scalar transformation λv of the vector itself, for all constants $\lambda > 0$.

These two challenges obstruct the use of many clustering algorithms for finding groups on WEB visitors based on their visitation paths (including k-MEANS and FUZZY-c-MEANS). The algorithms proposed to date [7,16,27,28,32] are all of quadratic time complexity (they essentially require computing the dissimilarity between all pairs of paths). These clustering efforts, although not scalable, have demonstrated the extensive benefits and sophisticated applications emerging from identifying groups of visitors to a WEB-site.

The implementation of $O(n\sqrt{n})$ time results in a dramatic improvement in CPU-time resources. Our implementation is much faster than previous matrix-based algorithms [13]. Just for the Usage dissimilarity metric the Matrix-Based algorithm requires over 18,000 CPU seconds (5 hrs!) with 590 users while our algorithms in crisp mode requires only 83 seconds (just over a minute) and in harmonic mode it requires 961 second (16 minutes). These results are on the same data set of logs identified with visitor and sessions used by Xiao et al [32]. Namely, we used the WEB-log data sets publicly available from the Boston University Computer Science Department.

To evaluate the quality of the clustering synthetic data sets are useful because it is possible to compare the results of the algorithms with the true clustering. Typically, synthetic data is generated from a mixture or from a set of k representatives by perturbing each slightly. The quality of the clustering is reflected by the proportion in which the clustering algorithm retrieves groups and identifies data items to their original group.

We reproduced to the best of our ability the synthetic generation suggested for the same task of clustering paths used by Shahabi et al [28]. Our crisp-version has already been shown to provide much better results than matrix-based alternatives [13] for the usage dissimilarity measure. In what follows, we discuss results comparing our harmonic EM type algorithm ($\omega^T = (1, 1/2, \ldots, 1/k)$ and its crisp EM type version ($\omega^T = e_i^T$) [14]. We used the usage-dissimilarity measure and other two measures, the frequency measure and the order measure [32]. The order measure is the same as the path measure [28]. Because our algorithms start with a random set of representatives, they were run each of them 5 times and confidence intervals are reported with 95% accuracy [14]. There are several issues we would like to comment on our results [14]. The first is that we were surprised that actually what the literature has claimed on the issue of features from paths towards dissimilarity measures is not reflected in our results. In fact, the more sophisticated the dissimilarity measure, the poorer the results. Quality was much more affected by the dissimilarity measure used than by the size of the data set or the clustering algorithm used. Our non-crisp algorithm does better, but we admit that for this data set the results are not dramatic. In fact, they are probably less impressive if one considers the CPU-time requirements [14]. The harmonic version is slower. It requires a factor of $O(k)$ more space and $O(k \log k)$ administrative work. However, the observed CPU times confirm the $O(n \log n)$ nature of our algorithms and that dissimilarity evaluation is the main cost. In fact, the usage and frequency dissimilarity functions can be computed in $O(\rho)$, where ρ is the average length of paths. However, the order dissimilarity function requires $\Omega(\rho^2)$ time to be computed.

We note that the confidence intervals for the harmonic version are smaller than for the crisp version. This indicates that harmonic is more robust to initialization. To explore further this issue we also performed on some initial experiments regarding the robustness to initialization of our algorithms. The experiment consisted of evaluating the discrepancy in clustering results between independent executions (with a different random seed) of the same algorithm. In our results [14] there is much less variance with the harmonic version. Given that the initialization is random, this suggests the algorithm finds high quality local optima with respect to its loss function. However, more thorough experimentation is required to confirm this suggestion.

We also point out that in parallel to k-MEANS, EXPECTATION MAXIMIZATION, and k-HARMONIC MEANS, our harmonic EM type algorithm may place two representatives very close together attracted by the same peak in frequency. However, the theoretical foundation provided here allows also to detect this and apply the "boosting" techniques as suggested for k-HARMONIC MEANS [34].

4   Final Remarks

We presented the theoretical framework for sub-quadratic clustering of paths with non-crisp classification. The experiments are not exhaustive [14] but they illustrate that there are benefits to be obtained with respect to quality with non-crisp classification. Moreover, they also reflect that there are trade-off to be investigated between the complexity of the dissimilarity function and its computational requirements. We indicated the possibility of hybridization between the discrete hill-climber type and the EM type. However, because our EM-methods are generic on the vector ω they offer a range of diversity for the computational requirements in this regard. For example, one can imagine a k'-nearest neighbor classification with $k' < k$. The vector ω would have entries equal to zero from the $(k'+1)$-th entry onwards. The nonzero entries can then be a harmonic average of the k' nearest neighbors or some other combination. Thus, this is a classification that incorporates the supervised-learning technique of nearest-neighbors [6] and reduces smoothly to crisp-classification with k' closer to 1.

We have illustrated the new clustering methods with similarity measures of interests between WEB visitors. Similarity measures proposed for analysis WEB visitation [16,27,28,32,33] pose a high-dimensional non-Euclidean clustering problem. This eliminates many clustering methods. Previously [13], we (and others [18]) provided a more detailed discussion of why density-based or hierarchical methods are unsuitable to clustering paths. Our methods here are fast and robust. They are applicable to any similarity measure and can dynamically track users with high efficiency. Moreover, we have generalized fuzzy-membership or probabilistic membership to non-crisp classification.

References

1. K. Alsabti, S. Ranka, and V. Singh. An efficient k-means clustering algorithm. *IPPS 11th Int. Parallel Processing Symp.*, 1998.
2. C. Bajaj. Proving geometric algorithm non-solvability: An application of factoring polynomials. *J. of Symbolic Computation*, 2:99–102, 1986.
3. M.J.A. Berry and G. Linoff. *Data Mining Techniques — for Marketing, Sales and Customer Support*. Wiley, NY, 1997.
4. J.P. Bigus. *Data Mining with Neural Networks: Solving Business Problems from Applciation Development to Decision Support*. McGraw-Hill, NY, 1996.
5. J. Borges and M. Levene. Mining assocaition rules in hypertext databases. *4th KDD*, 149–153, NY, 1998.
6. V. Cherkassky and F. Muller. *Learning from Data*. Wiley, NY, 1998.
7. C. R. Cunha & C. F. B. Jaccound. Determining www user's next access and its application to prefetching. *Int. Symp. Computers & Communication'97*, 1997.
8. P. Densham and G. Rushton. A more efficient heuristic for solving large p-median problems. *Papers in Regional Science*, 71:307–329, 1992.
9. V. Estivill-Castro & M.E. Houle. Robust clustering of large geo-referenced data sets. *3rd PAKDD-99*, 327–337. Springer-Verlag LNAI 1574, 1999.
10. V. Estivill-Castro and M.E. Houle. Fast randomized algorithms for robust estimation of location. *Int. Workshop on Temporal, Spatial and Spatio-Temporal Data Mining - TSDM2000, witht 4th PKDD*, 74–85, Lyon, 2000. LNAI 2007.
11. V. Estivill-Castro and A.T. Murray. Discovering associations in spatial data - an efficient medoid based approach. *2nd PAKDD-98*, 110–121, Melbourne, 1998. Springer-Verlag LNAI 1394.
12. V. Estivill-Castro and J. Yang. A fast and robust generl purpose clustering algorithm. *6th PRICAI-2000*, 208–218, Melbourne, 2000. Springer-Verlag LNAI 1886.
13. V. Estivill-Castro and J. Yang. Categorizing Visitors Dynamically by Fast and Robust Clustering of Access Logs *Asia-Pacific Conference on Web Intelligence WI-2001*. Maebashi City, Japan. 2001. N. Zhong and Y. Yao (eds) LNAI In press.

14. V. Estivill-Castro and J. Yang. Non-crisp clustering Web visitors by vast, convergent and robust algorithms on access logs. Tech. R. 2001-07, Dep. CS & SE, U. of Newcastle, www.cs.newcastle.edu.au/Dept/techrep.html.

15. M. Horn. Analysis and computation schemes for p-median heuristics. *Environment and Planning A*, 28:1699–1708, 1996.

16. T. Kato, H. Nakyama and Y. Yamane. Navigation analysis tool based on the correlation between contents and access patterns. Manuscript.
http://citeseer.nj.nec.com/354234.html.

17. M Lorr. *Cluster Analysis for Social Scientists*. Jossey-Bass, San Francisco, 1983.

18. T. Morzy, M. Wojciechowski, and Zakrzewicz. Scalabale hierarchical clustering methods for sequences of categorical values. D. Cheung, et al eds., *5th PAKDD*, 282–293, Hong Kong, 2001. LNAI 2035.

19. A.T. Murray. Spatial characteristics and comparisons of interaction and median clustering models. *Geographical Analysis*, 32:1–, 2000.

20. A.T. Murray and R.L. Church. Applying simulated annealing to location-planning models. *J. of Heuristics*, 2:31–53, 1996.

21. R.T. Ng and J. Han. Efficient and effective clustering methods for spatial data mining. *20th VLDB*, 144–155, 1994. Morgan Kaufmann.

22. G. Paliouras, C. Papatheodorou, V. Karkaletsis, and C. Spyropoulos. Clustering the users of large web sites into communities. P. Langley, ed., *17th Int. Conf. on Machine Learning*, 719–726, 2000. Morgan Kaufmann.

23. J. Pei, J. Han, B. Mortazavi-asl, and H. Zhu. Mining access patterns efficiently from web logas. *4th PAKDD*, 396–407, 2000. Springer-Verlag LNCS 1805.

24. D. Pelleg and A. Moore. X-means: Extending K-means with efficient estimation of the number of clusters. In P. Langley, ed., *17th Int. Conf. Machine Learning*, 727–734, CA, 2000. Morgan Kaufmann.

25. D.M. Pennock, E. Horvitz, S. Lawrence, and C.L. Giles. Collaborative filtering by personality diagnosis: A hybrid memory- and model-based approach. *16th Conf. on Uncertanity in Artificial Intelligence*, 473–840, 2000. Morgan Kaufmann.

26. M Perkowitz and O. Etzioni. Adaptive web sites: an AI challenge. *IJCAI*, 16–23, Nagoya, 1998.

27. M Perkowitz and O. Etzioni. Adaptive web sites: Automatically synthesizing web pages. *15th National C. on AI*, 727–732, Madison, July 1998. AAAI Press.

28. C. Shahabi, A. M. Zarkesh, J. Adibi, and V. Shah. Knowledge discovery from users web page navigation. *IEEE RIDE'97*, 20–31, 1997.

29. M. Spiliopoulou. Web usage mining for web site evaluation. *C. of the ACM*, 43:127–134, 2000.

30. J. Srivastava, R. Cooley, M. Deshpande, and P.-N. Tan. Web usage mining: Discovery and applications of usage patterns from web data. *SIGKDD Esplorations*, 1(2):12–23, January 2000.

31. M.B. Teitz and P. Bart. Heuristic methods for estimating the generalized vertex median of a weighted graph. *Operations Research*, 16:955–961, 1968.

32. J. Xiao, Y. Zhang, X. Jia, and T. Li. Measuring similarity of interests for clustering web-users. *12th ADC 2001*, 107–114, Gold Coast, IEEE Computer Society.

33. A.M. Zarkesh, J. Adibi, C. Shahabi, R. Sadri, and V. Shah. Analysis and design of server informative WWW-sites. *6th CIKM*, 254–261, Las Vegas, 1997. ACMPress.

34. B. Zhang, M. Hsu, and U. Dayal. K-harmonic means — a spatial clustering algorithm with boosting. *Int. Workshop on Temporal, Spatial and Spatio-Temporal Data Mining - TSDM2000, with 4th PKDD*, 31–42, Lyon, 2000. LNAI 2007.

Pattern Extraction for Time Series Classification

Pierre Geurts[*]

University of Liège, Department of Electrical and Computer Engineering
Institut Montefiore, Sart-Tilman B28, B4000 Liège, Belgium
geurts@montefiore.ulg.ac.be

Abstract. In this paper, we propose some new tools to allow machine learning classifiers to cope with time series data. We first argue that many time-series classification problems can be solved by detecting and combining local properties or patterns in time series. Then, a technique is proposed to find patterns which are useful for classification. These patterns are combined to build interpretable classification rules. Experiments, carried out on several artificial and real problems, highlight the interest of the approach both in terms of interpretability and accuracy of the induced classifiers.

1 Introduction

Nowadays, machine learning algorithms are becoming very mature and well understood. Unfortunately, most of the existing algorithms (if not all) are dedicated to simple data (numerical or symbolic) and are not adapted to exploit relationships among attributes (such as for example geometric or temporal structures). Yet, a lot of problems would be solved easily if we could take into account such relationships, e.g. temporal signals classification. While a laborious application of existing techniques will give satisfying results in many cases (our experiments confirm this), we believe that a lot of improvement could be gained by designing specific algorithms, at least in terms of interpretability and simplicity of the model, but probably also in terms of accuracy.

In this paper, the problem of time signals classification is tackled by means of the extraction of discriminative patterns from temporal signals. It is assumed that classification could be done by combining in a more or less complex way such patterns. For the aim of interpretability, decision trees are used as pattern combiners. The first section formally defines the problem of multivariate time-series classification and gives some examples of problems. Related work in the machine learning community is discussed here as well. In the next section, we experiment with two "naive" sets of features, often used as first means to handle time series with traditional algorithms. The third section is devoted to the description of our algorithm which is based on pattern extraction. The last section presents experiments with this method. Finally, we conclude with some comments and future work directions.

---

[*] Research fellow, FNRS

L. De Raedt and A. Siebes (Eds.): PKDD 2001, LNAI 2168, pp. 115–127, 2001.

2   The (Multivariate) Time-Series Classification Problem

2.1   Definition of the Problem

The time series classification problem is defined by the following elements:

- A universe U of objects representing dynamic system trajectories or scenarios. Each object[1], o, is observed for some finite period of time $[0, t_f(o)]$[2].
- Objects are described by a certain number of temporal candidate attributes which are functions of object and time, thus defined on $U \times [0, +\infty[$. We denote by $a(o, t)$ the value of the attribute a at time t for the object o.
- Each object is furthermore classified into one class, $c(o) \in \{c_1, ..., c_M\}$.

Given a random sample LS of objects from the universe, the goal of the machine learning algorithm is to find a function $f(o)$ which is as close as possible to the true classification $c(o)$. This function should depend only on attribute values (not on object), ie. $f(o) = f(\mathbf{a}(o, .))$ where $\mathbf{a}$ denotes the vector of attributes. The classification also should not depend on absolute time values. A consequence of this latter property is that the model should be able to classify every scenario whatever its duration of observation.

Note that alternative problems should also be addressed. For example, in [7], a temporal detection problem is defined where the goal is to find a function $f(o, t)$ of object and time which can detect as soon as possible scenarios of a given class from past and present attribute values only.

Temporal attributes have been defined here as continuous functions of time. However, in practice, signals need to be sampled for representation in computer memory. So, in fact, each scenario is described by the following sequence of vectors: $(\mathbf{a}(o, t_0(o)), \mathbf{a}(o, t_1(o)), ..., \mathbf{a}(o, t_n(o)))$ where $t_i(o) = i \cdot \triangle t(o)$ and $i = 0, 1, \cdots, n(o)$. The number of time samples, $n(o)$, may be object dependent.

2.2   Description of Some Problems

The possible application domains for time series classification are numerous: speech recognition, medical signal analysis, recognition of gestures, intrusion detection... In spite of this, it is difficult to find datasets which can be used to validate new methods. In this paper, we use three problems for evaluation. The first two datasets are artificial problems used by several researchers in the same context. The last one is a real problem of speech recognition.

Control Chart (CC). This dataset was proposed in [1] to validate clustering techniques and used in [2] for classification. Objects are described by one temporal attribute and classified into one of six possible classes (see [1] or [2] for more details). The dataset we use was obtained from the UCI KDD Archive [3] and contains 100 objects of each class. Each time series is defined by 60 time points.

---

[1] In what follows, we will use indifferently the terms scenario and object to denote an element of U.

[2] Without loss of generality we assume start time of scenario being always 0.

Cylinder-Bell-Funnel (CBF). This problem was first introduced in [12] and then used in [11,8,2] for validation. The goal is to separate three classes of object: cylinder(c), bell(b) and funnel(f). Each object is described by one temporal attribute given by:

$$a(o,t) = \begin{cases} (6 + \eta) \cdot \chi_{[a,b]}(t) + \epsilon(t) & \text{if } c(o) = c, \\ (6 + \eta) \cdot \chi_{[a,b]}(t) \cdot (t-a)/(b-a) + \epsilon(t) & \text{if } c(o) = b, \\ (6 + \eta) \cdot \chi_{[a,b]}(t) \cdot (b-t)/(b-a) + \epsilon(t) & \text{if } c(o) = f, \end{cases}$$

where $t \in [1, 128]$ and $\chi_{[a,b]}(t) = 1$ if $a \leq t \leq b$, 0 otherwise.

In the original problem, η and $\epsilon(t)$ are drawn from a standard normal distribution $N(0,1)$, a is an integer drawn uniformly from $[16, 32]$ and $b - a$ is an integer drawn uniformly from $[32, 96]$. Figure 1 shows an example of each class. As in [11], we generate 266 examples for each class using a time step of 1 (i.e. 128 time points per object).

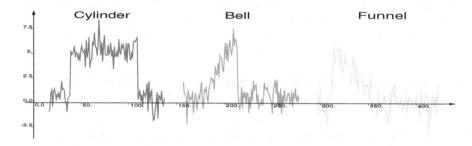

Fig. 1. An example of each class from the CBF dataset

This dataset attempts to catch some typical properties of time domain. Hence, the start time of events, a, is significantly randomized from one object to another. As we will argue later that our algorithm can cope with such temporal shifting of events, we generate another version of the same datasets by further emphasizing the temporal shifting. This time, a is drawn from $[0, 64]$ and $b - a$ is drawn from $[32, 64]$. We will call this dataset CBF-tr (for "CBF translated").

Japanese Vowels (JV). This dataset is also available in the UCI KDD Archive and was built by Kudo et al. [10] to validate their multidimensional curve classification system. The dataset records 640 time series corresponding to the successive utterance of two Japanese vowels by nine male speakers. Each object is described by 12 temporal attributes corresponding to 12 LPC spectrum coefficients. Each signal is represented in memory by between 7 to 29 time points. The goal of machine learning is to identify the correct speaker from this description.

2.3 Related Work in Machine Learning

Several machine learning approaches have been developed recently to solve the time series classification problem. Manganaris [11] for example constructs piecewise polynomial models for univariate signals and then extracts features from this representation for classification. Kadous [8] extracts parameterized events from signals. These events are clustered in the parameters space and the resulting prototypes are used as a basis for creating classifiers. Kudo et al. [10] transforms multivariate signals into binary vectors. Each element of this vector corresponds to one rectangular region of the space value-time and tells if the signal passes through this region. A method of their own, subclass, builds rules from these binary vectors. Gonzales et al. [2] extends (boosted) ILP systems with predicates that are suited for the task of time series classification.

All these approaches share some common characteristics. First, authors are all interested in getting interpretable rules more than in accuracy. We will give a justification for that in the next section. Second, they use some discretization techniques to reduce the search spaces for rules (from simple discretization to piecewise modeling or clustering). All of them extract rules which depend on absolute time value. This makes difficult the detection of properties which may occur at variable time position and can be a serious limitation to solve some problems (for example the CBF-tr problem). The technique we propose does not have this drawback.

3   Experiments with Naive Sampling and Classical Methods

Before starting with dedicated approaches for time series classification, it is interesting to see what can be done with classical machine learning algorithms and a naive approach to feature selection. To this end, experiments were carried out with two very simple sets of features:

- Sampled values of the time series at equally spaced instants. To handle time series of different durations, time instants are taken relative to the duration of the scenario. More precisely, if n is the number of time instants to take into account, each temporal attribute a gives rise to n scalar attributes given by: $a(o, t_f(o)\frac{i}{n-1})$, $i = 0, 1, \cdots, n-1$.
- Segmentation (also proposed in [8]). The time axis of each scenario is divided into n equal-length segments and the average value of each temporal attribute along these segments are taken as attributes.

The two approaches give $n \cdot m$ scalar attributes from m temporal ones. Note that while the first approach is fully independent of time, the second one takes into account the temporal ordering of values to compute their average and so is doing some noise filtering.

These two sets of attributes have been tried on the three problems described in Sect. 2.2 as inputs to three different learning algorithms: decision tree (the particular algorithm we used is described in [13]), decision tree boosting [5] and the one-nearest neighbor. Results in terms of error rates are summarized in Table 1 for increasing value of n. They were obtained by ten-fold cross-validation for the first three problems and by validation on an independent test set of size 370 for the last one[3] (JV). The best result is boldfaced in every row.

Table 1. Results with simple sampling methods

CC	Number of steps				
Sampling	3	5	10	30	60
DT	31.67 ± 4.94	17.00 ± 4.40	11.67 ± 4.08	8.17 ± 3.53	**6.83 ± 2.29**
Boosting	24.33 ± 4.67	12.33 ± 3.96	5.17 ± 3.20	2.00 ± 1.63	**1.50 ± 1.17**
1-NN	31.00 ± 4.72	17.00 ± 3.14	8.66 ± 3.78	1.50 ± 1.38	**1.83 ± 1.38**
Segment	3	5	10	30	60
DT	12.33 ± 4.73	16.33 ± 4.46	**3.50 ± 2.52**	7.50 ± 2.50	6.83 ± 2.29
Boosting	6.67 ± 4.01	11.83 ± 5.45	**1.50 ± 1.38**	2.00 ± 2.08	1.50 ± 1.17
1-NN	8.16 ± 4.24	12.00 ± 4.46	**0.50 ± 1.07**	1.33 ± 1.00	1.83 ± 1.38

CBF	Number of steps				
Sampling	8	16	32	64	128
DT	9.33 ± 3.35	7.83 ± 3.42	7.50 ± 2.61	**7.33 ± 2.49**	9.83 ± 3.83
Boosting	6.50 ± 3.02	4.00 ± 2.00	2.33 ± 1.70	**2.17 ± 1.83**	3.50 ± 2.17
1-NN	7.66 ± 4.16	3.83 ± 2.24	2.00 ± 1.63	1.33 ± 1.63	**1.16 ± 1.30**
Segment	8	16	32	64	128
DT	4.67 ± 2.45	**2.67 ± 1.33**	4.33 ± 2.38	7.67 ± 4.29	9.83 ± 3.83
Boosting	3.17 ± 1.57	**0.67 ± 1.11**	1.67 ± 1.83	2.17 ± 1.98	3.50 ± 2.17
1-NN	2.33 ± 2.00	**0.50 ± 0.76**	0.50 ± 1.07	1.00 ± 1.10	1.16 ± 1.30

CBF-tr	Number of steps				
Sampling	8	16	32	64	128
DT	**19.17 ± 3.18**	23.50 ± 6.81	20.67 ± 3.82	21.67 ± 3.80	23.83 ± 6.95
Boosting	14.17 ± 3.52	10.50 ± 4.54	6.67 ± 2.79	**5.00 ± 2.36**	7.17 ± 3.58
1-NN	19.33 ± 3.89	8.00 ± 4.70	5.33 ± 2.56	**3.50 ± 2.03**	3.83 ± 2.89
Segment	8	16	32	64	128
DT	14.17 ± 5.34	14.17 ± 4.55	12.83 ± 5.58	**12.67 ± 3.82**	23.83 ± 6.95
Boosting	12.67 ± 5.23	6.00 ± 3.27	**4.17 ± 1.86**	5.33 ± 2.08	7.17 ± 3.58
1-NN	12.00 ± 2.33	3.00 ± 2.66	**1.66 ± 1.82**	2.66 ± 1.52	3.83 ± 2.89

JV	Number of steps				
Sampling	2	3	5	7	
DT	14.86	**14.59**	19.46	21.08	
Boosting	6.76	**5.14**	5.68	6.22	
1-NN	**3.24**	3.24	3.24	3.78	
Segment	1	2	3	4	5
DT	18.11	17.30	**12.97**	19.46	17.03
Boosting	9.46	7.84	6.76	6.76	**6.22**
1-NN	6.49	**3.51**	3.51	3.78	4.05

---

[3] This division was suggested by the donors of this dataset [10]

There are several things to say about this experiment. There exists an optimal value of n which corresponds to the best tradeoff between bias and variance for each problem[4]. This optimal value could be automatically fixed by cross-validation. Segmentation rather than simple sampling is highly beneficial on all datasets except for the last one. The best error rates we get with this simple approach are very good with respect to previously published results on these problems (i.e. with dedicated temporal approaches). The best method is 1-NN on all problems. Decision trees do not work well while boosting is very effective. As boosting works mainly by reducing the variance of a classifier, the bad results of decision trees may be attributed to a high variance. Furthermore, their interpretability is also questionable because of the choice of attributes. Indeed, how to understand for example a rule like "if $a(o, 32) < 2.549$ and $a(o, 22) < 3.48$ then $c(o) = $ bell" which was induced from the CBF dataset? Although very simple and accurate, this rule does not make obvious the temporal increase of the signal peculiar to the bell class (see Fig. 1).

One conclusion of this experiment is that very good results can be obtained with simple feature sets but by sacrificing interpretability. This observation justifies the fact that most of the machine learning research on temporal data have focused on interpretability rather than on accuracy.

4   Pattern Extraction Technique

Why are the approaches adopted in the previous section not very appropriate? First, even if the learning algorithm gives interpretable results, the model will not be comprehensible anymore in terms of the temporal behavior of the system. Second, some very simple and common temporal features are not easily represented as a function of such attributes. For example, consider a set of sequences of n random numbers in $[0, 1]$, $\{a_1, a_2, ..., a_n\}$, and classify a sequence into the class c_1 if three consecutive numbers greater than 0.5 can be found in the sequence whatever the position. With a logical rule inducer (like decision trees) and using $a_1, a_2,...,a_n$ as input attributes, a way to represent such a classification is the following rule: if $(a_1 > 0.5$ and $a_2 > 0.5$ and $a_3 > 0.5)$ or $(a_2 > 0.5$ and $a_3 > 0.5$ and $a_4 > 0.5)$ or ... or $(a_{n-2} > 0.5$ and $a_{n-1} > 0.5$ and $a_n > 0.5)$ then return class c_1. Although the initial classification rule is very simple, the induced rule has to be very complex. This representation difficulty will result in a high variance of the resulting classifier and thus in poor accuracy. The use of variance reduction techniques like boosting and bagging often will not be enough to restore the accuracy and anyway will destroy interpretability.

In this paper, we propose to extend classifiers by allowing them to detect local shift invariant properties or patterns in time-series (like the one used to define the class c_1 in our example). The underlying hypothesis is that it is possible to classify a scenario by combining in a more or less complex way such pattern detections. In what follows, we first define what patterns are and how

---

[4] for a comprehensive explanation of the bias/variance dilemna, see for example [13]

to construct binary classification tests from them. Then, we propose to combine these binary tests into decision trees. In this context, piecewise constant
modeling is proposed to reduce the search space for candidate patterns.

Pattern Definition. A possible way to define a pattern is to use a limited
support reference signal and then say that the pattern is detected at a particular
position of a test signal if the distance between the reference signal and the test
signal at this position is less than a given threshold. In other words, denoting
by $p(.)$ a signal defined on the interval $[0, t_p]$ and by $a(.)$ a signal defined on the
interval $[0, t_a]$ with $t_a \geq t_p$, we would say that the pattern associated to $p(.)$ is
detected in $a(.)$ at time t' $(t_p \leq t' \leq t_a)$ if:

$$d(p(.), a(.), t') = \frac{1}{t_p} \int_{t'-t_p}^{t'} (p(t - t' + t_p) - a(t))^2 dt < d_p, \qquad (1)$$

where d_p is the minimal allowed distance to the pattern (euclidian distance). A
binary classification rule may be constructed from this pattern by means of the
following test:

$$T(o) = \text{True} \Leftrightarrow \exists t' \in [t_p, t_f(o)], : d(p(.), a(o, .), t') < d_p \qquad (2)$$

$$\Leftrightarrow [\min_{t' \in [t_p, t_f(o)]} d(p(.), a(o, .), t')] < d_p \qquad (3)$$

where a is a temporal attribute.

Integration with Decision Trees. As we are mainly interested in interpretable classifiers, the way we propose to combine these binary tests is to let
them appear as candidate tests during decision tree induction. Each step of decision tree induction consists in evaluating a set of candidate tests and choosing
the one which yields the best score to split the node (see [13] for more details).
In the present context, candidate tests are all possible triplets (a, p, d_p) where a
is a temporal candidate attribute.

Once we have chosen an attribute a and a pattern p, the value of d_p which
realizes the best score may be computed similarly as the optimum discretization
threshold for numerical attribute. Indeed, test (3) is equivalent to a test on the
new numerical attribute $a_n(o) = \min_{t'} d(p(.), a(o, .), t')$.

The number of candidate patterns $p(.)$ could be a priori huge. So, it is necessary to reduce the search space for candidate patterns. A first idea is to construct
patterns from subsignals extracted from the signals appearing in the learning set
(each one corresponding to temporal attributes of objects). However, it is still
impossible in practice to consider every such subsignal as a candidate pattern.
Even assuming a discrete time representation for the datasets, this step will remain prohibitive (e.g. there are 8256 different subseries in a time series of 128
points). Also, patterns extracted from raw signals may be too complex or too
noisy for interpretation. The solution adopted here is to first represent the signal
by some piecewise model and then use the discontinuity points of this model to
define interesting patterns. By choosing the complexity of the model (the number
of time axis pieces), we are thus able to fix the number of patterns to consider.

Table 2. Discretization of time signals by regression trees

Let us denote by $\text{mean}_{[t_1,t_2]}(a(.))$ and $\text{var}_{[t_1,t_2]}(a(.))$ respectively the mean and the variance of the signal $a(.)$ on the interval $[t_1, t_2]$:

$$\text{mean}_{[t_1,t_2]}(a(.)) = \frac{1}{t_2 - t_1} \int_{t_1}^{t_2} a(t)dt$$

$$\text{var}_{[t_1,t_2]}(a(.)) = \frac{1}{t_2 - t_1} \int_{t_1}^{t_2} (a(t) - \text{mean}_{[t_1,t_2]}(a(.)))^2 dt$$

To discretize $a(.)$ on $[t_1, t_2]$ with N_{max} pieces:

1. set $D = \{t_1, t_2\}$, the set of discontinuity points; set $L = \{[t_1, t_2]\}$, the set of intervals; set $\hat{a}(t) = \text{mean}_{[t_1,t_2]}a(.)$ on $[t_1, t_2]$, the model for $a(.)$;
2. set $N_p = 1$, the current number of time segments (pieces);
3. if $N_p = N_{max}$ then stop and return $\hat{a}(.)$;
4. find $[t_i, t_j]$ in L such that $(t_j - t_i).\text{var}_{[t_i,t_j]}(a(.))$ is maximal (best first strategy),
5. remove $[t_i, t_j]$ from L,
6. find $t^* \in [t_i, t_j]$ which maximizes the variance reduction:

$$\triangle\text{var}(t^*) = (t_j - t_i)\text{var}_{[t_i,t_j]}(a(.)) - (t^* - t_i)\text{var}_{[t_i,t^*]}(a(.)) - (t_j - t^*)\text{var}_{[t^*,t_j]}(a(.))$$

7. set $\hat{a}(t) = \text{mean}_{[t_i,t^*]}a(.)$ on $[t_i, t^*]$ and $\hat{a}(t) = \text{mean}_{[t^*,t_j]}a(.)$ on $[t^*, t_j]$;
8. $N_p = N_p + 1$; add $[t_i, t^*]$ and $[t^*, t_j]$ to L; add t^* to D.
9. go to step 3

Regression Tree Modeling. In this paper, a simple piecewise constant model is computed for each signal. Regression trees are used to build recursively this model. The exact algorithm is described in Table 2. It follows a best first strategy for the expansion of the tree and the number of segments (or terminal nodes) is fixed in advance. The discretization of an example signal in 5 segments is reproduced in the left part of Fig. 2.

From a discretized signal $\hat{a}(.)$, the set of candidate signals $p(.)$ is defined as follows:

$$P = \{p(.) \text{ on } [0, t_j - t_i]|t_i, t_j \in D, t_i < t_j, p(t) = \hat{a}(t_i + t)\},$$

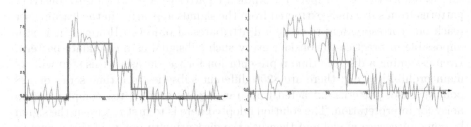

Fig. 2. Left, the regression tree modeling of a signal with 5 intervals. Right, the detection of a pattern extracted from this signal in another signal of the same class

where D is the set of discontinuity points defined in Table 2. The size of this set is $n \cdot (n+1)/2$ if n is the number of segments. The right part of Fig. 2 shows a pattern extracted from the left signal and its minimal distance position in another signal.

Node Splitting for Tree Growing. So, candidate signals $p(.)$ during node splitting will be extracted from piecewise constant modeling of learning set time series. Unfortunately, even with this discretization/segmentation, it will be intractable to consider every subsignals in the learning set, especially when the learning set is large. A simple solution to overcome this difficulty is to randomly sample a subset of the scenarios from the learning set as references for defining the subsequences. In our experiments, one scenario will be drawn from each class. This further simplification should not be limitative because interesting patterns are patterns typical of one class and these patterns (if they exist) will presumably appear in every scenario of the class. Eventually, our final search algorithm for candidate tests when splitting decision tree nodes is depicted in Table 3.

Table 3. Search algorithm for candidate tests during tree growing

For each temporal attribute a, and for each class c:

- select an objet o of class c from the current learning set,
- discretize the signal $a(o, .)$ to obtain $\hat{a}(o, .)$
- compute the set P of subsignals $p(.)$ from $\hat{a}(o, t)$
- for each signal $p(.) \in P$
  - compute the optimal threshold d_p,
  - if the score of this test is greater than the best score so far, retain the triplet $(a(.), p(.), d_p)$ as the best current test.

5   Experiments

We first experiment with the pattern extraction technique described in the previous section. Then, as a byproduct of regression tree modeling is a reduction of the space needed to store the learning set, we further test its combination with the nearest neighbor algorithm.

5.1   Decision Tree with Pattern Extraction

Experiments have been carried out in exactly the same test conditions as in Sect. 3. For regression tree modeling, increasing values of the number of time segments, N_{max}, were used (11 only for CC). Results are summarized in Table 4 and commented below.

Table 4. Results of decision tree with patterns

DB	Number of pieces			
	3	5	7	11
CC	**2.33 ± 1.70**	3.17 ± 2.03	3.33 ± 2.58	3.00 ± 1.63
CBF	4.00 ± 2.71	2.00 ± 1.45	**1.17 ± 1.67**	
CBF-TR	9.33 ± 5.68	3.83 ± 2.24	**2.33 ± 1.33**	
JV	22.97	21.62	**19.4**	

Accuracy. On the first three datasets, the new method gives significant improvements with respect to decision tree (compare with Table 1). As expected, the gain in accuracy is especially impressive on the CBF-tr problem (from 12.67 to 2.33). This problem is also the only one where our temporal approach is better than boosting with simple features. On JV, our approach does not improve accuracy with respect to naive sampling. Several explanations are possible. First, this is the only dataset with more than one attribute and our method is not able to capture properties distributed on several signals. Second, there are 9 classes and only 270 examples in this problem and the recursive partitioning of decision tree is known to suffer in such conditions. Third, it seems also that the temporal behavior is not very important in this problem, as 1-NN with only two values (the start and end values of each attribute) gives the best results (3.24 %).

From this experiment, the optimal number of segments appears to be problem dependent. In practice, we would thus need a way to tune this parameter. Besides cross-validation, various methods have been proposed to fix the number of segments for piecewise modeling (for example, the MDL principle in [11]). In our case, we could also take advantage of the pruning techniques (or stop-splitting criteria) in the context of regression tree induction. We have still to experiment with these methods.

Interpretability. By construction, the rules produced by our algorithm are very readable. For example, a decision tree induced from 500 examples of the CBF problem gives the very simple rules described visually at Fig. 3. The extracted patterns are confirmed by the definition of the problem. This decision tree gives an error rate of 1.3% on the 298 remaining examples. For comparison, a decision tree built from the mean values on 16 segments (the features set which yields the best result in Table 1) contains 17 tests and gives an error rate of 4.6%.

if p1 then funnel
else if p2 and p3 then bell
else if p2 and not p3 then funnel
otherwise cylinder

Fig. 3. classification rules for the CBF problems

5.2   Regression Tree Modeling with 1-NN

As the discretization by regression trees yields a compact version of the original time-series, it would be interesting to combine it into a nearest neighbor classifier. The main advantage will be a reduction of the space needed to memorize the learning set. The algorithm proceeds as follows. First, all signals in the learning set are discretized by regression trees using the same maximum number of pieces. Then, the distance between a test object o and an object o' of the learning set is defined by:

$$d(o,o') = \frac{1}{\min(t_f(o), t_f(o'))} \sum_{i=1}^{m} \int_{0}^{\min(t_f(o), t_f(o'))} (a_i(o,t) - \hat{a}_i(o',t))^2 dt. \quad (4)$$

So, discretized signals $\hat{a}_i(o', t)$ for learning set objects are compared to full signals for test objects. To deal with objects which are defined on different intervals, we simply truncate the longest one to the duration of the shortest one.

Experiments have been carried out with increasing values of the number of time segments (from 1 to 11). Results are reported in Table 5. On the first three problems, the accuracy is as good as the best accuracy which was obtained in Table 1 and the number of time segments to reach this accuracy is very small. The compression of the learning set is particularly impressive on the CC dataset where only three values are enough to reach an almost perfect accuracy. On the other hand, regression tree modeling decreases the accuracy on JV with respect to 1-NN and only two values per attribute. Again, the optimal number of pieces is problem dependent. In the context of 1-NN, leave-one-out is an obvious candidate method to determine this parameter.

Table 5. Results of 1-NN with regression tree modeling

DB	Number of pieces				
	1	3	5	7	11
CC	38.83 ± 9.40	0.50 ± 0.76	**0.17 ± 0.50**	0.33 ± 1.00	0.33 ± 0.67
CBF	46.17 ± 6.15	10.50 ± 2.69	1.33 ± 1.45	0.50 ± 0.76	**0.33 ± 0.67**
CBF-tr	43.00 ± 5.57	23.00 ± 7.18	4.50 ± 3.58	**2.33 ± 1.70**	2.50 ± 1.86
JV	11.35	5.67	4.86	**4.59**	4.59

6   Conclusion and Future Work

In this paper, we have presented a new tool to handle time series in classification problems. This tool is based on a piecewise constant modeling of temporal signals by regression trees. Patterns are extracted from these models and combined in decision trees to give interpretable rules. This approach has been compared to two "naive" feature selection techniques. The advantage of our technique in terms of interpretability is undeniable. In terms of accuracy, better results can be obtained by using either boosting or 1-NN with naive features. However, in some problems where start time of characteristic events are highly variable (like in CBF-tr), accuracy can be improved by pattern extraction. Eventually, even if our main goal was interpretability, our extended decision trees can also be combined in boosted classifiers where they are very unlikely to destroy accuracy with respect to the naive feature selection.

In the future, we will consider extensions of our method along several axis. First, there are still many possible improvements of the pattern extraction algorithm. For instance, we can experiment with other piecewise models (linear by hinges model, polynomial,...) or with more robust sampling strategies during node splitting. As already mentioned, we also need a way to automatically adapt the number of time segments during tree growing. Second, one limitation of our pattern definition is that it does not allow the detection of shrunk or extended versions of the reference pattern along the time axis. Several distances have been proposed to circumvent this problem, for example dynamic time warping [4,9] or probabilistic pattern matching [6]. We believe that such distances could be combined with our approach but at the price of a higher complexity. Eventually, there exist many problems where the exact ordering of patterns appearing in signals is crucial for classification. In these cases, the combination of patterns by simple logical rules would not be enough and dedicated methods should be developed which could take into account temporal constraints between patterns.

References

1. R. J. Alcock and Y. Manolopoulos. Time-series similarity queries employing a feature-based approach. In *Proc. of the 7th Hellenic Conference on Informatics*, Ioannina, Greece, 1999.
2. C. J. Alonso Gonzalez and Juan J. Rodriguez Diez. Time series classification by boosting interval based literals. *Inteligencia Artificial, Revista Iberoamericana de Inteligencia Artificial*, (11):2–11, 2000.
3. S. D. Bay. The UCI KDD archive, 1999. http://kdd.ics.uci.edu.
4. D. J. Berndt and J. Clifford. Finding patterns in time series: A dynamic programming approach. In *Advances in Knowledge discovery and data mining*. AAAI Press/MIT Press, 1996.
5. Y. Freund and R.E. Schapire. Experiments with a new boosting algorithm. In *Proc. of the 13th International Conference on Machine Learning*, 1996.
6. X. Ge and P. Smyth. Deformable markov model templates for time-series pattern matching. In *Proc. of the 6th Intl. Conf. on Knowledge Discovery and Data Mining (KDD)*, pages 81–90, Boston, MA, August 2000.
7. P. Geurts and L. Wehenkel. Early prediction of electric power system blackouts by temporal machine learning. In *Proc. of ICML-AAAI'98 Workshop on "AI Approaches to Times-series Analysis"*, Madison (Wisconsin), 1998.
8. M. W. Kadous. Learning comprehensible descriptions of multivariate time series. In *Proceedings of the Sixteenth International Conference on Machine Learning, ICML'99*, pages 454–463, Bled, Slovenia, 1999.
9. E. J. Keogh and M. J. Pazzani. Scaling up dynamic time warping for datamining applications. In *Proc. of the 6th Intl. Conf. on Knowledge Discovery and Data Mining (KDD)*, pages 285–289, Boston, MA, August 2000.

10. M. Kudo, J. Toyama, and M. Shimbo. Multidimensional curve classification using passing-through regions. *Pattern Recognition Letters*, 20(11-13):1103–1111, 1999.
11. S. Manganaris. *Supervised classification with temporal data*. PhD thesis, Vanderbilt University, 1997.
12. N. Saito. *Local feature extraction and its application using a library of bases*. PhD thesis, Department of Mathematics, Yale University, 1994.
13. L. Wehenkel. *Automatic learning techniques in power systems*. Kluwer Academic, Boston, 1998.

Specifying Mining Algorithms with Iterative User-Defined Aggregates: A Case Study

Fosca Giannotti[1], Giuseppe Manco[1], and Franco Turini[2]

[1] CNUCE-CNR - Via Alfieri 1 - 56010 Pisa Italy
{F.Giannotti,G.Manco}@cnuce.cnr.it
[2] Department of Computer Science - Corso Italia 40 - 56125 Pisa Italy
turini@DI.Unipi.IT

Abstract. We present a way of exploiting domain knowledge in the design and implementation of data mining algorithms, with special attention to frequent patterns discovery, within a deductive framework. In our framework domain knowledge is represented by deductive rules, and data mining algorithms are constructed by means of iterative user-defined aggregates. Iterative user-defined aggregates have a fixed scheme that allows the modularization of data mining algorithms, thus providing a way to exploit domain knowledge in the right point. As a case study, the paper presents user-defined aggregates for specifying a version of the apriori algorithm. Some performance analyses and comparisons are discussed in order to show the effectiveness of the approach.

1 Introduction and Motivations

The problem of incorporating data mining technology into query systems has been widely studied in the current literature [12,9,14,10]. In such a context, the idea of integrating data mining algorithms in a deductive environment [7,5] is very powerful, since it allows the direct exploitation of domain knowledge within the specification of the queries, the specification of ad-hoc interest measures that can help in evaluating the extracted knowledge, and the modelization of the interactive and iterative features of knowledge discovery in a uniform way. However, the main drawback of a deductive approach to data mining query languages concerns efficiency: a data mining algorithm can be worth substantial optimizations that come both from a smart constraining of the search space, and from the exploitation of efficient data structures. The case of association rules is a typical example of this. Association rules are computed from frequent itemsets, that actually can be efficiently computed by exploiting the *apriori property* [15], and by speeding-up comparisons and counting operations with the adoption of special data structures (e.g., lookup tables, hash trees, etc.). Detailed studies [1] have shown that a direct specification of the algorithms within a query language lacks of performance effectiveness.

A partial solution to this problem has been proposed in [5,14,2]. In these approaches, data mining algorithms are modeled as "black boxes" integrated within the system. The interaction between the data mining algorithm and the

L. De Raedt and A. Siebes (Eds.): PKDD 2001, LNAI 2168, pp. 128–139, 2001.
© Springer-Verlag Berlin Heidelberg 2001

query system is provided by defining a representation formalism of discovered patterns within the language, and by collecting the data to be mined in an ad-hoc format (a cache), directly accessed by the algorithm. However, such a decoupled approach has the main drawback of not allowing the tuning of the search on the basis of specific properties of the problem at hand. As an example, using black boxes we cannot directly exploit domain knowledge within the algorithm, nor we can "on-the-fly" evaluate interest measures of the discovered patterns.

The above considerations yield an apparent mismatch: it is unfeasible to specify directly and implement data mining algorithms using the query language itself, and by the converse it is inconvenient to integrate data mining algorithms within query languages as predefined modules. In this paper we propose to combine the advantages of the two approaches in a uniform way. Following the approach of [7,5], we adopt aggregates as an interface to mining tasks in a deductive database. Moreover, data mining algorithms are specified by means of *iterative* user-defined aggregates, i.e., aggregates that are computed using a fixed scheme. Such a feature allows to modularize data mining algorithm and integrate domain knowledge in the right points, thus allowing crucial domain-oriented optimizations.

On the other side, user-defined predicates can be implemented by means of *hot-spot refinements* [3,4]. That is, we can extend the deductive databases with new data types, (like in the case of object-relational data systems), that can be efficiently accessed and managed using ad-hoc methods. Such data types and methods can be implemented by the user-defined predicates, possibly in other programming languages, with a reasonable trade-off between specification and efficient implementation.

The main advantages of such an approach are twofold:

- on the one side, we maintain an adequate declarative approach to the specification of data mining algorithms.
- on the other side, we can exploit specific (physical) optimizations improving the performance of the algorithms exactly where they are needed.

As a case study, the paper presents how such a technique can be used to specify a version of the apriori algorithm, capable of taking into account domain knowledge in the pruning phase. We recall the **patterns** aggregate defined in [5], and provide a specification of such an aggregate as an iterative user-defined aggregate. Hence, we provide an effective implementation of the aggregate by exploiting user-defined predicates.

The paper is organized as follows. Section 2 introduces the notion of iterative user-defined aggregates, and justifies their use in the specification of data mining algorithms. In Sect. 3 we introduce the **patterns** iterative aggregate for mining frequent itemsets. In particular, we show how user-defined predicates can be exploited to efficiently implement the aggregate. Finally, in Sect. 4 some performance analyses and comparisons are discussed in order to show the effectiveness of the approach.

2   Iterative User-Defined Aggregates

In [11] we formalize the notion of logic-based knowledge discovery support environment, as a deductive database programming language that models inductive rules as well as deductive rules. Here, an inductive rule provides a smooth integration of data mining and querying. In [5,7] we propose the modeling of an inductive rule by means of *aggregate functions*. The capability of specifying (and efficiently computing) aggregates is very important in order to provide a basis of a logic-based knowledge discovery support environment. To this purpose, the Datalog++ logic-based database language [16,17,8] provides a general framework for dealing with user-defined aggregates. We use such aggregates as the means to introduce mining primitives into the query language.

In general, a *user-defined aggregate* [17] is defined as a *distributive* aggregate, i.e., a function f inductively defined over a (nondeterministically sorted) set S:

$$f(\{x\}) = g(x) \tag{1}$$
$$f(S \cup \{x\}) = h(f(S), x) \tag{2}$$

We can directly specify the base and inductive cases, by means of ad-hoc user-defined predicates `single`, `multi` and `return`, used implicitly in the evaluation of the aggregate rule

$$p(K_1, \ldots, K_m, \mathtt{aggr}\langle X \rangle) \leftarrow \mathtt{Rule\ body}.$$

In particular, `single(aggr, X, C)` associates to the first tuple X in the nondeterministic ordering a value, according to (1), and `multi(aggr, Old, X, New)` computes the value of the aggregate `aggr` associated to the current value X in the current ordering, by incrementally computing it from the previous value, according to (2).

However, in order to define complex aggregation functions, (such as mining functions), the main problem with the traditional user-defined aggregate model is the impossibility of defining more complex forms of aggregates than distributive ones. In many cases, even simple aggregates may require multiple steps over data in order to be computed. A simple way [6] of coping with the problem of multiple scans over data can be done by extending the specification of the aggregation rule, in order to impose some user-defined conditions for iterating the scan over data. The main scheme shown in [17] requires that the evaluation of the query $p(v_1, \ldots, v_m, v)$ is done by first compiling the above program, and then evaluating the query on the compiled program. In the compiling phase, the program is rewritten into an equivalent, fixed rule scheme, that depends upon the user-defined predicates `single`, `multi` and `return`.

In [6,11] we slightly modify such rewriting, by making the scheme dependent upon the new `iterate` user-defined predicate. Such predicate specifies the condition for iterating the aggregate computation: the activation (and evaluation) of such a rule is subject to the successful evaluation of the user-defined predicate `iterate`, so that any failure in evaluating it results in the termination of the computation.

Example 1. The computation of the absolute deviation $S_n = \sum_x |\overline{x} - x|$ of a set of n elements needs at least two scans over the data. Exploiting `iterate` predicate, we can define S_n as a user-defined predicate:

$$\text{single}(\text{abserr}, X, (\text{nil}, X, 1)).$$
$$\text{multi}(\text{abserr}, (\text{nil}, S, C), X, (\text{nil}, S + X, C + 1)).$$
$$\text{multi}(\text{abserr}, (M, D), X, (M, D + (M - X))) \leftarrow M > X.$$
$$\text{multi}(\text{abserr}, (M, D), X, (M, D + (X - M))) \leftarrow M \leq X.$$
$$\text{iterate}(\text{abserr}, (\text{nil}, S, C), (S/C, 0)).$$
$$\text{freturn}(\text{abserr}, (M, D), D).$$

The combined use of `multi` and `iterate` allows to define two scans over the data: the first scan is defined to compute the mean value, and the second one computes the sum of the absolute difference with the mean value.   ◁

Although the notion of iterative aggregate is in some sense orthogonal to the envisaged notion of inductive rule [11], the main motivation for introducing iterative aggregates is that the iterative schema shown above is common in many data mining algorithms. Usually, a typical data mining algorithm is an instance of an iterative schema where, at each iteration, some statistics are gathered from the data. The termination condition can be used to determine whether the extracted statistics are sufficient to the purpose of the task (i.e., they determine all the patterns), or whether no further statistics can be extracted.

Hence, the iterative schema discussed so far is a good candidate for specifying steps of data mining algorithms at low granularity levels. Relating aggregate specification with inductive rules makes it easy to provide an interface capable of specifying source data, knowledge extraction, background knowledge and interestingness measures. Moreover, we can specify the data mining task under consideration in detail, by exploiting ad-hoc definitions of `single`, `multi`, `iterate` and `return` iterative user-defined predicates.

3   The patterns Iterative Aggregate

In the following, we concentrate on the problem of mining frequent patterns from a dataset of transactions. We can integrate such mining task within the datalog++ database language, by means of a suitable inductive rule.

Definition 1 ([5]). *Given a relation* **r**, *the* **patterns** *aggregate is defined by the rule*

$$p(X_1, \ldots, X_n, \text{patterns}\langle(\text{min\_supp}, Y)\rangle) \leftarrow r(Z_1, \ldots, Z_m) \qquad (3)$$

where the variables $X_1, \ldots, X_n, Y$ are a rearranged subset of the variables $Z_1, \ldots, Z_m$ of **r**, `min_supp` is a value representing the minimum support threshold, and the Y variable denotes a set of elements. The aggregate **patterns** computes the set of predicates $p(t_1, \ldots, t_n, (s, f))$ where:

1. $t_1, \ldots, t_n$ are distinct instances of the variables $X_1, \ldots, X_n$, as resulting from the evaluation of r;
2. $s = \{l_1, \ldots, l_k\}$ is a subset of the value of Y in a tuple resulting from the evaluation of r;
3. f is the support of the set s, such that $f \geq min\_supp$.

$\square$

We can provide an explicit specification of the **patterns** aggregate in the above definition as an iterative aggregate. That is, we can directly implement an algorithm for computing frequent patterns, by defining the predicates **single**, **multi**, **return** and **iterate**.

The simplest specification adopts the purely declarative approach of *generating* all the possible itemsets, and then *testing* the frequency of the itemsets. It is easy to provide such a naive definition by means of the iterative schema proposed in Sect. 2:

$$\text{single}(\text{patterns}, (\text{Sp}, \text{S}), ((\text{Sp}, 1), \text{IS})) \qquad\qquad \leftarrow \text{subset}(\text{IS}, \text{S}).$$

$$\text{multi}(\text{patterns}, ((\text{Sp}, \text{N}), \_), (\text{Sp}, \text{S}), ((\text{Sp}, \text{N}+1), \text{IS})) \leftarrow \text{subset}(\text{IS}, \text{S}).$$
$$\text{multi}(\text{patterns}, ((\text{Sp}, \text{N}), \text{IS}), \_, (\text{Sp}, \text{IS})).$$

$$\text{multi}(\text{patterns}, (\text{Sp}, \text{IS}, \text{N}), (\_, \text{S}), (\text{Sp}, \text{IS}, \text{N}+1)) \qquad \leftarrow \text{subset}(\text{IS}, \text{S}).$$
$$\text{multi}(\text{patterns}, (\text{Sp}, \text{IS}, \text{N}), (\_, \text{S}), (\text{Sp}, \text{IS}, \text{N})) \qquad\qquad \leftarrow \neg\text{subset}(\text{IS}, \text{S}).$$

$$\text{iterate}(\text{patterns}, ((\text{Sp}, \text{N}), \text{IS}), (\text{Sp} \times \text{N}, \text{IS}, 0)).$$

$$\text{freturn}(\text{patterns}, (\text{Sp}, \text{IS}, \text{N}), (\text{IS}, \text{N})) \qquad\qquad \leftarrow \text{N} \geq \text{Sp}.$$

Such a specification works with two main iterations. In the first iteration (first three rules), the set of possible subsets are generated for each tuple in the dataset. The **iterate** predicate initializes the counter of each candidate itemset, and activates the computation of its frequency (performed by the remaining **multi** rules). The computation terminates when all itemsets frequencies have been computed, and frequent itemsets are returned as answers (by mean of the **freturn** rule). Notice that the **freturn** predicate defines the output format for the aggregation predicate: a suitable answer is a pair (Itemset, N) such that Itemset is an itemset of frequency $N > Sp$, where Sp is the minimal support required.

Clearly, the above implementation is extremely inefficient, since it checks the support of all the possible itemsets. More precisely, the aggregate computation generates $2^{|I|}$ sets of items, where I is the set of different items appearing in the tuples considered during the computation. As a consequence, no pruning strategy is exploited; namely, unfrequent subsets are discarded at the end of the computation of the frequencies of all the subsets. Moreover, no optimized data structure, capable of speeding-up the computation of some costly operations, is used.

A detailed analysis of the *Apriori* algorithm [15] shown in Fig. 1, however, suggests a smarter specification. Initially, the algorithm computes the candidate itemsets of size 1 (*init phase*: step 1). The core of the algorithm is then a loop,

Algorithm Apriori($\mathcal{B}$, σ);

Input: a set of transactions $\mathcal{B}$, a support threshold σ;
Output: a set $Result$ of frequent itemsets
Method: let initially $Result = \emptyset$, $k = 1$.
   1. $C_1 = \{a | a \in \mathcal{I}\}$;
   2. **while** $C_k \neq \emptyset$ **do**
   3.   **foreach** itemset $c \in C_k$ **do**
   4. $supp(c) = 0$;
   5.   **foreach** $b \in \mathcal{B}$ **do**
   6.   **foreach** $c \in C_k$ **such that** $c \subseteq b$ **do** $supp(c) + +$;
   7. $L_k := \{c \in C_k | \ supp(c) > \sigma\}$;
   8. $Result := Result \cup L_k$;
   9. $C_{k+1} := \{c_i \cup c_j | c_i, c_j \in L_k \wedge |c_i \cup c_j| = k+1 \wedge \forall c \subset c_i \cup c_j \text{ such that } |c| = k : c \in L_k\}$;
 10. $k := k + 1$;
 11. **end while**

Fig. 1. Apriori Algorithm for computing frequent itemsets

where the k-th iteration examines the set C_k of candidate itemsets of size k. During such an iteration the occurrences of each candidate itemset are computed scanning the data (*count phase*: steps 5-6). Unfrequent itemsets are then dropped (*prune phase*: step 7), and frequent ones are maintained in L_k. By exploiting the subset-frequency dependance, candidate itemsets of size $k + 1$ can be built from pairs of frequent itemsets of size k differing only in one position (*enhance phase*: step 9). Finally, $Result$ shall contain $\bigcup_k L_k$ (*itemsets phase*: step 8).

By exploiting iterative aggregates, we can directly specify all the phases of the algorithm. Initially, we specify the init phase,

$\text{single}(\text{patterns}, (\text{Sp}, \text{S}), ((\text{Sp}, 1), \text{IS}))$ $\leftarrow \text{single\_isets}(\text{S}, \text{IS}).$
$\text{multi}(\text{patterns}, ((\text{Sp}, \text{N}), \text{IS}), (\text{Sp}, \text{S}), ((\text{Sp}, \text{N} + 1), \text{ISS})) \leftarrow \text{single\_isets}(\text{S}, \text{SS}),$
                                                 $\text{union}(\text{SS}, \text{IS}, \text{ISS}).$

The subsequent iterations resemble the steps of the apriori algorithm, that is counting the candidate itemsets, pruning unfrequent candidates and generating new candidates:

$\text{iterate}(\text{patterns}, ((\text{Sp}, \text{N}), \text{S}), (\text{Sp} \times \text{N}, \text{S})).$
$\text{iterate}(\text{patterns}, (\text{Sp}, \text{S}), (\text{Sp}, \text{SS}))$ $\leftarrow \text{prune}(\text{Sp}, \text{S}, \text{IS}),$
                                        $\text{generate\_candidates}(\text{IS}, \text{SS}).$

$\text{multi}(\text{patterns}, (\text{Sp}, \text{IS}), (\_, \text{S}), (\text{Sp}, \text{ISS})) \leftarrow \text{count\_isets}(\text{IS}, \text{S}, \text{ISS}).$
$\text{freturn}(\text{patterns}, (\text{Sp}, \text{ISS}), (\text{IS}, \text{N})) \leftarrow \text{member}((\text{IS}, \text{N}), \text{ISS}), \text{N} \geq \text{Sp}.$

Such an approach exploits a substantial optimization, by avoiding to check a large portion of unfrequent itemsets. However, the implementation of the main operations of the algorithm is demanded to the predicates **singe_isets**, **prune**, **generate_candidates** and **count_isets**. As a consequence, the efficiency of the approach is parametric to the efficient implementation and evaluation of such predicates.

3.1   Exploiting User-Defined Predicates

In order to support complex database applications, most relational database systems support user-defined functions. Such functions can be invoked in queries, making it easier for developers to implement their applications with significantly greater efficiency. The adoption of such features in a logic-based system provides even greater impact, since they allow a user to develop large programs by *hot-spot refinement* [4]. The user writes a large datalog++ program, validates its correctness and identifies the hot-spots, i.e., predicates in the program that are highly time consuming. Then, he can rewrite those hot-spots more efficiently in a procedural language, such as C++, maintaining the rest of the program in datalog++.

The $\mathcal{LDL}$++ [17,16] implementation of datalog++ allows the definition of external predicates written in C++, by providing mechanisms to convert objects between the $\mathcal{LDL}$++ representation and the external representations. The ad-hoc use of such mechanisms reveals very useful to provide new data types inside the $\mathcal{LDL}$++ model, in the style of Object-relational databases. For example, a reference to a C++ object can be returned as an answer, or passed as input, and the management of such a user-defined object is demanded to a set of external predicates.

We adopt such a model to implement hot-spot refinements of frequent item-sets mining. In the following we describe the implementation of an enhanced version of the Apriori algorithm, described in Fig. 1, by means user-defined predicates. In practice, we extend the allowed types of the $\mathcal{LDL}$++ system to include more complex structures, and provide some built-in predicates that efficiently manipulate such structures:

$$\texttt{single}(\texttt{patterns}, (\texttt{Sp}, \texttt{S}), ((\texttt{Sp}, 1), \texttt{T})) \qquad \leftarrow \texttt{init}(\texttt{S}, \texttt{T}).$$

$$\texttt{multi}(\texttt{patterns}, ((\texttt{Sp}, \texttt{N}), \texttt{T}), (\texttt{Sp}, \texttt{S}), ((\texttt{Sp}, \texttt{N} + 1), \texttt{T})) \leftarrow \texttt{init}(\texttt{S}, \texttt{T}).$$

$$\texttt{iterate}(\texttt{patterns}, ((\texttt{Sp}, \texttt{N}), \texttt{T}), (\texttt{Sp} \times \texttt{N}, \texttt{T})) \qquad \leftarrow \texttt{prune}(\texttt{Sp}, \texttt{T}), \texttt{enhance}(\texttt{T}).$$

$$\texttt{multi}(\texttt{patterns}, (\texttt{Sp}, \texttt{T}), (\_, \texttt{S}), (\texttt{Sp}, \texttt{T})) \qquad \leftarrow \texttt{count}(\texttt{S}, \texttt{T}).$$

$$\texttt{iterate}(\texttt{patterns}, (\texttt{Sp}, \texttt{T}), (\texttt{Sp}, \texttt{T})) \qquad \leftarrow \texttt{prune}(\texttt{Sp}, \texttt{T}), \texttt{enhance}(\texttt{T}).$$

$$\texttt{freturn}(\texttt{patterns}, (\texttt{Sp}, \texttt{T}), (\texttt{I}, \texttt{S})) \qquad \leftarrow \texttt{itemset}(\texttt{T}, (\texttt{I}, \texttt{S})).$$

In such a schema, the variable T represents the reference to a structure of type *Hash-Tree* [15], which is essentially a prefix-tree with a hash table associated to each node. An edge is labelled with an item, so that paths from the root to an internal node represent itemsets. Figure 2 shows some example trees. Each node is labelled with a tag denoting the support of the itemset represented by the path from the root to the node. An additional tag denotes whether the node can generate new candidates. The predicates init, count, enhance, prune and itemset are *user-defined predicates* that implement, in C++, complex operators, exemplified in Fig. 2, over the given hash-tree. More specifically:

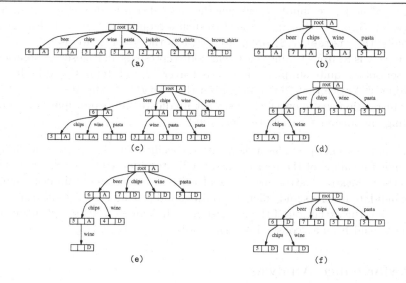

Fig. 2. a) Tree initialization. b) pruning. c) tree enhancement and counting. d) pruning. e) tree enhancement. f) cutting

- The `init(I,T)` predicate initializes and updates the frequencies of the 1-itemsets available from `I` in `T` (Fig. 2a). For each item found in the transaction `I`, either the item is already into the tree (in which case its counter is updated), or it is inserted and its counter set to 1.
- The `count(I,T)` predicate updates the frequencies of each itemset in `T` according to the transaction `I` (Fig. 2c). We define a simple recursive procedure that, starting from the first element of the current transaction, traverses the tree from the root to the leaves. When a leaf at a given level is found, the counter is incremented.
- The `prune(M,T)` predicate removes from `T` all the itemsets whose frequencies are less than `M` (Figs. 2b and d). Leaf nodes at a given depth (representing the size of the candidates) are removed if their support is lower than the given threshold.
- The `enhance(T)` predicates combines the frequent k-itemsets in `T` and generates the candidate $k+1$-itemsets. New candidates are generated in two step. In the first step, a leaf node is merged with each of its siblings, and new sons are generated. For example in Fig. 2e, the node labelled with `beer − chips` is merged with its sibling `beer − wine`, generating the new node labelled with `beer − chips − wine`. In order to ensure that every new node represents an actual candidate of size $n+1$, we need to check whether all the subsets of the itemset of size n are actually in the hash tree. Such an operation consists in a traversal of the tree from the enhanced node to the root node; for each

analyzed node, we simply check whether its subtree is also a subtree of its ancestor. Subtrees that do not satisfy such a requirement are cut (Fig. 2f).
- Finally, the itemset(T, S) predicate extracts the frequent itemset I (whose frequency is S) from T. Since each leaf node represents an itemset, generation of itemsets is quite simple. The tree is traversed and itemsets are built accordingly. Notice that, differently from the previous predicates, where only one invocation was allowed, the itemset predicate allows multiple calls, providing one answer for each itemset found.

The above schema provides a declarative specification that is parametric to the intended meaning of the user-defined predicates adopted. The schema minimalizes the "black-box" structure of the algorithm, needed to obtain fast counting of candidate itemsets and efficient pruning, and provides many opportunities of optimizing the execution of the algorithm both from a database optimization perspective and from a "constraints" embedding perspective [13].

4   Performance Analysis

In this section we analyze the impact of the architecture we described in the previous sections to the process of extracting association rules from data. The performance analysis that we undertook compared the effect of mining association rules according to four different architectural choices:

1. *DB2 Batch*, an Apriori implementation that retrieves data from a SQL DBMS, stores such data in an intermediate structure and then performs the basic steps of the algorithm using such structures. Such an implementation conforms to the Cache-Mine approach. The main motivation is to compare the effects of such an implementation with a similar one in the $\mathcal{LDL}$++ deductive database. Conceptually, such an implementation can be thought of as the architectural support for an SQL extension, like, e.g., the MINE RULE construct shown in [14].
2. *DB2 interactive*, an Apriori implementation in which data is read tuple by tuple from the DBMS. This approach is very easy to implement and manage, but has the main disadvantage of the large cost of context switching between the DBMS and the mining process. Since user-defined predicates need also such a context switching, it is interesting to see how the approach behaves compared to the $\mathcal{LDL}$++ approach.
3. $\mathcal{LDL}$++, the implementation of the rules mining aggregate patterns, by means of the iterative aggregate specified in the previous section.
4. a plain Apriori implementation (*Apriori* in the following), that reads data from a binary file. We used such an implementation to keep track of the actual computational effort of the algorithm on the given data size when no data retrieval and context switching overhead is present.

We tested the effect of a very simple form of mining query -one that is expressible also in SQL- that retrieves data from a single table and applies

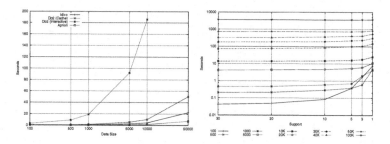

Fig. 3. Performance comparison and summary

the mining algorithm. In $\mathcal{LDL}++$ terms, the experiments were performed by querying `ans(min_supp, R)`, where `ans` was defined as

$$\texttt{ans}(S, \texttt{patterns}\langle\langle (S, \texttt{ItemSet}) \rangle\rangle) \leftarrow \texttt{transaction}(\texttt{ID}, \texttt{ItemSet}).$$

and the `transaction(ID, ItemSet)` relation is a materialized table.

In order to populate the `transaction` predicate (and its relational counterpart), we used the synthetic data generation utility described in [15, Sect. 2.4.3]. Data generation can be tuned according to the usual parameters: the number of transactions ($|\mathcal{D}|$), the average size of the transactions ($|T|$), the average size of the maximal potentially frequent itemsets ($|I|$), the number of maximal potentially frequent itemsets ($|\mathcal{I}|$), and the number of items (N). We fixed $|I|$ to 2, and $|T|$ to 10, since such parameters affect the size of the frequent itemsets. All the remaining parameters were adjusted according to increasing values of $\mathcal{D}$: as soon as $\mathcal{D}$ increases, $|\mathcal{I}|$ and N are increased as well.

The following figures show how the performances of the various solutions change according to increasing values of $\mathcal{D}$ and decreasing values of the support. Experiments were made on a Linux system with two 400Mhz Intel Pentium II processors, with 128Mb RAM. Alternatives 1 and 2 were implemented using the IBM DB2 universal database v6.1.

In Fig. 3 it can be seen that, as expected, the *DB2 (interactive)* solution gives the worst results: since a cursor is maintained against the internal buffer of the database server, the main contribution to the cost is given by the frequent context switching between the application and the database server [1]. Moreover, decreasing values of support strongly influence its performance: lower support values influence the size of the frequent patterns, and hence multiple scans over the data are required.

Figure 3 shows that the $\mathcal{LDL}++$ approach outperforms the *DB2 (Batch)* approach. However, as soon as the size of the dataset is increased, the difference between the two approaches tends to decrease: the graphs show that the $\mathcal{LDL}++$ performance gradually worsens, and we can expect that, for larger datasets, *DB2 (Batch)* can outperform $\mathcal{LDL}++$. Such a behavior finds its explanation in the processing overhead of the deductive system with respect to the relational system, which can be quantified, as expected, by a constant factor.

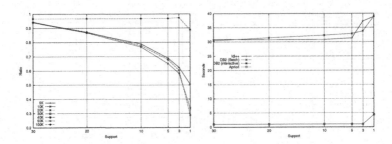

Fig. 4. Context switching overhead

The seconds graph in Fig. 3 summarizes the performance of the $\mathcal{LDL}$++ system for different values of the data size. The performance graph has a smooth (almost linear) curve. The ratio between the data preprocessing of $\mathcal{LDL}$++ and the application of the Apriori algorithm (i.e., the context switching overhead) is shown in Fig. 4. The ratio is 1 when the internal management phase is predominant with respect to the application of the algorithm. As we can see, this ratio is particularly high with the last dataset, that does not contain frequent itemsets (except for very low support values), and hence the predominant computational cost is due to context switching.

5   Conclusions and Future Work

Iterative aggregates have the advantage of allowing the specification of data mining tasks at the desired abstraction level: from a conceptual point of view, they allow a direct use of background knowledge in the algorithm specification; from a physical point of view, they give the opportunity of directly integrating proper knowledge extraction optimizations. In this paper we have shown how the basic framework allows physical optimizations: an in-depth study of how to provide high-level optimization by means of direct exploitation of background knowledge has to be performed.

The problem of tailoring optimization techniques to mining queries is a major research topic, in a database-oriented approach to data mining. It is not surprising that such a topic is even more substantial in deductive-based approaches, like the one presented in this paper. In [11] we have shown some examples of how a logic based language can benefit of a thorough modification of the underlying abstract machine, and how other interesting ways of coping with efficiency can be investigated (for example, by extracting expressive subsets of teh language viable for efficient implementation).

We are currently interested in formalizing such modifications in order to provide a mapping of deductive mining query specifications to query plan generations and optimizations.

References

1. R. Agrawal, S. Sarawagi, and S. Thomas. Integrating Association Rule Mining with Relational Database Systems: Alternatives and Implications. *Data Mining and Knowledge Discovery*, 4(3):89–125, 2000.
2. P. Alcamo, F. Domenichini, and F. Turini. An XML Based Environment in Support of the Overall KDD Process. In *Procs. of the 4th International Conference on Flexible Query Answering Systems (FQAS2000)*, Advances in Soft Computing, pages 413–424, 2000.
3. S. Chaudhuri and K. Shim. Optimization of Queries with User-Defined Predicates. *ACM Transactions on Database Systems*, 24(2):177–228, 1999.
4. D. Chimenti, R. Gamboa, and R. Krishnamurthy. Towards an Open Architecture for $\mathcal{LDL}$. In *Proc. 15th Int. Conf. on Very Large Data Bases (VLDB89)*, pages 195–204, 1989.
5. F. Giannotti and G. Manco. Querying Inductive Databases via Logic-Based User-Defined Aggregates. In *Proc. 3rd European Conference on Principles and Practices of Knowledge Discovery in Databases*, number 1704 in Lecture Notes on Artificial Intelligence, pages 125–135, September 1999.
6. F. Giannotti and G. Manco. Declarative Knowledge Extraction with Iterative User-Defined Aggregates. In *Procs. 4th International Conference on Flexible Query Answering Systems (FQAS2000)*, Advances in Soft Computing, pages 445–454, 2000.
7. F. Giannotti and G. Manco. Making Knowledge Extraction and Reasoning Closer. In *Proc. 4th Pacific-Asia Conference on Knowledge Discovery and Data Mining*, number 1805 in Lecture Notes in Computer Science, April 2000.
8. F. Giannotti, G. Manco, M. Nanni, and D .Pedreschi. Nondeterministic, Non-monotonic Logic Databases. *IEEE Trans. on Knowledge and Data Engineering*. To appear.
9. J. Han, Y. Fu, K. Koperski, W. Wang, and O. Zaiane. DMQL: A Data Mining Query Language for Relational Databases. In *SIGMOD'96 Workshop on Research Issues on Data Mining and Knowledge Discovery (DMKD'96)*, 1996.
10. T. Imielinski and A. Virmani. MSQL: A Query Language for Database Mining. *Data Mining and Knowledge Discovery*, 3(4):373–408, 1999.
11. G. Manco. *Foundations of a Logic-Based Framework for Intelligent Data Analysis*. PhD thesis, Department of Computer Science, University of Pisa, April 2001.
12. H. Mannila. Inductive databases and condensed representations for data mining. In *International Logic Programming Symposium*, pages 21–30, 1997.
13. R. Ng, L. V. S. Lakshmanan, J. Han, and A. Pang. Exploratory Mining and Pruning Optimizations of Constrained Associations Rules. In *Proc. ACM Conf. on Management of Data (SIGMOD98)*, June 1998.
14. S. Ceri R. Meo, G. Psaila. A New SQL-Like Operator for Mining Association Rules. In *Proc. 22th Int. Conf. on Very Large Data Bases (VLDB96)*, pages 122–133, 1996.
15. R. Srikant. *Fast Algorithms for Mining Association Rules and Sequential Patterns*. PhD thesis, University of Wisconsin-Madison, 1996.
16. C. Zaniolo, N. Arni, and K. Ong. Negation and Aggregates in Recursive Rules: The $\mathcal{LDL}$++ Approach. In *Proc. 3rd Int. Conf. on Deductive and Object-Oriented Databases (DOOD93)*, volume 760 of *Lecture Notes in Computer Science*, 1993.
17. C. Zaniolo and H. Wang. Logic-Based User-Defined Aggregates for the Next Generation of Database Systems. In *The Logic Programming Paradigm: Current Trends and Future Directions*. Springer-Verlag, Berlin, 1998.

Interesting Fuzzy Association Rules in Quantitative Databases

Jeannette M. de Graaf, Walter A. Kosters, and Jeroen J.W. Witteman

Leiden Institute of Advanced Computer Science
Universiteit Leiden
P.O. Box 9512, 2300 RA Leiden, The Netherlands
{graaf,kosters,jwittema}@liacs.nl

Abstract. In this paper we examine association rules and their interestingness. Usually these rules are discussed in the world of basket analysis. Instead of customer data we now study the situation with data records of a more general but fixed nature, incorporating quantitative (non-boolean) data. We propose a method for finding interesting rules with the help of fuzzy techniques and taxonomies for the items/attributes. Experiments show that the use of the proposed interestingness measure substantially decreases the number of rules.

1 Introduction

In this paper we study association rules, i.e., rules such as "if a person buys products a and b, then he or she also buys product c". Such a rule has a certain *support* (the number of records satisfying the rule, e.g., the number of people buying a, b and c) and *confidence* (the fraction of records containing the items from the "then part" out of those containing the items from the "if part"). In most practical situations an enormous number of these rules, usually consisting of two or three items, is present. One of the major problems is to decide which of these rules are interesting.

Association rules are of particular interest in the case of basket analysis, but also when more general so-called quantitative or categorical data are considered, cf. [17]. Here one can think of augmented basket data, where information on the customer or time stamps are added, but also on more general fixed format databases. For example, one can examine a car database with information on price, maximum speed, horsepower, number of doors and so on. But also quite different databases can be used, for instance web-log files. So instead of products we shall rather speak of items or attributes, and buying product a should be rephrased as having property a. We get rules like "if a car has four doors and is made in Europe, then it is expensive".

If we only consider the support of a rule, there is no emphasis on either "if part" or "then part", and in fact we rather examine the underlying *itemset*, in our first example $\{a, b, c\}$. A k-itemset consists of k elements. Such a set is called *frequent* if its support is larger than some threshold, which is given in advance. In this paper we focus on the support rather than the confidence.

L. De Raedt and A. Siebes (Eds.): PKDD 2001, LNAI 2168, pp. 140–151, 2001.
© Springer-Verlag Berlin Heidelberg 2001

In the sequel we shall define a precise notion of interestingness, based on hierarchies with respect to the items. Using both simple real life data and more complicated real life data we illustrate the relevance of this notion. Our goal is to find a moderate number of association rules describing the system at hand, where uninteresting rules that can be derived from others are discarded. Interestingness of itemsets based on a hierarchy for the items is also discussed in [16], where for a one taxonomy situation a different notion of lifting to parents is used. Several other measures of interestingness for the non-fuzzy case not involving taxonomies are mentioned in [2,3,6,10,15] and references in these papers; for a nice overview see [9].

We would like to thank Jan Niestadt, Daniel Palomo van Es and the referees for their helpful comments.

2 Fuzzy Approach

If one considers more general items/attributes, one has to deal with non-boolean values. Several approaches have been examined, each having its own merits and peculiarities. Two obvious methods are the usual boolean discretization (see [17]; note that this method suffers from the sharp boundary problem) and the fuzzy method. In this paper we focus on the fuzzy approach: split a non-boolean attribute into a (small) number of possible ranges called *fuzzified attributes*, and provide appropriate membership values (see [7,12,13]).

Some attributes naturally split into discrete values, for instance number of doors, giving a small number of crisp values. One can choose to add as many new items/attributes as there are values. It is also possible, in particular for two-valued attributes, to keep the boolean 0/1 notation. One has to keep in mind however that this gives rise to an asymmetry in the following sense: since only non-zero values will contribute, the rules found do not deal with "negative" information. For instance, if an attribute *Doors* has two possible values, 2 and 4, one can either split it into two new attributes *Doors2* and *Doors4* (notice that always exactly one of these will be true, so there is a clear negative dependency), or to keep only one attribute having the value 1 in the case of four doors; in this case rules with "having two doors" cannot easily be found.

An example for a more complex attribute is given in Fig. 1, where the attribute *Horsepower* is fuzzified into four regions. We can now say that a record has property a to a certain extent, e.g., a 68 *Horsepower* car has *Hp1* value 0.2 and *Hp2* value 0.8. In many situations the regions are chosen in such a way that for all values in the domain at most two membership values are non-zero. This approach is especially attractive, since it leads to hierarchies in a quite natural way: starting from basic ranges one can combine them into larger and larger ones in several ways, e.g., *Hp12* might be the union of *Hp1* and *Hp2*. Usually the membership values for the fuzzified attributes belonging to the same original attribute of a given record add to 1, as for the crisp case mentioned above. Note that the choice of the number of regions and the shape of the membership functions may be a difficult one. In this paper we use linear increase and decrease

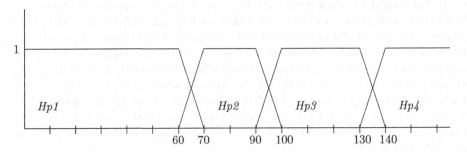

Fig. 1. Membership values for attribute *Horsepower*, split into four regions

functions for the boundaries of the regions. The fuzzifications are obtained manually; it is also possible to apply clustering algorithms to determine clusters, and then use these as a basis for the regions.

In a fuzzy context the support of an itemset should be understood in the following way: for every record in the database take the *product* of the membership values (that can be crisp) of the attributes under consideration, and sum these numbers. If we have n records, and if $\mu(i,j)$ denotes the membership value of the j-th (fuzzified) attribute of the i-th record, then the support of an itemset $A = \{a_{j_1}, a_{j_2}, \ldots, a_{j_k}\}$ is defined by

$$support(A) = \sum_{i=1}^{n} \prod_{\ell=1}^{k} \mu(i, j_\ell).$$

Notice that the usual 0/1 version is a special case. Here we mimic the well-known fuzzy AND: $\text{AND}(x, y) = x \cdot y$. Besides taking the product, there are also other possibilities for the fuzzy AND, for instance the often used minimum. The product however has a beneficial property, which is easily demonstrated with an example. Suppose that a car has *Hp1* value 0.2 and *Hp2* value 0.8 (the other *Hp* values being 0), and *Price1* value 0.4 and *Price2* value 0.6. Then it contributes to the combination $\{Hp1, Price1\}$ a value of $0.2 \cdot 0.4 = 0.08$, and similarly to the other three cross combinations values of 0.12, 0.32 and 0.48, respectively, the four of them adding to 1. The minimum would give 0.2, 0.2, 0.4 and 0.6, respectively, yielding a total contribution of $1.4 > 1$. In similar crisp situations every record of the database has a contribution of 1, and therefore we prefer the product.

Some simple example itemsets are $\{Milk, Bread\}$, $\{Milk, TimeEarly\}$ and $\{Expensive, Europe, Doors4\}$. Notice that the first one refers to the number of people buying both milk and bread, the second one measures the number of people buying milk early in the day (where *TimeEarly* is a fuzzified attribute), and the third one deals with the occurrence of expensive European cars having four doors in the current database.

In some situations it may occur that itemsets consisting of different "regions" of one and the same attribute have a somewhat high support, for instance the itemset $\{Hp1, Hp2\}$. This phenomenon indicates that many records lie in the intersection of these regions, and that the attribute needs to be fuzzified in yet another way.

3   Taxonomies

Now we suppose that a user defined *taxonomy* for the items is given, i.e., a categorization of the items/attributes is available. In this setting association rules may involve categories of attributes; abstraction from brands gives generalized rules, that are often more informative, intuitive and flexible. As mentioned before, also non-boolean attributes lead to natural hierarchies. Since the number of generated rules increases enormously, a notion of interestingness, cf. [8,16], is necessary to describe them. It might for instance be informative to know that people often buy milk early in the day; on a more detailed level one might detect that people who buy low fat milk often do so between 11 and 12 o'clock. The more detailed rule is only of interest if it deviates substantially from what is expected from the more general one. It might also be possible to get more grip on the possible splittings of quantitative attributes, cf. [14].

A taxonomy is a hierarchy in the form of a tree, where the original items are the leaves, and the root is the "item" *All*; see [5] for the non-quantitative situation. The (internal) nodes of the taxonomies are sets of original items, these being singleton sets; every parent is the union of his or her children. In the case of fuzzy attributes, the fuzzy value of a parent is the sum of those from its children (assuming that this sum is at most 1), which corresponds to the fuzzy OR: $\text{OR}(x, y) = \min(1, x + y)$. For example, the *Hp12* value for a 68 *Horsepower* car case is $0.2 + 0.8 = 1.0$. One can also consider the case where several taxonomies are given. In this setting, an itemset is allowed to be any set of nodes from arbitrary levels from the taxonomies. Often we will restrict an itemset to belong to a single taxonomy. The root *All* is the set of all original items, and is the root of all taxonomies at hand.

A simple example of a taxonomy for a car database, with attributes *Price1*, *Price2*, *Doors2*, *Doors4*, *Hp1*, *Hp2*, *Hp3* and *Hp4*, and aggregates *Price12*, *Hp12* and *Hp34*, is presented in Fig. 2.

4   Interestingness

An itemset (or rule) should be called *interesting* if it is in a way "special" with respect to what it is expected to be in the light of its parents. We first give some definitions concerning the connection between parent itemsets and their children.

4.1   Definitions

A *first generation ancestor itemset* of a given itemset is created by replacing one or more of its elements by their immediate parents in the taxonomy. For the

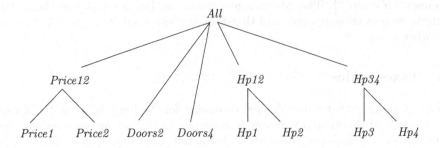

Fig. 2. Example – A simple taxonomy for a car database

moment we choose to stay within one taxonomy, but it is also possible to use several taxonomies simultaneously. The only difference in that case is that elements can have more than one parent. The support of an ancestor itemset gives rise to a prediction of the support of the k-itemset $\mathcal{I} = \{a_1, a_2, \ldots, a_k\}$ itself: suppose that the nodes $a_1, a_2, \ldots, a_\ell$ $(1 \le \ell \le k)$ are replaced by (*lifted* to) their ancestors $\widehat{a}_1, \widehat{a}_2, \ldots, \widehat{a}_\ell$ (in general not necessarily their parents: an ancestor of a is a node on the path from the root *All* to a, somewhere higher in the taxonomy) giving an itemset $\widehat{\mathcal{I}}$. Then the support of $\mathcal{I}$ is estimated by the support of $\widehat{\mathcal{I}}$ times the confidence of the rule "$\widehat{a}_1, \widehat{a}_2, \ldots, \widehat{a}_\ell$ implies $a_1, a_2, \ldots, a_\ell$":

$$EstimatedSupport_{\widehat{\mathcal{I}}}(\{a_1, a_2, \ldots, a_\ell, a_{\ell+1}, \ldots, a_k\}) =$$
$$Support(\{\widehat{a}_1, \widehat{a}_2, \ldots, \widehat{a}_\ell, a_{\ell+1} \ldots, a_k\}) \times \frac{Support(\{a_1, a_2, \ldots, a_\ell\})}{Support(\{\widehat{a}_1, \widehat{a}_2, \ldots, \widehat{a}_\ell\})}.$$

This estimate is based on the assumption that given the occurrence of the lifted items $\{\widehat{a}_1, \widehat{a}_2, \ldots, \widehat{a}_\ell\}$, the occurrences of $\{a_1, a_2, \ldots, a_\ell\}$ and $\{a_{\ell+1}, a_{\ell+2}, \ldots, a_k\}$ are independent events, see [5]. In fact, this is a simple application of conditional probabilities: if

$$P(\mathcal{I} \mid \widehat{a}_1, \widehat{a}_2, \ldots, \widehat{a}_\ell) =$$
$$P(a_1, a_2, \ldots, a_\ell \mid \widehat{a}_1, \widehat{a}_2, \ldots, \widehat{a}_\ell) \times P(a_{\ell+1}, \ldots, a_k \mid \widehat{a}_1, \widehat{a}_2, \ldots, \widehat{a}_\ell),$$

then

$$P(\mathcal{I}) = P(\widehat{a}_1, \widehat{a}_2, \ldots, \widehat{a}_\ell) \times P(\mathcal{I} \mid \widehat{a}_1, \widehat{a}_2, \ldots, \widehat{a}_\ell)$$
$$= P(\widehat{\mathcal{I}}) \times P(a_1, a_2, \ldots, a_\ell \mid \widehat{a}_1, \widehat{a}_2, \ldots, \widehat{a}_\ell),$$

where

$$P(a_1, a_2, \ldots, a_\ell \mid \widehat{a}_1, \widehat{a}_2, \ldots, \widehat{a}_\ell) = \frac{Support(\{a_1, a_2, \ldots, a_\ell\})}{Support(\{\widehat{a}_1, \widehat{a}_2, \ldots, \widehat{a}_\ell\})}.$$

Now an itemset is called *interesting* if and only if the predicted (fuzzy) supports based on all (but one as we shall see soon (∗)) of its first generation ancestor itemsets deviate substantially from its real (fuzzy) support. If there is at least one parent that predicts the child suitably well, this itemset is not interesting enough. The word "substantially" means that the predicted supports are *all* larger than the real support, or are *all* smaller than the real support, by at least some fixed factor. This factor is called the *interestingness threshold*. If all items from an itemset are lifted, estimated support and real support are exactly the same, so it makes sense to omit this prediction (see (∗)). Therefore 1-itemsets are always interesting, in particular the itemset {*All*} (which does not have ancestors): there is no way to predict their support. In order to give a complete description of the "rule database" it is sufficient to describe the interesting rules: the behaviour of the others can then be derived – if one remembers which ancestor itemset provided the best prediction.

4.2   More Details

The reasons that only first generation ancestor itemsets are used instead of arbitrary ancestors as in [16] (where the number of items in the two itemsets should also be the same) are the following. First, it severely restricts the number of sets that need to be examined. (Note that in a single taxonomy a k-itemset has $2^k - 2$ first generation ancestor itemsets in principle, the number of arbitrary ancestors being much higher; k is small in practice.) And second, if a set cannot be understood through any of its parents, but some grandparent does predict its support, in our opinion it still deserves attention.

Some problems arise during the lifting. In [5] the problem of several hierarchies (one item may contribute to several lifted ones at the same time, e.g., *Milk* is both *Dairy* and *Fluid*) is discussed. Another problem mentioned there is this: when lifting sibling attributes one gets itemsets of the form {*Child, Parent*}, e.g., {*Milk, Dairy*}. In [5] this was interpreted as the set {*Milk*}, since – logically speaking – buying milk is enough to satisfy both the milk and dairy requirements:

$$(Milk \text{ AND } Dairy) = (Milk \text{ AND } (Milk \text{ OR } \ldots)) = Milk.$$

In the fuzzy approach the lifting of siblings from one and the same original attribute (which only happens in rare situations) is treated in an analogous manner, using fuzzy AND and OR. For example, suppose that a car has *Hp1* value 0.2 and *Hp2* value 0.6 (this differs from the situation in Fig. 2 and in our experiments, where at most two membership values corresponding to one original attribute are non-zero), then its parent *Hp12* has value $0.2 + 0.6 = 0.8$, and its contribution to the itemset {*Hp2, Hp12*} equals $0.6 \cdot (0.2 + 0.6) = 0.48$. Note that this is analogous to the situation for crisp boolean attributes: for boolean x, y we have $x \wedge (y \vee x) = x$, leading to the interpretation mentioned in the beginning of this paragraph.

With respect to the partitioning of the attributes, either fuzzy or discrete, the notion of interestingness has yet another beneficial property. The support of an itemset may depend severely on the chosen partitioning. For instance, if a time period is split into periods of different sizes, the smaller ones will naturally have lower support. In the definition of *EstimatedSupport* the support of an itemset is estimated by the support of its parent multiplied by a factor that accounts for the relative size. The chosen partitioning is therefore of less importance than one would think at first sight, if interestingness is considered. But still it is necessary to carefully make this choice, since the domains should be split into discriminating understandable parts.

During experiments it sometimes occurred that itemsets containing some high supported item appeared to be interesting with respect to their first generation ancestor itemsets. From another point of view however, they might be considered not that interesting. For example, if an itemset $\{a\}$ has very high support, the itemsets $\{a, b, c\}$ and $\{b, c\}$ will probably have (nearly) the same support, and hence we feel that $\{a, b, c\}$ is not interesting. In general this phenomenon can be easily detected by checking whether the support of $\{a, b, c\}$ can be predicted through that of $\{b, c\}$. This corresponds to the situation where in the formula for the estimated support one particular item is lifted to the artificial item *All*. Because this easily computed extra interestingness measure improves the quality of the rules found, we added it in our experiments. This measure for interestingness is analogous to that in [3], where one or more items can be deleted from itemsets in order to check whether or not their support can be predicted from that of the smaller subsets. Finally, note that if in general one lifts to an attribute that is always 1, for instance the common ancestor of the different regions of fuzzified attributes, this corresponds to lifting to *All*.

5   Algorithms

The algorithms that find all interesting rules are straightforward. The well-known APRIORI algorithm from [1], or any of its refinements, provides a list of all association rules, or rather the underlying itemsets. This algorithm can be easily adapted to generate all rules including nodes from the taxonomy (for more details, see [16]), where special care has to be taken to avoid parent-child problems, and to the fuzzy situation (see [12]). Note that APRIORI works under the assumption that the support of a subset is always at least the support of any superset, which also holds in this generalized setting (all fuzzy membership values are at most 1 and we use multiplication as fuzzy AND; by the way, the frequently used minimum can also be chosen). In fact, if one augments the list of original items with all non-leaves from the taxonomy, the computations are straightforward. Once the list of all rules and their supports is known, it is easy to generate the interesting ones by just comparing supports for the appropriate rules. The order in which the computations are performed, is of no importance.

For every frequent itemset $\mathcal{I}$ all its first generation ancestor itemsets $\widehat{\mathcal{I}}$ are generated, and expected and real support are compared; we define the *support deviation* of $\mathcal{I}$ to be the smallest *interestingness ratio*

$$Support(\mathcal{I}) \; / \; EstimatedSupport_{\widehat{\mathcal{I}}}(\mathcal{I})$$

that occurs. If this support deviation is higher than the interestingness threshold, the itemset is called interesting. The frequent itemsets can be ordered with respect to this support deviation: the higher this ratio, the more interconnection occurs between the items involved. In fact, the assumption concerning the independence between lifted and non-lifted items clearly does not hold in that case, and an interesting connection is revealed. Of course it is also a possibility to look at overestimated supports – in many cases they are "complementary" to the underestimated ones. If necessary, the confidence can be used to turn the list of interesting itemsets into a list of interesting rules, further decreasing the number of interesting rules. Note that ancestors of frequent itemsets are automatically frequent, unless – as in [8] – different support thresholds are specified at different tree levels (if, e.g., {Milk, Bread} is frequent, {Dairy, Bread} should be frequent too in order to compute the support deviation).

The run time of the algorithms may – as usual – be long when the number of records is large and the minimum support threshold is low. In order to also get information on the bottom level, and not only on aggregate levels, this minimum support should be small enough. A run time of several hours was quite normal, most of it devoted to the computation of the frequent itemsets using the APRIORI algorithm. Once the rules/itemsets are computed, it is however easy to deal with different interestingness thresholds. This is an advantage over methods that detect interestingness during the computation of the frequent itemsets (cf. [3], where no taxonomies are used).

6 Experiments

In order to get a feeling for the ideas, we first present some details for a simple database consisting of descriptions of 205 cars, see [4]. We have clearly dependent attributes like *Price*, *MilesPerGallon*, *EngineSize* and *Horsepower* (an integer between 48 and 288, the median being 96). This last attribute may be fuzzified as in Fig. 1, where it is split into four regions, denoted by *Hp1*, *Hp2*, *Hp3* and *Hp4*. One might choose the regions in such a way that they all contain the same number of records – more or less (option **1**). Another option is to split the region simply into four equally large intervals (option **2**). We also examined a random fuzzification (option **3**). Of course there is quite a lot of freedom here, but an advantage of the fuzzy method is that slight changes do not lead to major differences (see, e.g., [12] for a comparison between crisp case and fuzzy case); as mentioned above, the interestingness corrects for different splittings to a certain extent. At aggregate levels we defined *Hp12* and *Hp34* as the "sum" of the first two regions, respectively the last two. In a similar way we also fuzzified the other attributes, all of them having four regions, region 1 corresponding to a low value, and so on. Furthermore we added the attributes *Doors2*, *Doors4* and *Turbo*, the last one being a boolean attribute.

Clear dependencies were easily detected in all cases, such as *Price4* and *Hp4* (more than expected), *Price4* and *MilesPerGallon4* (less than expected, but still enough to meet the support threshold), and *Price4* and *MilesPerGal-*

lon1 (more than expected). But also itemsets like {*Hp1*, *Price1*, *Doors2*} were found to be interesting for option **1**: all its eight parents (including those obtained by omitting an item) caused an interestingness ratio above 1.3. In Fig. 3 some results with respect to the number of rules are presented. The itemset {*Turbo*, *Hp34*, *Price34*} had support deviation 1.61, indicating that turbo engine cars occur quite often among cars with high values for *Horsepower* and *Price*; but it also means that among expensive turbo engine cars those with a high value for *Horsepower* occur more than expected. The support threshold was chosen to be 10%. Here the notation 22 / 137 means that 22 out of 137 itemsets are interesting. Note that option **2** leads to only 17 frequent 1-itemsets, due to the irregular distribution of the records over the equally sized intervals for the fuzzified attributes. We may conclude that a substantial reduction in the number of itemsets is obtained.

option for fuzzification	threshold for support deviation	1-itemsets	2-itemsets	3-itemsets	4-itemsets
1	1.3	27 / 27	34 / 137	24 / 185	14 / 103
	1.4	27 / 27	28 / 137	14 / 185	5 / 103
	1.5	27 / 27	22 / 137	11 / 185	4 / 103
	1.6	27 / 27	15 / 137	11 / 185	3 / 103
	1.7	27 / 27	9 / 137	4 / 185	1 / 103
	1.8	27 / 27	4 / 137	1 / 185	0 / 103
	1.9	27 / 27	4 / 137	0 / 185	0 / 103
	2.0	27 / 27	4 / 137	0 / 185	0 / 103
2	1.3	17 / 17	15 / 87	7 / 173	2 / 148
	1.4	17 / 17	13 / 87	5 / 173	1 / 148
	1.5	17 / 17	10 / 87	4 / 173	1 / 148
	1.6	17 / 17	9 / 87	4 / 173	1 / 148
	1.7	17 / 17	8 / 87	4 / 173	1 / 148
	1.8	17 / 17	7 / 87	2 / 173	1 / 148
	1.9	17 / 17	5 / 87	2 / 173	1 / 148
	2.0	17 / 17	4 / 87	2 / 173	1 / 148
3	1.3	24 / 24	20 / 109	12 / 162	4 / 108
	1.4	24 / 24	14 / 109	5 / 162	1 / 108
	1.5	24 / 24	13 / 109	5 / 162	1 / 108
	1.6	24 / 24	12 / 109	5 / 162	1 / 108
	1.7	24 / 24	10 / 109	5 / 162	1 / 108
	1.8	24 / 24	8 / 109	5 / 162	1 / 108
	1.9	24 / 24	7 / 109	4 / 162	1 / 108
	2.0	24 / 24	4 / 109	1 / 162	0 / 108

Fig. 3. Car database: number of interesting itemsets out of all frequent itemsets, for different fuzzifications and thresholds for the support deviation

Next we considered a much larger database, obtained from product and sales information from supermarket chains. For every product, and every time period, and for every chain, the number of sales is given – among other things. We restricted ourselves to one chain. The database consisted of 158,301 records, giving sales for 4,059 products over a period of three years (split into 39 periods).

We took minimum support 1%, leading to 163 frequent 1-itemsets, 378 frequent 2-itemsets and 102 frequent 3-itemsets. With a small interestingness threshold of 1.01, 162 2-itemsets were found to be interesting, and 46 3-itemsets. As in the previous example, some obvious itemsets were found quite easily. For example, {*BrandX*, *SmallBag*} and {*Mayonnaise*, *Jar*} were above expectation, with support deviations 3.50 and 2.85, respectively. Here *Mayonnaise* denotes a group of mayonnaise-like products, and *BrandX* consists of instant soups and sauces of a certain brand. The package clearly depends on the contents. Some interesting 3-itemsets were also discovered, for example {*BBQSauce*, *Bottle*, *Chili*} with support deviation 5.89. Apparently Chili taste in a bottle is even more frequent among other BBQ sauces.

It was much harder to find interesting itemsets containing time information, because the support of itemsets containing for example *Month4* were much smaller by nature than the ones mentioned in the previous paragraph. If one only examines the records corresponding to one category of products, for instance the BBQ sauces (for our database 21,450 records), it is possible to detect small differences in sales throughout the year. It appeared that in the third quarter of the year high sales were more frequent than expected, whereas low sales were more frequent than expected in the first quarter of the year.

Two important problems that arose are the following. Due to the fact that there were very many missing values in the database at hand, for some attributes it was hard to find a proper interpretation for the results. For the moment we chose not to skip the complete record; we ignored the missing fields when generating the frequent itemsets containing these fields. The second problem has to do with the fuzzifying process. In the database the number of products sold during some period in some supermarket chain is given. If one wants to fuzzify this number, one clearly has to take into account that notions like "many" or "few" severely depend on the product and the shop at hand. The usual data mining step that cleans the data has to be augmented with a process that handles this problem. For the current experiment we simply took global values, which seems justified because we deal with only one supermarket chain or even one category.

7   Conclusions and Further Research

We have presented a notion of interestingness for frequent itemsets in general fixed format databases with both quantitative, categorical and boolean attributes, using fuzzy techniques. Examples show that the number of itemsets found decreases substantially when restricted to interesting ones. It is in principle also possible to handle important attributes like time.

We would like to study this time dependency of itemsets further, for instance using time windows. It should also be possible to use the notion of interestingness for clustering techniques, cf. [11]. Other research issues are the handling of missing values and different fuzzifications. If for instance both price and sales attributes in a customer database are missing quite often, this might lead to an underestimated value for the support of itemsets containing both price and sales attributes. We would like to handle these kinds of problems, both in theoretical and practical respect.

Another problem is the following: it is sometimes necessary to split one and the same fuzzy attribute (like the number of sales in the second experiment) differently, depending on the record or the group of records. For example a sales of 1,000 may be "many" for *BrandX* but "few" for *BrandY*. It would be interesting to study different possibilities here, especially for practical situations. Finally we would like to get a better understanding of the missing value problem.

References

1. R. Agrawal, H. Mannila, R. Srikant, H. Toivonen, and A.I. Verkamo. Fast discovery of association rules. In U.M. Fayyad, G. Piatetsky-Shapiro, P. Smyth, and R. Uthurusamy, editors, *Advances in Knowledge Discovery and Data Mining*, pages 307–328. AAAI/MIT Press, 1996.

2. R.J. Bayardo Jr. and R. Agrawal. Mining the most interesting rules. In S. Chaudhuri and D. Madigan, editors, *Proceedings of the Fifth ACM SIGKDD International Conference on Knowledge Discovery and Data Mining*, pages 145–154. ACM Press, 1999.

3. R.J. Bayardo Jr., R. Agrawal, and D. Gunopulos. Constraint-based rule mining in large, dense databases. *Data Mining and Knowledge Discovery*, 4:217–240, 2000.

4. 1985 Auto Imports Database. Available at http://www.ics.uci.edu/~mlearn/.

5. J.M. de Graaf, W.A. Kosters, and J.J.W. Witteman. Interesting association rules in multiple taxonomies. In A. van den Bosch and H. Weigand, editors, *Proceedings of the Twelfth Belgium-Netherlands Artificial Intelligence Conference (BNAIC'00)*, pages 93–100, 2000.

6. A.A. Freitas. On objective measures of rule surprisingness. In J.M. Żytkov and A. Quafafou, editors, *Principles of Data Mining and Knowledge Discovery, Proceedings of the 2nd European Symposium (PKDD'98)*, Springer Lecture Notes in Computer Science 1510. Springer Verlag, 1998.

7. A. Fu, M. Wong, S. Sze, W. Wong, W. Wong, and W. Yu. Finding fuzzy sets for the mining of fuzzy association rules for numerical attributes. In *Proceedings of the First International Symposium on Intelligent Data Engineering and Learning (IDEAL'98)*, pages 263–268, 1998.

8. J. Han and Y. Fu. Mining multiple-level association rules in large databases. *IEEE Transactions on Knowledge and Data Engineering*, 11:798–804, 1999.

9. R.J. Hilderman and H.J. Hamilton. Heuristic measures of interestingness. In J. Żytkov and J. Rauch, editors, *Proceedings of the 3rd European Conference on the Priciples of Data Mining and Knowledge Discovery (PKDD'99)*, pages 232–241, 1999.

10. M. Klemettinen, H. Mannila, P. Ronkainen, H. Toivonen, and A.I. Verkamo. Finding interesting rules from large sets of discovered association rules. In *Proceedings of the Third International Conference on Information and Knowledge Management (CIKM'94)*, pages 401–407. ACM Press, 1994.

11. W.A. Kosters, E. Marchiori, and A. Oerlemans. Mining clusters with association rules. In D.J. Hand, J.N. Kok, and M.R. Berthold, editors, *Proceedings of the Third Symposium on Intelligent Data Analysis (IDA99)*, Springer Lecture Notes in Computer Science 1642, pages 39–50. Springer Verlag, 1999.

12. C. Kuok, A. Fu, and M. Wong. Mining fuzzy association rules in databases. *ACM SIGMOD Record*, 27:41–46, 1998.

13. J.-H. Lee and H. Lee-Kwang. An extension of association rules using fuzzy sets. In *The Seventh International Fuzzy Systems Association World Congress (IFSA'97)*, pages 399–402, 1997.

14. M.C. Ludl and G. Widmer. Relative unsupervised discretization for association rule mining. In D.A. Zighed, J. Komorowski, and J. Żytkov, editors, *Principles of Data Mining and Knowledge Discovery, Proceedings of the 4th European Conference (PKDD 2000)*, Springer Lecture Notes in Computer Science 1910, pages 148–158. Springer Verlag, 2000.

15. G. Piatetsky-Shapiro. Discovery, analysis, and presentation of strong rules. In G. Piatetsky-Shapiro and W.J. Frawley, editors, *Knowledge Discovery and Data Mining*, pages 229–248. MIT Press, 1991.

16. R. Srikant and R. Agrawal. Mining generalized association rules. In U. Dayal, P.M.D. Gray, and S. Nishio, editors, *Proceedings of the 21st VLDB Conference*, pages 407–419. Morgan Kaufmann, 1995.

17. R. Srikant and R. Agrawal. Mining quantitative association rules in large relational tables. In H. V. Jagadish and I.S. Mumick, editors, *Proceedings of the 1996 ACM SIGMOD International Conference on Management of Data*, pages 1–12, Montreal, Quebec, Canada, 1996.

Interestingness Measures for Fuzzy Association Rules

Attila Gyenesei and Jukka Teuhola

Turku Centre for Computer Science (TUCS)
University of Turku, Department of Computer Science
Lemminkäisenkatu 14, FIN-20520 Turku, Finland
{gyenesei,teuhola}@cs.utu.fi

Abstract. Data mining tries to discover interesting and surprising patterns among a given data set. An important task is to develop effective measures of interestingness for evaluating and ranking the discovered patterns. A good measure should give a high rank to patterns, which have strong evidence among data, but which yet are not too obvious. Thereby the initial set of patterns can be pruned before human inspection. In this paper we study interestingness measures for generalized quantitative association rules, where the attribute domains can be fuzzy. Several interestingness measures have been developed for the discrete case, and it turns out that many of them can be generalized to fuzzy association rules, as well. More precisely, our goal is to compare the fuzzy version of confidence to some other measures, which are based on statistics and information theory. Our experiments show that although the rankings of rules are relatively similar for most of the methods, also some anomalies occur. Our suggestion is that the information-theoretic measures are a good choice when estimating the interestingness of rules, both for fuzzy and non-fuzzy domains.

1 Introduction

Data mining, also referred to as knowledge discovery in databases, is concerned with the nontrivial extraction of implicit, previously unknown, and potentially useful information from data [14]. One major application domain of data mining is the analysis of transactional data. The problem of mining boolean association rules over basket data was first introduced in [1], and later broadened in [2], for the case of databases consisting of categorical attributes alone.

For example, in a database maintained by a supermarket, an association rule might be of the form:

"beer and potato chips → diapers (support: 2%, confidence: 73%)",

which means that 2% of all database transactions contain the data items beer, potato chips and diapers, and 73% of the transactions that have the items "beer" and "potato chips" also have the item "diapers" in them. The two percentage values are referred to as *support* and *confidence*, respectively.

L. De Raedt and A. Siebes (Eds.): PKDD 2001, LNAI 2168, pp. 152–164, 2001.

In practice the information in many, if not most, databases is not limited to categorical attributes (e.g. zip code, make of car), but also contains much quantitative data (e.g. age, income). The problem of mining quantitative association rules was introduced and an algorithm proposed in [17]. The algorithm involves discretizing the domains of quantitative attributes into intervals in order to reduce the domain into a categorical one. An example of such an association might be "10% of married people between 50 and 70 have at least 2 cars".

Without a priori knowledge, however, determining the right intervals can be a tricky and difficult task due to the "catch-22" situation, as called in [17], because of the effects of *small support* and *small confidence*. Moreover, these intervals may not be concise and meaningful enough for human experts to easily obtain nontrivial knowledge from those rules discovered.

Instead of using sharp intervals, fuzzy sets were suggested in [12] to represent intervals with non-sharp boundaries. The obtained rules are called fuzzy association rules. If meaningful linguistic terms are assigned to fuzzy sets, the fuzzy association rule is more understandable. The above example could be rephrased e.g. "10% of married old people have several cars". Algorithms for mining fuzzy association rules were proposed in ([9], [7]), but the problem is that an expert must provide the required fuzzy sets of the quantitative attributes and their corresponding membership functions. It is unrealistic to assume that experts can always provide the best fuzzy sets for fuzzy association rule mining. In [8], we tackled this problem and proposed a method to find the fuzzy sets for quantitative attributes by using clustering techniques.

It has been recognized that a discovery system can generate a large number of patterns, most of which are of no interest to the user. To be able to prune them, researchers have defined various measures of interestingness for patterns. The most popular are confidence and support [1], others include e.g. variance and chi-square (correlation) [13], entropy gain [13], laplace [5], and intensity of implication [4]. Properties of various measures were analyzed in [3]. An extensive survey of recently proposed interestingness measures is given in [10].

The term 'interestingness' is often used in a subjective sense, meaning the same as 'surprisingness'. Here we take the view that it should be also measurable in more precise terms. Although many interestingness measures have been developed for "discrete" domains, they are not directly applicable to other problem domains, such as fuzzy association rules. In this paper, we introduce generalizations of interestingness measures for fuzzy association rules, based on statistics and information theory. Especially, we present two new measures using the entropy concept. Our suggestion is that these information-theoretic measures are a good choice when estimating the interestingness of rules, both for fuzzy and non-fuzzy domains.

The rest of this paper is organized as follows. In the next section, we give a short summary of fuzzy association rules. Then we propose six measures for this fuzzy approach in Sect. 3. In Sect. 4 the experimental results are reported, comparing the proposed fuzzy interestingness measures. The paper ends with a brief conclusion in Sect. 5.

2   Fuzzy Association Rules

Let $I = \{i_1, i_2, \ldots, i_m\}$ be the complete set of attributes where each i_j ($1 \leq j \leq m$) denotes a categorical or quantitative attribute. Note that categories are a special case of quantitative attributes, and can be handled similarly. In [8], we proposed a method to find the fuzzy sets for each quantitative attribute by using clustering techniques. We defined the goodness index G for clustering scheme evaluation, based on two criteria: compactness and separation. The clustering process determines both the number (c) and centers $(r_i, i = 1, \ldots, c)$ of clusters. We divide the attribute interval into c sub-intervals around the cluster centers, with a coverage of p percent between two adjacent ones, and give each subinterval a symbolic name related to its position (Fig. 1). The non-fuzzy partitioning is obtained as a special case by setting p to zero.

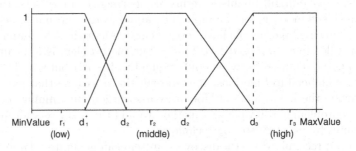

Fig. 1. Example of the proposed fuzzy partitions

For fuzzy set i, d_i^+ means the effective upper bound, and is given by:

$$d_i^+ = r_i + \frac{1}{100} \cdot \left(\frac{100 - p}{2}\right) \cdot (r_{i+1} - r_i),$$

where p is the overlap parameter in %, and r_i is the center of cluster i, $i = 1, 2, \ldots, c - 1$.

Similarly, for fuzzy set j, d_j^- means the effective lower bound, given by:

$$d_j^- = r_j - \frac{1}{100} \cdot \left(\frac{100 - p}{2}\right) \cdot (r_j - r_{j-1}),$$

where $j = 2, 3, \ldots, c$.

Then, we generate the corresponding membership function for each fuzzy set of a quantitative attribute; for formulas, see [8]. Finally, a new transformed (fuzzy) database D^T is generated from the original database by applying the discovered fuzzy sets and the membership values.

Given a database $D^T = \{t^1, t^2, \ldots, t^n\}$ with attributes I and the fuzzy sets $F(i_j)$ associated with attributes i_j in I, we use the following form for a fuzzy association rule [12]:

$$\text{If } X = \{x_1, x_2, \ldots, x_p\} \text{ is } A = \{a_1, a_2, \ldots, a_p\}$$
$$\text{then } Y = \{y_1, y_2, \ldots, y_q\} \text{ is } B = \{b_1, b_2, \ldots, b_q\},$$

where $a_i \in F(x_i)$, $i = 1, \ldots, p$, $b_j \in F(y_j)$, $j = 1, \ldots, q$. X and Y are ordered subsets of I and they are disjoint i.e. they share no common attributes. A and B contain the fuzzy sets associated with the corresponding attributes in X and Y. As in the binary association rule, "X is A" is called the *antecedent* of the rule while "Y is B" is called the *consequent* of the rule. We also denote $Z = X \cup Y = \{z_1, \ldots, z_{p+q}\}$ and $C = A \cup B = \{c_1, \ldots, c_{p+q}\}$.

3 Interestingness Measures for Fuzzy Association Rules

One problem area in knowledge discovery is the development of interestingness measures for ranking the usefulness and utility of discovered patterns and rules. In this section, we first describe the fuzzy itemset measures, then we propose six other candidate measures for fuzzy association rules. Three of these six are based on traditional statistics, and their non-fuzzy counterparts have occured many times in the literature. The three other measures, on the other hand, have their basis in the information theory, originally developed by Shannon, see e.g. [15]. Although our experiments in Sect. 4 do not show a big difference between the two categories of methods, we conjecture that the information-theoretic measures are in some cases better in capturing dependences among data. Another classification of measures would be on the basis of linear/nominal scale, but our formulations are such that this separation need not be explicit.

3.1 Fuzzy Itemset Measures

Let $D^T = \{t^1, t^2, \ldots, t^n\}$ be a database, where n denotes the total number of records ('transactions'). Let (Z, C) be an attribute-fuzzy set pair, where Z is an ordered set of attributes z_j and C is a corresponding set of fuzzy sets c_j. (From now on, we prefer to use the word "itemset" instead of "attribute-fuzzy set pair" for (Z, C) elements). If a fuzzy association rule $(X, A) \rightarrow (Y, B)$ is interesting, it should have enough fuzzy support $FS_{(Z,C)}$ and a high fuzzy confidence value $FC_{((X,A),(Y,B))}$, where $Z = X \cup Y$, $C = A \cup B$.

The fuzzy support value is calculated by multiplying the membership grade of each (z_j, c_j), summing them, then dividing the sum by the number of records [12]. We prefer the product operator as the fuzzy AND, instead of the normal minimum, because it better distinguishes high- and low-support transactions.

$$FS_{(Z,C)} = \frac{\sum_{i=1}^{n} \Pi_{j=1}^{m} (t^i [(z_j, c_j)])}{n},$$

where m is the number of items in itemset (Z, C).

The fuzzy confidence value is calculated as follows:

$$FC_{((X,A),(Y,B))} = \frac{FS_{(Z,C)}}{FS_{(X,A)}}.$$

Table 1. Part of database containing fuzzy membership

...	$(Balance, low)$	...	$(Income, low)$	...	$(Credit, low)$	$(Credit, high)$	...
	0.2		0.2		0.1	0.9	
	0.4		0.2		0.1	0.9	
...	0.9	...	0.8	...	0.7	0.3	...
	0.9		0.8		0.9	0.1	
	0.6		0.4		0.9	0.1	

Both of the above formulas are direct generalizations of the corresponding formulas for the non-fuzzy case [1].

We shall use the following two rules to demonstrate the calculation of interestingness measures. The data behind the rules are presented in Table 1.

Let $X = \{Balance, Income\}$, $A = \{low, low\}$, $Y = \{Credit\}$, $B = \{low\}$, and $\overline{B} = \{high\}$. Rule$_1$ $(X, A) \rightarrow (Y, B)$ is given by:

"If $Balance$ is low and $Income$ is low then $Credit$ is low",

and Rule$_2$ $(X, A) \rightarrow (Y, \overline{B})$ is phrased as:

"If $Balance$ is low and $Income$ is low then $Credit$ is $high$".

The consequents are thus complements of each other. From the table data, we can easily see that Rule$_1$ should be classified as 'valid', whereas Rule$_2$ should not. When introducing the different measures of interestingness, we will check, how they are able to confirm this observation.

Example 1. Fuzzy confidence does a good job in assessing the rules:

$$FC_{((X,A),(Y,B))} = \frac{0.004 + 0.008 + 0.504 + 0.648 + 0.216}{0.04 + 0.08 + 0.72 + 0.72 + 0.24} = 0.766$$

$$FC_{((X,A),(Y,\overline{B}))} = \frac{0.036 + 0.072 + 0.216 + 0.072 + 0.024}{0.04 + 0.08 + 0.72 + 0.72 + 0.24} = 0.233$$

For Rule$_1$, $FS_{(Y,B)} = 0.54$ and $FS_{(Z,C)} = 0.276$. Similarly, $FS_{(Y,\overline{B})} = 0.46$, and $FS_{(Z,C)} = 0.084$ for Rule$_2$. In both cases, $FS_{(X,A)} = 0.36$.

3.2   Fuzzy Covariance Measure

Covariance is one of the simplest measures of dependence, based on the co-occurrence of the antecedent (X, A) and consequent (Y, B). If they co-occur clearly more often than what can be expected in an independent case, then the rule $(X, A) \rightarrow (Y, B)$ is potentially interesting. Piatetsky-Shapiro called this measure a *rule-interest* function [14]. We extend it to the fuzzy case, and define the covariance measure as:

$$Cov_{((X,A),(Y,B))} = FS_{(Z,C)} - FS_{(X,A)} \cdot FS_{(Y,B)}.$$

Example 2. The covariance measures for our sample rules are:

$$Cov_{((X,A),(Y,B))} = 0.0816, \text{ and } Cov_{((X,A),(Y,\overline{B}))} = -0.0816.$$

3.3   Fuzzy Correlation Measure

Covariance has generally the drawback that it does not take distributions into consideration. Therefore, in statistics, it is more common to use so called correlation measure, where this drawback has been eliminated. Again, we have to generalize the non-fuzzy formula to the fuzzy case, and obtain:

$$Corr_{((X,A),(Y,B))} = \frac{Cov_{((X,A),(Y,B))}}{\sqrt{Var_{(X,A)} \cdot Var_{(Y,B)}}},$$

where

$$Var_{(X,A)} = FS_{(X,A)^2} - \left(FS_{(X,A)}\right)^2,$$

$$FS_{(X,A)^2} = \frac{\sum_{i=1}^{n} \left(\Pi_{j=1}^{m} t^i \left[(x_j, a_j)\right]\right)^2}{n},$$

similarly for (Y, B).

These definitions are extensions of the basic formulas of variance and covariance. The value of the fuzzy correlation ranges from -1 to 1. Only a positive value tells that the antecedent and consequent are related. The higher the value is, the more related they are.

Example 3. Again, applying the formula to our two sample rules, we obtain:

$$Corr_{((X,A),(Y,B))} = 0.738, \text{ and } Corr_{((X,A),(Y,\overline{B}))} = -0.738.$$

3.4   Fuzzy I-Measure

As an example of a more 'exotic' probability-based interestingness measure, we give the fuzzy version of a so-called *I-measure* suggested by Gray and Orlowska [6]. Though it has some structural similarity with correlation, we regard it rather as a heuristic measure. The fuzzy *I-measure* is defined as:

$$I_{((X,A),(Y,B))} = \left[\left(\frac{FS_{(Z,C)}}{FS_{(X,A)} \cdot FS_{(Y,B)}}\right)^k - 1\right] \cdot \left(FS_{(X,A)} \cdot FS_{(Y,B)}\right)^m,$$

where k and m are weight parameters of the two terms. A practical problem in applying this measure is the selection of these parameters.

Example 4. The *I-measure* values for our two sample rules (for $k = m = 2$) are:

$$I_{((X,A),(Y,B))} = 0.038, \text{ and } I_{((X,A),(Y,\overline{B}))} = -0.02.$$

In data mining, an association rule $X \rightarrow Y$ usually means that X implies Y and we cannot assume Y also implies X. Covariance, Correlation and *I-measure* are *symmetric* with respect to (X, A) and (Y, B). Thus, we can use them only as *non-directed* measures of dependence.

3.5   Fuzzy Unconditional Entropy (UE) Measure

Assume that we want to evaluate rule $(X, A) \rightarrow (Y, B)$, and denote $Z = X \cup Y$ and $C = A \cup B$. For (X, A), (Y, B), and (Z, C) we can calculate the probability of occurrence, based on the transactions. These are in fact the same as the (fuzzy) support $FS_{(X,A)}$, $FS_{(Y,B)}$, and $FS_{(Z,C)}$. If (X, A) and (Y, B) are independent, then it holds that

$$FS_{(Z,C)} = FS_{(X,A)} \cdot FS_{(Y,B)}.$$

However, if there is a dependence, then the equality does not hold. The degree of correlation can be measured as follows. We determine the information amount needed by assuming independence; we call this *independence entropy*, denoted $H_{((X,A);(Y,B))}$ and computed as follows:

$$H_{((X,A);(Y,B))} = - FS_{(Z,C)} \cdot \log_2 \left(FS_{(X,A)} \cdot FS_{(Y,B)} \right) - \\ - \left(1 - FS_{(Z,C)} \right) \cdot log_2 \left(1 - FS_{(X,A)} \cdot FS_{(Y,B)} \right).$$

This represents the amount of information needed per transaction, when using a (false) assumption of independence, applied when true probability is $FS_{(Z,C)}$. The true entropy of (Z, C) is computed as follows:

$$H_{(Z,C)} = -FS_{(Z,C)} \cdot \log_2 \left(FS_{(Z,C)} \right) - \left(1 - FS_{(Z,C)} \right) \cdot log_2 \left(1 - FS_{(Z,C)} \right).$$

Since this formula uses precise probabilities, its value is always smaller than or equal to the independence entropy. Moreover, their difference is larger when the dependence is higher. Therefore, we get a good measure of correlation as the difference, which we call *unconditional entropy (UE)*:

$$UE_{((X,A),(Y,B))} = H_{((X,A);(Y,B))} - H_{(Z,C)}.$$

Notice that although the measure is always non-negative, the related correlation can be either positive or negative, so that (X, A) and (Y, B) occur together either more or less frequently than in an independent case. Therefore, the true consequent of the (interesting) rule can be either (Y, B) or its complement. The latter holds if $FS_{(Z,C)} < FS_{(X,A)} \cdot FS_{(Y,B)}$, i.e. covariance is < 0.

Example 5. Let us compute the UE-values for our two sample rules:

$$UE_{((X,A),(Y,B))} = 0.878 - 0.850 = 0.028, \text{ and } UE_{((X,A),(Y,\overline{B}))} = 0.041.$$

Although the latter value is higher than the former, the condition $FS_{(Z,C)} = 0.084 < FS_{(X,A)} \cdot FS_{(Y,\overline{B})} = 0.36 \cdot 0.46 = 0.1656$ holds, and we conclude that Rule$_2$ is not valid. Instead, for Rule$_1$ $FS_{(Z,C)} = 0.276 > FS_{(X,A)} \cdot FS_{(Y,B)} = 0.1944$, so Rule$_1$ is a 'good' one.

3.6   Fuzzy Conditional Entropy (CE) Measure

UE-measure is analogous to the correlation of a rule in the sense that both formulas are symmetric with respect to (X, A) and (Y, B). We now develop another measure, which makes a distinction between the antecendent and consequent. Hereby we obtain an information-theoretic counterpart of confidence. The reasoning resembles the derivation of UE, but from the consequent's point of view. The unconditional entropy of (Y, B) is computed as follows:

$$H_{(Y,B)} = -FS_{(Y,B)} \cdot \log_2\left(FS_{(Y,B)}\right) - \left(1 - FS_{(Y,B)}\right) \cdot log_2\left(1 - FS_{(Y,B)}\right).$$

If (X, A) affects in some way on (Y, B), then the conditional probability. $P_{((Y,B)|(X,A))}$ is different from $P_{(Y,B)}$. Notice that the conditional probability is the same as (fuzzy) confidence $FC_{((X,A),(Y,B))}$, defined earlier. The conditional entropy is computed as

$$H_{((Y,B)|(X,A))} = - FC_{((X,A),(Y,B))} \cdot \log_2\left(FC_{((X,A),(Y,B))}\right) -$$
$$- \left(1 - FC_{((X,A),(Y,B))}\right) \cdot log_2\left(1 - FC_{((X,A),(Y,B))}\right).$$

Since the conditional entropy uses a more precise value for the probability of (Y, B) among the subset studied (transactions satisfying (X, A)), for 'true' rules, $H_{(Y,B)}$ should be larger than $H_{((Y,B)|(X,A))}$. Their difference represents the deviation from the independent case, and measures the dependence of (Y, B) on (X, A). The interestingness measure is thus defined as

$$CE_{((X,A),(Y,B))} = H_{(Y,B)} - H_{((Y,B)|(X,A))}.$$

The larger the value, the higher the dependence. As for UE, also here the actual consequent of a rule classified as *interesting* can be either (Y, B) or its complement. The latter holds if $FC_{((X,A),(Y,B))} < FS_{(Y,B)}$.

It should be noted that CE is similar to the *Theil* index [18], in the sense that both measure deviation from the expected entropy.

Example 6. The *CE-measure* gives the same value for both of our sample rules, because the consequents are complements to each other:

$$CE_{((X,A),(Y,B))} = CE_{((X,A),(Y,\overline{B}))} = 0.995 - 0.784 = 0.211.$$

This is just what should happen in information-theoretic sense. Our additional condition determines that Rule$_1$ is positive and Rule$_2$ is negative.

3.7   Fuzzy J-measure

Information theory has naturally been applied to measuring interestingness of rules before. One such measure, so called *J-measure*, was suggested by Smyth and Goodman [16]. It can be generalized to the fuzzy rules as follows:

$$J_{((X,A),(Y,B))} = FS_{(Y,B)} \cdot \left[\frac{FS_{(Z,C)}}{FS_{(Y,B)}} \cdot log_2\left(\frac{FS_{(Z,C)}}{FS_{(Y,B)} \cdot FS_{(X,A)}}\right) + \right.$$

$$+ \left(1 - \frac{FS_{(Z,C)}}{FS_{(Y,B)}}\right) \cdot log_2 \left(\frac{1 - \frac{FS_{(Z,C)}}{FS_{(Y,B)}}}{1 - FS_{(X,A)}}\right)\right]$$

The first term $FS_{(Y,B)}$ measures the generality of the rule. The term inside the square brackets measures the relative entropy of (Y, B) on (X, A), the similarity of two probability (support) distributions. Though the J-measure is different from our UE-measure, in experiments it gave rather similar rankings to rules (see next section).

Example 7. The J-measures for our two test rules are:

$$J_{((X,A),(Y,B))} = 0.037, \text{ and } J_{((X,A),(Y,\overline{B}))} = 0.050.$$

4   Experimental Results

We assessed the effectiveness of our interestingness measures by experimenting with a real-life dataset, which comes from a research by the U.S. Census Bureau. The data had 6 quantitative attributes. This database has been used in previous data mining research ([7], [8]) and will not be described again here.

Using support threshold = 20% and confidence threshold = 50%, we get exactly 20 rules, which are evaluated in the tests. Table 2 and Table 3 describe the calculated interestingness and the assigned ranks, respectively, as determined by the corresponding interestingness measure.

To quantify the extent of the ranking similarities between the seven measures, we computed the correlation coefficient for each pair of interestingness measures, see Table 4. The coefficients vary from a low 0.243 for the pair *Conf* and *I-measure*, to a high of 0.988 for the pair *UE-* and *J-measure*.

We found two distinct groups of measures, which are ranked similarly. One group consists of the non-directed measures *Cov, Corr, I-measure, UE-measure*, and *J-measure*. The other group consists of the directed measures *CE*, and *Conf*. However, there are no negative correlations between the two groups. Two representatives from both groups are shown in Fig. 2a and Fig. 2b.

At this point the reader may wonder, what advantage do information-theoretic measures give over statistical ones, if any. The difference comes e.g. in cases where support values are rather high. High support implies also a rather high confidence, even in a case where the antecedent and consequent are independent.

However, *CE* gives a value ≈ 0 in this case, pruning the rule. That will happen also with the 'symmetric' measures *Cov, Corr, I-measure*, and *UE-measure*, but their drawback is lack of direction. Thus, our conjecture is that *CE* is a good means of measuring the interestingness of rules.

5   Conclusion and Future Work

In this paper we have studied interestingness measures for generalized quantitative association rules, where the attribute domains can be fuzzy. We compared

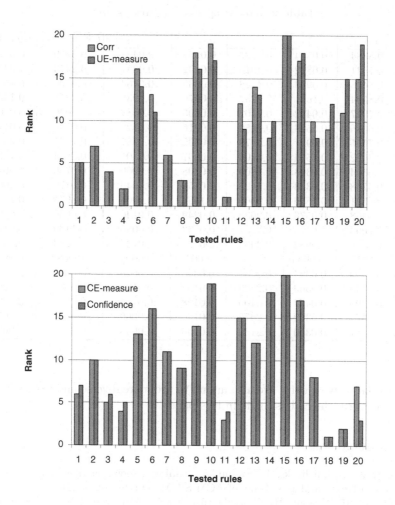

Fig. 2. Rankings of interestingness measures - (a) group$_1$, (b) group$_2$

the fuzzy version of confidence to six other measures, three of which were statistical, and the rest three were information-theoretic, based on the entropy concept.

The experiments show that rankings of rules are relatively similar for most of the methods, but also several inversions appeared in the ranking order. Scores of interestingness measures were used to compute the correlation coefficients, revealing two categories of measures, the directed and non-directed ones. We suggest that the information-theoretic measures are a good choice when estimating the interestingness of rules, both for fuzzy and non-fuzzy domains.

Here we compared the measures of interestingness only by means of numerical rankings, obtained from experiments. In the future, we plan to compare them

Table 2. Interestingness measures - scores

Rule	Conf	Cov	Corr	I-measure	UE-measure	CE-measure	J-measure
1	0.8384	0.0874	0.4522	0.0297	0.0427	0.3619	0.0524
2	0.7841	0.0812	0.4018	0.0292	0.0347	0.2473	0.0435
3	0.8418	0.0933	0.4728	0.0335	0.0464	0.3700	0.0580
4	0.8504	0.1601	0.7232	0.0970	0.0938	0.3911	0.1558
5	0.7067	0.0442	0.2102	0.0205	0.0081	0.1066	0.0102
6	0.6416	0.0528	0.2450	0.0216	0.0128	0.0586	0.0171
7	0.7655	0.0921	0.4273	0.0395	0.0387	0.2141	0.0519
8	0.8022	0.1514	0.6704	0.0967	0.0805	0.2824	0.1425
9	0.6804	0.0398	0.1809	0.0208	0.0060	0.0756	0.0080
10	0.5768	0.0338	0.1498	0.0150	0.0049	0.0170	0.0068
11	0.8521	0.1680	0.7560	0.1064	0.1005	0.3954	0.1751
12	0.6468	0.0576	0.2635	0.0249	0.0146	0.0630	0.0199
13	0.7093	0.0475	0.2231	0.0233	0.0090	0.1100	0.0116
14	0.5918	0.0682	0.3433	0.0522	0.0144	0.0244	0.0367
15	0.5117	-0.0064	-0.0316	-0.0046	0.0001	-0.0008	0.0003
16	0.6399	0.0394	0.2035	0.0340	0.0046	0.0369	0.0097
17	0.8148	0.0569	0.2923	0.0196	0.0172	0.2884	0.0200
18	0.9999	0.0474	0.3105	0.0198	0.0101	0.7274	0.0108
19	0.9679	0.0372	0.2675	0.0142	0.0066	0.5240	0.0070
20	0.9157	0.0340	0.2132	0.0166	0.0046	0.3118	0.0050

also by qualitative means. We also intend to use more diverse and extensive test data to confirm the claims made in this paper.

References

1. Agrawal, R., Imielinski, T., Swami, A.: Mining association rules between sets of items in large databases. Proc. of ACM SIGMOD (1993) 207–216
2. Agrawal, R., Srikant, R.: Fast algorithms for mining association rules in large databases. Proc. of the 20th VLDB Conference (1994) 487–499
3. Bayardo, R. J., Agrawal, R.: Mining the Most Interesting Rules. In Proc. of the 5th ACM SIGKDD (1999) 145–154
4. Bernadet M.: Basis of a Fuzzy Knowledge Discovery System. In Proc. of the 4th European Conference on PKDD (2000) 24–33
5. Clark, P., Boswell, P.: Rule Induction with CN2: Some Recent Improvements. In Machine Learning: Proc. of the Fifth European Conference (1991) 151–163
6. Gray, B., Orlowska, M.E.: Ccaiia: clustering categorical attributes into interesting association rules. In Proc. of the 2th Pacific-Asia Conf. on Knowledge Discovery and Data Mining (1998) 132–143
7. Gyenesei, A.: Mining Weighted Association Rules for Fuzzy Quantitative Items. In Proc. of the 4th European Conference on PKDD (2000) 416–423
8. Gyenesei, A.: Determining Fuzzy Sets for Quantitative Attributes in Data Mining Problems. Proc. of Advances in Fuzzy Systems and Evol. Comp. (2001) 48–53
9. Hong, T-P., Kuo, C-S, Chi, S-C.: Mining association rules from quantitative data. Intelligent Data Analysis 3 (5) (1999) 363–376

Table 3. Interestingness measures - ranks

Rule	Conf	Cov	Corr	I-measure	UE-measure	CE-measure	J-measure
1	7	6	5	8	5	6	5
2	10	7	7	9	7	10	7
3	6	4	4	7	4	5	4
4	5	2	2	2	2	4	2
5	13	14	16	14	14	13	14
6	16	11	13	12	11	16	11
7	11	5	6	5	6	11	6
8	9	3	3	3	3	9	3
9	14	15	18	13	16	14	16
10	19	19	19	18	17	19	18
11	4	1	1	1	1	3	1
12	15	9	12	10	9	15	10
13	12	12	14	11	13	12	12
14	18	8	8	4	10	18	8
15	20	20	20	20	20	20	20
16	17	16	17	6	18	17	15
17	8	10	10	16	8	8	9
18	1	13	9	15	12	1	13
19	2	17	11	19	15	2	17
20	3	18	15	17	19	7	19

Table 4. Correlation coefficients for interestingness measures

	Conf	Cov	Corr	I-measure	UE-measure	CE-measure	J-measure
Conf	-	0.378	0.500	0.243	0.359	0.949	0.300
Cov	0.378	-	0.987	0.945	0.975	0.372	0.967
Corr	0.500	0.987	-	0.915	0.957	0.495	0.940
I-measure	0.243	0.945	0.915	-	0.919	0.245	0.960
UE-measure	0.359	0.975	0.957	0.919	-	0.380	0.988
CE-measure	0.949	0.372	0.495	0.245	0.380	-	0.326
J-measure	0.300	0.967	0.940	0.960	0.988	0.326	-

10. Hilderman, R.J., Hamilton, H.J.: Knowledge discovery and interestingness measures: A survey. Technical Report CS 99-04, University of Regina, Canada (1999)
11. Kullback, S., Leibler, R.A.: On information and sufficiency. Annals of Mathematical Statistics, 22, (1951) 79–86
12. Kuok, C.M., Fu, A., Wong, M.H.: Fuzzy association rules in databases. In ACM SIGMOD Record 27(1),(1998) 41–46
13. Morishita, S.: On Classification and Regression. In Proc. of the First Int. Conf. on Discovery Science - LNAI 1532 (1998) 40–57
14. Piatetsky-Shapiro, G., Frawley, W.J.: Knowledge Discovery in Databases. Chapter 13. AAAI Press/The MIT Press, Menlo Park, California (1991)
15. Shannon, C.E., Weawer, W.: Introduction to Probability and Statistics for Scientists and Engineers. McGraw-Hill (1997)

16. Smyth, P., Goodman, R.M.: Rule induction using information theory. In Knowledge Discovery in Databases, AAAI/MIT Press (1991) 159–176
17. Srikant, R., Agrawal, R.: Mining quantitative association rules in large relation tables. Proc. of ACM SIGMOD (1996) 1–12
18. Theil, H.: Economics and information theory. North-Holland (1967)

A Data Set Oriented Approach for Clustering Algorithm Selection

Maria Halkich and Michalis Vazirgiannis

Department of Informatics
Athens University of Economics & Business
Patision 76, 10434, Athens, Greece (Hellas)
{mhalk,mvazirg}@aueb.gr

Abstract. In the last years the availability of huge transactional and experimental data sets and the arising requirements for data mining created needs for clustering algorithms that scale and can be applied in diverse domains. Thus, a variety of algorithms have been proposed which have application in different fields and may result in different partitioning of a data set, depending on the specific clustering criterion used. Moreover, since clustering is an unsupervised process, most of the algorithms are based on assumptions in order to define a partitioning of a data set. It is then obvious that in most applications the final clustering scheme requires some sort of evaluation.

In this paper we present a clustering validity procedure, which taking in account the inherent features of a data set evaluates the results of different clustering algorithms applied to it. A validity index, *S_Dbw*, is defined according to well-known clustering criteria so as to enable the selection of the algorithm providing the best partitioning of a data set. We evaluate the reliability of our approach both theoretically and experimentally, considering three representative clustering algorithms ran on synthetic and real data sets. It performed favorably in all studies, giving an indication of the algorithm that is suitable for the considered application.

1 Introduction & Motivation

Clustering is one of the most useful tasks in data mining process for discovering groups and identifying interesting distributions and patterns in the underlying data. Thus, the main concern in the clustering process is to reveal the organization of patterns into "sensible" groups, which allow us to discover similarities and differences, as well as to derive useful inferences about them [7].

In the literature a wide variety of algorithms have been proposed for different applications and sizes of data sets [14]. The application of an algorithm to a data set aims at, assuming that the data set offers such a clustering tendency, discovering its inherent partitions. However, the clustering process is perceived as an unsupervised process, since there are no predefined classes and no examples that would show what kind of desirable relations should be valid among the data [2]. Then, the various clustering algorithms are based on some assumptions in order to define a partitioning of a data set. As a consequence, they may behave in a different way depending on: i) the fea-

L. De Raedt and A. Siebes (Eds.): PKDD 2001, LNAI 2168, pp. 165–179, 2001.
© Springer-Verlag Berlin Heidelberg 2001

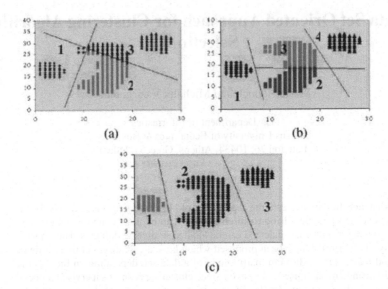

Fig. 1. A two dimensional data set partitioned into (a) three and (b) four clusters using K-Means (c) three clusters using DBSCAN

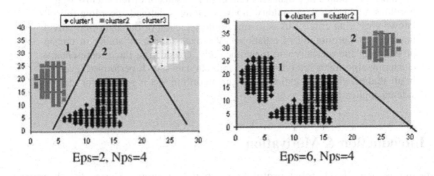

Fig. 2. The different partitions resulting from running DBSCAN with different input parameter values

tures of the data set (geometry and density distribution of clusters) and ii) the input parameters values.

Partitional algorithms such as K-means [2] are unable to handle noise and outliers and they are not suitable to discover clusters with non-convex shapes. Moreover, they are based on certain assumptions to partition a data set. They need to specify the number of clusters in advance except for CLARANS [11], which needs as input the maximum number of neighbors of a node as well as the number of local minima that will be found in order to define a partitioning of a data set. Also, *hierarchical algorithms* [9] proceed successively by either merging smaller clusters into larger ones or by splitting larger clusters. The result of these algorithms is a tree of clusters. Depending on the level at which we cut the tree, a different clustering of the data is obtained. On the other hand *density-based* [3, 4, 8] and *grid-based algorithms* [12] suitably handle arbitrary shaped collections of points (e.g. ellipsoidal, spiral, cylindrical) as well as clusters of different sizes. Moreover, they can efficiently separate noise (outliers). However, most of these algorithms are sensitive to some input parameters so as to require careful selection of their values.

It is obvious from above discussion that the final partition of a data set requires some sort of evaluation in most applications [16]. Then, an important issue in clustering is to find out the number of clusters that give the optimal partitioning (i.e, the partitioning that best fits the real partitions of the data set). Though this is an important problem that causes much discussion, the formal methods for finding the optimal number of clusters in a data set are few [10, 13, 14, 15]. Moreover, all clustering algorithms are not efficient for all applications, which is why a diverse of algorithms has been developed. Depending on the clustering criterion and the ability to handle the special requirements of an application a clustering algorithm can be considered more efficient in a certain context (e.g. spatial data, business, medicine etc). However, the issue of cluster validity is rather under-addressed in the area of databases and data mining applications, while there are no efforts regarding the evaluation of clustering schemes defined by different clustering algorithms.

Further more, in most algorithms' experimental evaluations [1, 4, 6, 7, 8, 11] 2D-data sets are used in order the reader is able to visually verify the validity of the results (i.e., how well the clustering algorithm discovered the clusters of the data set). It is clear that visualization of the data set is a crucial verification of the clustering results. In the case of large multidimensional data sets (e.g. more than three dimensions) effective visualization of the data set can be difficult. Moreover the perception of clusters using available visualization tools is a difficult task for the humans that are not accustomed to higher dimensional spaces.

Assuming that the data set includes distinct partitions (i.e., inherently supports clustering tendency), the above issues become very important. In the sequel, we show that different input parameters values of clustering algorithms may result in good or bad results in partitioning the data set. Moreover, it is clear that some algorithms may fail to discover the actual partitioning of a data set though the correct number of clusters is considered.

For instance in Fig. 1 and Fig. 2 we can see the way different algorithms (DBSCAN [4], K-Means [2]) partition a data set having different input parameter values. Moreover, it is clear from Fig. 1a that K-means may partition the data set into the correct number of clusters (i.e., three clusters) but in a wrong way. On the other hand, DBSCAN (see Fig. 1c) is more efficient since it partitioned the data set in the inherent three clusters under the consideration of the suitable input parameters' values. As it is evident, if there is no visual perception of the clusters it is impossible to assess the validity of the partitioning. It is important then to be able to choose the optimal partitioning of a data set as a result of applying different algorithms with different input parameter values.

What is then needed is a visual-aids-free assessment of some objective criterion, indicating the validity of the results of a clustering algorithm application on a potentially high dimensional data set. In this paper we propose an evaluation procedure based on a cluster validity index (S_Dbw). Assuming a data set S, the index enables the selection of the clustering algorithm and its input parameter values so as to result in the best partitioning of S.

The remainder of the paper is organized as follows. In the next section we motivate and define the validity index, while in Section 3 we provide a theoretical evaluation of S_Dbw based on its definition. Then, in Section 4 an experimental evaluation of our approach for selecting the algorithm that gives the optimal partitioning of a data set is presented. For the experimental study both synthetic and real data sets are used. We conclude in Section 5 by briefly presenting our contributions and indicate directions for further research.

2   Selecting the Best Algorithm

One of the most widely studied problems in area of knowledge discovery is the identification of clusters, i.e., dense region in multidimensional data sets. This is also the subject of cluster analysis. Clustering is perceived as a complicated problem since depending on the application domain and the feature of data the concept of cluster may be different. Thus to satisfy the requirements of diverse application domains, a multitude of clustering methods are developed and are available in the literature. However, the problem of selecting the algorithm that may result in the partitioning that best fits a data set is under-addressed. In the sequel, we present our approach and we define the validity index based on which we may evaluate the clustering schemes under consideration and select the one best fits the data.

2.1   An Approach of Clustering Schemes' Evaluation

The criteria widely accepted for evaluating the partitioning a data set are: i. the separation of the clusters, and ii. their compactness. In general terms we want clusters whose members have a high degree of similarity (or in geometrical terms are close to each other) while we want the clusters themselves to be widely spread.

As we have already mentioned, there are cases that an algorithm may falsely partition a data set, whereas only specific values for the algorithms' input parameters lead to optimal partitioning of the data set. Here the term "optimal" implies parameters that lead to partitions that are as close as possible (in terms of similarity) to the actual partitions of the data set.

Then our *objective* is the definition of a procedure for assessing the quality of partitioning as defined by a number of clustering algorithms. More specifically, a validity index is defined which based on the features of the clusters may evaluate the resulting clustering schemes as defined by the algorithm under consideration. Then, the algorithm and the respective set of input parameters resulting in the optimal partitioning of a data set may be selected.

Let a data set S and Alg={alg$_i$ | i=1,..,k} a set of widely known clustering algorithms. *Palg$_i$* denotes the set of input parameters of an algorithm, *alg$_i$*. Applying a clustering algorithm *alg$_i$* to S while their parameters take values in *Palg$_i$* a set of clustering schemes is defined, let Calg$_i$ ={c$_p$_alg$_i$|p∈ Palg$_i$}. Then, the clustering schemes are evaluated based on a validity index we define, S_Dbw. A list of the index values is maintained, denoted as *index,* for each set Calg$_i$ defined by the available algorithms. The main steps of our approach can be described as follows:

```
Step1. For all algᵢ∈Alg
    Step1.1 Define the range of values for Palgᵢ. Let [pₘₐₓ,
    pₘᵢₙ]
    Step1.2 For p =pₘᵢₙ to pₘₐₓ
            cₚ_algᵢ <- algᵢ (p);
            nc <- number of clusters in cₚ_algᵢ ;
            index[algᵢ].add(S_Dbw(nc));
        End for
    End for
Step2. index_opt <- minₐₗgᵢₑₐₗg{index[algᵢ]};
        opt_cl <- cₚ_algᵢ with S_Dbw value equal to index_opt;
        best_algᵢ <- algᵢ resulting in opt_cl;
```

In the sequel, we discuss in more detail the validity index which our approach use in order to select the clustering algorithm resulting in optimal partitioning of a data set.

2.2 Validity Index Definition

We define our validity index, S_Dbw, combining both clustering criteria (compactness and separation) taking also in account density. In the following we formalize our clustering validity index based on: i. clusters' compactness (in terms of intra-cluster variance), and ii. density between clusters (in terms of inter-cluster density).

Let $D=\{v_i|\ i=1,\dots, c\}$ a partitioning of a data set S into c clusters where v_i is the center of i cluster as it results from applying a clustering algorithm alg_j to S.

Let *stdev* the average standard deviation of clusters defined as:

$$stdev = \frac{1}{c}\sqrt{\sum_{i=1}^{c}\left\|\sigma(v_i)\right\|}\quad ^1$$

Then the overall inter-cluster density is defined as:

Definition 1. *Inter-cluster Density* (ID) - It evaluates the average density in the region among clusters in relation with the density of the clusters. The goal is the density among clusters to be significant low in comparison with the density in the considered clusters. Then, we can define inter-cluster density as follows:

$$Dens\_bw(c) = \frac{1}{c\cdot(c-1)}\sum_{i=1}^{c}\left(\sum_{\substack{j=1\\i\neq j}}^{c}\frac{density\,(u_{ij})}{\max\{density\,(v_i), density\,(v_j)\}}\right),\quad (1)$$

where v_i, v_j centers of clusters c_i, c_j, respectively and u_{ij} the middle point of the line segment defined by the clusters' centers v_i, v_j . The term *density(u)* is given by equation (2):

$$density(u\ ) = \sum_{l=1}^{n_{ij}} f(x_l, u\ ),\quad (2)$$

where n_{ij} = number of tuples that belong to the clusters c_i and c_j, *i.e.*, $x_l \in c_i \cup c_j \subseteq S$

---

[1] The term ‖x‖ is defined as : $\|x\| = (x^T x)^{1/2}$, where d dimension of x vector.

represents the number of points in the neighbourhood of u. In our work, the neighbourhood of a data point, u, is defined to be a hyper sphere with center u and radius the average standard deviation of the clusters, *stdev*. More specifically, the function $f(x,u)$ is defined as:

$$f(x,u) = \begin{cases} 0, & \text{if } d(x, u) > stdev \\ 1, & \text{otherwise} \end{cases} \tag{3}$$

It is obvious that a point belongs to the neighborhood of u if its distance from u is smaller than the average standard deviation of clusters. Here we assume that the data have been scaled to consider all dimensions (bringing them into comparable ranges) as equally important during the process of finding the neighbors of a multidimensional point [2].

Definition 2. *Intra-cluster variance - Average scattering for clusters.* The average scattering for clusters is defined as:

$$Scat(c) = \frac{\frac{1}{c}\sum_{i=1}^{c}\left\|\sigma(v_i)\right\|}{\left\|\sigma(X)\right\|} \tag{4}$$

The term $\sigma(X)$ is the variance of a data set; and its p_{th} dimension is defined as follows:

$$\sigma_x^p = \frac{1}{n}\sum_{k=1}^{n}\left(x_k^p - \overline{x}^p\right)^2 \tag{4a}$$

where $\overline{x}^p$ is the p_{th} dimension of $\overline{X} = \frac{1}{n}\sum_{k=1}^{n}x_k, \forall x_k \in X$ (4b)

The term $\sigma(v_i)$ is the variance of cluster c_i and its p_{th} dimension is given by

$$\sigma_{v_i}^p = \sum_{k=1}^{n_i}\left(x_k^p - v_i^p\right)^2 \Big/ n_i \tag{4c}$$

Then the validity index S_Dbw is defined as:
$$S\_Dbw = Scat(c) + Dens\_bw(c) \tag{5}$$

The definition of S_Dbw indicates that both criteria of "good" clustering (i.e., compactness and separation) are properly combined, enabling reliable evaluation of clustering results. The first term of S_Dbw, *Scat(c)*, indicates the average scattering within c clusters. A small value of this term is an indication of compact clusters. As the scattering within clusters increases (i.e., they become less compact) the value of *Scat(c)* also increases and therefore it is a good indication of the compactness of clusters. *Dens_bw(c)* indicates the average number of points between the *c* clusters (i.e., an indication of inter-cluster density) in relation with density within clusters. A small *Dens_bw(c)* value indicates well-separated clusters. The number of clusters, c, that minimizes the above index can be considered as an optimal value for the number of clusters present in the data set.

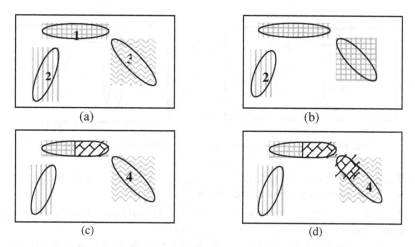

Fig. 3. A data set S partitioned in three (a) two (b) and four clusters (c, d)

3   Integrity Issues

In this section we evaluate the integrity of the validity index S_Dbw on which our approach based as regards their ability to select the best partitioning among these proposed by the clustering algorithms. In the following lemmas we summarize the different cases of clustering results giving also their respective proof sketches.

Let a data set S containing convex clusters (as in Fig.a) and various ways to partition it using different clustering algorithms (Figure 3b-d). Let the optimal (natural) partitioning of data set S (as it is appeared in Figure 3a) in three clusters. The number of clusters as it emanates from the case of optimal partitioning is further called "correct number of clusters". We assume that the data set is evenly distributed, i.e., on average similar number of data points are found for each surface unit in the clusters.

Lemma 1: *Assume a data set S with convex clusters and a clustering algorithm A applied repetitively to S, each time with different input parameter values P_i, resulting in different partitions D_i of S. The value of S_Dbw is minimized when the correct number of clusters is found.*

Proof: Let n be the correct number of clusters of the data set S corresponding to the partitioning D_1 (optimal partitioning of S): $D_1(n, S) = \{c_{D1i}\}$, i=1,..,n
and m the number of clusters of another partitioning D_2 of the same data set: $D_2(m, S) = \{c_{D2j}\}$, j=1,..,m.
Let S_Dbw_{D1} and S_Dbw_{D2} be the values of the validity index for the respective partitioning schemes. Then, we consider the following cases:

i) Assume D_2 to be a partitioning where more than the actual clusters are formed (i.e., m>n). Moreover, parts of the actual clusters (corresponding to D_1) are grouped into clusters of D_2 (as in Fig.d). Let $fC_{D1} = \{fc_{D1p} \mid p=1, \ldots, nfr1\ fc_{D1p} \subseteq c_{D1i}, i=1,\ldots,n\}$ a set of fractions of clusters in D_1. Similarly, we define $fC_{D2} = \{fc_{D2k} \mid k=1, \ldots, nfr2, fc_{D2k} \subseteq c_{D2j}, j=1,\ldots, m\}$. Then:

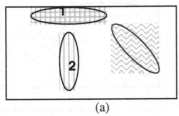 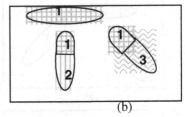

(a)   (b)

Fig. 4. A data set S partitioned correctly (a) and falsely (b) in three clusters

a) $\exists\ c_{D2j}$: $c_{D2i} = \cup fc_{D1p}$, where $p=p_1,....,\ p_n$, $p_1 >=1$ and $p_n<=$ nfr1, nfr1 is the number of considered fractions of clusters in D_1,

b) $\exists\ c_{D1i}$: $c_{D1i} = \cup fc_{D2k}$, where $k=k_1,....,\ k_n$, $k_1 >=1$ and $k_n<=$ nfr2, where nfr2 is the number of considered fractions of clusters in D_2,

In this case, some of the clusters in D_2 include regions of low density (for instance cluster 3 in Fig.d). Thus, the value of the first term of the index related to intra-cluster variance of D_2 increases as compared to the intra-cluster variance of D_1 (i.e., Scat(m) > Scat(n)). On the other hand, the second term (inter-cluster density) is also increasing as compared to the corresponding term of index for D_1 (i.e., Dens_bw(m) > Dens_bw(n)). This is because some of the clusters in D_1 are split and therefore there are border areas between clusters that are of high density (e.g., clusters 1 and 3 in Figure 3d). Then, since both S_Dbw terms regarding D_2 partitioning increase we conclude that $S\_Dbw_{D1} < S\_Dbw_{D2}$.

ii) Let D_2 be a partitioning where more clusters than in D_1 are formed (i.e., m>n). Also, we assume that at least one of the clusters in D_1 is split to more than one in D_2 while no parts of D_1 clusters are grouped into D_2 clusters (as in Fig.c), i.e., $\exists$ c_{D1i} : $c_{D1i} = \cup c_{D2j}$, $j=k_1,...,$ k and $k_1 >=1$, k <= m. In this case, the value of the first term of the index related to intra-cluster variance slightly decreases compared to the corresponding term of D_1 since the clusters in D_2 are more compact. As a consequence Scat(m)<=Scat(n). On the other hand, the second term (inter-cluster density) is increasing as some of the clusters in D_1 are split and therefore there are borders between clusters that are of high density (for instance clusters 1 and 3 in Fig.c). Then Dens(m) >> Dens(n). Based on the above discussion and taking in account that the increase of inter-cluster density is significantly higher than the decrease of intra-cluster variance we may conclude that $S\_Dbw_{D1} < S\_Dbw_{D2}$.

iii) Let D_2 be a partitioning with less clusters than in D_1 (m<n) and two or more of the clusters in D_1 are grouped to a cluster in D_2 (as in Fig.b.). Then, $\exists\ c_{D2j}$: $c_{D2j} = \cup c_{D1i}$, where $i=p_1, ..., $ p and $p_1 >= 1$, p <= n. In this case, the value of the first term of the index related to intra-cluster variance increases as compared to the value of corresponding term of D_1 since the clusters in D_2 contain regions of low density. As a consequence, Scat(m)>>Scat(n). On the other hand, the second term of the index (inter-cluster density) is slightly decreasing or remains vaguely the same as compared to the corresponding term of D_1 (i.e., Dens_bw(n)≡Dens_bw(m)). This is because similarly to the case of the D_1 partitioning (Figure 3a) there are no borders between clusters in D_2 that are of high density. Then, based on the above discussion and considering that the increase of intra-cluster variance is significantly higher than the decrease of inter-cluster density, we may conclude that $S\_Dbw_{D1} < S\_Dbw_{D2}$.

Lemma 2: *Assume a data set S containing convex clusters and a clustering algorithm A applied repetitively to S, each time with different parameter values P_i, resulting in different partitions D_i of S. For each D_i it is true that the correct number of clusters is found. The value S_Dbw is minimized when the optimal partitions are found for the correct number of clusters.*

Proof:. We consider D_2 to be a partitioning with the same number of clusters as the optimal one D1 (Figure 4a), (i.e., m=n). Furthermore, we assume that one or more of the actual clusters corresponding to D_1 are split and their parts are grouped into different clusters in D_2 (as in Fig. b). That is, if $fC_{D1} = \{fc_{D1p} \mid p=1, \ldots, nfr1$ $fc_{D1p} \subseteq c_{D1i}$, i=1,...,n} a set of clusters fractions in D_1 then $\exists$ c_{D2j}: $c_{D2j} = \cup fc_{D1i}$, i=p_1, ..., p and $p_1 >= 1$, p<=n. In this case, the clusters in D_2 contain regions of low density (e.g. cluster 1 in Figure 4b) and as a consequence the value of the first term of the index, intracluster variance, increases as compared to the corresponding term of D_1, i.e., Scat(m)>Scat(n). On the other hand, some of the clusters in D_2 are split and therefore there are border areas between clusters that are of high density (for instance clusters 1, 3 and 1, 2 in Fig. b). Therefore, the second term (inter-cluster density) of D_2 is also increasing as compared to the one of D_1, i.e., Dens_bw(m)>Dens_bw(n). Based on the above discussion it is obvious that $S\_Dbw_{D1} < S\_Dbw_{D2}$.

3.1   Time Complexity

The complexity of our approach depends on the complexity of the clustering algorithms used for defining the clustering schemes and the complexity of the validity index S_Dbw. More specifically, assume a set of clustering algorithms, Alg = {alg$_1$, ..., alg$_k$}. Considering the complexity of each of the algorithms, O(alg$_i$) (where, i =1, ..., k), we may define the complexity of the whole clustering process, i.e., the process for defining the clustering schemes based on the algorithms under consideration, let O(Alg). Moreover, the complexity of the index is based on its two terms as defined in (1) and (4). Assuming d is the number of attributes (data set dimension), c is the number of clusters, n is the number of database tuples. The intra-cluster variance complexity is O(ndc) while the complexity of inter-cluster density is O(ndc^2). Then S_Dbw complexity is O(ndc^2). Usually, $c, d << n$, therefore the complexity of our index for a specific clustering scheme is O(n). Finally, the complexity of the whole procedure for finding the clustering scheme best fitting a data set, S, among these proposed by the k algorithms and as a consequence to find the best clustering algorithm is O($O(Alg)+n$).

4   Experimental Evaluation

In this section, the proposed approach for selecting the clustering algorithm that results in the optimal clustering scheme for a data set is experimentally tested. In our study, we consider three well-known algorithms of different clustering categories, partitional, density-based and hierarchical (K-means, DBSCAN and CURE respectively). Also, we experiment with real and synthetic multidimensional data sets containing different number of clusters. In the sequel, due to lack of space, we present only some representative examples of our experimental study.

We consider two 2-dimensional data sets containing four and seven clusters respectively as Fig. 5, Fig. 6 depict. Applying the above mentioned clustering algorithms (i.e., K-means, DBSCAN and CURE) to these data sets three sets of clustering schemes are produced. Each of the clustering schemes' sets corresponds to the clustering results of an algorithm for different values of its input parameters. Then we evaluate the defined clustering schemes based on the proposed index, S_Dbw. The clustering scheme at which S_Dbw is minimized indicates the best partitioning of data set and as a consequence the best algorithm and its input parameters' values resulting in it.

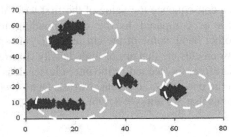

Fig. 5. DataSet1 - A Synthetic Data Set containing four clusters

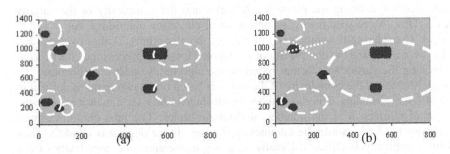

Fig. 6. DataSet2 – A partitioning of data set into seven clusters using (a) CURE or DBSCAN, (b) K-Means

Table 1 and Table 2 summarize the values of S_Dbw in each of the above cases. More specifically, Table 1 depicts that S_Dbw takes its minimum value when Data-Set1 is partitioned into four clusters (i.e., actual clusters in data set) no matter which algorithm is used. This means that according to our approach the optimal partitioning of DataSet1 is four clusters and all three algorithms partitioned it in a right way (i.e., they find the actual clusters in the data set). Figure 5 is a visualization of DataSet1 while the cycles indicate the proposed partitioning.

Table 1. The values of SD_bw for DataSet1 clustering schemes

No clusters	K-means		DBSCAN		CURE r =10, a=0.3	
	Input	S_Dbw Value	Input	S_Dbw Value	Input	S_Dbw Value
8	C=8	0.124		-	C=8	0.108
7	C=7	0.118		-	C=7	0.103
6	C=6	0.0712	Eps=20 MinPts=4	0.087	C=6	0.082
5	C=5	0.086	Eps=10 MinPts=10	0.086	C=5	0.091
4	**C=4**	**0.0104**	**Eps=40 MinPts=10**	**0.0104**	**C=4**	**0.0104**
3	C=3	0.0312	Eps=10 MinPts=15	0.031	C=3	0.031
2	C=2	0.1262	Eps=20 MinPts=15	0.1262	C=2	0.126

Table 2. The values of SD_bw for DataSet2 clustering schemes

No clusters	K-means		DBSCAN		CURE r =10, a=0.3	
	Input	S_Dbw Value	Input	S_Dbw Value	Input	S_Dbw Value
8	C=8	0.66	Eps=8 MinPts=10	0.0333	C=8	0.0517
7	C=7	0.6004	**Eps=20 MinPts=4**	**0.0009**	**C=7**	**0.0009**
6	C=6	0.575	Eps=80 MinPts=4	0.0018	C=6	0.0019
5	C=5	0.491		-	C=5	0.0051
4	C=4	0.365		-	C=4	0.032
3	C=3	0.045		-	C=3	0.073
2	C=2	0.854		-	C=2	0.796

Moreover, according to Table 2, in case of DataSet2, S_Dbw takes its minimum value for the partitioning of seven clusters defined by DBSCAN and CURE. This is also the number of actual clusters in the data set. Fig. a presents the partitioning of Dataset2 into seven clusters as defined by DBSCAN and CURE while the clustering result of K-Means into seven clusters is presented in Fig. b. It is obvious that K-Means fails to partition DataSet2 properly even in case that the correct number of clusters (i.e., c=7) is considered.

The value of our approach is more evident in case of multidimensional data sets where efficient visualization is difficult or even impossible. We consider two synthetic data sets, four- and six-dimensional (further referred as DataSet3 and DataSet4 respectively). We may discover four clusters in DataSet3 while the number of clusters occurred in DataSet4 is two. Assuming DataSet3 our approach proposes the partitioning of four clusters defined by DBSCAN and CURE as the best fitting the data under consideration. Four clusters is the value at which S_Dbw takes its minimum value (see Table 3) and it is also the actual number of clusters in data set. Similarly, in case of DataSet4 SD_bw takes its minimum value for the partitioning of two clusters defined by DBSCAN (see Table 4). Considering the clustering schemes proposed by CURE, S_Dbw is minimized when c=5. Thus, the best partitioning among these defined by CURE is five clusters. It is obvious that CURE seems to fail to partition Dataset4 in a right way, even in case that the actual number of clusters (i.e., two) is considered.

Table 3. The values of S_Dbw for 4D-data set clustering schemes

No clus-ters	K-means		DBSCAN		CURE r =10, a=0.3	
	Input	S_Dbw Value	Input	S_Dbw Value	Input	S_Dbw Value
9	C=9	2.3555556727820735E7	Eps=15 MinPts=4	0.042	C=9	0.2739
8	C=8	0.618	Eps=15 MinPts=10	0.226	C=8	0.256
7	C=7	1.295	-	-	C=7	0.1765
6	C=6	1800005.464	Eps=20 MinPts=4	0.0365	C=6	0.1899
5	C=5	1.02165327	Eps=10 MinPts=10	0.0311	C=5	0.0859
4	C=4	295333334.99	**Eps=40 MinPts=10**	**0.0013**	**C=4**	**0.0013**
3	C=3	1.031		-	C=3	0.0149
2	C=2	4.197		-	C=2	0.672

Table 4. The values of SD_bw for the 6D-data set clustering schemes

No clusters	K-means		DBSCAN		CURE r =10, a=0.3	
	Input	S_Dbw Value	Input	S_Dbw Value	Input	S_Dbw Value
8	C=8	0.689	-	-	C=8	0.291
7	C=7	0.653	-	-	C=7	0.338
6	C=6	0.662	-	-	C=6	0.322
5	C=5	0.669	-	-	C=5	0.239
4	C=4	0.58	Eps=5 MinPts=4	0.31	C=4	0.805
3	C=3	0.619	Eps=25 MinPts=4	0.233	C=3	1.401
2	C=2	0.114	**Eps=35 MinPts=4**	**0.096**	C=2	2.3249

Finally, we evaluate our approach using real data sets. One of the data sets, we studied, contains three parts of Greek roads network [17]. The roads are represented by their MBR approximations' vertices. Figure 7 is a visualization of this data. The

Table 5. The values of SD_bw for Real_Data1 (Figure 7)

No Clusters	K-means		DBSCAN		CURE r =10, a=0.3	
	Input	S_Dbw Value	Input	S_Dbw Value	Input	S_Dbw Value
8	C=8	0.179		-	C=8	0.1694
7	C=7	0.237		-	C=7	0.1914
6	C=6	0.343		-	C=6	0.2248
5	C=5	0.367		-	C=5	0.1621
4	C=4	0.35	Eps=50000 MinPts=10	0.192	C=4	0.1349
3	**C=3**	**0.083**	**Eps=30000 MinPts=10**	**0.084**	C=3	0.1086
2	C=2	0.918	Eps=10000 MinPts=10	0.891	C=2	1.0508

behaviour of S_Dbw regarding the different clustering schemes (i.e., number of clusters) defined by the above mentioned algorithms are depicted in Table 5. It is clear that S_Dbw indicates the correct number of clusters (three) as the best partitioning for the data set when K-Means or DBSCAN is used.

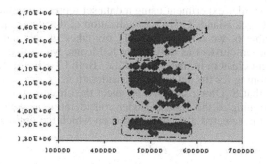

Fig. 7. Real_Data1- A data set representing a part of Greek network

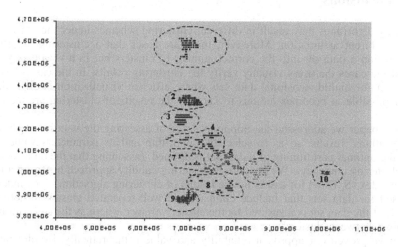

Fig. 8. Real_Data2 – A data set representing towns and villages of Greek islands

Table 6. The values of SD_bw for Real_Data2 (Figure 8)

No Clusters	K-means		DBSCAN		CURE r =10, a=0.3	
	Input	S_Dbw Value	Input	S_Dbw Value	Input	S_DbwValue
11	C=11	0.039	-	-	C=11	0.114
10	**C=10**	**0.0348**	Eps= 2000, MinPts=4	0.113	C=10	0.08
9	C=9	0.0503	Eps=2000 MinPts=10	0.072	C=9	0.049
8	C=8	0.088	Eps= 3000 MinPts=4	0.123	C=8	0.107
7	C=7	0.112	-	-	C=7	0.121
6	C=6	0.095	Eps=4000 MinPts=4	0.228	C=6	0.32
5	C=5	0.149	-	-	C=5	0.266
4	C=4	0.621	Eps=5000 MinPts=4	0.561	C=4	0.511
3	C=3	0.539	Eps=6000 MinPts=4	0.251	C=3	0.389
2	C=2	1.150	Eps=7000 MinPts=4	0.621	C=2	0.617

We carried out, a similar experiment using a data set representing the towns and villages of a group of Greek islands [17]. A visualization of this data is presented in Figure 8. Based on Table 6, we observe that SD_bw takes its minimum value for the clustering scheme of ten clusters as defined by K-Means, which is a "good" approximation of the inherent clusters in underlying data. Both CURE and DBSCAN fail to define a good partitioning for the data under consideration.

Then, it is clear that S_Dbw can assist to select the clustering algorithm resulting in the optimal partitioning of the data set under consideration as well as the input parameters' values of the selected algorithm based on which the optimal partitioning is defined.

5   Conclusions

Clustering algorithms may result in different clustering schemes under the consideration of different assumption. Moreover, there are cases that a clustering algorithm may partition a data set into the correct number of clusters but in a wrong way. In most of the cases the users visually verify the clustering results. In the case of voluminous and/or multidimensional data sets where efficient visualization is difficult or even impossible, it becomes tedious to know if the results of clustering are valid or not.

In this paper we addressed the important issue of assessing the validity of clustering algorithms' results, so as to select the algorithm and its parameters values for which the optimal partitioning of a data set is defined (assuming that the data set presents clustering tendency). We propose a clustering validity approach based on a new validity index (S_Dbw) for assessing the results of clustering algorithms. The index is optimised for data sets that include compact and well-separated clusters. The compactness of the data set is measured by the cluster variance where as the separation by the density between clusters.

We have proved our approach reliability and value i. theoretically, by illustrating the intuition behind it and ii. experimentally, using various data sets of non-standard (but in general non-convex) geometries covering also the multidimensional case. The index, as indicated by experiments, may always indicate the algorithm and the respective input parameters' values so as to find the inherent clusters for a data set.

Further Work. As we mentioned earlier the validity assessment index we proposed in this paper works better when the clusters are mostly compact. It does not work properly in the case of clusters of non-convex (i.e., rings) or extraordinarily curved geometry. We are going to work on this issue as the density and its continuity is not any more sufficient criteria. We plan an extension of this effort to be directed towards an integrated algorithm for cluster discovery putting emphasis on the geometric features of clusters, using sets of representative points, or even multidimensional curves rather than a single center point.

Acknowledgements. This work was supported by the General Secretariat for Research and Technology through the PENED ("99EΔ 85") project. We thank Y. Batistakis for his help in the experimental study. We are also grateful to C. Rodopoulos and C. Amanatidis for the implementation of CURE algorithm as well as to Drs Joerg Sander and Eui-Hong (Sam) Han for providing information and the source code for DBSCAN and CURE algorithms respectively.

References

1. Rakesh Agrawal, Johannes Gehrke, Dimitrios Gunopulos, Prabhakar Raghavan, "Automatic Subspace Clustering of High Dimensional Data for Data Mining Applications", *Proceedings of SIGMOD*, 1998.
2. Michael J. A. Berry, Gordon Linoff. Data Mining Techniques For marketing, Sales and Customer Support. John Willey & Sons, Inc, 1996.
3. Martin Ester, Hans-Peter Kriegel, Jorg Sander, Michael Wimmer, Xiaowei Xu. "Incremental Clustering for Mining in a Data Warehousing Environment", *Proceedings of 24th VLDB Conference*, New York, USA, 1998.
4. Martin Ester, Hans-Peter Kriegel, Jorg Sander, Xiaowei Xu. "A Density-Based Algorithm for Discovering Clusters in Large Spatial Databases with Noise", *Proceedings of 2nd Int. Conf. On Knowledge Discovery and Data Mining*, Portland, OR, pp. 226-231, 1996.
5. Usama M. Fayyad, Gregory Piatesky-Shapiro, Padhraic Smuth and Ramasamy Uthurusamy. *Advances in Knowledge Discovery and Data Mining*. AAAI Press 1996
6. Sudipto Guha, Rajeev Rastogi, Kyueseok Shim. "CURE: An Efficient Clustering Algorithm for Large Databases", *Published in the Proceedings of the ACM SIGMOD Conference*, 1998.
7. Sudipto Guha, Rajeev Rastogi, Kyueseok Shim. "ROCK: A Robust Clustering Algorithm for Categorical Attributes", *Published in the Proceedings of the IEEE Conference on Data Engineering*, 1999.
8. Alexander Hinneburg, Daniel Keim. "An Efficient Approach to Clustering in Large Multimedia Databases with Noise". *Proceeding of KDD '98*, 1998.
9. A.K Jain, M.N. Murty, P.J. Flyn. "Data Clustering: A Review", *ACM Computing Surveys*, Vol. 31, No3, September 1999.
10. Milligan, G.W. and Cooper, M.C. (1985), "An Examination of Procedures for Determining the Number of Clusters in a Data Set", *Psychometrika*, 50, 159-179.
11. Raymond Ng, Jiawei Han. "Efficient and Effective Clustering Methods for Spatial Data Mining". *Proceeding of the 20th VLDB Conference*, Santiago, Chile, 1994.
12. C. Sheikholeslami, S. Chatterjee, A. Zhang. "WaveCluster: A-MultiResolution Clustering Approach for Very Large Spatial Database". *Proceedings of 24th VLDB Conference, New York*, USA, 1998.
13. Sharma S.C. *Applied Multivariate Techniques*. John Willwy & Sons, 1996.
14. S. Theodoridis, K. Koutroubas. *Pattern recognition*, Academic Press, 1999
15. M. Halkidi, M. Vazirgiannis, I. Batistakis. "Quality scheme assessment in the clustering process", *In Proceedings of PKDD*, Lyon, France, 2000.
16. Ramze Rezaee, B.P.F. Lelieveldt, J.H.C Reiber. "A new cluster validity index for the fuzzy c-mean", *Pattern Recognition Letters*, 19, pp237-246, 1998.
17. Y. Theodoridis. Spatial Datasets: an "unofficial" collection. http://dias.cti.gr/~ytheod/research/datasets/spatial.html

Fusion of Meta-knowledge and Meta-data for Case-Based Model Selection

Melanie Hilario and Alexandros Kalousis

CUI - University of Geneva, CH-1211 Geneva 4
{hilario,kalousis}@cui.unige.ch

Abstract. Meta-learning for model selection, as reported in the symbolic machine learning community, can be described as follows. First, it is cast as a purely data-driven predictive task. Second, it typically relies on a mapping of dataset characteristics to some measure of generalization performance (e.g., error). Third, it tends to ignore the role of algorithm parameters by relying mostly on default settings. This paper describes a case-based system for model selection which combines knowledge and data in selecting a (set of) algorithm(s) to recommend for a given task. The knowledge consists mainly of the similarity measures used to retrieve records of past learning experiences as well as profiles of learning algorithms incorporated into the conceptual meta-model. In addition to the usual dataset characteristics and error rates, the case base includes objects describing the evaluation strategy and the learner parameters used. These have two major roles: they ensure valid and meaningful comparisons between independently reported findings, and they facilitate replication of past experiments. Finally, the case-based meta-learner can be used not only as a predictive tool but also as an exploratory tool for gaining further insight into previously tested algorithms and datasets.

1 Issues and Objectives

Broadly speaking, the *model selection* problem concerns the choice of an appropriate model for a given learning task. However, the term has been used with varying nuances, or at least shifting emphases, among the different communities now involved in data mining. The divergence seems to concern the level of generality at which one situates the search for the appropriate model. Among statisticians, model selection takes place *within* a given model family: it typically refers to the task of creating a fully specified instance of that family, called the fitted model, whose complexity has been fine-tuned to the problem at hand [9]. This convention has been carried over to neural network (NN) learning, where model complexity is a function of parameters specific to a family of network architectures – e.g., the number of hidden layers and units for feedforward NNs or the number of centers for Radial Basis Function Networks [15]. In the symbolic machine learning (ML) community, the term *model selection* designates the task of selecting a learning algorithm for a specific application; thus search is conducted in the space of all known or available model families and the selection of a learning algorithm circumscibes a model class or family from which

L. De Raedt and A. Siebes (Eds.): PKDD 2001, LNAI 2168, pp. 180–191, 2001.

the learned model will eventually emerge. However, the task of finding the most appropriate model instantiation from the selected family has been relatively neglected. In other words, ML researchers tend to end where statisticians and NN researchers tend to start. Thus, while the latter seldom envisage model selection beyond the frontiers of a specific model family (e.g. multilayer perceptrons), the former often overlook the role of model parameters when doing cross-algorithm comparisons; the Statlog [12] and Metal projects [11], for instance, have adopted the expedient of systematically evaluating learning algorithms with their default parameter settings. In the broader perspective of data mining, however, these diverse definitions should be seen as partial and complementary perspectives on a complex multifaceted task. *The first research objective of this work is to integrate the choice of learning methods as well as model parameters in a unified framework for model selection.*

Given that no learning algorithm can systematically outperform all others [17], the model selection problem arises anew with each learning task. The most common approach consists in experimenting with a number of alternative methods and models and then selecting one which maximizes certain performance measures. However, with the increasing number and diversity of learning methods available, exhaustive experimentation is simply out of the question. There is a need to limit the initial set of candidate algorithms on the basis of the given task or data, and one can legitimately hope that algorithms which have proved useful for a certain class of tasks will confirm their utility on other, similar tasks. Hence the idea that by examining results of past learning experiences, one might determine broad mappings between learning methods and task classes so that model selection does not start from scratch each time. Meta-learning is an attempt at automating the realization of this idea.

The meta-learning approach to model selection has been typically based on characterizations of the application dataset. In Statlog, meta-learning is a classification task which maps dataset attributes to a binary target variable indicating the applicability or non-applicability of a learning algorithm. Data characteristics can be descriptive summary statistics (e.g., number of classes, number of instances, average skew of predictive variables) or information-theoretic measures (e.g., average joint entropy of predictive and target variables). There have since been a number of attempts to extend or refine the Statlog approach. In the Metal project, for instance, datasets have also been characterized by the error rates observed when they are fed into simple and efficient learning algorithms called landmarkers (e.g., Naive Bayes or linear discriminants) [13]. However, the basic idea underlying the Statlog approach remains intact – i.e., that meta-attributes describing the application task/dataset suffice to predict the applicability or the relative performance of the candidate learning algorithms.

To broaden the range of meta-level predictors, we propose algorithm profiling as a complement to dataset characterization in general and to landmarking in particular. Landmarking uses specially selected learners to uncover information about the nature of the learning task or data. By contrast, algorithm profiling uses specially designed datasets to deliver information about a learning algorithm

– its bias/variance profile, scalability, tolerance to noise, irrelevant variables or missing data. While landmarking attempts to describe a dataset in terms of the areas of expertise to which it belongs (as witnessed by the landmarkers which perform well on it), algorithm profiling strives to describe in concrete, quantitative terms what makes up the region of expertise of a learning algorithm. *The second objective is to complement dataset characterizations with algorithm profiles as predictors in the meta-learning process.*

There is a fundamental difference between dataset and algorithm characterizations behind their apparent symmetry. Dataset characteristics are *meta-data* extracted from individual datasets whereas algorithm profiles embody *meta-knowledge* about learning algorithms which can be brought to bear on model selection over different datasets. The essential difference lies in the fact that algorithm characteristics have been derived via a process of abstraction and/or generalization. This generalized knowledge may be borrowed from the collective store of expertise in the domain or alternatively abstracted via controlled experimentation, as in the case of meta-attributes concerning sensitivity to missing or irrelevant data. In addition to prior meta-knowledge about learning/modelling tools, a domain expert's background knowledge of her application domain can be expressed in the form of constraints that should be taken into account in the search for an appropriate tool. *The third objective is to strike an effective and efficient balance between meta-learning and the use of prior (base- and meta-level) knowledge in the model selection process.*

With the introduction of prior knowledge about learning algorithms and application domains, meta-learning becomes a multi-relational task which calls for greater expressive power than that offered by attribute value vectors. In this paper we describe an object-oriented case-based meta-learning assistant which addresses the issues and objectives described above. Section 2 describes the knowledge embedded in the system's underlying conceptual (meta) model. Section 3 describes the current implementation – the extensive case base gathered to date as well as the different ways in which it can be exploited – and proposes a strategy for evaluating its incremental meta-learning capabilities. Section 4 summarizes and argues for its possible utility as a long-term meta-memory of machine learning experiments.

2   The Embedded Knowledge

This section focuses on the knowledge embedded in the meta-model of the learning process. A simplified view of the conceptual schema is shown in Fig. 1.

2.1   Modelling Processes

The core of the meta-model is the *modelling process*, which depicts a specific learning episode or experiment. It is described by a number of performance measures such as the error rate, the training/testing time, and the size of the learned model or hypothesis. More importantly, the ModProcess object is the hub

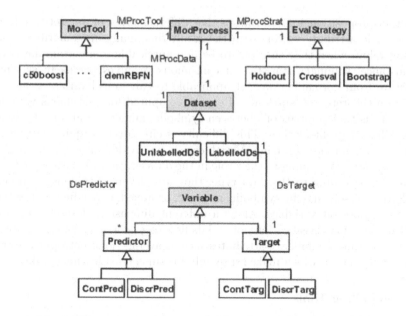

Fig. 1. The conceptual metamodel (see Sect. 2 for explanation)

which links together three main components according to a precise semantics: a modelling or learning tool (ModTool) is trained and tested on the given data (Dataset) following a particular evaluation strategy (EvalStrat). The structure and attributes of these three components comprise the background information which will be brought to bear in the meta-learning and model selection process.

2.2 Datasets

The object depicting a dataset can be seen as a simple, albeit extended, importation of the Statlog dataset characteristics. These will not be described here (see [12] for a detailed discussion); rather, we present several major extensions which have been made possible by the structured representation adopted. In the Statlog formalism, only summary statistics over all predictive variables of a dataset could be recorded; the consequence was that atypical variables (e.g., irrelevant variables) were impossible to detect since the symptoms of this atypicality (e.g., an extremely low measure of mutual information with the target variable) somehow got dissolved in the overall statistics (e.g., average mutual information). Such problems disappear in a multi-relational representation, where a dataset can be characterized more thoroughly by the collection of objects that describe its component variables.

In addition, both variables and datasets can be divided into subclasses and thus described only by features that are certain to make sense for the specific category in question. One persistent problem of meta-learning in Statlog and other propositional approaches is that different types of datasets are forced into a single attribute vector, with the result that many meta-attributes have missing values when they turn out to be non applicable to a certain data type. For instance, summary statistics of continuous variables (eg mean skewness, departure from normality) are not applicable to categorical variables; also, information theoretic measures are often not computed for continuous variables. The result is that comparisons between symbolic, numeric, and mixed datasets become highly problematical. This difficulty is circumvented quite naturally in a typed multi-relational setting. Variables can be divided into subclasses along two dimensions. According to their role in the dataset, they are either predictors or targets; according to the data type, they are either continuous or discrete. Similarly, datasets may be symbolic, numeric, or mixed, depending on the types of their component variables. Along a different dimension, datasets are either labelled (e.g., for classification) or unlabelled (e.g., for association). Labelled datasets contain a number of attributes such as average joint entropy or average mutual information which make sense only for supervised learning tasks.

2.3   Modelling Tools

The ModTool class subsumes any fully implemented modelling or learning method which can be used for supervised or unsupervised knowledge discovery from data. Each tool is formalized as a ModTool sublcass. The tools used in our initial study are C5.0 in its tree (c50tree) and rule (c50rule) versions, an oblique decision tree (ltree) [4], a sequential covering rule inducer (ripper) [3], the MLC++ implementations of Naive Bayes (mlcNB) and IB1 (mlcIB1) [7], Joao Gama's implementation of Fisher's linear discriminant (lindiscr), and the Clementine implementations of radial basis function networks (clemRBFN) and backpropagation in multilayer perceptrons (clemMLP)[1]. All learning tools inherit the meta-features defined for the ModTool class; in addition, each subclass has its specific attributes corresponding to the tool's user-tunable model and search parameters – e.g., pruning severity for (c50tree), the number of centers and their overlap for (clemRBFN). Each application of a learning tool is recorded as an instance of the corresponding subclass, and the actual parameters override the default values predefined in the conceptual schema.

There are no intermediate subhierarchies of modelling tools according to learning paradigm or computational approach. This design option has been taken deliberately: since the aim of our meta-learner is to discover mappings of data and task types onto classes of learners, we have avoided a priori classifications that may hinder the discovery of novel or unexpected affinities or clusters among learning methods. On the other hand, we have tried to embed as much knowledge as possible about the biases, strengths and weaknesses of each learning tool.

Representation and Approach. The simplest form of knowledge concerns the basic requirements, capabilities and limitations of each tool, which have

---

[1] The parenthesized names will be used throughout the rest of this paper to identify the specific implementations of the learning algorithms studied.

Table 1. Characterizing representation and approach of modeling tools

ModTool	Data	Inc	CH	VH	Par	Meth	Strat	Cum
c50rules	NS	N	Y	Seq	Sym	Logic	E	L
c50tree	NS	N	Y	Seq	Sym	Logic	E	L
clemMLP	NS	N	N	Par	NN	Thresh	E	M
clemRBFN	NS	N	N	Par	NN	Comp	E	M
lindiscr	NS	N	N	Par	Stat	Thresh	E	H
ltree	NS	N	N	SP	Sym	Logic	E	M
mlcib1	NS	Y	N	Par	Sym	Comp	L	M
mlcnb	NS	N	N	Par	Sym	Comp	E	H
ripper	NS	N	N	Seq	Sym	Logic	E	L

generally been gathered from algorithm specifications or instruction manuals of the implemented tool. Attributes in this group indicate the type of data (Data in Table 1) supported by a learning tool (N for numeric/continuous, S for symbolic/discrete, NS for both), whether the tool learns incrementally or not (Inc), or whether it can handle externally assigned costs (CH). These characteristics can be determined in a straightforward manner and they are usually invariant for all instantiations of a given learning tool.

As tool specifications provide only a minimal characterization of learner functionality, knowledge of less obvious features (see last five columns of Table 1) has been gathered mainly from cumulative results of past research. We borrowed the paradigm-based categorization of learning algorithms (Par) as symbolic, statistical, or connectionist as well as Langley's distinction between logical, competitive, and threshold-based learning approaches (Meth). From the point of view of learning strategy (Strat), modelling tools are either lazy or eager, depending on whether they simply store data, deferring learning until task execution time, or use given data to create a model in view of future task requests. Another dimension is the way a learner handles input variables in the generalization process (VH). Sequential algorithms (e.g., decision trees) examine one input variable at a time, while parallel algorithms examine all input variables simultaneously [14]. Neural networks are clearly parallel; so are instance-based learners and Naive Bayes classifiers, which aggregate distances or probabilities over all variable values simultaneously. A third, hybrid category includes algorithms such as oblique decision trees which alternate between sequential and simultaneous processing of variables depending on the data subset examined at a node.

An additional aspect of learning bias which has been brought to light by recent research is what Blockeel [2] calls cumulativity (Cum). This is a generalization of the statistical concept of additivity: two features are cumulative if their effects are mutually independent, so that their combined effect is the trivial composition of their separate effects. The cumulativity of learning algorithms is nothing more than their ability to handle cumulativity of features, which can be discretized roughly on a three-step scale. Linear regressors and discriminants are naturally situated on the high end of the scale; so is Naive Bayes with its assumption of the class-conditional independence of predictors (the product of

Table 2. Characterizing resilience of modeling tools

ModTool	Var	ErrSIrr	TimeSIrr	MCAR	MAR
c50rules	0.4503	0.0324	4.76	0.2475	0.2527
c50tree	0.4548	0.0337	4.26	0.2098	0.2094
clemMLP	0.4230	0.1292	378.25	?	?
clemRBFN	0.3626	0.0910	9595.93	?	?
lindiscr	0.2308	0.0351	4.92	0.1913	0.1624
ltree	0.4154	0.0413	14.57	0.1111	0.1251
mlcib1	0.3868	0.1347	56.98	0.2283	0.2292
mlcnb	0.2273	0	3.64	0.1073	0.0940
ripper	0.3862	0.0173	98.67	0.1310	0.1444

likelihoods and priors it maximizes translates directly to addivity of their respective logarithms). At the other extreme, sequential learners like decision trees and rule induction systems allow for maximal interaction between variables and therefore have low cumulativity. Instance-based learners and neural networks occupy the midpoint of the scale. Neural nets handle cumulativity by means of linear combinations while handling interaction by superposing multiple layers and using nonlinear threshold functions.

Resilience. A second group of characteristics concerns the resilience of a modelling tool, i.e., its capability of ensuring reliable performance despite variations in training conditions and especially in the training data. Resiliency characteristics reflect the sensitivity or tolerance of an algorithm to data characteristics or pathologies that are liable to affect performance adversely. Examples are stability, scalability, and resistance to noise, missing values, and irrelevant or redundant features. Contrary to representational and methodological meta-attributes, there is no consensus regarding the resilience of the ten learning tools included in our initial knowledge base. We thus undertook extensive experimental studies concerning their bias/variance trade-off and their sensitivity to missing values and irrelevant features.

Table 2 shows the results of these experiments. The column labelled Var gives the proportion of variance in the generalization error. This was obtained by applying Kohavi and Wolpert's bias-variance decomposition method for zero-one loss [8] to each tool, averaged over 40 datasets from the UCI Machine Learning Repository. Note that the variance measures given here concern each tool as applied with its default parameter settings. For instance, 0.4548 is the mean variance observed for Clementine RBF networks with the default number of hidden units, i.e., 20; variances have also been recorded as the number of hidden units is varied from 5 to 150. The next two columns quantfy a learner's sensitivity to irrelevant attributes as measured by its mean increase in generalization error (ErrSIrr) or in training time (TimeSIrr) for each additional percent of irrelevant attributes. These measures were obtained in a series of 10-fold cross-validation experiments on 43 UCI datasets; each learning algorithm was run with default parameters on the original datasets, then on 6 corrupted versions containing respectively 5%, 10%, 20%, 30%, 40%, and 50% irrelevant features. A full discussion of these experiments and the results is given in [5]. The last two columns depict mean increase in generalization error with each per cent increase in missing values – either values that are missing completely at random (MCAR) or missing at random (MAR). A value is said to be missing completely at random if its absence is completely independent of the dataset; it is missing at random if its absence depends, not on its own value, but on the value of some other attribute in the dataset [10]. Here again, we followed a strategy of "progressive corruption" to observe how learners cope with incomplete data. Generalization error was estimated for each learner on the original datasets, then on five increasingly incomplete versions from which 5%, 10%, 20%, 30%, and 40% of the feature values were deleted. For the MCAR series, feature values were deleted randomly following a uniform distribution; for the MAR series, values of selected features were deleted conditional on the values of other attributes. The interested reader is referred to [6] for details.

It should be stressed that all characteristics as well as any conclusions drawn about a modelling tool concern *the specific software implementation under study rather than the generic learning algorithm or method*. It is well known that the specification of an algorithm leaves considerable flexibility in implementation, and differences between implementations of the same algorithm can turn out to be as significant as differences between distinct methods or algorithms. Thus, while we have taken pains to include a wide variety of learning approaches in our study, the findings reported should not be extrapolated from the individual tool implementation to the generic method without utmost precaution.

Practicality. Finally, other features concern more practical issues of usability. They do not impact a learner's generalization performance but can be used to pre-select tools on the basis of user preferences. Examples of such characteristics are the comprehensibility of the method, the interpretability of the learned model, or the degree to which model and search parameters are handled automatically. Since values of these meta-characteristics are qualitative and highly subjective, we assigned 5-level ordinal values on what we deemed to be intuitively obvious grounds. For instance, parameter handling is rated very high for lindiscr, ltree, mlcib1, and mlcnb – tools which require absolutely no user-tuned parameter. When an algorithm involves user-tunable parameters, its rating depends on how well the algorithm performs without user intervention, that, when run with its default parameter settings. Thus c50tree and c50rules are marked high, clemMLP medium, and clemRBFN low (the default of 20 centers often leads to poor performance and even to downright failure to converge). As for method comprehensibility and result interpretability, we relied heavily on the Statlog characterization, since these are among the few characteristics that are intrinsic to the method and vary little across implementations. For instance, the neural network tools rate very low on both comprehensibility and interpretability; decision trees and rules rate high on both counts whereas for mlcib1, the method (learning by similarity) is easier to grasp than the 'model' (distance measures of nearest neighbors).

2.4   Evaluation Strategies

To ensure that all recorded learning episodes conform to the elementary rules of tool evaluation, each modelling process is associated with a fully specified evaluation strategy. Examples of generic strategies are simple holdout, cross-validation, bootstrap, and subsampling without replacement. Each has its own particular set of parameters: the proportion of the training set for holdout, the number of folds for cross-validation, or the number of replicates for bootstrap. Attributes common to all strategies are the number of trials (complete runs of the selected strategy) and the random seed used. Such detailed accounts have a two-fold motivation. First, we all know that the same method applied to the same dataset can lead to widely different performance measures, depending on whether these were estimated using simple holdout or leave-one-out cross-validation. Many of the cross-experimental comparisons reported in the literature deserve little credence for lack of evidence that performance measures were obtained under identical or at least comparable learning conditions. Secondly, information about the evaluation strategy followed in an experiment should be sufficiently precise and complete to allow for replication and take-up by other researchers.

3   The Implementation

3.1   The Case Base

The conceptual schema described in the preceding section has been implemented using CBR-Works Professional. Given the sheer volume of the collected metadata, interactive data entry was out of the question. A set of scripts was implemented to automate the translation of data characterization files as well as results of learning experiments into CBR-Works' Case Query Language. The current case base contains objects representing:

- more than 1350 datasets for classifications tasks (98 UCI and other benchmarks plus semi-artificial datasets generated from these for irrelevance and missing values experiments)
- around 37500 variables belonging to the above datasets
- around 11700 experiments involving the training and evaluation of 9 classification algorithms on the above datasets.

3.2   Exploitation Scenarios

The basic scenario follows the standard CBR cycle consisting of the four R's: retrieve, reuse, revise, retain [1]. A query case is entered in the form of a ModProcess object whose minimal content is a set of links to a three objects representing a dataset, a modelling tool, and an evaluation strategy. While the last two can be left completely unspecified, the application dataset should be fully characterized in the query case's Dataset object, itself linked to objects describing its component variables. Optionally, users can fill out slots of all the other objects of the query case in order to specify a set of constraints based on the nature of the application task or their own preferences. For instance, they can impose preferences on the incrementality, comprehensibility, or stability of a modelling tool by filling out the relevant slot of the ModTool object. In such cases, learner characteristics serve in prior model selection by restricting from the outset the space of tools to consider. Users can also use the ModProcess object to specify what they consider acceptable performance (e.g., a lower bound on the accuracy gain ratio or an upper bound on the error rate or the time to be spent in training or testing). The system retrieves k most similar cases (where k is a user-specified parameter), each of which can be taken as a combined recommendation for a modelling tool, its parameter settings, and an evaluation strategy. The user runs the recommended algorithms and the results are integrated into the case memory as k new cases and their associated objects. This basic scenario illustrates the use of standard CBR to incrementally improve model selection by learning from experience.

For case retrieval to work properly, additional domain-specific knowledge has been embedded in the similarity measures. While standard symmetric criteria work well with boolean or categorical meta-attributes such as learner incrementality, method, or cost handling ability, ordered features usually call for asymmetrical similarity criteria. Ordinal (including real) values specified in a query case are often meant as lower or upper bounds on the corresponding attribute. For instance, a user who requires medium interpretability of learned models would be even happier with high or very high interpretability. Similarly, an error specification of 0.2 in the query case should be taken to mean the highest acceptable error, with errors <0.2 getting proportionally higher similarity scores as they approach 0. On the contrary, an accuracy gain ratio of 0.1 should be interpreted as a minimum, with higher values becoming progressively more "similar " as they approach 1.

The reverse exploitation scenario illustrates the use of the system as an exploratory workbench which the user (who may happen to be a KDD researcher) can use to gain insights about learning tools of interest. In problem-solving cum learning mode, the goal is: Given this dataset, which modelling tool(s) should I use to get best results? In exploratory mode, the goal can be stated thus: Given this modelling tool, for which class(es) of tasks/data is it most appropriate? To chart the region of expertise of a learning algorithm, the user enters a query case consisting mainly of the learning algorithm and a bound on some performance measure (e.g., an error rate <learning algorithm's region of competence as defined by the performance criteria used.

3.3   Validating the System

We have described an initial implementation of a case-based assistant which recommends modelling tools for a given learning task. It provides decision support by incorporating meta-knowledge of the model selection problem into its basic learning mechanism. The goal is to develop a workbench for incremental meta-learning which is on the agenda for the third year of the Metal project.

To validate the system we need to set a baseline, i.e., measure the performance of the system with its initial knowledge and case base, and then evaluate its ability to improve performance with experience. We propose the following experimental setup: First, divide the exising meta-dataset into 3 roughly equal subsets (around 4500 learning episodes each) and prime the learner with subset 1. Second, use subset 2 to "grow" the system. Enter each case without the target performance measure (e.g., accuracy gain ratio) as a query, then compare system recommendations with known results and add the query case to the growing base. After addition of a fixed number of cases (e.g., 200), test the case base on subset 3 in view of plotting performance variation with experience.

4   Summary

We presented a case-based assistant for model selection which combines three major features. First, it combines knowledge of learning algorithms with dataset characteristics in order to facilitate model selection by focusing on the most promising tools on the basis of user specified constraints and preferences. Second, it incorporates a mechanism for distinguishing between different parameterizations of learning tools, thus extending model selection to cover both the choice of the learning algorithm and its specific parameter settings. Third, it integrates meta-data gathered from different learning experiences with meta-knowledge not only of learning algorithms but also of modelling processes, performance metrics and evaluation strategies. We are aware of no other system that has all these features simultaneously. As pointed out in the introduction, mainstream meta-learning for model selection has focused mainly on dataset characteristics as predictors of the appropriateness of candidate learning algorithms. Todorowski [16] has tried to go beyond summary dataset statistics and examine characteristics of the individual variables in the data in order to learn first-order model selection rules. However he does not incorporate knowledge of learning tools or their parameters.

We believe that the proposed system is not just useful for meta-learning but can also evolve into some kind of meta-memory of machine learning research. There is a need for a system that manages and maintains meta-knowledge induced from experimentation together with information about the experiments themselves. First, such a long-term memory would allow reliable cross-experimental comparisons. It is common practice among machine learning researchers to compare new observations on tool performance and efficiency with past findings; however, in the absence of clear indications concerning experimental conditions (parameter settings of the learning tools, evaluation strategies used, training and test sample sizes, statistical significance of results, etc.), there is no guarantee that the measures being compared are indeed comparable. Second, it would avoid redundant effort, as researchers pursuing an idea or hypothesis could first consult the store of accumulated knowledge before designing new experiments.

Acknowledgements. We are very grateful to Maria Malek, ESTI (France), for several fruitful discussions on the subject of CBR modelling. We also thank Johann Petrak of OFAI (Vienna) for his most useful experimentation scripts. The work reported in this paper was partly supported by a grant from the Swiss OFES in the framework of ESPRIT LTR Project METAL.

References

1. A. Agnar and E. Plaza. Case-based reasoning: Foundational issues, methodological variations, and system approaches. *AI Communications,* 7(1), 1994.
2. H. Blockeel. Cumulativity as inductive bias. In *Data Mining, Decision Support, Meta-Learning and ILP: Forum for Practical Problem Presentation and Prospective Solutions,* pages 61–70, Lyon, France, July 2000.
3. W. W. Cohen. Fast effective rule induction. In A. Prieditis and S. Russell, editors, *Proc. of the 11th International Conference on Machine Learning,* pages 115–123, Tahoe City, CA, 1995. Morgan Kaufmann.
4. J. Gama and P. Brazdil. Linear tree. *Intelligent Data Analysis,* 3:1–22, 1999.
5. M. Hilario and A. Kalousis. Quantifying the resilience of inductive classification algorithms. In *Principles of Data Mining and Knowledge Discovery. Proceedings of the 4th European Conference,* pages 106–115, Lyon, France, 2000. Springer-Verlag.
6. A. Kalousis and M. Hilario. Supervised knowledge discovery from incomplete data. In *International Conference on Data Mining,* Cambridge, UK, 2000.
7. R. Kohavi, G. John, R. Long, D. Manley, and K. Pfleger. MLC++: A machine learning library in C++. Technical report, CSD, Stanford University, August 1994. An abridged version of this report appears in AI'94: Tools in AI.
8. R. Kohavi and D. Wolpert. Bias plus variance decomposition for zero-one loss functions. In L. Saitta, editor, *Proc. of the 13th International Conference on Machine Learning,* pages 275–283, Bari (Italy), 1996. Morgan Kaufmann.
9. H. Linhart and W. Zucchini. *Model Selection.* J. Wiley, NY, 1986.
10. R. J. Little and D. B. Rubin. *Statistical Analysis with Missing Data.* Wiley, 1987.
11. MetaL Consortium. Project Homepage. http://www.metal-kdd.org/.
12. D. Michie, D. J. Spiegelhalter, and C. C. Taylor, editors. *Machine learning, neural and statistical classification.* Ellis-Horwood, 1994.
13. Bernhard Pfahringer, Hilan Bensusan, and Christophe Giraud-Carrier. Metalearning by landmarking various learning algorithms. In *Proc. Seventeenth International Conference on Machine Learning, ICML'2000,* pages 743–750, San Francisco, California, June 2000. Morgan Kaufmann.
14. J. R. Quinlan. Comparing connectionist and symbolic learning methods. In S. J. Hanson, G. A. Drastal, and R. L. Rivest, editors, *Computational Learning Theory and Natural Learning Systems,* volume I, chapter 15, pages 446–456. MIT Press, 1994.
15. B.D. Ripley. *Pattern Recognition and Neural Networks.* Cambridge U. Press, 1996.
16. L. Todorowski. Experiments in meta-level learning with ILP. In *International Workshop on Inductive Logic Programming,* Bled, Slovenia, 1999. Springer-Verlag.
17. D. Wolpert. The lack of a priori distinctions between learning algorithms. *Neural Computation,* 8(7):1381–1390, 1996.

Discovery of Temporal Patterns*
Learning Rules about the Qualitative Behaviour of Time Series

Frank Höppner

Department of Electrical Engineering and Computer Science
University of Applied Sciences, Emden
Constantiaplatz 4
D-26723 Emden, Germany
frank.hoeppner@ieee.org

Abstract. Recently, association rule mining has been generalized to the discovery of episodes in event sequences. In this paper, we additionally take durations into account and thus present a generalization to *time intervals*. We discover frequent temporal patterns in a single series of such labeled intervals, which we call a state sequence. A temporal pattern is defined as a set of states together with their interval relationships described in terms of Allen's interval logic, for instance "A before B, A overlaps C, C overlaps B" or equivalently "state A ends before state B starts, the gap is covered by state C". As an example we consider the problem of deriving local weather forecasting rules that allow us to conclude from the qualitative behaviour of the air-pressure curve to the wind-strength. Here, the states have been extracted automatically from (multivariate) time series and characterize the trend of the time series locally within the assigned time interval.

1 Introduction

To predict or forecast a system's behaviour in the near future it is probably best to develop a global model of the system and to estimate its parameters with the help of observations in the past. But the identification of such a model requires substantial knowledge about the whole system, which is absent in typical knowledge discovery applications. Nevertheless, we often expect certain relationships between measured variables and the systems behaviour in the future, may be we have already some snapshots of typical behaviour in mind, but we are far away from being able to model the system as a whole. Such *typical key situations* are often associated with a typical qualitative behaviour of measured variables, and consequently humans control technical systems often by simple visual inspection of displayed trends [4]. Examples of rules using qualitative descriptions of time-varying data can be found in the domain of medical diagnosis, material science

---

* This work has been supported by the Deutsche Forschungsgemeinschaft (DFG) under grant no. Kl 648/1.

L. De Raedt and A. Siebes (Eds.): PKDD 2001, LNAI 2168, pp. 192–203, 2001.

[6], diagnostics and supervision [11] or qualitative reasoning [12], to mention only a few. In this paper, we consider the problem of deriving such *local* rules inductively by observing the variables for a long period of time.

Why qualitative descriptions at all? The problem of finding common characteristics of multiple time series or different parts of the same series requires a notion of similarity. If a process is subject to variation in time (translation or dilation), those measures used traditionally for estimating similarity (e.g. pointwise Euclidean norm) will fail in providing useful hints about the time series similarity in terms of the cognitive perception of a human. This problem has been addressed by many authors in the literature, e.g. [1, 5]. Here we use qualitative descriptions to divide up the time series in small segments, each of it easy to grasp and understand by the human. Matching of time series is then performed on the basis of these labeled segments rather than on the raw time series. The basic descriptions can be defined a priori (for example "slightly increasing segment") [4, 14, 6], can be learned from a set of examples (labeled training set), or can be found automatically by means of clustering short subsequences [7]. Finally, we arrive at a sequence of labeled intervals: time intervals in which a certain condition holds in the original time series.

This paper considers the problem of discovering temporal relationships between primitive patterns in time series in a fairly general manner: The time series is turned into a sequence of labeled intervals in Sect. 2. A temporal pattern will be defined as a number of states (the primitive patterns) and their temporal relationship in terms of Allen's temporal logic [3] in Sect. 3. After discussing how to count patterns in an interval sequence in Sect. 4, we seek for frequent patterns in Sect. 5 in a fashion that is similar to the discovery of association rules [2], which has been extended to event sequences in [13, 15]. Given the frequent patterns, rules about temporal relationships can be derived. As an application of this algorithm, we consider the problem of finding rules about the qualitative behaviour of multivariate time series in Sect. 6.

2   State Sequences

Let $\mathcal{S}$ denote the set of all possible trends, properties, or states that we want to distinguish, for example "pressure goes down" or "water level is constant". A state $s \in \mathcal{S}$ holds during a period of time $[b, f)$ where b and f denote the *initial point* in time when we enter the state and the *final point* in time when the state no longer holds. A state sequence on $\mathcal{S}$ is a series of triples defining state intervals

$$(b_1, s_1, f_1), (b_2, s_2, f_2), (b_3, s_3, f_3), (b_4, s_4, f_4), \ldots$$

where $b_i \leq b_{i+1}$ and $b_i < f_i$ holds. We do not require that one state interval has ended before another state interval starts. This enables us to mix up several state sequences (possibly obtained from different sources) into a single state sequences.

However, we do require that every state (b_i, s, f_i) is *maximal* in the sense, that there is no (b_j, s, f_j) in the series such that $[b_i, f_i)$ and $[b_j, f_j)$ overlap or meet each other:

$$\forall (b_i, s_i, f_i), (b_j, s_j, f_j), i < j : f_i \le b_j \Rightarrow s_i \ne s_j \tag{1}$$

If (1) is violated, we can merge both state intervals and replace them by their union $(\min(b_i, b_j), s, \max(f_i, f_j))$.

3   Temporal Patterns

We use Allen's temporal interval logic [3] to describe the relation between state intervals. For any pair of intervals we have 13 possible relationships; they are illustrated in Fig. 1. For example, we say "A meets B" if interval A terminates at the same point in time at which B starts. The inverse relationship is "B is-met-by A". In the following we denote the set of interval relations as shown in the figure by $\mathcal{I}$.

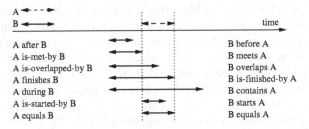

Fig. 1. Allen's interval relationships.

Given n state intervals (b_i, s_i, f_i), $1 \le i \le n$, we can capture their relative positions to each other by an $n \times n$ matrix R whose elements $R[i, j]$ describe the relationship between state interval i and j. As an example, let us consider the state sequence in Fig. 2. Obviously state A is always followed by B. And the lag between A and B is covered by state C. Below the state interval sequence both of these patterns are written as a matrix of interval relations. Formally, a temporal pattern of size n is defined by a pair (s, R), where $s : \{1, .., n\} \to \mathcal{S}$ maps index i to the corresponding state, and $R \in \mathcal{I}^{n \times n}$ denotes the relationship between $[b_i, f_i)$ and $[b_j, f_j)$[1]. By $\dim(P)$ we denote the dimension (number n of intervals) of the pattern P. If $\dim(P) = k$, we say that P is a k-pattern. Of course, many sets of state intervals map to the same temporal pattern. We say that the set of intervals $\{(b_i, s_i, f_i) \mid 1 \le i \le n\}$ is an *instance* of its temporal pattern (s, R). We define the space $TP(\mathcal{S})$ of temporal patterns over $\mathcal{S}$ informally as the space of all valid temporal patterns of arbitrary dimension[2].

---

[1] To determine the interval relationships we assume closed intervals $[b_i, f_i]$

[2] Conditions for a *valid* temporal pattern are, for instance, that $R[i, j]$ is always the inverse of $R[j, i]$.

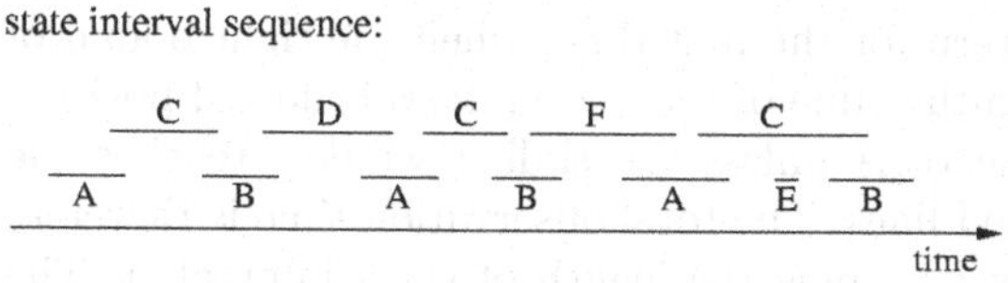

state interval sequence: temporal relations:

(abbreviations: a=after, b=before, o=overlaps, io=is-overlapped-by)

Fig. 2. Example for state interval patterns expressed as temporal relationships.

Next, we define a partial order $\sqsubseteq$ on temporal relations. We say that temporal relation (s_A, R_A) is subpattern of (s_B, R_B) (or $(s_A, R_A) \sqsubseteq (s_B, R_B)$), if $\dim(s_A, R_A) \leq \dim(s_B, R_B)$ and there is an injective mapping π : $\{1, .., \dim(s_A, R_A)\} \to \{1, .., \dim(s_B, R_B)\}$ such that

$$\forall i, j \in \{1, .., \dim(s_A, R_A)\} : R_A[i, j] = R_B[\pi(i), \pi(j)]$$

The relation $\sqsubseteq$ is reflexive and transitive, but not antisymmetric: we can have $(s_A, R_A) \sqsubseteq (s_B, R_B)$ and $(s_B, R_B) \sqsubseteq (s_A, R_A)$ without $s_A = s_B$ and $R_A = R_B$ due to a different state ordering. But permutating the states does not change the semantics of the temporal pattern. Therefore, we define $(s_A, R_A) \equiv (s_B, R_B) :\Leftrightarrow (s_A, R_A) \sqsubseteq (s_B, R_B) \wedge (s_B, R_B) \sqsubseteq (s_A, R_A)$ and consider the factorisation $\left(TP(S)/_{\equiv}, \sqsubseteq/_{\equiv}\right)$, where $\sqsubseteq$ has been generalized canonically to equivalence classes. Then, $\sqsubseteq/_{\equiv}$ is also antisymmetric and thus a partial order on (equivalence classes of) temporal patterns.

To simplify notation we pick a subset $NTP(S) \subseteq TP(S)$ of normalized temporal patterns such that $NTP(S)$ contains one element for each equivalence class of $TP(S)/_{\equiv}$ and $(NTP(S), \sqsubseteq)$ is isomorphic to $\left(TP(S)/_{\equiv}, \sqsubseteq/_{\equiv}\right)$. In the remainder, we will then use $(NTP(S), \sqsubseteq)$ synonymously to $\left(TP(S)/_{\equiv}, \sqsubseteq/_{\equiv}\right)$. Within each equivalence class, we can order the patterns lexicographically by initial time, final time, and state. This ordering is unique thanks to (1). We use the first pattern in this ordering as the representative of the class.

4   Occurrences of Temporal Patterns in State Sequences

To be considered interesting, a temporal pattern is limited in its extension, that is, the whole pattern has to be small enough to be observed by a (forgetful) operator. We therefore choose a maximum duration t_{max}, which serves as the width of a sliding window which is moved along the state sequences. We consider only those pattern instances that can be observed within this window. In a monitoring and control application, this threshold could be taken from the maximum history length that can be displayed on the monitor and thus be inspected by the operator.

We define the total time in which the pattern can be observed within the sliding window as the support $supp(P)$ of the pattern P. (Space limitations prohibit the justification of this choice, we refer the interested reader to [9].) Let us illustrate this definition with some examples in Fig. 3. In subfigure (a) we have a single state A. We see the pattern for the first time, when the right bound of the sliding window touches the initial time of the state interval (dotted position of sliding window). We can observe A unless the sliding window reaches the position that is drawn with dashed lines. The total observation time is therefore the length of the sliding window t_{max} plus the length of state interval A. The support (observation duration) is depicted at the bottom of the subfigure.

Subfigure (b) shows another example "A overlaps B". We can observe an instance of the pattern as soon as we can see state B and we loose it when A leaves the sliding window. If the pattern occurs multiple times, two things may happen: If there is a gap between the pattern instances, such that we loose the pattern in the meanwhile, then the support of the individual instances add up to the support of the pattern, as shown in subfigure (c). If there is no such gap (subfigure (d)), we see the pattern as soon as a first instance enters the sliding window until the last instance leaves the window. In the meantime, it does not matter *how many* instances are present, as long as there is at least one.

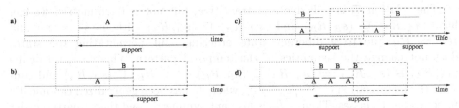

Fig. 3. Illustration of our notion of support.

If we divide the support of a pattern by the length of the state sequence plus the window width t_{max} we obtain the relative frequency p of the pattern: If we randomly select a window position we can observe the pattern with probability p. Also note that there is no need for discretization, we can handle time continuously by jumping from interval bound (initial or final time) to interval bound and integrating the support over the jump period. This is because observability of a pattern changes only if the sliding window meets one of the interval bounds.

5   Discovery of Temporal Rules

A pattern is called *frequent*, if its support exceeds a threshold $supp_{min}$. The task is to find all frequent temporal patterns in $NTP(\mathcal{S})$, from which we then create the temporal rules. To find all frequent patterns we start in a first database pass with the estimation of the support of every single state (also called candidate 1-patterns). After the kth run, we remove all candidates that have missed the minimum support and create out of the remaining frequent k-patterns a set of candidate $(k + 1)$-patterns whose support will be estimated in the next pass. This procedure is repeated until no more frequent patterns can be found. The fact that the support of a pattern is always less than or equal to the support of any of its subpatterns

$$\forall \text{patterns } P, Q : \quad Q \sqsubseteq P \Rightarrow \text{supp}(Q) \geq \text{supp}(P) \qquad (2)$$

guarantees that we do not miss any frequent patterns. At this level of detail the procedure is identical to association rule mining [2].

5.1 Candidate Generation

The number of potential candidates grows exponentially with the size k of the patterns. Efficient pruning techniques are therefore necessary to keep the increase in the number of candidates moderate. We use three different pruning techniques.

The technique that is used for the discovery of association rules [2] can still be applied to temporal patterns: Due to (2), every k-subpattern of a $(k+1)$-candidate must be frequent, otherwise the candidate itself cannot be frequent. To enumerate as few non-candidate $(k+1)$-patterns as possible, we join any two frequent k-patterns P and Q that share a common $(k-1)$-pattern as a prefix. Let us denote the remaining states in P and Q besides those in the prefix as p and q respectively. We denote the interval relationship between p and q in the candidate pattern $X = (s_X, R_X)$ as $R_X[k, k+1] = r$. Figure 4 illustrates how to build the $(k+1)$-pattern matrix R_X out of R_P and R_Q. Since R_P and R_Q are identical with respect to the first $k-1$ states in normalized form, the same is true for the new pattern X (indicated by the same submatrix A). The relationship between p and q and the first $k-1$ states can also be taken from R_P and R_Q. Thus, as we can see in Fig. 4(c), the only degree of freedom is r. From the $(k-1)$-pattern prefix and the two states p and q we thus can build up a $(k+1)$-pattern which is completely specified up to the relation between p and q.

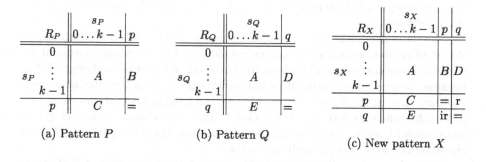

(a) Pattern P (b) Pattern Q (c) New pattern X

Fig. 4. Generating a candidate $(k+1)$-pattern X out of two k-patterns P and Q that are identical when restricted to the first $k-1$ states.

The freedom in choosing r yields 13 different patterns that might become candidate $(k+1)$-patterns, because there are 13 possible interval relationships. Since we can restrict ourselves without loss of generality to normalized patterns, the number of possible values for r reduces to a maximal number of 7. Before we check each of the seven $(k+1)$-patterns for frequent k-subpatterns, we apply another pruning technique based on the law of transitivity. For example, the two 2-patterns "A meets B" and "A meets C" share the primitive 1-pattern "A" as a common prefix. We have to fix the missing relationship between B and C to obtain a 3-candidate. The law of transitivity for interval relations [3] tells us that the possible set of interval relations is {is-started-by, equals, starts}. In normalized form, only 2 out of 7 possible relationships remain. In general, for each state $s(i)$ of the first $k-1$ states we apply Allen's transitivity table to the relationship between p and $s(i)$ ($R_P[k,i]$) and $s(i)$ and q ($R_Q[i,k]$). Only those values for r that do not contradict the results of the $k-1$ applications of the transitivity table yield a candidate pattern.

Finally, for every temporal pattern Q we maintain an *observed* and *expected* *support set* O_Q and E_Q, resp. The set O_Q contains all points in time that contribute to the support of the pattern Q, that is, all points in time in which the pattern can be observed in the sliding window. Before we consider a $(k+1)$-pattern P as a candidate pattern, we intersect[3] all sets O_Q of all k-subpatterns Q of P. The result gives us the expected support of P in E_P. The cardinality of E_P serves as a tighter upper bound of the support of P than $\min\{E_Q \mid Q \sqsubseteq P, \dim(Q) = k\}$ does. If it stays below supp_{min} the pattern cannot become a frequent pattern, therefore we do not consider it as a candidate.

5.2   Support Estimation

Again, due to space limitations we can give only a quick overview of the basic ideas, a more detailed report is currently in preparation (contact the author).

In order to estimate the support for the candidate patterns, we sweep through the state sequence and incrementally update the list of states which are currently visible in the sliding window. We also update the relation matrix for the states in the sliding window incrementally. By t_{act} we denote the right bound of the sliding window.

The set of candidate patterns is partitioned into three subsets, which we call the set of passive, active, and potential candidates. The set of passive candidates contains those candidates P that we do not expect in the current sliding window because the expected support does not contain the time of the current window position, that is, $t_{act} \notin E_P$. The set of potential candidates contains those candidates for which we have $t_{act} \in E_P$, that is, there is a chance of observing P in the window. Finally, the set of active patterns contains those patterns that are currently observable in the sliding window.

At the beginning all patterns are passive patterns. Associated with every pattern we have the set of expected support E_P, we therefore know in advance when the pattern will become a potential pattern, namely at *activation time* $a_P = \min\{t \mid t \in E_P\}$. If the set E_P is organized as a sorted list of intervals, the minimum is simply the left bound of the first interval in the list. We keep the set of passive patterns ordered by their activation time. Whenever t_{act} reaches the activation time of a pattern P, P becomes either a potential or active pattern, depending on whether P occurs in the sliding window or not. When P becomes

---

[3] The sets O_Q and E_Q can be organized as lists of intervals. The intersection is also a list of intervals. We only have to add up the interval lengths to obtain the cardinality.

a potential pattern, we remove the leading interval from the E_P list and store the *deactivation time* d_P (end of the interval), because at that time the pattern will fall back into the set of passive patterns.

A potential pattern P becomes a passive pattern if the fall back-time d_P has been reached by the sliding window. Whenever a new state interval enters the sliding window, we check for all potential patterns if an instance of the pattern can be found. (Since the set of potential pattern may become quite large, this is the most expensive operation.) If this is the case, the potential pattern becomes an active pattern, otherwise we keep it as a potential pattern. If a pattern instance has been found, we calculate the point in time when the pattern disappears and use it as the fall back-time for the active pattern.

Just like the set of passive patterns, the set of active patterns is sorted by their fall back-times. Whenever t_{act} reaches the fall back-time of an active pattern, we check whether a new pattern instance has entered the sliding window in the meanwhile. In this case the pattern remains an active pattern, but we update the fall back-time. Otherwise, depending on whether $d_P < t_{act}$ or not, the active pattern becomes a potential or passive pattern.

Whenever a pattern instance has been found, the support of the pattern is updated incrementally, that is, we insert the period of pattern observation (the support) into O_S. Since we have an upper bound of the remaining support (namely the cardinality of the continuously updated set E_P), we can perform a fourth online pruning test. If the support achieved so far (card(O_P)) plus the maximally remaining support (card(E_P)) drops below supp$_{min}$ we do not consider the pattern any longer. At the end of each database pass, the set E_P is empty and O_P contains the support of P, which is then subsequently used in the next candidate generation step for pruning.

5.3   Rule Generation

After having determined all frequent temporal patterns, we can construct rules $X \mapsto Y$ from every pair (X, Y) of frequent temporal patterns with $X \sqsubseteq Y$. We restrict ourselves to "forward rules", that is, rules that make conclusions in the future rather than in the past. If the confidence of the rule conf($A \to B$) = $\frac{\text{supp}(B)}{\text{supp}(A)}$ is greater than the minimal confidence, the rule is printed. Enumeration of all possible rules can be done efficiently using techniques described in [2].

5.4   Disjunctive Combination of Temporal Patterns

When analysing the rules obtained by the algorithm, we must keep in mind that we were seeking for the simple interval relationships only, that is, those relationships that consist of a single attribute $r \in \mathcal{I}$. If a process B is started some time after A has started, then this can result in a number of rules "$A \to B$" with temporal relationships *overlaps*, *meets*, and *before*. The confidence of the *true* relationship (which is in this case: A *overlaps/meets/before* B) might be very high, but the confidence values we observe for the three rules we have found are comparatively low. We are not allowed to add up the confidence values of all three rules in order to obtain the confidence of the composed rule. This would lead to an overestimation, because there might be sliding windows that contain multiple of these patterns simultaneously, and in this case we would count them twice (or more). Fortunately, it is possible to calculate the support of composed rules afterwards. The support of a pattern P which is a disjunction of two patterns Q and R can be calculated easily as $\text{supp}(P) = \text{card}(O_Q \cup O_R)$. The sets of observed support O_Q and O_R have been calculated already during the execution of the algorithm, all we have to do is to store the sets for later access. (Note that we cannot guarantee that we will find all frequent pattern compositions in this way. Several patterns that do not reach supp_{min} individually might fulfil this requirement after their combination.)

6   Evaluation and Discussion

We have examined air-pressure and wind strength/wind direction data from a small island in the northern sea[4]. From the time stamps we have also extracted the season. It is well known that local differences in air pressure are the cause for wind, therefore we should find some relationships between these variables. Although global weather forecast is (more or less) done perfectly by large-scale weather simulations, it is still not possible to precisely localize where a certain weather phenomenon will occur to which extent at what time. Rules about the qualitative behaviour of the air pressure curve indeed help sailors in short-term local weather forecasting [10].

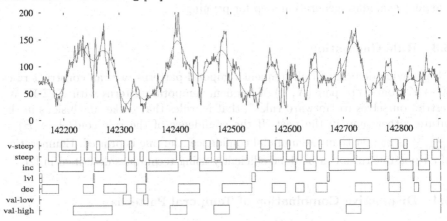

Fig. 5. Extracted features from time series: wind strength, Helgoland, April 1997.

The data has been measured hourly and we used 3, 6, and 9 years of data from 1991-1999 to test the algorithm. We have applied kernel smoothing in order to compensate for noise and to get more robust estimates of the first

---

[4] Helgoland, 54:11N 07:54O

and second derivative. Then, the smoothed series have been partitioned into primitive patterns like "increasing", "concave", "high-value", etc. See Fig. 5 for an example.

Table 1 shows the performance of the pattern mining algorithm with different average state densities, window widths, and state series lengths. The threshold $supp_{min}$ has been chosen to be 2% of the data period in all runs. The computation times ranged from a few seconds to 20 minutes on a 550 MHz Pentium III processor with 256MB main memory. We can see that the pruning techniques were quite efficient, besides a few exceptions, only 1-3% of all processed patterns became candidate patterns. The artificially generated data set has a rich pattern structure, on the average 45% of all candidates became frequent patterns. This value increases if we consider only runs with large window widths. If the state density D (average number of state intervals visible in the sliding window) is fixed, the run time is roughly linear in the size of the state series.

S	W	D	F	F/C	C/P	T	F	F/C	C/P	T	F	F/C	C/P	T
8	18	3.42	191	30.3	5.1	1.19	178	29.4	5.0	1.31	28	7.1	53.1	0.56
8	30	5.70	1,126	56.2	3.4	2.95	1,055	54.9	3.5	3.03	96	20.9	8.2	0.65
8	42	7.98	4,904	78.3	2.3	8.27	4,459	78.1	2.3	7.97	249	27.3	7.2	1.11
15	18	5.40	1,071	55.8	2.7	2.06	471	25.0	1.6	2.19	829	46.7	1.8	2.01
15	30	9.00	2,779	42.6	2.4	5.24	2,618	41.6	2.5	5.38	2,024	37.1	2.8	4.67
15	42	12.6	12,900	67.3	1.3	16.0	11,986	66.4	1.4	15.7	9,618	63.3	1.5	13.4
27	18	8.28	1,600	25.2	2.1	4.27	1,562	24.9	2.1	5.34	1,359	23.0	2.3	4.08
27	30	13.8	9,767	42.7	1.8	12.4	9,184	41.6	1.8	14.5	7,082	37.8	2.0	10.1
27	42	19.3	48,832	65.3	0.7	43.3	45,302	64.2	1.0	49.0	34,872	60.9	1.1	32.7

(a)   (b) years '97-'99   (c) years '94-'99   (d) years '91-'99

Table 1. Results of the algorithm. In all experiments the threshold $supp_{min}$ has been chosen to be 2% of the time series length (3, 6, and 9 years). Column S denotes the number distinct states in the series, column W denotes the window width (hours), column D the average state series density (average number of states visible in the window). Column F contains the number of frequent patterns, F/C the percentage of frequent patterns among candidate patterns, and C/P the percentage of candidate patterns among processed patterns (that is, candidate and pruned patterns). Column T shows the run time per 1000 state intervals in the series.

Due to the complexity of the temporal patterns, matching a k-pattern against the sliding window is $O(D^2)$. Therefore, the complexity of the analysis depends on all parameters that influence D, e.g. sliding window width, number and length of intervals generated from a time series, size of the set of labels, etc. Furthermore, if the sliding window content changes quickly, we have to check more frequently if potential candidates become active candidates. Another point is the number of "uninteresting" associations that are generated by the interval extraction: If the state series represents extracted local trends in time series it is natural that we observe many frequent patterns like "increasing segment before decreasing segment" or "concave before convex segment", and vice versa. These uninteresting frequent patterns can be combined to patterns with more than 2 states arbitrarily and have considerable impact on the number of frequent patterns (and thus on run-time).

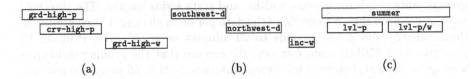

(a)   (b)   (c)

Fig. 6. Some exemplary rules. The bars indicate the temporal relationship between the intervals, their length has been chosen arbitrarily. The label in the bar describes a condition that holds in the interval (where **grd** denotes gradient, **crv** curvature, etc.).

Due to lack of space, here are only some exemplary rules. We have generated only those rules with a conclusion lying in the future (with respect to the intervals in the premise). Among them, there were many rules predicting a high gradient in wind strength, Fig. 6(a) shows one of them: If a period of highly increasing or decreasing air pressure overlaps a period of high curvature, it is very likely that the wind strength will change quickly (with a high gradient). The depicted rule occurs also with *during* and *meets* relationships between the air pressure states, so a disjunctive combination as described in Sect. 5.4 is promising. Figure 6(b) is an example for a rule that concludes from a change in wind direction to a strong change in wind strength. The rule in Fig. 6(c) tells us that stable weather (air pressure is nearly constant) is likely to be continued in summer, that is, a constant air pressure segment is followed by another constant air pressure period with low winds. Similar rules for other seasons can also be found, but with a much lower confidence value.

On the average, the confidence values of the rules are comparatively low (about 40-60% for the examples). This is because simple patterns (used in the premise) can be observed longer than complex patterns (patterns comprising premise and conclusion). To illustrate this, review Fig. 3(a)-(b), where the support of pattern "A" is greater than the support of pattern "A overlaps B", although A has the same length in both cases. This leads to confidence values below 1 even if every A overlaps a B in the examined state series. We are investigating on other measures for rule evaluation in [9].

7   Conclusion

We have proposed a technique for the discovery of temporal rules in state sequences, which might stem from multivariate time series for instance. The examples in Sect. 6 have shown that the proposed method is capable of finding meaningful rules that can be used as rules-of-thumb by a human, but also in a knowledge-based expert system. The rules can be easily interpreted by a domain expert, who can verify the rules or use them as an inspiration for further investigation. Even if there is already considerable background knowledge, the application of this method might be valuable if the known rules incorporate more variables than readily available. For instance, weather forecasting rules as discussed by Karnetzki [10] also use information about the general weather outlook (cloudiness) or information from the local weather forecasting station. Such information might be difficult to incorporate or expensive to measure, and in such a case one is interested in how much one can achieve by just using the available variables. Selection of the best rules gets further treatment in [9].

Acknowledgements. The author would like to thank Prof. F. Klawonn for critical review of this paper and the Deutsche Wetterdienst for providing the data.

References

[1] R. Agrawal, K.-L. Lin, H. S. Sawhney, and K. Shim. Fast similiarity search in the presence of noise, scaling, and translation in time-series databases. In *Proc. of the 21st Int. Conf. on Very Large Databases*, 1995.

[2] R. Agrawal, H. Mannila, R. Srikant, H. Toivonen, and A. I. Verkamo. Fast discovery of association rules. In [8], chapter 12, pages 307–328. MIT Press, 1996.

[3] J. F. Allen. Maintaing knowledge about temporal intervals. *Comm. ACM*, 26(11):832–843, 1983.

[4] B. R. Bakshi and G. Stephanopoulos. Reasoning in time: Modeling, analysis, and pattern recognition of temporal process trends. In *Advances in Chemical Engineering*, volume 22, pages 485–548. Academic Press, Inc., 1995.

[5] D. J. Berndt and J. Clifford. Finding patterns in time series: A dynamic programming approach. In [8], chapter 9, pages 229–248. MIT Press, 1996.

[6] A. C. Capelo, L. Ironi, and S. Tentoni. Automated mathematical modeling from experimental data: An application to material science. *IEEE Trans. on Systems, Man, and Cybernetics, Part C*, 28(3):356–370, Aug. 1998.

[7] G. Das, K.-I. Lin, H. Mannila, G. Renganathan, and P. Smyth. Rule discovery from time series. In *Proc. of the 4th Int. Conf. on Knowledge Discovery and Data Mining*, pages 16–22. AAAI Press, 1998.

[8] U. M. Fayyad, G. Piatetsky-Shapiro, P. Smyth, and R. Uthurusamy, editors. *Advances in Knowledge Discovery and Data Mining*. MIT Press, 1996.

[9] F. Höppner and F. Klawonn. Finding informative rules in interval sequences. In *Proc. of the 4th Int. Symp. on Intelligent Data Analysis*, Lissabon, Portugal, Sept. 2001. Springer.

[10] D. Karnetzki. *Luftdruck und Wetter*. Delius Klasing, 3 edition, 1999.

[11] K. B. Konstantinov and T. Yoshida. Real-time qualitative analysis of the temporal shapes of (bio)process variables. *Artificial Intelligence in Chemistry*, 38(11):1703–1715, Nov. 1992.

[12] B. Kuipers. *Qualitative Reasoning – Modeling and Simulation with Incomplete Knowledge*. MIT Press, 1994.

[13] H. Mannila, H. Toivonen, and A. I. Verkamo. Discovery of frequent episodes in event sequences. Technical Report 15, University of Helsinki, Finland, Feb. 1997.

[14] S. A. McIlraith. Qualitative data modeling: application of a mechanism for interpreting graphical data. *Computational Intelligence*, 5:111–120, 1989.

[15] R. Srikant and R. Agrawal. Mining sequential patterns: Generalizations and performance improvements. In *Proc. of the 5th Int. Conf. on Extending Database Technology*, Avignon, France, Mar. 1996.

Temporal Rule Discovery for Time-Series Satellite Images and Integration with RDB

Rie Honda[1] and Osamu Konishi[1]

Department of Mathematics and Information Science
Kochi University, Akebono-cyo 2-5-1 Kochi, 780-8520, JAPAN
{honda,konishi}@is.kochi-u.ac.jp
http://www.is.kochi-u.ac.jp

Abstract. Feature extraction and knowledge discovery from a large amount of image data such as remote sensing images have become highly required recent years. In this study, a framework for data mining from a set of time-series images including moving objects was presented. Time-series images are transformed into time-series cluster addresses by using clustering by two-stage SOM (Self-organizing map) and time-dependent association rules were extracted from it. Semantically indexed data and extracted rules are stored in the object-relational database, which allows high-level queries by entering SQL through the user interface. This method was applied to weather satellite cloud images taken by GMS-5 and its usefulness was evaluated.

1   Introduction

A huge amount of data has been stored in databases in the areas of business or science. Data mining or knowledge discovery from database (KDD) is a method for extracting unknown information such as rules and patterns from a large-scale database. The well-known data mining methods include decision tree, association rules [1] [2], classification, clustering, and time-series analysis [3], and there are some successful application studies for astronomical images such as SKICAT [5] and JARtool [4].

In our recent studies [7] [8], we have applied data mining methods such as clustering and association rules to a large number of time-series satellite weather images over the Japanese islands. Meteorological events are considered to be chaotic phenomena in that an object such as a mass of cloud changes its position and form continuously, and thus appropriate for experiments of spatial temporal data mining.

Features of our studies applied to the weather images are summarized as follows: application of data mining method to image classification and retrieval, feature description from time-series data, implementation of the result of classification as the user retrieval interface, and construction of the whole system as a domain-expert KDD supporting system.

We describe an overview of the system in Sect. 2. A clustering algorithm for time-sequential images and its experimental results are described in Sect. 3.

L. De Raedt and A. Siebes (Eds.): PKDD 2001, LNAI 2168, pp. 204–215, 2001.

Section 4 describes the algorithm of extraction of time-dependent association rules and its experimental results. Section 5 describes details of the construction of the database by using R-tree and the results of its implementation. Section 6 provides a conclusion.

2   System Overview

We constructed a weather image database that gathers the sequential changes of cloud images and aimed to construct the domain-expert analysis support system for these images. The flow of this system is shown in Fig. 1 and described as follows:

1. Clustering of frame images using a self-organizing map.
2. Transformation of time-series images into cluster address sequence.
3. Extraction of events and time-dependent rules from the time-sequential cluster addresses.
4. Indexing of events and rules by R-tree, and integration with the database.
5. Searching for time-sequential variation patterns and browsing of the retrieved data in the form of animation.

The above-described framework enables us to characterize enormous amount of images acquired at a regular time interval semi-automatically, and to retrieve the images by using the extracted rules. For example, this framework enables queries like "search for frequent events that occur between one typhoon and the next typhoon", or "search for a weather change such that a typhoon occurs within 10 days after a front and high pressure mass developed within the time interval of 5 days".

3   Time-Sequential Data Description by Using Clustering

3.1   Data Set Description

Satellite weather images, taken by GMS-5 and received at the Institute of Industrial Science of Tokyo University, are archived at the Kochi University weather page (http://weather.is.kochi-u.ac.jp). In this study, we used infrared band (IR1) images around Japanese islands, which reflect the cloud distribution very well. The size of image is 640-pixels in width and 480-pixels in height. Each image is taken every hour, and about 9000 images are archived every year.

We considered that conventional image processing methods might be unable to detect moving objects such as the cloud masses that change their position as time proceeds. Thus we used the following SOM-based method for the automatic clustering of images by taking the raster image intensity vectors as the inputs.

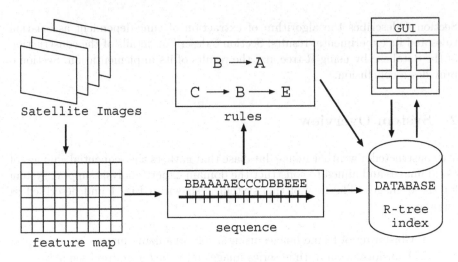

Fig. 1. Overview of the system.

3.2   Clustering and Kohonen's Self-Organizing Map

Kohonen's self-organizing map (SOM) [9] is a paradigm which was suggested in 1990, which has been widely used to provide a rough structure to a given non-structured information. The SOM is a two-layer network composed of a combination of the input layer and the competition layer that is trained through iterative non-supervised learning.

Each unit of the input layer and the competition layer has a vector whose components correspond to the input pattern elements. The algorithm of the SOM is described as follows: Let the input pattern vector $V \in R^n$ as $V = [v_1, v_2, v_3, \cdots, v_n]$, and the weight of union from the input vector to a unit i as $U_i = [u_{i1}, u_{i2}, u_{i3}, \cdots, u_{in}]$. Initial values of u_{ij} are given randomly. V is compared with all U_i, and the best matching unit which has the smallest Euclidean distance is determined and signified by the subscript c.

$$c = \mathrm{argmin}|V - U_i|. \tag{1}$$

Weight vectors of the unit c and its neighbors N_c, which is the area of $N \times N$ units around the unit c, are adjusted to increase the similarity as follows,

$$u_{ij}^{new} = \begin{cases} u_{ij}^{old} + \alpha(t)(v_j - u_{ij}) & (i \in N_c) \\ u_{ij}^{old} & (i \notin N_c), \end{cases} \tag{2}$$

where

$$\alpha(t) = \alpha_0 \left(1 - t/T\right), \tag{3}$$

$$N(t) = N_0 \left(1 - t/T\right). \tag{4}$$

The $\alpha(t)$ $N(t)$ are the learning rate and the size of neighbors at the time of t iterations, respectively, α_0 and N_0 is the initial learning rate and the size of

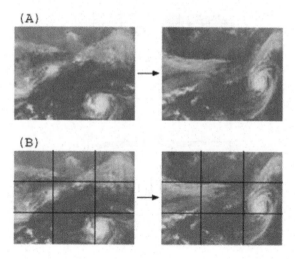

Fig. 2. Problem for clustering of weather images.

neighbors, and T is the total number of iterations of learning. The learning rate and the size of neighbor decreases as the learning proceeds to stabilize it.

The input signals V are classified into the activated (closest) unit U_c and projected onto the competition grids. The distance on the competition grids reflects the similarity between the patterns. After the training is completed, the obtained competition grids represent a natural relationship between the patterns of input signals entered into the network. Hereafter we call the competition grids obtained after the learning as the feature map.

3.3   Clustering by Two-Stage SOM

Figure 2 represents the problem of clustering of weather images. Two images in Fig. 2(A) are considered to have the same features of a typhoon and a front, although their forms and positions change as time proceeds. When we take the input vectors simply as the raster image intensity vectors, these images are classified into the different groups based on the spatial variations of intensity. We considered that this difficulty is avoided by dividing the images into blocks as shown in Fig. 2(B).

The procedure adopted here, named two-stage SOM, is shown in Fig. 3 schematically and described as follows:

stage 1 **Clustering of pattern cells**
  step 1 All Images are divided into $N \times M$ blocks.
  step 2 Learning by SOM is performed by entering the each block's raster image intensity vector as the input vector successively.
  step 3 Each block of the original images are projected onto the first SOM feature map and characterized with the closest unit address. We refer to this characterized blocks as the pattern cells.

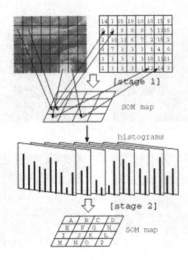

Fig. 3. Clustering of weather images by SOM.

stage 2 **Clustering of the images by using frequency histograms of pattern cells.**

step 1 Each image is transformed into the frequency histogram of the pattern cells.

step 2 The feature map of SOM is learned by entering each image's pattern cell frequency histogram as the input vector.

step 3 Each images are projected onto the second SOM feature map and characterized with the closest unit address.

Although the information of spatial distribution of pattern is lost by transforming images into frequency histograms of pattern cells (in step 1 of stage 2), this enables flexible classification of time-series images which have similar objects at different positions as shown in Fig. 2b as the same type of images.

Hereafter we refer the unit as the cluster, and express the cluster addresses by the characters of A, B, C, ···, P in the raster-scan order from the upper left corner to the lower right corner of 4×4 feature map.

3.4   Result of Experiments on Clustering

In the experiments, we sampled GMS-5 IR1 images with 8 hour time intervals obtained between 1997 and 1998, and composed two data set for 1997 and 1998 which include 1044 and 966 images, respectively. We defined number of blocks for each image to be 12 × 16, considering the typical size of cloud masses. The sizes of feature maps of both the first stage SOM and the second stage SOM are defined to be 4 × 4, which are determined by trial and error. Learning processes are iterated 8000-10000 times.

The result of the experiment shows that images including similar features are distributed into similar clusters. We describe clusters semantically by specifying

Table 1. Semantical description of each cluster

cluster address		season	prominent characteristics
1997	1998		
A	A,F,O	spring, summer	front, typhoon
J	H	spring, summer	rainy season's front, typhoon
N		spring, summer	high pressure, typhoon
B,C		spring autumn	high pressure in the west
		and low pressure in the east	
D,H	E	spring, autumn	band-like high-pressure
F	B	spring, autumn	front
P	B	spring, autumn	migratory anticyclone
I	J	summer	Pacific high pressure, front
M		summer	Pacific high pressure, typhoon
	C	summer	Pacific high-pressure
E	D	autumn	migratory anticyclone
G	P	autumn, winter	linear clouds
K,L	L,M	winter	winter type, whirl-like
		or linear cloud	
O	I,K,N	winter	cold front

Table 2. Accuracies of clustering

year	Recall	Precision
1997	86.0%(876/1022)	84.6%(876/1044)
1998	86.7%(838/945)	86.7%(838/966)

the season in which the clusters are observed, based on the frequency of each cluster every month, and by describing the representative object such as front or typhoon by means of visual observation of images in the cluster in a domain-expert like view. Table 1 shows the semantical descriptions of clusters for 1997 and 1998. The description of each clusters for 1998 is different from that for 1997 since we performed the SOM learning for these data sets independently. However, most of the groups are observed in both maps, thus the obtained result is meaningful even in the view of the domain-expert knowledge.

To evaluate the accuracy of clustering quantitatively, we defined the following parameters,

$$Recall = A/(A + B), Precision = A/(A + C), \qquad (5)$$

where A is the number of the relevant images classified into the cluster, B is the number of the relevant images classified into the other cluster, and C is the number of the nonrelevant images classified into the cluster. Relevance of images are evaluated by classifying the images visually.

Table 2 shows the values of recall for 1997 and 1998 to be 86.0% and 86.7%, respectively, and that the values of precision are 84.6% and 86.7%, respectively.

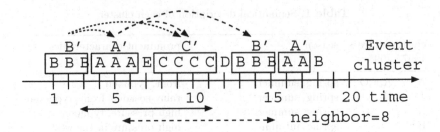

Fig. 4. Example of description of cluster sequence, event sequence, and extraction of time-dependent association rules.

These values indicate that two-stage SOM can successfully learn the features of weather images and can classify them with a high accuracy.

4   Time-Sequential Analysis and Extraction of Time-Dependent Association Rules

4.1   Time-Dependent Association Rule

In this study we extract time-dependent association rules such as "weather pattern B occurs after weather pattern A", which modify the episode rules [11] [12] using the concept of cohesion to evaluate its significance.

First we express the sequence of a weather pattern by $(A, 1), (A, 2), (C, 3), \cdots$ where each component is a pair of cluster address of image (obtained by SOM) and its observation time. Then we define the event e_i in the sequence as continuously occurring clusters, which is expressed by

$$e_i =< C_i, S_{if}, TS_i, TE_i > \quad (i = 1, \cdots, n), \tag{6}$$

where C_i is the cluster address, S_{if} is the continuity, TS_i is the starting time, and TE_i is the ending time. The sequence S is then represented by

$$S =< e_1, e_2, \cdots, e_n >, \tag{7}$$

where n is the total number of the events in the sequence. Figure 4 shows a representation of event sequence in the case of $S_{if} \geq 2$.

We extract the event pairs that occur closely in the sequence by introducing a local time window. Assuming the local time window with the length of *neighbor*, the simple local variation pattern E is represented by

$$E = \langle [e_i, e_j], neighbor \rangle \quad (i \in \{1, \cdots, n-1\}, j \in \{2, \cdots, n\}), \tag{8}$$

where $[e_i, e_j]$ is a combination of the two events e_i and e_j which satisfies $i < j$ and $TS_j - TE_i < neighbor$.

Although *neighbor* is an idea similar with a time window in episode rules [11] [12], we use this concept to extract only serial episodes such as $A \Rightarrow B$, excluding parallel episode rules and combination of serial/parallel episode rules which are included in [11] [12].

Furthermore we use the method of co-occurring term-pair for document analysis [10] to evaluate strength of correlation of event pairs which occurs in the local time window and to extract the prominent pairs as rules. The cohesion of the event e_i and e_j in a local time window is defined by

$$cohesion(e_i, e_j) = \frac{E_f(e_i, e_j)}{\sqrt{[f(e_i) \times f(e_j)]}}, \tag{9}$$

where $f(e_i)$ and $f(e_j)$ are the frequencies of e_i and e_j, respectively, and $E_f(e_i, e_j)$ is the frequency of the co-occurrence of both e_i and e_j in a local time window. The time-dependent association rules are extracted when the event pair has larger cohesion than the threshold.

The procedure of extraction of time-dependent association rules in each local time window with the length of *neighbor* is described in the following:

step 1 The frequency of each event $f(e)$ in a local time window is determined.

step 2 A combinational set of event pairs in a local time window are listed as rule candidates.

step 3 Candidate pairs are sorted lexicographically in regard to the first event and then the following event.

step 4 The same event pairs are bound, co-occurrence frequency of each candidate pair $E_f(e_i, e_j)$ is counted, and cohesion are calculated.

step 5 The event pairs that have larger cohesions than the threshold are extracted as rules.

It should be noted that extraction is performed for each local time window by sliding its position.

Strongly correlated event pairs have large *cohesion*s even if each event occurs less frequently. Inversely, weakly correlated event pairs have small *cohesion*s even if each event occurs very frequently.

4.2 Result of Experiments Regarding Time-Dependent Association Rules

We applied the above-described time-dependent association rule extraction to the sequence of cluster address obtained in 3.4. Here we take the threshold of cohesion of 0.4 and *neighbor* ranging from 10 to 50. Since we sampled images every 8 hours, the virtual length of *neighbor* is between 3.3 days and 16.7 days.

Table 3 shows the relationship between the size of *neighbor* and the number of extracted rules. Although the assessment of the contents of the extracted rules and development of its user-interface are ongoing issues, the result suggests the similar numbers of rules are extracted from the different year's data set, which indicates that our present method is useful and robust.

Table 3. Relationship between *neighbor* and number of rules.

neighbor	10	20	30	40	50
number of rules(1997)	17	63	116	165	207
number of rules(1998)	7	50	98	166	218

5   Integration of Extracted Rules and the Relational Database

We integrate image sequences and the extracted rules with the relational database and construct the system which supports analysis and discovery by domain-experts. Here we index the time sequences by using R-tree [6] to enable fast query operation.

5.1   Indexing by R-Tree

As shown in Fig. 5, there is a natural hierarchical enclosure relations between time sequences such as year, season, month, rule, and event. By using the method of R-tree [6], we can express these time sequences by the minimum bounding rectangles (defined by the staring time and the ending time of sequence) and store them into the hierarchical tree which reflects the enclosure relation. This enables fast query operation of weather patterns by using month or seasons as the search key.

5.2   Definition of Attributes

We stored extracted patterns in the following three tables: "series(l_term, r_term, cohesion, location, first, last)[1], "date_id (id, date), and "_series (term, first, last)[2] that represent contents of time-dependent rules, the relationship between image ID and the observation time, and the contents of time-dependent rule components (events), respectively.

5.3   Query by SQL

Storing extracted patterns in the database enables the secondary retrieval of the various complex patterns by using SQL statements. We show an example of complex queries and the corresponding SQL statement in the following:

---

[1] "l_term" and "r_term" are the cluster addresses of the first event and the second event of extracted rules, respectively, "location" is the reference to the R-tree rectangles, and "first" and "last" are the image IDs of the "l_term" starting point and the "r_term" ending point, respectively.

[2] "term" is the cluster number of the event, "first" and "last" are the image IDs of the starting point and the ending point of "term", respectively.

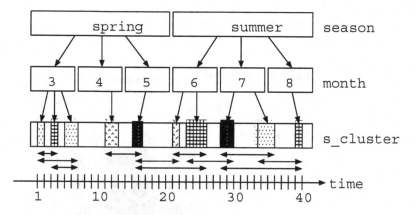

Fig. 5. Indexing by using R-tree, remarking at the continuing sequence. Arrows at the bottom represent minimum bounding boxes of rules.

"Search for a weather change in 1997 such that a typhoon occurred within 10 days after a front and a successive high pressure mass developed within the time interval of 5 days."

```
select t1.first, t2.last, t3.date, t4.date³
from series t1 , e_series t2 , date_id t3 , date_id t4
where ( t1.l_term = "A" or t1.l_term = "F" or t1.l_term = "I" or
t1.l_term = "J" or t1.l_term = "O") and ( t1.r_term = "B" or
t1.r_term = "C" or t1.r_term = "D" or t1.r_term = "H" or t1.r_term =
"I" or t1.r_term = "M" or t1.r_term = "N" ) and ( t2.term = "A" or
t2.term = "J" or t2.term = "M" or t2.term = "N") and (t1.last-t1.first
<15) and (t2.last- t1.first <30) and (t1.last <= t2.last) and t3.id
= t1.first and t4.id = t2.last
```

5.4   Result of Implementation and Issues in the Future Work

Figure 6 shows an example of the user interface of integrated KDD support system for weather information. Here we can retrieve the weather pattern by using the season, the first event and the second event as the search keys. Matched sequences are listed in the lower left frame, and by selecting one in the list, the corresponding weather variation is shown as an animation in the lower right frame. To deal with much more complex queries, we also prepare the user interface which accepts SQL query directly.

In this system, however, users are unable to operate the process of primary knowledge extraction by changing parameters such as the size of SOM, cohesion threshold, and the size of the local time window. There are two approaches to

---

[3] Note that time interval 1 in this SQL statement corresponds to 8 hours, and capital alphabets indicate the cluster addresses described in table 1.

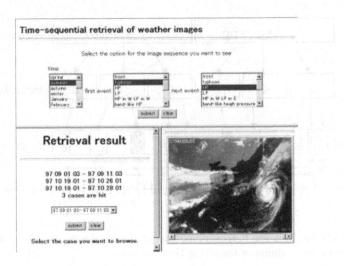

Fig. 6. Example of the result of retrieval from sequential image data.

solve this problem: one is incorporation of the optimization process of these parameters[4] and another is improvement of interactiveness of the user interface. Examination on both approaches will be one of most significant issues in the future work. Also we consider designing of the user interface to stimulate expert's natural discovery is also important. Furthermore, improvement of time sequential pattern analysis besides simple rule extraction will be significant to deal with temporal patterns more meaningful for domain-experts including prediction.

6   Conclusion

We applied clustering and time-dependent association rules to a large-scale content-based image database of weather satellite images. Each image is automatically classified by two-stage SOM. We also extracted unknown rules from time-sequential data expressed by a sequence of cluster addresses by using time-dependent association rules. Furthermore, we developed a knowledge discovery support system for domain experts, which retrieves image sequences using extracted events and association rules. From the perspective that high-level queries make the analysis easier, we stored the extracted rules in the database to admit sophisticated queries described by SQL. The retrieval responses to various queries shows the usefulness of this approach.

The framework presented in this study, clustering ⇒ transformation into time-sequential data ⇒ extraction of time-dependent association rules, is considered to be also useful in managing enormous multimedia data sets which include

---

[4] For examples, the algorithm of growing hierarchical SOM [13], which is capable of growing both in terms of map size as well as the three-dimensional tree structure, will be effective for the adaptation of map size. We would like to examine this algorithm in the future work.

sequential patterns such as video and audio information or result of numerical simulation.

Acknowledgements. The authors are grateful to Prof. T. Kikuchi for offering us well-prepared GMS-5 images, We also thank to K. Katayama, and H. Takimoto for their past contribution. This research is partly supported by grants-in-aid for intensive research(A)(1)(Project 10143102) from the Ministry of Education, Science, and Culture of Japan.

References

1. Agrawal, R., Imelinski, T., Swani, A.: Mining in association rules between sets of items in large database. Proc. ACM SIGMOD International Conference (1993) 207–216
2. Agrawal, R. and Srikant, R.: Fast Algorithms for mining association rules. Proceedings of 20th International Conference on VLDB (1994) 487–499.
3. Alex, A.F., Simon, H.L.: Mining very large databases with parallel processing. Kluwer Academic Publishers (1998)
4. Burl, M.C., Asker, L., Smyth, P., Fayyad, U.M., Perona, P., Crumpler, L., Aubele, J.: Learning to recognize volcanos on Venus. Machine Learning, Vol. 30, (2/3) (1998) 165–195
5. Fayyad, U.M., Djorgovski, S.G., Weir, N.: Automatic the analysis and cataloging of sky surveys. Advances in Knowledge Discovery and Data Mining, AAAI Press/MIT Press (1996) 471–493
6. Guttman, A.: R-trees: a dynamic index structure for spatial searching. Proc. ACM SIGMOD International Conference (1984) 47–57
7. Katayama, K., Konishi, O.: Construction satellite image databases for supporting knowledge discovery(in Japanese). Transaction of Information Processing Society of Japan, Vol. 40, SIG5(TOD2) (1999) 69–78
8. Katayama, K., Konishi, O.: Discovering co-occurencing patterns in event sequences (in Japanese). DEWS'99 (1999)
9. Kohonen, T.: Self-organizing maps. Springer (1995)
10. Konishi, O.: A statistically build knowledge based terminology construction system (in Japanese). Transaction of Information Processing Society of Japan, Vol. 30, 2 (1989) 179–189
11. Mannila, H., H. Tovinen and A. I. Verkano. Discovering frequent episodes in sequences. In First International Conference on Knowledge Discovery and Data Mining(KDD'95), AAAI Press (1995) 210–215
12. Mannila, H., Tovinen, H.: Discovering generalized episodes using minimal occurrences. In Proceeding of the Second International Conference on Knowledge Discovery and Data Mining(KDD'96), AAAI Press (1996) 146–151
13. Merkl, D. Rauber, A.: Uncovering the hierarchical structure of text archives by using unsupervised neural network with adaptive architecture. In PAKDD 2000 (2000) 384–395

Using Grammatical Inference to Automate Information Extraction from the Web

Theodore W. Hong and Keith L. Clark

Department of Computing
Imperial College of Science, Technology, and Medicine
180 Queen's Gate, London SW7 2BZ
United Kingdom
{twh1,klc}@doc.ic.ac.uk

Abstract. The World-Wide Web contains a wealth of semistructured information sources that often give partial/overlapping views on the same domains, such as real estate listings or book prices. These partial sources could be used more effectively if integrated into a single view; however, since they are typically formatted in diverse ways for human viewing, extracting their data for integration is a difficult challenge. Existing learning systems for this task generally use hardcoded *ad hoc* heuristics, are restricted in the domains and structures they can recognize, and/or require manual training. We describe a principled method for automatically generating extraction wrappers using grammatical inference that can recognize general structures and does not rely on manually-labelled examples. Domain-specific knowledge is explicitly separated out in the form of declarative rules. The method is demonstrated in a test setting by extracting real estate listings from web pages and integrating them into an interactive data visualization tool based on dynamic queries.

1 Introduction

The World-Wide Web contains a wealth of information resources, many of which can be considered as semistructured[1] data sources: that is, sources containing data that is fielded but not constrained by a global schema. For example, documents such as product catalogs, staff directories, and classified advertisement listings fall into this category. Often, multiple sources provide partial or overlapping views on the same underlying domain. As a result, there has been much interest in trying to combine and cross-reference disparate data sources into a single integrated view.

Parsing web pages for information extraction is a significant obstacle, however. Although the markup formatting of web sources provides some hints about their record and field structure, this structure is also obscured by the presentation aspects of formatting intended for human viewing and the wide variation in formats from site to site. Manually constructing extraction wrappers is tedious and time-consuming, because of the large number of sites to be covered and the need to keep up-to-date with frequent formatting changes.

L. De Raedt and A. Siebes (Eds.): PKDD 2001, LNAI 2168, pp. 216–227, 2001.
© Springer-Verlag Berlin Heidelberg 2001

We propose the use of grammatical inference to automate the construction of wrappers and facilitate the process of information extraction. Grammatical inference is a subfield of machine learning concerned with inferring formal descriptions of sets from examples. One application is the inference of formal grammars as generalized structural descriptions for documents.

By applying an inference algorithm to a training sample of web pages from a given site, we can learn a grammar describing their format structure. Using domain-specific knowledge encoded in declarative rules, we can identify productions corresponding to records and fields. The grammar can then be compiled into a wrapper which extracts data from those pages. Since the data pages on a given website typically follow a common site format, particularly if they are dynamically created from scripts, such wrappers should be able to operate on the rest of the pages as well.

This process can be largely automated, making it easy to re-generate wrappers when sites change formatting. Although others have explored the use of machine learning for wrapper creation, previous systems have generally relied on hardcoded *ad hoc* heuristics or the manual labelling of examples, and/or have been restricted in the domains and structures they can recognize. Our method is more principled, based on an objective method for inferring structure and a description language (context-free grammars) of high expressive power. We avoid manual intervention as far as possible and explicitly separate out domain-specific knowledge using declarative rules. These characteristics should make our system easier to use and more broadly applicable in different domains.

Taking the real estate domain as an example, we demonstrate the use of our approach to extract property listings from a set of mock web pages. We also briefly show an interactive data visualization tool based on dynamic queries for exploring the resulting high-dimensional data space.

The rest of this paper is organized as follows: in Sect. 2, we introduce the formal background to grammatical inference before describing our inference algorithm in Sect. 3. We then apply the algorithm to the real estate domain in Sect. 4. Related work is discussed in Sect. 5, and finally Sect. 6 gives conclusions and future work.

2   Grammatical Inference

Grammatical inference[17] is a class of inductive inference in which the target is a formal language (a set of strings over some alphabet Σ) and the hypothesis space is some family of grammars. The objective is to infer a consistent grammar for the unknown target language, given a finite set of examples.

The classical approach to grammatical inference was first given by Gold[13], who introduced the notion of *identification in the limit*. This notion is concerned with the limiting behavior of an inference algorithm on an infinite sequence of examples. Formally, a *complete presentation* of a language L is an infinite sequence of ordered pairs (w, l) in $\Sigma^* \times \{0,1\}$, where $l = 1$ if $l \in L$ and 0 otherwise, and every string $w \in \Sigma^*$ appears at least once. If an inference method

$\mathcal{M}$ is run on larger and larger initial segments of a complete presentation, it will generate an infinite sequence of guesses g_1, g_2, g_3, etc. $\mathcal{M}$ is said to *identify L in the limit* if there exists some number n such that all of the guesses g_i are the same for $i \geq n$, and g_n is equivalent to L.

This approach is not directly applicable to the web document task, since only positive examples are available (these being the actual documents existing at a site). Gold showed that any class of languages containing all the finite languages and at least one infinite language cannot be identified in the limit from only positive examples without negative ones. For example, the classes of regular and context-free languages both fit this criterion. The problem is that the task is under-constrained. Given only positive examples, the inferencer has no basis for choosing among hypotheses which are too general (e.g. the language consisting of all strings), too specific (e.g. the language consisting of exactly the examples seen so far), or somewhere in between.

3   Inference Algorithm

We approach the inference problem differently as a search for the *simplest* grammar which has a consistent *fit* with the provided sample, on the assumption that simple grammars are more likely to convey meaningful structure. We introduce a learning bias to constrain the search by starting from a specialized grammar which has high fit but low simplicity, and applying various transformations to generalize and simplify it while retaining fit. To guide this process, we take the set of *stochastic context-free grammars* as the hypothesis space and define a complexity function on it in terms of description length. Stochastic context-free grammars[4] are context-free grammars with probabilities attached to their productions. The probabilities aid inference by providing additional information about the relative weight of alternative productions—for example, given two alternatives for some nonterminal, are both equally important or is one likely to be just noise? This information is useful for assessing relative complexity and performing simplifications or extracting data later on.

3.1   Measuring Grammar Complexity

Let G be a stochastic context-free grammar with productions and associated probabilities given by:

$$
\begin{aligned}
X_1 &\rightarrow w_{11} \mid w_{12} \mid \ldots \mid w_{1,m_1} \quad [P_{11}, P_{12}, \ldots, P_{1,m_1}] \\
X_2 &\rightarrow w_{21} \mid w_{22} \mid \ldots \mid w_{2,m_2} \quad [P_{21}, P_{22}, \ldots, P_{2,m_2}] \\
&\vdots \\
X_n &\rightarrow w_{n1} \mid w_{n2} \mid \ldots \mid w_{n,m_n} \quad [P_{n1}, P_{n2}, \ldots, P_{n,m_n}] \, ,
\end{aligned}
\tag{1}
$$

where the X_i are nonterminals, the w_{ij} are alternatives, and the P_{ij} are the probabilities associated to those alternatives (i.e. $\sum_{j=1}^{m_n} P_{ij} = 1$ for each i).

Following Cook *et al.*[7], we define the complexity $C(G)$ as:

$$C(G) = \sum_{i=1}^{n} \sum_{j=1}^{m_n} - \log P_{ij} + c(w_{ij}) \tag{2}$$

where $c(w_{ij})$ is a second complexity function on the w_{ij} strings. This definition has the intuitively desirable properties that the complexity of G is the sum of the complexities of its productions and that the complexity of a production is the sum of the complexities of its alternatives. The complexity of an alternative has two components, the information-theoretic information content of its probability and the complexity of the string produced. Finally, the complexity of a string w is a function of its length and the proportions of distinct symbols in it:

$$c(w) = (K + 1) \log(K + 1) - \sum_{i=1}^{r} k_i \log k_i \tag{3}$$

where w has length K and contains r distinct symbols each occurring $k_1, k_2, \ldots,$ k_r times, respectively. Longer and more varied strings are rated more complex.

3.2   Inference as Search

We can formulate the goal of looking for the simplest consistent grammar as a search in the space of grammars where the cost function is the complexity function C. Our starting point is the overspecific grammar that simply generates the training set with perfect fit:

$$S \rightarrow w_1 \mid w_2 \mid \ldots \mid w_m \qquad [P_1, P_2, \ldots, P_m] \ , \tag{4}$$

where $w_1 \ldots w_m$ are the strings occurring in the set and $P_1 \ldots P_m$ are their relative frequencies. If all the strings are different, then the P_i will all be equal to $1/m$; however, the P_i may vary if some strings appear more than once in the set. This initial grammar will generally have very high complexity.

We can then perform a search by considering various transformation steps which might lower the complexity and generalize the grammar while retaining good fit. Some of the transformations used (again following [7]) are:

1. Substitution: If a substring s occurs multiple times in different alternatives (e.g. in the grammar $X_1 \rightarrow asb$, $X_2 \rightarrow csd$), create a new rule $Y \rightarrow s$ and replace all occurrences of s by Y's. This transformation helps identify subunits of structure. For example, when applied to the productions "John is eating cake" and "Mary is eating bread," it will separate "is eating" into another rule.

2. Disjunction: If two substrings s and t occur in similar contexts (e.g. in the grammar $X_1 \rightarrow asb$, $X_2 \rightarrow atb$), create a new rule $Y \rightarrow s \mid t$ and replace all occurrences of s and t by Y's. This transformation introduces generalization based on context. For example, when applied to the productions "John throws baseballs" and "John catches baseballs," it will propose "throws" and "catches" as alternatives for the same production.

3. Expansion: Remove a rule $Y \to s \mid t \mid \ldots \mid v$ by replacing every alternative that mentions Y with a set of alternatives in which Y is replaced with s, t, etc. This can reverse previous substitutions and disjunctions later on.
4. Truncation: Remove alternatives having very low probability and redistribute their probability among the remaining alternatives. This can be used to remove noise below some threshold.
5. Normalization: Merge redundant alternatives (e.g. $X \to s \mid s$) and drop productions that are inaccessible (cannot be reached from the start symbol) or blocking (result in some nonterminal that cannot be rewritten). This is often necessary to "clean up" grammars to show the full extent of simplification resulting from another transformation.

Other variations on these transformations are also considered. For practical reasons, since the branching factor of possible search steps can be very large (sometimes exceeding 100), we perform searching using a greedy deterministic hill-climbing strategy. Simulated annealing is another possibility we are examining.

3.3   Example: Parenthesis Expressions

To demonstrate the algorithm, we consider the language of balanced parenthesis strings. Take the set of all such strings up to length 6 as the training set, with frequencies as shown (to be justified later):

$$\text{sample} = \{(), ()(), (()), ()()(), ()(()), (())(), ((())), ((()))\} \tag{5}$$
$$[0.5, 0.125, 0.125, 0.0625, 0.03125, 0.03125, 0.0625, 0.0625] \ .$$

The initial grammar, with complexity 99.68, is:

$$S \to () \mid ()() \mid (()) \mid ()()() \mid ()(()) \mid (())() \mid ((())) \mid ((())) \tag{6}$$
$$[0.5, 0.125, 0.125, 0.0625, 0.03125, 0.03125, 0.0625, 0.0625] \ .$$

Ten substrings are candidates for substitution: (),)(, ((,)), ()(,)(), ((,)), ()(, and (()). The greatest reduction in complexity is obtained by substituting on (). Since it already appears as an alternative for S, we simply substitute S for () everywhere. The resulting grammar has complexity 88.09:

$$S \to () \mid SS \mid (S) \mid SSS \mid S(S) \mid (S)S \mid (SS) \mid ((S)) \tag{7}$$
$$[0.5, 0.125, 0.125, 0.0625, 0.03125, 0.03125, 0.0625, 0.0625] \ ,$$

Now the repeated substrings are SS, (S, S), and (S). Choosing (S) gives:

$$S \to () \mid SS \mid (S) \mid SSS \mid SS \mid SS \mid (SS) \mid (S) \tag{8}$$
$$[0.5, 0.125, 0.125, 0.0625, 0.03125, 0.03125, 0.0625, 0.0625] \ .$$

After normalizing by merging redundant alternatives and summing their associated probabilities, we obtain a grammar with complexity 42.19:

$$S \to () \mid SS \mid (S) \mid SSS \mid (SS) \tag{9}$$
$$[0.5, 0.1875, 0.1875, 0.0625, 0.0625] \ .$$

The final set of repeated substrings are SS, $(S$, and $S)$, of which SS lowers complexity the most. This gives:

$$S \to () \mid SS \mid (S) \mid SS \mid (S)$$
$$[0.5, 0.1875, 0.1875, 0.0625, 0.0625] \,, \tag{10}$$

which after normalizing is the usual grammar for the parenthesis language:

$$S \to () \mid SS \mid (S)$$
$$[0.5, 0.25, 0.25] \,. \tag{11}$$

The final complexity is 20.51. Notice that if these probabilities are used to generate a set of strings up to length 6, we recover the string frequencies in the original sample. In this example, only substitution and normalization operations were used, but in general other transformations may be needed as well.

4 Information Extraction

We tested our algorithm on a set of mock web pages containing London real estate listings. The pages all followed the same general layout (see Figs. 1 and 2) but contained varying numbers of listings on each page, some containing pictures of the described property and some without. The set of pages was taken as the training set and the algorithm attempted to construct a suitable description from which extraction wrappers could be generated.

4.1 Grammatical Inference Phase

The web pages in the training set were first converted to abstract strings over the alphabet {HTML tag types} ∪ {text}. This was done by discarding HTML attributes from the tags encountered, so that tags of the same type (e.g. anchor start tags) would be treated as the same alphabet symbol (e.g. a). Free text occurring between tags was converted to the symbol text. In using this transformation, we assume that structure is mainly present at the tag type level and focus on that level by ignoring variations in text and attributes (e.g. href values). For example, two contact links:

```
<hr><a href="mailto:sales@a.com">A-1 Realtors</a>
<hr><a href="mailto:help@b.com">Bee Estate Agents</a>
```

would both be transformed to the same abstract string, hr a text /a.

Each page string then became an alternative in the initial grammar, which had perfect fit but high complexity (1056.32):

$$S \to \begin{array}{l} \text{html head...table tr td b text /b br text.../html} \\ \mid \text{html head...table tr td img b text /b br.../html} \\ \mid etc. \end{array} \tag{12}$$

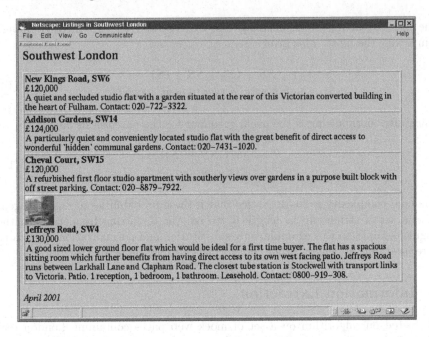

Fig. 1. A sample real estate listing page

```
<html><head>
<title>Listings in Southwest London</title>
</head>
<body>
<h1>Southwest London</h1>
<table border=1 width=100%>
<tr><td><b>New Kings Road, SW6</b><br>
&pound;120,000<br>
A quiet and secluded studio flat with a garden situated at
the rear of this Victorian converted building in the heart
of Fulham. Contact: 020-722-3322.
</td></tr>...
```

Fig. 2. Part of the HTML source for Fig. 1

The inference algorithm ran in five seconds on a Pentium 233 and examined 386 candidate grammars, lowering the complexity to a value of 119.19 (see Fig. 3 for the quality curve). The final grammar was:

$$
\begin{aligned}
S \rightarrow{}& \texttt{html head title text /title /head body h1 text /h1} \\
& \texttt{table } T \texttt{ /table p address text /address /body /html} \\
T \rightarrow{}& TT \mid \texttt{tr td } U \texttt{ b text /b br text br text /td /tr} \\
U \rightarrow{}& e \mid \texttt{img br .}
\end{aligned}
\tag{13}
$$

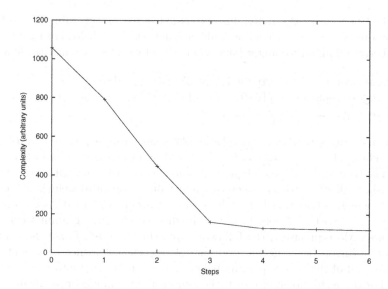

Fig. 3. Quality curve for the real estate grammar search

We can interpret this structure as follows. The start symbol S represents a complete page. A page begins with a fixed header, followed by one or more occurrences of T, each of which represents a single listing. A listing consists of a table row of data optionally containing an image U. Finally, the page is terminated by a fixed trailer.

In this process we have not made use of the DTD (document type definition) specification which defines the HTML language. Since by definition the HTML DTD is a general structure describing all HTML documents, it is not useful as a close fit to any particular set of pages. However, taking account of constraints from the DTD during transformations (for example, to keep blocks of elements from being split) might be a useful refinement to the algorithm. Alternately, a different approach altogether might be to start from the general HTML DTD and specialize it to the training set, rather than starting from a specific grammar and generalizing.

4.2   Domain-Specific Phase

The grammatical inference phase performs a coarse segmentation of the page into units of varying sizes, corresponding to different nonterminals. To complete the segmentation, we need to apply domain-specific knowledge to determine which units correspond to records and to segment the fields within records.

Domain knowledge is expressed as declarative information extraction rules for domain fields. Each rule consists of a field name and type plus a regular expression defining the context in which that field might appear. Rules are executed by applying the regular expression to a chunk of text. If a match is found, a specified portion of the matching text is extracted as the value of the field. Disjunctions can be used to define multiple contexts for a field. For example, in the real estate domain we might have a default set of rules such as the following:

```
number price    = (&pound;|&#163;|£){[0-9]+}
string telephone = {[0-9]+-[0-9]+-[0-9]+}
boolean garden   = garden|yard
```

The first rule says that a price looks like some form of pound sign followed by a number. The part of the match delimited by braces is returned as the field value. The second declares a telephone number as a string of digits interspersed with dashes, all of which becomes the field value. The third defines a boolean attribute which is true if either of the strings "garden" or "yard" is present.

These rules are then applied to the units discovered by the grammatical inference phase. More precisely, the following procedure is used. Parse the training pages according to the inferred grammar. For each occurrence of a nonterminal, collect all of the text appearing below it in the parse tree into an associated chunk. For the page shown in Fig. 1, the nonterminal S would be associated with one chunk containing all of the text on the page; T would be associated with four chunks, each containing the text of one listing; and U would be associated with four chunks containing no text.

Now apply the information extraction rules to each chunk. If a chunk yields multiple matches for several rules, as S does, it probably contains more than one record. However, if few or no rules match, as in U, the chunk is probably smaller than a record. The nonterminal matching the most rules without duplicate matches is assumed to correspond to a record—in this case, T.

4.3 Wrapper Generation Phase

Having identified the nonterminal T as corresponding to a listing record, we can now compile the grammar into a wrapper that extracts records from pages as chunks of text and applies domain rules to extract typed fields from those records. At this point, the user can manually add additional site-specific rules for fine-tuning. These rules may be optionally qualified by a piece number to restrict the match range to a particular piece (i.e. the section of text corresponding to a specific text symbol) within a chunk. For example, the following rules:

```
string address     = 1 : {.*},
string description = 3
```

specify that the address is the part of the first piece appearing before a comma, and that the description is the entire content of the third piece.

Running the wrapper on the sample page yields the records shown in Table 1. Once wrappers for all of the data sources to be used have been generated, the system can extract records from each and integrate the resulting data into a combined database. If a partial database is already available, it may be of use in helping to identify domain fields and formulate extraction rules for them.

Table 1. Partial listing of extracted records

Address	Price	Garden	Description
New Kings Road	120,000	yes	A quiet and secluded studio flat...
Addison Gardens	124,000	yes	A particularly quiet and convenient...
Cheval Court	120,000	yes	A refurbished first floor studio...
Jeffreys Road	130,000	no	A good sized lower ground floor...

Note that complete integration may not be possible, by nature of the data's origin in multiple collections of semistructured text. Some extraction rules may fail on some records, and not all fields may be present on all sites in the first place or even present in all records within a site. However, a mostly-complete overview can still be of significant value.

As a final step, this database can then be used as input into a data mining or information integration system. See for example [14], which describes an interactive real estate visualization system based on dynamic queries (see Fig. 4 for a screenshot). In this system, sliders continuously set selection criteria for properties (shown as color-coded points on a map) and can be used to naturally and rapidly explore the data space.

Although these preliminary results are qualitatively encouraging, more rigorous testing remains to be done to quantify performance on real-world data in terms of recognition rates, etc. Further work is also necessary to determine how robust the method is under different conditions and whether it might get stuck in local optima (switching to simulated annealing may be useful) or have difficulty identifying records properly.

5   Related Work

Ahonen[2] has used grammatical inference to generate structural descriptions for tagged SGML documents such as dictionaries and textbooks, while Freitag[10] explored the use of grammatical inference to find field boundaries in free text. A large amount of work has been done on developing inference algorithms; [17] presents a useful overview.

Work on integrating data from multiple websites has been carried out by a number of researchers. One of the first, Krulwich's BargainFinder[15], was able to scan product listings and prices from a set of on-line web stores and extract them into a unified ordered table. However, it was based entirely on hand-coded wrappers tailored specifically to each source site. ShopBot[9] went a step further by using various *ad hoc* heuristics to automate wrapper building for online stores, but was extremely domain-specific. Kushmerick[16] extended this work by defining some classes of wrappers that could be induced from labelled examples, while Ashish and Knoblock[3] built a toolkit for semi-automatically generating wrappers using hardcoded heuristics.

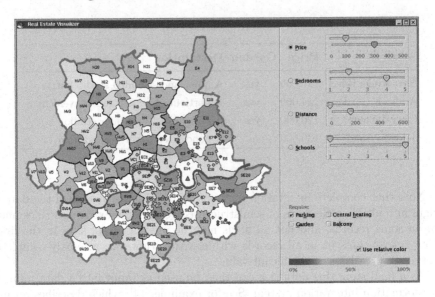

Fig. 4. Screenshot of an interactive real estate visualization system

Craven *et al.*[8] describe an inductive logic programming algorithm for learning wrappers, also using labelled examples. Cohen[6] introduced a method for
learning a general extraction procedure from pairs of page-specific wrappers and
the pages they wrap, although the method was restricted to simple list structures.
AutoWrapper[11] induces wrappers from unlabelled examples but is restricted
to simple table structures. Ghani *et al.*[12] combined extraction of data from corporate websites with data mining on the resulting information. The TSIMMIS
project[5] is another system aimed at integrating web data sources; however, its
main focus is on query planning and reasoning about source capabilities rather
than information extraction (performed by hand-coded wrappers).

6   Conclusions and Future Work

In conclusion, we have demonstrated a principled method for generating information extraction wrappers using grammatical inference that enables the integration of information from multiple web sources. Our approach does not require the
overhead of manually-labelled examples, should be applicable to general structures, and ought to be easily adaptable to a variety of domains using domain
knowledge expressed in simple declarative rules.

These are still preliminary results, and further work is necessary to test the
inference algorithm on more complicated web pages from real-world sources in
different domains, and to conduct a more rigorous quantitative evaluation. We
would also like to examine the use of simulated annealing in the search.

Acknowledgments. The first author acknowledges the support of the Marshall Aid Commemoration Commission. This material is based upon work supported under a National Science Foundation Graduate Fellowship.

References

1. S. Abiteboul, "Querying semi-structured data," in *Database Theory, 6th International Conference (ICDT '97)*, Delphi, Greece, 1–18. Springer (1997).
2. H. Ahonen, "Automatic generation of SGML content models," Electronic Publishing—Origination, Dissemination and Design **8**(2&3), 195–206 (1995).
3. N. Ashish and C.A. Knoblock, "Semi-automatic wrapper generation for Internet information sources," in *Second IFCIS International Conference on Cooperative Information Systems (CoopIS '97)*, Kiawah Island, SC, USA. IEEE-CS Press (1997).
4. J.K. Baker, "Trainable grammars for speech recognition," *Speech Communication Papers for the 97th Meeting of the Acoustical Society of America*, 547–550 (1979).
5. S. Chawathe, H. Garcia-Molina, J. Hammer, K. Ireland, Y. Papakonstantinou, J. Ullman, and J. Widom, "The TSIMMIS project: integration of heterogenous information sources," in *Proceedings of the 10th Meeting of the Information Processing Society of Japan (IPSJ '94)*, 7–18. (1994).
6. W.W. Cohen, "Recognizing structure in web pages using similarity queries," in *Proceedings of the Sixteenth National Conference on Artificial Intelligence (AAAI '99)*, Orlando, FL, USA. AAAI Press (1999).
7. C.M. Cook, A. Rosenfeld, and A.R. Aronson, "Grammatical inference by hill climbing," Informational Sciences **10**, 59–80 (1976).
8. M. Craven, D. DiPasquo, D. Freitag, A. McCallum, T. Mitchell, K. Nigam, and S. Slattery, "Learning to construct knowledge bases from the world wide web," Artificial Intelligence **118**, 69–113 (2000).
9. R. Doorenbos, O. Etzioni, and D. Weld, "A scalable comparison-shopping agent for the world-wide web," in *First International Conference on Autonomous Agents (Agents '97)*, Marina del Rey, CA, USA, 39–48. ACM Press (1997).
10. D. Freitag, "Using grammatical inference to improve precision in information extraction," in *ICML '97 Workshop on Automata Induction, Grammatical Inference, and Language Acquisition*, Nashville, TN, USA. (1997).
11. X. Gao and L. Sterling, "AutoWrapper: automatic wrapper generation for multiple online services," in *Asia Pacific Web Conference '99*, Hong Kong. (1999).
12. R. Ghani, R. Jones, D. Mladenić, K. Nigam, and S. Slattery, "Data mining on symbolic knowledge extracted from the web," in *KDD-2000 Workshop on Text Mining*, Boston, MA, USA. (2000).
13. E.M. Gold, "Language identification in the limit," Information and Control **10**, 447–474 (1967).
14. T. Hong, "Visualizing real estate property information on the web," *Information Visualization '99*. IEEE Computer Society, Los Alamitos, CA (1999).
15. B. Krulwich, "The BargainFinder agent: comparison price shopping on the Internet," in *Bots and Other Internet Beasties*. Sams Publishing (1996).
16. N. Kushmerick, "Wrapper induction: efficiency and expressiveness," Artificial Intelligence **118**, 15–68 (2000).
17. Y. Sakakibara, "Recent advances of grammatical inference," Theoretical Computer Science **185**, 15–45 (1997).

Biological Sequence Data Mining

Yuh-Jyh Hu

Computer and Information Science Department
National Chiao-Tung University
1001 Ta Shueh Rd., Hsinchu, Taiwan
yhu@cis.nctu.edu.tw

Abstract. Biologists have determined that the control and regulation of
gene expression is primarily determined by relatively short sequences in
the region surrounding a gene. These sequences vary in length, position,
redundancy, orientation, and bases. Finding these short sequences is a
fundamental problem in molecular biology with important applications.
Though there exist many different approaches to signal/motif (i.e. short
sequence) finding, in 2000 Pevzner and Sze reported that most current
motif finding algorithms are incapable of detecting the target signals in
their so-called Challenge Problem. In this paper, we show that using an
iterative-restart design, our new algorithm can correctly find the targets.
Furthermore, taking into account the fact that some transcription factors
form a dimer or even more complex structures, and transcription process
can sometimes involve multiple factors, we extend the original problem
to an even more challenging one. We address the issue of combinatorial
signals with gaps of variable lengths. To demonstrate the efficacy of our
algorithm, we tested it on a series of the original and the new challenge
problems, and compared it with some representative motif-finding algorithms. In addition, to verify its feasibility in real-world applications, we
also tested it on several regulatory families of yeast genes with known
motifs. The purpose of this paper is two-fold. One is to introduce an
improved biological data mining algorithm that is capable of dealing
with more variable regulatory signals in DNA sequences. The other is to
propose a new research direction for the general KDD community.

1 Introduction

Multiple various genome projects have generated an explosive amount of biosequence data; however, our biological knowledge has not been able to increase in
the same pace of the growth of biological data. This imbalance has stimulated
the development of many new methods and devices to address issues such as
annotation of new genes [1][2]. Once the Human Genome Project is completed,
it can be expected that related experiments will be carried out soon. The tough
computational challenges resulting from large-scale genomic experiments lie in
the specificity and complexity of the biological processes, e.g., how we identify
the genes directly involved in diseases, how these genes function, and how these
genes are regulated, etc. Answers to the questions above are absolutely related

L. De Raedt and A. Siebes (Eds.): PKDD 2001, LNAI 2168, pp. 228–240, 2001.
© Springer-Verlag Berlin Heidelberg 2001

to the future of health care and genomic medicine that will lead to personalized therapy. The success of the future health care will definitely affect the entire human race in terms of life quality and even life span. Though the content of this paper is focused on one specific biological problem, another important objective of this paper is to draw the attention of the general KDD community to a new research area which needs considerable efforts and novel techniques from a wide variety of research fields, including KDD.

A cluster of co-regulated genes isolated by gene expression measurements can only show which genes in a cell have similar reaction to a stimulus. What biologists further want to understand is the mechanism that is responsible for the coordinated responses. The cellular response to a stimulus is controlled by the action of transcription factors. A transcription factor, which itself is a special protein, recognizes a specific DNA sequence. It binds to this regulatory site to interact with RNA polymerase, and thus to activate or repress the expression of a selected set of target genes. Given a family of genes characterized by their common response to a perturbation, the problem we try to solve is to find these regulatory signals (aka motifs or patterns), i.e. transcription factor binding sites, that are shared by the control regions of these genes.

It has been determined that the control and regulation of gene expression is primarily determined by relatively short sequences in the region surrounding a gene. These sequences vary in length, position, redundancy, orientation, and bases. In any case these characteristics make the problem computationally difficult. For example, a typical problem would be: given 30 DNA sequences, each of length 800, find a common pattern of length 8. Let us simplify the problem, as many algorithms do, and assume the pattern occurs exactly once in each sequence. This means that there are approximately 800^{30} potential locations for a motif candidate. Research on finding subtle regulatory signals has been around for many years, and still draws a lot of attention because it is one of the most fundamental but important step in the study of genomics [3-9]. Despite that there already exist many various algorithms, this problem is nevertheless far from being resolved [10]. They found several widely used motif-finding algorithms failed on the Challenge Problem as follows.

Let $S = \{s_1, ..., s_t\}$ be a sample of t n-letter sequences. Each sequence contains an (l, d)-signal, i.e., a signal of length l with d mismatches. The problem is how to find the correct (l, d)-signal.

In their experiments, they implanted a (15,4)-signal in a sample of 20 sequences. To verify the effect of the sequence length, they varied n from 100 to 1000. The experimental results showed that as the sequence length increased, the performance of MEME [3], CONSENSUS [4] and the Gibbs sampler [5] decreased dramatically. There are two causes to their failures. First, the algorithms may lodge in local optima. The increase of the sequence length can incur more local optima, and further aggravates the problem. Second, they rely on the hope that the instances of the target signal appearing in the sample will reveal the signal itself. However, in the Challenge Problem, there are no exact signal occurrences in the sample, only variant instances with 4 mismatches instead. Pevzner and Sze proposed WINNOWER and SP-STAR to solve the Challenge Problem, but the applicability of WINNOWER is limited by its complexity and the performance of SP-STAR drops significantly like others as the sequence length increases.

Due to the fact that transcription factors may form a dimer or more complex structures, and some transcription initiations may require the binding of two or more transcription factors at the same time, we further extend the Challenge Problem by addressing the issue of combinatorial signals with gaps of variable lengths. Most of the current approaches can only find motifs consisting of continuous bases without gaps. Some methods have been proposed to deal with motifs or alignments with gaps, but they either limit the focus on fixed-gaps [11-13] or use other less expressive representations than the weight matrix, e.g., regular expression-like languages or the IUPAC code [14][15]. To alleviate the limitations of current approaches, we introduce a new algorithm called MERMAID, which adopts the matrix for motif representation, and is capable of dealing with gaps of variable lengths. This presentation expands upon work by others by combining multiple types of motif significance measures with an improved iterative sampling technique. We demonstrate its effectiveness in both the original and the extended Challenge Problems, and compare its performance with that of several other major motif finding algorithms. To verify its feasibility in real-world applications, we also tested MERMAID on many families of yeast genes that share known regulatory motifs.

2 Background

There are three main interrelated computational issues: the representation of a pattern, the definition of the objective function, and the search strategy. While we examine the algorithms on computational grounds, the final, gold-standard is how well the algorithm does at predicting motifs.

2.1 Representation

As the primary DNA sequences are described by a double-stranded string of nucleic bases {A,C,G,T}, the most basic pattern representation is the exact base string. Due to the complexity and flexibility of the motif binding mechanism, there is rarely any motif that can be exactly described by a string of nucleic bases. To obtain more flexibility, the IUPAC code was designed, which extends the expressiveness of the simple base string representation by including all disjunctions of nucleotides. In this language there is a new symbol for each possible disjunction, e.g. W represents A or T.

A more informative pattern representation is a probability matrix in which each element reflects the importance of the base at a particular position. Such matrices can be easily translated into the IUPAC code, while the converse is not true. These matrices are often transformed from the observed occurrence frequencies. For example, in the NIT regulatory family [6] which contains 7 members, a possible 6-base motif matrix is illustrated in Fig. 1. The normalized matrix is also shown in this figure.

```
A 0 7 0 7 7 0                 A 0.00 1.00 0.00 1.00 1.00 0.00
G 6 0 0 0 0 7  normalized to  G 0.86 0.00 0.00 0.00 0.00 1.00
C 1 0 0 0 0 0                 C 0.14 0.00 0.00 0.00 0.00 0.00
T 0 0 7 0 0 0                 T 0.00 0.00 1.00 0.00 0.00 0.00
```

Fig. 1. A 6-base Motif Matrix Example

2.2 Objective Function

The purpose of an objective function is to approximate the biological meanings of the patterns in terms of a mathematical function. The objective function are heuristics. Once the objective function is determined, the goal is to find those patterns with high objective function value. Different objective functions have been derived from the background knowledge, such as the secondary structures of homologous proteins, the relation between the energetic interactions among residues and the residue frequencies, etc [17][18]. Objective functions based on the information content or its variants were proposed [4][5]. Others evaluate the quality of the pattern by its likelihood or by some other measures of statistical significance [3][13].

Even though there are many different objective functions currently used, it is still unclear what is the most appropriate object function or the best representation for patterns that will correspond to biological significant motifs. More likely, additional knowledge will need to be incorporated to improve motif characterization. In the final analysis, the various algorithms can only produce candidate motifs that will require biological experiments to verify.

2.3 Search Strategy

If one adopts the exact string representation, then one can exhaustively check every possible candidate. However this approach is only able to identify short known motifs or partial long motifs [13]. Therefore, the primary representation used is a probability matrix [3][4][5][7]. Once one accepts a probability matrix as the representation, then there is no possibility for an exhaustive search. Initial approaches started with hill-climbing strategies, but these typically fell into local optimum. Standard approaches to repairing hill-climbing, such as beam and stochastic search, were tried next[4]. The current approaches involve a mixture of sampling and stochastic iterative improvement. This avoids the computational explosion and maintains or improves the ability to find motifs [3][5][7].

3   MERMAID: Matrix-Based Enumeration and Ranking of Motifs with gAps by an Iterative-Restart Design

According to the objective function they apply, most current approaches based on greedy or stochastic hill-climbing algorithms optimize the probability matrix with all positions within a sequence [4][5]. This is not only inefficient, but may also increase the chance of getting trapped in local optima in case of subtle signals contained in long sequences due to a greater number of similar random patterns coexisting in the sequences. To avoid this drawback, we can begin by allowing each substring of length l to be a candidate signal. We then convert this particular substring into a probability matrix, adopting an idea from [3]. This gives us a set of seed probability matrices to be used as starting points for iterative improvement. We use the seed probability matrix as a reference to locate the potential signal positions with match scores above some threshold. The optimization procedure only checks these potential positions instead of all possible locations in a sequence. By directing the attention to the patterns same as or close to the substring that is considered a motif candidate, we can significantly constrain the search space during the iterative improvement process.

Nevertheless, when the target signal is very subtle, e.g., (15,4)-signal, the way that we only consider the selected potential signal positions becomes biased. This bias is based on the assumption that the instances of the target signal existing in the sample have sufficient regularity so that we can finally derive the correct target signal from these instances through optimization. Unfortunately, this optimistic assumption does not hold if the regularity represented by the signal instances is inadequate to distinguish themselves from similar random patterns. As a consequence, the chance of mistaking random patterns for real signal instances gets higher. The optimization process may thus converge to other variant patterns than the correct signal.

When dealing with subtle signals, a stochastic approach is not guaranteed to find the correct target signal owing to the influence of similar random patterns. However, the pattern it converges to must be close to the target itself because the random patterns must carry some resemblance to the target signal; otherwise, they would not be selected to participate in the optimization process. Suppose the target signal is the most conserved pattern in the sample as usually expected and we use one signal instance as the seed for optimization. No matter what pattern it finally converges to, this pattern is at least closer to the target signal than the substring (i.e. the signal instance in the sample) used as the seed even if it is not the same as the target. Since the converged pattern is closer to the target signal, one way to further refine this pattern is to reuse it as a seed, and run through the optimization again. We can iteratively restart the optimization procedure with the refined pattern as a new seed until no improvement is shown. With this iterative restart strategy, we expect to successfully detect subtle signals like (l, d)-signals in the Challenge Problem.

Pevzner and Sze proposed some extension to SP-STAR to deal with gapped signals [10], but their method typically addressed the fixed-gap issue only. However, in some real domains, motifs may contain gaps of variable lengths, and simultaneous and proximal binding of two or more transcription factors may be required to initiate transcription[9][14]. Therefore, a natural extension to the Challenge Problem is to find combinatorial (l, d)-signals. A combinatorial (l, d)-signal signal may consist of multiple (l, d)-signals as its components, and the length of gap between two components may vary within a given range. For example, a (l, d)-$X(m, n)$-(l, d)-signal is one that has two (l, d)-signals with a gap of variable lengths between m and n bases. Note that the signal length and the number of mutations may be different in various components.

There are generally two approaches to finding combinatorial signals. The first is a two-phase approach. We find signal component candidates in the first phase. In the second phase, we use the component candidates to form and verify signal combinations [16]. This approach is effective when the signal components are significant enough *per se* so they can be identified in the first phase for later combination check. In cases that the signal components gain significance only in combinations, the former approach may overlook the interaction between components and thus fail to find meaningful combinations. To avoid this limitation, an alternative approach is to find combinatorial signals directly. We developed MERMAID (Matrix-based Enumeration and Ranking of Motifs with gAps by an Iterative-restart Design) to deal with subtle combinatorial signals.

The main process flow of MERMAID is divided into four steps. Given a biosequence family, it first translates substring combinations into matrices. We convert this particular substring into a probability matrix in two steps, adopting an idea from [3]. First we fix the probability of every base in the substring to some value $0 < X < 1$, and assign probabilities of the other bases according to $\frac{1-X}{4-1}$ (4 nucleic bases). Following Bailey and Elkan, we set X to 0.5. We also tried setting X to 0.6. The result showed no significant difference. Each matrix represents a component of a combinatorial motif. This step gives us a set of seed probability matrices to be used as starting points for iterative improvement. Second, it filters the potential motif positions in the family of sequences. Note that each single motif is derived from a substring combination. Thus, besides the matrices, MERMAID also keeps the locations of substrings for all potential motifs to deal with the flexible gaps. Third, given the set of potential motif positions that include the location of each motif component (i.e. substring), it performs an iterative stochastic optimization procedure to find motif candidates. Finally, it ranks and reports these candidates according to the motif significance that is based on the combination of different types of quality measures, including consus [4], multiplicity [6][13] and coverage [7]. The consus quality is derived from the relative entropy, which is used to measure how well a motif is conserved. The multiplicity is defined as the ratio of the number of motif occurrences in the family to that in the whole genome. This measures the representativeness of a motif in a family relative to the entire genome, and consequently, discounts motifs which are common everywhere, such as tandem repeats or poly A's. We define motif coverage as the ratio of the number of the sequences containing the motif to the total number of biosequences in the family. This reflects the importance of a motif's being commonly shared by functionally related family members. Due to limited space, please refer to [16] for more details.

A pseudocode description of the iterative-restart optimization procedure in MERMAID is given in Fig. 2. Let n be the sequence length. The pseudocode (4)-(9) scan the entire sample against each matrix m to find the highest match scoring substring combination in each sequence, locate the potential positions of the combinatorial motif, and form an initial matrix combination M. These totally take $O(n \cdot G^{N-1} \cdot |S|)$ operations, where G is the maximum gap range and N is the total number of motif components. Let p be the maximum number of potential positions in a sequence, p typically $\ll n$. The inner repeat-loop (10)-(14) takes $(p \cdot L)$ operations to check different positions, where L is a constant for the cycle limit. Pseudocode (15)-(19), which scan the entire sample against matrix M to isolate signal repeats, and form the final probability matrix FM, also take $O(n \cdot G^{N-1} \cdot |S|)$ operations. From above, the outer repeat-loop (3)-(21) totally takes $O(L(2n \cdot G^{N-1} \cdot |S| + pL)) = O(n \cdot G^{N-1} \cdot |S|)$. Now considering the outer for-loop (1)-(21) and (22)-(23), we conclude the whole procedure is bounded by $O(n \cdot G^{N-1} \cdot |S| \cdot n \cdot G^{N-1} \cdot |S|) = O((n \cdot G^{N-1} \cdot |S|)^2)$. When G and N are relatively small, $O((n \cdot G^{N-1} \cdot |S|)^2) = O((n \cdot |S|)^2)$, which is the same as MEME and SP-STAR, but lower than WINNOWER'S $O((n \cdot |S|)^{k+1})$, where k is the clique size, $k \geq 2$ in general.

4   Experimental Results

One of the goals of this paper is to demonstrate that enhanced by applying an iterative restart strategy, our new motif detection algorithm is able to find subtle signals, e.g. (15,4)-signal. Based on its definition, we reproduced the Challenge Problem, and used it to compare our new algorithm with others.

Pevzner and Sze's study [10] showed that for a (15,4)-signal, CONSENSUS, the Gibbs sampler and MEME start to break at sequence length 300-400bp. Their system called SP-STAR breaks at length 800 to 900, and their other algorithm named WINNOWER performs well through the whole range of lengths till 1000bp. Using the same data generator to create data samples (thanks to Sze for providing the program), we demonstrate our new algorithm is competitive with other systems. We tested MERMAID over eight samples, as Pevzner and Sze did, each containing 20 i.i.d. sequences of length 1000bp. The comparison of performance of the various algorithms is shown in Table 1. The numbers in Table 1 present the *performance coefficients* as defined in [10] averaged over eight samples. Let K be the set of known signal positions in a sample, and let P be the set of predicted positions. The *performance coefficient* is defined as $|K \cap P|/|K \cup P|$.

Moreover, in order to show that it is the synergy of the iterative restart strategy and the optimization procedure combined with the multiple objective functions in MERMAID that helps find the subtle signals, we implanted in the sample the motif found by MEME with minimum mismatches to the target signal at a random position. We then reran MEME. We repeated the above

Given: a set of biosequences, S
       the total width of a combinatorial motif, W (excluding gaps)
       the maximal gap range, G
       the number of components in a combinatorial motif, N
       the cycle limit, L
Return: a set of ranked motif candidates, C


```
(1)For each substring combo s in S Do
(2)   Set s to ss as a seed

(3)   Repeat
(4)      Translate each substring in ss into candidate probability
            matrix m via:
            m(i,base) = .50 if base occurs in position i
                      = .17 otherwise

(5)      Find highest match scoring substring combo in each sequence in S
(6)      Compute the mean of the highest match scores in S
(7)      For each sequence in S Do
(8)         Set Potential Positions to those with match score >= mean

(9)      Randomly choose a Potential Position in each sequence
            to initialize matrix combo M
(10)     Repeat
(11)        Randomly pick a sequence s in S
(12)        Check if M's significance can be improved by using a
               different Potential Position in s
(13)        Update matrix combo M
(14)     Until (no improvement in M's consensus) or (reach the
            cycle limit L)

(15)     Compute the mean of match scores of substring combo
            contributing to M
(16)     For each sequence s in S Do
(17)        Isolate motif repeats to those with match score >= mean
(18)     Form the final matrix combo FM with all repeats in S
(19)     Convert matrix combo FM into string combo ss as a new seed
(20)  Until (no improvement in FM's significance) or (reach the
         cycle limit L)
(21)  Put FM in C

(22)Sort all motif candidates in C according to significance
(23)Return C
```

Fig. 2. Pseudocode of MERMAID

Table 1. Comparison of performance for (15,4)-signals in 20 i.i.d. sequences of length 1000bp

CONSENSUS	Gibbs	MEME	MEME (w/ iterative restart)	oligonucleotide analysis	WINNOWER (clique size is 3)	SP-STAR	MERMAID
0.06	0.11	0.02	0.09	0.00	0.88	0.23	0.75

Table 2. Performance of MERMAID for (6,1)-X(m,n)-(6,1)-signal in 20 i.i.d. sequences of length 1000bp

$g = 3$	$g = 5$	$g = 7$	$g = 9$
0.91	0.88	0.90	0.56

process, and checked whether this iterative restart strategy alone could improve MEME's performance. The reason we tested MEME is that MERMAID adopts the same motif enumeration method as MEME. Since MEME exhaustively tests every substring in the sample, the implanted substring will be used as a seed in the next run. We only implanted the motif closest to the real signal (i.e., minimum mismatches) to ensure that the base distribution in the sample was nearly unchanged. Though we did not actually re-code MEME, this approximate simulation could still effectively reflect its performance. The result is also presented in Table 1.

Table 1 indicates that MERMAID outperforms CONSENSUS, the Gibbs sampler and MEME (with or w/o iterative restart) by a significant scale. Note that the performance coefficients of WINNOWER and SP-STAR reported in (Pevzner and Sze, 2000) are included only for reference because we did not have access to these two systems at the time. However, this indirect evidence may suggest that MERMAID performs better than SP-STAR, and is expected to be comparable with WINNOWER. We also tested MERMAID on ten real regulons collected by van Helden *et. al.* [6] to verify its usefulness in finding motifs in real-world domains. MERMAID successfully identified all the known motifs in each regulon.

For the extended Challenge Problem, we tested MERMAID on $(6, 1)$-$X(m, n)$-$(6, 1)$-signals in a set of 20 sequences of length 1000bp, where m and n were varied to form a gap ranging from three to nine bases. The experimental results are presented in Table 2, in which g presents the gap range. It shows that the performance of MERMAID is quite stable till the gap length reaches nine.

In addition to the artificial problem, we also tested MERMAID on several real regulons [13] in which the known binding sites have fixed gaps. The summary of the regulons is presented in Table 3, and we show the results in Table 4. In the fourth column of Table 4, the number within the brackets presents the rank of the signal found by MERMAID. Converting the matrices found into the IUPAC codes, we compared them with the published motifs, and found they have significant similarity. The known motifs in the regulatory families are all

Table 3. Summary of regulons used in the experiments

Family	Genes
GAL4	GAL1 GAL2 GAL7 GAL80 MEL1 GCY1
CAT8	ACR1 ICL1 MLS1 PCK1 FBP1
HAP1	CYB2 CYC1 CYC7 CTT1 CYT1 ERG11 HEM13 HMG1 ROX1
LEU3	GDH1 ILV1 LEU1 LEU2 LEU4
LYS	LYS1 LYS2 LYS4 LYS9 LYS20 LYS21
PPR1	URA1 URA3 URA4
PUT3	PUT1 PUT2

ranked in the top ten. The experimental results indicate MERMAID, which was originally developed to deal with variable gaps, also performs well on real domains where motifs have fixed gaps.

5   Conclusion and Future Work

In this paper we have described a new subtle signal detection algorithm called MERMAID, which iteratively restart a multi-strategy optimization procedure combined with complementary objective functions to find motifs. The experimental results show that the system performs significantly better than most current algorithms in the Challenge Problem. To argue the success of MERMAID is attributed to the synergy of iterative restart and other components in the system, i.e. optimization procedures and objective functions, we have demonstrated that simply attaching a iterative restart strategy with MEME shows little improvement.

The difficulty of finding the biologically meaningful motifs results from the variability in (1) the bases at each position in the motif, (2) the location of the motif in the sequence and (3) the multiplicity of motif occurrences within a given sequence. In addition, the short length of many biologically significant motifs and the fact that motifs gain biological significance only in combinations make them difficult to determine. MERMAID was developed to deal with subtle combinatorial signals. Our experiments showed MERMAID successfully detected combinatorial signals composed of proximal components as well as the known motifs with gaps in many real regulons of yeast genes.

For the future work, we aim to improve MERMAID in two directions. One is efficiency and the other is flexibility. First, the optimization process in MERMAID for a single candidate is independent of each other. Therefore, MERMAID can be easily implemented on a parallel or distributed system to improve its efficiency. Second, MERMAID only performs well on combinatorial signals with gaps within a relatively tight range. A wider range of gap length produces a

Table 4. Summary of MERMAID's analysis results in regulons

Family	Known Motifs	Dyad-Analysis by van Helden et. al.	MERMAID
GAL4	CGGRnnRCYnYnCCG	TCGGAn9TCCGA TCGGAn8CGCCGA CCGGAn9TCCGA	CGG-X(11)-CCG [1] A 0.0 0.0 0.0-X(11)-0.0 0.0 0.0 G 0.0 0.9 1.0-X(11)-0.0 0.0 1.0 C 1.0 0.1 0.0-X(11)-0.9 1.0 0.0 T 0.0 0.0 0.0-X(11)-0.1 0.0 0.0
CAT8	CGGnnnnnGGA	CGGn4ATGGAA	CGG-X(6)-GGA [1] A 0.0 0.0 0.0-X(6)-0.0 0.0 1.0 G 0.0 1.0 1.0-X(6)-1.0 1.0 0.0 C 1.0 0.0 0.0-X(6)-0.0 0.0 0.0 T 0.0 0.0 0.0-X(6)-0.0 0.0 0.0
HAP1	CGGnnnTAnCGG	GGAn5CGGC	CGG-X(6)-CGG [10] A 0.0 0.0 0.0-X(6)-0.0 0.0 0.0 G 0.3 0.8 0.9-X(6)-0.0 1.0 1.0 C 0.6 0.0 0.1-X(6)-1.0 0.0 0.0 T 0.1 0.2 0.0-X(6)-0.0 0.0 0.0
LEU3	RCCGGnnCCGGY	ACCGGCGCCGGT	GCCGG-X(2)-CCGGC [3] A 0.1 0.0 0.0 0.0 0.0-X(2)-0.1 0.0 0.0 0.0 0.4 G 0.8 0.0 0.0 0.8 0.9-X(2)-0.0 0.2 1.0 1.0 0.0 C 0.0 1.0 0.9 0.2 0.0-X(2)-0.9 0.8 0.0 0.0 0.6 T 0.1 0.0 0.1 0.0 0.1-X(2)-0.0 0.0 0.0 0.0 0.0
LYS	WWWTCCRnYGGAWWW	AAATTCCG	TTCCA-X(1)-CGGAA [10] A 0.0 0.0 0.1 0.0 0.5-X(1)-0.0 0.0 0.0 0.9 1.0 G 0.0 0.1 0.0 0.0 0.5-X(1)-0.1 1.0 1.0 0.1 0.0 C 0.0 0.1 0.9 1.0 0.0-X(1)-0.6 0.0 0.0 0.0 0.0 T 1.0 0.8 0.0 0.0 0.0-X(1)-0.3 0.0 0.0 0.0 0.0
PPR1	WYCGGnnWWYKCCGAW	CGGn6CCG	TTCGG-X(2)-AACCCCGAG [4] A 0.0 0.0 0.0 0.0 0.0-X(2)-1.0 0.7 0.0 0.0 0.0 0.0 0.0 0.4 0.0 G 0.0 0.0 0.0 1.0 1.0-X(2)-0.0 0.3 0.3 0.0 0.0 0.0 0.7 0.3 0.7 C 0.3 0.0 1.0 0.0 0.0-X(2)-0.0 0.0 0.7 1.0 0.7 1.0 0.3 0.3 0.0 T 0.7 1.0 0.0 0.0 0.0-X(2)-0.0 0.0 0.3 0.0 0.3 0.0 0.0 0.0 0.3
PUT3	YCGGAnGCGnAnnnCCGA CGGnAnGCnAnnnCCGA	CGGn10CCG	TCGG-X(10,11)-CCGA [1] A 0.0 0.0 0.0 0.0-X(10,11)-0.0 0.0 0.0 1.0 G 0.0 0.0 1.0 1.0-X(10,11)-0.0 0.0 1.0 0.0 C 0.0 1.0 0.0 0.0-X(10,11)-1.0 1.0 0.0 0.0 T 1.0 0.0 0.0 0.0-X(10,11)-0.0 0.0 0.0 0.0

larger search space for motif-finding algorithms, and in such cases, it is computationally prohibited to enumerate all possibilities exhaustively. We thus plan to apply a second stochastic sampling process to search through the space of variable gaps, and incorporate domain knowledge when available to constrain the search space.

References

[1] DeRisi, J., Iyer, V. and Brown, P., "Exploring the Metabolic and Genetic Control of Gene Expression on a Genomic Scale", *Science*, Vol 278, (1997) pp. 680-696.

[2] Wodicak, L., Dong, H., Mittmann, M., Ho, M. and Lockhart, D., "Genome-wide Expression Monitoring in Saccharomyces cerevisiae", *Nature Biotechnology*, Vol 15, (1997) pp. 1359-1367.

[3] Bailey, T. and Elkan, C., "Unsupervised Learning of Multiple Motifs in Biopolymers Using Expectation Maximization", *Machine Learning*, 21, (1995) pp. 51-80.

[4] Hertz, G., Hartzell III, G. and Stormo, G., "Identification of Consensus Patterns in Unaligned DNA Sequences Known to be Functionally Related", *Computer Applications in Biosciences*, Vol 6, No 2, (1990) pp. 81-92.

[5] Lawrence, C., Altschul, S., Boguski, M., Liu, J., Neuwald, A. and Wootton, J., "Detecting Subtle Sequence Signals: A Gibbs Sampling Strategy for Multiple Alignments", *Science*, Vol 262, (1993) pp. 208-214.

[6] van Helden, J., Andre, B, and Collado-Vides, J., "Extracting Regulatory Sites from the Upstream Region of Yeast Genes by Computational Analysis of Oligonucleotide Frequencies", *Journal of Molecular Biology*, 281, (1998) pp. 827-842.

[7] Hu, Y., Sandmeyer, S. and Kibler, D., "Detecting Motifs from Sequences", in Proceedings of the 16th International Conference on Machine Learning, (1999) pp. 181-190.

[8] Gelfand, M., Koonin, E. and Mironov, A., "Prediction of Transcription Regulatory Sites in Archaea by a Comparative Genomic Approach", *Nucleic Acids Research*, Vol 28(3), (2000), pp. 695-705.

[9] Li, M., Ma, B. and Wang, L. "Finding Similar Regions in Many Strings", in Proceedings of the 31st ACM Annual Symposium on Theory of Computing, (1999) pp. 473-482.

[10] Pevzner, P. and Sze, S. "Combinatorial Approaches to Finding Subtle Signals in DNA Sequences", in Proceedings of the 8th International Conference on Intelligent Systems for Molecular Biology, (2000).

[11] Rocke, E. and Tompa, M. "An Algorithm for Finding Novel Gapped Motifs in DNA Sequences", in *RECOMM-98*, (1998) pp. 228-233.

[12] Sinha, S. and Tompa, M. "A Statistical Method for Finding Transcription Binding Sites", in Proceedings of the 8th International Conference on Intelligent Systems for Molecular Biology, (2000).

[13] van Helden, J., Rios, A. F. and Collado-Vides, J., "Discovering Regulatory Elements in Non-coding Sequences by Analysis of Spaced Dyads", *Nucleic Acids Research*, Vol 28, (2000) pp. 1808-1818.

[14] Bairoch, A. "PROSITE: a dictionary of sites and patterns in proteins", Nucleic Acids Research, 20, (1992) pp. 2013-2018.

[15] Jonassen, I. "Methods for Finding Motifs in Sets of Related Biosequences", Dept. of Informatics, Univ. of Bergen, Norway, PhD thesis, 1996.

[16] Hu, Y., Sandmeyer, S., McLaughlin, C. and Kibler, D., "Combinatorial Motif Analysis and Hypothesis Generation on A Genomic Scale", *Bioinformatics*, Vol 16, (2000) pp. 222-232.

[17] Stormo, G. "Computer Methods for Analyzing Sequence Recognition of Nucleic Acids", Annual Review of Biophysic and Biophysical Chemistry, 17, (1988) p241-263.

[18] Lawrence, C. and Reilly, A. "An Expectation Maximization (EM) Algorithm for the Identification and Characterization of Common Sites in Unaligned Biopolymer Sequences", Protein: Structure Function and Genetics, 7, (1990) p41-51.

Implication-Based Fuzzy Association Rules

Eyke Hüllermeier

Statistics and Decision Theory
University of Paderborn, Germany
eyke@upb.de

Abstract. Fuzzy association rules provide a data mining tool which is especially interesting from a knowledge-representational point of view since fuzzy attribute values allow for expressing rules in terms of natural language. In this paper, we show that fuzzy associations can be interpreted in different ways and that the interpretation has a strong influence on their assessment and, hence, on the process of rule mining. We motivate the use of multiple-valued implication operators in order to model fuzzy association rules and propose quality measures suitable for this type of rule. Moreover, we introduce a semantic model of fuzzy association rules which suggests to consider them as a convex combination of simple association rules. This model provides a sound theoretical basis and gives an explicit meaning to fuzzy associations. Particularly, the aforementioned quality measures can be justified within this framework.

1 Introduction

Association rules, syntactically written $A \Rightarrow B$, provide a means for representing dependencies between attributes in databases. Typically, A and B denote sets of binary attributes, also called features or items. The intended meaning of a (binary) rule $A \Rightarrow B$ is that a transaction (a data record stored in the database) that contains the set of items A is likely to contain the items B as well. Several efficient algorithms for mining association rules in large databases have been devised [1, 19, 21]. Typically, such algorithms perform by generating a set of candidate rules from selected itemsets which are then filtered according to several quality criteria.

Generally, a database does not only contain binary attributes but also attributes with values ranging on (completely) ordered scales, e.g. cardinal or ordinal attributes. This has motivated a corresponding generalization of (binary) association rules. Typically, a *quantitative association rule* specifies attribute values by means of intervals, as e.g. in the simple rule "Employees at the age of 30 to 40 have incomes between $50,000 and $70,000."

This paper investigates *fuzzy association rules*, which are basically obtained by replacing intervals in quantitative rules by fuzzy sets (intervals). The use of fuzzy sets in connection with association rules – as with data mining in general [20] – has recently been motivated by several authors (e.g. [2, 3, 5–8, 13, 15, 23, 25]). Among other aspects, fuzzy sets avoid an arbitrary determination of crisp

L. De Raedt and A. Siebes (Eds.): PKDD 2001, LNAI 2168, pp. 241–252, 2001.

boundaries for intervals. Furthermore, fuzzy associations are very interesting from a knowledge representational point of view: The very idea of fuzzy sets is to act as an interface between a numeric scale and a symbolic scale which is usually composed of linguistic terms. Thus, the rules discovered in a database might be presented in a linguistic and hence comprehensible and user-friendly way. Example: "Middle-aged employees dispose of considerable incomes."

Even though fuzzy association rules have already been considered by some authors, the investigation of their semantics in the context of data mining has not received much attention as yet. This is somewhat surprising since a clear semantics is a necessary prerequisite, not only for the interpretation, but also for the rating and, hence, for the mining of fuzzy association rules.

The semantics of fuzzy associations and their assessment by means of adequate quality measures constitute the main topics of the paper. By way of background, Section 2 reviews the aforementioned types of association rules. In Section 3, we discuss quality measures for fuzzy associations. In this connection, it is shown that a generalization of (quantitative) association rules can proceed from different perspectives, which in turn suggest different types of measures. We especially motivate the use of multiple-valued implication operators in order to model fuzzy association rules. In Section 4, we introduce a semantic model of fuzzy associations which considers them as convex combinations of simple association rules. This model clarifies the meaning and provides a sound theoretical basis of fuzzy association rules. Particularly, the aforementioned quality measures can be justified within this framework.

2   Association Rules

2.1   Binary Association Rules

Consider an association rule of the form $A \Rightarrow B$, where A and B denote subsets of an underlying set $\mathcal{A}$ of *items* (which can be considered as binary attributes). As already said above, the intended meaning of $A \Rightarrow B$ is that a *transaction* $T \subset \mathcal{A}$ which contains the items in A is likely to contain the items in B as well.

In order to find "interesting" associations in a database D, a potential rule $A \Rightarrow B$ is generally rated according to several criteria, none of which should fall below a certain (user-defined) threshold. In common use are the following measures ($D_X \doteq \{T \in D \mid X \subset T\}$ denotes the transactions in the database D which contain the items $X \subset \mathcal{A}$, and $|D_X|$ is its cardinality):

- A measure of *support* defines the absolute number or the proportion of transactions in D containing $A \cup B$:

$$\mathsf{supp}(A \Rightarrow B) \doteq |D_{A \cup B}| \quad \text{or} \quad \mathsf{supp}(A \Rightarrow B) \doteq \frac{|D_{A \cup B}|}{|D|}. \tag{1}$$

- The *confidence* is the proportion of correct applications of the rule:

$$\mathsf{conf}(A \Rightarrow B) \doteq \frac{|D_{A \cup B}|}{|D_A|}. \tag{2}$$

– A rule $A \Rightarrow B$ should be interesting in the sense that it provides new information. That is, the occurrence of A should indeed have a positive influence on the occurrence of B. A common measure of the *interest* of a rule is

$$\text{int}(A \Rightarrow B) \doteq \frac{|D_{A \cup B}|}{|D_A|} - \frac{|D_B|}{|D|}. \tag{3}$$

This measure can be seen as an estimation of $\Pr(B \mid A) - \Pr(B)$, that is the increase in probability of B caused by the occurrence of A.

2.2   Quantitative Association Rules

In the above setting, a transaction T can be seen as a sequence $(x_1, \dots, x_m)$ of values of binary variables X_i with domain $\mathfrak{D}_{X_i} = \{0, 1\}$, where $x_i = T[X_i] = 1$ if the ith item X_i is contained in T and $x_i = 0$ otherwise. Now, let X and Y be quantitative attributes (such as age or income) with completely ordered domains $\mathfrak{D}_X$ and $\mathfrak{D}_Y$, respectively. Without loss of generality we can assume that $\mathfrak{D}_X, \mathfrak{D}_Y \subset \mathfrak{R}$. A quantitative association rule involving the variables X and Y is then of the following form:

$$A \Rightarrow B : \quad \text{If } X \in A = [x_1, x_2] \text{ then } Y \in B = [y_1, y_2], \tag{4}$$

where $x_1, x_2 \in \mathfrak{D}_X$ and $y_1, y_2 \in \mathfrak{D}_Y$. This approach can simply be generalized to the case where X and Y are multi-dimensional vectors and, hence, A and B hyper-rectangles rather than intervals. Subsequently, we proceed from fixed variables X and Y, and consider the database D as a collection of data points $(x, y) = (T[X], T[Y])$, i.e. as a projection of the original database.

Note that the quality measures from Section 2.1 are applicable in the quantitative case as well:[1]

$$\text{supp}(A \Rightarrow B) = |(\{(x, y) \in D \mid x \in A \wedge y \in B\}|, \tag{5}$$

$$\text{conf}(A \Rightarrow B) = \frac{|\{(x, y) \in D \mid x \in A \wedge y \in B\}|}{|\{(x, y) \in D \mid x \in A\}|}. \tag{6}$$

In fact, each interval $[x_1, x_2]$ does again define a binary attribute $X_{x_1, x_2} = \mathbb{I}_{[x_1, x_2]}$. Thus, not only the rating but also the mining of quantitative rules can be reduced to the mining of binary association rules, by simply transforming the numerical data into binary data [18, 22]. Still, finding a useful transformation (binarization) of the data is a non-trivial problem by itself which affects both, the efficiency of subsequently applied mining algorithms and the potential quality of discovered rules. Apart from data transformation methods, clustering techniques can be applied which create intervals and rules at the same time [16, 24].

---

[1] Subsequently we focus on *support* and *confidence* measures. The results can be transferred to other measures such as *interest* in a straightforward way.

2.3   Fuzzy Association Rules

Replacing the sets (intervals) A and B in (4) by fuzzy sets (intervals) leads to fuzzy (quantitative) association rules. Thus, a fuzzy association rule is understood as a rule of the form $A \Rightarrow B$, where A and B are now fuzzy subsets rather than crisp subsets of the domains $\mathfrak{D}_X$ and $\mathfrak{D}_Y$ of variables X and Y, respectively. We shall use the same notation for ordinary sets and fuzzy sets. Moreover, we shall not distinguish between a fuzzy set and its membership function, that is, $A(x)$ denotes the degree of membership of the element x in the fuzzy set A. Note that an ordinary set A can be considered as a "degenerate" fuzzy set with membership degrees $A(x) = \mathbb{I}_A(x) \in \{0, 1\}$.

3   Quality Measures for Fuzzy Association Rules

The standard approach to generalizing the quality measures for fuzzy association rules is to replace set-theoretic by fuzzy set-theoretic operations. The Cartesian product $A \times B$ of two fuzzy sets A and B is usually defined by the membership function $(x, y) \mapsto \min\{A(x), B(y)\}$. Moreover, the cardinality of a finite fuzzy set is simply the sum of its membership degrees [17]. Thus, (5) and (6) can be generalized as follows:

$$\mathsf{supp}(A \Rightarrow B) \doteq \sum_{(x,y)\in D} \min\{A(x), B(y)\}, \tag{7}$$

$$\mathsf{conf}(A \Rightarrow B) \doteq \frac{\sum_{(x,y)\in D} \min\{A(x), B(y)\}}{\sum_{(x,y)\in D} A(x)}. \tag{8}$$

Note that the support of $A \Rightarrow B$ corresponds to the sum of the *individual supports*, provided by tuples $(x, y) \in D$:[2]

$$\mathsf{supp}_{[x,y]}(A \Rightarrow B) = \min\{A(x), B(y)\}. \tag{9}$$

According to (9), (x, y) supports $A \Rightarrow B$ if both, $x \in A$ and $y \in B$.

3.1   Support

The fact that the antecedent A and the consequent B play symmetrical roles in (9) might appear strange. Indeed, a more logic-oriented approach to modeling a fuzzy rule "If X is A then Y is B" would use a generalized implication operator $\rightsquigarrow$, i.e. a mapping $[0, 1] \times [0, 1] \rightarrow [0, 1]$ which generalizes the classical material implication (particularly, $\rightsquigarrow$ is non-increasing in the first and non-decreasing in the second argument). Thus, individual support can be defined as

$$\mathsf{supp}_{[x,y]}(A \Rightarrow B) \doteq A(x) \rightsquigarrow B(y) \tag{10}$$

---

[2] See [12] for an alternative approach where the frequency of a fuzzy item is measured by a *fuzzy cardinality*, i.e. by a fuzzy (rather than by a crisp) number.

and, hence, the overall (now *asymmetric*) support as

$$\mathsf{supp}(A \Rightarrow B) \doteq \sum_{(x,y)\in D} A(x) \rightsquigarrow B(y). \tag{11}$$

In order to realize the difference between (9) and (10), consider a simple rule "$A \Rightarrow B$: If X is approximately 10 then Y is almost 0" defined by two fuzzy subsets of the non-negative integers,

$$A : x \mapsto \begin{cases} 1 - \frac{|10-x|}{5} & \text{if } 6 \le x \le 14 \\ 0 & \text{otherwise} \end{cases}, \quad B : y \mapsto \begin{cases} 1 - \frac{x}{5} & \text{if } 0 \le x \le 4 \\ 0 & \text{otherwise} \end{cases}.$$

To which degree does the tuple $(x, y) = (8, 3)$ support the above rule? According to (9), the support is 2/5, namely the minimum of the membership of 8 in A and the membership of 3 in B. According to (10) with $\rightsquigarrow$ the Goguen implication

$$\alpha \rightsquigarrow \beta \doteq \begin{cases} 1 & \text{if } \alpha = 0 \\ \min\{1, \beta/\alpha\} & \text{if } \alpha > 0 \end{cases}$$

the individual support is larger, namely 2/3. In fact, $(x, y) = (8, 3)$ does hardly violate (and hence supports) the rule in the sense of (10): It is true that $y = 3$ does not fully satisfy the conclusion part of the rule; however, since $x = 8$ does not fully meet the condition part either, it is actually not expected to do so.

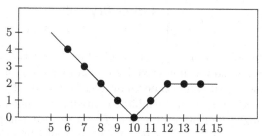

Fig. 1. A simple functional relation between two variables that can be described by means of a gradual fuzzy rule.

As can be seen, the definition of adequate quality measures for fuzzy association rules depends strongly on the interpretation of the rule.[3] For further illustration, consider the nine observations shown in Figure 1.[4] In the sense of (10), each of these observations does fully support the rule "If X is approximately 10 then Y is almost 0." In fact, this rule is actually interpreted as "The closer X

---

[3] Particularly, the strategy of first using (7) and (8) to find interesting fuzzy associations and then interpreting these rules as *implications* appears questionable [4].

[4] Needless to say, this is a somewhat artificial example not at all typical of data mining.

is to 10, the closer Y is to 0" or, more precisely, "The closer X is to 10, the more it is guaranteed that Y is close to 0." Therefore, (11) yields $\mathsf{supp}(A \Rightarrow B) = 9$. As opposed to this, the overall support is only 5 according to (7), since the individual support $\min\{A(x), B(y)\}$ which comes from a point (x, y) is bounded by $B(y)$, the closeness of y to 0. For instance, the support through $(6, 4)$ is only $1/5$ rather than 1. Note that, in the sense of (11), the support of the rule $A \Rightarrow B$ is larger than the support of $B \Rightarrow A$! This reflects the fact that the closeness of x to 10 is less guaranteed by the closeness of y to 0 than vice versa. For instance, $y = 2$ is "rather" close to 0, whereas $x = 14$ is only "more or less" close to 10, hence $\mathsf{supp}_{[2,14]}(B \Rightarrow A) = 1/3 < 1 = \mathsf{supp}_{[14,2]}(A \Rightarrow B)$.

The above example shows that the implication-based approach should be preferred whenever an association rule is thought of as expressing a gradual "the more ... the more ..."-relation between variables and all the more if this relation is not symmetric. For instance, the rule "Young people have low income" might actually be understood as "The younger a person, the lower the income," and this rule might well be distinguished from its inversion "The lower the income, the younger the person."

Concerning the adequacy of (11) as a support measure for association rules, two points deserve mentioning. Firstly, the concept of *support* in the context of association rules is actually intended as *non-trivial support*. Yet, the truth degree of a (generalized) implication $\alpha \rightsquigarrow \beta$ is 1 whenever $\alpha = 0$: From a logical point of view, a false premise entails any conclusion. That is, the rule $A \Rightarrow B$ would also be supported by those points (x, y) for which $x \notin A$. In order to avoid this effect, (10) can be modified as follows:

$$\mathsf{supp}_{[x,y]}(A \Rightarrow B) = \begin{cases} A(x) \rightsquigarrow B(y) & \text{if} \quad A(x) > 0 \\ 0 & \text{if} \quad A(x) = 0 \end{cases}. \tag{12}$$

According to (12), a point (x, y) supports a rule if both, it satisfies the rule (from a logical point of view) and it is non-trivial. Here, non-triviality is considered as a binary concept. However, it can also be quantified as a gradual property, namely as the degree to which x is in A. Combining satisfaction and non-triviality by means of a generalized logical conjunction $\top$, a so-called t-norm, then yields $\mathsf{supp}_{[x,y]}(A \Rightarrow B) = \top(A(x), A(x) \rightsquigarrow B(y))$. For example, by using the product operator as a special t-norm we obtain

$$\mathsf{supp}_{[x,y]}(A \Rightarrow B) = A(x) \cdot (A(x) \rightsquigarrow B(y)). \tag{13}$$

Note that (9), (12), and (13) are identical in the case where A and B are intervals, that is where $A(x), B(y) \in \{0, 1\}$.

The second point concerns the choice of the implication operator $\rightsquigarrow$. In fact, different types of implication operators exist which support different interpretations of a fuzzy rule [11]. The gradual "the more ... the more..."-interpretation discussed above is supported by so-called R(esiduated)-implications. An implication $\rightsquigarrow$ of this type can be derived from a t-norm $\top$ by residuation (hence the name):

$$\alpha \rightsquigarrow \beta \doteq \sup\{\gamma \in [0, 1] \mid \top(\alpha, \gamma) \leq \beta\}.$$

A second important class is given by so-called S(trong)-implications, which are defined by $\alpha \rightsquigarrow \beta \doteq n(\alpha) \oplus \beta$, where $\oplus$ is a t-conorm (a generalized disjunction) and n a strong (hence the name) negation. For example, taking $n(\cdot) = 1 - (\cdot)$ and $\oplus = \max$, one obtains the Kleene-Dienes implication $\alpha \rightsquigarrow \beta = \max\{1 - \alpha, \beta\}$.

S-implications support a different type of fuzzy rule, often referred to as *certainty rules*. Basically, they attach a level of uncertainty to the conclusion part of the rule, in correspondence with the truth degree of the condition part. These rules, however, appear less reasonable in the context of association rules. This can be exemplified by the Kleene-Dienes implication. For this operator, the truth degree is *lower-bounded* by $1 - A(x)$. Thus, (13) entails $\mathsf{supp}_{[x,y]}(A \Rightarrow B) \geq \min\{A(x), 1 - A(x)\}$ regardless of the value $B(y)$. For example, if $A(x) = 1/2$, then $\mathsf{supp}_{[x,y]}(A \Rightarrow B) = 1/2$, no matter whether $B(y)$ is $1/2$, $1/4$, or even 0. This contrasts with R-implications, for which $\beta = 0$ generally implies $\alpha \rightsquigarrow \beta = 0$.

3.2 Confidence

A measure of confidence of a fuzzy association rule can be derived from a corresponding measure of support. Indeed, in the non-fuzzy case, the confidence of $A \Rightarrow B$ is nothing else than the support of $A \Rightarrow B$ over the support of A, that is, the support of $A \Rightarrow \mathfrak{D}_Y$. Interestingly enough, however, the minimal confidence condition $\mathsf{conf}(A \Rightarrow B) \geq \Delta$ (where Δ is a user-specified threshold) can be interpreted in different ways, which in turn suggest different generalizations.

According to the aforementioned interpretation which relates the support of $A \Rightarrow B$ to the support of A, one obtains the generalized confidence measure

$$\mathsf{conf}(A \Rightarrow B) \doteq \frac{\sum_{(x,y)\in D} \mathsf{supp}_{[x,y]}(A \Rightarrow B)}{\sum_{(x,y)\in D} \mathsf{supp}_{[x,y]}(A \Rightarrow \mathfrak{D}_Y)}. \tag{14}$$

Note that $A(x) \rightsquigarrow \mathfrak{D}_Y(y) = A(x) \rightsquigarrow 1 = 1$ for all (x,y). Thus, the denominator in (14) simplifies to $\sum_{(x,y)\in D} \mathbb{I}_{(0,1]}(A(x))$ for (12) and $\sum_{(x,y)\in D} A(x)$ for (13).

A second possibility is to relate the support of $A \Rightarrow B$ to the support of $A \Rightarrow \neg B$. In this case, the minimal confidence condition means that the rule $A \Rightarrow B$ should be supported much better than $A \Rightarrow \neg B$:

$$\mathsf{conf}(A \Rightarrow B) = \frac{\sum_{(x,y)\in D} \mathsf{supp}_{[x,y]}(A \Rightarrow B)}{\sum_{(x,y)\in D} \mathsf{supp}_{[x,y]}(A \Rightarrow \neg B)}. \tag{15}$$

Note that $A(x) = \mathsf{supp}_{[x,y]}(A \Rightarrow \mathfrak{D}_Y) = \mathsf{supp}_{[x,y]}(A \Rightarrow B) + \mathsf{supp}_{[x,y]}(A \Rightarrow \neg B)$ for all (x,y) in the non-fuzzy case, which means that (14) and (15) are equivalent in the sense that one criterion can mimic the other one by adapting its threshold:

$$\frac{\mathsf{supp}(A \Rightarrow B)}{\mathsf{supp}(A \Rightarrow \mathfrak{D}_Y)} \geq \Delta \Leftrightarrow \frac{\mathsf{supp}(A \Rightarrow B)}{\mathsf{supp}(A \Rightarrow \neg B)} \geq \frac{\Delta}{1 - \Delta}.$$

4   Semantic Interpretation of Fuzzy Association Rules

In this section, we propose a semantic model of implication-based fuzzy rules which can directly be applied to fuzzy association rules. The idea is to represent a fuzzy rule as a collection of crisp (implication-based) rules. According to this model, a fuzzy association rule can be considered as a convex combination of non-fuzzy association rules. In this connection, we shall also justify the support measures (12) and (13).

4.1   Pure Gradual Rules

Consider two variables X and Y ranging on domains $\mathfrak{D}_X$ and $\mathfrak{D}_Y$, respectively. Moreover, let A and B denote fuzzy subsets of $\mathfrak{D}_X$ and $\mathfrak{D}_Y$. For the sake of simplicity, we assume the range of A and B to be a finite subset $\mathcal{L} \subset [0, 1]$. That is, membership degrees $A(x)$ and $B(y)$ are elements of $\mathcal{L} = \{\lambda_1, \dots, \lambda_n\}$, where $0 = \lambda_1 < \lambda_2 < \dots < \lambda_n = 1$.

A special type of fuzzy rule, called *pure* gradual rule [10], is obtained for the Rescher-Gaines implication

$$\alpha \rightarrow \beta \doteq \begin{cases} 1 & \text{if} \quad \alpha \leq \beta \\ 0 & \text{if} \quad \alpha > \beta \end{cases}. \tag{16}$$

A pure gradual rule does actually induce a *crisp* relation of admissible tuples (x, y). In fact, the fuzzy rule $A \Rightarrow B$, modeled by the implication (16), is equivalent to the following class of non-fuzzy constraints:

$$X \in A_\lambda \Rightarrow Y \in B_\lambda \qquad (\lambda \in \mathcal{L}) \tag{17}$$

where $A_\lambda = \{x \mid A(x) \geq \lambda\}$ is the λ-cut of A. Now, in some situations one might wish to modify the constraints (17), that is to weaken or to strengthen a conclusion $Y \in B_\lambda$ drawn from the condition $X \in A_\lambda$. This leads to a collection

$$X \in A_\lambda \Rightarrow Y \in B_{m(\lambda)} \qquad (\lambda \in \mathcal{L}) \tag{18}$$

of (non-fuzzy) constraints, where m is a mapping $\mathcal{L} \rightarrow \mathcal{L}$. These constraints can be written compactly in terms of membership functions as $m(A(X)) \leq B(Y)$, and correspond to the rule $A \Rightarrow B$ modeled by the *modified* Rescher-Gaines implication $\rightarrow_m$ with $\alpha \rightarrow_m \beta = 1$ of $m(\alpha) \leq \beta$ and 0 otherwise. Given two fuzzy sets A and B, we can thus associate a gradual rule $A \rightarrow_m B$ (which is short for: $A \Rightarrow B$ modeled by the implication $\rightarrow_m$) with each function $m : \mathcal{L} \rightarrow \mathcal{L}$. Note that m should be non-decreasing: If the premise $X \in A_\lambda$ entails the conclusion $Y \in B_{m(\lambda)}$, then a more restrictive premise $X \in A_{\lambda'}$ ($\lambda < \lambda'$) justifies this conclusion all the more, that is $m(\lambda) \leq m(\lambda')$. Thus, the scale $\mathcal{L}$ gives rise to the following class of gradual rules:

$$\mathcal{G} = \mathcal{G}_{A,B} = \{A \rightarrow_m B \mid m : \mathcal{L} \rightarrow \mathcal{L} \text{ is non-decreasing}\}. \tag{19}$$

4.2   Other Implication-Based Rules

The tuples (x, y) that satify a pure gradual rule $A \rightarrow_m B$ define an ordinary relation $\pi_m \subset \mathfrak{D}_X \times \mathfrak{D}_Y$:

$$\pi_m(x, y) = \begin{cases} 1 & \text{if} \quad m(A(x)) \leq B(y) \\ 0 & \text{if} \quad m(A(x)) > B(y) \end{cases}. \tag{20}$$

More generally, an implication operator $\rightsquigarrow$ induces a *fuzzy* relation $\pi_{\rightsquigarrow}$, where $\pi_{\rightsquigarrow}(x, y) = A(x) \rightsquigarrow B(y)$ is the degree of admissibility of (x, y). Subsequently, we assume a multiple-valued implication $\rightsquigarrow$ to be non-increasing in the first and non-decreasing in the second argument, and to satisfy the identity property: $\lambda \rightsquigarrow 1 = 1$ for all $\lambda \in \mathcal{L}$.

4.3   Randomized Gradual Rules

We are now going to establish a helpful relationship between an implication-based rule $A \rightsquigarrow B$, i.e. the rule $A \Rightarrow B$ modeled by the implication operator $\rightsquigarrow$, and the class (19) of pure gradual rules $A \rightarrow_m B$ associated with A and B.

Definition 1 (randomized rule). *A randomized rule associated with a conditional statement "If X is A then Y is B" is a tuple $(\mathcal{G}, p)$, where $\mathcal{G} = \mathcal{G}_{A,B}$ is the (finite) set of pure gradual rules (19) and p is a probability distribution on $\mathcal{G}$. Each rule $A \rightarrow_m B$ is identified by the corresponding function $m : \mathcal{L} \rightarrow \mathcal{L}$. Moreover, $p_m = p(A \rightarrow_m B)$ is interpreted as the probability (or, more generally, the weight) of the rule $A \rightarrow_m B$.*

Recall that each pure gradual rule $A \rightarrow_m B$ induces an admissible set (20) of tuples (x, y). Therefore, a randomized rule $(\mathcal{G}, p)$ gives rise to a *random set* over $\mathfrak{D}_X \times \mathfrak{D}_Y$ and, hence, induces the following fuzzy relation:

$$\pi_{(\mathcal{G}, p)} = \sum_{m \in \mathcal{G}} p_m \cdot \pi_m. \tag{21}$$

Moreover, (21) is completely determined by the following implication operator associated with $(\mathcal{G}, p)$:

$$\lambda_i \overset{(\mathcal{G}, p)}{\rightsquigarrow} \lambda_j = \sum_{m \in \mathcal{G} \, : \, m(\lambda_i) \leq \lambda_j} p_m. \tag{22}$$

Namely, $\pi_{(\mathcal{G}, p)}(x, y) = A(x) \overset{(\mathcal{G}, p)}{\rightsquigarrow} B(y)$ for all $(x, y) \in \mathfrak{D}_X \times \mathfrak{D}_Y$.

   Recall that a pure gradual rule corresponds to a collection of simple, non-fuzzy constraints and, hence, disposes of a very simple semantics. Since a random rule is a convex combination of pure gradual rules, it can also be interpreted in a very simple way. This lets the representation of a general implication-based fuzzy rule in terms of a random rule seem appealing. Concerning this representation, we have proved the following existence and uniqueness results [9]: For each implication operator $\rightsquigarrow$, a probability p exists such that the rule $A \rightsquigarrow B$ is equivalent to the randomized rule $(\mathcal{G}, p)$ in the sense that $\pi_{\rightsquigarrow} = \pi_{(\mathcal{G},p)}$. That is, the rule $A \rightsquigarrow B$ and the randomized rule $(\mathcal{G}, p)$ induce the same admissibility relation on $\mathfrak{D}_X \times \mathfrak{D}_Y$. Moreover, the probability p is guaranteed to be unique if the implication operator $\rightsquigarrow$ does not have a certain (strict) monotonicity property.

Theorem 1. *For each fuzzy rule $A \Rightarrow B$ formalized by means of an implication operator $\rightsquigarrow$ an equivalent random rule $(\mathcal{G}, p)$ exists. Moreover, the representation in terms of $(\mathcal{G}, p)$ is unique if the condition $\neg(\gamma_{kj} < \gamma_{ij} < \gamma_{il}) \vee \neg(\gamma_{kj} < \gamma_{kl} < \gamma_{il})$ holds for all $1 \leq i < k \leq n$ and $1 \leq j < l \leq l$, where $\gamma_{ij} = \lambda_i \rightsquigarrow \lambda_j$.*

4.4   Application to Association Rules

In Section 2, we have proposed to consider a fuzzy association $A \Rightarrow B$ as an implication-based (gradual) fuzzy rule. Referring to the above interpretation, a rule $A \Rightarrow B$ can hence be seen as a convex combination of simple or *pure gradual* association rules

$$A \rightarrow_m B \qquad (m \in \mathcal{G}), \tag{23}$$

weighted by the probability degrees p_m. Each of these gradual association rules in turn corresponds to a collection

$$A_\lambda \Rightarrow B_{m(\lambda)} \qquad (\lambda \in \mathcal{L}) \tag{24}$$

of ordinary association rules. In fact, if the level-cuts A_λ and $B_{m(\lambda)}$ of the fuzzy sets A and B are intervals, which holds true for commonly used membership functions, then (24) reduces to a class of interval-based association rules.

The interpretation as a randomized rule assigns an association rule a concrete meaning and might hence be helpful in connection with the acquisition (mining) and interpretation of such rules. Apart from this, it provides a basis for justifying quality measures for fuzzy association rules. In fact, proceeding from the convex combination of rules (23) it is obvious to define the support of $A \Rightarrow B$ as the convex combination of the supports of the rules $A \rightarrow_m B$:

$$\mathsf{supp}(A \Rightarrow B) = \sum_{m \in \mathcal{G}} p_m \cdot \mathsf{supp}(A \rightarrow_m B). \tag{25}$$

Thus, it remains to define the (non-trivial) support of a pure gradual association rule $A \rightarrow_m B$, that is of a collection of ordinary association rules (24). To which degree does a point (x, y) support this class of constraints? One possibility is to say that (x, y) supports $A \rightarrow_m B$ if it satisfies *all* individual constraints, and, furthermore, at least one of these constraints is non-trivial:

$$\mathsf{supp}_{[x,y]}(A \rightarrow_m B) = \begin{cases} 1 & \text{if } A(x) > 0 \wedge m(A(x)) \leq B(y) \\ 0 & \text{otherwise} \end{cases}. \tag{26}$$

A second possibility is to define $\mathsf{supp}_{[x,y]}(A \to_m B)$ as the sum of weights of those individual constraints which are indeed non-trivially satisfied:

$$\mathsf{supp}_{[x,y]}(A \to_m B) = \begin{cases} A(x) & \text{if } m(A(x)) \leq B(y) \\ 0 & \text{otherwise} \end{cases}. \tag{27}$$

It is readily verified that (26), in conjunction with (25), yields the support measure (12), and that (27) in place of (26) implies (13). This result provides a sound basis for these measures of (individual) support and, hence, for further quality measures derived from them.

5   Concluding Remarks

We have proposed an implication-based approach to fuzzy association rules as well as a semantic model which suggests of consider such rules as a convex combination of simple, non-fuzzy association rules. Thus, a fuzzy association can be seen as a compact representation of a class of simple rules. This model clarifies the meaning and provides a sound basis of fuzzy association rules.

The paper has mainly focused on theoretical foundations of fuzzy association rules. An important aspect of ongoing research is the practical realization of the results, that is the development of rule mining procedures. Our current implementation (not presented here due to space limitations, see [14]) is an extension of the APRIORI algorithm [1] which is able to cope with fuzzy attribute values and asymmetric support measures. This algorithm takes advantage of the fact that the support (13) of $A \Rightarrow B$ is *lower-bounded* by the support of the premise A: $\mathsf{supp}_{[x,y]}(A \Rightarrow B) = A(x) \cdot (A(x) \rightsquigarrow B(y)) \leq A(x)$. Consequently, the premise A of a minimally supported rule $A \Rightarrow B$ must be a frequent itemset or, put in a different way, the frequent itemsets (which can be found by APRIORI) constitute a superset of the condition parts of minimally supported association rules. Furthermore, the algorithm makes use of a monotonicity property for implications which is similar to the monotonicity property of frequent itemsets employed by APRIORI: $\mathsf{supp}(A \Rightarrow B) \leq \mathsf{supp}(A \Rightarrow B')$ for all $B' \subset B$. Thus, if $A \Rightarrow B$ satisfies the minimum support condition, the same condition holds for each rule $A \Rightarrow B'$ with $B' \subset B$. This provides the basis for filtering candidate rules (obtained by combining frequent itemsets A with conclusions B) in an efficient way.

References

1. R. Agrawal and S. Srikant. Fast algorithms for mining association rules. In *Proceedings of the 20th Conference on* VLDB, Santiago, Chile, 1994.
2. Wai-Ho Au and K.C.C. Chan. An effective algorithm for discovering fuzzy rules in relational databases. In *Proceedings* IEEE *World Congress on Computational Intelligence*, pages 1314 –1319, 1998.
3. Wai-Ho Au and K.C.C. Chan. FARM: A data mining system for discovering fuzzy association rules. In *Proceedings* FUZZ–IEEE–99, pages 1217 –1222, 1999.

4. M. Bernadet. Basis of a fuzzy knowledge discovery system. In D.A. Zighed, J. Komorowski, and J. Zytkow, editors, *Principles of Data Mining and Knowledge Discovery*, pages 24–33. Springer-Verlag, 2000.
5. K.C.C. Chan and Wai-Ho Au. Mining fuzzy association rules. In *Proceedings CIKM–97, 6th Int. Conf. on Inform. and Knowl. Management*, pages 10–14, 1997.
6. G. Chen, Q. Wei, and E.E. Kerre. Fuzzy data mining: Discovery of fuzzy generalized association rules. In G. Bordogna and G. Pasi, editors, *Recent Issues on Fuzzy Databases*. Springer-Verlag, 2000.
7. G. Chen, G. Wets, and K. Vanhoof. Representation and discovery of fuzzy association rules. Technical Report 00/01, ITEO Research Papers, 2000.
8. M. Delgado, D. Sanchez, and M.A. Vila. Acquisition of fuzzy association rules from medical data. In S. Barro and R. Marin, editors, *Fuzzy Logic in Medicine*. Physica Verlag, 2000.
9. D. Dubois, E. Hüllermeier, and H. Prade. Toward the representation of implicative fuzzy rules in terms of crisp rules. In *Proc. IFSA/NAFIPS-2001*, Vancouver, Canada, July 2001. To appear.
10. D. Dubois and H. Prade. Gradual inference rules in approximate reasoning. *Information Sciences*, 61(1,2):103–122, 1992.
11. D. Dubois and H. Prade. What are fuzzy rules and how to use them. *Fuzzy Sets and Systems*, 84:169–185, 1996.
12. D. Dubois and H. Prade. Fuzzy sets in data summaries – outline of a new approach. In *Proceedings IPMU-2000*, pages 1035–1040, Madrid, Spain, 2000.
13. A. Fu, M.H. Wong, S.C. Sze, W.C. Wong, W.L. Wong, and W.K Yu. Finding fuzzy sets for the mining of fuzzy association rules for numerical attributes. In *IDEAL–98, 1st Int. Symp. on Intell. Data Engineering and Learning*, pages 263–268, 1998.
14. E. Hüllermeier. Mining implication-based fuzzy association rules. Submitted.
15. C. Man Kuok, A. Fu, and M. Hon Wong. Mining fuzzy association rules in databases. *SIGMOD Record*, 27:41–46, 1998.
16. B. Lent, A. Swami, and J. Widom. Clustering association rules. In *Proceedings ICDE–97*, Birmingham, UK, 1997.
17. A. De Luca and S. Termini. Entropy of L-fuzzy sets. *Information and Control*, 24:55–73, 1974.
18. R.J. Miller and Y. Yang. Association rules over interval data. In *Proc. ACM SIGMOD Int. Conf. on Management of Data*, pages 452–461, 1997.
19. J.S. Park, M.S. Chen, and P.S. Yu. An efficient hash-based algorithm for mining association rules. In *ACM SIGMOD Int. Conf. on Management of Data*, 1995.
20. W. Pedrycz. Data mining and fuzzy modeling. In *Proc. of the Biennial Conference of the NAFIPS*, pages 263–267, Berkeley, CA, 1996.
21. A. Savasere, E. Omiecinski, and S. Navathe. An efficient algorithm for mining association rules in large databases. In *Proceedings VLDB–95*, Zurich, 1995.
22. R. Skrikant and R. Agrawal. Mining quantitative association rules in large relational tables. In *Proceedings of the ACM SIGMOD International Conference on Management of Data*, pages 1–12, 1996.
23. S. Ben Yahia and A. Jaoua. Mining linguistic summaries of databases using Lukasiewicz implication fuzzy functional dependency. In *Proceedings FUZZ–IEEE–99*, pages 1246 –1250, 1999.
24. Y. Yang and M. Singhal. Fuzzy functional dependencies and fuzzy association rules. In *Data Warehousing and Knowledge Discovery, Proceedings DAWAK–99*, pages 229–240. Springer-Verlag, 1999.
25. W. Zhang. Mining fuzzy quantitative association rules. In *Proc. 11th IEEE Int. Conf. on Tools with Artificial Intelligence*, Chicago, Illinois, 1999.

A General Measure of Rule Interestingness

Szymon Jaroszewicz and Dan A. Simovici

University of Massachusetts at Boston
Department of Mathematics and Computer Science
Boston, Massachusetts 02446, USA
{sj,dsim}@cs.umb.edu

Abstract. The paper presents a new general measure of rule interestingness. Many known measures such as chi-square, gini gain or entropy gain can be obtained from this measure by setting some numerical parameters, including the amount of trust we have in the estimation of the probability distribution of the data. Moreover, we show that there is a continuum of measures having chi-square, Gini gain and entropy gain as boundary cases. Therefore our measure generalizes both conditional and unconditional classical measures of interestingness. Properties and experimental evaluation of the new measure are also presented.

Keywords: interestingness measure, distribution, Kullback-Leibler divergence, Cziszar divergence, rule.

1 Introduction

Determining the interestingness of rules is an important data mining problem since many data mining algorithms produce enormous amounts of rules, making it difficult for the user to analyze them manually. Thus, it is important to establish some numerical interestingness measure for rules, which can help users to sort the discovered rules. A survey of such measures can be found in [1]. Here we concentrate on measures that assess how much knowledge we gain about the joint distribution of a set of attributes Q by knowing the joint distribution of some set of attributes P. Examples of such measures are *entropy gain, mutual information, Gini gain,* χ^2 [9,10,4,1,12,11]. The rules considered here are different from classical association rules studied in data mining, since we consider full joint distributions of both antecedent and consequent, while association rules consider only the probability of all attributes having some specified value. This approach has the advantage of applicability to mulitvalued attributes.

We show that all the above mentioned measures are special cases of a more general parametric measure of interestingness, and by varying two parameters, a family of measures can be obtained containing several well-known classical measures as special cases.

There is work done in machine learning and information theory literature [5, 6,15,3] on generalizing information-theoretical measures. However, all previous work is concerned with either unconditional or conditional measures, while this

L. De Raedt and A. Siebes (Eds.): PKDD 2001, LNAI 2168, pp. 253–265, 2001.

paper presents a generalization which includes family of intermediate measures, between conditional and unconditional ones, and shows a relation between these measures and the amount of trust we have in the estimate of probabilities from data. For example, we present a continuum of measures between χ^2 (unconditional measure), and the Gini gain (conditional measure). We show that the intermediate measures have many interesting properties which make them useful for rule evaluation.

Next, we give some essential definitions.

Definition 1. *A probability distribution is a matrix of the form*

$$\Delta = \begin{pmatrix} x_1 & \cdots & x_m \\ p_1 & \cdots & p_m \end{pmatrix},$$

where $p_i \geq 0$ for $1 \leq i \leq m$ and $\sum_{i=1}^m p_i = 1$.

Δ *is an uniform distribution if $p_1 = \cdots = p_m = \frac{1}{m}$. An m-valued uniform distribution will be denoted by $\mathcal{U}_m$.*

Let $\tau = (T, H, \rho)$ be a database table, where T is the name of the table, H is its heading, and ρ is its content. If $A \in H$ is an attribute of τ, the domain of A in τ is denoted by $\text{dom}(A)$. The projection of a tuple $t \in \rho$ on a set of attributes $L \subseteq H$ is denoted by $t[L]$. For more on relational notation and terminology see [14].

Definition 2. *The distribution of a set of attributes $L = \{A_1, \ldots, A_n\}$ is the matrix*

$$\Delta_{L,\tau} = \begin{pmatrix} \ell_1 & \cdots & \ell_r \\ p_1 & \cdots & p_r \end{pmatrix}, \tag{1}$$

where $r = \prod_{j=1}^n |\text{dom}(A_j)|$, $\ell_i \in \text{dom}(A_1) \times \cdots \times \text{dom}(A_n)$, and $p_i = \frac{|t \in \rho| t[L] = \ell_i|}{|\rho|}$ for $1 \leq i \leq r$.

The subscript τ will be omitted when the table τ is clear from context.

The *Havrda-Charvát α-entropy* of the attribute set L (see [7]) is defined as:

$$\mathcal{H}_\alpha(L) = \frac{1}{1-\alpha} \left(\sum_{j=1}^r p_j^\alpha - 1 \right).$$

The limit case, when α tends towards 1 yields the Shannon entropy $\mathcal{H}(L) = -\sum_{j=1}^r p_j \log p_j$. Another important case, the Gini index, is obtained when $\alpha = 2$ (see [1]) and is given by $\text{gini}(L) = 1 - \sum_{j=1}^r p_j^2$.

If L, K are two sets of attributes of a table τ that have the distributions

$$\Delta_L = \begin{pmatrix} l_1 & \cdots & l_m \\ p_1 & \cdots & p_m \end{pmatrix}, \text{ and } \Delta_K = \begin{pmatrix} k_1 & \cdots & k_n \\ q_1 & \cdots & q_n \end{pmatrix},$$

then the conditional Shannon entropy of L conditioned upon K is given by

$$\mathcal{H}(L|K) = -\sum_{i=1}^{m}\sum_{j=1}^{n} p_{ij} \log \frac{p_{ij}}{q_j},$$

where $p_{ij} = \frac{|\{t \in \rho | t[L] = \ell_i \text{ and } t[K] = k_j\}|}{|\rho|}$ for $1 \leq i \leq m$ and $1 \leq j \leq n$. Similarly, the Gini conditional index of these distributions is:

$$\text{gini}(L|K) = 1 - \sum_{i=1}^{m}\sum_{j=1}^{n} \frac{p_{ij}^2}{q_j}.$$

These definitions allow us to introduce the Shannon gain (called entropy gain in literature [9]) and the Gini gain defined as:

$$\text{gain}_{\text{gini}}(L, K) = \text{gini}(L) - \text{gini}(L|K),$$
$$\text{gain}_{\text{shannon}}(L, K) = \mathcal{H}(L) - \mathcal{H}(L|K)$$
$$= \mathcal{H}(L) + \mathcal{H}(K) - \mathcal{H}(LK), \qquad (2)$$

respectively, where LK is an abbreviation for $L \cup K$. Note that the Shannon gain is identical to the *mutual information* between attribute sets P and Q [9]. For the Gini gain we can write:

$$\text{gain}_{\text{gini}}(L, K) = \sum_{i=1}^{m}\sum_{j=1}^{n} \frac{p_{ij}^2}{q_j} - \sum_{i=1}^{m} p_i^2 \qquad (3)$$

The product of the distributions Δ_P, Δ_Q, where

$$\Delta_P = \begin{pmatrix} x_1 & \cdots & x_m \\ p_1 & \cdots & p_m \end{pmatrix}, \text{ and } \Delta_Q = \begin{pmatrix} y_1 & \cdots & y_n \\ q_1 & \cdots & q_n \end{pmatrix},$$

is the distribution

$$\Delta_P \times \Delta_Q = \begin{pmatrix} (x_1, y_1) & \cdots & (x_m, y_n) \\ p_1 q_1 & \cdots & p_m q_n \end{pmatrix}.$$

The attribute sets P, Q are *independent* if $\Delta_{PQ} = \Delta_P \times \Delta_Q$.

Definition 3. *A rule is a pair of attribute sets* (P, Q). *If* $P, Q \subseteq H$, *where* $\tau = (T, H, \rho)$ *is a table, then we refer to* (P, Q) *as a rule of* τ.

If (P, Q) *is a rule, then we refer to* P *as the* antecedent *and to* Q *as the* consequent *of the rule. A rule* (P, Q) *will be denoted, following the prevalent convention in the literature, by* $P \rightarrow Q$.

This broader definition of rules originates in [4], where rules were replaced by dependencies in order to capture statistical dependence in both the presence and absence of items in itemsets. The significance of this dependence was measured by the χ^2 test, and our approach is a further extension of that point of view.

The notion of *distribution divergence* is central to the rest of the paper.

Definition 4. *Let $\mathcal{D}$ be the class of distributions. A distribution divergence is a function $D : \mathcal{D} \times \mathcal{D} \longrightarrow \mathbb{R}$ such that:*

1. $D(\Delta, \Delta') \geq 0$ *and* $D(\Delta, \Delta') = 0$ *if and only if* $\Delta = \Delta'$ *for every* $\Delta, \Delta' \in \mathcal{D}$.
2. *When Δ' is fixed, $D(\Delta, \Delta')$ is a convex function of Δ; in other words, if $\Delta = a_1 \Delta_1 + \cdots + a_k \Delta_k$, where $a_1 + \ldots + a_k = 1$, then*

$$D(\Delta, \Delta') \geq \sum_{i=1}^{k} a_i D(\Delta_i, \Delta').$$

An important class of distribution divergences was obtained by Cziszar in [5] as: $D_\phi(\Delta, \Delta') = \sum_{i=1}^{n} q_i \phi \left(\frac{p_i}{q_i} \right)$, where

$$\Delta = \begin{pmatrix} k_1 & \cdots & k_n \\ p_1 & \cdots & p_n \end{pmatrix}, \text{ and } \Delta' = \begin{pmatrix} l_1 & \cdots & l_n \\ q_1 & \cdots & q_n \end{pmatrix},$$

are two distributions and $\phi : \mathbb{R} \longrightarrow \mathbb{R}$ is a twice differentiable convex function such that $\phi(1) = 0$. We will also make an additional assumption that $0 \cdot \phi(\frac{0}{0}) = 0$ to handle the case when for some i both p_i and q_i are zero. If for some i, $p_i > 0$, and $q_i = 0$ the value of $D_\phi(\Delta, \Delta')$ is undefined.

The Cziszar divergence satisfies properties (1) and (2) given above (see [7]).

The following result shows the invariance of Cziszar divergence with respect to distribution product:

Theorem 1. *For any distributions Γ, Δ, Δ' and any Cziszar divergence measure D_ϕ we have $D_\phi(\Gamma \times \Delta, \Gamma \times \Delta') = D_\phi(\Delta, \Delta')$.*

Depending on the choice of the function ϕ we obtain the divergences shown in the table below:

$\phi(x)$	$D(\Delta, \Delta')$	Divergence
$x \log x$	$p_i \log \frac{p_i}{q_i}$	Kullback-Leibler
$x^2 - x$	$\sum_{i=1}^{n} \frac{p_i^2}{q_i} - 1$	D_{χ^2}

Both the Kullback-Leibler divergence (also known as *crossentropy*), which we will denote by D_{KL} and the χ^2-divergence denoted by D_{χ^2} are special cases of the Havrda-Charvát divergence $D_{\mathcal{H}_\alpha}$ generated by $\phi(x) = \frac{x^\alpha - x}{\alpha - 1}$ [7]; specifically, D_{χ^2} is obtained by taking $\alpha = 2$, while D_{KL} is obtained as a limit case, when α tends towards 1.

It is easy to verify that

$$D_{\chi^2}(\Delta, \Delta') = \sum_{i=1}^{n} \frac{(p_i - q_i)^2}{q_i}.$$

Note that $|\rho| D_{\chi^2}$ equals the χ^2 dependency measure, well known from statistics [1].

2   Interestingness of Rules

The main goal of this paper is to present a unified approach to the notion of interestingness of rules. Let $r = P \to Q$ be a rule in a table $\tau = (T, H, \rho)$. To construct an interestingness measure we will use a Bayesian approach, in that we will consider an a posteriori distribution Θ of the consequent set of attributes Q.

The definition of an interestingness measure of r will be guided by two main considerations:

- The more the observed joint distribution of PQ diverges from the product distribution of P and the a posteriori distribution Θ of Q the more interesting the rule is. Note that $\Delta_{PQ} = \Delta_P \times \Theta$ corresponds to the situation when P and Q are independent and the observed distribution of Q is identical to the a posteriori distribution.
- The rule is not interesting if P, Q are independent. Therefore, we need to consider a correcting term in the definition of an interestingness measure that will decrease its value when Δ_Q is different from the a posteriori distribution.

The choice of the distribution Θ of the consequent Q of rules of the form $P \to Q$ can be made starting either from the content of the table, that is, adopting Δ_Q for Θ, or from some exterior information. For example, if Q is the sex attribute for a table that contains data concerning some experiment subjects, we can adopt as the a posteriori distribution either

$$\Delta_{sex} = \begin{pmatrix} \text{'F'} & \text{'M'} \\ 0.45 & 0.55 \end{pmatrix},$$

assuming that 45% of the individuals involved are female, or the distribution

$$\Delta_{gen\_pop} = \begin{pmatrix} \text{'F'} & \text{'M'} \\ 0.51 & 0.49 \end{pmatrix},$$

consistent with the general distribution of the sexes in the general population.

Moreover, we can use the Laplace estimator [10,16] (also known in literature as the m-estimate of probability) to obtain the a posteriori distribution

$$\Theta_m = \frac{|\rho|\Delta_Q + m\Theta_0}{|\rho| + m},$$

where Δ_Q is the distribution of Q that is extracted from a table τ, Θ_0 is the apriori distribution, $|\rho|$ is the size of the database, and the integer m represents the amount of trust we have in the prior distribution Θ_0. If $m = 0$, this means we completely ignore the a priori distribution, and $m \to \infty$ means that we have no trust in the data, and totaly rely on the prior distribution. To avoid using limits, we denote $a = \frac{|\rho|}{|\rho|+m}$, and write the Laplacian as a convex combination of the two distributions:

$$\Theta_a = a\Delta_Q + (1 - a)\Theta_0.$$

Now $a = 1$, and $a = 0$ correspond to cases $m = 0$, and $m \to \infty$ respectively.

Definition 5. *Let* $r : P \to Q$ *be a rule,* D *be some measure of divergence between distributions, and let* Θ *be a distribution.*

The measure of interestingness generated by D *and* Θ *is defined by*

$$\Upsilon_{D,\Theta}(r) = D(\Delta_{PQ}, \Delta_P \times \Theta) - D(\Delta_Q, \Theta).$$

In the above definition Θ represents the a posteriori distribution of Q, while Δ_Q is the distribution of Q observed from the data. The term $D(\Delta_Q, \Theta)$ measures the degree to which Δ_Q diverges from the prior distribution Θ, and $D(\Delta_{PQ}, \Delta_P \times \Theta)$ measures how far Δ_{PQ} diverges from the joint distribution of P and Q in case they were independent, and Q was distributed according to Θ.

The justification for the correcting term $D(\Delta_Q, \Theta)$ is given in the following theorem:

Theorem 2. *If* P *and* Q *are independent, and* D *is a Cziszar measure of divergence then* $\Upsilon_{D,\Theta}(P \to Q) = 0$.

Observe that if D is a Cziszar divergence $D = D_\phi$, then the invariance of these divergences implies:

$$\Upsilon_{D_\phi,\Theta}(P \to Q) = D_\phi(\Delta_{PQ}, \Delta_P \times \Theta) - D_\phi(\Delta_P \times \Delta_Q, \Delta_P \times \Theta).$$

3   Properties of the General Measure of Interestingness

Initially, we discuss several basic properties of the proposed measure.

Theorem 3. *If* D *is a Cziszar divergence, then*

$$\Upsilon_{D,\Delta_Q}(P \to Q) = \Upsilon_{D,\Delta_P}(Q \to P)$$

The above property means that when the a posteriori distribution of the consequent is always assumed equal to the distribution observed from data, then the measure is symmetric with respect to the direction of the rule, i.e. exchanging the antecedent and consequent does not change the value of the interestingness.

Theorem 4. *Let* D *be a Cziszar divergence. If* R *is a set of attributes independent of* P, *and jointly of* PQ, *then, for any* Θ *we have* $\Upsilon_{D,\Theta}(RP \to Q) = \Upsilon_{D,\Theta}(P \to Q)$.

If R *is a set of attributes independent of* Q, *and jointly of* PQ, *then* $\Upsilon_{D,\Delta_{RQ}}(P \to RQ) = \Upsilon_{D,\Delta_Q}(P \to Q)$.

The previous result gives a desirable property of $\Upsilon_{D,\Theta}$ since adding independent attributes should not affect rule's interestingness. In particular, when Θ equals the observed distribution of the consequent, then Υ is not affected by adding independent attributes to either the antecedent or the consequent.

Next, we consider several important special cases of the interestingness measure.

If the divergence D and the a priori distribution used in the definition of the interestingness measure are chosen appropriately, then the interestingness

$\Upsilon_{D,\Theta}(P \to Q)$ is proportional to a gain of the set of attributes of the consequent Q of the rule relative to the antecedent P. Both the Gini gain, $\text{gain}_{\text{gini}}(Q, P)$, and the entropy gain, $\text{gain}_{\text{shannon}}(Q, P)$, can be obtained by appropriate choice of D. Moreover a measure proportional to the χ^2 statistic can be obtained in that way.

Suppose that the attribute sets P, Q have the distributions

$$\Delta_P = \begin{pmatrix} x_1 & \cdots & x_m \\ p_1 & \cdots & p_m \end{pmatrix}, \text{ and } \Delta_Q = \begin{pmatrix} y_1 & \cdots & y_n \\ q_1 & \cdots & q_n \end{pmatrix}.$$

Let $\rho_{ij} = \{t \in \rho | t[P] = x_i \text{ and } t[Q] = y_j\}$ and let $p_{ij} = \frac{|\rho_{ij}|}{|\rho|}$ for $1 \leq i \leq m$ and $1 \leq j \leq n$.

Theorem 5. *Let* $P \longrightarrow Q$ *be a rule in the table* $\tau = (T, H, \rho)$. *If* $D = D_{\text{KL}}$ *then*

$$\Upsilon_{D,\Theta}(P \to Q) = \text{gain}_{\text{shannon}}(Q, P),$$

regardless of the choice of Θ.

The above theorem means that for the case D_{KL} the family of measures generated by Θ reduces to a single measure: the Shannon gain (mutual information). This is not the case for other divergences.

Theorem 6. *Let* $P \longrightarrow Q$ *be a rule in the table* $\tau = (T, H, \rho)$. *If* $D = D_{\chi^2}$ *and* $\Theta = \mathcal{U}_n$, *where* $n = |\text{dom}(Q)|$, *then*

$$\Upsilon_{D,\Theta}(P \to Q) = n \cdot \text{gain}_{\text{gini}}(Q, P).$$

Theorem 7. *We have* $\Upsilon_{D_{\chi^2}, \Delta_Q}(P \longrightarrow Q)$ *is proportional to* $\chi^2(P, Q)$, *the chi-squared statistics [1] for attribute sets* P, Q.

Note that above we treat attribute sets $P = \{A_1, \ldots, A_r\}$ and $Q = \{B_1, \ldots, B_s\}$ as single attributes with the domains given by (1). This is appropriate, since we are interested in how one *set* of attributes P influences another *set* of attributes Q. Another way, used in [4], is to compute $\chi^2(A_1, \ldots, A_r, B_1, \ldots, B_s)$, however this is not what we want.

The case when $D = D_{\chi^2}$ is of practical interest since it includes two widely used measures (χ^2, and $\text{gain}_{\text{gini}}$) as special cases, and allows for obtaining a continuum of measures "in between" the two.

Theorem 8 stated below shows that the generalized measure interestingness $\Upsilon_{D,\Theta}(P \to Q)$ is minimal when P and Q are independent and thus, it justifies our definition of this measure through variational considerations.

Theorem 8. *Let* $\Upsilon_{D,\Theta}$ *be the measure of interestingness generated by the a posteriori distribution* Θ *and the Kullback-Leibler divergence, or the* χ^2-*divergence and let* $P \to Q$ *be a rule. For any fixed attribute distribution* Δ_P, Δ_Q *and a fixed distribution* Θ, *the value of* $\Upsilon_{D,\Theta}(P \to Q)$ *is minimal (and equal to 0) if only if* $\Delta_{PQ} = \Delta_P \times \Delta_Q$, *i.e., when* P *and* Q *are independent.*

We saw that $\text{gain}_{\text{shannon}}$ and $\text{gain}_{\text{gini}}$ are equivalent to $\Upsilon_{D_{\text{KL}},\mathcal{U}_n}$ and $\Upsilon_{D_{\chi^2},\mathcal{U}_n}$, respectively. It is thus natural to define a notion of *gain* for any divergence D as

$$\text{gain}_D(P \to Q) = \Upsilon_{D,\mathcal{U}_n}(P \to Q).$$

Let $\Delta_Q|p_i$ denote the probability distribution of Q conditioned on $P = p_i$. For any Cziszar measure D_ϕ we have:

$$\text{gain}_{D_\phi}(P \to Q) = D_\phi(\Delta_{PQ}, \Delta_P \times \mathcal{U}_n) - D_\phi(\Delta_Q, \mathcal{U}_n)$$

$$= \sum_{i=1}^{m} p_i \sum_{j=1}^{n} \frac{1}{n} \phi\left(\frac{p_{ij}}{p_i \cdot \frac{1}{n}}\right) - D_\phi(\Delta_Q, \mathcal{U}_n)$$

$$= -\left[D_\phi(\Delta_Q, \mathcal{U}_n) - \sum_{i=1}^{m} p_i D_\phi(\Delta_Q|p_i, \mathcal{U}_n)\right].$$

As special cases $\text{gain}_{\text{gini}} \equiv \text{gain}_{\chi^2}$, and $\text{gain}_{\text{shannon}} \equiv \text{gain}_{\text{KL}}$.

A parameterized version of Υ that takes into account the degree of confidence in the distribution of the consequent as it results from the data is introduced next.

Let us define the probability distribution $\Theta_a, a \in [0, 1]$ by

$$\Theta_a = a\Delta_Q + (1 - a)\mathcal{U}_n.$$

The value of a expresses the amount of confidence we have in Δ_Q estimated from the data. The value $a = 1$ means total confidence, we assume the probability estimated from data as the true probability distribution of Q. On the other hand, $a = 0$ means that we have no confidence in the estimate and use some prior distribution of Q instead. In our case, the prior is the uniform distribution $\mathcal{U}_n$. Note that $\Theta_1 = \Delta_Q$, and $\Theta_0 = \mathcal{U}_n$.

We can now define

$$\Upsilon_{D,a} = \Upsilon_{D,\Theta_a}.$$

Note that when $D = D_{\chi^2}$, we have (up to a constant factor) both $\chi^2(P \to Q)$ and $\text{gini}_{\text{gain}}(P \to Q)$ as special cases of $\Upsilon_{D_{\chi^2},a}$. Moreover by taking different values of parameter a we can obtain a continuum of measures in between the two.

As noted before, both D_{χ^2} and D_{KL} divergence measures are special cases of Havrda-Charvát divergence $D_{\mathcal{H}_\alpha}$ for $\alpha \to 1$, and $\alpha = 2$ respectively. We can thus introduce $\Upsilon_{\alpha,a} = \Upsilon_{D_{\mathcal{H}_\alpha},\Theta_a}$, which allows us to obtain a family of interestingness measures, including (up to a constant factor) all three measures given in Sect. 3 as special cases, by simply changing two real valued parameters α and a.

Also note that for $a = 0$, we obtain a family of gains (as defined in Sect. 3) for all the Havrda-Charvát divergences.

4   Experimental Results

We evaluated the new measure on a simple synthetic dataset and on data from the UCI machine learning repository [2]. We concentrated on the case $D = D_{\chi^2}$, as potentially most useful in practice, and found interestingness of rules for different values of parameter a (see Sect. 3).

To ensure measures throughout the family handle obvious cases correctly, and to make it easy to observe properties of the measure for different values of parameter a we first evaluated the rules on a synthetic dataset with 3 attributes A, B, C and with known probabilistic dependencies between them.

Values of attributes A and B have been generated from known probability distributions:

$$\Delta_A = \begin{pmatrix} 0 & 1 & 2 \\ 0.1 & 0.5 & 0.4 \end{pmatrix}, \Delta_B = \begin{pmatrix} 0 & 1 \\ 0.2 & 0.8 \end{pmatrix}.$$

Attribute C depends on attribute A. Denote $\Delta_C|i$ the distribution of C conditioned upon $A = i$. We used

$$\Delta_C|0 = \begin{pmatrix} 0 & 1 \\ 0.2 & 0.8 \end{pmatrix}, \Delta_C|1 = \begin{pmatrix} 0 & 1 \\ 0.5 & 0.5 \end{pmatrix}, \Delta_C|2 = \begin{pmatrix} 0 & 1 \\ 0.7 & 0.3 \end{pmatrix},$$

One million data points have been generated according to this distribution, for a few values of a we sorted all possible rules based on their $\Upsilon_{D_{\chi^2},a}$ interestingness values. Results are given in Table 1.

1. Attribute B is totally independent of both A and C, so any rule containing only B as the antecedent or consequent should have interestingness 0. The experiments confirm this, for all values of parameter a such rules have interestingness close to zero, significantly lower than the interestingness of any other rules.
2. For $a = 0$ (the first quarter of the table) Υ becomes the Gini gain, a measure that is strongly asymmetric (and could thus suggest the direction of the dependence) and strongly affected by adding extra independent attributes to the consequent (which is undesirable).
3. For $a = 1$ (the last quarter of the table) Υ becomes (up to a constant factor) the χ^2 measure of dependence. This measure is totally symmetric and not affected by presence of independent attributes in either antecedent or consequent. Indeed, it can be seen that all rules involving A and C have the same interestingness regardless of the presence of B in the antecedent or consequent.
4. As a varies from 0 to 1 the intermediate measures can be seen to become more and more symmetric. Measures for a being close to but less than 1 could be of practical interest since they seem to 'combine the best of the two worlds', that is, are still asymmetric and pretty insensitive to presence of independent attributes in the consequent. E.g. for $a = 0.9$ all rules having A in the antecedent and C in the consequent have interestingness close to

Table 1. Rules on synthetic data ordered by $\Upsilon_{D_{\chi^2},a}$ for different values of a

rule	$\Upsilon_{D_{\chi^2},0}$	rule	$\Upsilon_{D_{\chi^2},0.5}$
$A{\to}BC$	0.122061	$A{\to}BC$	0.0989161
$C{\to}AB$	0.0896776	$AB{\to}C$	0.0898611
$AB{\to}C$	0.0896287	$A{\to}C$	0.089861
$A{\to}C$	0.0896287	$C{\to}AB$	0.0769886
$BC{\to}A$	0.065851	$BC{\to}A$	0.0683164
$C{\to}A$	0.0658484	$C{\to}A$	0.0683142
$B{\to}AC$	3.16585e-06	$B{\to}AC$	2.50502e-06
$B{\to}A$	2.7369e-06	$B{\to}A$	2.35091e-06
$AC{\to}B$	1.37659e-06	$AC{\to}B$	1.51849e-06
$A{\to}B$	1.32828e-06	$A{\to}B$	1.46355e-06
$B{\to}C$	1.70346e-07	$B{\to}C$	1.72781e-07
$C{\to}B$	1.10069e-07	$C{\to}B$	1.22814e-07

rule	$\Upsilon_{D_{\chi^2},0.9}$	rule	$\Upsilon_{D_{\chi^2},1}$
$A{\to}BC$	0.0908769	$BC{\to}A$	0.0905673
$AB{\to}C$	0.0903859	$A{\to}BC$	0.0905673
$A{\to}C$	0.0903859	$C{\to}AB$	0.0905654
$C{\to}AB$	0.0834734	$AB{\to}C$	0.0905654
$BC{\to}A$	0.082009	$A{\to}C$	0.0905653
$C{\to}A$	0.082007	$C{\to}A$	0.0905653
$B{\to}AC$	2.19739e-06	$AC{\to}B$	2.15872e-06
$B{\to}A$	2.12646e-06	$B{\to}AC$	2.15872e-06
$AC{\to}B$	1.95101e-06	$A{\to}B$	2.08117e-06
$A{\to}B$	1.87986e-06	$B{\to}A$	2.08017e-06
$B{\to}C$	1.73782e-07	$C{\to}B$	1.74126e-07
$C{\to}B$	1.57306e-07	$B{\to}C$	1.74126e-07

0.09, while rules having C in the antecedent and A in the consequent have all interestingness close to 0.082 regardless of the presence or absence of B in the consequents. So for $a = 0.9$ the intermediate measure correctly ranked the rules indicating the true direction of the relationship.

We then repeated the above experiment on data from the UCI machine learning repository [2]. Here we present results for the *agaricus-lepiota* database containing data on North American Mushrooms. To make the ruleset size manageable we restrict ourselves to rules involving the *class* attribute indicating whether the mushroom is edible or poisonous.

In the experiment we enumerated all rules involving up to 3 attributes and ranked them by interestingness for different values of parameter a. Top ten rules for each value of a are shown in Table 2. For $a = 1$ the symmetric rules were removed.

We noticed that for any value of a most of the rules involve the *odor* attribute. Indeed the inspection of data revealed that knowing the mushroom's odor allows for identifying its class with 98.5% accuracy, far better than for any other attribute.

Table 2. Rules on mushroom dataset ordered by $\Upsilon_{D_{\chi^2},a}$ for different values of a

rule	$\Upsilon_{D_{\chi^2},0}$
class→odor ring-type	9.84024
class→odor spore-print-color	9.16709
class→odor veil-color	8.22064
class→odor gill-attachment	8.2026
class→gill-color spore-print-color	7.82161
class→ring-type spore-print-color	7.62564
class→odor stalk-root	7.60198
class→gill-color ring-type	7.28972
class→odor stalk-color-above-ring	7.19584
class→odor stalk-color-below-ring	7.14197

rule	$\Upsilon_{D_{\chi^2},0.9}$
odor→class stalk-root	3.61877
class stalk-root→odor	3.2782
odor→class cap-color	2.59777
odor→class ring-type	2.54896
odor→class spore-print-color	2.54864
stalk-color-above-ring→class stalk-color-below-ring	2.47669
class cap-color→odor	2.46105
odor→class gill-color	2.45027
stalk-color-below-ring→class stalk-color-above-ring	2.38593
class spore-print-color→odor	2.35384

rule	$\Upsilon_{D_{\chi^2},1}$
class stalk-root→odor	4.11701
class stalk-color-below-ring→stalk-color-above-ring	3.38287
stalk-color-below-ring→class stalk-color-above-ring	3.37968
class ring-type→odor	2.98764
class cap-color→odor	2.85308
odor→class gill-color	2.82423
odor→class spore-print-color	2.56331
odor→class stalk-color-below-ring	2.44004
class stalk-color-above-ring→odor	2.42725
class gill-color→spore-print-color	2.42224

We note also that similar rules are ranked close to the top for all values of a, which proves that measures throughout the family identify dependencies correctly. From data omitted in the tables it can be observed that, as in the case of synthetic data, when a approaches 1 the measures become more and more symmetric and unaffected by independent attributes in the consequent.

It has been shown experimentally that measures throughout the Υ family are useful for discovering interesting dependencies among data attributes. By modifying a numerical attribute we can obtain a whole spectrum of measure of varying degree of symmetry and dependence on the presence of extra attributes in the rule consequent. Especially interesting seem to be measures with a parameter close to, but less than 1, which combine the relative robustness against extra independent attributes, while retaining the asymmetry suggesting the direction of the dependence.

5   Open Problems and Future Directions

Above we assumed complete confidence in the estimate of the distribution of P from the data. We may want to relax this restriction and assume that P has some a posteriori distribution Ψ (not necessarily equal to Δ_P), and Q the prior distribution Θ. We can then generalize Υ as $\Upsilon'_{D,\Theta,\Psi}(P \to Q) = D(\Delta_{PQ}, \Psi \times \Theta) - D(\Delta_Q, \Theta) - D(\Delta_P, \Psi)$. When $\Psi = \Delta_P$, Υ' reduces to Υ defined above. Some of the properties of Υ are preserved by this new definition. For example, if $D = D_{\mathrm{KL}}$, and P, Q be independent, then $\Upsilon'_{\Theta,\Psi,D}(P \to Q) = 0$. Also, if $P \longrightarrow Q$ is a rule in the table $\tau = (T, H, \rho)$ and $D = D_{\mathrm{KL}}$ then $\Upsilon'_{D,\Theta,\Psi}(P \to Q) = \mathrm{gain}_{\mathrm{shannon}}(Q, P)$ regardless of the choice of Θ and Ψ.

Further theoretical and experimental evaluation of the new measure is necessary. It would be of practical interest to find a modified general definition of gain that, being asymmetric, is not affected by adding independent attributes to the consequent.

As a primary application, we envision using the measure in association rule mining systems for sorting the discovered association rules. For this purpose it would be necessary to generalize the measure to express the interestingness of a rule with respect to a system of beliefs (that could be represented for example by a set of rules). Then, the rule would be considered interesting if its probability distribution would be significantly different from the one expected based on the set of beliefs. See [13] for a discussion of a similar problem.

Further work is necessary to assess the impact that the generalized measure would have on other common datamining tasks like attribute selection in decision trees. It might, for example, be beneficial to use values of parameter a close to 1 in the upper parts of the tree when large amount of data is still available, and decreasing the value of a at lower levels, where the amount of data is small and thus we have less confidence in the estimates of probabilities.

References

1. Bayardo R.J. and R. Agrawal, *Mining the Most Interesting Rules*, Proc. of the 5th ACM SIGKDD Int'l Conf. on Knowledge Discovery and Data Mining, pp. 145-154, August 1999.
2. Blake C.L., and Merz C.J. *UCI Repository of machine learning databases* Irvine, CA: University of California, Department of Information and Computer Science, http://www.ics.uci.edu/~mlearn/MLRepository.html
3. Chou P.A., *Optimal Partitioning for classification and regression trees* IEEE Trans. on Pattern Analysis and Machine Intelligence, PAMI-13(14):340–354, 1991.
4. Silverstein C., Brin S. and Motwani R., *Beyond Market Baskets: Generalizing Association Rules to Dependence Rules* Data Mining and Knowledge Discovery, 2(1998), pp. 39-68

5. Cziszar I., *A Class of Measures of Informativity of Observation Channels*, Periodic Math. Hungarica, 2:191-213, 1972.
6. Havrda J.H., Charvát F., *Quantification Methods of Classification Processes: Concepts of Structural α Entropy*, Kybernetica, 3:30-35, 1967.
7. Kapur J.N. and Kesavan H.K., *Entropy Optimization Principles with Applications*, Academic Press, San Diego, 1992.
8. Kvålseth T.O., *Entropy and Correlation: Some comments*, IEEE Trans. on Systems, Man and Cybernetics, SMC-17(3):517–519, 1987.
9. McEliece R.J. *The Theory of Information and Coding. A mathematical Framework for Communication*, Encyclopedia of Mathematics and its Applications, Addisson-Wesley, Reading Massachusetts, 1977.
10. Mitchell T.M.. *Machine Learning*, McGraw-Hill, ISBN: 0070428077.
11. Morimoto Y., Fukuda T., Matsuzawa H., Tokuyama T. and Yoda K. *Algorithms for Mining Association Rules for Binary Segmentations of Huge Categorical Databases*, Proc. of the 24th Conf. on Very Large Databases, pp. 380-391, 1998
12. Morishita S., *On Classification and Regression* Proc. of the First Int'l Conf. on Discovery Science — Lecture Notes in Artificial Intelligence 1532:40–57, 1998
13. Padmanabhan B. and Tuzhilin A. *Unexpectedness as a measure of interestingness in knowledge discovery* Decision and Support Systems 27(1999), pp. 303-318
14. Simovici, D. A. and Tenney R. L. *Relational Database Systems*, Academic Press, 1995, San Diego.
15. Wehenkel L., *On uncertainty Measures Used for Decision Tree Induction*, Info. Proc. and Manag. of Uncertainty in Knowledge-Based Systems (IPMU'96), July 1-5, 1996, Granada Spain, pp. 413–418.
16. Witten I.H., and Eibe F., *Data Mining, Practical Machine Learning and Techniques with JAVA Implementations*, Academic Press, San Diego, CA, 2000, ISBN: 1558605525.

Error Correcting Codes with Optimized Kullback-Leibler Distances for Text Categorization

Jörg Kindermann, Gerhard Paass, and Edda Leopold

GMD – German National Research Center for Information Technology
D-52754 Sankt Augustin

Abstract. We extend a multi-class categorization scheme proposed by Dietterich and Bakiri 1995 for binary classifiers, using error correcting codes. The extension comprises the computation of the codes by a simulated annealing algorithm and optimization of Kullback-Leibler (KL) category distances within the code-words. For the first time, we apply the scheme to text categorization with support vector machines (SVMs) on several large text corpora with more than 100 categories. The results are compared to 1-of-N coding (i.e. one SVM for each text category). We also investigate codes with optimized KL distance between the text categories which are merged in the code-words. We find that error correcting codes perform better than 1-of-N coding with increasing code length. For very long codes, the performance is in some cases further improved by KL-distance optimization.

1 Introduction

Automatic text categorization has become a vital topic in many text-mining applications. Imagine for example the automatic classification of Internet pages for a search engine database. There exist promising approaches to this task, among them, support vector machines (SVM) [9] are one of the most successful solutions. One remaining problem is however that SVM can only separate two classes at a time. Thus the traditional 1-of-n output coding scheme is applied in this case: n classes will need n classifiers to be trained independently. Early alternative solutions were published by Dietterich and Bakiri [4], and Vapnik [14, p438]. More recently, research in multi-class SVMs increased, see for example Guermeur et al. [7], Platt et al. [13], Crammer et al. [2], and Allwein et.al. [1].

Hsu and Lin [8] report that for many categories, multi-class solutions which construct a system of binary SVMs have advantages in computational resources over integrative extensions of SVM. It is therefore interesting to apply the approach of [4] to text categorization. Dietterich and Bakiri use a distributed output code. A second argument is that if the output code has more bits than needed to represent each class as a unique pattern, the additional bits may be used to correct classification errors. In this paper we investigate the potential of error correcting codes for text categorization with many categories. We extend the work in [4] by a simulated annealing algorithm for code generation and optimization of Kullback-Leibler (KL) category distances within the code-words.

L. De Raedt and A. Siebes (Eds.): PKDD 2001, LNAI 2168, pp. 266–276, 2001.

For the first time, we apply the scheme to text categorization on several large text corpora with 42 to 109 categories and up to 11 million running words. The results are compared to 1-of-N coding (i.e. one SVM for each text category).

2 The Text Corpora

Table 1 gives an overview over the quantitative properties of the four different text corpora we used. The columns have the following meaning: '# categories' is the number of categories to distinguish. '# documents' is the total number of texts in the corpus. '# types' is the total number of different words, or, more precisely, different alphanumeric strings including punctuation marks to be found in a corpus. '# tokens' is the number of running words in a corpus. 'min length' is the minimal length of a document in running words (tokens). Shorter documents were discarded from the corpus. 'min # docs per cat' is the minimal number of documents of a specific category to be found in the corpus. All categories with fewer documents were discarded. So each corpus was divided into n disjoint sets by its n remaining categories.

Table 1. Quantitative properties of the text corpora

corpus	# categories	# documents	# types	# tokens	min length	min # docs per cat.
bz	64	4366	103665	992483	200	10
reuters	42	10216	54832	887357	15	10
sjm	109	36431	254440	11163970	300	80
wsj	101	41838	203638	11989608	100	50

We did not apply any preprocessing steps such as stemming, elimination of stop-words, etc. to the corpora. Our research on text coding for SVMs in [11] indicated, that exhaustive inclusion of full word-forms, numbers and punctuation improves recognition rates. We now describe the contents of the four corpora:

- *bz:* Texts from the German newspaper "Berliner Zeitung". These texts were drawn from the online archive of the newspaper[1]. The categorization task here was to recognize the **author** of the document. There are 64 different authors in total. We choose this corpus, because we already had promising results for authorship attribution (see [3]).
- *reuters:* We used the Reuters-21578 dataset[2] compiled by David Lewis and originally collected by the Carnegie group from the Reuters newswire in 1987. The task was to recognize the correct topic out of 42 selected topics. We already used a smaller subset of the *reuters* corpus in a pilot study [10].

---

[1] see http://www.BerlinOnline.de

[2] (obtainable at http://www.research.att.com/~lewis/reuters21578.html)

- *sjm:* News articles from 1991 "San Jose Mercury News" from the TIPSTER database vol. 3. The TIPSTER catalogs are available from the Linguistic Data Consortium (http://www.ldc.upenn.edu) Each news document contains a list of manually-assigned codes for categories. To exclude problems of overlapping categories, we chose only the first item from the list as a label of the document.
- *wsj:* Newspaper texts from the "Wall Street Journal", 1990-92, from the TIPSTER database vol. 2. A for the preceding corpus we chose the first item from the list of categories for each text.

Figure 1 shows the type-frequency spectra of the corpora. It displays frequency on the x-axis and number of words with a given frequency on the y-axis. A small slope of the spectrum is an indicator of standardized language use in a text corpus (see [11] for details). With respect to this criterion, language use in the *bz* corpus appears to by more creative than in the others.

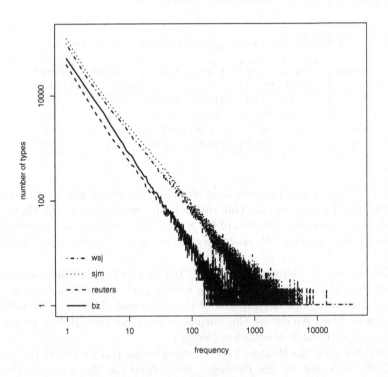

Fig. 1. Type-frequency spectra of the text corpora

3 Methods

3.1 Error Correcting Codes

Classification with error correcting codes can be seen "as a kind of communications problem in which the identity of the correct output class for a new example is being transmitted over a channel which consists of the input features, the training examples, and the learning algorithm" ([4, p266]). The classification of a new set of input features can no longer be determined from the output of one classifier. It is coded in a distributed representation of l outputs from *all* classifiers. Table 2 shows an example of an error correcting code for $n = 8$ classes with $l = 5$ code-words. The code-words are the columns of the table. Each classifier has to learn one of the code-words. This means, that the classifier should output a 1 for all input data belonging to one of the classes which are assigned 1 in the code-word of the classifier, and 0 in all other cases. The code for a specific class is to be found in the row of the table which is assigned to the class. The code length in bits is the number of code-words, 5 in our example. Note that at least $ceiling(log_2(n))$ code-words are required to distinguish n classes.

Table 2. Error correcting code for 8 classes with 5 code-words

class	code-word				
	1	2	3	4	5
1	0	0	0	1	1
2	0	0	1	0	1
3	0	1	0	0	1
4	0	1	1	0	0
5	1	0	0	1	0
6	1	1	0	1	1
7	1	1	1	0	1
8	1	1	1	1	0

Noise is introduced by the learning set, choice of features, and flaws of the learning algorithm. Noise may induce classification errors. But if there are more code-words than needed to distinguish n classes, i.e. $l >> log_2(n)$, we can use the additional bits to correct errors: If the output code does not match exactly one of the classes, take the class with minimal Hamming distance. If the minimum Hamming distance between class codes is d, we can in this way correct at least $\frac{d-1}{2}$ single bit errors (see [4, p.266]). It is therefore important to use codes with maximized Hamming distance for the classes.

There are several potential advantages in this approach: The number of required classifiers increases with $\mathcal{O}(log_2(n))$ only, and additional bits can be used for error correction.

We did not use the optimization criteria given by Dietterich and Bakiri to find optimal codes. Instead, we used simulated annealing to optimize a mix of Hamming distances of class codes, and of code-words. For a corpus with n

Table 3. Minimal Hamming distances for the *sjm*-codes

# code	min Hamming distance		KL-distance	
words	categories	code-words	random	optimized
54	21	48	4.080	4.054
81	34	46	4.085	4.059
109	47	43	4.084	4.066
164	75	40	4.084	4.072

categories to distinguish, we generated error correcting codes of four different sizes: $n \cdot 0.5$, $n \cdot 0.75$, $n \cdot 1.0$, and $n \cdot 1.5$, bits.

See Table 3 for the Hamming distances of a set of codes we used to categorize the *sjm*-corpus. For larger numbers of code-words, i.e. increasing l, the hamming distances grow. The reason is that the number of class codes to be generated remains constant ($n = 109$) and therefore we have more degrees of freedom to place the bits in the class codes. The Hamming distances of code-words decrease with increasing l. Here, we have constant length of code-words, but increasing numbers of them. Therefore we have decreasing degrees of freedom to design the code-words.

3.2   Optimized Kullback-Leibler Distance

The mapping of corpus categories onto error correcting codes has been arbitrary so far. Remember that each SVM in the classifier system has to implement categorization according to one code-*word*, i.e. a special column of the code matrix like the one shown in Table 2. This means that it has to recognize documents from each category labeled 1 in that column, and to reject all categories labeled 0.

Our hypothesis was that a reordering of classes such that more similar classes were grouped together in each of the code-words should improve the performance. We used the Kullback-Leibler test [6, p.57] to compute the distance $KLD(p_1, p_2)$ between two categories p_1 and p_2 as shown in equation 1.

$$KLD(p_1, p_2) \quad = \quad \sum_{i=1}^{n} p_1(i) \log\left(\frac{p_1(i)}{q(i)}\right) + \sum_{i=1}^{n} p_2(i) \log\left(\frac{p_2(i)}{q(i)}\right) \qquad (1)$$

$$q(i) = \frac{p_1(i) + p_2(i)}{2}$$

The two categories are represented by their word-frequency vectors p_1 and p_2 of length n. These vectors contain the frequencies of all types in the corpus, but the counts are restricted to documents which belong to the category in question. Therefore some values may be equal to 0.

The Kullback-Leibler Distance of a whole Matrix M of error-correcting codes is now computed by comparing the categories with label 1 against each other and also the categories with label 0. Let M_1 be the set of text categories which are labeled 1 in M and M_0 the set of text categories which are labeled 0 in M. Then we can define the Kullback-Leibler Distance of M as

$$KLD(M) = \frac{\sum_{p_i, p_j \in M_0} KLD(p_i, p_j)}{l_0 * (l_0 - 1) * 0.5} + \frac{\sum_{p_i, p_j \in M_1} KLD(p_i, p_j)}{l_1 * (l_1 - 1) * 0.5} \qquad (2)$$

l_0 is the number of elements in M_0, l_1 is the number of elements in M_1.

We tested optimization of $KLD(M)$ **after** generation of the code Matrix M, as well as simultaneous optimization of Hamming distance and Kullback-Leibler distances. In this paper we only report results on the simultaneous optimization, because the performance was better in general. See Table 3 for KLD values of the *sjm* corpus.

3.3   Support Vector Machines

Support Vector Machines (SVM) recently gained popularity in the learning community [14]. In its simplest linear form, an SVM is a hyperplane that separates a set of positive examples from a set of negative examples with maximum interclass distance, the *margin*.

The SVM can be extended to nonlinear models by mapping the input space into a very high-dimensional feature space chosen a priori. In this space the optimal separating hyperplane is constructed [14, p.421].

The distinctive advantage of the SVM for text categorization is its ability to process many thousand different inputs. This opens the opportunity to use all *words* in a text directly as features. For each word w_i the number of times of occurrence is recorded. Joachims [9] and also we [11] used the SVM for the classification of text into different topic categories. Dumais et al. [5] use linear SVM for text categorization because they are both accurate and fast. They are 35 times faster to train than the next most accurate (a decision tree) of the tested classifiers. They apply SVM to the *reuters* collection, e-mails and web pages.

3.4   Transformations of Frequency Vectors and Kernel Functions

The mapping of text to the SVM input space consists of three parts. First the type-frequencies (i.e. number of occurrences of words) are transformed by a bijective mapping. The resulting vector is multiplied by a vector of importance weights, and is finally normalized to unit length. We used those transformations that yielded the best results in [11].

We define the vector of logarithmic type frequencies of document d_i by

$$l_i \quad = \quad \left(\log\big(1 + f(w_1, d_i)\big), \ldots, \log\big(1 + f(w_n, d_i)\big) \right), \qquad (3)$$

where $f(w_k, d_i)$ is the frequency of occurrence of term w_k in document d_i, and n is the number of different terms in all documents of the collection. Logarithmic frequencies are combined with different importance weights. They are normalized with respect to L_2.

Importance weights can be used to quantify how specific a given type is to the documents of a text collection. A type which is evenly distributed across the document collection should be given a low importance weight because it is judged to be less specific for the documents it occurs in. A type which is used in only a few documents should be given a high importance weight. Redundancy quantifies the skewness of a probability distribution, and r_k is a measure of how much the distribution of a term w_k in the various documents deviates from the uniform distribution.

We therefore consider the empirical distribution of a type over the documents in the collection and define the importance weight of type w_k by

$$r_k \;=\; \log N + \sum_{i=1}^{N} \frac{f(w_k, d_i)}{f(w_k)} \log \frac{f(w_k, d_i)}{f(w_k)}, \tag{4}$$

where N is the number of documents in the collection. This yields a vector of importance weights for the whole document collection:

$$\mathbf{r} \;=\; (r_1, \ldots, r_n). \tag{5}$$

The advantage of redundancy over inverse document frequency is that it does not simply count the documents a type occurs in but takes into account the frequencies of occurrence in each of the document. The difference between redundancy and idf is larger for longer documents.

From the standpoint of the SVM learning algorithm the best normalization rule is the L_2-normalization because it yields the best error bounds. L_2-normalization has been used by Joachims [9] and Dumais et al. [5]. So the complete frequency transformation we used is defined as

$$\mathbf{x}_i \;=\; \frac{\mathbf{l}_i * \mathbf{r}}{\|\mathbf{l}_i * \mathbf{r}\|_{L_2}}$$

We used only the linear kernel function $K(\mathbf{x}, \mathbf{x}') = \mathbf{x} \cdot \mathbf{x}'$ of the SVM, because increased computing times prevented tests with nonlinear kernels. Furthermore linear kernels performed very well in our pilot study [10].

4   Performance Measures

We applied performance measures which are widely used in information retrieval, because we think they are more adequate to text categorization than plain error rates.

4.1   Definitions

Precision (equation 6) is the percentage of documents in the target category i of all those documents which are categorized (perhaps wrongly) as category i.

$$prc(i) = 100 * \frac{c_t(i)}{c_t(i) + e_o(i)}, \tag{6}$$

$$prc(i) = 0 \text{ if } c_t(i) = 0$$

Recall (equation 7) is the percentage of documents in target category i which are recognized correctly.

$$rec(i) = 100 * \frac{c_t(i)}{c_t(i) + e_t(i)} \tag{7}$$

$c_t(i)$ correctly categorized documents of target class
$e_t(i)$ wrongly categorized documents of target class
$c_o(i)$ correctly categorized documents of other classes
$e_o(i)$ wrongly categorized documents of other classes

Since *precision* and *recall* may be inadequate to measure the performance on very small categories, we also computed a performance measure combined from *precision* and *recall*. It is called the *F-measure* (see [12, p.269]):

$$F(i) = \left(\alpha \frac{1}{prc(i)} + (1 - \alpha)\frac{1}{rec(i)}\right)^{-1} \tag{8}$$

α is a weighting factor. In this paper we set $\alpha = 0.5$, because we wanted to put equal importance on both *precision* and *recall*. Thus we get $F(i) = 2 \cdot \frac{prc(i) \cdot rec(i)}{prc(i) + rec(i)}$ The mean performance over all N categories of a corpus is

$$prc = \sum_{i=1}^{N} p_t(i) \cdot prc(i) \tag{9}$$

$$rec = \sum_{i=1}^{N} p_t(i) \cdot rec(i) \tag{10}$$

$$F = \sum_{i=1}^{N} p_t(i) \cdot F(i) \tag{11}$$

$p_t(i)$ is the probability of occurrence of category i in the corpus. We determined $p_t(i)$ as the fraction of documents of category i in all documents of the corpus. Weighted in this way, prc, rec, and F again can vary between 0% and 100%.

4.2 Results

To exploit the training set S_0 of each corpus in a better way, we used the following *cross-testing* procedure. S_0 was randomly divided into 3 subsets S_1, S_2, S_3 of nearly equal size. Then three different SVM classification systems were determined using $S_0 \setminus S_i$ as training set and S_i was used as test set. The numbers of correctly and wrongly classified documents were added up yielding an effective test set of all documents in S_0. The SVM implementation of Joachims (http://ais.gmd.de/~thorsten/svm_light/) was used for our experiments.

Table 4 shows the mean performance with respect to *precision* (equation 9), *recall* (equation 10), and *F-measure* (equation 11). The first four rows give the values for the error correcting codes of different bit length (Sect. 3.1). The last row gives the value of the corresponding 1-of-N codes. The best values are printed in bold font. Table 5 shows the corresponding values for error correcting codes with optimized KL-distance.

In both tables the 1-of-N coding has better *precision* for corpora *bz* and *reuters* and better *recall* for for corpora *sjm* and *wsj*. The combined *F-measure* however is better for error correcting codes on all four corpora.

Comparing tables with and without KL-optimization, there is no clear tendency. It seems that for corpora *bz* and *sjm* there generally is a slight improvement. A slight degradation can be seen in most cases of *reuters* and *wsj*.

Table 6 shows the percentage of categories on which error correcting codes perform better than the 1-of-N code with respect to *precision* (equation 9), *recall* (equation 10), and *F-measure* (equation 11). Table 7 shows the corresponding percentages for error correcting codes with optimized KL-distance.

We observe converse trends for *precision* and *recall*: Those corpora with many good results for error correcting codes on *precision* tend to perform bad on *recall* and vice versa.

Comparing tables with and without KL-optimization, there is a mixed tendency for *precision* and *recall*. Regarding the *F-measure*, there is improvement for most KL-optimized codes.

5 Conclusion

We investigated the potential of error correcting codes for text categorization on several large text collections. The error correcting code classifier was implemented as a combination of binary SVMs. We compared the results with those of a 1-of-N classifier. The main result is that long error correcting codes perform better than 1-of-N codes for a combination of *precision* and *recall* error measures.

We also investigated the effects of optimization of the Kullback-Leibler distance of the text categories grouped together in the code-words. The classification performance could be improved slightly for the corpora *bz* and *sjm*, but the latter result seems to be of mostly theoretical interest.

Acknowledgments. We would like to thank Thorsten Joachims and Tamas Horvath for inspiring discussions on this topic.

Table 4. Mean performance on all corpora - *no* KL-optimization

code length	bz	reuters	sjm	wsj
50%	80.4	91.5	58.3	**59.0**
75%	79.8	91.4	57.7	58.6
100%	79.8	91.4	58.6	58.2
150%	79.6	91.8	**59.8**	58.7
1-of-n	**89.0**	**93.2**	53.2	47.6

precision

code length	bz	reuters	sjm	wsj
50%	78.2	**91.8**	58.5	57.7
75%	79.2	91.5	59.0	58.5
100%	79.7	91.5	59.8	58.3
150%	**80.2**	91.7	59.6	58.8
1-of-n	60.7	89.1	**63.9**	**69.0**

recall

code length	bz	reuters	sjm	wsj
50%	76.9	**91.4**	55.5	55.7
75%	76.8	91.0	55.5	56.5
100%	77.2	91.0	**56.5**	56.5
150%	**78.0**	91.3	56.1	**57.0**
1-of-n	69.5	90.4	55.9	54.9

F-measure

Table 5. Mean performance on all corpora - *with* KL-optimization.

code length	bz	reuters	sjm	wsj
50%	80.6	91.2	58.2	58.3
75%	80.3	91.2	58.4	**58.8**
100%	79.6	91.3	58.3	58.3
150%	80.9	91.5	**58.9**	58.7
1-of-n	**89.0**	**93.2**	53.2	47.6

precision

code length	bz	reuters	sjm	wsj
50%	79.0	91.4	58.7	57.5
75%	80.0	91.3	59.3	58.6
100%	80.4	91.5	59.7	58.6
150%	**80.7**	**91.6**	59.9	58.6
1-of-n	60.7	89.1	**63.9**	**69.0**

recall

code length	bz	reuters	sjm	wsj
50%	77.1	91.0	55.8	55.7
75%	78.0	90.9	55.8	**56.8**
100%	78.2	91.1	56.4	56.6
150%	**78.5**	**91.3**	**56.7**	**56.8**
1-of-n	69.5	90.4	55.9	54.9

F-measure

References

1. Erin L. Allwein, Robert E. Schapire, and Yoram Singer. Reducing multiclass to binary: A unifying approach for margin classifiers. In *Proc. 17th International Conf. on Machine Learning*, pages 9–16. Morgan Kaufmann, San Francisco, CA, 2000.

2. Koby Crammer and Yoram Singer. On the learnability and design of output codes for multiclass problems. In *Computational Learing Theory*, pages 35–46, 2000.

3. J. Diederich, K. Kindermann, E. Leopold, and G. Paass. Authorship attribution with support vector machines. *Applied Intelligence: The International Journal of Artificial Intelligence, Neural Networks, and Complex Problem-Solving Techniques*, 2001. in press.

4. T.G. Dietterich and G. Bakiri. Solving multiclass learning via error-correcting output codes. *Journal of Artificial Intelligence Research*, 2:263–286, 1995.

5. S. Dumais, J. Platt, D. Heckerman, and M. Sahami. Inductive learning algorithms and representations for text categorization. In *7th International Conference on Information and Knowledge Managment*, 1998.

6. Stephen E. Fienberg. *The analysis of cross-classified categorical data.* 1980.

Table 6. Percentage of categories on which EC-codes perform better than 1-of-N codes - *no* KL-optimization

code length	bz	reuters	sjm	wsj
50%	15.6	23.8	74.3	47.7
75%	20.3	14.3	83.2	60.6
100%	18.8	11.9	82.2	56.9
150%	17.2	23.8	89.1	63.3

precision

code length	bz	reuters	sjm	wsj
50%	84.4	66.7	17.8	44.0
75%	85.9	76.2	21.8	43.1
100%	90.6	83.3	16.8	48.6
150%	89.1	85.7	19.8	37.6

recall

code length	bz	reuters	sjm	wsj
50%	73.4	45.2	37.6	41.3
75%	75.0	52.4	43.6	45.9
100%	65.6	59.5	48.5	56.0
150%	75.0	69.0	60.4	46.8

F-measure

Table 7. Percentage of categories on which EC-codes perform better than 1-of-N codes - *with* KL-optimization

code length	bz	reuters	sjm	wsj
50%	20.3	14.3	73.3	56.0
75%	17.2	16.7	84.2	63.3
100%	14.1	19.0	83.2	58.7
150%	20.3	16.7	91.1	65.1

precision

code length	bz	reuters	sjm	wsj
50%	89.1	59.5	12.9	40.4
75%	90.6	78.6	15.8	40.4
100%	90.6	81.0	16.8	46.8
150%	95.3	92.9	12.9	51.4

recall

code length	bz	reuters	sjm	wsj
50%	79.7	31.0	35.6	45.0
75%	78.1	52.4	46.5	46.8
100%	75.0	61.9	47.5	57.8
150%	79.7	76.2	53.5	61.5

F-measure

7. Y. Guermeur, A. Eliseeff, and H. Paugam-Moisy. A new multi-class svm based on a uniform convergence result. In S.-I. Amari, C.L. Giles, M. Gori, and V. Piuri, editors, *Proceedings of the IEEE-INNS-ENNS International Joint Conference on Neural Networks IJCNN 2000*, pages IV–183 – IV–188, Los Alamitos, 2000. IEEE Computer Society.
8. C.-W. Hsu and C.J. Lin. A comparison on methods for multi-class support vector machines. unpulished manuscript, see http://www.csie.ntu.edu.tw/~cjlin/papers/multisvm.ps.gz, April 2001.
9. T. Joachims. Text categorization with support vector machines: Learning with many relevant features. In C. Nedellec and C. Rouveirol, editors, *European Conference on Machine Learning (ECML)*, 1998.
10. J. Kindermann, E. Leopold, and G. Paass. Multi-class classification with error correcting codes. Technical report, GMD, Oct 2000. Beiträge zum Treffen der GI Fachgruppe 1.1.3 Maschinelles Lernen.
11. E. Leopold and J. Kindermann. Text categorization with support vector machines. how to represent texts in input space? *Machine Learning*, 2001. in press.
12. C. Manning and H. Schütze. *Foundations of Statistical Natural Language Processing*. MIT Press, 1999.
13. J. Platt, N. Cristianini, and J. Shawe-Taylor. Large margin dags for multiclass classification. In *Advances in Neural Information Processing Systems 12*. MIT Press, 2000.
14. V. N. Vapnik. *Statistical Learning Theory*. Wiley, New York, 1998.

Propositionalisation and Aggregates

Arno J. Knobbe[1,2], Marc de Haas[3], and Arno Siebes[2]

[1]Kiminkii, P.O. box 171, NL-3990 DD Houten, The Netherlands, a.knobbe@kiminkii.com
[2]Utrecht University, P.O. box 80 089, NL-3508 TB Utrecht, The Netherlands
siebes@cs.uu.nl
[3]Perot Systems Nederland B.V., P.O. box 2729, NL-3800 GG Amersfoort, The Netherlands
marc.dehaas@ps.net

Abstract. The fact that data is scattered over many tables causes many problems in the practice of data mining. To deal with this problem, one either constructs a single table by hand, or one uses a Multi-Relational Data Mining algorithm. In this paper, we propose a different approach in which the single table is constructed automatically using aggregate functions, which repeatedly summarise information from different tables over associations in the datamodel. Following the construction of the single table, we apply traditional data mining algorithms. Next to an in-depth discussion of our approach, the paper presents results of experiments on three well-known data sets.

1 Introduction

An important practical problem in data mining is that we often want to find models and patterns over data that resides in multiple tables. This is solved by either constructing a single table by hand (deriving attributes from the other tables) or by using a Multi-Relational Data Mining or ILP approach. In this paper we propose another approach, viz., automatic construction of the single mining table using aggregates.

The motivation for the use of aggregates stems from the observation that the difficult case in constructing a single table is when there are one-to-many relationships between tables. The traditional way to summarise such relationships in Statistics and OLAP is through aggregates that are based on histograms, such as *count, sum, min, max*, and *avg*. We limit ourselves to these aggregates, but note that they can be applied recursively over a collection of relationships.

The idea of propositionalisation (the construction of one table) is not new. Several relatively successful algorithms have been proposed in the context of Inductive Logic Programming (ILP) [6, 12, 7, 1, 2]. A common aspect of these algorithms is that the derived table consists solely of binary features, each corresponding to a (promising) clause discovered by an ILP-algorithm. Especially for numerical attributes, our approach leads to a markedly different search space.

We illustrate our approach on three well-known data sets. The aim of these experiments is twofold. Firstly, to demonstrate the accuracy in a range of domains. Secondly, to illustrate the radically different way our approach models structured data, compared to ILP or MRDM approaches.

L. De Raedt and A. Siebes (Eds.): PKDD 2001, LNAI 2168, pp. 277-288, 2001.

The paper is organised as follows. First we discuss propositionalisation and aggregates in more detail. In particular we introduce the notion of depth, to illustrate the complexity of the search space. Next we introduce the RollUp algorithm that constructs the single table. Then we present the results of our experiments and the paper ends with a discussion and conclusions.

2 Propositionalisation

In this section we describe the basic concepts involved in propositionalisation, and provide some definitions. In this paper, we define propositionalisation as the process of transforming a multi-relational dataset, containing structured examples, into a propositional dataset with derived attribute-value features, describing the structural properties of the examples. The process can thus be thought of as summarising data stored in multiple tables in a single table (*the target table*) containing one record per example. The aim of this process, of course, is to pre-process multi-relational data for subsequent analysis by attribute-value learners.

We will be using this definition in the broadest sense. We will make no assumptions about the datatype of the derived attribute (binary, nominal, numeric, etc.) nor do we specify what language will be used to specify the propositional features. Traditionally, propositionalisation has been approached from an ILP standpoint with only binary features, expressed in first-order logic (FOL)[6, 7, 1, 2]. To our knowledge, the use of other aggregates than existence has been limited. One example is given in [4], which describes a propositionalisation-step where numeric attributes were defined for counts of different substructures. [5] also mentions aggregates as a means of establishing probabilistic relationships between objects in two tables. It is our aim to analyse the applicability of a broader range of aggregates.

With a growing availability of algorithms from the fields of ILP and Multi-Relational Data Mining (MRDM), one might wonder why such a cumbersome pre-processing step is desirable in the first place, instead of applying one of these algorithms to the multi-relational data directly. The following is a (possibly incomplete) list of reasons:

- Pragmatic choice for specific propositional techniques. People may wish to apply their favourite attribute-value learner, or only have access to commercial of-the-shelf Data Mining tools. Good examples can be found in the contributions to the financial dataset challenge at PKDD conferences [14].
- Superiority of propositional algorithms with respect to certain Machine Learning parameters. Although extra facilities are quickly being added to existing ILP engines, propositional algorithms still have a head-start where it concerns handling of numeric values, regression, distance measures, cumulativity etc.
- Greater speed of propositional algorithms. This advantage of course only holds if the preceding work for propositionalisation was limited, or performed only once and then reused during multiple attribute-value learning sessions.
- Advantages related to multiple consecutive learning steps. Because we are applying two learning steps, we are effectively combining two search strategies. The first step essentially transforms a multi-relational search space into a propositional one. The second step then uses these complex patterns to search deeper

than either step could achieve when applied in isolation. This issue is investigated in more detail in the remainder of this section.

The term propositionalisation leads to some confusion because, although it pertains to the initial step of flattening a multi-relational database, it is often used to indicate the whole approach, including the subsequent propositional learning step. Because we are mostly interested in the two steps in unison, and for the sake of discussion, we introduce the following generic algorithm. The name is taken from Czech, and indicates a two-step dance.

Polka (DB D; DM M; int r, p)
$\quad P := \text{MRDM}\ (D, M, r);$
$\quad R := \text{PDM}\ (P, p);$

The algorithm takes a database D and datamodel M (acting as declarative bias), and first applies a Multi-Relational Data Mining algorithm MRDM. The resulting propositional features P are then fed to a propositional Data Mining algorithm PDM, producing result R. We use the integers r and p very informally to identify the extent of the multi-relational and propositional search, respectively. Note that the propositionalisation step is independent of subsequent use in propositional learning.

In order to characterise more formally the extent of the search, we introduce three measures that are functions of the patterns that are considered. The values of the measures for the most complex patterns in the search space are then measures for the extent of the search algorithm. We can thus characterise both individual patterns, as well as algorithms. The definition is based on the graphical pattern language of Selection Graphs, introduced in [8], but can be re-written in terms of other languages such as FOL, relational algebra or SQL. We first repeat our basic definition of Selection Graphs.

Definition. A *selection graph* G is a pair (N, E), where N is a set of pairs (t, C), t is a table in the data model and C is a, possibly empty, set of conditions on attributes in t of type *t.a operator c*; the *operator* is one of the usual selection operators, $=$, $>$, etc. E is a set of triples (p, q, a) called *selection edges*, where p and q are selection nodes and a is an association between $p.t$ and $q.t$ in the data model. The selection graph contains at least one node n_0 (the root node) that corresponds to the target table t_0.

Now assume G is a Selection Graph.

Definition. variable-depth: $\quad d_v\ (G)$ equals the length of the longest path in G.

Definition. clause-depth: $\quad d_c\ (G)$ equals the sum of the number of non-root nodes, edges and conditions in G.

Definition. variable-width: $\quad w_v\ (G)$ equals the largest sum of the number of conditions and children per node, not including the root-node.

The intuition of these definitions is as follows. An algorithm searches *variable-deep*, if pieces of discovered substructure are refined by adding more substructure, resulting in chains of variables (edges in Selection Graphs). With each new variable, information from a new table is involved. An algorithm searches *clause-deep*, if it considers very specific patterns, regardless of the number of tables involved. Even propositional algorithms may produce clause-deep patterns that contain many conditions at the root-node and no other nodes. Rather than long chains of variables, *variable-wide* algorithms are concerned with the frequent reuse of a single variable. If information from a new table is included, it will be further refined by extra restrictions, either through conditions on this information, or through further substructure.

Example. The following Selection Graph, which refers to a 3-table database introduced in [8], identifies parents above 40 who have a child and bought a toy. The measures produce the following complexity characteristics:

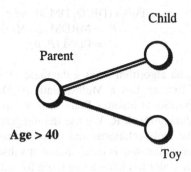

$$d_v(G)=1, d_c(G)=5, w_v(G)=0$$

The complexity measures can now be used to relate the search depth of Polka to the propositional and multi-relational algorithm it is made up of.

Lemma 1. d_v (Polka) = d_v (MRDM)
Lemma 2. d_c (Polka) = d_c (MRDM) · d_c (PDM)
Lemma 3. w_v (Polka) = w_v (MRDM)

Not surprisingly, the complexity of Polka depends largely on the complexity of the actual propositionalisation step. However, lemma 2 demonstrates that Polka considers very clause-deep patterns, in fact deeper than a multi-relational algorithm would consider in isolation. This is due to the combining of search spaces mentioned earlier. Later on we will examine the search restrictions that the use of aggregates have on the propositionalisation step and thus on Polka.

3   Aggregates

In the previous section we observed that an essential element of propositionalisation is the ability to summarise information distributed over several tables in the target table. We require functions that can reduce pieces of substructure to a single value, which describes some aspects of this substructure. Such functions are called aggregates. Having a set of well-chosen aggregates will allow us to describe the essence of the structural information over a wide variety of structures.

We define an aggregate as a function that takes as input a set of records in a database, related through the associations in the data model, and produces a single value as output. We will be using aggregates to project information stored in several tables on one of these tables, essentially adding virtual attributes to this table. In the case where the information is projected on the target table, and structural information belonging to an example is summarised as a new feature of that example, aggregates can be thought of as a form of feature construction.

Our broad definition includes aggregates of a great variety of complexity. An important aspect of the complexity of an aggregate is the number of (associations between) tables it involves. As each aggregate essentially considers a subset of the data model, we can use our 3 previously defined complexity-measures for data models to characterise aggregates. Specifically variable-depth is useful to classify aggregates. An aggregate of variable-depth 0 involves just one table, and is hence a case of propositional feature construction. In their basic usage, aggregates found in SQL (count, min, sum, etc.) have a variable-depth of 1, whereas variable-deeper aggregates represent some form of Multi-Relational pattern (benzene-rings in molecules, etc.). Using this classification of variable-depth we give some examples to illustrate the range of possibilities.

$d_v(A) = 0$:
- Propositions (adult == (age $\geq$ 18))
- Arithmetic functions (area == width·length)

$d_v(A) = 1$:
- Count, count with condition
- Count distinct
- Min, max, sum, avg
- Exists, exists with condition
- Select record (eldest son, first contract)
- Predominant value

$d_v(A) > 1$:
- Exists substructure
- Count substructure
- Conjunction of aggregates (maximum count of children)

Clearly the list of possible classes of aggregates is long, and the number of instances is infinite. In order to arrive at a practical and manageable solution for propositionalisation we will have to drastically limit the range of classes and instances. Apart from deterministic and heuristic rules to select good candidates, pragmatic limitations to a small set of aggregate classes are unavoidable. In this paper we have chosen to restrict ourselves to the classes available in SQL, and combinations thereof. The remainder of this paper further investigates the choice of instances.

4   Summarisation

We will be viewing the propositionalisation process as a series of steps in which information in one table is projected onto records in another table successively. Each association in the data model gives rise to one such step. The specifics of such a step, which we will refer to as summarisation, are the subject of this section.

Let us consider two tables P and Q, neither of which needs to be the target table, that are joined by an association A. By summarising over A, information can be added to P about the structural properties of A, as well as the data within Q. To summarise Q, a set of aggregates of variable-depth 1 are needed.

As was demonstrated before in [8], the multiplicity of association A influences the search space of multi-relational patterns involving A. The same is true for summarisation over A using aggregates. Our choice of aggregates depends on the multiplicity of A. In particular if we summarise Q over A only the multiplicity on the side of Q is relevant. This is because an association in general describes two relationships between the records in both tables, one for each direction. The following four options exist:

1   For every record in P there is but a single record in Q. This is basically a look-up over a foreign key relation and no aggregates are required. A simple join will add all non-key attributes of Q to P.

0..1   Similar to the 1 case, but now a look-up may fail because a record in P may not have a corresponding record in Q. An outer join is necessary, which fills in NULL values for missing records.

1..n   For every record in P, there is at least one record in Q. Aggregates are required in order to capture the information in the group of records belonging to a single record in P.

0..n   Similar to the 1..n case, but now the value of certain aggregates may be undefined due to empty groups. Special care will need to be taken to deal with the resulting NULL values.

Let us now consider the 1..n case in more detail. A imposes a grouping on the records in Q. For m records in P there will be m groups of records in Q. Because of the set-semantics of relational databases every group can be described by a collection of histograms or data-cubes. We can now view an aggregate instance as a function of one of these types of histograms. For example the *predominant* aggregate for an attribute $Q.a$ simply returns the value corresponding to the highest count in the histogram of $Q.a$. Note that m groups will produce m histograms and thus m values for one aggregate instance, one for each record in P. The notion of functions of histograms helps us to define relevant aggregate classes.

count. The *count* aggregate is the most obvious aggregate through its direct relation to histograms. The most basic instance without conditions simply returns the single value in the 0-dimensional histogram. Adding a single condition requires a 1-dimensional histogram of the attribute involved in the condition. For example the number of sons in a family can be computed from a histogram of gender of that family. An attribute with a cardinalty c will produce c aggregate instances of *count* with one condition. It is clear that the number of instances will explode if we allow even more conditions. As our final propositional dataset will then become impractically large we will have to restrict the number of instances. We will only consider counts with no condition and counts with one condition on nominal attributes. This implies that for the *count* aggregate $w_v \leq 1$.

There is some overlap in the patterns that can be expressed by using the *count* aggregate and those expressed in FOL. Testing for a count greater than zero obviously corresponds to existence. Testing for a count greater than some threshold t however, requires a clause-depth of $O(t^2)$ in FOL. With the less-than operator things become even worse for FOL representations as it requires the use of negation in a way that the language bias of many ILP algorithms does not cater for. The use of the *count* aggregate is clearly more powerful in these respects.

min and max. The two obvious aggregates for numeric attributes, *min* and *max*, exhibit similar behaviour. Again there is a trivial way of computing *min* and *max* from the histogram; the smallest and largest value for which there is a non-zero count, respectively. The *min* and *max* aggregates support another type of constraint commonly used in FOL-based algorithms, *existence* with a numeric constraint. The following proposition describes the correspondence between the minimum and maximum of a group of numbers, and the occurrence of particular values in the group.

Proposition.   Let B be a bag of real numbers, and t some real, then
$$\max (B) > t \quad \text{iff} \quad \exists v \in B : v > t,$$
$$\min (B) < t \quad \text{iff} \quad \exists v \in B : v < t.$$

This simply states that testing whether the maximum is greater than some threshold is equivalent to testing whether any value is greater than t. Analogous for *min*. It is important to note the combination of *max* and $>$, and *min* and $<$ respectively. If *max* were to be used in combination with $<$ or $=$ then the FOL equivalent would again require the use of negation. Such use of the *min* and *max* aggregate gives us a natural means of introducing the universal quantor $\forall$: all values are required to be above the minimum, or below the maximum. Another advantage of the *min* and *max* aggregate is that they each replace a set of binary *existence* aggregate instances (one for each threshold), making the propositional representation a lot more compact.

In short we can conclude that on the level of summarisation ($d_v = 1$) aggregates can express many of the concepts used in FOL. They can even express concepts that are hard or impossible to express in FOL. The most important limitation of our choice of aggregate instances is the number of attributes involved: $w_v \leq 1$. This restriction prevents the use of combinations of attributes which cause a combinatorial explosion of features [10].

5   The RollUp Algorithm

With the basic operations provided in the previous sections we can now define a basic propositionalisation algorithm. The algorithm will traverse the data model graph and repeatedly use the summarisation operation to project data from one table onto another, until all information has been aggregated at the target table. Although this repeated summarisation can be done in several ways, we will describe a basic algorithm, called RollUp.

The RollUp algorithm performs a depth-first search (DFS) through the data model, up to a specified depth. Whenever the recursive algorithm reaches its maximum depth or a leaf in the graph, it will "roll up" the relevant table by summarising it on the parent in the DFS tree. Internal nodes in the tree will again be summarised after all its children have been summarised. This means that attributes considered deep in the tree may be aggregated multiple times. The process continues until all tables are summarised on the target table. In combination with a propositional learner we have an instance of Polka. The following pseudo code describes RollUp more formally:

RollUp (Table T, Datamodel M, int d)
$V := T$;
if $d > 0$
    for all associations A from T in M
        $W := \text{RollUp}(T.\text{getTable}(A), M, d\text{-}1)$;
        $S := \text{Summarise}(W, A)$;
        $V.\text{add}(S)$;
return V;

The effect of RollUp is that each attribute appearing in a table other than the target table will appear several times in aggregated form in the resulting view. This multiple occurrence happens for two reasons. The first reason is that tables may occur multiple times in the DFS tree because they can be reached through multiple paths in the datamodel. Each path will produce a different aggregation of the available attributes. The second reason is related to the choices of aggregate class at each summarisation along a path in the datamodel. This choice, and the fact that aggregates may be combined in longer paths produces multiple occurrences of an attribute per path.

The variable-depth of the deepest feature is equal to the parameter d. Each feature corresponds to at most one attribute aggregated along a path of depth d_v. The clause-depth is therefore a linear function of the variable-depth. As each feature involves at most one attribute, and is aggregated along a path with no branches, the variable-width will always be either 0 or 1. This produces the following characteristics for RollUp. Use lemmas 1 to 3 to characterise Polka instantiated with RollUp.

Lemma 4. d_v (RollUp) = d
Lemma 5. d_c (RollUp) = $2 \cdot d_v$ (RollUp) + 1
Lemma 6. w_v (RollUp) = 1

6   Experiments

In order to acquire empirical knowledge about the effectiveness of our approach, we have tested RollUp on three well-known multi-relational datasets. These datasets were chosen because they show a variety of datamodels that occur frequently in many multi-relational problems. They are Musk [3], Mutagenesis [11], and Financial [14].

Each dataset was loaded in the RDBMS Oracle. The data was modelled in UML using the multi-relational modelling tool Tolkien (see [9]) and subsequently translated to CDBL. Based on this declarative bias, the RollUp module produced one database view for each dataset, containing the propositionalised data. This was then taken as input for the common Machine Learning procedure C5.0.

For quantitative comparison with other techniques, we have computed the average accuracy by leave-one-out cross-validation for Musk and Mutagenesis, and by 10-fold cross-validation for Financial.

6.1   Musk

The Musk´ database [3] describes molecules occurring in different conformations. Each molecule is either *musk* or *non-musk* and one of the conformations determines this property. Such a problem is known as a multiple-instance problem, and will be modelled by two tables **molecule** and **conformation**, joined by a one-to-many association. **Confirmation** contains a molecule identifier plus 166 continuous features. **Molecule** just contains the identifier and the class. We have analysed two datasets, MuskSmall, containing 92 molecules and 476 confirmations, and MuskLarge, containing 102 molecules and 6598 confirmations. The resulting table contains a total of 674 features.

Table 1 shows the results of RollUp compared to other, previously published results. The performance of RollUp is comparable to Tilde, but below that of special-purpose algorithms.

Table 1. Results on musk

Algorithm	MuskSmall	MuskLarge
Iterated-discrim APR	92.4%	89.2%
GFS elim kde APR	91.3%	80.4%
RollUp	**89.1%**	**77.5%**
Tilde	87.0%	79.4%
Back-propagation	75.0%	67.7%
C4.5	68.5%	58.8%

6.2   Mutagenesis

Similar to the Musk database, the Mutagenesis database describes molecules falling in two classes, *mutagenic* and *non-mutagenic*. However, this time structural information about the atoms and bonds that make up the compound are provided. As chemical compounds are essentially annotated graphs, this database is a good test-case for how well our approach deals with graph-data. The dataset we have analysed is known as the 'regression-friendly' dataset, and consists of 188 molecules. The database consists of 26 tables, of which three tables directly describe the graphical structure of the molecule (**molecule, atom** and **bond**). The remaining 23 tables describe the occurrence of predefined functional groups, such as benzene rings.

Four different experiments will be performed, using different settings, or so-called *backgrounds*. They will be referred to as experiment B1 to B4:

- B1: the atoms in the molecule are given, as well as the bonds between them; the type of each bond is given as well as the element and type of each atom.
- B2: as B1, but continuous values about the charge of atoms are added.
- B3: as B2, but two continuous values describing each molecule are added.
- B4: as B3, but knowledge about functional groups is added.

The largest resulting table, for B4, contains 309 constructed features.

Table 2 shows the results of RollUp compared to other, previously published results. Clearly RollUp outperforms the other methods on all backgrounds, except B4.

Most surprisingly, RollUp already performs well on B1, whereas the ILP methods seem to benefit from the propositional information provided in B3.

Table 2. Results on mutagenesis

	Progol	FOIL	Tilde	RollUp
B1	76%	61%	75%	86%
B2	81%	61%	79%	85%
B3	83%	83%	85%	89%
B4	88%	82%	86%	84%

Example. The following tree of the B3 experiment illustrates the use of aggregates for structural descriptions.

```
CNT_BOND =< 26
    PREDOMINANT_TYPE_ATOM [21 27] -> F
    PREDOMINANT_TYPE_ATOM 22 -> F
    PREDOMINANT_TYPE_ATOM 3
        MAX_CHARGE_ATOM =< 0.0
            PREDOMINANT_TYPE_BOND 7 -> F
            PREDOMINANT_TYPE_BOND 1 -> T
        MAX_CHARGE_ATOM  > 0.0 -> F
CNT_BOND  > 26
    LUMO =< -1.102
        LOGP =< 6.26 -> T
        LOGP  > 6.26 -> F
    LUMO  > -1.102 -> F
```

6.3 Financial

Our third database is taken from the Discovery Challenge organised at PKDD '99 and PKDD 2000 [14]. The database is based on data from a Czech bank. It describes the operations of 5369 clients holding 4500 accounts. The data is stored in 8 tables, 4 of which describe the usage of products, such as credit cards and loans. Three tables describe client and account information, and the remaining table contains demographic information about 77 Czech districts. We have chosen the **account** table as our target table. Although we thus have 4500 examples, the dataset contains a total of 1079680 records. Our aim was to determine the loan-quality of an account, that is the existence of a loan with status 'finished good loan' or 'running good loan'. The resulting table contains a total of 148 features.

A near perfect score of 99.9% was achieved on the Financial dataset. Due to the great variety of problem definitions described in the literature, quantitative comparisons with previous results are impossible. Similar (descriptive) analyses of loan-quality however never produced the pattern responsible for RollUp's performance. The aggregation approach proved particularly successful on the large **transaction** table (1056320 records). This table has sometimes been left out of other experiments due to scalability problems.

7   Discussion

The experimental results in the previous section demonstrate that our approach is at least competitive with existing multi-relational techniques, such as Progol and Tilde. Our approach has two major differences with these techniques, which may be the source of the good performance: the use of aggregates and the use of propositionalisation. Let us consider the contribution of each of these in turn.

Aggregates. There is an essential difference in the way a group of records is characterised by FOL and by aggregates. FOL characterisation are based on the occurrence of one or more records in the group with certain properties. Aggregates on the other hand typically describe the group as a whole; each record has some influence on the value of the aggregate. The result of this difference is that FOL and aggregates provide two unique feature-spaces to the learning procedure. Each feature-space has its advantages and disadvantages, and may be more or less suitable for the problem at hand.

Although the feature-spaces produced by FOL and aggregates have entirely different characteristics, there is still some overlap. As was shown in section 4, some aggregates are very similar in behaviour to FOL expressions. The common features in the two spaces typically

- select one or a few records in a group (*min* and $<$, *max* and $>$, *count* > 0 for some condition).
- involve a single attribute: $w_v \leq 1$
- have a relatively low variable-depth.

If these properties hold, aggregate-based learning procedures will generally perform better, as they can dispose of the common selective aggregates, as well as the complete aggregates such as *sum* and *avg*.

Datamodels with a low variable depth are quite common in database design, and are called star-shaped ($d_v = 1$) or snowflake schemata ($d_v > 1$). The Musk dataset is the most simple example of a star-shaped model. The datamodel of Mutagenesis consists for a large part of a star-shaped model, and Financial is essentially a snowflake schema. Many real-world datasets described in the literature as ILP applications essentially have such a manageable structure. Moreover, results on these datasets frequently exhibit the extra condition of $w_v \leq 1$. Some illustrative examples are given in [4, 13].

Propositionalisation. According to lemma 2, Polka has the ability to discovery patterns that have a bigger clause-depth than either of its steps has. This is demonstrated by the experiments with our particular instance of Polka. RollUp produces variable-deep and thus clause-deep features. These clause-deep features are combined in the decision tree. Some leafs represent very clause-deep patterns, even though their support is still sufficient. This is an advantage of Polka (propositionalisation + propositional learning) over multi-relational algorithms in general.

Next to advantages related to expressivity, there are more practical reasons for using Polka. Once the propositionalisation-stage is finished, a large part of the computationally expensive work is done, and the derived view can be analysed multiple times. This not only provides a greater efficiency, but gives the analyst more flexibility in choosing the right modelling technique from a large range of well-developed commercially available set of tools. The analyst can vary the style of analysis (trees, rules, neural, instance-based) as well as the paradigm (classification, regression).

8 Conclusion

We have presented a method that uses aggregates to propositionalise a multi-relational database, such that the resulting view can be analysed by existing propositional methods. The method uses information from the datamodel to guide a process of repeated summarisation of tables on other tables. The method has shown good performance on three well-known datasets, both in terms of accuracy as well as in terms of speed and flexibility.

The experimental findings are supported by theoretical results, which indicate the strength of this approach on so-called star-shaped or snowflake datamodels. We have also given evidence for why propositionalisation approaches in general may outperform ILP or MRDM systems, as was suggested before in the literature [4, 12].

References

1. Alphonse, É., Rouveirol, C. *Selective Propositionalization for Relational Learning*, In Proceedings of PKDD '99, 1999
2. Dehaspe, L., Toivonen, H., *Discovery of frequent Datalog patterns*, Data Mining and Knowledge Discovery 3(1), 1999
3. Dietterich, T.G., Lathrop, R.H., Lozano-Pérez, T., *Solving the multiple-instance problem with axis-parallel rectangles*, Artificial Intelligence, 89(1-2):31-71, 1997
4. Džeroski, S., Blockeel, H., Kompare, B., Kramer, S., Pfahringer, B., Van Laer, W., *Experiments in Predicting Biodegradability*, In Proceedings of ILP '99, 1999
5. Friedman, N., Getoor, L., Koller, D., Pfeffer, A., *Learning Probabilistic Relational Models*, In Proceedings of IJCAI '99, 1999
6. Kramer, S., *Relational Learning vs. Propositionalization*, Ph.D thesis, 1999
7. Kramer, S., Pfahringer, B., Helma, C., *Stochastic Propositionalization of non-determinate background knowledge*, In Proceedings of ILP '98, 1998
8. Knobbe, A.J., Blockeel, H., Siebes, A., Van der Wallen, D.M.G. *Multi-Relational Data Mining*, In Proceedings of Benelearn '99, 1999
9. Knobbe, A.J., Siebes, A., Blockeel, H., Van der Wallen, D.M.G., *Multi-Relational Data Mining, using UML for ILP*, In Proceedings of PKDD 2000, 2000
10. Lavrač, N., Džeroski, S., Grobelnik, M., *Learning nonrecursive definitions of relations with LINUS*, In Proceedings of EWSL'91, 1991
11. Srinivasan, A., King, R.D., *Feature construction with ILP: a study of quantitative predictions of biological activity by structural attributes*, In Proceedings of ILP '96, 1996
12. Srinivasan, A., King, R.D., Bristol, D.W., *An Assessment of ILP-Assisted Models for Toxicology and the PTE-3 Experiment*, In Proceedings of ILP '99, 1999
13. Todorovski, L., Džeroski, S., *Experiments in Meta-level Learning with ILP*, In Proceedings of PKDD '99, 1999
14. Workshop notes on Discovery Challenge PKDD '99, 1999

Algorithms for the Construction of Concept Lattices and Their Diagram Graphs

Sergei O. Kuznetsov[1] and Sergei A. Obiedkov[2]

[1]All-Russia Institute for Scientific and Technical Information (VINITI), Moscow, Russia
`serge@viniti.ru`
[2]Russian State University for the Humanities, Moscow, Russia
`bs-obj@east.ru`

Abstract. Several algorithms that generate the set of all formal concepts and graphs of line (Hasse) diagrams of concept lattices are considered. Some modifications of well-known algorithms are proposed. Algorithmic complexity of the algorithms is studied both theoretically (in the worst case) and experimentally. Conditions of preferable use of some algorithms are given in terms of density/sparsity of underlying formal contexts.

1 Introduction

Concept lattices proved to be a useful tool for machine learning and knowledge discovery in databases [3, 6, 9, 19, 22–24]. The problem of generating the set of all concepts and the diagram graph of the concept lattice is extensively studied in the literature [2-5, 7, 10, 11, 13, 16, 18–20]. It is known that the number of concepts can be exponential in the size of the input context (e.g., when the lattice is a Boolean one) and the problem of determining this number is #P-complete [15]. Therefore, from the standpoint of the worst-case complexity, an algorithm can be considered optimal if it generates the concept lattice in time and space linear in the number of all concepts (modulo a factor polynomial in the input size). On the other hand, "dense" contexts, which realize the worst case by bringing about exponential number of concepts, may occur not often in practice. Moreover, various implementation issues, such as dimension of a "typical" context, specificity of the operating system used, and so on, may be crucial for the practical evaluation of algorithms. In this article, we consider, both theoretically and experimentally, several algorithms that generate concept lattices for clearly specified data sets. In most cases, it was possible to improve the original versions of the algorithms. We present modifications of some algorithms and indicate conditions when some of them perform better than the others. Only a few known algorithms generating the concept set construct the graph of the line diagram. We modified some algorithms so that they can construct graphs of line diagrams.

The first comparative study of four algorithms constructing the concept set and the graph of the line diagram can be found in [13]. Descriptions of the algorithms are sometimes buggy and the description of the experimental tests lacks any information about data used for tests. The fact that the choice of an algorithm should depend on input data is not accounted for. Besides, only one of the algorithms considered in [13],

L. De Raedt and A. Siebes (Eds.): PKDD 2001, LNAI 2168, pp. 289–300, 2001.

namely that of Bordat [2], constructs the graph of the line diagram; thus, it is hard to compare its performance with that of the other algorithms.

A much more elaborate review can be found in [11] (where another algorithm is proposed). The authors of [11] consider algorithms that generate the graph of the line diagram. Algorithms that were not originally designed for this purpose are extended by the authors. Such extensions are not always efficient: for example, the time complexity of the version of the **Ganter** algorithm (called **Ganter-Allaoui**) dramatically increases with the growth of the context size. This drawback can be cancelled by the use of binary search in the list produced by the original **Ganter** algorithm. Tests were conducted only for contexts with small number of attributes per object as compared to the number of all attributes. Our experiments (we consider more algorithms) also show that the algorithm proposed in [11] performs better on such contexts than the others do [17]. However, for "dense" contexts, this algorithm performs worse than some other algorithms (details are found in [17]).

The paper is organized as follows. In Section 2, we give main definitions and an example. In Section 3, we give a survey of batch and incremental algorithms for constructing concept lattices and analyze their worst-case complexity. In Section 4, we consider results of experimental comparison of the algorithms.

2 Main Definitions

First, we introduce standard FCA notation [8], which will be used throughout the paper.

A *(formal) context* is a triple of sets (G, M, I), where G is called a set of objects, M is called a set of attributes, and $I \subseteq G \times M$. For $A \subseteq G$ and $B \subseteq M$: $A' = \{m \in M \mid \forall g \in A\ (gIm)\}$; $B' = \{g \in G \mid \forall m \in B\ (gIm)\}$. $''$ is a closure operator, i.e., it is monotone, extensive, and idempotent. A *(formal) concept* of a formal context (G, M, I) is a pair (A, B), where $A \subseteq G$, $B \subseteq M$, $A' = B$, and $B' = A$. The set A is called the *(formal) extent* and B the *(formal) intent* of the concept (A, B). For a context (G, M, I), a concept $X = (A, B)$ is *less general than or equal to* a concept $Y = (C, D)$ (or $X \leq Y$) if $A \subseteq C$ or, equivalently, $D \subseteq B$. Suppose that X and Y are concepts, $X \leq Y$, and there is no concept Z such that $Z \neq X$, $Z \neq Y$, $X \leq Z \leq Y$. Then X is called a *lower neighbor of Y*, and Y is called an *upper neighbor of X*. This relationship is denoted by $X \prec Y$. The set of all concepts of a formal context forms a complete lattice L [8]. The *graph of the line diagram* of a concept lattice (or simply a *diagram graph*) is the directed graph of the relation $\prec$. The *line diagram* is a plane embedding of a diagram graph where each concept vertex is always drawn above all its lower neighbors (thus, the arrows on the arcs become superfluous and can be omitted).

Example 1. Below we present a formal context with some elementary geometric figures and its line diagram. We shall sometimes omit parentheses and write, e.g., 12 instead of $\{1, 2\}$.

$G \setminus M$	a = 4 vertices	b = 3 vertices	c = has a right angle	d = all sides are equal
1	X		X	X
2	X		X	
3		X	X	
4		X		X

Fig. 1. A formal context

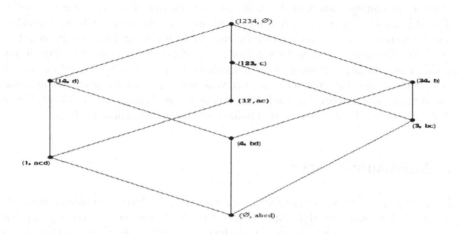

Fig. 2. The line diagram for the context from Fig. 1

Data structures that realize concept sets and diagram graphs of concept lattices are of great importance. Since their sizes can be exponentially large w.r.t. the input size, some their natural representations are not polynomially equivalent, as it is in the case of graphs. For example, the size of the incidence matrix of a diagram graph is quadratic w.r.t. the size of the incidence list of the diagram graph and thus cannot be reduced to the latter in time polynomial w.r.t. the input. Moreover, some important operations, such as find_concept, are performed for some representations (spanning trees [2, 10], ordered lists [7], CbO trees [16], 2-3 trees [1]) in polynomial time, but for some other representations (unordered lists) they can be performed only in exponential time. A representation of a concept lattice can be considered reasonable if its size cannot be exponentially compressed w.r.t. the input and allows the search for a particular concept in time polynomial in the input.

All the algorithms can be divided into two categories: incremental algorithms [3, 5, 11, 20], which, at the *i*th step, produce the concept set or the diagram graph for *i* first objects of the context, and batch ones, which build the concept set or its diagram graph for the whole context from scratch [2, 4, 7, 16, 18, 25]. Besides, any algorithm typically adheres to one of the two strategies: top–down (from the maximal extent to the minimal one) or bottom–up (from the minimal extent to the maximal one).

In many cases, we attempted to improve the efficiency of the original algorithms presented below. Only some of the original versions of the algorithms construct the diagram graph [2, 11, 18, 21]; it turned out that the other algorithms could be extended to construct the diagram graph within the same worst-case time complexity bounds. Some algorithms are given the name of their authors.

In the next section, we will discuss worst-case complexity bounds of the considered algorithms. Due to the possibility of the exponential output of the algorithms, it is reasonable to estimate their complexity not only in terms of the input and output size, but also in terms of (cumulative) delay. Recall that an algorithm for listing a family of combinatorial structures is said to have *polynomial delay* [14] if it executes at most polynomially many computation steps before either outputting each next structure or halting. Note that the worst-case complexity of an algorithm with polynomial delay is a linear function of the output size modulo some factor polynomial in the input size. A weaker notion of efficiency of listing algorithms was proposed in [12]. An algorithm is said to have a *cumulative delay d* if it is the case that at any point of time in any execution of the algorithm with any input p the total number of computation steps that have been executed is at most $d(p)$ plus the product of $d(p)$ and the number of structures that have been output so far. If $d(p)$ can be bounded by a polynomial of p, the algorithm is said to have a *polynomial cumulative delay*.

3   Algorithms: A Survey

Here we give a brief version of the survey found in [17]. First, we consider batch algorithms. The top-down algorithm **MI-tree** from [25] generates the concept set, but does not build the diagram graph. In **MI-tree**, every new concept is searched for in the set of all concepts generated so far. The top-down algorithm of Bordat [2] uses a tree (a "trie," cf. [1]) for fast storing and retrieval of concepts. Our version of this algorithm uses a technique that requires $O(|M|)$ time to realize whether a concept is generated for the first time without any search. An auxiliary tree, which is actually a spanning tree of the diagram graph, is used to construct the latter. $\mathbf{Ch}((A, B))$ is the set of children of the concept (A, B) in this tree; it consists of the lower neighbors of (A, B) generated for the first time.

```
Bordat
0. L := ∅
1. Process ((G, G'), G')
2. L is the concept set.

Process ((A, B), C)
1. L := L ∪ {(A, B)}
2. LN := LowerNeighbors ((A, B))
3. For each (D, E) ∈ LN
   3.1. If C ∩ E = B
```

```
3.1.1. C := C ∪ E
3.1.2. Process((D, E), C)
3.1.3. Ch((A, B)) := Ch((A, B)) ∪ {(D, E)}
3.2 Else
3.2.1. Find((G, G'), (D, E))
3.3. (A, B) is an upper neighbor of (D, E)
```

The full version of the algorithm can be found in [17]. The time complexity of the algorithm is $O(|G||M|^2|L|)$; its polynomial delay is $O(|G||M|^2)$.

The well-known algorithm proposed by Ganter computes closures for only some of subsets of G and uses an efficient canonicity test, which does not address the list of generated concepts. The subsets are considered in lexicographic order [7, 8]. The **Ganter** algorithm has polynomial delay $O(|G|^2|M|)$. Its complexity is $O(|G|^2|M||L|)$.

The **Close by One** (CbO) algorithm uses a notion of canonicity similar to that of **Ganter** and a similar method for selecting subsets. It employs an intermediate structure that helps to compute closures more efficiently using the generated concepts. Objects are assigned numbers; $g \prec h$ holds whenever the number of g is smaller than that of h. The **CbO** algorithm obtains a new concept from a concept (A, B) generated at a previous step by intersecting B with the intent of an object g that does not belong to A. The generation is considered canonical if the intersection is not contained in any object from $G \setminus A$ with smaller number than that of g. The algorithm repeatedly calls $Process(\{g\}, g, (\{g\}'', \{g\}'))$ for each object g.

```
Process(A, g, (C, D))                    C = A'', D = A'
1. If {h | h ∈ C \ A & h ≺ g} = ∅
  1.1. L := L ∪ {(C, D)}
  1.2. For each f ∈ {h | h ∈ G \ C & g ≺ h}
    1.2.1. Z := C ∪ {f}
    1.2.2. Y := D ∩ {f}'
    1.2.3. X := Y' (= Z ∪ {h | h ∈ G \ Z & Y ⊆ {h}'})
    1.2.4. Process(Z, f, (X, Y))
```

The CbO algorithm has polynomial delay $O(|G|^3|M|)$ and complexity $O(|G|^2|M||L|)$. To construct the diagram graph with the **CbO** algorithm, we use a tree, which is not a spanning tree of the diagram graph, but it agrees with the concept order.

The idea of the bottom-up algorithm in [18] is to generate the bottom concept and then, for each concept that is generated for the first time, generate all its upper neighbors. Lindig uses a tree of concepts that allows one to check whether some concept was generated earlier. The description of the tree is not detailed in [18], but it seems to be the spanning tree of the inverted diagram graph (i.e., with the root at the bottom of the diagram), similar to the tree from **Bordat**. Finding a concept in such a tree takes $O(|G||M|)$ time. In fact, this algorithm may be regarded as a bottom-up version of the **Bordat** algorithm. The time complexity of the algorithm is $O(|G|^2|M||L|)$. Its polynomial delay is $O(|G|^2|M|)$.

The **AI-tree** [25] and **Chein** [4] algorithms operate with extent–intent pairs and generate each new concept intent as the intersection of intents of two generated concepts. At every iteration step of the **Chein** algorithm, a new layer of concepts is created by intersecting pairs of concept intents from the current layer and the new intent is searched for in the new layer. We introduced several modifications [17] that made it possible to improve the performance of the algorithm. The time complexity of the modified algorithm is $O(|G|^3|M||L|)$; its polynomial delay is $O(|G|^3|M|)$.

Now we consider incremental algorithms, which cannot have polynomial delay. Nevertheless, all algorithms below have cumulative polynomial delay.

L. Nourine [21] proposes an algorithm for the construction of the lattice using a lexicographic tree with the best known worst-case complexity bound $O((|G| + |M|)|G||L|)$. Edges of the tree are labeled with attributes, and nodes are labeled with concepts whose intents consist of the attributes that label the edges leading from the root to the node. Clearly, some nodes do not have labels. First, the tree is constructed incrementally (similar to the **Norris** algorithm presented below). An intent of a new concept C is created by intersecting an object intent g' and the intent of a concept D created earlier, and the extent of C is formed by adding g to the extent of D; this takes $O(|M| + |G|)$ time. A new concept is searched for in the tree using the intent of the concept as the key; this search requires $O(|M|)$ time. When the tree is created, it is used to construct the diagram graph. For each concept C, its parents are sought for as follows. Counters are kept for every concept initialized to zero at the beginning of the process. For each object, the intersection of its intent and the concept intent is produced in $O(|M|)$ time. A concept D with the intent equal to this intersection is found in the tree in $O(|M|)$ time and the value in the counter increases; if the counter is equal to the difference between the cardinalities of the concepts C and D (i.e., the intersection of the intent of C and the intent of any object from D outside C is equal to the intent of D), the concept D is a parent of C.

The algorithm proposed by E. Norris [20] can be considered as an incremental analogue of the **CbO** algorithm. The concept tree (which is useful only for diagram construction) can be built as follows: first, there is only the dummy root; examine objects from G and for each concept of the tree check whether the object under consideration has all the attributes of the concept intent; if it does, add it to the extent; otherwise, form a new node and declare it a child node of the current one; the extent of the corresponding concept equals the extent of the parent node plus the object being examined; the intent is the intersection of this object intent and the parent intent; next, test the new node for the canonicity; if the test fails, remove it from the tree. The original version of the **Norris** algorithm from [20] does not construct the diagram graph. In this case, **Norris** is preferable to **CbO**, as the latter has to remember how the last concept was generated; this involves additional storage resources, as well as time expenses. The **Norris** algorithm does not maintain any auxiliary structure. Besides, the closure of an object set is never computed explicitly.

The algorithm proposed by Godin [11] has the worst-case time complexity quadratic in the number of concepts. This algorithm is based on the use of an efficiently computable hash-function f (which is actually the cardinality of an intent) defined on the set of concepts.

C. Dowling proposed an incremental algorithm for computing knowledge spaces [5]. A dual formulation of the algorithm allows generation of formal concepts. The worst-case complexity of the algorithm is $O(|M||G|^2|L|)$, the constants in this upper bound are large and in practice, the algorithm performs worse than other algorithms.

4   Results of Experimental Tests

The algorithms were implemented in C++. The tests were run on a Pentium II–300 computer, 256 MB RAM. Here, we present a number of charts that show how the execution time of the algorithms depends on various parameters. More charts can be found in [17].

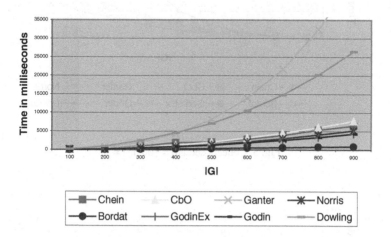

Fig. 3. Concept set: $|M| = 100$; $|g'| = 4$

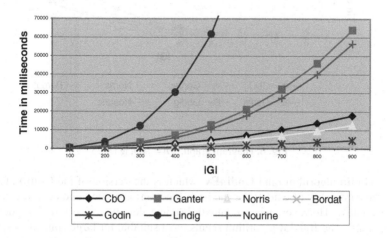

Fig. 4. Diagram graph: $|M| = 100$; $|g'| = 4$.

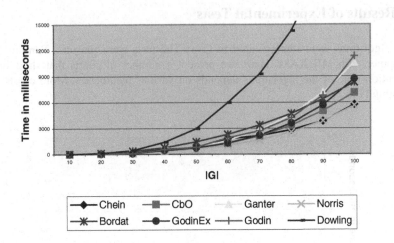

Fig. 5. Concept set: $|M| = 100$; $|g'| = 25$

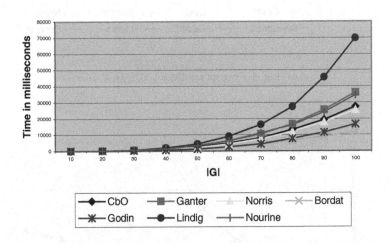

Fig. 6. Diagram graph: $|M| = 100$; $|g'| = 25$

The **Godin** algorithm (and **GodinEx**, which is the version of the **Godin** algorithm using the cardinality of extents for the hash-function) is a good choice in the case of a sparse context. However, when contexts become denser, its performance decreases dramatically. The **Bordat** algorithm seems most suitable for large contexts, especially if it is necessary to build the diagram graph. When $|G|$ is small, the **Bordat** algorithm runs several times slower than other algorithms, but, as $|G|$ grows, the difference between **Bordat** and other algorithms becomes smaller, and, in many cases, **Bordat** finally turns out to be the leader. For large and dense contexts, the fastest algorithms are bottom-up canonicity-based algorithms (**Norris, Ganter, CbO**).

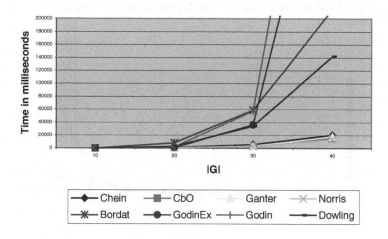

Fig. 7. Concept set: $|M| = 100$; $|g'| = 50$

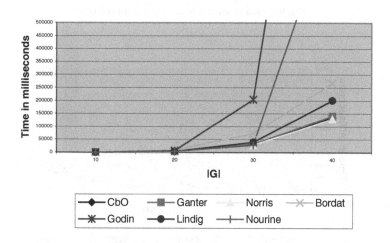

Fig. 8. Diagram graph: $|M| = 100$; $|g'| = 50$

It should be noted that the **Nourine** algorithm with the best worst-case time complexity did not show the best performance in our experiments: even when contexts of the form $(G, G, \neq)$ were processed (which corresponds to the worst case of Boolean concept lattice), it was inferior to the **Norris** algorithm. Probably, this can be accounted to the fact that we represent attribute sets by bit strings, which allows very efficient implementation of set-theoretical operations (32 attributes per one processor cycle); whereas searching in the Nourine-style lexicographic tree, one still should individually consider each attribute labeling edges.

Figures 9–10 show the execution time for the contexts of the form $(G, G, \neq)$ with $2^{|G|}$ concepts.

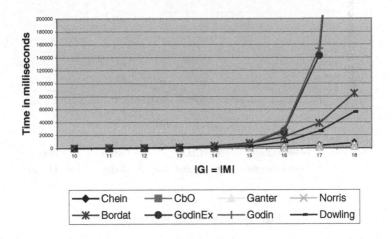

Fig. 9. Concept set: contexts of the form $(G, G, \neq)$

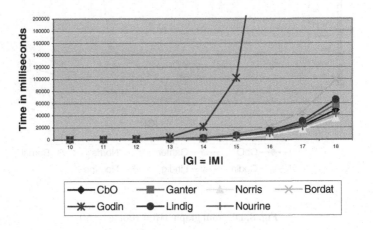

Fig. 10. Diagram graph: contexts of the form $(G, G, \neq)$

5 Conclusion

In this work, we attempted to compare some well-known algorithms for constructing concept lattices and their diagram graphs. A new algorithm was proposed in [22] quite recently, so we could not include it in our experiments. Its worst-time complexity is not better than that of the algorithms described above, but the authors report on its good practical performance for databases with very large number of objects. Comparing the performance of this algorithm with those considered above and testing the algorithms on large databases, including "classical" ones, will be the subject of the further work. We can also mention works [3, 19] where algorithms were applied for learning and data analysis, e.g., in [19] a **Bordat**-type algorithm was used. The description of the algorithm in [3] does not give details about the test for uniqueness of a generated concept, i.e., whether it is already in the list. As we have seen, this test is crucial for the efficiency of an algorithm.

The choice of the algorithm for construction of the concept set and diagram graph should be based on the properties of the input data. The general rule is as follows: the **Godin** algorithm should be used for small and sparse contexts; for dense contexts, the algorithms based on canonicity tests, linear in the number of output concepts, such as **Close by One, Norris,** and **Ganter,** should be used. The **Bordat** performs well on contexts of average density, especially, when the diagram graph is to be constructed.

As mentioned above, the experimental comparison of execution times of algorithms is implementation-dependent. To reduce this dependence, we implemented a program that made it possible to compare algorithms not only in the execution time, but also in the number of operations performed. Such comparison is both more reliable and more helpful, as it allows choosing an algorithm based on the computational complexity of the operations in particular implementation.

References

1. Aho, A.V., Hopcroft, J.E., Ullmann, J.D., Data Structures and Algorithms, Reading, Addison–Wesley (1983).
2. Bordat, J.P., Calcul pratique du treillis de Galois d'une correspondance, Math. Sci. Hum., no. 96, (1986) 31–47.
3. Carpineto, C., Giovanni, R., A Lattice Conceptual Clustering System and Its Application to Browsing Retrieval, Machine Learning, no. 24 (1996) 95–122.
4. Chein, M., Algorithme de recherche des sous-matrices premières d'une matrice, Bull. Math. Soc. Sci. Math. R.S. Roumanie, no. 13 (1969) 21–25.
5. Dowling, C.E., On the Irredundant Generation of Knowledge Spaces, J. Math. Psych., vol. 37, no. 1 (1993) 49-62.
6. Finn, V.K., Plausible Reasoning in Systems of JSM Type, Itogi Nauki i Tekhniki, Ser. Informatika, vol. 15 (1991) 54–101.
7. Ganter, B., Two Basic Algorithms in Concept Analysis, FB4-Preprint No. 831, TH Darmstadt (1984).
8. Ganter, B., Wille, R., Formal Concept Analysis. Mathematical Foundations, Springer, (1999).

9. Ganter B., Kuznetsov, S., Formalizing Hypotheses with Concepts, Proc. of the 8th International Conference on Conceptual Structures, ICCS 2000, Lecture Notes in Artificial Intelligence, vol. 1867 (2000) 342-356.

10. Ganter, B., Reuter, K., Finding All Closed Sets: A General Approach, Order, vol. 8, (1991) 283-290.

11. Godin, R., Missaoui, R., Alaoui, H., Incremental Concept Formation Algorithms Based on Galois Lattices, Computation Intelligence (1995).

12. Goldberg, L.A., Efficient Algorithms for Listing Combinatorial Structures, Cambridge University Press (1993).

13. Guénoche, A., Construction du treillis de Galois d'une relation binaire, Math. Inf. Sci. Hum., no. 109 (1990) 41–53.

14. Johnson, D.S., Yannakakis, M., Papadimitriou, C.H., On Generating all Maximal Independent Sets, Inf. Proc. Let., vol. 27 (1988) 119-123.

15. Kuznetsov, S.O., Interpretation on Graphs and Complexity Characteristics of a Search for Specific Patterns, Automatic Documentation and Mathematical Linguistics, vol. 24, no. 1 (1989) 37-45.

16. Kuznetsov, S.O., A Fast Algorithm for Computing All Intersections of Objects in a Finite Semi-lattice, Automatic Documentation and Mathematical Linguistics, vol. 27, no. 5 (1993) 11–21.

17. Kuznetsov, S.O., Obiedkov S.A., Algorithms for the Construction of the Set of All Concepts and Their Line Diagram, Preprint MATH-Al-05, TU-Dresden, June 2000.

18. Lindig, C., Algorithmen zur Begriffsanalyse und ihre Anwendung bei Softwarebibliotheken, (Dr.-Ing.) Dissertation, Techn. Univ. Braunschweig (1999).

19. Mephu Nguifo, E., Njiwoua, P., Using Lattice-Based Framework As a Tool for Feature Extraction, in Feature Extraction, Construction and Selection: A Data Mining Perspective, H. Liu and H. Motoda (eds.), Kluwer (1998).

20. Norris, E.M., An Algorithm for Computing the Maximal Rectangles in a Binary Relation, Revue Roumaine de Mathématiques Pures et Appliquées, no. 23(2) (1978) 243–250.

21. Nourine L., Raynaud O., A Fast Algorithm for Building Lattices, Information Processing Letters, vol. 71 (1999) 199-204.

22. Stumme G., Taouil R., Bastide Y., Pasquier N., Lakhal L., Fast Computation of Concept Lattices Using Data Mining Techniques, in Proc. 7th Int. Workshop on Knowledge Representation Meets Databases (KRDB 2000) 129-139.

23. Stumme G., Wille R., and Wille U., Conceptual Knowledge Discovery in Databases Using Formal Concept Analysis Methods, in Proc. 2nd European Symposium on Principles of Data Mining and Knowledge Discovery (PKDD'98).

24. Waiyamai K., Lakhal L., Knowledge Discovery from Very Large Databases Using Frequent Concept Lattices, in Proc. 11th European Conference on Machine Learning (ECML'2000), 437-445.

25. Zabezhailo, M.I., Ivashko, V.G., Kuznetsov, S.O., Mikheenkova, M.A., Khazanovskii, K.P., and Anshakov, O.M., Algorithms and Programs of the JSM-Method of Automatic Hypothesis Generation, Automatic Documentation and Mathematical Linguistics, vol. 21, no. 5 (1987) 1–14.

Data Reduction Using Multiple Models Integration

Aleksandar Lazarevic and Zoran Obradovic

Center for Information Science and Technology, Temple University,
Room 303, Wachman Hall (038-24),
1805 N. Broad Street, Philadelphia, PA 19122, USA
{aleks,zoran}@ist.temple.edu

Abstract. Large amount of available information does not necessarily imply that induction algorithms must use all this information. Samples often provide the same accuracy with less computational cost. We propose several effective techniques based on the idea of progressive sampling when progressively larger samples are used for training as long as model accuracy improves. Our sampling procedures combine all the models constructed on previously considered data samples. In addition to random sampling, controllable sampling based on the boosting algorithm is proposed, where the models are combined using a weighted voting. To improve model accuracy, an effective pruning technique for inaccurate models is also employed. Finally, a novel sampling procedure for spatial data domains is proposed, where the data examples are drawn not only according to the performance of previous models, but also according to the spatial correlation of data. Experiments performed on several data sets showed that the proposed sampling procedures outperformed standard progressive sampling in both the achieved accuracy and the level of data reduction.

1 Introduction

Many existing data analysis algorithms require all the data to be resident in a main memory, which is clearly untenable in many large databases nowadays. Even fast data mining algorithms designed to run in a main memory with a linear asymptotic time may be prohibitively slow, when data is stored on a disk, due to the many orders of magnitude difference between main and secondary memory retrieval time.

While data mining methods are faster when used on smaller data sets, the demand for accurate models often requires the use of large data sets that allow algorithms to discover complex structure and make accurate parameter estimates. Therefore, one of the most important data mining problems is to determine a reasonable upper bound of the data set size needed for building sufficiently accurate model. Oates and Jensen [1] found that increasing the amount of data used to build a model often results in a linear increase in model size, even when additional complexity causes no significant increase in model accuracy. Despite the promise of the better parameter estimation, models built with large amounts of data are often needlessly complex and cumbersome.

Data reduction can also be extremely helpful for data mining from very large distributed databases. In the contemporary data mining community, the majority of the

L. De Raedt and A. Siebes (Eds.): PKDD 2001, LNAI 2168, pp. 301-313, 2001.

work for learning in a distributed environment considers only two possibilities: moving all data into a centralized location for further processing, or leaving all data in place and producing local predictive models, which are later moved and combined via one of the standard machine learning methods [2]. With the emergence of new high-cost networks and huge amounts of collected data, the former approach may be too expensive, while the latter too inaccurate. Therefore, reducing the size of databases by several orders of magnitude and without loss of extractable information could speed up the data transfer for a more efficient and a more accurate centralized learning.

In this paper we propose a novel technique for data reduction based on the idea of progressive sampling [3]. Progressive sampling starts with a small sample in an initial iteration and uses progressively larger ones in subsequent iterations until model accuracy no longer improves. As a result, a near-optimal minimal size of the data set needed for efficient learning an acceptably accurate model is identified. Instead of constructing a single predictor on identified data set, our approach attempts to reuse the most accurate and sufficiently diverse classifiers built in sampling iterations and to combine their predictions. In order to further improve achieved prediction accuracy, we propose a weighted sampling, based on a boosting technique [4], where the prediction models in subsequent iterations are built on those examples on which the previous predictor had poor performance. Similar techniques of active or controllable sampling are related to windowing [5], wherein subsequent sampling chooses training instances for which the current model makes the largest errors. However, simple active sampling is notoriously ill behaved on noisy data, since subsequent samples contain increasing amount of noise and performance often decrease as sampling progresses [6].

In addition, both the number and the size of spatial databases are rapidly growing, because huge amounts of data have been collected in various GIS applications ranging from remote sensing and satellite telemetry systems, to computer cartography and environmental planning. Therefore the data reduction of very large spatial databases is of fundamental importance for efficient spatial data analysis. Hence, in this paper we also propose the method for efficient progressive sampling of spatial databases, where the sampling procedure is controlled not only by the accuracy of previous prediction models but also by considering spatially correlated data points. In our approach, the data points that are highly spatially correlated are not likely to be sampled together in the same sample, since they bear less useful data information than two non-correlated data points. The objective of this approach is to further reduce the size of spatial data set and to allow more efficient learning in such domains.

The proposed sampling methods applied to several very large data sets indicate that the both a general purpose and a spatial progressive sampling technique can learn faster than the standard progressive sampling [3], and also can outperform the standard progressive sampling in the achieved prediction accuracy.

2   Progressive Sampling

Given a data set with N examples, our goal is to determine its minimal size n_{min}, for which we aim to achieve a sufficiently accurate prediction model. The modification of geometric progressive sampling [3] is used in order to maximize accuracy of learned models. The central idea of the progressive sampling is to use a sampling schedule:

$$S = \{n_0, n_1, n_2, n_3, ..., n_k\} \tag{1}$$

where each n_i is an integer that specifies the size of a sample to be provided to a training algorithm at iteration i. Here, the n_i is defined as:

$$n_i = n_0 \cdot a^i \tag{2}$$

where a is a constant which defines how fast we increase the size of the sample presented to an induction algorithm during sampling iterations. The relationship between sample size and model accuracy is depicted by a learning curve (Fig. 1). The horizontal axis represents n, the number of instances in a given training set, that can vary between zero and the maximal number of instances N. The vertical axis represents the accuracy of the model produced by a training algorithm when given a training set with n instances. Learning curves typically have a steep slope portion early in the curve, a more gently sloping middle part, and a plateau late in the curve. The plateau occurs when adding additional data instances is not likely to significantly improve prediction. Depending on the data, the middle part and the plateau can be missing from the learning curve, when N is small. Conversely, the plateau region can constitute the majority of curves when N is very large. In a recent study of two large business data sets, Harris-Jones and Haines [7] found that learning curves reach a plateau quickly for some algorithms, but small accuracy improvements continue up to N for other algorithms.

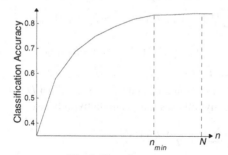

Fig. 1. Learning curve

The progressive sampling [3] was designed to increase the speed of inductive learning by providing roughly the same accuracy and using significantly smaller data sets than available. We used this idea to further increase the speed of inductive learning for very large databases and also to attempt to improve the total prediction accuracy.

3 Progressive Boosting

The proposed progressive boosting algorithm is based on an integration of Adaboost.M2 procedure [4] into the standard progressive sampling technique described at Section 2. The AdaBoost.M2 algorithm proceeds in a series of T rounds. In each round t, a weak learning algorithm is called and presented with a different distribution

D_t that is altered by emphasizing particular training examples. The distribution is updated to give wrong classifications higher weights than correct classifications. The entire weighted training set is given to the weak learner to compute the weak hypothesis h_t. At the end, all weak hypotheses are combined into a single hypothesis h_{fn}.

Instead of sampling the same number of data points at each boosting iteration t, our progressive boosting algorithm (Fig. 2) draws n_t data points ($n_t = n_0 \cdot a^{t-1}$) according to the sampling schedule S (equation 1). Therefore, we start with a small sample containing n_0 data points, and in each subsequent boosting round we increase the size of the sample used for learning a weak classifier L_t. Each weak classifier produces a weak hypothesis h_t. At the end of each boosting round t all weak hypotheses are combined into a single hypotheses H_t. However, the distribution for drawing data samples in subsequent sampling iterations is still updated according to the performance of a single classifier constructed in the current sampling iteration.

- Given: Set S $\{(x_1, y_1), \dots, (x_N, y_m)\}$ $x_i \in X$, with labels $y_i \in Y = \{1, \dots, C\}$
- Let B $= \{(i, y): i = 1, \dots, N, y \neq y_i\}$. Let $t = 0$.
- Initialize the distribution D_1 over the examples, such that $D_1(i) = 1/N$.
- *REPEAT*
1. $t = t + 1$
2. Draw a sample Q_t that contains $n_0 \cdot a^{t-1}$ data instances according to the distribution D_t.
3. Train a weak learner L_t using distribution D_t
4. Compute the pseudo-loss of hypothesis h_t:

$$\varepsilon_t = \frac{1}{2} \cdot \sum_{(i,y)\in B} D_t(i, y)(1 - h_t(x_i, y_i) + h_t(x_i, y))$$

5. Set $\beta_t = \varepsilon_t / (1 - \varepsilon_t)$ and $w_t = (1/2) \cdot (1 - h_t(x_i, y) + h_t(x_i, y_i))$
6. Update D_t: $D_{t+1}(i, y) = (D_t(i, y)/Z_t) \cdot \beta_t^{w_t}$

where Z_t is a normalization constant chosen such that D_{t+1} is a distribution.
7. Combine all weak hypotheses into a single hypothesis:

$$H_t = \arg\max_{y\in Y} \sum_{j=1}^{t} (\log\frac{1}{\beta_j}) \cdot h_j(x, y)$$

- *UNTIL* (accuracy of H_t is not significantly larger than accuracy of H_{t-1})
8. - Sort the classifiers from ensemble according to their accuracy.
    - *REPEAT* removing classifiers with accuracy less than prespecified threshold *UNTIL* there is no longer improvement in prediction accuracy

---

Fig. 2. The progressive boosting algorithm for data reduction

We always stop the progressive sampling procedure when the accuracy of the hypothesis H_t, obtained in the t-th sampling iteration, lies in 95% confidence interval of the prediction accuracy of hypothesis H_{t-1} achieved in the ($t-1$)-th sampling iteration:

$$acc(H_t) \in [acc(H_{t-1}), acc(H_{t-1}) + 1.645 \cdot \sqrt{\frac{acc(H_{t-1}) \cdot (1 - acc(H_{t-1}))}{N}}] \tag{3}$$

where $acc(H_j)$ represents classification accuracy achieved by hypothesis H_j constructed in j-th sampling iteration on the entire training set.

It is well known in machine learning theory that an ensemble of classifiers must be both diverse and accurate in order to improve the overall prediction accuracy. Diversity of classifiers is achieved by learning classifiers on different data sets obtained through weighted sampling in each sampling iteration. Nevertheless, some of the classifiers constructed in early sampling iterations may not be accurate enough due to insufficient number of data examples used for learning. Therefore, before combining the classifiers constructed in sampling iterations, we prune the classifier ensemble by removing all classifiers whose accuracy on a validation set is less than some prespecified threshold until the accuracy of the ensemble no longer improves. A validation set is determined before starting the sampling procedure as a 30% sample of the entire training data set. Assuming that the entire training set is much larger than the reduced data set used for learning, our choice of the validation sets should not introduce any significant unfair bias, since only the small fraction of data points from the reduced data set are included in the validation set. When the reduced data set is not significantly smaller than the entire training set, the unseen separated test and validation sets are used for estimating the accuracy of the proposed methods.

Since our goal is to identify a non-redundant representative subset, the usual way of drawing samples with replacement used in the AdaBoost.M2 procedure cannot be employed here. Therefore, the reminder stochastic sampling without replacement [8] is used, where the data examples cannot be sampled more than once. Therefore, as a representative subset we obtain a set of distinct data examples with no duplicates.

4 Spatial Progressive Boosting

Spatial data represent a collection of attributes whose dependence is strongly related to a spatial location where observations close to each other are more likely to be similar than observations widely separated in space. Explanatory attributes, as well as the target attribute in spatial data sets are very often highly spatially correlated. It is clear that data redundancy in spatial databases may be partially due to different reasons than in non-spatial data sets and therefore the standard sampling procedures may not be appropriate for spatial data sets.

In the most common geographic information science (GIS) applications the fixed-length grid is regular and therefore the standard method to determine the degree of correlation between neighboring points in such spatial data is to construct a correlogram [9]. The correlogram represents a plot of the autocorrelation coefficient computed as a function of separation distance between spatial data instances (Fig. 3). One of the main characteristics of the spatial correlogram is its range, which corresponds to a distance where spatial dependency starts to disappear, e.g. where the absolute value of the correlogram drops somewhere around 0.1.

Our spatial sampling procedure represents a modification of the proposed progressive boosting technique, described in Section 3. The general algorithm for progressive boosting, presented in Fig. 2 still remains the same, but the procedure for sampling the data examples in subsequent sampling iterations according to the given distribution is adapted to the spatial domain data. In standard sampling without replacement [8] when the data example is sampled once, it cannot be sampled again. In our spatial modification of sampling procedure, when a data instance (shown as O in Fig. 4) is drawn once, not only that instance cannot be sampled again but also all its neighboring points, represented with □ and ◊ in Fig. 4. How many neighbors are excluded from further sampling depends on the degree of correlation and also on the number of data points required to be drawn in current sampling iteration. If the number of points needed to be sampled prevails the number of available data examples for sampling, the farthest square of points (examples denoted as ◊ in Fig. 4) is then included in the set of examples available for sampling. This allows a more uniform sampling across the spatial data set, while still concentrating on more difficult examples for learning.

The spatial progressive boosting employs the same algorithm as one shown in Fig. 2, but uses our modified spatial sampling procedure.

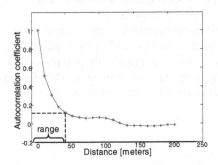

Fig. 3. A spatial correlogram with a 40 m range

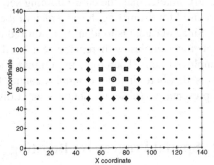

Fig. 4. The scheme for sampling data examples in spatial data sets

5 Experimental Results

An important issue in progressive sampling based techniques is the type of the model used for training through iterations. We used non-linear 2-layer feedforward neural network (NN) models that generally have a large variance, meaning that their accuracy can largely differ over different weight's initial conditions and choice of training data. In such situations using the progressive sampling procedure may effect in significant errors in the estimation of n_{min}. In order to alleviate the effect of neural network instability in our experiments, the prediction accuracy is averaged over 20 trials of the proposed algorithms, i.e. the sampling procedures are repeated 20 times and accuracies achieved at the same sampling round for all 20 trials are averaged. Since it is unlikely that the progressive sampling technique always stops at the same sampling iteration in each of these trials, we simply determined the number of sampling iterations in the first trial of progressive sampling technique, and all other trials for all sampling variants were repeated for such identified number of sampling iterations. To investigate real generalization properties of built NN models, we tested our classification models on the entire training set and on an unseen data with a similar distribution.

The number of hidden neurons in our NN models was equal to the number of input attributes. The NN classification models had the number of output nodes equal to the number of classes (3 in our experiments), where the class was predicted according to the output with the largest response. Resilient propagation (RP) [10] and Levenberg-Marquardt (LM) [11] algorithms were used for learning, although better prediction accuracies were achieved using the LM learning algorithm, and only those results are reported here. The LM algorithm is a variant of Newton's method, where the approximation of the Hessian matrix of mixed partial derivatives is obtained by averaging outer products of estimated gradients. This is very well suited for small to medium-size NN training through mean squared error minimization.

We performed our experiments on several large data sets. The first data set was generated using our spatial data simulator [12] such that the distributions of generated data resembled the distributions of real life spatial data. A square shaped spatial data of size 5120 meters x 5120 meters sampled on a relatively dense spatial grid (10meters x 10 meters) resulted in 262,144 (512^2) training instances. The obtained spatial data stemmed from a homogeneous distribution and had five continuous attributes and three equal size classes.

The second data set was Covertype data, currently one of the largest databases in the UCI Database Repository [13]. This spatial data set contains 581,012 examples with 54 attributes and 7 target classes and represents the forest cover type for 30 x 30 meter cells obtained from US Forest Service (USFS) Region 2 Resource Information System [14]. In Covertype data set, 40 attributes are binary columns representing soil type, 4 attributes are binary columns representing wilderness area, and the remaining 10 are continuous topographical attributes. Since training of a neural network classifier would be very slow if using all 40 attributes representing a soil type variable, we transformed them into 7 new ordered attributes. These 7 attributes were determined by computing relative frequencies of each of 7 classes in each of 40 soil types. Therefore, instead of using a single value for representing each soil type, we used a 7-dimensional vector with values that could be considered continuous and therefore more appropriate for use with neural networks. This resulted in the transformed data set with 21 attributes.

The experiments were also performed on Waveform and LED data sets from the UCI repository [13]. For the Waveform set, 100,000 instances with 21 continuous attributes and three equally sized classes were generated, while for the LED data set 50,000 examples were generated for training and 50,000 examples were generated for testing. Both training and test data sets had 7 binary attributes and 10 classes.

We first performed progressive sampling on all data sets, where in the schedule given in equation (2) we used $a = 2$. Therefore, randomly chosen data samples in subsequent sampling iterations were always twice larger than samples drawn in the previous iterations. Since in our sampling procedures all classifiers constructed in all previous sampling iterations are saved and together with the classifier from the current iteration are combined, we also used the *progressive bagging* scheme, where the classifiers constructed on randomly selected, progressively larger data samples were combined into an ensemble using the same combining weights. Finally, we performed our proposed progressive boosting technique for data reduction on all sets. The improvement of classification accuracy during the sampling iterations on all considered data sets is shown at Fig. 5.

In order to better compare our proposed sampling techniques with the progressive sampling, we stopped them in the same sampling iteration as we stopped the progressive sampling. In this way, we are able to examine two effects of data reduction techniques. First, we can observe what are the possible improvements in classification accuracy when the same size of data sample, necessary for constructing a sufficiently accurate model in progressive sampling, is used. Second, we are able to compare the level of data reduction by evaluating the sizes of data samples for which we achieve the same classification accuracy. The possible savings in processing time were not reported due to lack of space, although these savings are proportional to the level of data reduction since the time for training NN models is proportional to data set size. All results in Fig. 5 are shown starting from the second or third sampling iteration since all the methods achieved the similar accuracies in a first few iterations.

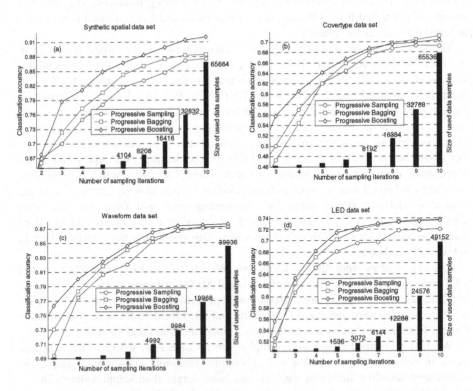

Fig. 5. The classification accuracy as a function of sample size for different progressive sampling techniques on four domains

Analyzing the charts in Fig. 5, it is evident that the sampling methods involving the proposed model integration showed improvements both in prediction accuracy and in achieved data reduction as compared to the standard progressive sampling. The improvement in achieved final prediction accuracy was evident for synthetic spatial, Covertype and LED data set, while the experiments performed on Waveform data sets resulted in similar final prediction accuracy for all proposed variants of sampling techniques probably due to high homogeneity of data. However, during the sampling (iterations 3 to 7, Fig. 5) progressive boosting was consistently achieving better prediction accuracy than progressive bagging, although this difference was fairly small. The dominance of progressive boosting can be explained by the fact that the sampling procedure employed in progressive boosting attempted to rank sampling data examples from those that are more difficult for learning to those that are easier. Therefore, all advantages of standard boosting were also integrated in our progressive boosting technique.

It is also evident that for the same level of data reduction (the same sampling iteration that corresponds to training data of the same size) the achieved prediction accuracy was significantly higher when using progressive boosting and even progressive bagging instead of standard progressive sampling (Fig. 5). In addition, the same prediction accuracy was achieved with much smaller data sets when using progressive boosting and bagging for data reduction instead of relaying on standard progressive sampling. For example, the prediction accuracy on the synthetic spatial data (Fig. 5a) that was achieved by progressive sampling technique with 65,664 examples (10 iterations), was also achieved by the progressive boosting with 8,208 examples (7 iterations). Hence, the gain of these three iterations was an about eight times smaller data set needed for progressive boosting as compared to the progressive sampling.

The level of data reduction for different sampling techniques may be compared if we measure the minimum data sets needed for achieving the same accuracy. This prediction accuracy is determined when no further significant improvements in accuracy, obtained by progressive sampling, is observed. For easier comparison, the size of a reduced data set used to obtain this accuracy by progressive sampling served as a basic reduction level, and then we compared the enhancements of other data reduction techniques. Table 1 shows the level of data reduction for three used data sets.

Table 1. The size of the data sets used for successful learning and their percentage of the original data set size when different sampling techniques are employed

Method ↓	Data set→	Synthetic Spatial	Covertype	LED	Waveform
Progressive Sampling	65,664 (25.1 %)	32,768 (5.6 %)	12,288 (25 %)	9,984 (9.9%)
Progressive Bagging	16,416 (6.3 %)	**8,192 (1.4 %)**	**3,072 (6.1 %)**	9,984 (9.9%)
Progressive Boosting	**8,208 (3.1 %)**	**8,192 (1.4 %)**	**1,536 (3.1 %)**	9,984 (9.9%)

It is evident from Table 1 that both sampling methods with model integration achieved better reduction performance than the standard progressive sampling. In model integration methods the reduced data set was four to eight times smaller than the reduced data set identified through standard progressive sampling. The only exception was the reduction of Waveform data sets (Table 1), where no additional reduction was achieved by combining different classifiers again due to high homogeneity of data. Nevertheless, when employing progressive boosting and progressive bagging techniques, there is an additional requirement to store all the previously constructed classifiers, or to save all data sets used for constructing these classifiers. Usually, storing only the constructed classifiers is beneficial when employing an ensemble to make a prediction on an unseen data set with a similar distribution. However, very often there is a need for storing all necessary data examples needed for constructing all the classifiers. Since we use geometric progressive sampling, where the data sample in subsequent sampling iteration is twice larger from the sample used at the previous iteration, the total size of all previous data samples cannot be larger than the size of the data sample used in the current sampling iteration. Therefore, even in this case, according to Table 1 we can still achieve a better level of data reduction than the standard progressive sampling.

We also performed experiments with pruning inaccurate classifiers constructed in progressive boosting iterations (Fig. 6). For geometric sampling schedule we again used $a = 2$. When pruning inaccurate classifiers, we always eliminated those classifiers that harmed the overall classification accuracy on the validation set. Again, the accuracies on the entire training set are shown starting from second iteration, since there was no pruning at the first iteration (Fig. 6).

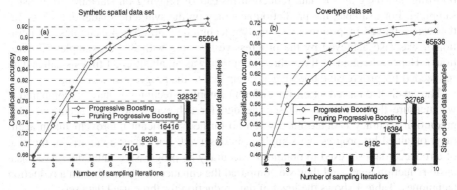

Fig. 6. The classification accuracy during the sampling iterations of progressive boosting and pruning progressive boosting

Results from the experiments presented in Fig. 6 indicate that pruning progressive boosting outperformed the progressive boosting technique both in achieved accuracy and in the level of data reduction for synthetic spatial and Covertype data sets. The enhancements of pruning progressive boosting on Waveform and LED data sets was insignificant as compared to the progressive boosting technique, and therefore these results are not presented here. It is evident from Fig. 6 that for synthetic spatial and Covertype data set the same prediction accuracy may be achieved much faster when pruning classifiers than without pruning. For example, accuracy of 92% for synthetic spatial data set was achieved by progressive boosting without pruning with 65,664 examples (iteration 11), while similar accuracy was achieved when pruning progressive boosting with 8,208 example (iteration 8), thus resulting in an eight times smaller data set. The same results can be observed for Covertype data set, where pruning progressive boosting again caused eight times smaller data set for the comparable prediction accuracy.

Finally, we performed the experiments for sampling spatial data using our proposed technique for spatial progressive boosting. Since the positions of data examples included in the form of x and y coordinates were only available for the synthetic spatial data set, but not for Covertype data set, the results are reported only for the synthetic spatial data (Fig. 7). The shown accuracy starts from the third sampling iteration due to similar performance of spatial and non-spatial sampling in the first two iterations.

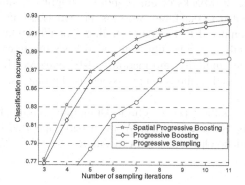

Fig. 7. The classification accuracy during the sampling iterations of spatial progressive boosting and standard progressive boosting on synthetic spatial data set

Fig. 7 shows that the spatial progressive boosting method, starting from the fourth iteration outperformed the regular progressive boosting in achieved prediction accuracy. In addition, for achieving accuracy of 92%, spatial progressive boosting needed four times smaller data set than the regular progressive boosting. One of the reasons for such a successful reduction of this data set is possibly in its high spatial correlation among observed attributes and a relatively dense spatial grid (10 x 10 meters).

6 Conclusions

Several new sampling procedures based on the progressive sampling idea are proposed. They are intended for an efficient reduction of very large and possibly spatial databases. Experimental results on several data sets indicate that the proposed sampling techniques can effectively achieve similar or even better prediction accuracy while obtaining a better data reduction than the standard progressive sampling technique. Depending on the data set, accuracy comparable to relying on the whole data set was achieved using 1.4% to 6.1% of the original data.

The question that naturally arises from this paper is a possible gain when comparing the proposed sampling techniques with the procedure of first performing the progressive sampling and then applying some of the methods for combining classifiers (bagging, boosting). First, our sampling techniques are faster since they do not require additional algorithm of combining classifiers. Second, our algorithms provide a better diversity of combined classifiers, since during the sampling iterations some of the instances difficult for learning were naturally included in the reduced data set by our algorithms while these may not be included in a final data set when performing standard progressive sampling. Finally, when using our algorithms, only a small number of data examples that are relatively easy for learning will be included in the reduced data set, unlike the progressive sampling where this number cannot be controlled. Our future work will address the significance of the difference between these two methods.

One of the possible drawbacks of our proposed sampling techniques that will be also carefully investigated in our future work, is an increased time required for controlled sampling as compared to random sampling. For reduction of heterogeneous data sets we are currently experimenting with radial basis functions, while for spatial data reduction different similarity information will be explored. In addition, we are also extending the proposed methods to regression-based problems.

Acknowledgment. The authors are grateful to Dragoljub Pokrajac for providing synthetic data and for his useful comments. Work in part supported by INEEL LDRD Program under DOE Idaho Operations Office Contract DE-AC07-99ID13727.

References

1.   Oates, T., Jansen, D.: Large Datasets Lead to Overly Complex Models: An Explanation and a Solution, *Proc. Fourth International Conference On Knowledge Discovery and Data Mining*, (1998), 294-298

2.   Grossman R, Turinsky A. A Framework for Finding Distributed Data Mining Strategies That Are Intermediate Between Centralized Strategies and In-Place Strategies, *KDD Workshop on Distributed Data Mining*, (2000)

3.   Provost, F., Jensen, D., Oates, T.: Efficient Progressive Sampling, *Proc. Fifth Int'l Conf. On Knowledge Discovery and Data Mining*, (1999), 23-32

4.   Freund, Y., and Schapire, R. E.: Experiments with a New Boosting Algorithm, in *Proc. of the 13th International Conference on Machine Learning*, (1996) 325-332

5.   Quinlan, J. R.: Learning Efficient Classification Procedures and their Application to Chess and Games, In Michalski, R., Carbonell, J., Mitchell, T. (eds.): Machine Learning. An Artificial Intelligence Approach, (1983), 463-482

6.   Fürnkranz, J.: Integrative windowing, *J. Artificial Intelligence & Research* 8, (1998), 129-164

7.   Harris-Jones, C., Haines, T.: Sample Size and Misclassification: Is More Always Better?, *Proc. Second International Conference on the Practical Application of Knowledge Discovery and Data Mining*, (1998)

8.   Goldberg, D.: Genetic Algorithms in Search, Optimization and Machine Learning, Addison-Wesley Reading, MA, (1989)

9.   Cressie, N.A.C., *Statistics for Spatial Data*, John Wiley & Sons, Inc., New York, 1993.

10.   Riedmiller, M., Braun, H.: A Direct Adaptive Method for Faster Backpropagation Learning: The RPROP Algorithm, *Proc. of the IEEE International Conference on Neural Networks*, (1993), 586–591

11. Hagan, M., Menhaj, M.B.: Training feedforward networks with the Marquardt algorithm. *IEEE Transactions on Neural Networks* 5, (1994) 989-993

12. Pokrajac D, Fiez T, Obradovic Z.: A Spatial Data Simulator for Agriculture Knowledge Discovery Applications, in review

13. Murphy, P.M., Aha, D.W., *UCI Repository of Machine Learning Databases,* Department of Information and Computer Science, University of California, Irvine, CA, (1999)

14. Blackard, J., *Comparison of Neural Networks and Discriminant Analysis in Predicting Forest Cover Types*, Ph.D. dissertation, Colorado State University, Fort Collins, (1998)

Discovering Fuzzy Classification Rules with Genetic Programming and Co-evolution

Roberto R.F. Mendes, Fabricio de B. Voznika, Alex A. Freitas, and Julio C. Nievola

PUC-PR
PPGIA - CCET
Av. Imaculada Conceição, 1155
Curitiba - PR, 80215-901 Brazil
{alex,nievola}@ppgia.pucpr.br
http://www.ppgia.pucpr.br/~alex
+55 41 330-1669

Abstract. In essence, data mining consists of extracting knowledge from data. This paper proposes a co-evolutionary system for discovering fuzzy classification rules. The system uses two evolutionary algorithms: a genetic programming (GP) algorithm evolving a population of fuzzy rule sets and a simple evolutionary algorithm evolving a population of membership function definitions. The two populations co-evolve, so that the final result of the co-evolutionary process is a fuzzy rule set and a set of membership function definitions which are well adapted to each other. In addition, our system also has some innovative ideas with respect to the encoding of GP individuals representing rule sets. The basic idea is that our individual encoding scheme incorporates several syntactical restrictions that facilitate the handling of rule sets in disjunctive normal form. We have also adapted GP operators to better work with the proposed individual encoding scheme.

1 Introduction

In the context of machine learning and data mining, one popular way of expressing knowledge consists of IF-THEN rules. This is due to the fact that they are intuitively comprehensible to a human being [5]. In addition, they represent independent units of knowledge, so that alterations can easily take place in their contents. IF-THEN rules are composed of two parts. The first part (IF component, or rule antecedent) corresponds to a conjunction of conditions that, if verified true, imply that the condition contained in the second part (THEN component, or rule consequent) is also considered true.

Rules in their classic format are appropriate when their conditions are constituted by discrete or categorical variables. However, the presence of continuous variables creates situations that thwart the common sense. Let's consider the rule: "IF age < 25 THEN safe_driver = no". The problem here is the sudden and unnatural transition between categories: an individual can be classified as not being a safe driver today but, in the following day, he might have completed 25 years and thus be classified as

L. De Raedt and A. Siebes (Eds.): PKDD 2001, LNAI 2168, pp. 314–325, 2001.

being a safe driver. This could lead a data mining system to completely different predictions in the interval of a single day. One promising alternative to work with continuous variables and to overcome this inconvenience is the use of fuzzy logic. Besides expressing knowledge in a more natural way, fuzzy logic is also a flexible and powerful method for uncertainty management [13], [6].

In the literature several techniques have been used for discovery of fuzzy IF-THEN rules. Several recent projects have proposed the use of evolutionary algorithms for fuzzy rule discovery [2], [10], [11], [19], [21], [17], because it allows a global search in the state space, increasing the probability of converging to the globally-optimal solution.

The main characteristic of our proposed system that makes it different from the above systems it that our system is based on the co-evolution of fuzzy rule sets and membership function definitions, using two separate populations, whereas in general the above projects are based on the evolution of a single population. The population of fuzzy rule sets is evolved by a Genetic Programming (GP) algorithm, whereas the population of membership function definitions is evolved by a simple evolutionary algorithm.

In addition, our system also has some innovative ideas with respect to the encoding of GP individuals representing rule sets. The basic idea is that our individual encoding scheme incorporates several syntactical restrictions that facilitate the handling of rule sets in disjunctive normal form. We have also adapted GP operators to better work with the proposed individual encoding scheme.

The remainder of this paper is organized as follows. Section 2 describes in detail our proposed co-evolutionary system. Section 3 discusses computational results. Finally, section 4 concludes the paper.

2 The Proposed Co-evolutionary System for Fuzzy Rule Discovery

2.1 An Overview of the System

This section presents an overview of our CEFR-MINER (Co-Evolutionary Fuzzy Rule Miner) system. CEFR-MINER is a system developed for the classification task of data mining. It consists of two co-evolving evolutionary algorithms. The first one is a Genetic Programming (GP) algorithm where each individual represents a fuzzy rule set. A GP individual specifies only the attribute-value pairs composing the rule conditions of that individual's rule set. The definitions of the membership functions necessary to interpret the fuzzy rule conditions of an individual are provided by the second population. The second algorithm is a simple evolutionary algorithm, which works with a "population" of a single individual. This population evolves via the principle of natural selection and application of mutation, but not crossover. This single individual specifies definitions of all the membership functions for all attributes being fuzzified (all originally continuous attributes). These definitions are used by the first population of GP individuals, as mentioned above. Note that categorical attributes are not fuzzified – their values are handled only by the GP population.

As a result, the system simultaneously evolves both fuzzy rule sets and membership function definitions specifically suited for the fuzzy rule sets. The main advantage of this co-evolutionary approach is that the fitness of a given set of membership function definitions is evaluated across several fuzzy rule sets, encoded into several different GP individuals, rather than on a single fuzzy set. This improves the robustness of that evaluation.

This basic idea of co-evolution for fuzzy-rule discovery has been recently proposed by [4]. The main differences between this work and our system are as follows. (a) Delgado et al.'s work uses three co-evolving populations and our work uses only two; (b) Delgado et al.'s work uses genetic algorithms for evolving two of its three populations. By contrast, we use genetic programming to evolve the rule set population; (c) our work addresses the classification task of data mining, whereas Delgado et al.'s work addresses the problem of numeric function approximation.

2.2 The Genetic Programming Population

2.2.1 Rule Representation
Our system follows the Pittsburgh approach [7] and thus each individual represents a set of rules. Each rule has the form: IF conditions THEN prediction. The prediction of the rule has the form: "goal attribute = class", where class is one of the values that can be taken on by the goal attribute. In each run of the system all individuals of the GP population are associated with the same prediction. Therefore, there is no need to explicitly encode this prediction into the genome of an individual. Since each run discovers rules predicting a single class, the system must be run c times, where c is the number of classes. Although this approach increases processing time, it has two important advantages: (a) it simplifies individual encoding; and (b) it avoids the problem of mating between individuals that predict different classes, which could produce low-quality offspring. Each individual actually corresponds to a set of rule antecedents encoded in disjunctive normal form (DNF), such as: (sore throat = true AND age = *low*) OR (headache = true AND NOT temperature = *low*).

In our system the function set contains the logical operators {AND, OR, NOT}. Since each individual represents fuzzy rules, a fuzzy version of these logical operators must be used. We have used the standard fuzzy AND (intersection), OR (union) and NOT (complement) operators [13]. More precisely, let $\mu_A(x)$ denote the membership degree of an element x in the fuzzy set A, i.e. the degree to which x belongs to the fuzzy set A. The standard AND of two fuzzy sets A and B, denoted A AND B, is defined as $\mu_{A\text{-AND-}B}(x) = \min[\mu_A(x), \mu_B(x)]$, where min denotes the minimum operator. The standard OR of two fuzzy sets A and B, denoted A OR B, is defined as $\mu_{A\text{-OR-}B}(x) = \max[\mu_A(x), \mu_B(x)]$, where max denotes the maximum operator. The standard NOT of a fuzzy set A, denoted NOT A, is defined as $\mu_{NOT\text{-}A}(x) = 1 - \mu_A(x)$.

The terminal set consists of all possible conditions of the form: "$\text{Attr}_i = \text{Val}_{ij}$", where Attr_i is the i-th attribute of the dataset. If attribute Attr_i is categorical, Val_{ij} is the j-th value of the domain of Attr_i. If attribute Attr_i is continuous - which means it is being fuzzified by the system - Val_{ij} is a linguistic value in {*low, medium, high*}. We use only three linguistic values in order to reduce the size of the search space.

In order to produce individual trees with only valid rule antecedents and in DNF we propose some syntactic restrictions in the tree representation, as follows: (a) the root node is always an OR node; (b) with the exception of the root node, each OR node must have as its parent another OR node, and can have as its children any kind of node; (c) each AND node must have as its parent either an OR node or another AND node, and can have as its children AND, NOT or terminal nodes; (d) a NOT node can have as its parent an OR node, an AND node or a NOT node; and it can have as its child either another NOT node or a terminal node (we allow conditions of the form "NOT NOT ..." to allow the possibility of a NOT being cancelled by another NOT as a result of genetic operators) and (e) there cannot be two or more terminal nodes referring to the same attribute in the same rule antecedent, since this would tend to produce invalid rule antecedents such as (sex = male AND sex = female). Fig. 1 shows an individual with five rule antecedents.

These syntactic constraints are enforced both when creating individuals of the initial population and when modifying individuals due to the action of a genetic operator. This approach can be regarded as a kind of strongly-typed GP [16] proposed specifically for the discovery of rule sets in disjunctive normal form, which makes it attractive for data mining applications.

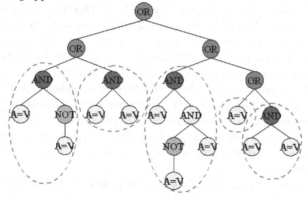

Fig. 1. A tree representing five rule antecedents

The main advantage of working with the DNF directly into the tree representation, rather than converting a rule set into DNF after GP has evolved, is that this makes it easier to fulfil the aforementioned restriction (e). Because of the hierarchical position of the nodes, it is easy to collect the terminal nodes of an individual rule, as shown in Fig. 1, in order to check whether or not a condition can be inserted into that rule.

Another possible approach to assure that the GP will run only with syntactically valid individuals would be to use a context-free grammar to implement the aforementioned syntactic restrictions. The drawback of this approach would be the difficulty in checking syntactic restriction (e), which would lead to an explosion of the number of production rules in the grammar. To avoid this, a logic grammar could be used [20], but this would introduce some complexity to the system. Thus, we have preferred the above-described direct implementation of syntactic constraints.

2.2.2 Selection and Genetic Operators

We use the tournament selection method, with tournament size 2 and with a simple extension: if two individuals have the same fitness, the one with smaller complexity is selected. Complexity is measured by the following formula [12]:

$$complexity = 2 \times number\_of\_rules + number\_of\_conditions . \qquad (1)$$

This extension was motivated by observations in our experiments: sometimes the two individuals competing in the tournament had the same fitness value, even though they were different individuals.

Once two individuals are selected crossover is performed in a similar way to conventional GP crossover, with the difference that in our case the crossover operator respects the above-discussed syntactic restrictions, in order to guarantee that crossover always generates syntactically-valid offspring. (If crossover cannot produce syntactically-valid individuals, the crossover operation fails and no children are produced.)

The current version of the system uses a crossover probability of 80%, a relatively common setting in the literature. However, in our system the offspring produced by crossover is not necessarily inserted into the population. Our population updating strategy is as follows. Once all crossovers have been performed, all the produced offspring are added to the population of individuals. Therefore, the population size is provisionally increased by 80%. Then all individuals are sorted by fitness value, and the worst individuals are removed from the population. The number of removed individuals is chosen in such a way that the number of individuals left in the population is always a constant population size, set to 250 individuals (an empirically-determined setting) in our experiments. We chose this population-updating strategy mainly because it increases selection pressure, in comparison with a conventional generational-replacement strategy. This is analogous to the $(\mu+\lambda)$-strategy employed in the second EA of this system, described in Section 2.3.2. The main difference is that here we use a $(\mu+\lambda)$ strategy on top of tournament selection, whereas the classic $(\mu+\lambda)$ strategy uses no such scheme.

Our system uses a mutation operator where a node is randomly chosen and then the subtree rooted at that node is replaced by another randomly-generated subtree. In the current version of the system an individual undergoes mutation with a probability of 20% (an empirically-determined setting), with just one exception. The best individual of each generation never undergoes mutation, so that its fitness will never be worsened.

2.2.3 Fitness Function

In order to calculate the fitness of a GP individual, the first step is to compute the following counters:

- *TP* (true positives) is the number of examples that are covered by at least one of the individual's rules and have the class predicted by those rules;
- *FP* (false positives) is the number of examples that are covered by at least one of the individual's rules but have a class different from the class predicted by those rules;
- *FN* (false negatives) is the number of examples that are not covered by any of the individual's rules but have the class predicted by those rules;

- *TN* (true negatives) is the number of examples that are not covered by any of the individual's rules and do not have the class predicted by those rules.

Note that the true positives and true negatives correspond to correct predictions made by the individual being evaluated, whereas the false positives and the false negatives correspond to wrong predictions made by that individual. In our system the fitness of a GP individual is computed by the following formula [9]:

$$(TP / (TP + FN)) \times (TN / (FP + TN)) . \tag{2}$$

In the data mining literature, in general it is implicitly assumed that the values of TP, FP, FN and TN are crisp. This very commonplace assumption is invalid in our case, since our system discovers fuzzy rules. In our system an example can be covered by a rule antecedent to a certain degree in the range [0..1], which corresponds to the membership degree of that example in that rule antecedent. Therefore, the system computes fuzzy values for TP, FP, FN and TN.

The membership degree of record r into the rule set encoded by the individual I is computed as follows. For each rule of I, the system computes the membership degree of r into each of the conditions of that rule. Then the membership degree for the entire rule antecedent is computed by a fuzzy AND of the membership degrees for all the rule conditions. This process is repeated for all the rules of the individual I. Then the membership degree of the entire rule set is computed by a fuzzy OR of the membership degrees for all the rules of I.

For instance, suppose a training example has the class predicted by the individual I's rules. Ideally, we would like that example to be covered by at least one of I's rules to a degree of 1, so that the entire rule set of I would cover that example to a degree of 1. Suppose that I has two rules, and that the current training example is covered by those rules to degrees of 0.6 and 0.8. Then the fuzzy OR would return a membership degree of 0.8 for the entire rule set. This means that the prediction made by the individual is 80% correct and 20% wrong. As a result, this example contributes a value of 0.8 for the number of true positives and a value of 0.2 for the number of false negatives.

2.2.4 Tree Pruning

Rule pruning is important not only in data mining [3] but also in GP, due to the well-known effects of code bloat [14], [1]. Code bloat has greatly affected our system's performance. In our initial experiments, with no pruning at all, some datasets required an unacceptable amount of running time. Therefore, we have designed an operator to prune GP trees. The basic idea of this operator is to randomly remove conditions from a rule with a null coverage – i.e. a rule which does not cover any record – until it covers at least one record or until all conditions are removed, which corresponds to removing the entire rule from its rule set.

More precisely, each rule of the individual is separated and evaluated by itself. The ones that have a null coverage will have some conditions dropped according to the following criteria:

- If a rule has more than 7 conditions, some conditions are randomly removed until the rule has between 5 and 7 conditions (a randomly chosen number). If even after this step the rule remains with a null coverage, the next criterion will be applied;

- If the number of conditions of a rule is less than or equal to 7, its conditions will be dropped randomly one by one until the rule covers at least one record or all of its conditions are dropped, removing the rule completely from the individual.

This operator is applied to an individual with a 20% probability. However, as an individual might be worsened by this operator, it is never applied to the best individual of the current generation. The motivation to apply the above operator only to 20% of the individuals is to save processing time, since this is a relatively computationally-expensive operator.

After the end of the evolution, the best individual also undergoes a different tree pruning. This operator removes two kinds of redundant rules: rules with a null coverage and duplicate rules. This final tree pruning does not alter the fitness of the individual, since the removal of null-coverage/duplicate rules does not alter the set of examples covered by an individual's rule set.

2.3   The "Population" of Membership Functions

As mentioned above, in our system the values of all continuous attributes are fuzzified into three linguistic values, namely low, medium, and high. These linguistics values are defined by trapezoidal membership functions. Each continuous attribute is associated with its own membership functions. Hence, the membership functions are dynamically evolved, modifying a set of parameters defining the membership functions, to get better adapted to their corresponding attribute. All the parameters of all membership functions are encoded into a single individual. This individual is considered as a "population" (in a loose sense of the term, of course) separated from the GP population. As mentioned in section 2.1, this single-individual population co-evolves with the GP population.

2.3.1   Individual Representation

The individual is divided into k parts (or "chromosomes", loosely speaking), where k is the number of attributes being fuzzified. Each chromosome consists of four genes, denoted $g1$, $g2$, $g3$ and $g4$, which collectively define the three membership functions (low, medium, and high) for the corresponding attribute, as shown in Fig. 2. Each gene represents an attribute value that is used to specify the coordinate of two trapezoid vertices belonging to a pair of "adjacent" membership functions. The system ensures that $g1 \leq g2 \leq g3 \leq g4$.

This individual representation has two advantages. First, it reduces the search space of the evolutionary algorithm and saves processing time, since the number of parameters to be optimized by the evolutionary algorithm is reduced. Second, this representation enforces some overlapping between "adjacent" membership functions and guarantees that, for each original value of the continuous attribute, the sum of its degrees of membership into the three linguistic values will be 1, which is intuitively sensible.

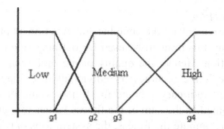

Fig. 2. Definition of 3 trapezoidal membership functions by 4 genes (g1, g2, g3, g4)

2.3.2 Evolutionary Algorithm to Evolve Membership Functions

Obviously, it is not possible to perform crossover in the single-individual "population" of membership functions. Therefore, the evolution of the single individual representing membership functions is the result of a simple evolutionary algorithm, which evolves by means of a ($\mu+\lambda$)-evolution strategy (more specifically the (1+5)-strategy), described as follows.

First of all, the individual is cloned 5 times. Each clone is an exact copy of the original individual. Then the system applies to each clone a relatively high rate of mutation. Each chromosome (i.e. a block of four contiguous genes, g1, g2, g3 and g4, defining the membership functions of a single attribute) has an 80% probability of undergoing a single-gene mutation. The mutation in question consists of adding or subtracting a small randomly-generated value to the current gene value. This has the effect of shifting the coordinate of the trapezoid vertices associated with that gene a little to the right or to the left.

Note that, since a chromosome has four genes and only one of those genes is mutated, a mutation rate of 80% per chromosome corresponds to a mutation rate of 20% per gene. Our motivation to use this relatively high mutation rate is the desire to perform a more global search in the space of candidate membership function definitions. If we used a much smaller mutation rate, say 1% or 0.1%, probably at most one gene of an entire individual (corresponding to all attributes being fuzzified) would be modified. This would correspond to a kind of local search, where a new candidate solution being evaluated (via fitness function) would differ from its "parent" solution by only one gene, without taking into account gene interactions. By contrast, in our (1+5)-evolution strategy scheme a new candidate solution being evaluated differs from its "parent" solution by several genes, and the effect of all these gene modifications is evaluated as a whole, taking into account gene interactions. This is important, since the attributes being fuzzified can interact in such a way that modifications in their membership functions should be evaluated as a whole. Actually, the ability to take into account attribute interactions can be considered one of the main motivations for using an evolutionary algorithm, rather than a local search algorithm.

In any case, once the 5 clones have undergone mutation, the 5 just-generated individuals are evaluated according to a fitness function – which is discussed in the next subsection. The best individual is kept and all others are discarded.

The number of clones (5) used in our experiments was empirically determined as a good trade-off between membership-function quality and processing time.

2.3.3 Fitness Function

Recall that the individual of the membership-function population represents definitions of membership functions to be used for defining rule antecedents being evolved by the GP population. Hence, the quality of the individual of the former population depends on the predictive accuracy of individuals of the latter population. More precisely, in our co-evolutionary scheme the fitness value of the membership-function individual is computed as the sum of the fitness values of a group of individuals of the GP population. To compute the fitness, the system uses only a small portion of the GP population – for the experiments reported in this paper we used the best five individuals – , in order to reduce processing time.

2.4 Classifying New Examples

Recall that a complete execution of our system generates one rule set for each class found in the data set. These rule sets are then used to classify the examples of the test set. For each test example the system computes the degree of membership of that example to each rule set (each one predicting a different class). Then the example is assigned the class of the rule set in which the example has the largest degree of membership. The accuracy rate on the test set is computed as the number of correctly classified test examples divided by the total number of test examples, as usual in the classification literature.

3 Computational Results

We have evaluated our system across four public-domain data sets from the UCI (University of California at Irvine) data set repository. These data sets are available from http://www.ics.uci.edu/~mlearn/MLRepository.html. Some of these data sets had a small number of records with unknown values. Since the current version of our system cannot cope with this problem, those records were removed. All the results reported below were produced by using a 10-fold cross-validation procedure [9].

In order to evaluate the performance of our system we have compared it to two other evolutionary systems found in the literature: ESIA [15] and BGP [18]. Both ESIA and BGP discover crisp rules. They were chosen for comparison because they have been applied to some of the data sets used in our experiments and because they have obtained good results in comparison with other data mining systems. The results for ESIA and BGP reported here are taken directly from the above-mentioned papers. The results for ESIA were also produced by 10-fold cross-validation, whereas the results for BGP were produced by generating 30 training and test sets.

As can be seen in Table 1, our system and ESIA obtained the same accuracy rate on the Iris data set. (The numbers between brackets for our system are standard deviations.) On the other two data sets (CRX and Heart), our system considerably outperforms ESIA. Our system outperforms BGP on the Iris data set, but BGP outperforms our system on the Ionosphere data set.

A possible explanation for the lower performance of the fuzzy rules discovered by our system in the Ionosphere data set is suggested by the large number (34) of continuous attributes in that data set. This suggests the possibility that the simple evolutionary algorithm described in section 2.3 has difficulty in coping with such a relatively high number of attributes being fuzzified. In other words, in this case the size of the search space may be too large for such a simple evolutionary algorithm. This hypothesis will be further investigated in future work.

Table 1. Accuracy rate (on test set), in %, of our system , ESIA and BGP

Data set	Our system	ESIA	BGP
CRX	84.7 (±3.5)	77.39	N/A
Heart (statlog)	82.2 (±7.1)	74.44	N/A
Ionosphere	88.6 (±6.0)	N/A	89.2
Iris	95.3 (±7.1)	95.33	94.1

Overall, we consider these results very promising, bearing in mind that, unlike ESIA and BGP, our system has the advantage of discovering fuzzy rules, which tend to be more intuitive for a user than the "hard" thresholds associated with continuous attributes in crisp rules. On the other hand, like most evolutionary algorithms, our co-evolutionary system needs a good amount of computational time to run. More precisely, a single iteration of cross-validation took a processing time varying from a couple of minutes for the Iris data set to about one hour for the CRX data set – results obtained for a dual-processor Pentium II 350. Shorter processing times may be obtained by the use of parallel data mining techniques [8], but this point is left for future research.

4 Conclusions and Future Research

We have proposed a co-evolutionary system for discovering fuzzy classification rules. The system uses two evolutionary algorithms: a genetic programming (GP) algorithm evolving a population of fuzzy rule sets and a simple evolutionary algorithm evolving a population of membership function definitions. The two populations co-evolve, so that the final result of the co-evolutionary process is a fuzzy rule set and a set of membership function definitions that are well adapted to each other.

The main advantage of this co-evolutionary approach is that the fitness of a given set of membership function definitions is evaluated across several fuzzy rule sets, encoded into several different GP individuals, rather than on a single fuzzy set. This makes that evaluation more robust. In order to mitigate the problem of long processing times, our system evaluates a set of membership function definitions only across the few best GP individuals.

In addition, our system also has some innovative ideas with respect to the encoding of GP individuals representing rule sets. The basic idea is that our individual encoding scheme incorporates several syntactical restrictions that facilitate the handling of rule sets in disjunctive normal form. We have also adapted GP operators to better work with the proposed individual encoding scheme.

We have evaluated our system across four public domain data sets and compared it with two other evolutionary systems (ESIA and BGP) found in the literature which used the same data sets. Our results can be summarized as follows:

(a) Our co-evolutionary system considerably outperforms ESIA in two out of three datasets and equals it in the other data set, with respect to predictive accuracy.

(b) Our system is competitive with BGP in two data sets. (In one data set our system outperforms BGP, whereas BGP outperforms our system in the other data set.)

(c) Our system has the advantage of discovering fuzzy rules, which tend to be more intuitive for the user than the crisp rules discovered by ESIA and BGP.

There are several directions for future research. For instance, the GP tree pruning operator currently used in our system is a "blind" operator, in the sense that tree nodes to be pruned are randomly chosen. It seems that a promising research direction would be to design a more "intelligent" pruning operator, which would choose the tree nodes to be pruned based on some estimate of the predictive power of those tree nodes.

Note that the above suggested research direction concerns improvement in the GP algorithm used by our system. However it seems that the most important point to investigate in future research is the performance of the simple evolutionary algorithm for evolving membership function definitions. It is possible that the current version of this algorithm is not robust enough to cope with data sets having a large number of attributes being fuzzified. This hypothesis must be further investigated in the future, which might lead to improvements in the current version of this simple evolutionary algorithm.

References

1. W. Banzhaf, P. Nordin, R.E. Keller, Francone FD Genetic Programming ~ an Introduction. Morgan Kaufmann, 1998.
2. P.J. Bentley. "Evolutionary, my dear Watson" - investigating committee-based evolution of fuzzy rules for the detection of suspicious insurance claims. Proc. Genetic and Evolutionary Computation Conf. (GECCO-2000), 702-709. Morgan Kaufmann, 2000.
3. L.A. Breslow and D.W. Aha. Simplifying decision trees: a survey. The Knowledge Engineering Review, 12(1), 1-40. Mar. 1997.
4. M. Delgado, F.V. Zuben and F. Gomide. Modular and hierarchical evolutionary design of fuzzy systems. Proc. Genetic and Evolutionary Computation Conf. (GECCO-99), 180-187. Morgan Kaufmann, 1999.
5. U.M. Fayyad, G. Piatetsky-Shapiro and P. Smyth. From data mining to knowledge discovery: an overview. In: U.M. Fayyad et al. (Eds.) Advances in Knowledge Discovery & Data Mining, 1-34. AAAI/MIT, 1996.
6. C.S. Fertig, A.A. Freitas, L.V.R. Arruda and C. Kaestner. A Fuzzy Beam-Search Rule Induction Algorithm. Principles of Data Mining and Knowledge Discovery (Proc. 3rd European Conf. - PKDD-99). Lecture Notes in Artificial Intelligence 1704, 341-347. Springer-Verlag, 1999.
7. A.A. Freitas. A survey of evolutionary algorithms for data mining and knowledge discovery. To appear in: A. Ghosh and S. Tsutsui. (Eds.) Advances in Evolutionary Computation. Springer-Verlag, 2001.
8. A.A. Freitas and S.H. Lavington. Mining Very Large Databases with Parallel Processing. Kluwer Academic Publishers, 1998.

9. D.J. Hand. Construction and Assessment of Classification Rules. John Wiley&Sons, 1997.
10. H. Ishibuchi and T. Nakashima. Linguistic rule extraction by genetics-based machine learning. Proc. Genetic and Evolutionary Computation Conf. (GECCO-2000), 195-202. Morgan Kaufmann, 2000.
11. H. Ishibuchi, T. Nakashima and T. Kuroda. A hybrid fuzzy GBML algorithm for designing compact fuzzy rule-based classification systems. Proc. 9th IEEE Int. Conf. Fuzzy Systems (FUZZ IEEE 2000), 706-711. San Antonio, TX, USA. May 2000.
12. C.Z. Janikow. A knowledge-intensive genetic algorithm for supervised learning. Machine Learning 13, 189-228. 1993.
13. G.J. Klir and B. Yuan. Fuzzy Sets and Fuzzy Logic. Prentice-Hall, 1995.
14. W.B. Langdon, T. Soule, R. Poli and J.A. Foster. The evolution of size and shape. In: L. Spector, W.B. Langdon, U-M. O'Reilly and P.J. Angeline. (Eds.) Advances in Genetic Programming Volume 3, 163-190. MIT Press, 1999.
15. J.J. Liu and J.T. Kwok. An Extended Genetic Rule Induction Algorithm. Proc. Congress on Evolutionary Computation (CEC-2000). La Jolla, CA, USA. July 2000.
16. D.J. Montana. Strongly typed genetic programming. Evolutionary Computation 3(2), 199-230. 1995.
17. C.A. Pena-Reyes and M. Sipper. Designing breast cancer diagnostic systems via a hybrid fuzzy-genetic methodology. Proc. 8th IEEE Int. Conf. Fuzzy Systems. 1999.
18. S.E. Rouwhorst and A.P.Engelbrecht. Searching the Forest: Using Decision Tree as Building Blocks for Evolutionary Search in Classification. Proc. Congress on Evolutionary Computation (CEC-2000), 633-638. La Jolla, CA, USA. July 2000.
19. D. Walter and C.K. Mohan. ClaDia: a fuzzy classifier system for disease diagnosis. Proc. Congress on Evolutionary Computation (CEC-2000), 1429-1435. La Jolla, CA. 2000.
20. M.L. Wong and K.S. Leung. Data Mining Using Grammar Based Genetic Programming and Applications. Kluwer, 2000.
21. N. Xiong and L. Litz. Generating linguistic fuzzy rules for pattern classification with genetic algorithms. Principles of Data Mining and Knowledge Discovery (Proc. PKDD-99) Lecture Notes in Artificial Intelligence 1704, 574-579. Springer-Verlag, 1999.

Sentence Filtering for Information Extraction in Genomics, a Classification Problem

Claire Nédellec[1], Mohamed Ould Abdel Vetah[1,2], and Philippe Bessières[3]

[1]LRI UMR 8623 CNRS, Université Paris-Sud, 91405 Orsay cedex
cn@lri.fr
[2]ValiGen SA, Tour Neptune, 92086 La-Défense
ould@lri.fr
[3] Mathématique, Informatique et Génome (MIG) INRA, 78026 Versailles cedex
philb@biotec.jouy.inra.fr

Abstract. In some domains, Information Extraction (IE) from texts requires syntactic and semantic parsing. This analysis is computationally expensive and IE is potentially noisy if it applies to the whole set of documents when the relevant information is sparse. A preprocessing phase that selects the fragments which are potentially relevant increases the efficiency of the IE process. This phase has to be fast and based on a shallow description of the texts. We applied various classification methods — IVI, a Naive Bayes learner and C4.5 — to this fragment filtering task in the domain of functional genomics. This paper describes the results of this study. We show that the IVI and Naive Bayes methods with feature selection gives the best results as compared with their results without feature selection and with C4.5 results.

1 Introduction

As an increasing amount of information becomes available in the form of electronic documents, the need for intelligent text processing makes shallow text understanding methods such as Information Extraction (IE) particularly useful. Up to now, IE has been restrictively defined by DARPA's MUC (Message Understanding Conference) program [10] as the task of extracting specific, well-defined types of information from natural language texts in restricted domains with the specific objective of filling pre-defined template slots and databases. We claim that in many domains, IE systems have to rely on deep analysis methods local to the relevant fragments. They should combine the semantic-conceptual analysis of text understanding methods and information extraction by pattern matching; in a first step the relevant textual fragments are filtered based on shallow criteria; in a second step, a representation of the content of the fragments is built by successive interpretation operations based on syntactico-semantic lexicon following a classical approach in text understanding, finally, extraction rules are applied to the resulting interpretations in order to identify the relevant information and store it in a database in the suitable format, usually by filling forms in the MUC

L. De Raedt and A. Siebes (Eds.): PKDD 2001, LNAI 2168, pp. 326-337, 2001.

case. These three steps differ by the nature of the knowledge that they exploit and by the complexity of the methods applied. The second step, that is, the syntactico-semantic parsing is the most expensive in terms of resources. The first step, i.e. the filtering of the relevant fragments, allows to limit that analysis to what is needed only, by focussing it on the fragments that potentially contain relevant information. This selection is even more crucial as the information to be extracted is sparser. The sparseness problem had been pointed out in previous research in IE [15] and [16] but no practical solution has been proposed. The main consequence is that the first step must be fast, even if this implies some lack of precision. It must thus be based on a shallow description of the text. The application of learning to the filtering of relevant fragments has received little attention in IE compared to other tasks such as learning for name entity recognition or learning extraction patterns [15, 16]. This lack of interest is due to the type of texts that are generally handled by IE, which are those proposed in the MUC competition. Those texts are usually short and the information to be extracted is generally dense, so that prefiltering is less or not needed at all. The type of information to be extracted such as company names or a seminar starting times often requires only a shallow analysis, the computational cost of which is low enough to avoid prefiltering. This is not the case in other IE tasks such as identifying gene interaction in functional genomics, the application that we describe here.

From a Machine Learning point of view, filtering can be viewed as a classification problem. Textual fragments have to be classified in two classes: potentially relevant for IE or not. The learning examples represent fragments, (sentences in this application) and the example attributes are the significant and the lemmatized words (in a canonical form) of the sentences. We compared experimentally the classification method IVI proposed in [12] for IE in functional genomics, a Naïve Bayes (NB) method [9], and a decision tree-based method, C4.5 [14], on three different datasets in functional genomics described in section 2. As a consequence of the example representation, the datasets are very sparse in the attribute space; the examples are described by few attributes. Thus, in addition to the basic methods, we studied the effect of feature selection as a preprocessing step. The objective of this study is to identify the best classification methods for filtering sentences in functional genomics and to characterize the corpora with respect to these methods. This paper reports our results on comparing classification methods. The methods and the evaluation protocol are detailed in section 3. Section 4 reports and discusses the experimental results. Future work is presented in section 5.

2   The Application Domain: Functional Genomics

2.1 A Genomics Point of View on IE

The application problem to which applying IE is here about modeling the gene interactions from text, in the domain of functional genomics. This problem has been previously described in [1, 12, 11, 18] among others. The existence of numerous scientific and technical domains sharing strong common aspects with functional genomics, from a document point of view, will allow adapting the methods developed here to other application domains. This is typically the case for related domains in biology, but more generally, the methods will be transposable and exploitable in any application of knowledge extraction from scientific and technical documents.

Modeling interactions between genes is of significant interest for biologists, because it is a prerequisite step towards the understanding of the cell functioning. To date, most of the biological knowledge about these interactions is not described into databanks, but only in the form of scientific summaries and articles. Therefore, their exploitation is a major milestone towards building models of interactions between genes. Actually, genome research projects have generated new experimental approaches like DNA chips at the level of the whole organisms. A research team is now able to quickly produce thousands of measurements. This very new context for biologists is calling for automatic extraction of knowledge from text, to be able to interpret and making sense of elementary measurements from the laboratory by linking them to scientific literature. The bibliographic databases can be searched via Internet using keyword queries that retrieve a superset of the relevant paper abstracts. For example, the query *"Bacillus subtilis transcription"* related to the gene interaction topic retrieves 2209 abstracts.

Extract of a MedLine abstract on Bacillus subtilis.

```
UI  - 99175219 [..]
AB  - [..] It is a critical regulator of cot genes encoding proteins
that form the spore coat late in development. Most cot genes, and the
gerE gene, are transcribed by sigmaK RNA polymerase. Previously, it
was shown that the GerE protein inhibits transcription in vitro of the
sigK gene encoding sigmaK. Here, we show that GerE binds near the sigK
transcriptional start site, [..]
```

Then the biologist has to identify the relevant fragments, (in bold-face in the example) in the abstracts and to extract the useful knowledge with respect to the goal of identifying gene interaction. Then, he has to represent it in a structured way so that it can be recorded in a database for further querying and processing. The more general goal is to identify all the interactions and molecular regulations and to build a functional network.

Example of a form filled with the information extracted from the sentence in the example.

Interaction	**Type**: negative		
	Agent: GerE protein		
	Target:	**Expression**	**Source**: sigK gene
			Product: sigmaK protein

This domain is representative of the scope of our study on automatizing filtering of relevant fragment for IE: the information to be extracted is local, mainly located in single sentences or part of sentences. It is very sparse in the document set. For instance, only 2.5 % (470) of the 20000 sentences contain relevant information on gene interaction in the 2209 *Bacillus subtilis* abstracts mentioned above. We contend that the information extraction has to rely on a deep analysis. Indeed previous approaches based on shallow descriptions of the texts (e. g. IE techniques such as transducers defined manually and based on significant verb and gene names [1, 11, 18]) or on statistic measures of keywords co-occurrences [12, 17] (e.g. information retrieval-based techniques) yield limited results with either a bad recall or a low precision. The following example illustrates some of the problems encountered:

"`GerE` `stimulates` `cotD` transcription and `inhibits` `cotA` transcription in vitro by sigma K RNA polymerase, as expected from in vivo studies, and, unexpectedly, profoundly `inhibits` in vitro transcription of the gene (`sigK`) that `encode` `sigma K`.".

The IE methods based on keywords or gene names (bold-face) and interaction verbs (framed) are not able to identify the inhibition interaction between `GerE` and `sigK` gene transcription (28 words far) or, if they will, also erroneously identify interactions between `cotD` and `sigK` and between `cotA` and `sigK`. Extracting relevant knowledge in the selected documents thus requires more complex IE methods such as syntaxico-semantic methods based on lexical and semantic resources specific to the domain[1]. The characteristics of this application thus perfectly fit the requirements for applying classification methods for filtering relevant text as an IE preprocessing step.

2.2 Textual Corpora and Learning Sets

The robustness of the classification methods has been evaluated with respect to different writing styles, different biological species, and then different gene interaction models. The classification methods chosen have been applied, evaluated and compared on three different datasets. These sets have been built from paper abstracts about three species: the first set, denoted *Dro*, is about a fly, *Drosophila melanogaster*[2], the second, denoted *Bs*, is about a bacterium, *Bacillus subtilis*[3] and the third, denoted *HM*, is about the mouse and the human[4]. They come from two bibliographic databases with different writing styles. The Dro dataset is from FlyBase, the database devoted to *Drosophila* genes. Its abstracts are concise, 2 or 3 sentences long, the sentences short and the syntax quite simple. The two others are from MedLine, the generalist biology bibliographic database. The abstracts of MedLine are longer, around 10 sentences, in more complex syntactic forms than those of FlyBase. The abstracts have been selected by the queries "*Bacillus subtilis transcription*" for Bs dataset and *Telomere, Apoptose, DNA replication, DNA repair, cell cycle control, two-hybrid* and *interaction* for HM. The examples sets have been selected in the abstracts under the locality assumption that the sentence level is the suitable granularity degree in this IE application, as it is often the case in Machine Learning for IE applications, [15] and [16]. It is assumed that the potentially relevant sentences in the Bs and HM sets contain at least two gene or protein names denoting the agents of the interaction as in previous work. In the Dro set as it has been provided to us, the sentences contain exactly two gene or protein names. This difference should not affect the filtering phase but the extraction phase only. The identification of gene names identification for the Dro and HM set has been done manually by LGPD-IBDM biologists. This manual selection results in 530 abstracts Dro set, and 105 abstracts and 962 sen-

---

[1] This is the goal of the Caderige project of which this research is part.

[2] The Dro example set has been provided as such by B. Jacq and V. Pillet from LGPD-IBDM.

[3] This set has been built by P. Bessières (MIG, INRA) in the Caderige project.

[4] It has been provided as such by the LGPD-IBDM and the ValiGen company.

tences for HM set that have been provided to us as such. This manual processing affects the classification results as it will be shown in section 4. The sentence selection for the Bs set has been automatically done with the help of a list of gene and protein names of *Bacillus subtilis* and their derivations provided by MIG and manually completed by new derivations observed in the corpus. The problem of the automatic identification of gene names in genomics document has been recently studied and recognized as a prerequisite for any further automatic document processing because of the lack of exhaustive dictionary and because of the varying notation [2, 5, 6, 13].

Table 1. Features of the example sets

	Dro	Bs	HM
Document data base	FlyBase	MedLine	
# bibliographic references	> 100 000	around 16 Millions	
# sentences per abstract	2, 3	approximatively 10	
species	*Drosophila*	*Bacillus subtilis*	mouse - human
# biblio. references to the species	20 300	15 213	4 067 879
# abstracts selected (queries)	20 300	2209	32448
# abstracts selected after manual step	530	Not relevant	105
# sentences in the abstracts	5 244	around 20 000	962
# sentences filtered (at least 2 gene names) = # examples	1197	932	407
# attributes	1701	2340	1789
# positive examples (PosEx)	653	470	240
# negative examples (NegEx)	544	462	167

Training example of Bs dataset built from the sentence, which illustrates Sect. 2.1

```
Example : addition stimulate transcription inhibit transcription
vitro RNA polymerase expected vivo study unexpectedly profoundly
inhibit vitro transcription gene encode
Class : Positive
```

The attributes that describe the learning examples represent the significant and lemmatized words of the sentences. They are boolean in the case of C4.5 and they represent the number of occurences in the sentence in the other cases, i.e, IVI and NB. The examples have been classified into the positive and the negative categories, i.e. describing *at least one* interaction (positive) or none at all (negative). The HM and Bs sentences have been lemmatized using Xerox shallow parser. Stopwords such as determinant have been removed as non-discriminant with the help of the list provided by Patrice Bonhomme (LORIA). It initially contains 620 words and it has been revised with respect to the application. After stopwords removal, the three example sets remain very sparse in the feature. Half of the attributes describe a single example. The capacity to deal with data sparseness was thus one of the criteria for choosing the classification methods.

3 Classification Methods

3.1 Method Descriptions

The classification method *IVI* had been applied to Dro dataset [12]. It is based on the example weight measure defined by (2), which is itself based on the attribute weight measure defined by (1) where $occ(Att_i, ex_j)$ represents the value, (i.e., the number of occurrences) of the attribute i for the example j. The class of the example is determined with respect to a threshold experimentally set to 0. Examples with weights above (resp. below) the threshold are classified as positive (resp. negative).

$$\text{Weight}(Att_i) = \frac{\sum_{ex_j^+ \in PosEx} occ(Att_i, ex_j^+) - \sum_{ex_j^- \in NegEx} occ(Att_i, ex_j^-)}{\sum_{ex_j \in Ex} occ(Att_i, ex_j)} \tag{1}$$

$$\text{IVI}(ex) = \sum_{i=1}^{|Att(Ex)|} \text{Weight}(Att_i) \tag{2}$$

The Naïve Bayes method (NB) as defined by [9], seemed to be suitable for the problem at hand because of the data sparseness in the attribute space. As IVI, NB estimates the probabilities for each attribute to describe positive examples and negative examples with respect to the number of their occurrences in the training set. The probability that a given example belongs to a given class is estimated by (4), the product of the probability estimations of the example attributes, given the class. The example is assigned to the class for which this probability is the highest.

$$\Pr(Att_j | Class_i) = \frac{\sum_{ex_k \in Class_i} occ(Att_j, ex_k)}{\sum_{l=1}^{|Class|} \sum_{ex_k \in Class_i} occ(Att_j, ex_k) + |Class|} \tag{3}$$

$$\Pr(ex | Class_i) = \prod_{j=1}^{|Att(ex)|} \Pr(Att_j | Class_i) \tag{4}$$

The Laplace law (3) yields better results here as compared with the basic estimate because its smoothing feature deals well with the data sparseness. The independence assumption of the attributes is obviously not verified here also previous work has shown surprisingly good performances of NB despite of this constrain [4]. The third class of methods applied is C4.5 and C4.5Rules. Compared to NB and IVI, the decision tree computed by C4.5 is more informative and explicit about the combination of attributes that denote interactions, and thus potentially on the phrases that could be useful for further information extraction.

3.2 Feature Selection

The data sparseness is potentially a drawback for C4.5 Feature selection appears here as a good way to filter the most relevant attributes for improving classification [19] but also for selecting the suitable corpus for other IE preprocessing tasks such as semantic class learning (Sect. 5). This latter goal has motivated the choice a filtering method for feature selection instead of a wrapper method selection [7], where the classification algorithms would be repeatedly applied and evaluated on attribute subsets in order to identify the best subset and the best classifier at the same time [8]. The measure of attribute relevance used here is based on (5). It measures the capacity of each attribute to characterize a class, independently of the other attributes and of the classification method. The attributes are all ranked according to this measure and the best of them are selected for describing the training sets (Sect. 4).

$$DiscrimP(Att) = \frac{\sum_{i=1}^{|Class|} Max\{Pr(Att,Cl_i), 1 - Pr(Att,Cl_i)\}}{|Class|} \quad (5)$$

3.3 Evaluation Metrics

The methods have been evaluated and compared with the usual criteria, that is, recall (7), precision (8), and the F-measure (9), computed for the three datasets.

$$Recall(Class_i) = \frac{|Ex \in Class_i \text{ and assigned to } Class_i|}{|Ex \in Class_i|} \quad (6)$$

$$Precision(Class_i) = \frac{|Ex \in Class_i \text{ and assigned to } Class_i|}{|Ex \text{ classified in } Class_i|} \quad (7)$$

$$F = \frac{(\beta^2 + 1) * Precision * Recall}{(\beta^2 * Precision) + Recall} \quad (8)$$

More attention is given to the results obtained for the positive class because the examples classified as positive only will be transferred to the IE component. The recall rate for this class should therefore be high even if this implies some lack of precision. The β factor of the F-measure has been experimentally set to 1.65 in order to favor the recall. IVI and BN have been evaluated by leave-one-out on each dataset. For performance reasons, C4.5 and C4.5Rules have been only trained on 90 % of the learning sets and tested on the remaining 10 %. The results presented here are computed as the average of the test results for ten independent partitions.

4   Evaluation

4.1   Comparison of the IVI, C4.5, and BN Methods

The first experiments allow the comparison of C4.5, C4.5Rules, NB and IVI on the three datasets (Table 2). As recall and precision computed for two classes yields to the same rates, they appear in a same line. NB has been applied here with the Laplace law. In the three cases, NB and IVI results are better than C4.5 and C4.5Rules results. This can be explained by the sparseness and the heterogeneity of the data. The global precision rate is 5 to 8 % higher and the precision rate for the positive class is 4 to 12 %

higher. However, the good behavior of the IVI-BN family is not verified by the recall rate for the positive on the Dro dataset: C4.5 recall rate is better than NB and IVI on this set (13 %) but worse on Bs' and HM's ones (-12 to -13 %). The origin of Dro dataset could explain these results: it comes from FlyBase where the sentences are much shorter than those of MedLine, from which Bs and HM are extracted. Thus Dro examples are described by *less attributes* although the ratio of the number of attributes to the examples is similar to Bs one. This could explain the overgenerality of C4.5 results on Dro set illustrated by the high recall and bad precision rates. The analysis of NB and IVI results shows that NB behaves slightly better at a global level.

Table 2. Comparison of C4.5, C4.5Rules, IVI and BN on the three datasets

Corpus	Dro				Bs				HM			
Method	C4.5	C4.5 R	BN	IVI	C4.5	C4.5 R	BN	IVI	C4.5	C4.5 R	BN	IVI
Recall Positive	**88,9** ±2.4	86,8 ±2.6	75,3 ±2.9	69,1 ±3.5	63,9 ±4.3	71,4 ±4.1	**85,7** ±3.2	82,6 ±3.4	88,3 ±4.1	84,5 ±4.1	**97,1** ±2.1	90 ±3.8
Precision Positive	68,1 ±3.6	70,5 ±3.5	82 ±3.2	**83,1** ±2.8	63,4 ±4.3	62,8 ±4.4	66,6 ±4.3	**67,4** ±4.2	63,7 ±6.1	64,2 ±6.1	68,5 ±5.9	**70,3** ±5.8
Recall-precision for all	72 ±2.5	73.6 ±2.5	**77,5** ±2.4	75,4 ±2.4	62,4 ±3.1	62,9 ±3.1	**71,1** ±2.9	71 ±2.9	63,7 ±4.1	63,4 ±4.7	**72** ±4.4	71,5 ±4.4

However, their behaviors on the positive examples are very different: NB achieves a higher recall than IVI (3 to 7 %) while IVI achieves a better precision than NB (1 to 2 %) but the difference is smaller. The higher recall and precision rates for positive on HM compared to Bs is explained by the way the HM set has been built. The selection of the sentences in the abstracts has been done manually by the biologists among a huge number of candidate sentences (Table 1) and the bias of the choice could explain the homogeneity of this dataset compared to Bs which has been selected automatically. This hypothesis has been confirmed by further experiments on the reusability of the classifiers learned from one corpus and tested on others. As a better recall is preferred in our application, the conclusion on these experiments is that NB should be preferred for data from MedLine (Bs and HM) while for FlyBase (Dro), it would depend on how much the IE component would be able to deal with sentences filtered with a low precision. C4.5 should be chosen if the best recall is preferable while BN should be chosen for its best recall-precision tradeoff.

4.2 Feature Selection

As described in Sect. 3, the attributes for each dataset have been ranked according to their relevance. For instance, the best attributes for the Dro set are, downstream, interact, modulate, autoregulate, and eliminate. The effect of feature selection on the learning results of IVI, NB and C4.5Rules methods has been evaluated by selecting the best n attributes, n varying from hundred to the total number of attributes, by increments of hundred.

4.2.1 Effect of Feature Selection on NB Results

For the three sets, the recall noticeably increases and the precision noticeably decreases with the number of relevant attributes selected, which is what is expected, (Fig. 2, Fig. 3 and Fig. 4). The F-measure increases in the first quarter, more or less stabilizes on a plateau on a half, slightly increasing since recall is predominant over precision in our setting of F-measure (section 3), and then decreases in the last quarter or fifth, after a small pick in the case of Dro and Bs sets. According to the F-measure, the best attribute selections in terms of the recall - precision compromise are thus at the end of the plateau around 3/4 - 4/5 of the total number of attributes. For the Dro set, it is around 1400 attributes and for Bs set it is around 1900 attributes. One can notice that the recall for positive examples for the Dro and Bs sets is 10 to 15 % higher than the global recall and that is the opposite for the precision, which is exactly what is desirable in our application.

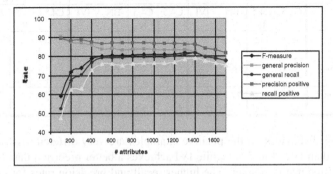

Fig. 2. NB classification results after feature selection on Dro set.

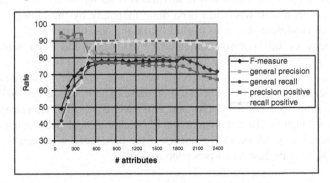

Fig. 3. NB classification results after feature selection on Bs set.

For the HM set, this phenomenon is even more noticeable: the recall of the positive is very high, close to 100 %, and 20 % higher than the global recall (Fig. 4). Compared to the other sets the plateau is more horizontal between 400 et 1900 attributes after a slight increase between 400 and 800, and there is no pick before the decrease, then the global recall-precision rate is stable between 800 and 1400 and all points are equivalent in this interval. This could be explained by the homogeneity of the HM dataset that affected the initial classification results in the same way (4.1).

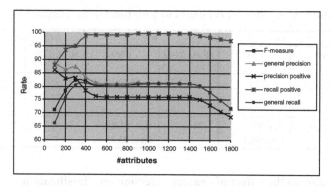

Fig. 4. NB classification results after feature selection on HM set

Table 3 presents a summary of the results obtained with NB without and after feature selection for the best attribute. NB results are improved by feature selection. The gain is very high for HM, around 10 %, less for Bs (6-7 %), and 4-5 % for Dro.

Table 3. Comparison of NB results with the best feature selection level

Dataset	Dro		Bs		HM	
# attrib- utes	all att. 1701	1400	all att. 2340	1800	All att. 1789	900-1300
Rec. Positive	75,3 ± 2.9	79±3.1	85,7±3.2	**90,8±2.6**	97,1±2.1	**99,6±0.8**
Prec. Positive	82 ±3.2	**86,4±2.6**	66,6±4.3	**74,1±4.00**	68,5±5.9	**76,1±5.4**
Prec.-Rec. for all classes	77,5 ±2.4	Rec. **81,8** ±2.2 Prec. **82,1** ± 2.2	71,1±2.9	Rec. **77,5**±2.7 Prec. **79,9**±2.6	72±4.4	Rec. **81,1** ±3.8 Prec. **81,3** ±3.8

4.2.2 Effect of Feature Selection on C4.5 and IVI Results

Similar experiments have been done with C4.5. There are summarized in Table 4.

Table 4. Comparison of C4.5 results with the best feature selection level

Dataset	Dro		Bs		HM	
# attributes	all at. 1701	1400	all at. 2340	1600	All at. 1789	1300
Recall Pos.	**86,8** ±2.6	84,5 ±2.8	**71,4** ±4.1	70,1 ±4.2	84,5 ±4.6	**84,6** ±4.6
Precision Pos.	70,5 ±3.5	**75**±3.33	62,8 ±4.4	**71,4** ±4.13	64,2 ±6.1	**78,8** ±4.6
Prec-Recall for all	73.7 ±2.5	**75,3** ±2.4	62,9± 3.1	**71,1**±3	63,4 ±4.7	**74,9** ±5.2

The conclusions are similar to NB ones: feature selection improves the global classification results for all sets, the global improvement is important for Bs and HM (9 %), and less for Dro (1,6 %) for the same reasons related to the origin of the corpora as previously pointed out.

The similar experiments done with IVI are summarized in Table 5. The improvement is higher for IVI than for the two other methods. Its range is between approximately +6 % for Dro, +10 % for Bs to +16 % for HM.

Table 5. Comparison of IVI results with the best feature selection level.

Dataset	Dro		Bs		HM	
# attributes	all at. 1701	1300	all at. 2340	1900	all at. 1789	1400
Recall Pos.	69 ±3.5	**77,9** ±3.2	82,6 ±3.42	**91,5**±2.5	90 ±3.8	**98,3** ±1.6
Prec. Pos.	83,6 ±2.9	**88,4** ±2.5	67,4 ±4.23	**78,3**±3.7	70,3 ±5.8	**83,4** ±4.7
Prec.-Rec. for all	75,4±2.4	Rec. **81,9**±2.2 Prec. **84,1**±2.1	71±2.9	Rec. **82,8**±2.4 Prec. **83,2**±2.4	71,5±4.4	Rec. **87,5**±1.6 Prec. **87,5**±4.7

4.2.3 Conclusion on the Effect of Feature Selection on Classification

The comparison between the experimental results with C4.5, NB and IVI for the best feature selection shows that IVI globally behaves better than the two others do. With respect to the recall rate for positive, NB behaves slightly better or similarly to IVI (1 to 2 %) while IVI precision rates are better than NB ones (2 to 7 %). Therefore, in the case where the good positive recall is preferred NB with feature selection should be chosen for all datasets except for those like Dro that are less sparse and more homogeneous and where C4.5 without feature selection is better. In the case where a best recall-precision compromise is preferred, IVI with feature selection should be applied.

5 Future Work

This research focuses on the classification of sentences represented by their significant and lemmatized words. The methods studied yield global recall and precision rates higher than 80 % and high recall rates for the positive class with feature selection by prefiltering. Other criteria should be tested for selecting the attributes, such as information gain and mutual information. Better results should also be obtained with classification with more information gain global measures that would take into account the dependency between the words which form significant noun phrases. For instance the results of the ongoing work at LIPN on the acquisition of terminology for gene interaction should reduce both the number of attributes and their dependency. We also plan to study the reduction of the number of attributes by replacing in the examples, the words by the concept (the semantic class) they belong to as learnt from a biological corpus. Moreover, classification should be improved by reducing the data heterogeneity by pre-clustering the examples; one classifier would then be learned per example cluster. From an IE point of view, the assumption that relevant sentences contain at least two gene or protein names should be relaxed. The attribute ranking will be used to identify automatically other potentially relevant sentences. Finally learning extraction rules requires semantic class acquisition. The attribute ranking will be also used to select the most relevant syntagms in the training corpora for learning semantic classes. Learning will thus focus on the potentially most relevant concepts with respect to the extraction task.

Acknowledgement. This work is financially supported by CNRS, INRA, INRIA and INSERM through *Caderige* contract. The authors thank V. Pillet, C. Brun and B. Jacq for the *Dro* and *HM* sets.

References

1. Blaschke C., Andrade M. A., Ouzounis C. and Valencia A., "Automatic Extraction of biological information from scientific text: protein-protein interactions", in Proc. of *ISMB'99*, 1999.
2. Collier N., Nobata C. and Tsujii, "Extracting the names of genes and gene products with a hidden Markov model. In Proc. *COLING'2000*, Saarbrück,, July-August 2000.
3. Craven M. and Kumlien J., "Constructing Biological Knowledge Bases by Extracting Information from Text Sources.", In Proc. of *ISMB'99*, 1999.
4. Domingos P. and Pazzani M., "Beyond independence: conditions for the optimality of the simple Bayesian classifier", in Proc. of *ICML'96*, Saitta L. (ed.), pp. 105-112, 1996.
5. Fukuda K., Tsunoda T., Tamura A. and Takagi T., "Toward Information Extraction: Identifying protein names from biological papers". In Proc. *PSB'98*, 1998.
6. Humphreys K., Demetriou G, and Gaizauskas R., "Two applications of information extraction to biological science article: enzyme interaction and protein structure". In Proc. of *PSB'2000*, vol.5, pp. 502-513, Honolulu, 2000.
7. John G. and Kohavi R., "Wrappers for feature subset selection", in *Artificial Intelligence Journal*, 1997.
8. Langley P. and Sage S., "Induction of selective Bayesian classifiers", in Proc. of UAI'94, Lopez de Mantaras R. (Ed.), pp. 399-406, Morgan Kaufmann, 1994.
9. Mitchell, T. M., *Machine Learning*, Mac Graw Hill, 1997.
10. Proceedings of the *Message Understanding Conference* (MUC-4-7), Morgan Kaufman, San Mateo, USA, 1992-98.
11. Ono T., Hishigaki H., Tanigami A., and Takagi T., "Automated extraction of information on protein-protein interactions from the biological literature". In Bioinformatics, vol 17 no 2 2001, pp. 155-161, 2001
12. Pillet V., Méthodologie d'extraction automatique d'information à partir de la littérature scientifique en vue d'alimenter un nouveau système d'information, thèse de l'Université de droit, d'économie et des sciences d'Aix-Marseille, 2000.
13. Proux, D., Rechenmann, F., Julliard, L., Pillet, V., Jacq, B., "Detecting Gene Symbols and Names in Biological Texts: A First Step toward Pertinent Information Extraction". In *Genome Informatics 1998*, S. Miyano and T. Takagi, (Eds), Universal Academy Press, Inc, Tokyo, Japan, pp. 72 - 80, 1998.
14. Quinlan J. R., *C4.5: Programs for Machine Learning*, Morgan Kaufmann, 1992.
15. Riloff E., "Automatically constructing a Dictionary for Information Extraction Tasks". In Proc. of *AAAI-93*, pp. 811-816, AAAI Press / The MIT Press, 1993.
16. Soderland S., "Learning Information Extraction Rules for Semi-Structured and Free Text" in *Machine Learning Journal*, vol 34, 1999.
17. Stapley B. J. and Benoit G., "Bibliometrics: Information Retrieval and Visualization from co-occurrence of gene names in MedLine abstracts". In Proc. of *PSB'2000*, 2000.
18. Thomas, J., Milward, D., Ouzounis C., Pulman S. and Caroll M., "Automatic Extraction of Protein Interactions from Scientific Abstracts". In Proc. of *PSB'2000*, vol.5, p. 502-513, Honolulu, 2000.
19. Yang Y. and Pedersen J., "A comparative study on feature selection in text categorization.", in Proc. of *ICML'97*, 1997. **Fehler! Textmarke nicht definiert.**

Text Categorization and Semantic Browsing with Self-Organizing Maps on Non-euclidean Spaces

Jörg Ontrup and Helge Ritter

Neuroinformatics Group
Faculty of Technology
Bielefeld University
D-33501 Bielefeld, Germany

Abstract. This paper introduces a new type of Self-Organizing Map (SOM) for Text Categorization and Semantic Browsing. We propose a "hyperbolic SOM" (HSOM) based on a regular tesselation of the hyperbolic plane, which is a non-euclidean space characterized by constant negative gaussian curvature. This approach is motivated by the observation that hyperbolic spaces possess a geometry where the size of a neighborhood around a point increases *exponentially* and therefore provides more freedom to map a complex information space such as language into spatial relations. These theoretical findings are supported by our experiments, which show that hyperbolic SOMs can successfully be applied to text categorization and yield results comparable to other state-of-the-art methods. Furthermore we demonstrate that the HSOM is able to map large text collections in a semantically meaningful way and therefore allows a "semantic browsing" of text databases.

1 Introduction

For many tasks of exploraty data analysis the creation of Self-Organizing Maps (SOM) for data visualization, as introduced by Kohonen more than a decade ago, has become a widely used tool in many fields [7].

So far, the overwhelming majority of SOM approaches have taken it for granted to use (some subregion of) a *flat space* as their data model and, motivated by its convenience for visualization, have favored the (suitably discretized) *euclidean plane* as their chief "canvas" for the generated mappings (for a few notable exceptions using tree- or hypercubical lattices see e. g. [1, 8, 14]).

However, even if our thinking is deeply entrenched with euclidean space, an obvious limiting factor is the rather restricted neighborhood that "fits" around a point on a euclidean 2d surface. Recently, it has been observed that a particular type of *non-euclidean spaces*, the *hyperbolic spaces* that are characterized by uniform negative curvature, are very well suited to overcome this limitation [9] since their geometry is such that the size of a neighborhood around a point increases *exponentially* with its radius r (while in a D-dimensional euclidean space the growth follows the much slower power law r^D). This exponential scaling behavior fits very nicely with the scaling behavior within hierarchical, tree-like

L. De Raedt and A. Siebes (Eds.): PKDD 2001, LNAI 2168, pp. 338–349, 2001.

structures, where the number of items r steps away from the root grows as b^r where b is the (average) branching factor. This interesting property of hyperbolic spaces has been exploited for creating novel displays of large hierarchical structures that are more accessible to visual inspection than in previous approaches [10].

Therefore, it appears very promising to use hyperbolic spaces also in conjunction with the SOM. The resulting *hyperbolic SOMs* (HSOMs) are based on a tesselation of the hyperbolic plane (or some higher-dimensional hyperbolic space) and their lattice neighborhood reflects the hyperbolic distance metric that is responsible for the non-intuitive properties of hyperbolic spaces.

Since the notion of non-euclidean spaces may be unfamiliar to many readers, we first give a brief account of some basic properties of hyperbolic spaces that are exploited for hyperbolic SOMs. We then illustrate the properties of hyperbolic SOMs with computer experiments focusing on the field of text-mining.

2 Hyperbolic Spaces

Surfaces that possess *negative gaussian curvature* locally resemble the shape of a "saddle", i. e., the negative curvature shows up as a local bending into opposite normal directions, as we move on orthogonal lines along the surface. This may make it intuitively plausible that on such surfaces the area (and also the circumference) of a circular neighborhood around a point can grow faster than in the uncurved case. Requiring a constant negative curvature everywhere, leads to a space known as the *hyperbolic plane H2* (with analogous generalizations to higher dimensions)[2, 20]. The geometry of H2 is a standard topic in *Riemannian geometry* (see, e. g. [19, 13]), and the relationships for the area A and the circumference C of a circle of radius r are given by

$$A = 4\pi \sinh^2(r/2), \; C = 2\pi \sinh(r) . \tag{1}$$

These formulae exhibit the highly remarkable property that both quantities grow *exponentially* with the radius r (whereas in the limit $r \to 0$ the curvature becomes insignificant and we recover the familiar laws for flat $I\!R^2$). It is this property that was observed in [9] to make hyperbolic spaces extremely useful for accommodating hierarchical structures: their neighborhoods are in a sense "much larger" than in the non-curved euclidean (or in the even "smaller" positively curved) spaces.

To use this potential for the SOM, we must solve two problems: (i) we must find suitable discretization lattices on H2 to which we can "attach" the SOM prototype vectors. (ii) after having constructed the SOM, we must somehow project the (hyperbolic!) lattice into "flat space" in order to be able to inspect the generated maps.

2.1 Projections of Hyperbolic Spaces

To construct an isometric (i. e., distance preserving) embedding of the hyperbolic plane into a "flat" space, we may use a *Minkowski space* [12]. In such a space, the squared distance d^2 between two points (x, y, u) and (x', y', u') is given by

$$d^2 = (x - x')^2 + (y - y')^2 - (u - u')^2 \tag{2}$$

i. e., it ceases to be positive definite. Still, this is a space with zero curvature and its somewhat peculiar distance measure allows to construct an *isometric* embedding of the hyperbolic plane H2, given by

$$x = \sinh(\rho)\cos(\phi), \; y = \sinh(\rho)\sin(\phi), \; u = \cosh(\rho), \tag{3}$$

where (ρ, ϕ) are polar coordinates on the H2 (note the close analogy of (3) with the formulas for the embedding of a sphere by means of spherical polar coordinates in $I\!R^3$!). Under this embedding, the hyperbolic plane appears as the surface M swept out by rotating the curve $u^2 = 1 + x^2 + y^2$ about the u-axis[1].

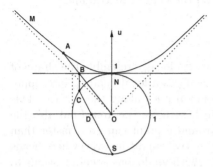

Fig. 1. Construction steps underlying *Klein* and *Poincaré*-models of the space H2

From this embedding, we can construct two further ones, the so-called *Klein model* and the *Poincaré model* [2, 3, 6](the latter will be used to visualize hyperbolic SOMs below). Both achieve a projection of the infinite H2 into the unit disk, however, at the price of distorting distances. The Klein model is obtained by projecting the points of M onto the plane $u = 1$ along rays passing through the origin O (see Fig. 1). Obviously, this projects all points of M into the "flat" unit disk $x^2 + y^2 < 1$ of $I\!R^2$. (e. g., $A \mapsto B$). The Poincaré Model results if we add two further steps: first a perpendicular projection of the Klein Model (e. g., a point B) onto the ("northern") surface of the unit sphere centered at the origin (point C), and then a stereographic projection of the "northern" hemisphere onto the unit circle about the origin in the ground plane $u = 0$ (point D). It turns out that the resulting projection of H2 has a number of pleasant properties, among them the preservation of angles and the mapping of shortest paths onto circular arcs belonging to circles that intersect the unit disk at right angles. Distances in the original H2 are strongly distorted in its Poincaré (and also in the Klein) image (cf. Eq. (5)), however, in a rather useful way: the mapping exhibits a strong "fisheye"-effect. The neighborhood of the H2 origin is mapped almost faithfully (up to a linear shrinkage factor of 2), while more distant regions become increasingly "squeezed". Since asymptotically the radial distances and the circumference grow both according to the same exponential law, the squeezing is "conformal", i. e., (sufficiently small) shapes painted onto H2 are not deformed, only their size shrinks with increasing distance from the origin.

---

[1] The alert reader may notice the absence of the previously described local saddle structure; this is a consequence of the use of a Minkowski metric for the embedding space, which is not completely compatible with our "euclidean" expectations.

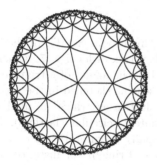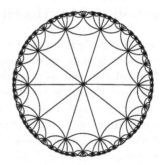

Fig. 2. Regular triangle tesselations of the hyperbolic plane, projected into the unit disk using the Poincaré mapping. The leftmost tesselation shows the case where the minimal number ($n = 7$) of equilateral triangles meet at each vertex and is best suited for the hyperbolic SOM, since tesselations for larger values of n (right: $n = 10$) lead to bigger triangles. In the Poincaré projection, only sides passing through the origin appear straight, all other sides appear as circular arcs, although in the original space all triangles are congruent.

By translating the original H2 the fisheye-fovea can be moved to any other part of H2, allowing to selectively zoom-in on interesting portions of a map painted on H2 while still keeping a coarser view of its surrounding context.

2.2 Tesselations of the Hyperbolic Plane

To complete the set-up for a hyperbolic SOM we still need an equivalent of a regular grid in the hyperbolic plane. We the following results [3, 11]: while the choices for tesselations with congruent polygons on the sphere and even in the plane such that each grid point is surrounded by the same number n of neighbors are severely limited (the only possible values for n being 3,4,5 on the sphere, and 3,4,6 in the plane), there is an infinite set of choices for the hyperbolic plane. In the following, we will restrict ourselves to lattices consisting of equilateral triangles only. In this case, there is for each $n \geq 7$ a regular tesselation such that each vertex is surrounded by n congruent equilateral triangles. Figure 2 shows two example tesselations (for the minimal value of $n = 7$ and for $n = 10$), using the Poincaré model for their visualization. While in Fig. 2 these tesselations appear non-uniform, this is only due to the fisheye effect of the Poincaré projection. In the original H2, each tesselation triangle has the same size, and this can be checked by re-projecting any distant part of the tesselation into the center of the Poincaré disk, after which it looks identical (up to a possible rotation) to the center of Fig. 3.

One way to generate these tesselations algorithmically is by repeated application of a suitable set of generators of their symmetry group to a (suitably sized, cf. below) "starting triangle", for more details cf [15].

3   Hyperbolic SOM Algorithm

We have now all ingredients required for a "hyperbolic SOM". In the following, we use the regular triangle tesselation with vertex order $n = 7$, which leads to the "finest" tesselation that is possible (in H2, the angles of a triangle uniquely determine its size). Using the construction scheme sketched in the previous section, we can organize the nodes of such a lattice as "rings" around an origin node (i. e., it is simplest to build approximately "circular" lattices). The numbers of nodes of such a lattice grows very rapidly (asymptotically exponentially) with the chosen lattice radius R (its number of rings). For instance, for $n = 7$, Table 1 shows the total number N_R of nodes of the resulting regular hyperbolic lattices with different radii ranging from $R = 1$ to $R = 10$. Each lattice node r carries a prototype vector $w_r \in \mathbb{R}^D$ from some D-dimensional feature space (if we wish to make any non-standard assumptions about the metric structure of this space, we would build this into the distance metric that is used for determining the best-match node). The SOM is then formed in the usual way, e. g., in on-line mode by repeatedly determining the winner node s and adjusting all nodes $r \in N(s, t)$ in a radial lattice neighborhood $N(s, t)$ around s according to the familiar rule

$$\Delta w_r = \eta h_{rs}(x - w_r) \qquad (4)$$

with $h_{rs} = \exp(-d^2(r, s)/2\sigma^2)$. However, since we now work on a hyperbolic lattice, we have to determine both the neighborhood $N(s, t)$ and the (squared) node distance $d^2(r, s)$ according to the natural metric that is inherited by the hyperbolic lattice.

Table 1. Node numbers N_R of hyperbolic triangle lattices with vertex order 7 for different numbers R of "node rings" around the origin.

R	1	2	3	4	5	6	7	8	9	10
N_R	8	29	85	232	617	1625	4264	11173	29261	76616

The simplest way to do this is to keep with each node r a complex number z_r to identify its position in the Poincaré model. The node distance is then given (using the Poincaré model, see e. g. [19]) as

$$d = 2\text{arctanh}\left(\left|\frac{z_r - z_s}{1 - \bar{z}_s \cdot z_r}\right|\right) . \qquad (5)$$

The neighborhood $N(t, s)$ can be defined as the subset of nodes within a certain graph distance (which is chosen as a small multiple of the neighborhood radius σ) around s.

Like the standard SOM, also the hyperbolic SOM can become trapped in topological defects. Therefore, it is also important here to control the neighborhood radius $\sigma(t)$ from an initially large to a final small value (for details on this and some further means to optimize convergence, see [15]).

4   Experiments

Some introductory experiments where several examples illustrate the favorable properties of the HSOM as compared to the "standard" euclidean SOM can be found in [15].

4.1   Text Categorization

While - similar as for the SOM [7] - a very high classification accuracy is of a secondary importance to visualization, a good classification performance is still important to obtain useful maps of text categories. With the ever growing amount of available information on the Internet, automatic text categorization based on machine learning techniques has become a key task where high-dimensional input spaces with few irrelevant features are involved [4]. Here the goal is the assignment of natural language documents to a number of predefined categories (each document d_j can belong to one, several or none of the categories c_i). Achieving a high classification accuracy is an important prerequisite for automating high volume information organization and management tasks.

Text Representation. In order to apply the HSOM to natural text categorization, we follow the widely used vector-space-model of Information Retrieval (IR). We applied a word stemming algorithm[2] such that for example the words "retrieved", "retrieval" and "retrieve" are mapped to the term "retrief". The value of f_i of the feature vector $\boldsymbol{f}(d_i)$ for document d_j is then determined by the frequency of which term t_i occurs in that document. Following standard practice [16] we choose a *term frequency* $\times$ *inverse document frequency* weighting scheme:

$$f_i = tf(t_i, j) \, log \left(\frac{N}{df(t_i)} \right) , \qquad (6)$$

where the term frequency $tf(t_i, j)$ denotes the number of times term t_i occurs in d_j, N the number of documents in the training set and $df(t_i)$ the document frequency of t_i, i. e. the number of documents t_i occurs in. Additionally, we built a stop list of the most and least frequent terms specific to the training set and omitted those from the feature vectors, since they have no descriptive function with respect to that text corpus.

HSOM Text Categorization. The HSOM can be utilised for text categorization in the following manner (Fig. 3). In a first step, the training set is used to adapt the weight vectors $\boldsymbol{w}_r$ according to (4). During the second step, the

---

[2] We applied the *triestem* function of the SMART system by G. Salton and C. Buckley (ftp://ftp.cs.cornell.edu/pub/smart/).

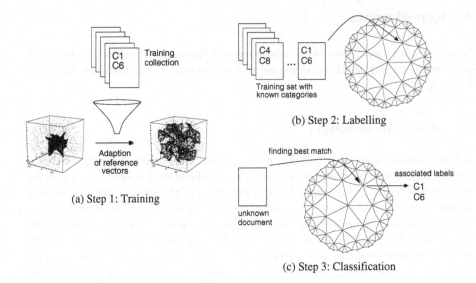

(b) Step 2: Labelling

(a) Step 1: Training

(c) Step 3: Classification

Fig. 3. Text categorization with the HSOM: First the training set is used to build an internal model of the collection represented by the HSOM's reference vectors. In *(b)* for each training document the winner nodes are labelled with the document's category. These labels are used in the classification step *(c)* where an unknown document is "thrown" onto the map and labelled with the categories of its corresponding best match node.

training set is mapped onto the HSOM lattice. To this end, for each training example d_j its best match node s is determined such that

$$|\boldsymbol{f}(d_j) - \boldsymbol{w}_s| \leqslant |\boldsymbol{f}(d_j) - \boldsymbol{w}_r| \quad \forall r , \tag{7}$$

where $\boldsymbol{f}(d_j)$ denotes the feature vector of document d_j, as described above. After all examples have been presented to the net, each node is labelled with the union U_r of all categories that belonged to the documents that were mapped to this node. A new, unknown text is then classified into the union U_s of categories which are associated with its winner node s selected in the HSOM. In order to evaluate the HSOM's categorization performance, we furthermore use $cos(\boldsymbol{w}_s, \boldsymbol{f}(d_j))$ as a confidence measure for the classification result.

Text Collection. The text collection consists of movie reviews taken from the rec.art.movies.reviews newsgroup. Genre information from the Internet Movie Database (http://www.imdb.com) was used to build a joined database containing the review texts plus the genres from their corresponding movies as the categories. To build the training text collection, for each of the most prominent 17 categories 20 movies were randomly selected. For each of these movies, 3 review texts were chosen by chance. Therefore, the training collection contained 1020 distinct documents. The test text collection was constructed in the same manner with the restriction that it must not contain any document of the training set. After word stemming and stop word removal we arrived at approximately 5000 distinct terms for the construction of the feature vectors.

Performance Evaluation. The classification effectiveness is commonly measured in terms of precision P and recall R [17], which can be estimated as

$$P_i = \frac{TP_i}{TP_i + FP_i}, \quad R_i = \frac{TP_i}{TP_i + FN_i}, \tag{8}$$

where TP_i and TN_i are the numbers of documents correctly classified, and correctly not classified to c_i, respectively. Analogous, FP_i and FN_i are the numbers of documents wrongly classified and not classified to c_i, respectively. By adjusting a threshold which is compared with the confidence value $cos(\boldsymbol{w}_s, \boldsymbol{f}(d_j))$ of the classifier, the number of retrieved documents can be controlled. In order to obtain an overall performance measure for all categories, we applied the *microaveraging* method [21]. Furthermore, the *breakeven* point of precision and recall, i. e. the value at which $P = R$ is a frequently given single number to measure the effectiveness determined by both values P and R [17].

In order to assess the HSOM's performance for text categorization, we have used a k-nearest neighbour (k-NN) classifier which was found to show very good results on text categorization tasks [21]. Apart from boosting methods [18] only support vector machines [5] have shown better performances. The confidence level of a k-NN classifier to assign document d_j to class c_i is

$$C_i^{k\text{-NN}}(d_j) = \sum_{d_z \in TR_k(d_j)} a_{iz} \cdot cos(d_j, d_z), \tag{9}$$

where $TR_k(d_j)$ is the set of k documents d_z for which $cos(d_j, d_z)$ is maximum. The assignment factor a_{iz} is 1, if d_z belongs to category c_i and 0 otherwise. According to [21, 5] we have chosen the $k = 30$ nearest neighbours.

Text Categorization Results. Precision-recall-diagrams for three categories and the microaveraged diagrams for all categories are shown in Fig. 4. The single category and microaveraged break-even points are layed out in Table 2.

It is notable that the HSOM performs significantly worse if only a few documents are recalled, but the precision in cases of high recall values is very close to that of the k-NN classifier. Since one is usually interested in high precision in conjunction with high recall, the suboptimal results for low recall values do not really affect the usefulness of the HSOM for the purpose of text categorization[3]. Thus, our results indicate that the HSOM does not perform better than a k-NN classifier, but it does not play significantly worse either. Since the main

---

[3] We also believe that a more clever heuristic than the simple distance to the bestmatch node in order to determine the evidence value of a classification will further improve accuracy for low retrieval rates.

purpose of the HSOM is the visualization of relationships between texts and text categories, we believe that the observed categorization performance of the HSOM compares sufficiently well with the more specialized (non-visualization) approaches to warrant its efficient use for creating insightful maps of large bodies of document data.

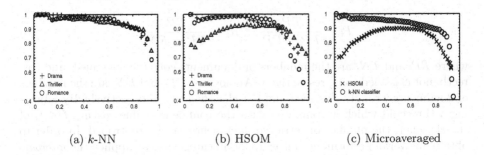

    (a) k-NN   (b) HSOM   (c) Microaveraged

Fig. 4. Precision-recall-diagrams for the three categories *Drama, Thriller* and *Romance. (a)* shows the results for the k-NN classifier, *(b)* for the HSOM. In *(c)* the microaveraged diagrams for both methods are shown.

Table 2. Precision-recall breakeven points for the most prominent categories. In most cases the k-NN performs better than the HSOM, but for the categories "Animation", "Fantasy" and "Musical" the HSOM yields better results.

	Action	Advent.	Animation	Comedy	Crime	Docum.	Drama	
HSOM	81.6	75.4	86.9	81.3	84.5	86.7	82.5	
k-NN	87.3	83.0	84.5	87.6	90.5	98.0	85.8	
	Fantasy	Horror	Musical	Mystery	Romance	Sci-Fi	Thriller	μ-avg.
HSOM	81.6	78.6	82.5	84.6	82.8	76.2	86.8	81.1
k-NN	75.0	88.9	81.2	86.1	87.8	89.3	89.1	86.4

4.2 Semantic Browsing

A major advantage of the HSOM is its remarkable capability to map high-dimensional similarity relationships to a low-dimensional space which can be more easily handled and interpreted by the human observer. This feature and the particular "fisheye" capability motivates our approach to visualize whole text collections with the HSOM. With just as little as 5 rings (c.f. Table 1), we can handle well over 500 prototype vectors which are able to represent different types of texts. The nodes are labelled with those document titles which resemble their prototype vectors most closely. We additionally map symbols to the nodes which correspond to the categories associated with the prototypes. We can now interactively change the visual focus to those regions which show an interesting structure. In Fig. 5(a) for example we have "zoomed" into a region of the map which indicated a cluster of "Animation" films. As a closer inspection shows, this region of the map resembles movie reviews all connected to Disney's typical animations released during Christmas time. In Fig. 5(b) the focal view was moved to a region connected to "Action" and "Fantasy" films. It does not only show the movies of the "Batman" series in a limited area of the map, but also a "Zorro" movie in the neigborhood - which makes a lot of sense, as the main characters of the films indeed have a semantic relation.

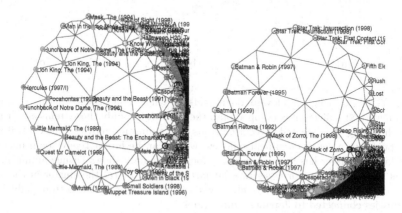

Fig. 5. By moving the visual focus of the HSOM, a large text collection can be browsed quite elegantly. In this example, the movie titles of their corresponding review texts (there might be several reviews for one movie) are mapped. In *(a)* reviews of Disney's animations have been moved into the centre, *(b)* shows a region of the map containing the "Batman" movies. Note, that the HSOM also mirrors the semantical connection between "Zorro" and "Batman".

As illustrated in Fig. 6, the HSOM might also be used to classify an unknown text by displaying its relationship to a previously acquired document collection. In this example an unknown review text for the film "Jurassic Park" was mapped. The map was then zoomed to that node which most closely resembled the given input text, which in this case was another review describing the same film. Note, that the neighborhood is occupied by reviews describing the sequel "The Lost World", respectively the "Dinosaurs" animation. By mapping a complete unknown document collection to a previously formed

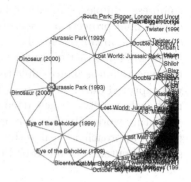

Fig. 6. Mapping a new text.

HSOM, relevant text documents can be discovered. In Fig. 7 the HSOM is used as a filter to display only those documents which belong to a semantic region of interest.

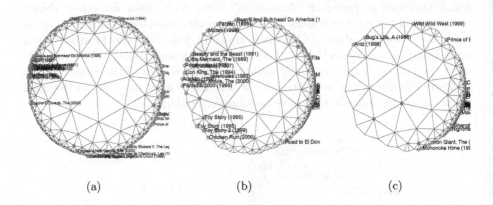

(a)   (b)   (c)

Fig. 7. Discovering of relevant documents in whole collections. In this example an unknown text collection is mapped onto the HSOM, but only those items are visualized which belong to a selected category, in this case animation movies. The central view in (a) points to a set of document clusters, which can be interactively zoom into. In (b) the largest cluster has been moved into focus. It mainly shows Disney animations and films from the "Toy story" series a bit farther down. In (c) the cluster in the top left contains "A Bug's Life" and "Antz", whereas the cluster in the bottom right belongs to movies connected to Japanese animations.

5   Discussion

Our results show that the HSOM is not only applicable to automated text categorization, but also specifically well suited to support "semantic browsing" in large document collections. Our first experiments indicate that the HSOM is able to exploit the peculiar geometric properties of hyperbolic space to successfully compress complex semantic relationships between text documents onto a two dimensional projection space. Additionally, the use of hyperbolic lattice topology for the arrangement of the HSOM nodes offers new and highly attractive features for interactive navigation in this way. Large document databases can be inspected at a glance while the HSOM provides additional information which was captured during a previous training step, allowing e. g. to rapidly visualize relationships between new documents and previously acquired collections.

Future work will address more sophisticated visualization strategies based on the new approach, as well as the evaluation for other widely used text collections, such as Reuters, Ohsumed or Pubmed.

References

1. D.S. Bradburn. Reducing transmission error effects using a self-organizing network. In *Proc. of the IJCNN89*, volume II, pages 531–538, San Diego, CA, 1989.
2. H. S. M. Coxeter. *Non Euclidean Geometry*. Univ. of Toronto Press, Toronto, 1957.

3. R. Fricke and F. Klein. *Vorlesungen über die Theorie der automorphen Funktionen*, volume 1. Teubner, Leipzig, 1897. Reprinted by Johnson Reprint, New York, 1965.

4. T. Joachims. Text categorization with support vector machines: Learning with many relevant features. Technical Report LS8-Report 23, Universität Dortmund, 1997.

5. T. Joachims. Text categorization with support vector machines: learning with many relevant features. In *Proceedings of ECML-98, 10th European Conference on Machine Learning*, number 1398, pages 137–142, Chemnitz, DE, 1998.

6. F. Klein and R. Fricke. *Vorlesungen über die Theorie der elliptischen Modulfunktionen*. Teubner, Leipzig, 1890. Reprinted by Johnson Reprint, New York, 1965.

7. T. Kohonen. *Self-Organizing Maps*. Springer Series in Information Sciences. Springer, second edition edition, 1997.

8. Pasi Koikkalainen and Erkki Oja. Self-organizing hierarchical feature maps. In *Proc. of the IJCNN 1990*, volume II, pages 279–285, 1990.

9. John Lamping and Ramana Rao. Laying out and visualizing large trees using a hyperbolic space. In *Proceedings of UIST'94*, pages 13–14, 1994.

10. John Lamping, Ramana Rao, and Peter Pirolli. A focus+content technique based on hyperbolic geometry for viewing large hierarchies. In *Proceedings of the ACM SIGCHI Conference on Human Factors in Computing Systems*, Denver, May 1995. ACM.

11. W. Magnus. *Noneuclidean Tesselations and Their Groups*. Academic Press, 1974.

12. Charles W. Misner, J. A. Wheeler, and Kip S. Thorne. *Gravitation*. Freeman, 1973.

13. Frank Morgan. *Riemannian Geometry: A Beginner's Guide*. Jones and Bartlett Publishers, Boston, London, 1993.

14. H. Ritter, T. Martinetz, and K. Schulten. *Neural Computation and Self-organizing Maps*. Addison Wesley Verlag, 1992.

15. Helge Ritter. Self-organizing maps in non-euclidian spaces. In E. Oja and S. Kaski, editors, *Kohonen Maps*, pages 97–108. Amer Elsevier, 1999.

16. G. Salton and C. Buckley. Term-weighting approaches in automatic text retrieval. *Information Processing and Management*, 24(5):513–523, 1988.

17. F. Sebastiani. Machine learning in automated text categorisation: a survey. Technical Report IEI-B4-31-1999, Istituto di Elaborazione dell'Informazione, Consiglio Nazionale delle Ricerche, Pisa, IT, 1999.

18. F. Sebastiani, A. Sperduti, and N. Valdambrini. An improved boosting algorithm and its application to automated text categorization. In *Proceedings of CIKM-00, 9th ACM International Conference on Information and Knowledge Management*, pages 78–85, 2000.

19. Karl Strubecker. *Differentialgeometrie III: Theorie der Flächenkrümmung*. Walter de Gruyter & Co, Berlin, 1969.

20. J.A. Thorpe. *Elementary Topics in Differential Geometry*. Springer-Verlag, New York, Heidelberg, Berlin, 1979.

21. Y. Yang. An evaluation of statistical approaches to text categorization. *Information Retrieval*, 1-2(1):69–90, 1999.

A Study on the Hierarchical Data Clustering Algorithm Based on Gravity Theory

Yen-Jen Oyang, Chien-Yu Chen, and Tsui-Wei Yang

Department of Computer Science and Information Engineering
National Taiwan University, Taipei, Taiwan
yjoyang@csie.ntu.edu.tw
cychen@mars.csie.ntu.edu.tw
lotte@mars.csie.ntu.edu.tw

Abstract. This paper discusses the clustering quality and complexities of the hierarchical data clustering algorithm based on gravity theory. The gravity-based clustering algorithm simulates how the given N nodes in a K-dimensional continuous vector space will cluster due to the gravity force, provided that each node is associated with a mass. One of the main issues studied in this paper is how the order of the distance term in the denominator of the gravity force formula impacts clustering quality. The study reveals that, among the hierarchical clustering algorithms invoked for comparison, only the gravity-based algorithm with a high order of the distance term neither has a bias towards spherical clusters nor suffers the well-known chaining effect. Since bias towards spherical clusters and the chaining effect are two major problems with respect to clustering quality, eliminating both implies that high clustering quality is achieved. As far as time complexity and space complexity are concerned, the gravity-based algorithm enjoys either lower time complexity or lower space complexity, when compared with the most well-known hierarchical data clustering algorithms except single-link.

Keywords: data clustering, agglomerative hierarchical clustering, gravity force.

1 Introduction

Data clustering is one of the most traditional and important issues in computer science [4, 7, 9, 10]. In recent years, due to emerging applications such as data mining and document clustering, data clustering has attracted a new round of attention in computer science research communities [3, 5, 6, 11, 14, 17, 19]. One traditional taxonomy of data clustering algorithms that work on data points in a K-dimensional continuous vector space is based on whether the algorithm yields a hierarchical clustering dendrogram or not [10]. One major advantage of the hierarchical clustering algorithms is that a hierarchical dendrogram is generated. This feature is very important for applications such as in biological, social, and behavior studies, due to the need to construct taxonomies [9]. Furthermore, as Jain, Murty, and Flynn summarized [10], hierarchical clustering algorithms are more versatile than non-hierarchical algorithms, or so-called partitional algorithms. For example, most partitional algorithms work well only on data sets containing isotropic clusters. Nevertheless, hierarchical clustering algorithms suffer higher time and space complexities [10]. Therefore, a latest

L. De Raedt and A. Siebes (Eds.): PKDD 2001, LNAI 2168, pp. 350–361, 2001.

trend is to integrate hierarchical and partitional clustering algorithms such as in BIRCH[19], CURE[5], and Chameleon[11]. In the kernel of these algorithms, a hierarchical clustering algorithm can be invoked to derive a dendrogram and to improve clustering quality. Due to this trend, it is expected that hierarchical clustering algorithms will continue to play an important role in applications that require a dendrogram. Furthermore, clustering quality becomes the prevailing concern in comparing various hierarchical clustering algorithms.

This paper discusses the clustering quality and complexities of the hierarchical data clustering algorithm based on gravity theory in physics. The gravity theory based clustering algorithm simulates how the given N nodes in a K-dimensional continuous vector space will cluster due to gravity force, provided that each node is associated with a mass. The idea of exploiting gravity theory in data clustering was first proposed by W. E. Wright in 1977 [16]. In the article, Wright discussed several factors that may impact clustering quality. Nevertheless, one crucial factor that was not addressed in Wright's article is the order of the distance term in the denominator of the gravity force formula. As we know, the order of the distance term is 2 for the gravity force. However, there are natural forces of which the magnitude of influence decreases much rapidly as distance increases. One such force is the strong force in atom nuclei. This observation inspired us to investigate the effect of the order of the distance term. In this paper, we still use the term "gravity force", even though we employ various orders of the distance term in the simulation model.

The experiments conducted in this study shows that the order of the distance term does have a significant impact on clustering quality. In particular, with a high order of the distance term, the gravity-based clustering algorithm neither has a bias towards spherical clusters nor suffers the well-known chaining effect [10,17]. Figure 1 exemplifies how bias towards spherical clusters impacts clustering quality. In Fig. 1, the data points at the two ends of the two dense regions are clustered. As will be shown in this paper, except the single-link algorithm, all the conventional hierarchical clustering algorithms studied in this paper as well as the gravity-based clustering algorithm with a low order of the distance term have a bias toward spherical clusters. On the other hand, the single-link algorithm suffers the well-known chaining effect. Since bias towards spherical clusters and the chaining effect are two common problems with respect to clustering quality, avoiding both implies that high clustering quality is achieved.

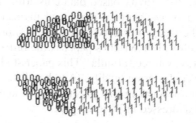

Fig. 1. An example of how a clustering algorithm with bias towards spherical clusters suffers poor clustering quality. The data points in the two clusters are marked by 0 and 1, respectively.

As Wright did not address time and space complexities of the gravity-based clustering algorithm, we conduct a detailed analysis in this paper. Table 1 compares the time complexity and space complexity between the gravity-based clustering algorithm and the most well-known hierarchical clustering algorithms [2, 10] that work in spaces of any degrees of dimension. The hierarchical clustering algorithms that work only in low-dimensional spaces [1, 12] are not included for comparison. The time and space complexities of the gravity-based algorithm reported in Table 1 are based on the simulation model employed in this paper, which is slightly different from the model employed in Wright's paper. Though Wright did not analyze the time and space complexities of his algorithm, our simulation results show that Wright's simulation model has the same orders of complexities as the simulation model employed in this paper. As Table 1 reveals, the gravity-based clustering algorithm enjoys either lower time complexity or space complexity, when compared with the most well-known hierarchical clustering algorithms except single-link.

In the following part of this paper, Sect. 2 elaborates how the gravity-based clustering algorithm works. Section 3 analyzes its time complexity and space complexity. Section 4 reports the experiments conducted to compare the gravity-based algorithm with the most well-known hierarchical clustering algorithms. Finally, concluding remarks are presented in Sect. 5.

Table 1. Time and space complexities of the gravity-based clustering algorithm and the most well-known hierarchical clustering algorithms.

Clustering Algorithm	Time complexity	Space complexity
The gravity-based algorithm	$O(N^2)$	$O(N)$
Single-Link [2]	$O(N^2)$	$O(N)$
Complete-Link [10, 13]	$O(N^2 \log N)$	$O(N^2)$
Centroid [2], Group Average [2]	$O(N^2 \log^2 N)$	$O(N)$

2 The Gravity-Based Clustering Algorithm

The simulation model that the gravity-based data clustering algorithm assumes is an analogy of how a number of water drops move and interact with each other in the cabin of a spacecraft. The main difference between the simulation model employed in this paper and that employed in Wright's paper is the order of the distance term in the denominator of the gravity force formula. This paper studies how different orders of the distance term impact clustering quality. Another difference is that the effect of air resistance is taken into account in this paper for guaranteeing termination of the algorithm, which was not addressed in Wright's paper.

Now, let us elaborate the simulation model employed in this paper. Due to the gravity force, the water drops in the cabin of a spacecraft will move toward each other. When these water drops move, they will also experience resistance due to the air in the cabin. Whenever two water drops hit, which means that the distance between these two drops is less than the lumped sum of their radii, they merge to form one new and larger water drop. In the simulation model, the merge of water drops corresponds to forming a new, one-level higher cluster that contains two existing clusters. The air resistance is intentionally included in the simulation model in order to guarantee that all these water drops eventually merge into one big drop regardless of how these water drops spread in the space initially. Before examining the details of the simulation algorithm, let us first discuss some important observations based on our physical knowledge.

Observation 1: As time elapses, the system can not continue to stay in a state in which there are two or more isolated water drops and all these water drops stand still.

Reason:

The system may enter such a state but will leave that state immediately due to gravity forces among these water drops.

Observation 2: As long as the system still contains two or more isolated water drops, the lumped sum of the dynamic energy and potential energy in the system will continue to decrease as time elapses.

Reason:

Due to Observation 1, if the system still contains two or more isolated water drops, then these water drops can not all stand still indefinitely. As some water drops move, the dynamic energy will gradually dissipate due to air resistance. Actually, the dissipated dynamic energy is turned to another form of energy. That is heat. Furthermore, as the dynamic energy in the system continues to dissipate, the potential energy in the system will gradually convert to dynamic energy. Since the dissipation of dynamic energy is a non-stopping process as long as there are two or more isolated water drops in the system. The lumped sum of dynamic energy and potential energy in the system will continue to decrease as time elapses.

Observation 3: Regardless of how the water drops spread in the space initially, all water drops will eventually merge into one big drop.

Reason:

Assume that there is an initial spreading of water drops such that the system never reaches a state in which all water drops merge into one big water drop. Let $ENG(t)$ denote the lumped sum of the potential energy and dynamic energy in the system. According to Observation 2, $ENG(t)$ is a monotonically decreasing function as long as there are two or more isolated water drops in the system. Since $ENG(t) \geq 0$ at any time, there is a number $a \geq 0$ such that $\lim_{t \to \infty} ENG(t) = a$. $\lim_{t \to \infty} ENG(t) = a$ implies $\lim_{t \to \infty} \dfrac{dENG(t)}{dt} = 0$. Because the air resistance force experienced by a moving water drop is proportional to the square of its moving velocity, $\lim_{t \to \infty} \dfrac{dENG(t)}{dt} = 0$ implies the velocities of all water drops will approach 0 as time elapses. However, just like the reason for Observation 1 above, the velocities of water drops can not all approach 0 as time elapses, because the gravity forces will accelerate them. Therefore, a contradiction would occur, if our assumption held. Hence, the system will eventually reach a state in which all water drops merge into one big drop.

The physical observations discussed above implies that the gravity-based data clustering algorithm based on simulating the physical system discussed above will eventually terminate. Following is a formal description of the simulation model.

1. Each of the N initial nodes in the K-dimensional space is associated with a mass M_0.

2. There are two forces applied to the nodes in the system. The first one is gravity force and the second one is air resistance.

3. The gravity force F_g applied to two nodes apart by a distance r is equal to:

$$F_g = \frac{C_g \times M_1 \times M_2}{r^k},$$

where C_g is a constant, M_1 and M_2 are the masses of these two nodes, and k is a positive integer.

4. The nodes will suffer air resistance when they move. The air resistance force F_r that a moving node experiences is equal to

$$F_r = C_r \times v^2,$$

where C_r is a constant and v is the velocity of the node.

5. At any time, if two nodes are apart by a distance less than the sum of their radii, then these two nodes will merge to form a new node with lumped mass. The radius of the new node is determined by the mass of the node and a given constant, which denotes the density of the material. As far as momentum is concerned, the momentum of the new node is equal to the addition of the momentums of the original nodes. The merge of two nodes corresponds to forming a new, one-level higher cluster that contains two existing clusters represented by the two original nodes.

Figure 2 shows the pseudo-code of the gravity-based clustering algorithm. Basically, the algorithm iteratively simulates the movement of each node during a time interval T and checks for possible merges. The algorithm terminates when all nodes merge into one big node.

```
W: the set containing all disjoint nodes.  At the beginning, W
contains all initial nodes.
Repeat

    For every  w_i ∈ W {

        calculate the acceleration of  w_i  based on the gravity

            forces applied on  w_i  by other nodes in  W and the mass of

            w_i ;

        calculate the new velocity of  w_i  based on its current ve-
            locity and acceleration;

        calculate the new position of  w_i  based on its current ve-
            locity;
    };
    For every pair of nodes  w_i , w_j ∈ W {

        if ( w_i and w_j  hit during the given time interval  T) {

            create a new cluster containing the clusters represented
                by  w_i  and  w_j ;

            merge  w_i  and  w_j  to form a new node  w_k  with lumped

                masses and merged momentum;
        };
    };
Until (W contains only one node);
```

Fig. 2. Pseudo-code of the gravity-based data clustering algorithm

3 Time and Space Complexity of the Gravity-Based Algorithm

We will employ a probability model to prove that the time complexity of the gravity-based data clustering algorithm is $O(N^2)$, where N is the number of nodes initially. The proof is based on the observation that the expected number of disjoint nodes remaining after each iteration of simulation decreases exponentially.

Assume that these N initial nodes randomly spreading in a K-dimensional Euclidian space bounded by $[X_{1l}, X_{1h}], [X_{2l}, X_{2h}], ..., [X_{kl}, X_{kh}]$, where X_{jl} and X_{jh} are the lower bound and upper bound in the j-th dimension, respectively. Depending on how these N nodes initially spread in the bounded space, the number of disjoint nodes remained after the i-th iteration of the gravity-based data clustering algorithm may differ. Let N_i denote the random variable that corresponds to the number of disjoint nodes after the i-th iteration of the gravity-based algorithm. It has been proved that all the nodes will eventually merge into one big node. Therefore, if the number initial nodes N and the boundary in the K-dimensional space are determined, then there exists an integer number S such that all nodes merge into one big node after S iterations of the gravity-based algorithm regardless of how these N nodes spread in the bounded space initially. Let $E[N_i]$ denote the expected value of random variable N_i and $q = $ Maximum($\dfrac{E[N_{i+1}]}{E[N_i]}$), where $0 \leq i < S\text{-}1$ and $E[N_0] = N$, $E[N_S] = 1$.

Then, we have $0 < q < 1$ and

$$E[N_i] \leq N \times q^i \tag{1}$$

One important attribute of q that we will exploit later is that q decreases as the number of initial nodes N increases, as long as the boundary in the K-dimensional space in which the initial nodes spread does not change with the value of N. As the number of nodes in a fixed-size space increases, the probability that two nodes hit during a time interval increases. As a result, q decreases as N increases.

To determine the time complexity of the graivity-based data clustering algorithm, we need to determine the number of operations performed in each iteration of the algorithm. In each iteration of the algorithm, we need to compute the distance between each pair of disjoint nodes and check for possible merges. The complexity of carrying out these two operations is in quadratic order. The complexities of all other operations executed in one iteration are in lower orders and thus can be ignored in determining time complexity. Therefore, the time complexity of the gravity-based data clustering algorithm is equal to

$\sum\limits_{i=0}^{S-1} E[C \times N_i^2]$, where C is a constant.

$$\sum_{i=0}^{S-1} E[C \times N_i^2] = C \times \sum_{i=0}^{S-1} E[N_i^2] = C \times \sum_{i=0}^{S-1} \sum_{l=1}^{N} \text{Probability}(N_i = l) \times l^2$$

$$\leq C \times \sum_{i=0}^{S-1} \sum_{l=1}^{N} \text{Probability}(N_i = l) \times l \times N = C \times N \times \sum_{i=0}^{S-1} \sum_{l=1}^{N} \text{Probability}(N_i = l) \times l$$

$$= C \times N \times \sum_{i=0}^{S-1} E[N_i] \leq C \times N \times \sum_{i=0}^{S-1} N \times q^i \text{ , according to (1) above}$$

$$= C \times N^2 \times \sum_{i=0}^{S-1} q^i = C \times \frac{1-q^S}{1-q} \times N^2$$

As elaborated earlier, q decreases as N increases and $0<q<1$. Therefore, term $\dfrac{1-q^S}{1-q}$ decreases as N increases and the time complexity of the gravity-based data clustering algorithm is $O(N^2)$. The space complexity of the algorithm is $O(N)$, because the space complexity of the hierarchical dendrogram built by the clustering algorithm is $O(N)$ and in each iteration we need to compute and store the location, velocity, and acceleration of each disjoint node.

4 Experimental Results

This section reports the experiments conducted to study how the gravity-based clustering algorithm performs in practice. The first part of this section reports how various algorithms perform with respect to clustering quality. The second part of this section reports the execution times of the gravity-based algorithm when running on real data sets. The clustering algorithms included in the clustering quality comparison are as follows:

(1)   the gravity-based clustering algorithm based on our simulation model with the order of the distance term set to 5;

(2)   the gravity-based clustering algorithm based on Wright's model with the order of the distance term set to 2;

(3)   four conventional hierarchical clustering algorithms: single-link[9, 10], complete-link[9, 10], group-average[9, 10], and centroid[9, 10].

Table 2 shows how the parameters in the gravity-based algorithms were set in these experiments. According to our experiences, the order of the distance term has the dominant effect on clustering quality. With the order of the distance term set to 5 or higher, the gravity-based clustering algorithm neither has a bias towards spherical clusters nor suffers the chaining effect. The settings of C_g, M_0, and T mainly affect how rapidly the nodes merge in iterations. Employing small values for these parameters may result in more iterations in simulation. Nevertheless, the effect does not change the order of the time complexity of the algorithm. It only affects a coefficient in the time complexity formula. The remaining two parameters, C_r and D_m, have essentially no effect on clustering quality or speed of converging as long as they are not set to some weird values. For example, the coefficient of air resistance should not be set so high that the nodes can hardly move and the material density of the nodes should not be set so high that all the nodes have virtually no volume and can hardly hit each other.

Table 2. The parameter settings in the gravity-based algorithms.

C_g : Gravity force coefficient	30
M_0 : Initial mass of each node	1
C_r : Air resistance coefficient	0.01
D_m : Material density of the node	1
T : Time interval of each iteration	1

(a) The simulation model employed in this paper

q : the order of the mass term	0
δ : the distance that the node with maximum velocity moves in one iteration	1

(b) Wright's simulation model

Figures 3~5 show three experiments conducted to study the clustering quality of different algorithms. These figures only plot the remaining clusters before the last merge of clusters is executed for better visualization quality. In these figures, different clusters are plotted using different marks. The experimental results presented in Fig. 3 show the effect caused by bias towards spherical clusters. As shown in Fig. 3, except the gravity-based algorithm with a high order of the distance term and the single-link algorithm, all other algorithms have a bias towards spherical clusters and generate clusters that contain data points from both separate dense regions. The experimental results presented in Fig. 4 show the well-known chaining effect. In this case, only the single-link algorithm suffers the chaining effect. As shown in Fig. 4b, the cluster containing the data points marked by "O" extends to both spheres. Fig. 5 shows a data set designed to test how each algorithm handle both bias towards spherical clusters and the chaining effect. As shown in Fig. 5, only the gravity-based algorithm with a high order of the distance term neither has a bias towards spherical clusters nor suffers the chaining effect.

We also use three 3-dimensional data sets to compare the clustering quality of various algorithms. Figure 6a depicts the shapes of the 3 data sets used in the experiments and the numbers of data points in these data sets, respectively. Figure 6b summarizes the clustering quality of various algorithms. Again, only the gravity-based algorithm with a high order of the distance term neither has a bias toward spherical clusters nor suffers the chaining effect.

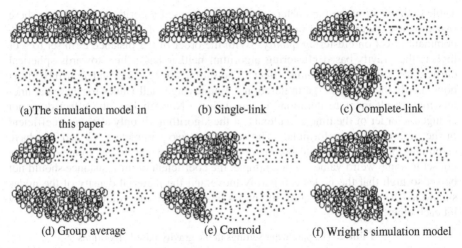

(a)The simulation model in this paper
(b) Single-link
(c) Complete-link

(d) Group average
(e) Centroid
(f) Wright's simulation model

Fig. 3. Clustering results of the first experiment

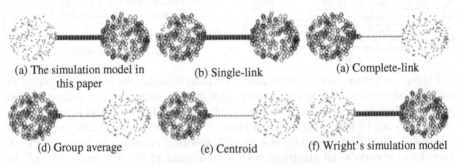

(a) The simulation model in this paper
(b) Single-link
(a) Complete-link

(d) Group average
(e) Centroid
(f) Wright's simulation model

Fig. 4. Clustering results of the second experiment

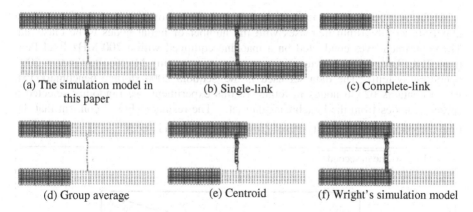

(a) The simulation model in this paper

(b) Single-link

(c) Complete-link

(d) Group average

(e) Centroid

(f) Wright's simulation model

Fig. 5. Clustering results of the third experiment

The experimental results above show that the gravity-based algorithm with a high order of the distance term is not biased towards spherical clusters. However, if the order of the distance term is low, then the situation may be different. We must resort to our physical intuition to explain this phenomenon. With a high order of the distance term, the influence of the gravity force decays rapidly as distance increases. Therefore, data points separated by a channel feel virtually no influence from each other.

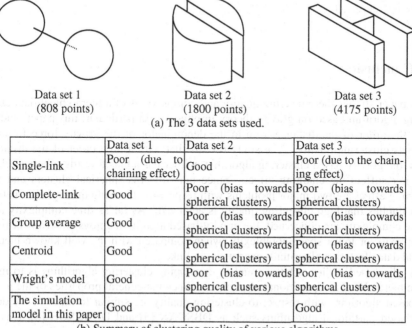

Data set 1
(808 points)

Data set 2
(1800 points)

Data set 3
(4175 points)

(a) The 3 data sets used.

	Data set 1	Data set 2	Data set 3
Single-link	Poor (due to chaining effect)	Good	Poor (due to the chaining effect)
Complete-link	Good	Poor (bias towards spherical clusters)	Poor (bias towards spherical clusters)
Group average	Good	Poor (bias towards spherical clusters)	Poor (bias towards spherical clusters)
Centroid	Good	Poor (bias towards spherical clusters)	Poor (bias towards spherical clusters)
Wright's model	Good	Poor (bias towards spherical clusters)	Poor (bias towards spherical clusters)
The simulation model in this paper	Good	Good	Good

(b) Summary of clustering quality of various algorithms

Fig. 6. The experiments conducted on 3-D data sets

As far as execution time is concerned, Fig. 7 shows how the execution time of the gravity-based algorithm increases with the number of initial nodes to be clustered. The experiment was conducted on a machine equipped with a 700-MHz Intel Pentium-III CPU and 786 Mbytes main memory and running Microsoft Window 2000 operating system. The data set used is the Sequoia 2000 storage benchmark[15], which contains 62556 nodes in total. In this experiment, we randomly selected a subset of nodes from the benchmark dataset. The results in Fig. 7 confirm that the time complexity of the gravity-based clustering algorithm is $O(N^2)$.

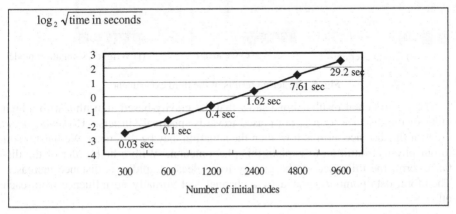

Fig. 7. Execution time of the gravity-based clustering algorithm versus the number of initial nodes to be clustered

5   Conclusions

This paper studies the clustering quality and complexities of a hierarchical data clustering algorithm based on gravity theory in physics. In particular, this paper studies how the order of the distance term in the denominator of the gravity force formula impacts clustering quality. The study reveals that with a high order of the distance term, the gravity-based clustering algorithm neither has a bias towards spherical clusters nor suffers the chaining effect. Since bias towards spherical clusters and the chaining effect are two major problems with respect to clustering quality, eliminating both implies that high clustering quality is achieved. As far as time complexity and space complexity are concerned, the gravity-based algorithm enjoys either lower time complexity or lower space complexity, when compared with the well-known hierarchical data clustering algorithms except single-link.

As discussed earlier, a latest trend in developing clustering algorithms is to integrate hierarchical and partitional algorithms. Since the general properties of the gravity-based algorithm with respect to clustering quality are similar to those of the density-based partitional algorithms such as DBSCAN [3] and DENCLUE [8], it is of interest to develop a hybrid algorithm that integrates the gravity-based algorithm and the density-based algorithm. In the hybrid algorithm, the gravity-based algorithm is invoked to derive the desired dendrogram. This is the follow-up work that we have been investigating.

References

1. Choudry, S. and N. Murty, *A divisive scheme for constructing minimal spanning trees in coordinate space*, Pattern Recognition Letters, volume 11 (1990), number 6 , pp. 385-389
2. D. Eppstein, *Fast hierarchical clustering and other applications of dynamic closest pairs*, The ACM Journal of Experimental Algorithmics, 5(1):1-23, Jun 2000
3. M. Ester, H.-P. Kriegel, J. Sander, X. Xu, *A density-based algorithm for discovering clusters in large spatial databases with noise*, Proceedings of 2nd International Conference on Knowledge Discovery and Data Mining (KDD-96), Aug. 1996.
4. B. Everitt, *Cluster analysis*, Halsted Press, 1980.
5. S. Guha, R. Rastogi, and K. Shim. *Cure: An efficient clustering algorithm for large databases*. In Proc. 1998 ACM-SIGMOD Int. Conf. Management of Data(SIGMOD'98), pages 73-84, Seattle, WA, June 1998.
6. S. Guha, R. Rastogi, and S. Kyuseok. *ROCK: A robust clustering algorithm for categorical attributes*. In Proceedings of ICDE'99, pp. 512-521, 1999.
7. J. Han, M. Kamber, *Data Mining: Concepts and Techniques*, Morgan Kaufmann Publishers, 2000
8. A. Hinneburg, and D. A. Keim, *An Efficient Approach to Clustering in Large Multimedia Databases with Noise*, Proceedings of the 4th International Conference on Knowledge Discovery and Data Mining, (KDD98), pp. 58-65, 1998.
9. A.K. Jain, R.C. Dubes, *Algorithms for clustering data*, Prentice Hall, 1988.
10. A.K. Jain, M.N. Murty, P.J. Flynn, *Data Clustering: A Review*, ACM Computing Surveys, Vol. 31, No. 3, pp.264-323, Sep. 1999.
11. G. Karypis, E.-H. Han, and V. Kumar. *CHAMELEON: A hierarchical clustering algorithm using dynamic modeling*. COMPUTER, 32:68-75, 1999
12. D. Krznaric and C. Levcopoulos, *Fast Algorithms for Complete Linkage Clustering*, Discrete & Computational Geometry, 19:131-145, 1998.
13. Kurita, T., *An efficient agglomerative clustering algorithm using a heap*, Pattern Recognition, volume 24 (1991), number 3 pp. 205-209
14. R.T. Ng, J. Han, *Efficient and Effective Clustering Methods for Spatial Data Mining*, VLDB'94, Proceedings of 20th International Conference on Very Large Data Bases, pp.144-155, Sep. 1994.
15. M. Stonebraker, J. Frew, K. Gardels and J. Meredith, *The Sequoia 2000 Storage Benchmark*, Proceedings of SIGMOD, pp. 2 – 11, 1993.
16. W.E. Wright, *Gravitational Clustering*, Pattern Recognition, 1977, Vol.9, pp. 151-166.
17. X. Xu, M. Ester, H.-P. Kriegel, J. Sander, *A distribution-based clustering algorithm for mining in large spatial databases*, In Proceedings of 14th International Conference on Data Engineering (ICDE'98), 1998.
18. Zamir, O. and O. Etzioni (1998). *Web document clustering: A feasibility demonstration*. In Proceedings of the 21th International ACM SIGIR Conference, pp. 46--54.
19. T. Zhang, R. Ramakrishnan, M. Livny, *BIRCH: An Efficient Data Clustering Method for Very Large Databases*, Proceedings of the 1996 ACM SIGMOD International Conference on Management of Data, pp.103-114, Jun. 1996.

Internet Document Filtering Using Fourier Domain Scoring

Laurence A.F. Park, Marimuthu Palaniswami, and Ramamohanarao Kotagiri

ARC Special Research Centre for Ultra-Broadband Information Networks
Department of Electrical & Elecronic Engineering
The University of Melbourne
Parkville, Victoria, Australia 3010
{lapark,swami,rao}@ee.mu.oz.au
http://www.ee.mu.oz.au/cubin

Abstract. Most search engines return a lot of unwanted information. A more thorough filtering process can be performed on this information to sort out the relevant documents. A new method called Frequency Domain Scoring (FDS), which is based on the Fourier Transform is proposed. FDS performs the filtering by examining the locality of the keywords throughout the documents. This is examined and compared to the well known techniques Latent Semantic Indexing (LSI) and Cosine measure. We found that FDS obtains better results of how relevant the document is to the query. The other two methods (cosine measure, LSI) do not perform as well mainly because they need a wider variety of documents to determine the topic.

1   Introduction

The ability of automatically classifying a document accurately has become an important issue in the past few years due to the exponential growth of the Internet and the availability of on-line information. Many methods such as topic identification have been tried by search engines creators and abused by web page writers who try their best to mislead the search engine so that their page appears at the top of the search results.

At present, the only way to find any useful information on the Internet is to use a search engine and manually sort through all of the results returned.

There has been a huge interest in relevant document retrieval, and several people have developed methods to allow the user to obtain the right information. For example, Spertus [10] uses different types of connectivity and spatial locality to detect relevant pages; Mladeniĉ [6] examines the pages previously visited by the user and uses these examples to learn what to retrieve in the future; Carrière et al. [3] calculates the score of a page based on how many relevant pages point to it through links; Ngu et al. [7] recommend that rather than search engines maintaining information about the entire Internet, each site should produce the information needed to produce better search results; Howe et al. [5] queries the

L. De Raedt and A. Siebes (Eds.): PKDD 2001, LNAI 2168, pp. 362–373, 2001.

existing range of search engines to obtain the best results from the collection of pages returned.

The method proposed here will examine the documents searched and try to find those with the topic requested by giving a score based on their spectrum, so that the user obtains the documents he/she truly requires.

This paper will proceed as follows, Sect. 2 contains a description of the document filtering process, Sect. 3 gives the problem formulation and explains how the current methods of filtering are not using all of the document information, Sect. 4 introduces the FDS method and explains how to calculate the score, Sect. 5 contains a short discussion on the computational complexity of the FDS method, Sect. 6 shows results from two separate experiments (one based on the TREC database and the other from three actual Internet searches) and gives an analysis of the results from both experiments, and finally the conclusion is given in Sect. 7.

2   Document Filtering

The objective of document filtering is to extract all of the relevant documents related to a certain topic from a set of documents of unknown topics. Examples of document filtering methods include the cosine measure, latent semantic indexing (LSI) and the new superior method Frequency Domain Scoring (FDS) introduced in this paper.

The methods used in this paper perform the filtering on a document set considered relevant by a selection of Internet search engines. Therefore the document filtering will be performed on a local machine rather than a remote machine.

Even though the trials were performed on the results of a few Internet search engines, these methods could easily be incorporated in the search engine itself.

3   Problem Formulation

Let $\mathcal{A}(t)$ be the entire collection of documents on the Internet at time t, where $\mathcal{A}(t) = \{d_0, d_1, \ldots, d_\mathcal{N}\}$ and $0 < \mathcal{N} < \infty$ is the number of documents on the Internet at time t. Each document d_n is represented as the tuple $\{i_n, \mathcal{L}_n\}$ where i is the information contained in document n and $\mathcal{L}_n \subset \mathcal{A}(t)$ is the set of documents which can be accessed through d_n via hypertext links.

There exists a set $\mathcal{R}_T \subset \mathcal{A}(t)$, where $\mathcal{R}_T$ is the set of all relevant documents to topic $T \in \mathbb{T}$ (the topic space). We want a function $\mathcal{S} : \mathbb{T} \rightarrow \mathcal{A}(t)$ such that $\mathcal{S}(T) = \mathcal{R}_T$. The current non-existence of the function $\mathcal{S}$ is the reason why search engines (which try to approximate $\mathcal{S}$) do not always return correct results. Internet search engines will give us a subset of $\mathcal{R}_T$ and a set of irrelevant information (related to the search topic T). This can be represented as $R_T \cup E_T$ where $R_T \subseteq \mathcal{R}_T$ and $E_T \subset \mathcal{A}(t)\backslash\mathcal{R}_T$.

Rather sifting through the entire collection of documents on the Internet ($\mathcal{A}(t)$), we will use the results from several search engines ($R_T \cup E_T$) and try to

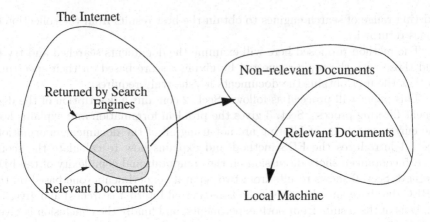

Fig. 1. This figure gives a visual example of the problem at hand. It can be seen that the set of documents returned by search engines contain irrelevant information. The problem is how do we extract the useful information from this set given to us

extract the set of documents R_T or remove the unwanted (irrelevant) E_T. This is shown in Fig. 1. This approach will lead to a good approximation of S.

Current searching methods use the following approach. By defining a function $g : \mathcal{A}(t) \to \mathbb{R}^{\mathcal{M}}$, we are able to represent $d_n \in \mathcal{A}(t)$ as an $\mathcal{M}$ dimensional vector in real space. The mapping is performed by treating each word in the document as a single dimension, the number of times that word appears in the document will be its value. Therefore

$$g(d_n) = \delta_n = \begin{bmatrix} c(d_n, w_1) \ c(d_n, w_2) \ldots c(d_n, w_{\mathcal{M}}) \end{bmatrix}^T \quad (1)$$

is a document vector, where $c(d_n, w_m) \in \mathbb{N}$ is the frequency count of word w_m, all w_m are unique and the dictionary contains $\mathcal{M}$ words. This document vector is then used to give the relevance for the document.

The above mapping of the document space into the M dimensional real space causes all of the important spatial information of the documents (the order of the words) to be lost. This also applies to the topic spatial information.

4   Frequency Domain Scoring

When a few key words are entered to search for, they are usually on the one topic. For example, if the words "aluminium cricket bat" is entered, we would expect to get documents on aluminium cricket bats. The classification methods listed so far would also return documents on cricket bats and aluminium.

To make use of the spatial information of the document, the vectors used here represent the positions of the search terms throughout the documents. Documents which have keywords appearing periodically and which contain the keywords together are given a higher relevance than the documents that have the keywords apart. To analyse the relative positions the vectors are mapped into the frequency domain.

Just as the discrete Fourier transform can map discrete time intervals in to the frequency domain, so to can it map discrete word spatial intervals into the frequency domain, as shown in Fig. 2

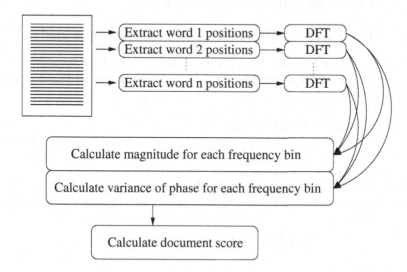

Fig. 2. This picture gives a visual example of how the Frequency Domain Scoring is performed. As shown, for each word in the search term, the document is split into equally sized bins. The value of each bin is the frequency of the word within that section of text. The DFT is performed and the magnitude and phase results are used to give the document score

By counting the number of appearances of a word in a document, we can treat the word position as the position in time. Performing the DFT allows us to observe the spectrum of the word. By splitting the spectrum into the magnitude and phase, we can see the power and delay of the word at certain frequencies.

By treating each word as a discrete time interval, we get a string of ones and zeros. To be more efficient, sequences of words can be clustered into bins (eg. the first fifty words in bin 1, the second fifty in bin 2, ...). This reduces the size of the input to the DFT and also gives larger counts than one in each bin.

Once the DFT is performed, the word spectrum shows the frequency components of which the word signal is made up. Each frequency component is a complex number of the form $H_f e^{i\phi_f}$ where $H_f \in \mathbb{R}$ represents the power of the frequency component f, and $\phi_f \in \mathbb{R}$ is the phase shift of f.

Terms made from several words are normally the topic of the document when the words appear close together and periodically. Therefore a document in which frequency f has a large magnitude (H_f) for all of the words from the set T, and the phases of each word from T are similar, then it is most likely that the T is a subset of the topic.

In mathematical terms, given a query T where

$$T = \{w_1, w_2, \ldots, w_M\} \tag{2}$$

we can define a counting function $\mathbf{cf} : \mathcal{A}(t) \times T \to \mathbb{R}^B$

$$\mathbf{cf}(d_n, w_m) = \left[c_1(d_n, w_m)/\beta \ c_2(d_n, w_m)/\beta \ \ldots \ c_B(d_n, w_m)/\beta \right] \tag{3}$$

where $c_b(d_n, w_m)$ is the count of word w_m in bin $1 \le b \le B$ of document d_n and β is the number of words per bin. The spectrum of $\mathbf{cf}$ can be found using the Fourier transform.

$$\mathcal{C}(d_n, w_m) = \mathcal{F}\left[\mathbf{cf}(d_n, w_m)\right] \tag{4}$$

$$= \left[H_1^{(n,m)} e^{i\phi_1^{(n,m)}} \ H_2^{(n,m)} e^{i\phi_2^{(n,m)}} \ \ldots \ H_B^{(n,m)} e^{i\phi_B^{(n,m)}} \right] \tag{5}$$

where $\mathcal{F}$ is the Fourier Transform, $H_b^{(n,m)} \in \mathbb{R}$ and $\phi_b^{(n,m)} \in \mathbb{R}$ are the magnitude and phase of the bth frequency bin from the nth document and mth word respectively. If

$$\mathrm{var}\left(\left\{ \phi_b^{(n,1)}, \phi_b^{(n,2)}, \ldots, \phi_b^{(n,M)} \right\} \right) < \epsilon \tag{6}$$

and

$$H_b^{(n,m)} > E \qquad \forall \ m \tag{7}$$

where ϵ is a small value and E is a large value, then more likely that $d_n \in \mathcal{R}_T$. Therefore we want to give a higher relevance score to those documents with a higher magnitude and lower variance in phase of each frequency component.

The measure of variance does not take into account the circular data of the phase (modulo 2π). To overcome this problem, a measure of precision (rather than variance, not to be confused with the precision measure of document retrieval) was used. If

$$\bar{C}_b^{(n)} = \frac{1}{M} \sum_{m=1}^{M} \cos \phi_b^{(n,m)} \qquad \text{and} \qquad \bar{S}_b^{(n)} = \frac{1}{M} \sum_{m=1}^{M} \sin \phi_b^{(n,m)} \tag{8}$$

then the precision ($\bar{r}$) and mean ($\bar{\phi}$) are defined by

$$\bar{C}_b^{(n)} = \bar{r}_b^{(n)} \cos \bar{\phi}_b^{(n)} \qquad \text{and} \qquad \bar{S}_b^{(n)} = \bar{r}_b^{(n)} \sin \bar{\phi}_b^{(n)} \tag{9}$$

so

$$\bar{r}_b^{(n)} = \sqrt{\left(\bar{C}_b^{(n)}\right)^2 + \left(\bar{S}_b^{(n)}\right)^2} \tag{10}$$

The precision has a range of $[0, 1]$, where 1 is maximum precision. The notion of precision of the phases can be seen in the visual example given in Fig. 3.

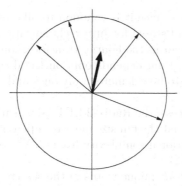

Fig. 3. This picture gives a visual example of how the precision function works. If each phase is considered as a unit vector (thin vectors) centered at zero, the precision will be the average of these vectors (thick vector)

This gives a score function of:

$$S_{\text{FDS}}(d_n, T) = \sum_{b=1}^{B} \bar{r}_b^{(n)} \log\left(\lambda + \sum_{m=1}^{M} \frac{H_b^{(n,m)}}{M}\right) \qquad (11)$$

where

$$\lambda = \begin{cases} 0 & \text{if } H_b^{(n,m)} = 0 \ \forall \ m \\ Q & \text{if } H_b^{(n,m)} \neq 0 \ \forall \ m \end{cases} \qquad (12)$$

where Q is a constant positive real number. Note that if the AC components are ignored, FDS will perform the same as the cosine measure. This is because $\bar{r}_1^{(n)} = 1$ for any n when $b = 1$. Therefore the cosine measure can be viewed as a special case of the FDS measure. By examining the spectrum of the words (and not just the count) we are able to obtain a better understanding of the content of the document.

The λ value was inserted to give a higher ranking to documents which contain all of the words in the query. This can be adjusted to suit the users preference.

5   Computational Complexity

Choosing an information retrieval method just because it gives accurate results is not sufficient. The methods have to be practical. This is why computational complexity comes into play when deciding which method is best. In most cases there is a trade off between speed and accuracy, where the level chosen should suit the user.

All methods suggested require scanning through the documents, word by word. This stage only depends on the length of the documents and has been omitted from the analysis since it is common to all methods. This process can also be pre-computed and stored for future classifications.

The FDS method performs the Fourier transforms on each word in the search query. Since the FDS method depends only on the document being processed, the spectral values have to be calculated only once and can then stored for later use.

To speed up the process, the Radix-2 FFT [8] was used. The only drawback to using this method is that the bin size must be a power of two ($B = 2^p$, $p \in \mathbb{N}$). This drops the computational complexity from $O(N^2)$ (direct DFT calculation) to $O\left(\frac{N}{2}\log_2 N\right)$ (Radix-2).

This implies that for M unique words in the search query, the time taken to calculate the score of one document will be in the order of $O\left(\frac{MN}{2}\log_2 N\right)$.

6   Results

We conducted two large experiments, one using the TREC database [11] and the other using a database of documents selected from the results of Internet search engines.

6.1   Preliminaries

To find how effective the FDS method was we compared the results given with trials using the cosine measure [12] and Latent Semantic Indexing (LSI) [1]. Pre-processing was performed on the data to make computation easier and give fairer results. This consisted of removing stop words, stemming, and using log-entropy normalisation (found in [4]). After performing several trials using different values of Q, it was chosen to be 1. The bin size was set to 16 to give a good tradeoff between accuracy and disk space. The document filtering methods FDS, cosine measure, and LSI are then performed to evaluate their relative merits.

The results (in table 2 and table 3) were evaluated by examining two accuracy measures of precision, which in the information retrieval sense, is the measure of the proportion of relevant documents to retrieved documents. The two measures are:

Average Precision This value is best explained by observing table 1.

R-Precision is the precision after the first R documents, where R is the number of relevant documents for that query.

The time taken to perform the ranking was very similar for each of the methods.

6.2   Methods Compared

Cosine Measure. The score for each document was calculated by finding the normalised dot product of the document vector (shown in equation 1 and the query vector. This method will be referred to as COS throughout this document.

Table 1. The average precision is calculated by first calculating the sub-precisions of each relevant document (shown on each line of the table). Sub-precision is found by including only the documents ranked higher than the selected relevant document

Relevant document number	Rank	Precision
1	r_1	$1/r_1$
2	r_2	$2/r_2$
3	r_3	$3/r_3$
$\vdots$	$\vdots$	$\vdots$
n	r_n	n/r_n

$$\text{Average Precision:} \quad \frac{\sum_{i=1}^{n} i/r_i}{n}$$

Latent Semantic Indexing. Latent Semantic Indexing produces document vectors of smaller dimension than the cosine measure, but closest to them in the least squares sense, via Singular Value Decomposition (SVD) [2]. This reduction of dimensionality reveals a latent structure of the documents that would not have been noticed otherwise. In this experiment, the dimension was reduced to 280.

Due to the large amounts of data and most of it being zeros, a sparse matrix data structure was used (found in [9]). Results were found by comparing each document vector to the query vector using the normalised dot product. The query vector was created by taking the average of the word vectors (produced by the SVD) that appeared in the search term. This method will be referred to as LSI throughout this document.

6.3   Experiment One: TREC Data

The TREC data [11] contains millions of documents from many different sources. This is useful to evaluate Internet search engines and searching tools for large databases. The method proposed in this paper is a refining process. It takes a subset of the whole data and extracts the truly relevant information from that. To emulate the process of the search engines, a number of random documents were chosen from the original data set, while making sure the documents classified relevant and irrelevant were included (shown in Fig. 4). The irrelevant documents are those that have been classified as relevant by other information retrieval methods but found to be wrong. By including these documents, the information retrieval methods applied here will be truly challenged. The results were evaluated using 'trec_eval', which was supplied by the TREC organisers.

The results from using the TREC data are shown in table 2. The data focused on was from the Associated Press document set, using queries 101 through to 200. Two experiments were run, the first processed 500 pseudo-random documents from the AP document set, the second processed 1000 documents.

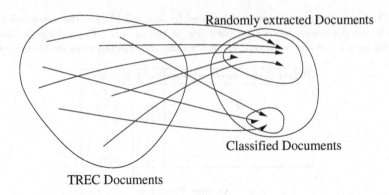

Fig. 4. To emulate the process of the search engines, a sample of relevant and irrelevant documents were taken from the TREC data set to feed into the document filtering process

It should be noted that it would have been very unlikely that any document contained every word in a selected query, due to the nature of the query. Rather than being a phrase or a few key words (which is what would be normally supplied to a search engine), the queries were structured into the form of a description of desired documents.

Table 2. Results given by trec_eval from a semi-random sample of documents using various filtering methods. FDS has the greatest precision for 500 documents and gives similar results to COS for 1000 documents

Method	500 documents		1000 documents	
	Average Precision	R-Precision	Average Precision	R-Precision
FDS	0.4439	0.3972	0.4560	0.3933
COS	0.4371	0.3830	0.4598	0.3930
LSI	0.3756	0.3508	0.3661	0.3508

The results show that FDS gives better results compared to the other methods. For all of the methods, the scores are low. A reason for this is the way the TREC queries are set up. A typical TREC query is of the form :

A {type of document} will identify {case 1} and {case 2} or ... but not ...

Therefore it requires parsing to obtain the keywords and anti-keywords. Some of the query results with lower precision did not contain examples. They only contained statements like "...contains information about a country...". The methods used contained no data on what country names are and so could not find the relevant documents.

6.4   Experiment Two: Internet Documents

The following results were obtained from a data set of documents returned from various search engines on the Internet after searching for three items with various degrees of difficulty. The query *"Aluminium Cricket Bat"* had only a few relevant documents, *"Bullet the blue sky mp3"* had some relevant documents, and *"Prank calls from Bart Simpson to Moe"* contained many relevant documents. The data was cleaned by extracting the text from the html structure, changing all the letters to lowercase, removing any stop-words (listed in a previously compiled list) and converting each word to its stem by using Porter's Stemming Algorithm.

The html documents were individually examined and assigned a label of *relevant* or *not relevant*. These were then compared with the score given by the listed methods (mentioned throughout the document). The results are presented in table 3 showing the method, the number of documents used, the number of relative documents, and the precision of the method for that search.

Table 3. This table shows how well the each method worked on different sets of documents retrieved from the Internet

Search for "Aluminium Cricket Bat"

Method	No. of Documents		Average Precision	R-Precision
	Total	Relevant		
FDS	120	2	0.5667	0.5000
COS	120	2	0.2857	0.5000
LSI	120	2	0.2845	0.5000

Search for "Bullet the blue sky mp3"

Method	No. of Documents		Average Precision	R-Precision
	Total	Relevant		
FDS	120	13	0.9822	0.9231
COS	120	13	0.7467	0.7692
LSI	120	13	0.6567	0.6923

Search for "Prank calls from Bart Simpson to Moe"

Method	No. of Documents		Average Precision	R-Precision
	Total	Relevant		
FDS	120	27	0.9279	0.9259
COS	120	27	0.7425	0.7778
LSI	120	27	0.7349	0.7778

By observing the results obtained, it can be seen that the FDS technique is a superior method and works far better than the LSI and COS document indexing schemes. This is due to the fact that FDS is able to extract more information from the documents. LSI and COS treat the documents as though they are a *'bag of words'*, while FDS observes any structures of the searched terms in the document. COS can be considered a special case of the FDS method, therefore FDS is expected to obtain better results.

7 Conclusion

While Internet search engines produce good results, they don't always give us exactly what we want. The proposed FDS method over comes this problem by filtering the results given by the search engines. The LSI and COS methods need a wide range of document types to really focus on the important documents. In this case most of the documents will be of the same class and therefore these methods will not work as well as the new FDS method.

LSI and COS methods could be considered sub-methods of FDS. LSI and COS methods consider only the DC components while FDS makes use of the full spectrum. This shows that LSI and COS do not require as much storage space for the calculations since it only takes a fraction of the data needed by FDS. But at the current rate in which storage media is growing in capacity, this is hardly an issue. The size of the stored information is proportional to the number of frequency components, which can be adjusted by changing the words per bin.

FDS can be implemented on the client side (as discussed throughout this document) or it could be implemented on the server side. It can easily be included in systems like Internet search engines since it is scalable (when extra documents are introduced into the database, the other documents are not affected), the frequency data can easily be put into an indexing table (current indexing tables only include the DC component, therefore FDS would be a simple extension of this), and the most important reason is that it gives excellent results. Including the FDS method in any search engine would boost the quality (in terms of results) of the search engine, and return a more relevant document set.

Acknowledgements. We would like to thank the ARC Special Research Centre for Ultra-Broadband Information Networks for their support and funding of this research.

References

1. M. W. Berry, S. T. Dumais, and G. W. O'Brien. Using linear algebra for intelligent information retrieval. Technical report, Computer Science Department, The University of Tennessee, Knoxville, TN, December 1994.
2. Michael W. Berry. *Large scale sparse singular value computations.* Department of Computer Science, University of Tennessee, 107 Ayres Hall, Knoxville, 1993.
3. S. Jeromy Carrière and Rick Kazman. Webquery: searching and visualising the web through connectivity. *Computer Networks and ISDN Systems*, 29:1257–1267, 1997.
4. Susan T. Dumais. Improving the retrieval of information from external sources. *Behaviour Research Methods, Instruments & Computers*, 23(2):229–236, 1991.
5. Adele E. Howe and Daniel Dreilinger. Savvysearch. *AI Magazine*, pages 19–25, Summer 1997.
6. Dunja Mladenič. Personal webwatcher: design and implementation. Technical report, Dept. for Intelligent Systems, J. Stefan Institute, Jamova 39, 11000 Ljubljana, Slovania, 1996.

7. Daniel Siaw Weng Ngu and Xindong Wu. Site helper: a localised agent that helps incremental exploration of the world wide web. *Computer Networks and ISDN Systems*, 29:1249–1255, 1997.

8. John G. Proakis and Dimitris G. Manolakis. *Digital signal processing : principles, algorithms, and applications*. Prentice-Hall, Inc, 3rd edition, 1996.

9. Yousef Saad. *Iterative methods for sparse linear systems*. PWS series in computer science. PWS Pub. Co., Boston, 1996.

10. Ellen Spertus. Parasite: mining structural information on the web. *Computer Networks and ISDN Systems*, 29:1205–1215, 1997.

11. National Institute Of Standards and Technology. Text retrieval conference (trec) http://trec.nist.gov/. World Wide Web, 2001.

12. Ian H. Witten, Alistair Moffat, and Timothy C. Bell. *Managing gigabytes : compressing and indexing documents and images*. Morgan Kaufmann Publishers, 1999.

Distinguishing Natural Language Processes on the Basis of fMRI-Measured Brain Activation

Francisco Pereira[1], Marcel Just[2], and Tom Mitchell[1]

[1] Computer Science Department
fpereira@cs.cmu.edu
[2] Psychology Department
Carnegie Mellon University
5000 Forbes Avenue
Pittsburgh, PA 15213
just+@andrew.cmu.edu

Abstract. We present a method for distinguishing two subtly different mental states, on the basis of the underlying brain activation measured with fMRI. The method uses a classifier to learn to distinguish between brain activation in a set of selected voxels (volume elements) during the processing of two types of sentences, namely ambiguous versus unambiguous sentences. The classifier is then used to distinguish the two states in untrained instances. The method can be generalized to accomplish knowledge discovery in cases where the contrasting brain activation profiles are not known a priori.

1 A fMRI Study of Sentence Processing

1.1 Introduction

This paper builds on an fMRI (functional Magnetic Resonance Imaging [2]) study of cortical activity during the reading of syntactically ambiguous sentences [3]. The latter are sentences in which a word can have one of two lexical and syntactic roles, and there is no disambiguating information in the context that precedes the ambiguity. However, the ambiguity is resolved by information occurring later in the sentence. For instance, in

The horse raced past the barn escaped from his trainer.

the meaning of the sentence is clear after the word "escaped" is reached. The ambiguity occurs at "raced", which is could be interpreted as either a past tense (preferred) or a past participle (unpreferred). An unambiguous sentence could be, for example

The experienced soldiers spoke about the dangers before the midnight raid.

where "spoke" is unambiguously the past tense form.

L. De Raedt and A. Siebes (Eds.): PKDD 2001, LNAI 2168, pp. 374–385, 2001.
© Springer-Verlag Berlin Heidelberg 2001

The study analyzed the activation in different parts of the brain every 1500 msec during the reading of ambiguous sentences and unambiguous control sentences. The analysis performed examined both the amount and location of such activation and the contrast between the two types of sentences, expressed in those terms.

One additional dimension of analysis could be the characterization of what is different between activation in the two experimental conditions. In addition to the amount of activation triggered, one might have to consider differences in the shape of the activation response, in localization (i.e. some points are only active in one of the conditions), and in timing. One could even consider the question of ascertaining whether there is more than one kind of cognitive process taking place.

But while it is relatively simple to test for such things as differing amounts of activation, that is not the case for the other questions. We propose a method for identifying specific locations in the brain where activation patterns are distinguishable across experimental conditions and, through that set of locations, allowing the discovery of answers to the questions above.

1.2 Syntactical Ambiguity Experiment

Let us take a closer look at what it means for a sentence to be ambiguous. The development of the sentence can be more or less surprising, and sentences taking the less likely meaning are called *ambiguous unpreferred* sentences. Ambiguous sentences which develop with the most predictable meaning are called *ambiguous preferred* sentences, and sentences without any ambiguity are *unambiguous* sentences. We shall concentrate on distinguishing ambiguous unpreferred and unambiguous sentences, and hence shall use the designations ambiguous/unambiguous from this point onwards.

The study above concentrated on two cortical areas known to be involved in sentence processing, the Left Inferior Frontal Gyrus (LIFG), also known as Broca's area, and the Left Superior Temporal Gyrus (LSTG)/ Left Posterior Middle and Superior Temporal Gyrus (LMTG), known as Wernicke's area. These will henceforth be referred to as Regions of Interest (ROIs). During sentence processing, these two areas showed a significant increase in activation when compared to their behavior during a control condition. It was also observed that brain activation went to a higher level, and remained at such a level for a longer period of time, during the processing of ambiguous sentences than it did during the processing of unambiguous sentences. As the processing of ambiguities leads to an increase in the demand for cognitive resources [3], such an increase results in additional cortical activity, which we are interested in characterizing.

1.3 Data Processing and Analysis

Each subject was presented a sequence of 20 trials (sentences), 10 ambiguous and 10 unambiguous, presented in a random order. Each trial consisted of the presentation of a sentence for 10 seconds, followed by a yes/no comprehension question. Cortical activity during the processing of each sentence was recorded every 1500 msec, providing a time series that constituted that basis of our data. The part of the brain under scrutiny is divided into a number of volume elements called *voxels*, measuring 3.125x3.125x5 mm. During the experiment, the *BOLD* (Blood Oxygen Level Dependent) signal at each voxel was measured every 1500 msec. This response is an indirect indicator of neural activity [2], and thus we will use the terms activity and amount of activation to refer to the level of the said response. An *image* is a set of such activation values, with one value per voxel. As images are acquired, the result is a succession of values for each voxel, containing its activation values at each instant of the experiment. The image are acquired not volumetrically but sequentially in slice planes 5 mm thick, with the acquisition of all 7 slices distributed over 1500 msec. The slight differences in acquisition time for the different slices is later corrected for by an interpolation technique.

The recordings available at each voxel will then consist of one time series of the activation for each sentence, as well some extra series corresponding to "baseline" activation during a control condition, during which the subject just fixates an asterisk instead of going through sentence-reading. Obviously, during the latter there should be no sentence-processing related activity.

The next step in the analysis was the identification of *active voxels*. These are voxels that display a significant activity in any of the experimental conditions. The activity during the experimental condition is gauged by comparing it with the one taking place during the control condition. This was done using a voxel-wise t-test comparing the activation level in the baseline condition and during all other conditions. A very high t threshold is used (equivalent to a Bonferroni correction for multiple comparisons) to identify voxels whose activation level during sentence processing differs significantly from their level during the control condition.

The time courses of the active voxels in a subject were then averaged across the 10 sentences of the same type and normalized as "percentage of activation above baseline". Afterwards, these were averaged across subjects. The end result was an average timecourse for every sentence trial, from which was obtained the average timecourse for each type of sentence. From analyses of variance of the data it was possible to conclude that brain activation went to a higher level, and remained at such a level for a longer period of time, during the processing of ambiguous sentences than it did during the processing of unambiguous sentences.

The expected model for this sentence processing task features each ROI recruiting voxels from a certain pool as resources for sentence processing in general. If a particular sentence demands more resources than are available in the pool (through its being ambiguous, for instance), more activity will be demanded from pool voxels and, eventually, other voxels might be recruited. We would like to extend this study by analyzing the degree and manner of involvement of these specially recruited voxels in the task being performed, and this effort will be described in Sect. 2.

2   Identifying Voxels with Varying Behaviour across Conditions

2.1   Our Approach and Related Work

The problem as we see it consists in ascertaining whether the behaviour of the BOLD response at some voxels is distinguishable between the two experimental conditions. If so, we would have candidate locations that might be supporting the additional activation required for processing ambiguous sentences, which could then be examined.

Currently, this question is addressed by identifying the most active voxels in two different experimental conditions, averaging their time series under each condition and then comparing the two averages. Identification of active voxels is done through a voxelwise t-test on one of the following: the difference between the mean activity during experimental and control conditions or the correlation of the voxel time series with a paradigmatic time series which corresponds to the expected response for voxels involved in the task.

A more agnostic approach is the clustering of the time series of all the voxels, guided either by known constraints on present cognitive processes or just using hierarchical clustering and using one of several possible metrics (see [7]). The centroids of the clusters thus found are then examined in the same way as the average time courses found through t-tests.

Yet another approach is to use a bayesian model of the fMRI signal at each voxel (see [4]). This can be used for questions beyond that of whether a given voxel is active or not, such as the influence of experimental condition on the parameters of the model, while being subject to assumptions regarding plausible signal shapes, noise and other factors.

A closer look at the t-test and clustering approaches will reveal that they give no guarantees of identifying voxels where the time series are different across experimental conditions. To see why consider that a high t-value for the contrast between experimental conditions and control only pertains to the mean activity and says nothing about the shape of the time series, which may be different for voxels that behave differently across the two experimental conditions In addition, the mean activity may be lower for such voxels than for the majority of voxels that accounts for the bulk of the activation.

If we were to user the t-test approach to test the mean during one experimental condition against the mean during another we would probably find that the means were too similar for strong results in most voxels where there is activity in both conditions. A clustering approach applied separately to each condition would still identify groups corresponding to the bulk of activation, which coincides in the two conditions.

The bayesian modelling approach allows for greater flexibility in that questions besides that of whether a voxel is active or not can be posed. In our case, the question would be whether the shape of the time series differs on a point by point basis across the two conditions. The caveat in this case is that the model pressuposes a certain BOLD response shape. Model fitting is accomplished by estimating the values of the model parameters from data. While this is fine for the bulk of the active voxels, which mainly share the same response shape, it might not work for voxels where the shapes of the response are unusual in one or both conditions. Moreover, prior information about response shape is, in many cases, derived from observations in areas such as motor cortex, which need not be exactly the same for areas performing cognitive functions such as language processing.

Therefore, we would like to find differences in time series for a given voxel in a way that is independent both of assumptions regarding response shape and of considerations about level of activity. We propose to use a classifier to learn the difference, through identification of the two types of sentences under consideration, ambiguous and unambiguous with two classes of examples to be learned, on a voxel by voxel basis. The features on which the learning will be based are the activation values recorded for each voxel at each time point during the processing of a sentence. The examples are the time series for each sentence for both conditions.

There are other possibilities for representation of the time courses. In the extreme, one might just consider the mean activity. Another possibility is to represent the time series as a number of adjacent temporal sections, in terms of which the activity is described, which is what is done for the bayesian modelling approach cited above. Yet another would be to obtain derived features such as spectra obtained via fourier or wavelet transforms and cast the learning problem in terms of them.

Our hope is that the degree of success of a classifier on a voxel can be taken as an estimate of how much the activity in the corresponding voxel differs between ambiguous and unambiguous sentences, the two experimental conditions. This, in turn, should be an indication of the degree of involvement of the voxel in specifically processing ambiguity.

2.2   Experimental Procedure

The data available for each voxel consists of 10 sentences per condition, where each sentence is a time series of 16 activation values (24 sec of data) captured during and immediately after the processing of a sentence. We used only values 4 to 13 in each token, eliminating the pre-rise and post-activity decay of the BOLD response. Each of the values in a token has been normalized as a percentage, referring to how much it was above the average base level of activation during the control condition of the experiment.

In classifier terms, this maps to 10 examples of each class, where each example is a series of 16 floating point values, available for every voxel in both ROIs for 6 subjects.

In addition, given the already small number of examples we would like to have as few features per example as possible, and thus 10 features were retained in the part of the series where differences are more likely, as mentioned above.

As what is needed is an estimate of how accurately the difference between conditions at a given voxel can be learned using a given classifier, we resort to leave-1-out cross validation over the 20 examples available, while taking care to balance the number of training examples across both classes. Initially, we create 10 random pairs with one example of each class. For each pair, we train on the remainder 18 examples, 9 of each class, and then test each of the examples of the pair. The estimate for attainable classifier accuracy for this voxel will be $\frac{\#of successes}{20}$.

The classifiers used in each voxel were a neural network (NN) with one sigmoidal hidden unit (see [6]), effectively doing logistic regression, and a linear kernel support vector machine (SVM) (see [5]). The choice of classifier was limited by the small number of examples available. We also tried other alternatives, such as SVMs with more complex kernels, NN with more hidden units and a simple k-nearest neighbour classifier. These were discarded because the performance was worse.

There are thus twelve sets of classification problems, with the set per each subject/ROI combination containing hundreds of classification problems, one per voxel. The output of the process is, for each subject and ROI, a list of voxels in that ROI ranked by decreasing classifier accuracy. Within groups of voxels with the same accuracy level, an additional ranking is performed based on "quality" of the classification (lowest mean squared error for NN or highest absolute value of the decision function for SVM). For each classifier, the process is run with different seeds for a number of times, the resulting rankings are averaged, and it is on these averaged lists that the analysis detailed below is performed.

2.3 Experimental Results

We found that it is possible to discriminate between activity in each of two experimental conditions for a small subset of the examined voxels. After applying the procedure described, we obtained consistent results across subjects and ROIs, in that a subset of 1% of the classifiers almost always has mean accuracy of 80% or more, for the best performing method (NN). The value of 1% typically corresponds to 3 to 7 voxels per subject/ROI (i.e. about 150 to 350 cubic mm) out of an anatomically huge volume of cortex. Considerations of how plausible the voxels found are from the psychological point of view are dealt with in the next section.

In each subject/ROI pair the distribution of accuracies is a unimodal curve centered around 50%, with a heavier tail for the higher accuracies and a smaller one for low accuracy voxels. Details about the distribution of the accuracy scores are discussed in the section that compares the results to a null model.

Because the goal was to find the relatively small group of voxels which activated differently during the processing of the two types of sentences, we will proceed considering only the top 1% most accurate voxels in each ROI and subject combination. Note that this number of voxels (3-7) is on the order of magnitude of the number of voxels believed to show real activation, typically demonstrated by their time-locking to the stimulus events and their signal amplitude in the experimental conditions, as detected through a t-test.

Table 1 details the mean accuracy attained in the top 1% group of voxels classified through each of the two methods. In addition, we were interested in finding out whether the voxels for which accuracy was greater using each method were the same, and thus the table contains the percentage of overlap between the groups. The comparison is made for the 6 subjects and 2 ROIs.

Table 1. Mean accuracy of the top 1% group selected using each classification method, as well as percentage of those belonging to the two groups

Subject#/ROI	Accuracy NN	Accuracy SVM	Overlap %
1-LIFG	0.82	0.80	0.50
1-LSTG	0.82	0.79	0.29
2-LIFG	0.78	0.72	0.00
2-LSTG	0.82	0.70	0.17
3-LIFG	0.82	0.81	0.25
3-LSTG	0.77	0.75	0.33
4-LIFG	0.85	0.78	0.67
4-LSTG	0.81	0.79	0.00
5-LIFG	0.86	0.76	0.00
5-LSTG	0.81	0.76	0.00
6-LIFG	0.81	0.83	0.33
6-LSTG	0.87	0.75	0.40
mean	0.82	0.77	0.25

The NN group had a mean accuracy ranging from 77% to 87% over subjects and ROIs, with an overall average of 82%, as displayed in the second column of Table 1. This means that a NN was capable of correctly distinguishing whether the subject had been reading an ambiguous or an unambiguous sentence on the basis of the fMRI activation data 82% of the time, on sentences on which it had not been trained, for each of these voxels. The SVM group had a mean accuracy ranging from 70% to 83%, averaging 77%. As this indicated some systematic difference between the two groups, we ran an ANOVA test on the difference in mean accuracy on the top 1% voxels between the two classifiers for all subjects/ROIs. In this test NN performed reliably better than SVM, across subjects and ROIs, at the 5% significance level, and therefore we will focus the rest of the paper on NN selected voxels.

Interestingly, there was not a great deal of overlap between the groups of most predictive voxels selected using each of the two methods, as evident in the mean overlap of 25%. This was unexpected, given that both methods resort to linear decision boundaries.

2.4   Comparison to a Null Model

As the classifiers for a few of the voxels considered do attain high levels of accuracy, we would like to demonstrate that that does not happen by chance.

In addition, we'd like to know for how many voxels can the effect be considered reliable.

Given the number of voxels involved and the procedure used, a classifier that guessed at random could conceivably attain relatively high accuracies in some small number of voxels. On the other hand, if we observed this happening for a large enough number of voxels, it would be less and less likely.

One way of testing this is to postulate a null model in which every voxel has the same inherent classifiability, and then examine what the probability of obtaining our accuracy results under that model is. By its being small it will be shown that the underlying model is not correct and that the inherent predictability at different voxels varies and can be high for a small group of them.

For a given voxel the accuracy of a classifier is an estimate of an underlying "true" accuracy attainable with that classifier. Given that the classifier is tested over 20 examples, the outcome can be seen as a sample from a binomial variable with 20 trials and probability of success equal to the underlying accuracy. In practice, the 20 trials are not independent, as they are a sequence of leave-1-out trials in which every pair of trials shares all but one training example. As performing the analysis in the latter case is far more complicated and would introduce details specific to the classification method used, we will proceed assuming independence. An empirical argument as to why the results thus obtained can still be used is given later.

Let us assume as a null hypothesis that the accuracy in each voxel is the same, and is some value close to 50%. The latter can be the empirical average of accuracies attained in most ROIs, which is indeed around that value.

We will examine the probability of the higher scores in a ROI under this model, assuming the ROI has n voxels:

$$Pr(1^{st}max \geq a) = 1 - Pr(max < a) = 1 - (cdf(a))^n$$

and, in general,

$$Pr(k^{th}max \geq a) = \Pi_{i=1}^{k}(1 - (cdf(a))^{n-i+1})$$

where $cdf(a) = Pr(X < a)$ when $X\ Binomial(20, \hat{p})$, with $\hat{p}$ being the mean observed accuracy across the ROI.

Under this model, we can calculate the probability that the kth high score would be observed, and thus declare the probability as significant (and unexpected under the model) if it falls belows a certain threshold. For our analysis we used this criterion, and considered an accuracy level significant if had a probability of 5% or less of occurring under the model.

Table 2 contains the results of this experiment discriminated by subject/ROI combination, with the number of voxels considered significant out of the total, the least accuracy attained on one of those voxels and the percentage of voxels out of the total that constitute the group.

As stated before, these results are related to a null model where we assume that the results of each of the 20 leave-1-out trials for a voxel are independent, for simplicity reasons. Treating the case where the trials are not independent is,

Table 2. Breakdown of the number of voxels with significant differences across conditions

Subject#ROI	#significant	out of	accuracy of lowest	top %
1-LIFG	2	395	90	0.5
1-LSTG	0	617	0	0.0
2-LIFG	0	257	0	0.0
2-LSTG	3	543	85	0.6
3-LIFG	3	329	85	0.9
3-LSTG	1	536	95	0.2
4-LIFG	3	257	85	1.2
4-LSTG	0	516	0	0.0
5-LIFG	3	244	85	1.2
5-LSTG	2	204	85	1.0
6-LIFG	1	269	90	0.4
6-LSTG	5	415	85	1.2

in our view, too complicated, so instead we decided to run an empirical test, as follows.

The same setup as for the NN experiments was used, but the data was randomized. Five of the ten examples in each class were selected at random and switched to the other class. In this fashion each classifier was guaranteed to have five correct examples in each class and five incorrect ones, and its expected accuracy should not be more than 50%. Note that this is a case where the results in each of the 20 leave-1-out trials are certainly not independent, as each pair of trials shares most of the training data. The same number of repetitions were made and the results were ranked in the same way as originally.

Looking at the number of voxels given by the null model procedure in the randomized results we notice that their accuracies are far below what could be attained by the null model outputting random classifications.

The point is that the few classification results on the table are deemed improbable under the null model with the independence assumption, and they are far more improbable under a true model where the expected accuracy is 50% and where maximum accuracy practically never rises above 70%. As a consequence, it is reasonable to think that the test based on the independence assumption is conservative.

Moreover, most of the subject/ROI combinations contain a few voxels that are significant by this criterion. Given that our wish is to narrow down the number of voxels to be manually examined, we feel that the possibility of allowing some false positives in the group is acceptable. Nevertheless, we will proceed by considering only the voxels deemed significant through the procedure above.

Our conclusion is that for most voxels there is no inherent discernibility, but that it very probably exists for at least a small subset of them, and that this warrants the exploration described in the previous sections.

2.5 Voxel Characteristics

The group of voxels in consideration in each subject/ROI was picked because the activity in each voxel was discernible across the two experimental conditions. This may have been so because of heightened activity during the processing of ambiguous sentences. However, it may also mean that what stands out is the level of activity during the processing of unambiguous sentences as being unusual.

There are also no guarantees that the identified voxels have a high degree of activation, at least on average. In fact, for each combination of subject and ROI, the group identified almost always has no voxels in common with the subset of the top 1% most active voxels for the same combination, as selected through a t-test. This t-test compares the mean activity during experimental conditions and during a control condition which acts as a baseline.

One possible application of being able to find this group of voxels is to identify common characteristics in their time courses, such as the onset and duration of higher activity in a given experimental condition.

There was no clear trend in the logistic regression coefficients found, which was our initial expectation and would allow us to target a specific temporal region as the source of the difference. In addition, some of the voxels found displayed higher activity for ambiguous sentences, others for unambiguous ones.

The voxels with higher activity in ambiguous sentences did correspond to our expectation of the type of voxel recruited when resource demands are extreme. This is reflected in their not showing a consistent higher activation throughout the task, but rather high activity intervention in short bursts, which presumably would be where resources are more demanded for the ambiguous sentences.

A tentative explanation for this would be that different sentences are not matched for length, and thus the ambiguity, and the corresponding demand for extra resources, can occur in different points in time. This contrasts with the voxels in the most active group, which display consistent high activity through-out most of the of the task, as they are involved in the main processing, and higher activity during processing of ambiguous sentences.

A serious objection may be that many of the voxels selected do not show a clear spatial distribution, contrary to what happens for the active voxels, which tend to cluster tightly and where activation spreads radially as demand increases. While a few are adjacent to such active voxel groups, most are set at locations further away (still inside the ROI). If we expect a model where activity percolates to neighbours from a centre as demand rises, then this is hard to explain.

There were not significant contrasts in accuracy across subjects, ROIs and experimental conditions (across sentences being tested).

2.6 Conclusion and Further Work

We have presented a novel method for identifying voxels with contrasting behaviors across experimental conditions in a fMRI study. Through its use it was possible to find a subset of such voxels in a real dataset.

Unfortunately, further analysis of this subset of voxels across subjects failed to reveal any striking temporal patterns of activity or contrasts in accuracy related to varying experimental variables (condition, subject, ROI). Many of the selected predicting voxels seem to have been picked for reasons not readily observable with the naked eye or easily relatable to the actual processing, which was our original hope. We are uncertain about what attributes of the time series of the predicting voxels are used by the classifier.

We do think, however, that the use of this method may be more successful in somewhat different studies. This would require alterations in experimental design so as to have sentences with similar lengths and positioning of ambiguity. Other possibilities lie in the use of alternative representations of the time series, be it through the use of composite features built from the initial series or through representations incorporating some prior assumptions regarding BOLD response shape. While limiting what can be learned, the latter might not be so restrictive as a full model of the response shape with parameters fitted to the data.

Another possibility would be to use the method to compare not two experimental conditions but all the conditions against the control condition. This could be used in place of t-tests for identifying active voxels as those where there is a greater contrast between activity during the experiment and activity during control, where the activity should be minimal and, above all, unstructured. The t-tests often performed for this purpose take into account solely the mean activity during experiment, and therefore our method would incorporate more information and possibly provide a better result. A completely different avenue rooted in the same idea would be the use of statistical tests of the difference between the distributions of time courses from the two classes for a given voxel (see, for instance, [9]).

Acknowledgments. Francisco Pereira was funded through a PhD scholarship from Fundação para a Ciência e Tecnologia, Portugal, for whose support he is exceedingly grateful. He would also like to thank Tom Minka and the anonymous reviewers for their precious comments and suggestions.

References

1. "Images of Mind", Posner, M.I, Raichle, M.E., W H Freeman (1997)
2. "Functional MRI", Moonen, C.T.W., Bandettini, P.A. (Eds.), Springer Verlag (2000)
3. "Ambiguity in the brain: How syntactically ambiguous sentences are processed.", Mason, R. A., Just, M. A., Keller, T. A., Carpenter, P. A., Manuscript submitted for publication (2001)
4. "Statistical Inference in Functional Magnetic Resonance Imaging", Genovese, C.R., Technical Report 674 (1999), Statistics Department, Carnegie Mellon University
5. "Making large-Scale SVM Learning Practical. Advances in Kernel Methods - Support Vector Learning", Joachims, T., B. Schölkopf and C. Burges and A. Smola (ed.) MIT Press (1999)
6. "Machine Learning", Mitchell, T., McGraw Hill (1997)
7. "On clustering fMRI time series", Goutte, C., Toft, P., Rostrup, E., Nielsen, F. Å., and Hansen, L. K., NeuroImage, 9(3):298-310.

8. "A neural network classifier for cerebral perfusion imaging", Chan KH, Johnson KA, Becker JA, Satlin A, Mendelson J, Garada B, Holman BL., Journal of Nuclear Medicine 35(5):771-4. (1994)
9. "Discrete Multivariate Analysis: Theory and Practice", Bishop, Y.M., Fienberg, S.E., Holland, P.W., MIT Press (1975)

Automatic Construction and Refinement of a Class Hierarchy over Multi-valued Data

Nathalie Pernelle, Marie-Christine Rousset, and Véronique Ventos

Université Paris-Sud
LRI Bat. 490
91 405 Orsay, France
{pernelle,mcr,ventos}@lri.fr

Abstract. In many applications, it becomes crucial to help users to access to a huge amount of data by clustering them in a small number of classes described at an appropriate level of abstraction. In this paper, we present an approach based on the use of two languages of description of classes for the automatic clustering of multi-valued data. The first language of classes has a high power of abstraction and guides the construction of a lattice of classes covering the whole set of the data. The second language, more expressive and more precise, is the basis for the refinement of a part of the lattice that the user wants to focus on.

1 Introduction

The main goal of our approach is to help users to access to a huge amount of multi-valued data by clustering them in a small number of classes organized in a hierarchy and described at an appropriate level of abstraction. The data (i.e. instances) we want to treat are described by a various set of attributes that can be multi-valued and each instance is labelled by the name of a basic type. The approach is based on the use of two languages of description of classes. The first language of classes has a high power of abstraction and guides the construction of a coarse lattice covering the whole set of the data. The second language, more expressive and more precise, is the basis for the refinement of a part of the lattice that the user wants to focus on. This second language actually allows us to distinguish new clusters. Besides, we exploit the fact that the data are labelled: we gather instances sharing the same label in basic classes and we construct clusters of basic classes rather than clusters of instances.

In Sect. 2, we present languages of instances and classes together with some basic operations used in the lattice construction steps. Section 3 describes the first clustering algorithm leading to the construction of a crude lattice. A part of this lattice may be refined using the second clustering algorithm described in Sect. 4. Our approach has been implemented and experimented on real data in the setting of the GAEL project which aims at building flexible electronic catalogs. Our experiments have been conducted on real data coming from the C/Net electronic catalog of computer products (http://www.cnet.com). Experimental results are presented in Sect. 5.

L. De Raedt and A. Siebes (Eds.): PKDD 2001, LNAI 2168, pp. 386–398, 2001.

2   Languages of Instances and Classes

In this section, we define the language of instances, $\mathcal{L}_1$, in which we describe multi-valued data, and the two languages of classes $\mathcal{L}_2$ and $\mathcal{L}_3$ that we use to describe classes over those data, at two levels of abstraction. First, we provide some notations and preliminaries.

2.1   Preliminaries and Notations

Given a language of instances, a language of classes $\mathcal{L}$ defines the expressions that are allowed as *class descriptions*. A class description is intended to represent in an abstract and concise way the properties that are common to the set of its instances. A *membership relation*, denoted by $isa_\mathcal{L}$, establishes the necessary connection between a given language of instances and an associated language of classes $\mathcal{L}$.

Definition 1 (Extension of a class description). *Let I be a set of instances, and C a $\mathcal{L}$ class description. The extension of C w.r.t I is the following set:*

$$ext_I(C) = \{i \in I \mid i\, isa_\mathcal{L}\, C\}$$

The subsumption relation is a preorder relation between class descriptions, induced by the inclusion relation between class extensions.

Definition 2 (Subsumption between classes). *Let C_1 and C_2 be two $\mathcal{L}$ class descriptions. C_1 is subsumed by C_2, denoted $C_1 \preceq_\mathcal{L} C_2$, iff for every set I of instances, $ext_I(C_1) \subseteq ext_I(C_2)$.*

In Sects. 2.3 and 2.4, we will provide a constructive characterization of subsumption for the two languages of classes that we consider.

The notion of *abstraction* of an instance in a language of classes $\mathcal{L}$ corresponds, when it exists, to the most specific class description in $\mathcal{L}$ which it is an instance of.

Definition 3 (Abstraction of an instance). *Let i be an instance, the $\mathcal{L}$ class description C is an* abstraction *of i in $\mathcal{L}$ (for short $C = abs_\mathcal{L}(i)$) iff*

1. *$i\, isa_\mathcal{L}\, C$, and*
2. *if D is a class description such that $i\, isa_\mathcal{L}\, D$, then $C \preceq_\mathcal{L} D$.*

The notion of *least common subsumer* will be the basis for gathering classes in our clustering algorithm.

Definition 4 (Least Common Subsumer).
Let $C_1, \ldots, C_n$ be class descriptions in $\mathcal{L}$. The $\mathcal{L}$ class description C is a least common subsumer *of $C_1, \ldots, C_n$ in $\mathcal{L}$ (for short $C = lcs_\mathcal{L}(C_1, \ldots, C_n)$) iff*

1. *$C_i \preceq_\mathcal{L} C$ for all $1 \leq i \leq n$, and*
2. *if D is a class description satisfying $C_i \preceq_\mathcal{L} D$ for all $1 \leq i \leq n$, then $C \preceq_\mathcal{L} D$*

2.2   The Language of Instances

The data that serve as instances of the classes that we build are typed (i.e., labelled by the name of a basic type) and described by a set of pairs (Attribute, Value). The attributes used for describing the data may vary from an item to another. In addition, an attribute can be multi-valued.

Definition 5 (Terms of $\mathcal{L}_1$). *Let $\mathcal{B}$ be a finite set of basic types, $\mathcal{A}$ a finite set of attributes, and $\mathcal{V}$ a set of values. A term of $\mathcal{L}_1$ is of the form:*

$$\{c, att_1 = V_1, \ldots, att_n = V_n\}$$

where $c \in \mathcal{B}$, $\forall i \in [1..n]$, $att_i \in \mathcal{A}$ and $V_i \subseteq \mathcal{V}$.

The description of an instance is a term of $\mathcal{L}_1$. For example, we can find a product in the C/Net catalog, whose $\mathcal{L}_1$ description is:

$\{RemovableDiskDrive, CD/DVD/Type=\{CDRW\},$
$StorageRemovableType=\{SuperDisk\}, Compatibility=\{MAC, PC\}\}$

In the following, we will consider that the type c of a $\mathcal{L}_1$ description is a boolean attribute.

2.3   The Language of Classes $\mathcal{L}_2$

Definition 6 (Class description in $\mathcal{L}_2$). *A $\mathcal{L}_2$ class description (of size n) is a tuple of attributes $\{att_1, \ldots, att_n\}$, where $\forall i \in [1..n]$, $att_i \in \mathcal{A}$.*

The connection between the language of instances $\mathcal{L}_1$ and the language of classes $\mathcal{L}_2$ is based on the following definition of the membership relation.

Definition 7 (Membership relation for $\mathcal{L}_2$). *Let i be an instance description in $\mathcal{L}_1$. Let C be a $\mathcal{L}_2$ class description: i is an instance of C iff every attribute appearing in C also appears in i.*

The following proposition, whose proof is straightforward, characterizes subsumption, least common subsumer and abstraction in $\mathcal{L}_2$.

Proposition 1 (Properties of $\mathcal{L}_2$).
- *Let C_1 and C_2 be two $\mathcal{L}_2$ class descriptions. $C_1 \preceq_{\mathcal{L}_2} C_2$ iff every attribute of C_2 is also an attribute of C_1.*
- *Let $\{att_1 = V_1, \ldots, att_n = V_n\}$ be an instance description in $\mathcal{L}_1$. Its abstraction in $\mathcal{L}_2$ is unique: it is $\{att_1, \ldots, att_n\}$.*
- *Let $C_1, \ldots, C_n$ be n $\mathcal{L}_2$ class descriptions. Their least common subsumer is unique: it is made of the set of attributes that are common to all the C_i's.*

2.4 The Language of Classes $\mathcal{L}_3$

$\mathcal{L}_3$ is richer than $\mathcal{L}_2$ on different aspects: it makes possible to restrict the possible values of an attribute ; it enables to distinguish the number of values of an attribute through different suffixes $(*, +, ?, \epsilon)$ whose notation is inspired by the one used in XML for describing document type definitions (DTDs), and whose formal semantics corresponds to standard description logics constructors.

Definition 8 (Class description in $\mathcal{L}_3$). *A $\mathcal{L}_3$ class description (of size n) is a tuple*

$$\{att_1^{suff_1} : V_1, \ldots, att_n^{suff_n} : Vn\}$$

where $\forall i \in [1..n]$, $att_i \in \mathcal{A}$, $V_i \subseteq \mathcal{V}$, and $suff_i \in \{*, +, ?, \epsilon\}$

The following definition formalizes the membership relation between an instance and a class description in $\mathcal{L}_3$.

Definition 9 (Membership relation for $\mathcal{L}_3$). *Let i be an instance description in $\mathcal{L}_1$. Let C be a $\mathcal{L}_3$ class description. i is an instance of C iff every attribute in i appears in C and for every term $att^{suff} : V$ appearing in C,*
- when $suff=*$, if there exists V' s.t $att=V' \in i$, then $V' \subseteq V$,
- when $suff=+$, there exists $V' \subseteq V$ s.t $att=V' \in i$,
- when $suff=?$, if there exists V' s.t $att=V' \in i$, then V' is a singleton and $V' \subseteq V$,
- when $suff=\epsilon$, there exists V' singleton s.t $V' \subseteq V$ and $att=V' \in i$.

The product described in 2.2 is an instance of the $\mathcal{L}_3$ class description C_1:

$\{RemovableDiskDrive^\epsilon : \{true\}, CD/DVD/ReadSpeed^? : \{20x, 32x, 24x\},$
$CD/DVD/Type^\epsilon : \{CDROM, CDRW\}, Compatibility^+ : \{MAC, PC\},$
$StorageRemovableType^\epsilon : \{SuperDisk, ZIP, JAZ\}\}$

It represents the set of products that have in their description *(i)* necessarily the monovalued and boolean attribute $RemovableDiskDrive$ whose value must be *true*, *(ii)* possibly the attribute $CD/DVD/ReadSpeed$, and if that is the case, this attribute is monovalued and its value belongs to the set $\{20x, 32x, 24x\}$, *(iii)* necessarily the attribute $CD/DVD/Type$, which is monovalued and takes its value in the set $\{CDROM, CDRW\}$, *(iv)* necessarily the attribute *Compatibility*, which can be multivalued and takes its value(s) in the set $\{MAC, PC\}$, *(v)* necessarily the attribute $StorageRemovableType$, which is monovalued and takes its value in the set $\{SuperDisk, ZIP, JAZ\}$.

The following propositions state the main properties of $\mathcal{L}_3$. Their proofs follow from results in tractable description logics where structural subsumption is complete.

Proposition 2 (Characterization of subsumption in $\mathcal{L}_3$). *Let C_1 and C_2 be two $\mathcal{L}_3$ class descriptions. $C_1 \preceq_{\mathcal{L}_3} C_2$ iff all the attributes appearing in C_1 appear also in C_2 and for every pair $att^{suff} : V$ appearing in C_2,*
- when $suff=*$, if there exists $att^{suff'} : V' \in C_1$, then $V' \subseteq V$,

- *when $suff$=+, there exists $V' \subseteq V$ s.t $att^+ : V' \in C_1$ or $att^\epsilon : V' \in C_1$*
- *when $suff$=?, if there exists $att^{suff'} : V' \in C_1$, then $suff'$=? or $suff'$=ϵ, and $V' \subseteq V$,*
- *when $suff$=ϵ, there exists V' s.t $V' \subseteq V$ and $att^\epsilon : V' \in C_1$.*

Proposition 3 (Characterization of abstraction in $\mathcal{L}_3$). *Let $\{att_1$=$V_1, \ldots, att_n$=$V_n\}$ be an instance description in $\mathcal{L}_1$. Its abstraction in $\mathcal{L}_3$ is unique: $abs_{\mathcal{L}_3} = \{att_1^{suff_1} : V_1, \ldots, att_n^{suff_n} : V_n\}$, where $\forall i \in [1..n]$, if $| V_i | \geq 2$ then $suff_i$=+ else $suff_i$=ϵ.*

Proposition 4 (Characterization of lcs in $\mathcal{L}_3$). *Let $C_1, \ldots, C_n$ be n $\mathcal{L}_3$ class descriptions. Let A be the set of attributes belonging to at least one description C_i. $C_1, \ldots, C_n$ have a unique least common subsumer in $\mathcal{L}_3$, whose description is characterized as follows:*

- *for every attribute $att \in A$, let V be the union of the sets of values associated with att in the class descriptions C_i's: $V = \bigcup_1^n \{v \in V_i \mid att^{suff} : V_i \in C_i\}$.*
  - *$att^\epsilon : V \in lcs(C_1, \ldots, C_n)$ iff $att^\epsilon : V_i \in C_i$ $\forall i \in [1..n]$.*
  - *$att^? : V \in lcs(C_1, \ldots, C_n)$ iff*
    $(\forall i \in [1..n]\ att^* : V_i \notin C_i$ and $att^+ : V_i \notin C_i)$, and
    - *either $\exists i \in [1..n]$ s.t. $att^? : V_i \in C_i$,*
    - *or $\exists i \in [1..n]$ s.t. $att^s : V' \notin C_i$ for any s.*
  - *$att^* : V \in lcs(C_1, \ldots, C_n)$ iff*
    - *either $\exists i \in [1..n]$ s.t. $att^* : V_i \in C_i$,*
    - *or $\exists i \in [1..n]$ s.t. $att^+ : V_i \in C_i$, and $\exists j \in [1..n]$ s.t. $att^? : V_j \in C_j$ or $att^{s'} : V' \notin C_j$ for any suffix s'.*
  - *$att^+ : V \in lcs(C_1, \ldots, C_n)$ iff*
    $\exists i \in [1..n]$ s.t. $att^+ : V_i \in C_i$ and $\forall j \in [1..n]$, $att^+ : V_j \in C_j$ or $att^\epsilon : V_j \in C_j$

For example, if C_2 is the $\mathcal{L}_3$ description:

　　$\{Compatibility^* : \{PC, Unix\}, StorageRemovableType^\epsilon : \{DAT\},$
　　$CompressedCapacity^\epsilon : \{8, 24, 32, 70\}\}$
$lcs(C_1, C_2)$=
　　$\{RemovableDiskDrive^? : \{true\}, CD/DVD/ReadSpeed^? : \{20x, 32x, 24x\},$
　　$CD/DVD/Type^? : \{CDROM, CDRW\}, Compatibility^* : \{MAC, PC, Unix\},$
　　$StorageRemovableType^\epsilon : \{SuperDisk, ZIP, JAZ, DAT\},$
　　$CompressedCapacity^? : \{8, 24, 32, 70\}\}$

3   Construction of a Lattice of $\mathcal{L}_2$ Classes

The goal is to structure a set of data described in $\mathcal{L}_1$ into clusters labelled by $\mathcal{L}_2$ descriptions, and organized in a lattice providing a browsable semantic interface facilitating the access to the data for end-users. We proceed in two steps:

1. In the first step, the data are partitioned according to their type: for each type c, we create a *basic class* named c. Its set of instances, denoted $inst(c)$, is the set of data of type c. Its $\mathcal{L}_2$ description, $desc(c)$, is obtained by computing the least common subsumer of the abstractions of its instances. The result of this step is a set $\mathcal{C}$ of basic classes and a set $\mathcal{A}$ of attributes supporting the $\mathcal{L}_2$ descriptions of the classes of $\mathcal{C}$. For each attribute a, the set $classes(a)$ of basic classes having a in their description is computed. This preliminary clustering step has a linear data complexity.

2. In the second step, a lattice of clusters is constructed by gathering basic classes according to similarities of their $\mathcal{L}_2$ descriptions. In this step, clusters are unions of basic classes. The computational complexity of this step does not depend on the number of initial data but only on the size of the $\mathcal{L}_2$ descriptions of basic classes.

We now detail this second step. A cluster $c_{i_1} \ldots c_{i_k}$ will appear in the lattice if the $\mathcal{L}_2$ descriptions of the classes $c_{i_1} \ldots c_{i_k}$ are judged similar enough to gather their instances. The similarity between class descriptions is stated by attributes in common. However, we take into account only attributes that do not occur in too many classes. For instance, the attribute *price* may appear in all the instances of a catalog describing products, and is therefore not useful to discriminate product descriptions. Among the set $\mathcal{A}$ of attributes, we select meaningful attributes as being the attributes $a \in \mathcal{A}$ such that $\frac{|classes(a)|}{|classes|} \leq s$ where s is a certain threshold (e.g., $s = 0.8$). Let $\mathcal{A}_0$ be the set of meaningful attributes. We redescribe all the basic classes in terms of the attributes of $\mathcal{A}_0$ only: for a basic class c, we call its *short description*, denoted $shortdesc(c)$, the $\mathcal{L}_2$ description of c restricted to the meaningful attributes: $shortdesc(c) = desc(c) \cap \mathcal{A}_0$.

Our clustering algorithm, $\mathcal{L}_2$-*Cluster*, is described in Algorithm 1. It is adapted from a frequent item set algorithm ([2]). It iteratively builds levels of clusters, starting with building the level of the coarsest clusters corresponding to unions of basic classes having atleast one attribute in common. Each iteration k is guided by attribute sets of increasing size k which, being common to some class descriptions, are the support of the creation of a potential node gathering those classes. Among those potential nodes, we effectively add to the lattice those whose $\mathcal{L}_2$ short description is equal to their k-support: the k-support of a node generated at iteration k is the k-itemset supporting the generation of that node. By doing so, we guarantee that the description of the nodes added to the lattice is strictly subsumed by those of their fathers.

Notation: We call a k-itemset a set of attributes of size k. We assume that attributes in itemsets are kept sorted in their lexicographic order. We use the notation $p[i]$ to represent the i-th attribute of the k-itemset p consisting of the attributes $p[1], \ldots, p[k]$ where $p[1] < \ldots < p[k]$.

Figure 1 shows the lattice returned by $\mathcal{L}_2$-*Cluster* when it is applied on $\mathcal{C} = \{c_1, c_2, c_3, c_4, c_5\}$ and $\mathcal{A} = \{a_1, a_2, a_3, a_4\}$ such that: $shortdesc(c_1) = \{a_1, a_2, a_3\}$ $shortdesc(c_2) = \{a_2\}$ $shortdesc(c_3) = \{a_1, a_3\}$ $shortdesc(c_4) = \{a_3, a_4\}$ $shortdesc(c_5) = \{a_1, a_3\}$

Algorithm 1. $\mathcal{L}_2$-Cluster

Require: a set $\mathcal{A}_0$ of meaningful attributes: for each $a \in \mathcal{A}_0$, $classes(a)$ is the set of basic classes of $\mathcal{C}$ whose $\mathcal{L}_2$ short description contains a.

Ensure: return a lattice organized in levels of nodes. Each node n is characterized by $classes(n)$: the basic classes it gathers, and $shortdesc(n)$: the least common subsumer of the short description of the basic classes of the cluster.

1: (* Initialization step gathering the biggest unions of classes having at least one attribute in common:*)
2: $\mathcal{A}_1 \leftarrow \mathcal{A}_0$, $level(1) \leftarrow \emptyset, \ldots, level(|\,\mathcal{C}\,|) \leftarrow \emptyset$
3: **for** every $a \in \mathcal{A}_1$ **do**
4:     let $classes(a) = \{c_1^a, \ldots, c_j^a\}$
5:     let $desc = lcs_{\mathcal{L}_2}(desc(c_1^a), \ldots, desc(c_j^a))$
6:     **if** $desc \cap \mathcal{A}_0 = \{a\}$ **then**
7:       add to $level(j)$ a node n such that:
          $classes(n) = \{c_1^a, \ldots, c_j^a\}$;
          $shortdesc(n) = desc \cap \mathcal{A}_0$;
          $node(\{a\}) = n$
8: $k \leftarrow 1$
9: (* Generation of new nodes supported by $k+1$-itemsets : *)
10: **repeat**
11:     **for** every pair $(p, q) \in \mathcal{A}_k$ **do**
12:       **if** $p[1] = q[1], \ldots, p[k-1] = q[k-1], p[k] < q[k]$ **then**
13:         let $newp = p \cup \{q[k]\}$, and let $\mathcal{S}_k$ be the set of k-subsets of $newp$.
14:         **if** $\mathcal{S}_k \subseteq \mathcal{A}_k$ and $classes(node(p)) \cap classes(q[k]) \neq \emptyset$ **then**
15:           add $newp$ to $\mathcal{A}_{k+1}$
16:           let $\{c_{i_1}, \ldots, c_{i_j}\}$ be $classes(node(p)) \cap classes(q[k])$
17:           let $desc = lcs_{\mathcal{L}_2}(desc(c_{i_1}), \ldots, desc(c_{i_j}))$
18:           **if** $desc = newp$ **then**
19:             add to $level(j)$ a node n such that:
                $classes(n) = \{c_{i_1}, \ldots, c_{i_j}\}$;
                $shortdesc(n) = desc$;
                $node(newp) = n$
20:     $k \leftarrow k + 1$
21: **until** $\mathcal{A}_k = \emptyset$
22: (* Creation of the lattice. For every node n, $Fathers(n)$ group the fathers of n among the nodes of greater levels:*)
23: Initialize $Fathers(n)$ and $AncNotFathers(n)$ to $\emptyset$ for every generated node n.
24: **for** $i = |\,\mathcal{C}\,| - 1$ **downto** 1 **do**
25:     **for** every node $n \in level(i)$ **do**
26:       **for** $j = i + 1$ to $|\,\mathcal{C}\,|$ **do**
27:         **for** every node $m \in level(j)$ **do**
28:           **if** $classes(n) \subset classes(m)$ and $m \notin AncNotFathers(n)$ **then**
29:             add m to $Fathers(n)$
30:             add $Fathers(m) \cup AncNotFathers(m)$ to $AncNotFathers(n)$

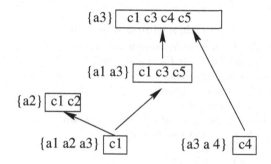

Fig. 1. Example of a lattice constructed by $\mathcal{L}_2$-Cluster

The following proposition summarizes the properties of the algorithm $\mathcal{L}_2$-Cluster.

Proposition 5 (Properties of $\mathcal{L}_2$-Cluster). *Let $\mathcal{H}$ be the lattice returned by $\mathcal{L}_2$-Cluster.*

- *For each node $n \in \mathcal{H}$, let shortdesc(n) and classes(n) be respectively the description and the set of basic classes returned by $\mathcal{L}_2$-Cluster:*

$$shortdesc(n) = lcs_{\mathcal{L}_2}(shortdesc(abst_{\mathcal{L}_2}(i_1)), \dots, shortdesc(abst_{\mathcal{L}_2}(i_k)))$$

where $\{i_1, \dots, i_k\} = \bigcup_{c \in classes(n)} inst(c)$.
- *$\mathcal{H}$ is a Galois lattice, i.e. for every node n, the pair (classes(n), shortdesc(n)) is maximal in the following sense: there is no $m \in \mathcal{H}$ such that classes(n) $\subset$ classes(m) and shortdesc(n) $=$ shortdesc(m), or shortdesc(n) $\prec$ shortdesc(m) and classes(n) $=$ classes(m).*

4   Refinement in $\mathcal{L}_3$

The goal of this step is to refine a part of the lattice $\mathcal{H}$ computed by $\mathcal{L}_2$-*Cluster* based on the more expressive language $\mathcal{L}_3$. This step is achieved after a user chooses one node *Fatn* and one of its descendants *Sonn* in $\mathcal{H}$. Algorithm 2 describes how new nodes are possibly added between *Sonn* and *Fatn*. Those new nodes correspond to clusters whose descriptions in $\mathcal{L}_2$ did not distinguish from those of *Fatn* or *Sonn*, while having distinct descriptions in $\mathcal{L}_3$. A closure operation on those nodes is necessary in order to make their $\mathcal{L}_3$ descriptions maximal w.r.t the union of basic classes which they gather. $\mathcal{L}_3$-*Cluster* applies after the descriptions in $\mathcal{L}_3$ (denoted *desc3* in Algorithm 2) have been computed for *Sonn* and *Fatn*. Those computations are least common subsumer calculations whose overall time cost is polynomial w.r.t to the size and the number of the instances of the basic classes involved in *Fatn*.

Let us illustrate the application of $\mathcal{L}_3$-Cluster on the nodes $c1\,c3\,c5$ and $c1$ of the lattice of Fig. 1, assuming that the $\mathcal{L}_3$ descriptions of the involved basic classes are:

Algorithm 2. $\mathcal{L}_3$-Cluster

Require: Two nodes $Fatn$ and $Sonn$ such that $classes(Sonn) \subset classes(Fatn)$.
Ensure: return a lattice between $Fatn$ and $Sonn$
1: L-Cl $\leftarrow \{classes(Fatn), classes(Sonn)\}$
2: LRes-Cl $\leftarrow$ L-Cl ; Nodes $\leftarrow \{Sonn\}$
3: **for** every node n $\in$ Nodes **do**
4:    **for** every class $c \in classes(Fatn) \setminus classes(n)$ **do**
5:       Change $\leftarrow$ false ; $classes \leftarrow classes(n) \cup \{c\}$
6:       **if** $classes \notin$ L-Cl **then**
7:          L-Cl $\leftarrow$ L-Cl $\cup \{classes\}$
8:          $desc3 \leftarrow lcs_{\mathcal{L}_3}(desc3(n), desc3(c))$
9:          (* Closure operation: *)
10:         **for** every class $Cl \in classes(Fatn) \setminus classes$ **do**
11:            **if** $desc3(Cl) \preceq_{\mathcal{L}_3} desc3$ **then**
12:               add Cl to $classes$; Change $\leftarrow$ true
13:         **if** $classes \notin$ LRes-Cl **then**
14:            add a node p to Nodes such that $classes(p)=classes$ and
               $desc3(p)=desc3$
15:            LRes-Cl $\leftarrow$ LRes-Cl $\cup \{classes(p)\}$
16:            **if** Change = true **then**
17:               L-Cl $\leftarrow$ L-Cl $\cup classes(p)$
18:   Suppress n from Nodes

$desc(c_1)=\{att_1^+ : \{v1, v3\}, att_2^+ : \{v2, v4\}, att_3^\epsilon : \{v6\}\}$ $desc(c_3)=\{att_1^\epsilon : \{v3\},$
$att_2^? : \{v4\}, att_3^\epsilon : \{v7\}\}$ $desc(c_5)=\{att_1^\epsilon : \{v5\}, att_3^\epsilon : \{v7, v8\}\}$.
LRes-Cl and L-Cl are initialized to $\{\{c1, c3, c5\}, \{c1\}\}$.
• Gathering $c3$ with $c1$ is considered first:
$desc3=\{att_1^+ : \{v1, v3\}, att_2^* : \{v2, v4\}, att_3^\epsilon : \{v6, v7\}\}$, $classes=\{c1, c3\}$
Since $desc3(c5)$ is not subsumed by $desc3$, the new node $c1c3$ is added.
LRes-Cl is updated to $\{\{c1, c3, c5\}, \{c1\}, \{c1, c3\}\}$.
• Gathering $c5$ with $c1$ is now considered:
$desc3=\{att_1^+ : \{v1, v3, v5\}, att_2^* : \{v2, v4\}, att_3^\epsilon : \{v6, v7, v8\}\}$, $classes=\{c1, c5\}$
Since $desc3(c3)$ is subsumed by $desc3$, $c3$ is added to $classes$, which is updated
to $\{c1, c3, c5\}$. The node corresponding to $c1\,c5$ is not added since it is not
closed, the node corresponding to its closure $c1\,c3\,c5$ is not added either because
$\{c1, c3, c5\}$ is already in LRes-Cl.

The following proposition summarizes the main properties of $\mathcal{L}_3$-*Cluster*.

Proposition 6 (Properties of $\mathcal{L}_3$-Cluster). *Let $\mathcal{C}_1$ be the set of basic classes
of the father node. Let $\mathcal{C}_2$ ($\mathcal{C}_2 \subset \mathcal{C}_1$) be the set of basic classes of the son node.
Let $\mathcal{H}_3$ be the lattice returned by $\mathcal{L}_3$-Cluster.*

– *For each node $n \in \mathcal{H}_3$, let $desc3(n)$ and $classes(n)$ be respectively the description and the set of basic classes returned by $\mathcal{L}_3$-Cluster:*

$$desc3(n) = lcs_{\mathcal{L}_3}(abst_{\mathcal{L}_3}(i_1), \ldots, abst_{\mathcal{L}_3}(i_k))$$

where $\{i_1, \ldots, i_k\} = \bigcup_{c \in classes(n)} inst(c).$

- $\mathcal{H}_3$ *is a complete Galois lattice, i.e. for every node n, the pair* $(classes(n),$ $desc3(n))$ *is maximal, and* $\mathcal{H}_3$ *contains every node verifying the maximality criteria and whose set of classes includes* C_2 *and are included in* C_1.

5 Complexity and Experimental Results

The following results come directly from known results in description logic and in Galois lattice. Since $\mathcal{L}_3$ is a subset of the C-CLASSIC description logic [7], the complexity of checking subsumption in $\mathcal{L}_3$ is quadratic w.r.t the maximal size of class descriptions and computing the lcs of $\mathcal{L}_3$ descriptions is linear in the number of descriptions and quadratic in their size. The worst time complexity of $\mathcal{L}_2$-Cluster is exponential in the maximal size of the basic classes $\mathcal{L}_2$ descriptions. The worst time complexity of $\mathcal{L}_3$-*Cluster* is exponential w.r.t $\mid classes(Fatn) \mid$ $- \mid classes(Sonn) \mid$.

We have evaluated our approach using a real dataset composed of 2274 computer products extracted from the C/Net catalog. Each product is described using a subset of 234 attributes, possibly multi-valued. There are 59 types of products and each product is labelled by one and only one type. The goal of the experiment was twofold: to assess the efficiency and the simplicity of the lattice for the first clustering step ($\mathcal{L}_2$-Cluster) and to show the accuracy of the refinement of a part of the lattice using the second clustering step ($\mathcal{L}_3$-Cluster).

In order to make the $\mathcal{L}_2$ lattice even simpler, the number of nodes obtained with $\mathcal{L}_2$-Cluster may be parametrized by a threshold n used to restrict the nodes that appear in the lattice to gather at least n basic classes ([13]). Figure 2 shows that, as it is mentionned in [15], this quantitative criteria allows us to significantly decrease the size of the lattice. Figure 3 illustrates the simplicity of the $\mathcal{L}_2$ descriptions and the significance of the nodes.

$\mathcal{L}_3$-Cluster allows to distinguish nodes that cannot be distinguished by $\mathcal{L}_2$-Cluster. For instance, if $\mathcal{L}_3$-Cluster is applied when an end-user chooses to refine the $\mathcal{L}_2$ lattice between the node (a) and the node (b) in Fig. 3, the aggregation of all types of drivers (i.e. *RemovableTapeDrive*, *RemovableDiskDrive* and *HardDiskDrive*) is part of the $\mathcal{L}_3$ lattice. This new cluster appears for the following reasons: no driver is described using the attributes *Stor.Controller/ RAIDLevel*, *Networking/DataLinkProtocol* or *Networking/Type* (those at-

Threshold	1	2	3	4	5
Number of nodes	119	60	24	13	9
Maximal depth	4	3	2	1	1
Running Times (s)	12.3	10.4	2.1	1.1	1

Fig. 2. Quantitative results of $\mathcal{L}_2$-Cluster

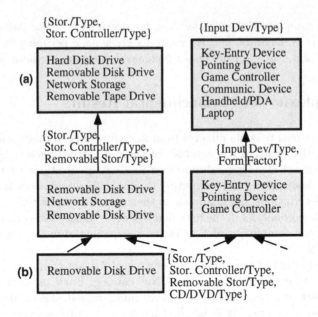

Fig. 3. A part of the $\mathcal{L}_2$ lattice for C/net (n=3)

tributes were optional in $\mathcal{L}_3$ description of (a)). In addition, the value $SCSI$ for the attribute $Stor.Controller/Type$ is not a possible value for a driver.

6   Conclusion and Discussion

This paper has proposed an approach to organize into clusters large sets of semistructured data. The scaling up of the approach is made possible because its complexity is remained in control in different ways: (1) the data are aggregated into basic classes and the clustering applies on the set of those basic classes instead of applying on the data set (2) the two-step clustering method first builds a coarse hierarchy, based on a simple language for describing the clusters, and uses a more elaborate language for refining a small subpart of the hierarchy delimited by two nodes.

Related Work: Our work can be compared with existing work in machine learning based on more expressive languages than propositional language and/or using a shift of representation. Most work on expressive languages has been developped in a supervised setting (e.g. Inductive Logic Programming), while little work exists in an unsupervised setting. We can cite KBG [4], TIC [5] and [11] which perform clustering in a relational setting. The main difference with our approach is that they use a distance as a numerical estimation of similarity. Although the best representation of a cluster is the least common subsumer of its instances, they approximate it numerically by the cluster centroid (i.e., the point that minimizes the sum of squared distances). The reason is that, in contrast with our setting where the lcs computation in $\mathcal{L}_3$ is polynomial, lcs computing in their first-order language may be exponential. KLUSTER [10] refines a basic taxonomy of concepts in the setting of a description logic for which computing lcs is polynomial. In KLUSTER, the clusters are not unions but subconcepts of primitive concepts, and the refinement aims at learning discriminating definitions of mutually disjoint subconcepts of a same concept. As for the use of a shift of representation, it is used in supervised learning in order to increase accuracy (i.e. the proportion of correctly predicted concepts in a set of test examples) [8,14] or to search efficiently a reduced space of concepts [9,6]. In unsupervised learning, shift of representational bias may be used to change the point of view about the data. For instance, Cluster/2 [12] provides a user with a set of parameters about his preferences on the concepts to be created. Finally, the two-step clustering approach proposed in [1] is similar in spirit with our clustering in $\mathcal{L}_2$ since it first identifies basic clusters (as high density clusters) before building more general clusters that are unions of those basic clusters.

Perspectives: We plan to extend our current work to take nested attributes and textual values into account in $\mathcal{L}_3$ in order to fully deal with XML data. Another relevant perspective of this work is the discovery of associations [3].

References

1. R. Agrawal, J. Gehrke, D. Gunopulos, and P. Raghavan. Automatic subspace clustering of high dimensional data for data mining applications. *SIGMOD Record*, 27:94–105, 1998.
2. R. Agrawal and R. Srikant. Fast algorithms for mining association rules. *VLDB-94*.
3. F. Baader Computing a minimal representation of the subsumption lattice of all conjunctions of concepts defined in a terminology. *KRUSE-95*.
4. G. Bisson. Conceptual clustering in a first order logic representation. *ECAI-92*.
5. H. Blockeel, L. De Raedt, and J. Ramon. Top-down induction of clustering trees. *ICML-98*.
6. P. Brézellec and H. Soldano. Tabata: a learning algorithm performing a bidirectional search in a reduced search space using a tabu strategy. *ECAI-98*.
7. W. W. Cohen and H. Hirsh. Learning the CLASSIC description logic: Theoretical and experimental results. *KR-94*.
8. W. Van de Velde. Learning through progressive refinement. *European Working Session on Learning (EWSL'98)*,Pitman editor.
9. J. Ganascia. Tdis: an algebraic formalization. *IJCAI-93*.
10. J. U. Kietz and K. Morik. A polynomial approach to the constructive induction of structural knowledge. *Machine Learning*, 14(2):193–217, 1994.
11. Mathias Kirsten and Stephan Wrobel. Extending k-means clustering to first-order representations. *ILP 2000*.
12. R.S. Michalski and R.E. Stepp. Learning from observation: Conceptual clustering. *Machine learning: An artificial intelligence approach Vol 1*, Morgan Kaufmann editor, 1983.

13. N. Pasquier, Y.Bastide, R.Taouil and L. Lakhal. Efficient mining of association rules using closed itemset lattices. *Information Systems (IS) Vol 24*, 1999.
14. P. E. Utgoff. Shift of bias for inductive concept learning. *Machine learning: An artificial intelligence approach Vol. 2*, Morgan Kaufmann editor, 1986.
15. R. Wille. Restructuring lattice theory. *Symposium on Ordered Sets*, Boston, 1982.

Comparison of Three Objective Functions for Conceptual Clustering

Céline Robardet* and Fabien Feschet

Laboratoire d'Analyse des Systèmes de Santé
Université Lyon 1
UMR 5823, bât 101, 43 bd du 11 nov. 1918
69622 Villeurbanne cedex
FRANCE

Abstract. Unsupervised clustering algorithms aims to synthesize a dataset such that similar objects are grouped together whereas dissimilar ones are separated. In the context of data analysis, it is often interesting to have tools for interpreting the result. There are some criteria for symbolic attributes which are based on the frequency estimation of the attribute-value pairs. Our point of view is to integrate the construction of the interpretation inside the clustering process. To do this, we propose an algorithm which provides two partitions, one on the set of objects and the second on the set of attribute-value pairs such that those two partitions are the most associated ones. In this article, we present a study of several functions for evaluating the intensity of this association.

Keywords. Unsupervised clustering, conceptual clustering, association measures.

1   Introduction

One of the main data mining process consists in reducing the dimension of a dataset to increase knowledge and understanding. When no prior information are available, unsupervised clustering can be used to discover the underlying structure of the data. Indeed, those algorithms aim to build a partition on the objects such that the *most* similar objects belong to a same cluster, and the *most* dissimilar belong to different clusters. Hence, those procedures synthesize the data into few clusters. There is however no consensus of the algorithm to use because there are many ways to evaluate the proximity between objects and the quality of a partition. Furthermore, the cardinality of the set of all possible partitions increases exponentially with the size n of the set of objects, which leads to use fastest but often rough approximated optimization procedures.

Among the algorithms, we can distinguish two main families. The first one gathers *numerical* algorithms. They can be characterized by the computation of

---

* Corresponding author, e-mail: robardet@univ-lyon1.fr

L. De Raedt and A. Siebes (Eds.): PKDD 2001, LNAI 2168, pp. 399–410, 2001.

a distance between pairs of objects. This synthesizes all the dimensions of the problem into a single one. The distance is used to construct the partition. For example in the K-MEANS algorithm [JD88], the distance is the Euclidean one computed between the descriptive vectors of the objects embedded in the metric space defined by the attributes. The objective function is equal to the sum over all the clusters of the intra-class variance. Unfortunately, this function favors over-cut partitions and it is necessary to fix the number K of clusters before using it. In the case of the EM algorithm [CS96], the distance is evaluated by a multivariate Gaussian density. At each step, the memberships of the objects to the different clusters are evaluated, just as the parameters of the Gaussian densities associated to each cluster. But this algorithm is still dependent on an *a priori* number of clusters.

Whereas *statistical* clustering methods are often constructed to process datasets described by continuous features, *conceptual* clustering methods mainly focus on symbolic features [TB01,BWL95]. They aim to provide a better integration between the clustering and the interpretation stages of the data analysis process. Each feature is an attribute of discrete type having several different values. Attribute-value pairs are used in the construction of the clustering. Those algorithms built a hierarchy of concepts using probabilistic representation based on a conditional probabilistic vector of the apparition of the several attribute-value pairs in the several clusters. In COBWEB [Fis87,Fis96], the objective function measures the average increase in the prediction of attribute-value pairs knowing the partition. The optimization procedure is incremental but order dependent.

Sharing the same aims than *conceptual* clustering (dealing with symbolic features and combining an interpretation with the obtained partition), we focus in this article on a non hierarchical approach of the problem. This type of methods consists in the construction of two linked partitions, called a bi-partition, one on the set of objects and the second one on the whole set of attribute-value pairs. The interest of such a method is to discover the underlying structure of the data on the point of view of the objects as well as the descriptors. Thus, we search a bi-partition such that a unique cluster of objects fits a unique cluster of attribute-value pairs and conversely. Consequently, each partition is an interpretation of the other one, making easier the understanding of the results. Such methods have already been built. The simultaneous clustering algorithm [Gov84] is an adaptation of the *nuées dynamiques* of Diday [CDG$^+$88] for symbolic data. It consists in searching a bi-partition with the partition of the set of objects in *a priori* K clusters and the partition of the attribute-value pairs in L clusters. An *ideal* binary table of dimensions $K \times L$ is constructed, such that the gap between the initial data table structured by the two partitions and the *ideal* table is minimized. This method needs to *a priori* fix the number of clusters (K, L) of the bi-partition and the iterative procedure leads to a local optimum. To avoid those drawbacks, we propose a new algorithm based on the optimization of an objective function which does not need to *a priori* fixed the number of clusters. We focus in this article on the construction of such a function.

The contributions of this paper are, first an algorithm without any prescribed number of clusters, second a modification of association measures on co-occurrence tables to increase their discrimination power, and third an empirical study showing the relevance of the approach.

2   An Algorithm for the Construction of a Bi-partition

A basic clustering algorithm consists in optimizing a function which rewards partitions with interested properties. To define our algorithm, we need to construct a function for evaluating the quality of a bi-partition. This function must favor bi-partitions which satisfy the following property,

Property The functional link, which allows to restore one partition on the basis of the knowledge of the second one, must be as strong as possible. Furthermore, both partitions of the bi-partition must have the same number of clusters.

We denote by f such a function over $\mathcal{P}_\mathcal{O} \times \mathcal{P}_\mathcal{Q}$, where $\mathcal{P}_\mathcal{O}$ is the set of partitions on the set of objects, and $\mathcal{P}_\mathcal{Q}$ is the set of partitions on the set of attribute-value pairs: $f : \mathcal{P}_\mathcal{O} \times \mathcal{P}_\mathcal{Q} \to \mathbb{R}$. Let us denote by P an element of $\mathcal{P}_\mathcal{O}$ and Q one of $\mathcal{P}_\mathcal{Q}$.

This function must satisfy some properties. Such properties have been defined in supervised clustering, where the function measures the agreement between two partitions of the same set: the one given by the *class variable* and the one constructed by the supervised clustering method. Those properties are the followings [BFOS84,Weh96]:

- The function is maximal when to each cluster of P (resp. Q) is associated one and only one cluster of Q (resp. P)
- When every clusters of P can be associated to each cluster of Q indiscriminately, then the objective function must be minimum.
- The function must be invariant under permutation of the clusters of $\mathcal{O}$ and under permutation of the clusters of $\mathcal{Q}$.
- The function must be able to compare two bi-partitions with different numbers of clusters.

Nevertheless, we must add two new properties due to the fact that in our problem none of the two partitions constituting a bi-partition is *a priori* fixed. The function must also check the two following ones when it is maximal:

- Each object of a cluster of P owns all the attribute-value pairs belonging to its associated cluster of Q.
- Each attribute-value pair of a cluster of Q is owned by all the objects of its associated cluster of P.

Having define the function f to evaluate the quality of a bi-partition, the clustering algorithm, we propose, is based on a *gradient like* optimization. We thus propose the following algorithm,

> *Let (P_0, Q_0) be a randomized initial bi-partition*
> *Repeat*
> $\quad Q_i$ *is fixed, we search* $P_{i+1} = \min\limits_{P_{i+1} \in \mathcal{P}_O} f(P_{i+1}, Q_i)$
> $\quad P_{i+1}$ *is fixed, we search* $Q_{i+1} = \min\limits_{Q_{i+1} \in \mathcal{P}_Q} f(P_{i+1}, Q_{i+1})$
> *Until a convergence criterion is met*

To modify a given bi-partition (P_i, Q_i), several ways are possible; either computing (P_{i+1}, Q_{i+1}) in one step, or computing (P_{i+1}, Q_{i+1}) in two steps as in the proposed algorithm. We choose this method to have a more tractable optimization problem and also, it is a way to fix one partition as a reference so to optimize the functional link with only one unknown.

3   The Kind of Functions to Use

The previous properties are partially satisfied by association measures, which have been built to evaluate the link between two attributes of discrete type. Those coefficients are widely used in supervised clustering [LdC96], whereas few unsupervised clustering algorithms used them. RIFFLE [MH91] uses Guttman's λ to measure the link between the partition (considered as an attribute) and each original discrete attribute. Such association measures can be adapted to be used as objective function in the search of a bi-partition.

The research of criteria, on one hand sufficiently complex to discriminate the different situations encountered and in the other hand sufficiently simple to allow intuitive interpretation, led to the creation of a lot of measures. Those measures have been constructed on contingency tables. After presenting some of them, we show how we construct the co-occurrence table and we modify them in the clustering context.

3.1   Some Association Measures

In the following of the paper, p_{ij} is an estimate of the probability that the value i of an attribute X, and the value j of an attribute Y arise simultaneously. n is the cardinal of the set of objects. (p_{ij}) define the so-called contingency table with $p_{.j} = \sum_i p_{ij}$ and $p_{i.} = \sum_j p_{ij}$ the margins.

A first group of association measures gather *divergence measures between probability distributions*. Those coefficients evaluate the association between a couple of attributes by measuring the gap between the current contingency table constructed on the two attributes, and the one obtained in case of independence. The situation of independence is easily characterized by $p_{ij} = p_{i.} \times p_{.j}$. A well-known measure of divergence is the χ^2,

$$\chi^2 = n \left[\sum_i \sum_j \frac{p_{ij}^2}{p_{i.} p_{.j}} - 1 \right]$$

This measure doesn't allow to compare contingency tables of different sizes (with different numbers of row and/or column), that is why we prefer to use a normalized version of this measure, the Tschuprow coefficient,

$$T = \sqrt{\frac{\chi^2}{n\sqrt{(p-1)(q-1)}}}$$

where p and q are the numbers of different values of each attributes.

A second class of measures gather *connection indices*. Those coefficients evaluate the gap with the situation of functional dependency characterized by a function f linking Y to X, $Y = f(X)$.

Goodman and Kruskal [GK54] built a family of such indices denoted by *measure of proportional reduction in error* (or PRE). Those coefficients have an easy interpretation due to the fact that they evaluate a prediction rule in terms of probability of error. The construction of such measures requires the definition of three elements:

- A prediction rule (C) of Y when X is known
- A prediction rule (I) of Y when X is unknown
- A measure of the error associated to the prediction rules

The PRE measure is then equal to:

$$\frac{error(I) - error(C)}{error(I)}$$

Guttman's λ is a PRE measure. It consists in predicting the value of an attribute by the most frequent one:

$$\lambda = \frac{(1 - \max_j p_{.j}) - \left(1 - \sum_i p_{i.} \max_j \frac{p_{.j}}{p_{i.}}\right)}{1 - \max_j p_{.j}}$$

Goodman and Kruskal proposed another more accurate coefficient called τ_b. Whereas λ focuses only on the most frequent value, τ_b measure takes into account all the structure of the distribution:

$$\tau_b = \frac{\sum_i \sum_j \frac{p_{ij}^2}{p_{i.}} - \sum_j p_{.j}^2}{1 - \sum_j p_{.j}^2}$$

This way to define connection indices can be generalized using the notion of uncertainties. We call uncertainty measure a concave function $I()$ on probability distributions. For example, the Shannon entropy $(-\sum_i p_i \log p_i)$, and the quadratic entropy $(2[1 - \sum p_i^2])$ belong to this class.

The gain of uncertainties allows to measure the reduction in error of the prediction of Y knowing X. It is equal to $\Delta I(Y \mid X) = I(P(Y)) - E_X[I(P(Y \mid X))]$.

We always have $\Delta I(Y \mid X) \geq 0$. Moreover, if X and Y are independent then $\Delta I(Y \mid X) = 0$. The converse is true if I is strictly concave. An index of connection is then defined by $C(Y \mid X) = \frac{\Delta I(Y \mid X)}{I(P(Y))}$.

The τ_b coefficient is obtained when $I\left(P\left(Y\right)\right) = 1 - \sum_j p_{.j}^2$ When using the Shannon entropy as $I\left(P\left(Y\right)\right)$, we obtain the uncertainty coefficient:

$$U = \frac{\sum_i p_{i.} \log p_{i.} + \sum_j p_{.j} \log p_{.j} - \sum_i \sum_j p_{ij} \log p_{ij}}{\sum_j p_{.j} \log p_{.j}}$$

3.2   How to Build the Co-occurrence Table

In our problem, we search a bi-partition constituted of two partitions such that their association is maximal. However, whereas the previous measures are based on contingency table, i.e. a table crossing two partitions on a same set, the partitions considered in our problem are built on separate sets which have a semantic link expressed through the data table. This link allows us to construct a co-occurrence table (η_{ij}). We consider h attributes V_i with values in a discrete space dom_i ($V_i : \mathcal{O} \to \mathrm{dom}_i$) and denote by $\mathcal{Q}$ the set of attribute-value pairs $\left(\mathcal{Q} = \biguplus_{i=1}^h \mathrm{dom}_i\right)$. Using the previous notations, we built a co-occurrence table between a partition $P = (P_1, \ldots, P_K)$ on the set $\mathcal{O}$ of objects and a partition $Q = (Q_1, \ldots, Q_K)$ on the set $\mathcal{Q}$ such that the elements of this table equal the number of attribute-value pairs of Q_j taken by the objects of P_i. More precisely,

$$\eta_{ij} = \sum_{x \in P_i} \sum_{y \in Q_j} \sum_{i=1}^h \delta_{V_i(x),y}$$

where δ is the Kronecker[1] symbol. We also use the following notations: $\eta_{i.} = \sum_{j=1}^K \eta_{ij}$, $\eta_{.j} = \sum_{i=1}^K \eta_{ij}$ and $\eta_{..} = \sum_{i=1}^K \sum_{j=1}^K \eta_{ij} = \sharp(\mathcal{O}) \times h$.

Then, we compute the previous measures by substituting in the formulas p_{ij}, $p_{i.}$, $p_{.j}$ and n by respectively η_{ij}, $\eta_{i.}$, $\eta_{.j}$ and $\eta_{..}$. Nevertheless, the computation of the *Uncertainty* coefficient requires the normalization of the co-occurrence table. That is why we divide every η_{ij} by $\eta_{..}$ when computing this coefficient.

3.3   Adaptation of Functions

Recall that the association measures only partially check the necessary properties. On a contingency table the notion of *purity* has no meaning whereas it is a key point in our problem when wanting to compare tables of different sizes. A cluster of objects is all the more *pure* since the objects have similar description on all the attributes. Similarly, a cluster of attribute-value pairs is all the more *pure* since the attribute-value pairs are taken by the same set of objects.

For example, we consider a data table composed of three *pure* clusters on objects and attribute-value pairs, and the perfect bi-partition associated (see Fig. 1 left). In this case, the association measure is maximum. If we merge two classes of objects, and the two associated classes of attribute-value pairs (see Fig. 1 right), the association measure is still maximum. Consequently, those two different situations are not discriminated by the measure.

---

[1] $\delta_{V_i(x),y} = 1$ if $V_i(x) = y$, $\delta_{V_i(x),y} = 0$ *otherwise*

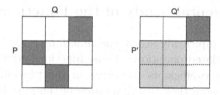

Fig. 1. A maximum value for two different situations

To overcome this drawback, we use a diversity measure between a cluster of objects and a cluster of attribute-value pairs to map η_{ij} into $[0,1]$ such that η_{ij} is maximum when the cluster is *pure*.

Since each object owns a unique value per attribute, η_{ij} is maximum when each object of P_i owns, for all the attributes represented in Q_j, a value belonging to Q_j. In this case, $\eta_{ij} = \sharp(P_i) \times \sum_i \left(1 - \delta_{V_i^{-1}(Q_j),\emptyset}\right)$, that is the number of objects times the number of different attributes belonging to Q_j. Thus in general η_{ij} divided by $\sharp(P_i) \times \sum_i \left(1 - \delta_{V_i^{-1}(Q_j),\emptyset}\right)$ belongs to $[0,1]$. However, this is not sufficient to discriminate the cases of Fig. 1. We must penalize Q_j with several values per attribute to solve the problem. We decide to penalize it by $\prod_{a \in H_j} \sharp(\mathrm{dom}_a \cap Q_j)$, with $H_j = \{a \in [1,h] \mid \mathrm{dom}_a \cap Q_j \neq \emptyset\}$. It is equal to one only when there is one value per attribute in Q_j and is greater than one otherwise.

Consequently to map η_{ij} into $[0,1]$, we replace η_{ij} by the following diversity measure in the co-occurrence table,

$$\frac{\eta_{ij}}{\sharp(P_i) \times \sum_i \left(1 - \delta_{V_i^{-1}(Q_j),\emptyset}\right) \times \prod_{a \in H_j} \sharp(\mathrm{dom}_a \cap Q_j)}$$

Nevertheless, modifying the values in the co-occurrence table does not influence the value of the association measure used. Indeed, association measures rely on the evaluation of the similarity between η_{ij} and $\eta_i.$ and/or $\eta._j$. That is why in order to take into account the effect of the diversity measure we have to compute a global index of diversity. It consists in the embedding of the co-occurrence table in the set of assignment matrices to force a functional link between the elements of a bi-partition. The set of possible assignment matrices $A = (A_{ij})$ contains all matrices such that

$$\forall i, \exists! j \quad such \quad that \quad A_{ij} = \eta_{ij} \neq 0 \quad and \quad \forall j, \exists! i \quad such \quad that \quad A_{ij} = \eta_{ij} \neq 0$$

Among the set of assignment matrices, we choose the one whose coefficients average is maximum. The global index of diversity is this average. Notice that the association measures belong to $[0,1]$ and that the average of (A_{ij}) also belongs to $[0,1]$. We thus weight the association measures by multiplying it by this global diversity index.

4   An Experimental Study of the Functions

In this section, we empirically study the functions regarding their capabilities to discriminate associated partitions. Those functions are the τ_b, the *Tschuprow* and the *Uncertainty* coefficients. Whereas in the previous section we modify those functions to ensure their discrimination of the *pure* bi-partition, we study in this section the regularity of those functions over others bi-partitions.

4.1   Study of the Quality Indices of the Partitions

In [RF00] we have proposed a graph theoretical approach to define an order on the set of partitions. It consists in constructing a data table such that there exist a bi-partition whose clusters are all pure. This bi-partition is then used as a reference called *ideal* bi-partition. A distance between each partition of $\mathcal{P}_\mathcal{O}$ and the partition on $\mathcal{O}$ belonging to the *ideal* bi-partition is then computed to order $\mathcal{P}_\mathcal{O}$. On a same manner, a distance between each partition of $\mathcal{P}_\mathcal{Q}$ and the partition on $\mathcal{Q}$ belonging to the *ideal* bi-partition is also computed. The distances used [RF00] are well discriminant and evaluate the proximity between two partitions in terms of similarity on the variables and objects shared between the closest clusters of both partitions.

That is why we study the discrimination power of a function on a set of partitions through the link between function's values and those orders on the set of partitions.

The following graphs represent the variations of the measures regarding the distance of the partitions to the associated *ideal* one. The partitions on the set of objects $\mathcal{O}$ are ordered on abscissa axis (right). On the ordinate axis (left) are ordered partitions on the set of attribute-value pairs $\mathcal{Q}$. On the z-axis is plotted the value of the function computed with the two partitions. The partitions are based on a 12×12 data table composed of three *pure* clusters on each set. In a first step, we have generated all the partitions on each set. But given the fact the number of partitions on each set is huge (more than 4 millions), we could not plot the graphs over the whole set of couples of partitions. That is why we selected a subset of 100 partitions in each set. We did not choose those partitions randomly for two reasons. First, if we pick up partitions in a uniform manner, we almost obtain partitions with *worst* values regarding the function and the distance. Indeed, among the 4 millions of partitions there are lots of bad ones. Secondly, we do not know the distribution of *good* partitions. Consequently, we chose partitions among the exhaustive set such that the partitions are well spread over the distance.

The Tschuprow measure (Fig. 2 left) seems smooth and regular over the couples of partitions. The incline of the surface is correctly oriented, with high values for *good* partitions and slow decrease towards the *bad* ones. Nevertheless, the slope is not very important. This could be an obstacle for the optimization procedure. In fact, in case of an optimization based on local (with respect to the distance) descent, the bumpiness of the function might be an obstacle. However, when considering stochastic procedures, like genetic algorithms, the slope of the

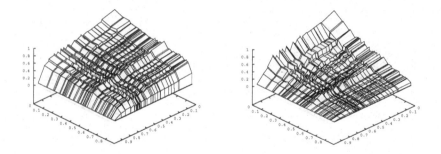

Fig. 2. Tschuprow and Tschuprow adapted

surface induces the survival of better individuals (with respect to the distance). There is a step in the border of the graph which means that a small increase of the quality of *very bad* partitions leads to an important increase of the objective measure. The modification of the measure (Fig. 2 right) globally increases the slope of the surface. Whereas the surface is a little bit more bumpy, the stochastic optimization should be more easy on this function.

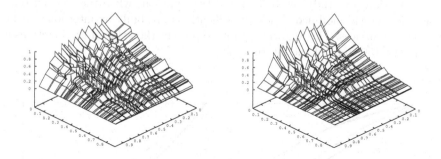

Fig. 3. τ_b (left) and τ_b adapted (right)

On Fig. 3 (left) we can see that the τ_b measure discriminates almost well the couples of partitions. The highest values of the function are obtained for *good* bi-partitions, and the values of the function decrease with the distance. The rough patches of the surface are more important than for the *Tschuprow* measure but the slope is much more important. The diversity coefficient (Fig. 3 right) flatten the surface partially erasing the bumps.

The results obtained with the *Uncertainty* measure (Fig. 4 left and right) are very similar to those given by the τ_b function. It is visually perceptible that

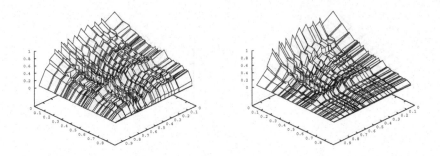

Fig. 4. Uncertainty coefficient original (left) and adapted (right)

those functions are similar each others and different to the *Tschuprow* measure. This is due to the fact that they do not evaluate the same property on the co-occurrence table. Whereas the *Tschuprow* evaluates the distance between the current table and the one corresponding to the independence situation, the two others evaluate the strength of the *functional* link between the two partitions.

4.2 Smoothness of the Functions

In this section, we study the behavior of the functions when the co-occurrence matrix is slightly modified. Those modifications are built by interpolation between two matrices. The following graphs represent the value of the functions at each of the 150 steps of the interpolation.

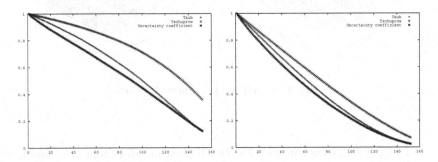

Fig. 5. Linear interpolation to Gaussian matrix non adapted vs adapted

In Fig. 5, we interpolate the matrix corresponding to the *ideal* bi-partition to a Gaussian modification of it. The interpolation is linear. We do this to measure the resistance of the function to a regular destruction of the functional link.

The three functions decrease quasi linearly (Fig. 5 left). This graph confirms that τ_b and *Uncertainty* coefficients have a similar behavior, which is rather different than those of the *Tschuprow* measure. Its decrease is slower regarding the two other functions. The diversity coefficient (Fig. 5 right) modifies the curves so that they have a similar linear slope.

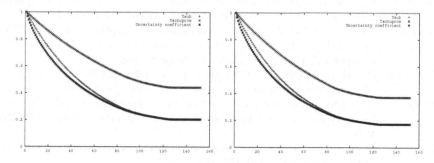

Fig. 6. Random interpolation to random matrix non adapted vs adapted

In Fig. 6, we interpolate the *ideal* co-occurrence matrix to a totally random one. The interpolation is linear for all cells of the matrix, but each cell has a randomly chosen number of steps. Consequently each cell of the matrix has its own speed of interpolation. This case is far less regular than the previous one.

Along the slight modifications of the matrix, the functions decrease more quickly than in the previous interpolation (Fig. 6 left). Nevertheless, the functions are still very smooth. The behavior of the functions is not affected by the diversity coefficient (Fig. 6 right).

Finally, the proposed modification of the association measures leads to an increase in their discrimination power but keeping their good behavior in resistance and regularity towards the measure of a functional link.

5   Conclusion and Perspective

In this article, we have presented an algorithm for finding bi-partition in unsupervised clustering. It is based on the search of a couple of the *most* associated partitions. Those partitions are based on the set of objects and the set of attribute-value pairs which are linked in the original dataset. In order to find this bi-partition, we propose three objective functions to optimize. We have adaptated the *Tschuprow*, the τ_b and the *Uncertainty* measures to the unsupervised clustering problem. The experimentation we provide, give two main information. First we notice that the τ_b measure and the *Uncertainty* coefficient have similar behaviors. The *Tschuprow* function is quite different, more smooth but may be less discriminant. Secondly, the application of the diversity coefficient we have introduced, to allow the functions to check all the required properties, slightly modify the functions. Globally, the functions are smoother and discriminant. In a further work we will present optimization procedures.

References

[BFOS84]   L. Breiman, J.H. Friedman, R.A. Olshen, and C.J. Stone. *Classification and Regression Trees*. Wadsworth International, California, 1984.

[BWL95]   G. Biswas, J. Weinberg, and C. Li. Iterate: a conceptual clustering method for knowledge discovery in databases. Technical report, Departement of Computer Science, Vanderbilt university, Nashville, 1995.

[CDG+88]   G. Celeux, E. Diday, G. Govaert, Y. Lechevallier, and H. Ralambondrainy. *Classification automatique des données*. Dunod, paris, 1988.

[CS96]   G. Celeux and G. Soromenho. An entropy criterion for assessing the number of clusters in a mixture model. *Journal of classification*, 13:195–212, 1996.

[Fis87]   D. H. Fisher. Knowledge acquisition via incremental conceptual clustering. *Machine Learning*, 2:139–172, 1987.

[Fis96]   D. H. Fisher. Iterative optimization and simplification of hierarchical clusterings. *Journal of Artificial Intelligence Research*, 4:147–180, 1996.

[GK54]   L. A. Goodman and W. H. Kruskal. Measures of association for cross classification. *Journal of the American Statistical Association*, 49:732–764, 1954.

[Gov84]   G. Govaert. Classification simultanée de tableaux binaires. In E. Diday, M. Jambu, L. Lebart, J. Pages, and R. Tomassone, editors, *Data analysis and informatics III*, pages 233–236. North Holland, 1984.

[JD88]   A. K. Jain and R. C. Dubes. *Algorithms for clustering data*. Prentice Hall, Englewood cliffs, New Jersey, 1988.

[LdC96]   I.C. Lerman and J. F. P. da Costa. Coefficients d'association et variables à très grand nombre de catégories dans les arbres de décision : application à l'identification de la structure secondaire d'une protéine. Technical Report 2803, INRIA, février 1996.

[MH91]   G. Matthews and J. Hearne. Clustering without a metric. *IEEE Transaction on pattern analysis and machine intelligence*, 13(2):175–184, 1991.

[RF00]   C. Robardet and F. Feschet. A new methodology to compare clustering algorithms. In H. Meng K. S. Leung, L. Chan, editor, *Intelligent data engineering and automated learning-IDEAL 2000*, number 1983 in LNCS. Springer-Verlag, 2000.

[TB01]   L. Talavera and J. Béjar. Generality-based conceptual clustering with probabilistic concepts. *IEEE Transactions on pattern analysis and machine intelligence*, 23(2):196–206, 2001.

[Weh96]   L. Wehenkel. On uncertainty measures used for decision tree induction. In *Info. Proc. and Manag. of Uncertainty*, pages 413–418, 1996.

Identification of ECG Arrhythmias Using Phase Space Reconstruction

Felice M. Roberts[1], Richard J. Povinelli[1], and Kristina M. Ropella[2]

[1] Department of Electrical and Computer Engineering, Marquette University, Milwaukee, WI
{felice.roberts,richard.povinelli}@mu.edu
[2] Department of Biomedical Engineering, Marquette University, Milwaukee, WI
k.ropella@marquette.edu

Abstract. Changes in the normal rhythmicity of a human heart may result in different cardiac arrhythmias, which may be immediately fatal or cause irreparable damage to the heart when sustained over long periods of time. The ability to automatically identify arrhythmias from ECG recordings is important for clinical diagnosis and treatment, as well as, for understanding the electrophysiological mechanisms of the arrhythmias. This paper proposes a novel approach to efficiently and accurately identify normal sinus rhythm and various ventricular arrhythmias through a combination of phase space reconstruction and machine learning techniques. Data was recorded from patients experiencing spontaneous arrhythmia, as well as, induced arrhythmia. The phase space attractors of the different rhythms were learned from both inter- and intra-patient arrhythmic episodes. Out-of-sample ECG rhythm recordings were classified using the learned attractor probability distributions with an overall accuracy of 83.0%.

1 Introduction

Thousands of deaths occur daily due to ventricular fibrillation (VF)[1]. Ventricular fibrillation is a disorganized, irregular heart rhythm that renders the heart incapable of pumping blood. It is fatal within minutes unless externally terminated by the passage of a large electrical current through the heart muscle. Automatic defibrillators, both internal and external to the body, have proven to be the only therapy for thousands of individuals whom experience ventricular arrhythmia. There is evidence [2] to suggest that the sooner electronic therapy is delivered following the onset of VF, the greater the success of terminating the arrhythmia, and thus, the greater the chance of survival. Defibrillators are required to classify a cardiac rhythm as life threatening before the device can deliver shock therapy; the patient is usually unconscious. Because of the hemodynamic consequences (i.e., the heart ceases to contract, thus no blood flows through the body) that accompany the onset of lethal VF, a preventive approach for treating ventricular arrhythmia is preferable, such as low-energy shock, pacing regimens and/or drug administration to prevent the fatal arrhythmia from occurring in the first place. Furthermore, there is evidence [3] to suggest that high-energy shocks delivered during lethal arrhythmia may be harmful to the myocardium. Thus, the ability to quickly identify and/or predict the impending onset of VF is highly desirable and may increase the alternate therapies available to treat an individual prone to VF.

L. De Raedt and A. Siebes (Eds.): PKDD 2001, LNAI 2168, pp. 411-423, 2001.
© Springer-Verlag Berlin Heidelberg 2001

Many of the current algorithms differentiate ventricular arrhythmias using classical signal processing techniques, i.e., threshold crossing intervals, autocorrelation, VF-filter, spectral analysis [4], time-frequency distributions [5], coherence analysis [6], and heart rate variability [7, 8]. In order to improve frequency resolution and minimize spectral leakage, these algorithms need five or more seconds of data when classifying the rhythms. This paper proposes that phase space embedding [9] combined with data mining techniques [10] can learn and accurately characterize chaotic attractors for the different ventricular tachyarrhythmias in short data intervals. Others who have used phase space techniques to study physiological changes in the heart include Bettermann and VanLeeuwen [11], who demonstrated that the changes in heart beat complexity between sleeping and waking states were not a simple function of the heart beat intervals, rather the changes in heart beat complexity were related to the existence of dynamic phases in heart period dynamics.

In this study, signals from two leads of a normal twelve lead ECG recording [12, 13] are transformed into a reconstructed state space, also called phase space. Attractors are learned for each of the following rhythms: sinus rhythm (SR), monomorphic ventricular tachycardia (MVT), polymorphic ventricular tachycardia (PVT), and ventricular fibrillation. A neural net is used to learn the attractors using features formed from the two-dimensional reconstructed phase space. Attractors are learned and tested from inter- and intra-patient data.

1.1 ECG Recording Overview

An ECG recording is a measure of the electrical activity of the heart from electrodes placed at specific locations on the torso. A synthesized surface recording of one heartbeat during SR can be seen in Figure 1. The cardiac cycle can be divided into several features. The main features are the P wave, PR interval, QRS complex, Q wave, ST segment, and T wave. Each of these components represents the electrical activity in the heart during a portion of the heartbeat [14].

- The P wave represents the depolarization of the atria.
- The PR interval represents the time of conduction from the onset of atrial activation to the onset of ventricular activation through the bundle of His.
- The QRS complex is a naming convention for the portion of the waveform representing the ventricular activation and completion.
- The ST segment serves as the isoelectric line from which amplitudes of other waveforms are measured, and also is important in identifying pathologies, such as myocardial infarctions (elevations) and ischemia (depressions).
- The T wave represents ventricular depolarization.

Recordings seen at different lead locations on the body may exhibit different morphological characteristics. Differences in the ECG recordings from one lead to another are a result of the electrodes being placed at different positions with respect to the heart. Thus the projection of the electrical potential at a point near the sinoatrial node would differ from that seen by an electrode near the atrioventricular node. Differences in recordings from one person to another may be due to the difference in the size of the hearts, the orientation of the heart in the body, exact lead location, and the healthiness of the heart itself.

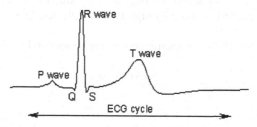

Fig. 1. Synthesized ECG recording for one heartbeat

2 Methods

2.1 Recordings

Simultaneous recordings of surface leads II and V1 of a normal 12 lead ECG [12, 13] were obtained from six patients using an electrophysiological recorder. These patients exhibited sustained monomorphic ventricular tachycardia, polymorphic ventricular tachycardia, ventricular fibrillation and/or any combination of these rhythms during electrophysiological testing (EP) and/or automatic implantable cardio-verter/defribrillator (AICD) implantation. None of the data was from healthy patients.

Two independent observers classified the ECG recordings as one of the following rhythms: VF, PVT, MVT, and SR. The criteria for classifying of the different rhythms were [15-17]:

- VF was defined by undulations that were irregular in timing and morphology without discrete QRS complexes, ST segments, or T waves with cycle length < 200 msec.
- PVT was defined as ventricular tachycardia having variable QRS morphology but with discrete QRS complexes with cycle length < 400 msec.
- MVT was defined as ventricular tachycardia having a constant QRS morphology with cycle length < 600 msec.
- SR was defined by rhythms exhibiting P waves, QRS complexes, ST segments, and T waves with no aberrant morphology interspersed in the data interval.

Ventricular tachycardia is most commonly associated in patients with coronary artery disease and prior myocardial infarctions. Patients with dilated cardiomyopathies, arrythmogenic right ventricular dysplasia, congenital heart disease, hypertrophic cardiomyopathy, or mitral valve prolapses experience VT. Infrequently VT occurs in patients without identifiable heart abnormalities[18]. Ventricular fibrillation occurs primarily in patients with transient or permanent conduction block. Patients experience VF under a variety of conditions, including: 1) electrically induced by a low-intensity stimulus delivered while the ventricles are repolarizing; 2) electrically induced by a burst (approximately 1 second duration) of 60 Hz AC current; 3) spontaneously induced due to ischemia leading to a conduction block; 4) reperfusion-induced; and 5) electrically induced by high-intensity electric shocks[16].

Examples of the different rhythm morphologies can be seen in Fig. 2.

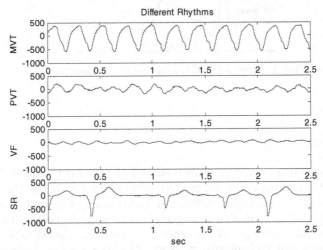

Fig. 2. Recording for individual examples of rhythm morphologies: monomorphic ventricular tachycardia (MVT), polymorphic ventricular tachycardia (PVT), ventricular fibrillation (VF), and sinus rhythm (SR)

2.2 Preprocessing

Data were antialiased filtered with a cutoff frequency of 200 Hz and subsequently digitized at 1,200 Hz. Up to 60 seconds of continuous data were digitized for each rhythm. In this study, the data was divided into 2.5-second contiguous intervals of MVT, PVT, VF or SR rhythms. The data were zero-meaned prior to further analysis.

2.3 Feature Identification

A two-dimensional phase space was constructed using the II and V1 ECG recordings. Figure 3 illustrates the generated phase space.

Each rhythm is attracted to a different subset of the phase space. This subset of the phase space is the attractor for that particular rhythm. Visually, one can differentiate the rhythm attractors in Fig. 3. However, for an automatic defibrillator to automatically classify rhythms, features must be determined that define each attractor. These features were generated using the following method.

```
Psuedo Code of Feature Identification
      Combine all lead II training intervals
      Take histogram of combined signals
      Determine boundary values that separate the com-
            bined data into 10 equally filled bins (each
            bin contains ~10% of data)
      Repeat for lead V1
      Using boundaries for each lead, create 100 regions
            in the phase space.
      For each individual training interval
      Determine percentage of data points in each region
```

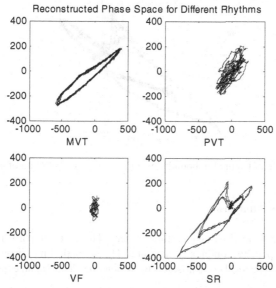

Fig. 3. Generated two-dimensional phase space for examples of MVT, PVT, VF, and SR. Notice that the different rhythms fill a different subset of the phase space

An example of the regions subdividing the phase space for an SR rhythm can be seen in Fig. 4.

2.4 Attractor Learning

The attractors were learned using neural networks with 100 inputs, one output, and two hidden layers. The first and second hidden layers consisted of 10 and 3 neurons with tan-sigmoid transfer functions, respectively. The output layer was a log-sigmoid neuron. The neural net was learned using the Levenberg-Marquardt algorithm in MATLAB. The inputs to the neural networks were the percentage of data points in each feature bin described in previously. Leave-one-out cross-validation [19] was used in the training and testing of the neural networks. Given an indexed data set

$\{d_i : i = 1, \dots, n\}$ containing n elements, n training/testing runs are performed. For the jth run, the test set is $\{d_j\}$ and the training set is $\{d_i : \forall i \neq j\}$.

Individual neural networks were used to classify each rhythm. The output of the neural net was rounded, in order that 1 classified the input data as the specific rhythm, 0 classified it as some other rhythm. For a patient exhibiting two different morphologies, two neural networks would be trained and tested to classify the ECG intervals. An example of the classifier architecture for Patient 2 can be seen in Fig. 5. To be a legitimate classification, only one neural network can classify the signal.

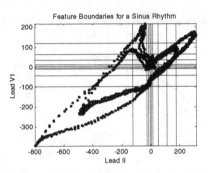

Fig. 4. Example of feature bin boundaries for a 2.5 second recording of sinus rhythm

2.5 Comparative Analysis

We compare our new method against three others. The first comparison is to a method based on the Lempel-Ziv complexity measure. The second comparison is to a method based on heart rate. The third comparison is to two independent human expert observers.

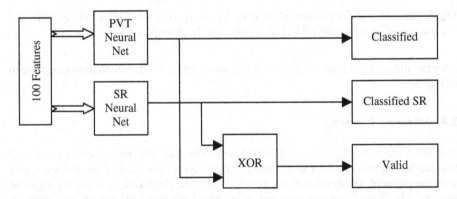

Fig. 5. Classifier architecture. The number of rhythm neural nets corresponds to the number of rhythms for a particular set of data. For sets of data with more than two rhythms to classify the XOR box is more complicated than a single exclusive OR

Zhang et al. [20] proposed a method for detecting MVT, VF, and SR using the Lempel-Ziv complexity measure. The complexity measure is a function of the number of patterns found in a string of threshold crossings. For each interval of data, a new threshold was calculated. As with the method proposed in this paper, Zhang's complexity measure does not need to detect the occurrences of beats. They used various interval lengths to determine the minimum amount of data needed to attain 100% training accuracy; no test accuracy was determined. A seven second interval was found to be the minimum length needed to correctly discriminating the three rhythms. For the rhythms (MVT, VF, and SR), intervals of length two and three seconds achieved training accuracies of (93.14%, 95.10%, and 98.04%) and (93.14%, 97.55%, and 95.59%), respectively. Zhang classified the rhythms using the following cutoff values for the complexity measures:

- SR – for complexity measures less than 0.150
- MVT – for complexity measures between 0.150 and 0.486
- VF – for complexity measures greater than 0.486.

Heart rate is used in many AICDs to discriminate one rhythm from another. Medtronic, Inc. a commercial maker of AICDs uses rate detection zones and different counts to detect and classify tachyarrhythmias [17]. AICDs count the number of beats in each detection zone, if a specified number of beats are within a particular zone without a SR rhythm beat being detected, the interval is marked as a tachyarrhythmia. Since the data intervals used are only two and half seconds long, there are not enough beats to be counted, so only the heart rate is used to classify the rhythm intervals. For each individual interval, thresholds for marking a new beat were set to 60% of the maximum amplitude of that interval.

3 Results

3.1 Data

Six patients comprised the study population. The heart rhythms exhibited by the six patients can be seen in Table 1. Four of the patients exhibited different combinations of two or three types of rhythms. The last two patients exhibited all four types of rhythms. Two independent observers performed the original rhythm classification.

Table 1. Patient and number of 2.5s rhythm intervals experienced

Patient	MVT	PVT	VF	SR
1			23	27
2		6	12	
3		23		30
4	15	8	4	
5	15	8	2	33
6	20	6	5	34

Overall inter-observer agreement for rhythm classification was 80.7%. The two observers conferred to reach consensus on the classification of the remaining 19.3%. The intervals used in this study were not meticulously selected to have comparable amplitudes, waveforms, and heart rates. The intervals were selected blindly from rhythms classified by the two observers.

3.2 Intra-patient Classification

For each patient, classifiers were created for each rhythm interval. The neural nets in the classifiers were able to learn the training data within approximately 20 epochs with 100% accuracy, with leave-one-out cross-validation. For the training data, the classifiers accurately identified rhythm type from 69.8% to 83.3% of the time with an overall average accuracy of 77.1%. The accuracy for each patient's classifier is listed in Table 2. Each classifier had four possible outputs:

- Correctly Classified – 2.5-second rhythm interval was classified correctly.
- Incorrectly Classified – 2.5-second rhythm interval was classified as a different rhythm.
- Undetermined (no classification) – 2.5-second rhythm interval was not classified.
- Undetermined (two classifications) – 2.5-second rhythm interval was classified as two rhythms (It should be noted that no rhythm interval was classified as more than two rhythms.)

Table 2. Intra-patient classifier accuracy

Patient	Correctly Classified	Incorrectly Classified	Undetermined (No classification)	Undetermined (2 classifications)	Percent Accuracy
1	41	1	2	6	82.0%
2	15	0	2	1	83.3%
3	37	3	8	5	69.8%
4	21	2	1	3	75.0%
5	44	5	3	6	75.8%
6	51	1	5	8	78.5%

3.3 Inter-patient Classification

All 271 data segments from the six patients were combined and classified. The training data was learned with 100% accuracy within approximately 30 epochs. Leave-one-out cross-validation was performed. The accuracy of classifying the 271 rhythm intervals was improved compared to the intra-patient classification accuracy. The classification accuracy for the 271 intervals was 83.0%, with the following breakdown of classification:

- 225 were correctly classified.
- 12 were incorrectly classified.
- 11 were undetermined due to no classification.
- 23 were undetermined due to two or more classifications (only one interval was classified as three separate rhythms).

The confusion matrix for the proposed method is given in Table 3. Recall because of the structure of the proposed classifier, a data interval may be under (no classification) or over (two or more classifications) classified, hence the total classifications in Table 3 is not 271.

Table 3. Confusion matrix for phase space classification method

| | Classified As | | | | Valid | |
	SR	MVT	PVT	VF	Classification	Accuracy
SR	117	1	7	6	109	87.9%
MVT	1	47	5	0	42	84.0%
PVT	3	4	45	2	39	76.5%
VF	2	0	6	38	35	76.1%

3.4 Complexity Measure Inter-patient Classification

Using the complexity measure algorithm from [20], the complexity measure for each interval was calculated. The distributions of the measures for the different rhythms are shown in Figure 5. It can be seen in the graph that unlike Zhang's training results there is no distinct separation between complexity measures of the different rhythms; nor were the values attained using this data within the same ranges as those determined by Zhang. The results are extremely poor as seen by the accuracies given in Table 4.

Table 4. Confusion matrix for complexity measure classification

| | Classified As | | | | |
	SR	MVT	PVT	VF	Accuracy
SR	116	8	0	0	93.5%
MVT	50	0	0	0	0%
PVT	51	0	0	0	0%
VF	38	8	0	0	0%

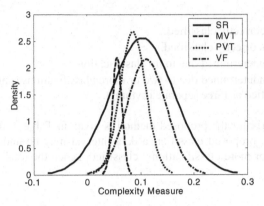

Fig. 6. Complexity measure distribution for the all four rhythm types

3.5 Heart Rate Inter-patient Classification

Classification using the heart rate had an overall accuracy of 62%. Misclassifications occurred in all rhythm intervals. The MVT intervals had the worst accuracy. The classification using heart rate can be seen in Table 5.

Table 5. Confusion matrix for heart rate classification

	Classified As				
	SR	MVT	PVT	VF	Accuracy
SR	83	38	3	0	66.9%
MVT	0	11	20	19	22.0%
PVT	0	0	40	11	78.4%
VF	0	1	1	44	95.6%

4 Discussion

Ideally, an implantable antitachycardia device should be capable of several modes of therapy including antitachycardia pacing, low-energy cardioversion, and high-energy defibrillation [21-23]. Patients requiring these types of therapy often experience more than one rhythm type. These different arrhythmias may require different therapies. However, for the several modes of therapy to be available in one device, detection algorithms must be able to accurately differentiate among various arrhythmias. The results from this preliminary study are encouraging for developing accurate detection algorithms among the various ventricular tachyarrhythmias. The ability to accurately classify rhythms experienced by individual patients more than 75% of the time is in close agreement with the classification of trained observers. The classification accuracy across all patients was better for the automated scheme than for the original classification by trained observers. The classification performed using the complexity measures of the rhythms was extremely poor. It is obvious that Zhang's threshold values are not generalizable. Even if new threshold values were determined for our data set, their classification method would perform poorly as can be seen in Fig. 6 by the strong overlapping of the classes.

Using the reconstructed phase space to classify out-of-sample ECG recordings performed better than the classification using the heart rate alone. This is due to several reasons. The first and foremost was part of the new algorithm's advantages is the ability to classify ECG rhythms in only 2.5 seconds. Most ICDs require 10 seconds to classify a tachyarrhythmia. Many of the commercial detection algorithms also allow the medical provider to determine templates for the patient's SR. As these were out-of-sample intervals no templates could be generated. Thus the detection of heartbeats ranged drastically from one interval to the next. Secondly, as stated previously, the morphology seen in an ECG recording is a function of the healthiness of the heart. And as each of these rhythms was recorded during electrophysiological testing (EP) and/or automatic implantable cardioverter/defibrillator (AICD) implantation, none of these hearts can be considered extremely healthy. Thus individual rhythms greatly vary from one patient to the next. For example during SR, one patient had T-waves whose amplitudes were as large as the QRS. The T-waves were counted as a new heartbeat, thus doubling the calculated heart rate. Finally, even though the data was zero-meaned linear trends were not removed from the intervals, thus fewer beats were counted.

Although the proposed method was accurate 83% of the time, if used in AICDs in its current form, the misclassification of SR and MVT as VF could cause a patient to receive an unnecessary defibrillation shock which has the possibility of being detrimental to the patient. Some of these false classifications were due to SR intervals in which the maximum amplitude of the signal was not very large, thus the phase space reconstruction of these non-fatal rhythms was very close to that of VF. Further improvement is still needed before these short intervals can be used in commercial applications, such as the development of multi-therapy implantable antitachycardia devices. The high classification accuracy of the proposed method within a short period of time reinforces the author's conjecture that phase space is a valid starting point in the classification of ventricular tachyarrhythmias. Other features will need to be added to the proposed method to improve the classification accuracy for short intervals of data. Further investigations for defining the rhythm attractors will incorporate time-delay and multi-dimensional phase spaces.

Future research into the identification of ventricular tachyarrhythmias may unveil electrophysiological mechanisms responsible for the onset and termination of fibrillatory rhythms. We hypothesize that the patterns of the quasi-periodic [24] attractors of heart rhythms change immediately prior to (within a 10-minute time period) the onset of a serious ventricular arrhythmia. Using these attractors, future research will focus on the transitions from one phase space attractor to another. This may reveal how changes in the attractor space correspond to heart rhythm changes, with the end goal being able to predict the onset of VF, thus improving available therapy and prevention.

References

[1] F. X. Witkowski, L. J. Leon, P. A. Penkoske, R. B. Clark, M. L. Spano, W. L. Ditto, and W. R. Giles, "A Method of Visualization of Ventricular Fibrillation: Design of a Cooled Fiberoptically Coupled Image Intensified CCD Data Acquisition System Incorporating Wavelet Shrinkage Based Adaptive Filtering," *American Institute of Physics*, vol. 8, pp. 94-102, 1998.

[2] E. Manios, G. Fenelon, T. Malacky, A. L. Fo, and P. Brugada, "Life Threatening Ventricular Arrhythmias in Patients with Minimal or no Structural Heart Disease: Experience with the Implantable Cardioverter Defibrillator," available at http://www.heartweb.org/heartweb/0197/icd0003.htm, 1997, cited December 2, 2000

[3] J. A. Stewart, "A More Effective Approach to In-Hospital Defibrillation," *Journal of Cardiovascular Nursing*, vol. 10, pp. 37-46, 1996.

[4] R. H. Clayton, A. Murray, and R. W. F. Campbell, "Comparison of Four Techniques for Recognition of Ventricular Fibrillation from the surface ECG," *Medical and Biological Engineering and Computing*, vol. 31, pp. 111-117, 1993.

[5] V. X. Afonso and W. J. Tompkins, "Detecting Ventricular Fibrillation," *IEEE Engineering in Medicine and Biology*, pp. 152-159, 1995.

[6] K. M. Ropella, J. M. Baerman, A. V. Sahakian, and S. Swiryn, "Differentiation of Ventricular Tachyarrhythmias," *Circulation*, vol. 82, pp. 2035-2043, 1990.

[7] S. Chen, N. V. Thakor, and M. M. Mower, "Analysis of Ventricular Arrhythmias: a Reliable Discrimination Technique," *Computers in Cardiology 1986*, pp. 179-182, 1986.

[8] A. Natarajan and N. V. Thakor, "A Sequential Hypothesis Testing Algorithm for Rapid Accurate Discrimination of Tachyarrhythmias," *Proceedings of the Annual Conference on Engineering in Medicine and Biology*, vol. 13, pp. 734-735, 1991.

[9] H. D. I. Abarbanel, *Analysis of Observed Chaotic Data*. New York, NY: Springer-Verlag New York, Inc., 1995.

[10] R. J. Povinelli, *Time Series Data Mining: Identifying Temporal Patterns for Characterization and Prediction of Time Series Events*, Dissertation, Marquette University, 1999.

[11] H. Bettermann and P. VanLeeuwen, "Evidence of Phase Transitions in Heart Period Dynamics," *Biological Cybernetics*, vol. 78, pp. 63-70, 1998.

[12] H. J. L. Marriott, *Practical Electrocardiography*, 7th ed. Baltimore, MD: Williams & Wilkins, 1983.

[13] A. E. Norman, *12 Lead ECG Interpretation: A self-Teaching Manual*. New York, NY: McGraw-Hill, Inc., 1992.

[14] R. M. Berne and M. N. Levy, *Physiology*, 3rd ed. Chicago, IL: Mosby Year Book, 1993.

[15] E. Braunwald, *Heart Disease. A Textbook of Cardiovascular Medicine*, 3 ed. Philadelphia: WB Saunders, 1988.

[16] J. L. Jones, "Ventricular Fibrillation," in *Implantable Cardioverter-Defibrillator*, I. Singer, Ed. Amonk, NY: Futura Publishing Company, Inc., 1994, pp. 43-67.

[17] W. H. Olson, "Tachyarrhythmia Sensing and Detection," in *Implantable Cardioverter-Defibrillator*, I. Singer, Ed. Amonk, NY: Futura Publishing Company, Inc., 1994, pp. 13-42.

[18] I. Singer, "Ventricular Tachycardia," in *Implantable Cardioverter-Defibrillator*, I. Singer, Ed. Amonk, NY: Futura Publishing Company, Inc., 1994, pp. 13-42.

[19] T. M. Mitchell, *Machine Learning*. Madison, WI: WCB McGraw-Hill, 1997.

[20] X.-S. Zhang, Y.-S. Zhu, N. V. Thakor, and Z.-Z. Wang, "Detecting Ventricular Tachycardia and Fibrillation by Complexity Measure," *IEEE Transactions on Biomedical Engineering*, vol. 46, pp. 548-555, 1999.

[21] D. P. Zipes, E. N. Prystowsky, W. M. Miles, and J. J. Heger, "Future Directions: Electrical Therapy for Cardiac Tachyarrhythmias," *PACE*, vol. 7, pp. 606-610, 1984.

[22] R. A. Winkle, "Electronic Control of Ventricular Tachyarrhythmias: Overview and Future Directions," *PACE*, vol. 7, pp. 1375-1379, 1984.

[23] A. S. Manolis, H. Rastegar, and N. A. M. Estes, "Automatic Implantable Cardioverter Defibrillator: Current Status," *JAMA*, vol. 262, pp. 1362-1368, 1989.

[24] E. Ott, *Chaos in Dynamical Systems*. New York, NY: Cambridge University Press, 1993.

Finding Association Rules That Trade Support Optimally against Confidence

Tobias Scheffer[1,2]

[1] University of Magdeburg, FIN/IWS, PO Box 4120, 39016 Magdeburg, Germany
[2] SemanticEdge, Kaiserin-Augusta-Allee 10-11, 10553 Berlin, Germany
`scheffer@iws.cs.uni-magdeburg.de`

Abstract. When evaluating association rules, rules that differ in both support and confidence have to compared; a larger support has to be traded against a higher confidence. The solution which we propose for this problem is to maximize the expected accuracy that the association rule will have for future data. In a Bayesian framework, we determine the contributions of confidence and support to the expected accuracy on future data. We present a fast algorithm that finds the n best rules which maximize the resulting criterion. The algorithm dynamically prunes redundant rules and parts of the hypothesis space that cannot contain better solutions than the best ones found so far. We evaluate the performance of the algorithm (relative to the Apriori algorithm) on realistic knowledge discovery problems.

1 Introduction

Association rules (*e.g.*, [1,5,2]), express regularities between sets of data items in a database. [Beer and TV magazine $\Rightarrow$ chips] is an example of an association rule and expresses that, in a particular store, all customers who buy beer and a TV magazine are also likely to buy chips. In contrast to classifiers, association rules do not make a prediction for *all* database records. When a customer does not buy beer and a magazine, then our example rule does *not* conjecture that he will not buy chips either. The number of database records for which a rule does predict the proper value of an attribute is called the *support* of that rule.

Associations rules may not be perfectly accurate. The fraction of database records for which the rules conjectures a correct attribute value, relative to the fraction of records for which it makes any prediction, is called the confidence. Note that the confidence is the relative frequency of a correct prediction on the data that is used for training. We expect the confidence (or accuracy) on unseen data to lie below that on average, in particular, when the support is small.

When deciding which rules to return, association rule algorithms need to take both confidence and support into account. Of course, we can find any number of rules with perfectly high confidence but support of only one or very few records. On the other hand, we can construct very general rules with large support but low confidence. The Apriori algorithm [2] possesses confidence and support thresholds and returns all rules which lie above these bounds. However,

L. De Raedt and A. Siebes (Eds.): PKDD 2001, LNAI 2168, pp. 424–435, 2001.
© Springer-Verlag Berlin Heidelberg 2001

a knowledge discovery system has to evaluate the interestingness of these rules and provide the user with a reasonable number of interesting rules.

Which rules are interesting to the user depends on the problem which the user wants to solve and hopes the rules to be helpful for. In many cases, the user will be interested in finding items that do not only happen to co-occur in the available data. He or she will rather be interested in finding items between which there is a connection in the underlying reality. Items that truly correlate, will most likely also correlate in future data. In statistics, confidence intervals (which bound the difference between relative frequencies and their probabilities) can be used to derive guarantees that empirical observations reflect existing regularities in the underlying reality, rather than occurring just by chance. The number of observation plays a crucial role; when a rule has a large support, then we can be much more certain that the observed confidence is close to the confidence that we can expect to see in future. This is one reason why association rules with very small support are considered less interesting.

In this paper, we propose a trade-off between confidence and support which is in a way optimal by maximizing the chance of correct predictions on unseen data. We concretize the problem setting in Sect. 2, and in Sect. 3 we present our resulting utility criterion. In Sect. 4, we present a fast algorithm that finds the n best association rules with respect to this criterion. We discuss the algorithm's mechanism for pruning regions of the hypothesis space that cannot contain solutions that are better than the ones found so far, as well as the technique used to delete redundant rules which are already implied by other rules. In Sect. 5, we evaluate our algorithm empirically. Section 6 concludes.

2 Preliminaries

Let D be a database consisting of one table over binary attributes $a_1, \ldots, a_k$, called items. In general, D has been generated by discretizing the attributes of a relation of an original database D'. For instance, when D' contains an attribute *income*, then D may contain binary attributes $0 \leq income \leq 20k$, $20k < income \leq 40k$, and so on. A *database record* $r \subseteq \{a_1, \ldots, a_k\}$ is the set of attributes that take value one in a focused row of the table D.

A database record r satisfies an item set $x \subseteq \{a_1, \ldots, a_k\}$ if $x \subseteq r$. The support $s(x)$ of an item set x is the number of records in D which satisfy x. Often, the *fraction* $\frac{s(x)}{|D|}$ of records in D that satisfy x is called the support of x. But since the database D is constant, these terms are equivalent.

An association rule $[x \Rightarrow y]$ with $x, y \subseteq \{a_1, \ldots, a_k\}$, $y \neq \emptyset$, and $x \cap y = \emptyset$ expresses a relationship between an item set x and a nonempty item set y. The intuitive semantic of the rule is that all records which satisfy x are predicted to also satisfy y. The confidence of the rule with respect to the (training) database D is $\hat{c}([x \Rightarrow y]) = \frac{s(x \cup y)}{s(x)}$ – that is, the ratio of correct predictions over all records for which a prediction is made.

The confidence is measured with respect to the database D that is used for training. Often, a user will assume that the resulting association rules provide information on the process that generated the database which will be valid in future, too. But the confidence on the training data is only an estimate of the rules' accuracy in the future, and since we search the space of association rules to maximize the confidence, the estimate is optimistically biased. We define the predictive accuracy $c([x \Rightarrow y])$ of a rule as the probability of a correct prediction with respect to the process underlying the database.

Definition 1. *Let D be a database the records r of which are generated by a static process P, let $[x \Rightarrow y]$ be an association rule. The predictive accuracy $c([x \Rightarrow y]) = Pr[r$ satisfies $y|r$ satisfies $x]$ is the conditional probability of $y \subseteq r$ given that $x \subseteq r$ when the distribution of r is governed by P.*

The confidence $\hat{c}([x \Rightarrow y])$ is the relative frequency of probability $c([x \Rightarrow y])$ for given database D. We now pose the *n most accurate association rules problem*.

Definition 2. *Given a database D (defined like above) and a set of database items a_1 through a_k, find n rules $h_1, \dots, h_n \in \{[x \Rightarrow y]|x, y \subseteq \{a_1, \dots, a_k\}; y \neq \emptyset; x \cap y = \emptyset\}$ which maximize the expected predictive accuracy $c([x \Rightarrow y])$.*

We formulate the problem such that the algorithm needs to return a fixed number of best association rules rather than all rules the utility of which exceeds a given threshold. We think that this setting is more appropriate in many situation because a threshold may not be easy to specify and a user may not be satisfied with either an empty or an outrageously large set of rules.

3   Bayesian Frequency Correction

In this section, we analyze how confidence and support contribute to the predictive accuracy. The intuitive idea is that we "mistrust" the confidence a little. How strongly we have to discount the confidence depends on the support – the greater the support, the more closely does the confidence relate to the predictive accuracy. In the Bayesian framework that we adopt, there is an exact solution as to how much we have to discount the confidence. We call this approach *Bayesian frequency correction* since the resulting formula (Equation 6) takes a confidence and "corrects" it by returning a somewhat lower predictive accuracy.

Suppose that we have a given association rule $[x \Rightarrow y]$ with observed confidence $\hat{c}([x \Rightarrow y])$. We can read $p(c([x \Rightarrow y])|\hat{c}([x \Rightarrow y]), s(x))$ as "P(predictive accuracy of $[x \Rightarrow y]$ given confidence of $[x \Rightarrow y]$ and support of x)". The intuition of our analysis is that application of Bayes' rule implies "P(predictive accuracy given confidence and support) $= P$(confidence given predictive accuracy and support)P(predictive accuracy)$/$ normalization constant". Note that the likelihood $P(\hat{c}|c, s)$ is simply the binomial distribution. (The target attributes of each record that is satisfied by x can be classified correctly or erroneously; the chance of a correct prediction is just the predictive accuracy c; this leads to a binomial distribution.) "P(predictive accuracy)", the prior in our equation, is the accuracy histogram over the space of all association rules. This histogram counts, for every accuracy c, the fraction of rules which possess that accuracy.

In Equation 1, we decompose the expectation by integrating over all possible values of $c([x \Rightarrow y])$. In Equation 2, we apply Bayes' rule. $\pi(c) = \frac{|\{[x \Rightarrow y] | c([x \Rightarrow y]) = c\}|}{|\{[x \Rightarrow y]\}|}$ is the accuracy histogram. It specifies the probability of drawing an association rule with accuracy c when drawing at random under uniform distribution from the space of association rules of length up to k.

$$E(c([x \Rightarrow y]) | \hat{c}([x \Rightarrow y]), s(x))$$

$$= \int cp(c([x \Rightarrow y]) = c | \hat{c}([x \Rightarrow y]), s(x)) dc \tag{1}$$

$$= \int c \frac{P(\hat{c}([x \Rightarrow y]) | c([x \Rightarrow y]) = c, s(x)) \pi(c)}{P(\hat{c}([x \Rightarrow y]) | s(x))} dc \tag{2}$$

In Equation 4, we apply Equation 2. Since, over all c, the distribution $p(c([x \Rightarrow y]) = c | \hat{c}([x \Rightarrow y]), s(x))$ has to integrate to one (Equation 3), we can treat $P(\hat{c}([x \Rightarrow y]) | c([x \Rightarrow y]), s(x))$ as a normalizing constant which we can determine uniquely in Equation 5.

$$\int p(c([x \Rightarrow y]) = c | \hat{c}([x \Rightarrow y]), s(x)) dc = 1 \tag{3}$$

$$\Leftrightarrow \int \frac{P(\hat{c}([x \Rightarrow y]) | c([x \Rightarrow y]) = c, s(x)) \pi(c)}{P(\hat{c}([x \Rightarrow y]) | s(x))} dc = 1 \tag{4}$$

$$\Leftrightarrow P(\hat{c}([x \Rightarrow y]) | s(x)) = \int P(\hat{c}([x \Rightarrow y]) | c([x \Rightarrow y]) = c, s(x)) \pi(c) dc \tag{5}$$

Combining Equations 2 and 5 we obtain Equation 6. In this equation, we also state that, when the accuracy c is given, the confidence $\hat{c}$ is governed by the binomial distribution which we write as $B[c, s](\hat{c})$. This requires us make the standard assumption of independent and identically distributed instances.

$$E(c([x \Rightarrow y]) | \hat{c}([x \Rightarrow y]), s(x)) = \frac{\int cB[c, s(x)](\hat{c}([x \Rightarrow y])) \pi(c) dc}{\int B[c, s(x)](\hat{c}([x \Rightarrow y])) \pi(c) dc} \tag{6}$$

We have now found a solution that quantifies $E(c([x \Rightarrow y]) | \hat{c}([x \Rightarrow y]), s(x))$, *the exact* expected predictive accuracy of an association rule $[x \Rightarrow y]$ with given confidence $\hat{c}$ and body support $s(x)$. Equation 6 thus quantifies just how strongly the confidence of a rule has to be corrected, given the support of that rule. Note that the solution depends on the prior $\pi(c)$ which is the histogram of accuracies of all association rules over the given items for the given database.

One way of treating such priors is to assume a certain standard distribution. Under a set of assumptions on the process that generated the database, $\pi(c)$ can be shown to be governed by a certain binomial distribution [9]. However, empirical studies (see Sect. 5 and Fig. 2a) show that the shape of the prior can deviate strongly from this binomial distributions. Reasonably accurate estimates can be obtained by following a Markov Chain Monte Carlo [4] approach to estimating the prior, using the available database (see Sect. 4). For an extended discussion of the complexity of estimating this distributions, see [9,6].

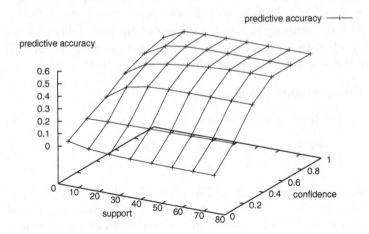

Fig. 1. Contributions of support $s(x)$ and confidence $\hat{c}([x \Rightarrow y])$ to predictive accuracy $c([x \Rightarrow y])$ of rule $[x \Rightarrow y]$

Example Curve. Figure 1 shows how expected predictive accuracy, confidence, and body support relate for the database that we also use for our experiments in Sect. 5, using 10 items. The predictive accuracy grows with both confidence and body support of the rule. When the confidence exceeds 0.5, then the predictive accuracy is lower than the confidence, depending on the support and on the histogram π of accuracies of association rules for this database.

4   Discovery of Association Rules

The Apriori algorithm [1] finds association rules in two steps. First, all item sets x with support of more then the fixed threshold "minsup" are found. Then, all item sets are split into left and right hand side x and y (in all possible ways) and the confidence of the rules $[x \Rightarrow y]$ is calculated as $\frac{s(x \cup y)}{s(x)}$. All rules with a confidence above the confidence threshold "minconf" are returned. Our algorithm differs from that scheme since we do not have fixed confidence and support thresholds. Instead, we want to find the n best rules.

In the first step, our algorithm estimates the prior $\pi(c)$. Then generation of frequent item sets, pruning the hypothesis space by dynamically adjusting the minsup threshold, generating association rules, and removing redundant association rules interleave. The algorithm is displayed in Table 1.

Estimating $\pi(c)$. We can estimate π by drawing many hypotheses at random under uniform distribution, measuring their confidence, and recording the resulting histogram. Algorithmically, we run a loop over the length of the rule

Table 1. Algorithm PredictiveApriori: discovery of n most predictive association rules

---

1. **Input:** n (desired number of association rules), database with items $a_1, \ldots, a_k$.
2. **Let** $\tau = 1$.
3. **For** $i = 1 \ldots k$ **Do:** Draw a number of association rules $[x \Rightarrow y]$ with i items at random. Measure their confidence (provided $s(x) > 0$). Let $\pi_i(c)$ be the distribution of confidences.
4. **For all** c, **Let** $\pi(c) = \dfrac{\sum_{i=1}^{k} \pi_i(c) \binom{k}{i}(2^i - 1)}{\sum_{i=1}^{k} \binom{k}{i}(2^i - 1)}$.
5. **Let** $X_0 = \{\emptyset\}$; **Let** $X_1 = \{\{a_1\}, \ldots, \{a_k\}\}$ be all item sets with one single element.
6. **For** $i = 1 \ldots k - 1$ **While** ($i = 1$ or $X_{i-1} \neq \emptyset$).
    a) **If** $i > 1$ **Then** determine the set of candidate item sets of length i as $X_i = \{x \cup x' | x, x' \in X_{i-1}, |x \cup x'| = i\}$. Generation of X_i can be optimized by considering only item sets x and $x' \in X_{i-1}$ that differ only in the element with highest item index. Eliminate double occurrences of item sets in X_i.
    b) Run a database pass and determine the support of the generated item sets. Eliminate item sets with support less than τ from X_i.
    c) **For all** $x \in X_i$ **Call RuleGen(x)**.
    d) **If** *best* has been changed, **Then Increase** τ to be the smallest number such that $E(c|1, \tau) > E(c(best[n])|\hat{c}(best[n]), s(best[n]))$ (refer to Equation 6). **If** $\tau >$ database size, **Then Exit**.
    e) **If** τ has been increased in the last step, **Then** eliminate all item sets from X_i which have support below τ.
7. **Output** $best[1] \ldots best[n]$, the list of the n best association rules.

Algorithm RuleGen(x) (generate all rules with body x)

10. **Let** γ be the smallest number such that $E(c|\gamma/s(x), s(x)) > E(c(best[n])|\hat{c}(best[n]), s(best[n]))$.
11. **For** $i = 1 \ldots k$ **With** $a_i \notin x$ **Do** (for all items not in x)
    a) **If** $i = 1$ **Then Let** $Y_1 = \{\{a_i\} | a_i \notin x\}$ (item sets with one element not in x).
    b) **Else Let** $Y_i = \{y \cup y' | y, y' \in Y_{i-1}, |y \cup y'| = i\}$ analogous to the generation of candidates in step 6a.
    c) **For all** $y \in Y_i$ **Do**
        i. Measure the support $s(x \cup y)$. **If** $s(x \cup y) \leq \gamma$, **Then** eliminate y from Y_i and **Continue** the for loop with the next y.
        ii. Equation 6 gives the predictive accuracy $E(c([x \Rightarrow y]) | s(x \cup y)/s(x), s(x))$.
        iii. **If** the predictive accuracy is among the n best found so far (recorded in *best*), **Then** update *best*, remove rules in *best* that are subsumed by other rules, and **Increase** γ to be the smallest number such that $E(c|\gamma/s(x), s(x)) \geq E(c(best[n])|\hat{c}(best[n]), s(best[n]))$.
12. **If** any subsumed rule has been erased in step 11(c)iii, **Then** recur from step 10.

and, given that length, draw a fixed number of rules. We determine the items and the split into body and head by drawing at random (Step 3). We have now drawn equally many rules for each size while the uniform distribution requires us to prefer long rules as there are many more long rules than there are short ones. There are $\binom{k}{i}$ item sets of size i over k database items, and given i items, there are $2^i - 1$ distinct association rules (each item can be located on the left or right hand side of the rule but the right hand side must be nonempty). Hence, Equation 7 gives the probability that exactly i items occur in a rule which is drawn at random under uniform distribution from the space of all association rules over k items.

$$P[i \text{ items}] = \frac{\binom{k}{i}(2^i - 1)}{\sum_{j=1}^{k} \binom{k}{j}(2^j - 1)} \tag{7}$$

In step 4 we apply a Markov Chain Monte Carlo style correction to the prior by weighting each prior for rule length i by the probability of a rule length of i.

Enumerating Item Sets with Dynamic Minsup Threshold. Similarly to the Apriori algorithm, the PredictiveApriori algorithm generates frequent item sets, but using a dynamically increasing minsup threshold τ. Note that we start with size zero (only the empty item set is contained in X_0). X_1 contains all item sets with one element. Given X_{i-1}, the algorithm computes X_i in step 6a just like Apriori does. An item set can only be frequent when all its subsets are frequent, too. We can thus generate X_i by only joining those elements of X_{i-1} which differ exactly in the last element (where last refers to the highest item index). Since all subsets of an element of X_i must be in X_{i-1}, the subsets that result from removing the last, or the last but one element must be in X_{i-1}, too. After running a database pass and measuring the support of each element of X_i, we can delete all those candidates that do not achieve the required support of τ.

We then call the RuleGen procedure in step 6c that generates all rules over body x, for each $x \in X_i$. The RuleGen procedure alters our array $best[1 \ldots n]$ which saves the best rules found so far. In step 6d, we refer to $best[n]$, meaning the nth best rule found so far. We now refer to Equation 6 again to determine the least support that the body of an association rule with perfect confidence must possess in order to exceed the predictive accuracy of the currently nth best rule. If that required support exceeds the database size we can exit because no such rule can exist. We delete all item sets in step 6e which lie below that new τ. Finally, we output the n best rules in step 7.

Generating All Rules over Given Body x. In step 10, we introduce a new accuracy threshold γ which quantifies the confidence that a rule with support $s(x)$ needs in order to be among the n best ones. We then start enumerating all possible heads y, taking into account in step 11 that body and head must be disjoint and generating candidates in step 11(b) analogous to step 6a. In step 11(c)i we calculate the support of $x \cup y$ for all heads y. When a rules lies among the best ones so far, we update $best$. We will not bother with rules that have a predictive accuracy below the accuracy of $best[n]$, so we increase γ. In step

11(c)iii, we delete rules from *best* which are subsumed by other rules. This may result in the unfortunate fact that rules which we dropped from *best* earlier, now belong to the n best rules again. So in step 11(c)iii we have to check this and recur from step 10 if necessary.

Removing Redundant Rules. Consider an association rule $[a \Rightarrow c, d]$. When this rule is satisfied by a database, then that database must also satisfy $[a, b \Rightarrow c, d]$, $[a \Rightarrow c]$, $[a \Rightarrow d]$, and many other rules. We write $[x \Rightarrow y] \models [x' \Rightarrow y']$ to express that any database that satisfies $[x \Rightarrow y]$ must also satisfy $[x' \Rightarrow y']$. Since we can generate exponentially many redundant rules that can be inferred from a more general rule, it is not desirable to present all these redundant rules to the user. Consider the example in Table 2 which shows the five most interesting rules generated by PredictiveApriori for the purchase database that we study in Sect. 5. The first and second rule in the bottom part are special cases of the third rule; the fourth and fifth rules are subsumed by the second rule of the top part. The top part shows the best rules with redundant variants removed.

Theorem 1. *We can decide whether a rule subsumes another rule by two simple subset tests:* $[x \Rightarrow y] \models [x' \Rightarrow y'] \Leftrightarrow x \subseteq x' \wedge y \supseteq y'$. *Moreover, if* $[x \Rightarrow y]$ *is supported by a database* D, *and* $[x \Rightarrow y] \models [x' \Rightarrow y']$ *then this database also supports* $[x' \Rightarrow y']$.

Proofs of Theorems 1 and 2 are left for the full paper. Theorem 1 says that $[x \Rightarrow y]$ subsumes $[x' \Rightarrow y']$ if and only if x is a *subset* of x' (weaker precondition) and y is a *superset* of y' (y predicts more attribute values than y'). We can then delete $[x' \Rightarrow y']$ because Theorem 1 says that from a more general rule we can infer that all subsumed rules must be satisfied, too. In order to assure that the n rules which the user is provided are not redundant specializations of each other, we test for subsumption in step 11(c)iii by performing the two subset tests that imply subsumption according to Theorem 1.

Theorem 2. *The PredictiveApriori algorithm (Table 1) returns* n *association rules* $[x_i \Rightarrow y_i]$ *with the following properties. (i) For all returned solutions* $[x \Rightarrow y]$, $[x' \Rightarrow y']$: $[x \Rightarrow y] \not\models [x' \Rightarrow y']$. *(ii) Subject to constraint (i), the returned rules maximize* $E(c[x_i \Rightarrow y_i] | \hat{c}([x_i \Rightarrow y_i]), s(x))$ *according to Equation 6.*

Improvements. Several improvements of the Apriori algorithm have been suggested that improve on the PredictiveApriori algorithm as well. The AprioriTid algorithm requires much fewer database passes by storing, for each database record, a list of item sets of length i which this record supports. From these lists, the support of each item set can easily be computed. In the next iteration, the list of item sets of length $i + 1$ that each transaction supports can be computed without accessing the database. We can expect this modification to enhance the overall performance when the database is very large but sparse. Further improvements can be obtained by using sampling techniques (*e.g.*, [11]).

Table 2. (Top) five best association rules when subsumed rules are removed; (bottom) five best rules when subsumed rules are not removed

[$\Rightarrow$ PanelID=9 ProductGroup=84]
$E(c \mid \hat{c} = 1, s = 10000) = 1$
[Location=market_4 $\Rightarrow$ PanelID=9, ProductGroup=84, Container=nonreuseable]
$E(c \mid \hat{c} = 1, s = 1410) = 1$
[Location=market_6 $\Rightarrow$ PanelID=9, ProductGroup=84, Container=nonreuseable]
$E(c \mid \hat{c} = 1, s = 1193) = 1$
[Location=market_1 $\Rightarrow$ PanelID=9, ProductGroup=84, Container=nonreuseable]
$E(c \mid \hat{c} = 1, s = 1025) = 1$
[Manufacturer=producer_18 $\Rightarrow$ PanelID=9, ProductGroup=84, Type=0, Container=nonreuseable]
$E(c \mid \hat{c} = 1, s = 1804) = 1$

[$\Rightarrow$ PanelID=9]	$E(c \mid \hat{c} = 1, s = 10000) = 1$
[$\Rightarrow$ ProductGroup=84]	$E(c \mid \hat{c} = 1, s = 10000) = 1$
[$\Rightarrow$ PanelID=9, ProductGroup=84]	$E(c \mid \hat{c} = 1, s = 10000) = 1$
[Location=market_4 $\Rightarrow$ PanelID=9]	$E(c \mid \hat{c} = 1, s = 1410) = 1$
[Location=market_4 $\Rightarrow$ ProductGroup=84]	$E(c \mid \hat{c} = 1, s = 1410) = 1$

5   Experiments

For our experiments, we used a database of 14,000 fruit juice purchase transactions, and the mailing campaign data used for the KDD cup 1998. Each transaction of the fruit juice dtabase is described by 29 real valued and string valued attributes which specify properties of the purchased juice as well as attributes of the customer (*e.g.*, age and job). By binarizing the attributes and considering only a subset of the binary attributes, we varied the number of items during the experiments. For instance, we transformed the attribute "ContainerSize" into five binary attributes, "ContainerSize ≤ 0.3", "$0.3 <$ ContainerSize ≤ 0.5", etc.

Figure 2a shows the prior $\pi(c)$ as estimated by the algorithm in step 3 for several numbers of items. Figure 1 shows the predictive accuracy for this prior, depending on the confidence and the body support. Table 2 (top) shows the five best association rules found for the fruit juice problem by the PredictiveApriori algorithm. The rules say that all transactions are performed under PanelID 9 and refer to product group 84 (fruit juice purchases). Apparently, markets 1, 4, and 6 only sell non-reuseable bottles (in contrast to the refillable bottles sold by most german supermarkets). Producer 18 does not sell refillable bottles either.

In order to compare the performance of Apriori and PredictiveApriori, we need to find a uniform measure that is independent of implementation details. For Apriori, we count how many association rules have to be compared against the minconf threshold (this number is independent of the actual minconf threshold). We can determine this number from the item sets without actually enumerating all rules. For PredictiveApriori, we measure for how many rules we need to determine the predictive accuracy by evaluating Equation 6.

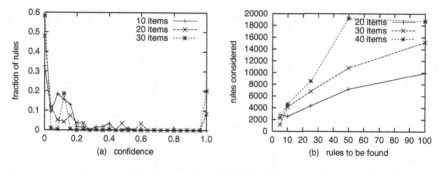

Fig. 2. (a) Confidence prior π for various numbers of items. (b) Number of rules that PredictiveApriori has to consider dependent on the number n of desired solutions

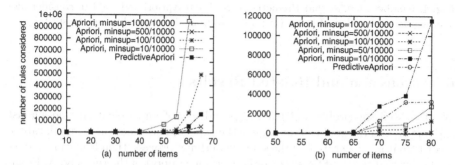

Fig. 3. Time complexity of PredictiveApriori and Apriori, depending on the number of items and (in case of Apriori) of minsup (a) fruit juice problem, (b) KDD cup 1998

The performance of Apriori depends crucially on the choice of the support threshold "minsup". In Fig. 3, we compare the computational expenses imposed by PredictiveApriori (10 best solutions) to the complexity of Apriori for several different minsup thresholds and numbers of items for both the fruit juice and the KDD cup database. The time required by Apriori grows rapidly with decreasing minsup values. Among the 25 best solutions for the juice problem found by PredictiveApriori we can see rules with body support and confidence of 92. In order to find such special but accurate rules, Apriori would run many times as long as PredictiveApriori. Figure 2b shows how the complexity increases with the number of desired solutions. The increase is only sub-linear. Figure 4 shows extended comparisons of the Apriori and PredictiveApriori performance for the fruit juice problem. The horizontal lines show the time required by PredictiveApriori for the given number of database items ($n = 10$ best solutions). The curves show how the time required by Apriori depends on the minsup support threshold. Apriori is faster for large thresholds since it then searches only a small fraction of the space of association rules.

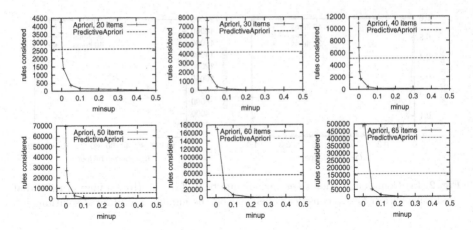

Fig. 4. Number of rules that PredictiveApriori and Apriori and need to consider, depending on the number of items (in case of Apriori also depending on minsup)

6   Discussion and Related Results

We discussed the problem of trading confidence of an association rule against support. When the goal is to maximize the expected accuracy on future database records that are generated by the same underlying process, then Equation 6 gives us the optimal trade-off between confidence and support of the rule's body. Equation 6 results from a Bayesian analysis of the predictive accuracy; it is based on the assumption that the database records are independent and identically distributed and requires us to estimate the confidence prior. The PredictiveApriori algorithm does this using a MCMC approach [4].

The Bayesian frequency correction approach that eliminates the optimistical bias of high confidences relates to an analysis of classification algorithms [8] that yields a parameter-free regularization criterion for decision tree algorithms [10]. The PredictiveApriori algorithm returns the n rules which maximize the expected accuracy; the user only has to specify how many rules he or she wants to be presented. This is perhaps a more natural parameter than minsup and minconf, required by the Apriori algorithm.

The algorithm also checks the rules for redundancies. It has a bias towards returning general rules and eliminating all rules which are entailed by equally accurate, more general ones. Guided by similar ideas, the Midos algorithm [12] performs a similarity test for hypotheses. In [13], a rule discovery algorithm is discussed that selects from classes of redundant rules the most simple, rather than the most general ones. For example, given two equally accurate rules $[a \Rightarrow b]$ and $[a \Rightarrow b, c]$ PredictiveApriori would prefer the latter which predicts more values whereas [13] would prefer the shorter first one.

The favorable computational performance of the PredictiveApriori algorithm can be credited to the dynamic pruning technique that uses an upper bound on the accuracy of all rules over supersets of a given item set. Very large parts of the search space can thus be excluded. A similar idea is realized in Midos [12].

Many optimizations of the Apriori algorithm have been proposed which have helped this algorithm gain its huge practical relevance. These include the AprioriTid approach for minimizing the number of database passes [2], and sampling approaches for estimating the support of item sets [2,11]. In particular, efficient search for frequent itemsets has been addressed intensely and successfully [7, 3,14]. Many of these improvements can, and should be, applied to the PredictiveApriori algorithm as well.

References

1. R. Agrawal, T. Imielinski, and A. Swami. Mining association rules between sets of items in large databases. In *ACM SIGMOD Conference on Management of Data*, pages 207–216, 1993.
2. R. Agrawal, H. Mannila, R. Srikant, H. Toivonen, and A. Verkamo. Fast discovery of association rules. In *Advances in Knowledge Discovery and Data Mining*, 1996.
3. S. Brin, R. Motwani, J. Ullmann, and S. Tsur. Dynamic itemset counting and implication rules for market basket data. In *Proceedings of the ACM SIGMOD Conference on Managament of Data*, 1997.
4. W. Gilks, S. Richardson, and D. Spiegelhalter, editors. *Markov Chain Monte Carlo in Practice*. Chapman & Hall, 1995.
5. M. Klemettinen, H. Mannila, P. Ronkainen, H.Toivonen, and A. I. Verkamo. Finding interesting rules from large sets of discovered associacion rules. *Proc. Third International Conference on Information and Knowledge Management*, 1994.
6. J. Langford and D. McAllester. Computable shell decomposition bounds. In *Proceedings of the International Conference on Computational Learning Theory*, 2000.
7. D. Lin and Z. Kedem. Pincer search: a new algorithm for discovering the maximum frequent set. In *Proceedings of the International Conference on Extending Database Technology*, 1998.
8. T. Scheffer. *Error Estimation and Model Selection*. Infix Publisher, Sankt Augustin, 1999.
9. T. Scheffer. Average-case analysis of classification algorithms for boolean functions and decision trees. In *Proceedings of the International Conference on Algorithmic Learning Theory*, 2000.
10. T. Scheffer. Nonparametric regularization of decision trees. In *Proceedings of the European Conference on Machine Learning*, 2000.
11. T. Scheffer and S. Wrobel. A sequential sampling algorithm for a general class of utility functions. In *Proceedings of the International Conference on Knowledge Discovery and Data Mining*, 2000.
12. S. Wrobel. Inductive logic programming for knowledge discovery in databases. In Sašo Džeroski and Nada Lavrač, editors, *Relational Data Mining*, 2001.
13. M. Zaki. Generating non-redundant association rules. In *Proceedings of the International Conference on Knowledge Discovery and Data Mining*, 2000.
14. M. Zaki and C. Hiao. Charm: an efficient algorithm for closed association rule mining. Technical Report 99-10, Rensselaer Polytechnic Institute, 1999.

Bloomy Decision Tree for Multi-objective Classification

Einoshin Suzuki, Masafumi Gotoh, and Yuta Choki

Division of Electrical and Computer Engineering
Yokohama National University, Japan
{suzuki,dandy,choki}@slab.dnj.ynu.ac.jp

Abstract. This paper presents a novel decision-tree induction for a multi-objective data set, i.e. a data set with a multi-dimensional class. Inductive decision-tree learning is one of the frequently-used methods for a single-objective data set, i.e. a data set with a single-dimensional class. However, in a real data analysis, we usually have multiple objectives, and a classifier which explains them simultaneously would be useful and would exhibit higher readability. A conventional decision-tree inducer requires transformation of a multi-dimensional class into a single-dimensional class, but such a transformation can considerably worsen both accuracy and readability. In order to circumvent this problem we propose a bloomy decision tree which deals with a multi-dimensional class without such transformations. A bloomy decision tree has a set of split nodes each of which splits examples according to their attribute values, and a set of flower nodes each of which predicts a class dimension of examples. A flower node appears not only at the fringe of a tree but also inside a tree. Our pruning is executed during tree construction, and evaluates each class dimension based on Cramér's V. The proposed method has been implemented as D3-B (Decision tree in Bloom), and tested with eleven data sets. The experiments showed that D3-B has higher accuracies in nine data sets than C4.5 and tied with it in the other two data sets. In terms of readability, D3-B has a smaller number of split nodes in all data sets, and thus outperforms C4.5.

1 Introduction

Given a set of training examples, learning from examples aims at constructing a classifier which predicts the class of an unseen example. Here, learning from examples assumes that each example has a single-dimensional class, and can thus be called as single-objective. Inductive decision-tree learning [2,10,11] has been successfully used in various fields as one of the most useful methods in learning from examples.

In dealing with real data, however, we often have multiple objectives, and may wish to predict a multi-dimensional class [3,4]. Building a separate decision tree for each objective would be problematic in terms of readability because decision trees differ in their structures and in their split attributes, and are thus difficult to be compared. A single classifier which predicts this multi-dimensional class

L. De Raedt and A. Siebes (Eds.): PKDD 2001, LNAI 2168, pp. 436–447, 2001.

would be more useful. For example, suppose an analyst constructing a classifier from an agricultural data set about various crops. Rather than having a decision tree which predicts only corn, the analyst would prefer a decision tree which predicts corn and wheat simultaneously since it would be comprehensible.

In such a case, a conventional decision-tree learning algorithm can construct a classifier if the multi-dimensional class is transformed into a single-dimensional class. This idea is described in [3,4] briefly without experimental justification[1]. However, a transformation without loss of information, such as assigning a new class value to each combination of class values, considerably increases the number of class values. This tendency causes a fragmentation problem [11]: each class value has only a few training examples in a split node at the bottom of a decision tree, and appropriate selection of an attribute would be difficult. A transformation with loss of information such as principle component analysis [6, 7] could overlook useful knowledge.

In order to circumvent this problem we propose a bloomy decision tree in which each class dimension is independently predicted by a flower node. Since a flower node can be constructed inside a tree, the number of class dimensions gradually decreases as an example descend the tree. This corresponds to coping with the fragmentation problem by simplifying the classification task in order to construct a small decision tree with high accuracy. We have implemented an induction algorithm of bloomy decision trees as D3-B (Decision tree in Bloom), and demonstrate its effectiveness as a multi-objective classifier with eleven data sets.

2   Decision Tree

In this section, we give a simple explanation of inductive decision-tree learning [2,10,11]. For various problems in this field, please refer to a recent survey [9].

2.1   Construction of a Decision Tree

A decision tree represents a tree-structured classifier which consists of a set of nodes and a set of edges. A node is either a split node which tests an attribute or a leaf node which predicts a class of an example. Given an unseen example, a split node assigns the example to one of its subtrees according to the value of its attribute, and a leaf node predicts the class value of the example.

The input to a decision-tree inducer is a set E of examples. An example e_i has n attribute values $a_{1i}, a_{2i}, \cdots, a_{ni}$ for attributes $a_1, a_2, \cdots, a_n$ and a class value c_i to a class c, and is represented as $e_i = (a_{1i}, a_{2i}, \cdots, a_{ni}, c_i)$.

---

[1] Caruana formalized a learning problem with multiple objectives as multitask learning [3,4], which includes our multi-objective classification. He almost exclusively worked with neural networks, and only dropped a few remarks about decision trees. His remarks mainly concern proposal of novel split criteria, and no proposals are given for knowledge representation.

A decision tree is typically constructed by a recursive split of example space with a divide and conquer method. The split typically employs greedy search, and, for each split node, the best attribute is selected as the attribute of the node based on an evaluation function. We will explain a typical function in Sect. 2.2. The class value of a leaf node is determined if all training examples in the node have the same class value. If a leaf node has no training examples, the most frequent class value of examples in its parent is assigned as the class value of the leaf. If the training examples in a split node can no longer be split, the node becomes a leaf node and the most frequent class value of examples in the node is assigned as the class value of the leaf. Here, a decision tree which perfectly predicts the class of a training example tends to perform poorly for test examples. A procedure called pruning replaces a subtree which is judged irrelevant in the prediction with a leaf node. We will explain a pruning method in Sect. 2.3.

2.2   Attribute Selection

Here, we explain gain ratio [10,11] as one of the evaluation criteria. Gain ratio $G(a, c, E)$ is a criterion based on mutual entropy of an attribute a and the class c for a set E of examples. Let $|E|$, $E_{a=i}$, and $E_{c=i}$ be the number of examples in E, the set of examples each of which satisfies $a = i$ in E, and the set of examples each of which satisfies $c = i$ in E respectively, then

$$G(a, c, E) \equiv \frac{H(c, E) - J(a, c, E)}{H(a, E)} \tag{1}$$

where

$$H(c, E) \equiv -\sum_i \frac{|E_{c=i}|}{|E|} \log_2 \left(\frac{|E_{c=i}|}{|E|} \right) \tag{2}$$

$$J(a, c, E) \equiv \sum_i \frac{|E_{a=i}|}{|E|} H(c, E_{a=i}) \tag{3}$$

2.3   Pruning

Pruning can be classified as either pre-pruning, which is executed during tree construction, or post-pruning, which is executed after tree construction [8,10, 11]. Compared with post-pruning, pre-pruning is time-efficient since it does not require construction of a complete tree. However, experimental evidence shows that pre-pruning leads to low accuracy [8], and most decision-tree inducers employ post-pruning.

Pruning based on χ^2 is employed in decision-tree inducers such as ID3 [10]. This method first calculates a χ^2 value $\chi^2(a, c, E)$ of an attribute a and the class c for a set E of examples in a node. Let $E_{a=i,c=j}$ be the set of examples each of which satisfies both $a = i$ and $c = j$ in E, then

$$\chi^2(a, c, E) \equiv \sum_i \sum_j \frac{(|E_{a=i,c=j}| - \epsilon_{a=i,c=j}(E))^2}{\epsilon_{a=i,c=j}(E)} \tag{4}$$

where

$$\epsilon_{a=i,c=j}(E) \equiv \frac{|E_{a=i}||E_{c=j}|}{|E|} \tag{5}$$

Let $\chi_r^2(\alpha)$ be a χ^2 value with a degree of freedom r and a significance level α, then when $\chi^2(a, c, E)$ is smaller than a threshold $\chi_r^2(\alpha)$, the attribute a and the class c are considered to have no relevance, and the split node is replaced by a leaf node. A shortcoming of this approach is that $\chi^2(a, c, E)$ tends to be overly large when the number of examples in the training set is large, and a decision tree is often under-pruned [8].

3   Bloomy Decision Tree for Multi-objective Classification

3.1   Bloomy Decision Tree

In a data set E for multi-objective classification, i.e. with a multi-dimensional class, each example e_i has n attribute values $a_{1i}, a_{2i}, \cdots, a_{ni}$ for attributes $a_1, a_2, \cdots, a_n$, and m class values $(c_{1i}, c_{2i}, \cdots, c_{mi})$ for a m-dimensional class $(c_1, c_2, \cdots, c_m)$.

The problems in Sect. 1 have led us to invent a bloomy decision tree for multi-objective classification. In a decision tree for multi-objective classification, several class dimensions can be predicted accurately even at an internal node. A bloomy decision tree predicts such dimensions in an internal node which is called a flower node, and typically reduces the number of class dimensions to be predicted as an example descends the tree from its root to one of its leaves. This corresponds to simplifying a multi-objective classification downward a decision tree, and can be considered as an efficient solution to the fragmentation problem described in Sect. 1. A bloomy decision tree is expected to show high accuracy with a simpler structure compared with a conventional decision tree. A flower node corresponds to a leaf node which predicts a set of class dimensions, and appears not only at the fringe of a tree but also inside a tree.

Similar to a conventional decision tree, a bloomy decision tree T has a recursive tree structure. A node N of a bloomy decision tree T is classified as either a flower node N_{bloom} which predicts values of a set of class dimensions, or a split node N_{split} which splits examples according to their attribute values. Figure 1 shows an example of a bloomy decision tree for a 2-dimensional class (c_1, c_2), where an oval and a rectangle represent a flower node and a split node respectively. Note that a flower node appears inside the tree since a class dimension is predicted as $c_1 = $ p for examples each of which satisfies $Attribute1$ =Y.

A root node of a bloomy decision tree is a split node. A split node N_{split} has an attribute a which is selected according to a procedure in the next section. Let the number of values for an attribute a be v_a, then there are v_a child nodes for N_{split}, and each child node is assigned a subset $E_{a=a_i}$ where a_i is the i-th value of a. A child node of N_{split} is either a split node or a flower node.

A flower node N_{bloom} consists of l $(\leq m)$ petals $p_1, p_2, \cdots, p_l$ each of which predicts a class dimension. Alternatively, a petal p_i represents that a predicted

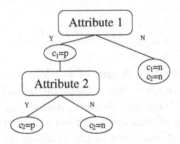

Fig. 1. Example of a bloomy decision tree

value is assigned to a class dimension c_j. The predicted value of c_j is fixed in the petal and remain unchanged in the child nodes of N_{bloom}. If some of the class dimensions remain unpredicted in N_{bloom}, N_{bloom} has a child node which is a split node. Note that a flower node can be an internal node as well as a leaf node.

3.2 Attribute Selection

Similar to the construction of a decision tree, we employ a divide and conquer method based on an attribute selection function $F(a, E)$. Gain ratio presented in Sect. 2.2 is an evaluation function for a single-dimensional class, and cannot be employed without modification. In this paper, we employ the add-sum $F(a, E)$ of gain ratio $G(a, c_j, E)$ for each class dimension c_j.

$$F(a, E) \equiv \sum_{c_j} G(a, c_j, E) \tag{6}$$

Given a set E of training examples, the attribute a which maximizes $F(a, E)$ is selected in a split node. We call this approach as the add-sum criterion.

Instead of using the add-sum of gain ratios, we can also consider their product or the add-sum of their squares, which we call the product criterion and the squares-sum criterion respectively. However, the product criterion would be overly pessimistic, avoiding an attribute which has at least a nearly-zero gain ratio. The squares-sum criterion, on the other hand, would be overly optimistic, preferring an attribute which relies on a few large gain ratios. The former neglects an attribute which works well for a subset of dimensions, and the latter criterion is typically dominated by outliers. Therefore, we use the add-sum criterion in our approach. Note that this analysis could be justified experimentally under various settings, but we leave this for future work due to space constraint.

3.3 Pruning

In order to obtain an accurate classifier for all class dimensions, each dimension should be evaluated independently. Our method employs pre-pruning for each dimension immediately after constructing a split node, and assigns a predicted value for a dimension which is pruned.

As explained in Sect. 2.3, χ^2 pruning tends to produce an overly large decision tree when the number of examples in the training set is large. Therefore, we use Cramér's V [7] to cope with this problem. Cramér's V $V(a, c_j, E)$ is an index of relevance of an attribute a and a class dimension c_j for a set E of examples.

$$V(a, c_j, E) \equiv \sqrt{\frac{\chi^2(a, c_j, E)}{|E|(\min(v_a, q(c_j)) - 1)}} \tag{7}$$

where $q(c_j)$ is the number of values of c_j. This index satisfies $0 \leq V(a, c_j, E) \leq 1$.

Since this index is, unlike χ^2, simply employed to compare its value and has no theoretical interpretation, we use the following value $V_r(a, c_j, E_Z, \alpha)$ as a threshold for pruning.

$$V_r(a, c_j, E_Z, \alpha) \equiv \sqrt{\frac{\chi_r^2(\alpha)}{|E_Z|(\min(v_a, q(c_j)) - 1)}} \tag{8}$$

where $|E_Z|$ is the expected number of examples assigned to the split node. Let $|E_P|$ and $|N_{PC}|$ be the number of examples in the parent split node and the number of child nodes of the parent split node respectively, then

$$|E_Z| \equiv \frac{|E_P|}{|N_{PC}|} \tag{9}$$

For a root node, we define that $|E_P|$ is equivalent to the number of training examples in the data set. In our method, a split node is pruned with respect to a dimension c_j if $V(a, c_j, E) < V_r(a, c_j, E_Z, \alpha)$, and decision-tree construction is continued with the remaining dimensions of the class.

As explained in Sect. 2.3, post-pruning produces an accurate tree but is time-consuming [8]. Our method, unlike a conventional decision-tree inducer, continues construction of a decision tree with the remaining dimensions even after pruning. Therefore, we do not employ post-pruning since it requires iterations of construction and pruning, and is thus time-consuming.

4 D3-B

4.1 Construction of a Bloomy Decision Tree

We have implemented our method as D3-B. Its algorithm is shown below, where each attribute and each class dimension is assumed to have a discrete value. Given a set E of examples, D3-B outputs a bloomy decision tree T using *D3-B*(training set).

Given a set E of examples, algorithm *D3-B* recursively constructs a bloomy decision tree T with a divide and conquer method. If the training set E in a node can no longer be divided, we add, to T, a flower node which predicts all dimensions in E. We define that a node can no longer be divided if and only if at least one of the following conditions hold: 1) no class dimension in E, 2) values of each class dimension are identical, or 3) E is empty. A predicted value is the majority of E if E is non-empty, otherwise the majority of the training set.

If E can be divided, an attribute a is first selected according to the procedure described in Sect. 3.2. Next, based on the pruning procedure which will be described in the next section, a set P of class dimensions to be pruned are obtained. If P is non-empty, we add, to T, a flower node which predicts the class dimensions in P, and those class dimensions are deleted from E. From Sect. 3.1, in this case, there is only one child node, which will be constructed by $D3\text{-}B(E)$. For instance, in Fig. 1 c_1 was pruned at the left child of the root node. If P is empty, child nodes are constructed by $D3\text{-}B(E_{a=v})$ for each value v of a.

Algorithm: $D3\text{-}B(E)$
Input: data set E
Return value: bloomy decision tree T
begin
If ((E can no longer be split) **and** (E has a class dimension))
    Add a flower node which predicts all class dimensions in E to T
Else
  begin
    $a \leftarrow \arg\max_{a'} F(a', E)$
    $P \leftarrow Prune(E, a)$
    If(P is non-empty)
      begin
      Add a flower node which predicts class dimensions in P to T
      Delete class dimensions in P from E
      Construct a child node of T by $D3\text{-}B(E)$
      end
    Else
      Foreach(value v of attribute a)
        Construct child nodes of T by $D3\text{-}B(E_{a=v})$
  end
Return T
end

4.2 Pruning of a Bloomy Decision Tree

Given a set E of examples and a selected attribute a, our algorithm returns a set P of class dimensions each of which should be predicted in the node. For each dimension c_i in E, the following procedure checks the pruning condition explained in Sect. 3.3, and adds the class dimension if it satisfies the condition to P. This procedure is done in lexical order of class dimensions for simplicity, and a class dimension c_i which satisfies the condition is not employed in the calculation of $V(a, c_j, E)$ and $V_r(a, c_j, E_Z, \alpha)$ for a subsequent class dimension c_j.

Procedure: Prune(E,a)
Input: data set E, selected attribute a
Return value: a set of class dimensions P
begin
$P \leftarrow \phi$
Foreach(class dimension c_i in E)
  If($V(a, c_i, E) < V_r(a, c_i, E_Z, \alpha)$)
    begin
      $P \leftarrow P \cup \{c_i\}$
    c_i is not employed in the calculation of $V(a, c_j, E)$ and $V_r(a, c_j, E_Z, \alpha)$ for a
subsequent class dimension c_j
    end
Return P
end

5 Experimental Evaluation

5.1 Conditions of Experiments

We demonstrate the effectiveness of D3-B as a multi-objective classifier by experiments with eleven data sets. In the rest of this paper, thresholds for pruning were settled with $r = 1$ and $\alpha = 5\%$.

"Agriculture" is a series of data sets which describe agricultural statistics for 3,246 municipalities in Japan. In this experiment, we employed the 1991 version. Each example is represented by 37 attributes such as areas, populations, financial statistics, and industrial statistics; and has a 25-dimensional class about gross products of crops. A continuous attribute was first discretized with equal-frequency method [5] of five bins. We employed a simple class-blind discretization method, rather than a class-driven discretization method, for the sake of simplicity and speed-up. Before discretization, we visualized distributions of values for several attributes, and chose the number five arbitrarily. A continuous class dimension was first discretized with equal-frequency method of two bins. The number two was chosen after we observed poor performance of induction algorithms with five bins. We consider that information contained in this data set is insufficient in order to learn a classifier which correctly predicts a fine-defined multi-dimensional class.

"Kiosk" is a data set which describes inventories about 52 kinds of merchandise in 232 shops of a Japanese company in 1994. In this data set, each kind of merchandise has at least 83 zeros. In discretizing a continuous attribute, we treated 0 as a value, and applied equal-frequency method of three bins to the other values. The number three was chosen because only a small number of examples were used in the discretizing procedure.

The other nine data sets comes from the UCI Repository [1]. We discretized a continuous attribute with equal-frequency method of four bins, where a missing value was left unchanged. The number four was chosen due to the wide variety of attributes concerning distributions of values: the distribution was relatively balanced for some attributes such as those in "Agriculture", and was skewed for other attributes such as those in "Kiosk".

For each data set, 100 multi-objective classification tasks were settled. For each classification task except for those with the agriculture data, we chose six attributes randomly, and regarded them as a 6-dimensional class. In choosing these attributes for UCI data sets, we considered their appropriateness as a class dimension. For each attribute, a single-objective classification task was settled, and an attribute with which C4.5[11]'s accuracy is less than 63.5% with 5-fold cross-validation was ignored in selecting a class dimension. As the result, the Australian data and the mushroom data have only 28 ($= {}_8C_6$) possible sets of 6-class tasks, so we checked all these 28 tasks instead of randomly-chosen 100 tasks for these data sets. For the agriculture data, we employed the 25-dimensional class. Initial experiments revealed that 3.0 % difference for average accuracy and 1.5 difference for average number of nodes can be each considered as significant.

Note that, in practice, a class dimension should be settled in terms of its importance in the domain. An interesting research avenue would be to measure effectiveness of learning algorithms by constructing a class attribute with attributes that can be more naturally used as a class dimension, in the sense that their prediction is useful for the user.

In order to evaluate the effectiveness of our approach, we compared D3-B with six learning algorithms including C4.5 and variants of D3-B. In the experiments, average accuracies for class dimensions and average number of split nodes were measured by 5-fold cross-validation as evaluation indices. First, C4.5 was chosen as the representative of conventional decision-tree inducers. In applying C4.5, a multi-dimensional class was transformed to a single-dimensional class by assigning a new class value to each combination of class values. Second, D3-B was also applied to data sets each of which was produced with this transformation in order to evaluate the effectiveness of flower nodes. Third, in order to evaluate the effectiveness of Cramér's V pruning, we also employed D3-B with χ^2 pruning. Fourth and fifth, the add-sum criterion in Sect. 3.2 was evaluated by using D3-Bs with the product criterion and the squares-sum criterion. Sixth, we compared D3-B with a method which constructs a decision tree for each class dimension.

5.2   Experimental Results

Figure 2a shows the accuracies and the numbers of split nodes of D3-B and C4.5. Concerning accuracy, our method outperforms C4.5 in nine data sets by 3.4 % - 19.3 %, and approximately ties with it in the other two data sets (our advantage is less than 2.4 %). Concerning the number of split nodes, D3-B constructs smaller trees in all data sets by 9.1 - 452.9. This shows that our D3-B outperforms C4.5 in accuracy and readability due to its appropriateness to a multi-objective classification task.

Figure 2b shows the effect of flower nodes on the accuracy and the number of split nodes. Concerning the accuracy, D3-B outperforms D3-B without flower nodes in "hepatitis", "Australian", and "German" by 7.9 % - 11.8 %; and ap-

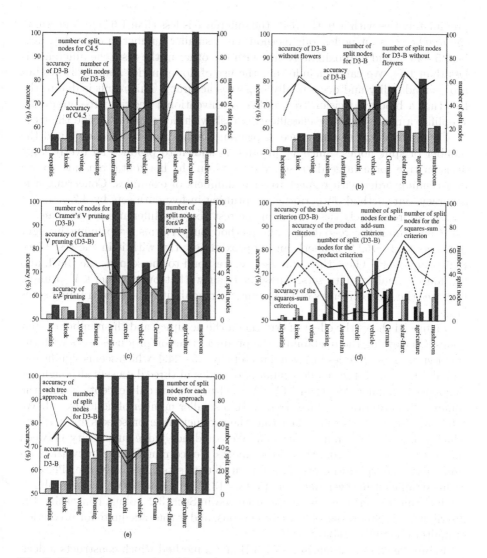

Fig. 2. Experimental results. (a) Accuracies and numbers of split nodes of D3-B and C4.5. For C4.5, the numbers of nodes for "vehicle", "German", and "agriculture" are 109, 152, and 468 respectively. (b) Effect of flower nodes on the accuracies and the numbers of split nodes. (c) Accuracies and numbers of split nodes of D3-Bs with Cramér's V pruning and χ^2 pruning. The numbers of nodes of the latter method for "Australian", "credit", "German", and "mushroom" are 132, 125, 179, and 103 respectively. (d) Accuracies and numbers of split nodes of D3-Bs with the add-sum criterion, the product criterion, and the squares-sum criterion. (e) Comparison of D3-B and a method which constructs a decision tree for each class dimension. The numbers of nodes of the latter method for "housing", "Australian", "credit", and "vehicle" are 101, 144, 143, and 119 respectively. Note that this comparison should be treated differently since the latter method constructs multiple trees.

proximately ties with it in the rest (the difference is less than 1.6 %). Concerning the number of split nodes, our method has a smaller number in eight data sets by 3.5 - 45.5, and approximately ties with the other in the rest (the difference is less than 1.7). We can conclude that the use of flower nodes almost always improves readability and occasionally improves accuracy. This result is due to the fact that a bloomy decision tree, unlike a conventional decision tree, gradually simplifies a multi-objective classification task with flower nodes inside the tree.

Figure 2c shows the influence of pruning methods on the accuracy and the number of split nodes. Since χ^2 pruning is known to produce an overly large decision tree for a large data set, data sets on the horizontal axis are sorted in ascending order with respect to their numbers of examples. Concerning the accuracy, our method outperforms χ^2 pruning in five data sets by 3.7 % - 12.4 %, and approximately ties with it in the rest six (the difference is less than 1.1 %). Concerning the readability, our method outperforms χ^2 pruning in eight data sets (7.2 - 152.8 smaller), and approximately ties with it in the rest three (0.6 - 2.9 larger). These three data sets correspond to the second, the third, and the fourth smallest data sets. These facts show that our Cramér's V pruning tolerates the ineffectiveness of χ^2 pruning in readability when the training set is large.

Figure 2d shows the effect of criteria on the accuracy and the number of split nodes. Concerning the readability, the product criterion produces trees with the smallest number of nodes in seven data sets by 7.5 - 24.4, which seems significant, and also trees with the smallest number of nodes in three data sets although the difference is smaller (less than 1.6). "Agriculture" is the only exception since the squares-sum criterion produces trees with a smaller number of nodes by 4.4. We attribute these results to the fact that the product criterion selects an attribute which splits all class dimensions well. We could not judge superiority between the other two criteria from these experiments. Concerning the accuracy, the add-sum criterion outperforms other criteria in all data sets. Especially, the difference seems significant in seven data sets (4.9% - 13.7%). We attribute these results to the fact that our criterion is, as we discussed in Sect. 3.2, robust concerning the distribution of gain ratios of class dimensions, and is thus adequate for prediction of multi-objective classification.

Figure 2e shows comparison of D3-B and a method which constructs a decision tree for each class dimension. We see that the differences of accuracies seem not significant since they are less than 2.7% in all data sets. For readability, however, D3-B always constructs a smaller tree (the difference is at least 6.6, which seems significant). We consider that these results are due to the fact that D3-B constructs a single tree while the other method constructs multiple trees. Moreover, as we mentioned in Sect 1, readability is much worse than it appears in the latter method since analysis based on multiple trees is difficult.

We also investigated these methods by varying the number m of class dimensions from two to five. Our method typically has no clear advantage for $m = 2$, but gradually outperforms other methods as m increases. It should be noted that no clear difference was observed for relatively "easy" data sets such as "housing". We didn't tried for $m \geq 7$ to avoid the effect that the number of attributes becomes smaller as m increases.

From these results, the superiority of our method in accuracy and/or readability has been empirically proved against other methods. We consider that this superiority demonstrate that our proposals of the flower node, the add-sum criterion, and the Cramér's V pruning are effective in multi-objective classification.

6   Conclusion

In this paper, we proposed a learning algorithm for a novel decision tree from a multi-objective data set. Conventional learning algorithms are ineffective in constructing an accurate and readable decision tree in multi-objective classification. Our D3-B constructs a single classifier: a bloomy decision tree for such a data set. In a bloomy decision tree, the number of class dimensions gradually decreases by the use of flower nodes inside the tree. Experiments with eleven data sets showed that our D3-B, compared with C4.5 and other methods, typically constructs more accurate and/or smaller trees.

References

1. Blake, C., Keogh, E., and Merz, C. J.: UCI Repository of Machine Learning Databases, http://www.ics.uci.edu/~mlearn/MLRepository.html, Univ. California, Irvine, Dept. Information and Computer Science (1998).
2. Breiman, L., Friedman, J., Olshen, R., and Stone, C. A.: *Classification and Regression Trees*, Chapman & Hall, New York (1984).
3. Caruana, R.: "Multitask Learning", *Machine Learning*, Vol. 28, No. 1, pp. 41–75 (1997).
4. Caruana, R.: "Multitask Learning", *Ph. D. Thesis, CMU-CS-97-203*, School of Computer Science, Carnegie Mellon Univ., Pittsburgh, Pa. (1997).
5. Dougherty, J., Kohavi, R., and Sahami M.: "Supervised and Unsupervised Discretization of Continuous Features", *Proc. Twelfth Int'l Conf. on Machine Learning (ICML)*, pp. 194–202 (1995).
6. Forouraghi, B., Schmerr, L. W., and Prabhu, G. M.: "Induction of Multivariate Regression Trees for Design Optimization", *Proc. Twelfth Nat'l Conf. on Artificial Intelligence (AAAI)*, pp. 607–612 (1994).
7. Kendall, M. G.: *Multivariate Analysis, second edition*, Charles Griffin, High Wycombe, England (1980).
8. Mingers, J.: "An Empirical Comparison of Pruning Methods for Decision-Tree Induction", *Machine Learning*, Vol. 4, No. 2, pp. 227–243 (1989).
9. Murthy, S. K.: "Automatic Construction of Decision Trees from Data: A Multi-Disciplinary Survey", *Data Mining and Knowledge Discovery*, Vol. 2, No. 4, pp. 345–389 (1998).
10. Quinlan, J. R.: "Induction of Decision Trees", *Machine Learning*, Vol. 1, No. 1, pp. 81–106 (1986).
11. Quinlan, J. R.: *C4.5: Programs for Machine Learning*, Morgan Kaufmann, San Mateo, Calif. (1993).

Discovery of Temporal Knowledge in Medical Time-Series Databases Using Moving Average, Multiscale Matching, and Rule Induction

Shusaku Tsumoto

Department of Medicine Informatics, Shimane Medical University, School of Medicine
89-1 Enya-cho Izumo City, Shimane 693-8501 Japan
tsumoto@computer.org

Abstract. Since hospital information systems have been introduced in large hospitals, a large amount of data, including laboratory examinations, have been stored as temporal databases. The characteristics of these temporal databases are: (1) Each record are inhomogeneous with respect to time-series, including short-term effects and long-term effects. (2) Each record has more than 1000 attributes when a patient is followed for more than one year. (3) When a patient is admitted for a long time, a large amount of data is stored in a very short term. Even medical experts cannot deal with these large databases, the interest in mining some useful information from the data are growing. In this paper, we introduce a combination of extended moving average method, multiscale matching and rule induction method to discover new knowledge in medical temporal databases. This method was applied to a medical dataset, the results of which show that interesting knowledge is discovered from each database.

1 Introduction

Since hospital information systems have been introduced in large hospitals, a large amount of data, including laboratory examinations, have been stored as temporal databases [15]. For example, in a university hospital, where more than 1000 patients visit from Monday to Friday, a database system stores more than 1 GB numerical data of laboratory examinations. Thus, it is highly expected that data mining methods will find interesting patterns from databases because medical experts cannot deal with those large amount of data. The characteristics of these temporal databases are: (1) Each record are inhomogeneous with respect to time-series, including short-term effects and long-term effects. (2) Each record has more than 1000 attributes when a patient is followed for more than one year. (3) When a patient is admitted for a long time, a large amount of data is stored in a very short term. Even medical experts cannot deal with these large temporal databases, the interest in mining some useful information from the data are growing.

In this paper, we introduce a rule discovery method, combined with extended moving average method, multiscale matching for qualitative trend to discover

L. De Raedt and A. Siebes (Eds.): PKDD 2001, LNAI 2168, pp. 448–459, 2001.

new knowledge in medical temporal databases. In this system, extended moving average method and multi-scale matching are used for preprocessing, to deal with irregularity of each temporal data. Using several parameters for time-scaling, given by users, this moving average method generates a new database for each time scale with summarized attributes. For matching time sequences, multiscale matching was applied. Then, rule induction method is applied to each new database with summarized attributes. This method was applied to two medical datasets, the results of which show that interesting knowledge is discovered from each database.

This paper is organized as follows. Section 2 introduces the definition of probabilistic rules. Section 3 discusses the characteristics of temporal databases in hospital information systems. Section 4 presents extended moving average method. Section 5 introduces second preprocessing methods to extract qualitative trend and rule discovery method with qualitative trend. Section 6 shows experimental results. Section 7 gives a brief discusson of the total method. Finally, Section 8 concludes this paper.

2   Probabilistic Rules and Conditional Probabilities

Before discussing temporal knowledge discovery, we first discuss the characteristics of probabilistic rules. In this section, we use the following notations introduced by Grzymala-Busse and Skowron [11], which are based on rough set theory [10].

Let U denote a nonempty, finite set called the universe and A denote a nonempty, finite set of attributes, i.e., $a : U \to V_a$ for $a \in A$, where V_a is called the domain of a, respectively.Then, a decision table is defined as an information system, $A = (U, A \cup \{d\})$. The atomic formulae over $B \subseteq A \cup \{d\}$ and V are expressions of the form $[a = v]$, called descriptors over B, where $a \in B$ and $v \in V_a$. The set $F(B, V)$ of formulas over B is the least set containing all atomic formulas over B and closed with respect to disjunction, conjunction and negation. For each $f \in F(B, V)$, f_A denote the meaning of f in A, i.e., the set of all objects in U with property f, defined inductively as follows.

1. If f is of the form $[a = v]$ then, $f_A = \{s \in U | a(s) = v\}$
2. $(f \wedge g)_A = f_A \cap g_A; (f \vee g)_A = f_A \vee g_A; (\neg f)_A = U - f_a$

By the use of the framework above, classification accuracy and coverage, or true positive rate is defined as follows.

Let R and D denote a formula in $F(B, V)$ and a set of objects which belong to a decision d. Classification accuracy and coverage(true positive rate) for $R \to d$ is defined as:

$$\alpha_R(D) = \frac{|R_A \cap D|}{|R_A|}(= P(D|R)), \text{ and } \kappa_R(D) = \frac{|R_A \cap D|}{|D|}(= P(R|D)),$$

where $|S|$, $\alpha_R(D)(= P(D|R))$, $\kappa_R(D)(= P(R|D))$ and P(S) denote the cardinality of a set S, a classification accuracy of R as to classification of D and coverage (a true positive rate of R to D), and probability of S, respectively.

By the use of accuracy and coverage, a probabilistic rule is defined as:

$$R \overset{\alpha,\kappa}{\rightarrow} d \quad s.t. \ R = \wedge_j [a_j = v_k], \alpha_R(D)(= P(D|R)) \geq \delta_\alpha$$
$$\text{and } \kappa_R(D)(= P(R|D)) \geq \delta_\kappa,$$

For further information about these probabilistic rules, reader may refer to [14].

3 Temporal Databases in Hospital Information Systems

Since incorporating temporal aspects into databases is still an ongoing research issue in database area [1], temporal data are stored as a table in hospital information systems(H.I.S.). Table 1 shows a typical example of medical data, which is retrieved from H.I.S. The first column denotes the ID number of each patient, and the second one denotes the date when the datasets in this row is examined. Each row with the same ID number describes the results of laboratory examinations, which were taken on the date in the second column. For example, the second row shows the data of the patient ID 1 on 04/19/1986. This simple database show the following characteristics of medical temporal database:

(1) The Number of Attributes Are Too Many. Even though the dataset of a patient focuses on the transition of each examination (attribute), it would be difficult to see its trend when the patient is followed for a long time. If one wants to see the long-term interaction between attributes, it would be almost impossible. In order to solve this problems, most of H.I.S. systems provide several graphical interfaces to capture temporal trends [15]. However, the interactions among more than three attributes are difficult to be studied even if visualization interfaces are used.

(2) Irregularity of Temporal Intervals. Temporal intervals are irregular. Although most of the patients will come to the hospital every two weeks or one month, physicians may not make laboratory tests at each time. When a patient has a acute fit or suffers from acute diseases, such as pneumonia, laboratory examinations will be made every one to three days. On the other hand, when his/her status is stable, these test may not be made for a long time. Patient ID 1 is a typical example. Between 04/30 and 05/08/1986, he suffered from a pneumonia and was admitted to a hospital. Then, during the therapeutic procedure, laboratory tests were made every a few days. On the other hand, when he was stable, such tests were ordered every one or two year.

(3) Missing Values. In addition to irregularity of temporal intervals, datasets have many missing values. Even though medical experts will make laboratory examinations, they may not take the same tests in each instant. Patient ID 1 in Table 1 is a typical example. On 05/06/1986, medical physician selected a specific test to confirm his diagnosis. So, he will not choose other tests. On 01/09/1989, he focused only on GOT, not other tests. In this way, missing values will be observed very often in clinical situations.

Table 1. An example of temporal database

ID	Date	GOT	GPT	LDH	γ-GTP	TP	edema	$\cdots$
1	19860419	24	12	152	63	7.5	-	$\cdots$
1	19860430	25	12	162	76	7.9	+	$\cdots$
1	19860502	22	8	144	68	7.0	+	$\cdots$
1	19860506							$\cdots$
1	19860508	22	13	156	66	7.6	-	$\cdots$
1	19880826	23	17	142	89	7.7	-	$\cdots$
1	19890109	32					-	$\cdots$
1	19910304	20	15	369	139	6.9	+	$\cdots$
2	19810511	20	15	369	139	6.9	-	$\cdots$
2	19810713	22	14	177	49	7.9	-	$\cdots$
2	19880826	23	17	142	89	7.7	-	$\cdots$
2	19890109	32					-	$\cdots$

$\cdots$

These characteristics have already been discussed in KDD area [5]. However, in real-world domains, especially domains in which follow-up studies are crucial, such as medical domains, these ill-posed situations will be distinguished. If one wants to describe each patient (record) as one row, then each row have too many attributes, which depends on how many times laboratory examinations are made for each patient. It is notable that although the above discussions are made according to the medical situations, similar situations may occur in other domains with long-term follow-up studies.

4   Extended Moving Average Methods

4.1   Moving Average Methods

Averaging mean methods have been introduced in statistical analysis [6]. Temporal data often suffers from noise, which will be observed as a spike or sharp wave during a very short period, typically at one instant. Averaging mean methods remove such an incidental effect and make temporal sequences smoother.

With one parameter w, called *window*, moving average $\hat{y}_w$ is defined as follows:

$$\hat{y}_w = \sum_{j=1}^{w} y_j.$$

For example, in the case of GOT of patient ID 1, y_5 is calculated as: $\hat{y}_5 = (24 + 25 + 22 + 22 + 22)/5 = 23.0$. It is easy to see that $\hat{y}_w$ will remove the noise effect which continue less than w points.

The advantage of moving average method is that it enables to remove the noise effect when inputs are given periodically [6]. For example, when some tests are measured every several days[1], the moving average method is useful

---
[1] This condition guarantees that measurement is approximately continuous

to remove the noise and to extract periodical domains. However, in real-world domains, inputs are not always periodical, as shown in Table 1. Thus, when applied time-series are irregular or discrete, ordinary moving average methods are powerless. Another disadvantage of this method is that it cannot be applicable to categorical attributes. In the case of numerical attributes, average can be used as a summarized statistic. On the other hand, such average cannot be defined for categorical attributes.

Thus, we introduce the extended averaging method to solve these two problems in the subsequent subsections.

4.2   Extended Moving Average for Continuous Attributes

In this extension, we first focus on how moving average methods remove noise. The key idea is that a window parameter w is closely related with periodicity. If w is larger, then the periodical behavior whose time-constant is lower than w will be removed. Usually, a spike by noise is observed as a single event and this effect will be removed when w is taken as a large value. Thus, the choice of w separates different kinds of time-constant behavior in each attribute and in the extreme case when w is equal to total number of temporal events, all the temporal behavior will be removed. We refer to this extreme case as $w = \infty$.

The extended moving average method is executed as follows: first calculates y_∞ for an attribute y. Second, the method outputs its maximum and minimum values. Then, according to the selected values for w, a set of sequence $\{y_w(i)\}$ for each record is calculated. For example, if $\{w\}$ is equal to $\{10$ years, 5 years, 1 year, 3 months, 2 weeks$\}$, then for each element in $\{w\}$, the method uses the time-stamp attribute for calculation of each $\{y_w(i)\}$ in order to deal with irregularities.

In the case of Table 1, when w is taken as 1 year, all the rows are aggregated into several components as shown in Table 2. From this aggregation, a sequence y_w for each attribute is calculated as in Table 3.

Table 2. Aggregation for $w = 1$ (year)

ID	Date	GOT	GPT	LDH	γ-GTP	TP	edema	$\cdots$
1	19860419	24	12	152	63	7.5	-	$\cdots$
1	19860430	25	12	162	76	7.9	+	$\cdots$
1	19860502	22	8	144	68	7.0	+	$\cdots$
1	19860506							$\cdots$
1	19860508	22	13	156	66	7.6	-	$\cdots$
1	19880826	23	17	142	89	7.7	-	$\cdots$
1	19890109	32					-	$\cdots$
1	19910304	20	15	369	139	6.9	+	$\cdots$

$\cdots$

Table 3. Moving average for $w = 1$ (year)

ID	Period	GOT	GPT	LDH	γ-GTP	TP	edema	$\cdots$
1	1	23.25	11.25	153.5	68.25	7.5	?	$\cdots$
1	2	23	17	142	89	7.7	?	$\cdots$
1	3	32					?	$\cdots$
1	4						?	$\cdots$
1	5	20	15	369	139	6.9	?	$\cdots$
1	∞	24	12.83	187.5	83.5	7.43	?	$\cdots$
	$\cdots$							

The selection of w can be automated. The simplest way to calculate w is to use the power of natural number, such as 2. For example, we can use 2^n as the window length: 2, 4, 8, 16,...... Using this scale, two weeks, three months, one year correspond to $16 = 2^4$, $64 = 2^6$, $256 = 2^8$.

4.3   Categorical Attributes

One of the disadvantages of moving average method is that it cannot deal with categorical attributes. To solve this problem, we will classify categorical attributes into three types, whose information should be given by users. The first type is *constant*, which will not change during the follow-up period. The second type is *ranking*, which is used to rank the status of a patient. The third type is *variable*, which will change temporally, but ranking is not useful. For the first type, extended moving average method will not be applied. For the second one, integer will be assigned to each rank and extended moving average method for continuous attributes is applied. On the other hand, for the third one, the temporal behavior of attributes is transformed into statistics as follows.

First, the occurence of each category (value) is counted for each window. For example, in Table 2, *edema* is a binary attribute and variable. In the first window, an attribute *edema* takes $\{-,+,+,-\}$.[2] So, the occurence of $-$ and $+$ are 2 and 2, respectively. Then, each conditional probability will be calculated. In the above example, probabilities are equal to $p(-|w_1) = 2/4$ and $p(+|w_1) = 2/4$. Finally, for each probability, a new attribute is appended to the table (Table 4).

Summary of Extended Moving Average. All the process of extended moving average is used to construct a new table for each window parameter as the first preprocessing. Then, second preprocessing method will be applied to newly generated tables. The first preprocessing method is summarized as shown in Fig. 1.

---

[2] Missing values are ignored for counting.

Table 4. Final table with moving average for $w = 1$ (year)

ID	Period	GOT	GPT	LDH	γ-GTP	TP	edema(+)	edema(-)	$\cdots$
1	1	23.25	11.25	153.5	68.25	7.5	0.5	0.5	$\cdots$
1	2	23	17	142	89	7.7	0.0	1.0	$\cdots$
1	3	32					0.0	1.0	$\cdots$
1	4						0.0	1.0	$\cdots$
1	5	20	15	369	139	6.9	1.0	0.0	$\cdots$
1	∞	24	12.83	187.5	83.5	7.43	0.43	0.57	$\cdots$

$\cdots$

1. Repeat for each w in List L_w,
   a) Select an attribute in a List L_a;
      i. If an attribute is numerical, then calculate moving average for w;
      ii. If an attribute is constant, then break;
      iii. If an attribute is rank, then assign integer to each ranking; calculate moving average for w;
      iv. If an attribute is variable, calculate accuracy and coverage of each category;
   b) If L_a is not empty, goto (a).
   c) Construct a new table with each moving average.
2. Construct a table for $w = \infty$.

Fig. 1. First preprocessing method

5 Second Preprocessing and Rule Discovery

5.1 Summarizing Temporal Sequences

From the data table after processing extended moving average methods, several preprocessing methods may be applied in order for users to detect the temporal trends in each attribute. One way is discretization of time-series by clustering introduced by Das [4]. This method transforms time-series into symbols representing qualitative trends by using a similarity measure. Then, time-series data is represented as a symbolic sequence. After this preprocessing, rule discovery method is applied to this sequential data. Another way is to find auto-regression equations from the sequence of averaging means. Then, these quantitative equations can be directly used to extract knowledge or their qualitative interpretation may be used and rule discovery [3], other machine learning methods [7], or rough set method [12] can be applied to extract qualitative knowledge.

In this research, we adopt two modes and transforms databases into two forms: one mode is applying temporal abstraction method [9] with multiscale matching [8] as second preprocessing and transforms all continuous attributes into temporal sequences. The other mode is applying rule discovery to the data after the first preprocessing without second one. The reason why we adopted these two mode is that we focus not only on temporal behavior of each attribute, but also on association among several attributes. Although Miksch's method [9] and Das's approach [4] are very efficient to extract knowledge about transition, they cannot focus on association between attributes in an efficient way. For the latter purpose, much simpler rule discovery algorithm are preferred.

5.2   Continuous Attributes and Qualitative Trend

To characterize the deviation and temporal change of continuous attributes, we introduce standardization of continuous attributes. For this, we only needs the total average $\hat{y}_\infty$ and its standardization σ_∞. With these parameters, standardized value is obtained as:

$$z_w = \frac{y_w - \hat{y}_\infty}{\sigma_\infty}.$$

The reason why standardization is introduced is that it makes comparison between continuous attributes much easier and clearer, especially, statistic theory guarantees that the coefficients of a auto-regression equation can be compared with those of another equation [6].

After calculating the standardized values, an extraction algorithm for qualitative trends is applied [9] with multiscale matching briefly shown in the next subsection.

This method is processed as follows: First, this method uses data smoothing with window parameters. Secondly, smoothed values for each attributes are classified into seven categories given as domain knowledge about laboratory test values: extremely low, substantially low, slightly low, normal range, slightly high, substantially high, and extremely high. With these categories, qualitative trends are calculated and classified into the following ten categories by using guideline rules: decrease too fast(A1), normal decrease(A2), decrease too slow(A3), zero change(ZA), dangerous increase(C), increase too fast(B1), normal increase(B2), increase too slow(B3), dangerous decrease(D). For matching temporal sequences with guideline rules, multiscale matching method is applied. For example, if the value of some laboratory tests change from substantially high to normal range within a very short time, the qualitative trend will be classified into A1(decrease too fast). For further information, please refer to [9].

5.3   Multiscale Matching

Multiscale matching is based on two basic ideas: the first one is to use the curvature of the curve to detect the points of inflection. The second idea is to use the scale factor to calculate the curvature of the smoothed curve [8]. The curvature is given as:

$$c(t) = \frac{y''}{(1 + (y')^2)^{3/2}},$$

where $y' = dy/dt$ and $y'' = d^2y/dt^2$. In order to compute the curvature of the curve at varying levels of detail, function y is convolved with a one-dimensional

Gaussian kernel $g(t, \sigma)$ of the width (scaling factor) σ:

$$g(t, \sigma) = \frac{1}{\sigma\sqrt{2\pi}} e^{-t^2/2\sigma^2}.$$

$Y(t, \sigma)$, the convolution of $y(t)$ is defined as:

$$Y(t, \sigma) = y(t) \otimes g(t, \sigma) = \int_{-\infty}^{\infty} y(t) \frac{1}{\sigma\sqrt{2\pi}} e^{-t^2/2\sigma^2} du.$$

According to the characteristics of the convolution, the derivative and the second derivative is calculated as:

$$Y'(t, \sigma) = y(t) \otimes \frac{\partial g(t, \sigma)}{\partial t} \quad and \quad Y''(t, \sigma) = y(t) \otimes \frac{\partial^2 g(t, \sigma)}{\partial t^2}$$

Using $Y(t, \sigma)$, $Y'(t, \sigma)$ and $Y''(t, \sigma)$, we can calculate the curvature of a given curve for each value of σ within one window w:

$$c(t) = \frac{y(t) \otimes \dfrac{\partial^2 g(t, \sigma)}{\partial t^2}}{\left(1 + \left(y(t) \otimes \dfrac{\partial g(t, \sigma)}{\partial t}\right)^2\right)^{3/2}}$$

This gives a sequence of the value of curvature for each time series. If two time series sequence is similar with respect to temporal change, two sequences of curvature will be similar. Furthermore, since we calculate the curvature for each scaling factor, we can compare between these sequences from the local level to global level. For further information, please refer to [8] and [9].

5.4 Rule Discovery Algorithm

For rule discovery, a simple rule induction algorithm discussed in [13] is applied, where continuous attributes are transformed into categorical attributes with a cut-off point. As discussed in Sect. 3, moving average method will remove the temporal effect shorter than a window parameter. Thus, $w = \infty$ will remove all the temporal effect, so this moving average can be viewed as data without any temporal characteristics. If rule discovery is applied to this data, it will generate rules which represents non-temporal association between attributes. In this way, data after processing w-moving average is used to discover association with w or longer time-effect. Ideally, from $w = \infty$ down to $w = 1$, we decompose all the independent time-effect associations between attributes. However, the time-constant in which users are interested will be limited and the moving average method shown in Sect. 3 uses a set of w given by users. Thus, application of rule discovery to each table will generate a sequence of temporal associations between attributes. If some temporal associations will be different from associations with $w = \infty$, then these specific relations will be related with a new discovery.

5.5 Summary of Second Preprocessing and Rule Discovery

Second preprocessing method and rule discovery are summarized as shown in Fig. 2.

1. Calculate $\hat{y}_\infty$ and σ_∞ from the table of $w = \infty$;
2. Repeat for each w in List L_w;
   (w is sorted in a descending order.)
   a) Select a table of w: T_w;
       i. Standardize continuous and ranking attributes;
       ii. Calculate qualitative trends for continuous and ranking attributes with multiscale matching;
       iii. Construct a new table for qualitative trends;
       iv. Apply rule discovery method for temporal sequences;
   b) Apply rule induction methods to the original table T_w;

Fig. 2. Second preprocessing and rule discovery

6   Experimental Results: Discovered Results in CVD

The above rule discovery system was applied to a clinical database on cerebrovascular diseases (CVD), which has 2610 records, described by 12 classes. Each record followed up at least 10 years and the averaged number of attributes are 2715. A list of w, $\{w\}$ was set to $\{10$ years, 5 years, 1 year, 3 months, 2 weeks$\}$ and thresholds, δ_α and δ_κ were set to 0.60 and 0.30,respectively. One of the most important problems in CVD is whether CVD patients will suffer from mental disorders or dementia and how long it takes each patient to reach the status of dementia.

6.1   Non-temporal Knowledge

Concerning the database on CVD, several interesting rules are derived. The most interesting results are the following positive and negative rules for thalamus hemorrhage:

$$[Sex = Female] \wedge [Hemiparesis = Left] \wedge [LOC : positive] \rightarrow Thalamus$$
$$(accuracy : 0.62, coverage : 0.33),$$
$$[Risk : Hypertension] \wedge [Sensory = no] \rightarrow Putamen$$
$$(accuracy : 0.65, coverage : 0.43),$$

Interestingly, LOC(loss of consciousness) under the condition of $[Sex = Female] \wedge [Hemiparesis = Left]$ is an important factor to diagnose thalamic damage. In this domain, any strong correlations between these attributes and others, like MND, have not been found yet. It will be our future work to find what factor will be behind these rules. However, these rules do not include the relations between dementia and brain functions.

Short-Term Effect. As short-term rules, the following interesting rules are discovered:

$$[Gastro : A1] \wedge [Quadriceps : A1] \rightarrow [Dementia : A2]$$
$$(accuracy : 0.71, coverage : 0.31, w = 3(months)),$$
$$[Gastro : D] \wedge [TA : D] \rightarrow [Dementia : A2]$$
$$(accuracy : 0.74, coverage : 0.32, w = 3(months)).$$

These rules suggests that the rapid decrease of muscle power in the lower extremities are weakly related with the appearance of dementia. However, these knowledge has never been reported and further investigation is required for interpretation.

Long-Term Effect. As long-term rules, the following interesting rules are discovered:

$$[JointPosition : A3] \wedge [Quadriceps : A3] \rightarrow [Dementia : A3]$$
$$(accuracy : 0.61, coverage : 0.35, w = 1(year)),$$
$$[Gastro : A3] \wedge [Vibration : A3] \rightarrow [Dementia : A3]$$
$$(accuracy : 0.87, coverage : 0.33, w = 1(year)).$$

These rules suggests that combination of the decrease of muscle power in the lower extremities and the increase of sensory disturbance are weakly related with the appearance of dementia. However, these knowledge has neither been reported and further investigation is required for interpretation.

7 Discussion

This paper introduces combination of extended moving average methods as first preprocessing, extraction of qualitative trend as second preprocessing and rule discovery. As discussed in Sects. 3 and 4, this approach is inspired by rule discovery in time series introduced by Das [4]. However, the main differences between Das's approach and our approach are the following.

1. For smoothing data, extended moving average method is introduced.
2. The system incorporates domain knowledge about a continous attribute to detect its qualitative trend.
3. Qualitative trend are calculated for each time-constant.
4. Rules are discovered with respect to not only associations between qualitative trends but also non-temporal associations.

Using these methods, the system discovered several interesting patterns in a clinical database of different time constant.

The disadvantage of this approach is that the program is not good at extracting periodical behavior of disease processes, or the recurrence of some diseases because the qualitative trends do not support the detection of cycles in temporal behavior of attributes. For these periodical processes, auto-regressive function analysis is much more useful [6]. It will be our future work to extend our approach so that it can deal with periodicity more clearly.

8   Conclusion

In this paper, we introduce a combination of extended moving average method, multiscale matching and rule induction method, to discover new knowledge in temporal databases. In the system, extended moving average method are used for preprocessing, to deal with irregularity of each temporal data. Using several parameters for time-scaling with multiscale matching, given by users, this moving average method generates a new database for each time scale with summarized attributes. Then, rule induction method is applied to each new database with summarized attributes. This method was applied to two medical datasets, the results of which show that interesting knowledge is discovered from each database.

References

1. Abiteboul, S., Hull, R., and Vianu, V. *Foundations of Databases*, Addison-Wesley, New York, 1995.
2. Adams, R.D. and Victor, M. *Principles of Neurology*, 5th edition, McGraw-Hill, NY, 1993.
3. Agrawal, R., Imielinski, T., and Swami, A., Mining association rules between sets of items in large databases, in *Proceedings of the 1993 International Conference on Management of Data (SIGMOD 93)*, pp. 207-216, 1993.
4. Das, G., Lin, K.I., Mannila, H., Renganathan, G. and Smyth, P. Rule discovery from time series. In: *Proceedings of Fourth International Conference on Knowledge Discovery and Data Mining*, pp.16-22, 1998.
5. Fayyad, U.M., et al.(eds.)., *Advances in Knowledge Discovery and Data Mining*, AAAI Press, 1996.
6. Hamilton, J.D. *Time Series Analysis*, Princeton University Press, 1994.
7. Langley, P. *Elements of Machine Learning*, Morgan Kaufmann, CA, 1996.
8. Mokhtarian, F. and Mackworth, A. Scale-Based Description and Recognition of Planar Curves and Two-Dimensional Shapes. *IEEE Trans. Pattern. Anal. Machine Intell.*, **PAMI-8**, pp.34-43, 1986.
9. Miksch, S., Horn, W., Popow, C., and Paky, F. Utilizing temporal data abstraction for data validation and therapy planning for artificially ventilated newborn infants. *Artificial Intelligentce in Medicine*, **8**, 543-576, 1996.
10. Pawlak, Z., *Rough Sets*. Kluwer Academic Publishers, Dordrecht, 1991.
11. Skowron, A. and Grzymala-Busse, J. From rough set theory to evidence theory. In: Yager, R., Fedrizzi, M. and Kacprzyk, J.(eds.) *Advances in the Dempster-Shafer Theory of Evidence*, pp.193-236, John Wiley & Sons, New York, 1994.
12. Tsumoto, S. and Tanaka, H., PRIMEROSE: Probabilistic Rule Induction Method based on Rough Sets and Resampling Methods. *Computational Intelligence*, **11**, 389-405, 1995.
13. Tsumoto, S. Knowledge Discovery in Medical MultiDatabases: A Rough Set Approach, *Proceedings of PKDD99*(in this issue), 1999.
14. Tsumoto, S. Mining Positive and Negative Knowledge in Clinical Databases based on Rough Set Model. *Proceedings of PKDD2001*.
15. Van Bemmel,J. and Musen, M. A. *Handbook of Medical Informatics*, Springer-Verlag, New York, 1997.

Mining Positive and Negative Knowledge in Clinical Databases Based on Rough Set Model

Shusaku Tsumoto

Department of Medicine Informatics, Shimane Medical University, School of Medicine
89-1 Enya-cho Izumo City, Shimane 693-8501 Japan
tsumoto@computer.org

Abstract. One of the most important problems on rule induction methods is that extracted rules partially represent information on experts' decision processes, which makes rule interpretation by domain experts difficult. In order to solve this problem, the characteristics of medical reasoning is discussed positive and negative rules are introduced which model medical experts' rules. Then, for induction of positive and negative rules, two search algorithms are provided. The proposed rule induction method was evaluated on medical databases, the experimental results of which show that induced rules correctly represented experts' knowledge and several interesting patterns were discovered.

1 Introduction

Rule induction methods are classified into two categories, induction of deterministic rules and probabilistic ones [1,2,3,4]. On one hand, Deterministic rules are described as *if-then* rules, which can be viewed as propositions. From the set-theoretical point of view, a set of examples supporting the conditional part of a deterministic rule, denoted by C, is a subset of a set whose examples belongs to the consequence part, denoted by D. That is, the relation $C \subseteq D$ holds and deterministic rules are supported only by positive examples in a dataset. On the other hand, probabilistic rules are if-then rules with probabilistic information [4]. From the set-theoretical point of view, C is not a subset, but closely overlapped with D. That is, the relations $C \cap D \neq \phi$ and $|C \cap D|/|C| \geq \delta$ will hold in this case.[1] Thus, probabilistic rules are supported by a large number of positive examples and a small number of negative examples. The common feature of both deterministic and probabilistic rules is that they will deduce their consequence positively if an example satisfies their conditional parts. We call the reasoning by these rules *positive reasoning*.

However, medical experts do not use only positive reasoning but also *negative reasoning* for selection of candidates, which is represented as if-then rules whose consequences include negative terms. For example, when a patient who complains of headache does not have a throbbing pain, migraine should not be

---

[1] The threshold δ is the degree of the closeness of overlapping sets, which will be given by domain experts. For more information, please refer to Sect. 3.

L. De Raedt and A. Siebes (Eds.): PKDD 2001, LNAI 2168, pp. 460–471, 2001.
© Springer-Verlag Berlin Heidelberg 2001

suspected with a high probability. Thus, negative reasoning also plays an important role in cutting the search space of a differential diagnosis process [4]. Thus, medical reasoning includes both positive and negative reasoning, though conventional rule induction methods do not reflect this aspect. This is one of the reasons why medical experts have difficulties in interpreting induced rules and the interpretation of rules for a discovery procedure does not easily proceed. Therefore, negative rules should be induced from databases in order not only to induce rules reflecting experts' decision processes, but also to induce rules which will be easier for domain experts to interpret, both of which are important to enhance the discovery process done by the corporation of medical experts and computers.

In this paper, first, the characteristics of medical reasoning are focused on and two kinds of rules, positive rules and negative rules are introduced as a model of medical reasoning. Interestingly, from the set-theoretical point of view, sets of examples supporting both rules correspond to the lower and upper approximation in rough sets [2]. On the other hand, from the viewpoint of propositional logic, both positive and negative rules are defined as classical propositions, or deterministic rules with two probabilistic measures, classification accuracy and coverage. Second, two algorithms for induction of positive and negative rules are introduced, defined as search procedures by using accuracy and coverage as evaluation indices. Finally, the proposed method was evaluated on several medical databases, the experimental results of which show that induced rules correctly represented experts' knowledge and several interesting patterns were discovered.

2   Focusing Mechanism

One of the characteristics in medical reasoning is a focusing mechanism, which is used to select the final diagnosis from many candidates [4]. For example, in differential diagnosis of headache, more than 60 diseases will be checked by present history, physical examinations and laboratory examinations. In diagnostic procedures, a candidate is excluded if a symptom necessary to diagnose is not observed.

This style of reasoning consists of the following two kinds of reasoning processes: exclusive reasoning and inclusive reasoning.[2] The diagnostic procedure will proceed as follows: first, exclusive reasoning excludes a disease from candidates when a patient does not have a symptom which is necessary to diagnose that disease. Secondly, inclusive reasoning suspects a disease in the output of the exclusive process when a patient has symptoms specific to a disease. These two steps are modelled as usage of two kinds of rules, negative rules (or exclusive rules) and positive rules, the former of which corresponds to exclusive reasoning and the latter of which corresponds to inclusive reasoning. In the next two subsections, these two rules are represented as special kinds of probabilistic rules.

---

[2] Relations this diagnostic model with another diagnostic model are discussed in [5].

3 Definition of Rules

3.1 Rough Sets

In the following sections, we use the following notations introduced by Grzymala-Busse and Skowron [6], which are based on rough set theory [2]. These notations are illustrated by a small database shown in Table 1, collecting the patients who complained of headache.

Table 1. An example of database

No.	age	location	nature	prodrome	nausea	M1	class
1	50-59	occular	persistent	no	no	yes	m.c.h.
2	40-49	whole	persistent	no	no	yes	m.c.h.
3	40-49	lateral	throbbing	no	yes	no	migra
4	40-49	whole	throbbing	yes	yes	no	migra
5	40-49	whole	radiating	no	no	yes	m.c.h.
6	50-59	whole	persistent	no	yes	yes	psycho

DEFINITIONS. M1: tenderness of M1, m.c.h.: muscle contraction headache, migra: migraine, psycho: psychological pain.

Let U denote a nonempty, finite set called the universe and A denote a nonempty, finite set of attributes, i.e., $a : U \to V_a$ for $a \in A$, where V_a is called the domain of a, respectively.Then, a decision table is defined as an information system, $A = (U, A \cup \{d\})$. For example, Table 1 is an information system with $U = \{1, 2, 3, 4, 5, 6\}$ and $A = \{age, location, nature, prodrome, nausea, M1\}$ and $d = class$. For $location \in A$, $V_{location}$ is defined as $\{occular, lateral, whole\}$.

The atomic formulae over $B \subseteq A \cup \{d\}$ and V are expressions of the form $[a = v]$, called descriptors over B, where $a \in B$ and $v \in V_a$. The set $F(B, V)$ of formulas over B is the least set containing all atomic formulas over B and closed with respect to disjunction, conjunction and negation. For example, $[location = occular]$ is a descriptor of B.

For each $f \in F(B, V)$, f_A denote the meaning of f in A, i.e., the set of all objects in U with property f, defined inductively as follows.

1. If f is of the form $[a = v]$ then, $f_A = \{s \in U | a(s) = v\}$
2. $(f \wedge g)_A = f_A \cap g_A$; $(f \vee g)_A = f_A \vee g_A$; $(\neg f)_A = U - f_a$

For example, $f = [location = whole]$ and $f_A = \{2, 4, 5, 6\}$. As an example of a conjunctive formula, $g = [location = whole] \wedge [nausea = no]$ is a descriptor of U and f_A is equal to $g_{location,nausea} = \{2, 5\}$.

3.2   Classification Accuracy and Coverage

Definition of Accuracy and Coverage. By the use of the framework above, classification accuracy and coverage, or true positive rate is defined as follows.

Definition 1.
Let R and D denote a formula in $F(B, V)$ and a set of objects which belong to a decision d. Classification accuracy and coverage(true positive rate) for $R \to d$ is defined as:

$$\alpha_R(D) = \frac{|R_A \cap D|}{|R_A|} (= P(D|R)), \text{ and}$$

$$\kappa_R(D) = \frac{|R_A \cap D|}{|D|} (= P(R|D)),$$

where $|S|$, $\alpha_R(D)$, $\kappa_R(D)$ and P(S) denote the cardinality of a set S, a classification accuracy of R as to classification of D and coverage (a true positive rate of R to D), and probability of S, respectively.

In the above example, when R and D are set to $[nau = 1]$ and $[class = migraine]$, $\alpha_R(D) = 2/3 = 0.67$ and $\kappa_R(D) = 2/2 = 1.0$.

It is notable that $\alpha_R(D)$ measures the degree of the sufficiency of a proposition, $R \to D$, and that $\kappa_R(D)$ measures the degree of its necessity. For example, if $\alpha_R(D)$ is equal to 1.0, then $R \to D$ is true. On the other hand, if $\kappa_R(D)$ is equal to 1.0, then $D \to R$ is true. Thus, if both measures are 1.0, then $R \leftrightarrow D$.

3.3   Probabilistic Rules

By the use of accuracy and coverage, a probabilistic rule is defined as:

$$R \xrightarrow{\alpha, \kappa} d \quad s.t. \ R = \wedge_j [a_j = v_k], \alpha_R(D) \geq \delta_\alpha$$
$$\text{and } \kappa_R(D) \geq \delta_\kappa,$$

This rule is a kind of probabilistic proposition with two statistical measures, which is an extension of Ziarko's variable precision model(VPRS) [9].[3]

It is also notable that both a positive rule and a negative rule are defined as special cases of this rule, as shown in the next subsections.

3.4   Positive Rules

A positive rule is defined as a rule supported by only positive examples, the classification accuracy of which is equal to 1.0. It is notable that the set supporting this rule corresponds to a subset of the lower approximation of a target concept, which is introduced in rough sets [2]. Thus, a positive rule is represented as:

$$R \to d \quad s.t. \quad R = \wedge_j [a_j = v_k], \quad \alpha_R(D) = 1.0$$

---

[3] This probabilistic rule is also a kind of *Rough Modus Ponens* [10].

In the above example, one positive rule of "m.c.h." (muscle contraction headache) is:

$$[nausea = no] \rightarrow m.c.h. \quad \alpha = 3/3 = 1.0.$$

This positive rule is often called a deterministic rule. However, in this paper, we use a term, positive (deterministic) rules, because a deterministic rule which is supported only by negative examples, called a negative rule, is introduced as in the next subsection.

3.5 Negative Rules

Before defining a negative rule, let us first introduce an exclusive rule, the contrapositive of a negative rule [4]. An exclusive rule is defined as a rule supported by all the positive examples, the coverage of which is equal to 1.0.[4] It is notable that the set supporting an exclusive rule corresponds to the upper approximation of a target concept, which is introduced in rough sets [2]. Thus, an exclusive rule is represented as:

$$R \rightarrow d \quad s.t. \quad R = \vee_j [a_j = v_k], \quad \kappa_R(D) = 1.0.$$

In the above example, the exclusive rule of "m.c.h." is:

$$[M1 = yes] \vee [nau = no] \rightarrow m.c.h. \quad \kappa = 1.0,$$

From the viewpoint of propositional logic, an exclusive rule should be represented as:

$$d \rightarrow \vee_j [a_j = v_k],$$

because the condition of an exclusive rule corresponds to the necessity condition of conclusion d. Thus, it is easy to see that a negative rule is defined as the contrapositive of an exclusive rule:

$$\wedge_j \neg [a_j = v_k] \rightarrow \neg d,$$

which means that if a case does not satisfy any attribute value pairs in the condition of a negative rules, then we can exclude a decision d from candidates. For example, the negative rule of m.c.h. is:

$$\neg [M1 = yes] \wedge \neg [nausea = no] \rightarrow \neg m.c.h.$$

In summary, a negative rule is defined as:

$$\wedge_j \neg [a_j = v_k] \rightarrow \neg d \quad s.t. \quad \forall [a_j = v_k] \, \kappa_{[a_j = v_k]}(D) = 1.0,$$

where D denotes a set of samples which belong to a class d.

Negative rules should be also included in a category of deterministic rules, since their coverage, a measure of negative concepts is equal to 1.0. It is also notable that the set supporting a negative rule corresponds to a subset of negative region, which is introduced in rough sets [2].

---

[4] An exclusive rule represents the necessity condition of a decision.

4   Algorithms for Rule Induction

The contrapositive of a negative rule, an exclusive rule is induced as an exclusive rule by the modification of the algorithm introduced in PRIMEROSE-REX [4], as shown in Fig. 1. This algorithm will work as follows. (1)First, it selects a descriptor $[a_i = v_j]$ from the list of attribute-value pairs, denoted by L. (2) Then, it checks whether this descriptor overlaps with a set of positive examples, denoted by D. (3) If so, this descriptor is included into a list of candidates for positive rules and the algorithm checks whether its coverage is equal to 1.0 or not. If the coverage is equal to 1.0, then this descriptor is added to $R_e r$, the formula for the conditional part of the exclusive rule of D. (4) Then, $[a_i = v_j]$ is deleted from the list L. This procedure, from (1) to (4) will continue unless L is empty. (5) Finally, when L is empty, this algorithm generates negative rules by taking the contrapositive of induced exclusive rules.

On the other hand, positive rules are induced as inclusive rules by the algorithm introduced in PRIMEROSE-REX [4], as shown in Fig. 2. For induction of positive rules, the threshold of accuracy and coverage is set to 1.0 and 0.0, respectively.

This algorithm works in the following way. (1) First, it substitutes L_1, which denotes a list of formula composed of only one descriptor, with the list L_{er} generated by the former algorithm shown in Fig. 1. (2) Then, until L_1 becomes empty, the following procedures will continue: (a) A formula $[a_i = v_j]$ is removed from L_1. (b) Then, the algorithm checks whether $\alpha_R(D)$ is larger than the threshold or not. (For induction of positive rules, this is equal to checking whether $\alpha_R(D)$ is equal to 1.0 or not.) If so, then this formula is included a list of the conditional part of positive rules. Otherwise, it will be included into M, which is used for making conjunction. (3) When L_1 is empty, the next list L_2 is generated from the list M.

5   Experimental Results

For experimental evaluation, a new system, called PRIMEROSE-REX2 (Probabilistic Rule Induction Method for Rules of Expert System ver 2.0), was developed, where the algorithms discussed in Sect. 4 were implemented.

PRIMEROSE-REX2 was applied to the following three medical domains: headache(RHINOS domain), whose training samples consist of 52119 samples, 45 classes and 147 attributes, cerebulovasular diseases(CVD), whose training samples consist of 7620 samples, 22 classes and 285 attributes, and meningitis, whose training samples consists of 1211 samples, 4 classes and 41 attributes (Table 2).

For evaluation, we used the following two types of experiments. One experiment was to evaluate the predictive accuracy by using the cross-validation method, which is often used in the machine learning literature [7]. The other experiment was to evaluate induced rules by medical experts and to check whether these rules led to a new discovery.

procedure *Exclusive and Negative Rules*;
  var
    L : *List*;
      /* A list of elementary attribute-value pairs */
  begin
    $L := P_0$;
    /* P_0: A list of elementary attribute-value pairs given in a database */
    while $(L \neq \{\})$ **do**
      begin
        Select one pair $[a_i = v_j]$ from L;
        if $([a_i = v_j]_A \cap D \neq \phi)$ **then do** /* D: positive examples of a target class d */
          begin
            $L_{ir} := L_{ir} + [a_i = v_j]$;   /* Candidates for Positive Rules */
            if $(\kappa_{[a_i=v_j]}(D) = 1.0)$
            then $R_{er} := R_{er} \wedge [a_i = v_j]$;
              /* Include $[a_i = v_j]$ into the formula of Exclusive Rule */
          end
        $L := L - [a_i = v_j]$;
      end
    Construct Negative Rules:
      Take the contrapositive of R_{er}.
  end {*Exclusive and Negative Rules*};

Fig. 1. Induction of exclusive and negative rules

Table 2. Databases

Domain	Samples	Classes	Attributes
Headache	52119	45	147
CVD	7620	22	285
Meningitis	1211	4	41

5.1 Performance of Rules Obtained

For comparison of performance, The experiments were performed by the following four procedures. First, rules were acquired manually from experts. Second, the datasets were randomly splits into new training samples and new test samples. Third, PRIMEROSE-REX2, conventional rule induction methods, AQ15 [1] and C4.5 [3] were applied to the new training samples for rule generation. Fourth, the induced rules and rules acquired from experts were tested by the new test samples. The second to fourth were repeated for 100 times and average all the classification accuracy over 100 trials. This process is a variant of repeated 2-fold cross-validation, introduced in [4].

Experimental results(performance) are shown in Table 3. The first and second row show the results obtained by using PRIMEROSE-REX2: the results in the first row were derived by using both positive and negative rules and those in the second row were derived by only positive rules. The third row shows the results

```
procedure Positive Rules;
  var
    i : integer;    M, L_i : List;
  begin
    L_1 := L_{ir};
    /* L_{ir}: A list of candidates generated by induction of exclusive rules */
    i := 1;    M := {};
    for i := 1 to n do
    /* n: Total number of attributes given
        in a database */
      begin
        while ( L_i ≠ {} ) do
          begin
            Select one pair R = ∧[a_i = v_j] from L_i;
            L_i := L_i − {R};
            if    (α_R(D) > δ_α)
              then  do S_{ir} := S_{ir} + {R};
            /* Include R in a list of the Positive Rules */
              else M := M + {R};
          end
        L_{i+1} := (A list of the whole combination of the conjunction formulae in M);
      end
  end {Positive Rules};
```

Fig. 2. Induction of positive rules

derived from medical experts. For comparison, we compare the classification accuracy of C4.5 and AQ-15, which is shown in the fourth and the fifth row. These

Table 3. Experimental results (accuracy: averaged)

Method	Headache	CVD	Meningitis
PRIMEROSE-REX2 (Positive+Negative)	91.3%	89.3%	92.5%
PRIMEROSE-REX2 (Positive)	68.3%	71.3%	74.5%
Experts	95.0%	92.9%	93.2%
C4.5	85.8%	79.7%	81.4%
AQ15	86.2%	78.9%	82.5%

results show that the combination of positive and negative rules outperforms positive rules, although it is a little worse than medical experts' rules.

5.2   What Is Discovered?

Positive Rules in Meningitis. In the domain of meningitis, the following positive rules, which medical experts do not expect, are obtained.

$$[WBC < 12000] \wedge [Sex = Female] \wedge [Age < 40]$$
$$\wedge [CSF\_CELL < 1000] \rightarrow Virus$$
$$[Age \geq 40] \wedge [WBC \geq 8000] \wedge [Sex = Male]$$
$$\wedge [CSF\_CELL \geq 1000] \rightarrow Bacteria$$

The former rule means that if WBC(White Blood Cell Count) is less than 12000, the Sex of a patient is FEMALE, the Age is less than 40 and CSF_CELL (Cell count of Cerebulospinal Fluid), then the type of meningitis is Virus. The latter one means that the Age of a patient is less than 40, WBC is larger than 8000, the Sex is Male, and CSF_CELL is larger than 1000, then the type of meningitis is Bacteria.

The most interesting points are that these rules included information about age and sex, which often seems to be unimportant attributes for differential diagnosis of meningitis. The first discovery was that women did not often suffer from bacterial infection, compared with men, since such relationships between sex and meningitis has not been discussed in medical context [11]. By the close examination of the database of meningitis, it was found that most of the above patients suffered from chronic diseases, such as DM, LC, and sinusitis, which are the risk factors of bacterial meningitis. The second discovery was that [age < 40] was also an important factor not to suspect viral meningitis, which also matches the fact that most old people suffer from chronic diseases.

These results were also re-evaluated in medical practice. Recently, the above two rules were checked by additional 21 cases who suffered from meningitis (15 cases: viral and 6 cases: bacterial meningitis.) Surprisingly, the above rules misclassified only three cases (two are viral, and the other is bacterial), that is, the total accuracy was equal to $18/21 = 85.7\%$ and the accuracies for viral and bacterial meningitis were equal to $13/15 = 86.7\%$ and $5/6 = 83.3\%$. The reasons of misclassification were the following: a case of bacterial infection was a patient who had a severe immunodeficiency, although he is very young. Two cases of viral infection were patients who also suffered from herpes zoster. It is notable that even those misclassification cases could be explained from the viewpoint of the immunodeficiency: that is, it was confirmed that immunodeficiency is a key word for meningitis.

The validation of these rules is still ongoing, which will be reported in the near future.

Positive and Negative Rules in CVD. Concerning the database on CVD, several interesting rules were derived. The most interesting results were the following positive and negative rules for thalamus hemorrhage:

$$[Sex = Female] \wedge [Hemiparesis = Left]$$
$$\wedge [LOC : positive] \rightarrow Thalamus$$
$$\neg [Risk : Hypertension] \wedge \neg [Sensory = no]$$
$$\rightarrow \neg Thalamus$$

The former rule means that if the Sex of a patient is female and he/she suffered from the left hemiparesis([Hemiparesis=Left]) and loss of consciousness

([LOC:positive]), then the focus of CVD is Thalamus. The latter rule means that if he/she neither suffers from hypertension ([Risk: Hypertension]) nor suffers from sensory disturbance([Sensory=no]), then the focus of CVD is Thalamus.

Interestingly, LOC(loss of consciousness) under the condition of $[Sex = Female] \wedge [Hemiparesis = Left]$ was found to be an important factor to diagnose thalamic damage. In this domain, any strong correlations between these attributes and others, like the database of meningitis, have not been found yet. It will be our future work to find what factor is behind these rules.

5.3   Rule Discovery as Knowledge Acquisition

Expert System: RH. Another point of discovery of rules is automated knowledge acquisition from databases. Knowledge acquisition is referred to as a bottleneck problem in development of expert systems [12], which has not fully been solved and is expected to be solved by induction of rules from databases. However, there are few papers which discusses the evaluation of discovered rules from the viewpoint of knowledge acquisition [13].

For this purpose, we have developed an expert system, called RH(Rule-based system for Headache) by using the acquired knowledge.[5] RH consists of two parts. Firstly, RH requires inputs and applies exclusive and negative rules to select candidates (focusing mechanism). Then, RH requires additional inputs and applies positive rules for differential diagnosis between selected candidates. Finally, RH outputs diagnostic conclusions.

Evaluation of RH. RH was evaluated in clinical practice with respect to its classification accuracy by using 930 patients who came to the outpatient clinic after the development of this system. Experimental results about classification accuracy are shown in Table 4. The first and second row show the performance of rules obtained by using PRIMROSE-REX2: the results in the first row are derived by using both positive and negative rules and those in the second row are derived by only positive rules. The third and fourth row show the results derived by using both positive and negative rules and those by positive rules acquired directly from a medical experts. These results show that the combination of positive and negative rules outperforms positive rules and gains almost the same performance as those experts .

6   Conclusions

In this paper, the characteristics of two measures, classification accuracy and coverage are discussed, which shows that both measures are dual and that accuracy and coverage are measures of both positive and negative rules, respectively.

---

[5] The reason why we select the domain of headache is that we formerly developed an expert system RHINOS (Rule-based Headache INformation Organizing System), which makes a differential diagnosis in headache [14,15]. In this system, it takes about six months to acquire knowledge from domain experts.

Table 4. Evaluation of RH (accuracy: averaged)

Method	Accuracy
PRIMEROSE-REX2 (Positive and Negative)	91.4% (851/930)
PRIMEROSE-REX (Positive)	78.5% (729/930)
RHINOS (Positive and Negative)	93.5% (864/930)
RHINOS (Positive)	82.8% (765/930)

Then, an algorithm for induction of positive and negative rules is introduced. The proposed method was evaluated on medical databases, the experimental results of which show that induced rules correctly represented experts' knowledge and several interesting patterns were discovered.

References

1. Michalski RS, Mozetic I, Hong J, and Lavrac N: The Multi-Purpose Incremental Learning System AQ15 and its Testing Application to Three Medical Domains. *Proceedings of the fifth National Conference on Artificial Intelligence*, AAAI Press, Palo Alto CA, pp 1041-1045, 1986.
2. Pawlak Z: *Rough Sets*. Kluwer Academic Publishers, Dordrecht, 1991.
3. Quinlan JR: *C4.5 - Programs for Machine Learning*. Morgan Kaufmann, Palo Alto CA, 1993.
4. Tsumoto S and Tanaka H: Automated Discovery of Medical Expert System Rules from Clinical Databases based on Rough Sets. In: *Proceedings of the Second International Conference on Knowledge Discovery and Data Mining 96*, AAAI Press, Palo Alto CA, pp.63-69, 1996.
5. Tsumoto S: Modelling Medical Diagnostic Rules based on Rough Sets. In: Polkowski L and Skowron A (Eds): *Rough Sets and Current Trends in Computing*, Lecture Note in Artificial Intelligence **1424**, 1998.
6. Skowron, A. and Grzymala-Busse, J. From rough set theory to evidence theory. In: Yager, R., Fedrizzi, M. and Kacprzyk, J.(eds.) *Advances in the Dempster-Shafer Theory of Evidence*, pp.193-236, John Wiley & Sons, New York, 1994.
7. Shavlik JW and Dietterich TG(Eds): *Readings in Machine Learning*. Morgan Kaufmann, Palo Alto CA, 1990.
8. Rissanen J: *Stochastic Complexity in Statistical Inquiry*. World Scientific, Singapore, 1989.
9. Ziarko W: Variable Precision Rough Set Model. *Journal of Computer and System Sciences* **46**:39-59, 1993.
10. Pawlak Z: Rough Modus Ponens. In: *Proceedings of International Conference on Information Processing and Management of Uncertainty in Knowledge-Based Systems 98*, Paris, 1998.
11. Adams RD and Victor M: *Principles of Neurology*, 5th edition. McGraw-Hill, New York, 1993.
12. Buchnan BG and Shortliffe EH(Eds): *Rule-Based Expert Systems*. Addison-Wesley, 1984.
13. Tsumoto S: Automated Extraction of Medical Expert System Rules from Clinical Databases based on Rough Set Theory. *Journal of Information Sciences*, **112**, 67-84, 1998.

14. Matsumura Y, Matsunaga T, Hata Y, Kimura M, Matsumura H: Consultation system for diagnoses of headache and facial pain: RHINOS. *Medical Informatics* **11**: 145-157, 1988.
15. Matsumura Y, Matsunaga T, Maeda Y, Tsumoto S, Matsumura H, Kimura M: Consultation System for Diagnosis of Headache and Facial Pain: "RHINOS". *Proceedings of Logic Prgram Conferences*, pp.287-298, 1985.

The TwoKey Plot for Multiple Association Rules Control

Antony Unwin[2], Heike Hofmann[1], and Klaus Bernt[2]

[1] AT&T Research, Florham Park NJ 09732, USA
heike@att.research.com
[2] Department of Computer-Oriented Statistics and Data Analysis University of
Augsburg, 86135 Augsburg, Germany
{antony.unwin,klaus.bernt}@math.uni-augsburg.de

Abstract. Association rules have been popular in theory, though it is
unclear how much success they have had in practice. Very many association rules are found in any application by any approach and they require
effective pruning and filtering. There has been much research in this
area recently, but less with the goal of providing a global overview and
summary of all rules, which may then be used to explore the rules and
to evaluate their worth. The unusual feature of association rules is that
those with the highest objective values for the two key criteria (support
and confidence) are not usually those with the most subjective interest
(because we know the obvious results already). The TwoKey plot is a way
of displaying all discovered association rules at once, while also providing
the means to review and manage them. It is a powerful tool in order to get
a first overview of the distribution of confidence and support. Features
such as separate groups of rules or outliers are detected immediately. By
exploiting various ancestor relationship structures among the rules, we
can use the TwoKey Plot also as a visual assessment tool, closely related
to pruning methods – e.g. those proposed by Bing Liu (1999). The concept will be illustrated using the interactive software MARC (Multiple
Association Rules Control).

1 Introduction

Analysis by association rules is one of a number of techniques in the field of Data
Mining, the study of very large data sets. Simple methods like Association Rules
are popular because they can be applied to such large data sets, while some
more traditional statistical methods do not scale up. It is typical of Data Mining
analyses that very many results are produced, not only through the application
of a single method but also because several different techniques may be applied.
Tools for organising and managing large numbers of results are very necessary
and some of the ideas in this paper will apply to results from other Data Mining
approaches as well.

Association rules were introduced formally by Agrawal et al (1993) and have
been discussed widely since (see Bruzzese & Davino (2001) or Hofmann & Wilhelm (2001) for recent references). They are a simple approach to analysing the

L. De Raedt and A. Siebes (Eds.): PKDD 2001, LNAI 2168, pp. 472–483, 2001.
© Springer-Verlag Berlin Heidelberg 2001

association between large numbers of categorical variables and part of their attraction is that the method is easy to explain and that individual results are readily understandable. What is not so easy to deal with is that for any realistic data set there are two main problems: firstly, that far too many association rules tend to be reported and most software packages just display them all in a fairly incomprehensible long list (see Table 1 for the first lines from a typical example); secondly, that the obvious way round the first problem "to just report the 'best' rules discovered" doesn't work. Association rules that are best on the two key criteria of support and confidence are likely to be trivial or well known already. The most interesting rules will tend to be ones, which have good, but not outstanding, values for support and confidence. Unfortunately, there will usually be a large number of these. There has been research on pruning and filtering sets of rules, but while these methods look promising they still leave many rules to be evaluated. Background information has to be brought into play and it makes sense to try to concentrate on discussing a small group of rules. Some of these will have high criteria values, but be of no practical application. What remains will ideally be of value to the data set owners.

Table 1. Sample output from association rules software. (Only the first four rules found are shown, there are many more to follow!)

age>33 & weeks worked in year>8 → income=50000+
  [Cov=0.307 (91870); Sup=0.051 (15308); Conf= 0.167; Lift=2.69]
age>33 & wage/hour≤0 & weeks worked in year>8 → income=50000+
  [Cov=0.277 (82808); Sup=0.049 (14634); Conf=0.177; Lift=2.85]
age>33 & hispanic origin=All other & weeks worked in year>8 → income=50000+
  [Cov=0.276 (82712); Sup=0.049 (14585); Conf=0.176; Lift=2.84]
age>33 & wage/hour≤0 & hispanic origin=All other & weeks worked in year>8
                                                        → income=50000+
  [Cov=0.248 (74276); Sup=0.047 (13931); Conf= 0.188; Lift=3.02]

2 Analysis by Association Rules

It is assumed that the data set comprises 0/1 variables reflecting the absence or presence of attributes in transactions. For non-binary data we will assume an appropriate recoding. An association rule [Agrawal et al., 1993] is defined as an implication of the form $X \rightarrow Y$, where X and Y are mutually exclusive itemsets. An association rule $X \rightarrow Y$ holds with confidence $c = c(X, Y)$, if $c\%$ of transactions in the data set that contain X also contain Y. $X \rightarrow Y$ has support $s = s(X, Y)$ in the data set, if $s\%$ of transactions contain X and Y. Confidence is equivalent to the conditional probability of Y given X. Support is equivalent to the joint probability of X and Y. In this paper we shall restrict ourselves to rules with single item conclusions (i.e. the itemset Y on the Right Hand Side always contains just one item) for expository purposes. Simple rules with just one assumption (when itemset X on the Left Hand Side has only one member) will be referred to as level two rules, because two items are involved. By extension, a rule with $(m-1)$ assumptions on the LHS will be a level m rule.

All Association Rules software will produce some kind of listing of rules (as in Table 1) and most packages will also provide summaries. Few appear to offer substantial organisation and management capabilities. To emphasise how important this is, it is worth noting that 5807 rules of between 2 and 8 levels were found for the 34 variable data set considered in this paper, even though support had to be more than 60% and confidence higher than 80%. The MARC software produces an initial summary window giving the parameter values chosen, the number of rules found (in total and by level) and a listing of the individual variables with their frequency of occurrence and the numbers of rules in which they are involved as either assumption or conclusion. There is also a set of controls to enable flexible selections of variables for detailed analysis and the capability to sort on any of the numbers produced. Sorting is a much-underrated facility in statistical software. That the rules should be sorted on confidence and support is obvious, but sorting on variables is also informative for grouping rules with the same variables as assumptions or conclusions.

3   Data Set Description

Association rules are supposed to be ideal for analysing market basket data, that is customer shopping transactions. Which products are bought together is an important question for store management. These data sets have large numbers of products (just think of how many different products your local supermarket stocks) and almost all are bought relatively rarely. Either the method is successful, but the results have not been released for reasons of confidentiality, or there has been less practical application of this kind than theoretical development.

Like most other researchers in this field we have therefore not analysed a real market basket data set (there are several analyses of artificial data sets in the literature) but have experimented with applying the method of association rules to another kind of binary data. The data set contains information on birdsbreeding habits by geographic region [Buckland et al., 1990]. 395 regions in North East Scotland were classified as breeding or non-breeding grounds for each of 34 different kinds of bird. There is interest in which groups of birds breed in the same regions. Do some birds share the same breeding grounds? Does the breeding presence of certain birds imply that a further species breeds there too? While this data set is not large and does not have a large number of variables, it is a real data set and it is both interesting to see what association rules might suggest and also as an example to illustrate how large numbers of rule results can be displayed and analysed.

One unexpected result of the analysis was the realisation that not only is effective post-filtering essential to cut down the number of rules discovered to a manageable group, but that pre-filtering is necessary as well. The high support threshold chosen immediately excluded all birds, which bred in less than 60% of the regions from being in any of the rules, whether as assumption or conclusion. In many ways it is the rarer birds, which are more interesting. Setting the support threshold much lower and then selecting the rules in which the rarer birds were conclusions would always be possible, but huge numbers of rules of no interest would be produced. It is more practical to both lower the threshold and to have the option of excluding the more frequent birds from appearing as conclusions in any rules.

4   What Is a TwoKey Plot?

A TwoKey plot shows the two keys of confidence and support for all discovered association rules. Its lower limits are determined by the threshold criteria specified by the user. In Fig. 1 these were a minimum support of 60% and a min-

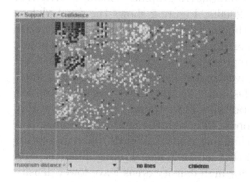

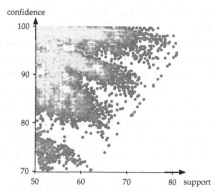

Fig. 1. A scatterplot of all 5807 rules found. No density estimation has been used. In the colour version the points are coloured by the level of the rule and this is partially seen in the shading

Fig. 2. MANET plot of confidence against support with pointsize = 2 and maximum brightness at pixels with 12 or more points

imum confidence of 80%. The maximum values are, of course, potentially 100% and this may be reached on the Y axis (confidence). It is more than a standard scatterplot because it has extensive interactive features, but it is more than an interactive scatterplot, because it has tools specifically designed for association rules. A TwoKey plot includes basic interactive features (see Unwin [1999]) such as querying (to find out which rules are represented), zooming (to study a subset of rules in more detail), selecting (to highlight rules of certain types) and linking (to garner information from other displays). There are also density estimation tools and line connections to display relationships between rules.

Several features can be identified in Fig. 1. The darker points on the right are all 2-level rules. They form straight lines because the LHS assumption is the same in all cases. The reason for this is simple. For an association rule $X \rightarrow Y$

the fraction of confidence and support is constant in X, i.e. for each LHS X, there is a straight line, on which all data points $X \to Y$ appear with increasing confidences (starting from the origin).

In Fig. 1 there are three blocks of rules, which have the appearance of clouds moving to the left leaving exhaust trails behind them. Rules involving a particular variable as conclusion will sometimes be in just one of these blocks. This arises when there is at least one good 2 level rule (i.e. good for that conclusion) and adding further assumptions lowers support but adds little to confidence.

The colour coding of rule levels is very informative in an initial overview. Low-level rules tend to be to the right (high support) and lower (less confidence), but individual rules of different types then stand out, especially higher-level rules with more support. To get an impression of how many rules are located in different areas of the plot, a density estimation version of the display is needed (without therefore the colour coding of levels). This cannot yet be carried out in MARC, but is available in the general interactive graphics software, MANET, written by Heike Hofmann [Hofmann, 2000b]. Figure 2 shows the same plot as Fig. 1 but in MANET and with a fast (though crude) density estimate. There are two parameters controlling the density estimation, the size r of individual points and an upper limit L on the density represented. In Fig. 1 $r = 2$ and $L = 12$. Each pixel at which 12 or more points overlap is coloured bright white and lower densities are shaded in a proportional fashion. (At many locations in the top left hand corner of the plot there are substantially more than 12 rules, as is readily found by direct querying of the locations). Although the method is simple, it is fast enough to be interactive so that changing r and L reveals different aspects of the density of rules. This is particularly useful when examining different parts of the plot. Parameter values suitable for high density areas leave lower density areas looking quite uniform and vice versa.

TwoKey plots can be used as standard interactive displays, where they may be linked to other graphic displays of the data: a barchart of level (for the same reason as the colour coding above), barcharts of the individual variables (to show in which groups of rules variables are involved) or mosaic plots [Hofmann, 2000a] of combinations of the variables (to select rules with certain combinations or, more usefully, to show which combinations arise in a selected group of rules). Linking is a powerful two-way tool. The information it delivers depends on the diagram where you make the selection and which diagrams you link to. Graphical interaction provides an easily understandable interface to the results for smaller numbers of variables. For working with larger numbers, the control window in MARC is more suitable, where many variables can be selected simultaneously. It could be argued that detailed interactive approaches are most relevant when studying subsets of results after extensive filtering, but both kinds of selection facilities should be provided. Using subjective filtering (e.g. just display the rules with a particular conclusion or display all rules involving any of a subset of variables) is an effective exploratory tool, but remains subjective. Selection rules based on objective filtering criteria must still be added, but it is not yet clear which. There are several promising alternatives and they need to be put into a common framework. We envisage a three-part process:

1. Draw the TwoKey plot for all rules to gain a global overview.
2. Apply one or more "objective" filtering rules to reduce the number of rules under consideration.
3. Use subjective selection tools to uncover the most interesting rules amongst the remainder. This would not be a rigid three-stage process, but a continuing exploration to identify rules and subgroups of rules that are worth following up.

In an interactive environment of linked graphics (Becker et al 1987, Unwin et al 1996, Theus 1996, Wilhelm 2000), further information can be brought into consideration using selection & highlighting.

In this data set, spatial information about the items is available. We can extract two rules and have a closer look at them. The rules Mallard → Pheasant (54.4, 81.4) and Blue Tit, Curlew, Great Finch, Oystercatcher, Wren → Pheasant (50.1, 97.1) are shown on the corresponding map (see Fig. 3).

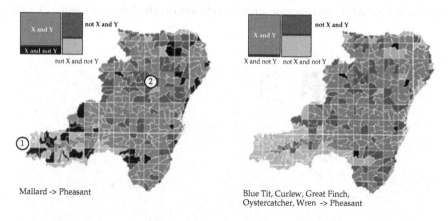

Fig. 3. Maps of the bird watching area. Gray shading corresponds to different combination of presence/absence of left and right hand side of rules

Gray shading is used to encode different combinations of left and right hand side of two rules. Areas, in which both birds of left and right hand side of the rules have been observed are coloured middle gray, areas, in which only birds from the right hand side but not of the left hand side have been observed are coloured black. The darkish gray represents all those areas where birds of the right hand side are present, but not all birds of the left hand side have been observed.

In this example you can see, that the simple rule Mallard → Pheasant shows some spatial relationship: several areas in the south-eastern part of the map are falsely assigned to Pheasant (marked by the circled 1), whereas the rule misses out some areas in the centre (marked by 2). This problem is overcome by the more specific rule shown on the right of Fig. 3. The areas in the south-eastern part are fitted nicely by it and the rule detects most of the areas in the centre, too.

Using interactive graphics opens the way to find structural behaviour in association rules, e.g. separate spatial clusters or subgroups among the target population.

5   Special Tools in TwoKey Plots for Analysing Association Rules

5.1   Children and Descendants

Given a typical simple two level rule that $X \to Y$, it is clearly worth investigating what happens when more conditions are added to the left hand side. $X \to Y$ could be an obvious relationship and we might be interested in seeing how it might be extended. In MARC's TwoKey plot you can select any rules (not just two level rules) and have lines drawn from each rule to its immediate children. A child is defined as having one more condition on the left hand side. Figure 4

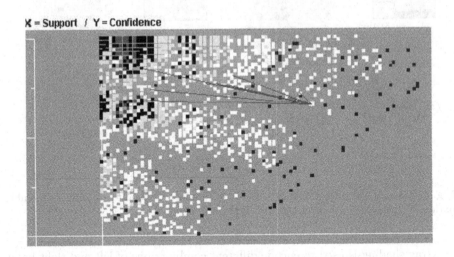

Fig. 4. The children of a 3-level rule have been linked by lines to the rule

shows a plot of this kind with one three level rule selected. Naturally, only rule children are shown which have sufficient confidence and support values to appear in the plot. It is immediately clear which additional group of rules it might be worth looking at if we start from the selected rule. All rule children must lie to the left (they cannot have higher support) and only rules with higher confidence will be worth considering. There are likely to be two kinds: a few rules which have somewhat higher confidence, but only a little less support and some rules which have a lot less support, but rather more confidence. It very much depends on the client's goals and the particular rules, which group might be more important. We will have a closer look at this situation in Sect. 6. In Fig. 4 we can see that only 3 children are worth considering and they have very different reductions in support. Note that the display would also make clear if there were a number of closely related alternatives or if one rule child was substantially better than the others. It is possible in MARC to display descendants of 2 or more generations, but the display rapidly becomes unclear. It is a topic of current research to see how this might be improved.

5.2 Parents and Ancestors

Just as it can be informative to study rule descendants, it is helpful to be able to examine rule predecessors. For a single m level rule there can be at most (m - 1) parents. Lines may of course be drawn in MARC from selected rules to their parents. Parents must lie to the right (higher support). A rule with a parent with higher confidence will not be a good rule. There is an argument for filtering out all such rules, but, initially at any rate, it seems appropriate to display all rules that pass the user-specified thresholds.

5.3 Neighbours

Individual association rules are rather blinkered. They tell you nothing about closely related rules. Relatives cover one form of closeness, but the term neighbour is used in MARC to cover all others.

A rule R2: $X' \to Y'$ is a neighbour of distance d of another rule R1: $X \to Y$ if one of the following holds (where a step is an addition or a deletion):

(a) the RHS is the same ($Y' = Y$) and the LHS's are d steps apart;
(b) the RHS is different and the LHSs are $d - 2$ steps apart.

With this definition the only immediate neighbours ($d = 1$) are parents and children. Rules with only the RHS different are neighbours of distance 2.

Linking neighbours of a selected rule by lines in MARC helps in various ways. For instance, for distance $d = 2$, the rules on a straight line are those with the same assumptions but different conclusions. The other rules of the same colour have the same conclusion but one different assumption. The remaining rules of different colours have the same conclusion but either two fewer assumptions (grandparents) or two more (grandchildren).

MARC produces tables of results for the selected subgroup of rules to provide a textual overview to complement the graphic display. Further developments will include the incorporation of statistical tests in these tables to identify rules, which are "significantly" different from the originally selected rules, and this may also be colour-coded on the lines in the graphic display. Significance would only be used as a rough guideline. The interdependence of the tests and the multiple testing involved precludes anything more, but it is valuable to attempt to assess relationships in a formal statistical way.

6   Relationships among Rules

Selecting rules from the set of results is a crucial issue, with the help of inter-active selection methods and linking we have a lot more choices for criteria of acceptance, all of which may be sensible in the background of a specific application.

Of particular interest is, how we may compare rules of the form $X_1 \to Y$ and $X_2 \to Y$, where the first rule has higher confidence, but less support than the second rule. Is there a way to tell, which of these rules is "better" than the other?

Between each two of the rules in fig. 5 that fulfill an ancestor relationship a line is drawn.

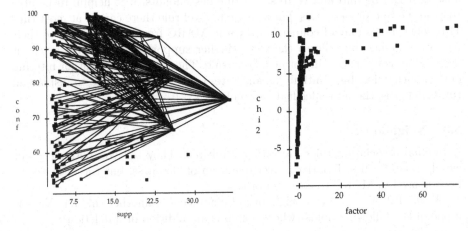

Fig. 5. Lines between each ances-
tor/successor pair of rules

Fig. 6. Slope sl between two related
rules vs. their test-statistic T

For these lines, the angle between a rule and its successor is of interest: it is clear, that an angle $\leq 0°$ connects a rule to a successor with less confidence - something, which marks the successor rule as a total failure. Lines with a very steep angle, on the other hand, show those successors, which have only little less support than their ancestor but more confidence.

Can the angles of these lines therefore be exploited for a visual pruning mecha-nism? For this, we have a look at the (negative) slope sl between $X \to Z(s_1, c_1)$ and its successor $X \cap Y \to Z(s_2, c_2)$:

$$sl = \tan(\alpha) = \frac{c_2 - c_1}{s_1 - s_2}$$

This expression for the slope between two related rules recalls another test-statistic, which is used widely for pruning rules based on their ancestor relationship structure [Bing Liu et al., 1999]: Let T be the test statistic of $P(Z \mid X, Y)$ vs $P(Z \mid X, \neg Y)$:

$$T = \sqrt{nP(X)} \frac{P(Y \cap Z \mid X) - P(Y \mid X)P(Z \mid X)}{\sqrt{P(Z \mid X)P(\neg Z \mid X) \cdot P(Y \mid X)P(\neg Y \mid X)}}$$

T is approximately normally distributed (it's the square root of a χ^2 test of conditional independence of Y and Z given X). Prominent features in Fig. 6 are the strong linear relationship between the lower values of the statistics and the cloud of points with high slope. Within this cloud of points, T and sl do take very different values. The two rules mined from the SAS Assoc Data, herring & baguette $\to$ heineken and chicken & coke & sardines $\to$ heineken, have similar values in T, but different slope values:

rule	ancestor	T	sl
herring&baguette $\to$ heineken	baguette $\to$ heineken	10.72	4.13
chicken&coke&sardines $\to$ heineken	chicken&coke $\to$ heineken	10.82	71.41

In order to explain the differences in T and slope, we rewrite the slope as:

$$sl = [P(Y \cap Z \mid X) - P(Y \mid X)P(Z \mid X)] \cdot \frac{1}{P(Y \mid X)P(X \cap Z \cap \neg Y)}.$$

The first term of this product gives a measure for the conditional independence of Y and Z given X and is well known from the test statistic T. The second term is more tricky: $P(Y|X)$ will be large, if $P(X \cap \neg Y)$ is small; this measures the loss in the support of $X \to Z$ by adding the item Y. $P(X \cap Z \cap \neg Y)$ is linear in the number of result hits that are thrown away by adding Y.

Some properties of the slope:

- according to the value of the slope that rule $X \cap Y \to Z$ is chosen, which cuts off small slices from the support while gaining maximum confidence.
- It ignores the values of the ancestor rule $X \to Z$.
- It's not additive:

$$sl_3 \le sl_1 + sl_2,$$

where sl_1 is the slope between rules $X \to Z$ and $\to Z$, sl_2 is the slope between rules $X \cap Y \to Z$ and $X \to Z$ and sl_3 is the slope between rules $X \cap Y \to Z$ and $\to Z$,

For each ancestor rule, the results of sl and T show a strong linear relationship (cf. Fig. 7).

Conclusion: for single ancestor rules the results from the test statistic and the slope are approximately linear dependent. The angles between the ancestor rule and its successsors therefore may be used as a measure for the strength of a successor rule. This leads to the following criterion: A rule $X \cap Y_1 \to Z$ is dominated by a rule $X \cap Y_2 \to Z$,

$$\Longleftrightarrow sl(X \cap Y_1 \to Z) < sl(X \cap Y_2 \to Z)$$

$$\Longleftrightarrow \frac{P(Z \mid X, Y_2) - P(Z \mid X)}{P(Z \cap X) - P(Z \cap X \cap Y_2)} > \frac{P(Z \mid X, Y_1) - P(Z \mid X)}{P(Z \cap X) - P(Z \cap X \cap Y_1)}.$$

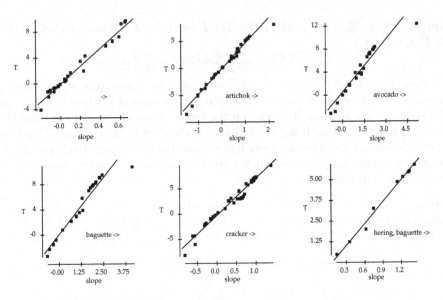

Fig. 7. Linear dependencies between sl and T for fixed ancestors

7   Summary

The concept of TwoKey Plots is a very simple but very effective one. It has been introduced as a means of providing a global overview of large amounts of association rules discovered in an analysis and of providing the tools to explore and evaluate them. The range and flexibility of the resulting graphic displays make this a very attractive method for working with association rules.

Data Mining methods can produce many different outputs and these need to be organised, managed and filtered. Pruning or filtering methods are an important first step, but they leave many rules still to be assessed. Exploiting the ancestor relationship structure of rules gives a visual approach to filter out potentially interesting rules. Here, we have seen that a visual analysis of the standard ancestor-successor relationship coincides with a χ^2-test of independence as proposed by Bing et al (1999).

The effective application of any method of analysis lies in the combination of objective results and subjective knowledge. The TwoKey plot is a step in this direction for association rules. Its particular strength lies in interactivity, so that users can incorporate both their background knowledge and their foreground goals in evaluating the rules that have been discovered.

Software. The MARC (Multiple Association Rules Control) software used for the work in this paper is being developed by the authors at Augsburg. Klaus Bernt is responsible for the system design and programming. MARC is written in Java and it is planned to make the software available to other researchers in the near future. (Check our website www1.math.uni-augsburg.de for further details.) Like all Augsburg software, MARC is named after a painter close to the Impressionists. Franz Marc was born in Munich, near to Augsburg, and was an influential member of the Blaue Reiter group.

References

[Agrawal et al., 1993] Agrawal R., Imielinski T. & Swami A. (1993) *Mining Associations between Sets of Items in Massive Databases.* Proc. of the ACM-SIGMOD 1993 Int'l Conference on Management of Data, Washington D.C., pp. 207 - 216.

[Becker et al., 1987] Becker R.A., Cleveland W.S. & Wilks A. (1987) Dynamic Graphics For Data Analysis. In: Cleveland & McGill, 1988, pp.1-50.

[Bing Liu et al., 1999] Bing Liu, Wynne Hsu & Yiming Ma (1999) Pruning and Summarizing the Discovered Association Rules. In Proc. of the 5th ACM SIGKDD Conference: KDD99, pp.125-134, 1999.

[Buckland et al., 1990] Buckland, S.T., Bell, M.V. and Picozzi, N. (eds) (1990) The Birds of North-East Scotland. North-East Scotland Bird Club, Aberdeen. 473pp.

[Bruzzese & Davino, 2001] Bruzzese, D., Davino, C. (2001) Statistical Pruning of Discovered Association Rules. Computational Statistics (to be published)

[Cleveland & McGill, 1988] Cleveland W. & McGill R. (1988) Dynamic Graphics for Statistics. Pacific Grove, CA: Wadsworth & Brooks, Inc.

[Hofmann, 2000a] Hofmann H. (2000) Exploring categorical data: interactive mosaic plots. Metrika, 51(1), 11-26.

[Hofmann, 2000b] Hofmann H. (2000) MANET www1.math.uni-augsburg.de/Manet/. In Augsburg: Rosuda.

[Hofmann et al., 2000] Hofmann H., Siebes A., Wilhelm A. (2000) Visualizing Association Rules with Interactive Mosaic Plots, In Proc. of the 6th Int'l Conference of SigKDD, pp. 227-235.

[Hofmann & Wilhelm, 2001] Hofmann, H., Wilhelm, A. (2001) Visual Comparison of Association Rules. Computational Statistics (to be published)

[Mannila H., 1997] Mannila, H (1997) Methods and Problems in Data Mining. In F. Afrati Kolaitis, P. (Ed.), International Conference on Database Theory, . Delphi: Springer.

[Piatetsky-Shapiro & Masand, 1999] Piatetsky-Shapiro, G. & Masand, B. (1999) Estimating Campaign Benefits and Modeling Lift. In 5th ACM SIGKDD, (pp. 185-193).

[Theus, 1996] Theus M. (1996) Theorie und Anwendung Interaktiver Statistischer Graphik. Augsburger mathematisch-naturwissenschaftliche Schriften, **14**, Wißner Verlag, Ausgburg, Germany.

[Unwin, 1999] Unwin, A. R. (1999) Requirements for interactive graphics software for exploratory data analysis. Computational Statistics, 14, 7-22.

[Unwin et al., 1996] Unwin A. R., Hawkins G. Hofmann H. & Siegl B. (1996) Interactive Graphics for Data Sets with Missing Values - MANET. Journal of Computational and Graphical Statistics, *5*, 2, pp. 113 - 122.

[Wilhelm, 2000] Wilhelm A. (2000) Interactive Statistical Graphics: The Paradigm of Linked Views. Habilitationsschrift, Universität Augsburg.

Lightweight Collaborative Filtering Method for Binary-Encoded Data

Sholom M. Weiss and Nitin Indurkhya

IBM T.J. Watson Research Center
P.O Box 218, Yorktown Heights, NY 10598, USA
sholom@us.ibm.com, nitin@data-miner.com

Abstract. A lightweight method for collaborative filtering is described that processes binary encoded data. Examples of transactions that can be described in this manner are items purchased by customers or web pages visited by individuals. As with all collaborative filtering, the objective is to match a person's records to customers with similar records. For example, based on prior purchases of a customer, one might recommend new items for purchase by examining stored records of other customers who made similar purchases. Because the data are binary (true-or-false) encoded, and not ranked preferences on a numerical scale, efficient and lightweight schemes are described for compactly storing data, computing similarities between new and stored records, and making recommendations tailored to an individual.

1 Introduction

Recommendation systems provide a type of customization that has become popular on the internet. Most search engines use them to group relevant documents. Some newspapers allow news customization. E-commerce sites recommend purchases based on preferences of their other customers. The main advantages of recommendation systems stem from ostensibly better targeted promotions. This promises higher sales, more advertising revenues, less search by customers to get what they want, and greater customer loyalty.

Collaborative filtering [1] is one class of recommendation systems that mimics word-of-mouth recommendations. An related task is to compare two people and assess how closely they resemble one another. The general concept of nearest-neighbor methods, matching a new instance to similar stored instances, is well-known [2]. Collaborative filtering methods use this fundamental concept, but differ in the how data are encoded, how similarity is computed, and how recommendations are computed.

We describe a lightweight method for collaborative filtering that processes binary-encoded data. Examples of transactions that can be described in this manner are items purchased by customers or web pages visited by individuals. As with all collaborative filtering, the objective is to match a person's records to customers with similar records. For example, based on prior purchases of a customer, one might recommend new items for purchase by examining stored

L. De Raedt and A. Siebes (Eds.): PKDD 2001, LNAI 2168, pp. 484–491, 2001.

records of other customers who made similar purchases. Because the data are binary (true-or-false) encoded, and not ranked preferences on a numerical scale, efficient and lightweight schemes are described for compactly storing data, computing similarities between new and stored records, and making recommendations tailored to an individual. Our preliminary results are promising and competitive with published benchmarks.

2 Methods

The collaborative filtering problem we looked at is a generic task that occurs in many applications. A specific example is recommending pages to a user surfing the web. We shall describe our algorithm within the context of this application where the attributes are the pages visited by users (and so we shall use "page" and "attribute" interchangeably). The value-attribute for a user simply records whether or not the user visited the corresponding page. Hence the data we are concerned with is purely binary.

In the simplest scoring scheme, recommendations might be made based on a linear weighted combination of other people's preferences. Most popular are memory-based methods. Complex model-based approaches such as Bayesian networks have also been explored [3]. We examined variations of a far simpler scheme. The basic idea is as follows:

1. find the k nearest neighbors to the new (test) case
2. collect all attributes of these neighbors that don't occur in the test case
3. rank these attributes by frequency of occurrence among the k neighbors.

In measuring distance between cases, we compute a score that measures similarity, the higher the score, the greater the similarity. For each training case, count the number of positive attributes in common with the test case. We add a small bonus for each page: the reciprocal of the number of training cases in which this page appears. This ensures that rare pages get a higher bonus than "popular" pages. As an example, suppose a new example has visited 5 webpages. We look at the stored examples to find similar examples. The most similar examples would match in all 5 webpages. Their scores would be 5 plus the value of the pre-computed bonuses for each of those pages. The score would ignore any negative distance that could be computed from pages visited in the stored examples but not visited by the new example.

Further improvements might be obtained by modifying step 2 slightly and splitting an example's vote. Instead of considering all attributes of all neighbors equally, we instead assign 1 vote for each neighbor, and split that vote among its attributes. The intuition behind this is that if a neighbor makes only one recommendation, it is more important than a recommendation made by a neighbor that makes 10 recommendations. This affects the frequency of occurrence and alters the ranking of the recommended attributes in the ranked list.

Another change we consider is to also measure the degree of similarity among neighbors' scores. Attributes of closer neighbors might be assigned a higher weight than those far away. We do this by using a weight of 1 for the closest neighbor(s), and a proportionally smaller weight for neighbors further away. The weight is the ratio of the score of a case to the highest score.

The overall algorithm is shown in Fig. 1. It follows the 3 steps listed earlier. Scoring a case involves computing a function $pv(j)$ for each attribute. This function measures the apriori predictive value of the attribute and is computed once at the start. Note the two modifications to the basic algorithm corresponding to vote splitting and relative similarity.

In order to compute the scores and tally the frequencies efficiently, the sample of cases are stored as follows:

- **Case List.** Here the cases are stored sequentially as a series of numbers corresponding to the *positive* attributes in the case. All cases are stored in a single vector, with another vector pointing to the start of each case. Table 1 shows an example of how the cases are implemented using two lists. The first case consists of positive attributes 2 and 5. The second case consists of positive attributes 1, 7, 21 and 43. The third case begins with the attribute 2.

Table 1. Example of case list implementation

case vector	2 5 1 7 21 43 2 ...
start vector	1 3 7 ...

- **Inverse List.** Here we record a series of numbers corresponding to the cases in which a specific positive attribute occurs. All attribute mappings to examples can be stored sequentially in a single vector, with another vector pointing to the start of each attribute. Table 2 shows an example of how this is done. The first attribute occurs in cases 2 and 50, the second attribute occurs in cases 1, 3 and 45.

Table 2. Example of inverse list implementation

inverse vector	2 50 1 3 45 ...
attribute start vector	1 3 6 ...

The case list is used to compute the frequencies; the inverse list is used to compute the scores. Both the lists are computed once, at the start. Following that, the scores and frequencies can be computed very efficiently.

```
Input: C {new case represented by M attributes C(1), ... C(m)},
       D {Historical data of n cases, D1 ... Dn}
Output: A {Ranked list of attributes}

Begin
  For j = 1 to m do
      df = number of cases in D where attribute j appears;
      pv(j) = 1 + 1/df;
  done
  score(Di) = 0 for i=1,n
  rank(j) = 0 for j=1,m
  For j = 1 to m do
      If (C(j) == 0) continue;
      // examine only attributes that are positive for the new case
      For i = 1 to n do
         If (Di(j) == 0) continue;
         // score a case only if it shares an attribute with new case
      score(Di) += pv(j);
      done
  done
  T = select k cases with highest scores in D;
  For j = 1 to m do
      If (C(j) == 1) continue;
      // examine only attributes that are NOT positive for new case
      For i = 1 to k do
          // increase count of those attributes that are in top-k cases
          If (Ti(j) == 1)
            rank(j) += 1;
          // MODIFICATION 1 (vote splitting): rank(j) += 1/sum(Ti);
          // where sum(case) is the number of positive attributes
              in case
          // MODIFICATION 2 (relative similarity): rank(j) +=
             (1/sum(Ti))*xscore(Ti)
          // where xscore(Ti) = score(Ti)/score(T1)
      done
  done
  Output = small subset of attributes with highest rank(j);;
End
```

Fig. 1. The lightweight collaborative filtering algorithm

3   Results

Our work is a followup to [3] which reports on empirical results using Bayesian networks and memory-based methods for three datasets. Our experiments were performed on the msweb dataset.

The problem we looked at is a generic task that occurs in many applications: recommending pages to a user surfing the web. The msweb data of users visiting pages at the Microsoft website can be viewed in this manner. The data is pre-divided into 32711 training cases and 5000 test cases, and 298 attributes. A case can be seen as a user and an attribute can be seen as a webpage visited by the user. [3] report a variety of experiments in which some attributes in the test cases are predicted by models based on the training data. One of the scenarios is as follows: in each test case, a visited page is randomly selected and "hidden". Based on the other attributes, the models learned from the training data attempt to recommend pages to visit. The models are evaluated by assessing how well they do in predicting the "hidden" page. Since our experiments require that test cases have 2 or more visited pages, the test cases used are a subset of the full set – 3453 cases.

Since the models typically make a ranked list of recommendations, [3] use an R-metric to measure the quality of the recommendation. The R-metric is specified in Equations 1 and 2. Here, R_a is the expected utility measuring how likely it is that the user will visit an item on the ranked list, with an exponential decay in likelihood for successive items, and is based on the user a's votes $v_{a,j}$, on item j. R_a^{max} is the maximum achievable utility and normalizing with it helps us consider results independent of sample sizes and the number of recommendations made. The higher the rank of the "hidden" page in the list of recommendations, the higher the value of the R-metric.

$$R_a = \sum_j \frac{max(v_{a,j} - d, 0)}{2^{(j-1)/(\alpha-1)}} \qquad (1)$$

$$R = 100 \frac{\sum_a R_a}{\sum_a R_a^{max}} \qquad (2)$$

Table 3 summarizes the results obtained for several Model-based and Memory-based methods. The static ranked list simply recommends based on popularity and without considering the known votes. As such it serves as a baseline. Bayesian Clustering and Bayesian Networks are relatively complex Bayesian models [4]. The Correlation method [5] is further enhanced by the use of inverse user frequency, default voting and case amplification. Vector similarity [6] are enhanced by the use of inverse user frequency transformations as well. The three versions of the lightweight algorithm differ in the rank computation as described in Fig. 1. Except for the two Bayesian methods, all the other methods are memory-based methods.

The results in Table 3 are for the best variation of each method. Clearly the parameters of each method need to be optimized carefully. The performance of the lightweight method depends on k, the number of neighbors used. Fig. 3

Table 3. Summary of results on MSWEB data

Collaborative Filtering Method	R-metric
Static Ranked List	49.77
Bayesian Clustering	59.42
Vector Similarity	61.70
Correlation	63.59
Bayesian Network	66.69
Basic Lightweight	61.76
Lightweight with vote splitting	64.35
Lightweight with vote splitting and relative similarity	64.60

Table 4. Top x recommendations

x	1	5	10
accuracy	.3165	.7387	.8412

shows the result of varying k for each of the three variations. For a vote-splitting strategy, higher values of k are helpful. For the basic algorithm,, beyond a lesser number of k, the performance gains are marginal.

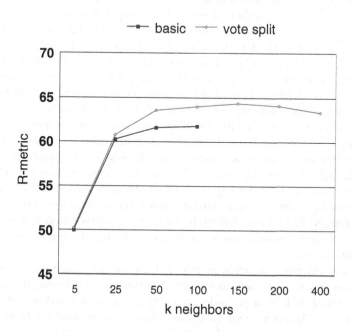

Fig. 2. Effect of k on performance of the lightweight method

4 Discussion

The experiments suggest that our lightweight collaborative filtering method can be competitive with published results for far more complicated models. A lightweight algorithm, analogous to our basic collaborative filtering algorithm, has been extensively tested for information retrieval and document matching [7]. An earlier study showed that in an IR environment, where more than one recommendation is made, simpler algorithms can be surprisingly effective [8].

We relied on published results for the alternative, highly specialized collaborative filtering methods. Our method is restricted to applications that are represented in binary form. Most real-world collaborative filtering methods expect ranked data, where a user is asked to rate products, for example on a scale of 1 to 5. Far fewer benchmark datasets for binary data are publicly available. In the future, we can expect interest in binary representations to increase because greater automation is achieved without users manually assigned ratings.

The paucity of publicly available datasets with binary encodings limited our evaluation to one well-known dataset. Clearly, this is a weakness of the evaluation of our method. In the original study [3], several scenarios were examined including fixing the number of given items to 2, 5 or 10, each simulating different levels of information. Still, these variations are all taken from the same data, and the simulations create an unnatural set of data, all with the same number of positive features. We chose to use the one testing variation, all-but-one, that encompasses the variable scenarios of the unmodified snapshot of users.

Because memory-based methods, like our lightweight method, have complexity $O(n)$, where n is the number of examples, many researchers have shifted attention from instance-based techniques to model-based techniques [9] [10]. We are not presenting our method as the best or as the most run-time efficient under all circumstances. Belief and dependency networks have many desirable properties, along with issues of complex representations and training. Our lightweight method is trivial to implement, mostly processes vectors sequentially, and operates in an environment where almost every attribute is measured as zero. These conditions lend themselves to relatively efficient implementations until the number of instances grows very large. Even then, experimentation may show that predictive performance reaches a plateau at a relatively small sample size of N cases. For example, on this dataset, much more data were originally available, but experimental results did not improve much with more data [9]. The simplicity of the lightweight method along with its binary vector representation, and its application without formal training to derive an intermediate model, may make it a suitable for some recommendation systems, including those with very large numbers of attributes.

Collaborative filtering matches an individual's history to users with similar records. An alternative approach to recommendations is item-based [10]. There, the top matches of each item are independently precomputed and stored (as in book retailers like Amazon), and only this information is used for tailoring a recommendation. Such an approach is efficient, has shown some good results, but has less potential for personalized recommendations.

Many collaborative filtering algorithms, including our lightweight algorithm, ignore the sequence order of user-actions. Alternative algorithms, such as Markov models, can capture such information, which potentially can yield improved performance [11]. However, such models can become extremely complex, especially in higher dimensions, where either a long sequence of actions is traced or the space of recommendations is very large.

The R-metric is effective in measuring performance over a ranked list of recommendations. It rewards those recommendations that are correct and highly ranked, and it penalizes those recommendations that appear at the bottom of the list. We used the R-metric to facilitate comparisons to published results. Other metrics can also be examined. We measured the accuracy of finding the "hidden" page among the top x recommendations. This is shown in Table 4. An advantage of this metric is that by examining the trend for different values of x, one can get a good idea of the quality of the solution.

Like search engines, the lightweight collaborative filtering algorithm uses an inverted list for efficient processing of sparse data. It requires very little data preparation and has a compact codebase. As such, it may prove highly desirable for applications that naturally fit a binary-encoded data representation.

References

1. D. Goldberg, D. Nichols, B. Oki, and D. Terry. Using collaborative filtering to weave an information tapestry. *CACM*, 35(12):61–70, 1992.
2. T. Cover and P. Hart. Nearest neighbour pattern classification. *IEEE Transactions on Information Theory*, 13:21–27, 1967.
3. J. Breese, D. Heckerman, and C. Kadie. Empirical analysis of predictive algorithms for collaborative filtering. In *Proceedings of the Fourteenth Conference on Uncertainty in AI*, 1998.
4. D. Chickering, D. Heckerman, and C. Meek. A bayesian approach to learning bayesian networks with local structure. In *Proceedings of the Thirteenth Conference on Uncertainty in AI*, 1997.
5. P. Resnick, N. Iacovou, M. Suchak, P Bergstrom, and J. Riedl. Grouplens: An open architecture for collaborative filtering of netnews. In *Proceedings of the ACM Conference on Computer Supported Cooperative Work*, pages 175–186, 1994.
6. G. Salton and M. McGill. *Introduction to Modern Information Retrieval*. McGraw-Hill, New York, 1983.
7. S. Weiss, H. White, and C. Apté. Lightweight document clustering. In *Proceedings of PKDD-2000*, pages 665–672. Springer, 2000.
8. S. Weiss, B. White, C. Apte, and F. Damerau. Lightweight document matching for help-desk applications. *IEEE Intelligent Systems*, pages 57–61, 2000.
9. D. Heckerman, D. Chickering, C. Meek, R. Rounthwaite, and C. Kadie. Dependency networks for inference, collaborative filtering and data visualization. *Journal of Machine Learning Research*, 1:49–75, 2000.
10. G. Karypis. Evaluation of item-based top-n recommendation algorithms. Technical Report 046, Department of Computer Science, University of Minnesota, 2000.
11. M. Deshpande and G. Karypis. Selective markov models for predicting web-page accesses. In *Proceedings of SIAM Data Mining Conference*, 2001.

Support Vectors for Reinforcement Learning

Thomas G. Dietterich and Xin Wang

Oregon State University, Corvallis, Oregon, USA
tgd@cs.orst.edu
http://www.cs.orst.edu/~tgd

Abstract. Support vector machines introduced three important innovations to machine learning research: (a) the application of mathematical programming algorithms to solve optimization problems in machine learning, (b) the control of overfitting by maximizing the margin, and (c) the use of Mercer kernels to convert linear separators into non-linear decision boundaries in implicit spaces. Despite their attractiveness in classification and regression, support vector methods have not been applied to the problem of value function approximation in reinforcement learning. This paper presents three ways of combining linear programming with kernel methods to find value function approximations for reinforcement learning. One formulation is based on the standard approach to SVM regression; the second is based on the Bellman equation; and the third seeks only to ensure that good actions have an advantage over bad actions. All formulations attempt to minimize the norm of the weight vector while fitting the data, which corresponds to maximizing the margin in standard SVM classification. Experiments in a difficult, synthetic maze problem show that all three formulations give excellent performance. However, the third formulation is much more efficient to train and also converges more reliably. Unlike policy gradient and temporal difference methods, the kernel methods described here can easily adjust the complexity of the function approximator to fit the complexity of the value function.

L. De Raedt and A. Siebes (Eds.): PKDD 2001, LNAI 2168, p. 492, 2001.
© Springer-Verlag Berlin Heidelberg 2001

Combining Discrete Algorithmic and Probabilistic Approaches in Data Mining

Heikki Mannila

Nokia Research Center and Helsinki University of Technology

Abstract. Data mining research has approached the problems of analyzing large data sets in two ways. Simplifying a lot, the approaches can be characterized as follows. The database approach has concentrated on figuring out what types of summaries can be computed fast, and then finding ways of using those summaries. The model-based approach has focused on first finding useful model classes and then fast ways of fitting those models. In this talk I discuss some examples of both and describe some recent developments which try to combine the two approaches.

L. De Raedt and A. Siebes (Eds.): PKDD 2001, LNAI 2168, p. 493, 2001.
© Springer-Verlag Berlin Heidelberg 2001

Statistification or Mystification? The Need for Statistical Thought in Visual Data Mining

Antony Unwin

Augsburg University

Abstract. Many graphics are used for decoration rather than for conveying information. Some purport to display information, but provide insufficient supporting evidence. Others are so laden with information that it is hard to see either the wood or the trees. Analysing large data sets is difficult and requires technically efficient procedures and statistically sound methods to generate informative visualisations. Results from big data sets are statistics and they should be statistically justified. Graphics on their own are indicative, but not substantive. They should inform and neither confuse nor mystify.

This paper will NOT introduce any new innovative graphics, but will discuss the statistification of graphics – why and how statistical content should be added to graphic displays of large data sets. (There will, however, be illustrations of the Ugly, the Bad and the possibly Good.)

L. De Raedt and A. Siebes (Eds.): PKDD 2001, LNAI 2168, p. 494, 2001.
© Springer-Verlag Berlin Heidelberg 2001

The Musical Expression Project:
A Challenge for Machine Learning
and Knowledge Discovery

Gerhard Widmer

Dept. of Medical Cybernetics and Artificial Intelligence, University of Vienna, and
Austrian Research Institute for Artificial Intelligence, Vienna
gerhard@ai.univie.ac.at

Abstract. This paper reports on a long-term inter-disciplinary research project that aims at analysing the complex phenomenon of *expressive music performance* with machine learning and data mining methods. The goals and general research framework of the project are briefly explained, and then a number of challenges to machine learning (and also to computational music analysis) are discussed that arise from the complexity and multi-dimensionality of the musical phenomenon being studied. We also briefly report on first experiments that address some of these issues.

1 Introduction

This paper presents a long-term inter-disciplinary research project situated at the intersection of musicology and Artificial Intelligence. The goal is to develop and use machine learning and data mining methods to study the complex phenomenon of *expressive music performance* (or *musical expression*, for short). Formulating formal, quantitative models of expressive performance is one of the big open research problems in contemporary (empirical and cognitive) musicology. Our project develops a new direction in this field: we use *inductive learning techniques* to discover general and valid expression principles from (large amounts of) real performance data. The project, financed by a generous research grant by the Austrian Federal Government, started in early 1999 and is intended to last at least six years. The research is truly inter-disciplinary, involving both musicologists and AI researchers. We also expect to contribute new results to both disciplines involved, and our first experimental results show that this is realistic — for instance, in [26] both a new, general rule learning algorithm and some interesting, novel musical discoveries are presented.

In recent years, there has been an increasing number of attempts, in the field of empirical musicology, to formulate quantitative, mathematical or computational models of (aspects of) expressive performance (e.g., [1, 12, 13, 16–21]). This work has produced a wealth of detailed hypotheses and insights, but has often been based on rather limited sets of performance data (which were sometimes also produced under 'laboratory conditions'). What distinguishes our project is the use of large amounts of 'real-world' data, and the application of inductive

L. De Raedt and A. Siebes (Eds.): PKDD 2001, LNAI 2168, pp. 495–506, 2001.

learning methods to discover interesting and possibly novel patterns and regularities in the data. In short, we aim at performing the most data-intensive investigations ever done in musical expression research.

The purpose of the present paper is to give an overview of the project and its current state, and to discuss the challenges that this application problem presents to machine learning and knowledge discovery. In section 2, we explain the basic notions of expressive music performance. Section 3 sketches the general research framework of the project and briefly touches upon the enormous difficulties involved in data acquisition and preparation (an aspect often neglected in machine learning publications). Section 4 looks at the problem from a machine learning point of view and discusses some of the particular challenges posed by the complex nature of the target phenomenon. Section 5 briefly summarizes some interesting results obtained so far and talks about some of our ongoing research.

2   Expressive Music Performance

When played exactly as notated in the musical score, a piece of music would sound utterly mechanical and lifeless; it is both unmusical and physically impossible for a musician to perform a piece with perfectly constant tempo, even loudness, etc. What makes a piece of music come alive (and what makes some performers famous) is the art of *music interpretation*, that is, the artist's understanding of the structure and 'meaning' of a piece of music, and his/her (conscious or unconscious) expression of this understanding via *expressive performance*: a performer shapes a piece by continuously varying important parameters like tempo, dynamics (loudness), articulation, etc., speeding up at some places, slowing down at others, stressing certain notes or passages by various means, and so on. It is this shaping that can turn a lifeless piece of music into a moving experience, and that also makes both the composer's and the performer's ideas clear to the listener. What types of parameters are at a performer's disposal partly depends on the instrument being played, but the most important dimensions are *tempo* and *timing*, *dynamics* (variations in loudness), and *articulation* (basically, the way successive notes are connected).

Expressive music performance plays a central role in our current musical culture, and musicologists are showing increased interest in understanding exactly what it is that artists do when they play music. Are there explainable and quantifiable principles that govern expressive performance? To what extent and how are 'acceptable' performances determined by the (structure of the) music? What are the cognitive principles that govern the production (in the performer) and the perception (in the listener) of expressive performances? And what does this have to do with how we experience music?

Our project hopes to contribute to answering the first two of these questions. We collect precise measurements of performances by skilled musicians, and try to detect patterns and regularities (and intelligible characterizations of these) via inductive learning. As we also enable the computer to recognize structural aspects of the music, potential relationships between expressive patterns and musical structure should emerge naturally from these investigations.

This approach is based on earlier work by the author [23, 24], where it was shown that given some knowledge about musical structure, a computer can indeed learn general performance rules that produce rather sensible 'interpretations' of musical pieces. The central problem with these early studies was a lack of real performance data (the investigations were based largely on performances by the author himself). In our current work, we go beyond this by working with large collections of performances by skilled musicians, recorded on special instruments (pianos) that precisely measure and record each action of the performer. Ideally, we would also like to study the performance style of famous artists, on the basis of, e.g., audio CDs, but that will depend on the availability of computational methods for precise musical information extraction from audio, which is still an open problem in signal processing.

3   The Project: A High-level View

To give the reader an impression of the complexity of such a 'real-world' knowledge discovery project, Fig. 1 sketches the overall structure of our approach. As explained above, the basic goal is to take recordings of pieces as played by musicians, measure the 'expressive' aspects (e.g., tempo fluctuations) in these, and apply some machine learning algorithms to these measurements in order to induce general, predictive models of various aspects of expressive performance (e.g., a set of classification or regression rules that predict the tempo deviations a pianist is likely to apply to a given piece). These models must then be validated, e.g., by comparing them to theories in the musicological literature, by applying them to new pieces and analysing the musical quality of the resulting computer-generated performances, and, of course, by measuring their generalization accuracy on unseen data. All this is sketched in the lower half of Fig.1.

However, the story is much more complex. The problems involved in acquiring and pre-processing the data turned out to be formidable and forced us to develop a whole range of novel music analysis algorithms. And since we spent so much effort on these issues, I take the liberty of at least briefly mentioning them here.

3.1   Data Acquisition

The first problem was obtaining high-quality performances by human musicians (e.g., pianists) in machine-readable form. There are currently no signal processing algorithms that can extract the precise details of a performance from audio signals, so we cannot use sound recordings (e.g., audio CDs) as a data source. Our current source of information is the Boesendorfer SE290, a high-class concert grand piano that precisely measures every key, hammer, and pedal movement and records these measurements in a symbolic form similar to MIDI (though with higher precision). We did eventually manage to get large sets of performances that had been recorded on this instrument by a number of excellent pianists.

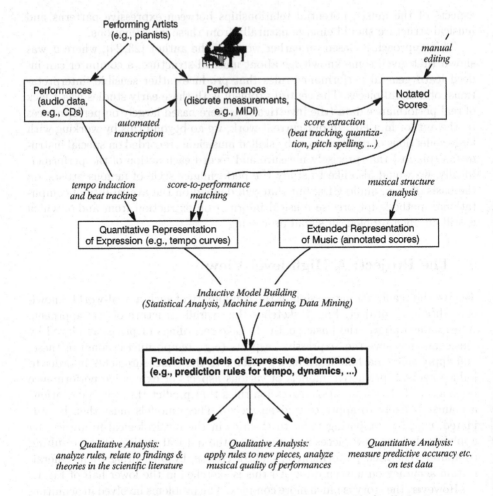

Fig. 1. The research framework: a sketch of data processing/analysis steps.

For instance, we currently have performances of 17 complete piano sonatas by W.A. Mozart as played by a highly skilled concert pianist. This data set corresponds to some 5 1/2 hours of music and contains around 150.000 notes. We also have performances, by a famous Russian pianist, of essentially the entire piano works by Frédéric Chopin (more than 9 hours of music, 300.000 notes, 2 million pedal measurements). This is a huge amount of data indeed; in fact, it is by far the largest collection of detailed performance measurements that has ever been compiled and studied in expression research.

Another line of current research, which cannot be discussed here, concerns the extraction of performance information directly from *digital audio* data, e.g., audio CDs [9] (see top left corner in Fig. 1). This will eventually allow us to also study at least certain limited aspects of expression in arbitrary recordings by famous artists.

3.2   Data Preprocessing

Preprocessing these data to make them usable for analysis and machine learning is a formidable task. What we need is not only the performances (i.e., information about how the notes were played), but also the notated music score (i.e., information about how the notes 'should be' played) and the exact note-to-note correspondence between the two. Manually coding musical scores consisting of tens of thousands of notes is not feasible; in order to get at the scores, we had to develop computational methods for extracting (re-constructing) the score information from the expressive performances themselves. The result is a whole range of new algorithms for music analysis problems like *beat induction* and *tempo tracking* i.e., inferring the metrical structure of the piece in the face of (sometimes rather extreme) tempo changes [10, 11], *quantization*, i.e., inferring the 'intended' onset times and durations of notes in the underlying score [2], and inducing the *correct enharmonic spelling* of notes (e.g., G♯ vs. A♭) [3], which is not merely an aesthetic issue, but absolutely vital for the correct interpretation of a musical passage.

The 'raw' score files extracted by these algorithms from the performance data (up to now, some 150.000 lines of text) still needed to be manually corrected and further annotated. And finally, the resulting score files were matched, in a semi-automatic process, with the performance files to establish the exact note-to-note correspondence; thousands of notes were manually identified and labelled as missing or extraneous (most of these are related to ornaments like trills etc.). From this information we could then finally compute all the detailed aspects of a performer's expressive playing (e.g., tempo changes, articulation details etc.) that serve as training data in the inductive learning process.

3.3   Enhancing the Data: Musical Structure Analysis

The next problem concerns the representation of the music. What we are searching for are systematic connections between the *structure* of the music (e.g., harmonic, metrical, and phrase structure) and patterns in the performances (e.g., a gradual rise in loudness (*crescendo*) over a given phrase). The representation of the musical pieces must therefore be extended with an explicit description of certain structural aspects. Again, a complete manual analysis of a large number of complex pieces is infeasible or at least highly impractical, so there is a need for computational methods. In the context of our project, we have developed a number of new music analysis algorithms that make explicit different structural aspects of a piece such as its segment structure [5], categories of melodic motifs and their recurrence [6], and various types of common melodic, harmonic, and rhythmic patterns, as postulated by music theorists [15]. These algorithms are of general interest to musicology, as they constitute formal computational models of aspects of musical structure understanding that had not hitherto been sufficiently formalized in music theory. The analyses computed by these tools can be used as additional descriptors in the representation of musical pieces.

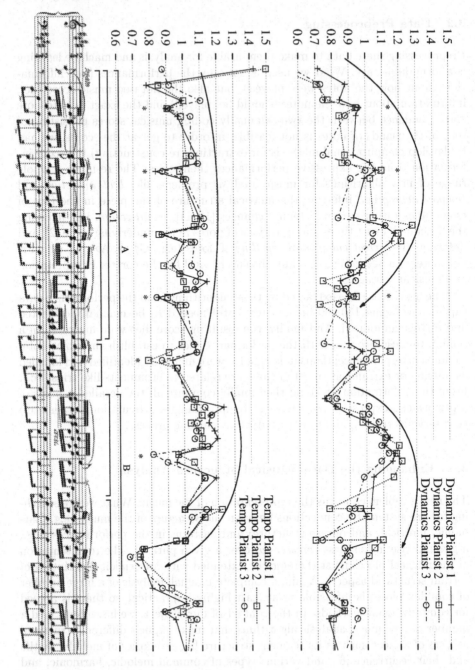

Fig. 2. Frédéric Chopin, Etude Op.10 No.3, mm.1–9, as played by three different pianists: dynamics (relative to average dynamics of entire piece) and tempo (relative to average tempo) of the melody.

4   Challenges to Machine Learning

The result of all these efforts are training data as exemplified in Fig. 2, which shows the dynamics and tempo deviations extracted from performances, by three different pianists, of a well-known piece by Frédéric Chopin. For the moment, we restrict our attention to how the *melodies* of the pieces are played (and neglect more complex aspects like interactions between different voices of a piece). All the three expression dimensions that we are currently studying — tempo/timing, dynamics, and articulation — can then be represented as curves that associate a particular tempo, loudness, or relative duration value with each melody note. Fig. 2 also contains a number of annotations added by the author to highlight different structural aspects of both the piece itself, and the performances. These will be of help in the following discussion.

The first question one might ask is: is there something to be learned at all? Isn't expressive performance something intangible, something that reflects the artistic uniqueness of a performer and thus necessarily escapes any attempt at formalisation or explanation? A look at Fig. 2 reassures us: there are, of course, individual differences in the interpretations by the three pianists, but there are also very clear commonalities in the three curves. In other words, there seem to be some strong common principles at work that lead performers to do things in a similar way. And these common performance patterns must somehow be determined by the structure of the music being played.

In fact, this situation affords opportunities for at least two different types of learning. The one that better fits the 'traditional' inductive learning setting is learning to characterise and predict the *commonalities* between performances. In the simplest case, a learner that is given different performances of the same piece can be expected to find descriptions of those patterns that are common to most of the performances, and treat those situations where the individual performers differ as *noise*.[1] Characterising common performance patterns that point to some fundamental underlying principles is indeed the primary goal of our project. But it would also be interesting to try to learn about characteristic *differences* between individual artists. Here, the problem is not to find out where two performers differ — that is directly obvious from the data — but to find classes of situations in which there is a *systematic* and *explicitly characteriseable* difference in behaviour. This might be a novel problem for machine learning.

A related question is *how much* we can expect to learn and formalise. Clearly, we cannot expect artists to be entirely predictable. We will have to make do with models that explain only a (possibly small) fraction of the observed phenomena. This requirement favours learners that, rather than trying to cover all of the instance space, can focus on those subspaces where something can be learned and produce models that clearly indicate when something is outside their area of expertise. Some interesting results along these lines are reported in [26].

---

[1] 'Real' noise (in the sense of mistakes or inaccuracies by the performer) is not much of a problem — high-class pianists are extremely precise, both in terms of motor control and in terms of their memory and capacity to reproduce particular expressive patterns over repeated performances.

Another fundamental question is: what are the target concepts? And that relates to a number of deep problems concerning representation, abstraction level, and context. At first sight, the curves in Fig. 2 are reminiscent of *time series*, which suggests the use of methods from time series analysis and forecasting. However, this is an inappropriate view. It is not so much the past states that determine how a curve is going to continue into the future; it is the structure of the underlying musical piece that partly determines what 'shapes' or 'envelopes' (in tempo, dynamics, etc.) a performer will apply to the music. The question then arises as to what exactly the scope of these 'shapes' is, and what the structural units in the music are to which these 'shapes' are applied — in other words, what is the appropriate *abstraction level*?

Actually, musical expression is a *multi-level phenomenon*. Good performances exhibit structure at several levels. Local deviations expressing detailed nuances (e.g., the stressing of a particular note) will be embedded in more extended, higher-level expressive shapes, such as a general *accelerando–ritardando* (speeding up – slowing down) over an entire phrase. For instance, the expression curves in Fig. 2 exhibit both local, note-level (see notes marked by asterisks) and more global structural patterns (e.g., a clear *crescendo–decrescendo* applied the medium-level phrase A.1 (dynamics curve), and an ever so slight *accelerando–ritardando* over phrase A in the tempo dimension). Thus, it will be necessary to learn models at different structural abstraction levels, which introduces the additional problems of discerning and separating multiple pattern levels in given training observations, and of combining learned models of different granularity at prediction time. Moreover, apart from the note and the phrase levels, there may be other, intermediate structural units relevant to explaining certain aspects of the curves. Discovering these is an intriguing musicological problem. One of our plans here is to study the utility of new *substructure discovery algorithms* [8].

Generally, the *representation* problem is a non-trivial one. There are many conceptual frameworks in which music can be described. Finding the most appropriate music-structural descriptors is a question of musicological interest. Systematic experimentation with different music-theoretic vocabularies will be necessary to identify these. In addition, the representation should capture the relevant *context* of notes and musical structures, which is a tricky issue not only because we do not know exactly how large this context should be, but also because there are also some highly *non-local* effects at work (e.g., when the recurrence of a melodic motif prompts the performer to 'fall back' into a previous pattern). As for the essentially *relational* nature of music, which would suggest the use of first-order logic for knowledge representation and Inductive Logic Programming for learning, it will be a matter of experimentation to study the trade-off between the increase in expressive power and the increase in search complexity implied by the use of ILP algorithms (see [14]).

Another interesting observation, which may be a source of new learning problems, is that the different target dimensions are very likely to *interact* or be *inter-dependent*. The performances in Fig.2 exhibit some clear parallels between dynamics and tempo, particularly in the case of some local deviations. For instance, there seems to be a strong correlation between dynamic emphasis and individual note lengthening (see the events marked by asterisks in Fig. 2). At a higher level, one could construe a certain parallelism between the dynamics and tempo shapes of the second of the high-level phrases (B) (see the arcs in the dynamics and tempo plots), which would confirm a general hypothesis by musicologists.[2] In general, performers have different means of stressing musical passages, by combining timing, dynamics, and articulation in certain ways. This suggests that expressive performance might be an ideal candidate domain for *multi-task learning* [7], where multiple learning tasks are pursued in parallel using a shared representation, which presumably enables the learner to transfer information between different related problems. Moreover, we would be interested in an explicit *characterisation* of the connection between, say, timing and dynamics, if there is one. This seems to be a new type of learning problem.

And finally, there is the *evaluation* problem. How is one to evaluate and quantify the validity of a given theory in a domain where there is no unique 'correct' solution (there are usually many 'acceptable' ways of performing a piece)? The empirical evaluation methods used in machine learning (measuring classification accuracy and prediction error on unseen data, estimating true error via cross-validation etc.) do have their place here, but they need to be complemented with more music-specific methods that, while avoiding to make judgments concerning the musical or aesthetic quality of a performance, do account for musical aspects of a model's predictions. This is a challenging research question for musicology and is beyond the scope of the present paper.

5   First Results and Ongoing Research

It is only rather recently that we have begun to perform systematic learning experiments with the huge data collections mentioned in section 3.1, so most of the above questions and challenges are still open. Our investigations so far have mostly concentrated on the *note level*, i.e., on describing and predicting how individual notes will be played, given various features of the notes and their immediate context. Here is a brief list of the most interesting results so far:

Basic learnability: In a first suite of experiments [25], we succeeded in showing that even at the level of individual notes, there is structure that can be learned. Standard inductive learners managed to predict the performer's choices with better than chance probability. Extented feature selection experiments showed that different sets of music-theoretic descriptors are relevant for different expressive dimensions (timing, dynamics, articulation).

New rule learning algorithm: Based on experiences gathered in these initial investigations, we developed a new rule learning algorithm named PLCG that can find simple partial theories in complex data where neither high coverage nor high precision can be expected. The PLCG algorithm and some

---

[2] In fact, this parallelism becomes clearer once certain local distortions and artifacts in the expression curves (caused, e.g., by the grace notes in bars 7 and 8) are removed.

experiments with it are described in more detail elsewhere in this volume [26].

Partial note-level rule model: PLCG has discovered a number of surprisingly simple and surprisingly general and robust[3] note-level expression principles [27, 28]. These rules are currently investigated more closely from a musicological perspective; some of them will probably form the nucleus of a quantitative rule-based model of note-level timing and articulation.

Learning at higher structural levels: In some limited earlier studies [23, 24], we had already found indications that learning at multiple structural levels does indeed improve the results (and the musical quality of the resulting computer-generated performances) considerably. However, the definitions of these higher musical levels and particularly the methods for combining learned theories of different granularity were very *ad hoc*, and the training material was extremely limited. We are currently developing a more principled approach.

Discovering stylistic differences: Regarding the possibility of discovering *stylistic differences* between different performers, we had obtained first indirect positive evidence in an early experiment that involved performances of the same piece by both the famous Vladimir Horowitz and a number of advanced piano students [22]. There it turned out that rules learned from Horowitz yielded a significantly higher predictive accuracy on other Horowitz data than on the student data, and vice versa. Recently, we have started new focussed investigations on this issue, with the aim of finding *characterisations* of these differences. This can be done with standard inductive rule learning algorithms, but requires the design of a different type of learning scenario. In a small initial experiment, several interesting rules were discovered that might describe characteristic differences in behaviour between the two great pianists Alfred Cortot and V. Horowitz. But the data were much too limited to permit general conclusions. We are now planning to repeat this type of experiments with a much more extended data set.

Machine learning for structural music analysis: And finally, computational music research offers many other opportunities for machine learning that are not necessarily related to the performance issue itself. There are many problems in *automated structural music analysis* for which there are as yet no reliable algorithms (e.g., harmonic analysis, phrase structure analysis, etc.) and which could benefit from inductive learning. For instance, we have developed an algorithm for finding classes of musical motifs and for elucidating the motivic structure of a piece, based on a new *clustering method*. This algorithm has been shown to be capable of reproducing motivic analyses by human musicologists of such complex pieces as Schumann's *Träumerei* and Debussy's *Syrinx* [6], and of predicting the categorizations made by human listeners [4].

---

[3] For instance, 4 simple timing rules turn out to be sufficient for correctly predicting more than 20% of a pianist's local *ritardandi*, and these rules seem to generalize well to music of different styles.

Obviously, these are just first steps in a long research journey that should take us closer to our final goal — a quantitative, composite computational theory that explains as much as possible of the various dimensions of expressive music performance, and the interactions between them — and that will force us to address a number of novel machine learning problems on the way. This is a long-term undertaking, and we would like to extend an invitation to motivated young researchers to join our project team and work with us towards this goal.

Acknowledgements

The project is made possible by a very generous START Research Prize by the Austrian Federal Government, administered by the Austrian *Fonds zur Förderung der Wissenschaftlichen Forschung (FWF)* (project no. Y99-INF). Additional support for our research on machine learning and music is provided by the European project HPRN-CT-2000-00115 (MOSART). The Austrian Research Institute for Artificial Intelligence acknowledges basic financial support by the Austrian Federal Ministry for Education, Science, and Culture. I would like to thank my colleagues Emilios Cambouropoulos, Simon Dixon, and Werner Goebl for their cooperation and many fruitful and enjoyable discussions.

References

1. Bresin, R. (2000). *Virtual Virtuosity: Studies in Automatic Music Performance.* Doctoral Dissertation, Royal Institute of Technology (KTH), Stockholm, Sweden.
2. Cambouropoulos, E. (2000). From MIDI to Traditional Musical Notation. In *Proceedings of the AAAI'2000 Workshop on Artificial Intelligence and Music,* 17th National Conference on Artificial Intelligence (AAAI'2000), Austin, TX. Menlo Park, CA: AAAI Press.
3. Cambouropoulos, E. (2001). Automatic Pitch Spelling: From Numbers to Sharps and Flats. In *Proceedings of the 8th Brazilian Symposium on Computer Music,* Fortaleza, Brazil.
4. Cambouropoulos, E. (2001). Melodic Cue Abstraction, Similarity, and Category Formation: A Formal Model. *Music Perception,* 18(3) (in press).
5. Cambouropoulos, E. (2001). The Local Boundary Detection Model (LBDM) and its Application in the Study of Expressive Timing. In *Proceedings of the International Computer Music Conference (ICMC'2001).* San Francisco, CA: International Computer Music Association.
6. Cambouropoulos, E. and Widmer, G. (2000). Automatic Motivic Analysis via Melodic Clustering. *Journal of New Music Research,* 29(4) (in press).
7. Caruana, R. (1997). Multitask Learning. *Machine Learning* 28(1), 41–75.
8. De Raedt, L. & Kramer, S. (2001). The Levelwise Versionspace Algorithm and its Application to Molecular Fragment Finding. In *Proceedings of the 17th International Joint Conference on Artificial Intelligence (IJCAI-01),* Seattle, WA.
9. Dixon, S. (2000). Extraction of Musical Performance Parameters from Audio Data. In *Proceedings of the First IEEE Pacific-Rim Conference on Multimedia (PCM 2000),* Sydney, Australia.

10. Dixon, S. (2001). Automatic Extraction of Tempo and Beat from Expressive Performances. *Journal of New Music Research* (in press).
11. Dixon, S. and Cambouropoulos, E. (2000). Beat Tracking with Musical Knowledge. In *Proceedings of the 14th European Conference on Artificial Intelligence (ECAI-2000)*, Berlin. IOS Press, Amsterdam.
12. Friberg, A. (1995). *A Quantitative Rule System for Musical Performance*. Ph.D. dissertation, Department of Speech Communication and Music Acoustics, Royal Institute of Technology (KTH), Stockholm.
13. Friberg, A., Bresin, R., Frydén, L., and Sundberg, J. (1998). Musical Punctuation on the Microlevel: Automatic Identification and Performance of Small Melodic Units. *Journal of New Music Research* 27(3), 271–292.
14. Kramer, S. (1999). *Relational Learning vs. Propositionalization. Investigations in Inductive Logic Programming and Propositional Machine Learning*. Ph.D. thesis, Technical University of Vienna.
15. Narmour, E. (1992). *The Analysis and Cognition of Melodic Complexity: The Implication-Realization Model*. Chicago, IL: University of Chicago Press.
16. Palmer, C. (1988). *Timing in Skilled Piano Performance*. Ph.D. Dissertation, Cornell University.
17. Repp, B. (1992). Diversity and Commonality in Music Performance: An Analysis of Timing Microstructure in Schumann's 'Träumerei'. *Journal of the Acoustical Society of America* 92(5), 2546–2568.
18. Shaffer, L.H. (1980). Analyzing Piano Performance: A Study of Concert Pianists. In G.Stelnmach and J. Requin (eds.), *Tutorials in Motor Behavior*. Amsterdam: North-Holland.
19. Sundberg, J., Friberg, A., and Frydén, L. (1991). Common Secrets of Musicians and Listeners: An Analysis-by-Synthesis Study of Musical Performance. In P. Howell, R. West & I. Cross (eds.), *Representing Musical Structure*. London: Academic Press.
20. Todd, N. (1989). Towards a Cognitive Theory of Expression: The Performance and Perception of Rubato. *Contemporary Music Review, vol. 4*, pp. 405–416.
21. Todd, N. (1992). The Dynamics of Dynamics: A Model of Musical Expression. *Journal of the Acoustical Society of America* 91, pp.3540–3550.
22. Widmer, G. (1996). What Is It That Makes It a Horowitz? Empirical Musicology via Machine Learning. In *Proceedings of the 12th European Conference on Artificial Intelligence (ECAI-96)*, Budapest. Wiley & Sons, Chichester, UK.
23. Widmer, G. (1996). Learning Expressive Performance: The Structure-Level Approach. *Journal of New Music Research* 25(2), pp. 179-205.
24. Widmer, G. (1998). Applications of Machine Learning to Music Research: Empirical Investigations into the Phenomenon of Musical Expression. In R.S. Michalski, I. Bratko and M. Kubat (eds.), *Machine Learning, Data Mining and Knowledge Discovery: Methods and Applications*. Chichester, UK: Wiley & Sons.
25. Widmer, G. (2000). Large-scale Induction of Expressive Performance Rules: First Quantitative Results. In *Proceedings of the International Computer Music Conference (ICMC'2000)*. San Francisco, CA: International Computer Music Association.
26. Widmer, G. (2001). Discovering Strong Principles of Expressive Music Performance with the PLCG Rule Learning Strategy. In *Proceedings of the 11th European Conference on Machine Learning (ECML'01)*, Freiburg. Berlin: Springer Verlag.
27. Widmer, G. (2001). Inductive Learning of General and Robust Local Expression Principles. In *Proceedings of the International Computer Music Conference (ICMC'2001)*. San Francisco, CA: International Computer Music Association.
28. Widmer, G. (2001). *Machine Discoveries: Some Simple, Robust Local Expression Principles*. Submitted.

Scalability, Search, and Sampling: From Smart Algorithms to Active Discovery

Stefan Wrobel

Otto-von-Guericke-Universität Magdeburg
School of Computer Science, IWS
Knowledge Discovery and Machine Learning Group
http://kd.cs.uni-magdeburg.de
P.O.Box 4120, Universitätsplatz 2
39016 Magdeburg, Germany
wrobel@iws.cs.uni-magdeburg.de

Abstract. The focus on *scalability* to very large datasets has been a distinguishing feature of the KDD endeavour right from the start of the area. In the present stage of its development, the field has begun to seriously approach the issue, and a number of different techniques for scaling up KDD algorithms have emerged. Traditionally, such techniques are concentrating on the *search* aspects of the problem, employing algorithmic techniques to avoid searching parts of the space or to speed up processing by exploiting properties of the underlying host systems. Such techniques guarantee perfect correctness of solutions, but can never reach sublinear complexity. In contrast, researchers have recently begun to take a fresh and principled look at stochastic *sampling* techniques which give only an approximate quality guarantee, but can make runtimes almost independent of the size of the database at hand. In the talk, we give an overview of both of these classes of approaches, focusing on individual examples from our own work for more detailed illustrations of how such techniques work. We briefly outline how *active learning* elements may enhance KDD approaches in the future.

L. De Raedt and A. Siebes (Eds.): PKDD 2001, LNAI 2168, p. 507, 2001.
© Springer-Verlag Berlin Heidelberg 2001

Author Index

Lecture Notes in Artificial Intelligence (LNAI)

Lecture Notes in Computer Science